Strategies
of Argument

Strategies
of Argument

STUART HIRSCHBERG

Rutgers: The State University
of New Jersey, Newark

Macmillan Publishing Company
NEW YORK

Editor: Eben Ludlow
Production Supervisor: Charlotte Hyland
Production Manager: Richard C. Fischer
Text Designer: Marysarah Quinn
Cover Designer: Patrice Fodero
Cover Art: Reginald Wickham
Illustrations: Vantage Art, Inc.

This book was set in Palatino by Digitype and printed and bound by Arcata/Halliday. The cover was printed by Phoenix Color Corp.
Acknowledgments appear on pages 800–801, which constitute a continuation of the copyright page.

Macmillan Publishing Company
866 Third Avenue, New York, New York 10022

Collier Macmillan Canada, Inc.

Library of Congress Cataloging-in-Publication Data

Strategies of argument / [edited by] Stuart Hirschberg.
    p. cm.
  A selection of reprints of articles originally published from 1921
to 1989.
  Includes index.
  ISBN 0-02-354773-1
  1. College readers.   2. English language — Rhetoric.
I. Hirschberg, Stuart.
PE1417.S768   1990
808'.0427 — dc20   89-35727
                   CIP

Printing: 1 2 3 4 5 6 7   Year: 0 1 2 3 4 5 6

For
David and Ida
Etta and Sam

Preface

Strategies of Argument is both a reader and a rhetoric on argument. This book has two aims: to provide a range of engaging and enlightening arguments on timely and timeless issues, and to offer instruction on understanding, analyzing, and evaluating different types of arguments, with guidance on writing effective arguments.

As a Rhetoric

Chapters 1, 2, 3, and 4 introduce students to the skills of critical reading, note-taking, summarizing, and the basic strategies of argument, in order to show them how to identify central ideas and techniques as a first step in understanding and analyzing arguments. The discussion, based on the Stephen Toulmin model of claim, warrant, backing, support, and qualifier, examines different kinds of arguments, explores basic argumentative strategies, and places particular emphasis on the importance of underlying assumptions, definition, and types of evidence in different disciplines. The uses (and abuses) of logic and language in argument are discussed in depth. Selections illustrating points in the discussion are on topics ranging from the serious — questions on AIDS, treatment of the disabled, and censorship — to lighter analyses of workaholism and an amusing parody of Wagnerian opera.

Chapter 5 provides guidance in writing effective arguments using a process model and discusses the important points of invention strategies, arriving at a thesis, adapting arguments for different audiences, using an outline, and revising a rough draft. The important role of critical thinking in bridging the gap between analyzing someone else's argument and generating one's own ideas is examined in detail. Students are introduced to the criteria important in evaluating the arguments of others and are provided a sample student evaluation of an argument. The three short arguments for analysis with which the chapter ends include a tongue-in-cheek look at societal stereotyping of overweight people, a comparison of Eastern and Western methods of punishment, and an account of the dangers data bases can pose to individual privacy.

Chapter 6 takes students step by step through the process of writing a research paper and covers the crucial aspects of formulating a thesis statement, using the library, evaluating source materials, note-taking procedures, quoting, writing and revising a rough draft, and using the new MLA and APA styles of documentation. All examples from the card catalog, periodical and newspaper indexes, and other sources are those that were actually used in producing the sample student research paper.

As a Reader

Chapter 7 provides opposing viewpoints on sixteen controversial issues such as abortion, bilingualism, animal experimentation, and genetic engineering. These thirty-two selections represent arguments in important areas including law, medicine, ethics, science, government, and the environment.

In Chapters 8 through 10, three thematic clusters provide multiple perspectives and in-depth views on the contemporary topics of corporate responsibility, drug addiction, and the media. In Chapter 8 ("Business"), readings range from a classic justification of the free-market system by Milton Friedman to pro–con arguments on farm policy and the moral and legal obligations of corporations. In Chapter 9 ("Addictions"), selections explore America's monumental drug problem, the use of steroids by athletes, and arguments for and against mandatory drug testing. Chapter 10 ("Media") provides selections on a wide range of lively topics including media ministries, rock music and videos, and television's unsuspected and damaging effects on the viewing public.

The broad range of subjects and points of view, and the varying levels of difficulty should accommodate a variety of teaching approaches and provide jumping-off points for further research. The annotated table of contents identifies the subject, purpose, and central idea of each selection.

End-of-selection questions explore the substance of each reading and its argumentative strategies. These questions are intended to engage students' interest in the key issues in the text and to direct their attention to the ways that authors adapt their arguments for specific audiences. Some of the end-of-selection questions might best be handled by analytical essays that evaluate the author's purpose in writing the selection, underlying assumption, tone or "voice" chosen, and success in adapting the presentation for a particular audience or occasion.

When the author's purpose in these selections is to argue for the acceptance of a proposition or persuade his or her audience to take or approve an action, the student's analysis can assess the author's use of evidence (both for and against the position being presented) and his or her reasoning (is it clear, logical, compelling, and so forth). When the author's purpose is to demonstrate how to solve a problem or relate how a problem was solved, the student's analysis can address questions of (1) whether there is a clear definition of the problem, (2) whether there is sufficient background presented to understand why there is a problem and what previous attempts have been made to solve it, and (3) why the solution of this problem would be important.

These selections also reveal that the assumptions underlying a particular article are very closely tied in with the author's purpose. For this reason some questions ask students to draw up a list of these assumptions before deciding what the author's purpose might be. Once the assumptions are identified, students can compare the author's assumptions with their own beliefs, determine whether the assumptions are commonly held, and thus be in a better position to evaluate the validity of the author's statements.

Other questions direct attention toward the tone or voice the author chooses to project to the audience. Questions also ask students to evaluate this aspect of arguments by focusing on the writer's choice of words, sentence structure, use of punctuation, choice of person, and success in matching the tone of the article with the subject, the audience, and the occasion.

The wide range of selections in *Strategies of Argument* should give students ample opportunity to see how writers seek to persuade different audiences, including the general public, scholars, or professionals in a particular field of study.

For every set of opposing viewpoints there are writing suggestions designed to encourage students to compare and evaluate how writers discussing the same issue adapt basic argumentative strategies for different audiences.

Instructor's Manual

An accompanying *Instructor's Manual* provides (1) strategies for teaching argumentative writing, (2) suggested answers to the end-of-selection questions, and (3) supplemental bibliographies of books and periodicals for students who wish to follow up on any of the opposing viewpoints or in-depth thematic units for their research papers.

Acknowledgments

My special thanks go to the following teachers of composition for their helpful suggestions: Frederick J. Antczak, University of Iowa; William R. Cantrall, Chicago State University; Lester Faigley, University of Texas at Austin; Gerald Levin, Emeritus, University of Akron; and Marcia MacLennan, Kansas Wesleyan University.

I am especially grateful to my editor at Macmillan, Eben W. Ludlow, for his usual professionalism, inestimable help, and amazing patience. I owe much to John Sollami, Sally Robertson, and the able staff at Macmillan, particularly Janice Marie Johnson, Charlotte Hyland, and M. V. Callcott, for their tireless efforts in miraculously transforming the manuscript into this book. Finally, heartfelt thanks to my wife Terry for her "Assistance-in-Emergency" (see Robert Benchley's *Opera Synopsis* in Chapter 4).

Contents

3   The Role of Logic in Argument   137

4   The Role of Language in Argument   172

Part Two
Pro and Con Arguments

underscore the psychologically destructive effects of
prohibiting children from speaking Spanish in
elementary schools.

Part Three
Different Perspectives on Current Issues

PART ONE

The Elements of Argument

1

Understanding Arguments

"Whether our argument concerns public affairs or some other subject we must know some, if not all, of the facts about the subject on which we are to speak and argue. Otherwise, we can have no materials out of which to construct arguments."
— **ARISTOTLE**, *Rhetoric*

The Nature of Argument

Some of the most interesting and effective writing you will encounter takes the form of arguments that seek to persuade a specific audience of the validity of a proposition or claim through logical reasoning supported by facts, examples, data, or other kinds of evidence. Formal arguments differ from assertions based on likes and dislikes or personal opinion. Unlike questions of personal taste, arguments rest on evidence, whether in the form of facts, examples, the testimony of experts, or statistics, that can be brought forward to prove or disprove objectively the thesis in question.

Although the two are frequently confused, argumentation differs from persuasion. Argument is a form of discourse in which statements are offered in support of a claim or proposition. Argument is based on a rational appeal to the understanding and builds its case on a network of logical connections.

The term *argument* also refers to the practice of giving reasons to convince or persuade an audience to accept a claim or proposition. Argument is a form of advocacy and a process of reasoning designed to support a claim. Making an assertion, offering a hypothesis, presenting a claim, and putting forward a moral objection are all ways of arguing. Thus, the process of argument is valuable because it provides an arena for testing the validity, truth, or probability of specific ideas, propositions, and claims.

Whereas argument presents reasons and evidence to gain an audience's intellectual agreement with the validity of a proposition, persuasion also includes appeals to the emotional needs and values of an audience to move them to approve an action or to take an action that the writer recommends. In argument, the audience's agreement with the truth of the claim has more to do with the soundness of the evidence than with the audience's response to the speaker's character and personality. Because of this, arguments are usually addressed to a general, unspecified audience, whereas persuasion is usually keyed to the beliefs, prejudices, interests, values, and needs of a specific audience. For example, political speeches employing persuasive appeals are usually keyed to the specific needs of an immediate audience. Persuasion is influenced by the audience's sense of the speaker's character, presence, and reputation. The difference between argument and persuasion can be clearly seen by comparing the following two short paragraphs.

Kirkpatrick Sale in his book *Human Scale* (1980) cites the results of various studies as evidence to support his claim that smaller communities are more neighborly and healthier places in which to live:

> There is another way of coming at the question of the human limits of a community. Hans Blumenfeld, the urban planner, suggests starting with the idea of the size at which "every person knows every other person by face, by voice, and by name" and adds, "I would say that it begins to fade out in villages with much more than 500 or 600 population." Constantine Doxiadis, after reducing thousands of data from various centuries, came to the conclusion that what he called the "small neighborhood" would hold approximately 250 people, a large neighborhood some 1,500, with an average around 800–900. Gordon Rattray Taylor, the British science writer, has estimated that there is a "natural social unit" for humans, defined by "the largest group in which every individual can form some personal estimate of the significance of a majority of the other individuals in the group, in relation to himself," and he holds that the maximum size of such a group, depending on geography and ease of contact, is about 1200 people.

Henry Fairlie, on the other hand, in *The Spoiled Child of the Western World* (1976) claims that life in a small community is subject to intrusion and loss of privacy and characterizes the typical village shop as follows:

> But the village shop, as one knew it personally, and as one can read about it in fiction, was usually an unattractive place, and frequently a malignant one. The gossip which was exchanged was, as often as not, inaccurate and cruel. Although there were exceptions, one's main memory of the village shopkeeper, man and wife, is of faces which were hard and sharp and mean, leaning forward to whisper in ears that were cocked and turned to hear all that they could of the misfortunes or the disgrace of a neighbour. Whisper! Whisper! Whisper! This has always been the chief commodity of the village shop.

And not only whispers, because the village shopkeeper, informed or misinformed, could always apply sanctions against those to whom disgrace or misfortune was imputed.

Notice how Sale relies on evidence and the testimony of experts to support his claim that small communities promote peace, social harmony, trust, and well-being. The information is objectively verifiable and the character of Sale as a person is less important than the facts he presents to support his thesis or claim.

By contrast, Fairlie's description of the stifling character of small town life is communicated by picturesque language that is designed to appeal to the imagination and arouse the emotions of his audience against this life. The audience's sense of Fairlie, as a person, is important since his own observations are presented as a source of evidence drawn from his past experiences. There is no objective evidence as such in this passage. Fairlie's ability to appeal to the emotions of his audience through skillful use of provocative language is the only evidence he presents. Yet it would be difficult to say which of these two passages is more persuasive. The point here is that the difference between argument and persuasion is one of degree. Arguments tend to emphasize appeals to logic, whereas persuasion tries to sway an audience through a calculated manipulation of the audience's needs and values. Real world arguments, however, should be a blend of the two.

Rhetoric and Persuasion

Rhetoric came into existence as a specific field of study in the early part of the fifth century B.C. in Sicily to enable ordinary citizens to make an effective case concerning why they should be entitled to recover property that had been seized by a dictatorial tyrant. The claimants had to present their case without supporting documentation and construct an argument solely on the basis of inference and probability. This emphasis on discovering, arranging, and presenting arguments to enhance the probability of a claim defines the distinctive nature of persuasive discourse from this beginning to the present day.

The term *rhetoric* has acquired negative connotations of language calculated to deceive; "mere rhetoric" is associated with stylistic flourishes devoid of content, or empty talk without action. It was not always thus. For Aristotle, rhetoric meant discovering all the available means of persuasion in any given situation where the truth could not be known for certain (Aristotle, *Rhetoric*, Book I, Chapter 1, lines 26–27). Aristotle, of course, excluded coercive or violent means and concerned himself solely with systematic and skillful efforts that one person could use to get another to think in a certain way.

Rhetoric in its original context referred to the process of seeking out the best arguments, arranging them in the most effective way, and presenting them in the manner best calculated to win agreement from a particular audience.

Rhetoric is concerned with those questions in the realm of the contingent where the truth is not able to be known. (Aristotle, *Rhetoric*, Book I, Chapter 2, line 15). It is up to arguers on all sides of the issues to find the most effective means for persuading audiences to believe or at least consider the probable truth of their claims.

Normally, the kinds of questions dealt with are those that are open to different interpretations; rhetoric, therefore, is concerned with the methods or strategies arguers may use in seeking acceptance of their position from an audience. Aristotle said there are three means by which people could persuade each other to adopt a certain point of view or approve a course of action. Broadly stated, these three elements — which are all present in some degree in every successful instance of persuasion — he identified as (1) the appeal to the audience's reason (*logos*), (2) the appeal to the audience's emotions (*pathos*), and (3) the degree of confidence that the speaker's character or personality could inspire in the audience (*ethos*) (Aristotle, *Rhetoric*, Book I, Chapter 2, lines 1–4).

The goal of all three of these appeals is the same although each takes a different approach to achieve the same end of persuading or increasing the credibility or probable truth of the claim. The appeal to the audience's reason (*logos*) is often associated with formal logic and the citation of relevant facts and objective evidence (statistics, case histories, surveys, facts, examples, precedents). Well-constructed arguments that genuinely appeal to reason are indeed persuasive. And even though Aristotle made the point that appeals to an audience's deepest desires, needs, and values need not be deceptive, arguers soon became aware that appeals to the emotions, such as fear, greed, love of comfort, desire for status, or paranoia toward outsiders (*pathos*) could substitute for appeals to reason especially in those cases where the persuader had little evidence or lacked the skill necessary to construct a logical argument. The third means Aristotle identified (*ethos*) depended on the degree to which the arguer could win the confidence of the audience. The credibility and persuasiveness of the arguer's claims would be in direct proportion to the audience's view of the speaker or writer as a person of good sense, good moral character, and good intentions (Aristotle, *Rhetoric*, Book I, Chapter 2, line 13).

It is in the context of these three methods that we will discuss arguments, what makes some persuasive, others ineffective, some legitimate, and others deceptive, and look at the separate elements that collectively comprise effective argumentation. Even though at points we may, for the sake of clarity, discuss elements of argumentation separate from elements of persuasion, the two are inextricably intertwined in any successful instance of persuasion.

The purpose, then, of argument is to persuade an audience to accept the validity or probability of an idea, proposition, or claim. Essentially, a claim is an assertion that would be met with skepticism if it were not supported with sound evidence and logical reasoning. Argument plays a key role for writers who use the forums provided by newspapers, popular magazines, as well as the more specialized literary and scientific journals to persuade colleagues and the general public alike of the truth of their ideas, discoveries, viewpoints, and conclusions. Argument is useful for students as well, as a vital element in debate and writing argumentative essays, and it is an indispensable skill simply if one is to be a well-informed citizen.

Perhaps no issue in recent times illustrates the need to distinguish between the factual nature of a situation and the emotions it arouses as has the AIDS crisis. Almost every aspect connected with this disease elicits questions that can be answered in so many ways that proponents of different answers invariably find themselves constructing arguments to support their positions.

On June 2, 1987, the United States Senate unanimously approved a bill that would require AIDS testing for immigrants (the military was already screening applicants for the presence of the AIDS virus). Should testing of prospective marriage applicants for the AIDS virus be mandatory, like compulsory testing for syphilis? Should hospital patients be routinely tested to detect the presence of AIDS antibodies? Is it desirable or possible to guarantee the confidentiality of test results? What will be the direct and indirect costs of AIDS, and who should absorb the high cost of treatment, experimental therapies, and research? Should insurance companies be allowed to test for AIDS? How can the public be protected while preserving the civil rights of carriers of the virus so that they are not discriminated against by employers, landlords, insurance companies, and public schools? For example, should children with AIDS be allowed to attend public schools? When Clifford and Louise Ray tried to send their three AIDS-infected sons to public school (boys who, as hemophiliacs, had contracted the virus through blood transfusions before screening of the blood supply became mandatory in 1984), neighbors turned against them, their house was burned down, and they were forced to leave Arcadia, Florida. How have patterns of sexual behavior (homosexual and heterosexual) changed in response to the AIDS epidemic?

What arguments are advanced for and against the designation of hospitals in specific neighborhoods as centers solely for the treatment of AIDS victims? Perhaps the most controversial questions of all are those that pertain to society's attitude toward homosexuals, who are those most likely (although by no means exclusively) to contract and die from this inexorably fatal disease. For example, how would proposals recommending that homosexuals be barred from jobs as bartenders, waiters, food handlers, attendants at health care facilities, teachers, and employees at day-care centers come into direct conflict with "right to work" laws? Has the government's willingness to spend money on treatment centers, preventive education, and biomedical research been so slow to get off the ground because a majority of the victims are seen as disposable citizens (homosexuals, the poor, blacks, Hispanics, intravenous drug users)?

Every one of these questions (and untold others) is already or will soon become the center of an argument by individuals and groups who disagree about the basic facts, and offer various hypotheses as to what caused the AIDS epidemic and what the consequences will be. (Some claim that by 1991, 179,000 Americans will have died from AIDS.) The nature of the issue has provoked groups from every sector of American life to make value judgments and advocate various social, sexual, legal, medical, and educational policies.

A writer presenting an argument must keep an open mind, consider points of view other than his or her own, define or stipulate the meaning for key terms in the argument, and present a clear statement of the thesis. The writer must present the argument in logical order, cite the best and most relevant evidence, statistics, examples, and testimony available, state assumptions when necessary, draw conclusions that seem plausible and are consistent with the known facts, and effectively use rhetorical strategies to adapt the argument for a given audience.

Critical Reading for Ideas and Organization

One of the most important skills to have in your repertoire is the ability to survey unfamiliar articles, essays, or excerpts and come away with an accurate understanding of what the author wanted to communicate and how the material is organized. On the first and in subsequent readings of any of the selections in this text, especially the longer ones, pay particular attention to the title, look for introductory and concluding paragraphs (with special emphasis on the author's statement or restatement of central ideas), identify the headings and subheadings (and determine the relationship between these and the title), and identify any unusual terms necessary to fully understand the author's concepts.

As you work your way through an essay, you might look for cues to enable you to recognize the main parts of the argument or help you perceive the overall organization of the article. Once you find the main thesis, underline it. Then work your way through fairly rapidly, identifying the main ideas and the sequence in which they are presented. As you identify an important idea, ask yourself how this idea relates to the thesis statement you underlined or to the idea expressed in the title.

You might also wish to underline the topic sentence of each paragraph or section (since key ideas are often developed over the course of several paragraphs). Jot it down in your own words in the margin, identify supporting statements and evidence (such as examples, statistics, and testimony of authorities), and try to discover how the author organizes the material to support the development of important ideas. To identify supporting material, look for any ideas more specific than the main idea that is used to support it. Also look for instances where the author uses examples, descriptions, statistics, quotations from authorities, comparisons, or graphs to make the main idea clearer or prove it to be true.

Pay particular attention to important transitional words, phrases, or paragraphs to better see the relationships between major sections of the selection. Noticing how certain words or phrases act as transitions to link paragraphs or sections together will dramatically improve your reading comprehension. Also look for section summaries where the author draws together several preceding ideas.

Writers use certain words to signal the starting point of an argument. If you detect any of the following terms, look for the main idea they introduce:

since, because, for, as, follows from, as shown by, inasmuch as, otherwise, as indicated by, the reason is that, for the reason that, may be inferred from, may be derived from, may be deduced from, in view of the fact that

An especially important category of words is that which includes signals that the author will be stating a conclusion. Words to look for are:

therefore, hence, thus, so, accordingly, in consequence, it follows that, we may infer, I conclude that, in conclusion, in summary, which shows that, which means that, and which entails, consequently, proves that, as a result, which implies that, which allows us to infer, points to the conclusion that

You may find it helpful to create a running dialogue with the author in the margins, posing and then trying to answer basic questions as to *who, what, where, when,* and *why,* along with observations on how the main idea of the article is related to the title. These notes can later be used to evaluate how effectively any specific section contributes to the overall line of thought.

Paraphrasing and summarizing are other useful skills that will enhance your critical reading abilities.

PARAPHRASING

A skill closely related to summarizing, paraphrasing also requires you to restate the thoughts of the author in your own words. Unlike the shorter summary, a sentence by sentence paraphrase will be approximately the same length as the original. The ability to restate the thoughts, ideas, and opinions of the author in your own words clearly demonstrates that you understand what you have read. In both summarizing and paraphrasing, it is a good idea to check what you have written against the original to see whether you have inadvertently left out anything important.

SUMMARIZING

The value of summarizing is that it requires you to pay close attention to the reading in order to distinguish the main points from the supporting details. Summarizing tests your understanding of the material by requiring you to restate, concisely, the author's main ideas in your own words. First, create a list comprised of sentences that express in your own words the essential idea of each paragraph, or each group of related paragraphs. Your previous underlining of topic sentences, main ideas, and key terms (as part of the process of critical reading) will help you follow the author's line of thought. Whittle down this list still further by eliminating repetitive ideas. Then formulate a thesis statement that expresses the main idea behind the article. Start your summary with this thesis statement and combine your notes so that the summary flows together and reads easily.

Remember that summaries should be much shorter than the original text (whether the original is one page or twenty pages long) and should accurately reflect the central ideas of the article in as few words as possible. Try not to intrude your own opinions or critical evaluations into the summary. Besides requiring you to read the original piece more closely, summaries are necessary first steps in developing papers that synthesize materials from different sources. The test for a good summary, of course, is whether a person reading it without having read the original article would get an accurate, balanced, and complete account of the original material.

To illustrate, here are two paragraphs from an argument titled "The Politics of AIDS" (1984), by Kenneth W. Payne and Stephen J. Risch, that show how public reaction and political responses to diseases depend on the status of the group affected, not merely on the medical facts:

> To date, the majority of victims of AIDS have been homosexual or bisexual men (72%); intravenous drug users (17%); Haitians (4%); and hemophiliacs (1%). Unfortunately, three of these groups in particular—homosexual/bisexual men, drug users, and Haitian immigrants—are stigmatized, even regarded by some as disposable populations. Classified as "high risk" for contracting AIDS, members of these groups have become victims of a "double stigma," at once social and medical pariahs. One recent article referred to hemophiliacs and others who have contracted AIDS via blood transfusions as "innocent bystanders caught in the path of [this] new disease." Al-

though much is known about viruses, bacteria, and "germs" as causative agents in disease, people still ask the age-old question, "Why
me?" when struck down with sickness. This singularity-of-misfortune notion seeks not an impersonal germ as the cause, but some
more personal explanation, whether one extracted from Biblical
dogma or modern psychiatric notions. In either case, responsibility
for the disease is often laid at the victim's doorstep. A very close fit is
made here between the disease and the victim. People are even led to
believe that disease agents made rational choices—they seek out
"proper victims." As Joan Ablon noted about other stigmatized conditions, the illness becomes a crime in the eyes of society—and, by
extension, the victims of the illness, criminals. The fact that homosexuals have been most affected by the AIDS epidemic makes it easy to
posit a Christian theory of divine retribution: the victim has gotten
what he deserves.

The following short summary of this passage restates the authors'
main ideas without adding any comments that express personal feelings
or responses to the ideas presented. Keep in mind that the purpose of a
summary or concise restatement of the author's ideas in your own words
is to test your understanding of the material:

**Of the four groups most afflicted with AIDS (homosexual men,
intravenous drug users, Haitians, and hemophiliacs), society extends sympathy only to hemophiliacs as innocent victims. Since
most AIDS victims are already regarded as "disposable populations," they are doubly stigmatized because society views the
illness in their case as being a just punishment for their lifestyles.**

Although some other features of the original passage might have
been mentioned, such as that not only hemophiliacs but also all others
who "have contracted AIDS via blood transfusions" are viewed by
society as "innocent victims," this is still an effective summary. Whereas
the original is approximately 150 words, the summary of 55 words
accurately and fairly expresses the main ideas in the original. Summarizing and careful reading both lead to a clearer understanding of the ideas
being presented.

TWO SHORT ARGUMENTS FOR CRITICAL READING

Patrick J. Buchanan and J. Gordon Muir

Gay Times and Diseases

To see how one would go about reading an unfamiliar argument for its main ideas here is an article, "Gay Times and Diseases," (1984), by Patrick J. Buchanan, a nationally syndicated columnist, and J. Gordon Muir, a medical researcher. This article first appeared in The American Spectator *(August 1984). As you read, jot down points that would be useful in constructing a rough summary. Try to identify the essential points of the argument and note where Buchanan and Muir take into account views opposite to their own.*

1   AIDS, acquired immune deficiency syndrome, the killer disease that has claimed 4600 victims—40 percent of whom are already dead—is but the tip of an immense iceberg. Within the homosexual community, there are today incubating pandemic, rare, and exotic diseases with a time-bomb potential of exploding into the general population. Without descending into clinical detail, some concept of the "gay life style" needs to be understood. Its essence is random, repeated, anonymous sex— runaway promiscuity. The chapel of this new faith has been the bath house.

2   According to Dr. Kinsey, the *average* homosexual has 1000 sex partners in a lifetime. *Village Voice* put the figure at 1600. One activist has said that 10,000 sex partners in the lifetime of a "very active" homosexual would not be extraordinary. (Frank Sinatra was once quoted as saying that had he romanced half as many women as gossip-mongers contended, he would be speaking from a jar at the Harvard Medical School.) Many gays visit these bath houses two and three times a week, where ten contacts a night are not uncommon. A study a decade ago found that more than half the active gay males (Lesbians have more enduring relationships) engaged in group sex at least once a month.

3   As a consequence of this jack-rabbitry, young men living the gay life in America's large cities are infecting and re-infecting one another with a

variety of diseases that suggests that the proper term to describe their behavior is suicidal. By the precise way in which they define themselves, they are killing themselves.

That realization is hitting the Gay Community. A year ago, a co-author of this article was denounced as a "homophobe" by Governor Cuomo and Mayor Koch for suggesting that Gotham's bath houses be shut down as a health hazard during Gay Pride Week. Early this year, San Francisco homosexuals themselves took the lead in demanding a municipal decree outlawing sex in the city's baths. As one gay writer told the *Washington Post:* "You can take away AIDS and you're still looking at a community that happens to be a diseased community. I'm sorry. The bulk of your venereal diseases now reside within the gay community. The bulk of enteric (intestinal) diseases is now within the gay community."   4

When it comes to health, declares the *Medical Tribune,* the gay life is "no bed of roses." It never was—notwithstanding the mendacious propaganda of gay activists to paint homosexuality as a natural and healthy alternative. Laboring under this self-generated delusion, hundreds of thousands of young men have been indulging themselves in what *Newsweek* termed a "carefree sexual adventure, a headlong libido." Well, the adventure is ending—and it is revealed for what it always was: an egregious assault upon the ecology of the human body. Call it nature's retribution, God's will, the wages of sin, paying the piper, ecological kickback, whatever phraseology you prefer. The facts demonstrate that promiscuous homosexual conduct is utterly destructive of human health.   5

This is not to disavow sympathy for those horribly caught up in the most highly publicized consequence of the homosexual life style—AIDS. There are few sadder or more pathetic human tragedies than the stories of young men trying to cope with the sudden crushing agony of discovering that they have this inexorably fatal disease. An element of that tragedy is that the victims were lied to—consistently. As one 28-year-old AIDS victim from New York City told *Newsweek:* "The belief that was handed to me was that sex was liberating and more sex was more liberating." Nobody told that young man, now under a sentence of death, that his life style and his body were on a fatal collision course.   6

The AIDS epidemic has been the single most prominent factor in blowing apart the "natural alternative" myth about homosexuality—a myth that should have been dispelled before the first AIDS case came to light. But organized medicine has been timid to the point of cowardice in speaking openly about the health consequences of homosexual practice. Why? Quite simple. Warning people about the health hazards of promiscuous eating or drinking is sound advice. Warning people about the health hazards of promiscuous or unnatural sexual activity is not advice. It is "moralizing." And moralizing is wrong!   7

As a consequence of this "conspiracy of silence" in the medical   8 community — one physician's phrase — tens of thousands of young men joyously embarked upon their pleasure cruises, ignorant of the fate awaiting them at journey's end — while the science pages of the fashionable press were given over to learned discussion of the medical consequences of exhaled cigarette smoke upon the non-smoking passengers of United Airlines.

9   The real story is that there are several epidemics running loose, not all of them permanently confined to the gay community. They have been largely or solely caused, and perpetuated, by the growing urban population of active gays whose modal form of sexual behavior is impersonal, repeated, random, and anonymous sex. (The typical AIDS victim admits to five different sex encounters monthly.)

10   How did gays get led into this mess? Again, very simple: They followed leaders who spouted slogans and cliches about "rights." They took intellectual comfort from harebrained psychologists who peddled nonsense in the guise of learning. When George Will, in a 1977 *Newsweek* column, suggested that homosexuality was "an injury to healthy functioning," gay leaders John O'Leary and Bruce Voeller screamed "outrage" at this "unsupported and totally false statement." Shortly thereafter, gay history professor Martin Duberman, challenging the view that homosexuality was abnormal, wrote in *Skeptic* that "almost all the recent scientific literature . . . points to exactly the opposite conclusion." (Duberman did not indicate what scientific literature he had been reading.)

11   Some of the most profound rot on the subject was penned back in 1975 in *Psychology Today* by San Francisco psychologist Mark Freedman (a founding member of the Association of Gay Psychologists):

> . . . homosexuality in some cases can lead to better-than-average functioning and to a fuller realization of certain fundamental values.
>
> Gay people . . . commonly decide to have sex for the sake of sex . . . The prospective partners don't have to feign love or any other emotion . . . Moreover, gay men are more comfortable engaging in group sex than nongay men, and group sex in my opinion offers pleasures that are impossible for couples.
>
> Gay people constitute a large and varied group and they are capable of providing new kinds of personal fulfillment and social vitality.

12   With this sort of science-fiction in vogue, gay liberation became glamorous. The movement demanded all manner of reform: That sex education courses in public schools taught by gays portray homosexuality as a valid, healthy life style. That gay love stories be available in libraries and schools.

One goal the gay movement sought desperately was removal of the   13
term "homosexuality" as a category of mental disorder from the diagnostic manual of the American Psychiatric Association. This they
achieved. The APA had probably never before seen such pressure, but
that is a story in itself. The APA capitulated. In an attempt at explanation
the APA said, "No doubt homosexual activist groups will claim that
psychiatry has at last recognized that homosexuality is as 'normal' as
heterosexuality. They will be wrong. In removing homosexuality *per se*
from the nomenclature we are only recognizing that by itself homosexuality does not meet the criteria for being considered a psychiatric disorder." *Time* magazine called the APA's action "an awkward compromise by a confused and defensive profession." That the APA was
confused and defensive should be no surprise. So was almost everyone
else.

Despite intense pressure to recognize homosexuality (and its model   14
sex practices) as normal human behavior, a few in the medical profession
refused to capitulate. In a letter to *Patient Care*, Prof. James Kurfees of the
University of Louisville School of Medicine declared himself "appalled"
at the way "this deviant sexual behavior is now dignified with more and
more pseudoscience. Most of the homosexuals I have known have been
pretty miserable, unhappy misfits." A 1982 report by the American
Medical Association's council on scientific affairs stated that "Any person, of whatever sexual preference, who shows a dominant pattern of
frequent sexual activity with many partners who are and will remain
strangers, presents evidence of shallow, narcissistic, impersonal, often
compulsively driven genital rather than person-oriented sex and is almost always regarded as pathological."

A recent signed editorial in the *Southern Medical Journal* refers to the   15
homosexual disease epidemics as a "kickback." Quoting from the book
Homosexuality and the Law: From Condemnation to Celebration, the author
notes that "The law on homosexuality is changing rapidly. It is moving
from condemnation to legitimation and next . . . to sponsorship." Even
now, he points out, we have such things as "Gay Pride Month, with
notable politicians lending their support to gays by marching with them
down public thoroughfares." The author proceeds to ask the key
question:

> If we act as empirical scientists, can we not see the implications of
> the data before us? If homosexuality, or even just male homosexu-
> ality, is "OK," then why the high prevalence of associated com-
> plications both in general and especially with regard to AIDS?
> Might not these "complications" be "consequences"? Might it be
> that our society's approval of homosexuality is an error and that
> the unsubtle words of wisdom of the Bible are frightfully correct?

The writer adds that "from an empirical medical perspective alone,   16
current scientific observation seems to require the conclusion that homo-

sexuality is a pathologic condition . . . certain cause and effect data are convincing—so convincing that health care providers, in this age of unbridled enthusiasm for preventive medicine, would do well to seek reversal treatment for their homosexual patients just as vigorously as they would for alcoholics or heavy cigarette smokers, for what may not be treated might well be avoided." (Although life-style changes for homosexuals appear to be difficult, there is good evidence they are not impossible.) . . .

17   Ninety percent of AIDS victims are sexually active homosexual males or intravenous drug users. Most other victims have been infected by secondary spread from these groups: recipients of blood transfusions or blood components (e.g., hemophiliacs among whom AIDS is now the second most common cause of death); women who have had sexual contact with infected bisexual males; and a few children born to such women. AIDS has occurred in Haitians (about 6 percent of cases) causing them to be listed as a risk group, but there is strong evidence that in these people AIDS had its origin in the gay clubs of Haiti frequented by young poor Haitian male prostitutes and vacationing U.S. gays.

18   So far there are over 4,000 confirmed cases of AIDS in the U.S. It is estimated that there are 20,000 to 40,000 persons with pre-AIDS (i.e., with some of the early signs, such as swollen lymph glands) and no one can be sure how many persons with no symptoms are incubating the disease. John Maddox, editor of *Nature*, describes the situation as "chilling." According to *Newsweek*, Dr. Donald Abrams of San Francisco General Hospital "estimates that 25 percent of gay men in San Francisco now have lymphadenopathy." If this represents an early stage of AIDS (and there is evidence that it does and that it is infective), then, short of some dramatic behavioral change, the gay community may self-destruct.

19   The cause of AIDS may recently have been discovered by Dr. Robert Gallo and his research team at the National Institutes of Health. The suspected culprit is a virus designated HTLV-3. This agent may or may not be the sole cause. Some research physicians believe the announcement of this finding was grossly premature, spurred by what the *New York Times* called "a private competition—for fame, prizes, new research funds."

20   If HTLV-3, frequently found in pre-AIDS patients, is indeed the cause of AIDS, this is a truly ominous finding. *For HTLV-3 has been detected in 75 percent of patients with pre-AIDS and no less than 35 percent of symptomless homosexuals.* Whether or not it is the cause, it appears to be a reliable marker for infected donor blood—a positive finding, which could provide a means to protect the blood supply at the staggering cost of 23 million blood tests per year. However, talk of a cure resulting from this research is nonsense; and talk of a vaccine should await confirmation of Gallo's research.

21   The nation's blood supply also appears to have been contaminated by

homosexual donors, though the present risk of contracting AIDS from a one- or two-unit blood transfusion is low — about one in 100,000. Hemophiliacs, deriving blood components from several thousand units at a time, are at much greater risk. Other ways the AIDS *may* spill over into the general population would theoretically be similar to those applying to hepatitis B. Thus health-care professionals are at some risk as, conversely, are patients in the care of certain homosexually active health-care professionals. So far this problem hasn't materialized, but AIDS is a new disease with a long incubation period (up to four years).

If the AIDS agent is indeed a virus, a worrisome possibility is that   22
changes in virulence will take place, now that the disease is in the amplification system of homosexual promiscuity. It may be that the AIDS agent underwent some change in 1979 that triggered the sudden appearance of the current epidemic. John Maddox asks, "May [it] change again, becoming in the process a more generalized infection of people?" In the microbial world there are precedents. God forbid that such a thing should happen. The result could well be the real "final epidemic" (the description given by a group of physicians to the effects of a nuclear exchange between the U.S. and the USSR). The continuation of human life on this planet would then depend on the rapid development of an AIDS vaccine to protect those not yet infected. This isn't scare talk. The question was raised by the editor of one of the world's leading scientific journals.

Gay leaders, while demanding massive government spending to find   23
an AIDS "cure," are advising gays only to be more careful in their sexual practices. Picture, if you can, the vaulted gothic chapel of the Union Theological Seminary in upper Manhattan with speakers for the Gay Men's Health Crisis standing below a large carved crucifix, graphically explaining the elements of low-risk sex and distributing pamphlets advising the assembled to "shower with your partner as part of your foreplay to check for sores, swollen glands, etc., of which he may not be aware."

Hepatitis B, once uncommon in this country, has become epidemic   24
among active homosexuals. The virus agent is carried in blood, semen, saliva, and possibly in mucus, urine, and sweat. No effective treatment exists for this liver infection, which can progress to cirrhosis and cancer. Transmission through infected semen explains its prevalence in the gay community. One study found that nearly 50 percent of homosexuals with a history of more than 40 sexual partners had evidence of previous infection. Another study of homosexual men in Amsterdam showed evidence of previous infection in over 60 percent — and an annual attack rate of about 30 percent among the previously uninfected . . .

Another equally serious type of hepatitis, for which there are no tests   25
or vaccines, is hepatitis non-A, non-B. An intelligent guess would be that this disease has been propagated in the homosexual community the same way as hepatitis B. Two viruses are possibly involved: They are

believed to be the main cause of chronic liver disease in hemophiliacs and of post-transfusion hepatitis. (The problems visited on hemophiliacs by homosexual blood donors through AIDS, and possibly through hepatitis non-A, non-B, have yet to evoke any large measure of contrition from the gay activists whose greatest concern has been with the ethical issue of anonymity attending blood-screening procedures.)

26   Then there is the "Gay Bowel Syndrome," a group of rare bowel diseases, previously considered "tropical," now epidemic in urban gay communities. These are a particular cause for concern because they can be transmitted by fecal contamination. All it requires is unclean hands in contact with food or water. Inside a population of sexually active gays where oro-anal contact is reportedly practiced by 70–75 percent it is hardly surprising that the increase in these diseases has been described as "explosive." . . .

27   A 1979 study of gay men in New York City turned up an infection rate of 39 percent for amebiasis or giardiasis (that was using only a single fecal specimen; three are usually required to be sure of not missing the diagnosis).

28   Back in 1974 shigellosis began to turn up as a common homosexual infection, first in San Francisco and later in New York, London, and elsewhere. In 1976 physicians at the New York hospital found that 57 percent of cases of shigellosis, not related to foreign travel, were in homosexuals, who made up only 2.5 percent of the patients.

29   Hepatitis A is also common in homosexuals. Among gay men attending a venereal disease clinic in Seattle there was evidence of previous hepatitis A infection in 30 percent. The yearly attack rate was about 22 percent.

30   A public health debacle is here in the making. The *New England Journal of Medicine* reported in 1980 that in San Francisco *an average of 10 percent of persons reported as having amebiasis, giardiases, or shigellosis were employed as food handlers.* Between 60 percent and 70 percent of these persons were homosexuals.

31   Clearly, homosexuals no more belong in the food-handling business than they do in the blood banks. As Dr. Selma Dritz of the San Francisco Department of Public Health wrote in the *Western Journal of Medicine* in 1982, "special precautions are required to protect the public from [carriers] who work as food handlers, bartenders, attendants in medical care facilities, and as teachers and aides in day-care centers for infants and young children." Common sense suggests that sexually active gays have no business in any of these occupations.

32   Finally, gonorrhea is also rampant in the homosexual community. In one large survey of U.S. gays, 40 percent reported known infection with gonorrhea. Common homosexual varieties of this disease (oral and rectal) are also more difficult to detect and treat. Antibiotic-resistant gonococci are now making an appearance; the pharmaceutical industry is only about one drug ahead of these strains, and there is no guarantee it will remain so.

Syphilis, an old disease that was in decline, is also making a come- 33
back. In the same gay survey, 13.5 percent reported a previous infection
with syphilis. Among gays attending saunas in Amsterdam there was
evidence of old or recent syphilis in 34 percent; only half the men were
aware of their infection.

It is self-evident that gay sexual practices are an assault upon the 34
ecology of the human body, that the gay communities of America's cities
are polluted with disease. With respect to AIDS, there exists a potential
for disaster.

The general public has been grossly deceived about the gravity of this 35
homosexually engendered public health menace. Hollywood and the
media under the tutelage of the Gay Media Task Force have done their
part, portraying gays in programs like "Dynasty" as all-American types
with boy-next-door good looks. Of the movie *Partners,* Richard Schickel
wrote: "Like all the other pictures, in what looks like a trend . . . it
shows homosexuality neutrally, as just another fact one is likely to
encounter." Of the movie *Making Love,* he added, "the people who made
this picture are determined to prove that 'nice boys' do, that homosexuals can be as well-adjusted and as middle-class as anyone else."

According to *TV Guide,* we can expect to see many more "almost 36
commonplace" gay characters. "'We're very pleased,' says Chris Uszler,
chairperson of the Alliance for Gay Artists . . . 'there are [going to be]
more of what we call "happens-to-be-gay" characters.'"

Perhaps so, Chris. Still, one is reminded of the observation of the 37
nineteenth-century historian J.A. Froude: "One lesson, and one lesson
only, history may be said to repeat with distinctness [and that is] that the
world is built somehow on moral foundations."

A rough summary of Buchanan and Muir's article, using no more
than two complete sentences to summarize each of the ten sections,
might appear as follows. Numbers show which paragraphs are summarized from the article:

1–5   Since the presence of AIDS and other diseases that are killing
      homosexuals could spread into the general population, the es-
      sence of the "gay life-style" needs to be understood. The results
      of studies by Dr. Kinsey and the *Village Voice* suggest that the
      promiscuous, random, repeated, anonymous nature of sexual
      activity among homosexuals, who infect and reinfect one an-
      other, is a suicidal form of behavior that is ample evidence that
      the life-styles of gays is destructive of human health.

6–8   Victims of AIDS were deceived by leaders of the gay rights
      movement who promulgated the myth that homosexuality was
      a healthy "natural alternative" and encouraged promiscuous
      sexual behavior. Although the medical community should have
      warned homosexuals about the dire health consequences of

their life-style, they were slow in speaking out because they feared being accused of moralizing.

9–12   Because of the growing population of active gays in large cities, several epidemics are now no longer confined to the homosexual population. These epidemics are caused and perpetuated by the growing population of active gays who were led by activists who clamored for "rights" and were misinformed by researchers who themselves were gay.

13–16   Despite the fact that the American Psychiatric Association, under considerable pressure from the gay movement, removed the term *homosexuality* from its category of mental disorders, many psychiatrists still believe that compulsive homosexual promiscuity is pathological.

17   Ninety percent of AIDS victims are homosexuals and there is reason to believe that AIDS was first transmitted via gay clubs in Haiti and then spread rapidly throughout the gay community in the United States.

18–20   It is estimated that up to 40,000 people may be incubating AIDS and, according to Dr. Robert Gallo, the cause of the disease may be a deadly virus designated HTLV-3, "detected in 75% of patients with pre-AIDS and no less than 35% of symptomless homosexuals."

21–23   AIDS poses a grave danger of contaminating the general public through the national blood supply. Infected patients can transmit it to health-care professionals who in turn can transmit it to noninfected patients. If the AIDS virus were to mutate the results could be even more devastating to everyone than the current epidemic.

24–25   Other diseases that were once uncommon (such as types of hepatitis) for which there are no treatments or vaccines have also risen to epidemic proportions in the homosexual community. Despite these facts, gay activists are still primarily concerned with ethical issues of disclosure of test results following blood-screening procedures.

26–31   Because of the high prevalence of diseases that can be transmitted by unclean hands coming in touch with food or water, homosexuals should not be employed in any occupations that involve handling food, or in blood banks, schools, or medical facilities.

32–37   The devastating epidemics from which the gay community suffers is overwhelming evidence that homosexuality is a destructive life-style. Because of the danger that AIDS poses to the general population, it is important for the public to recognize the extent to which it has been deceived by the media, including Hollywood, in their depiction of homosexuality as an essentially normal and healthy way of life.

Buchanan and Muir's thesis or principal claim is that the AIDS epidemic is ample evidence that the gay life-style is unnatural and destructive to human health, contrary to the myth of the "natural alternative" espoused by gay rights leaders, psychologists, and the media. This central thesis is supported by a number of specific reasons and facts that might be listed as follows:

1. The presence of AIDS is the result of its transmission via the random, promiscuous, repeated, anonymous sexual activities of homosexuals.
2. Victims of AIDS were deceived by leaders of the gay rights movement into believing that promiscuous sexual behavior was liberating.
3. The APA under pressure from the gay movement removed the term *homosexuality* from its category of mental disorders and thereby made it appear as a viable and acceptable life-style.
4. Ninety percent of AIDS victims are homosexuals.
5. Other diseases that were once rare (such as types of hepatitis) have risen to epidemic proportions in the gay community.
6. The media, including Hollywood, have deceived the public in depicting homosexuality as an essentially normal, healthy way of life.

Each of these points is necessary to Buchanan and Muir's overall conclusion that the blame for the AIDS epidemic rests squarely with the leaders of the gay rights movement who advocated a promiscuous homosexual life-style, as well as with psychologists and the media who promulgated the acceptability of homosexuality as "normal behavior." If these reasons were to be presented in the form of a single concise paragraph, Buchanan and Muir's argument might look something like this:

The acceptance of homosexuality as a "natural alternative" led to an increase in promiscuity among gays that has caused the spread of many sexually transmitted diseases, of which the most deadly is AIDS. The victims of AIDS were themselves led astray by gay activists, the media, and the APA who redefined homosexuality as normal behavior. Ninety percent of AIDS victims are homosexuals, and other rare diseases such as hepatitis B are now epidemic in the gay community. There is a grave danger of AIDS spreading throughout the entire population through an infected national blood supply. Because certain diseases now epidemic in the gay

community can be transmitted by contact with food, water, or
blood, homosexuals should be banned from donating blood or
working in the food-handling or medical service fields. The AIDS
epidemic offers proof that homosexuality is a self-destructive and
unnatural form of behavior that has created a potentially catastrophic health problem for the general population.

Whether or not you agree with the conclusions reached by Buchanan
and Muir, you will be in a better position to write your own argument if
you have first developed the ability to read critically and summarize
accurately.

Questions for Discussion and Writing

1. What reasons do Buchanan and Muir advance to support their
contention that the existence of AIDS itself is evidence against the gay
life-style?

2. What different kinds of evidence do Buchanan and Muir offer to
support their assertion that the gay life-style can be characterized as
one of "random, repeated, anonymous sex—[and] runaway
promiscuity" (para. 1)?

3. To what extent are Buchanan and Muir more concerned with the
public health implications of AIDS than with passing moral judgment?

4. How do Buchanan and Muir structure their argument so as to lay
the blame for the AIDS epidemic on those leaders of the gay rights
movement who, in their view, have advocated a promiscuous
homosexual life-style? What effect do Buchanan and Muir produce by
not blaming the victims who have been led astray, in terms of gaining
acceptance for their position by their audience?

5. Why, in Buchanan and Muir's view, has the medical establishment
been more reticent in offering advice against homosexual practices
than against smoking, excessive eating, and drinking?

6. Buchanan and Muir fault Martin Duberman (para. 10) for not citing
specific sources. Do Buchanan and Muir do this themselves anywhere
in their argument? If so, where?

7. Although the APA (para. 13) declined to define homosexuality as a
mental disorder, how do Buchanan and Muir interpret this fact as
further evidence to support their own views that there is "intense
pressure to recognize homosexuality . . . as normal human behavior"?

8. How does paragraph 15 put forward the essential thesis that Buchanan and Muir's article explores?

9. What connection of causes and effects do Buchanan and Muir sketch out (para. 17) in describing an epidemiological model for the spread of AIDS?

10. Although they disclaim any effort to use scare tactics, are there points raised by Buchanan and Muir that might indeed have this effect on an audience? Specifically, what is the effect in their argument of discussing possible mutation of the AIDS virus, and possible contamination of the national blood supply?

11. What function does Buchanan and Muir's discussion of other diseases, such as hepatitis B and gonorrhea, have in supporting their main thesis that societal permission to practice homosexuality has led to the current threat of a sexually transmitted epidemic?

12. From what types of occupations would Buchanan and Muir bar homosexuals? How would Buchanan and Muir's recommendations come into conflict with existing right-to-work laws?

13. Evaluate the effectiveness of paragraphs 34 and 35 in restating Buchanan and Muir's principal thesis. In Buchanan and Muir's opinion, how have Hollywood and the other media helped to promulgate a myth concerning the gay life-style that has resulted in a homosexually engendered public health menace?

Kenneth W. Payne and
Stephen J. Risch

The Politics of AIDS

An issue as controversial as AIDS elicits a wide range of viewpoints. Two paragraphs from the following article, "The Politics of AIDS," by Kenneth W. Payne, a medical anthropologist, and Stephen J. Risch, who teaches biology at the University of California, Berkeley (originally published in Science for the People *[September/October 1984]) were used earlier in the section on summarizing; the text that follows is in its complete form, with only minor exceptions. Payne and Risch offer an analysis of the AIDS crisis and reach conclusions that are quite different from those reached by Buchanan and Muir in their article "Gay Times and Diseases."*

1   Disease is an analytic prism for cultural understanding. Entire mythologies build up, not only about a disease itself, but about the individuals bearing the disease. Social images, stereotypes, and official fictions come to be perpetuated by the media as the facts of the disease. The more virulent the disease, the greater its social importance. Diseases of no known cause or cure, especially, strike at the very depths of our fears.

2   Medical factors alone do not determine the course of public health events. Attitudes toward particular diseases closely reflect general attitudes of the times in which such diseases occur. From the Renaissance until the 18th century, for instance, syphilis carried none of the stigma that later was attached to it, for those were years of "tolerance in sex matters." With Victorian morality, attitudes towards syphilis changed.

3   Public reaction and political responses to diseases are also dependent on the status of the groups most affected by the disease. Whether the disease is perceived as a public health problem or as a problem for the victims themselves, is not grounded in scientific fact, but in social reality: "How much of a national scientific effort we devote to fighting an illness is a reflection of the political value we attach to it and its victims." A disease which clearly illustrates the interaction between social forces and medicine is Acquired Immune Deficiency Syndrome (AIDS), which has grown into the nation's "Number One Public Health Priority" since its identification in 1981. Only recently have we begun to understand what causes it, although we do not yet know how to cure it, where it began, or

how it works. This has spawned a climate of uncertainty in which misinformation abounds and attempts to curb the spread of the syndrome encounter resistance and challenge. Attitudes towards AIDS can tell us much about current social climate. The epidemic allows us to peer beneath the veneer of tolerance of diversity so loudly proclaimed in the mass media and view the deeply conservative feelings of our time.

To date, the majority of victims of AIDS have been homosexual or bisexual men (72%); intravenous drug users (17%); Haitians (4%); and hemophiliacs (1%). Unfortunately, three of these groups in particular — homosexual/bisexual men, drug users, and Haitian immigrants — are stigmatized, even regarded by some as disposable populations. Classified as "high risk" for contracting AIDS, members of these groups have become victims of a "double stigma," at once social and medical pariahs. One recent article referred to hemophiliacs and others who have contracted AIDS via blood transfusions as "innocent bystanders caught in the path of [this] new disease." 4

Although much is known about viruses, bacteria, and "germs" as causative agents in disease, people still ask the age-old question, "Why me?" when struck down with sickness. This singularity-of-misfortune notion seeks not an impersonal germ as the cause, but some more personal explanation, whether one extracted from Biblical dogma or modern psychiatric notions. In either case, responsibility for the disease is often laid at the victim's doorstep. A very close fit is made here between the disease and the victim. People are even led to believe that disease agents make rational choices — they seek out "proper victims." As Joan Ablon noted about other stigmatized conditions, the illness becomes a crime in the eyes of society — and, by extension, the victims of the illness, criminals. The fact that homosexuals have been most affected by the AIDS epidemic makes it easy to posit a Christian theory of divine retribution: the victim has gotten what he deserves. 5

An AIDS "personality" has been sought among AIDS patients, and the press has suggested that alienation, personal inability to cope with stress, and shame are contributory to AIDS. It has even been posited that "the disease is 'chosen' at a profound, unconscious 'level' as a dramatic form of protest." 6

Homosexuality has long received widespread opprobrium in the U.S. In response, Gays have kept their sexuality underground, finally surfacing in some areas during the increasingly liberal climate of the 1960s and early 1970s. With the advent of AIDS, media attention has brought Gay sexuality up for discussion in nearly everyone's home. The "darker" side of homosexuality (e.g. sex clubs, orgy rooms) has been exposed to public scrutiny. Absurd statistics intended to shock the public have been quoted, suggesting that the "average" number of sexual partners in the life of the "average" active male homosexual is more than 1,600. 7

The medical/scientific establishment has yet to publish for general 8 consumption a comprehensive profile of the individuals stricken with AIDS, although it is well over three years (and over 5,000 U.S. victims) since the epidemic was first recognized and monitored. The profile presented in the popular media is blurred—the image is one of a highly promiscuous man who uses recreational drugs and has repeatedly abused his health. This profile contrasts dramatically with those AIDS victims whose lives and experiences have been chronicled in the Gay press, or who have been interviewed in the popular press as well. Instead of statistical data, Gays have had to rely on anecdotes. For every report of an AIDS victim who lived in the fast lane (with alcohol and drug abuse, poor sleep patterns, poor diet, etc.), most Gays have heard of exceptions, where someone has lived a moderate lifestyle, one similar to their own, perhaps even a monogamous lifestyle.

9　　　　That AIDS has appeared in these conservative times seems especially unfortunate. "Just as society was ready to grant that homosexuality is not a disease, it is seized with the idea that homosexuality breeds disease." AIDS is described in many circles as a disease of sexual expression, a narcissistic neurosis of sorts, the consequence of enslavement to one's desires. The public's anxiety over AIDS has begun to generate a climate that could lead to erosion of many of the civil rights that Gays have gained over the last 15 years.

10　　　　Politicians and preachers have evinced a special interest in AIDS. "For them, it represents opportunity—opportunity for politicians to score political points with homosexuals, and for preachers to score moral points against them." Recently, Phyllis Schlafly's publication, *The Eagle Forum*, used AIDS for political manipulation. In an article titled, "The ERA-Gay-AIDS Connection," she claimed that, were the ERA ratified, the American family would have no protection against AIDS. AIDS was also used by California Senator H.L. Richardson (R) to defeat Assembly Bill 1, which would have placed homosexuals under the protection of the fair employment statutes by adding them to the list of minorities in the anti-discrimination codes. In a letter to members of the Judiciary Committee, Richardson cited "real medical problems" in the homosexual community that would place everyone in potential grave jeopardy. Homophobic propaganda exploiting AIDS also appeared in Texas, where Representative Bill Ceverha worked on House Bill 2138, designed to prevent and deter homosexual conduct which could "destroy the public health of the State of Texas" by causing the transmission of AIDS.

11　　　　The media have offered considerable in-depth coverage of the AIDS crisis, but the coverage has oscillated between sensationalism and assurances that all will soon be under control by scientists. Although AIDS has continued to spread unabated, the impression given by a longitudinal study of the media's coverage of the epidemic is that AIDS, somehow, is less of a problem today. Left with the impression that the media coverage of the epidemic is proportionate to the threat of the disease, the public has been misled. So-called "break-throughs" in AIDS treatment or in understanding the etiology of the disease receive front page and prime time coverage. But there is rarely any follow-up of these leads, which are mostly false starts: "Poppers Causes AIDS," "Homosexual Intercourse Linked to AIDS," "Interferon Checks the Progress of AIDS."

Gay groups have been forced for their own good to monitor the   12
media's presentation of AIDS information for accuracy and timeliness, trying to maintain a balance between public education and hysteria. Certain facts have had to be continuously underlined:

- AIDS is not a "Gay" disease. The connection between AIDS and homosexuality has become a verbal reflex. This is unfortunate, because it has impressed upon the public the erroneous idea that AIDS is *only* a homosexual affliction. That intravenous drug users and Haitians constitute the next largest affected groups only serves to underscore the belief that AIDS affects outcast groups, disenfranchised peoples, and that, with luck, the disease could be contained among these peoples. The only outpourings of public concern and sympathy came with the recognition of a small percentage of AIDS victims who "unwittingly" contracted the disease, namely, hemophiliacs and blood transfusion recipients. Heterosexuals *can* get the disease.

- AIDS is not a "plague." Calling AIDS a "plague" conjures up images of a medieval scourge, unchecked contagions sweeping the land and annihilating the population. AIDS is a devastating disease (43.5% of reported cases are dead already), but the number of individuals affected thus far barely constitutes an epidemic, let alone a plague. The fact remains that, uncharacteristic of a plague, AIDS has proven rather difficult to transmit.

AIDS research is unique since it is the first time the medical estab-   13
lishment has had to deal with a national crisis that primarily affects a highly stigmatized group. Although Gay activists complained that the government was committing far too few funds to deal adequately with the health crisis, such suppositions were dismissed by the popular press as the pleadings of special interest groups until the release in 1983 of a House Committee on Government Operations Report, "The Federal Response to AIDS." The report, which described in detail the internal memos of the U.S. Department of Health and Human Services on AIDS research financing, found that the government responded far too slowly to the AIDS outbreak in 1981, and that the research funding that finally came was dictated by narrow political and budget "constraints," rather than by the advice of health experts. . . .

14   The federal and state monies now finally going to AIDS research are
nearly all earmarked for strictly biologically-oriented investigations (e.g.
What is the causative agent? How can the syndrome be treated?). Of 20
grants (totalling nearly $4 million) announced in February 1984, for New
York State – financed research, only one grant was awarded for a preventative study, and no money was allocated for educational assess-
ments. This has not been the most effective or judicious expenditure of
funds if the immediate goal is to stop the spread of the epidemic and
help those who already have the disease. The biological questions are
important, but too little money has been spent on public education and
prevention, despite the fact that very early in the epidemic most researchers suspected that the disease could be sexually transmitted, and
that Gay people could arm themselves with the information necessary to
make educated decisions regarding certain sexual practices.

15   Only in a few large urban centers where Gay people are politically
organized (e.g. New York and San Francisco) has there been a significant
effort to educate the Gay community about preventative measures. This
was possible only with funds solicited directly from the Gay community
and by intense pressure on local governments to generate money for
education. Chicago has yet to allocate any funds for public education,
while Los Angeles got its AIDS program off the ground only in the Fall of
1983. New York City, with about one-half of the nation's AIDS cases,
has still spent only $1 million for its non-hospital health activities relat-
ing to AIDS.

16   The rapidity with which the medical establishment successfully laid
claim to the available research money reflects both its opportunism and
its lobbying power. Because of the severity of the problem, it was quite
clear that there were going to be large amounts of research money
available, at least eventually. In today's tight funding market, research
priorities often are dictated by funding levels. There are now many
laboratories receiving AIDS money that previously had only the most
peripheral association with AIDS research. The recent congressional
report noted that only 10% of the money given to nongovernmental
researchers for AIDS went to scientists specifically investigating the
syndrome. The remaining 90% comprised previously awarded grants to
investigators who devoted 20% or less of their funds to AIDS research.

17   Another factor motivating the medical community's interest in AIDS
was that the disease raised some very exciting scientific questions, especially in the area of immunology. There were clearly careers to be made
— tenure, promotion, international recognition. Already there is evidence that some laboratories are not openly sharing their research findings or adequately recognizing the findings of others, in obvious competition for medical fame. For example, nearly a year after a French team at
the Pasteur Institute in Paris published an article in the widely read
journal, *Science,* on their discovery of T-lymphotropic viruses (LAV) in

AIDS cases, American researchers, led by Dr. Gallo, admitted the importance of LAV and the probability that this virus was identical to one that they, too, had isolated, grown, and named HTLV-III. Why the French discovery was not fully appreciated earlier is curious. Dr. Roger W. Enlow of the New York City Department of Health observed:

> . . . it is inconceivable to me that Dr. Gallo and his coworkers have been to date unable to consider LAV as fully as his other isolates. LAV has been available to him repeatedly. . . . Evidence that these viral isolates and others from around the world are one and the same would add essential evidence that these isolates cause the disease we now call "AIDS." Withholding or obscuring of such information is reprehensible behavior of the gravest sort. Such can not be tolerated one moment by a civilized society and thwarts the pursuit of truly meaningful scientific collaboration and inquiry.

"Everybody sees a Nobel Prize in this, of course," said Warren Winkelstein of the University of California, Berkeley, the recipient of a $3 million federal grant for AIDS research. "But that's not bad — that means you'll get the best minds in the country working on this." . . .

AIDS is a "medical profession's free-for-all." Treatments depend on "what clinic one stumbles on, what doctor he happens on, what hospital he gets delivered to, and who is funding what program with whatever experimental drug company's largesse." . . . 18

The moral value we attach to a disease also affects the extent to which its victims receive proper medical attention. Patient management is adversely affected by the attitudes of medical staff about the culpability of their patients. Persons not responsible for their illness are regarded as "legitimate," whereas those regarded as somehow responsible for their illness come to be viewed as unworthy. As such, the latter are subjected to less-than-optimal care. This has been illustrated in the case of anorexia nervosa, another disease believed by many to be self-induced. The literature on anorexia nervosa indicates that the victims are the brunt of hospital gossip, that many are purposely neglected, and that some are even abused by their nurses. AIDS is widely regarded as a disease one has brought on oneself, and hence one in which the victims should expect neither sympathy nor help from the public coffers. 19

Doctors themselves have decried what they see to be the abuse of the medical system by homosexuals. They cite high recidivism rates (e.g. multiple cases of sexually transmitted diseases within a single year's time or multiple hospital admissions for one infection after another) to support their case. One San Diego physician recently charged that Gays were demanding taxpayers' money to save themselves from their own frivolous indiscretions. Another doctor recently justified discrimination against homosexuals as "reasonable" since "their activity not only is 20

harmful to themselves but risks the health of the society they live in."
This accusation of culpability could also be leveled at victims of other
diseases proven to be the direct consequences of lifestyle choices, such as
victims of lung cancer due to cigarette smoking, or of liver cancer related
to alcohol abuse. The underlying homophobia in the case of AIDS is all
too apparent. . . .

21   All diseases occur in a political context and an appropriate analysis of
any major disease can tell us much about the medical establishment and
the larger society. But the particular attributes of AIDS — its high mortality, epidemic status, poorly understood biology, and, most importantly,
the stigmatized nature of the groups it affects — make an analysis of
AIDS especially revealing.

22   Despite the vast resources available in the U.S., the response to AIDS
on the part of the government and the research community has been
relatively slow and disorganized. . . .

23   Within the medical research establishment itself, there have been
competitive struggles over funds and intellectual turf, with examples of
laboratories withholding information or refusing to publicly acknowledge the contributions of other research groups. The result has been
slower progress than should have been the case. While one could say
that this happens after the discovery of any new disease in our system,
AIDS is much more than just a lesson in the normal operation of the U.S.
medical system. Because almost 95% of its victims are stigmatized, the
response to AIDS has revealed a tremendous amount about how the
medical system, and society at large, responds to the needs of its dispos-
sessed. Since by far the largest group affected were homosexual and
bisexual, here is a special message about the prevalence and impact of
homophobia. The 1960s and 1970s saw tremendous gains made by Gays
in winning basic civil and human rights. AIDS has clearly demonstrated
that beneath a veneer of social tolerance lies widespread, virulent homophobia, and that it can surface at the slightest excuse. The medical
struggle against AIDS will be won long before we can wipe out the social
attitudes that have hindered a humane and timely response to this
epidemic.

Payne and Risch believe that the AIDS crisis has been distorted and
exploited to suit the needs of politicians, preachers, the media, and
medical researchers. They assert that all these groups "politicize" AIDS
to fit their own preconceived agendas.

If we wished to write a rough summary to clarify how this idea was
developed by taking a closer look at the reasons and evidence Payne and
Risch advanced to support their thesis, the results might appear as
follows. The numbers refer to paragraphs in the article:

   1 Mythologies about incurable diseases and about the individuals
      bearing these diseases show how easily health issues can be-

come controversial social issues when the public's attitude toward the disease is distorted by preconceptions about the victims.

2–3　The extent to which political responses to victims of diseases depend on the public's already existing attitude toward the status of the victims can be measured by looking closely at society's response to AIDS.

4–5　Of the four groups most afflicted with AIDS (homosexual men, intravenous drug users, Haitians, and hemophiliacs) society extends sympathy only to hemophiliacs as innocent victims. Since most AIDS victims are already regarded as "disposable populations," they are doubly stigmatized because society views the illness in their case as being a just punishment for their life-styles.

6　The desire to blame the victim has reached such a point that the media have gone so far as to suggest that individuals unconsciously chose to contract AIDS as a "dramatic form of protest" against being homosexual.

7–8　With the advent of AIDS, homosexuality has been propelled into the limelight. Unfortunately, since the medical community has been remiss in providing clear factual information, the press has presented outrageously inaccurate statistics that contrast sharply with the real life-styles of actual victims.

9–10　Ironically, AIDS appeared just as homosexuals were being accepted into the mainstream of society and granted their civil rights; politicians and preachers quickly exploited AIDS to reestablish latent homophobia.

11–12　The media have exploited AIDS by providing superficial sensationalized stories that promote public hysteria and misconceptions: statistically, AIDS is not a plague, does not affect only homosexuals, is hard to transmit, and barely qualifies as an epidemic.

13–18　Because AIDS is a disease which affects an already stigmatized population, the government and the medical establishment have been slow to allocate money for AIDS research. The little money allocated has gone to groups that have just recently jumped on the bandwagon and almost no money is used to treat those already infected or for preventive education. Prevention programs are only set up in areas where the gay community has supplied most of the funds and has put pressure on local government.

19　The medical establishment has exploited AIDS by viewing the finding of a cure as the ultimate prize and researchers compete with each other for federal funding. The finding of a cure is actually hindered because competing researchers do not share the results found in their respective studies.

20–22   AIDS treatment is very much a product of chance, as it varies according to the attitude of the medical staff of various facilities. Some doctors blame homosexuals for AIDS and are sympathetic only toward innocent victims such as hemophiliacs.

23   Overall, the slow and disorganized response of the government and medical community to AIDS, and the exploitation of the crisis by the media, preachers, and politicans reveal how quickly latent homophobia can reemerge and erode the political gains made by a whole group in a seemingly tolerant and progressive society.

Payne and Risch's conclusion that preventive education and biomedical research have been hampered because AIDS victims are seen as disposable citizens is startling and requires good reasons and evidence to make it credible. Try your hand at analyzing this argument using the following questions and writing suggestions to guide you.

Questions for Discussion and Writing

1. Using either the rough summary above or one you make up yourself, write a single coherent paragraph summarizing Payne and Risch's argument in less than 150 words. Be sure to check your summary against the original article so that you do not omit essential points.

2. What reasons do the authors present to support their thesis that "public reaction and political responses to diseases" are "dependent on the status of the groups most affected by the disease"?

3. Summarize the argument presented in paragraphs 4 and 5 in your own words and explain the phenomenon known as "blaming the victim."

4. According to the authors, how might the special medical treatments required by AIDS victims serve as an excuse to reinforce existing social stigmas?

5. What is the phenomenon of homophobia and what examples do the authors present to support their contention that "it can surface at the slightest excuse"?

6. Evaluate the authors' presentation of arguments opposite to their

own position. What are these arguments, and what counterarguments do Payne and Risch give?

7. What reasons do the authors present to support their thesis that groups with many different interests (the media, politicians, preachers, medical researchers) distort the phenomenon of AIDS to suit their own agendas?

8. To what extent does the fact that both authors have extensive backgrounds in the biological sciences show itself in the kinds of examples they introduce? Which of these examples do you find especially informative in clarifying their thesis that AIDS has become a political football?

2

Strategies of Argument

Introduction

What we usually call an *argument* is not the same thing as a formal written argument. Arguments in everyday life are usually spontaneous, often illogical, and usually not well thought through. Yet the goal of everyday debates is often the same as the most elegant, well-reasoned argument — persuasion of an audience to come around to your point of view. A well-reasoned argument not only makes a claim but presents reasons and evidence necessary to convince an audience that the claim is true. Arguments arise in any situation where a wide range of responses are possible. The most obvious example might be a court of law. The prosecution and the defense each tell their side of the story or their version of events. The judge or jury, acting as an audience, then decides which version of the events seems more plausible. As with a formal argument, the legal system requires evidence to meet certain standards and draws a distinction between admissible and inadmissible evidence. Expert witnesses also play the same role in the court as they do in a written argument. The adversary nature of the legal system assumes, as does a formal argument, that any reason that survives all objections raised against it is a valid one. Many other professions besides the law, such as journalism, science, and business, also depend on the formulation of convincing arguments to win an audience's assent. What all arguments have in common is the need to persuade an audience by means of exact and careful reasoning that a specific claim or assertion is true.

The basic elements to be considered in any argument include (1) the claim or proposition the audience is to consider, (2) the evidence, support, or grounds the writer will have to produce to back up the claim, and (3) the warrant, the underlying assumption (an idea we all agree upon before the argument begins), belief, or rule that spells out the relationship between the claim and the evidence offered to support it. For example, if advertisers claim that their baked ham can be used to make a great sandwich, the evidence might be the results of a survey comparing their brand of ham with a competitor's, but the warrant or assumption (implicit in this case) is that a sandwich is comprised of a filling — such as slices of baked ham — between two pieces of bread. The advertisers are relying on the audience's knowing what a sandwich is. In other cases where the audience might be unfamiliar with rules it is assumed everyone knows, the warrant might have to be spelled out explicitly.

For example, a writer putting together a guidebook for travelers to Thailand would spell out rules and customs tourists would be wise to observe. She might warn tourists never to touch anyone—especially children—on the head since Thais consider it to be the dwelling place of the soul. Other Thai customs based on assumptions every Thai knows but the tourist might not could, for example, necessitate explicitly warning the traveler never to cross the legs with one foot resting on the other knee. The feet are considered the lowliest part of the body and pointing at anyone with your foot, even if inadvertently, is taken as an insult. Other customs could be assumed to be more self-evident—such as showing disrespect to images or statues of Buddha—and the warrants for them would not have to be spelled out explicitly for those of other religions.

Thus, any argument recommending certain kinds of behavior in Thailand would have to make explicit the underlying warrant rather than taking it for granted that readers would connect the evidence to the claim in the same way as would the writer. A traveler would need to understand the rationale or underlying principles of Thai culture in order to know how to act correctly. The assumptions or rules about what constitutes proper behavior assures (or warrants) the claim or advice about what is considered correct behavior in different circumstances.

In our example, the writer might quote authorities, cite anecdotes of travelers' experiences, and appeal to the need of travelers not to embarrass themselves when traveling in other cultures. In other arguments, support can also take the form of specific facts, data, statistics, personal testimony, results of experiments or surveys, and appeals to the emotions, needs, and values of the audience. The character of the author of the guidebook would also support the claim insofar as the reader perceived her as a seasoned traveler, familiar with the values and customs of different cultures. Both the citation of evidence and the appeal to needs and values of an audience are valid means by which writers support claims.

Kinds of Claims

The proposition that we wish our audience to agree with or act upon is called a claim. The claim is expressed as the thesis statement. Claims can be classified according to the kinds of questions that they answer.

I. Factual Claim: Prices of generic drugs are often well below those of leading brands.
Claims of fact seek to answer the question, what is the nature of [something]?

II. Causal Claim: Sex differences cause differences in mathematical ability.
Claims about cause or consequence try to answer the questions, what caused [something] to be the way it is? or what will happen as a result of [something]?

III. Value Claim: Affirmative action is morally justifiable.
Claims of value seek to answer the question, is [something] good or bad, right or wrong, moral or immoral, practical or impractical? These types of claims make value judgments.

IV. Policy Claim: Automobiles should not be allowed in Yellowstone National Park.
Claims about policy try to answer the question, what ought, should, or must we do about [something]? Claims of policy frequently appear as arguments that propose specific actions or policies as the best way to solve problems.

Claims may be phrased to suggest that there are certain kinds of conditions or limitations that prevent the claim from being advanced unconditionally. These qualifiers often take the form of adverbial phrases (*presumably, in all probability, apparently,*) that indicate the provisional nature of the claim. In other cases, writers try to specify the sort of restrictions that limit the conditions under which the claim is true. For example, Dorothy Collier, in "Where Is My Child?" (*The London Sunday Times* [1977]), concludes her argument with a policy recommendation that includes a qualification. Collier, as a mother who has given up her son for adoption, believes that the natural parents should have the right to learn the identity and whereabouts of their children even though they have given them up for adoption. She argues the case on the grounds that adopted children have the right to learn who their natural parents are. She is careful to phrase her policy claim so that the reader understands she would apply the same restrictions as now govern the disclosure of information to adopted children:

> The law applies only to the child [the Children Act signed into law November 26, 1976, that permits adopted people to gain access to their own birth records and thus to find out who they are]. He has all the rights and all the initiatives. If my son, the child that I bore, is dead, I am denied even the right to know where his body lies. I cannot believe that that right should be abrogated by the stroke of the pen at the time when the mind has ceased to function. I believe firmly that, with the same safeguards as now apply to the children, the right to know, the right to acquire basic information, should be granted to the natural parents of adopted persons.

How Collier qualifies her claim can be seen in the following sentence (the qualifying phrase is emphasized):

Policy Claim: I believe firmly that, **with the same safeguards as now apply to the children,** the right to know, the right to acquire basic information, should be granted to the natural parents of adopted persons.

Although we can more clearly see the distinctive qualities of each of these four types of claims (factual, causal, value, and policy) by discussing them separately, arguments frequently rely on more than just one type of claim. For example, Lori B. Andrews in an article titled "My Body, My Property" (*Hastings Center Report* [1986]) creates an argument that recommends changing the current system of voluntary donation of body parts (used in organ transplants) to permit the creation of a commercial market in organs and tissues (a claim about policy). In the course of her argument, Andrews defends the right of patients to sell their own body parts (a claim about value), defines the important difference between "regenerative" and "nonregenerative" organs and tissues (a claim about meaning), and discusses the benefits of such a market to donors, to recipients, and to society as a whole (a claim about consequences).

The Goals of Claims

Different kinds of arguments seek to accomplish different objectives or goals. Generally speaking, four kinds of goals can be identified:

FACTUAL CLAIMS DEFINE AND DRAW DISTINCTIONS

Arguments that define and draw distinctions must identify the unique properties of the idea, term, or phenomenon being defined in a way that clearly distinguishes it from all other things with which it might be confused. Arguments that assert that a situation should be characterized in a certain way must identify the most important feature or crucial aspect of any situation, phenomenon, event, or idea.

Some arguments arise because of a lack of consensus as to what commonly used terms actually mean. For example, in medicine, new technologies for prolonging life make it necessary to agree on what the terms *life* and *death* mean in this new context. Since machines can now prevent cessation of respiration, the traditional definition of death — as occurring when respiration ceases and the heart stops beating — must be stipulated as occurring with *brain death*. In these cases, decisions as to when to terminate life support or to remove organs for transplantation will obviously depend on which definition is applied. Thus, an argument seeking to establish what is most essential about the subject will often depend on the definition of a key term or concept.

For example, an argument against deinstitutionalization of the mentally ill might begin with a factual claim intended to establish the essential nature of one particular kind of mental illness: "schizophrenia is a mental disorder." In this case, the factual claim could easily be verified by citing the official definition published in the *Diagnostic Manual of the American Psychiatric Association.*

In Chapter 1, Buchanan and Muir discuss the significance of the removal of another controversial term, *homosexuality*, as a category of mental disorder from this same manual. They quote the American Psychiatric Association's statement that "in removing 'homosexuality' *per se* from the nomenclature we are only recognizing that by itself homosexuality does not meet the criteria for being a psychiatric disorder." Despite the qualified nature of the American Psychiatric Association's statement, Buchanan and Muir are critical of the association for "redefining" homosexuality in a way that tends to legitimize it.

In addition to citing testimony of responsible authorities, claims of fact can also be verified by citing evidence in the form of examples, statistics, and empirical generalizations. For example, Timothy Ashby, in his article "A Nine Point Strategy for Dealing with Castro" (*Backgrounder* [November 21, 1985]), makes the claim: "Cuba is a Latin American military power second only to Brazil." Ashby supports his claim with statistics showing that Cuba has "regular armed forces exceeding 225,000 personnel and a militia that numbers nearly a million." Of course, to fully develop his case, Ashby would need to verify these statistics and provide comparable data on military personnel and militia in Brazil.

Evaluating the Reliability of Sources of Information

The persuasiveness of factual claims not only depends on specific reasons and evidence given to support the claim but on the reliability of the source of the information. The reliability of an authority depends on how reliable this expert has been in the past, and on his or her ability to make accurate observations and draw sound conclusions. Both the way information is selected and the way judgments are made must be free from bias. For this reason, it is important to be able to distinguish statements that you merely believe to be true from those that you know to be true. You might try to do this with the following two descriptions of a Suzuki Samurai truck. The first paragraph appears as the advertising copy in the August 1988 issue of *Motor Trend*:

IT HAS FUN WRITTEN ALL OVER IT.

—Take off your top with two piece removable hardtop.
—Haul your things around on a handy luggage rack.
—Fog lamps make great evening wear.
—Pull out of trouble with heavy duty compact winch.
—Protect your funmobile with durable brush guard.
—The Samurai logo. It has fun all over it.

The fun thing about a Suzuki Samurai™ is that you can give it a personality all your own. Genuine Suzuki accessories for America's favorite 4 × 4. We've got all kinds to choose from for the Suzuki look you want. Tops. Racks. Lamps. Western mirrors. Chrome bumpers. More. Make it sporty. Make it outdoorsy. Make it rugged. Make it yours. So go out and get a pure Suzuki. And make it your Suzuki.

The next series of paragraphs contain an evaluation of the Suzuki Samurai that appeared in the July 1988 issue of *Consumer Reports:*

Early this year a staff member was driving our new *Suzuki Samurai* slowly, in second gear, along a snow-covered dirt road leading to our auto test track when he felt the tires grab in a rut worn by earlier traffic. The driver turned the wheel to the right to steer clear. The front wheels pulled out of the rut and climbed approximately six inches up a ridge of plowed snow at the side of the road. Then, as the driver tried to straighten the wheels, the *Suzuki* flopped over on its side.

The driver climbed out uninjured, but with new respect for the laws of physics.

The laws of physics say a vehicle with a high center of gravity is more likely to roll over than a vehicle with a low center of gravity. All four-wheel-drive utility vehicles have a higher center of gravity than passenger cars, a consequence of the extra ground clearance needed when driving on rough terrain rather than a paved road.

The laws of physics say a *narrow* vehicle with a high center of gravity is more likely to roll over than a wider vehicle with a high center of gravity. The *Suzuki Samurai* is one of the narrowest vehicles on the road. Its "tread" width—the distance from the center of the left front wheel to the center of the right front wheel—measures only 51.2 inches.

A *short* narrow vehicle with a high center of gravity is more likely to roll over than a longer narrow vehicle with a high center of gravity. The *Suzuki Samurai* is also one of the shortest vehicles on the road, only 80 inches between the centers of the front and rear wheels.

Finally, a light vehicle is more likely to tip over than a heavy vehicle, other things being equal. The *Suzuki* weighs 950 pounds less than the *Jeep Wrangler,* the small utility vehicle that's closest to it in general configuration. It weighs 1220 pounds less than the *Jeep Cherokee* and 1590 pounds less than the *Isuzu Trooper II*, the two larger utility vehicles tested for this report.

Given their physical characteristics, it's not surprising that utility vehicles roll over two to three times more frequently than do passenger cars and small pickup trucks, the second most hazardous types of vehicle.

When the Insurance Institute for Highway Safety analyzed auto-accident fatalities in one- to three-year-old cars and trucks for the years 1981 to 1985, it found that occupants of small utility vehicles were being killed at the rate of 5.7 for every 10,000 vehicles registered. For small passenger cars and small pickups, the rate was about 2.4 deaths per 10,000; for large cars, about 1.2 deaths per 10,000.

The *Suzuki Samurai* was not marketed in the U.S. during the years those accident fatalities were occurring. However, it is rapidly compiling mortality statistics all its own.

The Center for Auto Safety, a nonprofit consumer group, says it has received reports of 20 *Suzuki Samurai* rollover accidents resulting in 21 injuries and four deaths. It has also received reports of six rollovers in variants of the *Samurai*, such as the *Suzuki SJ410*, which is sold in Hawaii and the Virgin Islands; those resulted in seven injuries and one death. The National Highway Traffic Safety Administration has received 44 reports of *Samurai* rollovers, resulting in 16 deaths.

That's an ominous record of rollovers, considering that there are only 150,000 *Samurais* on U.S. roads so far, and that many of them have been in use for less than a year.

The physical characteristics of four-wheel-drive utility vehicles, the accident statistics, and our own experience were very much on the minds of our auto testers as they prepared to run the *Suzuki Samurai* the *Jeep Wrangler,* the *Isuzu Trooper II*, and the *Jeep Cherokee* through their paces.

Our regular test program includes a maneuver designed to see how controllable a car remains when a driver is forced to steer sharply—to avoid, say, a child who unexpectedly darted into the road. To simulate that kind of sudden emergency, our drivers run each car through a lane-changing course marked off by traffic cones. One cone blocks the right-hand lane, a stand-in for the obstacle to be avoided. The drivers begin their left turn out of the lane 60 feet before the obstacle. They then must steer sharply enough to get back into the lane no more than 60 feet beyond the obstacle.

Our test drivers take the cars through the course at increasingly higher speeds, noting how fast they can swerve around the obstacle without knocking over cones and without losing control.

The cars get the benefit of the doubt in this test. We run the test on dry pavement with expert drivers who've steered through the course hundreds of times before. The drivers don't brake while steering, as a nonprofessional driver might in an emergency, so the cars aren't forced into premature skids or spins. Nor do they accelerate. This "accident-avoidance maneuver" realistically simulates a situation that could confront any driver any day. We never attempt unrealistic stunts, such as U-turns at high speeds.

Most vehicles weave through the course easily up to about 50 mph, then start hitting cones or skidding at some point above 50 mph. During the 10 years we've used this test, no vehicle we've tested — and these have included many vans and small trucks with high centers of gravity — has threatened to roll over.

In our judgment, the *Suzuki Samurai* is so likely to roll over during a maneuver that could be demanded of any car at any time that it is unfit for its intended use. We therefore judge it Not Acceptable.

A rollover in a *Suzuki Samurai* would be even more dangerous than a rollover in a passenger car. Utility vehicles such as the *Suzuki* are not required to meet Federal safety standards for side-impact and rollover protection, which cover only passenger cars. Although widely advertised, sold, and used as a passenger car — indeed, as a car in which "to have a ball," as the advertising trade press puts it — the *Suzuki* we tested has no rollbar to reinforce its hardtop, as the *Jeep Wrangler* does.

Soon after our tests were complete, we called the results to the attention of the National Highway Traffic Safety Administration, in an effort to warn those who might have been considering a *Suzuki* before this issue of CONSUMER REPORTS came out. We have also petitioned NHTSA to establish minimum stability standards for all vehicles, so that cars and trucks as tippy as the *Suzuki Samurai* can no longer be sold here.

In comparing these two accounts of the Suzuki Samurai truck, we notice that the same vehicle is viewed very differently by the advertisers trying to sell their product and by the editors of *Consumer Reports*, a magazine that tests products and reports the findings. As you can see, if we are to accurately evaluate the source of information we must be aware of the vested interests of the people reporting the information. We must also understand how these interests or purposes may have influenced the way the information has been presented. The key questions to ask in determining reliability of sources of information are:

1. How knowledgeable or experienced is the source?
2. What sort of track record does the source of information have — that is, how reliable has this source been in the past?
3. Was the source able to make accurate observations in this particular case?
4. How could this information be objectively verified?
5. Do you have reason to believe that the information is incomplete or has been distorted by the self-interests of those relaying the information?

A useful procedure by which to evaluate arguments is (1) to draw up a list of all the factual statements made in the course of the article, (2) to describe, next to each statement, how this fact is verified, and (3) to evaluate the reliability of the source.

For example, let's say you were reading an article that claimed "big business does not control America." You would put this statement in your first column. Next you would look through the article for support for this claim. In this case, you would find the statement:

> [F]ewer of us who are employed are working for "big companies" than in 1976 (32% worked for a company with over 250 employees in 1976; 30% in 1982, the latest year for which figures are available).

The documentation for this source establishes that it was drawn from the *Statistical Abstract of the United States 1985*. You would record this fact in your second column. Since this document was published by the Bureau of the Census, an agency in the United States Department of Commerce, you would be justified in considering it a reliable source, and note the fact in the third column.

Distinguishing between Fact and Opinion

When reading arguments, it is important to be able to distinguish between statements of fact and statements of opinion. Statements of fact relate information that is widely accepted and objectively verifiable; facts are used as evidence to support claims. By contrast, an opinion is a personal interpretation of data that should not be mistaken by the reader for objective evidence. For example, consider the following claim:

> The primary fact of American life is that the nation's gross national product — our economic pie — is no longer growing as fast as it once did.

This statement could be verified or refuted on the basis of objective data. By contrast, here is an opinion presented as a statement of fact:

> There is a social upper class in the United States that is a ruling class by virtue of its dominant role in the economy and government.

This statement presents an opinion that is merely the writer's own interpretation of evidence that another writer might interpret quite differently. It should not be mistaken by the reader for a statement of fact. A reader who could not distinguish between statements of fact and interpretations or opinions disguised as statements of facts would be at a severe disadvantage in understanding the argument.

To take another case, consider the statement:

> In 1979, the federal deficit was about $74 billion.

This statement is a factual claim that could be verified by objective data. On the other hand, consider the claim:

The federal deficit will destroy America's economy.

Those who are apprehensive about large deficits would concur; those who saw some benefit in large federal deficits would disagree. Nonetheless, the statement is only the writer's interpretation and, as such, is still open to debate. In any case, the reader should be on guard against statements of opinion presented in the guise of facts.

CAUSAL CLAIMS IDENTIFY POSSIBLE CAUSES FOR A GIVEN EFFECT OR POSSIBLE EFFECTS FOR A GIVEN CAUSE

Claims about causation assert that two events do not merely appear together but are in fact causally connected. That is, the writer argues that one event is caused by another or will cause another to occur. Whatever form they take, all causal arguments must demonstrate the means (sometimes called the *agency*) by which an effect could have been produced. For example, a writer who claimed that "cancer is caused by industrial chemicals" would be obligated to show the means by which specific industrial chemicals could produce certain kinds of cancer.

Causal arguments also offer plausible explanations as to the cause or causes of a series of events or a trend. A trend is the prevailing tendency of general direction of a phenomenon that takes an irregular course, like the upward or downward trend of the stock market, or the growing tendency to ban smoking in the workplace.

For example, Lou Harris, the pollster, in *Inside America* (1987), identifies a dramatic upward trend in arts attendance:

From the mid-1970s to the mid-1980s, arts attendance in this country literally exploded.

To support this statement, Harris cites results of opinion surveys conducted by his organization establishing that the number of people who (1) attended the movies went up from 70 percent to 78 percent, (2) attended live performances of plays, musical comedies, and other forms of theater rose during the same period from 53 percent to 67 percent, and (3) attended live music performances by popular singers, bands, and rock groups increased over the decade from 46 percent to 60 percent. In his view, a plausible explanation of this trend is that the upsurge in arts attendance is probably a reaction to increased societal pressure to make money as well as "an expression of creativity in an era marked by conformity."

Arguments over causation (such as "is cancer caused by industrial chemicals?") arise because there may be several possible causes for a given effect or a number of possible effects for a given cause. An argument that attempts to demonstrate a causal connection between cancer and industrial chemicals would have to show that a particular cause or combination of causes was capable of producing the effect in question.

A causal argument must present plausible grounds to support a claim as to why something happened or why something will happen. Writers may work backwards from a given effect and attempt to demonstrate what cause or chain of causes could have produced the observed effect, or show how further effects could follow from a known cause. To see how this works, let's examine the following section drawn from William J. Darby's article "The Benefits of Drink" (*Human Nature* [November 1978]). The author, an emeritus professor of biochemistry at the Vanderbilt University School of Medicine, argues that persons who drink moderately tend to live longer than persons who abstain totally from drinking alcoholic beverages:

> Klatsky and his colleagues evaluated the medical histories of 120,000 patients and found that moderate alcohol users were 30 percent less likely to have heart attacks than were non-drinking patients or matched controls or so-called risk controls — people who suffer from diabetes, hypertension, obesity, high serum cholesterol, or who smoke. (All of these factors are associated with increased risk of heart attacks.)
>
> It was found that non-drinkers run a significantly greater risk of myocardial infarction than do users of alcohol. This finding was independent of age, sex, or prior related disease. In each of the groups of drinkers — those who drank up to two drinks daily, those who drank three or more drinks daily, and even those who drank six or more drinks per day — fewer heart attacks occurred than among the abstainers. The investigators concluded that "abstinence from alcohol may be a new risk factor." In a subsequent report from Massachusetts, where investigators studied 399 cases of infarction and evaluated 2,486 case histories, evidence persisted of a lower rate of heart attacks in subjects who consumed six or more drinks per day.

To substantiate his claim that contrary to popular belief moderate drinking is basically a healthy activity, Darby cites the results of several studies that seem to suggest that a causal argument could be made that alcohol consumption reduces the risk of heart attack in moderate drinkers. He cites a continuing study by Arthur Klatsky at the Kaiser-Permanente Medical Center in Oakland, California. (Klatsky first analyzed 464 heart attack patients and found that a large majority of them were persons who rarely or never consumed alcohol. He then broadened his study to 120,000 patients and found that moderate drinkers were 30 percent less likely to have heart attacks than teetotalers.) Darby also uses statistics drawn from a subsequent study to support his causal analysis. (For a fuller analysis of how writers use statistics to support a claim, see the discussion under "Support" later in this chapter.) A medical report in Massachusetts that included studies of 399 heart attack cases and 2,486 case histories found that the rate of heart attacks was significantly lower in persons who consumed six or more drinks in one day. It was especially important that Darby provide objective evidence since his claim and its accompanying implication (that people who abstain from alcohol are actually at greater risk of having a heart attack than those who consume three to six drinks daily) is so controversial.

The rhetorical strategies that come into play in causal analysis require the writer to describe the subject in question, identify and discuss probable causes, provide reasons and evidence to support the causal claim, and consider and reject alternative explanations. Some writers reverse the sequence so that their own argument for a probable cause follows a thorough evaluation and rejection of competing explanations.

One way to substantiate a causal claim entails citing statistical evidence showing that a correlation exists between an increase or decrease of the stipulated cause and a simultaneous change in the effect. Demonstrating correlations remains one of the most difficult kinds of causal arguments. As Darrell Huff and Irving Geis, authors of *How to Lie with Statistics* (1954) have observed:

> Take the figures that show the suicide rate to be at its maximum rate in June. Do suicides produce June brides—or do June weddings precipitate suicides of the jilted? A somewhat more convincing (though equally unproved) explanation is that the fellow who licks his depression all through the winter with the thought that things will look rosier in the spring gives up when June comes and he still feels terrible.

Simply because two things change at the same time does not mean that there is causal correlation between them, that is, that the change in one has caused the change in the other.

Many studies in the social sciences investigate causal correlations. For example, the social psychologists John M. Darley and Bibb Latané, in "Why People Don't Help in a Crisis" (*Psychology Today* [1968]), described experiments to identify what factors cause people, when part of a group, to be less likely to aid the same victims of street crime they would have helped on a one-to-one basis. Darley and Latané discovered a clear correlation between the numbers of people witnessing an emergency and the willingness of any one individual to come to the aid of the victim. Surprisingly, the more people in a group, the less likely any one person was to volunteer to help the victim. One such factor was peer pressure:

> A person trying to interpret a situation often looks at those around him to see how he should react. If everyone else is calm and indifferent, he will tend to remain so; if everyone else is reacting strongly, he is likely to become aroused. This tendency is not merely slavish conformity; ordinarily we derive much valuable information about

new situations from how others around us behave. It's a rare traveler, who, in picking a roadside restaurant, chooses to stop at one where no other cars appear in the parking lot.

Darley and Latané's classic experiment disclosed a significant correlation between a measurable cause (number of bystanders) and an observable effect (willingness of any one individual to aid the victim). Causal analysis is an important tool used by researchers to discover the means by which social pressures control the behavior of people in groups. In this case, Darley and Latané's results challenged the traditional idea that apathy is the reason bystanders are unwilling to help victims of street crime.

Because of the complexity of causal relationships, writers must try to identify as precisely as possible the contributory factors in any causal sequence. The direct or immediate causes of the event are those most likely to have triggered the actual event, yet behind direct causes may lie indirect or remote causes that set the stage or create the framework in which the event could occur. Immediate or precipitating causes are those that can be identified as occurring just before the event, phenomenon, or trend. On the other hand, remote, indirect, or background causes occur in the past well before the actual event takes place.

For example, Aldous Huxley, political essayist and author of *Brave New World* (1932), distinguished between predisposing and triggering causes to explain why one segment of the German population was so easily swayed by Hitler's rhetoric:

> Hitler made his strongest appeal to those members of the lower middle class who had been ruined by the inflation of 1923, and then ruined all over again by the depression of 1929 and the following years. "The masses" of whom he speaks were these bewildered, frustrated and chronically anxious millions. To make them more masslike, more homogeneously subhuman, he assembled them, by the thousands and the tens of thousands, in vast halls and arenas, where individuals could lose their personal identity, even their elementary humanity, and be merged with the crowd. . . .

In this passage from "Propaganda Under a Dictatorship" in *Brave New World Revisited* (1958), Huxley uses causal analysis to emphasize that the people most likely to yield to propaganda were those whose security had been destroyed by previous financial disasters. That is, previous cycles of financial instability (the disastrous inflation of 1923 and the depression of 1929) played a crucial role in predisposing the lower middle classes, those whose security was most affected by the financial turmoil, to become receptive to Hitler's propaganda. Hitler, says Huxley, used techniques of propaganda—mass marches, repetition of slogans, scapegoating—to manipulate the segment of the population that was the least secure and most fearful.

Long-term future effects are much more difficult to make a case for than are short-term, immediate effects. Determining with any degree of certainty that X caused Y is more complicated in situations where one cause may have produced multiple effects or the same effect could have been produced by multiple causes.

For example, David Hilfiker in "A Doctor's View of Modern Medicine" (*The New York Times Magazine*, February 23, 1986) analyzes a number of causes that have, in his words, resulted in "private medicine's abandonment of the poor." As part of his analysis identifying the cause that, in his view, plays the dominant role, Hilfiker must consider and evaluate all possible causes as well:

> There are of course many complex factors that have precipitated private medicine's abandonment of the poor. The urbanization and anonymity of the poor, the increasingly technological nature of medicine and the bureaucratic capriciousness of public medical assistance —all these serve to make private physicians feel less responsible for the medical needs of those who cannot afford the going rate.
>
> But the cause that is probably most obvious to the lay public is singularly invisible to the medical community: Medicine is less and less rooted in service and more and more based in money. With many wonderful exceptions all over the country, American physicians as a whole have been turned away from the ideals of service by an idolatry of money. Physicians are too seldom servants and too often entrepreneurs. A profitable practice has become primary. The change has been so dramatic and so far-reaching that most of us do not even recognize that a transformation has taken place, that there might be an alternative. We simply take it for granted that economic factors will be primary even for the physician.

In his article Hilfiker draws on his own experience as a practicing physician to illustrate how a variety of pressures transformed him from a caring physician into a businessman concerned only with the efficient management of his office and medical practice. The fact that the average medical student can accrue up to $100,000 of debt, coupled with the increasing cost of malpractice insurance and the enormous amounts of money necessary to set up and maintain an office are identified by Hilfiker as contributory causes in transforming the practice of medicine into just another profit-oriented business. Hilfiker then cites a range of effects (including the use of ever more costly "procedures" and the assembly-line approach of seeing thirty or more patients a day) that dramatically illustrate the negative consequences for patients when doctors become little more than businessmen.

Causal arguments can get off the track when writers confuse sequence with causation. Events that merely follow each other in sequence should not be confused with true cause and effect. Simply because A preceded B does not necessarily mean that A caused B. This confusion of antecedent or correlation with causation is called the *post hoc* fallacy, from the Latin *post hoc, ergo propter hoc* (literally, after this, therefore because of this).

Darrell Huff and Irving Geis, mentioned earlier, provide an amusing example of one form the *post hoc* fallacy can take:

> As an instance of the nonsense or spurious correlation that is a real statistical fact, someone has gleefully pointed to this: There is a close relationship between the salaries of Presbyterian ministers in Massachusetts and the price of rum in Havana.
>
> Which is the cause and which the effect? In other words, are the ministers benefiting from the rum trade or supporting it? All right. That's so farfetched that it is ridiculous at a glance. But watch out for other applications of post hoc logic that differ from this one only in being more subtle. In the case of the ministers and the rum it is easy to see that both figures are growing because of the influence of a third factor: the historic and world-wide rise in the price level of practically everything.

The confusion here is based on the erroneous assumption that simply because two events occur in the same time period there is also a cause and effect relationship. Many common superstitions are a result of this fallacy. For example, a person who walked under a ladder and then, ten minutes later, tripped and fell, might attribute the fall to walking under the ladder. To avoid falling for the *post hoc* fallacy, writers need to examine every cause and effect relationship carefully.

Writers should also be wary of attempting to oversimplify events that have complex causes. A common error is to mistake a necessary condition for a sufficient one. A necessary condition is one that must be present if the effect is to occur. For example, if electricity is considered a cause for light in an electric bulb, then without electricity there can be no light. A sufficient conition is a condition in whose presence the effect will always occur. Using our example, a worn filament is a sufficient condition for the light to go out. But a worn filament is not a necessary condition; the light could also go out if the power lines were down due to a storm. To take another example, most people would agree that buying a lottery ticket is a necessary condition to winning a prize. That is, you cannot win without having bought a ticket. It is equally obvious that buying a lottery ticket, while necessary, does not of itself cause one to win the prize. By contrast, buying a lottery ticket with the correct numbers is a sufficient condition to cause one to win the prize — that is, it is a condition that will always ensure that the effect will occur.

Causes and effects can occur in connecting sequences of "chains of causation," where each effect itself becomes the cause of a further effect. Causal arguments must demonstrate how each cause produces an effect that then acts as a cause of a further effect. This type of causal argument often takes the form of a conditional prediction: if X happens then Y will occur.

For example, Carl Sagan's argument in "The Nuclear Winter" (*Parade Magazine* [1983]) is developed around the following conditional claim:

Nuclear winter would be the result of even a small-scale nuclear war.

Sagan must show how an effect that has never been observed could be produced. Most people would not be convinced that the most devastating effect of even a small-scale nuclear war would be mass starvation. Yet Sagan's research leads him to conclude that this would be the ultimate consequence of any nuclear exchange:

In the baseline case, land temperatures, except for narrow strips of coastline, dropped to minus 25 Celsius (minus 13 degree Fahrenheit) and stayed below freezing for months—even for a summer war . . . Because the temperatures would drop so catastrophically, virtually all crops and farm animals, at least in the Northern Hemisphere, would be destroyed, as would most varieties of uncultivated or domesticated food supplies. Most of the human survivors would starve.

In Sagan's analysis, the fatal chain of consequences that even a small-scale nuclear war would produce begins with (1) dust lofted into the atmosphere, producing (2) a greater than expected drop in global temperatures, lasting (3) much longer than anticipated, and resulting in (4) the extinction of crops and animals and (5) mass starvation among human beings. In the article from which this passage is taken Sagan draws on many kinds of evidence, including the computer's ability to simulate hypothetical scenarios, to support the "nuclear-winter" hypothesis. Because of the hypothetical nature of this thesis, Sagan is obligated to show how the ecosystem is much more vulnerable—and the consequences of even a small-scale nuclear war much more extreme—than scientists previously believed.

VALUE CLAIMS MAKE VALUE JUDGMENTS

As distinct from arguments that debate matters of fact, value arguments apply ethical, moral, aesthetic, or utilitarian criteria to produce judgments that measure a subject against an ideal standard. For example, consider the following cases:

A sportswriter evaluates two teams and says that one has a better chance of winning the pennant because of better pitching.
A writer for *Consumer Reports* evaluates different brands of microwave ovens and selects the best.

A student writes an analysis arguing that the latest novel by a
writer is her best work yet.
A critic writes a review evaluating a new restaurant, movie, or
software program.

In all these cases, the writers are not merely expressing personal taste,
but are making a reasoned judgment based on identifiable standards of
value. Writers of value arguments must demonstrate that the standard
being used as the yardstick is an appropriate one, and must provide a
convincing argument with reasons and evidence in order to influence the
readers' judgment and perception of the subject. For example, a writer
who contended that bilingual education was or was not worthwhile, or
that euthanasia was or was not immoral, would be obligated to present
clearly the ideal standard against which the subject was being evaluated.
Arguments that evaluate whether something is good or bad must provide (1) sufficient and verifiable evidence of a phenomenon and (2) an
appropriate standard by which to measure value.

Writers frequently use comparison and contrast as a rhetorical strategy in organizing value arguments. Whether the comparison is between
two books, two candidates, two kinds of automobiles, or any two subjects in the same class or category, evaluations are structured so that one
choice is clearly seen as superior to the other when the two are directly
compared. To get a more accurate idea of how writers use this strategy,
consider the following argument by Jennifer James, a social anthropologist. James presents her case in the article "The Prostitute as Victim"
(1978):

> Violations of the prostitution statutes account for approximately 30%
> of most women's jail populations. Convicted prostitutes serve long
> jail sentences compared to other misdemeanants such as shoplifters
> or those involved in larceny or assault. The judicial attitude repre-
> sented by these sentencing patterns has no justification when consid-
> ered in reference to the traditional legal concerns of danger to person
> or property loss. Nor does the large number of women arrested for
> prostitution indicate the commitment of the criminal justice system to
> an effective realistic campaign to eliminate prostitution. Each act of
> prostitution, after all, requires at least two participants: a seller and a
> buyer. Despite this incontrovertible fact, the arrest rate for customers
> is only two for every eight prostitutes arrested (*Uniform Crime Reports,*
> 1976). It has been estimated that about 20% of the male population
> has some contact with prostitutes, and yet the prostitutes seem to
> bear virtually the entire weight of legal reprisals. Since the prostitu-
> tion laws in almost every state are neutral on their face, holding the
> prostitute and the customer equally culpable, the figures prove that
> prostitutes are the victims of discriminatory law enforcement.
>
> The traditional justification for discriminatory enforcement of
> prostitution laws was stated by K. David in 1937:
>> The professional prostitute, being a social outcast, may be

periodically punished without disturbing the usual course of society; no one misses her while she is serving out her term — no one, at least, about whom society has any concern. The man [customer], however, is something more than a partner in an immoral act; he discharges important social and business relations. . . . He cannot be imprisoned without deranging society. . . .

In this society, there are some behaviors which are considered acceptable for men but not for women. Prostitutes are women who are simultaneously rewarded and punished for choosing to earn their living through patterns of behavior that are unacceptable for members of their sex. In other words, prostitutes are the victims of sex-role stereotyping. . . . Men who purchase the services of prostitutes are still considered normal (nondeviant), even though their action may be seen as unpalatable, or even immoral, according to the personal standards of the observer. . . . Men are expected to have a wide variety of sexual needs and to actively seek fulfillment of those needs. As part of that search, men are allowed to illegally purchase the sexual services of women with relative impunity, as arrest statistics demonstrate. . . . The provisions of sexual services to males by women is, in contrast, clearly labeled deviant. Males break few social rules in patronizing a prostitute; females break almost all the rules in becoming prostitutes. Streetwalkers, in particular, place themselves at the wrong end of the whore-madonna spectrum: they accept money for sex, they are promiscuous, they are not in love with their customers, they are not subtle, and they engage in "abnormal" or deviant sex acts — acts which "respectable" women are not expected to accept.

James identifies the essential issue as one of equal treatment under the law. Her strategy is to contrast how the law treats prostitutes in comparison with their clients. The fact that the arrest rate for customers is only "two for every eight prostitutes arrested" indicates that prostitutes are discriminated against by being treated much more harshly than their customers. James then speculates on why this discriminatory attitude exists and finds that it has its roots in the different value judgments society makes about the social worth of the prostitute in comparison with the presumed higher value of her customer as a contributing member of society.

Although the concept of equal protection under the law is a value standard with which few people would disagree, it is important to recognize that different people bring different value standards to bear within the same situation and therefore may produce very different value judgments. For example, a solution that might be perfectly acceptable on pragmatic or utilitarian grounds might be unacceptable or even repugnant when judged by moral or aesthetic standards. For this reason, it is important for readers to identify the particular value system the writer is using as a criterion.

Value systems shape perceptions by influencing what people see, how they make sense out of what they see, and, most important, how they interpret what they see. When people bring different value systems to the same situation, they perceive and understand the same events in radically different ways. Personal feelings, expectations, and interests strongly influence how people interpret events.

Michael Novak makes this point in his article "The Poor and Latin America" (*The Atlantic Monthly* [March 1982]):

> Latin Americans do not value the same moral qualities North Americans do. The two cultures see the world quite differently. Latin Americans seem to feel inferior to North Americans in practical matters but superior in spiritual ones. In Latin American experience, powerful personages control almost everything. From this experience, it is easy to imagine that the whole world must work this way, and to project such expectations upon North America. It must be said, then, that relations between North and South America are emotional as well as economic. The "Catholic" aristocratic ethic of Latin America places more emphasis on luck, heroism, status, and *figura* than the relatively "Protestant" ethic of North America, which values diligence, regularity, and the responsible seizure of opportunity. Given two such different ways of looking at the world, intense love-hate relations are bound to develop.

As Novak's article illustrates, we should try to become aware of the extent to which value systems, our own and those of others, influence and shape our perceptions. This is crucial in arguments when we discover our own perception differs drastically from that of others when we are seeing the same events. In these cases, we need to take a close look at the reasons and evidence that support the beliefs and decide whether the information on which the beliefs are based is reliable. This is one important function value arguments perform: they challenge us to examine underlying assumptions that ordinarily remain unquestioned by forcing us to justify our view of the world.

POLICY CLAIMS MAKE RECOMMENDATIONS

In addition to arguments that characterize situations, make value judgments, or seek to establish causes or consequences, there are arguments that recommend policy changes. Many arguments in law and politics are of this kind, as are proposals in the fields of business, science, and technology.

A policy argument concerns itself first with establishing that a problem exists that is serious enough to need solving. The writer then analyzes the problem to discover the causes of the problem, puts forward a specific solution to the problem, and creates an argument that demonstrates that the proposed solution is workable (that is, can be implemented) and is superior to other proposed solutions.

Frequently the proposed solution is put in the form of a recommendation using the terms *should, ought,* or *must.* For example, Siegfried and Therese Englemann in their book *Give Your Child a Superior Mind* (1981) argue that "parents *should* provide pre-school academic instruction for their children."

Likewise, an advocate for teaching creationism in the public schools might phrase the recommendation thus: "public schools *ought* to give equal weight to the teaching of creationism and the theory of evolution in the classrooms."

So, too, a staunch backer of drug testing might propose: "athletes competing in international sports events *must* be tested for steroids and other drugs."

Ideally, a policy argument should demonstrate that the way things are currently being done is producing negative consequences and that the recommended action or policy change would be capable of producing better results. For example, Dorothy W. Nelson, a judge in the United States Court of Appeals for the Ninth Circuit, in an article titled "Abolish the Blight of Plea Bargaining" (*The Christian Science Monitor* [February 12, 1979]) provides the following analysis to support her policy claim that "plea bargaining is a distorted and disgraceful blight on our criminal justice system which ought to be abolished":

> The prison conversations, a review of the empirical data available, and a conviction that there are alternative procedures available lead me to conclude that plea bargaining is a distorted and disgraceful blight on our criminal justice system which ought to be abolished. Admittedly, it would be folly to declare the abolition of plea bargaining merely to have the practice displaced to an earlier stage of the criminal justice system, or increased reliance on tacit rather than explicit plea bargaining. It is possible, however, to eliminate the bargaining or "bartering," as some would term it, through an expanded form of the felony preliminary hearing.

Nelson first defines the nature of the problem, demonstrates that it is serious enough to need solving, modifies her claim to take into account the counterclaim about the negative consequences of abolishing plea bargaining, and suggests a solution that, from her perspective, would provide a workable alternative to the current procedure.

Nelson's argument is typical in that it employs a problem–solution format. The author first defines the problem to be solved, carefully assesses alternative solutions (which she does in the full article), and then recommends and defends a particular course of action that will solve the problem more effectively than will other proposed ways.

Besides meeting the specific requirements of the problem-solving situation, solutions must be feasible, effective, and attractive to the audience to whom they are proposed. A writer of policy arguments must be sensitive to the needs and values of those whom he or she is attempting to influence. The audience must feel that the writer understands both the problem's causes and its consequences, is familiar with the history of past efforts to deal with it, and is united with them in their desire to remedy the problem.

For example, notice how Richard N. Goodwin devotes much of his article "Money Has Corrupted the Legislative Process" (*The Los Angeles Times* [December 12, 1985]) to demonstrating that a serious problem exists whose solution should be a matter of vital concern to his audience. He presents evidence to show that American government is being held hostage by special interest political action committee (PAC) groups. Implicit in Goodwin's article is the impression that he identifies with his reading public and is speaking out as any one of them might if he or she knew all the facts of the situation:

> Power of wealth has [with honorable exceptions] achieved dominion over the legislative process and, hence, the conduct of democratic government. . . .
>
> The principal instrument of this dominion is the political action committee, or PAC, which collects money from its members and gives it to the constitutional guardians of the public trust — members of Congress and aspirants to Congress.
>
> Most of these committees belong to economic interests that have an important stake in the actions of government — insurance companies, real-estate developers, chemical and drug companies, for example. In less than a decade they have become the single most important force in the contest for federal office. . . . PAC money is neither a "gift" nor a "contribution."
>
> It is an investment. The PACs expect recipients to give careful, and usually favorable, consideration to legislation that affects their economic well-being. Being experienced investors, they generally get what they expect. . . .
>
> The meaning of the PACs is clear. Congress is not *influenced* by special interests. Congress does not *represent* special interests. Congress is *owned* by special interests. Morally the system is bribery. It is not criminal only because those who make the laws are themselves accomplices. Government is for sale. But the bids are sealed, and the prices are very high. There is an easy way out: Eliminate PACs. We should place a rigorous ceiling on all congressional campaigns, allocate public funds to finance campaigns and require television stations — the most costly component of modern political campaigns — to give a specified amount of air time to candidates.

As Goodwin's article illustrates, persuading readers to accept a recommendation not only means telling them what the best solution would be but also showing them through specific examples or hypothetical scenarios just how the solution would operate in practice. A writer who helps the reader visualize how the solution would work goes a long way toward refuting objections that the proposed solution might not be feasible, effective, or attractive, is too costly, or simply will not solve the problem.

It is important to keep in mind that because policy arguments are basically designed to motivate people to act, or to approve of an action that has been taken, the writer must make every attempt to make the audience aware of just how serious the problem really is. It must be serious enough to warrant doing something about it. For this reason, writers often begin by pointing out the negative consequences of failing to solve the problem and also provide an account of past attempts to solve the same problem.

Next, writers propose a solution and evaluate it against alternative solutions, giving sound reasons for rejecting the alternative solutions. It is important that the writer be willing to admit honestly that difficulties could arise in carrying out his or her proposed solution and be willing to modify it in light of valid suggestions made by others.

Since policy arguments require not merely agreement, but action on the part of the audience, it is crucial for writers to try to anticipate how readers may react to the proposed solution. By putting yourself into the position of those you wish to persuade, you can generate a list of objections that might be made to your proposed solution. Would your critics reject your recommendation on any of the following grounds: your proposed action is too expensive, inefficient, unworkable, impractical, disrupting to the status quo, or unacceptable on the grounds that it is morally offensive or aesthetically unappealing?

Equally important as any substantive concerns, writers of policy arguments would be wise to adopt an appropriate tone for their argument. Usually the purposes of a policy argument are best served if the writer presents himself or herself as a reasonable person of good character who is well informed on the issue in question and who is sensitive to the needs and concerns of the audience.

Support

EVIDENCE

Every assertion or claim put forward in an argument should be supported by appropriate, authoritative, and timely evidence. Evidence can appear in a variety of forms, including examples drawn from personal experience, hypothetical cases, analogies, the testimony of experts, or statistical data. Readers expect that evidence cited to substantiate or refute assertions will be sound, accurate, and relevant, and that conclusions will be drawn logically from this evidence. Readers also expect that a writer arguing in support of a proposition will acknowledge and answer objections put forth by the opposing side in addition to providing compelling evidence to support his or her own position.

Examples Drawn from Personal Experience

Providing good examples is an essential part of effective argumentative writing. A single well-chosen example, or a range of illustrations, can provide clear cases which illustrate, document, and substantiate a writer's thesis. The report of a memorable incident, an account drawn from records, eyewitness reports, or a personal narrative account of a crucial incident, are all important ways examples can serve to document the authenticity of the writer's thesis. For example, Loren C. Eiseley begins his review of Rachel Carson's *Silent Spring*, "Using a Plague to Fight a Plague" (1962), by drawing on personal experience to underscore the issue that is at the heart of Carson's book — the threat the widespread use of chemical pesticide poses to the environment:

> A few days ago I stood amidst the marshes of a well-known wildlife refuge. As I studied a group of herons through my glasses, there floated by the margin of my vision the soapy, unsightly froth of a detergent discharged into the slough's backwaters from some source upstream. Here nature, at first glance, seemed green and uncontaminated. As I left, however, I could not help wondering how long it would be before seeping industrial wastes destroyed the water — life on which those birds subsisted — how long it would be before poisonous and vacant mudflats had replaced the chirping frogs and waving cattails I loved to visit. I thought also of a sparkling stream in the Middle West in which, as a small boy, I used to catch sunfish, but which today is a muddy, lifeless treacle filled with oil from a nearby pumping station. No living thing now haunts its polluted waters.
>
> These two episodes out of my experiences are trifling, however, compared with that virulent facet of man's activities treated in Rachel Carson's latest book. It is a devastating, heavily documented, relentless attack upon human carelessness, greed, and irresponsibility — an irresponsibility that has let loose upon man and the countryside a flood of dangerous chemicals in a situation which, as Miss Carson states, is without parallel in medical history. "No one," she adds, "yet knows what the ultimate consequences may be."

These observations serve to illustrate the thesis of Carson's book and provide a context for Eiseley's discussion. It is significant that ecological effects documented by Carson are also confirmed by Eiseley's observations made by him in two widely different areas of the country. His observations dramatize the consequences of chemical dumping and establish that the phenomenon identified by Carson has not occurred in just one section of the country; chemical pesticides pose a widespread threat to the environment.

One extremely effective way of substantiating a claim is by using a *case history* that is, an in-depth account of the experience of one person that typifies the experience of many people in the same situation. The following account drawn from Michael Harrington's acclaimed sociological study, *The Other America: Poverty in the United States* (1969), uses one woman's experiences to typify the plight of a whole class of older citizens:

Sometimes in the course of an official Government report, a human being will suddenly emerge from the shadows of statistics and analyses. This happened in a summary statement of the Senate Subcommittee on the Problems of the Aged and Aging in 1960. Louise W— comes to life: Louise W—, age 73, lives by herself in a single furnished room on the third floor of a rooming house located in a substandard section of the city. In this one room, she cooks, eats and sleeps. She shares a bathroom with other lodgers. Widowed at 64, she has few friends remaining from her younger years. Those who do remain do not live near her, and it is difficult for her to see them. She feels that the other older men and women living in the same rooming house are not good enough for her company (conversations with these persons reveal that they have the same attitude, too: their fellow inhabitants are not good enough for them either).

And so she stays confined to her one room and the bathroom shared by nine other people. When the weather is warm enough, she ventures down the long flight of stairs about once a week for a walk to the corner and back. Louise W— is symbolic of a growing and intense problem in American society. The nation venerates youth, yet the proportion of the population over sixty-five years of age is increasing. For many of these older people, their declining years are without dignity. They have no function; they are sick; they are without money. Millions of them wear out the last days of their existence in small apartments, in rooming houses, in nursing homes.

This is no country for old men. The physical humiliation and the loneliness are real, but to them is added the indignity of living in a society that is obsessed by youth and tries to ignore age. These people are caught, as one witness before the Senate Committee testified, in a triple "chain of causality": they are plagued by ill health; they do not have enough money; and they are socially isolated. Some of them are new entrants to the world of the other America, drifting down from a working life of decent wages to an old age of dependency and social workers. A good many are old and poor because they were young and poor, middle-aged and poor. Taken together, they constitute a section of the culture of poverty with over 8,000,000 inhabitants.

The example of Louise W— serves as anecdotal proof that illustrates Harrington's claim that many of the elderly are among the most poverty-stricken people in the country. He shows, graphically and vividly, that many older people face a future very unlike the popular depiction of the "golden years."

Hypothetical Cases (Scenarios and "What if" Situations)

All examples need not be real. In some types of causal arguments where no real and observable effects can be cited as examples, the writer is obliged to show how an effect that has never been observed is possible or could be produced. In these circumstances, hypothetical examples are useful in clarifying possible future consequences. For example, in "The Case for Torture" (*Newsweek*, 1982). Michael Levin argues that in certain circumstances torture is "not merely permissible but morally mandatory." Levin uses a series of hypothetical examples to support this assertion. Levin's strategy is to begin with a very extreme hypothetical example of a terrorist who has "hidden an atomic bomb on Manhattan Island" in order to compel the reader to examine her own assumptions as to whether or not torture is, if ever, permissible:

Suppose a terrorist had hidden an atomic bomb on Manhattan Island which will detonate at noon on July 4 unless . . . (here follow the usual demands for money and release of his friends from jail). Suppose, further, that he is caught at 10 A.M. of the fateful day, but— preferring death to failure—won't disclose where the bomb is. What do we do? If we follow due process—wait for his lawyer, arraign him—millions of people will die. If the only way to save those lives is to subject the terrorist to the most excruciating possible pain, what grounds can there be for not doing so? I suggest there are none. In any case, I ask you to face the question with an open mind. Torturing the terrorist is unconstitutional? Probably. But millions of lives surely outweigh constitutionality. Torture is barbaric? Mass murder is far more barbaric. Indeed, letting millions of innocents die in deference to one who flaunts his guilt is moral cowardice, an unwillingness to dirty one's hands. If you caught the terrorist, could you sleep nights knowing that millions died because you couldn't bring yourself to apply the electrodes?

Once you concede that torture is justified in extreme cases, you have admitted that the decision to use torture is a matter of balancing innocent lives against the means needed to save them. You must now face more realistic cases involving more modest numbers. Someone plants a bomb on a jumbo jet. He alone can disarm it, and his demands cannot be met (or if they can, we refuse to set a precedent by yielding to his threats). Surely we can, we must, do anything to the extortionist to save the passengers. How can we tell 300, or 100, or 10 people who never asked to be put in danger, "I'm sorry, you'll have to die in agony, we just couldn't bring ourselves to . . . "

Here are the results of an informal poll about a third, hypothetical, case. Suppose a terrorist group kidnapped a newborn baby from a hospital. I asked four mothers if they would approve of torturing kidnappers if that were necessary to get their own newborns back. All said yes, the most "liberal" adding that she would administer it herself.

Levin's strategy is extremely effective. If a reader accepts the use of torture in some cases, then he or she would have to consider more seriously whether torture is appropriate in nonhypothetical cases in real life. If torture is acceptable (1) to save the lives of millions of people from an atomic bomb hidden by terrorists, or (2) to save a few hundred people from a terrorist bomb on a jumbo jet, or (3) to save the life of one newborn child from kidnappers, then the reader must confront the question as to when torture is *not* appropriate. Levin imaginatively uses these scenarios to probe the issue and to compel his readers to seriously consider his claim that "the decision to use torture is a matter of balancing innocent lives against the means necessary to save them." Note how Levin uses results of an "informal poll" to suggest that even apart from extreme hypothetical cases torture remains a viable option for those mothers whose children's lives are at stake. Levin's argumentative strategy is to work from extreme cases to more realistic ones, saying in effect, "If you agree with my first and second examples, then you must agree with my third." These invented episodes have the effect of provoking his audience to think beyond immediate responses and really consider whether or not torture is ever permissible.

Analogies

Analogies are useful for bringing out convincing similarities between ideas, situations, and people in order to persuade an audience that if two things are similar in a number of observed respects, they may well be similar in other ways as well. The distinguished philosopher David Hume observed that "in reality all arguments from experience are founded on the similarity which we discover among natural objects, and by which we are induced to expect effects similar to those which we have found to follow from such objects." Analogy is effective as a rhetorical strategy in that it persuades an audience if two subjects share a number of specific observable qualities then they may probably share some unobserved qualities as well.

Analogies are an unparalleled means of clarifying complex ideas and abstract concepts. For example, the historian Arnold J. Toynbee employs an unusual analogy in "Challenge and Response" (from *A Study of History* [1946]) to illuminate his thesis that societies become civilizations when their normal routine is challenged by an outside force. The crucial difference Toynbee discovered between primitive and higher cultures is that primitive societies remain static, whereas higher cultures respond creatively to challenge:

> Primitive societies as we know them by direct observation, may be likened to people lying torpid upon a ledge on a mountainside with a precipice below and a precipice above; civilizations may be likened to companions of these sleepers who have just risen to their feet and

have started to climb up the face of the cliff above . . . we can observe that, for every single one now strenuously climbing, twice that number . . . have fallen back onto the ledge defeated.

Toynbee's analogy of cliff climbers and ledge sitters is meant to reflect the contrast between dynamic civilizations on the one hand and stagnant cultures on the other. In his analogy, societies are represented by the dormant sleepers. The ledge below is the past they have risen above. The precipice above them is the next plateau they must reach to become flourishing civilizations. The analogy captures the readiness of some societies to risk a possible fall in order to leave the relative safety of the ledge and climb the precipice in search of the ledge above.

The preceding example illustrates one important aspect of creating effective analogies: every analogy is useful until the differences between the things being compared become greater than the similarities. Arguments based on analogy, however compelling, interesting, and imaginative the analogy might be, can only strive to demonstrate a high degree of probability, not absolute certainty. For this reason, the criteria for evaluating analogical arguments depend on comparing the number of respects in which the two subjects are said to be similar or analogous with the number of respects in which they are said to differ. A strong analogy will be persuasive to the extent that the number of qualities shared by two subjects far outweigh the differences. Correspondingly, many points of difference between the two subjects greatly weakens the analogical argument by reducing the audience's perception that the two things are probably alike in many ways.

In the law, strong analogies serve as proof. When lawyers cite previously decided cases as legal precedents to argue that a case in question should be decided along the lines of the earlier cases, they are reasoning from strong analogies. For example, a lawyer might cite the *Miranda* case (Supreme Court decision, 1966) as a precedent in arguing that the defendant in the present case should not be tried since he was not advised of his rights (as the *Miranda* decision requires). The use of legal precedent in the courtroom is a form of reasoning from analogy. Lawyers may argue that the present case should be dismissed since a previous case was also dismissed on the same grounds. Such straightforward reasoning assumes that enough similarities between two cases exist to support the claim that what was true of one case is also true of the other.

By contrast, weak or figurative analogies can clarify or illustrate, but cannot serve as evidence to support a claim. For example, a striking figurative analogy by Isaac Asimov in "Science and Beauty" (1983) dramatically clarifies his claim of an intimate and precarious interrelationship between all living things and their environment:

In fact, we can pursue the analogy. A man is composed of 50 trillion cells of a variety of types, all interrelated and interdependent. Loss of some of those cells, such as those making up an entire leg, will seriously handicap all the rest of the organism: serious damage to a relatively few cells in an organ, such as the heart or kidneys, may end by killing all 50 trillion.

In the same way, on a planetary scale, the chopping down of an entire forest may not threaten Earth's life in general, but it will produce serious changes in the life forms of the region and even in the nature of the water runoff and, therefore, in the details of geological structure.

Asimov's analogy is designed to persuade his readers that many parallels exist between the life processes of a person and the life processes of the planet Earth. Asimov's analogy is quite effective as a way of clarifying the issues involved and alerting the audience to the vulnerability of the planet to environmental disturbance.

To discover if you can tell whether an analogy is strong enough to support a claim, consider the following argument from "The Scourge of This Society Is Drug Abuse: Testing is Clearly an Idea Whose Time Has Come" (*Miami Herald*, March, 1986) by John Underwood:

> For if a drug test is an invasion of privacy, what is a blood test? A man's blood is certainly as private as his urine, and even if it might, in its course or of its type, communicate a deadly disease or produce a deformed child, the testing of it most assuredly requires an invasion. The common good, and every state in the union, nevertheless requires blood tests. Try to get a marriage license without one. Moreover, what is an eye test if not (by short extension of ACLU logic) an invasion of privacy? On the common sense basis that we already wreak havoc on our highways without allowing the physically disabled behind the wheels of our killer vehicles, the common good calls for eye tests. Try getting a driver's license without one.
>
> And what about the lie tests that are burgeoning in popularity as a means of screening security risks in both the government and private sectors? Is a lie test an invasion of privacy? Is a man's brain as sacred as his bladder, regardless of how much or little can be found in either? You betcha. What could be more intrusive than poking around in a man's thought processes. But we allow it. The common good demands it.

Underwood argues that drugs have caused such damage to society that civil liberties groups are wrong to stand in the way of drug testing. He argues by analogy that just as eye tests, blood tests, and lie detector tests are widely accepted even though they invade privacy, so widespread drug testing should be instituted although it admittedly is also an invasion of privacy.

On first reading, Underwood's use of an analogy seems rooted in real similarities in comparable situations. The analogy, however, breaks down in a number of respects: the results of blood tests and eye tests are used to diagnose illness or cite deficiencies which can then be remedied.

In other words, the results of these tests are used for the benefit of the person being tested. By contrast, a urinanalysis drug test has only one purpose, to identify a drug abuser to his or her employer or the government. The results are not used to benefit the person being tested and may even be used to the detriment of that person. In short, information derived from the test is used against the person being tested.

Lie detector tests seem to offer a closer analogy. Here, however, Underwood does not take into account the fact that the results from lie detector tests are not admissible as evidence in court. Thus, a crucial number of differences weaken his argument and greatly undercut the validity of his conclusion.

Testimony of Experts

The testimony of experts is an invaluable way of quickly demonstrating that the conclusions one has reached about a given issue are independently subscribed to by renowned authorities in the field. Writers rely on the opinion of authorities when their own ability to draw conclusions based on firsthand observations is limited. The authorities are presumed to have expertise based on many years of research and greater familiarity with the issues under investigation. The opinion of experts is no substitute for the process of reasoning by which you have arrived at your conclusion, but a well-known authority can add considerable weight to your opinion and a dimension of objective credibility to the argument.

When deciding whether to quote an authority consider the following guidelines:

1. The expert must be an authority in the field.
2. His or her testimony must be free from bias and result from free and open inquiry that is subject to public verification.
3. The opinion must be timely and not open to question on the grounds that it might have been true in the past but is no longer relevant.

For example, in "Ethical and Surgical Considerations in the Care of the Newborn with Congenital Abnormalities" (1982), by C. Everett Koop, a pediatric surgeon who was Surgeon General of the United States until 1989, Koop assails the medical profession for giving in to demands by families that treatment be withheld from newborns with severe birth defects:

> If any group of physicians knows what can be accomplished by surgery on the handicapped newborn—and the proper support of the patient and his family in subsequent years—it is pediatric surgeons. Drs. Anthony Shaw, Judson G. Randolph, and Barbara Manard surveyed members of the surgical section of the American Academy of Pediatrics in reference to the management of newborns with handicaps. Of the 400 pediatric surgeons queried, 267 (67 percent)

completed questionnaires. A separate group of 308 pediatricians completed 190 questionnaires (62 percent). The first question was, "Do you believe that the life of each and every newborn infant should be saved if it is within our ability to do so?" Eighty percent of those surgeons with my kind of background answered no.

Although the pediatricians quoted by Koop hold an opinion opposite to his own, he cites their opinion as evidence precisely because these pediatricians are experts in their field, their opinion is timely, and what they say can be objectively verified.

Three Forms Expert Opinion Can Take. The opinion of experts offers an interpretation of a set of facts. The interpretation can take one of three forms: the expert (1) points out a causal connection, (2) offers a solution to a problem, or (3) offers a prediction about the future. Correspondingly, writers can use these "expert opinions" to support a causal claim (that is, to document the existence of causal correlation or connection), to support a proposed solution to a problem, or to authenticate the reliability of a prediction.

1. Pointing out a causal connection. For example, a writer wishing to support a claim that where you live influences your chances of getting cancer might quote Samuel S. Epstein, a professor of occupational and environmental medicine at the University of Illinois Medical Center, in "The Cancer-Producing Society" (*Science For the People* [July 1976]):

> A recent National Cancer Institute (NCI) atlas on cancer mortality rates, in different counties, has demonstrated marked geographical clustering of rates for various organs in the U.S. with populations in heavily industrialized areas. Such data suggest associations between cancer rates in the general community and the proximity of residence to certain industries.

The writer would probably mention Epstein's credentials and, to further enhance the credibility of his source, might cite the fact that Epstein's efforts were responsible for the enactment of legislation to control toxic substances.

2. Offering a solution to a problem. Besides citing experts to document the existence of causal connections, writers look to authorities for solutions to problems. For example, the philosopher Peter Singer's article "Rich and Poor" (1979) might be cited to support an argument that rich nations should help poor ones since they can do so at a relatively low cost to themselves:

> Death and disease apart, absolute poverty remains a miserable condition of life, with inadequate food, shelter, clothing, sanitation,

health services and education. According to World Bank estimates which define absolute poverty in terms of income levels insufficient to provide adequate nutrition, something like 800 million people — almost 40 percent of the people of developing countries — live in absolute poverty. Absolute poverty is probably the principal cause of human misery today.

This is the background situation, the situation that prevails on our planet all the time. It does not make headlines. People died from malnutrition and related diseases yesterday, and more will die tomorrow. The occasional droughts, cyclones, earthquakes and floods that take the lives of tens of thousands in one place and at one time are more newsworthy. They add greatly to the total amount of human suffering; but it is wrong to assume that when there are no major calamities reported, all is well.

The problem is not that the world cannot produce enough to feed and shelter its people. People in the poor countries consume, on average, 400 lbs. of grain a year, while North Americans average more than 2000 lbs. The difference is caused by the fact that in the rich countries we feed most of our grain to animals, converting it into meat, milk and eggs. Because this is an inefficient process, wasting up to 95 percent of the food value of the animal feed, people in rich countries are responsible for the consumption of far more food than those in poor countries who eat few animal products. If we stopped feeding animals on grains, soybeans and fishmeal the amount of food saved would — if distributed to those who need it — be more than enough to end hunger throughout the world.

Note how the expert opinion here takes the form of a solution offered to the problem of world hunger.

3. Making a prediction. A third form in which the testimony of authorities can be used to support a claim is as a prediction. For example, a writer who argued against continued reliance on fossil fuels, because of the resulting increase in carbon dioxide concentration in the air, might quote the opinion of the meteorologist Harold W. Bernard, Jr., from *The Greenhouse Effect* (1980):

CO_2 allows sunshine to heat the earth but then traps much of the heat near the earth's surface, rather than permitting it to radiate back to space. This *greenhouse* effect warms the earth. This is not a problem, of course, as long as the amount of CO_2 in the air remains fairly constant; the amounts of incoming sunshine and outgoing heat remain in balance, and our climate remains relatively comfortable.

However, the amount of atmospheric CO_2 is increasing, and most scientists fear that this may lead to a significant warming of the earth's climate. Current estimates suggest that CO_2 induced warming may account for about a 1.8° F rise in global temperature by early next century. Within a hundred years, global warming could be on the order of 11° F, with temperature increases in polar regions as much as three times that.

The opinion of a meteorologist provides a highly credible source for the prediction of how increasing atmospheric carbon dioxide levels would lead to major alterations in weather patterns that would drastically affect climate (as the United States began to witness in the unusually hot and dry summer of 1988) and perhaps melt part of the polar ice caps resulting in flooding of low-lying coastal areas on all continents. Keep in mind that the opinion of experts, however credible, is still only an interpretation of a set of facts. Other authorities might presumably reach diametrically opposite conclusions from the same evidence. This is why an argument should never be based on the opinion of experts alone. The writer should first create an independent, well-reasoned argument that can stand on its own and only then add the testimony of experts to strengthen the case.

Statistics

Statistical evidence is among the most compelling kinds of proof a writer can offer to support a thesis. To be effective, statistical data should be drawn from recent data and be as up-to-date as possible. It is important that statistics come from reliable and verifiable sources such as the United States Bureau of the Census, the Bureau of Labor, documented surveys conducted by well-established research centers or universities, or from well-known polling organizations like those of Lou Harris, Burns and Roper, and George Gallup. Statistical data are useful in many kinds of argument because of the ease with which comparative differences can be evaluated in quantifiable form. For example, in an argument that the insanity defense is little more than a legal ploy mostly used to favor white, upper-middle-class defendants, Jonathan Rowe, in "Why Liberals Should Hate the Insanity Defense," (*The Washington Monthly* [May 1984]), cites available statistics to prove that the insanity defense is not employed in the majority of prosecutions:

> The insanity defense looms a good deal larger in our minds than it does in actual life. Somewhere between 1,000 and 2,000 criminals make use of it each year, or about 1 percent to 2 percent of felonies that go to trial (over 90 percent in many jurisdictions are plea-bargained before trial). The issue is important not because it arises frequently, but because it tends to arise in the most serious crimes: think of Son of Sam, for example, or the Hillside Strangler. Such people tend to be dangerous, and their trials attract so much publicity that they put our entire system of justice to a test.

It is important for Rowe to establish that the insanity defense is only rarely used since his argument recommends abolishing it in its present form. The way statistical evidence is used will depend on the nature of the claim. Evidence in the form of statistics may provide stronger support for a writer's claim than anecdotal cases or hypothetical examples.

Statistics are especially useful in arguments where writers use inductive reasoning (drawing an inference from specific cases) to support a generalization extrapolated from a representative sampling of all the evidence that might be examined. As with other uses of evidence in inductive reasoning, writers must be careful not to draw conclusions, even from reliable, objectively verifiable statistics, that go so far beyond what the available evidence warrants as to seem improbable. Perhaps the most famous illustration of unwarranted generalization from a relatively small sample was the erroneous prediction in the 1948 presidential election that the Republican governor of New York, Thomas E. Dewey, would definitely defeat the incumbent Democrat, Harry S Truman. Unfortunately for the pollsters, the poll on which this prediction was made was drawn from an inadequate sample and did not represent the entire voting population. Since any prediction based on polls is essentially an inference drawn from a number of individual cases, this claim or conclusion will become more probable as the size of the sample becomes greater. An inference, therefore, is a generalization capable of being expressed in quantitative or statistical terms. For example, William J. Darby (whose study we have looked at earlier in this chapter as an example of a causal argument) in "The Benefits of Drink" (*Human Nature* [1978]) cites a study of 120,000 patients that discovered moderate drinkers were 30 percent less likely to have heart attacks than were teetotalers:

> A recent study by Arthur L. Klatsky and his colleagues at the Kaiser-Permanente Medical Center in Oakland, California, offers new evidence that moderate drinking may serve as a deterrent to heart attacks. They studied 464 patients who had been hospitalized with a first myocardial infarction (heart attack) and discovered that an unusually large proportion were teetotalers. Their curiosity aroused, Klatsky and his colleagues evaluated the medical histories of 120,000 patients and found that moderate alcohol users were 30 percent less likely to have heart attacks than were non-drinking patients or matched controls or so-called risk controls — people who suffer from diabetes, hypertension, obesity, high serum cholesterol, or who smoke. (All of these factors are associated with increased risk of heart attacks.)

Notice how the conclusion uses statistics to quantify the generalization as to the mitigating effects of moderate drinking. In essence, the writer is saying, "Based on these 120,000 instances, I'm reasonably certain that similar results would be obtained in comparable studies on other groups of patients."

Three Types of Averages: The Arithmetic Mean, Median, and the Mode. When a writer supports a claim by referring to the "average" he or she is purposely selecting a specific value to represent the qualities of a whole aggregate of things. But it is important for the reader to realize that there is more than one type of average and to know the writer has used the right kind to support his or her claim. There are three main types of averages, called (1) the *mean,* (2) the *median,* and (3) the *mode.* Each has its own characteristics and the values they represent can, in different situations, be quite different from one another. The most commonly used kind of average is the *arithmetic mean*—or, as it is commonly called, the mean. To calculate it, you simply add up all the numerical values and divide by the total number. The resulting average is the arithmetic mean.

1. *The arithmetic mean.* One example of the mean might be in baseball, where a player's batting average shows statistically how often the batter has successfully hit the ball in comparison with the total number of times he has had at bat. While this kind of an average is useful for giving a sense of where the "center of gravity" of any set (total number of times at bat, in this case) is located, the useful information drawn from this type of average can be distorted by very large or very small instances averaged in with all the others. For example, a brokerage firm, in order to recruit account executive trainees, advertises that the average starting salary for new employees is $36,000 a year. Only later might a new account executive discover that the $36,000 was derived by averaging in the $108,000 starting salary of a senior account executive with ten years' experience (transferring in from another firm) along with the $18,000 starting salary of four new account executive trainees. Here, the average of $36,000 is reached by adding $108,000 + (4 × $18,000) (equaling $180,000) divided by the five new employees.

2. *The median.* Other ways of measuring the average would have provided prospective employees with a much more realistic figure of what starting salary they could expect. One of these more accurate kinds of averages is the median. The median is usually the central value in a set of values. The median also establishes a dividing line that separates higher from lower values in a set of numbers. In the preceding case, the median starting salary would be $18,000 (while the average or mean was $36,000). As the following list shows, the median establishes a dividing line with two salaries above and two salaries below:

$108,000
$18,000
$18,000 (the median)
$18,000
$18,000

3. *The mode.* Another way of arriving at an average that is useful for interpretive purposes is the mode. The mode is the value that occurs most frequently in any series of numbers. In the preceding case, more new employees (four out of five) start at $18,000 a year than any other amount; hence, $18,000 is the modal income. In this case, the median and the mode are both more reliable indicators for a prospective new

employee than the more commonly relied upon average arithmetical mean. This case illustrates how important it is for readers to understand what kind of average writers are using to substantiate a claim. Keep in mind that the three uses of the word *average* in the preceding example all draw different conclusions from the exact same information. The median is a much more representative measure than the mean or average because in any example extremely high or extremely low readings on the scale will distort the average but not the median. The mode is a good way to keep track of the frequency and occurrence of any phenomenon.

Using Charts and Graphs. Evidence drawn from statistical data can be expressed and presented in charts, graphs, or percentages. The reader should determine whether conclusions drawn from statistics are consistent with other evidence in the argument.

Statistical information can be represented in a variety of graphic forms. For example, Figure 2.1 shows how the statistical breakdown of responses to the question "Should people who are carriers of genetic diseases be allowed to have children?" might be represented in a *pie chart.*

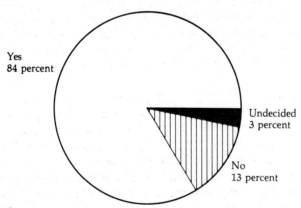

FIGURE 2.1
Should People Who Are Carriers of
Genetic Diseases Be Allowed to
Have Children? (Source: Adapted
from Lou Harris, Inside Ameria,
Vintage Books, 1987, p. 139.
Business Week/Harris Poll
conducted by Lou Harris &
Associates for Business Week, *Nov.*
1–4, 1985—national cross-section
of 1,254 adults.)

Statistical information can also appear in a *bar chart*. Figure 2.2 shows how the answer to the question "Would you engage in illegal insider trading if you got a tip?" might be shown.

The way statistical information is presented in graphic form can create, intentionally or unintentionally, a misleading impression. Examine the way the following two line graphs represent the exact same information. The first graph (Figure 2.3) is designed to create the impression that not much is going on: over a twelve month period the line marking changes in millions of dollars barely manages to creep up from January to December.

Now look at the way the second graph (Figure 2.4) represents the same facts. By making the vertical axis cover a fraction of what it covered in the first graph, an erroneous impression is created by the way the graph line zooms into the stratosphere. From this graph, it appears that millions of dollars have been made. For these reasons, it is important to look at the scale used on each axis of a graph.

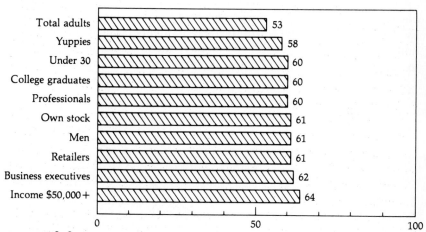

FIGURE 2.2
Would You Engage in Illegal Insider Trading If You Got A Tip? (Source: Adapted from Lou Harris, Inside America, Vintage Books, *1987, p. 110. Business Week/Harris Poll conducted by Lou Harris & Associates for* Business Week, *August 5–11, 1986—national cross section of 1,248 adults.)*

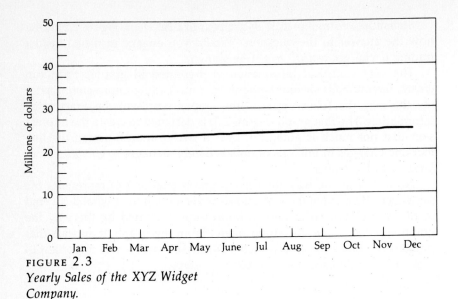

FIGURE 2.3
*Yearly Sales of the XYZ Widget
Company.*

The context in which statistics are presented is important. For example, the National Safety Council urges people to buckle up their seat belts by announcing "80 percent of all fatal accidents occur five miles from home." Reading this, you're liable to have the mistaken impression that the area surrounding your house is more dangerous than other areas

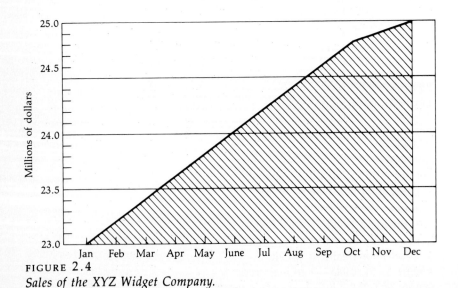

FIGURE 2.4
Sales of the XYZ Widget Company.

where you drive. Do you literally have to don a helmet and a flak jacket along with your seat belt whenever you enter this "danger zone"? What this public service announcement neglects to add is that 80 percent of *all* driving is done within five miles of where you live, which explains why 80 percent of all accidents, fatal and otherwise, occur in this area. The statistics themselves are true but a proper context for evaluating what they mean has been omitted.

To evaluate the validity of a survey, readers should be aware of the size of the sample used to compile the data and the methods used to assure a fair cross section of the population under study. Opinion can be manipulated through seemingly impressive statistics where the sampling procedure used is subtly biased to support a preconceived opinion. For example, someone who reads that "nine out of ten dentists who recommend chewing gum, recommend XYZ gum" will probably overlook the key phrase "who recommend chewing gum." The statistics themselves might be true, but the sample has been skewed to survey only those dentists who recommend chewing gum, an atypical and miniscule subgroup of all dentists.

The most reliable technique for avoiding an error in sampling is to make sure the poll or study surveys a representative cross section of all those who might be polled. To ensure fairness, the sample must be random so that even if every individual cannot be polled, each member of the population has exactly the same chance of being included in the sample as any other.

This type of sampling procedure relies upon probability principles. It is implemented by dividing the population into separate categories or *strata*. People interviewed are selected solely on a chance basis within each stratified category (for example, people who live in a certain part of town, or who earn a certain amount of money, or have reached a certain level of education). The theory behind probability sampling is really quite straightforward. If one had a large barrel containing 10,000 marbles, half of which were red and half of which were blue, and wished to draw a probability sample of 200 marbles, one might draw the first marble while blindfolded to make sure that the marbles all stood an equal chance of being drawn. The barrel would be shaken after each trial to ensure that in subsequent drawings all the marbles still had an equal chance of being selected. The law of probability states that if this procedure were repeated an infinite number of times, the 200 marbles selected would be fairly close to a 50–50 division, with approximately 100 of them being red and 100 of them being blue. The next most likely combination would be either 99 red and 101 blue or 99 blue and 101 red. The next most likely combination after that would be 98 red and 102 blue or 98 blue and 102 red, and so on. The most unlikely combination would produce 200 marbles that were either all red or all blue.

For the same reason, if each member of a population being surveyed has an equal chance of being selected, probability theory states that the sample will wind up being sufficiently representative to provide an accurate index of the whole population. In practice, the expense of surveying a large number of people means that the size of the sample is frequently less than might be optimally desirable since the larger the sample the smaller the sampling error that can be expected. *Sampling error* refers to the degree to which the results in the sample can be expected to differ from what the results would be if everyone in the population had been selected. It is expressed in terms of a range of percentage points above and below a reported percentage. For example, a survey based on 1,000 interviews might show that a candidate for governor might expect to be supported by 50 percent of the population. The margin of sampling error might be reported as plus or minus 4 percent. This means that if everyone in the population had been interviewed, rather than only 1,000, the actual results might see the candidate supported by as few as 46 percent of the people or as many as 54 percent. If the election were really close, a completely different outcome could be possible within the sampling error.

Therefore, any sampling procedure that automatically excludes any portion of the population is going to produce unrepresentative results of the kind that led pollsters to predict erroneously that Dewey would defeat Truman in the 1948 presidential election. The surveys that are used as evidence must be ones in which great efforts were made to ensure that all parts of the population are represented and not some arbitrarily selected group. It is also important to determine that those drawing up the survey have no vested interest in the outcome.

Thus, statistics play an important role in arguments where claims must be substantiated by reference to a number of cases where it would be impractical to test a whole population. At the same time, readers of arguments must be aware of the dangers of accepting statistics at face value without understanding both the procedures and the motives of those who gathered and interpreted the data.

Warrants

In everyday speech a "warranted" or "unwarranted" conclusion refers to the fact that some ways of connecting claims with supporting evidence are legitimate whereas others are not. For this reason, a third important element, in addition to the claim and the support, in understanding arguments, is the warrant. All claims are based on warrants or underlying assumptions. For an argument to be persuasive, both the writer and the audience must share the same underlying assumptions or beliefs regarding the issue. Moreover, the audience must agree with, or at least let pass unchallenged, the idea that a particular kind of evidence can be used in a specific way to support the claim. The warrant actually functions to guarantee the relationship between the claim and the support. Warrants guarantee (the ancient form of the word *guarantee* is *warrant*) that the evidence offered can really be used to support the claim in question.

Warrants provide a means of testing how the facts (in the form of statistics, real or hypothetical examples, expert opinion, and so on) are connected to a particular claim. If the support offered to prove the claim is relevant, then the warrant (in the form of a statute, precedent, rule, or principle) authorizes the writer to move from the evidence to the conclusion.

Warrants can take a variety of forms in different fields. In the law, warrants take the form of legal principles, statutes, licenses, or permits. The idea underlying a warrant survives today in the familiar term *arrest warrant*. In the natural and physical sciences, warrants take the form of scientific laws, formulas, and methods of calculation. In all these fields, warrants reflect acceptable methods of relating the evidence to the claim or chief assertion.

For example, in the law the warrant is an explicit statute laying out the specific circumstances under which someone can be found guilty of an offense. The warrant permits the judge or the court to conclude that a particular defendant is guilty of an offense if supporting evidence has been submitted and verified.

In other fields, like natural sciences and mathematics, warrants may take the form of relevant formulas that are used to confirm or reject a hypothesis or claim on the basis of evidence produced by experimentation and research. Within these fields warrants appear as commonly accepted principles or "laws." For example, Boyle's law in thermodynamics states that at relatively low pressures the pressure of an ideal gas kept at constant temperature varies inversely with the volume of the gas. Likewise, Einstein's discovery of the relationship between mass and energy is contained in the famous equation or law $E = mc^2$.

In other fields, medicine, for example, warrants derive more from principles generalized from the practitioner's past experience than from formulas as such. A doctor making a diagnosis of a seven-year-old patient's illness might discover an unusual rash of raised, circular, small red spots and measure an elevated temperature. Based on principles generalized from past experience, the doctor concludes that the patient has probably caught measles. To see how the warrant serves as a kind of rule dictating how the evidence (rash, elevated temperature) should be related to the particular claim (the patient has caught measles), examine the following analysis of the reasoning underlying the doctor's diagnosis:

a rash of raised, circular,
small red spots and high
temperature are the symptoms
of measles, particularly in five-to seven-
year-old children

[the warrant in the form of a general principle]

this 7-year-old patient has a
rash of raised, circular, - - - - - - - - - - - - - - - - - -> patient has measles
small red spots and high
temperature

[evidence, or all the facts   [conclusion or claim]
about this particular situation]

The warrant here is drawn from general principles of the kind that might be familiar to the doctor from past experience and from information provided by a medical textbook.

UNDERLYING ASSUMPTIONS

Warrants can be either explicit or implicit; that is, they can take the form of set rules or simply be assumptions and beliefs that both the writer and the audience share. Whereas warrants take the form of broad generalizations, rules of thumb, or general principles that could apply to various circumstances, claims and support always apply to specific events and circumstances. In law or the sciences, warrants are generalizations based on extensive experience and data. Outside these formal fields of study, in everyday conversation, warrants take the form of beliefs, assumptions, or rule-of-thumb generalizations.

As with all other generalizations, warrants must ultimately rest on relevant facts and evidence. If the warrant or underlying assumption in an argument is challenged, the writer may have to produce some of the primary information or backing on which the warrant itself is based. This is important because people often bring different assumptions to the same situation without realizing it. For example, in her book *When Society Becomes an Addict* (1987), Anne Wilson Schaef, a psychotherapist, describes an episode of how two people "read" the same situation in different ways because of their different underlying assumptions:

> During one of my workshops an incident occurred that illustrates
> this lack of clarity very aptly. We had baked apples for dinner. I was
> too full to eat mine, so I took it back to the cottage I was sharing with

another staff member and put it in the refrigerator, planning to eat it at my leisure. Since it was obviously mine, it did not occur to me that my cabin mate would eat it.

Later, when I went to get my apple, it was gone. My cabin mate — a compulsive overeater — had, in fact, gobbled it down. I did not appreciate that, and I said so. Her response was, "I assumed you didn't want it since you hadn't eaten it." She had made two assumptions, neither of which she checked out with me: first, that I didn't want the apple, and second, that it was okay for her to eat it. Then she had used her assumptions to support her distorted thinking and feed her compulsive eating habit.

Identifying underlying beliefs is essential since many writers erroneously take it for granted that they and the audience share a common point of view. An audience that notices that they and the writer do not share the same assumptions might require the author to back up the warrant, since from the audience's point of view the warrant might be questionable.

Assumptions in an argument often remain implicit when the writer feels that the audience shares his or her underlying beliefs. If the audience already agrees with these beliefs, the writer can feel comfortable in bringing forth reasons to support the claim. The contrary is true in those arguments where the writer feels the audience may not share his or her basic values. In these cases, an assumption that might prove controversial may need to be stated explicitly and defended at the outset. The writer must win a hearing for the assumption on which the argument is based before going on to present evidence that specifically bears on the question or exact point that is the subject of the argument.

Not all warrants will be explicitly stated in the course of an argument. Sometimes the writer will not explicitly state the warrant because she feels that both she and the audience share a common perspective on the issue. In effect, the writer is depending on the audience to mentally supply the implicit warrant to connect the evidence with the claim. This is especially true when writers argue before partisan audiences who already share the same beliefs and can be depended upon to bring the same set of assumptions or warrants to the situation. For example, a lottery equipment manufacturer arguing for a national lottery before fellow manufacturers of lottery ticket printing equipment will not have to state or defend the assumption that a national lottery will mean more business for lottery equipment manufacturers. His audience can be depended upon to interpret any evidence he presents in the light of this implicit warrant.

In other cases, the warrants will not be explictly stated because the writer does not want the audience to be aware that they disagree on underlying assumptions. Such was the case in the baked apple incident where the cabin mate did not ask if she could eat the apple because she did not want to risk hearing that she could not.

EVALUATING WARRANTS

Before you can evaluate the effectiveness of any particular warrant, you need to be able to identify all the warrants in any argument and to make explicit those that lie hidden beneath the surface. Writers must inquire (1) whether the warrant expresses a reliable generalization and (2) whether this generalization authorizes the connection between the facts and the conclusion in this particular case.

Evaluating how warrants work in a given argumentative situation means discovering whether the writer has used the correct kind of warrant to connect the evidence to the claim or has connected the evidence to the claim in the correct way. The first point has to do with the relevance of the evidence. The second concerns the quality of the writer's reasoning or use of logic.

A listing of the six main kinds of warrants writers use in creating arguments follows. The particular kind of warrant selected depends on the nature of the argument, the type of claim (of fact, causation, value, or policy), as well as the specific audience addressed or the context in which the argument is formulated.

Types of Warrants

Generalization Warrant. A generalization warrant authorizes the movement from a number of specific examples offered as evidence to a generalization offered as a conclusion. The generalization warrant asserts that what is true of a sample is probably true of a group as a whole. The examples used must meet the test of being sufficiently representative, properly selected, and timely.

For example, Sigmund Freud, in his classic essay "Typical Dreams (*Basic Writings of Sigmund Freud* [1938]) brings forward a whole range of examples from the dreams of children that illustrate one common theme —the death or disappearance of brothers or sisters. From these numerous case histories, Freud generalizes that children's dreams often reveal sibling rivalry, albeit in a disguised form. Freud's claim of the existence of sibling rivalry is an inference that should be verifiable as well in dreams of children whom Freud has not observed.

Looked at in terms of claim, support, and warrant, the argument appears this way:

CLAIM: Children's dreams often reveal sibling rivalry in disguised form.

SUPPORT: In numerous case histories, the dreams of children always have one common theme — the death or disappearance of brothers and sisters.

GENERALIZATION WARRANT: What is true of this sample can be taken to be true of the whole group.

Everyday reasoning closely resembles arguments from generalizations as do arguments whose claims are based on polls or surveys. For example, the Harris survey, or the Gallup opinion poll, generalizes from results drawn from a sample cross section of from 1,200 to 1,500 adults to infer what is true of the entire population. If the sample, by a margin of 80 percent to 20 percent, holds the view that "American business is not paying its fair share of taxes," Gallup will predict that this opinion would also be true in the same proportion if every adult in the United States were polled.

Cause and Effect Warrant. Reasoning from cause assumes that one event can produce another. Causal generalization stipulates that if a particular cause is observed, a particular effect can be expected to follow. Conversely, the causal warrant may state that if a certain effect is observed, a particular cause may be assumed to have preceded it. Causal warrants may extend to chains of causation as well as multiple causes or multiple effects. For example, Wilson Bryan Key, a professor of communications, wanted to discover why many viewers of William Friedkin's movie *The Exorcist* became fearful, angry, and physically sick after seeing the film. As reported in his book *Media Sexploitation* (1976), Key discovered that Friedkin had accompanied the images on the screen with a sound track in which sounds of squealing pigs and the buzzing of infuriated bees were recorded at a level below the audience's conscious awareness. Key argues that this subliminal use of sound, though not consciously perceived, created an undertone of fear that amplified the frightening nature of the images on the screen. He interviewed theater staff who heard the sound track before they actually viewed the film and discovered that they often experienced the same reactions of hysteria and anxiety as did members of the audience who saw *and* heard the movie. In outline form, Key's causal argument might look like this (notice that the warrant acts as the cause while the claim expresses the effect):

CLAIM: The anxiety of audiences watching *The Exorcist* was, in part, an unconscious reaction to the sounds of squealing pigs and infuriated bees interwoven into the sound track at a subliminal level.

SUPPORT: Theater staff who heard only the sound track of the movie experienced reactions of hysteria and anxiety. Friedkin admitted that he interwove sounds of pigs and bees in a way that coordinated with the visual images.

CAUSAL WARRANT: Even if the sounds were not consciously perceived, people instinctively fear the sounds of squealing pigs and infuriated bees.

Sign Warrant. Arguments based on sign warrants point to a particular sign to support a claim that a certain event, condition, or situation exists. For example, a doctor may be reasoning from sign when he cites certain observable characteristics to justify the diagnosis that a patient is suffering from a particular disease. Anne Wilson Schaef uses the same reasoning process in *When Society Becomes an Addict* (1987):

> An addiction is any process over which we are powerless. It takes control of us, causing us to do and think things that are inconsistent with our personal values and leading us to become progressively more compulsive and obsessive. A sure sign of an addiction is the sudden need to deceive ourselves and others — to lie, deny, and cover up. An addiction is anything we feel *tempted* to lie about.

Although one could certainly dispute her definition of addiction, Schaef clearly reasons from signs (need to lie, deny, and cover up) to support a claim about the presence of the phenomenon (addiction) to which the sign refers.

The philosopher C. S. Peirce defines *sign* this way: "a sign is something which stands to somebody for something else, in some respect or capacity." We reason from sign anytime we drive down the highway, see a sign indicating a winding road, and slow down. The sign is used as a reliable indicator that a condition (a winding road) is or will be present. We do the same thing when we check our wallet before entering a restaurant in front of which we see a long green awning and a doorman. The fancy facade is a usually reliable indicator that the restaurant is expensive.

In law, the concept of circumstantial evidence is based on the idea of reasoning from sign. A case may be constructed on a network of circumstantial facts based on the assumption or warrant that the defendant exhibits all the signs — that have been reliable indicators in past cases — of having committed the crime. In economics, economists look for signs of health or weakness in the nation's economy. These financial indicators (balance of trade, housing starts, unemployment figures, etc.) are believed to indicate the presence of a corresponding economic condition.

In "Notes on Class" (1980) Paul Fussell creates an amusing argument, based on a sign warrant, by pointing to features that he believes define different class levels in American society:

> Facade study is a badly neglected anthropological field. As we work down from the (largely white-painted) bank-like facades of the Upper and Upper Middle Classes, we encounter such Middle and Prole conventions as these, which I rank in order of social status:
> *Middle*
> 1. A potted tree on either side of the front door, and the more pointy and symmetrical the better.

2. A large rectangular picture-window in a split-level "ranch" house, displaying a table-lamp between two side curtains. The cellophane on the lampshade must be visibly inviolate.

3. Two chairs, usually metal with pipe arms, disposed on the front porch as a "conversation group," in stubborn defiance of the traffic thundering past.

High-Prole

4. Religious shrines in the garden, which if small and understated, are slightly higher class than

Mid-Prole

5. Plaster gnomes and flamingos, and blue or lavender shiny spheres supported by fluted cast-concrete pedestals.

Low-Prole

6. Defunct truck tires painted white and enclosing flower beds. (Auto tires are a grade higher.)

7. Flower-bed designs worked in dead light bulbs or the butts of disused beer bottles.

> The Destitute have no facades to decorate, and of course the Bottom Out-of-Sights, being invisible, have none either, although both these classes can occasionally help others decorate theirs— painting tires white on an hourly basis, for example, or even watering and fertilizing the potted trees of the Middle Class.

Reduced to its essentials, Fussell's argument might look like this:

CLAIM: Although we like to pretend that American society is classless, "facade study" reveals a hierarchical class structure in American culture.

SUPPORT: Symmetrical plants, large rectangular picture windows, two chairs in middle-class homes; religious shrines in high-prole homes; plaster gnomes and flamingos in mid-prole homes; painted truck tires and designs worked into disused beer bottles in low-prole homes, and so on.

SIGN WARRANT: Statues, objects, and assorted bric-a-brac in front of people's houses are reliable signs of the social class to which they belong.

Much of advertising attempts to appropriate this form of reasoning to persuade potential customers to purchase a product. Advertisers are very clever in using warrants from sign in persuading audiences that purchasing, wearing, or using a particular product will enable the purchaser to partake of the reality (such as wealth, beauty, or health) of which the sign is an indicator. For example, an ad for expensive crystal glasses directed toward prospective brides might show a diamond ring and a wedding veil alongside the glasses. The ring and the veil are signs standing for marriage. The technique of advertising is based, in large part, on correlating attainable tangible objects with difficult to obtain feelings, moods, attitudes, and conditions. The advertiser can depend on the consumer reasoning from sign that the purchase of the attainable will be accompanied by the difficult to obtain. For example, an ad for an expensive watch might show it on a night table alongside a gold money clip holding a stack of $100 bills. Reasoning from sign, the consumer might conclude that the purchase of this watch (as a sign of the possessions of a wealthy person) would somehow enable him or her to possess other items associated with wealth.

Analogy Warrant. Reasoning from analogy assumes that there are sufficient similarities between two things to warrant the claim that what is true of one can reasonably be expected to be true of the other. Anytime we look forward to reading a new novel by an author whose previous books we read and enjoyed, or seeing a new movie by a favorite director, we are reasoning by analogy. We infer that the new book or movie will resemble the works we previously enjoyed.

It is important that shared characteristics be directly relevant to the claim and that no important differences exist that would undermine or weaken the analogy. For example, if a car manufacturer issues a recall of a certain model because a structural weakness in the frame has led rear bumpers to fall off, then it can reasonably be assumed that other cars of the same make and model are likely to develop the same problem. This would hold true despite differences in appearance or options. Since structural weakness in one model can reasonably be expected to be true of other cars in the line, the shared characteristics are directly relevant to the claim.

The more the analogy departs from the literally shared resemblances, the less useful it will be in supporting a claim. This is not to say that such analogies cannot be extraordinarily helpful in describing or explaining some point, but these analogies, sometimes called *figurative analogies*, cannot actually serve to warrant a claim. For example, Martin J. Rees and Joseph Silk writing in *Scientific American* ("The Origin of Galaxies" [August 1969]) formulated a figurative analogy to describe the phenomenon of an expanding universe:

> Perhaps the most startling discovery made in astronomy this century is that the universe is populated by billions of galaxies and that they are systematically receding from one another, like raisins in an expanding pudding.

The authors are not suggesting that the universe *is* an expanding pudding with raisins, but are simply using a figurative analogy to describe and explain an otherwise hard-to-grasp concept. It is important for any reader of an argument using analogies to evaluate just how the analogy is being used. The question to ask is: does the analogy simply describe or explain something or does it actually support an inference and thereby warrant the claim?

Consider how David J. Armor, a professor, uses an analogy warrant in his argument against mandatory school busing in Statements Submitted to Committee on the Judiciary (U.S. Senate, Hearings on the Fourteenth Amendment and School Busing, 97th Congress, 1st Session, May 14, 1981):

> The school busing issue has been with us now for over ten years, and it shows no signs of abating. Massive mandatory busing has been ordered recently by courts in Los Angeles, Columbus (Ohio), and St. Louis; and major busing lawsuits are still pending in San Diego, Cincinnati, Kansas City (Missouri), and Indianapolis. Clearly, court-ordered busing is alive and well. This is a remarkable achievement for the most unpopular, least successful, and most harmful national policy since Prohibition.
>
> At the outset let me say I fully agree with the Supreme Court's policy that intentional segregation of the schools is prohibited by the United States constitution. Moreover, racial isolation and discrimination do exist in American society and in the schools, and these conditions should be combated wherever they are found.
>
> The real issue is the method chosen by the courts to remedy segregation. The courts adopted mandatory busing because they believed it to be the most effective way to end racial isolation. Therefore, it was also seen as the best way to end the harmful effects of segregation on race relations and on the educational opportunity of minority students. But, just as Prohibition was not a feasible remedy for alcohol abuse, so mandatory busing is not a feasible remedy for school segregation. Like Prohibition, the policy is not merely ineffective; it is counterproductive.

In schematic form the argument would appear this way:

CLAIM: Mandatory busing is an ineffective and undesirable remedy for racial segregation in the school systems.

SUPPORT: Like Prohibition, mandatory busing is not merely ineffective: it is counterproductive.

ANALOGY WARRANT: Prohibition as an intended solution that proved ineffective is comparable and analogous to the use of mandatory busing to solve the problem of racial segregation.

Armor's argument depends on the analogy warrant or assumption that court-ordered school busing is analogous to Prohibition. For him, similarities between the two are more significant than the obvious differences. An opponent would assert that the fundamental dissimilarities between the two programs makes any attempt to compare them unwarranted.

Authority Warrant. Reasoning from authority presumes that the authority cited is in fact qualified to express an expert opinion on the subject of the claim. If the authority were to be challenged the writer would have to supply backing for the warrant in the form of credentials and expertise that would qualify the authority in the particular circumstances.

In evaluating an argument based on authority, determine if the writer clearly connects the claim and the authority's area of expertise. Also, try to determine whether the authority is acknowledged as such by other experts in the field and has made his or her investigations recently. Of course, the authority must be explicitly identified and not referred to as simply "a well-known expert." As an illustration, consider how Monroe Freedman uses the testimony of widely respected figures, in *Lawyers Ethics in an Adversary System* (1975), to support his controversial claim that a lawyer's first obligation is to protect his or her client, not to search for the truth:

> Thus, the defense lawyer's professional obligation may well be to advise the client to withhold the truth. As Justice Jackson said: "any lawyer worth his salt will tell the suspect in no uncertain terms to make no statement to police under any circumstances." Similarly, the defense lawyer is obligated to prevent the introduction of evidence that may be wholly reliable, such as a murder weapon seized in violation of the Fourth Amendment, or a truthful but involuntary confession. Justice White has observed that although law enforcement officials must be dedicated to using only truthful evidence, "defense counsel has no comparable obligation to ascertain or present the truth. Our system assigns him a different mission. . . . We . . . insist that he defend his client whether he is innocent or guilty."
>
> Such conduct by defense counsel does not constitute obstruction of justice. On the contrary, it is "part of the duty imposed on the most honorable defense counsel," from whom "we countenance or require conduct which in many instances has little, if any, relation to the search for truth." The same observation has been made by Justice Harlan, who noted that "in fulfilling his professional responsibilities," the lawyer "of necessity may become an obstacle to truthfinding." Chief Justice Warren, too, has recognized that when the criminal defense attorney successfully obstructs efforts by the government to elicit truthful evidence in ways that violate constitutional rights, the attorney is "merely exercising . . . good professional judgment," and "carrying out what he is sworn to do under his oath — to protect to the extent of his ability the rights of his client." Chief Justice Warren concluded: "In fulfilling this responsibility the attorney plays a vital role in the administration of criminal justice under our Constitution."
>
> Obviously, such eminent jurists would not arrive lightly at the conclusion that an officer of the court has a professional obligation to place obstacles in the path of truth. Their reasons, again, go back to the nature of our system of criminal justice and go to the fundamentals of our system of government. Before we will permit the state to

deprive any person of life, liberty, or property, we require that certain processes be duly followed which ensure regard for the dignity of the individual, irrespective of the impact of those processes upon the determination of truth.

Freedman's point is that a lawyer may advise his or her client to lie in those situations where disclosure of the truth will hurt the client. To support his claim that an attorney's main duty is to the client, not to the truth as such, Freedman cites the expert testimony of Supreme Court justices Jackson, White, Harlan, and Warren. Because each of these figures is a widely respected legal authority, their statements can be expected to persuade the reader to accept the claim. The three elements function as follows:

CLAIM: The defense lawyer's professional obligation may be to advise the client to withhold the truth.

SUPPORT: Supreme Court justices Jackson, White, Harlan, and Warren testify that this behavior is appropriate.

AUTHORITY WARRANT: The expert opinion of Supreme Court justices on matters of the law carries considerable weight because they are the nation's foremost legal authorities.

Also, notice how Freedman structures the argument to end with the remarks of the most important legal authority, the Chief Justice of the Supreme Court.

Value Warrant. Value warrants are moral or ethical principles or beliefs that the writer hopes will be shared by the audience. It is especially important that the value the warrant expresses be relevant to the claim and be a belief that the intended audience will perceive as important. Value warrants are frequently unexpressed in arguments and readers must make every effort to make explicit the value, principle, or belief, that the writer may have taken for granted. Value warrants function exactly as any other kind of warrant to guarantee a connection between the claim and the evidence. Value warrants frequently embody ethical principles that designate certain kinds of actions as right or wrong, acceptable or unacceptable, or stipulate what should be considered as good or bad, or express the standards by which some actions should be considered good or bad, preferable or objectionable. In some cases these value warrants will express societal concensus about the ethical propriety of certain kinds of actions. In other cases they may express a personal, rather than universal, moral value.

In the following paragraph from "Abolish the Insanity Defense?— Not Yet," (*Rutgers Law Review* [1973]) John Monahan uses a value warrant to explain how the insanity defense is based on an underlying belief that people who are incapable of knowing the meaning or consequences of their actions should not be punished:

> The existing Anglo-American system of criminal justice is based on a model of man as a responsible agent with a free will. The insanity defense is closely tied to this model. Oversimplifying somewhat, "the defense of insanity rests upon the assumption that insanity negates free will, and the law does not punish people who lack the capacity for choice."
>
> If an individual has a complete inability to know the nature and quality of the act he has committed, that is, if he is insane by M'Naghten standards, then, it is argued, he is incapable of forming the cognitive or mental component (intent, recklessness, etc.) which is part of the definition of much serious crime. Since the insane person is held to be incapable of forming normal cognition, and since cognitive ability is part of the definition of crime, he has a complete defense to much criminal prosecution.

Split into the three elements, Monahan's case would appear thus:

CLAIM: A particular defendant should not be prosecuted as if he or she were consciously aware of the meaning or consequences of the crime.

SUPPORT: The defendant can be shown to be insane by M'Naghten standards.

VALUE WARRANT: The law does not punish people who lack the capacity for choice.

This argument is unusual in that it rests on a basic assumption on which the entire system of criminal law is built but it reaches a conclusion with which increasing numbers of people disagree. When reading any argument based on a value warrant, try to identify any assumptions or unexamined beliefs that the writer expects the audience to share. Ask yourself how this assumption supports the author's purpose. Then compare this assumption (you may need to state it explicitly if the author does not) with your own beliefs on the issue, and decide whether the warrant, in fact, (1) is reliable and (2) actually applies to the particular case.

Audience

Most of the things people write are written with the expectation that someone will read what they have written. Since each audience has its own characteristic concerns and values, writers must be acutely sensitive to the audience's special needs. Without knowing what was important to an audience, it would be difficult for writers to assess what kinds of arguments, evidence, and supporting material a particular audience would be likely to find convincing.

Writers should try to identify who the audience is or is likely to be by creating an audience profile. For example, how might the audience, from its point of view, define the issue at the center of the argument? If the audience sees the issue differently, is there anything the writer can do to take this into account while characterizing the problem or issue? The key question is, how can the writer create a common meeting ground?

Matching the argument to the audience is largely a matter of figuring out what particular argumentative strategy would work best with a particular audience. In a typical persuasion situation, the writer is trying to influence readers who have not made up their minds on the topic and can be presumed to have open minds or at least to be neutral on the issue.

In this situation, the writer can announce the thesis of the argument at the outset and then present reasons and evidence in a straightforward way. The writer is obliged to present, directly and without apology, the most timely, up-to-date, and relevant information and the most cogent arguments he or she can muster.

In other situations, the writer attempts to persuade an audience that has already formed strong opinions and beliefs. Clearly, different tactics are required. For example, the writer might wish to present both sides of the argument before announcing the thesis. Or he might consider using deductive reasoning as a rhetorical strategy to win his audience's agreement to certain *premises* and then show how the conclusion must necessarily follow.

For many writers, a reasonable goal is not so much to change the readers' minds as to persuade them to give the writer's opposing point of view a fair hearing. The writer's goal is to get the audience to see the issue from a point of view or perspective different from their customary one.

There are a number of ways to enhance the probability that the writer's argument will address the readers' special concerns. But before this can happen, the writer must be able to define the issue in a way that will appeal to the audience's needs and values. At the very least, the writer must recognize and acknowledge the legitimacy of the audience's feelings on the issue. It is naive to assume that an audience will be persuaded by an argument, however well written or well supported, that fails to take into account psychological factors that can prevent each side from "hearing" the other.

One of the most useful attempts to study the factors that block communication is by the prominent psychologist, Carl R. Rogers. His article "Communication: Its Blocking and Its Facilitation," originally a paper delivered at Northwestern University's Centennial Conference on Communications, October 11, 1951, points out that people on both sides of an argument characteristically tend to dig in their heels and simply seek to justify their own opinion.

There are a variety of psychological reasons that explain this intransigent mind set. First of all, people tend to identify with their positions on issues and are not able to separate themselves from their opinions. This automatic preference for one's own opinions makes it impossible to allow oneself to even consider another point of view. Because people identify with their opinions, they feel the need to defend their positions no matter how weak because in essence they are defending themselves against what they perceive to be a personal attack.

This basic frame of mind brings with it the tendency to rationalize. Rationalization is a self-deceptive form of reasoning in which evidence is distorted to fit a previously formed opinion. By contrast, authentic reasoning relies on logic and evidence to reveal a conclusion that may or may not agree with the preconceived opinion. Rogers has studied how the need to defend one's personal values and self-image shuts out potentially useful ideas. To get beyond these limitations Rogers recommends the following exercise:

> The next time you get into an argument with your wife, or your friend, or with a small group of friends, just stop the discussion for a moment and for an experiment, institute this rule. "Each person can speak up for himself only *after* he has first restated the ideas and feelings of the previous speaker accurately, and to that speaker's satisfaction." You see what this would mean. It would simply mean that before presenting your own point of view it would be necessary for you to really achieve the other speaker's frame of reference — to understand his thoughts and feelings so well that you could summarize them for him. . . . Once you have been able to see the other's point of view, your own comments will have to be drastically revised. You will also find the emotion going out of the discussion, the differences being reduced, and those differences which remain being of a rational and understandable sort.

This intriguing method of introducing some psychological perspective makes it more likely that the writer will be able to define the issue at the center of the argument in terms that reflect the values and beliefs of the audience. That is, by being able to summarize impartially an opponent's viewpoint on an issue, in language that the opponent would consider a fair restatement of the issue, the writer immeasurably increases the chances of reaching a middle ground. As Rogers observes:

> Real communication occurs and this evaluative tendency is avoided when we listen with understanding. What does that mean? It means *to see the expressed idea and attitude from the other person's point of*

*view, to sense how it feels to him, to achieve his frame of reference in
regard to the thing he is talking about.*

Also, having a sense of the audience's values will allow the writer to
allude to common experiences related to the issue. A knowledge of the
readers' special concerns can suggest the kinds of hypothetical scenarios
the writer might introduce to persuade the audience. In any case, it is
important that writers make every attempt to adapt the argument to the
needs and values of their particular audience. It is also crucial to set
realistic persuasion goals in the context of the particular situation.

If the argument is well-formulated, with effective examples, evidence, and cogent reasons, most audiences will want to try out the new
viewpoint, even if it means suspending their own views on the subject in
the meantime. They will try on for size the writer's perspective simply to
have the experience of seeing things from a different angle.

BACKING

Sometimes merely considering the argument as it appears to an audience
will not be sufficient. It is at this point that the concept of *backing*
becomes important. An audience may not be satisfied that the warrant
used to connect the evidence or grounds to the claim is an appropriate
one to apply to the present case. Backing supplies additional evidence
necessary to support the warrant, and provides the assurance that the
assumptions used in formulating the argument really rest on solid and
trustworthy grounds. Of course, not all arguments will require the writer
to produce the broader foundation of backing. Only when readers can be
presumed to view the claims of an argument with doubt or skepticism
need backing be produced. For example, you and a friend might be
arguing over whether a particular tennis player would win Wimbleton.
You might claim that player X was a sure bet to win Wimbleton this year
and back up your claim with statistics about the relative strengths of the
serve and volley game of this year's crop of tournament players. You
might even state your warrant in the form of an assumption that "only a
tennis player who had a strong serve and volley game has a real chance
to take the Wimbleton title."

At this point, your skeptical friend might question the validity of your
assumption. You would then have to produce the backing on which your
warrant rests to clarify your claim and answer your friend's doubts. In
this case, backing might take the form of an analysis of the serve and
volley game of past winners of Wimbleton. Thus, warrants or assumptions that are not accepted by your audience at face value must be
supported to clarify and substantiate the underlying structure of your
claim.

Backing is required often enough so that it should be considered a basic part of any argument, satisfying the doubts of an audience that wants to know that the writer can, if challenged, provide further support.

QUALIFIERS

Another way writers take audiences into account is by using what are called *qualifiers*. Realistically, no claim is ever presented in a vacuum. The qualifier represents the writer's assessment of the relative strength or weakness of the claim. Qualifiers express limitations that may have to be attached to a claim in order to pass scrutiny of a particular audience. Frequently qualifiers take the form of phrases such as *in all probability, very likely, presumably,* or *very possibly.*

For example, let's say you're having a discussion with a friend about computer software and you want to recommend the use of a new spreadsheet program. Rather than making your recommendation in an unqualified way without conditions or restrictions, you phrase your recommendation so as to indicate the kind of strength you wish to be attributed to your claim. To do this you need to include a qualifying word or phrase such as "program X, *as far as I can tell,* will make the job much easier." In this way, arguers take their audiences into account by modifying a claim to include a restriction whose effect is to enhance the persuasiveness of the message.

REBUTTALS OR EXCEPTIONS

While the addition of *backing* and *qualifiers* to the basic structure of claim–support–warrant goes a long way to adapting an argument to cope with the contrary beliefs, expectations, or skepticism of an audience, writers are aware that one further element is required to create a persuasive case. This element, called the *rebuttal* or *exception,* arises from the writer's responsibility in confronting special circumstances or extraordinary instances that challenge the claim being made. Inserting the rebuttal or exception into the structure of the argument enhances the persuasiveness of the claim by honestly recognizing that there may be some particularly exceptional circumstances under which the claim could not be directly supported by the grounds. For example, a typical use of the rebuttal or exception is in the form of warnings printed by pharmaceutical companies regarding contraindications or situations where an otherwise safe-to-prescribe drug should not be used. This type of argument might appear as follows:

GROUNDS: This patient is on a weight control program.

BACKING: Clinical experience shows that—

WARRANT: As part of a weight control program, D-amphetamine may be prescribed.

QUALIFIER: It appears very likely that—

CLAIM: This patient needs D-amphetamine as part of a weight control program.

REBUTTAL OR EXCEPTION: Unless the patient has a history of heart disease, high blood pressure, thyroid disease, glaucoma, or is allergic to any amphetamine or has a history of abusing amphetamine medications, or is pregnant (because of possible links to birth defects).

To illustrate how backing, qualifiers, and rebuttals work in a real situation, consider the following speech given by Bruce Springsteen at the induction of Roy Orbison into the Rock and Roll Hall of Fame, January 21, 1987 (*Roy Orbison In Dreams* [1987]):

In 1970, I rode for 15 hours in the back of a U-Haul truck to open for Roy Orbison at the Nashville Music Fair. It was a summer night and I was 20 years old and he came out in dark glasses, a dark suit and he played some dark music.

In 74, just prior to going in the studio to make *Born To Run*, I was looking at Duane Eddy for his guitar sound and I was listening to a collection of Phil Spector records and I was listening to Roy Orbison's *All-Time Greatest Hits*. I'd lay in bed at night with just the lights of my stereo on and I'd hear *Cryin', Love Hurts, Runnin' Scared, Only The Lonely* and *It's Over* fillin' my room. Some rock 'n' roll reinforces friendship and community, but for me, Roy's ballads were always best when you were alone and in the dark. Roy scrapped the idea that you need verse-chorus-verse-chorus-bridge-verse-chorus to have a hit.

His arrangements were complex and operatic, they had rhythm and movement and they addressed the underside of pop romance. They were scary. His voice was unearthly.

He had the ability, like all great rock 'n' rollers, to sound like he'd dropped in from another planet and yet get the stuff that was right to the heart of what you were livin' in today, and that was how he opened up your vision. He made a little town in New Jersey feel as big as the sound of his records.

I always remember layin' in bed and right at the end of *It's Over*, when he hits that note where it sounds like the world's going to end, I'd be laying there promising myself that I was never going to go outside again and never going to talk to another woman.

Right about that time my needle would slip back to the first cut and I'd hear . . . (the opening riff to) Pretty Woman/I don't believe you/You're not the truth/No one could look as good as you. And that was when I understood.

I carry his records with me when I go on tour today, and I'll always remember what he means to me and what he meant to me when I was young and afraid to love.

In 75, when I went into the studio to make *Born To Run*, I wanted to make a record with words like Bob Dylan that sounded like Phil Spector, but most of all I wanted to sing like Roy Orbison. Now everybody knows that nobody sings like Roy Orbison.

The two opening paragraphs let the audience see Orbison from Springsteen's perspective like two snapshots in time. The first reveals the difference in stature between Orbison and the young Springsteen who "rode for 15 hours in the back of a U-Haul truck" to open for Orbison. The second lets the audience know how important Orbison's music was to Springsteen just before he recorded his own very successful album, *Born to Run*. The heart of the speech is really an argument. The claim appears in the sentence:

Some rock 'n' roll reinforces friendship and community, but for me, Roy's ballads were always best when you were alone and in the dark.

Notice how this assertion is qualified by the words "for me" and includes an exception that anticipates an implied objection: "some rock 'n' roll reinforces friendship and community."

The evidence to support the basic claim that "Roy's ballads were always best when you were alone and in the dark" can be found in the following paragraph:

His arrangements were complex and operatic, they had rhythm and movement and they addressed the underside of pop romance. They were scary. His voice was unearthly.

He had the ability, like all great rock 'n' rollers, to sound like he'd dropped in from another planet and yet get the stuff that was right to the heart of what you were livin' in today, and that was how he opened up your vision. He made a little town in New Jersey feel as big as the sound of his records.

The warrant or assumption that links the assertion with the evidence that supports it might be stated as follows:

Great rock 'n' roll ballads let you know you are not alone, not the only person who has suffered, and help you get beyond the suffering.

At this point, the argument as such is complete, but notice how Springsteen intuitively adds what might be considered *backing* to clarify and support his implicit warrant for those members of the audience who might feel differently about what great rock 'n' roll ballads should be. The *backing* appears in the form of Springsteen's personal recollections that reveal how important Orbison's music was for him in echoing his own heartache and getting him beyond it to love again:

> I always remember layin' in bed and right at the end of *It's Over*, when he hits that note where it sounds like the world's going to end, I'd be laying there promising myself that I was never going to go outside again and never going to talk to another woman.
>
> Right about that time my needle would slip back to the first cut and I'd hear . . . (the opening riff to) Pretty Woman/I don't believe you/You're not the truth/No one could look as good as you. And that was when I understood.
>
> I carry his records with me when I go on tour today, and I'll always remember what he means to me and what he meant to me when I was young and afraid to love.

The argument now complete, Springsteen ends by evoking the opening paragraphs, almost as if the speech itself were a kind of song, ending with his now wiser perspective that "now everybody knows that nobody sings like Roy Orbison."

Arguing Across the Disciplines

Some of the most interesting and effective writing in various disciplines takes the form of arguments that seek to persuade a specific audience (colleagues, fellow researchers, or the general public) of the validity of a proposition or claim through logical reasoning supported by facts, examples, or other kinds of evidence. Writers and researchers in all academic disciplines often are compelled to convince others of the validity of their ideas and discoveries. Discussion and debate accompany the development of central ideas, concepts, and laws in all fields of study. Writers in the liberal arts, the political and social sciences, and the physical and natural sciences use strategies of argument to support new interpretations of known facts or establish plausible cases for new hypotheses.

Although arguments explore important issues and espouse specific theories, the forms in which they appear vary according to the style and format of the individual discipline. Evidence in different disciplines can appear in a variety of formats, including the interpretation of statistics, laws, precedents, or the citation of authorities. The means used in constructing arguments depend on the audience within the discipline being addressed, the nature of the thesis being proposed, and the accepted methodology for that particular discipline.

The kinds of knowledge sought and the procedures used by the political and social sciences are quite different from those of the liberal arts. These disciplines have, to a large extent, adapted the techniques and objectives of the physical and natural sciences to study how human beings interact within the context of social, political, business, legal, psychological, and cultural relationships.

The types of information sought and the methods employed within the domain of the sciences aim at providing an accurate, systematic, and comprehensive account of the world around us, as well as a framework within which new hypotheses can be put forward and evaluated.

In the liberal arts, critics evaluate and interpret works of art, review music, dance, drama, and film, and write literary analyses. Philosophers probe the moral and ethical implications of people's actions and advocate specific ways of meeting the ethical challenges posed by new technologies. Historians interpret political, military, and constitutional events, analyze their causes, and theorize about how the past influences the present.

In the political and social sciences, lawyers and constitutional scholars argue for specific ways of applying legal and constitutional theory to everyday problems. Economists debate issues related to changes wrought by technology, distribution of income, unemployment, and commerce. Political scientists look into how effectively governments initiate and manage social change and ask basic questions about the limits of governmental intrusion into individual rights. Sociologists analyze statistics and trends to evaluate how successfully institutions accommodate social change.

In the sciences, biologists, as well as biochemists, zoologists, botanists, and other natural scientists, propose theories to explain the interdependence of living things and their natural environment. Psychologists champion hypotheses based on physiological, experimental, social, and clinical research to explain various aspects of human behavior. Physicists, as well as mathematicians, astronomers, engineers, and computer scientists, put forward and defend hypotheses about the basic laws underlying the manifestations of the physical world, from the microscopic to the cosmic.

Like general arguments, the structure of arguments within the disciplines requires (1) a clear statement of a proposition or claim, (2) grounds that are relevant to the claim and sufficient to support it, and (3) a warrant based on solid backing that guarantees the appropriateness and applicability of the grounds in supporting the claim. So, too, appropriate qualifiers or possible exceptions to the claim must be stated as part of the argument.

We can appreciate the relevance of claims only in the context of the requirements of the larger fields within which the claims are advanced. That is, there are certain defining features and distinctive goals of each discipline that determine which items, data, or evidence will be seen as relevant to the claim. Training in different fields consists in learning what kinds of evidence are accepted as appropriate in supporting claims within that particular field. (The following discussions applying the Toulmin model to a range of disciplines have been adapted from Stephen Toulmin, Richard Rieke, and Allan Janik, *An Introduction to Reasoning* (1984). Future in-text citations refer to this source; page numbers are given in parentheses.)

Different fields have different concepts of what constitutes evidence to be introduced to support a claim. Grounds, evidence, and data that are appropriate in a legal argument will be of a different kind and will be judged differently from evidence in a scientific argument or in an argument in the arts. As in general arguments, warrants in the disciplines are statements, formulas, and rules that authorize the way evidence (all data: pertinent information, all that is known about a situation, the known variables, and so on) can be interpreted so as to justify the conclusion reached or the claim being made.

In fields such as natural and physical sciences, computer science, engineering, and mathematics, warrants most frequently take the form of exact formulas used to convert raw data (in the form of known variables) into a significant conclusion (50). In mathematics, for example, the circumference of a circle can be discovered by applying a relevant formula, πr^2. For example, if the radius was measured at 3 feet you would apply the formula multiplying pi times 9 to discover the value of the circumference. Of course, many more complex formulas govern other applied and theoretical sciences. These warrants are known, reliable, exact, and can be depended upon.

By contrast, the law, assuming there is no disagreement about what the facts of the situation are, applies warrants in the form of relevant statues or precedents to discover whether one has or has not violated the law in a given situation (51).

As in general arguments, warrants are backed up in different ways. In science, the backing is the theoretical and experimental basis on which the warrant relies for its authority. In law, all the legal history of a particular statute would constitute the backing (whereas the warrant would be the statute that is appropriate to apply in that particular case).

In medicine, the backing for a diagnosis would be all the research that the physician might consult to make sure that the diagnosis was based on a generalization (the warrant) that provided the most accurate interpretation of the facts (symptoms, results of laboratory work, past medical history, etc.) of a particular case (53). Backing in all disciplines always refers to the underlying body of research in that specific field that justifies using a particular warrant (67).

Professional training is designed to familiarize students with concepts of evidence and with how the methodology of any particular field is related to its larger purposes or goals. Apprenticeship in various disciplines involves the process of discovering what warrants are appropriate to apply in different circumstances. In many fields, warrants do not take the form of exact formulas or statutes, but rather are general principles, capable of being learned only through years of experience in that field. For example, in medicine, a skillful diagnostician draws on years of accumulated experience as well as information learned in medical school.

The way a veterinarian reaches a conclusion is characteristic of medical diagnoses. In *All Creatures Great and Small* (1972), James Herriot diagnoses the true causes of a cow's sudden illness:

> I have a vivid recollection of a summer evening when I had to carry out a rumenotomy on a cow. As a rule, I was inclined to play for time when I suspected a foreign body—there were so many other conditions with similar symptoms that I was never in a hurry to make a hole in the animal's side. But this time diagnosis was easy; the sudden fall in milk yield, loss of cudding; grunting, and the rigid sunken-eyed appearance of the cow. And to clinch it the farmer told me he had been repairing a hen house in the cow pasture—nailing up loose boards. I knew where one of the nails had gone.

The way Herriot reaches his conclusion is characteristic of a veterinary or medical diagnosis. Herriot is able to relate the meaning of the signs of illness the cow displays to general principles drawn from his experience and presumably from veterinary textbooks. In effect, he says, these kinds of symptoms can mean the cow has ingested a foreign body like a nail, and in this particular case there is a good chance that is what happened. Therefore, he concludes that a rumenotomy, or surgical incision to remove a foreign body, should be performed.

Broken down into the separate elements in the argument, Herriot's line of thought appears as follows:

GROUNDS: Sudden fall in milk yield, loss of cudding, grunting, rigid sunken-eyed appearance, nails used to repair loose boards in a hen house in the cow pasture.

WARRANT: A cow that swallows a foreign body like a nail can be expected to display characteristic symptoms of sudden fall in milk yield, and so forth.

CLAIM (**expressed as a diagnosis**): The cow needs a rumenotomy to remove the foreign body.

QUALIFIER OR EXCEPTION: Unless it can be established that the cow definitely did not swallow one of the loose nails.

Because the purposes or goals of different disciplines are different, each field brings different perspectives to bear, even when viewing the same subject. By examining how various disciplines look at what appears to be the same thing, we can see how the same phenomenon becomes, in effect, a different object of inquiry according to the conceptual framework within which it is investigated. For example, a psychiatrist, Judith L. Rapoport, has looked at the life and music of the early twentieth-century French composer Erik Satie (*The Boy Who Couldn't Stop Washing*) (1989) as part of her study of obsessive compulsive disorder (OCD). Those suffering from OCD are compelled to repeat certain acts over and over again, whether it be washing, counting, checking, or other more elaborate rituals:

> Although he lived alone in Paris and at times in great poverty, he dressed fastidiously and his personal trappings were typical of OCD. No one was allowed to enter his room during his life. When he died, his wardrobe was found to contain a dozen identical new suits, shirts, collars, hats, walking sticks, and a cigar box was found with several thousand pieces of paper with the same symbols and inscriptions. All of them, for some unknown reason, about Charlemagne. Satie's OCD may have also influenced his music, although this is less clear. Satie's "trinitarian obsession" as musicologists refer to it was manifested in his works which were frequently conceived in groups of three. Within his music, Satie wrote he intended to present different views on a theme. Almost always, three were offered, the three *Gymnopedies* the best known.

By contrast, Joseph Machlis, a musicologist (writing in the *Introduction to Contemporary Music* [1961]), views Satie and the same work, *Gymnopedies*, within the completely different conceptual framework of his discipline. For example:

> Satie is best known to the public for his early piano pieces: the *Sarabandes* (1887), *Gymnopedies* (1887) and *Gnossiennes* (1890). Each set contains three dance pieces in the composer's characteristic manner. These works anticipate certain procedures that later became associated with Debussy, notably the unconventional handling of unresolved chords of the ninth, the modal idiom, and the movement of the harmony in parallel block-like formations.
>
> This music has a grave simplicity. It displays certain hallmarks of Satie's style: short symmetrical phrases repeated over and over; an airy melodic line, with an easy swing; limpid harmony, whose modal character is brought into focus at the cadences; lightness of texture and establishment at the outset of a rhythmic pattern that persists throughout.

Professionals in other disciplines have also studied Satie from their perspective, including the relationship between his emergence in the Rosicrucian Sect and his association with innovative movements in the world of art — cubism, dadaism, and surrealism.

ARGUING IN THE ARTS

The essential nature of the arts is to provide insight into the human condition, that is, to communicate what being human actually means, and how humanity appears at different times under different social conditions. The ultimate criteria by which works of art (both creative and interpretive) are judged is how well this is done without falsifying or distorting the human condition. This primary concern with the often inexpressible qualitative sense of the human experience defines both the kinds of problems as well as the methods used to address them within the arts.

For the artist, the question is how well the techniques of the craft have been used to bring the audience into direct contact with the internal real-life experiences each artist tries to express. Thus, arguments at this level are often technical over the best means of achieving a desired effect (352). We can see this at work in Tom Wolfe's "Why Aren't They Writing the Great American Novel Anymore?" *Esquire* (1972), where Wolfe analyzes how dissatisfaction with traditional techniques led innovative journalists to incorporate many of the narrative techniques of fiction—scene-by-scene construction, personal viewpoint, details of furnishings, clothes, social status, eccentric punctuation, slang and the vernaculars of different subcultures—to enhance their ability to report on human experience. In schematic form, Wolfe's argument appears as follows:

GROUNDS: You, as a nonfiction writer, want to achieve the effects of immediacy, concrete reality, emotional involvement, and a gripping or absorbing quality.

BACKING: The technical experiments and innovations of Fielding, Smollett, Balzac, Dickens, and Gogel have established that:

WARRANT: In the genre of fiction writing an effective way of introducing realism is to introduce (1) scene-by-scene construction, (2) realistic dialogue, (3) third-person point of view, and (4) a record of people's everyday gestures, habits, manners, customs, styles of furniture, clothing, decoration, styles of traveling, eating, keeping house, modes of behaving toward children, superiors, inferiors, plus various looks, glances, poses, styles of walking, and other details symbolic of the entire pattern of behavior through which people express their position in the world.

CLAIM: You, as a nonfiction writer, should try to use all the techniques of novelists to obtain the effects of immediacy, concrete reality, emotional involvement, and a gripping or absorbing quality.

The audiences for whom the arts are created judge an artist's work from a different perspective (353). For the audience, the key question is how effectively the artist's work succeeds in deepening, enriching, or extending the sense of being human and conveying insight into human nature. As representative of and mediator for the audience's reactions, the critic or reviewer evaluates the work of art or artist's performance. For example, in "The Boo Taboo" (*New York Magazine* [1987]) the acerbic theater critic John Simon offers this evaluation of Richard Tucker's performance in the opera *Carmen*:

> The most illuminating occurrence for me was a recent Saturday matinee at the Met. It was Barrault's wretched staging of *Carmen*, with Richard Tucker as Don Jose. Now Tucker had once been in possession of a good, strong voice; but he had never been a genuine artist with a sense of shading, expressive range, a feeling for the emotional depth of the part or the language in which he was singing. By this time, with even his basic organ gone, Tucker is long overdue for retirement. In this Don Jose, Tucker's voice was as off as it had been for years, his phrasing as unlovely as it had always been. Visually, he was a geriatric travesty; histrionically, even by the shockingly low standards of operatic acting, a farce. Even his French was, let us say, hyper-Tourelian. After he got through mangling the Flower Song, and after the orchestra was through as well, I added to the general applause three loud *phooeys* — a *phooey* cuts through applause better than a boo or hiss.

When each of the elements in Simon's critique is identified, the outline of his argument appears this way:

GROUNDS: Tucker's basic singing voice although once good and strong was gone. His phrasing was unlovely, visually he was a geriatric travesty, his acting fell below even the "shockingly low standards of operatic acting." His French was not authentic. He mangled the "Flower Song" from *Carmen*.

BACKING: Viewers, listeners, and critics of operatic performances have generally agreed that:

WARRANT: Good operatic singing requires a strong voice, a sense of shading, and expressive range, a feeling for the emotional depth of the part or the language in which the performer is singing, appropriate visual appearance, and competent acting ability.

CLAIM: Richard Tucker should not be performing since he can no longer meet the standards required for professional operatic singing.

QUALIFIER OR EXCEPTION: Despite the fact that there was general applause for Tucker's performance.

The broadest perspectives are brought to bear by academic disciplines in the liberal arts that interpret the meaning of an individual work as it relates to other works of that type and to the historical context in which it was produced (354). For example, the art historian Alan Wallach views particular paintings by William L. Haney and Jan van Eyck as they relate to larger social and cultural contexts. Open-endedness of interpretive issues and problems are characteristic of the humanities and liberal arts. That is, although arguments take the form of interpretations (however well supported and effective the arguments may be) they do not foreclose the possibility of new, different, and equally convincing interpretations in the future. Reduced to its essentials, Wallach's argument in "William L. Haney and Jan van Eyck" (1984) appears like this:

GROUNDS: In Haney's *The Root of it All*, the gold ring of the American Stock Exchange is drastically foreshortened and made to resemble a casino gambling table. Haney further complicates things by placing near the front of the gold ring an anamorphoric image of a black man's severed head. . . . Another composite technique Haney shares with van Eyck is a picture within a picture. Van Eyck's *Giovanni Arnolfini and His Bride* contains a convex mirror at the rear of the marriage chamber which reflects in extraordinary detail the couple and the otherwise invisible witnesses to the scene. In *A Present Tense of Extinct Too*, Haney's painting of a CBS sound stage, five television monitors play a similar role, commenting on the picture and augmenting its meaning with images of the Vietnam War, a nineteenth-century buffalo hunt, a mushroom cloud, and so on.

WARRANT: Artists, even those who live centuries apart, belonging to different worlds and different social conditions, often use the same techniques to express artistic judgments about the societies in which they live.

CLAIM: Both Haney and van Eyck solved problems of showing how spirituality was ruthlessly subordinated to materialism by (1) creating the illusion of unified compositions that break down upon closer inspection, (2) using architecture surrounding figures to bring together seemingly unrelated scenes, (3) using the technique of painting a picture within a picture, and (4) employing submerged symbolism to comment on the materialism of their respective societies.

ARGUING IN ETHICS

Originally a branch of philosophy, the field of ethics as a discipline in its own right has grown increasingly important as society has become more specialized and technological. As people are more locked into specialized roles and see things only from narrow viewpoints, an ethical view is required as a counterbalance so that they can evaluate the consequences of their actions in relation to society as a whole.

Ethics as a field tries to mediate claims between traditional professional or societal demands and those larger overriding human concerns by providing a systematic procedure that makes it possible to discover which course of action, among many choices, is preferable. Because ethical dilemmas involve a choice of actions, the ability to create hypothetical or "what if" situations is invaluable as it allows one to construct different scenarios in which the effects of different kinds of choices can be dramatized. A consideration of ethical choices should always involve understanding the consequences of choices for all those who will be affected.

Ethics is concerned with questions of what should be done because it seeks to investigate what kinds of actions are acceptable or unacceptable, right or wrong, good or bad, when judged according to a specified moral or ethical criterion. Thus, typical ethical arguments require the writer to apply a general ethical principle in the form of a warrant to discover whether an action that has already happened or is being considered is good or bad, desirable or regrettable, and is to be chosen or avoided (402–3).

We can see how this works by examining the argument made by Terence Cardinal Cooke in an address delivered to the First Annual American Health Congress (1972) (reprinted at the end of this chapter). Cooke argues that doctors, nurses, and other health-care professionals need to think about their professional obligations in light of equally compelling ethical and moral considerations. The occasion prompting Cooke's speech was the imminent passage of a "death with dignity" bill in the state legislature that would require health care professionals to take an active role in disconnecting life-support systems of terminally ill patients (without any immediate family with whom to confer) whose life, in the opinion of three physicians, was meaningless.

This is a typical ethical argument in that Cooke is addressing a conflict between a role health care professionals would be obligated to play and equally compelling moral considerations. Cooke argues that medical professionals should not be put in a situation where they are able to "play God" and decide when a patient's life is or is not meaningful.

The ethical principle Cooke applies as a warrant is based on the assumption that life is a God-given gift and that no human being has the right to take the life of another regardless of the circumstances. Represented in outline form, Cooke's argument appears thus:

GROUNDS: Allowing "death with dignity" would become an accepted part of health care professionals' duties because the state legislature was considering a bill stating that any disabled person with no immediate family, and for whom, in the opinion of three physicians, the prolongation of life would be meaningless, could be granted "death with dignity."

WARRANT: Permitting a patient's life to be terminated on the grounds that it is meaningless is against the law of God and should be justly labeled as "murdering a human being."

CLAIM: Health care professionals should not be party to a practice labeled "death with dignity" because it is against the law of God and constitutes murder.

ARGUING IN HISTORY

History explains how the present has been affected by the past and provides a clear account of the conditions in which societies have lived. Historical research brings to life important military, social, economic, and political events from the past. To create a persuasive reconstruction of past events, historians need to examine a wide range of records (private journals, letters, newspaper accounts, photographs if available, and other primary documents from the period under study), as well as secondary documents (such as interpretations of the same events by other historians). In seeking to delineate a plausible explanation for past events, historians may also draw on the information and research methods of political science (which studies how governments manage their affairs), sociology (which investigates the relationships between individuals and institutions in society), anthropology and archeology (which reconstruct past cultures and inquire into why they have different customs and patterns of development), and psychology (which studies human behavior). Historians may also use statistical and computer analyses to form a more accurate picture of past events.

The methods of inquiry used in history attempt to provide a clear picture of who, what, where, when, and how events took place. Some historians go beyond these basic issues and offer interpretations of why the events took place. Arguments in history often take the form of revising older interpretations or taking into account new information that forces a reevaluation of previously held beliefs. For example, in *The Peculiar Institution: Slavery in the Ante-Bellum South* (1956), Kenneth M. Stampp, a distinguished American historian, has investigated the relationship between the southern plantation system and slavery. In contrast to previous historians, such as Ulrich B. Phillips in *American Negro Slavery* (1918), who claimed that slavery was part of the social structure of the plantation system, Stampp asserted that a shortage of labor and a desire to increase profits were the real reasons behind the phenomenon of slave labor.

In one section of his book—"To Make Them Stand in Fear"— Stampp uses a variety of source documents, including recorded testimony of slave owners in Mississippi, South Carolina, North Carolina, and Virginia, as well as quotations from the actual manuals written to advise plantation owners on the management of slaves, to support his analysis of conditioning procedures used to instill fear and dependency in newly arrived blacks. In outline form Stampp's argument appears as follows:

GROUNDS: The manual "Discourses on the management of slaves" provided specific instructions on all phases of the "programming process." Stampp identifies five separate steps: (1) establishment of strict discipline modeled on army regulations, (2) implanting in the bondsman a consciousness of inferiority, (3) instilling a sense of awe at the master's enormous power, (4) persuading the bondsman to value the success of the master's enterprise, and (5) creating a habit of perfect dependence.

WARRANT: The study of original source documents provides valuable new information with which to reevaluate and revise previously held interpretations of events in history. (The warrant expresses the methodology underlying the concept of historical revisionism practiced by Stampp.)

CLAIM: Contrary to historical interpretations that view slavery as an integral component of the plantation system, original source documents reveal a calculated effort on the part of slave owners to transform newly arrived blacks into slaves who would be psychologically conditioned to believe that what was good for the plantation owners was good for them as well.

ARGUING IN LAW

Features of legal arguments are determined by the purpose of the law, that is, to provide protection for individuals in society and for society as a whole. Accordingly, legal decisions have to do with protecting life and liberty, property, public order, and providing systematic guidelines in ensuring the performance of contractual relationships (281).

The law provides a procedure for reaching decisions that is binding on all parties. Beyond the immediate goal of reaching decisions, the law strives to make decisions that are consistent with previous statutes, codes, and precedents, and with what society considers to be fair, equitable, and just (284). As with other arguments, the process of legal reasoning depends on the interplay between evidence or grounds and claims and warrants to produce the legal decision expressed as a claim. For example, the features of a regular legal argument can be seen in the following hypothetical case: A man whose name is Dan Webster petitions the court to have his name legally changed to 666. Dan Webster testifies that the number 666 has great personal meaning for him, but that the State Motor Vehicle Bureau would not agree to accept the name 666 without a legal name change. In analytical form, the legal argument would look like this:

GROUNDS: A man whose name is Dan Webster petitions the court to have his name legally changed to 666. Dan Webster testified that the number 666 had great personal meaning for him, but that the State Motor Vehicle Bureau would not agree to accept the name 666 without a legal name change.

WARRANT: Laws governing name changes passed by the state where Dan Webster resides require names to be changed to ones comprised of letters.

CLAIM: Dan Webster should not be allowed to change his name legally to 666.

QUALIFIER OR EXCEPTION: Unless Dan Webster wishes to change his name to a spelled out version of Six Six Six.

In court, legal reasoning makes use of an adversarial procedure where two opposing parties present the strongest case they can assemble for their proposed claims. Each party tells its story, or version of the truth, and the court (judge or jury) decides which version is more credible (284). The court chooses between the two opposing versions rather than working out a negotiated settlement that would be acceptable to both parties. The adversary character of legal reasoning can be seen in other legal forums where arguments are heard, such as in congressional hearings where individuals provide competing versions of the facts.

The examination of evidence is at the center of legal reasoning. Evidence is entered in the form of exhibits. Letters, documents, contracts, tape recordings, videotapes, and a wide range of physical evidence is then evaluated to see whose claim it best supports (302).

Evidence or grounds can also take the form of testimony of witnesses, to be tested by cross-examination, or of the expert opinion of authorities, that is also subjected to cross-examination. Cross-examination is an important feature of legal reasoning, as are rules governing what evidence the jury will or will not be allowed to hear (302). For example, evidence cannot be admitted from certain kinds of protected relationships (doctor – patient, lawyer – client, priest – parishioner, husband – wife). In other cases, the court must rule whether particular circumstantial or hearsay evidence is admissible.

As with other types of arguments, a range of warrants specific to the law authorize a connection between the claim and the evidence (304). Some warrants justify the use of expert testimony (for example, taking the form of an assumption that the testimony of a person with extensive experience and expertise in a particular field can be taken as authoritative). Other legal warrants justify the use of circumstantial, physical evidence to reach a conclusion. Still others take the form of particular cases to be used as precedents in reaching a decision on a current case (307).

In all disciplines a distinction is usually drawn between arguments that rely on laws, rules, procedures, accepted ways of thinking, and formulas and those arguments that challenge the very procedures or rules used in arriving at judgments. This latter kind of argument challenges the accepted methodology, the theoretical model upon which the discipline is based, whereas regular legal arguments simply apply the rules (308).

To see how rule-setting decisions become precedents that lawyers can use in ordinary legal arguments, we might examine the legal reasoning underlying the historic 1954 Supreme Court ruling on segregation in public schools (*Brown* v. *Board of Education of Topeka*). The decision was written by Earl Warren, then Chief Justice of the Supreme Court. In outline form, Warren's decision on behalf of the Court appears this way:

GROUNDS: Warren cites the results of psychological studies showing that segregated schools instill a sense of inferiority, retard mental development, and deprive the children of minority groups of equal educational opportunities.

WARRANT: A crucial clause in the Fourteenth Amendment, namely "no state shall . . . deny to any person within its jurisdiction the equal protection of the laws," empowers the court to evaluate how well states manage the important function of education for citizens.

CLAIM: Warren concluded that "in the field of public education the doctrine of 'separate but equal' has no place." The Court ruled that separate educational facilities are inherently unequal and found that segregation in the public schools deprives children of minorities of the educational opportunities they should rightfully enjoy under the Fourteenth Amendment.

An argument like this that challenges the very interpretation of what the law is, is obviously of a different order than an argument that simply applies accepted rules or methodology. This Supreme Court decision served as a catalyst for the civil rights movement, bringing about a series of public demonstrations, marches, and sit-ins, that, in conjunction with changes in the law, permanently altered existing social attitudes toward the acceptibility of racial discrimination.

ARGUING IN BUSINESS

Every phase of business production—finance, research and development, purchasing, marketing, and organizational development—entails a variety of decisions. Business in the present context refers to the part of the economy that provides goods and services for society.

Arguments in business differ from arguments advanced by scientists, historians, literary critics, ethicists, and so forth, in several important respects. Because the goal of business is to make a profit, arguments tend to focus on questions of tactics or strategy in accomplishing this purpose.

In contrast to law, where arguments take place in an adversary framework, business and management decisions require all the parties involved to arrive at a consensus or practical compromise (370). Furthermore, most business decisions have to be made within a certain time. Not to decide within the time available is equivalent to not making the decision at all. Moreover, business decisions sometimes have to be made despite the fact that circumstances are not completely understood or information is incomplete. In this respect, business decisions are unlike those arguments advanced by historians and scientists where time constraints play almost no part and where the emphasis is on taking as much time as necessary to understand circumstances as fully as possible (371).

The forums within which business arguments take place include board room conferences, stockholder meetings, consultations between managers, and any other administrative setting where management must explain the basis of its decision to others both inside and outside the company—that is, to employees, stockholders, and government officials (370).

Claims in business take the form of policy recommendations. These proposals may concern actions that should be taken to introduce a new product or service, decisions as to whether to invest in a new plant, and proposals covering a wide range of issues (383). For example, should the company branch out, change its pricing strategies? How should it best respond to the marketing strategies of the competition? What use should be made of market research data in order to market a product more effectively? Most business arguments are utilitarian, short- or medium-term proposals, and are concerned with questions of strategies and tactics rather than discussions of ultimate goals and purposes.

Grounds or support in business arguments consists of all the information on which claims can be based (383–4). This includes economic information, data gleaned from market research, as well as relevant government regulations. Information used to support claims frequently appears as a detailed breakdown of all types of expenses (administrative, market research, and costs of development). Business today also avails itself of a whole range of systematized information in the form of data bases.

The manipulation of information in business uses a problem-solving model that defines the nature of the problem, uses a variety of search techniques (brainstorming, breaking the problem into subproblems, and so forth) and generates a list of alternative solutions. The most feasible solution is presented as a proposal or claim. Solutions are evaluated in terms of what constitutes the best match of the company's resources and proven competence consistent with government regulations and expectations of society.

Most business warrants relate directly to the underlying purpose of business itself, that is, whatever promises to produce a greater profit consistent with the proven methods should be selected from any field of alternatives (385–6). Likewise, whatever promises to lessen the cost of operation in producing a product or service, or promises to promote the more efficient functioning of the company should be chosen from any field of alternatives.

We can see these basic elements operating in a typical situation where a municipality has entered into a long-term agreement to have trash collected by a private contractor. Town officials must now decide whether to sell their own equipment (trucks, shovels, plows) that the municipality no longer needs for the present and probably will not need for some years in the future.

Arguments in favor of selling the equipment emphasize the cost of maintaining and repairing it and the revenue its sale could generate. Arguments against selling the equipment refer to the experience of other municipalities that, having sold their trucks, and so on, were at the mercy of the contractor when the agreement came up for renegotiation. Ultimately, the municipality officials decided not to sell in order to avoid a situation where they would be dependent on private contractors who would know they would be forced to pay because they could not provide the service themselves. In outline form, the argument appears as follows:

GROUNDS: The projected cost of maintaining the equipment, the revenue its sale would generate, and the projected costs of keeping a private contractor to collect the trash.

BACKING: Precedents are provided by other municipalities who initially entered into long-term service contracts because of low prices, sold their equipment, and subsequently were at the mercy of contractors who raised their prices dramatically when the service agreement came up for renewal.

WARRANT: In the short term the sale would produce apparent savings, but in the long term it might prove very costly. In weighing two alternatives, long-term disadvantages outweigh short-term advantages.

CLAIM: The municipality should keep its equipment (trucks, plows, etc.) rather than put it up for sale.

QUALIFIERS OR EXCEPTIONS: Unless unforeseen costs in maintenance and storage become excessive.

Business in a Changing Environment

Recent times have seen a change in societal expectations about business that have created what might be called a new theoretical model for this discipline. Whereas traditional obligations for businesses ended with making profits, new expectations mean that business has to change accordingly if it is to fulfill its underlying mandate of responding to society's needs (380). The question as to whether or not business should assume social responsibilities beyond basic obligations to earn a profit is increasingly the subject of debate.

A traditionalist like Milton Friedman in "The Social Responsibility of Business is to Increase Its Profits" (reprinted in Chapter Eight) claims that economic values should be the only criteria to which businesses should be held accountable. From this viewpoint, money used to meet social responsibilities is money taken illegally from shareholders that must be recovered through higher product costs. If these firms were attempting to compete with other companies internationally, they would be at a severe disadvantage. Moreover, says Friedman, businessmen and women should not assume governmental functions and try to determine how resources should best be allocated.

The opposing position is well presented by Robert Almeder in "Morality in the Marketplace" (also in Chapter Eight). Almeder asserts that as society's needs and expectations change, businesses must change accordingly. It is not inconceivable that a corporation's efforts to be socially responsible will gain more customers ultimately and make more money in the long run precisely because of the good will generated by the company's actions. More pragmatically, says Almeder, businesses that do not act in a socially responsible manner will compel the government to step in and regulate them on behalf of society. Thus, his position is that social irresponsibility on the part of businesses is not only self-destructive but will be unprofitable in the long run.

Business must also fulfill its obligation to consumers through truth in advertising, warranty service, and by not producing products that pose a danger to the consumers. In relation to stockholders, there are standards of financial disclosure that must be met. At the same time, management's new relationship with labor has led to pension plans, concern for occupational health and safety issues, and profit-sharing plans. Many businesses now routinely fulfill obligations to minorities in terms of training and equal opportunity employment and some businesses participate in solving community problems, establishing health care facilities, and participating in other local projects. How great the change in underlying warrants has been can be seen by comparing, in diagram form, the same set of circumstances when applying first the traditional warrant and then one in which the newer assumption has been used:

GROUNDS: The Alaska reserves of untapped oil constitute the largest single remaining source of energy-producing fossil fuel left available to the United States.

WARRANT (traditional): The dependence of society on fossil fuel for energy requires the exploitation of any domestic energy source that is discovered.

CLAIM: Oil companies must be granted the right to drill for oil in the Alaska oil reserve.

Observe how a change in the underlying assumption or warrant would produce a completely opposite conclusion. This warrant, if commonly accepted, would bring about a major paradigm shift in the world of business.

GROUNDS: The Alaska reserves of untapped oil constitute the largest single remaining source of energy-producing fossil fuel left available to the United States.

WARRANT (new): The long-term impact of the burning of fossil fuels on the environment (including the greenhouse effect) requires oil companies to act in such a way that harm is not caused to society as a whole.

CLAIM: Oil companies must not be granted the right to drill for oil in the Alaska oil reserve.

ARGUING IN THE SOCIAL SCIENCES

The social sciences are often referred to as the behavioral sciences because they focus on what can be observed objectively about human beings—their actions, or behavior. These disciplines seek to discover causal connections (sometimes expressed as statistical laws) that have both descriptive and predictive value, and that can be confirmed or refuted by data from subsequent research.

The social sciences have adapted in some measure both the techniques and the objectives of the physical and natural sciences in order to study how human beings interact in the context of social, political, business, legal, psychological, and cultural relationships.

To ensure an objectivity comparable to that of the physical and natural sciences, social science researchers rely on statistical surveys, questionnaires, and other data-gathering techniques. Social scientists draw upon a whole range of theoretical models to explain human behavior and explore how individual behavior may be conditioned by expectations of the surrounding culture. The range of theories available often raises the question as to which theoretical model should be applied to explain the data in question. Social scientists strive to achieve results in quantifiable and repeatable form so that other researchers can repeat and thereby confirm the validity of the results of their experiments.

The ways in which social sciences have adapted methodology from the natural and physical sciences can be seen in the procedures social scientists use for gathering evidence through observation and controlled experiments. First and foremost, social sciences (including sociology, psychology, anthropology, archeology, education, economics, political sciences, business and management, and so forth) emphasize the importance of systematic and objective observation of events and people recorded in concrete language, without interposing any personal opinion as to motives. Events and human behavior must be recorded as objectively as possible so other social scientists can verify the observations and authenticate the findings. Of course, some social sciences such as archeology have to gather information after the event has taken place and must gather data in the form of artifacts and records.

To look at this methodology more closely, we might examine its use in sociology, a discipline that is concerned with the observation, description, and explanation of the behavior of people in groups. Sociologists investigate institutions within society, their origins, their capacity for accommodating social change, and the mechanisms within them that influence the behavior of individuals.

Questions to be answered or problems to be solved are expressed in the form of hypotheses whose validity can be measured by empirical means. For example, in a classic experiment John Darley and Bibb Latané used small groups of people to test their "diffusion of responsibility" theory to solve the problem of why people don't help in a crisis. By varying the number of people who thought others also were aware of a crisis, Darley and Latané demonstrated in quantifiable form a plausible mechanism to explain the real causes of seeming apathy in bystanders.

Since it would be impractical for social scientists to test everyone in a particular population in order to gather evidence, researchers test a sample or small group of people from a specific population. Darley and Latané's research took the typical form of an experimental study in which they manipulated one variable (the number of people in the group in a room filling with smoke) and observed the effect on a second variable (the likelihood of any of the subjects reporting the smoke to an external authority).

The professional journal in which the results of their study appeared is an appropriate forum within which arguments can be tested and evaluated. By studying the methodology of this experiment, other researchers could set up comparable experiments to test for themselves the validity of Darley and Latané's conclusions. The authors explain the design of the experiment, the hypothesis being tested, and the results in a brief abstract that precedes their article, "Group Inhibition of Bystander Intervention in Emergencies" (1968):

> Male undergraduates found themselves in a smoke-filling room, either alone, with 2 non-reacting others, or in groups of 3. Ss [subjects] were less likely to report the smoke when in the presence of passive others (10%) or in groups of 3 (38% of groups) than when alone (75%). These results seemed to have been mediated by the way Ss interpreted the ambiguous situation; seeing other people remaining passive led Ss to decide the smoke was not dangerous.

In outline form, Darley and Latané's argument appears as follows:

GROUNDS: Male undergraduates found themselves in a smoke-filling room, either alone, with two nonreacting others, or in groups of three. Ss (subjects) were less likely to report the smoke when in the presence of passive others (10 percent) or in groups of three (38 percent of groups) than when alone (75 percent).

BACKING: Prior research by social psychologists (Darley and Latané, Latané and D. C. Glass, S. Schacter, E. Goffman, R. Brown) makes it probable that the diffusion of responsibility model determines how people in groups react to a crisis.

WARRANT: The diffusion of responsibility hypothesis states that if an individual is alone when an emergency occurs, he or she feels solely responsible. When others are present, individuals feel that their own responsibility for taking action is lessened, making them less likely to help.

CLAIM: The behavior of the people in the situation is explained by the diffusion of responsibility model. As Darley and Latané conclude, "seeing other people remaining passive led Ss to decide the smoke was not dangerous."

QUALIFIERS OR EXCEPTIONS: (1) Unless Ss felt the presence of others increased their collective ability to cope with fire, and therefore were less afraid *because* they were in a group, or (2) unless desire to hide fear and exhibit bravery compels people to appear less apprehensive when others are watching.

ARGUING IN THE SCIENCES

The types of information sought and the methods employed within the domain of the sciences aim at providing an accurate, systematic, and comprehensive account of the world around us as well as a framework within which new hypotheses can be put forward and evaluated (315).

The forums in which argumentation takes place in the sciences include professional meetings, refereed journals, and conferences. These public forums guarantee that all ideas will be tested to determine their underlying validity.

Scientists, even those on the losing side of an argument, have a common interest in gaining a more accurate picture of the natural world, its origin, makeup, and functioning (317). Thus, the putting forth and disputing of claims is not an end in itself as it is in the law, but a means to clarify and improve a picture of the world.

The way science solves problems and generates new knowledge can be seen by examining procedures used by the biologists Arthur D. Hasler and James A. Larsen in "The Homing Salmon" (1955). Their experiments solved the mystery of how salmon could find their way back to the exact streams where they were born, even from distances as great as 900 miles, by pinpointing the role played by the salmon's olfactory sense.

Well-documented observations based on the recovery of tagged salmon in the streams where they were originally born had established that the homing instinct was a scientific problem worth investigating. For scientists, observation plays a crucial role in identifying mysterious phenomena or anomalies (319). The question of how salmon remember their birthplace and find their way back to the stream in which they were born, sometimes from great distances, is an enigma which has fascinated naturalists for many years.

Once observations show the existence of a problem needing explanation, scientists formulate a tentative explanation or hypothesis to account for this otherwise inexplicable event.

Scientists then design specific experiments to measure in objective and quantifiable form whether the hypothesis provides an adequate explanation of the phenomenon. A scientific hypothesis, if true, should have both descriptive and predictive value. That is, it must accurately predict that in particular circumstances (that other scientists can duplicate) certain kinds of measurable effects can be observed. These effects should confirm the truth of the hypothesis.

For this reason, the design of the experiment is the essential feature of scientific research. The experiment should make it possible to isolate, control, and measure the role played by one key variable. In Hasler and Larsen's experiment, half of a group of salmon were marked and deprived of their olfactory sense and the other half were used as a control group. When all the salmon were released downstream, it was determined that the control group correctly returned as usual to the original stream whereas the "odor-blinded" fish migrated in random fashion "picking the wrong stream as often as the right one."

The way in which evidence or grounds, warrants, and claims play a part in scientific problem-solving as a method of inquiring into the truth (as opposed to advocating a position, as in the law) can be seen in the following outline:

GROUNDS:

"We took water from two creeks in Wisconsin and investigated whether fish could learn to discriminate between them. Our subjects, first minnows, then salmon, were indeed able to detect a difference. If, however, we destroyed a fish's nose tissue, it was no longer able to distinguish between the two water samples. Chemical analysis indicated that the only major difference between the two waters lay in the organic material. By testing the fish with various fractions of the water, separated by distillation, we confirmed that the identifying material was some volatile organic substance. The idea that fish are guided by odors in their migrations was further supported by a field test. From each of the two different branches of the Issaquah River in the state of Washington, we took a number of sexually ripe silver salmon which had come home to spawn. We then plugged with cotton the noses of half the fish in each group and placed all the salmon in the river below the fork to make the upstream run again. Most of the fish with unplugged noses swam back to the stream they had selected the first time. But the 'odor-blinded' fish migrated back in random fashion, picking the wrong stream as often as the right one."

BACKING: The experience of scientists in developing systematic procedures for testing hypotheses that claim to account for otherwise inexplicable phenomena.

WARRANT: The established procedures of scientific research state that the results of an experiment designed in such a way as to make it possible to isolate, control, and measure the role played by one key variable can be reliably depended upon to explain and predict a previously inexplicable phenomenon.

CLAIM **(takes the form of a clear-cut working hypothesis for investigating the mystery of the homing salmon):**

"We can suppose that every little stream has its own characteristic odor, which stays the same year after year; that young salmon become conditioned to this odor before they go to sea; that they remember the odor as they grow to maturity, and that they are able to find it and follow it to its source when they come back upstream to spawn."

QUALIFIER OR EXCEPTION: **Unless the salmon's homing instincts are due to other causes such as salinity, water temperature, or the earth's magnetic field, and so forth.**

Sometimes the anomalies observed and theories formulated to explain them are in such conflict with existing paradigms or agreed-upon scientific laws that they demand the establishment of new theoretical models to guide further research (328–9). Charles Darwin's observations *On the Origin of Species By Means of Natural Selection* (1859) in the Galapagos Islands of adaptive mutations in finches, tortoises, and other species ultimately led him to formulate a theory of evolution that proposed that both humans and apes evolved from a common primate ancestor. By challenging existing theories and replacing them with a new theoretical model, Darwin advanced all of science.

THREE SHORT ARGUMENTS FOR ANALYSIS

Mike Jackman

Enabling the Disabled

This article originally appeared in Perspectives *(Spring/Winter 1983). Mike Jackman is a partner of Phase Two Strategies, a management consulting firm specializing in strategic communications planning and corporate positioning. He is the author of* Macmillan's Book of Business and Economic Quotations *(1984). In "Enabling the Disabled," Jackman draws on a wide range of examples that dramatize the nature of the physical, legal, and psychological obstacles disabled people must confront in our society. The author shows how an insidious form of discrimination disguised as paternalism discourages the disabled from becoming productive and then how this "catch 22" situation is used to perpetuate the stereotype that the disabled cannot care for themselves.*

You step into an elevator to go to your job interview, but you can't   1
see the button to push for the fifth floor.

An emergency room doctor is injecting you with an antibiotic to   2
which you're allergic but you can't protest because the hospital has no
sign language interpreter.

It's Saturday night and a friend asks you out but you know that many   3
bars, nightclubs and theaters will turn you away because you're considered a fire hazard.

You're disabled. What did you expect anyway?   4

Facing higher rates of unemployment and poverty than any other   5
group of Americans, disabled adults have less access to decent schooling,
housing, work and transportation than anyone in this country, including
non-citizens.

We're very young when we first learn that the rights of citizenship   6
are universal, that they're not conditional on religion, race or sex. But we
never question the more subtle conditions and being disabled is one of
them.

Being disabled means considering whether to protest when a restau-   7 rant turns you away because your presence might disturb the other patrons. Being disabled means working in back rooms, because you might disrupt the office work routine or force your employer to modify the workplace.

8   Being disabled means settling for a limited existence because society is unwilling to pay what it costs to guarantee your right to participate. It means accepting hundreds of barriers to independence and dignity.

9   To most of us, the idea of barriers probably suggests the battle for physical access to public facilities. Physical access is a convenient rallying point for the disability rights movement because it is the most visible. The fact that it is still controversial is a sign of our limited commitment to this country's 36 million disabled citizens.

10   There are however, far more barriers for disabled people and most of them are invisible to those who are not disabled—barriers that political activism and Federal legislation have only recently begun to dismantle, such as barriers to the basic need for housing.

11   In a western city, a landlord refused to rent an apartment to a blind professional woman. How could he be sure she wouldn't start a fire trying to cook herself a meal, he asked?

12   In another major city, a man confined to a wheelchair was prohibited from renting a second-floor apartment because the elevator would have been his only exit, violating a city fire ordinance.

13   One suburban man, diagnosed as schizophrenic, received heavy medication causing severe relaxation of his facial muscles. His landlord, saying that he bothered other tenants, evicted the man from his apartment. Like hundreds of other disabled people, he is appealing to government housing bodies before filing suit.

14   Invisible communications barriers also abound. In a midwestern city, a totally deaf man sued his town because he was unable to communicate with the fire and police department emergency operators—a requirement mandated by telecommunications and disability rights legislation.

15   A woman enrolled at a state teachers college was temporarily speech-imparied after her first two years. University officials told her she would not be able to pursue a full teaching credential, only a limited degree. Seeking recourse through the grievance process, she is appealing on the grounds of both state and Federal violations.

16   In an eastern city, a woman psychotherapist afflicted with cerebral palsy was accepted into a private institute to obtain a doctorate in psychology. After successfully completing a year of coursework, the institute would not readmit her for the second year claiming that her disability would interfere with her ability to relate to patients. Appealing to the state human rights commission, she is reliving the similar experiences of blacks who once had to fight for the right to practice as therapists.

17   Many cases, particularly in education, are examples of direct violations of Federal and State disability rights legislation. Typical is the

instance of a grade school student who is suing his principal who refused to let him into a regular class despite the fact that the student does not require any adaptive assistance.

Air transportation for those in wheelchairs presents both bureaucratic   18
and civil rights conflicts. A paraplegic Vietnam veteran is suing a major US airline company for what he claims is a discriminatory and humiliating policy. The airline, following its own internal policy and not an FAA regulation, requires that all wheelchair passengers must have a blanket underneath them when sitting in an airline seat so airline personnel can carry off the passenger during a safety evacuation. The veteran claims the airline is really worried that paraplegics are incontinent and that the blanket policy deals neither with his safety nor his needs as a passenger.

And if you're blind and require a guide dog, you would be advised to   19
not go to Hawaii for a short vacation. A regulation in that island state requires a 120 day quarantine for entering dogs, including guide dogs. The dog's owner is also required to foot the $466 bill for the quarantine. A blind guide dog owner may stay with his or her dog in a special compound (where gates are locked after hours) during the quarantine period.

Most conflicts between institutions and disabled people do not go to   20
court; lawyers sooner or later confront the clear mandate of Federal legislation. As a result, out-of-court settlements, resolutions and administrative grievances are the usual avenues for recourse.

At the base of all invisible barriers for the disabled is an insidious   21
paternalism: the attitude that disability means incompetence, that disabled people will always need the able-bodied to care for them because they are flawed and incapable of caring for themselves.

The attitude that disability is a flaw rather than a human variation   22
implies that it is the burden of the disabled to adjust to the lives of the majority, that society has no burden to accommodate its members' differing needs. As black and women's groups have discovered, the paternalistic parent-child relationship destroys individual identity and self-esteem. It also robs its victims of the power to compete with other groups in the struggle to shape public policy.

Historically denied the rights to attend school, hold a job, marry and   23
have children, the disabled have also been denied the opportunity to improve their political status. Physical and communication barriers and arbitrarily defined standards of mental competence have traditionally deprived disabled people of the right to vote.

The barrier of paternalism has its roots in a series of myths and   24
stereotypes that able-bodied people have about disabled people. These myths are also widely shared by disabled people who have been socialized to accept this society's definition of the disabled as helpless, unproductive and incompetent.

Like racists, able-bodied people see the results of discrimination and   25
confuse them with the results of physical disability. Since disabled peo-

ple rarely hold good jobs, they must be incapable of having careers. Disabled people are rarely seen or heard so they must have little to contribute to the world.

26   The 1973 Rehabilitation Act was the first crack in this pervasive attitude. Section 504 of the act, in words almost identical to those of Title VI of the 1964 Civil Rights Act, guaranteed specific civil rights for disabled people which up until then had only been generally inferred from the 13th and 14th amendments.

27   Unlike civil rights legislation affecting blacks and women, Section 504 predated any widespread public pressure for change. "Federal law is the only major reason you're seeing more workers who are disabled," says Robert Funk, executive director of the Disability Rights Education and Defense Fund (DREDF). "Public attitudes are still the worst barrier."

28   The passage of the Rehabilitation Act was the first time the Federal government officially acknowledged that disabled people as a group were being discriminated against. It reflected an expanding social consciousness on the part of legislators, though not necessarily on the part of the general public.

29   Indifference to the disabled became charitable paternalism, an approach that still dominates the thinking of the public and of government officials who see disability as more of an administrative challenge rather than a legislative and moral concern. And there will be little impetus for such officials to change their views as long as so many disabled remain invisible.

30   The isolation of disabled people is the result of the same out-of-sight, out-of-mind mentality that has always allowed us to institutionalize people who are different. The immediate causes of isolation are multiple, from poor outreach by public agencies to both the physical and hidden barriers that keep most disabled people off the streets. This not only isolates disabled adults from the social mainstream, it also separates disabled people from one another.

31   "Seeing another disabled person is a rare event," says Funk. "And when you do meet another disabled person, the conversation is usually a technological exchange about special equipment or services. The lack of information is a barrier to self-sufficiency."

32   For any disenfranchised group of people to become an effective political force, it must escape the exploitative and immobilizing hold of paternalism. But disabled people must first break down their own barriers.

33   Having announced in Section 504 that those receiving Federal financial assistance could not discriminate on the basis of handicap, it took Congress four more years to put teeth into the law. Compliance regulations were issued in 1977 only after months of protests and sit-ins by disabled people—the first time in U.S. history the disabled had mounted a political effort commanding national attention.

Arguing that court-enforced compliance would be costly and lengthy, 34
the Department of Education set up a more passive system to enforce
Section 504, a kind of voluntary compliance. To monitor compliance, the
government actually funded a national program that would train local
disabled people—who had previous legal background—in the gentle
art of persuading Federal funding recipients to comply with Section 504.

One major organization charged with the task of training these local 35
volunteers was the Disability Rights Education and Defense Fund. Based
in Berkeley, California, DREDF was founded in 1979 to establish and
protect the constitutional rights of disabled people. It has trained nearly
3,000 disabled people and their families in 24 western and mid-western
states, teaching them to apply Section 504 to issues that include equal
access to employment, education and social services.

This system of training helped create a broad-based disability rights 36
movement with a nationwide network of disabled people who were
committed to a civil rights agenda on behalf of their peers. Even more
significant, the new disability rights network brought all disability-re-
lated organizations closer to one another. "Now you have a coalition of
all types of disabled people," says Funk. "Many of us who get together
have nothing in common except the legal status of disability." According
to Funk, the isolation that used to exist among disability groups is rapidly
disappearing as organizations that serve specialized constituent concerns
see that they face similar civil rights barriers.

This new emphasis on civil rights has not replaced the traditional 37
efforts to improve services and access. The disability rights movement,
however, has established a new standard by which all progress could be
measured, a standard allowing the disabled to be viewed as people with
full civil rights. The movement also forced local and Federal policy
makers to see disabled people as full citizens and to respond to them as
such.

Physical access is important both as a real issue and as a symbolic 38
rallying point for the disability rights movement. Is a building's owner
willing to make modifications necessary for disabled people to lead
integrated lives in a society that prizes mobility and communication?
That most such commitments are highly visible when enacted—ramps,
special buses, lower water fountains, Braille numbers in elevators—has
given them a strategic significance in the emerging disability rights
movement that extends beyond their immediate importance. But this
visibility has also had its drawbacks. A new ramp or renovated restroom
gives the public the false impression that adequate physical access has
been established. For disabled people, the barriers that remain far outnumber the victories.

Air travel for people in wheelchairs poses fundamental problems. 39
Because motorized chairs have acid batteries, they can't be taken on
airplanes. At $3,000 apiece, who can afford to have a second motorized
wheelchair waiting in the next city?

40   Since airplane aisles make it impossible to get to the restroom, you must decide whether or not to test your bladder's tolerance for pain or to have someone carry you to the restroom.

41   Whether you're blind, deaf or in a wheelchair, choosing and ordering the food you want in a cafeteria line is guess-work at best. Using a standard public telephone ranges from difficult to impossible (a deaf person can't hear on that equipment, a blind person has difficulty dialing and someone in a wheelchair can't reach the receiver in a phone booth) despite the proven cost-effectiveness of new architectural and communications technology such as open cubicles, touchtone phones and devices that allow some deaf persons to communicate. And every library and supermarket poses its own logistical problems.

42   Americans watch at least 40 hours of television a week. It's a national institution and social lubricant. For those with impaired hearing, *watching* television is most of the experience. Only a handful of programs (mostly PBS) are captioned for deaf people. The television industry, which consistently has one of the highest returns on shareholder equity of any industry, says captioning is too expensive to provide for the 11 million Americans with hearing problems.

43   In fact, almost any routine activity — shopping, visiting, working, and going out at night — represents a series of barriers for the disabled person.

44   Those barriers even extend to our ultimate right — voting. In colonial days, voting was limited to white male property owners. While subsequent court decisions have established that voting "is preservative of all rights," only recently has the unrestricted exercise of this right become a reality for millions of Americans. The last class of citizens still seeking to achieve full protection of its right to vote is the disabled.

45   Polling places are usually inaccessible; ballots aren't available in Braille; poll workers cannot communicate in sign language; and thousands of people are forbidden to vote because they don't meet arbitrarily determined standards of mental competence (a category that includes most mentally retarded people.)

46   Recent court decisions have not been helpful. There have been three Federal cases dealing directly with voting rights, none later than 1975. Filed on claims of denial of equal protection, all three claims were denied by the courts. While the courts agreed that access to polling places and the lack of Braille ballots for secret voting constituted a burdened right, they have said that the economic and administrative interests of the state justify such barriers to voting rights.

47   While voting is a crucial right, in America jobs are a major source of status, dignity and self-esteem. "What do you do?" is a conversational staple. To contribute to society and support yourself is as prized today as it was in colonial days when the New World meant opportunity.

48   If a disabled person is lucky enough to have received an equal education, he or she will face the most demoralizing barrier of all —

getting a job. The disincentives to looking for work are many. Besides the usual physical barriers, Federal benefits policies actually penalize people who take the risk of looking for work.

Many disabled people receive some combination of state and Federal   49
benefits in the form of Supplemental Security Income (SSI) or Social Security Disability Income (SSDI). When SSI recipients go to work, benefit payments are discontinued after a nine-month trial period. But if you should lose a job, you can't reapply for SSI since you've proven by working that you're no longer disabled. To be eligible again, you must prove you are *more* disabled than you were before you took the job. Even if you do make it through this punitive process, you will have to wait from six months to two years before you are again eligible for SSI, Medicare and other benefit programs.

In California, disabled people can work and receive SSI payments on   50
a sliding scale that moves up or down with their employment status. No other state has a similar program. In a country where individualism and self-sufficiency are prized, disabled people must gamble on poverty with every attempt at real independence. How many of us would be willing to take the risk?

Assume that you are an able-bodied person making enough money to   51
live on. Imagine your present household budget — car, food, rent, clothes, medical expenses. If you're like most people, every penny is accounted for. In fact, you're probably close to the credit limit on your charge card.

Now you become disabled. Your medical costs go up, especially since   52
you can't get medical insurance anymore. You'll probably need to buy special equipment or modify your home or apartment to accommodate your disability. If you need help getting ready for work, you'll have to hire a part-time attendant. You're way over budget but you've just started. At work, you'll either be laid off, demoted or at best, passed over for promotion. Your expenses increase as your income falls.

So being disabled is expensive. That's why more than one in three   53
disabled people live below the poverty line. Ironically, some agencies estimate that *half* of all disabled people qualified to work are unemployed.

But employment is no picnic either. For every dollar earned by an   54
able-bodied white male, a disabled white male makes 60 cents, a disabled black male makes 25 cents and a disabled black female makes about 12 cents.

Can disability rights survive the budget process? Who decides that it's   55
too expensive to design airplanes for disabled people? Who decides that disabled children must lower their expectations about adulthood?

Many public officials still see the civil rights mandate of disability   56
legislation as social services or regulatory law. And with the highest budget deficit and unemployment rate since World War II, some people are saying that we can't afford disability rights.

57   Congress did not pass the Rehabilitation Act to increase the GNP, although putting disabled people to work would help do just that. Section 504 and P.L. 94–142 were enacted for the same reason as the 13th and 14th amendments — to remove the legal barriers of discrimination. And while that's being done, it's up to all of us to remove those other barriers to the handicapped — the hidden ones.

Sample Analysis

CLAIM: Jackman claims that the disabled are victims of an insidious form of discrimination. Because of the stereotyped way in which they are viewed, society, despite its overt attitude of concern, actually discourages the disabled from becoming productive. The tragedy, says Jackman, is that the disabled internalize this perception, begin to see themselves as helpless, and fail to become productive. This, in turn, strengthens the societal stereotype that the disabled "will always need the able-bodied to care for them because they are flawed and incapable of caring for themselves."

GROUNDS: Jackman opens his essay with everyday instances (not being able to see the numbers in an elevator, being turned away from various public places, trying to rent an apartment) that allow his readers to empathize with the kinds of obstacles disabled people face daily. To back up his claim, Jackman cites a broad range of discriminatory regulations (governing guide dogs, motorized wheel chairs, and so on) as evidence of continuing discrimination against the disabled in areas of employment, housing, voting, transportation, and education. Jackman further supports his claim by citing statistics as to the number of cents on the dollar ("a disabled white male makes 60 cents, a disabled black male makes 25 cents and a disabled black female makes about 12 cents") the disabled can earn when compared to the able-bodied.

   To show how the stereotype arises from perception rather than reality, Jackman makes extremely effective use of cases where people who were in no way disabled and subsequently became handicapped (although still quite competent) were treated with exactly the same prejudices as those who are born disabled.

WARRANT: The principle to which Jackman appeals is the concept that discrimination against the disabled should be as illegal as discrimination against any other minority.

PERSUADING THE AUDIENCE: Jackman appeals to his audience's sense of fair play: all people should be given equal opportunity to prove themselves, none should be treated unfairly, be forced to live less productive lives than they are capable of, or be discriminated against in opportunities for employment, housing, and education.

Jackman's article is not only addressed to the able-bodied who have no conception of what life as a disabled person is like, but to the handicapped as well.

This article urges the handicapped to believe in themselves and see themselves as competent to deal with their own lives. Jackman wishes to make the general public aware of how stereotyped assumptions about the disabled are governed by an insidious form of paternalism and to urge the public to see the disabled in more realistic terms.

Questions for Discussion and Writing

1. What types of situations does Jackman present that might be hypothetical for most of his readers, but that are very real for disabled persons, to make his audience realize the nature of the obstacles disabled people face every day?

2. How does Jackman use the opening paragraphs of his argument to launch a two-pronged assault on society's attitudes toward the disabled? How does his discussion of the subtle psychological aspects of discrimination strengthen his analysis of outward discrimination in areas of employment, housing, voting, transportation, and schooling? Describe the psychologically insidious results when disabled men and women accept as valid society's assumptions and perceptions about them.

3. In what way does Jackman's use of examples of people who were in no way incapacitated and then became disabled prove his thesis about the way in which society views the disabled? Why are these examples particularly effective in strengthening his assertions about the way people are treated who were disabled from birth?

4. How does society's treatment of the disabled start a vicious cycle that reduces the scope of activities and the quality of the lives of the disabled, which are then used as arguments to perpetuate the stereotype that the disabled are incompetent and "will always need the able-bodied to care for them because they are flawed and incapable of caring for themselves"?

5. What examples of actual rules and regulations that are applied to the disabled are especially effective in supporting Jackman's thesis? For instance, what are the implications of Hawaii's quarantine requirements (para. 18)?

6. What facts, figures, and statistical evidence does Jackman give to support specific assertions throughout his essay?

7. What is the history and significance of the 1973 Rehabilitation Act, specifically section 504? In a paragraph, summarize the effects that Jackman says this piece of legislation has had in producing equal access to employment, education, and social services for the disabled.

8. Evaluate the effectiveness of the title "Enabling the Disabled" in conveying Jackman's arguments about what kinds of measures should be taken to remove barriers faced by the disabled.

9. How does Jackman's essay contain arguments addressed to two different kinds of audiences—the general public, and the disabled? Discuss the extent to which Jackman's argument might be capable of bringing about greater public awareness of the serious problems faced by the disabled and, as important, changing the false perceptions the disabled may have about themselves?

10. If you have ever been temporarily physically incapacitated, or have a disability, write an essay that will help your audience to understand your plight and the visible and subtle psychological aspects of discrimination that the disabled must endure every day.

Gilbert Cant

Deciding When Death Is Better Than Life

Gilbert Cant is a journalist whose articles have appeared in The New York Times Magazine *and* Good Housekeeping. *"Deciding When Death Is Better than Life" first appeared in* Time *(July 16, 1973). Cant brings forward two cases that dramatize the issues involved in the euthanasia debate and argues that mercy killing, in some circumstances, is not only morally permissible but humane. Cant's discussion makes it clear why new developments in biomedical technologies require us to rethink commonly accepted definitions of death.*

George Zygmaniak. 26. . . . as he lay in a hospital bed last month in Neptune, N.J., paralyzed from the neck down because of a motorcycle accident, felt that he was a broken piece of machinery. He was ready to go. He begged his brother Lester, 23, to kill him. According to police, Lester complied—using a sawed-off shotgun at close range. Lester, who had enjoyed an unusually close relationship with his brother, has been charged with first-degree murder. 1

Last December Eugene Bauer, 59, was admitted to Nassau County Medical Center on Long Island with cancer of the throat. Five days later he was in a coma and given only two days to live. Then, charges the district attorney, Dr. Vincent A. Montemarano, 33, injected an overdose of potassium chloride into Bauer's veins. Bauer died within five minutes. Montemarano listed the cause of death as cancer but prosecutors now say that it was a "mercy killing" and have accused the doctor of murder. 2

The two cases underscore the growing emotional controversy over euthanasia ("mercy killing") and the so-called right to die—that is, the right to slip from life with a minimum of pain for both the patient and his family. No one seriously advocates the impulsive taking of life, as in the Zygmaniak shooting. A person suddenly crippled, no matter how severely, may yet show unpredictable improvement or regain at least a will to live. Whether or not to speed the passage of a fatally ill patient is a far subtler question. The headlong advances of medical science make the issue constantly more complex for patients and their families, for doctors and hospitals, for theologians and lawyers. 3

The doctor's dilemma—how long to prolong life after all hope of 4 recovery has gone—has some of its roots in half-legendary events of 2,400 years ago. When Hippocrates, the "Father of Medicine," sat under his giant plane tree on the Aegean island of Kos euthanasia (from the Greek meaning "a good death") was widely practiced and took many different forms. But from beneath that plane tree came words that have been immortalized in the physician's Hippocratic oath, part of which reads: "I will neither give a deadly drug to anybody, if asked for, nor will I make a suggestion to this effect."

5   Down the centuries, this has been interpreted by most physicians to mean that they must not give a patient a fatal overdose, no matter how terrible his pain or how hopeless his prospects. Today many scholars contend that the origin of this item in the oath has been misinterpreted. Most likely it was designed to keep the physician from becoming an accomplice of palace poisoners or of a man seeking to get rid of a wife.

6   The most emphatic opponents of euthanasia have been clergymen, of nearly all denominations. Churchmen protest that if a doctor decides when a patient is to die, he is playing God. Many physicians still share this objection. However much they may enjoy a secret feeling of divinity when dispensing miraculous cures, to play the angel of death is understandably repugnant. Moreover, as psychoanalysts point out, they are chillingly reminded of their own mortality.

7   At a recent conference chaired by the Roman Catholic Archbishop of Westminster, Dr. W. F. Anderson of Glasgow University, a professor of geriatric medicine, called euthanasia "medicated manslaughter." Modern drugs, he argued, can keep a patient sufficiently pain-free to make mercy killing, in effect, obsolete. Perhaps. There is no doubt, however, that a panoply of new techniques and equipment can be and often are used to keep alive people who are both hopelessly ill and cruelly debilitated. Artificial respirators, blood-matching and transfusion systems, a variety of fluids that can safely be given intravenously to medicate, nourish and maintain electrolyte balance—these and many other lifesavers give doctors astonishing powers.

8   Until about 25 years ago, the alternatives facing a doctor treating a terminally ill patient were relatively clear. He could let nature take its sometimes harsh course, or he could administer a fatal dose of some normally beneficent drug. To resort to the drug would be to commit what is called active euthanasia. In virtually all Western countries, that act is still legally considered homicide (though juries rarely convict in such cases).

9   On the record, physicians are all but unanimous in insisting that they never perform active euthanasia, for to do so is a crime. Off the record, some will admit that they have sometimes hastened death by giving an overdose of the medicine they had been administering previously. How many such cases there are can never be known.

10   Now, with wondrous machines for prolonging a sort of life, there is

another set of choices. Should the patient's heart or lung function be artifically sustained for weeks or months? Should he be kept technically alive by physicochemical legerdemain, even if he has become a mere collection of organs and tissue rather than a whole man? If a decision is made not to attempt extraordinary measures, or if, at some point, the life-preserving machinery is shut off, then a previously unknown act is being committed. It may properly be called passive euthanasia. The patient is allowed to die instead of being maintained as a laboratory specimen.

While legal purists complain that euthanasia and the right to die 11 peacefully are separate issues, the fact is that they are converging. With the increasing use of extraordinary measures, the occasions for passive euthanasia are becoming more frequent. The question of whether terminal suffering can be shortened by active or passive means is often highly technical — depending on the type of ailment. Thus the distinctions are becoming blurred, particularly for laymen.

No dicta from ancient Greece can neatly fit the modern logistics of 12 death. Until this century, death was a relatively common event in the household, particularly among farm families. Today more than 70% of deaths in American cities occur in hospitals or nursing homes. Both medical care and death have been institutionalized, made remote and impersonal. In major medical centers the family doctor is elbowed out by specialists and house physicians who have their elaborate and expensive gadgets. The tendency is to use them.

"The idea of not prolonging life unnecessarily has always been more 13 widely accepted outside the medical profession than within it," says a leading Protestant (United Church of Christ) theologian, University of Chicago's Dr. James Gustafson. "Now a lot of physicians are rebelling against the triumphalism inherent in the medical profession, against his sustaining of life at all costs. But different doctors bring different considerations to bear. The research-oriented physician is more concerned with developing future treatments, while the patient-oriented physician is more willing to allow patients to make their own choices."

House-staff physicians, says Tufts University's Dr. Melvin J. Krant in 14 *Prism*, an A.M.A. publication, "deal with the fatally ill as if they were entirely divorced from their own human ecology. The search for absolute biological knowledge precludes a search for existential or symbolic knowledge and the patient is deprived of his own singular humanism." The house staff, Krant says, assumes "that the patient always prefers life over death at any cost, and a patient who balks at a procedure is often viewed as a psychiatric problem."

Technical wizardry has, in fact, necessitated a new definition of 15 death. For thousands of years it had been accepted that death occurred when heart action and breathing ceased. This was essentially true, because the brain died minutes after the heart stopped. But with machines, it is now possible to keep the brain "alive" almost indefinitely. With the machines unplugged, it would soon die. In cases where the brain ceases to function first, heart and lung activity can be artificially maintained. While legal definitions of death lag far behind medical advances, today's criterion is, in most instances, the absence of brain activity for 24 hours.

16   The question then, in the words of Harvard Neurologist Robert Schwab, is "Who decides to pull the plug and when?" Cutting off the machines — or avoiding their use at all — is indeed passive euthanasia. But it is an ethical decision — not murder, or any other crime, in any legal code. So stern a guardian of traditional morality as Pope Pius XII declared that life need not be prolonged by extraordinary means.

17   But Pius insisted, as have most other moralists, that life must be maintained if it is possible to do so by ordinary means — that is, feeding, usual drug treatment, care and shelter. This attitude is supported by history. It would have been tragic, in 1922, to hasten the end of diabetics, for the medical use of insulin had just been discovered. Similar advances have lifted the death sentence for victims of hydrocephalus and acute childhood leukemia. But such breakthroughs are rare. For the aged and patients in severely deteriorated condition, the time for miracles has probably passed.

18   Faced with a painful and tenuous future and an all-too-tangible present crisis, how does the doctor decide what to do? Does he make the decision alone? Dr. Malcolm Todd, president-elect of the American Medical Association, wants doctors to have help at least in formulating a general policy. He proposes a commission of laymen, clergy, lawyers and physicians. "Society has changed," says Todd. "It's up to society to decide." The desire to share the responsibility is reasonable, but it is unlikely that any commission could write guidelines to cover adequately all situations. In individual cases, of course, many doctors consult the patient's relatives. But the family is likely to be heavily influenced by the physician's prognosis. More often than not, it must be a lonely decision made by one or two doctors.

19   Some conscientious physicians may not even be certain when they have resorted to euthanasia. Says Dr. Richard Kessler, associate dean of Northwestern University Medical School: "There's no single rule you can apply. For me it is always an intensely personal, highly emotional, largely unconscious, quasi-religious battle. I have never said to myself in cold analytic fashion, 'Here are the factors, this is the way they add up, so now I'm going to pull the plug.' Yet I and most doctors I know have acted in ways which would possibly shorten certain illnesses — without ever verbalizing it to ourselves or anyone else."

20   Kessler's ambivalence is shared by Father Richard McCormick of Loyola University's School of Theology. There are cases, McCormick observes, where the line is hard to draw. One example: a Baltimore couple who let their mongoloid baby die of starvation by refusing permission for an operation to open his digestive tract. The operation might

have been considered an ordinary means of treatment, if the child had not been a mongoloid. "In cases like that," says McCormick, "you're passing judgment on what quality of life that person will have. And once you pass judgment that certain kinds of life are not worth living, the possible sequence is horrifying. In Nazi Germany they went from mental defectives to political enemies to whole races of people. This kind of judgment leads to the kind of mentality that makes such things possible."

For cases where the line is unclear between ordinary and extraordi- 21
nary means, Roman Catholic theology offers an escape clause: the principle of double effect. If the physician's intention is to relieve pain, he may administer increasing doses of morphine, knowing full well that he will eventually reach a lethal dosage.

When Sigmund Freud was 83, he had suffered from cancer of the jaw 22
for 16 years and undergone 33 operations. "Now it is nothing but torture," he concluded, "and makes no sense any more." He had a pact with Max Schur, his physician. "When he was again in agony," Schur reported, "I gave him two centigrams of morphine. I repeated this dose after about twelve hours. He lapsed into a coma and did not wake up again." Freud died with dignity at his chosen time.

Dr. Schur's decision was, in the end, relatively easy. More often, 23
there are unavoidable uncertainties in both active and passive euthanasia. Doctors may disagree over a prognosis. A patient may be so depressed by pain that one day he wants out, while the next day, with some surcease, he has a renewed will to live. There is the problem of heirs who may be thinking more of the estate than of the patient when the time to pull the plug is discussed. Doctors will have to live with these gray areas, perhaps indefinitely. Attempts to legalize active euthanasia —under severe restrictions—have failed in the U.S. and Britain but will doubtless be revived. The fundamental question, however, is humane rather than legal. To die as Freud died should be the right of Everyman.

Sample Analysis

CLAIM: Cant asserts that mercy killing is not only morally permissible, but humane.

GROUNDS: The reasons and evidence Cant brings forward to support his claim are of various kinds. He cites the cases of George Zygmaniak and Eugene Bauer to illustrate the principle that mercy killing, in some circumstances, is done out of compassion to shorten periods of suffering and give those who wish it "death with dignity." Cant also cites new developments in biomedical technology that make it possible to sustain respiration and heartbeat indefinitely even when there is no brain activity. Under these conditions, the concept of "life" has no meaning and it would be unjust to deny "death with dignity" to such a person, especially if they had previously given voluntary consent to disconnecting life support systems.

WARRANT: Cant appeals to the basic principles that: (1) people should have a basic right to make decisions about their own lives and deaths and (2) allowing a terminally-ill or irreparably injured patient to die is morally permissible when there is no chance that the person will again be able to have a meaningful existence.

PERSUADING THE AUDIENCE: Cant's argument addressed to the general public begins with a discussion of two cases that dramatize the issues involved in the euthanasia debate. These real-life examples encompass voluntary and non-voluntary instances of mercy killing. A major element of Cant's argument has to do with establishing that an individual's wish to "die with dignity" must be respected. The concept of what constitutes a meaningful human existence plays a vital role in Cant's argument. The idea of "death with dignity" is set against portrayals of how machines keep people alive, prolong suffering of the terminally-ill, destroy self-respect, and erode human dignity. Cant's main argumentative strategy consists of getting his audience to identify with the people whose situations he describes, including Freud, who made arrangements to "die with dignity" because his mouth cancer had made it impossible to live what he considered a meaningful life.

Questions for Discussion and Writing

1. How does Cant use the two cases of Zygmaniak and Bauer to represent the two ends of a spectrum of possibility where on one hand death was brought about by violent means and on the other hand resulted from non-violent means? Keep in mind that *euthanasia* derives from the Greek word meaning "good or happy death" and in both cases the "murderers" believed they were saving others from further pain and acted out of compassion.

2. What information does Cant provide to suggest that the commonly accepted definition of death may no longer be adequate?

3. Is there any reason to believe that the distinction between active and passive euthanasia, that is, between killing and letting die, is meaningful once it is obvious that a patient does not wish to continue to live? To discover your own views on whether killing a patient can ever be morally justifiable, consider the following scenario: someone quite close to you is in great pain, paralyzed, and, according to the doctors, will die within a month. This person wants to die and

beseeches you to give him or her a lethal drug. What would you do? You may consider the scenario once with the condition that no one will ever discover what you have done and again with the constraint that someone will discover your role.

4. How have new developments in biomedical technologies made it necessary to address the issue of when extraordinary measures should or should not be used to keep someone alive who would have died, as a matter of course, before these new technologies came into existence? How would you define the difference between "active" and "passive" euthanasia?

5. How does Cant make use of comments by Pope Pius XII to support his argument, although, as he says, "the most emphatic opponents of euthanasia have been clergymen of all denominations"?

6. What reasons are given by Father Richard McCormick to support his claim that allowing death decisions (in the case of a Baltimore couple who let their mongoloid baby die of starvation) can lead to the active extermination of "whole races of people," as was seen in Nazi Germany?

7. How does Cant use the case of Sigmund Freud as an illustration of "death with dignity"?

8. In what way did this article change your views or contribute to the development of your views of euthanasia? In an essay, discuss any of the main issues of euthanasia by considering some of the following questions: (*a*) Do individuals have a basic right to decide about their own lives and deaths, as dramatized in the play *Whose Life Is It Anyway*? This might translate into the question: do people have a right to refuse life-sustaining treatment? (*b*) Is there such a thing as "death with dignity"? (*c*) How is it possible to know when consent to die is given rationally and voluntarily? (*d*) Isn't it true that doctors make mistakes in diagnoses and prognoses? (*e*) Is the "sanctity of life" more important than the "quality of life"? For example, is allowing a seriously defective infant to die morally permissible or prohibited in circumstances where there is no possibility for a meaningful human existence? (*f*) Who actually should be given the power to make such life and death decisions—the physician, patient, family, clergymen, or a board composed of any combination of these?

Terence Cardinal Cooke

Address Delivered to the First Annual American Health Congress

---

Terence Cardinal Cooke was Archbishop of New York. During his life, Cooke led a vigorous campaign against legalizing abortion. The following selection was given as an address delivered to the First Annual American Health Congress in Chicago (August 8, 1972). Archbishop Cooke uses the occasion of addressing an audience of health care professionals to make the case that mercy killing ought not to be considered under any circumstances. He is concerned that doctors and nurses around the country would become responsible for deciding which people deserve to live and argues that medical professionals should not be able to play God.

1   The theme of this Congress—Health and the Quality of Life—prompts me to offer a number of reflections concerning the question of "values, both changing and unchanging in the field of health." I am thinking particularly of the basic principles that underlie the phrase—*The Quality of Life.* In recent years, there has been considerable attention focused on improving the quality of life for all Americans. This has generated a new spirit of ecological concern, as well as an effort in law and social policy to improve the total environment in which our lives are lived. At the same time there arises a real danger—and that is, the serious threat of deciding that some lives are not of sufficient quality to merit society's concern and protection.

2   If there is to be a real quality to life, there first must be full recognition of the dignity inherent in every human life. Whatever might arise to modify or redefine values which are changeable, we must never lose sight of those values which are changeless. And paramount among these changeless values is the essential God-given dignity present in every human life at every stage and in every condition. Whatever winds of change may alter one philosophy or another, human life *is* an all important value as it comes from the Hands of God.

Reverence for Life

A society such as ours which prides itself on the affirmation of the   3
equality of all must constantly be on its guard to protect that equality for
each. It cannot allow respect for life to be removed from even the
smallest segment of our population. We cannot—we must not—allow
any human being to stand outside the pale of our respect for life.

Albert Schweitzer, who gave so much of his own life for others,   4
phrased it very movingly when he said: "If a man loses his reverence for
any part of life, he will lose his reverence for *all* life."

I am very concerned lest in some ways we are losing part of our   5
reverence for life. In the dynamics of American society today, this essential and changeless value is indeed assaulted in the pressure cooker of
social change. Although I believe that human life begins at the moment
of conception, I have seen the destruction of that life legally sanctioned
in parts of our country, including, I am sad to say, my own state of New
York, where legalized abortion has already claimed almost a half million
innocent lives.

We have seen the tragedy of the destruction of life in many war-torn   6
parts of the world.

We have seen the death of mind and body and spirit suffered by so   7
many through the evil of drug abuse.

We have seen oppressive limitations placed on the lives of the poor   8
and the lower middle class by inadequate housing, education, employment, and yes, even inadequate health care.

We have seen far too many men, women, and children suffer—and   9
we have seen the value and the very basic respect for their human lives
threatened and assailed. Yet we believe that the right to life is a sacred
and inalienable right, and we hold this truth to be changeless.

Every man, woman and child has dignity; every life has dignity. That   10
dignity must not only be recognized, it must also be protected.

A particular opportunity to protect the God-given dignity of life is   11
available to all of you in the field of health care. For you, death is a
constant, always near at hand in your work. You see it come swiftly and
unexpectedly; you see it come slowly and lingeringly. But come it does
and you sense its presence. As much as anyone, and more than most,
you deal with the incurably ill, the elderly and the dying.

Americans recently have become more sensitive to the subject of   12
dying. The media, state legislators, community organizations, all have
expressed interest in the dignity of the incurably ill and the dying. Our
society's concern for the quality of life has been broadened to encompass
a special concern for the dignity of death. But it seems to me that as yet
the meaning of the phrase, *death with dignity*, has not been fully
explored.

13   There are some who equate "death with dignity" with allowing a person to die comfortably when death is inevitable. But, there are others who mean by "death with dignity" the direct termination of a person's life.

14   I believe that directly to take one's own life or to permit another person to do [so] is contrary to nature and against the law of God. I also believe that to deprive the deformed, the mentally ill and those who suffer from incurable disease, of their lives, as though these people and their lives are somehow inferior in value and in dignity, is a crime which offends all humanity.

15   The philosophical principles behind the euthanasia movement are utilitarian and materialistic and they run contrary to the Judaeo-Christian tradition which respects the sacredness and dignity of all human life.

16   Recently, a so-called model bill was introduced in one of our state legislatures providing that "If any person is disabled and there is no (immediate family) — death with dignity shall be granted — if in the opinion of three physicians the prolongation of life is meaningless." But who is to decide the definition of the key terms of the proposed statute — when is a man disabled, and who is to decide when life ceases to be meaningful? This bill would have destroyed innocent life through the application of a totally materialistic and utilitarian misconception of the quality of life, masked and sugar-coated in the language of seemingly humane terminology. Although the Florida bill was defeated in Committee, it was only a recent skirmish in the new wave of attacks against life itself in our nation.

17   Legislation similar to this had already been enacted in Germany in 1943 when Pope Pius XII said what needs to be repeated today in America:

18   "We see the bodily deformed, the insane and those suffering from hereditary disease at times deprived of their lives, as though they were a useless burden to society. And this procedure is hailed by some as a new discovery of human progress and as something that is altogether justified by the common good. Yet what sane man does not recognize that this not only violates the natural and Divine Law written in the heart of every man, but flies in the face of every sensibility of civilized humanity?"

19   The American Declaration of Independence testifies to values that are changeless and it speaks of life as an inalienable right. Basically, the Declaration of Independence states that the human right to life is beyond recall by anyone — individuals, physicians, or legal statutes.

20   Human life is a God-given gift. It is an innate right bestowed by the Creator. If there is to be any real *death* with dignity, every person's innate right to *life* must be respected. But in our technological society, there is a tendency to adopt a limited view of man, to see man only for what he does or produces and to overlook the source of man's dignity — the fact that he is made in the image of God and that, from the moment of conception to the moment of death, he is worthy of the full support of

the human family of which he is a member. No reason, however alleg-edly humanitarian, can deny that right: not medical reasons, not family reasons, not social reasons, not reasons of alleviating suffering. No one can or should take innocent human life.

The current interest in euthanasia is related to recent remarkable   21
advances in the field of medical science. Modern discoveries of "miracle drugs" have tempered the ravages of tuberculosis, influenza and pneumonia—once the leading causes of death in our country. Refined medical skills and technical advancements have also aided in the control of fatal diseases and the consequent prolongation of life. At the same time, while the life expectancy of man has doubled in the past one hundred years in our land, the specter of dying from long-term degener-ative illnesses such as heart disease and cancer is an ever increasing reality. Nevertheless, we cannot overlook the fact that the continuing progress of medical science and technology offers to patients so afflicted the hope of newly discovered cures. Furthermore, prolonged treatment of the dying patient immeasurably aids the medical profession to com-prehend and hopefully one day conquer presently incurable diseases.

As members of one human family we are reminded that there is a   22
responsibility on the part of all of us to insure that there is dignity both in living and in dying. In the case of the incurably ill, the dying, those suffering terminal disease, there is much that we can do that will harmo-nize with the respect due the individual and yet alleviate his pain, both physical and mental.

It goes without saying that if the patient reasonably desires extra-   23
ordinary medical procedures, they should not be denied him. And, of course, in no case would it be justifiable to withhold ordinary medical procedures from any patient. Euthanasia or "mercy killing" in all its forms is contrary to nature and against the law of God.

There is no doubt that at times the application of these principles may   24
be difficult and perplexing, but these problems cannot be solved apart from moral principles and changeless spiritual values.

To a very real degree we all share one another's burdens and respon-   25
sibilities. Whether we be legislators or jurists, physicians or surgeons, nurses or technicians, attorneys or counselors, ministers or priests, we cannot retreat from invoking moral principles in dealing with the com-plex and grave problems which confront our society today. Those who for even the most humanitarian of reasons would relegate to men or to institutions the decision as to who will live and who will die run counter to the whole civilized tradition of Western man. The right to life is a fundamental, a basic right inherent in each individual. It comes from no man or no institution; it can be taken away by no man or no institution. Too much is at stake—the future of our nation, the welfare of our families and the hope of a tomorrow for young and old.

Real "death with dignity" respects each individual as he approaches   26
death. It provides that he be subjected to no unnecessary procedures. It

allows for alleviation of his pain. It gives to him the opportunity to put his house in order spiritually and temporally and to be at peace.

27   The changeless value which I urge we all support is described by Moses in the Old Testament as follows: "I have set before you life and death . . . therefore choose life that you and your descendants may live." (Deut. 30, 19)

28   I hope and pray that our leaders and our society will heed those words of a great Hebrew prophet and indeed choose life, thus really bringing the blessings of the true quality of life to a generation which shall remain faithful to this most basic of human values.

Sample Analysis

CLAIM: Cooke claims that health care professionals should not be party to a practice labeled "death with dignity" because it is against the law of God and constitutes murder.

GROUNDS: The grounds of Cooke's argument include known information that allowing "death with dignity" could become an accepted part of health care professionals' duties because a state's legislature was considering a bill stating that any disabled person with no immediate family, and for whom, in the opinion of three physicians, the prolongation of life would be meaningless, could be granted "death with dignity." The reasons Cooke presents include: (1) the idea that human beings, even health care professionals, should not be put in the position of playing God by deciding who should die, (2) there is always a chance of "newly discovered cures," and (3) permitting non-voluntary deaths to occur could lead to abuses of the kind legalized in Germany in 1943.

WARRANT: Permitting a patient's life to be terminated on the grounds that it is meaningless is against the law of God and should be justly labeled as "murdering a human being."

PERSUADING THE AUDIENCE: Cooke adapts his argument to the specific occasion of delivering an address to the First Annual American Health Congress. Cooke tells his audience that if a proposed bill were to be enacted, doctors and nurses would become responsible for deciding who deserved to live. He claims that health care professionals need to think about the moral issues involved. He reminds his audience that only God gives life and human beings should not take it upon themselves to play God by withdrawing life-sustaining medical care. Cooke redefines the phrase "death with dignity" to mean that a patient's humanity should be respected as that person approaches death. Cooke also raises the possibility that there is always a chance of a new cure being discovered that, however slight, should not be discounted. Interestingly, Cooke does not risk alienating his audience of doctors and nurses by reminding them that doctors make mistakes and that diagnoses may be wrong. A powerful component of Cooke's argument is made up of emotional appeals using language that evokes the *Declaration of Independence* to underscore his thesis that euthanasia is not only a crime against God, but also a practice that goes against the fundamental tenets of American society.

Questions for Discussion and Writing

1. Evaluate Cooke's claim (citing Albert Schweitzer) that "If a man loses his reverence for any part of life, he will lose his reverence for *all* life," and that this in turn will lead to the diminution of respect for life throughout society.

2. How does the tone of Cooke's argument reflect the fact that he is an archbishop of the Catholic church? Specifically, what word choices, ideas, and themes contribute to the "voice" he projects in this capacity?

3. How does Cooke's argument turn on the central issue that "human life *is* an all important value as it comes from the Hands of God"? That is, discuss how the acknowledgment that only God gives life is a changeless value that precludes permitting changing social concepts to "allow respect for life to be removed from even the smallest segment of our population"?

4. How does Cooke acknowledge the particular importance of euthanasia as an issue that must be especially relevant to the audience of health care professionals he is addressing? Why would physicians, nurses, and other health care professionals need to think about facing the central moral issues in light of new legislation which, if passed, would provide that "if any person is disabled and there is no immediate family — death with dignity shall be granted — if in the opinion of three physicians the prolongation of life is meaningless"?

5. How does Cooke's reference to the American *Declaration of Independence* contribute to his principal argument that "the right to life is a sacred and inalienable right, and we hold this truth to be changeless"? How does Cooke's language itself echo the original document? Specifically, how does Cooke use language drawn from the *Declaration of Independence* to support his thesis that euthanasia is not only a crime against God but is a crime against the fundamental tenets of American society?

6. How does Cooke's reference to the "hope of newly discovered cures" support his main argument? Isn't there usually a great lapse of

time between a medical breakthrough and the widespread availability of the cure? How is this a different kind of argument from the one that states that "Euthanasia or 'mercy killing' in all its forms is contrary to nature and against the law of God"?

7. How does Cooke's argument take up the phrase "death with dignity" and redefine it to support his own thesis?

8. Compare and contrast what Cant means when he uses the phrase "death with dignity" with what Cooke means when he uses the same phrase. How does each writer attempt to achieve a victory by definition by the way he interprets the meaning of this phrase?

9. If you were incurably ill, slowly dying, and suffering great pain that could only intermittently be alleviated by drugs, would you prefer that extraordinary measures be taken to keep you alive? If you were too sick to make your wishes known, who would you want to speak for you, Cant or Cooke? Discuss your decision and the reasons behind it in an essay. Some considerations to weigh in the balance include (a) possible medical costs, (b) the feelings of family and friends, (c) the desire not to be dependent on others, (d) the fear of becoming totally helpless and losing control over your intellectual and physical faculties, (e) the possibility, however slight, of a cure being discovered in a short time.

3

The Role of Logic in Argument

Why study logic? The answer is simply that most audiences expect an argument to rest on a rational foundation, and logic is the method used to study the nature and features of effective reasoning. Although the study of logic is often opposed to emotional appeals by which writers persuade their audiences, arguments that ring true are usually based on clear reasoning. The following discussion may not help you become the ever-logical Vulcan, Mr. Spock, but it will spell out the distinctive features of correct reasoning and show some signs with which you can recognize arguments based on faulty logic. Traditionally, the study of logic has centered on two methods of reasoning, induction and deduction, and the analysis of fallacies that short-circuit the rules of logic.

Methods of Reasoning

INDUCTIVE REASONING

Reasoning that moves from the observation of specific cases to the formulation of a hypothesis is called inductive reasoning (from the Latin *in ducere,* to lead toward). Inductive reasoning depends on drawing inferences from particular cases to support a generalization or claim about what is true of all these kinds of cases (including those that have not been observed).

Many inferences we draw every day follow this pattern. For example, if three friends tell you independently of each other that a particular movie is worth seeing, you infer that the movie in question is probably good. Or, if you bought two pairs of the same brand of shoes on two separate occasions and found them to be comfortable, you might reasonably infer that a third pair of the same brand would prove equally satisfactory. Drawing inferences about a movie you have not yet seen or shoes you have not yet bought typically involves what is called an *inductive leap.* Thus, inductive reasoning strives toward a high degree of probability, rather than absolute certainty.

The ability to generalize is a fundamental reasoning skill based on discerning common qualities shared by groups of things. For example, consider this traditional form of inductive reasoning:

> Fred is human and mortal.
> John is human and mortal.
> Mary is human and mortal.
> Therefore it is reasonable to infer that all human beings are mortal.

Since it would be impossible to observe every human being in the world, the inductively reached conclusion can only suggest what is probably true (even if the conclusion in this particular case seems certain). Inductive reasoning extrapolates that all human beings are mortal based on the three particular cases that have actually been observed.

Because inductive reasoning generalizes from specific cases, the conclusion will be stronger in proportion to the number of relevant examples the writer can cite to support it. Arguments based on atypical or sparse examples will be less convincing than those based on conclusions drawn from a greater number of representative examples.

Conclusions reached by inductive reasoning can only be stated in terms of relative certainty because it is unlikely that all instances in a particular class of things can ever be observed. A generalization based on the observation of any phenomenon, from a virus to a spiral nebulae, does not rule out the chance that new observations made in the future will require the formulation of totally new hypotheses.

Writers use inductive reasoning to draw inferences from evidence in order to convince an audience to accept a claim. Evidence may take the form of historical documents, laboratory experiments, data from surveys, the results of reports, personal observations, and the testimony of authorities. When our ability to draw conclusions based on firsthand observations is limited, we frequently rely on the opinion of authorities whose field of expertise includes a greater depth of knowledge about the instances, examples, or case histories under investigation.

Writers draw on specific cases and a wide range of empirical evidence to form a generalization that asserts what is true of specific instances is also true of the whole. As an argumentative strategy, the more different kinds of evidence used as the basis of an inductive generalization, the stronger the argument will be. An argument that generalizes from a variety of sources including personal experience, observation, the results of experiments, statistics, and historical research will provide stronger support for a generalization from an audience's point of view than an argument than generalizes from fewer kinds of evidence.

Because inductive reasoning makes predictions or draws inferences about an entire class of things, writers must be careful not to draw conclusions from so limited a sample that these conclusions extend far beyond what the available evidence warrants and thus seem improbable.

The process of forming a generalization always involves making this inductive leap.

There are three main kinds of inductive reasoning: (1) sampling, (2) analogy, and (3) causal generalization.

Sampling

Inductive generalizations depend on a process known as *sampling*, based on the selection of a sample drawn from a group. The sample must be drawn so as accurately to represent the composition and makeup of the entire group from which it is taken. All other things being equal, the larger the sample, the more probable it is that important characteristics in the larger population will be represented. For example, if the subject of a study were a small town with a population of 10,000, the sample should not be less than 500 townspeople lest the sample not be broad enough to be significant. Furthermore, because the townspeople that comprise the whole population can be categorized into different subgroups or strata, a reliable sampling must reflect that stratification. No survey of townspeople should fail to take into account small but important segments of different racial, cultural, or ethnic groups. The sample procedure should be random to ensure that a true cross section of townspeople is selected to represent the entire group about which the generalization or prediction is made. Just how this works can be seen on election nights, right after the polls have closed, when commentators report that "on the basis of a very small percentage of the vote" in sample precincts, candidate X or Y is declared the winner. More often than not these predictions turn out to be correct because the sample precincts accurately represent the district, state, or region as a whole.

The sample (1) must be randomly selected, (2) must be broad enough to be significant, and (3) must accurately reflect the general population from which it is taken. Evidence presented to support an inductive generalization must be clearly relevant to the conclusion drawn, objectively presented, and supported strongly enough to withstand challenges from opposing evidence. This last point is crucial since writers of arguments must always assume that evidence can be brought forward to challenge their conclusions.

Analogy

Arguments from analogy rely on inductive reasoning to suggest that things or events that are alike in some ways are probably similar in other ways as well. The use of analogy in argument differs from the purely illustrative use of analogy to clarify subjects that otherwise might prove to be hard to visualize or be difficult to understand. For example, in his book *The Revolution Begins* (1979), Christopher Evans uses an ingenious analogy to help his readers realize the incredible processing speeds of which modern integrated circuits are capable:

Imagine a British billionaire who decides that he is going to hand out
a pound note to everyone who comes up to him—just one pound
each. A long line forms and the billionaire starts handing out his
pounds. He moves quickly and manages to get rid of them at the rate
of one every ten seconds, but being human he can only keep it up for
eight hours a day, five days a week. How long will it take him to
dispose of his billion? . . . Does it seem conceivable, for example,
that the billionaire could have started as far back as the Battle of
Waterloo? Well, in fact he would have had to start before that. The
Great Fire of London? No, he would have been counting away while
Old St Paul's blazed. The execution of Anne Boleyn? No, he would
have been counting then too. Agincourt? No. Battle of Hastings? No,
further still. To cut a long story short, you would have to go back to
the year 640 or thereabouts before you would see the billionaire
handing over his first pound note. But that is just a taste of the cake.
A billion times per second is no longer considered to be anything like
the upper limit of computer processing speeds.

Think how very difficult it would be to try to imagine this mind-boggling
speed without Evans' clever and entertaining analogy.

A writer uses analogy for argumentative (rather than descriptive or
illustrative) purposes to show how evidence serves to support a particular conclusion. An instance of arguing by analogy can be observed in
Abraham Lincoln's famous rebuttal silencing critics who condemned his
administration for dragging its heels in settling the Civil War. Notice how
Lincoln structures the analogy to bring out similarities between his own
situation and the one faced by Blondin (the famous tightrope walker who
crossed Niagara Falls three separate times—in 1855, 1859, and again in
1860):

Gentlemen, I want you to suppose a case for a moment. Suppose that
all the property you were worth was in gold, and you had put it in the
hands of Blondin, the famous rope-walker, to carry across the Niagara Falls on a tightrope. Would you shake the rope while he was
passing over it, or keep shouting to him, "Blondin, stoop a little more!
Go a little faster!"? No, I am sure you would not. You would hold
your breath as well as your tongue, and keep your hand off until he
was safely over. Now, the Government is in the same situation. It is
carrying an immense weight across a stormy ocean. Untold treasures
are in its hands. It is doing the best it can. Don't badger it! Just keep
still, and it will get you safely over.

Lincoln asserts that none of the spectators would have dreamt of
distracting Blondin while he was attempting to cross the falls. Nor would
anyone in the audience have dared to "shake the rope" while Blondin
was crossing the falls, especially since Lincoln has stipulated that Blondin is carrying "all the property you were worth . . . in gold." Next,
Lincoln points out the similarities between Blondin's situation and the
government's own precarious circumstances. Lincoln says that the gov-

ernment, too, is walking a tightrope bearing the burden of seeking to resolve the Civil War. Lincoln concludes that "it [his administration] is doing the best it can." The inductive inference based on the number of ways in which the two situations are analogous is quite clear: critics should refrain from "shaking the rope" and let Lincoln strive to settle the war as he sees fit. Doubtless Lincoln did not depend on this analogy alone to make the case against interference, but most likely supported the same conclusion with other evidence (reports from generals in the field, attempts at behind-the-scenes negotiations, and so on). Although some analogical arguments are better than others, it is important to remember that, like other forms of inductive reasoning, the conclusions are probable, not certain.

Causal Generalization

Causal analysis attempts to persuade an audience that one event caused another. Like other kinds of inductive reasoning, causal analysis aims at establishing probability rather than certainty. Writers may work backward from a given effect and seek to discover what might have caused it or work forward and predict what further effects will flow from the known cause. Argument based on causal analysis must identify as precisely as possible the contributory factors in any causal chain of events. The direct or immediate causes of the event are those that are likely to have triggered the actual event. Yet behind the direct causes may lie indirect or remote causes that set the stage or create the framework in which the event could occur.

It often helps to distinguish between several meanings of the word *cause*. First, the concept of cause may refer to a *necessary condition* that must be present if a specific effect is to occur. For example, buying a lottery ticket is a necessary condition for winning the lottery. Yet a necessary condition does not by itself guarantee the effect will occur. For the effect to be produced, there must be a *sufficient condition*, that is, a condition in whose presence the effect will always occur. If, for example, you bought a lottery ticket with the winning numbers, that alone would be a sufficient condition to ensure the effect (winning the lottery).

A claim that one event could have caused another is expressed as a generalization. This generalization either explains why an event has happened or predicts why it will happen in the future. For example, a medical writer, Judith Glassman, in "Beating the Odds" (*New Age Journal* [November 1985]) asserts that there is a direct relationship between emotional states of patients and the immune responses of the body. She argues that attitudes directly affect the body's response to disease. She cites research to support her claim that studies show a clear causal relationship between mental states and cancer survival:

> The widely influential Simontons [oncologist Carl Simonton and psychotherapist Stephanie Simonton-Ashley] use an amalgam of group

therapy, meditation, and visualization—teaching their patients to picture their cancer cells as weak and disorganized and their treatment and immune systems as powerful. The Simontons' method has amassed impressive statistics. Of 240 incurable patients treated between 1973 and 1979, the median survival time was double the national average, and 10% of those patients had dramatic remissions.

Glassman concludes that the median survival time of double the national average for this group is directly due to the Simonton method for altering the attitudes of cancer patients. This kind of claim would require the author to demonstrate that the technique of changing attitudes was capable of producing these results.

Readers might also expect Glassman to demonstrate exactly how a change in attitudes affects the body's ability to fight cancer. Readers might also wonder whether the attitude change in the patients was the real cause of their high survival rate or whether it just preceded it in time. Might not the connection be just coincidental? Was the Simonton method the only cause of higher survival rates in this group? Might not there be other causes of equal or greater importance, such as a change in diet? A complete causal analysis would be more persuasive if it covered these points.

DEDUCTIVE REASONING

Deductive reasoning is a method of reasoning that complements inductive reasoning. Rather than moving from the evidence provided by specific cases to a conclusion, deduction allows us to infer the validity of a particular case from generalizations or *premisses*. The generalization "therefore it is reasonable to infer that all human beings are mortal" can be used deductively to predict that all as yet unobserved human beings will also be mortal. The classic form illustrating the relationship between the *premisses* and the conclusion is known as a *syllogism*:

MAJOR PREMISS: All human beings are mortal.

MINOR PREMISS: John is a human being.

CONCLUSION: Therefore, John is mortal.

Notice how deductive reasoning applies a general statement to a particular case to draw a logical conclusion (whereas inductive reasoning uses individual cases, facts, and examples to create a hypothesis or generalization). The statements on which deductive reasoning is based appear as categorical propositions or *laws*. If inferences from the original statements or *premisses* are drawn correctly according to the rules of logic then the conclusion is valid.

In contrast to inductive reasoning (which draws inferences or generalizes from specific cases), deductive reasoning (from the Latin *de ducere*, to lead from) draws inferences from statements called *premisses* that are assumed to be true or "self-evident." Conclusions drawn via deductive reasoning are both logically necessary and certain (in contrast to the merely probable conclusions reached via inductive reasoning).

Deductive logic assumes that the truth of the *premisses* is sufficient to establish the truth of the conclusion. No external evidence is required beyond the statements from which the conclusion is drawn. The conclusion is logically certain or valid because it follows necessarily from the *premisses*. The term *validity* here refers only to the way in which the conclusion is drawn. If either the major or the minor *premiss* is not true, then the conclusion, although logically valid, will not be true either.

It is frequently overlooked that many of the self-evident truths taken as *premisses* in deductive reasoning are generalizations that have been previously established by inductive reasoning from empirical evidence and observation. **The process of inductive reasoning supplies the generalizations that appear as the starting point or major *premiss* in deductive reasoning.**

To see how this works examine the following passage from Arthur Conan Doyle's story "The Red Headed League" (1892), one of the innumerable exploits of his legendary character Sherlock Holmes:

> "How, in the name of good fortune, did you know all that, Mr. Holmes?" he asked.
> "How, did you know, for example, that I did manual labor? It's true as gospel, for I began as a ship's carpenter."
> "Your hands, my dear sir. Your right hand is quite a size larger than your left. You have worked with it and the muscles are more developed."

Diagrammed in the form of a syllogism Holmes's reasoning might appear thus:

MAJOR PREMISS: All men in whom at least one hand has more developed muscles do manual labor.

MINOR PREMISS: This man's right hand is a size larger than his left and the muscles are much more developed.

CONCLUSION: Therefore, this man has done manual labor.

This deductive syllogism is comprised of a major *premiss* that generalizes about an entire group or class, a minor *premiss* that identifies the individual as a member of that class, and a conclusion expressing the inference that what is true of all manual laborers must be true of the man Holmes has encountered.

The major *premiss* is a generalization reached by Holmes inductively; after all, Holmes had observed many instances where the hand muscles of manual laborers were more highly developed than the average person's. The minor *premiss* places this particular man in the general category of all those whose hands exhibit signs of unusual muscular development. The conclusion Holmes draws is valid in its reasoning; that is, his process of reasoning from the *premisses* to the conclusion is correct. However, if one or both of the *premisses* were false, the argument would be untrue even though the process of reasoning is correct and the conclusion is validly drawn.

For example, Holmes's major *premiss* might be untrue; perhaps there are men whose right hands are more muscular than their left who do not do manual labor. For instance, squash or tennis might produce unusual muscular development of the one hand used to grip the racquet. His minor *premiss* could also have been untrue. For example, the "manual laborer" might have actually been Moriarty, Holmes's arch nemesis in disguise, wearing a prosthetic device to lead Holmes to his erroneous conclusion.

It is important to understand how conclusions reached through inductive reasoning are used as major *premisses* in deductive reasoning. For example, a naturalist who observed a great number of snowflakes might generalize that since every snowflake he observed had six sides, all snowflakes probably have six sides. This generalization would then appear in deductive reasoning as the major *premiss*: "All snowflakes have six sides." The minor *premiss* would then assert something about a particular member of this class of objects. For example: "This is a snowflake." Given the major *premiss* and the minor *premiss*, the deductive conclusion is that: "This snowflake has six sides." Notice how the syllogism would go awry if the minor *"premiss"* were stated as "this has six sides." In this case the object might be an innovative hexagonal container, but the only conclusion allowed by the syllogism would be an erroneous one, that is, "this is a snowflake."

Conclusions reached through deductive reasoning are only as correct as the truth of the *premisses*. If some snowflakes had eight sides, then the conclusion that this particular snowflake has six sides would be less certain. Deductive reasoning can go wrong in other ways. Suppose what our naturalist mistook for a snowflake was actually a bit of duck down that had floated by and stuck to the window; in this case, the minor *premiss* ("this is a snowflake") would be incorrect. Since the minor *premiss* would then no longer refer to a member of the class of snowflakes, any conclusion drawn would likewise be untrue.

Since major *premisses* are often assumed to express self-evident truths, value arguments use deductive reasoning. In these arguments, the major *premiss* states an absolute moral or ethical obligation. The minor *premiss* specifies an instance or individual that falls within the scope of this obligation. The conclusion connects the general obligation to the individual case.

For example, the following syllogism illustrates how an absolute moral obligation can be applied to a specific case to produce a value judgment (adapted from "Medical Paternalism," by Allen E. Buchanan, in *Paternalism*, edited by Rolf Sartorius [1983]):

MAJOR PREMISS: The physician's duty — to which he or she is bound by the oath of Hippocrates — is to prevent or at least minimize harm to his or her patient.

MINOR PREMISS: Giving the patient information X will do greater harm to the patient on balance than withholding the information will.

CONCLUSION: Therefore, it is the physician's duty to withhold information X from the patient.

This example illustrates that deductive reasoning is useful in developing an argument leading to a conclusion that would be disputed if it were presented as a starting point. Deductive reasoning allows the writer to build an argument step by step that will lead an audience to consider the possibility of a claim they might have rejected initially. In this case the claim is that in certain circumstances physicians are justified in withholding information from patients even if it means deceiving them.

The syllogisms we have been discussing are known as *categorical* syllogisms because the major *premiss* sets up classes or categories ("all snowflakes," "all men" in the Sherlock Holmes syllogism, and "all physicians"). The minor *premiss* identifies an individual or instance as part of that class and the conclusion affirms that the specific case shares characteristics with the general class. Within the syllogism, logicians have identified elements in each of the terms:

       middle term   major term
MAJOR PREMISS: Hindus believe in reincarnation.

       minor term   middle term
MINOR PREMISS: Professor Godbole is a Hindu.

       minor term   major term
CONCLUSION: Therefore, Professor Godbole believes in reincarnation.

In this syllogism, the major and minor *premisses* are statements or propositions that provide the evidence for the conclusion. The major term describes the largest class in the syllogism and occurs once in the major *premiss* and then again in the conclusion. The middle term describes the class that appears in both the major *premiss* and in the minor *premiss* but never appears in the conclusion. The minor term describes the specific case, instance, individual, or group about which the generalization is being made. It occurs once in the minor *premiss* and always appears as the subject of the conclusion. In the syllogism just presented the major term is "[belief in] reincarnation," the minor term is "Professor Godbole," and the middle term is "Hindu." This syllogism is valid in the way the conclusion is deductively reached. Given these *premisses* no other conclusion could be drawn.

Notice how the major *premiss* expresses a belief that is taken as self-evident about the relationship between two classes or two groups. The broadest group comprises all people who believe in reincarnation. The major *premiss* states that within this broad category are all Hindus. The minor *premiss* then stipulates that a specific person, object, or group is related to one of the classes or broad categories identified in the major *premiss*. In the case presented, the minor *premiss* states that Professor Godbole, as an individual, belongs to the broader category of Hindus. The conclusion then draws an inference: what is true of all Hindus must also be true of an individual belonging to that group. Thus, the conclusion follows logically that Professor Godbole believes in reincarnation.

Except for the ever logical Mr. Spock of *Star Trek* fame, most people do not think in the form of syllogisms. It is far more common to leave out the major *premiss* and only mention the minor *premiss* and the conclusion. The resulting abbreviated syllogism is called an *enthymeme*. An enthymeme takes for granted the assumption or unexpressed major *premiss*. For example, Charles de Gaulle was quoted in *Newsweek*, October 1, 1962, as saying "how can you be expected to govern a country that has 246 kinds of cheese?" De Gaulle takes for granted the unexpressed major *premiss* that might be stated as: any country whose citizens have hundreds of preferences in cheese is unlikely to unite behind one political leader.

It is often helpful to make the unexpressed major *premiss* explicit in order to evaluate the soundness of different parts of the argument. For example, suppose you and a friend were driving past a factory and your friend said: "Look at the picket line over there; there must be a strike at the factory." The unexpressed major *premiss* here would be that picket lines are present only at strikes. The *premiss* expresses a sign warrant: a picket line indicates the presence of a strike.

Consider how deductive reasoning works in the following argument, "Nuclear Power: The Fifth Horseman" (1976) by Denis Hayes:

> Increased deployment of nuclear power must lead to a more authoritarian society. Reliance upon nuclear power as the principal source of energy is probably possible only in a totalitarian state. Nobel Prize–winning physicist Hannes Alfven has described the requirements of a

stable nuclear state in striking terms: Fission energy is safe only if a number of critical devices work as they should, if a number of people in key positions follow all of their instructions, if there is no sabotage, no hijacking of transports, if no reactor fuel processing plant or waste repository anywhere in the world is situated in a region of riots or guerrilla activity, and no revolution or war—even a "conventional one"—takes place in these regions. The enormous quantities of extremely dangerous material must not get into the hands of ignorant people or desperados. . . .

Nuclear power is viable only under conditions of absolute stability. The nuclear option requires guaranteed quiescence—internationally and in perpetuity. Widespread surveillance and police infiltration of all dissident organizations will become social imperatives, as will deployment of a paramilitary nuclear police force to safeguard every facet of the massive and labyrinthine fissile fuel cycle.

Diagrammed as a syllogism, Hayes's argument would appear this way:

major term   middle term
MAJOR PREMISS: Nuclear power is viable only under conditions of absolute stability.
Minor term
MINOR PREMISS: Widespread surveillance and police infiltration of dissident organizations and deployment of a paramilitary police force are
middle term
required to produce absolute stability.
minor term
CONCLUSION: Therefore, a more authoritarian society (with widespread
major term
surveillance) will result from increased reliance on nuclear power.

Hayes uses deductive reasoning to try to persuade his audience to accept the claim that "increased deployment of nuclear power must lead to a more authoritarian society." His major *premiss* states the assumed truth that "nuclear power is viable only under conditions of absolute stability." Hayes then builds his argument on this *premiss* as follows: (1) nuclear power is viable only under conditions of absolute security and (2) absolute security can be achieved only by widespread surveillance, police infiltration, and deployment of a paramilitary nuclear police force. From these *premisses* Hayes draws the conclusion that (3) increased deployment of nuclear power must lead to a more authoritarian society.

As we have seen, deductive reasoning is useful as a rhetorical strategy in situations when an audience might reject a conclusion if it were stated at the outset. A writer who can get an audience to agree with the assumptions on which the argument is based stands a better chance of getting them to agree with the conclusion if he or she can show how this conclusion follows logically from the *premisses*.

Logical Fallacies

Inappropriate use of strategies of argument can result in arguments that give the appearance of being persuasive but use incorrect ways of reasoning. These methods of pseudo-reasoning often seem quite persuasive because although they appear to be logical, they usually appeal to emotions, prejudices, and existing beliefs.

Writers should be able to identify certain common fallacies both in their own works and in the arguments of others. A familiarity with the main types of fallacies can keep writers from being misled by them. Although we often think of fallacies as being intentionally contrived to lend plausibility to an unsound argument, they may occur accidentally without the writer's awareness. In either case, understanding how arguments go wrong is just as important as being able to understand the correct relationship among claims, evidence, underlying assumptions, and other elements of sound arguments.

The following discussion covers the more commonly occurring fallacies that persistently undermine sound reasoning.

FALLACIES THAT RESULT WHEN NO REAL EVIDENCE IS PRESENTED TO SUPPORT THE CLAIM

Begging the Question (*Petitio Principii*, Circular Reasoning)

This fallacy occurs when a writer doesn't bring forward evidence to support the claim but simply repeats the main assertion in a disguised form. The argument assumes as already proven the claim that the argument exists to prove. What is offered as proof is only a restatement of the proposition or claim in other words. For example, note the circular pattern of reasoning in the following dialogue:

How do you know God exists?
It says so in the Bible.
How do you know the Bible is a reliable source?
Because the Bible is the divinely inspired word of God.

Another form of *begging the question* is *circular definition*, which defines a term by offering a synonym or restatement in other words of the term to be defined. For example, a hero is one who is heroic, hiccup is the sound made by hiccuping, or fermentation is the process of fermenting.

Question-Begging Epithets

This common fallacy occurs in arguments when the writer inserts loaded terms or phrases whose connotations (positive or negative) substitute for the logic of the argument. These phrases often substitute clichéd or stereotyped judgments for sound reasoning. For example, "creeping socialism," "bleeding heart liberal," "city slicker," "country bumpkin," "corrupt politicians," and "irresponsible teenagers."

FALLACIES THAT RESULT WHEN THE EVIDENCE IS NOT RELEVANT TO THE CLAIM

Red Herring (*Ignoratio Elenchi*, Arguing Off the Point)

Writers introduce a *red herring* into an argument when they bring in a point that is tangential or irrelevant to the issue under dispute. The picturesque name stems from the days when it was believed that a pack of hounds would be diverted from following the scent if a herring with its accompanying strong odor were dragged across the trail in front of them. So, too, the *red herring* is a tactic arguers may use to divert the attention of the audience from their pursuit of the real issue at hand. A debate over possible effects on children of witnessing violence on television would *argue off the point* if the arguer started discussing possible dangers of low-level radiation emanating from television screens.

Non Sequitur

Another fallacy where the evidence introduced to support the claim is not directly relevant to the claim is the non sequitur, meaning literally, it does not follow. For example, the statement "My parents raised Golden Retrievers; therefore, I'm against wearing real fur" may make sense to the person making the statement. However, there is no logical connection between being opposed to killing animals to use their skin for coats and the fact that one's parents raised dogs of any kind.

Straw Man

The *straw man* fallacy diverts attention from the real issue onto an easily demolished target. A writer using the *straw man* fallacy would like the audience to believe the original argument has been disproved when the *straw man* is knocked down. A blatant example of the *straw man* fallacy took place in Richard Nixon's "Checkers" speech, one of the most famous instances of public persuasion in this century. Nixon appeared on television on September 23, 1952, to defend himself against accusations that he had used a political fund for his own personal use. Nixon's situation was especially precarious because Dwight Eisenhower was considering taking him off the Republican ticket as his vice-presidential running mate in the upcoming election. The speech was enormously effective and elicited over two million favorable telegrams from people all over the country. Nixon volunteered the information that "I probably should tell you [about this] because if I don't they'll probably be saying this about me too" as if to suggest that accepting the gift of a puppy, Checkers, was equal in seriousness to dipping into the public coffers. Nixon's strategy of bringing up and then replying to a charge no one had made had the effect of suggesting that all the other charges made against him were equally baseless and absurd.

Inappropriate Use of Authorities *(Argumentum ad Verecundiam)*

This fallacy frequently is the basis of much advertising featuring testimonials or endorsements by sports figures, movie stars, and other celebrities. The value of expert opinion is that it allows the writer to support conclusions with testimony of someone whose professional expertise is based on greater experience with the issue in question. The opposite of this would be the citation of an authority outside the field that adds nothing in support of the claim. A baseball player might be very credible on the subject of bats, baseballs, and gloves. Yet the same baseball player's endorsement of snow tires, extolling their tread pattern and triple-ply construction, would project him as an authority in an area unrelated to his expertise.

Ad Hominem *(Argument Against the Person)*

There are two forms that this fallacy can take. In the first, called the *abusive argumentum ad hominem,* the writer attacks the character of the person or his or her personal life rather than providing compelling evidence to disprove the person's argument.

For example, Ashley Montagu, in "Frank Lloyd Wright" (*The American Way of Life* [1967]) veers in the direction of ad hominem when he asserts that Wright's architectural theory and practice were determined by his physical stature: "Wright built houses for cave-dwellers, troglodytes, it would almost seem as a practical joke . . . being a short man Wright designed his rooms with very low ceilings." So, too, William J. Darby in his review of Rachel Carson's *Silent Spring,* titled "Silence, Miss Carson," (*Chemical and Engineering News* [October, 1962]) verges on ad hominem when he says "it is doubtful that many readers can bear to wade through its high-pitched sequence of anxieties."

Ad hominem arguments are not off the issue when the character of the person is directly connected to the issue in question. Thus, an argument made by a chief executive officer or a senior partner against certain business practices such as insider trading, would gain or lose credibility according to the business ethics of the speaker. In this case, it would not be inappropriate for a counterargument to refer to the character of the speaker, especially if it could be shown that the official in question had undisclosed personal interests linked to the acceptance of his argument. Most frequently, however, ad hominem argument reflects the inability of the writer to refute points raised by the opposition.

A variation of ad hominem is called the *genetic fallacy*, which seeks to disprove an argument by condemning its source or genesis rather than disproving the position itself. Another variation is sometimes referred to as *guilt by association*, which seeks to discredit a claim by linking the person with an already discredited group or a group about whom the audience can be expected to hold a low opinion. For example, Andrew H. Merton writes in the prologue to his book *Enemies of Choice* (1981):

> In its emotional appeals and its disregard of logic, the right-to-life movement resembles many other oppressive crusades in human history, from the earliest witch hunts to the Spanish inquisition to the Nazis persecution of Jews and other *untermenschen* (subhumans). All were based on false logic, and all resulted in widespread misery and loss of freedom. The right-to-life movement differs from these others only in sublety; it does not directly name the object of its ire — primarily women — but instead would set severe limits on their liberty in the name of saving fetuses.

Here, Merton is using *guilt by association* to put forward evidence that is not directly relevant to the claim. He is trying to manipulate his audience into feeling the way he does by linking anti-abortion groups with discredited groups about which the audience already has negative feelings.

Argument from Ignorance (*Argumentum ad Ignorantiam*)

This particular fallacy occurs in arguments where the writer's claim is supported by the reason that since "no one knows" what happened or will happen in a given situation, the thesis should be accepted as true. The fact that a hypothesis has not been conclusively proven or disproven cannot itself be used as evidence to support a claim. This fallacy proceeds from the claim that a proposition is true until it is proved false, or false until it is proved true. For example, to argue that UFOs exist on the grounds that no one has ever succeeded in proving they do not, or that there must be ghosts since no one has ever succeeded in disproving their existence is to commit this fallacy. In short, the failure to draw a conclusion cannot be used as ground for a conclusion.

Appeal to the People (*Argumentum ad Populum,* **Folksy Appeal, Patriotic, Provincialism, Majority Opinion, Popularity in Numbers, Bandwagon, Status, Snob Appeal, Common Practice**)

This fallacy takes the form of an emotional appeal to the feelings people have for country, class, national identity, or religious affiliation. For example, a political propagandist might appeal to biases, irrational fears, and prejudices by substituting emotional responses for a reasoned set of arguments on the issue. The *ad populum* appeal can take a folksy turn. In fact this variation is called "just plain folks." Here, the arguer seeks to gain the confidence of his or her audience by seeming to appear as just an ordinary, down-to-earth person whose values are the same as those of most other people.

This appeal is frequently encountered in political campaigns as well as in the world of advertising. For example, Lee Iacocca appeared in Chrysler ads saying in essence that the purchase of an American-made Chrysler was an act of good citizenship. Conversely, not buying a Chrysler might be unpatriotic. To take another case, in the past, Betty Crocker was once presented as "the first lady of desserts."

Sometimes this fallacy takes the form of an appeal to majority opinion, or the idea that the supposed popularity of an idea or product should be sufficient to support its claim. Sometimes this is called the *bandwagon effect,* as in the claim "this product is used in 70 million homes, shouldn't it be used in yours?" Of course, the corollary is that this idea is believed by x number of millions of people, so shouldn't you believe it too?

Advertisers use a variation of this tactic when they appeal to consumers to buy a product by using *snob appeal* or an *appeal to status.* The subgroup here are those who are "in the know." Perhaps the earliest example of the use of *snob appeal* is in an advertisement carried in 1710 in *The Spectator.* The tooth powder so advertised was described as "an Incomparable Powder for cleaning Teeth, which has given great satisfaction to most of the nobility and gentry in England." So, too, today status ads for perfume, Scotch, luxury cars, suggest to readers that by purchasing the product they, too, will be rubbing shoulders with the rich and famous trendsetters.

The fallacy of reasoning underlying these kinds of ads is sometimes called the *fallacy of the undistributed middle term.* This common fallacy can be seen when conclusions draw a wider inference than is warranted by the facts that have been stated. Using our 1710 advertisement, we might diagram the deductive logic as a syllogism designed to expose the flaw in the argument:

MAJOR PREMISS: All members of the nobility and gentry in England use X brand of toothpowder.

MINOR PREMISS: All members of the French Court use X brand of toothpowder.

CONCLUSION: Therefore, all members of the French Court are members of the nobility and gentry in England.

Obviously, the conclusion is not necessarily true. The confusion results from the use of the middle term "X brand of toothpowder" in both of the *premises*; but this term is undistributed because it does not appear in the conclusion. The argument has failed to establish that the minor term "all members of the French Court" falls within the major term "all members of the nobility and gentry in England." In advertising, this translates into the mistaken perception that because wealthy people buy a particular kind of very expensive watch, you will be one of them if you too purchase this watch. When put in this blatant form the fallacy becomes obvious, but advertisers concentrate on the ambiguous area of wishes and fantasies where simply believing something makes it seem true.

Appeal to Pity (*Argumentum ad Misericordiam,* Appeal to Compassion)

This fallacy occurs when the arguer seeks to evoke and play on feelings of pity to get his audience to let emotions rather than reason persuade them to accept a conclusion. Again, it should be said that *appeals to compassion* in and of themselves are not necessarily wrong. This fallacy occurs when the arguer seeks to settle a factual matter by using irrelevant appeals to sentiment. Perhaps the most outrageous example is the proverbial case of a defendant on trial for murdering his parents who proceeds to throw himself on the mercy of the court on the grounds that he is now an orphan.

Appeal to Force (*Argumentum ad Baculum,* Scare Tactics)

An *appeal to force* is encountered in those arguments that seek to intimidate the audience into compliance or hold up the threat of force to compel acceptance of a claim. The threats posed can include moral or psychological threats as well as ones of physical violence or economic retaliation. For example, Yoshi Tsurumi writing in *The World Policy Journal* (Spring 1987) argues that the United States should not restrict Japanese imports:

> There's nothing wrong with pressing Japan to open markets that remain closed, but the U.S. cannot expect simply to bully its way to competitiveness. The U.S. needs to recognize that it can no longer dictate the rules of international competition, especially now that it is so dependent on Japanese capital to revive its industries.

It's hard to miss the iron hand in the velvet glove here. In politics, the threat of war, in religion, the threat of everlasting damnation (as in Jonathan Edward's sermon "Sinners in the Hands of an Angry God"

[1741]) have their counterparts in *scare tactics* used in advertising. For example, an advertising agency head, in the early days of advertising, once proposed an ad based on *scare tactics* for baby food that copywriter Helen Woodward, as quoted by Stuart Ewen in *Captains of Consciousness* (1976), describes as follows:

> "Give 'em the figures about the baby death rate—but don't say it flatly. You know if you just put a lot of figures in front of a woman she passes you by. If we only had the nerve to put a hearse in the ad, you couldn't keep the women away from the food." One such ad did appear. Although there was no hearse, the illustration showed an ominously empty pair of baby shoes.

The unsubtle implication is that her baby will die unless the mother buys a particular brand of baby food.

FALLACIES THAT RESULT WHEN INSUFFICIENT EVIDENCE IS OFFERED TO SUPPORT A CLAIM

Hasty Generalization *(Jumping to Conclusions)*

One of the most common forms of *hasty generalization* involves jumping to a conclusion based on too few instances or inadequate samples. The strength of generalization is that it allows conclusions to be drawn about an entire group or whole category of things based on inferences drawn from observation and analysis of a representative sample. When great care is not taken in selecting the sample or when the sample does not truly represent the entire group, a fallacy of *hasty generalization* can result.

1. *Generalizing from too few instances.* You would be jumping to a conclusion if you concluded that Maine's summers are always hot and humid based on a week's vacation during an uncharacteristically hot, humid spell.

2. *Generalizing from atypical or unrepresentative examples.* If you read Jerzy Kosinski's novella *Being There* and concluded on the basis of this one story that all his other novels were equally lighthearted, witty, and whimsical, you would be forming a hasty generalization about all his novels based on an atypical example. His other novels, including *The Painted Bird, Steps, Pinball, The Devil Tree, Cockpit, Blind Date,* and *The Hermit of 69th Street,* are rather somber, and are centered around the theme of individual survival in a hostile environment.

3. *Stereotyping.* A particularly irrational form of generalizing is called stereotyping. A stereotype is a kind of hasty generalization that expresses a rigid belief about all people in a group based on insufficient evidence,

generalized from some members of the group. The logical fallacy involved is moving from some to all in a way that does not take into account individual differences.

Fallacy of Accident (Sweeping Generalization)

A *fallacy of accident* is directly opposite to *hasty generalization*. It arises from the assumption that if rules exist there can be no exceptions and often takes the form of a *sweeping generalization* that fails to take into account cases that are clearly exceptions to the rule. The failure to take into account special circumstances or a particular case, that is, the refusal to admit that circumstances can alter the rule, might result in a *sweeping generalization*. A *sweeping generalization* can take one of two forms: (1) an assertion that something is always good even in circumstances where it clearly is not, or (2) something is invariably bad even in situations where it might do some good. For example, most people would agree with the statement that "sunshine contributes to good health," but if this generalization were extended to say that "therefore even people who are fair-skinned or allergic should sit in the sun for hours," the writer would be applying a generalization to a specific case whose circumstances prevent the general rule from applying. Conversely, many people would agree with the statement that "marijuana is a harmful drug with negative consequences," but if the writer were then to argue that "therefore marijuana should never be used even for patients suffering from glaucoma," this would be an unjustified application of the general rule to circumstance clearly regarded as an exception.

FALLACIES THAT RESULT FROM UNWARRANTED ASSUMPTIONS

Fallacies resulting from unwarranted assumptions take a variety of forms.

Oversimplification of Causes

This fallacy results when writers assume that complex events can be explained by pointing to one single cause. For example, a writer might oversimplify the causes of hyperactivity in children by singling out sugar-laden junk foods as the only important factor. Yet researchers have discovered that metabolism and heredity are just as important.

Complex Questions

The fallacy of the *complex question* occurs when the arguer poses the question in such a manner as to assume or make the unwarranted assumption that an implicit unasked question has already been answered. The most famous example of this fallacy is "Have you stopped beating your wife?" Sometimes this fallacy is called a *loaded question* for obvious reasons, since it presumes that the person has already been asked the question "Do you beat your wife?" has answered "Yes," and is now answering whether or not he still continues this practice. Trick questions of this kind make it impossible to give a simple *yes* or *no* answer. *Complex questions* enter into legal proceedings when a prosecuting attorney asks a witness, "Where did you hide the axe you used as the murder weapon?" Questions like these can best be handled by separating the issues involved and treating them as two separate questions.

False Dilemma *(Either/Or, Black/White Fallacy)*

This fallacy results from an unwarranted assumption that there are only two choices in a particular situation. The writer puts the audience in the position of having to pick between one or another of these extreme alternatives. This bumper sticker mentality purveys a simplistic view of the world in terms of black and white, right or wrong extremes. For example, Noel Keane, the attorney who pioneered the practice of surrogate motherhood, in his book coauthored with Dennis L. Breo, *The Surrogate Mother* (1981), characterizes the phenomenon as follows:

> With surrogate mothers, we are talking about giving life. Those who want to deny life can practice contraception or obtain an abortion.

Keane's characterization suggests that only these two alternatives exist to the problem and does not mention other alternatives, including adoption. Keane's persuasive intent here seems to be to characterize the situation in such extreme terms that surrogate parenting seems by contrast to be a more viable option than it otherwise might be. This fallacy depends on the audience accepting the unwarranted assumption that no other options exist, including the alternative of not having to make a choice at all.

False Cause

Overlooking a Common Cause. This fallacy results from the failure to recognize that two seemingly related events may both be effects of a third common cause.

Suppose, as Darrell Huff (mentioned earlier) has pointed out, someone observes that "there is a close relationship between the salaries of Presbyterian ministers in Massachusetts and the price of rum in Havana." Huff asks, "Which is the cause and which the effect? In other words are the ministers benefiting from the rum trade or supporting it?" The inference that these two events are connected is improbable, and it is much more likely as Huff observes that "in the case of the ministers and the rum it is easy to see that both figures are growing because of the influence of a third factor: the historic and worldwide rise in the price level of practically everything."

Confusing Temporal Succession with Causal Sequence (Post Hoc Ergo Propter Hoc). This fallacy (from the Latin, "after this, therefore because of this") confuses sequence with causation and infers that simply because B follows A that A has caused B. The cause–effect nature of the relationship is spurious. For example, Roger Blough, former president of U.S. Steel Corporation, once observed that "steel prices cause inflation like wet sidewalks cause rain" (*Forbes* [August 1, 1967]).

Darrell Huff and Irving Geis, in *How to Lie with Statistics* (1954), provide an amusing example of this kind of false correlation:

> The conviction of the people among the New Hebrides [is] that body lice produce good health. Observation over the centuries had taught them that people in good health usually had lice and sick people very often did not. The observation itself was accurate and sound, as observations made informally over the years surprisingly often are. Not so much can be said for the conclusion to which these primitive people came from their evidence: lice make a man healthy. Everybody should have them . . . more sophisticated observers finally got things straightened out in the New Hebrides. As it turned out, almost everybody in those circles had lice most of the time. It was, you might say, the normal condition of man. When, however, anyone took a fever (quite possibly carried to him by those same lice) and his body became too hot for comfortable habitation, the lice left. There you have cause and effect altogether confusingly distorted, reversed and intermingled.

The nearness or proximity of events may suggest that a causal relationship exists between the two events in question, but true causation always involves the presence of a means (sometimes called *agency*) by which the first event can be demonstrated to have caused the second event.

Mistaking Statistical Correlations for Causal Connections

Simply because two events are linked statistically does not mean that one event has caused the other. The fallacy results from mistaking coincidence for causation. For example, *Science Digest* (August, 1988) featured this tongue-in-cheek account of the discovery of a correlation between storks and babies:

> In 1980, there were 1,000 pairs of breeding storks in West Germany, about half the 1965 census. Helmut Sies of the University of Dusseldorf in West Germany has uncovered a possible clue to that country's falling birth rate: there are not enough storks to go around. Between 1965 and 1980, the decline in the West German birth rate almost exactly matched the decline in brooding [breeding] storks, an explanation that, as Sies says, "every child knows makes sense."

Obviously, it would take more than a statistical correlation between a decline in number of breeding storks and numbers of children to establish that one produced the other. As with the post hoc fallacy, what is required is a demonstration of a means or *agency* by which one event could have caused the other. Even though this is a lighthearted example, many serious arguments rely on statistical correlations to prove a causal relationship. For example, arguments as to whether high blood cholesterol causes heart disease, or whether cigarette smoking causes lung cancer, depend on statistical correlations.

Slippery Slope

This fallacy results when writers assume that X will set in motion a series of events that lead to a catastrophe without demonstrating how one step would lead to the next. An example of a *slippery slope* is this turn-of-the-century forecast of the dire consequences of the women's suffrage movement by Henry T. Finck in *The Independent* (January 31, 1901):

> Woman's participation in political life . . . would involve the domestic calamity of a deserted home and the loss of the womanly qualities for which refined men adore women and marry them. . . . Doctors tell us, too, that thousands of children would be harmed or killed before birth by the injurious effect of untimely political excitement on their mothers.

Faulty Analogy

Faulty analogy results from the unwarranted assumption that because two things are comparable in some respects, it can be assumed that they are comparable in other ways as well. For example, John McMurtry, a former linebacker who became a professor of philosophy, in his article "Kill 'Em! Crush 'Em! Eat 'Em Raw!" (*Maclean's* [October, 1971]) formulates an analogy between football and war to support his thesis that violence in football might not be a side effect of the game but rather its main point. McMurtry's tactics are based on getting his audience to agree, point by point, that since football and war are so similar in many obvious respects, they may be similar in less obvious ways as well — as expressions of innate human aggression:

> The family resemblance between football and war is, indeed, striking. Their languages are similar: "field general," "long bomb," "blitz," "take a shot," "front line," "pursuit," "good hit," "the draft" and so on. Their principles and practices are alike: mass hysteria, the art of intimidation, absolute command and total obedience, territorial aggression, censorship, inflated insignia and propaganda, blackboard manoeuvres and strategies, drill, uniforms, formations, marching bands and training camps. And the virtues they celebrate are almost identical: hyper-aggressiveness, coolness under fire and suicidal bravery.

Some readers may feel that in his zeal to condemn violence in football, McMurtry has gotten carried away with his analogy. Admittedly violence in sports is a major problem, but it is not on the same level as war. And it may be true that McMurtry makes a valid point, that violence for its own sake is beginning to eclipse other aspects of football, but the differences between war and football are greater than the similarities. After all, war is something that takes place between countries or nations rather than between individuals or small groups. Furthermore, football games don't include taking prisoners of war from the other team nor do the football players get killed during the course of the game. At first McMurtry's analogy might seem convincing, but when significant differences begin to outweigh the similarities the result is a false analogy.

FALLACIES THAT RESULT FROM THE USE OF AMBIGUOUS TERMS OR PHRASES

This class of fallacies occurs when the same word takes on different meanings within the course of the argument. These fallacies may also arise quite unintentionally when the writer has not clearly defined terms crucial to the argument.

Fallacy of Equivocation

This fallacy occurs whenever the writer allows a key term to take on different meanings at different points in the argument. For example, if, in the course of an argument, the writer asserts "the law is on my side," it would be difficult to tell whether the writer meant *law* in the sense of legal statutes, administrative regulations, common law, or constitutional law. Perhaps the writer might even have meant *higher law* in the sense of a moral principle or a divine imperative of the kind contained in the Bible or the Koran. Obviously, important terms need careful definition. Otherwise the argument will quickly unravel because of lack of clarity.

Equivocation has a lighter side when the writer exploits a shift in meaning for humorous effects. For example, Zsa Zsa Gabor was quoted in *Newsweek* (March 28, 1960) as saying that "a man in love is incomplete until he has married. Then he's finished." Gabor's amusing aphorism relies on two different connotations of the word "complete."

A classic example of *equivocation* used for comic effect occurs in Shakespeare's play *Hamlet*, Act V, Scene I. Hamlet has returned secretly to Denmark and he and his friend Horatio observe a grave being dug in the churchyard by a jocular gravedigger:

HAMLET. . . . Whose grave's this sirrah?
CLOWN. Mine, Sir.
[Sings] O, a pit of clay for to be made for such a guest is meet.
HAMLET. I think it be thine indeed, for thou liest in't.

CLOWN.   You lie out on't, sir, and therefore 'tis not yours. For my part, I do not lie in't, yet it is mine.

HAMLET.   Thou dost lie in't, to be in't and say it is thine. 'Tis for the dead, not for the quick; therefore thou liest.

CLOWN.   'Tis a quick lie, sir; 'twill away again from me to you.

HAMLET.   What man dost thou dig it for?

CLOWN.   For no man, sir.

HAMLET.   What woman then?

CLOWN.   For none neither.

HAMLET.   Who is to be buried in't?

CLOWN.   One that was a woman, sir; but, rest her soul, she's dead.

HAMLET.   How absolute the knave is! We must speak by the card, or equivocation will undo us.

The comic effects of this passage are due to the double meaning of the word *lie*, and the pun on the word *quick* (which not only means *swiftly* but *living* as well). So, too, the shift of meaning of the word *man* (referring to both males and human beings) is the source of witty repartee. Hamlet aptly observes on all matters of ambiguity, "we must speak by the card [that is, exactly] or equivocation will undo us."

Fallacy of Amphiboly

The *fallacy of amphiboly* can occur through faulty punctuation, faulty grammar, or the awkward or careless way in which words are put together. In this case, ambiguity doesn't stem from a term having two meanings, but from faulty syntax or a confusing grammatical structure. A classic example is a bequest that was worded "I hereby leave $20,000 to my cousins Philip Horton and George Matthews." Imagine being the executor of the estate trying to decide whether this bequest meant (1) each cousin should receive $20,000 or (2) $20,000 should be divided so that each cousin would receive $10,000. The *New Yorker* magazine frequently features amusing examples of unintended meaning created by careless placement of words — for instance, "Do taxidermists make the most effective decoys?" to which the *New Yorker* (July 18, 1988) replied, "Only when you can get them to hold still."

In the following speech, taken from Willard R. Espy, *The Garden of Eloquence* (1983), notice how the meaning of the first paragraph is reversed when the same passage is punctuated differently:

Ladies and gentlemen, I bring you a man among men. He is out of place when among cheaters and scoundrels. He feels quite at home when surrounded by persons of integrity. He is uncomfortable when not helping others. He is perfectly satisfied when his fellow human beings are happy. He tries to make changes in order for the country to be a better place. He should leave us this evening with feelings of disgust at ineptitude and a desire to do better. I present to you Mr. John Smith.

But somehow the master of ceremonies, or perhaps his secretary, mispunctuated the passage, and it came out this way:

> Ladies and gentlemen, I bring you a man. Among men, he is out of place. When among cheaters and scoundrels, he feels quite at home. When surrounded by persons of integrity, he is uncomfortable. When not helping others, he is perfectly satisfied. When his fellow human beings are happy, he tries to make changes. In order for the country to be a better place, he should leave us this evening. With feelings of disgust at ineptitude and a desire to do better, I present to you Mr. John Smith.

Fallacy of Accent

The *fallacy of accent* occurs whenever a secondary meaning is communicated (1) as a result of misplaced emphasis, or (2) when an entirely different meaning is created by taking words out of their original context.

Misplaced Emphasis or Accent. For example, the *Philadelphia Inquirer* magazine (cited in *Quarterly Review of Doublespeak* [April 1987]) carried an account of a sign that appeared in a restaurant that said "Managers Shrimp Special: All you can eat—\$5.95." After a couple had eaten the first serving of shrimp they ordered more—only to be told that they couldn't have anymore. When the customer pointed out the sign in the window, he was told, "The manager says that's all you *can* eat."

Words Taken Out of Context. The original review of a science fiction film called *The Big Yolk* might appear as follows: "This movie is based on the premise that a big uncracked egg is approaching Earth from outer space and threatens to submerge all the inhabitants in yolk. This so-called film is an astounding bore, it is not capable of holding the attention of a gnat, and is for all audiences whose I.Q.'s are below the level of house plants. Do anything rather than see this colossal bomb of a movie." Taken out of context, for publicity purposes, this review might become: "Astounding, . . . capable of holding the attention of . . . all audiences . . . do see this colossal . . . movie."

Fallacies of Composition and Division

The *fallacy of composition* occurs when an inference is drawn about the qualities of a group as a whole based on the evaluations of individual members. For example, the owner of a basketball franchise might pay an enormous amount of money to fill each position on the team with the best players money can buy. Yet the team composed of these high-priced superstars would not necessarily be the best basketball team in the country. This fallacy overlooks the fact that qualities of the individual parts do not automatically extend to the whole.

To take a hypothetical example, if your favorite foods were chocolate ice cream, tuna fish, tomatoes, and corn, the *fallacy of composition* would imply that a casserole dish combining all your favorite ingredients would be your favorite dish. Inferring that the dish comprised of these ingredients would be even better than the individual parts would be erroneous, and inedible.

The *fallacy of division* is the opposite of the *fallacy of composition* and occurs when an inference is drawn about the qualities of the parts based on something that is valid for the whole. Simply because a cake is round does not mean that it can be inferred that each piece of the cake also must be round.

TWO SHORT ARGUMENTS FOR ANALYSIS

Susan Jacoby

Unfair Game

Susan Jacoby has written extensively about women's subjects in the
New York Times *and* McCalls. *Many pieces have been collected in
her book* The Possible She *(1979). The following essay was originally
published in the "Hers" column of* The New York Times *(1978).
Jacoby voices a complaint that despite, or perhaps because of, the
sexual revolution unescorted women are considered fair game and are
subjected to undesired and unsolicited sexual advances. Notice how
Jacoby uses examples drawn from her everyday experiences to reach
her conclusion.*

My friend and I, two women obviously engrossed in conversation, 1
are sitting at a corner table in the crowded Oak Room of the Plaza at ten
o'clock on a Tuesday night. A man materializes and interrupts us with
the snappy opening line, "A good woman is hard to find."

We say nothing, hoping he will disappear back into his bottle. But he 2
fancies himself as our genie and asks, "Are you visiting?" Still we say
nothing. Finally my friend looks up and says, "We live here." She and I
look at each other, the thread of our conversation snapped, our thoughts
focused on how to get rid of this intruder. In a minute, if something isn't
done, he will scrunch down next to me on the banquette and start
offering to buy us drinks.

"Would you leave us alone, please," I say in a loud but reasonably 3
polite voice. He looks slightly offended but goes on with his bright social
patter. I become more explicit. "We don't want to talk to you, we didn't
ask you over here, and we want to be alone. Go away." This time he
directs his full attention to me—and he is mad. "All right, all right,
excuse me." He pushes up the corners of his mouth in a Howdy Doody
smile. "You ought to try smiling. You might even be pretty if you smiled
once in a while."

At last the man leaves. He goes back to his buddy at the bar. I watch 4
them out of the corner of my eye, and he gestures angrily at me for at
least fifteen minutes. When he passes our table on the way out of the

room, this well-dressed, obviously affluent man mutters, "Good-bye, bitch," under his breath.

5   Why is this man calling me names? Because I have asserted my right to sit at a table in a public place without being drawn into a sexual flirtation. Because he has been told, in no uncertain terms, that two attractive women prefer each other's company to his.

6   This sort of experience is an old story to any woman who travels, eats, or drinks — for business or pleasure — without a male escort. In Holiday Inns and at the Plaza, on buses and airplanes, in tourist and first class, a woman is always thought to be looking for a man in addition to whatever else she may be doing. The man who barged in on us at the bar would never have broken into the conversation of two men, and it goes without saying that he wouldn't have imposed himself on a man and a woman who were having a drink. But two women at a table are an entirely different matter. Fair game.

7   This might be viewed as a relatively small flaw in the order of the universe — something in a class with an airline losing luggage or a computer fouling up a bank statement. Except a computer doesn't foul up your bank account every month and an airline doesn't lose your suitcase every time you fly. But if you are an independent woman, you have to spend a certain amount of energy, day in and day out, in order to go about your business without being bothered by strange men.

8   On airplanes, I am a close-mouthed traveler. As soon as the "No Smoking" sign is turned off, I usually pull some papers out of my briefcase and start working. Work helps me forget that I am scared of flying. When I am sitting next to a woman, she quickly realizes from my monosyllabic replies that I don't want to chat during the flight. Most men, though, are not content to be ignored.

9   Once I was flying from New York to San Antonio on a plane that was scheduled to stop in Dallas. My seatmate was an advertising executive who kept questioning me about what I was doing and who remained undiscouraged by my terse replies until I ostentatiously covered myself with a blanket and shut my eyes. When the plane started its descent into Dallas, he made his move.

10   "You don't really have to get to San Antonio today, do you?"

11   "Yes."

12   "Come on, change your ticket. Spend the evening with me here. I'm staying at a wonderful hotel, with a pool, we could go dancing . . ."

13   "No."

14   "Well, you can't blame a man for trying."

15   I do blame a man for trying in this situation . . . for suggesting that a woman change her work and travel plans to spend a night with a perfect stranger in whom she had displayed no personal interest. The "no personal interest" is crucial; I wouldn't have blamed the man for trying if I had been stroking his cheek and complaining about my dull social life.

There is a nice postscript to this story. Several months later, I was   16
walking my dog in Carl Schurz Park when I ran into my erstwhile
seatmate, who was taking a stroll with his wife and children. He recognized me, all right, and was trying to avoid me when I went over and
courteously reintroduced myself. I reminded him that we had been on
the same flight to Dallas. "Oh yes," he said. "As I recall you were going
on to somewhere else." "San Antonio," I said. "I was in a hurry that
day."

The code of feminine politeness, instilled in girlhood, is no help in   17
dealing with the unwanted approaches of strange men. Our mothers
didn't teach us to tell a man to get lost; they told us to smile and hint that
we'd be just delighted to spend time with the gentleman if we didn't
have other commitments. The man in the Oak Room bar would not be
put off by a demure lowering of eyelids; he had to be told, roughly and
loudly, that his presence was a nuisance.

Not that I am necessarily against men and women picking each other   18
up in public places. In most instances, a modicum of sensitivity will tell a
woman or a man whether someone is open to approaches.

Mistakes can easily be corrected by the kind of courtesy so many   19
people have abandoned since the "sexual revolution." One summer
evening, I was whiling away a half hour in the outdoor bar of the
Stanhope Hotel. I was alone, dressed up, having a drink before going on
to meet someone in a restaurant. A man at the next table asked, "If
you're not busy, would you like to have a drink with me?" I told him I
was sorry but I would be leaving shortly. "Excuse me for disturbing
you," he said, turning back to his own drink. Simple courtesy. No insults
and no hurt feelings.

One friend suggested that I might have avoided the incident in the   20
Oak Room by going to the Palm Court instead. It's true that the Palm
Court is a traditional meeting place for unescorted ladies. But I don't like
violins when I want to talk. And I wanted to sit in a large, comfortable
leather chair. Why should I have to hide among the potted palms to
avoid men who think I'm looking for something else?

Sample Analysis

CLAIM: Jacoby argues that our society is unfair to women, despite the
changes brought about by the sexual revolution and advances toward
equal opportunity in the workplace. Nonetheless, the psychological attitudes of men toward women still remain in the Dark Ages. Men must
realize that women sitting alone in public places should not be subjected
to unwanted advances on the erroneous assumption that unescorted
women are always looking for escorts for the evening.

GROUNDS: Jacoby presents evidence to support her claim that men are, for the most part, still operating according to older conventions. She draws on examples from her everyday experience. On an airplane trip, while she was immersed in work, the man sitting next to her boorishly insisted on making a pass. At another time in the Oak Room of the Plaza Hotel, she and a friend wished to talk privately while having drinks and were accosted by a man who did not want to leave them alone. A third incident illustrates the more enlightened code: Jacoby politely rejected the advances of a man at the Stanhope Hotel who then simply apologized and left her alone. This last case serves to show that Jacoby does not object to men picking up women if the women have no objection. What she really minds is men who refuse to take no for an answer, who still believe that women who say no really mean yes. Jacoby's claim is related to the idea expressed in the title, women if unescorted should not be considered fair game to be picked up by men.

WARRANT: The principle to which Jacoby appeals to assure that her audience will draw the same conclusions from her experiences that she does is the rule that social relationships should be initiated only when both parties are interested. Jacoby relies on this warrant to connect both the two cases of unwanted attention and the example of courteous behavior to the claim that a woman should have the right to be left alone if she so chooses.

PERSUADING THE AUDIENCE: Jacoby's article is addressed to an audience comprised of both men and women. Jacoby appeals to the values of her audience in terms of the principle that respecting another person's privacy and a code of basic human decency in relationships is never out of date. Jacoby wishes to persuade men not to mistake isolation for invitation and to assure women that they have every right to go places alone without being subjected to unwanted advances from men. The formal elements of her argument are strengthened by Jacoby's tone, that of an intelligent, self-assured, independent woman who is expressing a strong sense of indignation at a common attitude in society. She appeals directly to the audience's sense of how unfair it is that advances in the workplace have not been matched by equally progressive attitudes in relationships between the sexes.

Questions for Discussion and Writing

1. Evaluate the significance of the title of the essay. How is the concept of fair game connected to Jacoby's argument?

2. Jacoby says that it is widely assumed in our society that "a woman is always thought to be looking for a man in addition to whatever

else she may be doing." What examples based on her personal experiences does she offer that support this assertion?

3. Write a short paragraph describing Jacoby's personality as it comes through from her essay. What measures does she use to establish herself as a trustworthy observer?

4. Evaluate Jacoby's argument that one cause of the problem she describes is due, in part, to the fact that girls are taught to invite, and not refuse attention and advances from men. To what extent do you find Jacoby's observation to be true?

5. Although few people would disagree with Jacoby's basic wish for more considerate treatment of women by men, several opposing arguments might be developed from her essay. Write a paragraph arguing that the sexual revolution either has or has not made it more likely that the types of objectionable advances Jacoby describes will occur.

6. How is the construction of Jacoby's argument based on inductive reasoning? Does she provide a sufficient number of representative examples to support her argument? Are there too few or atypical examples used to justify an inductive leap, reasoning from a few examples to what Jacoby says is true of a whole class?

7. How does the example of the behavior of the gentleman in the Stanhope Hotel (para. 19) serve as evidence to support her thesis that the presence or absence of personal interest should be the ultimate criterion in governing social interactions between men and women?

8. Have you ever been in a situation that you now recognize as essentially similar to the ones Jacoby describes? Discuss your experiences either from the perspective of being a woman who was the object in an "unfair game" or from the viewpoint of a male who misperceived a woman's independent behavior for an invitation.

John Milton

Areopagitica: Defense of Books

"Defense of Books" is from Areopagitica: A Speech for the Liberty of Unlicensed Printing, *to the Parliament of England. John Milton named his 1644 pamphlet* Areopagitica *after a speech of the same name delivered by Isocrates, an Athenian orator (436–338 B.C.), imploring his fellow Athenians to rid themselves of political weaknesses in their society and return to the true democracy, including the freedom to write, speak, and publish freely. Milton urges his contemporaries to emulate the policy of the Greeks and censor only those books that are atheistic or libelous. Surprisingly, most people believed Milton's argument to be against all censorship, which it clearly is not. In 1643, Presbyterians in power in Parliament tried to quiet the opposition by imposing censorship. Milton uses sound argumentative strategy by arguing passionately against censorship before publication, although permitting the later suppression of books found to endanger religion and morality. Milton creates an inventive analogy between killing a man and censoring a book; the argument that some books are worth more than some lives is so unusual that it compels his audience to really think about his basic proposition. Also, notice how Milton begins by conceding that it is important for the church and the commonwealth to "have a vigilant eye" on books. By agreeing to this opposing viewpoint, Milton steers the discussion away from a direct confrontation so that he can get a hearing for his argument and have the chance to persuade his audience.*

1   I deny not, but that it is of greatest concernment in the Church and Commonwealth, to have a vigilant eye how books demean themselves as well as men; and thereafter to confine, imprison, and do sharpest justice on them as malefactors. For books are not absolutely dead things, but do contain a potency of life in them to be as active as that soul was whose progeny they are; nay, they do preserve as in a vial the purest efficacy and extraction of that living intellect that bred them. I know they are as lively, and as vigorously productive, as those fabulous dragon's teeth; and being sown up and down, may chance to spring up armed men. And yet, on the other hand, unless wariness be used, as good almost kill a man as kill a good book. Who kills a man kills a reasonable creature, God's image; but he who destroys a good book, kills reason itself, kills the image of God, as it were in the eye. Many a man lives a burden to the

earth; but a good book is the precious life-blood of a master spirit, embalmed and treasured up on purpose to a life beyond life. 'Tis true, no age can restore a life, whereof perhaps there is no great loss; and revolutions of ages do not oft recover the loss of a rejected truth, for the want of which whole nations fare the worse.

We should be wary therefore what persecutions we raise against the 2 living labours of public men, how we spill that seasoned life of man, preserved and stored up in books; since we see a kind of homicide may be thus committed, sometimes a martyrdom, and if it extend to the whole impression, a kind of massacre; whereof the execution ends not in the slaying of an elemental life, but strikes at that ethereal and fifth essence, the breath of reason itself, slays an immortality rather than a life. But lest I should be condemned of introducing licence, while I oppose licensing, I refuse not the pains to be so much historical, as will serve to show what hath been done by ancient and famous commonwealths against this disorder, till the very time that this project of licensing crept out of the inquisition, was catched up by our prelates, and hath caught some of our presbyters.

In Athens, where books and wits were ever busier than in any other 3 part of Greece, I find but only two sorts of writings which the magistrate cared to take notice of; those either blasphemous and atheistical, or libellous. Thus the books of Protagoras were by the judges of Areopagus commanded to be burnt, and himself banished the territory for a discourse begun with his confessing not to know 'whether there were gods, or whether not.' And against defaming, it was agreed that none should be traduced by name, as was the manner of Vetus Comoedia, whereby we may guess how they censured libelling. And this course was quick enough, as Cicero writes, to quell both the desperate wits of other atheists, and the open way of defaming, as the event showed. Of other sects and opinions, though tending to voluptuousness, and the denying of Divine Providence, they took no heed.

Therefore we do not read that either Epicurus, or that libertine school 4 of Cyrene, or what the Cynic impudence uttered, was ever questioned by the laws. Neither is it recorded that the writings of those old comedians were suppressed, though the acting of them were forbid; and that Plato commended the reading of Aristophanes, the loosest of them all, to his royal scholar Dionysius, is commonly known, and may be excused, if holy Chrysostom, as is reported, nightly studied so much the same author and had the art to cleanse a scurrilous vehemence into the style of a rousing sermon.

Sample Analysis

CLAIM: Milton maintains that books are not inanimate objects but contain a potency of life expressing the essential thoughts of those who wrote them. In this sense, books are alive because ideas spring from them, embody living truth, and therefore "killing" a book through prevention of publication, censorship, or withdrawal from circulation is a kind of murder that is in some ways worse than homicide.

GROUNDS: The grounds of Milton's argument takes two forms. The first form of support is an unexpected analogy that is as persuasive as it is surprising. Books are living in the sense that they contain the immortal spirit of those who created them. Thus, killing a book deprives the world of ideas that might have been of enormous value to society. The second form of support is based on historical precedent. Milton urges his contemporaries to follow the ancient example of the Athenians, who censored only those books that were judged blasphemous or libelous. Milton cites works by Epicurus and Aristophanes as examples of ancient writers his contemporaries would never have known if they had been censored.

WARRANT: Milton relies on two kinds of warrants. He draws on an analogy warrant that books can be seen as possessing a potency of life as if they were living beings; therefore, censoring a book is like killing a man. He also draws on an authority warrant when he cites practices and authors in Athenian society, knowing that his contemporaries would view such cases as authoritative.

PERSUADING THE AUDIENCE: Milton begins by conceding it is important for the church and commonwealth "to have a vigilant eye" on books, that is, for the church and state to be aware of publications. His persuasive strategy is designed to avoid a direct confrontation with his audience and present his position as a reasonable one. Milton appeals directly to his audience's sense that a civilized society should seek a middle course, on the one hand, eliminating the chance that people will come into contact with offensive, corrupting, or dangerous materials, while on the other hand, preserving the valuable concept of freedom of choice to reject or accept a published idea. A civilized society should provide freedom to people to make up their own minds. He presents his case as a reasonable alternative to complete freedom of publication or to blanket censorship. He urges his contemporaries to emulate policies of the ancient Greeks and censor only those books that are atheistic or libelous.

Questions for Discussion and Writing

1. Why does Milton start out by conceding that it is important for the church and the commonwealth to "have a vigilant eye" on books as well as men?

2. What reasons does Milton present to support his thesis that "books are not absolutely dead things, but do contain a potency of life in them"?

3. Why, according to Milton, may the "killing" of a book (that is, preventing it from being published, or censoring it after it has been published) in some circumstances do as much injury as murdering a human being? In what way does Milton's argument depend on the systematic elaboration of an analogy for its effect?

4. Does Milton's argument that some books are to be valued more than even the lives of some men strike you as fanciful, persuasive, and effective in conveying his thesis because of or despite the very outrageousness of his claim? If you disagree, write an essay explaining why no book (remember, this would include the Bible, the Koran, the Bhagavad Gita, as well as *Valley of the Dolls*) would ever be as valuable as a human life.

5. What contrast in concepts does Milton bring together in paragraph 2 when he says, "But lest I should be condemned of introducing licence, while I oppose licensing . . ."?

6. Summarize paragraphs 3 and 4. How does the evidence drawn from practices in ancient Greece support Milton's argument against censorship? Keep in mind that Milton named his 1644 essay *Areopagitica* after a speech of the same name delivered by Isocrates, an Athenian orator (436–338 B.C.), imploring his fellow Athenians to rid themselves of political weaknesses in their society and return to the true democracy, including the freedom to write, speak, and publish freely. Areopagus was the name of a hill west of the Acropolis in Athens where a high tribunal met to decide criminal cases, including homicide, and to deliberate questions of morality.

7. How might Milton's argument be analyzed as an example of deductive reasoning? Specifically, how does Milton build his argument on the *premisses* that an inanimate object, a book, is capable of transmitting truth to future generations and that some books are worth more than some human lives?

8. In a short essay discuss whether there are any kinds of books, other than pornography, whose publication ought not to be permitted. For instance, do books that claim the Holocaust never happened give the impression to the uninformed that known historical events never existed? Do books of this kind do such damage by lending the appearance of legitimacy to an issue as to warrant their being censored?

4

The Role of Language in Argument

The words a writer uses play a vital role in making any argument more effective for a given audience. By adapting the style of the argument to a particular audience, writers can increase their chances of not only getting a fair hearing for their case, but also convincing the audience to share their outlook. For some audiences, tone, style, and syntax that are colloquial may work best. For others, a more formal, literary style may be more appropriate. Of all the stylistic means a writer can use to develop an argument, three areas deserve a close look: (1) definition, (2) tone, and (3) persuasive techniques. Definition covers broad questions of what kind of boundaries a writer chooses to draw around the issue, as well as specific meanings of key terms. Tone reveals a writer's attitude toward the subject, and persuasive techniques include every means a writer uses to encourage an audience to share this viewpoint.

Definition

PURPOSES AND USES OF DEFINITION

Definition is the method of clarifying the meaning of words that are vague or ambiguous. These words may be important terms either in the claim of the argument or elsewhere in the essay. In other cases, you may wish to devote an entire essay to exploring all the connotations and denotations that have accrued to an unusual or controversial term, or challenge preconceptions attached to a familiar term.

In everyday life, arguments on a whole range of issues are really arguments about how terms ought to be defined. There are several reasons why writers should clarify the basic nature of key terms on which an argument depends. First of all, as a practical matter the audience must understand what the writer means by certain unfamiliar terms crucial to the argument before they can even begin seriously considering the writer's thesis, or the evidence brought forward to support the claim. The writer must define ambiguous terms that might be mistaken to mean something other than what he or she intended. Otherwise audiences may bring their own assumptions, preconceptions, and associations to the meaning of the terms in question. Definition offers writers a method by which to clarify the meaning of a term so that it will be free from extraneous associations and undesired connotations.

For example, an argument as to whether the government should censor pornographic materials would have to clarify exactly what is meant by such terms as *pornographic* or *obscene*. In *Roth* v. *U.S.* (1957), the United States Supreme Court defined "obscene and pornographic" material as material that is "patently offensive because it affronts contemporary community standards relating to the description or representation of sexual matters in a way that appeals only to 'prurient interests' and is without 'social value.'" Critics have responded that the Supreme Court's definition has itself raised questions as to just how key terms such as *community*, *prurience*, and *social value*, in turn, ought to be defined. How is one really to gauge a community's standards — through a poll, or the testimony of leading citizens? And what type of "community" did the Supreme Court have in mind — a neighborhood, a town, a city, an entire county, state, or region of the country? Moreover, might not an evaluation of what constitutes prurience be merely a matter of personal taste? And how is one to identify characteristics that make it possible to say a work has or has not social value?

Likewise, an argument focusing on any of a number of issues surrounding organ transplantation would have to stipulate what is meant by the concept of death. A clear definition of death is important since new developments in biomedical technology now make it possible to sustain life by artificial means long after an individual would normally have died. The crux of the issue is that someone who would have been declared dead in the past might now be declared living. Until recently, the courts would have relied on the traditional definition of death as "the cessation of life; the ceasing to exist; defined by physicians as a total stoppage of the circulation of blood and a cessation of the animal and vital functions consequent thereon such as respiration, pulsation, etc." (*Black's Law Dictionary*, revised Fourth Edition [1968]).

In other words, death was defined as occurring only when respiration and circulation of blood ceased. New machines, however, can sustain heartbeat and respiration indefinitely even in individuals who show no signs of brain activity. For this reason, the Ad Hoc Committee of the Harvard Medical School, in "A Definition of Irreversible Coma" (1968), proposed a new definition of death based on the criterion of irreversible coma. From the committee's point of view, this more accurate definition makes it possible to determine if and when respirators and other devices should be withdrawn, when a patient should be considered dead, and at what point still viable organs might be removed for transplantation.

Besides eliminating ambiguity, vagueness, or defining a term important to the development of the argument, definitions in argument can be used to influence the attitudes of an audience toward a particular issue. Definition becomes important in arguments where the ability to control the way a central term is perceived is equivalent to winning the argument. A writer who convinces an audience that abortion should be "defined" (and perceived) as synonymous with murder has won the debate. Definition of controversial terms not only defines the terms but effectively shapes how people will perceive the issue.

For example, during hearings by the Hawaiian State Legislature on a proposal to abolish the state's law against abortion, the following letter appeared in the February 14, 1970, *Honolulu Advertiser*:

> Dear Sir: You ask me how I stand on abortion. Let me answer forthrightly and without equivocation.
>
> If by abortion you mean the murdering of defenseless human beings; the denial of rights to the youngest of our citizens; the promotion of promiscuity among our shiftless and valueless youth and the rejection of Life, Liberty and the Pursuit of Happiness — then, Sir, be assured that I shall never waver in my opposition, so help me God. But, Sir, if by abortion you mean the granting of equal rights to all our citizens regardless of race, color or sex; the elimination of evil and vile institutions preying upon desperate and hopeless women; a chance for all our youth to be wanted and loved; and, above all, that God-given right for all citizens to act in accordance with the dictates of their own conscience — then, Sir, let me promise you as a patriot and a humanist that I shall never be persuaded to forego my pursuit of these most basic human rights.
>
> Thank you for asking my position on this most crucial issue and let me again assure you of the steadfastness of my stand.
>
> Mahalo and Aloha Nui.

Definitions can not only change perceptions of an event by influencing the attitudes and emotions of an audience but can affect the perception of facts as well. For example, in "The Shrinking Middle Class" (*New England Economic Review* [September/October 1986]) Katharine L. Bradbury, an economist with the Federal Reserve Bank of Boston, addresses the question whether the middle class is shrinking, that is, whether there was a decline in the percentage of families with middle-class incomes between 1973 and 1984. Her argument must first establish what she means by the term *middle class*. She writes:

> . . . the family income range from $20,000 to $49,999 in 1984 dollars is used to define the middle class in this study. This choice implies that one-half of families are in the middle class, about one-third have lower incomes and the remainder (roughly 15%) have higher incomes.

Bradbury explains the limitations of using a simple money income cutoff to define the middle class. She is aware that families of different sizes have different income requirements to achieve the same standard of living, and that living costs vary with regional location. Based on her definition of middle class she reports:

> . . . using this definition the fraction of families with middle class incomes did indeed decline between 1973 and 1984, from 53% to less than 48%. Most of the decline in the middle class share was picked up by the lower income class which increased from 32% of families to 36%; the upper income class grew slightly, from 15% to 16%.

She employs this particular definition and the accompanying evidence to support her claim that "increasing affluence was not the general case between 1973 and 1984." Of course, a different definition of what constitutes middle class would not only alter an audience's perception but would change the "facts" in question and alter any conclusions that might be drawn. For example, in an election year both political parties might be expected to define middle class in a way that was favorable to their candidate.

It is important for the writer to establish clearly a set of criteria and list distinctive characteristics of the term in question, especially if the definition is really an argument for a different interpretation of the term. For example, the following discussion from *Re-making Love: The Feminization of Sex* (1986) by Barbara Ehrenreich, Elizabeth Hess, and Gloria Jacobs calls into question the conventional definition of *sex*. They argue for a reinterpretation of the traditional definition of sex and present a rationale for asking the reader to accept this new definition:

> First, we challenged the old definition of sex as a physical act. Sex, or "normal sex," as defined by the medical experts and accepted by mainstream middle-class culture, was a two-act drama of foreplay and intercourse which culminated in male orgasm and at least a display of female appreciation. We rejected this version of sex as narrow, male-centered, [and] unsatisfying. In its single-mindedness and phallocentrism, this form of sex does imitate rape; it cannot help but remind us of the dangers and ambiguities of heterosexuality. At best, it reminds us simply of work: "Sex," as narrowly and traditionally defined, is obsessive, repetitive, and symbolically (if not actually) tied to the work of reproduction. We insisted on a broader, more playful notion of sex, more compatible with women's broader erotic possibilities, more respectful of women's needs. Our success in redefining sex can be measured not only in the reported proliferation of "variations" (not all of which are women's innovations, of course) or surveys documenting changes in sexual routine and practice, but in expectations: Twenty years ago the woman dissatisfied with sex was made to believe she was lacking something; the woman who selfishly advanced her own pleasure was made to worry about being less than

normal. Today, it is the woman whose marriage still confines her to phallo-centered sex who knows she is missing something; and it is the woman who does not know how to negotiate or find her own way to pleasure who wonders if she is different, abnormal.

Notice how the authors set up a standard, identify criteria, apply them to traditional ideas about sex, and argue that their view is much better suited to characterize the changes wrought by the sexual revolution. In many arguments that seek to persuade an audience to reject or adopt certain values, definition is a way of identifying those criteria that ought to be used in making value judgments. That is, definition is not required because the terms are vague or ambiguous, but rather because the writer rejects familiar and traditional standards and argues for the acceptance of a new set of criteria.

METHODS OF DEFINING TERMS

There are a variety of strategies writers can use, either singly or in combination, for defining terms. A description of eight of these strategies follows.

Synonyms

One of the simplest methods of defining words is to cite a synonym, that is, another word that has the same meaning. Thus, a writer who wanted to convey the meaning of *feast* might cite a synonym such as *banquet*. By the same token, a writer who wished to communicate the meaning of *labyrinth* could use the synonym *maze*. This method is efficient and workable but cannot always be used because many words have no exact synonyms. For example, most people, if asked to give a synonym for *teepee*, would say *tent*. Yet the meaning of the word teepee is not accurately reflected by the synonym tent since a tent is made of canvas and a teepee is an American Indian tent made from animal skins.

For a more useful way of defining terms we need to look at the method first discussed by Aristotle in the *Topica* (one of his treatises on logic), still in use today to define terms in dictionaries.

Dictionary or Lexical

This method, sometimes called analytical definition, puts the thing to be defined into a *genus* or general class and then gives the *differentiae*, or distinguishing features that differentiate the subject being defined from all other things in its class with which it might be confused. For example, a *teepee* is defined by *Webster's New Collegiate Dictionary* as "an American Indian skin-tent." The modifiers "American Indian" and "skin" are necessary to distinguish this particular type of tent from all other kinds of tent (for example, a canvas Army tent) in the same general class. The terms used to define a word should be more specific, clear, and familiar than the actual term in question. Of course, there are many cases where a dictionary definition will not be adequate because the dictionary does not delve into specific criteria, characteristics, and qualities a writer might need to explore in the course of developing an argument. In these cases, the unabridged *Old English Dictionary* may prove useful because this voluminous work gives examples, in context, of how the word has been used down through the centuries.

Etymological

Often a fascinating light is thrown on the meaning of words by studying their etymology, that is, by tracing a word to its origin and following its shift of meaning or acquisition of connotative meanings through the years. For example, William Safire, in *William Safire on Language* (1980), traces the derivation of the word *welfare*:

> When words die, they deserve a decent burial, or at least a respectful obituary. One noun bit the dust recently, at least in government usage, and it is herein bid adieu. The noun is "welfare," as in "Department of Health, Education and Welfare." This fine old word was born before 1303, the offspring of the Middle English *wel*, meaning "wish" or "will," and *faren*, meaning "to go on a journey." In its youth, the word enjoyed a period on the stage: "Study for the people's welfare," Warwick advised Henry VI in Shakespeare's play. In middle age, the word was used in the same sense but with more of a governmental connotation, beginning in a 1904 *Century* magazine article about the "welfare manager . . . a recognized intermediary between employers and employees." About that time, *The Westminster Gazette* was pinpointing its sociological birthplace: "The home of the 'welfare policy' is the city of Dayton, Ohio." According to the etymologist Sir Ernest Weekly, "*Welfare*, as in 'child welfare,' 'welfare center' and so forth, was first used in this sense in Ohio in 1904."

Figurative Language — Metaphors, Similes, and Analogies

Figurative language is used by writers who wish to define a term in order to persuade an audience to agree with their point of view. This form of definition uses metaphors, similes, and analogies to place a thing in its class and identify atypical properties. For example, Len Deighton, in his book *Mexico Set* (1985), writes:

> In Mexico an air conditioner is called a politician because it makes a lot of noise but doesn't work very well.

In each of the following cases, the writers use an extended metaphor, simile, or analogy to clarify the meaning of a term.

"Politics is the art of looking for trouble, finding it everywhere, diagnosing it incorrectly, and applying the wrong remedies." (Groucho Marx)

"Money is like manure. If you spread it around, it does a lot of good, but if you pile it up in one place it stinks like hell." (Clint W. Murchison, Texas financier)

"Suicide is a permanent solution to a temporary problem." (Phil Donahue, NBC, May 23, 1984)

"Golf is a good walk spoiled." (Mark Twain)

"A Jewish man with parents alive is a 15-year-old boy." (Philip Roth, *Portnoy's Complaint*, [1969])

"An actor's a guy who, if you ain't talking about him, ain't listening." (Marlon Brando, *British Vogue*, August 1974)

Stipulation

A stipulative definition proposes a meaning for a term that it did not have before being given it by the definition. In some cases, the writer introduces a brand new term and stipulates that, at least for the purposes of the argument, it is to carry a specific meaning. For example, Peter Singer, the director of the Monash Center for Human Bio-ethics, coins the word *speciesism* by analogy with *racism* or *sexism*. This term characterizes an attitude that leads scientists involved in animal experimentation to rationalize their cruelty toward the animals used in their tests on the grounds that human beings, as the apex of all species, have every right to sacrifice other species to obtain information useful to humans. Singer feels that a new term is necessary to dramatize the low value industrial societies place on animal life. He stipulates the definition of speciesism to set the parameters of the debate in a way favorable to his viewpoint.

In other cases, the writer uses a term that has been coined to characterize a situation so as both to identify it and to express a judgment about it. One such term is *greenmail* (by analogy with *blackmail*). For example, Gerald L. Houseman argues in "The Merger Game Starts with Deception" (1986) that the use of greenmail has allowed corporate raiders like Carl Icahn, Rupert Murdoch, the Bass Brothers, T. Boone Pickens, and Ivan Boesky, among others, to accumulate millions of dollars at the expense of workers, stockholders, and the general public:

Many offers to take over a company (so-called "tender offers") are made with little or no thought of actually taking it over. The objective in these cases is to threaten the board and management but, after a variety of financial and legal skirmishes, to withdraw—if the company will pay off with "greenmail." Greenmail, technically speaking, is the premium over market value paid by a company to the raider for its own stock in order to obtain withdrawal from a proxy fight (the fight for control of the firm). Let us assume a market value of $40 per share. The stock goes to $52 on the news of the take-over attempt. . . . When this occurs, a contract is drawn up which guarantees that the raider will not try to do this again for a set number of years. In exchange for this agreement, he sells his stock back to the company for a price of, say, $62. (The terms of the agreement outlined in this example are quite typical.) The take-over artist, or "broker," which is his usual title, has been well rewarded for notifying the SEC about buying into the company "for investment purposes" and for carrying out a war of nerves against the firm.

Notice how Houseman not only defines greenmail but explains how it operates and identifies the ways in which it is damaging to the entire economy of the country. Those who favor takeovers, acquisitions, mergers, and leveraged buyouts on the grounds that such mergers are necessary if the United States is to remain competitive in the world market, would not use the term *greenmail* because of its negative associations with *blackmail*. They would probably refer to the same events as "financial restructuring."

In still other cases, the writer stipulates an unconventional meaning for a traditional term (as Barbara Ehrenreich, Elizabeth Hess, and Gloria Jacobs do for the word *sex*) to steer the argument in a direction favorable to his or her viewpoint. For example, William F. Buckley's argument in *Execution Eve* (1972) against those "abolitionists" who favor eliminating capital punishment turns on his unconventional definition of the words *cruel and unusual* punishment. Buckley argues that capital punishment is by no means cruel and unusual (the Eighth Amendment to the U.S. Constitution expressly forbids "cruel and unusual" punishment) and goes on to stipulate his own definition for these terms. Buckley interprets the word *unusual* to mean simply *uncommon* or *infrequent*, in contrast to the framers of the Constitution who used it to refer to bizarre methods of execution like death by public stoning, by the guillotine, and so on. Similarly, of the meaning of the word *cruel*, Buckley says:

Capital punishment is cruel. That is a historical judgment. But the Constitution suggests that what must be proscribed as cruel is (a) a particularly painful way of inflicting death or (b) a particularly undeserved death: and the death penalty, as such, offends neither of these criteria and cannot therefore be regarded as objectively cruel.

While not everyone will be persuaded to accept Buckley's stipulated definitions of these words, we can see how he uses them to control and limit the argument.

Negation

Another useful strategy for defining a term is to specify what it is not. For example, Paul Theroux in *The Old Patagonian Express* (1979) provides this definition by negation of a *good flight*:

> You define a good flight by negatives: you didn't get hijacked, you didn't crash, you didn't throw up, you weren't late, you weren't nauseated by the food so you are grateful.

In another case, Gloria Steinem uses a negative definition to define *writing*:

> Writing is the only thing that, when I do it, I don't feel I should be doing something else.

Negative definitions do not release the writer from the responsibility of providing a positive definition of the term, but definition by negation is often a helpful first step in clearing away false assumptions. For example, Jesse Jackson uses both a negative definition and a figurative definition this way:

> America is not like a blanket — one piece of unbroken cloth, the same color, the same texture, the same size. America is more like a quilt — many patches, many pieces, many colors, many sizes, all woven and held together by a common thread.

Example

Good examples are an essential part of effective writing. Nowhere is this more true than when a writer wishes to define an abstract term. Well-chosen examples are especially useful in clarifying the meaning of a term because they provide readers with a context in which to understand it. Examples may take the form of anecdotes, case histories, in-depth interviews, statistics, or even hypothetical cases that illuminate the meaning of the term in question. For instance, when Erwin Wickert in *The Middle Kingdom: Inside China Today* (1981) discusses contemporary Chinese culture, he offers clear-cut examples to illustrate the nature and meaning of *shame* in Chinese society, past and present:

> Thus the courts of ancient times did not so much punish a crime definable in terms of evidence as penalize the state of mind that led to its perpetration. Judicial verdicts and sentences are still coloured by this attitude. In the penal code of the *Qing* dynasty, which remained valid until the beginning of the twentieth century, forty lashes were prescribed as the punishment for "shameless conduct." Shameless conduct itself remained undefined because everyone knew what it

was. We, on the other hand, live in a shameless society, where it would be difficult to reach a consensus about what is shameless and what is not.

The more abstract the concept the more important it is for the writer to provide a wide range of representative examples to clarify the meaning of the term. These examples may be drawn from personal observation, history, law, literature, or indeed any field so long as they are effective in clarifying the meaning of the term(s) to the audience. Down through the ages, the persuasive use of examples to define key terms can be seen in the writings and teachings of philosophers, poets, and preachers. For instance, St. Paul (in I Corinthians, Chapter 13) in his definition of the spiritual dimensions of love uses a range of examples, both real and hypothetical, along with synonyms and figurative language, to define a heightened state of being:

And now I will show you the best way of all. I may speak in tongues of men or of angels, but if I am without love, I am a sounding gong or a clanging cymbal. I may have the gift of prophecy, and know every hidden truth; I may have faith strong enough to move mountains; but if I have no love, I am nothing. I may dole out all I possess, or even give my body to be burnt, but if I have no love, I am none the better. Love is patient; love is kind and envies no one. Love is never boastful, nor conceited, nor rude; never selfish, not quick to take offence. Love keeps no score of wrongs; does not gloat over other men's sins, but delights in the truth. There is nothing love cannot face; there is no limit to its faith, its hope, and its endurance. Love will never come to an end. Are these prophets? their work will be over. Are there tongues of ecstasy? they will cease. Is there knowledge? it will vanish away; for our knowledge and our prophecy alike are partial, and the partial vanishes when wholeness comes. When I was a child my speech, my outlook, and my thoughts were all childish. When I grew up, I had finished with childish things. Now we see only puzzling reflections in a mirror, but then we shall see face to face. My knowledge now is partial; then it will be whole, like God's knowledge of me. In a word, there are three things that last for ever: faith, hope, and love; but the greatest of them all is love.

Modern readers might recognize this as a current translation from the New English Bible. In the past, the translation of this same passage in the King James Version of the Bible renders the same word (*agape* in Greek) as *charity*. Without Paul's powerful examples, it would be difficult to see what he means by *love*. The examples broaden the range of associations and make the meaning of the term resonate through specific cases. Paul's definition of love suggests a spiritual depth and richness that goes far beyond what most people normally associate with the term.

Extended Definition

An extended definition differs from other methods for defining terms because it is usually much longer and brings into play a greater variety of methods used. This type of definition expands on or uses any or all of the definition strategies previously discussed to clarify and define the basic nature of any idea, term, condition, or phenomenon. The length can range from several paragraphs to a complete essay or conceivably an entire book. In this sense, St. Paul's definition of love is an extended definition.

An extended definition can become synonymous with the definition essay in which a writer delves more deeply into a concept by looking at its historical connotations and variations in meaning from culture to culture. For example, Terence McLaughlin, a member of the Royal Institute of Chemistry in Great Britain and an authority on the problems of pollution, devoted an entire book, *Dirt: A Social History As Seen Through the Uses and Abuses of Dirt* (1971), to this unlikely subject. The following essay originally appeared as the introduction to this book and addresses the question "what is dirt" by using various strategies for defining terms. McLaughlin explains that what may be offensive to one culture may be desirable to another. As you read through this essay, notice how McLaughlin relies on specific details and graphic language and structures sentences as comparisons to show that what is considered clean in one situation is considered dirty in another. Also, notice how his extended definition relates the concept of dirt to pollution (para. 4), ritual defilement (para. 5), and contamination (para. 13):

Dirt is evidence of the imperfections of life, a constant reminder of change and decay. It is the dark side of all human activities — human, because it is only in our judgements that things are dirty: there is no such material as absolute dirt. Earth, in the garden, is a valuable support and nourishment for plants, and gardeners often run it through their fingers lovingly; earth on the carpet is dirt. A pile of dung, to the dungbeetle, is food and shelter for a large family; a pile of dung to the Public Health Inspector, is a Nuisance. Soup in a plate, before we eat it, is food; the traces that we leave on the plate imperceptibly become dirt. Lipstick on a girl's lips may make her boy-friend more anxious to touch them with his own lips; lipstick on a cup will probably make him refuse to touch it.

Because of this relativity, because dirt can be almost anything that we choose to call dirt, it has often been defined as "matter out of place." This fits the "earth (garden)/earth (carpet)" difference quite well, but it is not really very useful as a definition. A sock on the grand piano or a book in a pile of plates may be untidy, and they are certainly out of place, but they are not necessarily dirty. To be dirt, the material has to be hard to remove and unpleasant. If you sit on the beach, particularly if you bathe, sand will stick to you, but not many people would classify this as *dirt*, mainly because it brushes off so easily. However, if, as often happens the sand is covered with oil, tar, or sewage, and this sticks to you, it is definitely dirt.

Sartre, in his major philosophical work on Existentialism, *L'Etre et le Neant*,[1] presents a long discussion on the nature of sliminess or stickiness which has quite a lot to do with our ideas of dirt. He points out that quite small children who presumably have not yet learned any notions of cleanliness, and cannot yet be worried by germs, still tend to recognize that slimy things are unpleasant. It is because slimy things are clinging that we dislike them—they hold on to us even when we should like to let them go, and like an unpleasant travelling companion or an obscene telephone caller, seem to be trying to involve us in themselves. "If an object which I hold in my hands is solid," says Sartre, "I can let go when I please. . . . Yet here is the slimy reversing the terms . . . I open my hands, I want to let go of the slimy material and it sticks to me, it draws me, it sucks me. Its mode of being is neither the reassuring inertia of the solid nor a dynamism like that in water which is exhausted in fleeing from me. It is a soft yielding action, a moist and feminine sucking, it *lives* obscurely under my fingers. . . . "

This is the feeling of *pollution*, the kind of experience where something dirty has attached itself to us and we cannot get rid of the traces, however hard we try. Ritual defilement is one aspect of this feeling, and one which provides an enormous field of study for anthropologists (when they are not engaged in their favourite activity of reviling one another), but powerful irrational feelings of defilement exist in the most sophisticated societies. Try serving soup in a chamber-pot. However clean it may be, and however much a certain type of guest may find it "amusing," there will be a very real uneasiness about the juxtaposition. There are some kinds of dirt that we treat, in practice, as irremovable—as in the case of the old lady who was unlucky enough to drop her false teeth down the lavatory, where they were flushed into the sewer. When a search failed to find them, she heaved a sigh of relief. "I would never have fancied them again," she said, and most people would agree.

Even things which in themselves are clean, but can be associated with dirt, tend to be suspect. Vance Packard, in *The Hidden Persuaders*,[2] quotes the sad story of a company who tried to boost their sales of soup mix by offering free nylon stockings. The scheme was a complete fiasco. ". . . people seeing the offer were offended. Subconsciously they associated feet and soup and were alienated because they didn't like the idea of feet being in their soup." Faced by such reactions from industrialized society, we are in a better position to understand such primitive taboos as the fact that, for instance, a

[1] In English, this major work of the French Existentialist philosopher Jean Paul Sartre (1905–1980) was translated as *Being and Nothingness*.
[2] This 1957 work investigates techniques that advertisers use to manipulate the public into buying products.

woman of the Lele tribe who is menstruating must not cook for her husband or even poke the fire that is used for cooking.

Sartre, in his analysis, goes on to discuss the fear and disgust inspired by slimy things. When we touch them, they not only cling to us, but the boundary line between ourselves and the slime is blurred —if we dip our fingers in oil or honey (Sartre's favourite exemplar— it is difficult to tell whether he likes honey or dislikes it so intensely as to have a fixation about it) it hangs in strings from our fingers, our hands seem to be dissolving in it: "To touch slime is to risk being dissolved in sliminess. Now this dissolution by itself is frightening enough . . . but it is still more frightening in that the metamorphosis is not just into a *thing* (bad as that would be) but into slime. . . ."

There is a feeling of helplessness when you are faced by something slimy: the real horror to some of eating oysters is that, once the *thing* is in your mouth, there is no way of avoiding eating all of it. Other food of a strange character may be sampled in nibbles or sips, and if it is too distasteful you can stop; oysters take over the situation as the dominant partner. The same applies to the raw herrings beloved by the Dutch. Unfortunately for our peace of mind, most of the products of the human body are slimy—saliva, mucus, excrement, pus, semen, blood, lymph—and even honest sweat gets sticky by evaporation. "If I can fervently drink his tears," wrote Genet,[3] "Why not so the limpid drop on the end of his nose?" And the answer is quite clear. The drop on the end of his nose is slimy. We do not wish to be associated so closely and so permanently with other human beings. Their various slimy secretions will pollute us, will bring us into a closer and more permanent relationship with them than we should wish.

Of course, our own secretions are different. We have learned to live with them. We do not object to our own saliva, for instance, but the idea of someone else's saliva touching us is usually repellant, just as we do not like to think of cooks tasting the food which we are going to eat. Brahmins[4] carry this even further, and do not like their own saliva to touch their skin: if a Brahmin accidentally touches his fingers to his lips he must bathe or at least change his clothes, and this means that he has to eat by effectively throwing the food into his mouth. Spitting on other people is a sign of great loathing, and being spat on is extremely humiliating and disgusting, despite the fact that the saliva is mostly water. There was an old music-hall joke about a man called away from a public-house bar, leaving a glass on the counter; to protect his drink he put up a little notice saying, "I have spat in this beer." When he returned the drink was still there, but there was an addition to the notice: "So have I."

We are tolerant of our own bodily functions and smells, like Mr. Bloom in *Ulysses*[5] reading *Tidbits* in the outside privy—"He read on,

---

[3]The French playwright and novelist (1910–).
[4]The highest caste in Hindu society.
[5]A groundbreaking novel (published in 1922) by Irish novelist, poet, and playwright James Joyce (1882–1941).

seated calm above his own rising smell"—and the Icelanders have a coarse but accurate proverb, that every man likes the smell of his own farts, but too much evidence of other people's bodily function is "dirty."

We can extend some tolerance to the people we love, because the sense of close contact and lasting association is not then a matter of pollution. Lovers can share a cup or a bath with one another, and not worry about the close contact that this implies, but we do not extend this tolerance to the rest of humanity. Indeed, the whole act of sexual intercourse, without the tolerance induced by love and respect, would be hopelessly polluting and grotesque. Those who find it difficult to reconcile themselves to human contact often consider love-making a disgusting affair, like the lady who wrote to the *Bristol Evening Post* some years ago:

> Sex used to be treated with decent reticence—now it is discussed openly. This sort of thing can do immense harm. The moral standards accepted as "normal" by most young people today are a case in point.
>
> Why our all-wise Creator should have chosen such a distasteful—even disgusting—means of reproducing humanity is a thing that I, personally, have never been able to understand.

Where the tolerance stops is a matter of taste. Those couples whose desire to "merge" into one another is greater than their innate or acquired fear of pollution may resort to practices that appear "dirty" to other people. Krafft-Ebing[6] in the *Psychopathia Sexualis*, deals with the curious deviation of *coprolegny*, where people derive sexual pleasure from licking or touching the bodily secretions of others, including excrement. Bizarre as this habit may seem . . . dirt is an entirely relative concept, and . . . there is no limit to the strangeness of people's attitudes to it. Coprophilia, the love of filth, can take all forms, from Aubrey Beardsley's[7] joking reference to it in *Under the Hill* and *Venus and Tannhauser*, where it seems to be introduced out of a scholarly wish to include *everything*, to a complete acceptance and even enjoyment of living conditions and bodily habits that seem disgusting.

On this crowded planet, it is very difficult to get away from contact with other people, and the traces they leave behind. In the countryside, if we settle down to rest or picnic, we do not consider pine cones, dead sticks, leaves, pebbles, earth, or anything else *natural* strewn over the ground as dirt, or even as litter, and we are not likely to be very worried even by rabbit droppings and other traces of animal life, but paper bags, beer cans, and other signs of human life make us annoyed, and human excrement left in the open will probably make us look for another place to sit. It is the human traces that we object to, because we fear contamination, a kind of magical power

[6]Richard von Krafft-Ebing (1840–1902) was one of the earliest investigators of deviant sexual behavior.
[7]Aubrey Beardsley (1872–1898) was an English artist and writer.

that these traces might exert on us if we happened to touch them or even smell them. We dislike the feeling that these unknown people who have been in the place before us may somehow infect us with their own diseases and shortcomings, and their lives may be permanently entwined with ours, just as the Thieves in Circle VIII of the *Inferno*[8] lose their individual likenesses and are constantly melting one into another. This is not just a fear of germs, for the feelings date from pre-Pasteur days, and are shared, or even intensified, in primitive societies where no notions of the germ theory exist. "And this shall be his uncleanness in his issue whether his flesh run with his issue, or his flesh be stopped from his issue, it is his uncleanness. Every bed, whereon he lieth that hath the issue, is unclean: and every thing, whereon he sitteth, shall be unclean. And whosoever toucheth his bed shall wash his clothes, and bathe himself in water, and be unclean until the even. . . . " And so on in *Leviticus* chapters xi to xv, in passages that the well-known Biblical interpreter Nathan Micklem[9] has called "the least attractive in the whole Bible. To the modern reader there is much in them that is meaningless or repulsive." Of course we know now that such regulations helped to prevent the spread of infectious diseases, and that the orthodox Jews who followed these hygienic laws managed to survive plague periods and other epidemics better than the mass of the population, but the founders of the law were working only on instinct and the formalization of instinct that we call ritual. The Jewish hygienic rules may be stricter than many other systems, but they are not different in kind. An orthodox Jew's abstention from pork is no more logical or illogical than his Christian neighbour's abstention from dog or cat; both feelings are deeply held, and have nothing to do with the habits of the animals themselves. Those writers who try to explain away such customs as the results of semi-scientific investigation often say that Jews abstain from pork because the pig is dirty, or because pork is more liable to *Salmonella* infection than other meat. Both statements are true, but if these were the only reasons, Jews and Christians should be eating cats, who have very clean habits, or guinea-pigs, who keep themselves free from vermin. The purely hygienic laws, about leprosy, skin diseases, menstruation, and discharges from the body, are not based on bacteriology, they are based on avoidance of defilement by other people.

We are all jealous of our "one-ness," our individuality, and we resent and fear any situation that forces us to become intimate, in the real sense of the word, with another person against our will. Contamination by other people is what we really fear about dirt: Sartre says in *Huis Clos*[10] that Hell is other people. Dirt is also other people.

---

[8]The region designated as Hell in Dante Alighieri's (1265–1321) epic allegory, *Divine Comedy*.
[9]A noted professor of theology at Oxford University (1888–1977).
[10]Jean Paul Sartre's play *No Exit* (1944).

McLaughlin begins his definition of dirt with a number of observations from everyday experience which illustrate his claim that "there is no such material as absolute dirt." He shows that what is considered dirt changes with a changing viewpoint, with the passage of time, and with location (for example, lipstick on a girl's lips versus lipstick on a cup, or soup at the beginning of a meal versus leftover soup after the meal). After showing that context, time, location, and viewpoint are all important in determining what is considered dirt, McLaughlin explores the relation between dirt and the concepts of pollution, ritual defilement, and contamination. The idea of *pollution* is that something dirty has attached itself to something else and can't be gotten rid of. *Ritual defilement* occurs when something dirty is used where normally a clean item would be required. *Contamination* also refers to a feeling of personal disgust tinged with helplessness about something dirty attaching itself to us that cannot be gotten rid of. In McLaughlin's view, all three concepts reflect a fear of dirt attaching itself to us in different ways.

To support his analysis he quotes from philosophical works by the French existentialist Jean Paul Sartre as well as from research done by Vance Packard in *The Hidden Persuaders* (1957) on the psychological dimension of marketing. The fact that McLaughlin can document his thesis from such diverse sources adds credibility to his claim that the universal abhorrence of coming into contact with what is considered dirt is basically a fear of having one's individuality infringed upon. In this sense, the reaction to dirt is a defensive measure by the Ego to maintain our individuality. McLaughlin continues his exploration into the meaning of dirt by citing a wide range of sources including the French dramatist Jean Genet, Brahmin religious customs, the predilections of Leopold Bloom in James Joyce's novel *Ulysses*, the work of German psychiatrist Richard von Krafft-Ebing, and nineteenth-century English artist and writer Aubrey Beardsley. All these sources testify to divergent attitudes toward dirt and support McLaughlin's principal claim that the concept of dirt is a relative one.

McLaughlin then draws attention to the relationship between overpopulation and the fear of contamination and cites an example of a picnic to illustrate that people dislike human litter but not that left by animals. He examines pertinent sections from the Old Testament and suggests that the hygienic laws of the Hebrews had their basis in the same instinct to avoid contamination that underlies a universal human repugnance toward dirt. His conclusion is that people fear dirt because it represents a compromising of our "individuality." McLaughlin concludes that "contamination by other people is what we really fear about dirt." Throughout his essay, McLaughlin reveals distinctive characteristics of what he is defining. He cites an extraordinary range of examples that provide concrete, easy-to-understand illustrations, and are invaluable in supporting his evolving definition. His definition is stipulative to the extent that he is trying to persuade his audience to accept a definition of dirt that is really quite different from the conventional one. Overall, McLaughlin's essay expands on the simple definition of dirt as "matter out of place" to develop a definition that illuminates the human need to maintain an individual identity.

Tone

Tone is a vital element in the audience's perception of the author. In the *Rhetoric*, Aristotle discussed how an audience's confidence in the character and credibility of the writer or speaker was a key element in persuading them to accept a claim. He emphasized that the audience would most likely reach their estimate of the writer or speaker's character not so much from what they already knew about the writer, which might be very little, but from the speech itself. This is why the question of tone is crucial. Aristotle believed that credibility was created by the audience's perception of the writer or speaker as a person of good sense, moral integrity, and good intentions. Good sense might be shown by the writer's knowledge of the subject, adherence to the principles of correct reasoning, and judgment in organizing a persuasive case. The more intangible qualities of character might be gauged from the writer's respect for commonly accepted values and unwillingness to use deceptive reasoning simply to win a point.

The most appropriate tone is usually a reasonable one. A reasonable tone shows that the writer cares about the subject under discussion and is sensitive to the needs and concerns of the audience.

Tone is produced by the combined effect of word choice, sentence structure, and the writer's success in adapting her or his particular "voice" to suit the subject, the audience, and the occasion. Choosing between a casual or formal tone might be compared to choosing between wearing jeans or a tuxedo to a party. Most likely, the choice of clothes would fall somewhere in the middle. So, too, the most useful tone is neither undisciplined nor formal and pretentious, but one that creates an impression of a reasonable person calmly discussing issues in a natural voice.

When we try to identify and analyze the tone of a work, we are seeking to hear the "voice" of the author in order to understand how he or she intended the work to be perceived. Tone indicates the author's attitude toward both the subject and the audience. Tone is a projection of the writer's self. The entire essay or argument creates an impression of the writer as a certain kind of person. It is important for writers to know what image of themselves they are projecting in their writing. Writers should consciously decide on what kind of style and tone would best suit the audience, the occasion, and the specific subject matter of the argument. Although a casual tone might be suited for a conversation between friends, the same tone would be inappropriate for an argument designed to convince an audience to accept the validity of a claim.

For example, consider the tone of George F. Will's comment in his essay "Government, Economy Linked":

> The government in its wisdom considers ice a "food product." This means that Antarctica is one of the world's foremost food producers.

Will's point is that the government has inappropriately included ice in its classification of "food products." His purpose in writing is to persuade his audience to protest this senseless bureaucratic categorization. That much is obvious. What is less obvious but is just as important is the tone of Will's comment. His tone reveals a well-developed sarcastic sense of humor, a dry wit, common sense, and a readiness to spot bureaucratic absurdities. Beyond this, we can sense Will's basic conservative position that big government should not wield too much power.

Of all the characteristics of tone the first and most important to audiences is clarity. Write so that nothing you put down can be misunderstood. Use a natural rather than an artificial vocabulary. Adopt a tone that reinforces what you want your audience to think and feel about the issue. Keep in mind that insight, wit, and sensitivity are always appreciated.

Certain kinds of tone are more difficult for apprentice writers to manage successfully. A writer who is flippant will run the risk of not having the argument taken seriously by the audience. Arrogance, belligerence, and anger are usually inappropriate in argumentative essays. Even if you are indignant and outraged, make sure you have evidence to back up your emotional stance or else you will appear self-righteous and pompous. By the same token, steer away from special pleading, sentimentality, and an apologetic "poor me" tone—you want the audience to agree with your views, not to feel sorry for you. Keep out buzz words or question-begging epithets ("bleeding heart liberal" or "mindless fundamentalist") that some writers use as shortcuts to establish identification with readers instead of arguing logically and backing up their position with facts and evidence.

IRONY

A particular kind of tone encountered in many arguments is called irony. Writers adopt this rhetorical strategy to express a discrepancy between opposites, between the ideal and the real, between the literal and the implied, and, most often, to highlight a disparity between the way things are and the way the writer thinks things ought to be.

Sometimes it is difficult to pick up the fact that not everything a writer says is intended to be taken literally. Authors will occasionally say the opposite of what they mean to catch the attention of the reader. Often the first response to an ironic statement or idea is "Can the writer really be serious?" If your response to an argument is such, look for clues meant to signal you that the writer means the opposite of what is being said. Irony draws the reader into a kind of secret collaboration with the author in a way that very few other rhetorical strategies can accomplish. One clear signal the author is being ironic is a noticeable disparity between the tone and the subject.

For example, in Jonathan Swift's "A Modest Proposal" (1729) the tone in which the narrator speaks is reasonable, matter of fact, and totally at odds with his recommendation that Ireland solve its overpopulation problem by encouraging poor people to sell their babies as food to the wealthy:

> I shall now therefore humbly propose my own thoughts, which I hope will not be liable to the least objection.
>
> I have been assured by a very knowing American of my acquaintance in London, that a young healthy child well nursed is at a year old a most delicious, nourishing, and wholesome food, whether stewed, roasted, baked, or boiled, and I make no doubt that it will equally serve in a fricassee, or a ragout.
>
> I do therefore humbly offer it to public consideration, that of the hundred and twenty thousand children already computed, twenty thousand may be reserved for breed, whereof only one fourth part to be males, which is more than we allow to sheep, black-cattle, or swine, and my reason is that these children are seldom the fruits of marriage, a circumstance not much regarded by our savages, therefore one male will be sufficient to serve four females. That the remaining hundred thousand may at a year old be offered in sale to the persons of quality, and fortune, through the kingdom, always advising the mother to let them suck plentifully in the last month, so as to render them plump, and fat for a good table. A child will make two dishes at an entertainment for friends, and when the family dines alone, the fore or hind quarter will make a reasonable dish, and seasoned with a little pepper or salt will be very good boiled on the fourth day, especially in winter.
>
> I have reckoned upon a medium [average], that a child just born will weigh 12 pounds, and in a solar year if tolerably nursed increaseth to 28 pounds.
>
> I grant this food will be somewhat dear, and therefore very proper for landlords, who, as they have already devoured most of the parents, seem to have the best title to the children.

You may have noticed the practical, down-to-earth, and understated voice with which the narrator enumerates the financial and culinary advantages of his proposed "solution." The discrepancy between his matter-of-fact tone and the outrageous content is a clear signal that the writer means the exact opposite of what is being said. If you missed Swift's signals, you might even think he was being serious!

SATIRE

Satire is an enduring form of argument that uses parody, irony, and caricature to poke fun at a subject, idea, or person. The question of tone is especially important in satire. The satirist frequently creates a "mask" or *persona* that is very different from the author's real voice in order to shock the audience into a new awareness about an established institution or custom. As we have seen, in "A Modest Proposal," Swift creates the persona of a reasonable, seemingly well-intentioned bureaucrat who proposes, in an offhand way, that Ireland solve its economic problems by slaughtering and exporting one-year-old children as foodstuffs. To mistake the voice as that of Swift's would be to miss the ironic contrast between what is said and what is meant. As with other works that rely on irony, the writer must be in full control of the material no matter how strongly he or she feels personally. Satiric works initially seem quite plausible, coherent, and even persuasive on the surface until the reader notices that the writer intends the work to be read ironically.

Enduring satirical works include Aristophanes' *The Birds*, Samuel Johnson's *Rasselas*, Voltaire's *Candide*, Swift's *Gulliver's Travels*, Mark Twain's *A Connecticut Yankee in King Arthur's Court*, and Joseph Heller's *Catch 22*. These works assail folly, greed, corruption, pride, self-righteous complacency, hypocrisy, and other permanent targets of the satirists' pen. In "Opera Synopsis" (at the end of this chapter) Robert Benchley presents a hilarious parody of Wagnerian opera in the guise of a seemingly straightforward, matter-of-fact plot synopsis.

Language and Persuasion

—*"And the Lord said: 'go to, let us go down, and there confound their language, that they may not understand one another's speech.'"* Genesis 11:7

LANGUAGE SHAPES THOUGHT

Language clearly has an influence on our beliefs and actions. Those who have an interest in persuading us to believe or buy something are quite skillful in using language to persuade. Thus, if we are more aware of how others, including politicians and advertisers, use language to manipulate our behavior, the less likely it becomes that we can be deceived into doing things against our own best interests.

Emotionally Charged Language

Emotionally charged language is a principal means by which language affects perceptions. Basically, emotive language is designed to elicit certain feelings in an audience.

For example, imagine you saw your three-year-old child playing next to the stove, in danger of tipping over a pan of boiling water. Consider how different your reactions would sound using nonemotive language and emotive language to express your concern:

> Please get away from the stove. It is dangerous to play near the stove when something is cooking. You might get burned

> My God, you're going to get burned! Get away from there!

Or consider the difference in impact of a factual and an emotive account of the same event:

> Rutgers wins over Penn State
> Rutgers clobbers Penn State

The sports page abounds with accounts of one team *shooting down, jolting, blasting, mauling, bombing,* or *outslugging* another team. Sportswriters purposely choose those verbs that will produce the most dramatic effect, such as, "the Devils submerge the Penguins." The feelings evoked in the reader are as important as the scores of the games.

Connotations of Words

The connotations of words are often far more persuasive than their explicit or primary meanings. For example, the connotations of *home* suggest qualities of security, comfort, affection, and caring, that ultimately are far more persuasive in influencing perception than the simple denotative meaning of the word.

In the hands of a skilled writer, connotations can be used to arouse positive or negative emotions toward the subject. For example, think of the different feelings you would have about the following subjects depending on which words the writer used:

> *Youthful offender* instead of *juvenile delinquent*
> *Perspire* instead of *sweat*
> *Sanitation engineers* instead of *garbage collectors*
> *Pass away* instead of *die*
> *Full-figured* instead of *fat*

Celebrities often change their names to avoid negative connotations or to elicit positive associations from audiences. To see how this works, compare the person's real name with his or her stage name:

Frances Gumm	Judy Garland
Marion Morrison	John Wayne
Leonard Slye	Roy Rogers
Henry John Deutschendorf, Jr.	John Denver
Issur Danielovitch Demsky	Kirk Douglas
Doris Kappelhoff	Doris Day
Archibald Leach	Cary Grant
Robert Zimmerman	Bob Dylan
Steveland Judkins Morris	Stevie Wonder
Marvin Lee Aday	Meat Loaf
Reginald Kenneth Dwight	Elton John

So, too, advertisers spend considerable time, money, and effort in formulating brand names for products that are designed to trigger favorable connotations. Fashion and cosmetic industries take great care in naming their products. Plain brown carpeting might be marketed as Coffee Buff, Berber Beige, or Plantation Amber. Likewise, red lipstick might be marketed under the brand names of Red, Hot and Blue, Fire and Ice, or Roseberry. In automotive advertising car names play an important role in manipulating the emotions of the car-buying public. To appeal to the need for status, cars are named Regal, Le Baron, and Grand Marquis. To conjure up places where the wealthy congregate, cars are named Riviera, Capri, Monte Carlo, and Fifth Avenue. To evoke feelings of freedom, uninhibited expression, and power, cars take on real and mythological animal names as in Skyhawk, Mustang, Cougar, AMC Eagle, Firebird, and Thunderbird.

Sometimes brand names can take on unintended negative connotations, especially when product names are translated into other languages to be marketed in other countries. Occasionally the original English name takes on entirely different connotations in a different culture. For example, in "What's In a Name?" (*Big Business Blunders* [1983]), David A. Ricks points out that Ford's Pinto was introduced in Brazil under its English name. After Ford discovered that Pinto in Portuguese slang meant "a small male appendage" the company changed the car's name to Corcel (*horse* in Portuguese). In another case, a foreign company introduced its chocolate concoction with the unappetizing English name of Zit. To avoid such negative connotations, companies often conduct extensive research to produce names like Kodak and Exxon that can be pronounced but have no specific meanings in any language.

Euphemisms

Euphemism comes from the Greek ("to speak well of" or "to use words of good omen"); Originally these words were used to placate the gods.

Euphemistic language is used to make things seem better than they are, smooth over, and present activities in a more favorable light. More commonly, euphemisms are used to avoid taboo subjects. For example, in ancient Greece, baby boys were encouraged to call their genitals their "kokko," their "laloo," or their "lizard." Roman nannies taught little girls to call their genitals their "piggy." In the nineteenth century, Victorians used a wide range of euphemisms to avoid explicit references to sex, birth, and bodily functions. Trousers were called "unmentionables," sexual organs became "private parts" and the birth of a baby became the arrival of "the little stranger" or "the patter of tiny feet."

Today, poverty has replaced sex and bodily functions as a taboo subject. The result of using euphemisms to disguise reality was the point of a 1965 Jules Feiffer cartoon quoted in *Safire's Political Dictionary*, (1978) which read:

> I used to think I was poor. Then they told me I wasn't poor, I was needy. They told me it was self-defeating to think of myself as needy, I was deprived. Then they told me underprivileged was overused. I was disadvantaged. I still don't have a dime. But I have a great vocabulary.

A principal subject of euphemisms is death, whose implacable reality has been skirted by such phrases as the following:

> to go to a better place, just reward, with God, cash in one's chips, to pop off, to croak, cross over, go to the hereafter, join one's ancestors, meet the grim reaper, go to the last roundup, bite the dust, pass out of the picture, and slip away

In fact, the systematic use of language to mask the reality of death has been the subject of satiric novels like Evelyn Waugh's *The Loved One* (1948) and exposés like Jessica Mitford's *The American Way of Death* (1963). In this profession, the word *coffin* has long since been displaced by the term *casket*, a shroud is called a "slumber robe" and the room in which the dead body is viewed is called the "slumber room" or the "reposing room."

We can see euphemism at work when the Russian government claims that it has eliminated prostitution, while acknowledging that there are "priestesses of love," "night stalkers," "ladies of easy virtue," and "ladies who take tips" walking the streets of Moscow and other cities (*The Philadelphia Inquirer*, cited in *Quarterly Review of Doublespeak* [April 1987]). In all these cases, euphemisms are designed to foster favorable perceptions, or at least to neutralize unfavorable ones — as, for example, referring to abortion as "pregnancy reduction" (*Atlanta Constitution*, cited in *Quarterly Review of Doublespeak* [April 1988]).

The Language of Advertising

Of all the techniques advertisers use to influence what people believe and how they spend their money, none is more basic than the use of so-called *weasel* words. This term was popularized by Theodore Roosevelt in a speech he gave in St. Louis, May 31, 1916, when he commented that notes from the Department of State were filled with *weasel* words that retract the meaning of the words they are next to just as a weasel sucks the meat out of the egg.

In modern advertising parlance, a *weasel* word has come to mean any qualifier or comparative that is used to imply a positive quality that cannot be stated as a fact, because it cannot be substantiated. For example, if an ad claims a toothpaste will "help" stop cavities it does not obligate the manufacturer to substantiate this claim. So, too, if a product is advertised as "fighting" germs, the equivocal claim hides the fact that the product may fight and lose. The words *virtually* (as in "virtually spotless") and *up to* or *for as long as* (as in "stops coughs up to eight hours") also remove any legal obligation on the part of the manufacturer to justify the claim.

Other favorite words in the ad man's repertoire, such as *free* and *new*, are useful in selling everything from cat food to political candidates.

Slanting

Information that is edited to reflect a particular point of view is referred to as being *slanted*. Slanting can take the form of selecting facts to purposely mislead, quoting out of context, or presenting facts in a biased way. We might easily accept these biased characterizations without thinking them through. For example, *question-begging epithets* like *flaming liberal* or *arch conservative* attempt to slip value judgments past the reader disguised as objective descriptions.

Slanting can also result from apparently innocuous word choices, use of quotation marks around a word, or exclamation points that draw special attention!!!

People employ a subtle form of slanting when they use words like *nothing but, only, just, mere, little more than, nothing more than*, or some other disparaging qualifier. For example, "her speech was *mere* rhetoric," "he is *only* an adolescent," "she's *just* a freshman," or "she's *little more than* a secretary."

Labels that Stereotype

How a person or event is labeled influences the readers' or listeners' perception of what is being described. Labels can be damaging because they classify people in ways that stereotype or stigmatize. The label creates a stereotyped picture that portrays the person only in terms of a single trait. Perhaps the most dangerous thing about stereotypes is that they create a mind-set that makes it impossible to accept people as they really are. Stereotypes distort our perceptions and make it impossible to acknowledge experiences that conflict with the stereotype. If your expectations about members of an entire group are shaped by a stereotyped view, research shows you are more likely to disregard contradictory evidence in order to avoid giving up the stereotype.

Labels act as filters that screen out everything that does not confirm the stereotype. For example, let's say you were asked to complete any of the following statements:

Southerners are . . .	Easterners are . . .
Texans are . . .	Hairdressers are . . .
Rock stars are . . .	Football players are . . .

Each completed statement reveals one of your attitudes or beliefs. If you were then asked to write down whatever experiences you have had that justify or explain this attitude, you might discover that your ideas are based to a much greater extent on portrayals and labels conveyed by the media rather than on your own personal experiences.

One of the most interesting studies of how proper names (literally, how we are labeled) evoke stereotypes that operate without our being aware of them was conducted by Gordon W. Allport (*The Nature of Prejudice* [1954]):

Thirty photographs of college girls were shown on a screen to 150 students. The subjects rated the girls on a scale from one to five for *beauty, intelligence, character, ambition, general likability.* Two months later the same subjects were asked to rate the same photographs and fifteen additional ones (introduced to complicate the memory factor). This time five of the original photographs were given Jewish surnames (Cohen, Kantor, etc.), five Italian (Valenti, etc.), and five Irish (O'Brien, etc.); and the remaining girls were given names chosen from the signers of the Declaration of Independence and from the Social Register (Davis, Adams, Clark, etc.).

When Jewish names were attached to photographs there occurred the following changes in ratings:

decrease in liking
decrease in character
decrease in beauty
increase in intelligence
increase in ambition

For those photographs given Italian names there occurred:

decrease in liking
decrease in character
decrease in beauty
decrease in intelligence

Thus a mere proper name leads to prejudgments of personal attributes.

The unconscious assumptions triggered by students' names meant that each person was no longer perceived as being a complete human being. The label set up expectations that would block any conflicting new information and make it probable that only information that could be interpreted to support the preconception would be believed. It is for these reasons that all labels designed to persuade us must be carefully identified and analyzed.

Sexist, Racist, and Agist Language

One form discriminatory labeling takes is in sexist language, that is, any language that expresses a stereotyped attitude that presumes the inherent superiority of one sex over the other. As with other kinds of labeling, those placed in the devalued categories are, by definition, stigmatized and treated as less than fully human. Language can also discriminate by omission. For example, the way the English language has tended to make women seem invisible is addressed by Elaine Morgan in the opening chapter, "The Man-Made Myth," of her book *The Descent of Woman* (1972):

> All this may sound like a mere linguist quibble or a piece of feminist petulance. If you stay with me, I hope to convince you it's neither. I believe the deeply rooted semantic confusion between "man" as a male and "man" as a species has been fed back into and vitiated a great deal of the speculation that goes on about the origins, development, and nature of the human race.
>
> A very high proportion of the thinking on these topics is androcentric (male-centered) in the same way as pre-Copernican thinking was geocentric. It's just as hard for man to break the habit of thinking of himself as central to the species as it was to break the habit of thinking of himself as central to the universe. He sees himself quite unconsciously as the main line of evolution, with a female satellite revolving around him as the moon revolves around the earth. This not only causes him to overlook valuable clues to our ancestry, but sometimes leads him into making statements that are arrant and demonstrable nonsense.
>
> The longer I went on reading his own books about himself, the more I longed to find a volume that would begin: "When the first ancestor of the human race descended from the trees, she had not yet developed the mighty brain that was to distinguish her so sharply from all other species. . . ."
>
> Of course, she was no more the first ancestor than he was—but she was no *less* the first ancestor, either. She was there all along, contributing half the genes to each succeeding generation. Most of the books forget about her for most of the time. They drag her onstage rather suddenly for the obligatory chapter on Sex and Repro-

duction, and then say: "All right, love, you can go now," while they get on with the real meaty stuff about the Mighty Hunter with his lovely new weapons and his lovely new straight legs racing across the Pleistocene plains. Any modifications in her morphology are taken to be imitations of the Hunter's evolution, or else designed solely for his delectation.

Casey Miller and Kate Swift suggest in *Words and Women* (1976) that the abbreviation *Miss* (from the seventh-century noun *mistress*) had evolved as a "means of distinguishing married from unmarried women." They believe it came into popular use as a way of supplying:

> at least a modicum of information about a woman's sexual availability, and it applied not so subtle social pressure toward marriage by lumping single women with the young and inexperienced . . . [in this way] the needs of the patriarchy were served when a woman's availability for her primary role as helper and sexual partner was made an integral part of her identity—in effect, a part of her name.

The marriage-neutral term *Ms.* was introduced to remedy this problem. As Miller and Swift note, "the abbreviation Ms. has been around as a title of courtesy at least since the 1940's, but it was largely unused until two things happened: the growth of direct mail selling made the abbreviation an effective time and money saver, and a significant number of women began to object to being labeled to their (presumed) marital status."

The prospect of changing attitudes by changing language (or reflecting changed attitudes in new terminology) has resulted in the *The Government's Dictionary of Occupational Titles* (1977) replacing potentially discriminatory job titles with sex-neutral terms. For example, *telephone linemen* has been replaced by *telephone line installers, firemen* are now listed as *firefighters, airline stewardesses* are now *flight attendants,* and *policewoman* has become simply *police officer.*

Historically, stigmatization always precedes disenfranchisement. Haig A. Bosmajian in "Defining the American Indian" (*The Speech Teacher* [March 1973]) reminds us that "one of the first important acts of an oppressor is to redefine the oppressed victims he intends to jail or eradicate so that they will be looked upon as creatures warranting suppression and in some cases separation and annihilation."

Agist stereotypes, that is, the negative labels used to refer to old age, are as destructive as racist or sexist language. Referring to elderly women as *biddy* or *hag* or to elderly men as *codger, coot, geezer,* or *fogey,* fosters a conception of the elderly as senile, incapable of learning new things, and antiquated. These labels promote a notion of the elderly that makes it difficult for the young and middle-aged to identify with them as human beings. Agist language encourages discriminatory reactions toward the elderly and reinforces a negative self-image among older people. The mechanisms involved are identical to those of racism (based on differences in skin color) or sexism (based on differences in gender). As in these cases, the use of dehumanizing language paves the way for discounting the elderly and treating them as second-class citizens. This issue has been studied by Frank Nuessel in "Old Age Needs a New Name but Don't Look for It in Websters" (*Aging* [August/September 1984]) who concludes that "in this regard the extensive, pejorative, and agist vocabulary of the English language constitutes a verbal record of this society's fear of getting old."

Words that Create Images

The ability to create compelling images in picturesque language is an important element in communicating a writer's thoughts, feelings, and experiences. For example, consider how picturesque terms are often used by wine experts to describe different kinds of wines. A wine might be said to be *robust* or *mellow* or *round*; a beaujolais might be described as "witty" or "an amusing little wine" or "a delightful wine."

The way a writer chooses to describe something expresses an opinion that is capable of persuading an audience. In the following description of London, H. G. Wells selects details that reinforce the dominant impression he has of the city, organizes these details in terms of his main impression, and creates a vivid word picture that allows the reader to see the city as Wells does: "London, like a bowl of viscid human fluid, boils sullenly over the rim of its encircling hills and slops messily and uglily into the home counties."

Notice how Wells' picturesque description of London's urban sprawl relies on words whose emotive effect is enhanced by his skillful use of picturesque language. The fact that Wells does not make a formal claim does not lessen the impact of this description. The word picture itself expresses his opinion. Or consider how Fred Allen's opinion of Hollywood is strengthened by the unusual image he creates: "You can take all the sincerity in Hollywood, place it in the navel of a fruit fly, and still have room enough for three caraway seeds and a producer's heart."

Creating a vivid picture or image in an audience's mind requires writers to use metaphors and similes (and other figures of speech). Imagery works by evoking a vivid picture in the audience's imagination. A simile compares one object or experience to another using *like* or *as*. For example, if you wrote that "on a trip home the train was crowded and the passengers were packed in like sardines," your audience would be expected to understand the idea rather than to literally assume you were accompanied in the train by sardines. A metaphor applies a word or phrase to an object it does not literally denote in order to suggest the comparison. Thus, if you looked into the crowded train and yelled, "Hey, you sardines," most people on the train would know what you meant.

To be effective, metaphors must look at things in a fresh light to let the reader see a familiar subject in a new way. As George Orwell observed in *Politics and the English Language* (1946), "the sole aim of a metaphor is to call up a visual image." Metaphors when they are first conceived can call up pictures in the mind, but worn out metaphors lack the power to summon these images. What is meant by an effective metaphor can be illustrated by two short descriptions drawn from Henry Allen's "The Corps" (*The Washington Post* [March 1972]). In describing the Marine Corps drill instructors at the Marine boot camp, Parris Island, South Carolina, Allen notes "the wry ferocity drill instructors cultivate, the squinted eyes and the mouth about as generous as a snapping turtle's, and the jut-jawed arrogance of their back-of-the throat voices."

Of one particularly feared D.I., Allen writes, "He is seething, he is rabid, he is wound up tight as a golf ball, with more adrenalin surging through his hypothalmus than any corner slum rat." And of the new recruits, Allen comments, "fat and forlorn, they look like 60 sex perverts trapped by a lynch mob."

Slang

> — *"I have seen the future and it is slang."* — Eric Overmeyer, On the
> Verge (1986)

A particularly vivid, playful, and ephemeral form of picturesque language is called *slang*. Slang does not take itself seriously, and expresses itself in down-to-earth, direct idioms. Many slang expressions use picturesque language metaphorically. For example, consider the range of terms used to describe drinking too much:

> blitzed, bombed, blotto, zonked, plastered, tanked, embalmed, sauced, juiced, corked, shellacked, hung over, tight, tipsy, smashed

How slang is created can be seen in the origin of the term *hype* (hyping a movie, product, book). The term originated as an abbreviation at the turn of the century for a hypodermic needle. *Hype* gradually lost its connection with an actual hypodermic needle but retained the idea of injecting or infusing. Today it refers to artificially stimulated public relations phenomena designed to generate publicity and sales.

Clichés

Words that, through overuse, lose their power to evoke concrete images become clichés. A cliché is a trite, time-worn expression or outworn phrase that has become commonplace or lost its freshness. Initially, each of the following descriptions of mental deficiency probably seemed quite inventive the first time it was used:

> not playing with a full deck, front porch light is out, out to lunch, asleep at the switch, off his rocker

The fact that these clichés are used so much has made them predictable. Metaphors that are no longer relevant, stereotyped expressions, and overused idioms no longer have the ability to conjure up an image in the hearer's mind. They have been used so often that they become a ready-made way of substituting a phrase to avoid thinking, as in the following list of clichés about money:

> as sound as a dollar, it's money in the bank, don't sell yourself short, stop on a dime, a penny for your thoughts, pay your dues, take it at face value, put your two cents in, worth one's weight in gold

Some clichés depend on effects of alliteration and rhyming to produce sets of words that are easy to remember: bag and baggage, wishy washy, safe and sound, high and dry, fair and square, wear and tear. Other clichés use two words where one would be sufficient: ways and means, null and void, six of one and half a dozen of the other. Still other clichés are really overused similes:

> clean as a whistle, dead as a doornail, cool as a cucumber, fit as a fiddle, flat as a pancake, free as a bird, fresh as a daisy, good as gold, hard as nails, light as a feather, mad as a march hare, quiet as a mouse, slippery as an eel, ugly as sin, sweet as sugar

An even greater sin than using stale metaphors is using them incorrectly, as John Simon complained of the film critic Rex Reed in "Why Reed Can't Write" (*Paradigms Lost* [1980]):

> Reed's brain is incapable of grasping how metaphors work. In perusing some of Reed's pieces in *Vogue* I came upon some truly remarkable formulations. For example: "the note of reigning terror is struck in the first scene (a dull woman's body is being examined by a Fascist doctor)." A dull corpse? How many witty ones has Reed known? But a corpse so dull as to strike a note of terror? That *is* dull, even for a corpse.

Abstract and Concrete Language

Abstract and concrete language plays a crucial role in argument. Concrete words refer to actual things, instances, or experiences. Writers require abstractions, by contrast, in order to generalize about experience and discuss qualities or characteristics apart from specific objects or to sum up the qualities of whole classes of things. For example, we have been using the term *warrant* to refer to the rules or principles that allow conclusions to be connected to evidence. The term is used to convey an abstract idea. Yet originally the term *warrant* referred to a literal document (as in *arrest warrant* or *search warrant*) that gave the possessor authority to take an action. In this book, the term *warrant* preserves the essential idea — of justifying an action (in argument, drawing a conclusion) by referring to a particular principle that authorizes connecting evidence to a claim.

Without being able to call upon abstractions with which to generalize we would find ourselves in a situation similar to the one described by Jonathan Swift in Book III of *Gulliver's Travels* (1727). There, Gulliver, on a visit to a "school of languages," learns of a "Scheme for Entirely Abolishing All Words Whatsoever." The rationale behind this unlikely enterprise is that "since words are only names for things, it would be more convenient for all men to carry about them, such things as were necessary to express the particular business they are to discourse on." Thus, instead of speaking, citizens would carry sacks filled with the physical objects about which they wished to converse and a "conversation" would appear as follows:

> If a man's business be very great and of various kinds, he must be obliged in proportion to carry a greater bundle of Things upon his back unless he can afford one or two strong servants to attend him. I have often beheld two of those sages almost sinking under the weight of their packs like peddlars among us who when they meet in the streets would lay down their loads, open their sacks and hold conversation for an hour together, then put up their implements, help each other to resume their burdens and take their leave.

This amusing caricature of a conversation without speech dramatizes the disadvantages of being unable to use abstractions to symbolize qualities or express ideas.

People frequently misunderstand each other's arguments because key terms evoke entirely different specifics (or referents) for the writer than they do for the audience. The chances for communicating improve if the writer attempts to discover what the key terms being used in the argument actually mean to the audience. For example, if a physician was trying to persuade a physicist, a botanist, and an astronomer to change their views on the probable effects of a nuclear winter and used the term *node*, she would know she was referring to a term in anatomy describing a concentrated swelling, as in *lymph node*. However, the physicist would most likely know the term only as a reference to the point in a string where the least vibration occurs, the botanist might think the physician meant the stem joint out of which a leaf grows, and the astronomer might conjecture the physician was talking about a point where the earth's orbit appears to cross the sun's apparent path.

Although it would be quite literally impossible to think without being able to generalize, it is clear that any argument requires a balance between the use of abstract terms to make generalizations and concrete or literal terms to provide supporting details and evidence.

Concrete terms provide specific details that allow the writer to focus the audience's attention on all the particulars of the case on which generalizations are based. Without a specific frame of reference and supporting details, examples, and anecdotes, abstract terms can be used to conceal rather than to reveal and clarify. In "Politics and the American Language" (*The American Scholar* [1974]) the eminent historian Arthur Schlesinger, Jr. observed that the use of abstractions in politics has long been a problem:

> So words, divorced from objects, became instruments less of communication than of deception. Unscrupulous orators stood abstractions on their head and transmuted them into their opposites, aiming to please one faction by the sound and the contending faction by the meaning. They did not always succeed. "The word *liberty* in the mouth of Webster," Emerson wrote with contempt after the Compromise of 1850, "sounds like the word *love* in the mouth of a courtezan." Watching Henry Kissinger babbling about his honor at his famous Salzburg press conference, one was irresistibly reminded of another of Emerson's nonchalant observations: "The louder he talked of his honor, the faster we counted our spoons."

Jargon

An important kind of language often encountered in arguments within specialized fields is jargon. Basically, jargon is the specialized language of a trade, field, or profession. It provides a shorthand way of quickly communicating a lot of information. For example, in publishing, horror stories combined with romantic melodrama are called "creepy weepys," and historical romances filled with sex and violence to stimulate sales are known as "bodice rippers." In police work, officers refer to confiscated drug money as "dead presidents."

The word *jargon* comes from the fifteenth-century French term *jargoun* (twittering or jibberish). In its original context, *jargoun* referred to the secret language criminals used to communicate with each other without being understood by the authorities. The impenetrable nature of jargon makes it all too easy to use it to disguise the inner workings of a particular trade or profession or to avoid being held accountable.

Part of the function of jargon is to make the ordinary seem extraordinary and to give an air of importance to everyday situations encountered in different fields. For example, Diane Johnson in "Doctor Talk" (*The New Republic* [1979]) reports that new physicians have been told to use "scientific-sounding euphemisms" in the presence of patients. An alcoholic patient might be told he was suffering from "hyper-ingestion of ethynol." The use of specialized terms is not only part of the medical shorthand doctors use in communicating with each other but such jargon has the added benefit of impressing patients, forestalling counterarguments (how can the patient argue without knowing what the terms mean?), and justifying larger fees.

In military jargon, descriptions of objects are blown out of proportion to warrant higher procurement costs. For example, an ordinary pencil is a "portable, handheld communications inscriber" (*Quarterly Review of Doublespeak* [January 1984] quoting Senator Ted Stevens of Alaska), a toothpick is a "wood interdental stimulator" (*Quarterly Review of Doublespeak* [October 1983]) and a shovel is a "combat emplacement evacuator" (in Hugh Rawson, *A Dictionary of Euphemisms and Other Doubletalk* [1981]).

We can see the same desire to make high-sounding utterances at work in many other fields as well. For example, *The New York Times* (February 4, 1987) reports on a New York artist, William Quinn, who teaches a course entitled "Meeting People at the Great Museums." According to Quinn, an important part of the course is acquiring a basic but critical vocabulary for discussing art. Thus, at the conclusion of the course, a student would not say, "It just looks like a mess to me" when speaking of Jackson Pollock's "Autumn Rhythm (Number 20)." Instead, the student would say, "Although the words poured and dripped are commonly used to describe Mr. Pollock's unorthodox creative process, they hardly suggest the diversity of Mr. Pollock's movements, namely flicking, splattering and dribbling" (cited in *Quarterly Review of Doublespeak* [October 1987]).

Lawyers, along with academicians, scientists, and bureaucrats, have their own trade talk that often presents what would normally be easy to grasp in language that mystifies and obscures. For example, the *New Haven* (Connecticut) *Register* (August 9, 1986) reports that the estate of a man who was killed when a barn collapsed on him is bringing a suit against the owners of the barn. The legalese of the suit states that the man's death "destroyed his capacity to carry on life's activities, resulting in loss and damage to his estate." According to the suit, death also "curtailed his earning capacity" and caused him to lose "the joy of life." (cited in *Quarterly Review of Doublespeak* [October 1987]).

Propaganda: The Language of Doublespeak

Ultimately, it is the intention with which words are used that determines whether any of the techniques already discussed, such as slanting, labeling, and emotionally loaded language, pose a political danger. Of themselves, strategies of persuasion are neither good nor bad, it is the purpose for which they are employed that makes them unethical and offensive. It is for this reason that the techniques of rhetorical persuasion have been decried throughout the ages. Aldous Huxley in "Propaganda Under a

Dictatorship" in *Brave New World Revisited* (1958) discussed how the manipulation of language through propaganda techniques in Nazi Germany conditioned thoughts and behavior. Some of the key techniques identified by Huxley included the use of slogans, unqualified assertions, and sweeping generalizations. Huxley notes that Hitler had said "all effective propaganda must be confined to a few bare necessities and then must be expressed in a few stereotyped formulas. . . . Only constant repetition will finally succeed in imprinting an idea upon the memory of a crowd." Hitler knew that any lie can seem to be the truth if it is repeated often enough. Repeated exposure encourages a sense of acceptance and familiarity with the slogan. Hitler's use of propaganda required that all statements be made without qualification.

George Orwell commented frequently on the dangers posed by political propaganda. In his novel *1984* he coined the term *doublespeak* to show how political language could be used to deceive, beg the question, and avoid responsibility.

Doublespeak can take forms that can range from the innocuous, such as Lt. Colonel Oliver North's intention to give "a non-visual slide show," (cited in *Quarterly Review of Doublespeak* [January 1988]) to the deceptive and dangerous, such as the Pentagon's reference to the neutron bomb as "an efficient nuclear weapon that eliminates an enemy with a minimum degree of damage to friendly territory." Or consider a statement by the U.S. Army that "we do not call it 'killing,' we call it 'servicing the target'" (cited in *Quarterly Review of Doublespeak* [January 1988]). In each of these cases language is used against itself to distort and manipulate rather than to communicate.

Intensifying and Downplaying: Strategies for Persuasion

One of the most valuable ways of analyzing forms of public persuasion was suggested by Hugh Rank in "Teaching about Public Persuasion: Rationale and a Schema" (1976). Rank won the 1976 *Orwell Award* (presented by the Committee on Public Doublespeak) for his "Intensifying/Downplaying Schema." Rank observed that all acts of public persuasion are variations of what he terms *intensifying* and *downplaying*.

Persuaders use intensifying and downplaying in the following ways: (1) to intensify, focus on, or draw attention to anything that would make their case look good; (2) to intensify, focus on, or draw attention to anything that would make counterclaims or their opponent's arguments look bad; (3) to downplay, dismiss, or divert attention from any weak points that would make their case look bad; and (4) to downplay, dismiss, or divert attention from anything that would make their opponent's case look good.

What is meant by intensifying and downplaying can be seen by comparing the words a country uses to refer to actions of the enemy (by intensifying) with those words it uses to describe its own identical activities (by downplaying):

INTENSIFYING	DOWNPLAYING
Bombing	Air support
Spying	Intelligence gathering
Invasion	Pacification
Infiltration	Reinforcement
Retreat	Strategic withdrawal

The calculated manipulation and conditioning of thought and behavior by propaganda experts is now a fact of everyday life. Professional persuaders have an unequal advantage over those whom they seek to influence and persuade. By contrast, the average citizen has never received any training in critically examining the various techniques professional persuaders use.

The three basic techniques of intensification are (1) repetition, (2) association, and (3) composition.

Repetition. Slogans, unqualified assertions, and sweeping generalizations will seem more true if they are constantly repeated. Much of commercial advertising is built on the repetition of slogans, product logos, and brand names. Political campaigns rely on repetition of candidates' names and messages over the airwaves and on posters and bumper stickers.

Association. Intensifying by association is a technique that is also known as virtue (or guilt) by association. This strategy depends on linking an idea, person, or product with something already loved or admired (or hated and despised) by the intended audience. That is, an idea, person, or product, is put into a context that already has an emotional significance for the intended audience. Once market researchers discover needs and values of a target audience, political campaigns and advertising for commercial products can exploit the audience's needs by linking their idea, candidate, or product to values already known to be appealing to the audience. Much of advertising exploits this technique of correlating feelings and emotions with purchasable objects.

Composition. A message gains intensity when it is arranged in a clearly perceivable pattern. Arranging the message can rely on the traditional rhetorical patterns (comparison and contrast, cause and effect, process analysis, classification, analogy, narration, description, and exemplification) as well as inductive or deductive logic or any other distinctive way of grouping elements of the message.

The three basic techniques of downplaying are (1) omission, (2) diversion, and (3) confusion.

Omission. If persuaders wish to downplay or divert attention away from an issue that is felt to be potentially damaging to their purposes, they can use the opposite of each of the intensifying techniques. If repetition is an effective way to intensify, persuaders can downplay by omitting, biasing, or slanting. Omissions can range from euphemisms that downplay serious issues to overt censorship.

Diversion. Just as persuaders intensify by associating, they can downplay by diverting attention through an emphasis on unimportant or unrelated side issues. Many of these tactics, already discussed in the section on logical fallacies in Chapter 3 include the *red herring, non sequitur, straw man, argumentum ad hominem, argumentum ad populum, argumentum ad misericordiam* or *appeal to pity, argumentum ad baculum* or *appeal to force, circular reasoning* or *begging the question*, and *appeal to ignorance*. All these techniques are used to divert or distract attention from the main issues to peripheral or entirely unrelated issues.

Confusion. Just as a message gains intensity when it is well structured and coherent, so persuaders can downplay by using a variety of techniques designed to obscure or cloud the points at issue. These techniques include the calculated use of faulty logic, including the *fallacy of complex question, false dilemma, false cause, post hoc, slippery slope,* and *faulty analogy.* Downplaying via confusion also results from the use of ambiguous terms or phrases as in the fallacies of *equivocation, amphiboly,* and *accent,* as well as the use of bureaucratese, medicalese, legalese, pentagonese, and all other jargons used to obscure or cloud the real issues.

We should realize that all these strategies of intensifying and downplaying can take place *simultaneously* during any attempt to persuade.

To see how this works in practice, we can apply Rank's "Intensifying/Downplaying Schema" to a set of pro–con arguments from Chapter 7.

In "The Case of the Non-Unanimous Jury" by Charles Sevilla and "Justice Can Be Served Despite Dissenting Votes" by Robert E. Jones, the point at issue is whether unanimous juries are necessary to the process of reaching fair verdicts. Sevilla *intensifies the virtues of his argument* by using the movie *Twelve Angry Men* to dramatically illustrate how the need for a unanimous verdict compels juries to review facts and evidence carefully. Sevilla uses this classic movie to illustrate his claim that the current system offers a better chance for a correct result by offering dissenters the opportunity to argue points in testimony that other jurors may have missed.

At the same time, Sevilla *intensifies negative aspects of his opponent's* (Jones') *argument* by arguing that despite the current system innocent people are still convicted; therefore, eliminating the requirement for unanimous verdicts (as Jones recommends) would lead to more mistaken convictions. Sevilla also claims that removing the need for dissenting jurors to justify their decisions would compromise a crucial element of our justice system. Simultaneously, Sevilla *downplays points on which his case might be vulnerable* by claiming that hung juries are statistically such a small fraction of all cases that they do not warrant changing the system and losing the benefits of a unanimous verdict. At the same time, he concedes that requirements for unanimity can lead to inconclusive results but asserts that no verdict is better than an erroneous one. Last, he *downplays what might be seen as a positive point for the other side* by suggesting that if Jones is so interested in saving money, why not do away with trials altogether (*reductio ad absurdum*).

By contrast, Jones, arguing the opposite position, *intensifies the virtues of his own argument* by citing his own twenty years' experience as a trial judge overseeing civil cases where verdicts were reached by ten out of twelve jurors, and not one person convicted by a nonunanimous jury was later found to be innocent. Jones also aids his case by presenting an accurate summary of Sevilla's argument, thereby enhancing his credibility as a thoughtful and objective person taking the opponent's position into account. Jones *intensifies weak points of Sevilla's argument* by asserting that trials may be aborted by one or two kook jurors whose irrationality does not blossom until after the jury is locked up for deliberation.

At the same time Jones *downplays points on which he might be vulnerable* by failing to mention that the mock trials set up to compare unanimous with nonunanimous verdicts were not designed to test for the blossoming of kook jurors. Last, he *downplays what might be seen as good points of his opponent's argument* by arguing that, Henry Fonda notwithstanding, it is improbable that one juror could convince eleven others, as depicted in *Twelve Angry Men*. Jones also *downplays or undercuts his opponent's claim* of infrequent hung juries by citing research and mock trials to prove that hung juries happen often enough to justify judicial reform.

As a final illustration of the broad applicability of the intensify/downplay method of analysis for arguments and speeches meant to persuade, we will consider one of the most famous cases of public persuasion in this century — Richard Nixon's "Checkers" speech. Before the speech was broadcast on radio and television in Los Angeles, on September 23, 1952, Dwight Eisenhower, an immensely popular Republican presidential candidate, was going to dump Nixon as his running mate because of accusations that Nixon had accepted $18,000 in personal gifts from lobbyists. Nixon appealed for one last chance to go on television and make his case before the American public. After the speech, two million favorable telegrams were received and Nixon stayed on the ticket. This speech accomplished what it set out to do — it neutralized the charges against him and brought about a favorable public image of Nixon. After disclosing his financial assets, Nixon concluded:

> . . . That's what we have and that's what we owe. It isn't very much.
>
> But, Pat and I have the satisfaction that every dime that we've got is honestly ours. I should say this, that Pat doesn't have a mink coat, but she does have a respectable Republican cloth coat.
>
> And I always tell her that she'd look good in anything. One other

thing I probably should tell you because if I don't they'll probably be saying this about me too. We did get something, a gift, after the election. A man down in Texas heard Pat on the radio mention the fact that our two youngsters would like to have a dog. And, believe it or not, the day before we left in this campaign trip, we got a message from Union Station in Baltimore saying they had a package for us. We went down to get it. You know what it was. It was a little cocker spaniel dog in a crate that he sent all the way from Texas. Black and white spotted. And our little girl Tricia the 6 year old, named it "Checkers." And you know, the kids like all kids, love the dog and I just want to say this, right now, that regardless of what they say about it, we're going to keep it.

It isn't easy to come before a nationwide audience and bare your life as I have done. But I want to say some things before I conclude that I think most of you will agree on. Mr. Mitchell, the Chairman of the Democratic National Committee, made the statement that if a man couldn't afford to be in the United States Senate he shouldn't run for the Senate. And, I just want to make my position clear. I don't agree with Mr. Mitchell when he says that only a rich man should serve his government in the U.S. Senate or in the Congress. I don't believe that represents the thinking of the Democratic Party. And, I know that it doesn't represent the thinking of the Republican Party.

I believe that it's fine that a man like Governor Stevenson who inherited a fortune from his father can run for President. But I also feel that it is essential in this country of ours that a man of modest means can also run for President. Because you know, remember Abraham Lincoln, you remember what he said "God must have loved the common people, he made so many of them." And now I am going to suggest some courses of conduct. First of all, you have read in the papers about other funds now, Mr. Stevenson apparently had a couple, one of them in which a group of business people paid and helped to supplement the salaries of state employees. Here is where the money went directly into their pockets. And I think what Mr. Stevenson should do should be to come before the American people as I have, give the names of the people that contributed to that fund, give the names of the people who put this money into their pockets at the same time that they were receiving money from their state government and see what favors, if any, they gave out for that. I don't condemn Mr. Stevenson for what he did, but until the facts are in, there is a doubt that will be raised. And as far as Mr. Sparkman is concerned, I would suggest the same thing. He's had his wife on the payroll. I don't condemn him for that, but I think that he should come before the American people and indicate what outside sources of income he has had. I would suggest that under the circumstances both Mr. Sparkman and Mr. Stevenson should come before the American people as I have and make complete financial statements as to their financial history. And, if they don't, it will be an admission that they have something to hide. And, I think you will agree with me. Because folks, remember, a man that's to be President of the U.S., a man that's to be Vice President of the U.S. must have the confidence of all the people. And, that's why I'm doing what I'm doing and that's why I suggest that Mr. Stevenson and Mr. Spark-men, since they are under attack, should do what they're doing [sic].

Now, let me say this, I know that this is not the last of the smears. In spite of my explanation tonight, other smears will be made. Others have been made in the past. And the purpose of the smears, I know, is this—to silence me, to make me let up. Well, they just don't know who they're dealing with. I'm going to tell you this. I remember in the dark days of the Hiss case, some of the same columnists, some of the same radio commentators who are attacking me now, and misrepresenting my position, were violently opposing me at the time I was after Alger Hiss. But I continued to fight because I knew I was right and I can say to this great television and radio audience that I have no apologies to the American people for my part in putting Alger Hiss where he is today. And as far as this is concerned, I intend to continue to fight. Why do I feel so deeply, why do I feel that in spite of the smears, the misunderstandings, the necessity for a man to come up here and bare his soul as I have? Why is it necessary for me to continue this fight? I want to tell you why, because you see, I love my country and I think my country is in danger and I think the only man that can save America at this time is the man that's running for President on my ticket, Dwight Eisenhower.

A breakdown of this speech using the intensify/downplay schema might appear as follows:

1. Nixon intensifies positive features in the following lines:
    a. "But, Pat and I have the satisfaction that every dime that we've got is honestly ours."
    b. "Pat doesn't have a mink coat, but she does have a respectable Republican cloth coat."[Virtue by association.]
    c. "And I always tell her that she'd look good in anything."
    d. "It was a little cocker spaniel dog . . . named . . . 'Checkers.' And you know, the kids like all kids, love the dog and I just want to say this, right now, that regardless of what they say about it, we're going to keep it." [Virtue by association; i.e., loves his children who love dogs, wouldn't hurt his children by sending Checkers back, implies opponents would take his children's puppy away; name Checkers has folksy connotation of people playing checkers.]
    e. "a man of modest means can also run for President." [Just plain folks appeal.]
    f. "Because you know, remember Abraham Lincoln, you remember what he said 'God must have loved the common people . . . '" [Virtue by association, plain folks appeal and suggests a link with a respected Republican president.]
    g. "I think the only man that can save America at this time is the man that's running for President on my [sic] ticket, Dwight

Eisenhower." [Virtue by association with a person already loved and admired by the voting public; although perhaps a slip of the tongue, note how Nixon, who is the vice-presidential candidate, makes himself as important as the respected and very popular presidential candidate.]

2. Nixon intensifies the points on which his opponents might be vulnerable:

   a. "and I just want to say this, right now, that regardless of what they say about it, we're going to keep it." [Wouldn't hurt his children by sending Checkers back, with the clear implication that his opponents would.]

   b. "I don't agree with Mr. Mitchell when he says that only a rich man should serve his government in the U.S. Senate or in the Congress." [Characterizing himself as poor but honest in contrast to rich elitist Democrats.]

   c. "Mr. Stevenson apparently had a couple [of funds] . . . where the money went directly into their pockets."

   d. "I don't condemn Mr. Stevenson for what he did, but until the facts are in, there is a doubt that will be raised. And as far as Mr. Sparkman is concerned, I would suggest the same thing. He's had his wife on the payroll. I don't condemn him for that . . . " [Presented as a search for the truth, Nixon accrues the added benefit of appearing to be nonjudgmental; he raises the issue while at the same time appears to deny he is doing so.]

   e. "I know that this is not the last of the smears. In spite of my explanation tonight, other smears will be made. Others have been made in the past. And the purpose of the smears . . . " [Technique of repetition, characterizing the accusation that prompted this speech as a smear.]

3. Nixon downplays potential weaknesses in his own position:

   a. "It isn't very much." [Diminishes importance of financial holdings; by implication, he would be richer if he had really been accepting money.]

   b. "One other thing I probably should tell you because if I don't they'll probably be saying this about me too." [A classic straw man maneuver since no one had or conceivably would accuse him of accepting a puppy for his little girls as a payoff.]

   c. "Because you know, remember Abraham Lincoln, you remember what he said 'God must have loved the common people . . . '" [Diverting attention with an unrelated *argumentum ad populum*.]

   d. "Mr. Sparkman and Mr. Stevenson should come before the American people as I have and make complete financial statement as to their financial history. And, if they don't, it will be an admission that they have something to hide." [Diverting attention to Stevenson and Sparkman who Nixon characterizes as being under a cloud of guilt.]

e. "And the purpose of the smears, I know, is this — to silence me, to make me let up. Well, they just don't know who they're dealing with. I'm going to tell you this. I remember in the dark days of the Hiss case, some of the same columnists, some of the same radio commentators who are attacking me now, and misrepresenting my position, were violently opposing me at the time I was after Alger Hiss." [Diversion by attributing a false cause to confuse the issue; diversion by introducing a red herring converts the charge of financial impropriety being made against him into an occasion for characterizing "some" of his accusers as un-American.]

f. "In spite of the smears, the misunderstandings, the necessity for a man to come up here and bare his soul as I have." [Diversion through appeal to pity, fused with the common man theme.]

g. "Why is it necessary for me to continue this fight. I want to tell you why, because you see, I love my country and I think my country is in danger . . . " [Scare tactics combined with elevation of his campaign for the vice-presidency into a holy cause to save the country.]

4. Nixon downplays what some might consider to be a point in Stevenson's favor, i.e., a man or woman wealthy at the time he or she took office might be seen as less likely to exploit power for financial gain.

a. "I believe that it's fine that a man like Governor Stevenson who inherited a fortune from his father can run for President." [In light of his earlier condemnation of Mitchell for implying that "only a rich man should serve his government" this statement is transparently false.]

TWO SHORT ARGUMENTS FOR ANALYSIS

Marilyn Machlowitz

What Is Workaholism?

*This opening chapter, "What Is Workaholism?" from Marilyn Mach-
lowitz's book* Workaholics *(1980) presents the results of extensive
research and interviews to dispel the popular stereotype that workaholism is an addiction much like alcoholism. Machlowitz believes it is
important to provide a more accurate definition to dispel negative
connotations of the term* workaholism. *She cites a range of case
histories including those of a surgeon, playwright, janitor, and U.S.
Senator to show that workaholics are often productive and happy.*

As retirees rapidly come to realize, a job provides a lot more than just   1
a paycheck. Jobs structure people's time. They permit regular interpersonal interaction and provide a sense of identity, self-esteem, and self-
respect. But for all these positive effects attributed to working, alienated
workers have received far more of scholars' attention than have their
highly absorbed counterparts, the workaholics.

The popular press has paid some attention to work addicts. It's an   2
unusual business magazine that doesn't mention the word at least once
per issue. One career guide advises job applicants to answer the inevitable question "What are your weaknesses?" with a quality that is apt to be
attractive to a prospective employer. It tells readers to say, "I'm such a
workaholic that I tend to get completely caught up in my work." And a
woman's magazine told its readers to end a summer or vacation romance
by warning men about being a workaholic back at home.

But there is scant scientific research on workaholics. My own master's   3
thesis and doctoral dissertation were the first systematic studies of the
phenomenon. My best estimate suggests that workaholics comprise no
more than 5 percent of the adult population. They probably make up a
slightly higher percentage of the workforce, since workaholics are the
least likely to be unemployed. Somehow, it seems, workaholics have
overcome or averted the difficulties and dissatisfactions that plague
today's workers. Perhaps, once workaholism is better understood, it will
be possible to use the experience of the work addict to enrich and

enhance the working lives of others. But first we need to dispel some of the negative attitudes we have about workaholics.

4   Most descriptions of the phenomenon do not define workaholism as much as they denigrate and deride workaholics. Lotte Bailyn of M.I.T. described the workaholic as the "victim of a newly recognized social disease presumably responsible for the disintegration of the family, [and] for severe distortion of full personal development." Likewise, a respected *New York Times* writer, Charlotte Curtis, portrayed the workaholic as someone who was "anxious, guilt-ridden, insecure, or self-righteous about . . . work . . . a slave to a set schedule, merciless in his demands upon himself for peak performance . . . compulsively over-committed."

5   The word "workaholism" owes its origin, as well as its negative overtones to "alcoholism." What distinguishes workaholism from other addictions is that workaholism is sometimes considered a virtue, while others, such as alcoholism, or drug addiction, are invariably considered vices.

6   Yet workaholics are usually portrayed as a miserable lot. This bias stems from the ways we learn about them. The clergy hears their confessions; physicians and therapists, their complaints; and judges, their divorces. The few articles about workaholics that have appeared in scientific journals typically emphasize the psychosocial problems of specific patients. The workaholics that I interviewed had few such problems.

7   Another major bias against workaholics are the beliefs of nonworkaholics. People who work to live cannot understand those who live to work and love it. They watch in amazement and wonder about those who delight in what they do. Workaholics' unorthodox attitude — that their work is so much fun they'd probably do it for free — causes non-workaholics to question their own situation. The latter group begins to worry "What's wrong with my job?" or, worse, "What's wrong with me?" To resolve these feelings, nonworkaholics resort to denouncing workaholics rather than running down themselves. They say, "Sure, workaholics are successful at work, but aren't they really ruining the rest of their lives?" This logic is akin to that of "Lucky in cards, unlucky in love" and equally untrue. Satisfaction with work and with life are more apt to be intertwined than mutually exclusive.

8   Workaholism is almost exclusively American, but it is also un-American. You are *supposed* to lead lives that are well-rounded, balanced, and more "normal" than those of workaholics. Sure, you should go to work weekdays, but you better not spend evenings and weekends at work, as well. Those times should be spent with the family or playing ball or seeing friends or gardening. Have you ever heard of a beauty pageant contestant who couldn't list at least half a dozen hobbies, from basket weaving to opera singing? In contrast, when faced with an employment application, a workaholic might have to leave that item blank. Workaholics are more willing to settle for excellence in one endeavor and to

admit that they are inept and uninterested in anything else. As playwright Neil Simon said (italics mine). "I wish I *could* do other things well
besides write. . . . play an instrument, learn other languages, cook, ski.
My greatest sense of accomplishment is that I didn't waste time *trying* to
learn those things."

Nor is it American to like your job that much, and those who do are   9
suspect. To look forward to Monday instead of Friday is regarded as
strange and even abnormal. Production workers attach posters to their
machines that say "Hang in there; Friday's coming." In the executive
suites such signs are understandably absent, but sentiments like "Thank
God It's Friday" are frequently heard.

As a result, workaholics are often openly maligned. A top health   10
insurance organization placed a full-page magazine ad warning of the
alleged health hazards and related costs of working too hard. The photo
featured an angry-looking man with a cigarette dangling from his lips
and butts spilling out of an overflowing ashtray; his tie loosened, his
collar undone, his shirt straining at his paunch, a styrofoam coffee cup in
one hand and several others strewn about an incredibly cluttered desk.
The headline read, "He's working twelve hours a day to increase the cost
of health care." The copy continued, "In the Horatio Alger story the hero
works day and night to get ahead and everybody looks up to him with
admiration. Now, millions of Americans are following this example. . . . We're not asking you to stop working. Just try not to overdo it.
And when you see someone who things he's Horatio Alger, don't think
of him as a hero. Think of him as a villain."

Most workaholics won't admit that's what they are because the word   11
has such negative connotations. In fact, so many of the people I interviewed objected to the word that I frequently substituted other phrases
("the role of work in the lives of successful hard workers") when talking
to them. Everyone I interviewed acknowledged that they had been
accused of being a workaholic. And almost all admitted that my characteristics of workaholism came a little too close for comfort. As television
anchorwoman Jessica Savitch wrote me, "I do not like the label since it
conjures up a negative addiction such as alcoholic. But the qualities you
ascribe to a workaholic are qualities I seek and admire in others."

Now everyone, however, dismisses workaholics as dismal or danger-   12
ous. When a young mathematician heard I was writing a book about
workaholics, he eagerly asked me, "Does your book tell how to become
one?" And, indeed, in certain governmental, professional, and academic
circles, workaholism has managed to develop considerable cachet. In,
say, Washington, D.C., New York City, or Cambridge, Massachusetts,
you can hear quite a few people claim to be workaholics. I, for one, doubt
that too many of them really are simply because they brag about it. Real
workaholics will doubt, demur, or deny outright that that's what they
are.

Then, too, workaholics do not necessarily recognize or realize just   13 how hard they do work. But they don't mind working hard. While the masses may moan and grumble about having to work hard, workaholics enjoy and exult in it. In fact, Dr. John Rhoads, a psychiatrist on the faculty of Duke University, maintains that it is almost axiomatic that those who complain of being overworked are not. For example, Dick Vermeil, head coach of Philadelphia's pro football team, the Eagles, and a man who is invariably called a workaholic, told me, "I don't actually know what the word means, but I am tired of its being used in describing my personality. I do what I'm doing because I enjoy it very much and really don't consider it hard work."

14   While workaholics do work hard, not all hard workers are workaholics. I will use the word workaholic to describe those whose desire to work long and hard is intrinsic and whose work habits almost always exceed the prescriptions of the job they do and the expectations of the people with whom or for whom they work. But the first characteristic is the real determinant. What truly distinguishes workaholics from other hard workers is that the others work only to please a boss, earn a promotion, or meet a deadline. Moonlighters, for example, may work sixteen hours a day merely to make ends meet, but most of them stop working multiple shifts as soon as their financial circumstances permit. Accountants, too, may sometimes seem to work non-stop, but most slow down markedly after April 15th. For workaholics, on the other hand, the workload seldom lightens, for they don't *want* to work less. As Senator William Proxmire has found, "The less I work, the less I enjoy it."

15   Time spent working would be an appealing index of workaholism, but it would also be a misleading measure. Although workaholics may work from 5 A.M. to 9 P.M. instead of the more usual 9 A.M. to 5 P.M., the hours they work are not the *sine qua non* of workaholism. It is in fact preferable to view workaholism as an approach or an attitude toward working than as an amount of time at work. Workaholics will continue to think about work when they're not working — even at moments that are, well, inappropriate. One energy specialist recalls dreaming about Con Ed and seeing barrels of oil in her sleep. One research and development director mentally designs new studies while making love to his wife.

16   But numbers and totals do count: Workaholics are given to counting their work hours and especially their achievements. Dr. Denton Cooley, the founder and chief surgeon of the Texas Heart Institute of Houston, enclosed a six-page vitae and a two-page biography with his finished questionnaire, which was handwritten in the illegible scrawl for which physicians are famous. The vitae listed a string of international honors; the biography, his achievements: By 1978, Cooley had performed over 30,000 open heart operations, more than any other surgeon in the world. He and his staff perform 25 to 30 such operations a day. An aide explains:

> I don't think you'll talk to anyone who likes to operate more than Cooley. People like him don't go into medicine for mankind. They

do it because they like it. I mean he could relax, he doesn't need the money. His dad was a successful dentist who invested very widely in Houston real estate. And Denton's surgical fees are more than one million dollars a year. But he just wouldn't be happy if he couldn't operate every day. Hell, I've seen him call in from a morning meeting in New York to set up an afternoon surgery schedule. The guy is hooked.

Dr. Cooley defended his dedication far more simply. He works as he does, he said, "because I enjoy it."

Workaholism is not restricted to hospital corridors, Congressional   17
offices, or elegant executive suites. While we sneer at it in corporate executives, workaholism is something we've come to accept — and even admire — in artists, and it is what we expect of our personal physicians. It is also part and parcel of our image of most scientists, such as Edison and Einstein. As Wilfred J. Corrigan, former chairman of Fairchild Camera and Instrument Corporation told *Business Week*, "A lot of people in this industry are totally involved with their work. Everyone sees this as appropriate for an artist painting the Sistine chapel or an author writing a novel. But in science and technology, there are times when you just don't want to go home."

Although I interviewed far more white collar than blue collar   18
workers, I found that workaholics exist in every occupation, from managers and doctors to secretaries and assembly line workers. One man had a combined M.D.–Ph.D.; another had only a high school diploma. A friend once described her apartment building's janitor as a workaholic. "I feel very fortunate," she said, "to have a super who's a compulsive worker. He won't even stop and talk. Occasionally, he'll have a conversation with someone while he's sweeping the sidewalk."

Nor is workaholism restricted to just one sex. While women have   19
been almost completely overlooked in the little that has been written about workaholism, there have always been women workaholics. If housework, for instance, were rightfully regarded as work, generations of compulsive cleaners could be considered workaholics. And so would the tireless organizers of charity events. Today, women's workaholism is merely more apparent, since more and more women work outside their homes.

Dr. Helen De Rosis, associate clinical professor of psychiatry at New   20
York University School of Medicine and the author of several books about women, cautions against confusing women workaholics with the so-called Superwomen. A Superwoman tries to be Supermom and Superwife as well as Superworker. Superwoman, according to syndicated columnist Ellen Goodman, is not only a Wonder Woman at work but an elegant dresser and an excellent cook as well. Her kids do not subsist on cold cereal: Superwoman gets up at the crack of dawn to make them a hot, nutritious, and nitrite-free breakfast. Her husband has a delicious dinner every night: She not only has time to get the groceries, but to

whip up gourmet delights, courtesy of Julia Child and Cuisinart. Her relationship with her children is characterized, of course, by the *quality* —not by the quantity—of the time she spends with them. Similarly, her marriage can only be called a meaningful relationship. She and her husband are not only each other's best friend but also ecstatic lovers, because Superwoman is never too tired at night. Instead, she is, in the words of Ellen Goodman, "multiorgasmic until midnight."

21   According to Dr. De Rosis, whose books include *Women and Anxiety*, Superwomen and workaholics share a basic similarity: Both use their work as a defense against anxiety. While workaholics appear to enjoy their work, Dr. De Rosis explains that the enjoyment they experience is distinct from the pleasure felt by women who are able to shift their priorities for different occasions. "The workaholic can't do this. She can't say, 'Today I'll stay home because my child is sick.' She can't make that decision."

22   Nor should women workaholics be mistaken for women who must do double time to make up for sex-related obstacles in their careers. When Monica Bauer joined Xerox in 1966, she found that she "really did have to put in more time than my male associates just to get the information." Back then, Bauer was excluded from the "old boy network" and other informal channels of communication and had no "new girl network" to turn to. The times have changed, but Bauer's drive shows no decline. She continues to put in long days at Xerox, where she is now manager of low volume products and pricing, and recently completed an M.B.A. at the University of Rochester while working full-time.

23   So, despite the fact that workaholics come from all classes, sexes, and occupations, they all share one over-riding passion: work. After interviewing more than one hundred work addicts over several years, I have some good news and some bad news. The good news is that as a group, workaholics are surprisingly happy. They are doing exactly what they love—work—and they can't seem to get enough of it. If the circumstances are right—that is, if their jobs fit and their families are accommodating—then workaholics can be astonishingly productive. But here's the bad news: The people who work with and live with workaholics often suffer. Adjusting to the frenetic schedule of a workaholic is not easy and only rarely rewarding. At work these addicts are often demanding and sometimes not very effective. At home, well, you'll seldom find a workaholic at home. The tensions implicit in this rather unbalanced life-style cause very real dilemmas for those involved, and a good part of this book is about those problems.

Sample Analysis

CLAIM: Workaholism, says Machlowitz, is not an addiction like alcoholism. Workaholics do not have miserable personal lives, are actually quite happy and productive, and should not be subjected to ridicule or stereo-typed as obsessive killjoys.

GROUNDS: Machlowitz cites many well-known individuals (Neil Simon, Dick Vermeil, William Proxmire, and others) from a wide range of prc-fessions to support her claim. Her examples show that workaholics do not work to please bosses, earn promotions, or meet deadlines, but instead work only to satisfy themselves. Other cases serve to dispel the common misconception that workaholics are not blue-collar workers.

WARRANT: It is unfair to characterize productive behavior as if it were as addictive, debilitating, and detrimental as alcoholism.

PERSUADING THE AUDIENCE: Machlowitz's task in presenting the argu-ment is made more difficult because she is going against the value assumptions of her audience, namely, that in American culture life should be well-rounded, balancing work during the day with participa-tion in hobbies and other activities at night and on the weekends. Machlowitz is also swimming against the current if we assume people usually dislike their jobs whereas workaholics cannot get enough of theirs. If Machlowitz's argument were successful, the relatively small five percent of the population who might be workaholics, and feel bad about themselves because of societal labeling, would feel better about their behavior; the larger percentage of the audience who might have held a negative view of workaholics might be persuaded to be more tolerant of them.

Questions for Discussion and Writing

1. According to Machlowitz, what would be the benefits of coming to a better understanding of the characteristics that collectively define someone as a workaholic?

2. One of Machlowitz's unquestioned assumptions is that workaholism is a positive phenomenon. Where in her article does this positive view of workaholism emerge? What arguments does she cite that characterize workaholism as a negative form of behavior? What evidence does she present to refute popular conceptions that workaholism is an addiction even though its effects might not be as detrimental as excessive drinking, eating, smoking, or the use of drugs?

3. How has the fact that workaholics tend to concentrate on achieving excellence in one endeavor to the exclusion of the traditional well-rounded, balanced range of activities made them more susceptible to accusations of being "abnormal"? What assumptions characteristic of American culture does Machlowitz identify as the cause of this negative perception?

4. What is the phenomenon of labeling, and what is its connection to stereotyping? How does Machlowitz apply the concept of labeling to the popular perceptions of workaholics? What other examples can you think of where how an occupation is labeled has the effect of reinforcing positive or negative connotations? For example, what effect is produced by saying someone's occupation is that of a "landscape engineer" or "sanitation engineer" instead of gardener or garbage collector?

5. What examples does Machlowitz give to support her characterization of workaholics as people who find it difficult to do nothing, who work long hours, get very little sleep, don't take vacations, avoid retirement, work on weekends and holidays, and seem really to enjoy their work? How do these traits fit her definition of a workaholic as one "whose desire to work long and hard is intrinsic and whose work habits almost always exceed the prescriptions of the job they do and the expectations of the people with whom or for whom they work"?

6. Evaluate Machlowitz's use of testimony by Neil Simon, Dick Vermeil, William Proxmire, Wilfred J. Corrigan, and others to support her analysis. How does the fact that many of the people she quotes are famous and from a wide range of occupations strengthen her argument?

7. How does Machlowitz widen the scope of her argument by applying her thesis to both white-collar workers and blue-collar workers and to women as well as men?

8. What distinctions does Machlowitz draw between workaholics and the popular stereotype of the so-called superwoman? Although the superwoman, who is a "wonder woman at work . . . elegant dresser . . . excellent cook . . . best friend . . . ecstatic lover," might be confused with the workaholic, Machlowitz asserts that there are very basic differences between them. What are these differences and why are they important to Machlowitz's argument?

9. In a paragraph, discuss the extent to which you might now be, or have the potential to be, a workaholic. Since only five percent of the population is characterized in this way, explain why this particular style of life might or might not appeal to you.

10. If you had to choose between having an interesting, financially rewarding career with an unsatisfying personal life or a boring, low

paying job with a deeply satisfying personal life, which would you choose and why?

11. Would you choose to win a lottery guaranteeing you an annual income of $75,000 per year (after taxes) for twenty years if a condition of your winning was that you could not work during the twenty years?

Robert Benchley

Opera Synopsis

Robert Benchley was an American actor, humorist, author, and member of the notorious Algonquin Round Table along with Dorothy Parker, James Thurber, Robert Sherwood, and George Kaufman. He is best known for his books of humorous essays, including Twenty Thousand Leagues Under the Sea; or, David Copperfield (1928), and My Ten Years in a Quandry, and How It Grew (1936). Benchley won an academy award for the short film How to Sleep. "Opera Synopsis" is drawn from The Benchley Roundup (1922). An opera synopsis is given to audiences at performances of grand opera because operas are usually performed in foreign languages. A synopsis is intended to help the audience understand the action and the relationships of characters. Many operas, however, have plots that are so complex that even in synopsis form they do not make any sense. Benchley gleefully satirizes many of the outer trappings of grand opera, pokes fun (through the use of non sequiturs) at their convoluted narratives, masterfully exploits the comic potential of characters' names (Zweiback, Strudel, Schmalz, etc.), and ridicules the pretentiousness of this form of "high culture."

DIE MEISTER-GENOSSENSCHAFT

SCENE: *The Forests of Germany.*
TIME: *Antiquity.*

Cast

STRUDEL, *God of Rain*	Basso
SCHMALZ, *God of Slight Drizzle*	Tenor
IMMERGLÜCK, *Goddess of the Six Primary Colors*	Soprano
LUDWIG DAS EIWEISS, *the Knight of the Iron Duck*	Baritone
THE WOODPECKER	Soprano

Argument

1   The basis of "Die Meister-Genossenschaft" is an old legend of Germany which tells how the Whale got his Stomach.

ACT I

The Rhine at Low Tide Just Below Weldschnoffen.—Immerglück has   2
grown weary of always sitting on the same rock with the same fishes
swimming by every day, and sends for Schwül to suggest something to
do. Schwül asks her how she would like to have pass before her all the
wonders of the world fashioned by the hand of man. She says, rotten.
He then suggests that Ringblattz, son of Pflucht, be made to appear
before her and fight a mortal combat with the Iron Duck. This pleases
Immerglück and she summons to her the four dwarfs: Hot Water, Cold
Water, Cool, and Cloudy. She bids them bring Ringblattz to her. They
refuse, because Pflucht has at one time rescued them from being buried
alive by acorns, and, in a rage, Immerglück strikes them all dead with a
thunderbolt.

ACT 2

A Mountain Pass—Repenting of her deed, Immerglück has sought   3
advice of the giants, Offen and Besitz, and they tell her that she must
procure the magic zither which confers upon its owner the power to go
to sleep while apparently carrying on a conversation. This magic zither
has been hidden for three hundred centuries in an old bureau drawer,
guarded by the Iron Duck, and, although many have attempted to rescue
it, all have died of a strange ailment just as success was within their
grasp.

But Immerglück calls to her side Dampfboot, the tinsmith of the gods,   4
and bids him make for her a tarnhelm or invisible cap which will enable
her to talk to people without their understanding a word she says. For a
dollar and a half extra Dampfboot throws in a magic ring which renders
its wearer insensible. Thus armed, Immerglück starts out for Walhalla,
humming to herself.

ACT 3

The Forest Before the Iron Duck's Bureau Drawer.—Merglitz, who has   5
up till this time held his peace, now descends from a balloon and
demands the release of Betty. It has been the will of Wotan that Mergli-
tyz and Betty should meet on earth and hate each other like poison, but
Zweiback, the druggist of the gods, has disobeyed and concocted a
love-potion which has rendered the young couple very unpleasant company. Wotan, enraged, destroys them with a protracted heat spell.

Encouraged by this sudden turn of affairs, Immerglück comes to   6
earth in a boat drawn by four white Holsteins, and, seated alone on a
rock, remembers aloud to herself the days when she was a girl. Pilgrims

from Augenblick, on their way to worship at the shrine of Schmürr, hear the sound of reminiscence coming from the rock and stop in their march to sing a hymn of praise for the drying-up of the crops. They do not recognize Immerglück, as she has her hair done differently, and think that she is a beggar girl selling pencils.

7   In the meantime, Ragel, the papercutter of the gods, has fashioned himself a sword on the forge of Schmalz, and has called the weapon "Assistance-in-Emergency." Armed with "Assistance-in-Emergency" he comes to earth, determined to slay the Iron Duck and carry off the beautiful Irma.

8   But Frimsel overhears the plan and has a drink brewed which is given to Ragel in a golden goblet and which, when drunk, makes him forget his past and causes him to believe that he is Schnorr, the God of Fun. While laboring under this spell, Ragel has a funeral pyre built on the summit of a high mountain and, after lighting it, climbs on top of it with a mandolin which he plays until he is consumed.

9   Immerglück never marries.

Sample Analysis

CLAIM: Benchley suggests that grand opera, despite the reverence with which it is viewed, has nonsensical story lines, makes illogical use of legends, is set in vague time frames, has unrelated subplots, and superfluous characters. Moreover, librettists contrive such convoluted plots that they must resort to magic and potions to resolve their complicated story lines.

GROUNDS: Benchley's evidence takes the form of a parody of specific features of grand opera. For example, in his version the treasure is hidden in a bureau drawer, and characters' names (Zweibach, druggist of the gods; Strudel, god of rain; Schmalz, god of slight drizzle; Immerglück, goddess of the six primary colors) parody the names usually given to heroes and heroines in grand opera. Benchley also parodies the conventions that govern operatic story lines (a love potion that makes couples hate each other), and includes a scenario where the second act has nothing to do with the first act.

WARRANT: The principle to which Benchley is appealing is a traditional one for satire. Pretentious forms of art deserve to be punctured now and then, especially if it can be done without malice.

PERSUADING THE AUDIENCE: Benchley appeals directly to the audience's sense of being able to laugh at something that is usually taken seriously. The method he chooses (writing his own opera synopsis) is an effective one, disguising his objections in an amusing package. How many opera lovers would be persuaded by Benchley's humor is of course open to question.

Questions for Discussion and Writing

1. How does Benchley's satiric technique depend on extending traditional ideas to absurd lengths in order to parody the usual conventions of legends? What's so funny about locating treasure in a bureau drawer (where people hide keys) instead of in the middle of the forest?

2. Why does Benchley never mention the music which an opera lover would find so compelling? Why does he choose to concentrate on the aspects of the opera that can be ridiculed? What would be the counterargument by a Wagnerian opera lover to Benchley's essay?

3. How does Benchley's "Opera Synopsis" use ridicule, exaggeration, and irony to parody conventional aspects of traditional grand opera? For example, how does Benchley use modern professions to satirize the tradition that the gods are always attended by servants?

4. How does Benchley exploit the comic potential of the names of dwarfs and gods to poke fun at the traditional names of gods in grand opera?

5. Do the characters and action that take place in Act II and Act III have anything to do with previous acts?

6. How does Benchley poke fun at the nonsensical narratives and story lines of grand opera? For instance, what is the effect of introducing characters with distinctive modern names (Betty) in the midst of characters whose names derive from mythological or legendary sources?

7. Discuss Benchley's attitude toward audiences who applaud, shout "Bravo," and hold grand opera in great esteem although the stories make no sense, characters drop in out of the blue, and librettists resolve complicated plots by resorting to magic powers and potions.

8. How does each of the following reverse traditional expectations: (1) praises and hymns are sung to the dying of the crops, (2) love potions make couples hate each other, and (3) Immerglück never marries.

9. How does naming characters after foods such as (1) Zweibach, (2)

strudel, and (3) schmalz contribute to the comic effect? Zweibach is a dry cracker given to babies to teeth on, strudel is a multilayered pastry filled with fruit, and schmalz is chicken fat.

10. Try your hand at writing your own opera synopsis based on a real opera or even a play or movie whose story line lends itself to Benchley's type of parody. For example, you might want to spoof any Wagnerian opera, *The Wizard of Oz*, or any of the classic Humphrey Bogart films such as *The Maltese Falcon*. If unsure of exactly how to proceed with this assignment, you might check any back issue of *MAD Magazine*, which would be of great "Assistance-in-Emergency."

5

Strategies for Writing Arguments

The process of writing an argument essay is similar to writing other kinds of essays in that it requires you to find a subject, define your approach to the topic, establish a thesis sentence, decide on your purpose, identify your audience, plan your essay (with or without an informal outline), write a rough draft, revise, edit, and proofread to produce a final paper.

Argumentative essays differ from other kinds of essays in that they are designed to achieve at least one of the following purposes: (1) persuade others to accept your position on a clearly defined issue, (2) accept your argument refuting someone else's position, or (3) endorse a solution you propose to a problem.

The process of writing can best be thought of as a series of operations you perform. These actions or steps encompass prewriting activities that precede the first draft, including a variety of invention strategies useful for discovering a topic, identifying your purpose, analyzing your audience, and organizing the material before writing a first draft.

Although this chapter will spell out the different steps in the writing process, writers know that it is impossible to take a prescriptive approach to writing. Writing is a recursive process without clearly defined beginnings and endings. You should feel free to do any of the following steps in a different order from the way they are presented or to return to any of the earlier steps at any time. You should also feel free to follow the developing idea in whatever direction it may lead, whether or not it means departing from some predetermined sequence of steps. You may discover, as many writers do, that the act of writing requires you to substantially rethink your thesis and perhaps even change your entire essay as you discover a new topic or come to a radically different conclusion about your original topic. What is valuable about the process approach is that it gives you many opportunities to get a clear idea of what you want to write about and a way to test your developing essay in order to correct basic oversights and add new insights.

Prewriting

Finding something to write about (if you have not been assigned a topic in class) can be helped along if you consider some of the following sources for likely argumentative essay subjects.

Differences of opinion on issues with friends are a potential starting point, as are other issues drawn from your personal experiences. For example, you might address a problem that needs solving. How should fraternities deal with the alcohol-related problems that have caused injuries and deaths during fraternity hazings? Is the problem so unsolvable that colleges should even consider banning fraternities from their campuses?

You might begin with experiences that frustrate you or make you dissatisfied with the way things are being done. What do you complain about a lot? You might propose that your school provide more parking facilities for students since there is always a rush for the few spaces that are available.

For another source, you might consider topics of current controversy reported in the news. For example, in a 1988 book Albert Goldman wrote a biography of John Lennon that portrays Lennon as a heroin addict and a bisexual. The remaining members of the Beatles and Yoko Ono have protested Goldman's unsavory characterization of Lennon, especially since none of them was interviewed by Goldman for the book. You might wish to argue that something should be done to change the current libel laws to protect deceased celebrities and other people who cannot defend themselves.

Consider issues that have come up in reading you have done for other courses. In a psychology course you might have read different arguments by Desmond Morris, Ashley Montagu, or Sigmund Freud claiming that human aggression is either innate or learned. Your thesis could be that human aggression is not genetically determined but is a form of learned behavior.

The issue you choose to write about must be genuinely debatable. Rule out arguments over facts that could be settled by looking in a reference book. Also eliminate questions of personal taste. What you are looking for is an issue about which knowledgeable people disagree. The assumption is that if people who know a lot about the issue disagree, then the facts of the situation can be interpreted in different ways, and therefore that issue would make a good, debatable subject to explore in your essay. For example, people still disagree about whether the Supreme Court 1966 Miranda decision (which requires the police to inform those being arrested of their right to remain silent unless an attorney is present) should be amended to make it less likely that hard-core criminals can be released on procedural technicalities. You might wish to argue that the Miranda decision should be modified to rectify this problem.

SELECTING AN ISSUE

To get started, you might begin by listing possible topics you already know about. For example, you might have been in Little League and experienced a lot of pressure to compete, both from the coaches and from your parents. Some children later think the experience was worthwhile, whereas others think the pressure parents put on them to win was too traumatic. If you felt this latter way, you might make a case that parents who wish to live vicariously through their children's successes put an unfair burden on their children.

The next step in selecting an issue is to consider whether it requires research just to find out what is entailed. You might need to discover the range of arguments that already exist to determine what your own position might be. For example, police officers occasionally pose as students to find out who is using and selling drugs on campus. What exactly does the law say on this issue? Where does posing as an undercover student leave off and entrapment begin?

When considering controversial issues, list what people who know something about the issue have said on either side. For example, you might be interested in the arguments as to whether prayer should be allowed in public schools. As reported in the newspapers, former U.S. Senator John East, Republican from North Carolina, claims it is basically up to the states to decide whether or not to permit voluntary school prayer. On the other hand, former Senator Lowell Weicker, Republican from Connecticut, argues that putting any requirement in place for school prayer would go against the separation of church and state spelled out in the First Amendment ("Congress shall make no law respecting an establishment of religion"). You might want to look into this issue to find out who makes a better case.

To discover whether you have found a genuinely debatable topic, consider whether the same facts are open to more than one interpretation. Most college students have heard about the increasing incidence of date rape (a recent study suggests one out of six female college students have faced this problem) where women are not attacked by some anonymous stranger but by their dates or romantic acquaintances. Yet many of these men do not see themselves as rapists. The question of what is considered permissible sexually in the context of modern male–female relationships has contributed to the problem. For instance, men who hold traditional views of sex roles may believe that if the woman asks a man for a date, goes to his apartment, or allows him to pay for all expenses, a sexual invitation is implied that the woman has no right to withdraw. The whole question is obviously subject to more than one interpretation.

Genuinely debatable topics spring from situations where people bring two competing sets of values to the same situation, perhaps without even being aware of it. Thus, a tradition of the Christmas season may have been a manger scene in front of the town hall, yet, recently, groups have protested that having such a scene on a municipally owned piece of property violates the First Amendment's "establishment clause" separating church and state. This is an emotional issue precisely because people are bringing competing sets of values to bear on the same set of circumstances.

You might consider moral questions you have debated with friends regarding what is right and what is wrong. What if you discover that athletes at your school are receiving special academic tutoring that is not equally available to other students, or that a particular athlete has received an under-the-table cash payment to induce him or her to attend a particular college. Although you can appreciate that college athletics bring big money and prestige to schools, you may wish to argue that school administrations apply one set of standards to athletes and another to all the other students.

Aside from maintaining an inquisitive perspective to discover a potential starting point for your essay, you might be the type of person who wonders what caused certain things to be the way they are. Let's say you lived abroad and recently immigrated to the United States or that your grandparents and other relatives came from another culture. You might wonder why the elderly are often treated as disposable citizens in the United States when they are treated with veneration and respect in many other cultures. Why should this be so? You might wish to argue a thesis that many people would find controversial: our culture does not value old people because many are poor and cannot afford to participate in the consumer culture. You might develop your thesis by looking at how our culture encourages young people starting out in life to assume debt of monumental proportions. You might further claim that since old people are unwilling or unable to take on large debts, they are automatically viewed as second-class citizens.

You might consider what started a fad. For example, what explains the increase in popularity of "new age" fads such as channeling, crystal healing, flower essences, and reflexology. Or you might consider what started a certain trend. For example, statistics show an increasing trend in the numbers of children who are abused physically and emotionally each year. Are more accurate identification procedures responsible for the greater numbers of cases reported or are greater numbers of children actually being abused? If the latter, what is causing this trend to accelerate?

You might be aware of implications or far-reaching effects about which others seem unaware. For example, you read that crops are going to be sprayed with biogenetically produced frost-inhibiting bacteria. You wonder what precautions have been taken to prevent this and other genetically engineered substances from wreaking havoc on the environment.

Even if you are not assigned a specific subject, topics that can become sources of good arguments are all around you. All that is required is that you discover a situation that is subject to more than one interpretation and where it is probable that neither side has a lock on the truth. For example, you read about a case where strict Christian Scientists would not permit doctors to give a blood transfusion to their severely injured child. The hospital appealed to a judge who allowed the transfusion despite the parents' religious convictions. Who made the correct decision in this case? Do you think the court was warranted in overstepping the parents' wishes?

INVENTION STRATEGIES

After selecting the issue that is most interesting to you from your list, excluding those that are too broad, are matters of fact, or are simple disagreements over personal preferences, consider whether this issue can be investigated within the amount of time you have to write about it and within the number of pages you have been assigned.

At this point, you might wish to consider any or all of the following invention strategies that have proved useful to many writers in discovering their particular aspect of a topic, and how best to approach it in developing an essay. The basic invention strategies we will discuss include:

1. Free-writing
2. Five *W*'s
3. Cubing
4. Writing a dialogue
5. Discovering the pros and cons

Free-Writing

Free-writing is a technique for setting down whatever occurs to you on the topic within a few minutes to a half hour. There are no restrictions whatsoever as to what can or cannot be put down. Free-writing serves a sound psychological purpose. It lets you find out what you already know about the issue without imposing any editorial constraints on your thought processes. Simply free-associate everything you think of that has to do with this issue. Write without stopping to edit or correct. The only rule is to keep writing without stopping to think or to be critical about what you are writing. You will find that your thought processes will function more fully and creatively when you are not being critical. Also, the very act of expressing your thoughts in writing compels you to clarify what you think. Simply free-associate, allowing your mind to come up with any thoughts without stopping to censor, evaluate, or edit them. Don't worry about spelling or punctuation or rules of grammar.

Free-writing is meant to be casual, informal, and tentative. You write to define the issue. Your goal is to get as clear a perception as you can of the key aspects of the issue in order to discover how you should focus your argument. For example, let's say that in your social psychology class you read an account of the Kitty Genovese case (in which a young woman was stabbed to death while her neighbors watched and did not call the police) and have decided to try to focus on the components of the case to discover a genuinely debatable topic.

Your free-writing might appear thus:

Why would 38 people ignore a woman's cries for help, maybe afraid to get involved, what were they thinking, hassles with the police, legal proceedings, open court and criminal would get off and come back and kill them, what did they say to themselves, why did they do nothing, isn't plausible that all 38 were apathetic, maybe each thought another called police, rationalize not doing anything wonder if the number of people has anything to do with the decision, how aware were these people of each other.

Five *W*'s

Next, you might wish to ask and answer questions journalists often use to define what can be known about the subject.

WHO is involved in this situation?
WHAT is at stake? WHAT action or outcome is hanging in the balance?
WHERE did the action take place?
WHEN did the action take place?
WHY is what happened an important issue?

In the above case, your answers might be:

WHO — 38 people, Kitty Genovese, the murderer
WHAT — Kitty Genovese is attacked as she returns home from work at 3 A.M. 38 of her neighbors in Kew Gardens, New York come to their windows when she cries out in terror. Not one comes to her assistance even though her assailant takes one-half hour to murder her. The murderer is twice frightened away and returns. No one so much as calls the police. She dies.
WHEN — 1968
WHERE — apartment building in Kew Gardens, Queens, New York.
WHY — why did none of the 38 people help the woman or call the police at any time during the 35 minutes? Why did the witnesses continue to look out of their windows at the scene only to ignore what was happening?

Cubing

The next step is to explore your topic from different angles. Cubing is an invention strategy to help you generate and develop material for your essay by looking at an issue from several angles. Cubing requires you to take the topic and write for a few minutes from each of the following perspectives.

1. What is the issue connected to or related to? What does this issue bring to mind, what common elements does this situation share with other situations that I am familiar with?
Your answer might be:

For me, the issue is connected with urban violence, crime in the subways, and the baffling question why people don't help victims of crime.

2. What is the issue similar to or different from? What distinguishes this situation from other situations that at first glance might look very similar?
Your answer might be:

Is this situation similar to the Holocaust? Does it involve the same phenomenon of being indifferent to what is happening to people around you? On the other hand, it is different from the Holocaust because then the German state acted criminally and here the government is against the criminal. It seems more similar to other cases of bystander noninvolvement, for example, subway riders not coming to the assistance of fellow passengers, even after the attackers have left the subway car.

3. Analyze the different elements involved. Break the topic into its component parts. How might the same event appear through the eyes of each of the people involved? How do they relate to each other?
Your answer might be:

By running away, the killer revealed he could have been scared off and it would not have taken very much to scare him. If the people watching literally did anything at all, the murder would not have taken place. There was no way for the people in the apartment building to know if the person being murdered was a friend or not. She could have been someone they knew. Or was there enough light to recognize her and no one cared that she was being murdered since they did not know her personally. Has our society made life so difficult for witnesses, in terms of police lineups, testimony in open court, endless trial delays, taking time off from work, that witnesses end up being victims of the system? The key point is that, psychologically, 38 people from very different backgrounds shared something in common that prevented all of them from taking any action. What could this be?

4. Define the issue. The purpose of defining is to try to arrive at a working definition of the topic. What are the distinctive elements in this particular situation that give it its unique quality or meaning? Try to isolate the most important qualities of the issue and discuss what they mean. Write for a few minutes. (You can use any of the techniques under "Definition" in Chapter 4.

Your answer might be:

Why didn't any of the 38 witnesses feel a sense of personal responsibility and intervene or at least call the police? Were they merely indifferent to the violence they were watching? Does living in a city make you not care about what is happening to others? Would I react the same way they did in the same situation? If asked before the event, most of the 38 people would probably have said they would have helped the victim, or at least called the police before this incident. What caused all of them not to do anything? So, the issue is what prevented each of them individually and collectively from acting?

Writing a Dialogue

Writing a dialogue is another invention strategy useful in discovering what is at stake in the issue. You invent a drama in which you discuss the issue from both sides, playing yourself as well as a devil's advocate to fairly represent different viewpoints. This technique depends on your ability to create an imaginary dialogue where you take both sides. To get started, you might wish to use a tape recorder and then transcribe your dialogue later. We all have had the experience of rehearsing conversations in order to clarify what we would say in different situations, and how we would answer someone who held the opposite view.

To construct the dialogue, simply begin by making an assertion that expresses your view on any aspect of the issue. Then swing around and put yourself in the position of someone who had an opposing viewpoint. Next, put down what you would reply as yourself. Then challenge that view by putting yourself in the frame of mind of your opponent who views the issue from a totally different angle or perspective. The technique is an old one, used by Socrates (as reported by Plato in the *Dialogues*) to challenge people to discover whether they had good reasons for supporting their beliefs. Being cross-examined forces you to look critically at assumptions you might take for granted, and pressures you to come up with reasons to support your views. Any reason able to survive objections raised by an opponent would qualify as a sound reason with which to support your belief.

You will know you are on the right track when the dialogue assumes a momentum of its own. It is important to avoid getting bogged down. If you get stuck, ask yourself a question, taking the part of the other person. You will find this a valuable technique for anticipating the counterarguments of those who would react negatively to the points you raise.

After you create your informal dialogue, you will want to identify and rank the reasons you have discovered on both sides of the issue from weakest to strongest.

For example, what follows is an imaginary dialogue between you and you-as-your-opponent. Your purpose in making up this dialogue was to systematically focus on each aspect of the topic of the Kitty Genovese case in order to discover a point of view to encapsulate in your thesis statement.

OPPONENT: The issue is apathy; people simply didn't care.

YOU: People were not apathetic, they were aware and did care, but were inhibited from acting.

OPPONENT: Maybe they rationalized not acting because each person believed someone else had called the police.

YOU: It's just not credible that in a group of 38 people not one person would care that someone was screaming for help while being murdered. It is much more likely that people did care but were afraid to get involved for some reason.

OPPONENT: I understand why they would be afraid to go down there and confront a killer personally, but why would they be afraid to call the police?

YOU: It isn't so simple as calling the police. They knew they would have to identify themselves, testify in open court, and if the killer got off or got out of jail he could return to kill them.

OPPONENT: Not true. All they had to do was phone in without giving a name and the police still would have come. How do you explain that?

YOU: You're right. Good point. Maybe each witness thought someone else had called the police and rationalized not calling for that reason.

OPPONENT: That might seem plausible at first but what about when they saw that the police did not arrive and the murderer returned, was frightened away again, and returned again. Remember, this whole attack took over 35 minutes.

YOU: Let's look at it from another angle. Would any one of these people have called if they thought they were the only witness and saw a crime being committed and knew they were the only one who could possibly stop it or report it to the police? I don't have any hard evidence, but I think chances would have been 38 times greater if any one of them thought they were the only one.

OPPONENT: So, you're saying that a number of people, all of whom were aware of each other's presence, are less likely to help a victim of street crime than they would be if they knew they were the only one who could call the police.

YOU: I guess that's what I mean. People are social animals and the behavior of individuals in a group is strongly influenced by the behavior of the group as a whole. I guess that's my thesis:

I think the 38 people who witnessed the murder of Kitty Genovese were inhibited from helping because as time went on it became obvious that the group had decided not to call the police, so ironically the longer the attack went on, the less likely it was anyone would call.

Discovering the Pros and Cons

The activities of note-gathering and exploration in free-writing, answering the five questions, cubing, and writing your own dialogue, should provide you with enough material to start looking at the issue in an organized way. You may find that your dialogue has given you some idea of how you would want to go about advancing your views and how you would defend your reasons if someone with an opposing viewpoint challenged them.

You should now be ready to prepare a list of pro and con points on each side, along with accompanying reasons.

List these reasons in two columns under pro and con headings and then arrange each list of reasons from weakest to strongest or vice versa. From the range of reasons on both sides of the issue, you should be able to discover the idea you believe will be important enough to serve as a focus of your argument. This idea should be expressed in one sentence (called *a thesis statement*) that asserts your view on the issue.

For example: A student who wished to explore the phenomenon of ESP (extra sensory perception) and look into the case that could be made for and against its existence might use all the previous invention strategies (free-writing, five W's, cubing, and dialogue) to generate the following list of points for and against the existence of ESP:

PRO
1. Premonitions of disaster, feelings of déjà vu, and strange coincidences suggest ESP exists.

CON
1. Belief in ESP gives people a sense of power, leads them to think the future can be predicted and controlled, and boosts their egos—who wouldn't want to believe in ESP?

PRO

2. One of the conditions of having ESP is that you cannot use it for personal gain.

CON

2. If ESP existed, those who had it would be multimillionaires and would be able to prove it was true.

PRO

3. The evidence found to prove the existence of any new phenomenon in the past has always been scant and the existence of the phenomenon difficult to prove. For example, Galileo was almost killed when he suggested that the sun, not the earth, was at the center of the solar system. When Louis Pasteur introduced his germ theory, medical men scoffed at it as being a "ridiculous fiction."

CON

3. No one has been able to demonstrate the existence of ESP under research conditions. A phenomenon that cannot be replicated in the laboratory does not exist, for scientific purposes.

From this list of reasons, the student chose the concept of being able to replicate ESP under laboratory conditions as the focus of her argument. Her tentative thesis statement would read as follows:

All so-called demonstrations of the existence of ESP simply don't meet any of the criteria required for scientific research.

Notice that the thesis statement is phrased as a complete sentence and is stated in a way that would allow an opponent to be able to make a case for the opposite point of view. For example, in the above instance, an opponent might take the contrary position that laboratory replications of ESP really do meet the traditional criteria required of all scientific research. To test whether your thesis statement will allow you to create an argument, turn it around and see if you can make a case from the opposite side.

ARRIVING AT A THESIS

It may take several tries to arrive at a clear and supportable thesis statement. Arriving at a thesis involves discovering an idea you think is important enough to serve as the focus of your essay. The thesis is stated in the form of a single sentence that asserts your personal response to an issue that others might respond to in different ways. If, for example, the issue was euthanasia, your response might be that "mercy killing, in some circumstances, is not only morally permissible but a humane course of action." Or, you might wish to assert the contrary, that "mercy killing, under any circumstances, is not morally permissible."

If the issue were the crime-stoppers program, your thesis might be "crime-stoppers has proved its value in solving crimes, recovering property, and obtaining convictions in cases that previously baffled investigators." By contrast, you might wish to argue the opposite position, that is, "crime-stoppers should be abolished on the grounds that it invites the erosion of vital civil liberties guaranteed by the Sixth Amendment's provision against anonymous accusations."

The thesis usually is not the first thought that springs to mind on an issue; it should not be an automatic response but rather an idea you have carefully considered. The thesis is an idea that you have arrived at by thinking through an issue or problem until you feel you have come up with an opinion capable of being substantiated with good reasons. Of course, it won't be until you get into the actual process of writing the essay that you will discover whether you have enough good reasons and supporting evidence to persuade your audience to agree with your thesis.

The thesis statement should be phrased as an assertion that makes a claim of fact (what is it?), value (is it good or bad?), causation (what caused it?), or policy (what should be done about it?). For example, the thesis statement "mercy killing, under any circumstances, is not morally permissible" expresses a value judgment that requires the writer to persuade the audience to agree with a set of moral criteria, and then to judge the phenomenon of mercy killing accordingly.

Obviously, it is helpful to figure out what kind of question your thesis, and consequently your entire essay, will answer since the methods by which your essay will be developed are keyed to the specific goal you have in mind. The kind of evidence you would use and how you would develop your argument would, of course, depend on your specific thesis, but here are some examples of different kinds of thesis statements along with possible ways of developing them.

1. A thesis statement that makes a *factual claim:* "Nearly three-quarters of the American people believe in some form of life after death." To develop a factual claim like this you would probably need to cite evidence provided by reputable public opinion polls such as those conducted by Lou Harris or the George Gallup organization.

2. A thesis statement that makes a *causal claim:* "De-institutionalization programs by the nation's hospitals is the major cause of the hundreds of thousands of homeless people wandering the streets of our major cities." Notice how the thesis statement implies how the paper should be organized. The author would need to show what the hospital policy was before, why it was changed, and exactly what effects the

change produced. It is important not to assume that your thesis statement is permanent. In this case, the writer discovered midway into the process of writing the essay that a big part of the homeless population in our big cities were the unemployed and all those who simply could not afford the price of housing. This meant that the thesis would have to be modified, restated, or perhaps even scrapped entirely.

3. A thesis statement that makes a *value claim:* "Hollywood stars and producers should not be treated preferentially by being allowed to work off drug sentences in community service whereas ordinary people convicted of the same crimes would have to serve jail time." Notice how this thesis statement implies that the paper should be organized around a comparison showing how Hollywood stars are treated in contrast to how ordinary people are treated who have committed the same drug-related crimes.

4. A thesis statement that makes a *policy claim:* "Since the federal government already requires health warnings on every pack of cigarettes and forbids advertising of cigarettes on radio and television, tax money should not be used to subsidize tobacco growers." The argument here is a recommendation based on what the writer perceives as an inadvisable government policy.

A good thesis statement is like a schematic blueprint of a building that shows what the building will look like before money, effort, and time are spent on its construction. By the same token, it makes more sense to put in extra time in drafting your thesis statement than in having to spend extra time later extensively rewriting your entire essay hoping that some central point or thesis will emerge. For instance, a student's essay (see Chapter 6, "Writing a Research Paper") was originally organized around the thesis that:

> In order to combat the drug problem, the federal government should encourage crop substitution in countries where drugs are produced, impose mandatory random drug testing in the workplace, and spend more money on treatment centers and preventive mass education programs.

As it stands, this thesis statement has no central focus. An essay organized around it would go off in all directions. But this would become apparent only after the student had spent considerable time and effort. Think of how much more efficient it would be to revise the thesis statement so that everything in the essay would tie into one central point. In its revised form the thesis statement reads as follows:

> Short of changing society's attitude toward using drugs, only federally funded mass education stands a real chance of stopping the drug epidemic.

The thesis should express the idea that you would want your audience to reach after they had read through your entire essay. Place the thesis statement in the first paragraph or group of paragraphs so that your readers will be able to evaluate each of the reasons you present to support your thesis and be better able to perceive the relationship between these reasons and the main idea of your argument.

MAKING UP AN OUTLINE

If you have a workable thesis that expresses the conclusion you would want your audience to reach, consider whether it is capable of being adequately supported with evidence in the form of examples, statistics, or expert testimony. An easy way to do this, and at the same time to see what the structure of the paper you intend to write will look like, is to draw up an outline before writing the rough draft. For example, the outline of the student paper in Chapter 6, with the kinds of evidence brought in to support each idea, appears as follows:

    I. Current theories explaining widespread drug use.
      —supported by evidence in the form of expert opinions by a psychologist and a sociologist

   II. Increasing drug use in the success-oriented areas of sports, finance, and entertainment.
      —supported by evidence of personal testimony, sports medicine experts, interviews, and surveys

  III. Unsuccessful efforts of the government to stop the drug epidemic.
      —supported by statistics, reports by government agencies, testimony of psychologists and lawyers, and court cases

  IV. The crucial role of education in preventing drug abuse.
      —supported by government supplied statistics

Even if it is only an informal outline, as long as it sets the boundaries for different sections of your paper it will prove invaluable as a blueprint in pointing out structural weaknesses in the organization of your essay. The outline might reveal that two short, partially developed sections in the argument might be better joined together as one complete, fully developed section. Likewise, your outline may disclose an overly long section that might be more effective if it were split into two or more shorter paragraphs. Check your outline to make sure your essay has covered all the important points necessary to the development of your argument.

CHOICES IN ORGANIZING YOUR ESSAY

The choices open to the writer in organizing an argumentative essay depend on the nature of the thesis and the specific writing task it entails. The traditional argumentative essay has three parts: the introduction, the middle or body, and the conclusion.

Writing the Introduction

The function of the initial paragraph or introduction is to engage the reader in the central issue and to present your claim regarding the question at hand. If you intend to disagree with widely held views or if the nature of the issue is complex or unfamiliar to your readers, you might wish to use the first few paragraphs to briefly summarize relevant background information before explicitly stating your thesis.

Some writers find it valuable to use the opening paragraphs to briefly acknowledge commonly held views opposed to the position taken in the essay. The introduction alerts readers to the fact that the writer is aware of opposite views and plans to rebut them while providing reasons and evidence supporting his or her own argument as the essay advances. By helping your readers to understand how you will organize your argument you are providing them with a map to follow in reading your essay.

Some writers find that a brief story or anecdote is an ideal way to focus the audience's attention on the subject. For example, Walter Berns introduces his argument for capital punishment "Crime and the Morality of the Death Penalty" (from *For Capital Punishment* [1979]) with an amusing anecdote that focuses the attention of the audience on the issue of capital punishment in a memorable way:

> It must be one of the oldest jokes in circulation. In the dark of a wild night a ship strikes a rock and sinks, but one of its sailors clings desperately to a piece of wreckage and is eventually cast up exhausted on an unknown and deserted beach. In the morning, he struggles to his feet and, rubbing his salt-encrusted eyes, looks around to learn where he is. The only human thing he sees is a gallows. "Thank God," he exclaims, "civilization."
> There cannot be many of us who have not heard this story or, when we first heard it, laughed at it. The sailor's reaction was, we think, absurd. Yet, however old the story, the fact is that the gallows has not been abolished in the United States even yet, and we count ourselves among the civilized peoples of the world. Moreover, the attempt to have it abolished by the U.S. Supreme Court may only have succeeded in strengthening its structure.

Other writers use the strategy of opening with an especially apt quotation. Henry David Thoreau opens his famous essay "Civil Disobedience" (1849) with a quotation that sets the stage for his defense of individual conscience on the grounds that when conflicts arise between citizens and the government, "we should be men first and subjects afterward":

> I heartily accept the motto, "That government is best which governs least"; and I should like to see it acted up to more rapidly and systematically. Carried out, it finally amounts to this, which also I believe — "That government is best which governs not at all"; and when men are prepared for it, that will be the kind of government which they will have. Government is at best but an expedient; but most governments are usually, and all governments are sometimes, inexpedient.

Still other writers draw us in by beginning with a personal narrative, as does Richard Rodriguez in "Aria: A Memoir of a Bilingual Childhood" (1980):

> I remember, to start with, that day in Sacramento, in a California now nearly thirty years past, when I first entered a classroom — able to understand about fifty stray English words. The third of four children, I had been preceded by my older brother and sister to a neighborhood Roman Catholic school.

Another effective way to begin is by setting the stage or describing the setting as a backdrop against which to see the conflict the argument will explore. For example, this is the way Byron Dorgan opens his essay "America's Real Farm Problem: It Can Be Solved" (1983):

> Recent scenes from America's farm belt seem like a grainy film clip from the thirties. Young families putting their home and farm machinery on the auction block. Men, choked with emotion, breaking down in tears as they describe their plight. Angry farmers organizing, getting madder and madder. It's not as bad as the thirties yet, no governor has called out the National Guard to stop the foreclosures, the way North Dakota's William "Wild Bill" Langer did in 1933. But the pain is running deep. Losing a farm is not like having a new Chevrolet or a color TV repossessed. In many cases, what's lost is land that's been in the family for generations — and a way of life that for many is the only one they've ever known or wanted.

Writers may also choose to introduce their arguments in many other ways by defining key terms, offering a prediction, posing a thoughtful question, or using a touch of humor. William Ryan begins an argument (*Blaming the Victim* [1971]) whose thesis is that the poor are blamed for their own poverty with an amusing, but all too true, story:

Twenty years ago, Zero Mostel used to do a sketch in which he impersonated a Dixiecrat Senator conducting an investigation of the origins of World War II. At the climax of the sketch, the Senator boomed out, in an excruciating mixture of triumph and suspicion, "what was Pearl Harbor *doing* in the Pacific?" This is an extreme example of Blaming the Victim.

Titles. Even though your introductory paragraph is the most logical place to state your thesis, you can also put the central assertion of your essay in the title. Suzanne Britt does this in the title of her essay "That Lean and Hungry Look." You might recognize this title as a line from Shakespeare's play *Julius Caesar* (III.iv.5) expressing Caesar's mistrust of Cassius, one of the conspirators. The title immediately alerts readers to Britt's distrust of thin people in her witty defense of "chubbies."

It is best to avoid lengthy and overcomplicated titles that suggest a long, dreary road ahead. Titles do not necessarily have to contain the writer's thesis but should refer to the subject of the essay. For example, one would surmise correctly that William C. Martin's article "The God Hucksters of the Radio" was fashioned as an exposé of religious broadcasters who con the public.

Writing the Middle of the Essay

The middle or body of the essay presents and develops the main points of the argument in the order previewed in the introduction. The reasons presented by the writer will be those already preselected as the strongest from the prewriting activities. The middle also must identify counterarguments, state them fairly, and either modify the argument to accommodate them or refute them by presenting convincing reasons.

Any one of the argumentative strategies discussed in Chapter 2 may be used to develop the main body of the argument. That is, the writer may use causal analyses, definitions, comparisons, exemplification, or any other of the many other approaches available.

Writing the Conclusion

The conclusion of an argumentative essay may serve a variety of purposes. The writer may restate the thesis after reviewing the most convincing points in the argument. The writer may also choose to support a recommendation by closing with an appeal to the needs and values of the specific audience being addressed. In some cases, the conclusion itself may contain the strongest reasons and supporting evidence of the entire paper. Whatever ending is chosen, it is important for the reader to feel that the essay has completed all the important lines of thought the writer has set out to develop. This sense of closure can be achieved in many different ways. The following examples illustrate but a few.

The conclusion can echo the ideas in the opening paragraph. For instance, here are the introduction and the conclusion of an argument "Computer Monitoring and Other Dirty Tricks" (1985) by 9 to 5, National Association of Working Women, a group who claims that computer monitoring of office workers increases stress and threatens to reestablish an electronic version of "nineteenth-century garment industry sweat shops":

Introduction:

> From "Chuckle Pops" to electronic surveillance, office computers are being used in absurd and even threatening ways. Today there's a host of computer tools that allow managers to keep tabs on office workers to an extent that was never before possible. The goal is to increase productivity. The results range from the benign to the malevolent but they all add up to the same thing: miserable working conditions for office workers. We call these tools computer dirty tricks, and they are being played on many of the 13 million men and women who work on VDTs [video display terminals or computer screens].

Conclusion (note how this final paragraph recaps the opening):

> When, as a data processor tells us, her VDT flashes the message, "You're not working as fast as the person next to you," or when a claims processor logs in in the morning and the screen informs her that she's been fired, it may seem like some bad practical joke. But surveillance, work speed-ups, stress-related heart diseases and possible violation of Constitutional rights are dirty tricks in our book.
> And they are not acceptable in the office.

Another strategy writers use is to end on a note of reaffirmation and challenge, as does Edward Abbey in his argument in "The Right to Arms" (1979), arguing that those countries where citizens are prohibited from owning guns are, for the most part, oppressive police states:

> If guns are outlawed, only the government will have guns. Only the police, the secret police, the military. The hired servants of our rulers. Only the government—and a few outlaws. I intend to be among the outlaws.

Still another way to conclude an argumentative essay is with irony or a striking paradox. For example, C. R. Creekmore cites Brendan Gill in his argument "Cities Won't Drive You Crazy" (*Psychology Today* [1985]) to support his claim that, contrary to popular belief, cities are far better places in which to live than rural areas:

"It is a power that gives them the means of meeting the city on its own fierce terms of constant stress. And it is profoundly the case that your true (urbanite) rejoices in stress; the crowds, the dirt, the stench, the noise. Instead of depressing him, they urge him onto an unexpected 'high,' a state of euphoria in which the loftiest of ambitions seems readily attainable."

The most traditional kind of ending is one that sums up the points raised in the argument and brings the essay to a focused conclusion. We can see this in Betty Winston Baye's last paragraph of "You Men Want It Both Ways" (1985), an argument that states men may say they want educated and independent women but in reality they feel threatened by the prospect of a truly equal partner:

> There are dozens of other ways that men send out mixed signals to the women in their lives and show, through their words and deeds, that they really want it both ways. They want us to drive the car—but from the backseat. Mostly what they want is for things to be the way they used to be. That, however, is a pipe dream. Black women, like their counterparts of other races, are liberating their minds and their bodies from the shackles of the past. Increasingly, women are refusing to waste their lives trying to decode men's mixed messages and buying into some man's macho fantasies. Instead, many women who are or want to be high achievers are accepting the fact that the price of success may be temporary loneliness. And even that loneliness is relative, since many of us have learned that having a man isn't all there is to life.

Modifying the Basic Format According to the Kind of Argument

This basic format can be easily modified to accommodate different kinds of arguments. For example, if the argument makes a value judgment the introduction can describe the subject to be evaluated, provide background discussion, discuss the criteria being applied, and present the writer's opinion on the issue. In some cases the writer may have to stipulate a meaning for key terms (such as *euthanasia*) that appear in the claim.

The middle portion of the essay presents reasons that support the value judgment with persuasive evidence that backs up the reasons. Often an evaluation essay or value argument relies on comparison to establish that something is either good or bad as compared to something else. The middle portion may also contain a critical analysis of opposing value judgments along with reasons why the writer's value judgment should be accepted as more compelling.

The conclusion should allude to reasons developed within the essay and end on a note of commonality, by emphasizing the concerns, values, and beliefs shared with the audience.

If the argument focuses on a causal claim, the introduction must first describe the phenomenon and demonstrate its importance for the audience by using statistics, authoritative testimony, or illustrative examples.

The main portion of the essay identifies the probable causes of a single event or chain of events, distinguishing immediate causes from those that are remote. Like other forms of argument a causal claim requires the writer to consider alternative causes and give sound reasons for rejecting them.

The conclusion follows the pattern of other kinds of arguments. The writer concludes the essay by restating important points and by emphasizing how they support the thesis. The conclusion should convey a feeling of closure on the issue.

For policy arguments, a different plan of organization is required. Policy arguments are usually arranged in a problem-solution format that concludes with an appeal for action. Although the basic plan can be as simple as demonstrating the existence of a problem, proposing a solution, and providing reasons supported by evidence to accept the solution, a fully developed policy argument should delve into a whole range of related issues. The statement of the problem must show that the problem exists and is serious enough to need solving by documenting negative effects the problem is causing. In some cases, the writer might discuss the consequences of failing to solve the problem. Next, the writer must identify the cause of the problem, determining who or what has caused it, and provide a history of the problem, including a discussion of past efforts to solve it.

The writer is obliged not only to present reasons showing why the solution is practical but also to present and refute counter objections that may be made to the proposed solution.

The conclusion should stress that the solution is the best, feasible alternative, and may also make an appeal to the audience to act upon the writer's recommendation.

AUDIENCE

The specific audience for whom you are writing your argumentative essay determines, to some extent, what reasons you present to support your claim.

Unless you have inquired into what beliefs and attitudes your audience already holds, you won't be able to determine the best way to present your argument. Try to estimate how much the audience knows about the issue in question. If they are unfamiliar with the issue, you might provide a brief summary of background information to give them a more complete context in which to appreciate why this particular issue is an important one. If your audience already knows something about the issue, how do they feel about it?

For most writers, the simplest procedure consists of imagining yourself as part of the audience and then asking what would be necessary to convince you to agree with the assertion stated in the thesis. By being your own most critical reader, you can assess the credibility of the reasons that it would take to change your attitudes. From this viewpoint, you can evaluate whether the reasons given are adequate. If you are not persuaded, consider what better reasons and what additional evidence would convince you.

To understand what writers do to increase the chances that an argument will be accepted by the audience for whom it is intended, we might use a simple analogy: Writing an argumentative essay is rather like cooking and serving a meal. Just as the process of writing an essay moves through the stages of prewriting, writing, and revising, the process of preparing a meal moves through the stages of planning the meal, cooking the food, and serving it in an appetizing way.

Audience considerations play an important part in both processes. Both processes require the writer or chef to look at actions performed in the present with reference to what will be required in the future. The writer uses a variety of invention strategies to generate a thesis while looking at the thesis from the perspective of how well it will serve as a focus for a rough draft. The writer also evaluates the thesis in light of the purpose of the whole essay and the particular audience for whom it is intended. Only by looking to the end point of what can be accomplished by addressing this particular audience can the writer avoid formulating an unrealistic thesis. So, too, the chef looks ahead to the particular audience during the planning stages. Who the audience is and what the occasion is will alter the decision of what to cook. Without these considerations, the chef might begin to prepare a rib roast for vegetarians. The early decision of what to cook then determines what kitchen utensils will be needed, what will be kept out, and what will be put away.

To continue our analogy, the prewriting stage would be equivalent to preparing the food to be cooked — cleaning, washing, and cutting up the ingredients.

For the writer, the next stage, writing the first draft, involves combining the thesis, an outline of the organization of the paper, and any notes generated in the prewriting stage, while keeping in mind the particular needs, values, and concerns of the audience for whom the argument is being written. The order in which the writer raises points, the kinds of examples a particular audience would find effective, and questions of tone can be correctly gauged only by keeping in mind potential audience reactions.

Analogously, the chef might have to cook the food in a certain way to meet the unique requirements of his or her audience. This involves thinking of what you would do for others that you might not do for yourself. For instance, the chef would not be able to use salt to season food for people who were on low sodium diets.

For the writer, the third stage, revising, encompasses everything that must be done in terms of transforming the essay to make it easier to understand and more presentable. This can only be done effectively by keeping in mind how the particular audience for whom the essay is being written would react. Revising ambiguous words or unclear phrases and garbled sentences, checking to see that the essay has an attention-getting introduction and an effective conclusion, adding transition sentences to help the audience see the relationship between sections of the argument, and making final adjustments to the tone of the paper are some of the basic things writers do to modify first drafts to make arguments more persuasive for specific audiences.

By the same token, the chef might originally have been concerned only with transforming raw ingredients into cooked food, but at a certain point the issue becomes one of presentation—how the food will be served, what sort of sauces and garnishes will accompany it, how it will be carved, arranged, and so forth, for the enjoyment of those who will consume it.

At this later stage, all the ingredients acquire a significance based not only on what will be needed to transform these raw ingredients into cooked food, but into food to be served and appreciated by an audience.

To summarize, a traditional or "product approach" to writing or cooking would simply take the form of "do this at this stage" and "do this at that stage"; the "process approach," on the other hand, looks beyond the materials to the underlying psychological processes that must accompany the outward transformation of ingredients. At each stage of cooking a meal, the cook's perspective of the ingredients and what is required changes. So, too, the writer knows that you cannot speak of a completed piece of writing without taking into account the people who are going to read it.

This internal aspect of writing requires that you sometimes look forward and sometimes look backward, even though what goes on externally only appears to go forward step by step. Psychologically, the writer, like the chef, performs each action while keeping the big picture in mind so that he or she is always a step ahead mentally of the actual steps being performed.

The most important shift in perspective relates to seeing what is being prepared from the potential audience's point of view. In our analogy, the chef's attitude toward the food changes so that he or she no longer sees only the ingredients being transformed into this or that kind of a dish, but now perceives the task as one of making the food acceptable to others in terms of their needs, their anticipated expectations, and satisfactions. The chef must see the meal as having a new significance, no longer looking at it for itself, alone but for what it is able to give those who will eat it.

So, too, the writer must be able to look at the work as it is being written from the perspective of those who will read and "digest" it, and do everything forseeable to facilitate the audience being able to assimilate the essay and take away favorable impressions.

Writing the First Draft

As you begin putting your first draft on paper, you might find the following suggestions useful:

1. Give yourself enough time to write the rough draft so that you'll have time to look it over and make necessary changes.
2. Try not to get bogged down by questions of spelling and punctuation when you are putting the first draft together.
3. If you are not sure about spelling, punctuation, or a question of grammar, simply mark the spot and come back to it later.
4. Don't erase what you write. Instead, cross out lightly so that you can still use it later if you want to.
5. Keep in mind that this draft is temporary, discardable, and revel in the fact that for once neatness does *not* count.
6. Don't get hung up on how to open or close your argument. Just concentrate on stating your thesis and laying out the points and evidence that support it.
7. If you lose the thread of your argument, or find that you have hit the proverbial brick wall, you might want to take some time off and come back to it later. If this doesn't work, go back to notes you accumulated during the prewriting and invention stages and try to find another aspect to the topic that might prove more productive.

The rough draft is the place to put on paper the progression of reasons and supporting evidence that your readers will need to come to the conclusion you stated as your thesis at the outset. Since the purpose of the argument is to win people over to your side, it is important to look at your rough draft from the audience's point of view.

Whereas the introduction or opening paragraphs state the nature of the problem and may briefly touch on opposing arguments, the body of the essay creates a structure of assertions or claims backed up by evidence in the form of examples, statistics, or the testimony of experts. The exact order in which you acknowledge and respond to counterarguments will, of course, depend on the kind of argument you are presenting.

When you suspect your audience does not share your viewpoint your argument should be presented in the spirit of a mutual search for the best reasons to support your claim rather than in a spirit of trouncing the opposition. Your goal should be to present your argument as an open-minded inquiry, expressed in a reasonable tone, for people who may not share your views initially but who you assume will be fair enough to acknowledge any good reasons brought forward to support your argument.

Conclude your essay with the strongest and most persuasive reasons for your point of view.

With audiences who agree with you or who are neutral on the issue, choose the opposite method of organization. Begin the main part of your essay with the strongest reasons you have in order to reinforce the audience's attitudes and win their assent as quickly as you can.

You must make it as easy as possible for your audience to see the relationship among the different parts of your essay so that they can reach the conclusion stated in the thesis sentence at the outset of your argument.

Revising, Rewriting, and Editing

Although revision is often discussed as if it were something you do after writing your essay, it is actually part of the continuous editing process that goes on as you write your paper. Each time you change a word to improve how a sentence sounds, or make your essay more coherent by changing the order in which reasons are presented, or pursue any promising idea that may not have been apparent when you began writing, you are revising your essay.

Read your essay aloud so that you can hear how your writing sounds. Your ear will often tell you what your eye will not. As you listen to what you have written, you may hear inconsistencies in grammar, usage, and syntax that escaped your notice. Reading your work aloud is also a good way to discover repetitious words, sentence fragments, and run-ons.

In looking over your paper for stylistic flaws, be on the lookout for inappropriate, emotionally charged language, melodramatic figures of speech, and flowery metaphors. Writers who hold strong opinions are understandably susceptible to such linguistic excesses; argument is a dramatic form and tends to bring out the theatrical tendencies in some writers.

Ask whether the issues in your argument are raised in the best possible order. Could any paragraph or group of paragraphs be better placed elsewhere? Would some other arrangement contribute more effectively to the overall sense of the paper as expressed in the thesis? The type of development your paper should follow will depend in large part on your thesis, but certain general criteria should be met:

1. Have you offered sufficient evidence to support your assertions?
2. If your approach requires you to attack the credibility of an opposing viewpoint, have you summarized the opposing position before countering its main assertions?
3. Have you effectively questioned the assumptions underlying the opposing argument, disputed the validity of the evidence cited, and pointed out logical fallacies in the process by which the conclusions were reached?
4. Did you support your recommendations or proposed solutions with logical reasoning and compelling evidence?

If this seems like a tall order, keep in mind that all argument papers and to a lesser extent all research papers are expected to take into account diverse opinions on the subject. What would someone who holds a view opposite to your own have to say about your argument? What about the assumptions underlying your argument? Does any portion of your essay depend on shaky assumptions, whether implicit or explicitly stated, that would not withstand close scrutiny? Consider whether some of the assumptions you take for granted need to be explicitly stated for your audience.

Often writers are so immersed in formulating the argument that they omit transitional words and connecting phrases that readers will need to understand the relationship between different parts of the essay. These connections may seem self-evident to you, but the reader needs explicitly stated signaling words to perceive more accurately the underlying organization of your essay. Also, you may have inserted words and phrases that give the appearance of logical connections where none exist. Don't be fooled into thinking a generous sprinkling of *thuses*, *therefores*, and *moreovers* will lend an aura of coherence to your paper. The contrary is true. Inappropriate use of these words will alert the reader that all is not well and that your conclusions may not really follow from an adequate developed line of reasoning.

REFUTING ARGUMENTS

An important aspect of writing arguments depends on the ability to refute opposing views. In fact, some arguments are entirely refutations of the opposition's argument.

An analysis of someone else's argument, like any argument of your own, must center around a thesis or central assertion. When you evaluate another's argument the thesis will be your overall assessment of how convincingly the author has succeeded in bringing forward good reasons and persuasive evidence to justify the conclusions reached. Your thesis should not express your opinion of the issue but rather should be an objective evaluation of the skill with which the author uses different strategies of argumentation to present his or her case.

How Critical Thinking Can Be Used to Bridge the Gap between Analyzing Someone Else's Argument and Inventing Your Own

If you have never gone through the process of analyzing someone else's argument before creating your own, you might find it difficult to know what to look for. Fortunately, there are a number of strategies you can use both for analyzing someone else's argument and for inventing material for your own. For example, you might analyze someone else's argument to determine what the purpose of the author was and how well he or she accomplished it. You might describe the author's tone or voice and try to assess how much it contributed. How effectively does the writer use authorities, statistics, or examples to support the claim? Does the author identify the assumptions or warrants on which the argument is based, and are they ones with which you agree or disagree? To what extent does the author use the emotional connotations of language to try to persuade his or her audience? Do you see anything unworkable or disadvantageous about the solutions offered as an answer to the problem the essay addresses? All these and many other ways of analyzing someone else's argument can be used to create your own case. The entire range of strategies has come to be known collectively as *critical thinking*, which differs from taking things for granted or taking things at face value.

Critical thinking involves becoming aware of the reasoning processes other people use and that you yourself use in thinking about experiences. The central element in critical thinking is the ability to critically evaluate information. This means you must be able to identify the main idea underlying someone else's argument, locate the reasons and evidence that support the idea, be able to express the idea in your own words, and evaluate how well (in terms of formal strategies of argument) the author makes his or her case. You must also be able to see the relationship between the main idea and other things that you already know.

We think critically when we change our views about something from what we first thought. Critical thinking not only involves being willing to change your views when the evidence warrants it, but encompasses being able to see how the same phenomenon can be viewed very differently by people with different perspectives. For example, you might have seen a movie and not liked it initially and then seen it later on television and found it more enjoyable. By the same token, a first reaction of not liking someone you met might have been an automatic response. On reflection, you might have later changed your attitude.

In a different context, thinking critically means being open to new perspectives that add something to your understanding. First, of course, you must be aware of the angle from which you view events and your own preconceptions, expectations, and biases. Critical thinking makes it possible to generate ideas when you take the trouble to review what you think you already know. Often we discover we have been passively taking in information and making other people's beliefs our own without exploring or testing them. If someone else's argument makes you rethink things and examine reasons you have for holding beliefs, you will discover material enough for more essays than you will ever have time to write. In this sense, critical thinking means becoming aware of how you react to an issue. Of course, you must be honest enough to modify your views, if the evidence warrants it, as you go about the process of examining, questioning, and inquiring into the issue at stake in someone else's argument.

What follows are several kinds of strategies you can use as you analyze someone else's argument to generate material for your own:

1. What is missing in the argument? The first strategy involves paying attention not to what the argument says but what it does not say. This search for what is missing in an argument can turn up some valuable clues for generating your own. Information that does not appear and is not mentioned is often just as significant as the information as the writer chose to include. First, you must have already summarized the main points in the article. Then, make up another list of points that are not discussed, that is, information that you would have expected an article of this kind to have covered or touched on but that is missing. Write down the reasons why this missing material has been omitted, censored, or downplayed. What possible purpose could the author have had? As you look deeper below the surface of the argument, not for what is there but for what is missing, look at other techniques the writer may be using to lead you away from these areas. Specifically, is the writer using any logical fallacies (such as begging the question, attacking a straw man, or arguing *ad hominem*) to divert your attention? As you consider this other information you would expect to find but that is not there, look for vested interests or biases that could explain why information of a certain kind is missing.

2. Since an essential element in critical thinking is becoming aware of what you don't know about a subject, a second strategy is to analyze someone else's argument in terms of what you already know and what you didn't know about the issue. To do this, simply make a list of what concepts were already familiar to you and a second list of information or concepts that were new to you. Then write down three to five questions you would like answered about this new information and make a list of possible sources you might consult. You might also wish to turn to the research chapter (Chapter 6) for guidance on how to use the resources in your library.

3. As a third strategy, you might consider whether the argument you are evaluating presents a solution to a problem. List the short-term and long-term effects or consequences of the action the writer recommends. You might wish to evaluate the solution to see whether positive short-

term benefits are offset by possible negative long-term consequences not mentioned by the author. This might provide you with a starting point for your own argument.

4. After clearly stating what the author's position on an issue is, try to imagine other people who would view the same issue very differently. How would the concerns of these people be different from those of the writer? Try to think of as many different people representing as many different perspectives as you can. Now, try to think of a solution that would satisfy both the author and at least one other person who holds a different viewpoint. Imagine you are an arbitrator negotiating an agreement. How would your recommendation require both parties to compromise and reach an agreement? What would each party have to trade off? What lesser demands would you recommend that each give up to get most of what he or she wants? People with different views should not simply be diametrically opposed to the author's views or there will be no basis upon which to reach a compromise.

5. As an alternative to the previous strategy, if the writer whose argument you are analyzing recommends a solution, list all the alternatives you can think of that the person may have overlooked. In this case your own argument might be constructed as setting forth this better alternative to the one recommended by the writer.

6. If, after analyzing someone else's argument, you have come up with a solution you think is better, draw up a list of all the ways you would be able to tell if the solution had worked once it had been put into action. If you can put down a list of specific, concrete circumstances that would indicate the solution is working, you can use these to generate hypothetical examples that will support your own argument.

Another element of critical thinking requires you to relate your own ideas to those of the person who wrote the argument you are reading. You can use this to generate material for your own essay if you can evaluate your own attitudes at the same time that you are evaluating someone else's argument. The more you are challenged, or even threatened by what the person says, the greater your opportunity to use the conflict, tension, or discomfort being produced to look at your own values and beliefs.

Does the writer you are analyzing make assumptions about human nature, society, religion, or culture, that are different from your own? In what way do they differ? Keep in mind that you wouldn't even be aware you had these assumptions if you weren't analyzing why someone else's assumptions are making you uncomfortable. Essentially, this is how the analytical process can be used as an opportunity for critical thinking. The extent to which the argument you are reading forces you to question your own highly personal beliefs and values, or provides you with new perspectives you can use to change your own point of view, depends solely on how you react. The encounter with someone who makes a compelling case for something you do not believe can be unsettling because it forces you to examine the reasons underlying your own beliefs. The point is that you can use any discomfort creatively as an opportunity to engage the issue.

To do this, of course, you must be able (1) to identify the basic issues at stake, (2) to summarize in your own words the main points of the arguments, (3) to understand why the writer used particular kinds of evidence to support this specific viewpoint. Most important, use the occasion of analyzing someone else's argument as an opportunity to critically examine your own beliefs. Read critically and try to be aware of your own attitudes as they emerge while you are responding to someone else's argument. To help you do this, some specific guidelines follow.

When evaluating someone else's argument, consider what the author's purpose was in writing the argument. Was it to inform, explain, solve a problem, make a recommendation, amuse, enlighten, or some combination of these goals? How is the tone or voice the author projects toward the audience related to his or her purpose in writing the argument? Did the author take into account what the audience already knew or would want to know about the subject? What strategies did the author use to adapt his or her presentation for a particular audience and what kinds of changes would the author have to make in adapting the same viewpoint for a different audience?

You may find it helpful to write a short summary after each major section to determine if you understand the argument. These summaries can then serve as a basis for an analysis of how successfully the author employs reasons, examples, statistics, and expert testimony to support and develop the main points of the argument.

For example, if the argument you are analyzing cites authorities to support a claim, assess whether the authorities bring the most timely opinion to bear on the subject, display any obvious biases, and determine whether they are experts in that particular field. Watch for experts described as "often quoted" or "highly placed reliable sources" without accompanying names, credentials, or appropriate documentation. If the experts cited offer what purports to be a reliable interpretation of facts, consider whether the writer also quotes equally trustworthy experts who hold opposing views.

If statistics are cited to support a point, judge whether they derive from verifiable and trustworthy sources. Also, evaluate whether the author has interpreted them in ways that are beneficial to his or her argument, whereas someone who held an opposing view could interpret them quite differently. If real-life examples are presented to support the author's opinions, determine whether they are representative or are too atypical to be used as evidence. If the author relies on hypothetical examples or analogies to dramatize ideas that otherwise would be hard to grasp, judge whether these examples are too farfetched to back up the claims being made. If the argument being evaluated depends on the stipulated definition of a term that might be defined in different ways, check whether the author provides clear reasons to indicate why one definition rather than another is preferable.

As you list observations about the various elements of the argument you are analyzing, take a closer look at the assumptions underlying the argument and see if you can locate and distinguish between those assumptions that are explicitly stated and those that are implicit. Once the author's assumptions are identified, you can compare them with your own beliefs about the subject, determine whether these assumptions are commonly held, and make a judgment as to their validity. Would you readily agree with these assumptions? If not, has the author provided sound reasons and supporting evidence to persuade you to change your mind?

A signal that the writer is relying more on implicit assumptions than on evidence, statistics, expert testimony, logic, and sound reasoning is the frequent use of words whose emotional connotations are meant to prejudice the reader into automatically agreeing with the author's viewpoint. When you come across one of these loaded terms or phrases, or question-begging epithets, ask yourself whether you agree with the writer's characterizations. Are the assumptions underlying these characterizations supported independently by real reasons and examples elsewhere in the article? When looking for a conclusion, try to identify pivotal terms (*because, likewise, consequently*) that indicate the writer is bringing together various elements of the argument to support an inference or generalization. Is the conclusion warranted by the preceding facts and reasons?

The arguments you are evaluating may not appear legitimate, may contain flawed reasoning, be impractical, or otherwise may pose unrealistic or unworkable alternatives. To refute these kinds of arguments look carefully to see whether the claim is based on implausible warrants or assumptions, whether the proposed solutions would produce disadvantageous effects, whether evidence cited to support the claim is irrelevant or insufficient, or whether the logic underlying the reasoning is faulty. For a discussion of the most common logical fallacies, see Chapter 3. Bring the same standards to bear on an argument you are evaluating that you would on an argument you were writing. In this case, your argument will be developed as a critique or an evaluation of someone else's argument.

An Argument with a Student's Evaluation of It

The following argument, "The Business World as a Hunting Ground," comprises a chapter in Esther Vilar's *The Manipulated Man* (1971). The chapter is followed by student Helene Santos' evaluation.

Esther Vilar

The Business World as a Hunting Ground

Born of German parents in 1935 in Buenos Aires, Esther Vilar received a medical degree from the University of Buenos Aires. After moving to Munich, Germany, she practiced as a physician and now works as a free-lance writer. This chapter, "The Business World as a Hunting Ground," (from The Manipulated Man [1972]*) has as its thesis that men from earliest childhood are manipulated by women, first by their mothers, then by their wives. Vilar says "only women can break this vicious cycle of exploitation. But they will not break it, for they have no rational reason for doing so. Thus, the world will continue to sink into a kitchy, barbaric, and feebleminded morass of femininity."*

There are many women who take their place in the working world of today. Secretaries and shop assistants, factory workers and stewardesses —not to mention those countless hearty young women who populate the colleges and universities in ever-increasing numbers. One might even get the impression that woman's nature had undergone a radical change in the last twenty years. Today's young women appear to be less unfair than their mothers. They seem to have decided—perhaps out of pity for their victims—not to exploit men any more, but to become, in truth, their partners.

The impression is deceptive. The only truly important act in any woman's life is the selection of the right partner. In any other choice she can afford to make a mistake. Consequently, she will look for a man where he works or studies and where she can best observe and judge the necessary masculine qualities she values. Offices, factories, colleges, and universities are, to her, nothing but gigantic marriage markets.

The particular field chosen by any young woman as a hunting ground will depend to a large extent on the level of income of the man who has previously been her slave, in other words, her father. The daughters of men in the upper income brackets will choose colleges or universities. These offer the best chances of capturing a man who will earn enough to maintain the standards she has already acquired. Besides, a period of study for form's sake is much more convenient than a temporary employment. Girls from less-well-off homes will have to go into factories, shops, offices, or hospitals for a time—but again with the same purpose in mind. None of them intend to stay in these jobs for long. They will continue only until marriage—or, in cases of hardship, till pregnancy. This offers woman one important advantage: any woman who marries nowadays has given up her studies or her job "for the sake of the man of her choice"—and "sacrifices" of this nature create obligations.

4   Therefore, when women work and study, it merely serves to falsify statistics and furthermore to enslave men more hopelessly than ever, because education and the professions mean something very different when applied to women as opposed to men.

5   When a man works it is a matter of life and death, and, as a rule, the first years of his life are decisive. Any man of twenty-five who is not well on his way up the ladder can be considered, to all intents and purposes, a hopeless case. At this stage, all his faculties are being developed, and the fight with his competitors is a fight to the death. Behind a mask of business friendship, he is constantly on the watch for any sign of superiority in one of his associates, and he will note its appearance with anxiety. If this same associate shows signs of weakness or indecision, it must be taken advantage of at once. Yet man is only a tiny cog in a gigantic business machine, he himself being in effect exploited at every turn. When he drives others, he drives himself most of all. His orders are really orders from above, passed on by him. If the men at the top occasionally take time to praise him, it is not in order to make him happy: it is only to spur him on, to stimulate him to greater effort. For man, who was brought up to be proud and honorable, every working day is merely an endless series of humiliations. He shows enthusiasm for products he finds useless, he laughs at jokes he finds tasteless, he expresses opinions which are not his own. Not for a moment is he allowed to forget that the merest oversight may mean demotion, that one slip of the tongue may spell the end of his career.

6   Yet woman, who is the prime cause of all these struggles, and under whose very eyes these fights take place, just stands aside and watches. Going to work means to her flirting and dates, teasing and banter, with the odd bit of "labor" done for the sake of appearances—work for which, as a rule, she has no responsibility. She knows that she is only marking time, and even if she does have to go on working for one reason or another, at least she has had years of pleasant dreams. She watches men's battles from a safe distance, occasionally applauding one of the contestants, encouraging or scolding, and while she makes their coffee, opens their mail, or listens to their telephone conversations, she is cold-bloodedly taking her pick. The moment she has found "Mr. Right," she retires gracefully, leaving the field open to her successors.

7   The same applies to university education. American colleges admit more and more women, but the percentage who actually complete their courses is less than before the Second World War. They sit happily in lectures designing their spring wardrobe and between classes flirt with

the boys. With their scarlet nails carefully protected by transparent rubber gloves, they play around with corpses in the dissecting rooms, while their male colleagues realize their whole future is at stake. If a woman leaves the university with an engagement ring on her finger, she has earned her degree; man has hardly begun when he obtains his diploma. Degrees are, after all, easy to come by — you have only to memorize. How many examiners can tell the difference between real knowledge and bluff? Man, however, has to *understand* his subject as well. His later success will depend on whether his knowledge is well-founded; his later prestige will be built on this, and often other people's lives are dependent on it.

None of these battles exists for woman. If she breaks off her studies   8
and marries a university lecturer, she has achieved the same level as he has without exerting herself. As the wife of a factory owner she is treated with greater respect than he is (and not as somebody who at best would be employable on the assembly line in the same factory). As a wife she always has the same standard of living and social prestige and has to do nothing to maintain them — as he does. For this reason the quickest way to succeed is always to marry a successful man. She does not win him by her industry, ambition, or perseverance — but simply through an attractive appearance.

We have already seen what demands the well-trained man makes   9
on a woman's appearance. The best women trainers — without the least effort — catch the most successful fighters among men. The so-called "beautiful" women are usually those who have had an easy life from their childhood days and therefore have less reason than others to develop their intellectual gifts (intelligence is developed only through competition); it follows as a logical consequence that very successful men usually have abysmally stupid wives (unless, of course, one considers woman's skill at transforming herself into bait for man a feat of intelligence).

It has almost become a commonplace that a really successful man, be   10
he a company director, financier, shipping magnate, or orchestra conductor, will, when he reaches the zenith of his career, marry a beautiful model — usually his second or third wife. Men who have inherited money often take such a supergirl as their first wife — although she will be exchanged over the years for another. Yet, as a rule, models are women of little education who have not even finished school and who have nothing to do until they marry but look beautiful and pose becomingly in front of a camera. But they are "beautiful" — and that makes them potentially rich.

As soon as a woman has caught her man, she "gives up her career for   11
love" — or, at least, that is what she will tell him. After all, he could hardly be flattered by the thought that she had been saved in the nick of time from having to sweat her way through examinations. He would much rather get drunk on the idea of the love "that knows no compro-

mise," which this woman pretends to feel for him. Who knows, he thinks, she might have become a famous surgeon (celebrated prima ballerina, brilliant journalist), and she has given it all up for him. He would never believe that she preferred to be the wife of a famous surgeon, to have his income and prestige without having either the work or the responsibility. Therefore, he resolves to make her life at his side as comfortable as possible to compensate for her great sacrifice.

12   A small percentage (ten to twenty percent) of women students in industrial countries of the West do, in fact, obtain their degrees before they get married. Despite occasional exceptions, they are, as a rule, less attractive and have failed to catch a suitable provider while still in school. But then, this degree will automatically raise their market value, for there are certain types of men who feel bolstered if their wife has a degree — providing they have one themselves. It is clear evidence of his own cleverness if such a highly educated woman is interested in him. If by chance this female mastermind happens to be sexy, he will be beside himself with joy.

13   But not for long. Even women doctors, women sociologists, and women lawyers "sacrifice" their careers for their men, or at least set them aside. They withdraw into suburban ranch houses, have children, plant flower beds, and fill their homes with the usual trash. Within a few years these new entertainments obliterate the small amount of "expert knowledge," learned by rote, of course, and they become exactly like their female neighbors.

by Helene Santos

Are Men Really the Slaves of Women?

What follows is a student's analysis of Vilar's essay:

In "The Business World as a Hunting Ground," Vilar   1
substitutes catchy phrases for evidence to develop her
argument that women seek an education or employment to
find husbands. Vilar claims that women seek education
or employment to reach this objective because
"offices, factories, colleges and universities are,
to her, nothing but gigantic marriage markets."

Vilar says that women have to do nothing other than   2
marry someone who will support them for the rest of
their lives. Vilar claims that "as soon as a woman has
caught her man she 'gives up her career for love'—or,
at least, that is what she will tell him." Upon hearing
this, the husband, in Vilar's view, is so flattered and
guilt-ridden that "he resolves to make her life at his
side as comfortable as possible to compensate for her
great sacrifice."

Vilar fails to provide objective evidence such as   3
surveys, interviews, or case histories, to support her
thesis that women have no goals other than finding
"Mr. Right." For example, Vilar presents no
documentation to support her claim that the percentage
of women who graduated from American colleges are
"less than before the Second World War." The reader
has to depend on Vilar's interpretation because she
doesn't give any statistics. She bases her argument on
erroneous assumptions and unexamined beliefs. How can
Vilar possibly claim to know what motivates all women?

First Vilar asserts that the motivation of men and   4
women towards work and education is radically
different. She maintains that men view employment and
higher education as serious tasks on which their future
lives will depend, whereas women see work and study as
games to be played while seeking a husband.

5   Furthermore, Vilar says that because of their
    different attitudes towards education, men and women
    develop different levels of intelligence. Women, she
    claims, merely have to memorize enough to get by while
    man have to understand the material on which their
    future careers depend. Vilar assumes that no men
    memorize their way through school, and no women
    understand what they study unless, as she claims, they
    are so unattractive that they can't find a man to
    support them and must become intelligent in order to
    survive. Innate intelligence exists and does not
    develop out of the blue at the age of nineteen because
    one cannot find a husband. Such simplistic reasoning
    is characteristic of Vilar's argument.

6   Vilar believes that women attend universities solely
    to find men. In her view, men achieve social status
    through their careers whereas women marry to better
    themselves. For this reason, she thinks women work to
    observe more closely the money-making potential of
    prospective husbands. Vilar uses the phrase ''hunting
    ground'' to express her thesis that women view the
    workplace and universities as ''arenas'' in which to
    ''capture'' their ''prey.'' She describes men as having
    to struggle in a highly competitive work environment
    while women watch the battle, ''cold-bloodedly''
    taking their pick. Vilar asserts that for a woman,
    sex-appeal is a commodity that can be translated into
    marriage and a life of ease. Vilar fails to cite even
    one case history that might support these claims.

7   Women at work, according to Vilar, will be less capable
    as employees since husband ''hunting'' and not work is
    their primary objective. She uses phrases like ''odd
    bit of 'labor' done for the sake of appearances'' and
    ''for a time'' to imply that women are not serious about
    their jobs. Vilar says that for women work means
    flirting and dates. What of those dedicated and skilled
    women who take their jobs seriously? How would Vilar
    account for these women?

8   Moreover, Vilar would have us believe that women choose
    low-paying jobs with little responsibility because
    they do not take work seriously. Her tactic of
    ''blaming the victim'' fails to acknowledge that very
    often women are excluded from executive positions and

must take menial jobs in order to survive. Vilar often confuses cause and effect in this way.

Vilar's stereotyped view of women as sex objects 9
doesn't take into account that beauty is in the "eye
of the beholder," and more a matter of subjective
choice than Vilar assumes. She also stereotypes men by
portraying them as witless dupes who believe their
wives have given up possible careers as famous
surgeons, celebrated ballerinas, or brilliant
journalists to marry them.

Vilar claims that "very successful men usually have 10
abysmally stupid wives." She reaches this conclusion
through a parody of reasoning that runs as follows: (1)
"intelligence is developed only through
competition," (2) "so-called 'beautiful'
women . . . have had an easy life from their childhood
days," (3) "those who have had an easy life . . . have
less reason . . . to develop their intellectual
gifts," (4) "an attractive appearance" acts as
"bait" for a "really successful man," therefore (5)
"very successful men usually have abysmally stupid
wives." Why must beauty and intelligence be mutually
exclusive?

Vilar bases her argument on unexamined assumptions. 11
For instance, she assumes that no woman wants to be
single. She also assumes that no man wants to be married
and therefore must be manipulated into a lifetime
"obligation." Vilar ignores the many men who want to
get married and the large number of women who want to
remain single in order to pursue their education and
careers.

Vilar claims that women obtain degrees in order to 12
"raise their market value" or because they are so
unattractive that they cannot find a man to support
them. From this, she mistakenly concludes that only
unattractive women go on to have successful careers.
She also fails to mention the large number of women who
complete their degrees after getting married and
overlooks the many women who return to work after
marriage. In her view, only wives of unsuccessful
husbands return to work after marriage.

13 Vilar discounts objections to her argument by using phrases like "might . . . get the impression," "appear" and "seem." In this way, she suggests that those who believe opposing arguments are being fooled and only she is telling the truth.

14 Instead of citing evidence, examples, statistics, testimony, quotations, and surveys, as support for her claims, Vilar uses imaginative metaphors such as "hunting ground," "prey," "victim," "arena," "capturing," "cold-bloodedly," and "slave." Her strategy is to use words to create images whose connotations imply foregone conclusions. For example, she states, "the particular field chosen by any young woman as a hunting ground will depend to a large extent on the level of income of the man who has previously been her slave, in other words, her father." This statement appears to convey a conclusion, but is actually "begging the question." A closer look reveals Vilar's circular reasoning: Vilar asserts as a proven fact what the argument itself exists to prove-- "all men are slaves of women."

15 Despite Vilar's catchy phrases and stylistic flair, the lack of any objective evidence to prove her assertions makes it impossible to perceive her as a reliable observer or take her views seriously. Vilar presents herself as a hard-working, truly emancipated woman surrounded by silly, conniving women who giggle, flirt, play games, and "design their spring wardrobes" while sizing up their "prey."

16 Perhaps women do view the "business world as a hunting ground," but they are "hunting" things other than husbands such as self-esteem and rewarding careers.

This student has done an excellent job in analyzing Esther Vilar's "The Business World as a Hunting Ground":

1. The title of the essay "Are Men Really the Slaves of Women?" is effective in suggesting both the subject and the writer's skeptical attitude.
2. Santos identifies the subject, author, and title of the article early on and announces the thesis of her essay in the first sentence.
3. She skillfully summarizes Vilar's chief claims in order to give her readers a necessary background against which to understand her analysis and evaluation.

4. She considers and evaluates all of Vilar's main points, identifying contradictions in Vilar's reasoning.

5. She does an exceptionally good job of locating and analyzing the implicit assumptions in Vilar's argument.

6. Santos adroitly incorporates a few brief quotations to let the reader hear Vilar's voice at crucial points in her analysis. This is especially effective when she turns her attention to questions of word choice and emotionally loaded language in Vilar's essay.

7. Her essay has a sensible, easy-to-recognize, consistent organization. She analyzes Vilar's essay without getting sidetracked.

8. Santos' conclusion ties up all the loose ends with some stylistic grace using the metaphor of a "business world as a hunting ground" to challenge Vilar's main *premiss.*

9. One area for improvement in Santos' essay is sentence structure. Several of the extremely long sentences might be divided into shorter, clearer sentences. Another problem that could be easily corrected is her unvaried use of "Vilar" to begin sentences. Simply varying the opening of sentences with "she," "the author," "the writer," or "Ms. Vilar" would solve the problem.

THREE SHORT ARGUMENTS
FOR ANALYSIS

Suzanne Britt

That Lean and Hungry Look

Suzanne Britt's "That Lean and Hungry Look" first appeared in Newsweek *(October, 9, 1978). Britt teaches writing at Meredith College and at the Divinity School at Duke University. She writes a weekly newspaper column and is author of* Show and Tell *(a collection of essays) and* Skinny People Are Dull and Crunch like Carrots. *This engaging essay defends fat people against being stereotyped by our society. Britt contends that fat people have the ability to see all sides of an issue and have a better grasp of reality than do thin people who tend to believe in simplistic answers to complex problems. Many of Britt's conclusions are drawn by means of a deductive process of reasoning. She asserts that fat people are jolly, knowledgeable, convivial, and better equipped than thin people to deal with life's mysteries.*

1   Caesar was right. Thin people need watching. I've been watching them for most of my adult life, and I don't like what I see. When these narrow fellows spring at me, I quiver to my toes. Thin people come in all personalities, most of them menacing. You've got your "together" thin person, your mechanical thin person, your condescending thin person, your tsk-tsk thin person, your efficiency-expert thin person. All of them are dangerous.

2   In the first place, thin people aren't fun. They don't know how to goof off, at least in the best, fat sense of the word. They've always got to be adoing. Give them a coffee break, and they'll jog around the block. Supply them with a quiet evening at home, and they'll fix the screen door and lick S&H green stamps. They say things like "there aren't enough hours in the day." Fat people never say that. Fat people think the day is too damn long already.

3   Thin people make me tired. They've got speedy little metabolisms that cause them to bustle briskly. They're forever rubbing their bony

hands together and eyeing new problems to "tackle." I like to surround myself with sluggish, inert, easygoing fat people, the kind who believe that if you clean it up today, it'll just get dirty again tomorrow.

Some people say the business about the jolly fat person is a myth, 4 that all of us chubbies are neurotic, sick, sad people. I disagree. Fat people may not be chortling all day long, but they're a hell of a lot *nicer* than the wizened and shriveled. Thin people turn surly, mean and hard at a young age because they never learn the value of a hot-fudge sundae for easing tension. Thin people don't like gooey soft things because they themselves are neither gooey nor soft. They are crunchy and dull, like carrots. They go straight to the heart of the matter while fat people let things stay all blurry and hazy and vague, the way things actually are. Thin people want to face the truth. Fat people know there is no truth. One of my thin friends is always staring at complex, unsolvable problems and saying, "The key thing is . . ." Fat people never say that. They know there isn't any such thing as the key thing about anything.

Thin people believe in logic. Fat people see all sides. The sides fat 5 people see are rounded blobs, usually gray, always nebulous and truly not worth worrying about. But the thin person persists. "If you consume more calories than you burn," says one of my thin friends, "you will gain weight. It's that simple." Fat people always grin when they hear statements like that. They know better.

Fat people realize that life is illogical and unfair. They know very well 6 that God is not in his heaven and all is not right with the world. If God was up there, fat people could have two doughnuts and a big orange drink anytime they wanted.

Thin people have a long list of logical things they are always spouting 7 off to me. They hold up one finger at a time as they reel off these things, so I won't lose track. They speak slowly as if to a young child. The list is long and full of holes. It contains tidbits like "get a grip on yourself," "cigarettes kill," "cholesterol clogs," "fit as a fiddle," "ducks in a row," "organize" and "sound fiscal management." Phrases like that.

They think these 2,000 point plans lead to happiness. Fat people 8 know happiness is elusive at best and even if they could get the kind thin people talk about, they wouldn't want it. Wisely, fat people see that such programs are too dull, too hard, too off the mark. They are never better than a whole cheesecake.

Fat people know all about the mystery of life. They are the ones 9 acquainted with the night, with luck, with fate, with playing it by ear. One thin person I know once suggested that we arrange all the parts of a jigsaw puzzle into groups according to size, shape and color. He figured this would cut the time needed to complete the puzzle by at least 50 per cent. I said I wouldn't do it. One, I like to muddle through. Two, what good would it do to finish early? Three, the jigsaw puzzle isn't the important thing. The important thing is the fun of four people (one thin person included) sitting around a card table, working a jigsaw puzzle.

My thin friend had no use for my list. Instead of joining us, he went outside and mulched the boxwoods. The three remaining fat people finished the puzzle and made chocolate, double-fudged brownies to celebrate.

10   The main problem with thin people is they oppress. Their good intentions, bony torsos, tight ships, neat corners, cerebral machinations and pat solutions loom like dark clouds over the loose, comfortable, spread-out, soft world of the fat. Long after fat people have removed their coats and shoes and put their feet up on the coffee table, thin people are still sitting on the edge of the sofa, looking neat as a pin, discussing rutabagas. Fat people are heavily into fits of laughter, slapping their thighs and whooping it up, while thin people are still politely waiting for the punch line.

11   Thin people are downers. They like math and mortality and reasoned evaluation of the limitations of human beings. They have their skinny little acts together. They expound, prognose, probe and prick.

12   Fat people are convivial. They will like you even if you're irregular and have acne. They will come up with a good reason why you never wrote the great American novel. They will cry in your beer with you. They will put your name in the pot. They will let you off the hook. Fat people will gab, giggle, guffaw, gallumph, gyrate and gossip. They are gluttonous and goodly and great. What you want when you're down is soft and jiggly, not muscled and stable. Fat people know this. Fat people have plenty of room. Fat people will take you in.

Sample Analysis

CLAIM: Britt claims the stereotyped view of fat people as lazy, poorly adjusted, and unhappy with themselves is off the mark. Britt argues that in reality fat people have their priorities straight, don't oversimplify things, or see the world in a rigidly organized manner as do thin people. Consequently they enjoy a happier and more fulfilling life.

GROUNDS: Evidence in this essay takes a variety of forms, including a quote from Shakespeare's *Julius Caesar* as its title to support Britt's claim that thin people are pessimistic, power hungry, and not to be trusted. Her strategy consists in playing off the virtues of fat people as convivial, warm, open, against the lack of these qualities in thin people who, by contrast, are characterized as dull, worrying about nonexistent problems, and too defensive, paranoid, and rigid to enjoy themselves.

WARRANT: The value warrant that Britt appeals to in moving from the support to the claim is the assumption that many qualities, such as warmth, compassion, kindness, sense of humor, and tolerance, are far more important than superficial appearance.

PERSUADING THE AUDIENCE: There are few segments in the audience to whom Britt's winning good humor would not appeal, irrespective of what shape they are in. Addressing a culture that, for the most part, believes that "thin is in" requires Britt to describe those who are thin as possessing unappealing characteristics. Few people would wish to see themselves as oversimplifying things, being dull, seeing the world in a rigidly organized manner, believing in simplistic answers to complex problems, or being obsessive and morose.

That segment of the audience unhappy about being fat, which diets, exercises, and takes appetite suppressants, might welcome a defender and vicariously enjoy Britt's characterization of thin people. Those people who are fat and feel good about it (and either cannot lose weight or don't care to try) would find much to praise in this essay. Doubtless, some thin people will take offense; others will perceive obesity as symptomatic of some deeply rooted psychological problem. Other thin people will continue to see themselves as svelte, suave, and sprightly despite Britt's arguments; a few thin readers will be won over to Britt's viewpoint and will hurry to the nearest fast food emporium.

Questions for Discussion and Writing

1. How does Britt use a phrase from Shakespeare's play, *Julius Caesar* (and the supporting reference "Caesar was right"), to put forward an opinion about thin people that the rest of her essay will attempt to establish? How is the original context of the quote related to Britt's use of it?

2. Choose any two sections of Britt's essay and state her arguments in the form of syllogisms. Keep in mind that her arguments are often stated in the form of incomplete or abbreviated syllogisms, called *enthymemes,* which will require you to explicitly formulate the two premises on which she bases specific conclusions. For example, in paragraph 2, what major and minor *premisses* lead her to the conclusion that "thin people aren't fun"?

3. How does Britt deal with the counterarguments that the "jolly fat person is a myth" and "all of us chubbies are neurotic, sick, sad people"?

4. Evaluate the quality of Britt's reasoning in defending fat people against societal stereotyping. Keep in mind that there are lazy thin people and energetic fat people.

5. What reasons does Britt give to support her view that fat people have a less simplistic and better grasp of reality, than do thin people?

6. Summarize the list of attributes that Britt uses to characterize thin people on the one hand and fat people on the other. Whether or not you agree with her, write an essay in which you defend thin people while keeping in mind that there are just as many stereotypes about them as there are about fat people. Compare your essay to Britt's and decide who makes a better case.

7. If the person to whom you were engaged suddenly, inexplicably, and permanently became very thin or very fat, would you still go through with the wedding? Explain your answer in two short paragraphs exploring both possibilities.

8. To what extent do cultural attitudes shape our perception of fat or thin people? Keep in mind that in some cultures, past and present, food is (or was) very hard to come by, and being fat is a sign of prosperity and wealth. Also, remember that different aesthetic standards have applied at different times; for example, the women painted by Rubens were considered very beautiful because they were large and voluptuous.

9. Discuss how the tone of this essay reinforces the validity of Britt's assertions. That is, in what way does Britt's tone create the impression that she is a jolly, kind, and compassionate (except toward thin people) person with a great sense of humor?

Stephen Chapman

The Prisoner's Dilemma

Stephen Chapman has served as the associate editor of the New Republic *and as a columnist with the* Chicago Tribune. *In "The Prisoner's Dilemma" (which first appeared in the* New Republic *[March 8, 1980]) Chapman calls into question the widely held assumption that the system of imprisonment as punishment employed in the West is more humane and less barbaric than the methods of punishment (including flogging, stoning, amputation) practiced in Eastern Islamic cultures.*

If the punitive laws of Islam were applied for only one year, all the devastating injustices would be uprooted. Misdeeds must be punished by the law of retaliation: cut off the hands of the thief; kill the murderers; flog the adulterous woman or man. Your concerns, your "humanitarian" scruples are more childish than reasonable. Under the terms of Koranic law, any judge fulfilling the seven requirements (that he have reached puberty, be a believer, know the Koranic laws perfectly, be just, and not be affected by amnesia, or be a bastard, or be of the female sex) is qualified to be a judge in any type of case. He can thus judge and dispose of twenty trials in a single day, whereas the Occidental justice may take years to argue them out.

—from *Sayings of the Ayatollah Khomeini* (Bantam Books)

One of the amusements of life in the modern West is the opportunity 1 to observe the barbaric rituals of countries that are attached to the customs of the dark ages. Take Pakistan, for example, our newest ally and client state in Asia. Last October President Zia, in harmony with the Islamic fervor that is sweeping his part of the world, revived the traditional Moslem practice of flogging lawbreakers in public. In Pakistan, this qualified as mass entertainment, and no fewer than 10,000 law-abiding Pakistanis turned out to see justice done to 26 convicts. To Western sensibilities the spectacle seemed barbaric—both in the sense of cruel and in the sense of pre-civilized. In keeping with Islamic custom each of the unfortunates—who had been caught in prostitution raids the previous night and summarily convicted and sentenced—was stripped down to a pair of white shorts, which were painted with a red stripe across the buttocks (the target). Then he was shackled against an easel, with pads thoughtfully placed over the kidneys to prevent injury. The floggers were muscular, fierce-looking sorts—convicted murderers, as it happens—who paraded around the flogging platform in colorful loin-cloths. When the time for the ceremony began, one of the floggers took a running start and brought a five-foot stave down across the first victim's buttocks, eliciting screams from the convict and murmurs from the audience. Each of the 26 received from five to 15 lashes. One had to be carried from the stage unconscious.

2   Flogging is one of the punishments stipulated by Koranic law, which has made it a popular penological device in several Moslem countries, including Pakistan, Saudi Arabia, and, most recently, the ayatollah's Iran. Flogging, or *ta'zir*, is the general punishment prescribed for offenses that don't carry an explicit Koranic penalty. Some crimes carry automatic *hadd* punishments—stoning or scourging (a severe whipping) for illicit sex, scourging for drinking alcoholic beverages, amputation of the hands for theft. Other crimes—as varied as murder and abandoning Islam—carry the death penalty (usually carried out in public). Colorful practices like these have given the Islamic world an image in the West, as described by historian G. H. Jansen, "of blood dripping from the stumps of amputated hands and from the striped backs of malefactors, and piles of stones barely concealing the battered bodies of adulterous couples." Jansen, whose book *Militant Islam* is generally effusive in its praise of Islamic practices, grows squeamish when considering devices like flogging, amputation, and stoning. But they are given enthusiastic endorsement by the Koran itself.

3   Such traditions, we all must agree, are no sign of an advanced civilization. In the West, we have replaced these various punishments (including the death penalty in most cases) with a single device. Our custom is to confine criminals in prison for varying lengths of time. In Illinois, a reasonably typical state, grand theft carries a punishment of three to five years; armed robbery can get you from six to 30. The lowest form of felony theft is punishable by one to three years in prison. Most states impose longer sentences on habitual offenders. In Kentucky, for example, habitual offenders can be sentenced to life in prison. Other states are less brazen, preferring the more genteel sounding "indeterminate sentence," which allows parole boards to keep inmates locked up for as long as life. It was under an indeterminate sentence of one to 14 years that George Jackson served 12 years in California prisons for committing a $70 armed robbery. Under a Texas law imposing an automatic life sentence for a third felony conviction, a man was sent to jail for life last year because of three thefts adding up to less than $300 in property value. Texas also is famous for occasionally imposing extravagantly long sentences, often running into hundreds or thousands of years. This gives Texas a leg up on Maryland, which used to sentence some criminals to life plus a day—a distinctive if superfluous flourish.

4   The punishment *intended* by Western societies in sending their criminals to prison is the loss of freedom. But, as everyone knows, the actual punishment in most American prisons is of a wholly different order. The

February 2 riot at New Mexico's state prison in Santa Fe, one of several bloody prison riots in the nine years since the Attica bloodbath, once again dramatized the conditions of life in an American prison. Four hundred prisoners seized control of the prison before dawn. By sunset the next day 33 inmates had died at the hands of other convicts and another 40 people (including five guards) had been seriously hurt. Macabre stories came out of prisoners being hanged, murdered with blowtorches, decapitated, tortured, and mutilated in a variety of gruesome ways by drug-crazed rioters.

The Santa Fe penitentiary was typical of most maximum-security   5
facilities, with prisoners subject to overcrowding, filthy conditions, and routine violence. It also housed first-time, non-violent offenders, like check forgers and drug dealers, with murderers serving life sentences. In a recent lawsuit, the American Civil Liberties Union called the prison "totally unfit for human habitation." But the ACLU says New Mexico's penitentiary is far from the nation's worst.

That American prisons are a disgrace is taken for granted by experts   6
of every ideological stripe. Conservative James Q. Wilson has criticized our "crowded, antiquated prisons that require men and women to live in fear of one another and to suffer not only deprivation of liberty but a brutalizing regimen." Leftist Jessica Mitford has called our prisons "the ultimate expression of injustice and inhumanity." In 1973 a national commission concluded that "the American correctional system today appears to offer minimum protection to the public and maximum harm to the offender." Federal courts have ruled that confinement in prisons in 16 different states violates the constitutional ban on "cruel and unusual punishment."

What are the advantages of being a convicted criminal in an ad-   7
vanced culture? First there is the overcrowding in prisons. One Tennessee prison, for example, has a capacity of 806, according to accepted space standards, but it houses 2300 inmates. One Louisiana facility has confined four and five prisoners in a single six-foot-by-six-foot cell. Then there is the disease caused by overcrowding, unsanitary conditions, and poor or inadequate medical care. A federal appeals court noted that the Tennessee prison had suffered frequent outbreaks of infectious diseases like hepatitis and tuberculosis. But the most distinctive element of American prison life is its constant violence. In his book *Criminal Violence, Criminal Justice,* Charles Silberman noted that in one Louisiana prison, there were 211 stabbings in only three years, 11 of them fatal. There were 15 slayings in a prison in Massachusetts between 1972 and 1975. According to a federal court, in Alabama's penitentiaries (as in many others), "robbery, rape, extortion, theft and assault are everyday occurrences."

At least in regard to cruelty, it's not at all clear that the system of   8
punishment that has evolved in the West is less barbaric than the grotes-

que practices of Islam. Skeptical? Ask yourself: would you rather be subjected to a few minutes of intense pain and considerable public humiliation, or to be locked away for two or three years in a prison cell crowded with ill-tempered sociopaths? Would you rather lose a hand or spend 10 years or more in a typical state prison? I have taken my own survey on this matter. I have found no one who does not find the Islamic system hideous. And I have found no one who, given the choices mentioned above, would not prefer its penalties to our own.

9   The great divergence between Western and Islamic fashions in punishment is relatively recent. Until roughly the end of the 18th century, criminals in Western countries rarely were sent to prison. Instead they were subjected to an ingenious assortment of penalties. Many perpetrators of a variety of crimes simply were executed, usually by some imaginative and extremely unpleasant method involving prolonged torture, such as breaking on the wheel, burning at the stake, or drawing and quartering. Michel Foucault's book *Discipline and Punish: The Birth of the Prison* notes one form of capital punishment in which the condemned man's "belly was opened up, his entrails quickly ripped out, so that he had time to see them, with his own eyes, being thrown on the fire; in which he was finally decapitated and his body quartered." Some criminals were forced to serve on slave galleys. But in most cases various corporal measures such as pillorying, flogging, and branding sufficed.

10   In time, however, public sentiment recoiled against these measures. They were replaced by imprisonment, which was thought to have two advantages. First, it was considered to be more humane. Second, and more important, prison was supposed to hold out the possibility of rehabilitation — purging the criminal of his criminality — something that less civilized punishments did not even aspire to. An 1854 report by inspectors of the Pennsylvania prison system illustrates the hopes nurtured by humanitarian reformers:

> Depraved tendencies, characteristic of the convict, have been restrained by the absence of vicious association, and in the mild teaching of Christianity, the unhappy criminal finds a solace for an involuntary exile from the comforts of social life. If hungry, he is fed; if naked, he is clothed; if destitute of the first rudiments of education, he is taught to read and write; and if he has never been blessed with a means of livelihood, he is schooled in a mechanical art, which in after life may be to him the source of profit and respectability. Employment is not his toil nor labor, weariness. He embraces them with alacrity, as contributing to his moral and mental elevation.

11   Imprisonment is now the universal method of punishing criminals in the United States. It is thought to perform five functions, each of which has been given a label by criminologists. First, there is simple *retribution*: punishing the lawbreaker to serve society's sense of justice and to satisfy

the victims' desire for revenge. Second, there is *specific deterrence:* discouraging the offender from misbehaving in the future. Third, *general deterrence:* using the offender as an example to discourage others from turning to crime. Fourth, *prevention:* at least during the time he is kept off the streets, the criminal cannot victimize other members of society. Finally, and most important, there is *rehabilitation:* reforming the criminal so that when he returns to society he will be inclined to obey the laws and able to make an honest living.

How satisfactorily do American prisons perform by these criteria?   12
Well, of course, they do punish. But on the other scores they don't do so well. Their effect in discouraging future criminality by the prisoner or others is the subject of much debate, but the soaring rates of the last 20 years suggest that prisons are not a dramatically effectively deterrent to criminal behavior. Prisons do isolate convicted criminals, but only to divert crime from ordinary citizens to prison guards and fellow inmates. Almost no one contends anymore that prisons rehabilitate their inmates. If anything, they probably impede rehabilitation by forcing inmates into prolonged and almost exclusive association with other criminals. And prisons cost a lost of money. Housing a typical prisoner in a typical prison costs far more than a stint at a top university. This cost would be justified if prisons did the job they were intended for. But it is clear to all that prisons fail on the very grounds — humanity and hope of rehabilitation — that caused them to replace earlier, cheaper forms of punishment.

The universal acknowledgment that prisons do not rehabilitate crimi-   13
nals has produced two responses. The first is to retain the hope of rehabilitation but do away with imprisonment as much as possible and replace it with various forms of "alternative treatment," such as psychotherapy, supervised probation, and vocational training. Psychiatrist Karl Menninger, one of the principal critics of American penology, has suggested even more unconventional approaches, such as "a new job opportunity or a vacation trip, a course of reducing exercises, a cosmetic surgical operation or a herniotomy, some night school courses, a wedding in the family (even one for the patient!), an inspiring sermon." The starry-eyed approach naturally has produced a backlash from critics on the right, who think that it's time to abandon the goal of rehabilitation. They argue that prisons perform an important service just by keeping criminals off the streets, and thus should be used with that purpose in mind.

So the debate continues to rage in all the same old ruts. No one, of   14
course, would think of copying the medieval practices of Islamic nations and experimenting with punishments such as flogging and amputation. But let us consider them anyway. How do they compare with our American prison system in achieving the ostensible objectives of punishment? First, do they punish? Obviously they do, and in a uniquely painful and memorable way. Of course any sensible person, given the choice, would

prefer suffering these punishments to years of incarceration in a typical American prison. But presumably no Western penologist would criticize Islamic punishments on the grounds that they are not barbaric enough. Do they deter crime? Yes, and probably more effectively than sending convicts off to prison. Now we read about a prison sentence in the newspaper, then think no more about the criminal's payment for his crimes until, perhaps, years later we read a small item reporting his release. By contrast, one can easily imagine the vivid impression it would leave to be wandering through a local shopping center and to stumble onto the scene of some poor wretch being lustily flogged. And the occasional sight of an habitual offender walking around with a bloody stump at the end of his arm no doubt also would serve as a forceful reminder that crime does not pay.

15   Do flogging and amputation discourage recidivism? No one knows whether the scars on his back would dissuade a criminal from risking another crime, but it is hard to imagine that corporal measures could stimulate a higher rate of recidivism that already exists. Islamic forms of punishment do not serve the favorite new right goal of simply isolating criminals from the rest of society, but they may achieve the same purpose of making further crimes impossible. In the movie *Bonnie and Clyde*, Warren Beatty successfully robs a bank with his arm in a sling, but this must be dismissed as artistic license. It must be extraordinarily difficult, at the very least, to perform much violent crime with only one hand.

16   Do these medieval forms of punishment rehabilitate the criminal? Plainly not. But long prison terms do not rehabilitate either. And it is just as plain that typical Islamic punishments are no crueler to the convict than incarceration in the typical American state prison.

17   Of course there are other reasons besides its bizarre forms of punishment that the Islamic system of justice seems uncivilized to the Western mind. One is the absence of due process. Another is the long list of offenses — such as drinking, adultery, blasphemy, "profiteering," and so on — that can bring on conviction and punishment. A third is all the ritualistic mumbojumbo in pronouncements of Islamic law (like that talk about puberty and amnesia in the ayatollah's quotation at the beginning of this article). Even in these matters, however, a little cultural modesty is called for. The vast majority of American criminals are convicted and sentenced as a result of plea bargaining, in which due process plays almost no role. It has been only half a century since a wave of religious fundamentalism stirred this country to outlaw the consumption of alcoholic beverages. Most states also still have laws imposing austere constraints on sexual conduct. Only two weeks ago the *Washington Post* reported that the FBI had spent two and a half years and untold amounts of money to break up a nationwide pornography ring. Flogging the clients of prostitutes, as the Pakistanis did, does seem silly. But only a few months ago Mayor Koch of New York was proposing that clients caught in his own city have their names broadcast by radio stations. We

are not so far advanced on such matters as we often like to think. Finally, my lawyer friends assure me that the rules of jurisdiction for American courts contain plenty of petty requirements and bizarre distinctions that would sound silly enough to foreign ears.

Perhaps it sounds barbaric to talk of flogging and amputation, and perhaps it is. But our system of punishment also is barbaric, and proba-18 bly more so. Only cultural smugness about their system and willfull ignorance about our own make it easy to regard the one as cruel and the other as civilized. We inflict our cruelties away from public view, while nations like Pakistan stage them in front of 10,000 onlookers. Their outrages are visible; ours are not. Most Americans can live their lives for years without having their peace of mind disturbed by the knowledge of what goes on in our prisons. To choose imprisonment over flogging and amputation is not to choose human kindness over cruelty, but merely to prefer that our cruelties be kept out of sight, and out of mind.

Public flogging and amputation may be more barbaric forms of pun-19 ishment than imprisonment, even if they are not more cruel. Society may pay a higher price for them, even if the particular criminal does not. Revulsion against officially sanctioned violence and infliction of pain derives from something deeply ingrained in the Western conscience, and clearly it is something admirable. Grotesque displays of the sort that occur in Islamic countries probably breed a greater tolerance for physical cruelty, for example, which prisons do not do precisely because they conceal their cruelties. In fact it is our admirable intolerance for calculated violence that makes it necessary for us to conceal what we have not been able to do away with. In a way this is a good thing, since it holds out the hope that we may eventually find a way to do away with it. But in another way it is a bad thing, since it permits us to congratulate ourselves on our civilized humanitarianism while violating its norms in this one area of our national life.

Sample Analysis

CLAIM: Although we prefer to believe that punishment in modern western cultures is less barbaric than in some Islamic nations, Chapman points out that prisons in the West are overcrowded, violent, unsanitary, and inhuman places in which to be confined. Thus the West, suggests Chapman, can make no claim of moral superiority over the East in these matters.

GROUNDS: Chapman cites increasing crime rates over the last twenty years to support his claim that prison sentences do not deter crime. He also compares specific Eastern methods of public flogging, stoning, and scourging to the Western methods based on confinement (where inmates are routinely subjected to abuse and violence from inmates and guards alike) in terms of how well or poorly each system achieves goals of retribution, deterrence, and rehabilitation.

WARRANT: Chapman connects the evidence to the claim by appealing to the value warrant that a system that subjects prisoners to dehumanizing conditions over years in private is just as barbaric as one that subjects prisoners to a quick, humiliating, painful punishment in public. An implied second warrant is that a system of punishment that fails to achieve its stated goals should be reformed.

PERSUADING THE AUDIENCE: A civilized society likes to believe that its methods of punishing criminals are less cruel, more humane, and more effective than methods employed in cultures commonly perceived as less advanced. As a way of approaching the issue of prison reform, Chapman's rhetorical strategy ("your left hand or a decade in an American penitentiary, you decide") is highly effective in getting the audience to question its assumptions that Western practices of punishment are more civilized than those in other cultures. Readers of the *New Republic* for which this article was originally written might be expected to favor prison reform and would appreciate Chapman's unusual approach to this issue. Some members of the audience might even respond to the stated "dilemma" by choosing a quick flogging in public over a long drawn out confinement in dehumanizing conditions.

Questions for Discussion and Writing

1. How do practices of punishment in Eastern cultures differ from those in Western societies?

2. According to Chapman, in western culture there are five functions that imprisonment is thought to achieve: (1) retribution, (2) specific deterrence, (3) general deterrence, (4) prevention, and (5) rehabilitation. Summarize Chapman's arguments as to how satisfactorily American prisons perform these functions. Do you agree with his conclusion that "at least in regard to cruelty, it's not at all clear that the system of punishment that has evolved in the West is less barbaric than the grotesque practices of Islam"?

3. In a few short paragraphs indicate which system of justice, Eastern or Western, strikes you as being more inhumane and backward. Keep in mind Chapman's ironic portrayal of the "advantages of being a convicted criminal in an advanced culture" (para. 7).

4. What relationship does Chapman's depiction of different methods

of punishment in Eastern and Western cultures have to do with the title of his essay, "The Prisoner's Dilemma"? What exactly is the dilemma facing a hypothetical prisoner?

5. Write an essay that answers Chapman's question, "would you rather be subjected to a few minutes of intense pain and considerable public humiliation, or be locked away for two or three years in a prison cell crowded with ill-tempered sociopaths" (para. 8)?

6. What in your opinion is the significance of the fact that in the West punishment is private (i.e., culprits are sent to prison where they are kept out of the mainstream and confined for varying lengths of time) whereas in Eastern cultures punishment is public (the criminal is forced to suffer humiliation and violent physical punishment before a public audience)? How does this difference raise the question of what punishment is for, that is, what purpose it serves in Eastern versus Western cultures? Why is it significant that the nature and form of punishment in the West follows secular guidelines while in Islamic cultures punishment follows injunctions stipulated by Koranic law?

7. What is the relationship of the excerpt from *Sayings of the Ayatollah Khomeini* to Chapman's article?

8. How does Chapman use the rhetorical technique of comparison and contrast to organize his essay? To understand the structure better you might wish to create a topic outline to see clearly how specific portions of the article support one side or the other.

9. How is Chapman's attitude revealed both in the tone of the essay and in the title he has given it, "The Prisoner's Dilemma?"

10. If you wish to do a research paper on this topic, you might want to read any of the following books: Andrew Von Hirsh, *Doing Justice: The Choice of Punishments* (1976); Graeme Newman, *Just and Painful: A Case for Corporal Punishment of Criminals (1983);* Michel Foucault, *Discipline and Punish* (1977); Jessica Mitford, *Kind and Usual Punishment* (1973).

David Burnham

Surveillance

David Burnham's investigative skills have won him many awards as a reporter for UPI, Newsweek, CBS, and The New York Times. *His articles on police corruption in New York City, based in part on information from Frank Serpico and David Durk, were the basis for the movie* Serpico, *starring Al Pacino (1973), and led to the formation of the KNAPP Commission and reform of the New York police department. While working on a story about health and safety problems at the Kerr-McGee plutonium factory in Oklahoma, Burnham arranged a meeting with Karen Silkwood, a worker at the plant. Silkwood died under mysterious circumstances in a car crash on her way to that meeting. Her story was the basis for the movie* Silkwood, *starring Meryl Streep and Cher (1984).*

Burnham has always sought to alert the public to the increasing political dangers of new technologies and electronic surveillance. In this chapter from The Rise of the Computer State *(1983), Burnham interweaves personal narratives (obtained through interviews) and government records to document how information collected by the Census Bureau was used by the U.S. military in identifying and imprisoning 112,000 Japanese-Americans during World War II (despite a provision in the bureau's charter to prevent information from being turned against those from whom it was collected). Burnham uses this incident to alert the public to the danger that information collected by the government for benign purposes can subsequently be misused to violate guaranteed constitutional rights.*

> The right to be left alone — the most comprehensive of rights, and the right most valued by civilized men.
>
> —Louis D. Brandeis

1   Hiroshi Kashiwagi stood on the makeshift speaker's platform, the flatbed of a huge army truck. Painted in undulating camouflage patterns of tan and green and gray, the truck was out of place in the busy parking lot of the Tan Foran Shopping Center, just beyond the first range of hills south of San Francisco. Very few of the Sunday shoppers on that warm spring morning in 1981 stopped to hear the speaker's message.

2   But the small audience sitting in the folding chairs near the truck

listened intently as Kashiwagi read his memorial poem "A Meeting at Tule Lake." Tule Lake was one of the ten internment camps established by the United States at the beginning of World War II to hold 112,000 Japanese Americans — a majority of them native-born citizens — driven from their homes in California, Oregon and Washington. And the Tan Foran Shopping Center where the audience gathered to hear the poet was of special interest too. Four decades before it had been a racetrack that had been swiftly converted into an emergency assembly area where 8,033 Japanese Americans from the San Francisco area were held behind barbed-wire fences until they were shipped to the permanent detention centers such as Tule Lake.

Kashiwagi, wearing blue jeans, a plaid shirt and a tan jockey's cap, read his poem with melodic intensity: 3

"We are driven inside . . .
For three years or more,
For three years or more.
To see again the barbed-wire fence,
The guard towers, the MPs, the machine guns,
The bayonets, the tanks, the mess halls, the latrine.
It's right to know the bitter cold of winter,
The dust storms. How can we forget the sand, the sand?
Biting into our skin, filling our eyes and nose and mouth and ears,
Graying our hair in an instant.
How can we forget the sand, the sand?
It's right to recall the directives, their threats and lies, the meetings,
    the strikes, the resistance, the arrests, stockades, violent attacks,
    murder.
Derangement. Derangement. Pain, grief, separation.
Departure. Informers, recriminations, disagreements.
Loyalty, disloyalty. Yes, yes. No, no, no. Yes."

Kashiwagi's passionate words on that sunny February afternoon marked the day thirty-eight years before when President Roosevelt signed Executive Order 9066, a regulation effectively authorizing the army to remove all people of Japanese ancestry from the West Coast. The president's order has long been recognized as setting in motion the single most massive civil-rights violation in the history of the United States. What has not been celebrated, however, is how an early version of the computer contributed to this dark moment.   4

First a brief outline of the incarceration itself. This extraordinary breach in the constitutional rights of 112,000 persons of Japanese descent frequently has been excused as a necessity of war. But the available evidence puts this reassuring assumption in doubt. J. Edgar Hoover, for example, contended that the Federal Bureau of Investigation could keep the relatively small number of serious Japanese suspects under direct   5 surveillance and that the demand for the evacuation of all Japanese Americans was "based primarily upon public political pressure rather than upon factual data."

6   Curtis B. Munson, a respected troubleshooter in the State Department, was appointed by President Roosevelt several months before Pearl Harbor specifically to investigate the loyalty of Japanese Americans. His report, kept secret until well after World War II, concluded: "For the most part the local Japanese are loyal to the United States or, at worst, hope that by remaining quiet they can avoid concentration camps or irresponsible mobs. We do not believe that they would be at the least any more disloyal than any other racial group in the United States with whom we went to war."

7   Commander K. D. Ringle, intelligence chief for the Southern California Naval District, agreed with Munson's analysis. He said a mass evacuation was "unwarranted" and argued that the question of what to do about the Japanese people living in the United States had been "magnified out of true proportion because of the physical characteristics of the people."

8   The intelligence officer's concern about the impact of racial prejudice on the government's policy was valid. Consider the argument for forced removal by the young attorney general of California. "When we are dealing with the Caucasian race we have methods that will test the loyalty of them. . . . But when we deal with the Japanese we are in an entirely different field and we cannot form an opinion that we believe to be sound." The author of this openly racist remark later earned a reputation as one of America's most liberal judges after he was appointed Chief Justice of the U.S. Supreme Court. His name was Earl Warren.

9   President Roosevelt came down on the side of the U.S. Army and the local politicians such as Warren. On February 19, 1942, he signed an order authorizing the secretary of the army to establish "military areas" from which all persons who did not have permission to enter could be excluded as a military necessity. The first action under the executive order was the expulsion of the entire Japanese American community from Terminal Island near Los Angeles on February 25 through 27. Armed soldiers marched into the old fishing village and ordered all persons of Japanese ancestry to leave their homes. A substantial majority of the refugees were citizens of the United States who had been born here. A large number were infants, children and women. No hearings were held. No charges were brought.

10   The initial targets were the Japanese Americans living close to the Pacific Ocean. But gradually the government campaign began to move inland. During the summer of 1942, the notices went up on the telephone polls around Fresno, California. A family named Okamura — three children, their parents and two grandparents — made hurried arrangements to leave their forty-acre farm.

11   "I was confused and terrified," recalls Raymond Okamura, then

eleven years old. "I didn't know what was happening to us on the trip to Arizona. It took four days. We had to keep the shades down in the railroad car and the train was locked and guarded. When we finally got to the Gila River Concentration Camp, it was hot and windy. We believe the dusty windstorms there probably were the cause of my grandfather's death about two weeks after we got to the camp."

Okamura has a round, gently smiling face, short cropped hair, and a   12
soft voice. He now lives in Berkeley with his wife and three children and works as a chemist with the California Health Department. He is obsessed by what the government did to his people. Okamura was the principal organizer of the memorial service at the Tan Foran Shopping Center. He also is the person who by persistent inquiry forced the Census Bureau, after forty years of evasion, to disclose the details of how it provided the army with material from the 1940 census to help in the roundup of the Japanese.

The Census Bureau data, recorded on punch cards that could be   13
quickly tabulated by a kind of mechanical computer, was used in the roundup despite a provision in the bureau's legal charter that said "in no case shall information furnished under the authority of this act be used to the detriment of the person or persons to whom such information relates."

The Census Bureau's admission was made in a letter from Vincent   14
Barabba, the director of the agency under both President Nixon and President Carter, in response to repeated inquiries from Okamura. The punch cards given the army, Barabba acknowledged, "provided sufficient geographical information to use for planning purposes in the evacuation program."

But the government official sought to obscure the significance of his   15
admission by informing Okamura that the Census Bureau cards had "contained no names or other identifiers for individuals." This same point was emphasized by the bureau in 1980 during an intense advertising campaign designed to persuade the American people of the sanctity of information given the bureau just before its most recent census. In one television spot, in fact, the Census Bureau proudly proclaimed that at the beginning of World War II the secretary of war had tried to persuade the bureau to disclose the names and addresses of all Japanese Americans living on the West Coast.

"In spite of the national emergency — and the hysteria — the bu-   16
reau's decision not to supply this information was upheld," the advertisement claimed.

Barabba's defense, while technically accurate, was misleading and   17
irrelevant. First of all, on at least one occasion when under pressure from the military the Census Bureau *did* provide law-enforcement officials with the names and addresses of individuals. This happened during World War I when the Justice Department was trying to track down and prosecute young men who were dodging the draft.

18   Second, and most important, in the age of the computer, aggregate information can be just as dangerous as information that is attached to an individual's name. A young lawyer from Texas named Tom Clark was the Justice Department's coordinator of alien control at the beginning of World War II. Clark subsequently was named attorney general and then associate justice of the Supreme Court. In an interview that is part of the Earl Warren Oral Liberty Project at the University of California at Berkeley, Clark described how he used the Census Bureau's aggregate information to round up the Japanese. It is worth noting that Clark, unlike Warren, later expressed deep personal regret about his involvement in the mass incarceration.

19   The Census Bureau, Clark explained, "would lay out on a table various city blocks where the Japanese lived and they would tell me how many were living in each block. Then the army engineers prepared housing; we started with the Santa Anita racetrack and turned the stalls into nice apartments. The army would designate certain blocks where the Japanese lived. A processing station, as it was called, would then be opened up in the designated area, and all the persons of Japanese descent were directed to report to that station and to bring with them all electronic devices such as radios, as well as firearms and anything of that nature. On the day that the army selected for removal, these people would report to the processing station with their clothing, personal effects, etc., and the army would move them by bus or by train to the camp where they were to stay for the duration."

20   So much for the benign quality of aggregate information. A second defense offered by Barabba was that the Census Bureau had been authorized to do whatever was necessary for the war effort by the Second War Powers Act. The law in question was introduced on January 22, 1942, passed by Congress on March 19 and signed by President Roosevelt on March 27. "But the Census Bureau," Okamura observed, "started releasing information on Japanese Americans to other agencies as early as December 17, 1941, well before the bill was introduced and over three months before the law took effect."

21   In the fall of 1981, the National Commission on Wartime Relocation and Internment of Civilians held a hearing in Washington to examine the circumstances of the roundup forty years before. One witness was Calvert L. Dedrick, a white-haired, blue-eyed statistician and sociologist who had been in charge of the project that used census material to tell the army exactly how many Japanese lived within each of its evacuation areas.

22   Dedrick told the commission that early in 1942 he had organized a mapping unit, an analytical unit, a tabulating unit and what was "in effect a war room, where we kept the officers in charge up-to-date as to where people were, how many were moving back and forth under permits of one kind or another."

Now retired, the elderly gentleman was proud of his work for the   23
army and insistent that it had not violated the law. One commission
member, however, Judge William Marutani of the Pennsylvania Court of
Common Pleas, was skeptical. In response to the judge's questions,
Dedrick offered an analogy about a current situation that the judge did
not find reassuring.

"The fact that there are so many Cubans living in Miami is a census   24
fact, a statistical fact, and if something happens to the Cubans in Miami
that is not our fault," Dedrick contended.

"Well, I don't want to prolong our discussion, but I cannot help but   25
make one comment," Judge Marutani replied. "That perhaps if I was a
Cuban-American and the Census Bureau came around, and particularly
if I lived in South Florida, I might leave the space blank or put something
other than Cuban with this type of interpretation."

"Then, sir," Dedrick replied, "you would be in violation of federal   26
law."

"Well, that would be better than being jailed for certain," the judge   27
shot back.

When the Supreme Court of the United States reviewed the issue   28
during the heat of World War II, however, a majority of the judges did
not share Judge Marutani's feelings. By a margin of six to three, in a
decision handed down in 1944, the Supreme Court held that the massed
incarceration of the people of Japanese ancestry was constitutional. Justice Owen J. Roberts was one of the three dissenters. He wrote that the
real purpose of the army regulation issued under President Roosevelt's
executive order was to lock up the defendants "in a concentration
camp." Justice Frank Murphy offered a second dissenting opinion.
"Being an obvious racial discrimination, the order deprives all those
within its scope of equal protection of the laws as guaranteed by the Fifth
Amendment."

At the Tan Foran Shopping Center almost four decades later, the   29
reedy sound of Japanese music and the nostalgic beat of such World War
II hit tunes as Glenn Miller's "In the Mood" shared equal time in the
loudspeakers set up by the memorial committee. Ray Okamura, despite
his anger, remained guardedly optimistic. The only hope, he said, "is the
attitude of the people in charge. This depends upon the public mood:
whether the public will stand for certain actions. The people of California were fully aware that the Japanese Americans were being locked up.
And they supported it. If the people had understood the true dangers,
the general erosion of freedom implied by the mass incarceration of the
Japanese Americans, it could have been halted."

In an extraordinarily complex world, however, understanding the   30
dangers can be hard. It is not easy, for example, to understand how
aggregate and statistical information can be used by a large organization
to control and manipulate people. It also is hard to comprehend just how

easy it is for a government agency or corporation to collect information for one purpose, often benign, and then use it for another purpose, sometimes malignant.

Sample Analysis

CLAIM: With the increasing technological ability to compile data bases and dossiers on individuals, Burnham argues that government must exercise every precaution to see that information gathered for a benign purpose is not used against those from whom the information was taken.

GROUND: The initial quotation by Justice Brandeis establishes the context. Burnham cites arguments in favor of confinement advanced by Earl Warren, quotes firsthand narratives to add a personal dimension, and explores the backgrounds of President Roosevelt's decision in the context of an election year (and against pragmatic counterarguments advanced by J. Edgar Hoover). Burnham describes in depth how private Census Bureau information on ancestry was used by the military in locating Japanese-Americans on the West Coast for internment.

WARRANT: Here, the warrant is the principle by which the Census Bureau was supposed to have been administered: "in no case shall information furnished under the authority of this act be used to the detriment of the person or persons to whom such information relates."

PERSUADING THE AUDIENCE: A commonly held value in this country is that the government or a corporation should not collect information under false pretenses and then use it against the people from whom it was taken. This view could be expected to prevail despite recognition that the government does need to gather and maintain accurate statistical information. The key question, however (and one whose significance has intensified with the increased use of computers to create data bases), is: at what point does the government's responsibility to the general public (however it conceives of that duty) come into conflict with the implied constitutional right (stated by Supreme Court Justice Brandeis) of the individual to "privacy."

Questions for Discussion and Writing

1. How does the initial quotation from former Supreme Court Justice Louis D. Brandeis create a conceptual framework for Burnham's essay? How does Burnham's use of the Brandeis quotation help establish the tone of the article and reveal at the outset his attitude toward the subject?

2. Were you surprised to discover that the argument (para. 8) for the forced removal of Japanese-Americans into internment camps was put forward by Earl Warren, then the "young attorney general of California"? Explain your reaction in light of Earl Warren's role as Chief Justice of the Supreme Court in the 1954 *Brown* v. *Board of Topeka* decision against public school desegregation.

3. What role do personal narratives by Kashiwagi and Okamura play in the development of Burnham's argument? What additional dimension do they add?

4. What kinds of pressures for and against internment does Burnham explore in the context of his argument? Evaluate the extent to which the decision by President Roosevelt (Executive Order 9066 "authorizing the army to remove all people of Japanese ancestry from the West Coast") was the result of political pressures, as distinct from considerations of national security. Specifically, how does Burnham use J. Edgar Hoover's opinion — that it was entirely feasible for the FBI to keep watch on particular Japanese-Americans whose actions posed a conceivable threat without herding a whole section off the population into internment camps — to imply that Roosevelt's decision for internment reflected political considerations rather than demands of national security?

5. In what specific way was information "recorded on punch cards that could be quickly tabulated by a kind of mechanical computer" used to assist the military in identifying and incarcerating 112,000 persons of Japanese descent?

6. Did Burnham's inclusion of the dialogue between Judge William Marutani and Calvert L. Dedrick (paras. 24–27) lead you to believe that what happened to Japanese-Americans might happen just as easily to Cubans living in south Florida? In what ways are the situations similar and in what ways are they different? To what extent do you think that the issue raised in this exchange explains why such a low percentage of illegal aliens have taken advantage of the government's offer of amnesty? Why would so many people think it might be better to continue to take their chances, without registering, than come forward?

7. How does Burnham's description of the willingness of the Census Bureau — under pressure from the military — to provide law enforcement officials with the names and addresses of persons of Japanese descent illustrate his thesis: "computerized information makes it easy for a government agency or corporation to collect

information for one purpose, often benign, and then use it for another purpose, sometimes malignant."

8. After reading Burnham's essay, write an essay that addresses the central issue of how to determine when legitimate needs to gather and maintain accurate statistical information on the population at large comes into conflict with existing constitutional rights against surveillance and the misuse of that information. For example, the national health service has a need to have accurate up-to-date statistics on how many people have AIDS or AIDS-related disorders, whereas individuals may well fear that results of blood tests and other hospital records, obtained confidentially, might be used to deny them employment, insurance, housing, and routinely available benefits that are the rights of all citizens.

9. Look through your wallet and describe all the places where information about you might be recorded in computer data banks.

10. If you wish to do a research paper on this topic, you might wish to read any of the following books: Joseph Weisenbaum, *Computer Power and Computer Reason* (1976); John Wicklein, *Electronic Nightmare: The New Communication and Freedom* (1979); Alan F. Westin and Michael A. Baker, *Databanks in a Free Society: Computers, Record-Keeping and Privacy* (1972); Frank J. Donner, *The Age of Surveillance* (1980).

6

Writing a Research Paper

The research paper (sometimes called the *library paper, term paper,* or *source paper*) contains the results of your investigation of an important question through an orderly and close examination of a broad range of available sources. Ideally the results of your research will shed new light on the subject of the inquiry. The process of writing a research paper is an invaluable opportunity for you to develop the ability to discover and limit a research topic, gain skill in using the library, evaluate the usefulness of source materials, read critically, take worthwhile notes, organize information in the arrangement that best illuminates the answer to the research question, and become proficient in putting together and documenting the results of an extended and systematic study.

Choosing a Topic

The process of discovering a topic and narrowing it down to a manageable issue that you can focus on and adequately investigate for a paper of seven to ten pages in the time available involves several steps. If you have not been assigned a topic and are free to choose any topic you wish, ask yourself what issues you deeply care about or what problems urgently need solutions. Feel free to draw on your own personal experience for clues as to what issues, problems, ideas, or concerns you might like to explore. If you have only a general subject in mind, try the invention technique called *brainstorming*. Simply set aside a block of time of from ten to thirty minutes, sit down with some paper and pencils, and without paying any attention to spelling or grammar list all the possibilities that come to mind on the question or problem. Don't be critical of what you are writing. Go ahead and put down everything about the subject that might hold the key to a problem worth solving or an issue worth arguing about. Give yourself reasons why the subject would be important enough to occupy your time or how your audience might benefit from knowing more about the subject. You might also want to consider using other invention strategies (the five W's, cubing, or writing a dialogue) discussed in Chapter 5.

One of the following topics might serve as a starting point for your research paper. The list is useful because in each case a wide range of books, articles, and other source materials are available.

Victims' compensation laws
Technological advances in robot production
Prescription drug abuse
World money crisis
Nuclear balance of terror
Patterns of tourism: Who's going where?
The creationism debate
History of any "ism" (communism, romanticism, and so forth)
Behavior modification: Stop smoking, overeating, insomnia
How are recent changes within the Catholic church received?
Astrology debunked
Origin of social rituals: Cocktail parties
Rites of passage in primitive and civilized cultures
History of a famous rock band: Rolling Stones, the E Street Band,
the Traveling Wilbury's, Tom Petty and the Heartbreakers
Some aspect of mythology
What do apprentices do in various fields: Electrician, plumber,
police officer, priest, and so on
Organ transplants
Washington lobbyists
Customs of hospitality around the world
Biological warfare
What's involved in voodoo?
Themes in the work of any artist, cartoonist, illustrator
The right to die issue: a dilemma for religion, law, and medicine
Examining the effectiveness of the prison system
Uses and abuses of hypnotism
Occupational hazards
The sharp rise in teenage pregnancies
The potential of cable television
Freedom of the press: right or privilege?
The role of Amnesty International
Changes in courtship over the past fifty years
Advice columnists: who do they help?
Psychotherapists on the radio: helpful or harmful?
The Vietnam legacy: vets, MIAs, Agent Orange, the boat people
Orbiting inhabited earth satellites: What's on the drawing board?
Is America in the grip of a cocaine epidemic?
Architectural styles: By century, by region of the country.
Fashion industry fads: why do they change?
Television violence and its effect on children
Unlocking the mysteries of sleep: Why do we dream?
Teenage alcohol abuse
Changing the Social Security system
Response of men to women in the military
Mainstreaming: handicapped children in regular classes

Alternate energy technologies: Using wind, water, and sun
Rights of Smokers versus Rights of Non-Smokers
The problem of nuclear waste disposal
Is one individual's "cult" another's religion?
What the new statistics on violent crimes show
Forecasting weather disasters
Signs of the physical fitness boom
Why are children running away at the rate of one million a year?
Broadening the definition of the family: childless couples, single parents, communal families, and so on
Preventing, diagnosing, and treating child abuse
Cancer victims and unorthodox treatment: breakthrough or deception?
Benefits and perils of gene splicing
The FDA's drug approval procedure: careful or just bureaucratic?
America's fascination with New Age fads: crystals and spirit channeling, and so on
New mass transit systems
How the family changes when husband and wife both work
Legalized gambling: fiscal panacea or corrupting influence?
Socialized medicine: will it work in the United States?
The two happiest days in the life of a boat owner
Patenting an invention
Security and safety at rock concerts
History of the Nobel Prize, the Pulitzer Prize, the Academy Awards
Ridiculous old laws still on the books
New developments in the automotive field
Should children be prosecuted as adults for serious crimes?
How do fraternities/sororities help later in life?
Experiments on the intelligence of dolphins
Famous misers
Funeral practices: ancient and modern
The latest chapter in the history of affirmative action
Nostrodamus: prophet or fraud?
Famous court cases
Central America: the domino theory
Life in the suburbs: still the dream?

FINDING A QUESTION TO ANSWER

Preparing a research paper requires you to select a subject and come up with a question on it that you would like to answer in a certain number of pages, given the resources of your library and the time available to you. For this reason, the research process begins with careful considera-tion of a wide range of thought-provoking questions connected with your subject. If, for example, you were assigned the broad subject of "drug use and drug addiction in contemporary society," each question you thought of would limit this wide-ranging subject to a more manageable topic. Some interesting questions that might be asked on this subject are:

1. What has caused such a massive upswing of drug use in our society?
2. Are legal drugs less addictive or less dangerous than illegal drugs?
3. Should marijuana use be decriminalized?
4. How dependent are the economies of other countries on the billions of dollars generated by producing cocaine that is sold in the United States?
5. Does mandatory drug testing provide reliable results? Does it violate the Fourth Amendment guarantee against "illegal search and seizure" and constitute an invasion of privacy?
6. What level of success has been achieved by the voluntary "just say no" program?
7. Are athletes coerced into using performance-enhancing drugs, such as steroids, in order to remain competitive?
8. What part do drugs play in highly competitive areas such as professional sports, the entertainment industry, and the financial world?
9. How do drugs affect the central nervous system?
10. What part have hallucinogenic substances played in religions down through the ages?

Some topics, such as in question 10, are still too wide-ranging to be researched within the time available. Other topics, such as in question 9, would be too difficult since it would require you to possess a high level of technical information. Still other topics, such as in question 6, might be a subject on which sufficient information is not readily available or be too narrow to be the subject of a research paper. Since the process of writing a research paper often discloses unsuspected relationships, you may discover that different questions focus on different but related aspects of the same topic.

For example, questions 1, 7, and 8 might be combined as a question that asked "What part does the idea of competition and winning at all costs play in the massive upswing in drug use in professional sports, the entertainment industry, and the world of finance?" Or the research process might create the possibility for an interesting comparative analysis (combining questions 4, 5, and 6) expressed in the question "Are attempts to curtail the demand side of drug use through 'just say no' programs and mandatory drug testing more effective than governmental efforts to limit the supply side of drug trafficking by encouraging other countries to grow crops other than coca?"

DETERMINING WHETHER RELEVANT SOURCES EXIST

From all the questions you have generated on a subject, choose several that seem especially interesting. The next step is to determine whether adequate material exists in the library to produce a well-researched paper drawn from a variety of relevant sources. Avoid topics that are either so new or so old that sources may not be readily available. Some questions such as the more factual ones will have already been answered. You might discover that a certain percentage of the cocaine coming to the United States is grown in Peru, Bolivia, and Colombia, or that the government spends a certain amount on drug treatment programs. These and any other questions that have already been answered must be eliminated from contention. Only those questions for which satisfactory answers have not been found should be considered as possible topics for your research paper.

The Preliminary Thesis Statement

The question around which your paper is organized should be stated in the form of a tentative thesis, as a declarative sentence. The thesis statement represents your view on the subject and is stated in such a way that it is apparent to your readers that your research paper will make a case for this point of view.

The thesis statement will provide a way to test the usefulness of source materials and acts to focus your research so that you do not waste time reading and taking notes on material unrelated to your topic. To be effective, your thesis statement should contain your opinion on the subject, much as the thesis statement of an argumentative essay presents the viewpoint you hope to persuade others to accept. Don't feel that you are locked into a specific formulation of your thesis statement. At this point it is just a means to guide your reading and note taking. What you discover may require you to substantially alter the scope or direction of your paper. If this occurs, you will need to revise your thesis statement accordingly.

The search for a thesis statement is a valuable means of organizing your thinking. Once you hit upon it you can use this single sentence to test every piece of information you discover in your reading. If your thesis were: "drugs pose such a threat to society that mandatory drug testing should be instituted in schools as well as the workplace," this sentence would define the central idea around which your paper would be organized. The process of finding materials and sources, taking notes, and writing a rough draft would be guided by this sentence. Revising the rough draft would mean eliminating everything in the paper that did not support, illuminate, substantiate, or explain this central idea. For these reasons, the thesis statement is the single most important sentence in the paper. In fact, you might want to write it out on a three-by-five card and look at it frequently while investigating what sources are available in the library.

Using the Library

The essence of the research process depends on your skill in finding what others have written on your topic. Certain basic general reference works in your library are of great value in providing an informative, balanced overview of your research topic. General works, including encyclopedias, dictionaries, and handbooks can give you a balanced idea of accepted views of your subject and make your research easier. Most of these works can be found in the library's reference room and must be used there.

MAJOR ENCYCLOPEDIAS

The encyclopedia is the most useful general reference work. Articles written by specialists in particular fields cover general, national, religious, and special topics. Although the articles are relatively short you will find a comprehensive, carefully selected and well-balanced overview of most subjects.

In most cases one of the following encyclopedias will provide you with the background information you need:

Chambers Encyclopedia
Collier's Encyclopedia
Encyclopedia Americana
Encyclopedia Britannica
New Columbia Encyclopedia

In addition, there are encyclopedias that deal with special subjects whose usefulness is often nearly as great as that of the general encyclopedias:

Dictionary of American History
Encyclopedia of World Art
Encyclopedia of World Literature in the 20th Century
The International Encyclopedia of the Social Sciences
The McGraw-Hill Encyclopedia of Science and Technology

To make full use of the information contained in encyclopedias it is often necessary to consult a separate index, usually contained in the last volume. This main index will provide you with all the cross-references to your topic. For most students the short list of other works, or bibliography, on the same subject at the end of most articles is the ideal starting point for further research. It is a good idea to consult more than one encyclopedia on your topic since the same subject may be treated differently in each one.

OTHER ENCYCLOPEDIAS AND HANDBOOKS

The following list provides many of the standard general reference works you will need to get you started with background information in almost any field.

ALMANACS, YEARBOOKS, AND COMPILATIONS OF FACTS
The American Annual (1923–date)
The Book of Lists
CBS News Almanac (1976–date)
Collier's Yearbook (1939–date)
Facts on File (1940–date)
Statistical Abstract of the United States (1878–date)
The World Almanac and Book of Facts (1868–date)
Year Book of World Affairs (1947–date)

ART AND ARCHITECTURE
Britannica Encyclopedia of American Art (1973)
Encyclopedia of World Art, 15 vols. (1959–1968)
Larousse Encyclopedia of Byzantine and Medieval Art (1963)
Larousse Encyclopedia of Modern Art (1965)
Larousse Encyclopedia of Prehistoric and Ancient Art, rev. ed. (1966)

ASTRONOMY
Cambridge Encyclopedia of Astronomy (1977)

BIOGRAPHY
Chamber's Biographical Dictionary, ed. J. O. Thorne, rev. ed. (1969)
Current Biography (1940–date)
Dictionary of American Biography, 22 vols. (1928–1958)
International Who's Who (1935–date)
Leslie, Stephen, and Sidney Lee, eds., *Dictionary of National Biography* [British], 63 vols. (1885–1901); reissued 22 vols. (1908–1909; suppl. to 1963)
The National Cyclopaedia of American Biography (1893–date)
Notable American Women 1607–1950, (1971)
Who's Who in America (1899–date)

BIOLOGY
Gray, Peter, ed., *Encyclopedia of Biological Sciences*, 2d ed. (1970)

BUSINESS AND ECONOMICS
Clark, Donald T., and Bert A. Gottfried, *University Dictionary of Business and Finance* (1974)
Douglas Greenwald, *The McGraw-Hill Dictionary of Modern Economics*, 2d ed. (1973)

Heyel, Carl, ed, *The Encyclopedia of Management*, 2d ed. (1973)
Nemmers, Erwin E., ed., *Dictionary of Economics and Business*, 4th enl. ed. (1978)

CHEMISTRY
Hampel, Clifford A., and Gessner G. Hawley, eds., *Encyclopedia of Chemistry*, 3rd ed. (1973)

DICTIONARIES
Hayakawa, S. I., *Modern Guide to Synonyms and Related Words* (1969)
A New English Dictionary on Historical Principles (also called *The Oxford English Dictionary*), 12 vols. and suppl. (1888–1933)
Partridge, Eric, *A Dictionary of Slang and Unconventional English*, 7th ed., 2 vols. (1970)
Webster's New Dictionary of Synonyms (1973)

DRAMA
Fidell, Estelle A., and D. M. Peake, eds., *Play Index* (1949–1973)
Hartnoll, Phyllis, ed., *The Oxford Companion to the Theater*, 3d ed. (1967)
Matlaw, Myron, *Modern World Drama: An Encyclopedia.* (1972)
McGraw-Hill Encyclopedia of World Drama. 4 vols. (1972)

EDUCATION
Encyclopedia of Education, ed. Lee C. Deighton et al. 10 vols. (1971)
International Yearbook of Education (1948–date)

ENGINEERING
Perry, Robert H., ed., *Engineering Manual: A Practical Reference of Design*, 3d ed. (1976)
Schenck, Hilbert, *Introduction to the Engineering Research Project* (1969)

ENVIRONMENTAL SCIENCE
Encyclopedia of Ecology, ed. Bernhard Grzimek (1976)
Lapedes, Daniel N., ed., *Encyclopedia of Environmental Science* (1974)

FOLKLORE AND MYTHOLOGY
Frazer, Sir James G., *The Golden Bough: A Study in Magic and Religion*, 12 vols. (1907–1915; suppl. 1936, 1955)
Larousse World Mythology (1968)
Thompson, Stith, *Motif-Index of Folk Literature*, rev. ed., 6 vols. (1955–1958)

GEOGRAPHY
May, Herbert G., and G. H. Hunt, *The Oxford Bible Atlas*, 2d ed (1974)
National Geographic Atlas of the World, 4th ed. (1975)
Shepherd, William R., ed., *Historical Atlas*, 9th ed. (1964)
The Time Atlas of the World, comprehensive ed. (1975)
Webster's New Geographical Dictionary, rev. ed. (1972)

HISTORY
Freidel, Frank, and Richard K. Showman, eds., *Harvard Guide to American History*, rev. ed., 2 vols. (1974)

Langer, William L., ed. *Encyclopedia of World History: Ancient, Medieval, and Modern Chronologically Arranged*, 5th ed. Boston (1974)
Morris, Richard B., *Encyclopedia of American History*, rev. ed. (1970)
Poulton, Helen J., and M. S. Howland, *The Historian's Handbook* (1972)
New Cambridge Modern History, ed G. R. Potter, 14 vols. (1970)

LANGUAGE AND LINGUISTICS
Hayes, Curtis W., J. Ornstein, and W. Gage. *The ABC's of Languages and Linguistics*, rev. ed. (1977)

LIBRARY
Encyclopedia of Library and Information Science (1968–)

LITERATURE
Baugh, Albert C., *A Literary History of England*, 2d ed. (1967)
Bede, Jean-Albert, and W. Edgerton, eds., *Columbia Dictionary of Modern European Literature*, 2d ed. (1980)
Feder, Lillian, ed., *Crowell's Handbook of Classical Literature* (1964)
Hornstein, Lillian H., ed., *The Reader's Companion to World Literature*, rev. ed. (1973)
Leary, Lewis, *Articles on American Literature; 1950–1967* (1970)
The Oxford Companion to English Literature, ed. Paul Harvey, Rev. ed. Dorothy Eagle (1967)
Spiller, Robert E., et al., *The Literary History of the United States*, 4th ed. 2 vols. (1974)
Whitlow, Roger, *Black American Literature* (1973)
Woodress, James, ed., *American Fiction 1900–50: A Guide to Information Sources* (1974)

MEDIA
Educational Media Year Book 1980, 6th ed., ed James W. Brown and Shirley N. Brown (1980)

MUSIC
New Grove Dictionary of Music and Musicians, 20 vols. (1980)
The New Oxford History of Music, 10 vols. (1954–)
Westrup, J. A., and F. L. Harrison, *New College Encyclopedia of Music*, rev. ed. (1976)

PHILOSOPHY
Copleston, Frederick, *A History of Philosophy*, 9 vols. (1976)
Edwards, Paul, ed., *Encyclopedia of Philosophy*, 4 vols. (1973)
Russell, Bertrand, *A History of Western Philosophy* (1945)

PHYSICS
Encyclopedia Dictionary of Physics
Fluegge, E., ed., *Encyclopedia of Physics*, 54 vols. (1957–)

POLITICAL SCIENCE AND SOCIAL SCIENCE
Freides, Thelma, *Literature and Bibliography of the Social Sciences* (1973)

Hoselitz, Bert F., ed., *A Reader's Guide to the Social Sciences*, rev. ed. (1972)
Klein, Barry T., ed. *Reference Encyclopedia of the American Indian*, 2d ed. (1973–1974)
Plano, Jack C., and Milton Greenberg, *American Political Dictionary*, 5th ed. (1979)
Sills, David L., ed., *International Encyclopedia of the Social Sciences*, 17 vols. (1968)
Smith, Edward C., and Arnold J. Zurcher, eds., *Dictionary of American Politics*, 2d ed. (1968)
Yearbook of World Affairs (1947–) (Annual)

PSYCHOLOGY
Bachrach, Arthur J., *Psychological Research: An Introduction*, 3d ed. (1974)
Eysenck, H. J., ed. *Encyclopedia of Psychology*, 2d ed. 3 vols. (1979)
Grinstein, Alexander, *Index of Psychoanalytic Writings* (1956–date)

QUOTATIONS
Bartlett, John, and E. M. Beck, *Familiar Quotations*, 14th ed. (1968)
Mencken, H. L., *A New Dictionary of Quotations* (1942)
Smith, William G., and F. P. Wilson, *The Oxford Dictionary of English Proverbs*, 3d ed. (1970)

RELIGION
Cross, F. L., and Elizabeth A. Livingstone, *The Oxford Dictionary of the Christian Church* (1974)
Hick, John, ed., *Philosophy of Religion*, 2d ed. (1973)
Mead, Frank Spencer, *Handbook of Denominations in the United States*, 6th ed. (1975)
Parrinder, Geoffrey, *A Dictionary of Non-Christian Religions* (1973)

SCIENCE AND TECHNOLOGY
McGraw-Hill Encyclopedia of Science and Technology, 3d ed., 15 vols. (1971)
Van Nostrand's Scientific Encyclopedia, 4th ed. (1968)

SOCIOLOGY AND ANTHROPOLOGY
Encyclopedia of Anthropology, eds. David E. Hunter and Philip Whitten (1976)
Encyclopedia of Social Work, ed. John Turner (1977)
Encyclopedia of Sociology, ed. Gayle Johnson (1974)

SPORTS AND PASTIMES
Arlott, John, ed., *The Oxford Companion to Sports and Games* (1975)
Hollander, Zander, *Great American Athletes of the 20th Century* (1972)
Hollander, Zander, ed., *The Modern Encyclopedia of Basketball*, rev. ed. (1973)
Menke, Frank G., *The Encyclopedia of Sport*, 5th ed., by Roger Treat (1974)
Quercetani, Roberto L., *A World History of Track and Field Athletics, 1864–1964* (1964)
Reeves, Fred, *A Baseball Handbook* (1973)
Styer, Robert A., *Encyclopedia of Hockey*, rev. ed. (1973)
Treat, Roger, ed., *Encyclopedia of Football*, 12th ed., rev. (1974)

Among the more important books devoted to the lives of people of accomplishment are the *Dictionary of National Biography* (DNB) and the

Dictionary of American Biography (DAB). Biographical sketches of living people can be found in *Current Biography* and *Who's Who in America*. If your paper concerns a historical figure you might wish to consult *Who Was Who in America*. Also, there are biographical works that feature people from particular nationalities and professions. There are guides to musicians, artists, and nationally prominent figures in sports and politics. One of the most useful guides is a compiled series called *Contemporary Authors* that covers more than 85,000 authors who are alive or who have died since 1960.

HOW TO LOCATE BIOGRAPHICAL INFORMATION

If what you need is a brief outline of a person's life, you can get the basic facts quickly and conveniently by using a biographical dictionary. The selection of a biographical source depends on the type of information the researcher knows about the person he or she is investigating. For example:

1. If a person's nationality is not known, an international biographical dictionary should be consulted first.
2. If it is known that a person is no longer living, a retrospective source should be consulted first.
3. If it is known that a person is living, a current source should be consulted first.
4. If a person's profession is known, a biographical source for his or her profession should be consulted first.

The following annotated entries give examples of the types of biographical sources available for consultation. They are listed beginning with the more general and working down to the most specific.

INTERNATIONAL BIOGRAPHICAL SOURCES
Chamber's Biographical Dictionary (1970)
A British publication that includes 1970 biographies "of all nations and all times."
Lipschutz, Mark R., and Kent R. Rasmussen, *Dictionary of African Historical Biography* (1978)
Approximately 800 biographical sketches of historical figures. Excludes individuals who became prominent only after 1960. Bibliographic references. Thematic subject index. Variant name index.

DICTIONARIES
Dictionary of World History (1973)
Alphabetical dictionary of world history up to the end of 1970. Some emphasis on Britain and the United States. Emphasis on political, social, and economic events. Bibliographical references at end of longer entries. Index.

NATIONAL BIOGRAPHICAL SOURCES — United States
(Retrospective)
Dictionary of American Biography (1928–1937)
A twenty-volume set that gives nearly 15,000 long evaluations of those "who
  have made some significant contribution to American life." United States
  (contemporary).
Sharp, Harold S., *Footnotes to American History: A Bibliographic Source Book*
  (1977)
Lists 313 events, many of the general interest category (for example, The Salem
  Witchcraft Trials, The Tweed Ring, The Scopes Monkey Trial, The Patty Hearst
  Trials.) Narratives are followed by selective bibliographies. Chronological ar-
  rangement; index.

BIOGRAPHICAL SOURCES
National Cyclopaedia of American Biography (1892–)
More comprehensive, albeit less scholarly, than the *Dictionary of American Biog-
  raphy*. Nonalphabetical arrangement. Illustrated. Cumulative index volumes.
Who's Who in America (1879–) (Biennial)
Gives brief descriptive sketches with addresses of biographees.
Who's Who of American Women (1958–) (Biennial)
Provides brief descriptive sketches, exclusively of women. To locate biographies
  of other nationals, check the card catalog under the appropriate subjects. For
  example:
  Canada — Biography
  China — Biography
  Great Britain — Biography

CURRENT SOURCES
Current Biography (1940–) (Monthly)
A well-indexed tool giving biographies of people in the news. Includes portraits.

PROFESSIONS
Biographies of people can be retrieved by professions in the card catalog by
  looking up the appropriate subjects. For example:
  Artists — Biography
  Who's Who in American Art (1935–) (Biennial)
  Limited to American artists.

AUTHORS – Biography
Twentieth Century Authors (1942)
With its 1955 supplement over 2,500 authors of all nations are covered. Includes
  some portraits.

SCIENTISTS — Biography
American Men and Women of Science (1973)
Comprised of eight volumes with six being devoted to the physical and biological
  sciences, the other two to the social and behavioral sciences.

INDEXES
Biography Index (1947–) (Quarterly)

Worldwide in coverage and unlimited in time, covers people from many different fields of endeavor.

Often you will need to know the exact meaning of specialized terms that you come across in your research. Or you may need to know how the meaning of a particular word has developed and changed from the time it was first employed. In both cases, dictionaries of various kinds can be consulted. For example, *Webster's Collegiate Dictionary*, which is condensed from the unabridged *Webster's Third New International Dictionary*, is quite adequate for describing contemporary American word meanings. Under a typical word entry, you will find many kinds of information.

The American Heritage Dictionary of the English Language, the *Funk and Wagnall's Standard College Dictionary*, and the *Random House Dictionary of the English Language* are other popular and useful dictionaries providing helpful information on the origins, meanings, usage, and status of hundreds of thousands of words. On the other hand, you may need to use a specialized dictionary for technical terms that are not found in these general dictionaries. For example, if you need definitions of key terms in political science, sociology, social anthropology, economics, and social psychology you might consult Julius Gould and William L. Kolb's *A Dictionary of the Social Sciences* (1964) which contains long scholarly definitions of approximately 1,000 concepts and terms along with discussions of usage.

The dictionary that dwarfs all the others is the *Oxford English Dictionary*, in thirteen volumes. It deals with the history of the meanings of words over the centuries and cites actual examples. (The *OED*, as it is abbreviated, is also available in a two-volume reduced-type edition.) In 1986, a four-volume supplement to this work was completed. If you examine the *OED*, analyzing a word entry or comparing it to the *Webster's Third*, you will find that the *OED* gives illustrations of the usage of words from the time they first appeared to the present.

In addition to the dictionaries listed above, there are bilingual dictionaries as well as those that deal primarily with synonyms and current usage.

USING THE CARD CATALOG

The card catalog of your college library is a record of all the books and other materials available in that library. While libraries vary in their holdings, types of materials located in your library that are listed in the card catalog usually include books, newspapers and periodicals (but not articles in them), theses and dissertations, some government documents (most are not listed), and multimedia items including records, cassettes, and filmstrips. Materials usually not listed in the card catalog include college catalogs and annual corporation reports.

Libraries traditionally use one of two systems for classifying information, the Dewey decimal system and the Library of Congress system. The Dewey decimal system classifies books numerically into ten categories that are further broken down into decimals:

000 General Works
100 Philosophy and Related Disciplines
200 Religion
300 Social Sciences
400 Language
500 Pure Science
600 Technology (Applied Science)
700 The Arts
800 Literature and Rhetoric
900 General Geography and History

The system often used in most university and college libraries is the Library of Congress system. This system classifies books according to the alphabet using numbers for further subdivisions:

A　General Works, Polygraphy
B　Philosophy, Psychology, and Religion
C　Auxiliary Sciences of History
D　General and Old World History (except America)
E-F American History
G　Geography, Anthropology, Manners and Customs, Folklore, Recreation
H　Social Science, Statistics, Economics, Sociology
J　Political Science
K　Law
L　Education
M　Music
N　Fine Arts
P　Language and Literature
Q　Science
R　Medicine
S　Agriculture, Plant and Animal Industry, Fish Culture, Fisheries, Hunting, Game Protection
T　Technology
U　Military Science
V　Naval Science
Z　Bibliography and Library Science

The card catalog in the library organizes and presents information on each book in a variety of ways. Each book is listed alphabetically on a separate card according to title, subject, and author. An especially useful benefit of using the card catalog is that lists of related subject headings and cross-listed subject areas on the cards make it easy to continue searching for relevant source materials.

The card catalog is usually divided into two alphabetical sections: the author/title catalog and the subject catalog.

Authors are usually individuals (such as Freud, Sigmund), but they may also be corporate bodies such as government agencies, business firms, institutions, or associations (such as U.S. Central Intelligence Agency, General Motors Corporation, American Medical Association). When trying to locate an entry in the card catalog, keep in mind the following filing guidelines:

1. Alphabetization is word-by-word and letter-by-letter within a word. Owing to the rule that nothing comes before something, New York is filed ahead of Newark (the space in New York comes before the *a* in Newark). If, however, you were looking for Newyork, then Newark would come first.
2. Numerals in titles are filed as if written out (for example, *2001: A Space Odyssey* is filed as *Two Thousand One: A Space Odyssey*).
3. Articles (*a, an, the,* and their foreign language equivalents) are disregarded in filing when they come at the beginning of titles (for example, *A Night to Remember* is filed under *N*).
4. Names beginning with "Mc" or "Mac" are filed as "Mac" (for example, McNamara precedes MacRae).
5. Cards beginning with initials are filed before any other cards beginning with the same letter (for example, DNA is filed before Darwin, Charles).
6. Common abbreviations are arranged as though spelled out (for example, Dr. is filed as Doctor, Mrs. is filed as Mistress, Mlle. is filed as Mademoiselle).

The subject catalog is used to locate library holdings (1) on a certain topic (such as Psychology, Hot Dog Rolls, Railroad Travel) or (2) about a certain person, place, or group (such as Shakespeare, William; Africa; Pueblo Indians). Usually subjects are listed in a specific rather than a general form (for example, for material on basketball, see Basketball in preference to Sports).

Each book in the library will have a minimum of three cards—an author card, a title card, and a subject card. Books that have more than one author will have an additional card for each author. Moreover, the same book may be listed under several subject cards. Figure 6.1 shows four sample cards for Andrew Weil and Winifred Rosen's book *Chocolate to Morphine: Understanding Mind-Active Drugs.* A sample author card for Winifred Rosen is not shown. Notice that except for a different heading, the information on each card is identical and includes the title of the book, the author (in this case, two coauthors), the city where it was

Alternate subject card

DRUGS—POPULAR WORKS.

RM
315
.W44
1983

Weil, Andrew.
    Chocolate to morphine : understanding mind-active drugs / Andrew Weil and Winifred Rosen. — Boston : Houghton Mifflin, 1983.
      228 p. : ill. ; 24 cm.
      Includes bibliographical references and index.
      ISBN 0-395-33108-0

      1. Psychotropic drugs. 2. Drugs—Popular works. I. Rosen, Winifred, 1943-   II. Title

Subject card

PSYCHOTROPIC DRUGS.

RM
315
.W44
1983

Weil, Andrew.
    Chocolate to morphine : understanding mind-active drugs / Andrew Weil and Winifred Rosen. — Boston : Houghton Mifflin, 1983.
      228 p. : ill. ; 24 cm.
      Includes bibliographical references and index.
      ISBN 0-395-33108-0

      1. Psychotropic drugs. 2. Drugs—Popular works. I. Rosen, Winifred, 1943-   II. Title

Author card

RM
315
.W44
1983

Weil, Andrew.
    Chocolate to morphine : understanding mind-active drugs / Andrew Weil and Winifred Rosen. — Boston : Houghton Mifflin, 1983.
      228 p. : ill. ; 24 cm.
      Includes bibliographical references and index.
      ISBN 0-395-33108-0

      1. Psychotropic drugs. 2. Drugs—Popular works. I. Rosen, Winifred, 1943-   II. Title

Title card

RM
315
.W44
1983

Chocolate to morphine
Weil, Andrew.
    Chocolate to morphine : understanding mind-active drugs / Andrew Weil and Winifred Rosen. — Boston : Houghton Mifflin, 1983.
      228 p. : ill. ; 24 cm.
      Includes bibliographical references and index.
      ISBN 0-395-33108-0

      1. Psychotropic drugs. 2. Drugs—Popular works. I. Rosen, Winifred, 1943-   II. Title

Library of Congress call number

Book title

Book length

Headings under which book can be found

Publication date

Book size

Authors/editors

Publisher

Bibliography and index

FIGURE 6.1
Sample of Entries In The Card Catalog.

published, the publisher, the date of publication, the number of pages, an abbreviation (ill.) indicating illustrations, the size of the book (24 cm.), and the fact that the book contains both a bibliography and an index. Notice also that the call number appears in the upper left-hand corner on all four cards. The same call number is also found on the spine of the book itself.

The *Library of Congress Subject Headings*, an indispensable resource for all researchers, provides a complete list of all the headings used for entering materials in the catalog. These headings not only reflect the actual vocabulary used to file materials in the card catalog, but they can be used to continue your search for information related to your topic. For example, you might see the following entry:

> **Drugs and youth** (*Indirect*)
> *sa* Alcohol and youth
>   Narcotics and youth
>   Smoking and youth
> *x*   Counter culture
>   Youth and drugs
> *xx* Drug abuse

The bold-faced heading is an entry you would look for in the card catalog. Headings listed as *sa* (see also) and *xx* indicate other headings under which material would be listed, if your library has holdings on that subject. The *x* indicates an unused heading. A skillful researcher can take advantage of these headings to broaden or narrow the search for materials to form the basis of a working bibliography.

USING THE COMPUTER CATALOG

In addition to the traditional card catalog many libraries have begun to use other means of cataloging information, including the COM (Computer Outform Microfilm) catalog, sometimes nicknamed "Comcat" on microfilm or microfiche. In newer systems, information on library holdings is available through an on-line computer catalog that also provides subscribers (at a fee, sometimes hefty) with access to a number of on-line data-base services. The most widely used services available in university libraries are BRS (Bibliographic Retrieval Service), DIALOG (which provides access to more than 250 data bases), COMPUSERV (for business information), LEXIS (for legal information), THE SOURCE (for business information), NEXIS (for news and public affairs), RLIN (Research Libraries Information Network), OCLC (On Line Computer Library Center), and ERIC (Educational Research Information Center). Since computer searching can become very expensive very quickly you must work out a strategy in advance so that you can request specific information with exact terms or *descriptors*. Once your search discloses potential leads you can get a printout of citations you can follow up later. The advantage of computer searching, when done correctly, is that you can quickly receive information that would take you many hours or even days to obtain on your own.

USING PERIODICAL INDEXES

One of the major resources of any college or research library is its periodical and serial holdings. The latest scientific and technological information is usually first available in journals, proceedings of conferences, or society bulletins before the same material appears in book form. The same is true of much of the specialized work in the humanities and social sciences. The student who wishes to keep up-to-date on various subjects should be aware of the current content of periodicals. Periodicals can refer to any work that appears regularly in print and that has the same title for successive issues. They can be issues of newspapers, of popular magazines such as *Newsweek* or *Sports Illustrated*, or of professional journals such as the *American Journal of Psychology*, published for people in the field.

In putting together your research paper you will most likely use many kinds of sources. Your library's card catalog will give you access to all of the books in the various collections, including the reference room. It will not tell you, however, where to locate the various magazines, journals, and newspapers that your library receives and stores. These are listed separately in what are called *indexes*.

An index is an alphabetical listing of subject and author entries used to locate articles in periodicals. An index is valuable only if it is up-to-date; virtually all appear at least annually, but most are quarterly, and some appear more frequently. The most commonly used index to periodicals—itself a periodical—is the *Reader's Guide to Periodical Literature*, which indexes more than 150 general magazines and journals by subject and by author. By learning how to use this index you will automatically be learning how to use many other more specialized indexes, such as the *Social Sciences Index* and the *Humanities Index*, which are similarly arranged. Figure 6.2 shows a portion of the listings under "drug abuse" from the February 1987 issue, along with annotations to demonstrate how abbreviations and headings are used.

Although *The Reader's Guide to Periodical Literature* is the best place to start gathering sources on your topic, the nature of the research paper requires you to move beyond these general sources to more specialized ones. In this case, *The Social Sciences Index* would be an ideal next place to look since it includes specialized investigations into relationships between drugs and society. Figure 6.3 shows some of the listings in the part of the index that provides information on studies produced in one year on drugs and athletes, children, crime, employment, Indians, police, the handicapped, women, and youth.

FEBRUARY 1987

Drug abuse—Conferences—*cont.*
Preparatory body for international drug conference calls for draft outline of future activities. il *UN Chron* 23:84 Ap '86
History
A Yale drug historian sniffs something familiar in today's cocaine craze [interview with D. Musto] M. Wilheim. il por *People Wkly* 26:155-6+ N 24 '86
International aspects
Threat to health from drugs termed 'narco-terrorism'. *World Health* p30 Ag/S '86
Rehabilitation
See also
Hale House (New York, N.Y.)
Acupuncture used to help crack addicts. *Jet* 71:36 D 22 '86
A life of lies, a dance with death—a recovering addict talks about the cost of crack. A. Abrahams. il *People Wkly* 26:93-4+ N 3 '86
Unhooking from drugs. il *Changing Times* 40:113-18+ O '86
Testing
The battle over drug testing [privacy issue] I. R. Kaufman. il *N Y Times Mag* p52+ O 19 '86
Busting the drug testers [faculty lab results] S. Budiansky. il *U S News; World Rep* 101:70 O 20 '86
Can test positive for pot by just being near smoke. *Jet* 71:31 D 15 '86
Courts foil schools' efforts to detect drugs. T. J. Flygare. *Phi Delta Kappa* 68:329-30 D '86
Danforth urges rules for drug testing of airline employees. *Aviat Week Space Technol* 125:47 D 1 '86
Disputed tactics in the war on drugs. M. Gray. il *Macleans* 99:55 O 13 '86
In-school drug tests: right or wrong? K. Henderson. *Seventeen* 45:84 D '86
NCAA prepares to test athletes for drug use. *Jet* 71:51 O 13 '86
A new focus on drugs. W. Hoffer. il *Nations Bus* 74:57-9 D '86
No racial bias found in Cleveland drug case [surprise urine testing of police] *Jet* 71:22 N 10 '86
"Obsolete" amendments [mandatory drug testing] D. E. Petzal. *Field Stream* 91:23+ D '86
Reaganites at risk. R. Vigilante. il *Natl Rev* 38:31-2+ D 5'86
Test cases. *Time* 128:35 D 15 '86
Testing hair can detect cocaine use, researchers. *Jet* 71:53 N 10 '86
This is what you thought: 56% say no to drug testing [results of survey] *Glamour* 84:103 N '86
Anecdotes, facetiae, satire, etc.
Our Puritan dilemma. J. Morley. *New Repub* 195:13-14 D 1 '86

Article title
Author
Issue date
Periodical title
Page reference
Volume number
Illustrations
Special feature

FIGURE 6.2
Sample Page from The Reader's Guide to Periodical Literature

(continued)

Western Europe
AIDS increases among addicts in Europe. il
World Health p30 N '86
Drug addicts *See* Drug abuse
Drug control *See* Narcotics laws and
regulations
Drug delivery systems in the body *See*
Drugs—Dosage forms
Drug education
Federal government should set standards
for states on drug education: Dukakis
[Massachusetts program] *Phi Delta
Kappan* 68:172 O '86
Len Bias' mom lectures on Christ, woes
of drugs. por *Jet* 71:50 O '86

FIGURE 6.2 CONTINUED

The *Social Sciences Index* and *The Humanities Index*, which covers scholarly journals, are both more specialized than *The Reader's Guide to Periodical Literature*. As you narrow your topic, however, you will find that you need to search more specialized bibliographies and indexes that provide up-to-date information on highly specific subject areas. The following have proven to be the most valuable; they are listed according to liberal arts, political and social sciences, natural and physical sciences and technology.

LIBERAL ARTS
Abstracts of English Studies
Art Index
Biography Index
Cumulated Dramatic Index
Film Literature Index
A Guide to Critical Reviews
Historical Abstracts
International Index to Film Periodicals
MLA International Bibliography
Music Index
Philosophy Index
Poole's Index for Periodical Literature
Religion Index

POLITICAL AND SOCIAL SCIENCES
Abstracts in Anthropology
American Statistical Index
Business Periodicals Index
Current Index to Journals in Education (CIJE)
Education Index
GEO Abstracts
Index to Legal Periodicals
International Political Science Abstracts
Monthly Catalog of United States Government Publications

(continued on page 310)

SOCIAL SCIENCES INDEX

Drugs, Nonprescription
Correlates of mothers' use of medications for their children. L. A. Maiman and others. *Soc Sci Med* 22 no1:41-51 '86

Drugs (Muscle relaxants) *See* Muscle relaxants — Subject heading

Drugs and athletes —
Article title — Banning drugs in sports: a skeptical view. N. Fost. *Hastings Cent Rep* 16:5-10 Ag '86 — Journal title

Volume number —
Drugs and children — Author
Reliability and discriminant validity of the children's drug-use survey. E. R. Oetting and others. bibl *Psychol Rep* 56:751-6 Je '85 — Issue date

Page reference —

Drugs and crime
Expensive drug use and illegal income: a test of explanatory hypotheses. J. J. Collins and others. bibl *Criminology* 23:743-64 N '85

Drugs and employment
Drugs at work; high on the firm's time. *Economist* 300:65 S 27 '86

Drugs and Indians *See* Indians of North America—Drug abuse

Drugs and police
Drug abuse by police officers [panel discussion] *Police Chief* 53:71-84 Mr '86 — Article type
Drug screening programs. W. C. Summers. *Police Chief* 53:12 O '86
IACP announces drug testing policy. *Police Chief* 53:22 + O '86
Police and drug testing: a look at some issues. J. K. Stewart. *Police Chief* 53:27 + O '86 — Continued in later pages
Urinalysis drug testing programs for law enforcement. J. Higginbotham. *FBI Law Enforc Bull* 55:25-30 O '86; 55:25-30 N '86; 56:16-21 Ja '87

Drugs and the handicapped
Substance abuse among people with disabilities: a problem of too much accessibility. B. G. Greer. bibl *J Rehabil* 52:34-8 Ja/Mr '86 — Bibliography

Drugs and women
Contraceptive practices among female heroin addicts. N. Ralph and C. Spigner. *Am J Public Health* 76:1016-17 Ag '86; Discussion. 76:1460 D '86
Masculinity-femininity scale of the MMPI and intellectual functioning of female addicts. Z. Z. Cernovsky. bibl *J clin Psychol* 42:310-12 Mr '86

Drugs and youth
Assessment of refusal skill in minority youth. J. K. Bobo and others. bibl il *Psychol Rep* 57:1187-91 D '85 pt2
Drug abuse resistance education: a police officer-taught drug prevention program. D. F. Gates. il *Police Chief* 53:54 + O '86
Drugs in schools: combining efforts to protect our children. W. J. Bennett. il *Police Chief* 53:50-2 O '86 — Illustrations

FIGURE 6.3
Sample Page from The Social
Sciences Index

Psychological Abstracts
Physical Education/Sports Index
Public Affairs Information Service Bulletin
Sociological Abstracts
United Nations Document Index

NATURAL AND PHYSICAL SCIENCES AND TECHNOLOGY
Applied Science and Technology Index
Biological and Agricultural Index
Chemical Abstracts
Computer and Control Abstracts
Energy Index
Engineering Index
Food Science and Technology Abstracts
General Science Index
Physics Abstracts
Pollution Abstracts

Chapters in books can be found in the *Essay and General Literature Index*. To find books on a given subject, try *Books in Print: Subjects*. Remember that "out of print" books are not contained in this volume, but they may be listed in the card catalogue. When you have discovered many promising titles of books but don't have the time to pursue each and every one, consult the *Book Review Index, Index to Book Reviews in the Humanities,* or the *Book Review Digest*. The *Book Review Digest* is both a digest and index of selected reviews of fiction and nonfiction works. More than 6,000 books a year are covered. Excerpts from the book reviews are given, as well as bibliographic information for locating the reviews in full. This work is arranged alphabetically by author with a subject and title index.

The *Book Review Index* is an index to reviews in more than 200 English language journals in the humanities and social sciences. It is arranged alphabetically by author or by title of the book being reviewed and does not contain abstracts. The *Index to Book Reviews in the Humanities* covers books on art and architecture, biography, drama and dance, folklore, history, language, literature, music, philosophy, travel, and adventure. Through 1962 only reviews in English are indexed. Beginning January 1963 indexes also review in foreign languages. Reviews are arranged alphabetically by author.

The *Library Journal Book Review* also contains full reprints of book reviews as they originally appeared in the *Library Journal*. Current fiction and nonfiction titles are included. An author-title index accompanies each annual volume. Another valuable resource, the *Social Sciences and Humanities Index* (formerly titled *International Index to Periodicals*), indexes about 200 scholarly journals in the humanities and social sciences. Reviews are often cited under author and subject entries.

A compilation of all *New York Times Sunday Book Review Magazines* published since 1896 appears in the *New York Times Book Review*. Individual reviews may be located by consulting the *New York Times Index*. When using the *New York Times Index*, book reviews may be located under the heading "Book Reviews." Citations are arranged under this heading by author. Exact references to page, date, and column of the *New York Times* are given.

If the book you are looking for is very recent and is not listed in *Book Review Digest* or other indexes, try the *New York Times Book Review*, *The Times Literary Supplement*, or the *Library Journal*. Reviews will help you determine if the book has been favorably received and will give you a concise overview of the subject and the author's viewpoint. Figure 6.4 illustrates the 1984 *Book Review Digest*'s listing of reviews that appeared for *Chocolate to Morphine: Understanding Mind-Active Drugs*, by Andrew Weil and Winifred Rosen.

The best way to find out about a new reference tool such as an index is to read its preface. Unlike the card catalog, which conveniently cross-lists all possible leads, reference indexes may rely only on subject or author listings. Reading the preface will tell you how the index is organized and what materials, subjects, and time periods it includes. All indexing services list articles under subjects and many list them by author, usually in one alphabetical sequence.

When using indexes, jot down the author, title of the article, complete journal title, volume number, page numbers, and date of the issue. If the journal title is abbreviated, use the list in the front of the index to find the complete title. To find out if your library holds the periodical you need, consult a list of currently received periodicals, usually kept as a computer printout or a microfiche list (if available) at the periodical services department or the reference desk.

USING NEWSPAPER INDEXES

A concise, objective, and thorough account of all significant international, national, and general news is available in *The New York Times Index*. Entries drawn from the news and editorial matter of the final late city edition of the *Times* are arranged alphabetically under specific subject headings. Summaries of news stories are published in supplements every two weeks and are combined into one volume at the end of every year. Annual volumes of the index have appeared since 1913.

To use the index simply choose the volume from the year in which you think the subject of your research paper might have appeared in the news. Look through the index for references to your subject. You will notice that entries end with abbreviations that tell you the date, page, and column on or in which the story originally appeared. You may then wish to obtain a copy of the microfilm edition of *The New York Times* and look at it through a microfilm viewer to get the complete story as it

BOOK REVIEW DIGEST 1984

Author, book title —— **WEIL, ANDREW.** Chocolate to morphine; understanding mind-active drugs; [by] Andrew Weil and Winifred Rosen. 228p il $16.95; pa $8.95 1983 Houghton Mifflin —— Publication facts

Library of Congress —— 613.8   1. Drugs
classification
number   ——   ISBN 0-395-33108-0; 0-395-33190-0 (pa)
LC 82-12112 ——
—— Library of Congress call number

International
Standard
Book Number

The authors "discuss many substances that are frequently abused, telling what it feels like to take them, what they do to the body, the dangers involved, and how to avoid dependence." (Libr J) Glossary. Index. —— Summary

"It is hard to reach teenagers with counsel about drugs, but Weil (a doctor) and Rosen (a young-adult writer) may do it with this book. (Adults, however, may find it shocking.) The authors don't condemn all drugs but claim that almost any drug can be used wisely if its effects and the reasons for taking it are properly understood, whether it be caffeine, alcohol, PCP, or pot. . . Although some may think the authors too permissive, they don't advocate drug use; they do supply the kind of information young people need in order to make up their own minds in a drug- ridden society." —— Excerpt from review

Journal title ——

Volume number ——

Page reference ——

Libr J 108:596 Mr 15 '83. Peggy Champlin (140w)

—— Reviewer

—— Issue date

"For those who wish to hear strong anti-drug statements, parts of the book will be disturbing. Readers must judge the book as a whole and avoid the temptation to single out statements that fit preconceived ideas or offend their values. Some readers may interpret the casual and open discussion of drug effects and safe usage as promotion or indirect approval of casual drug use. This is not the message, although I am concerned that the young or less sophisticated reader may interpret the book in this manner. However, this is not necessarily a fault. Parents and teachers must be involved, give guidance, and be prepared to express their views and values to teenage readers. . . The information is accurate and easy to read, and the authors' case descriptions are realistic, uncomfortably realistic. The more accurate your knowledge of drugs is, the better your decisions will be." *Sci Books Films* 19:89 N/D '83. Steven W. Mann (200w)

Review length ——

FIGURE 6.4
Sample Page from Book Review Digest

appeared on that date. Through the microfilm editions you can gain access to international, national, and general news stories going back to 1851.

The New York Times Index provides not only a subject and chronological guide to events but also summaries of *Times* articles and items. Other indexes are available for the *Wall Street Journal* and the *Christian Science Monitor*. Information on articles in the *Chicago Tribune*, the *Los Angeles Times*, the *New Orleans Times-Picayune*, and the *Washington Post* can be located in the *Newspaper Index*.

USING ABSTRACTS

An abstract has the same information as an index and is used in the same way to locate articles in periodicals, but an abstract also provides a brief summary of the contents for each article it lists. There are comprehensive abstracting services for major subject areas including:

Abstracts in Anthropology
Biological Abstracts
Chemical Abstracts
Historical Abstracts
Physics Abstracts
Psychological Abstracts
Sociological Abstracts
Women's Studies Abstract

An abstract is a bibliographic tool that serves as both an index and a source of concise summaries of original articles. *Psychological Abstracts* (1927–) is one of the most important bibliographies of the world's literature in psychology and related disciplines. It contains listings of books, journal articles, and dissertations with signed abstracts. Abstracts are arranged in seventeen major classification categories. There are author indexes, and, beginning in 1983, brief subject indexes to each issue number as well as full author and subject indexes to each volume.

If you were looking for an article by a particular author you would use the *Cumulated Author Index*. If you were looking for an article on a particular subject you would use the *Cumulated Subject Index*. You would notice that the *Psychological Abstracts Cumulated Index* covers all the materials that have appeared under an author's name or under a subject during the time period listed on the spine of the volume. Thus, if the author's name appears in the *Cumulated Author Index, 1972–74* or *1969– 71*, there will also be the title of his article and the name of the journal in which it appeared as well as the *Psychological Abstracts* volume number and abstract number.

When looking for a subject, find the terms that best describe the material. List these terms. Look through the *Cumulated Subject Index* for each subject. If the desired terminology is found, there will be a brief sentence or phrase describing the articles and giving an abstract number. Copy this information. Do not omit the *Psychological Abstracts* volume number. Next search the annual bound *Indexes of Psychological Abstracts*.

Use either an author or subject approach. Record the abstract numbers and do not forget to include the year and issue number of *Psychological Abstracts.*

After finding an appropriate list of abstract numbers, refer to the proper volume of *Psychological Abstracts*, which are usually located in the periodical collection. Journals are usually shelved here in strict alphabetic order by title from A to Z, with *Psychological Abstracts* toward the end of the collection.

The abstract found under the number written down contains the author's name, the title of the article, the name of the journal, and the issue in which the article appeared. This is followed by the abstract itself, which is a brief description of the article.

Copy the complete citation of the article you wish to read and consult the alphabetic periodicals holdings list, which will be on a printout or on microfiche. If your library received that periodical for the year and issue you need, you would then look for it in alphabetic title order on the bound periodical shelves. In the case of a book or dissertation listing, you would consult the card catalog or ask for help from a reference librarian. Figure 6.5 shows a sample page of summaries from *Psychological Abstracts* along with annotations designed to help you use this essential resource.

USING FIELD RESEARCH—INTERVIEWS

For some research papers you may wish to go beyond the sources available to you in the library (such as *The Gallup Opinion Index*, 1956, containing results of national public opinion surveys on topics of current interest, including presidential popularity, elections, and important international and domestic issues); you may wish to conduct interviews or surveys whose results will play a significant role in your research.

For example, faculty members from different specialized fields of study will probably be glad to share their expertise. Or you may want to interview someone whose experiences provide valuable insights into the subject of your study. In any case, you must plan your interview ahead of time by first finding out from your instructor whether information gained from interviews would be considered acceptable and appropriate for the particular assignment. You should have the questions you want to ask already formulated. Carefully check them to see whether you have unintentionally worded them in such a way as to elicit certain answers. What you want are open, honest, and informative responses. If you would like to use a tape recorder, first clear this with the person you plan to interview. Plan to take accurate notes during the interview, including key words and phrases, to make it easier to recall the substance of the interview later. After the interview, review your notes as soon as you can and put down a few sentences that summarize the most important

1032. **Rubio Perez, A. M. et al.** (Facultad de Medicina, Valladolid, Spain) Estudio comparativo del consumo de drogas del medio universitario de Cordoba y Valladolid. [Comparative study of drug use among students at the Universities of Cordoba and Valladolid.] (Span) *Psicopatologia.* 1984 (Oct–Dec), Vol 4(4), 373–384. —Administered a modified test of psychiatric disorders to a sample of medical and nursing students from the Universities of Cordoba and Valladolid as part of an epidemiological survey on drug usage. The test contained 80 questions on individual, familial, and social traits and on attitudes toward disease and drug use. 1,107 tests from Cordoba and 823 from Valladolid were analyzed. Results were shown as percentages or as means plus or minus standard deviations. Statistical analyses were performed with an unpaired t-test or chi-square test. Analgesic drug use by nursing students (15%) was lower than that by medical students (21%). 50% of Ss used stimulants, but amphetamines were used by no more than 10% of the medical students and 3% of the nursing students. Only 1% of the Ss used amphetamines to help them perform better on tests. Hypnotics were used more in clinical than preclinical years. 16.6% of the sample used cannabis–related drugs (mainly hashish in Cordoba and marihuana in Valladolid). The decrease in tobacco smokers in the general population was confirmed in the sample. More Ss from Cordoba (70%) than Valladolid (53%) consumed alcoholic beverages. (English abstract) (8 ref)

Language of article

Summary is in English

Author's institutional affiliation

1033. **Siegel, Ronald K.** (VA Branch, Los Angeles, CA) **Cocaine and the privileged class: A review of historical and contemporary images.** *Advances in Alcohol & Substance Abuse.* 1984(Win), Vol 4(2), 37–49. —Discusses the belief that cocaine is a drug associated with privilege and the privileged class, which is frequently cited as a motivating factor for nonmedical use. This association, part myth and part reality, has influenced the perception of cocaine as a glamorous and exotic drug, a drug immune to serious problems, a drug for the successful and wealthy, and, hence, a privileged drug. The origins and development of this myth are examined in terms of both historical and contemporary images in the arts and the media. Alternative competing images of cocaine as a drug associated with severe dependency and toxicity are discussed in terms of their past and future trends. (38 ref)—*Journal abstract.*

Entry number corresponding to number from subject index

Journal title

Issue date

Article title

Page reference

Volume and issue number

Bibliography includes 38 sources

FIGURE 6.5
Sample Page of Summaries from
Psychological Abstracts

points. Don't forget to record the date, time, full name, and title, if any, of the person you have interviewed.

Drawing Up a Working Bibliography

The working bibliography contains the results of your search to discover which books, periodicals, abstracts, newspapers, and other source materials held by the library will be useful in formulating an answer to the question expressed in the thesis statement. The working or preliminary bibliography should be considered a flexible rather than fixed list of sources. You can add new source materials or discard those found to be irrelevant.

When you have finished your paper you will be ready to make up a final bibliography listing only those works actually cited. A separate 3-by-5 or 4-by-6 bibliography card needs to be created for each source. This card should record the library call number, the complete title of the work, the author's full name, and the place, date, and publisher of the work. A bibliography card for an article in a journal, periodical, or magazine should record the complete name of the author, the title of the article, the name of the journal or magazine, the volume number, the day, month, and year of publication (if given), and the complete run of page numbers of the article.

On the same card, jot down your impression of how the source might be used in your paper, or where it might fit into the overall investigation. Ask yourself how the source will help you to answer the thesis question or add to your total knowledge of the issue.

Drawing Up a Working Outline

Before you start taking notes but after you have drawn up the working bibliography is a good time to start a working outline. It is important to have a working outline at this point. Otherwise, you might spend more time than necessary reading and taking extensive notes only to discover that you have no effective means of separating notes that bear directly on the topic from those that are irrelevant. The headings for this preliminary outline may reflect important aspects of the topic that you have discovered by looking through the *Library of Congress List of Subject Headings*, the headings and subheadings listed in indexes, and tables of contents of books on the subject for which you have created bibliography cards.

Headings are best arranged in an order that develops the topic in the direction suggested by the thesis statement. If your thesis statement was "Short of changing society's attitudes toward drug use, only federally funded mass education stands a real chance of stopping the drug epidemic," the headings in your preliminary outline might read:

I. Current theories explaining widespread drug use
II. Evidence of increasing drug use in the success-oriented areas of sports, entertainment, and finance
III. Unsuccessful efforts of the government to stop the drug epidemic
IV. The crucial role of education in preventing drug abuse

EVALUATING SOURCE MATERIALS

Creating a working outline makes the process of taking notes more efficient. By consulting the outline headings you will be able to tell quickly if a source from which notes are to be taken might prove useful.

After determining that sufficient source materials exist, with your preliminary bibliography and outline in hand, you can begin to evaluate the quality of the source materials by answering the following questions:

1. Does the information presented in the source material bear directly on the question the paper will answer?
2. Does the author have appropriate credentials, experience, or expertise in the field?
3. Is the author's research timely or has it been superceded by more recent research?
4. Are the conclusions presented by the author clearly drawn from well-documented and reliable evidence?
5. Does the book, chapter in a book, article from a magazine or journal, or other source contain a sufficient amount of discussion to warrant its use as a source from which notes will be taken? (Frequently, the best way to determine this for a book is by checking the page numbers on the subject listed in the index. An index entry on "crop substitution programs in Peru" on pages 17–28 would be a more useful source than the same entry followed by pages 17, 28. The first entry covers a discussion of twelve pages whereas the second indicates that the entire book touches on the subject on only two separate pages.)

Note-taking Procedures

To be useful, notes should be legible, written on one side of 4-by-6 index cards, and contain information from only one source per card. Each card should include the title of the work from which the note was taken, along with exact page numbers, placed in the upper right-hand corner.

In the upper left-hand corner, write a short phrase identifying the particular aspect of the research question to which the note relates. Frequently
this key phrase will be closely related to one of the headings in your
working outline. The actual note should be clearly written, preferably in
ink, in the center of the card.

Only information on the source and the exact page number need
appear on the card since you have already made up a card with complete
bibliographical information. If you are using more than one work by the
same author, however, put an abbreviation of the title along with the
author's last name and the page number to avoid confusing this note
with others drawn from a different work by the same author.

THE VALUE OF DIFFERENT KINDS OF NOTES

Different kinds of notes serve different purposes. Notes can take the
form of (1) paraphrases, (2) summaries, (3) quotations, or (4) factual
references.

Paraphrases

Paraphrasing requires you to restate the thoughts of the author in
your own words. Unlike the shorter summary, a sentence-by-sentence
paraphrase will be approximately the same length as the original; the
thoughts will be the author's, but the language in which these thoughts
are expressed will be your own. A research paper, of course, requires you
to footnote any paraphrased material to indicate its source. If you can
restate the thoughts, ideas, and opinions of the author in your own
words, you demonstrate that you have understood what you have read.
In both summarizing and paraphrasing it is a good idea to check what
you have written down against the original to see whether you have
inadvertently left out anything important.

For example, here is an original passage from Andrew Weil and
Winifred Rosen's chapter from *Chocolate to Morphine*:

> Many drug users talk about getting high. Highs are states of con-
> sciousness marked by feelings of euphoria, lightness, self-transcen-
> dence, concentration, and energy. People who never take drugs also
> seek out highs. In fact, having high experiences from time to time
> may be necessary to our physical and mental health, just as dreaming
> at night seems to be vital to our well-being. Perhaps that is why a
> desire to alter normal consciousness exists in everyone and why
> people pursue the experiences even though there are sometimes un-
> comfortable side effects.

The paraphrased entry on a note card might appear this way:

· ·

Innate need to alter   **Weil & Rosen,** *Chocolate,*
consciousness   **page 15**

Drugs allow the user to experience a feeling of vitality, excitement,
loss of ego, and a heightened sense of well-being. Since people all
over the world engage in non drug-taking activities to produce this
state, we might conclude that human beings have an innate need
to alter consciousness that is so strong it will make people overlook
possible bad reactions produced by the drugs.

· ·

Notice how paraphrasing makes the writer think about the ideas in order
to express them in different words. Paraphrasing is a way of thinking
through the subject, and in so doing you automatically must take into
account what others have had to say about it. Remember that since you
are using someone else's ideas, facts, and research as a basis for your
own paper, you must always provide a reference indicating your source.
Restating another person's thoughts in your own words not only demonstrates that you have really understood what you read, but means that
your paper will not be simply a patchwork of connected quotations of
many different styles.

Summaries

Summaries are also written in your own words, but unlike paraphrases they tend to be shorter than the original. The length of your
summary does not depend on the length of the original passage. A
summary simply presents your concise restatement of the author's main
ideas. It is important to be careful not to change ideas when you com-
press and condense them. For example, here is a passage from Philip
Slater's article "Want-creation Fuels Americans' Addictiveness" (1984):

But in our society we spend billions each year creating want. Cove-
tousness, discontent and greed are taught to our children, drummed
into them—they are bombarded with it. Not only through advertising, but in the feverish emphasis on success, on winning at all costs,
on being the center of attention through one kind of performance or
another, on being the first at something—no matter how silly or
stupid ("The Guinness Book of Records"). We are an addictive society. Addiction is a state of wanting. It is a condition in which the
individual feels he or she is incomplete, inadequate, lacking, not
whole, and can only be made whole by the addition of something
external.

Compressed into a note card summary, the above passage might appear:

. . . .

Society encourages   Slater, "Want-Creation" page 7
want-creation

Our society encourages drug use by constantly pushing people to be successful, to win, and to be the best. This emphasis on competition and success makes people feel inadequate and leads them to believe that drugs can remedy the societally induced feelings of dissatisfaction.

. . . .

Quotations

A third type of note card involves direct quotation, or copying the author's words exactly as they appear in the original. Unlike paraphrase or summary, you are putting down the exact words of your original source. Quotation marks at the beginning and end remind you that this is a word-for-word copy, including original punctuation and mistakes, if any. Basically, you directly quote a source that you consider especially important, concise, or vivid and want to present in the author's words directly to the reader. Perhaps you discover that the original idea loses its force when you try to paraphrase or summarize it. Or perhaps the distinctive style in which the idea is expressed is unique and memorable. These are all good reasons for directly quoting. But the most important reason for using direct quotation is that your opinion without the support of the quotation will carry less weight and be less persuasive.

For example, here is what a note card looks like that is directly quoting from a *Wall Street Journal* article "High Fliers: Use of Cocaine Grows Among Top Traders in Financial Centers" (September 12, 1983):

. . . .

Cocaine use in financial   WSJ, page 1
centers

"In Chicago, cocaine use is spreading in the city's commodities trading and financial centers. 'A few people take a toot before the trading session and maybe a few times during the day,' says one member of the Chicago Board of Trade, himself a user. 'It's like drinking coffee.' He estimates that 10% of the traders and brokers he knows use cocaine on the job."

. . . .

Notes where you directly quote an author's actual words exactly as they appear in the original should comprise no more than 15 percent of all your note cards. Although it might seem simpler initially to put down many quotations, you will only be postponing the moment when you have to reread, summarize, comment on, or evaluate each of these quotations. Remember, your research paper should not appear to be little more than a patchwork of stitched together quoted sources. You would be better off summarizing as many passages as early as possible rather than using your time copying down lengthy quotations that you will not be able to use. The only time quotations should be taken down is when the author's wording is so unique and authoritative that a summary would fail to do it justice.

Notice how each of the preceding examples of note cards not only put the author's last name and shortened title of the work in the upper right-hand corner but also record the page where the original information appeared. Exact page numbers are necessary since this information will appear in parentheses, according to the new Modern Language Association style of documentation (discussed later in this chapter).

Also, observe that the upper left-hand corner of each note card contains a concise key phrase to remind you how you might want to use this information. You should write down this key phrase before you take the time and effort to put down the entire note. Doing this will compel you to evaluate how useful the information on the card will be. This key phrase will come in handy when you're working with more than thirty cards because it will save you from having to reread the entire contents of each card when you are organizing them into groups before writing a rough draft. Whenever possible, try to see if the key phrase corresponds to an existing heading from your working outline. Doing this will prevent you from taking notes that are off the subject.

Factual References

Other note cards may be used for recording your own ideas or for keeping track of significant facts you will use to document assertions in your paper. For example, you might record the percentage of Bolivia's gross national product accounted for by cocaine production, or the fact that according to the National Narcotics Intelligence Consumer's Commission "6% of U.S. cocaine users consume 60% of the cocaine" produced in Bolivia, Peru, and Colombia.

Such hard statistical data serve an important function in substantiating your claims. Keep in mind that only one piece of information, whether it is a summary, quotation, combined note (your summary + a short quotation), fact, or observation should be recorded on each note card.

THE DANGERS OF UNDOCUMENTED SOURCES

The very nature of the research paper requires you to document all information taken from sources, whether in the form of quotations, paraphrases, summaries, or factual references. This is important even if you are not using the exact language used by the author. It means that you must provide an in-text reference specifying the author, title of the work, and location within the work where the reference can be found. For this reason it is important that you accurately note down the source, including specific page numbers, on each note card you write. Not to do this may later lead you to believe that these were your own ideas and you may fail to acknowledge that this information derives from an external source. Be especially careful in making sure you have included quotation marks so that you do not, however unintentionally, mistake someone else's words for your own and not give proper credit. It is preferable to overdocument sources that could have been assumed to fall in the category of general knowledge than to underdocument sources and raise the question of plagiarism.

USING YOUR NOTES TO REFINE THE THESIS STATEMENT

After quotations, facts, summaries of source materials, and your own ideas have been entered as separate items on individual note cards, take a close look at your thesis to determine whether your research has turned up information that will require you to rephrase your original statement. Suppose your original thesis was: "Moderate alcohol consumption reduces the risk of heart attacks, promotes healthier social relationships, and contributes to longevity." But after looking through your note cards you realized that the evidence of traumatic lifelong effects suffered by children of alcoholic parents contradicts the portion of your original claim that stated that moderate alcohol use "promotes healthier social relationships." In this case, you would have to revise your original thesis to bring it into line with the new evidence your research has unearthed. When you cross-check your thesis statement against your notes you will often discover that new information will require you to revise your original assertion.

USING YOUR NOTES TO CREATE AN OUTLINE

Once you are satisfied that your note cards are complete, you need to sort them to discover the arrangement that will best allow you to develop a coherent structure for the entire paper. To do this, group together index cards with the same or similar headings (indicated in the upper left-hand corner).

These groups represent sections of your paper that should be placed in a logical and coherent order. Since there are so many ways you can arrange the sections, it is imperative that you let your thesis statement suggest the direction you should take in developing your topic. Perhaps the most useful for research papers that present and defend an assertion is the problem–solution format. The first section of the paper defines the nature of the problem and offers evidence of its seriousness. This section may also investigate different hypotheses put forward to explain the causes of the problem. In the middle section the writer considers the advantages and disadvantages of alternative solutions. The final section of the paper presents the writer's own recommendation and supports it with appropriate reasons and evidence.

For example, the sample student paper at the end of this chapter, "Why Doesn't the Government 'Just Say Yes' to Funding Prevention Programs Against Drug Abuse?" is organized around the thesis that "short of changing society's attitudes toward using drugs, only federally funded mass education stands a real chance of stopping the drug epidemic." For this student, the note cards he had taken were most effectively organized as follows:

1. Causal explanations put forward to explain widespread drug use in contemporary American society
2. The effects of cocaine use in professional sports, on Wall Street, and in Hollywood
3. Why are attempts to stop the flow of drugs from the supply side by arresting the dealers, intercepting the drugs, and encouraging crop substitution ineffective?
4. Why are attempts to stop drug use by mandatory drug-testing ineffective?
5. Why government funded mass education is a solution that might work

The sequence in which these groups of note cards are arranged follows a straightforward pattern. The student first defines the nature of the problem, considers theories put forward to explain what might be causing it, examines the effects the problem is having on different areas of society, considers the merits of various solutions put forward to deal with the problem, states his objection to these proposed solutions, and lastly presents arguments that support his recommended solution.

Once the note cards have been organized in groups that define the individual sections of the paper, and cards within groups have been arranged in a sequence that defines the order in which information will be developed within sections, the key phrases on each of the note cards can be used to create a complete outline. You may decide to use a general heading or a key phrase that appears frequently in each group as a main heading in your outline. For example, "causal explanations put forward to explain widespread drug use in contemporary American society" accurately reflects the content of note cards in the first section of the paper. Once the cards with similar content have been grouped together, the outline created from the headings gives you an accurate picture of the order, arrangement, and divisions of the sections of your paper. For example, here is what an outline for the paper appearing at the end of the chapter would look like:

I.   Current theories explaining widespread drug use
     A.   Weil and Rosen's theory of "innate need"
     B.   Philip Slater's theory of societal pressure
II. Evidence of increasing drug use in the success-oriented areas of sports, finance, and entertainment
     A.   the effects of cocaine use in professional sports
     B.   the effects of cocaine use on Wall Street
     C.   the effects of cocaine use in Hollywood
III. Unsuccessful efforts of the government to stop the drug epidemic
     A.   Unsuccessful attempts on the "supply" side
          1.   arresting the dealers
          2.   intercepting the drugs
          3.   encouraging crop substitution in countries where produced
     B.   Ineffective attempts to stop drug use on the "demand" side
          1.   mandatory drug testing
          2.   voluntary "just say no" programs
          3.   drug treatment programs
IV. The crucial role of education in preventing drug abuse
     A.   Reduced funding for drug education programs
     B.   A recommendation for increased governmental support of mass education programs

The benefit of creating an outline from your note cards is that it allows you to tinker with different arrangements for the material in your paper. Does any section need to be filled out with more supporting evidence? You can easily spot gaps where information is needed. By the same token, you can see whether you have taken notes that don't bear directly on your thesis, are extraneous, and should be eliminated.

Test the ideas expressed in the headings against your thesis statement. Material that does not illuminate, support, develop, or explain the main idea should be omitted. Are there approximately the same number of note cards for each major section? Use your outline to check whether individual sections provide equal levels of support to develop the entire paper. If any sections are insufficiently developed, you may need to return to the library to gather more material.

Creating the Rough Draft

Different choices are available in writing a rough draft. Many students find it helpful to compose the introduction first, informing readers in a straightforward way of what issue, topic, or idea the paper will cover. Asking a provocative question catches the audience's attention and challenges them to reexamine their unquestioned assumptions and beliefs on the subject. Another effective way of introducing readers to the issue is with a brief review of the controversy that gives a historical context in which to understand the discussion.

A dramatic or attention-getting quotation is another method skilled writers use to capture the audience's attention. For example, a paper exploring the relationship between writing and alcoholism might begin with a quote by Horace: "no poems can please nor live long which are written by water drinkers" (Horace 65–8 B.C. from *Epistles*, I, 19).

The introduction not only states the question at issue, but should also tell the reader how you plan to demonstrate the validity of your hypothesis. If you wish you may include some general comments as to the kinds of sources you intend to use, and give an overview of the approach you intend to follow in developing your argument. Before beginning to write the main portion of your paper be sure to have your outline and note cards in front of you. Detach each group of note cards and spread them out in front of you so you can clearly see the contents of each card. In the rough draft your only concern is with writing or typing the information from your note cards in a coherent order, using the information on each card to illustrate, explain, or substantiate headings from your outline. Don't be concerned about questions of style or grammar. Your primary goal should be to get down the ideas in your outline and support them with the specific quotations, summaries, facts, and observations written on your cards. As you write, be sure to leave extra space between lines and a wide margin on both sides that will give you room to add corrections or make changes in the original text.

Frequently compare what you are writing against the note cards and outline to check that you have not omitted any important points or supporting evidence. Check the wording of any quotations you have copied from your note cards to make sure you have not unintentionally omitted any of the original wording.

Quotations are useful when you wish to support, illustrate, or document important points by citing the opinions of experts or authorities in the field. Quotations are also useful when the language in which ideas are expressed is so vivid, unique, or memorable that a summary or paraphrase would fail to do justice to the original passage. Although most of your paper should be written in your own words, there are occasions when it is important for your readers to hear the voice of your original sources. Quotations of less than four lines are normally run into the text but separated from it by sets of double quotation marks. Unless what you quote can be made grammatically part of your own sentence you must reproduce all punctuation and capitalization exactly as it appears in the original. If you change the capitalization to make the quote part of your own sentence, be sure to check that your introductory phrase and what you are quoting combine to make a complete sentence with the same verb tenses. For example:

> Weil and Rosen's research has led them to conclude that many religions have used marijuana, alcohol, and other psychoactive drugs to enable followers to "transcend their sense of separateness and feel more at one with nature, God and the supernatural."

Quotations of more than four lines should be separated from the text, single spaced, and indented. No quotation marks are necessary as the form here indicates that you are quoting.

The wording of the quotation should be exactly as it appears in the original except that occasionally you may have to insert a word or phrase to correct or clarify the original passage. Words or phrases so added should be placed in brackets to indicate that these are editorial emendations. You may want to add a word or phrase when a word in the original passage is misspelled, when you wish to supply specific names that clarify an unclear pronoun reference, and when you wish to indicate that you have underlined part of a quotation for emphasis. For example, if the original quote was "Coca's being grown all over Brazil, Venezuela, and Argentina too, according to the State Department's Bureau of International Matters," you might feel it necessary to clarify how the production of a coca crop is related to cocaine. An interpolation to clarify the meaning of the original appears in enclosed square brackets:

> Coca's [from which cocaine is made] being grown all over Brazil, Venezuela, and Argentina too, according to the State Department's Bureau of International Matters.

The Latin word *sic* (thus or so) also can be placed in brackets after misspelled words, or words or phrases that are incorrectly used, to let the reader know that the error is in the original material, not in your restatement.

Whenever you omit a part of a sentence from the original you must indicate your omission with an ellipsis (three spaced periods) placed where the omitted passage occurred. If the ellipsis appears at the end of a sentence, these three periods appear in addition to any punctuation in the original. For example:

Cocaine is one way a growing segment of our society is finding escape from the tedium of daily life. And fame and stardom can be just as tedious as anything else. . . .

If the sentence ends in a question mark your quote should end with three spaced periods and a question mark. If the sentence ends in a period, as in the example above, place the ellipsis at the end after one additional period indicating the end of the original sentence. Omission of material in a sentence beginning a quotation should be indicated by three spaced periods, as follows:

. . . Contac, Sudafed, certain diet pills, decongestants, and heart and asthma medications can register as amphetamines on the test.

Omission of material from a sentence within a quotation is indicated as follows:

Anti-inflammatory drugs and common pain killers, including Datril . . . and Nuprin, mimic marijuana.

If what you are quoting is a phrase from a sentence, it should be enclosed in quotation marks and unobtrusively blended into your own sentence, making sure that the syntax of the quote and the syntax of your original sentence are in agreement. When you are quoting a passage that you must put within double quotation marks and that also itself contains a quotation, the double quotation marks appearing in the original should be changed to single quotation marks. For example:

Knowledgeable insiders note the change, "'Cocaine is a negotiable instrument in this town,' said one veteran producer, familiar with drug dealing."

This rule applies only to sentences that are run into the text. Quotations of more than four lines should be separated, single-spaced, and set off from the text as a block without being enclosed in quotation marks. Quoted material within the block quotation should be enclosed in double quotation marks even if the source quoted uses single quotation marks. For example:

Perhaps the most sinister aspect of the growing use of cocaine in the TV industry is the way it is used as a medium of exchange. "Cocaine is a negotiable instrument in this town," said one veteran producer, familiar with drug dealing.

As important as quotations are, they should never exceed 15 percent of your original paper and should be used only in circumstances in which nothing else would substantiate, illustrate, clarify, or dramatize a point as effectively.

While writing the rough draft, look at what you have put down from the reader's perspective. Would a change in the order of the presentation make your ideas clearer?

One of the most important things you can do to help the reader understand the main idea of your paper is to use clear transitional words, phrases, and sentences to signal how parts of the paper are connected to each other. Even though the ideas are presented in an order that is clear to you, you must make every effort to help your reader understand the organization of your paper and perceive relationships between the sections. Short transitional phrases, or even short paragraphs, are invaluable in informing the reader how paragraphs are related to each other. These guide words serve as explicit directions signaling the relationship between paragraphs and sections.

Transitions may be of several kinds. Some signal your reader that you are following a chronological order with words such as *now, when, before, after, during, while, next, finally, later, meanwhile,* and *soon.* Other linking words express causal relationships, such as *as a result, since, consequently, because, therefore,* and *thus.* Still other guide words express intensification, such as *furthermore, really, in addition, ultimately,* or *moreover.* Some express limitation, restriction, or concession, such as *although, yet, however, even though, still, despite, but,* or *granted.*

One especially effective kind of transition is an introductory phrase or short transitional paragraph that refers back to prior material while also serving as a connecting bridge into the next section. These short connecting paragraphs allow the writer to sum up the ideas in one section before going on to the next.

As with the introduction, there are many choices available when deciding how to end your paper. If your paper has investigated a problem and considered alternative solutions offered by others, your conclusion might present your own solution along with evidence and reasons required to ensure its acceptance. Some writers prefer to end their papers, especially those that deal with complex issues, with a thought-provoking question intended to keep readers thinking about the implications of the issue. Other writers prefer to use the conclusion to suggest how the issue in question relates to a wider context. Most frequently, however, writers briefly enumerate the most important points turned up by their research and emphasize how these points prove the validity of the idea expressed by the thesis statement in the introduction.

Revising the Rough Draft into a Final Draft

Careful revision of your rough draft can make your paper many times better. James Michener said, "I have never thought of myself as a good writer. Anyone who wants reassurance of that should read one of my first drafts. But I'm one of the world's great revisers."

Transforming a rough draft into a final draft entails testing everything that you have put down — every sentence, every paragraph, every section — to see whether it relates to the central idea expressed in your thesis statement. In fact, some writers find it helpful to write the thesis statement on a separate piece of paper and place it where they can see it while they rewrite their rough draft. Revising consists of eliminating everything from your paper that does not substantiate, exemplify, or explain this thesis sentence.

To evaluate whether any passage really contributes to substantiating or developing the idea contained in the thesis statement try to see your paper from the viewpoint of a prospective reader. What passages, words, or sentences would the reader see as unnecessary or confusing? At what points would your reader require additional examples or evidence to emphasize an idea, or more effective transitions to signal the relationship between different parts of your paper? Revision is best carried out by going through your paper several times, looking for different kinds of things to improve each time. The first reading should be used to improve the paper's overall organization. Is there any section that would be better placed elsewhere? You may want to rearrange paragraphs if you discover that a change in the order of presentation will make your ideas clearer. Do transitions effectively signal your reader where a paragraph fits in the total organization of the paper? You might need to write short transitional paragraphs, often no longer than a single sentence, to guide your reader smoothly from one section to the next. Transitions should be unobtrusive and make it possible for your reader to follow your line of thought.

If you are satisfied with the overall presentation of your ideas, next consider all the things that might be improved *within* paragraphs. Does each paragraph center around one idea that is clearly related to one aspect of your paper's thesis? Do other sentences in your paragraph clarify this idea by explaining or presenting evidence to support it? Keep in mind that each paragraph must contain a major idea stated in the topic sentence and supporting sentences that clarify or explain the topic sentence. You may find that some sentences in your paragraphs do not support or illustrate the idea in the topic sentence. Go ahead and delete them.

In addition to relevancy, your paragraphs should be checked to see whether they are equally well developed and supported with effective samples, evidence, and quotations from source documents. Some paragraphs might be so long that they will have to be divided into several shorter paragraphs, each of which must still have its own topic sentence. Conversely, a series of short paragraphs without topic sentences might be consolidated into one coherent paragraph with a topic sentence.

Test your paragraphs for unity and coherence by asking yourself whether these sentences provide facts and details that would lead a reasonable person to believe the truth of your topic sentence. Evidence that illustrates the central idea in your paragraphs can take the form of examples, statistics, citation of authorities, illustrative analogies, or anything else that presents specific, interesting, and relevant information. Also, consider whether you might arrange supporting sentences in a more sensible and logical order.

STYLE

Consider how your choice of words can be improved. Choose words that express clearly, simply, and concretely what you mean to say. Just as every paragraph must clearly support the development of the paper's thesis, and just as every sentence within a paragraph must support, illustrate, or clarify that paragraph's topic sentence, so every word in a sentence must be necessary to express that sentence's thought.

When you revise to improve style, go through your paper looking for sentences that might be recast in the active voice. First, find the verb, ask who is doing what to whom, and rewrite the sentence to conform to the basic subject-verb-object (or complement) pattern. When you find prepositional phrases that wander off from the trunk of your sentence, prune them back.

Change your method of editing by reading your paper aloud. Do you hear any sentences that you would not understand if you had not written them? Does the introduction of your paper immediately capture your interest? If you find the opening superfluous, imagine how your readers will feel. The beginnings of most rough drafts are notoriously expendable. Is it easy to tell how the paper is organized at first glance, or do you need to insert clearer signposts letting your reader know that you are defending a thesis, making a value judgment, or recommending a certain course of action to solve a problem? Does each section of your paper contain enough different kinds of evidence from a variety of sources to substantiate your points?

Do any of the sections of your paper bore you to tears? If it fails to keep your interest, pity your audience. See if you can improve these sections through clever analogies, attention-getting quotations, and unusual and interesting examples. There is no law that research papers must be dull.

Don't be afraid to experiment with language. Substitute down-to-earth words for abstract jargon. Cut through the fog. Say it simply by using single words for the following circumlocutions:

although	for	in spite of the fact that
because	for	due to the fact that
where	for	in the place that

if	for	in the event that
after	for	at the conclusion of
now	for	at this point in time
when	for	at the time that

Do you hear any clichés, hackneyed expressions, or trite phrases that could be rewritten in your own voice to express your ideas, insights, and opinions? Most importantly, are all the words you have written really necessary? Any words that do not make your thoughts clearer to the reader should be eliminated.

Next, reread your paper, this time double-checking whether you have accurately transcribed the information from your note cards. If you have combined direct quotations from one source with supporting interpretations from other sources, make sure that you have not omitted any necessary documentation. Is every source you have cited also included in the list of works cited or bibliography that will be turned in along with your paper?

Are there places where additional direct quotations are necessary to give your ideas greater weight, conviction, and validity? Have you remembered to indicate clearly the source of every quotation at the point where it is introduced in your paper? Check whether in recopying information from your note cards you have mistaken a quotation for your own words.

Using the New MLA and APA Styles to Document the Manuscript

In 1984 the Modern Language Association (MLA) introduced a radically simplified method of documenting sources. In this new system of crediting sources any quotation, fact, line of poetry, or other source you would normally document with a footnote or endnote is followed by parentheses with the author's last name and the page reference. The paper that appears at the end of this chapter uses this new system. If the author's name is mentioned in the sentence, you need only provide the page number in parentheses. For example, notice the following sentence taken from the sample student research paper:

> Murray takes the opposite view, claiming that coaches have been known to coerce players into using drugs in order to perform better (28).

The parenthetical reference indicates that this citation refers to material taken from page 28 of a work by Thomas H. Murray. A complete reference on the page listing works cited at the end of the paper gives all necessary information:

Murray, Thomas. "The Coercive Power of Drugs in Sports." *The Hastings Center Report* 13 (1983): 24–30.

Complete information for correct models of documentation is provided by the *MLA Handbook for Writers of Research Papers, Theses, and Dissertations,* second edition (1984). Although most humanities courses will require you to follow the style described by the *MLA handbook,* most scientific and technical courses require quite different procedures of documentation. Instructors in the social sciences will require the style set forth in the *Publication Manual of the American Psychological Association* [APA], third edition (1983). The bibliographical documentation of the APA style is similar to the MLA from but differs from it in some important respects. In the following list of examples, the most commonly encountered forms of citation are listed for a wide variety of references. In each set, the MLA form appears first, followed by the style recommended by the APA.

An article in a Journal with Continuous Pagination of the Volume for That Particular Year
Rockas, Leo. "A Dialogue on Dialogue." *College English* 41 (1980): 570–80.
Rockas, L. (1980). A dialogue on dialogue. *College English, 41,* 570–80.

The issue number is not mentioned because the volume is continuously paginated throughout the year; hence, only the volume number (41) is necessary.

An Article from a Magazine Issued Weekly
Sanders, Sol W. "The Vietnam Shadow Over Policy for El Salvador." *Business Week* 16 Mar. 1981: 52.

Note that all months except May, June, and July are abbreviated in MLA.

Sanders, S. W. (1981, March 16). The Vietnam shadow over policy for El Salvador. *Business Week,* p. 52.

A Book by a Single Author
Shishka, Bob. *An Introduction to Broadcasting.* Chicago: Wade Press, 1980.
Shishka, B. (1980). *An introduction to broadcasting.* Chicago: Wade Press.

A Book by Two or Three Authors
Murphy, Mark, and Rhea White. *Psychic Side of Sports.* Reading: Addison-Wesley, 1979.

Only the first author's name, as it is given on the title page, appears — last name first.

Murphy, M. & White, R. (1979). *Psychic side of sports.* Reading, Ma.: Addison-Wesley.

A Book by More than Three Authors or Editors
Allen, David Yale, et al. *Classic Cars.* London: Macmillan, 1978.
Allen, D. Y., Collins, B., Mirsky, S., & Powell, R. T. (1978). *Classic cars.* London: Macmillan.

A Book by a Corporate Author
Modern Language Association. *MLA Handbook for Writers of Research Papers, Theses, and Dissertations.* 2nd ed. New York: Modern Language Association, 1984.
Modern Language Association. (1984). *MLA handbook for writers of research papers, theses, and dissertations* (2nd ed.). New York: Author.

APA substitutes *Author* for the publisher's name when a book is published by its author.

A Collection of Essays by Different Authors Compiled by an Editor
Sebok, Ted, ed. *How Animals Communicate.* Bloomington; Indiana University Press, 1977.
Sebok, T. (Ed.). (1977). *How animals communicate.* Bloomington: Indiana University Press.

A Work in an Anthology
Arnold, Charles. "How Monkeys Use Sign Language." *How Animals Communicate.* Ed. Ted Sebok. Bloomington: Indiana UP, 1977. 40–50.
Arnold, C. (1977). How monkeys use sign language. In T. Sebok (Ed.), *How animals communicate.* (pp. 40–50). Bloomington, IN: Indiana University Press.

A Book that Is Translated with Both the Author and Translator Named
Fernandez, Ruth. *The Architectural Heritage of the Moors.* Trans. Wanda Garcia. London: Routledge, 1980.
Fernandez, R. (1980). *The architectural heritage of the moors* (W. Garcia, Trans.). London: Routledge. (Original work published 1976)

A Book by Two or Three Authors; a Revised or Later Edition
Reichman, Stuart, and Marsha Deez. *The Washington Lobbyist.* 5th ed. New York: Harcourt, 1978.
Reichman, S., & Deez, M. (1978). *The Washington lobbyist* (5th ed.). New York: Harcourt.

A Book Published in More than One Volume
Thorndike, Lynn. *A History of Magic and Experimental Science.* 3 vols. New York: Columbia UP, 1941.
Thorndike, L. (1941). *A history of magic and experimental science.* (Vols. 1–3). New York: Columbia University Press.

A Republished or Reprinted Book
Nilsson, Martin P. *Greek Folk Religion.* 1940. Philadelphia: University of Pennsylvania Press, 1972.
Nilsson, M. P. (1972). *Greek folk religion.* Philadelphia: University of Pennsylvania Press. (Original work published 1940)

A Newspaper Article
Petzinger, Thomas J., Gary Putka, and Stephen J. Sansweet. "High Fliers." *Wall Street Journal* 12 Sept. 1983, sec. 1: 1+.
Petzinger, T. J., G. Putka, & S. J. Sansweet. (1983, September 12). High fliers. *Wall Street Journal*, sec. 1, pp. 1, 7.

A Book Review
Bill Katz. Rev. of *Norman Rockwell: My Adventures as an Illustrator*, by Norman Rockwell. *Library Journal* 85 (1960): 648.
Katz, B. (1960). [Review of *Norman Rockwell: My adventures as an illustrator*]. *Library Journal, 85*, 648.

Some Less Common Bibliographic Forms

A Book Published as a Volume in a Series
Hochberg, Julian E. *Perception*. Vol. 7 of *Foundations of Modern Psychology Series*. 22 vols. Englewood Cliffs: Prentice Hall, 1964.
Hochberg, J. E. (1964). *Perception. Vol. 7. Foundations of modern psychology series*. Englewood Cliffs: Prentice Hall.

A Lecture or Publicly Delivered Paper
Flaye, Sue. "Zen Buddhism and Psychotherapy." Conference on Zen Buddhism. Fargo, 17 March 1988.
Flaye, S. (1988, March). *Zen buddhism and psychotherapy*. Paper presented at the Conference on Zen Buddhism, Fargo.

A Personal Interview
Gold, Mark. Personal interview. December 2, 1987.

The name of the person interviewed should appear first, followed by the kind of interview (personal, telephone) as well as the date.

Gold, M. (1987, December 2). [Unpublished personal interview].

A Reference to an Article from Dissertation Abstracts
Knutt, Meg. "The Many Masks of Ted Hughes." *DAI* 44 (1984): 474B. Albion University.
Knutt, M. (1984). The many masks of Ted Hughes. *DAI, 44*, 474B.

An Introduction, Foreword, Preface, or Afterword of a Book
Wise, Robert. Foreword. *The Film Director*. By Richard L. Bare. New York: Macmillan, 1971. ii–v.
Wise, R. (1971). Foreword. In R. L. Bare, *The film director*. New York: Macmillan, ii–v.

A Radio or Television Program
Egypt: Quest for Eternity. National Geographic Society. PBS. WNET, Newark. 28 February 1982.

National Geographic Society. (1982, February 28). *Egypt: Quest for Eternity*. Newark: PBS.

A Reference to a Recording
Richardson, Sir Ralph. *The Poetry of Blake*. Caedmon, TC 1101, 1958.
Richardson, R. (1958). *The poetry of Blake*. New York: Caedmon.

A Government Publication of the Executive Branch
United States. Bureau of the Budget. *Special Analysis: Budget of the United States, Fiscal Year 1967*. Washington: GPO, 1966.
United States. Bureau of the Budget. (1966). *Special analysis: Budget of the United States, fiscal year 1967*. Washington, DC: U.S. Government Printing Office.

Preparing the Manuscript

1. Type your paper on good quality 8½-by-11-inch white paper.
2. Make sure you have a copy for yourself.
3. Type on only one side of each page.
4. Leave at least a 1- to 1½-inch margin at the top, bottom, left-hand, and right-hand sides of each page.
5. Your paper, including bibliography, should be double spaced.
6. Indent each paragraph consistently, whether you indent five, six, or seven spaces. Quotations of more than four lines should be separated, single-spaced and set off from the text as a block without being enclosed in quotation marks.
7. Starting with the second page, number each page consecutively in the upper right-hand corner. Type your last name in the upper left-hand corner of each page, including pages of your bibliography and footnotes.
8. The title page should display your name, your teacher's name, the course name and number, and the date submitted as well as the full title of your research paper.
9. To facilitate the reading of your paper, fasten it in a plastic folder or with a paper clip.
10. If required by your teacher, make sure you have turned in all your note cards, bibliography cards, and outline with your final copy.
11. Proofread your paper and make any last-minute corrections neatly in ink.

What follows is a sample research paper, annotated to illustrate typical features.

Double space.———— Jack Manion
                   Professor Kent
                   English 102
                   March 17, 1989

                   Why Doesn't the Government "Just Say Yes" to Preventative
                                Education Against Drug Abuse?

Introduction of   The phenomenon of drug abuse now poses a grave threat to our country. The
the topic as a   extent of damage caused by drugs in terms of lives and lost productivity is
problem to be   staggering. From elementary school students to the executive suites of Wall
solved.   Street, the insidious effects of the drug epidemic has left no area of American
Student states   society untouched. In light of the obvious magnitude of this problem, why isn't
thesis.   more being done to educate young people as to the nature and dangers of taking
                   drugs? All the solutions that have been put forward are plagued with many
                   obvious disadvantages. In my view, the government should institute a massive
                   preventative education program to help children and teenagers understand the
                   dangers of using drugs.

                     Why drug use should have escalated so radically in the 1980's and become
                   such a big part of our society is a question that many have tried to answer.
                   Perhaps if we understood the reasons why so many are taking drugs, the
                   solutions proposed would be more effective.

                     Andrew Weil, a professor of addiction studies at the University of Arizona,
                   and Winifred Rosen, suggest that the need to alter consciousness is
                   necessary to physical and psychological well-being; they assert that the
                   need to transcend the monotony of everyday life and feel at one with the
                   universe is basic to human nature:

Block quotation   Human beings are pleasure-seeking animals who are very inventive
single spaced,   when it comes to finding new ways to excite their senses and gratify
indented and   their appetites. . . . Because drugs can, temporarily at least, make the
centered.   ordinary extraordinary, many people seek them out and consume them
                       in an effort to get more out of life (18).

                     Weil and Rosen assert that since people all over the world engage in these
                   activities, human beings are not culturally influenced to use drugs but
                   rather have an innate need to alter consciousness.

                     A more credible explanation for this widespread problem is offered by
                   the sociologist, Philip Slater, who claims that our culture conditions us
                   through advertising to expect that our problems will be resolved within

minutes. This leads to an inability to tolerate frustration and to the belief that all problems are susceptible to an immediate "quick fix" (7).

Slater reveals that as society's values and norms have changed, fashions in drug use have also changed. After World War II, alcohol use was promoted through images of the "typical suburban alcoholic of the forties and fifties and the wealthy drunks glamorized by Hollywood" (7). Economic class and social values determine the kind of substances or drugs to which people become addicted. Slater observes that "marijuana and psychedelics" were used by the sixties generation, whereas "cocaine [is] for modern Yuppies" and "heroin [is used by] the hopeless of all periods" (7).

Slater's conclusion is a very persuasive one. Advertising constantly bombards us with messages that we can cope only by using some substance or product. Although we may flatter ourselves that "we may be smart enough not to believe the silly claims of the individual ad, but can we escape the underlying message on which all of them agree? . . . Can we reasonably complain about the amount of addiction in our society when we teach it every day" (8)?

No one would dispute the fact that drugs have had a profound impact on our society. Crime, much of it drug-related, has gone up dramatically in the last twenty years. Newspapers are filled with stories of those who have had their lives ruined because of their addiction to drugs. Cocaine, in particular, has spread to almost every sector of American life. The extent to which drug use has escalated can be judged by examining its effects in three different areas in our society: in the field of sports, in the financial sector, and in the entertainment industry.

Athletes use drugs for many of the reasons identified by Slater—to remain competitive and to win at all costs. Thomas H. Murray, a professor of ethics and public policy at the University of Texas, points out that many athletes are coerced into using drugs in order to remain competitive with other athletes who are willing to risk addiction by taking performance-enhancing drugs (27). Still other athletes take drugs to numb the pain of injuries and risk permanent physical damage in order to remain competitive.

This practice is defended by Norman Fost who claims that performance-enhancing drugs pose no higher health risks than taking vitamins. He says that athletes, in any case, always have free choice as to whether or not to use drugs (7). Murray takes the opposite view, claiming

Material inserted to clarify put in brackets.

Student's summary of opposing viewpoints with analysis of underlying assumptions.

that coaches have been known to coerce players into using drugs in order to
perform better (28). It is significant that both Murray and Fost take it for
granted that the pressure to win is the main cause of drug use by athletes.

Peter Gent, a former offensive-end for the Dallas Cowboys, and author of
North Dallas Forty, notes that drugs are not only used to enhance
performance on the field, but are used after the game as well to celebrate a
win or numb the pain of a loss. Gent theorizes that:

> Cocaine is one way a growing segment of our society is finding
> escape from the tedium of daily life. And fame and stardom can be
> just as tedious as anything else . . . . Today's players seem to be
> using cocaine to avoid the awful pain of coming down after the
> tremendous high of game day (15).

— Ellipsis shows omitted material.

A producer of television shows, Frank Swertlow, reveals that drugs,
especially cocaine, have permeated the entertainment industry. Swertlow
observes that:

> Perhaps the most sinister aspect of the growing use of cocaine in
> the TV industry is the way it is used as a medium of exchange.
> "Cocaine is a negotiable instrument in this town," said one veteran
> producer, familiar with drug dealing. "You might not be able to pay
> a writer or an actor or a director a bonus; so you pay him in
> cocaine" (10).

Actors under pressure need cocaine to perform. Writers take cocaine because
they believe it makes them more creative. Production budgets are frequently
altered to accommodate drug costs. Swertlow reports that some producers are
successful in getting contracts for their TV pilots solely because of their
ability to procure and supply "coke" (12).

Paradoxically, the public continues to admire many of these actors, writers,
and producers while disparaging the dismal quality of shows that,
ironically, are the result of such widespread cocaine use.

As an article in the Wall Street Journal makes clear, cocaine use has
spread beyond the football field and the silver screen to the world of finance. The
dimensions of the problem are startling:

> In Chicago, cocaine use is spreading in the city's commodities
> trading and financial centers. "A few people take a toot before the
> trading session and maybe a few times during the day," says one
> member of the Chicago Board of Trade, himself a user. "It's like
> drinking coffee." He estimates that 10% of the traders and brokers
> he knows use cocaine on the job (Petzinger, Putka, and Sansweet 1).

— Quoted matter within block quotation enclosed in double quotation marks.

Manion 4

The use of drugs by athletes or entertainers may be disturbing but it is not as alarming as the spectre of drug use by brokers, and managers of large portfolios containing the pension funds for millions of Americans. Apparently, those in charge of the securities and financial services industry react in much the same way as do the owners of NFL teams when cocaine use is exposed. It is first denied and when overwhelming evidence is presented, cocaine abuse is treated simply as "an image problem" (Petzinger, Putka, and Sansweet 22).

— Author(s) not cited in text are in parenthesis.

Like athletes and actors, traders use cocaine to eliminate any feelings of inadequacy and to feel more successful. While it is true that people in professional sports, in the entertainment industry, and on Wall Street are under tremendous pressure to succeed, these areas simply reflect more intensely the pressures put on everyone in our society.

Hundreds of times each day we are urged to buy, eat, drink, or use products that will instantly make us better-looking, sexier, younger, healthier, more successful and more desirable. Slater appears absolutely correct when he asserts that our society glorifies drug use.

Of course, it is ironic that people in the United States hold other countries responsible for the widespread use of drugs when the real reasons for increasing drug use are inherent in our society's values. In essence, we are falling back on the same "quick fix" mentality that created the problem in our attempts to stop drug abuse.

The solutions that have been tried thus far—like arresting the dealers, intercepting the flow of drugs or encouraging crop substitution in countries where drugs are grown—have proven ineffective, according to the Editors of <u>Dollars & Sense</u>. They point out that many countries in South and Central America are heavily dependent on the revenues produced by the coca crops (from which cocaine is made) for a significant percentage of their national income (Editors 6). The profits to be had from growing coca plants are as much as 29 times greater (up to $4,000 an acre) than money which could be earned from such legal crops as corn, rice, and barley ($140 an acre). One-fourth of Bolivia's gross national product is based on cocaine and 100,000 Bolivians are employed in the cocaine industry.

— Student analyzes solutions tried thus far.

Moreover, America remains the primary market for cocaine since according to the National Narcotics Intelligence Consumers Commission "6 percent of U.S. cocaine users consume 60% of the cocaine" produced in these countries. The conclusion is inescapable: cocaine addiction is almost exclusively the

Manion 5

"property" of American society (Editors 7). Even more disturbing, the amount of cocaine available is now greater than the demand for it. The cocaine industry has responded by producing "crack," a cheaper, much more concentrated, highly addicting and deadly form of cocaine (Editors 7).

Tragically, efforts to educate people to stay away from drugs have been undercut; the budget for drug education programs has been reduced during the Reagan administration "from 14 million in 1981 to less than 3 million in 1985," and proposed funding for drug-treatment programs is no higher than what it was in 1980 (Editors 8).

If economic pressures have doomed attempts to solve the problem from the "supply" side, attempts to solve the problem from the "demand" side have centered around the idea of mandatory drug-testing. Advocates make the case that although drug-testing is intrusive, it is necessary as a means of protecting society against a problem that has reached epidemic proportions.

Anne Marie O'Keefe, a psychologist and lawyer who specializes in health issues, argues that urinalysis violates the basic Fourth Amendment guarantees against "unreasonable search and seizure" (38). She objects to mandatory drug-testing by employers on the grounds that the use of the results of drug-testing to evaluate employees, when no shortcomings in job performance are evident, is a breach of constitutionally guaranteed civil rights. O'Keefe states that statistics show drug-testing to be, on the whole, highly inaccurate, producing both "false negative" results and "false positive" results often leading to job loss (35). She cites studies to prove that many over-the-counter drugs give erroneous "false positive" indications of drug use. For example:

> . . . Contact, Sudafed, certain diet pills, decongestants, and heart and asthma medications can register as amphetamines on the test. Cough syrups containing dextromethorphan can cross-react as opiates, and some antibiotics show up as cocaine. . . . Even poppy seeds, which actually contain traces of morphine, and some herbal teas containing traces of cocaine can cause positive test results for these drugs (35).

The right to privacy is a key issue in the whole controversy surrounding drug-testing. Even if the results could be confirmed, what worries most people is the possibility that the test results would not be kept confidential, regardless of the promises of the government or private employers. These issues were at the center of a case in the Carlstadt-East Rutherford School System in New Jersey where students were going to be required to take mandatory urinalysis tests.

Student cites evidence to support thesis.

Student incorporates quotation into syntax of the sentence.

Manion 6

School officials claimed their policy of mandatory physical examinations would be enacted to determine whether students had "'any physical defects, illnesses or communicable diseases'" (qtd. in Flygare 329). The proposed test included provisions for testing students for drug use. The students brought suit against the school board, arguing that "under the subterfuge of a forced medical examination" drug-testing violated Fourth Amendment rights prohibiting unreasonable "search and seizure" (329).

Lawyers for the students argued that the small percentage of students (28 out of 520) referred for counseling for drug related problems did not constitute evidence of a genuine need to institute mandatory testing for the entire student body. The New Jersey State Court decided mandatory drug-testing was unconstitutional on the grounds that the "'comprehensive medical examinations violated the reasonable privacy expectations of school children'" (qtd. in Flygare 329).

This case illustrates some of the legal and ethical problems produced by society's attempt to deal with the drug crisis solely through the "quick fix" of mandatory drug-testing. But surprisingly, little has been done to deal with the underlying causes. The Editors of Dollars & Sense report that "the Reagan administration has substantially cut funding" for "drug treatment programs (to help heavy users) and [for] preventative education." They also note that "instead of these programs, the administration has made 'voluntary' drug-testing and Nancy Reagan's 'just say no' clubs the real center pieces of its demand-side strategy" (Editors 8).

— Student cites an indirect source for a quotation.

By not understanding that the place where you stand the best chance of stopping drug abuse is in the schools when people are most vulnerable to peer pressure and form lifelong habits, the government's reduction of funds is clearly ill-advised and short-sighted. Clearly, the single most important action the government should take would be to support mass-education programs to prevent children and teenagers from getting involved with drugs in the first place. The efforts might be modeled on the same kinds of programs that successfully educated the public about the dangers of cigarette smoking. The latest report by the Surgeon General states that cigarettes are as addicting as other drugs. Yet, millions of people have stopped smoking because of these programs. Doubtless, there are significant differences between taking drugs and smoking cigarettes, but the fact remains that preventative education programs are one of the few potentially workable solutions that has not been seriously supported.

— Student concludes that preventative mass education is the best solution.

Manion 7

Works Cited

Editors of Dollars & Sense Magazine. "White Lines, Bottom Lines:
Profile of a Mature Industry." Dollars & Sense Dec. 1986:
6-8.

— Five spaces

Flygare, Thomas J. "Courts Foil Schools' Efforts to Detect Drugs."
Phi Delta Kappan 68 (1986): 329-30.

Fost, Norman. "Banning Drugs in Sports: A Skeptical View." The
Hastings Center Report 16 (1986): 5-10.

— Article in a journal with continuous pagination for that year.

Gent, Peter. "Between the White Lines: The NFL Cocaine War." The
Dallas Times Herald 4 Sept. 1983, Magazine: 13-15.

Murray, Thomas H. "The Coercive Power of Drugs in Sports." The
Hastings Center Report 13 (1983): 24-30.

O'Keefe, Anne Marie. "The Case vs Drug Testing." Psychology Today
June 1987: 34-38.

— Article in a journal with separate pagination for each issue.

Petzinger, Thomas J., Gary Putka, and Stephen J. Sansweet. "High
Fliers." Wall Street Journal 12 Sept. 1983, sec. 1: 1+.

Slater, Philip. "Want-Creation Fuels Americans' Addictiveness." St.
Paul Pioneer Dispatch 6 Sept. 1984, sec. 1: 7.

— A signed article in a daily newspaper.

Swertlow, Frank. "Hollywood's Cocaine Connection." TV Guide
28 Feb. 1981: 7-12.

Weil, Andrew and Winifred Rosen. Chocolate to Morphine:
Understanding Mind-Active Drugs. Boston: Houghton Mifflin,
1983.

— A book by two authors.

PART TWO

Pro and Con Arguments

7

Pro and Con Arguments on Controversial Questions

Introduction

This chapter contains paired pro and con selections on various topics to show how the same issue can be viewed from opposite perspectives.

The selections illustrate a wide range of situations where the same sets of facts are subject to more than one interpretation, where people disagree about the way a problem should be solved, or where people bring two competing sets of values to bear on a single subject. The format is also intended to help stimulate and structure discussions by encouraging thinking about an issue in the context of readings that dramatize specific points and counterpoints. Besides helping you to understand the issue and its practical and theoretical implications, the pro–con format will enhance your understanding of one of the oldest procedures logicians and philosophers, such as Socrates, have used down through the ages.

Socrates believed that the most productive dialogues are those in which evidence for all points of view is critically examined and considered in a point-counterpoint fashion. Socrates' use of opposing positions for discussion is called a *dialectic,* and the famous Socratic dialogues capture the give and take of conversation between Socrates and his companions on a whole range of issues. These dialogues introduced an invaluable way of thinking about things that was not geared toward right answers or facts that could be memorized. Each issue was considered to be open-ended and discussable from different viewpoints. The emphasis was on learning how to evaluate information from opposing perspectives.

The following chapter is meant to engage you in a series of "dialogues" on controversial questions and you will find it rewarding only to the extent that you actively enter into the debates, weighing the significance of various arguments and the varying styles of rhetorical persuasion.

The sixteen debates that follow cover a wide range of classic and contemporary issues including gun control, black English, the new woman, pornography, the abominable snowman, a 1929-style crash, abortion, feeding the hungry masses, capital punishment, government, bilingualism, sexual harassment, unanimous juries, animal experimentation, South Africa, and genetic engineering.

These pro and con debates will acquaint you with a wide range of issues and problems and show you that for each issue there are at least two proposed solutions, perspectives, or alternative remedies. Many of the issues debated are in areas where there are no simple answers, or where the resolution involves hard choices and necessary compromises. Every attempt has been made to present the strongest, most cogent argument put forward on each side of the issue, and to present them in this adversarial way to sharpen your awareness of the dilemmas involved.

For each set of arguments, headnotes identify the points at issue, provide background on the individual writers, and give information on where and when the article or chapter was first published.

One of the benefits of entering into any of the following debates, by reading the articles and answering the end-of-selection questions, is that it will enhance your critical thinking skills. You will discover how to distinguish between fact and opinion, recognize an author's bias, identify logical fallacies and faulty reasoning, develop skill in making judgments and drawing logical conclusions, evaluate the accuracy and completeness of information presented, and clarify your own ideas on the issue.

GUN CONTROL

Edward Abbey

The Right to Arms

Edward Abbey is a former ranger for the National Park Service whose books include the novels Fire on the Mountain *(1963),* The Monkey Wrench Gang *(1975), and* Good News *(1980) as well as several collections of essays including, most recently,* Beyond the Wall: Essays From the Outside *(1984). "The Right to Arms" originally appeared in Abbey's Road (1979). Abbey argues that gun regulation is the first step toward authoritarian rule. He cites examples to show that governments that currently have or have had gun control laws are for the most part oppressive and tyrannical states whose citizens have no recourse against the crimes committed by the regime in power.*

If guns are outlawed
Only outlaws will have guns
(True? False? Maybe?)

1   Meaning weapons. The right to own, keep, and bear arms. A sword and a lance, or a bow and a quiverful of arrows. A crossbow and darts. Or in our time, a rifle and a handgun and a cache of ammunition. Firearms.

2   In medieval England a peasant caught with a sword in his possession would be strung up on a gibbet and left there for the crows. Swords were for gentlemen only. (*Gentlemen!*) Only members of the ruling class were entitled to own and bear weapons. For obvious reasons. Even bows and arrows were outlawed—see Robin Hood. When the peasants attempted to rebel, as they did in England and Germany and other European countries from time to time, they had to fight with sickles, bog hoes, clubs—no match for the sword-wielding armored cavalry of the nobility.

3   In Nazi Germany the possession of firearms by a private citizen of the Third Reich was considered a crime against the state; the statutory penalty was death—by hanging. Or beheading. In the Soviet Union, as in Czarist Russia, the manufacture, distribution, and ownership of firearms have always been monopolies of the state, strictly controlled and supervised. Any unauthorized citizen found with guns in his home by

the OGPU or the KGB is automatically suspected of subversive intentions and subject to severe penalties. Except for the landowning aristocracy, who alone among the population were allowed the privilege of owning firearms, for only they were privileged to hunt, the ownership of weapons never did become a widespread tradition in Russia. And Russia has always been an autocracy — or at best, as today, an oligarchy.

4   In Uganda, Brazil, Iran, Paraguay, South Africa — wherever a few rule many — the possession of weapons is restricted to the ruling class and to their supporting apparatus: the military, the police, the secret police. In Chile and Argentina at this very hour men and women are being tortured by the most up-to-date CIA methods in the effort to force them to reveal the location of their hidden weapons. Their guns, their rifles. Their arms. And we can be certain that the Communist masters of modern China will never pass out firearms to *their* 800 million subjects. Only in Cuba, among dictatorships, where Fidel's revolution apparently still enjoys popular support, does there seem to exist a true citizen's militia.

5   There must be a moral in all this. When I try to think of a nation that has maintained its independence over centuries, and where the citizens still retain their rights as free and independent people, not many come to mind. I think of Switzerland. Of Norway, Sweden, Denmark, Finland. The British Commonwealth. France, Italy. And of our United States.

6   When Tell shot the apple from his son's head, he reserved in hand a second arrow, it may be remembered, for the Austrian tyrant Gessler. And got him too, shortly afterward. Switzerland has been a free country since 1390. In Switzerland basic national decisions are made by initiative and referendum — direct democracy — and in some cantons by open-air meetings in which all voters participate. Every Swiss male serves a year in the Swiss Army and at the end of the year takes his government rifle home with him — where he keeps it for the rest of his life. One of my father's grandfathers came from Canton Bern.

7   There must be a meaning in this. I don't think I'm a gun fanatic. I own a couple of small-caliber weapons, but seldom take them off the wall. I gave up deer hunting fifteen years ago, when the hunters began to outnumber the deer. I am a member of the National Rifle Association, but certainly no John Bircher. I'm a liberal — and proud of it. Nevertheless, I am opposed, absolutely, to every move the state makes to restrict my right to buy, own, possess, and carry a firearm. Whether shotgun, rifle, or handgun.

8   Of course, we can agree to a few commonsense limitations. Guns should not be sold to children, to the certifiably insane, or to convicted criminals. Other than that, we must regard with extreme suspicion any effort by the government — local, state, or national — to control our right to arms. The registration of firearms is the first step toward confiscation. The confiscation of weapons would be a major and probably fatal step

into authoritarian rule—the domination of most of us by a new order of "gentlemen." By a new and harder oligarchy.

The tank, the B-52, the fighter-bomber, the state-controlled police   9
and military are the weapons of dictatorship. The rifle is the weapon of democracy. Not for nothing was the revolver called an "equalizer." *Egalité* implies *liberté*. And always will. Let us hope our weapons are never needed—but do not forget what the common people of this nation knew when they demanded the Bill of Rights: An armed citizenry is the first defense, the best defense, and the final defense against tyranny.

If guns are outlawed, only the government will have guns. Only the   10
police, the secret police, the military. The hired servants of our rulers. Only the government—and a few outlaws. I intend to be among the outlaws.

Questions for Discussion and Writing

1. What reasons does Abbey present to support his argument against gun control? How does Abbey's citation of historical and current regimes, such as those of Nazi Germany, the USSR, China, and Chile, illustrate his claim that "wherever a few rule many—the possession of weapons is restricted to the ruling class and to their supporting apparatus: the military, the police, the secret police"?

2. What is the relationship between the italicized lines with which the essay opens and Abbey's thesis? Specifically, how does Abbey's argument take the often heard statement against gun regulation and give it a novel twist that forms the thesis of his argument, namely "If guns are outlawed, only . . . the police, the secret police, the military" will have guns?

3. Abbey mentions many governments, countries, regimes, mottos (*egalité* and *liberté*), and folk heroes (William Tell, Robin Hood). How do these references serve to support the thesis of Abbey's argument? How does Abbey use the strategy of "virtue by association" by mentioning Robin Hood and William Tell as examples of legendary heroes who carried and used their own weapons? How does Abbey attempt to change the negative connotations firearms generate by associating them with positive images? Why is it significant that these heroes are populist leaders, defenders of the rights of the people against evil governments?

4. How does Abbey's depiction of himself ("I don't think I'm a gun fanatic. . . . I'm a liberal") help make his argument more effective?

How is his depiction of himself as a liberal intended to persuade his audience that he is concerned about the rights of citizens? How is his strategy of portraying himself as a decent, average citizen (while at the same time depicting the government as a potential dictatorship seeking to take away his rights) intended to influence his readers? What effect is his mentioning that he stopped hunting when the numbers of hunters outnumbered the deer intended to have? Collectively, how are all of these means of presenting himself intended to enhance his credibility?

5. Evaluate Abbey's argument in a short essay. If you were in favor of gun control would any of the points in his chapter make you rethink your position? To what extent are you convinced that those governments that seek to enforce their will by force of arms instead of mutual consent are governments that want to disarm the citizenry? Is it a flaw, in your opinion, that Abbey fails to draw a distinction between handguns and other firearms? Would his argument have been more effective had he done so?

6. If Abbey had his way and all the people in a neighborhood were armed and began patrolling the streets as a citizen's militia, would society become more or less violent than it is currently? Discuss your reaction.

Adam Smith

Fifty Million Handguns

Adam Smith is a pseudonym of George J. Goodman, graduate of Harvard and former Rhodes scholar. The author of several novels and screenplays, he is best known for work he has published as "Adam Smith," the name he borrowed from a renowned eighteenth-century economist. He writes about business and finance for Esquire, For- tune, *and* New York Magazine *and was moved to write about gun control after a good friend, Michael Halberstam, was murdered in 1981. Smith draws on his own personal experience and uses statistics to advocate the banning of handguns as the first important step in eliminating the onslaught of random violence afflicting American society. Smith's argument for the elimination of handguns owned by private citizens is strengthened by the fact that he once saw the issue from the perspective of gun owners like those he is now trying to persuade. "Fifty Million Handguns" first appeared in* Esquire *(1981).*

"You people," said my Texas host, "do not understand guns or gun   1
people." By "you people" he meant not just me, whom he happened to
be addressing, but anyone from a large eastern or midwestern city. My
Texas host is a very successful businessman, an intelligent man. "There
are two cultures," he said, "and the nongun culture looks down on the
gun culture."

My Texas host had assumed—correctly—that I do not spend a lot of   2
time with guns. The last one I knew intimately was a semi-automatic
M-14, and, as any veteran knows, the Army bids you call it a weapon,
not a gun. I once had to take that weapon apart and reassemble it
blindfolded, and I liked it better than the heavy old M-1. We were also
given a passing introduction to the Russian Kalashnikov and the AK-47,
the Chinese copy of that automatic weapon, presumably so we could use
these products of our Russian and Chinese enemies if the need arose. I
remember that you could drop a Kalashnikov in the mud and pick it up
and it would still fire. I also remember blowing up a section of railroad
track using only an alarm clock, a primer cord, and a plastic called C–4.
The day our little class blew up the track at Fort Bragg was rather fun.
These experiences give me some credibility with friends from the "gun
culture." (Otherwise, they have no lasting social utility whatsoever.) And
I do not share the fear of guns—at least of "long guns," rifles and
shotguns—that some of my college-educated city-dweller friends have,

perhaps because of my onetime intimacy with that Army rifle, whose serial number I still know.

3   In the gun culture, said my Texas host, a boy is given a .22 rifle around the age of twelve, a shotgun at fourteen, and a .30–caliber rifle at sixteen. The young man is taught to use and respect these instruments. My Texas host showed me a paragraph in a book by Herman Kahn in which Kahn describes the presentation of the .22 as a rite of passage, like a confirmation or a bar mitzvah. "Young persons who are given guns," he wrote, "go through an immediate maturing experience because they are thereby given a genuine and significant responsibility." Any adult from the gun culture, whether or not he is a relative, can admonish any young person who appears to be careless with his weapon. Thus, says Kahn, the gun-culture children take on "enlarging and maturing responsibilities" that their coddled upper-middleclass counterparts from the nongun culture do not share. The children of my Texas host said "sir" to their father and "ma'am" to their mother.

4   I do not mean to argue with the rite-of-passage theory. I am quite willing to grant it. I bring it up because the subjects of guns and gun control are very emotional ones, and if we are to solve the problems associated with them, we need to arrive at a consensus within and between gun and nongun cultures in our country.

5   Please note that the rite-of-passage gifts are shotguns and rifles. Long guns have sporting uses. Nobody gives a child a handgun, and nobody shoots a flying duck with a .38 revolver. Handguns have only one purpose.

6   Some months ago, a college friend of mine surprised a burglar in his home in Washington, D.C. Michael Halberstam was a cardiologist, a writer, and a contributor to this magazine. The burglar shot Halberstam, but Halberstam ran him down with his car on the street outside before he died, and the case received widespread press. I began to work on this column, in high anger, right after his death. A few days later, John Lennon was killed in New York. These two dreadful murders produced an outpouring of grief, followed immediately by intense anger and the demand that something be done, that Congress pass a gun-control law. The National Rifle Association was quick to point out that a gun-control law would not have prevented either death; Halberstam's killer had already violated a whole slew of existing laws, and Lennon's was clearly sufficiently deranged or determined to kill him under any gun law. The National Rifle Association claims a million members, and it is a highly organized lobby. Its Political Victory Fund "works for the defeat of antigun candidates and for the support and election of progun office seekers." Let us grant the National Rifle Association position that the accused killers in these two recent spectacular shootings might not have been deterred even by severe gun restrictions.

7   In the course of researching this column, I talked to representatives of both the progun and the antigun lobbies. Anomalies abound. Sam Fields,

a spokesman for the National Coalition to Ban Handguns, is an expert rifleman who was given a gun at age thirteen by his father, a New York City policeman. The progun banner is frequently carried by Don Kates Jr., who describes himself as a liberal, a former civil rights worker, and a professor of constitutional law. Fields and Kates have debated each other frequently. Given their backgrounds, one might expect their positions to be reversed.

Some of the progun arguments run as follows: 8

Guns don't kill people, people kill people. Gun laws do not deter 9
criminals. (A 1976 University of Wisconsin study of gun laws concluded that "gun control laws have no individual or collective effect in reducing the rate of violent crime.") A mandatory sentence for carrying an unlicensed gun, says Kates, would punish the "ordinary decent citizens in high-crime areas who carry guns illegally because police protection is inadequate and they don't have the special influence necessary to get a 'carry' permit." There are fifty million handguns out there in the United States already; unless you were to use a giant magnet, there is no way to retrieve them. The majority of people do not want guns banned. A ban on handguns would be like Prohibition — widely disregarded, unenforceable, and corrosive to the nation's sense of moral order. Federal registration is the beginning of federal tyranny; we might someday need to use those guns against the government.

Some of the antigun arguments go as follows: 10

People kill people, but handguns make it easier. When other 11
weapons (knives, for instance) are used, the consequences are not so often deadly. Strangling or stabbing someone takes a different degree of energy and intent than pulling a trigger. Registration will not interfere with hunting and other rifle sports but will simply exercise control over who can carry handguns. Ordinary people do not carry handguns. If a burglar has a gun in his hand, it is quite insane for you to shoot it out with him, as if you were in a quick-draw contest in the Wild West. Half of all the guns used in crimes are stolen; 70 percent of the stolen guns are handguns. In other words, the supply of handguns used by criminals already comes to a great extent from the households these guns were supposed to protect.

"I'll tell you one thing," said a lieutenant on the local police force in 12
my town. "You should never put that decal in your window, the one that says THIS HOUSE IS PROTECTED BY AN ARMED CITIZEN. The gun owners love them, but that sign is just an invitation that says 'Come and rob my guns.' Television sets and stereos are fenced at a discount; guns can actually be fenced at a premium. The burglar doesn't want to meet you. I have had a burglar tell me, 'If I wanted to meet people, I would have been a mugger.'"

After a recent wave of burglaries, the weekly newspaper in my town 13
published a front-page story. "Do not buy a gun — you're more likely to shoot yourself than a burglar," it said. At first the police agreed with that

sentiment. Later, they took a slightly different line. "There is more danger from people having accidents or their kids getting hold of those guns than any service in defending their houses; but there was a flap when the paper printed that, so now we don't say anything," said my local police lieutenant. "If you want to own a gun legally, okay. Just be careful and know the laws."

14   What police departments tell inquiring citizens seems to depend not only on the local laws but also on whether or not that particular police department belongs to the gun culture.

15   Some of the crime statistics underlying the gun arguments are surprising. Is crime-ridden New York City the toughest place in the country? No: your chances of being murdered are higher in Columbus, Georgia, in Pine Bluff, Arkansas, and in Houston, Texas, among others. Some of the statistics are merely appalling: we had roughly ten thousand handgun deaths last year. The British had forty. In 1978, there were 18,714 Americans murdered. Sixty-four percent were killed with handguns. In that same year, *we had more killings with handguns by children ten years old and younger than the British had by killers of all ages.* The Canadians had 579 homicides last year, we had more than twenty thousand.

16   H. Rap Brown, the Sixties activist, once said, "Violence is as American as apple pie." I guess it is. We think fondly of Butch Cassidy and the Sundance Kid; we do not remember the names of the trainmen and the bank clerks they shot. Four of our Presidents have died violently; the British have never had a prime minister assassinated. *Life* magazine paid $8,000 to Halberstam's accused killer for photos of his boyhood. Now he will be famous, like Son of Sam. The list could go on and on.

17   I am willing to grant to the gunners a shotgun in every closet. Shotguns are not used much in armed robberies, or even by citizens in arguments with each other. A shotgun is a better home-defense item anyway, say my police friends, if only because you have to be very accurate with a handgun to knock a man down with one. But the arguments over which kinds of guns are best only demonstrate how dangerously bankrupt our whole society is in ideas on personal safety.

18   Our First Lady has a handgun.

19   Would registry of handguns stop the criminal from carrying the unregistered gun? No, and it might afflict the householder with some extra red tape. However, there is a valid argument for registry. Such a law might have no immediate effect, but we have to begin somewhere. We license automobiles and drivers. That does not stop automobile deaths, but surely the highways would be even more dangerous if populated with unlicensed drivers and uninspected cars. The fifty million handguns outstanding have not caused the crime rate to go down. Another two million handguns will be sold this year, and I will bet that the crime rate still does not go down.

20   Our national behavior is considered close to insane by some of the other advanced industrial nations. We have gotten so accustomed to

crime and violence that we have begun to take them for granted; thus we are surprised to learn that the taxi drivers in Tokyo carry far more than five dollars in cash, that you can walk safely around the streets of Japan's largest cities, and that Japan's crime rate is going *down*. I know there are cultural differences; I am told that in Japan the criminal is expected to turn himself in so as not to shame his parents. Can we imagine that as a solution to crime here?

In a way, the tragic killings of Michael Halberstam and John Lennon have distracted us from a larger and more complex problem. There is a wave of grief, a wave of anger — and then things go right on as they did before. We become inured to the violence and dulled to the outrage. Perhaps, indeed, no legislation could stop murders like these, and perhaps national gun legislation would not produce overnight change. The hard work is not just to get the gunners to join in; the hard work is to do something about our ragged system of criminal justice, to shore up our declining faith in the institutions that are supposed to protect us, and to promote the notion that people should take responsibility for their own actions.

What makes us so different from the Japanese and the British and the Canadians? They are not armed, as we are, yet their streets and houses are far safer. Should we not be asking ourselves some sober questions about whether we are living the way we want to?

Questions for Discussion and Writing

1. How does Smith use the distinction between "the gun culture" and the "nongun culture" to develop his argument in favor of gun control?

2. What is the purpose of Smith's discussion of his previous experience with the M-14 and exposure to a variety of other weapons when he was in the army?

3. How are the murders of David Halberstam (Smith's college friend) and John Lennon related to the larger argument Smith is making?

4. Why, according to Smith, do police departments not like the idea of private citizens owning guns?

5. How does Smith use statistics (in the title and elsewhere) to develop the readers' awareness of the more important role guns play in American culture compared to the role they play in England, Canada, and Japan? Specifically, how does the comparative light thrown by these statistics support Smith's assertion that there is something seriously wrong with America's addiction to a "gun culture"?

6. Evaluate the degree to which Smith's argument serves his

announced purpose (stated as "we need to arrive at a concensus within and between gun and nongun cultures in our country"). What trade-offs does he offer in order to persuade people to give up handguns? To what extend does his essay present a moderate position?

7. How does Smith's strategy of presenting himself as a moderate advocating a compromise position toward gun control make it more likely that his arguments will be favorably received by those normally opposed to any form of gun regulation? Why would Smith's audience be more likely to accept a recommendation from someone whose experiences are essentially the same as theirs?

8. What effect is produced by Smith presenting the arguments for both sides on the issue before proposing his own recommendation?

9. How does Smith make skillful use of factual evidence and personal experience in exploring the question of gun control within the larger context of America's societal problems?

10. Draw up a list of pros and cons of the respective merits of Abbey's and Smith's arguments. Who, in your opinion, presents a stronger case? Use this list to explain your answer in a short essay.

11. Compare and evaluate the different means Abbey and Smith use in supporting their assertions. Specifically, compare and contrast Abbey's use of hypothetical examples to sketch out a menacing future with Smith's use of real evidence grounded in personal experience and statistics. In your opinion, is Abbey's position weakened because he does not grapple with the crucial differences between handguns and other firearms? Is Abbey's appeal to latent paranoia about the possibility of America turning into a totalitarian state as effective as Smith's more moderate stance? Smith is willing to make some concessions and does not insist on complete elimination of private ownership of guns; he is willing to allow shotgun and rifle ownership for hunting.

12. Draw on your own personal experience, if appropriate, to evaluate Abbey's and Smith's characterizations of the "gun culture." Which description in your opinion seems to be more accurate?

13. Formulate your own argument expressing your views on the gun control issue. Incorporate a summary of the argument of either Smith or Abbey and explain why you were not convinced by the other side's argument. Be sure to consider to what extent your own views on gun control were modified by either Abbey's or Smith's argument.

BLACK ENGLISH

James Baldwin

If Black English Isn't a Language, Then Tell Me, What Is?

James Baldwin's "If Black English Isn't a Language, Then Tell Me, What Is?" originally appeared on the Op-ed page of The New York Times *(July 29, 1979). The distinguished American essayist, novelist, and playwright is author of many books including* The Fire Next Time *(1963),* Notes of a Native Son *(1956), and* Just Above My Head *(1979). In this article Baldwin formulates an impassioned defense of the role played by black English as a "political instrument," "a proof of power," and "the most vivid crucial key to identity." He relates the development of black English to the history and experience of blacks in the United States and uses a stipulated definition of "language" to develop his claim that black English is a language, not merely a dialect. Baldwin doesn't suggest that black English be spoken instead of* standard English *but that it be accepted as a different but equal language.*

ST. PAUL DE VENCE, France—The argument concerning the use, 1
or the status, or the reality of black English is rooted in American history and has absolutely nothing to do with the question the argument supposes itself to be posing. The argument has nothing to do with language itself but with the *role* of language. Language, incontestably, reveals the speaker. Language, also, far more dubiously, is meant to define the other—and, in this case, the other is refusing to be defined by a language that has never been able to recognize him.

People evolve a language in order to describe and thus control their 2
circumstances, or in order not to be submerged by a reality that they cannot articulate. (And, if they cannot articulate it, they *are* submerged.) A Frenchman living in Paris speaks a subtly and crucially different language from that of the man living in Marseilles; neither sounds very much like a man living in Quebec; and they would all have great difficulty in apprehending what the man from Guadeloupe, or Martinique, is saying, to say nothing of the man from Senegal—although the "common" language of all these areas is French. But each has paid, and is paying, a different price for this "common" language, in which, as it

turns out, they are not saying, and cannot be saying, the same things: They each have very different realities to articulate, or control.

3   What joins all languages, and all men, is the necessity to confront life, in order, not inconceivably, to outwit death: The price for this is the acceptance, and achievement, of one's temporal identity. So that, for example, though it is not taught in the schools (and this has the potential of becoming a political issue) the south of France still clings to its ancient and musical Provençal, which resists being described as a "dialect." And much of the tension in the Basque countries, and in Wales, is due to the Basque and Welsh determination not to allow their languages to be destroyed. This determination also feeds the flames in Ireland for among the many indignities the Irish have been forced to undergo at English hands is the English contempt for their language.

4   It goes without saying, then, that language is also a political instrument, means, and proof of power. It is the most vivid and crucial key to identity: it reveals the private identity, and connects one with, or divorces one from the larger, public, or communal identity. There have been, and are, times, and places, when to speak a certain language could be dangerous, even fatal. Or, one may speak the same language, but in such a way that one's antecedents are revealed, or (one hopes) hidden. This is true in France, and is absolutely true in England: The range (and reign) of accents on that damp little island make England coherent for the English and totally incomprehensible for everyone else. To open your mouth in England is (if I may use black English) to "put your business in the street": You have confessed your parents, your youth, your school, your salary, your self-esteem, and, alas, your future.

5   Now, I do not know what white Americans would sound like if there had never been any black people in the United states, but they would not sound the way they sound. *Jazz*, for example, is a very specific sexual term, as in *jazz me, baby*, but white people purified it into the Jazz Age. *Sock it to me*, which means, roughly, the same thing, has been adopted by Nathaniel Hawthorne's descendants with no qualms or hesitations at all, along with *let it all hang out* and *right on! Beat to his socks*, which was once the black's most total and despairing image of poverty, was transformed into a thing called the Beat Generation, which phenomenon was, largely, composed of *uptight*, middle-class white people, imitating poverty, trying to *get down*, to get *with it*, doing their *thing*, doing their despairing best to be *funky*, which we, the blacks, never dreamed of doing—we *were* funky, baby, like *funk* was going out of style.

6   Now, no one can eat his cake, and have it, too, and it is late in the day to attempt to penalize black people for having created a language that permits the nation its only glimpse of reality, a language without which the nation would be even more *whipped* than it is.

7   I say that this present skirmish is rooted in American history, and it is. Black English is the creation of the black diaspora. Blacks came to the United States chained to each other, but from different tribes: Neither

could speak the other's language. If two black people, at that bitter hour of the world's history, had been able to speak to each other, the institution of chattel slavery could never have lasted as long as it did. Subsequently, the slave was given, under the eye, and the gun, of his master, Congo Square, and the Bible — or, in other words, and under these conditions, the slave began the formation of the black church, and it is within this unprecedented tabernacle that black English began to be formed. This was not, merely, as in the European example, the adoption of a foreign tongue, but an alchemy that transformed ancient elements into a new language: *A language comes into existence by means of brutal necessity, and the rules of the language are dictated by what the language must convey.*

There was a moment, in time, and in this place, when my brother, or   8
my mother, or my father, or my sister, had to convey to me, for example, the danger in which I was standing from the white man standing just behind me, and to convey this with a speed, and in a language, that the white man could not possibly understand, and that, indeed, he cannot understand, until today. He cannot afford to understand it. This understanding would reveal to him too much about himself, and smash that mirror before which he has been frozen for so long.

Now, if this passion, this skill, this (to quote Toni Morrison) "sheer   9
intelligence," this incredible music, the mighty achievement of having brought a people utterly unknown to, or despised by "history" — to have brought this people to their present, troubled, troubling, and unassailable and unanswerable place — if this absolutely unprecedented journey does not indicate that black English is a language, I am curious to know what definition of language is to be trusted.

A people at the center of the Western world, and in the midst of so   10
hostile a population, has not endured and transcended by means of what is patronizingly called a "dialect." We, the blacks, are in trouble, certainly, but we are not doomed, and we are not inarticulate because we are not compelled to defend a morality that we know to be a lie.

The brutal truth is that the bulk of the white people in America never   11
had any interest in educating black people, except as this could serve white purposes. It is not the black child's language that is in question, it is not his language that is despised: It is his experience. A child cannot be taught by anyone who despises him, and a child cannot afford to be fooled. A child cannot be taught by anyone whose demand, essentially, is that the child repudiate his experience, and all that gives him sustenance, and enter a limbo in which he will no longer be black, and in which he knows that he can never become white. Black people have lost too many black children that way.

And, after all, finally, in a country with standards so untrustworthy,   12
a country that makes heroes of so many criminal mediocrities, a country unable to face why so many of the nonwhite are in prison, or on the needle, or standing, futureless, in the streets — it may very well be that

both the child and his elder have concluded that they have nothing whatever to learn from the people of a country that has managed to learn so little.

Questions for Discussion and Writing

1. How does Baldwin develop his argument by stipulating a definition of language that states that only a language rather than a dialect made it possible for blacks to survive? Specifically, how was black English created as a form of communication between blacks who were brought from different tribes in Africa and did not speak the same language?

2. In essence, what is Baldwin's thesis about the role of language? In what way is language a "political instrument," a "proof of power," and "the most vivid and crucial key to identity"?

3. According to Baldwin, what special contributions to the language have been made by black people in the United States?

4. How does Baldwin use examples of the experiences of those who still speak varieties of French, Basque, Welsh, and Irish (Gaelic) to stress the importance of political and cultural contexts on questions of linguistic acceptability? How does dialect serve to confirm or reject identity of certain groups?

5. What role did black English play in Baldwin's own life in enabling him to survive?

6. What role did the evolution of black English play in establishing and consolidating a common identity for "blacks [who] came to the United States chained to each other, but from different tribes"?

7. What reasons does Baldwin offer to support his thesis that black English is a language and not "what is patronizingly called a 'dialect'?"

8. What would happen to blacks, according to Baldwin, if their children were taught to repudiate black English?

9. For a research project, investigate the connection between Baldwin's novels and his assertion that language is a "political instrument" and a "proof of power." To what extent do his novels deal with the issues of identity and collective history?

10. For a research project, read any of the novels of Toni Morrison, including *Song of Solomon* (1977) and *Beloved* (1988), and discuss the role of black English in these novels. Would these works have been as effective had Morrison substituted standard English for black English? Write an essay using these novels as examples to evaluate the validity of Baldwin's thesis.

John Simon

Playing Tennis Without a Net

John Simon, the witty and influential drama critic of New York
Magazine, *argues in "Playing Tennis Without a Net" (from Paradigms Lost [1980], a collection of essays assailing linguistic abuses)
against accepting any dialect, including black English, as an equivalent to Standard English. Simon uses an analogy to argue that just as a
game of tennis requires rules so language needs a set of commonly
accepted standards to permit effective and unambiguous communication. If everyone spoke in a private language, says Simon, we would
have equality, but also chaos. Simon asserts that dialects are often less
clear than Standard English because words and phrases in dialect can
have multiple meanings.*

1   The National Council of Teachers of English is about to debate once
again at its 1979 annual meeting in New York a resolution passed in a
1974 business meeting of the Conference on College Composition and
Communication that accepted as valid "all the regional, ethnic, and
social dialects of American English." The C.C.C.C. voted, in other words,
to make acceptable in schools and colleges any kind of English that until
recently was called substandard, although the N.C.T.E. then added an
equivocal codicil stating that there was "a distinction between spoken
and written English." The document justifying this resolution is a special
issue of the journal *College Composition and Communication* entitled
"Students' Right to Their Own Language."

2   The first and most obvious flaw in all this is the N.C.T.E.'s jesuitical
assumption that one can differentiate between spoken and written
English — that one can tell students that "I be baaad" (meaning "I am
good") is acceptable when spoken but inadequate when written. There is
enough schizophrenia on the rampage in the world without nurturing
further forms of it in the classroom. But the very ideas behind the
resolution and the brochure that is meant to proselytize for them strike
me as not a little absurd and, ultimately, pernicious.

3   The committee to which we owe the C.C.C.C. language statement
consists of a baker's dozen of academics, apparently carefully chosen to
represent both renowned and obscure institutions and to include
women, blacks, Hispanics, and teachers at community colleges. Nothing
could be more democratic. In the introduction to the eighteen-page
double-column statement, the committee permits itself a rare irony:

"Lack of reliable information . . . seldom prevents people from discussing language questions with an air of absolute authority." To prove their own authoritativeness, the committee members helped one of their number, Jenefer Giannasi (whose Christian name reads rather as if she didn't know how to spell it), compile a thirteen-page single-column bibliography, containing mostly items on sociolinguistics, descriptive linguistics, and such—my favorite being "Davis, Philip W.: *Modern Theories of Language,*" which deals with "the theories of Saussure, Hjelmslev Bloomfield, the Post-Bloomfieldians, and the Prague School; tagmemics; Firthian linguistics; stratificational grammar; transformational generative grammar." Nevertheless, Miss Giannasi and her colleagues write things like "a controversy which must be faced before staff can react to students' needs," which is rather like what you hear from medical receptionists: "Doctor will see you now." Clearly, there are cases where neither Bloomfield nor the Post-Bloomfieldians, to say nothing of tagmemics, prove to be of much help.

But right at the beginning, our committee commits an error in logic 4 that is considerable for such valiant structural linguists. The committee bemoans the fact that all kinds of people—"businessmen, politicians, parents, and the students themselves"—insist "that the values taught by the schools must reflect the prejudices held by the public." It soon becomes apparent that what these people want and agitate for through their representatives on various boards is nothing more or less than what has generally been called Standard English, which the committee prefers to call edited written English or edited American English (E.A.E.). In its democratic, pluralistic zeal, the committee obviously reprehends what I am still quite happy to call Standard English for being "Anglo" and ignoring, indeed affronting, the customs and needs of "the people," many of whom belong to black, Latin-American, or other ethnic groups. Yet, clearly, businessmen, politicians, parents, and students themselves (not to mention the historians, mathematicians, and nurses adduced earlier in the pamphlet) include a lot of people, probably at least as many as there are members of various ethnic groups. Why then should *their* traditions and demands be ignored?

The point, of course, is that everyone has a right to his ignorance and 5 no one is compelled to become educated. But everyone is then also entitled to suffer the consequences of choosing not to become educated. This is very different, needless to say, from having been discouraged from becoming educated or from, worse yet, having been deliberately prevented from so becoming. But when I read our supposed educators' statement that "we need to discover whether our attitudes toward 'educated English' are based on some inherent superiority of the dialect itself or on the social prestige of those who use it," I begin to despair. Could anything be sadder than the fact that those quotation marks around educated English come from the pen of an educator—someone who ought to be proud of the fact that generations of educators have labored to develop and codify that English? Yet now the C.C.C.C.'ers act as if there were something fishy and indecent about all this, something to condescend to with quotation marks, because, as they later put it, it is merely the dialect of the middle class. The poor old middle class, by the way, gets it coming and going. After centuries of kicks from above, it can now look forward to centuries of kicks from below.

6   And we read on: "We need to ask ourselves whether our rejection of students who do not adopt the dialect most familiar to us is based on any real merit in our dialect or whether we are actually rejecting the students themselves, rejecting them because of their racial, social, and cultural origins." Not only is ignorance going to be defended on the sacred ground of the right to nonconformity, but also it will be upheld on the still more sacred grounds of antiracism and antielitism. Under the circumstances, it is not surprising to find our committee arguing forthwith that "Mary daddy home" is just as comprehensible and good as "Mary's daddy is at home" and that "the grammar of one American dialect may require 'he is' in the third person singular present tense; the grammar of another dialect may require 'he be' in that slot."

7   Of course, what is the use of arguing with English teachers who pronounce "Mary daddy home" equally clear as "Mary's daddy is at home"? The former concatenation of words (it would be preposterous to call it a construction) could just as easily mean "the home of Mary's daddy" or "Mary's daddy had gone home" or God only knows what else. (Or perhaps I should write "Don't nobody but God know that," which our authors find "just as clear" and "in certain circumstances [unspecified] more emphatic.") It may be true that we can gradually figure out from the context what was meant, but why should we have to make such an effort? And suppose the speaker were trying to discuss more complicated matters with that kind of grammar. Where would *that* conversation lead?

8   As for "I be," "you be," "he be," etc., which should give us all the heebie-jeebies, these may indeed be comprehensible, but they go against all accepted classical and modern grammars and are the product not of a language with roots in history but of ignorance of how language works. It may be a regrettable ignorance, innocent and touching, one that unjust past social conditions cruelly imposed on people. But it *is* ignorance, and bowing down to it, accepting it as correct and perhaps even better than established usage, is not going to help matters. On the contrary, that way lies chaos. The point is that if you allow this or that departure from traditional grammar, everything becomes permissible — as, indeed, it has become, which is why we are in the present pickle.

9   Here is what our C.C.C.C.'ers have to say about this: "Once a teacher understands the arbitrary nature of the oral and written forms, the pronunciation or spelling of a word becomes less important than whether it communicates what the student wants to say. In speech,

*PO*lice communicates as well as po*LICE*, and in writing, 'pollice' is no insurmountable barrier to communication, although all three variations might momentarily distract a person unfamiliar with the variant." One difficulty with addressing oneself thoroughly to the absurdity of this pamphlet is that where every sentence, like the above, pullulates with logical and moral errors, one doesn't know where to begin with a rebuttal.

To start with, what does the crucial but glided-over term "less impor-   10 tant" mean to the committee? Should pronunciation and spelling mistakes be ignored entirely? Almost entirely? On alternate Tuesdays only? Should they be punished with merely one stroke of the ferule, as opposed to two for physical assault on the teacher? Furthermore, why should people have to be distracted even momentarily by having to figure out what other people are saying? There are situations in which these could cause serious damage. But, above all, language is not just a matter of communication. It is a way of expressing one's fastidiousness, elegance, and imaginativeness; it is also a way of displaying one's control over a medium, just as a fine horseman displays his horsemanship by the way he sits in the saddle and handles his horse. Even a person who desperately hangs on to the matio of his mount might make it from point A to point B, but that doesn't make him an equestrian.

The basic contradiction in which the committee wallows is this: on   11 the one hand, we are told that blacks and Chicanos and other minorities cannot be expected to know and speak the "dialect" of the established "Anglo" middle class and that we must have sympathy and respect for their dialects; on the other hand, we are told that these youngsters are just as bright as anybody else and can learn correct E.A.E. as easily as anyone. I am willing to give credence to either of these assertions, but I find it difficult to accept *both*. Thus we find our C.C.C.C.'ers declaring on page 7 that "dialect itself is not an impediment to reading" and "cannot be posited as a reason for a student's failure to be able to read E.A.E." But on page 12 we read: "Standardized tests depend on verbal fluency, both in reading the directions and in giving the answers, so even slight variations in dialect may penalize students by slowing them down." Well now, which will it be?

Again, we are told on page 6 that "dialect switching . . . becomes   12 progressively more difficult as the speaker grows older." But on page 16 we read that "it is unreasonable for teachers to insist that students make phonemic shifts, which we as adults have difficulty in making." Well, if it's so much easier for young people to learn, why can't their elders expect them to do so? It is, however, useless to expect anything resembling logic from people who could write the following: "All languages are the product of the same instrument, namely, the human brain. It follows, then, that all Languages and all dialects are essentially the same in their deep structure, regardless of how varied the surface structure might be. [This is equal to saying that the human brain is the human brain.]" And with this, the committee thinks that it has proved that all dialects are equally good.

13   But they are not—just as all human brains are not equally good, a simple fact that in their democratic, egalitarian frenzy the C.C.C.C.'ers cannot admit. Indeed, they will go so far as to assert that "if speakers of a great variety of American dialects do master E.A.E.—from Senator Sam Ervin to Senator Edward Kennedy, from Ernest Hemingway to William Faulkner—there is no reason to assume that dialects such as urban black and Chicano impede the child's ability to learn to write E.A.E. while countless others do not." Notice the choice of people of outstanding intellectual gifts or at least of privileged background from earliest childhood: these are not typical cases and so prove nothing. And just as individual situations vary, so do the circumstances behind dialects. For instance, the kinds of English that blacks and Chicanos speak are based on underlying thought structures that are not native and idiomatic but derived from African languages and from Spanish—and not the best Spanish at that—and so are not germane to the English language at all.

14   The disingenuousness of the committee is downright insidious. It argues that "just as most Americans added 'sputnik' to their vocabularies a decade or more ago, so speakers of other dialects can add such words as 'periostitis' or 'interosculate' whenever their interests demand it." Consider: "Sputnik" was at that time in every headline, in every news broadcast everywhere. The other two terms will always be abstruse for the average citizen, and "interosculate" is almost ridiculous—no doubt deliberately chosen for that reason.

15   With similar dishonesty, the committee perceives an analogy between fighting "he be" and "he don't" and the alleged efforts of yesteryear's teachers to prevent accreditation of "jazz," "lariat," and "kosher." But, clearly there are no more proper ways of saying "lariat" or "jazz" or "kosher," whereas there are such things as "he is" and "he doesn't." In fact, one wonders why people who believe so fanatically in the rights, if not indeed the superiority, of other dialects chose to cast their tract in E.A.E., especially since they are not particularly good at it. They write "alternate approaches" for "alternative approaches"; "because 'Johnny can't read' doesn't mean that Johnny is immature" for "that 'Johnny can't read,'" etc.; "different than" for "different from"; "equally as willing" for "equally willing"; and are capable of writing sentences like "Classroom reading materials can be employed to further our students' reading ability and, at the same time, can familiarize them with other varieties of English." Who would want to familiarize reading materials ("them") with varieties of English? Or take this alleged sentence: "For example, an unfamiliar speech rhythm and resulting pronunciation while ignoring the content of the message." And in the very next sentence (page 4) there is a "they" for which there is no antecedent.

16   "E.A.E. allows much less variety than the spoken forms," the

C.C.C.C.'ers pronounce. But that is just the point: to speak correctly yet with individualism and variety is, to adapt Frost's old trope, to play a good game of tennis with the net up; without a net, anyone can perform all kinds of meaningless prodigies. In any case, the point of language is not simply to communicate but to communicate with originality and imaginativeness — within the bounds of propriety. Otherwise, as Stéphane Mallarmé so wisely observed, "it might suffice by way of exchanging human thought to take or put into another's hand silently a coin." When language becomes a mere convenience, like the mute passing of money from hand to hand, it ceases to have any aesthetic or, indeed, humanistic value. And when accepted language begins to model itself on what a culturally underprivileged group or individual says, it becomes a parochialism. This is the very opposite of an ecumenical language, which is perhaps difficult to master, but which, once mastered, unites all its initiates in a common pursuit and a shared beauty.

Questions for Discussion and Writing

1. How is Simon's argument based on the assumption that language should provide an effective method of communicating with others of different backgrounds? How does it rely on the idea that the whole concept of education depends on the creation of a society in which citizens can communicate with each other?

2. Which specific words and phrases reveal Simon's attitude toward the proposal put forward by the C.C.C.C.? Identify these and write a short analysis of Simon's tone as it shapes the overall emotional cast of his argument. Are the judgments expressed by these emotionally loaded terms adequately supported by reasons and evidence elsewhere in Simon's essay?

3. What reasons does Simon advance to support his thesis that the NCTE's resolution is "not a little absurd and, ultimately, pernicious"?

4. What specific examples of poor writing and illogical thought does Simon present to discount the value of the recommendations put forward by the committee?

5. Why does Simon find it ironic that recommendations proposed by the committee should come from English teachers who are part of "generations of educators [who] have labored to develop and codify that English"? How does the fact that this issue arose originally in the context of a National Council of Teachers of English meeting illuminate Simon's defense of Standard English?

6. How does Simon use the fact that the phrase "Mary daddy home"

can convey different meanings to different audiences to illustrate his basic objection to the NCTE committee's proposal accepting "as valid 'all the regional, ethnic, and social dialects of American English'"? Specifically, how is Simon's analysis of this and other phrases related to his general objection to the acceptance of dialect as equivalent to Standard English? For example, assess the validity of his argument: "why should people have to be distracted even momentarily by having to figure out what other people are saying?"

7. Implicit in Simon's argument is his belief that only Standard English allows writers a way of expressing themselves with "fastidiousness, elegance, and imaginativeness." Is there any obvious reason why a skilled writer (for example, Toni Morrison or Maya Angelou) could not use dialect just as effectively as Standard English to achieve the same results?

8. How does Simon use the image of a horseman to present an argument by analogy? Specifically, in what way does the difference between an amateur horseman getting from point A to point B by hanging on for dear life and a skilled horseman who maneuvers the horse gracefully dramatize Simon's assertion that there are real differences between using Standard English or a dialect to communicate? How is this analogy related to Simon's assertion that extra effort is necessary to interpret a dialect because words and phrases can have multiple meanings?

9. In what specific cases does Simon object to what he perceives to be the use of faulty analogies offered as evidence by the committee to promote the acceptance of dialectic phrases such as "he be" and "he don't"?

10. How does Simon use examples of faulty syntax drawn from the committee's own writing to discount their recommendations?

11. How does the meaning of the title "Playing Tennis Without a Net" underscore Simon's principal argument? In what way does the presence of a net in tennis or of rules in language provide a standard by which the skill, originality, and creativity in playing tennis or communicating can be judged?

12. In an essay, compare and contrast the arguments of Simon and Baldwin. Pay particular attention to the idea that conflicts about accepting any dialect as the equivalent of Standard English are always implicitly connected to the acceptance or rejection of the group to which the dialect belongs. In your opinion, would Baldwin really

want black English to be accepted as the equivalent of Standard English and to be widely used? You might address the point of why Baldwin chooses Standard English to present his case for the acceptance of black English. Be sure to evaluate Simon's central assertion that although a Standard English phrase has a single relatively clear-cut meaning, one dialect phrase could be understood in many different ways by a nonnative speaker.

THE NEW WOMAN

Betty Winston Baye

You Men Want It Both Ways!

Betty Winston Baye is a reporter for the Courier Journal *in Louisville, Kentucky, and the author of* The Africans *(1983). "You Men Want It Both Ways!" appeared in* Essence *(July 1985). Baye argues that although men claim they want educated, independent, money-earning women, their egos cannot handle a true equal. Baye asserts that men really wish to continue the traditional unequal division of labor in the household.*

1   I thought the 1980's would be different, especially after the revolutionary sixties, when it was common to hear some Black men hollering about how Black women should walk ten paces behind their "kings" and have babies for the revolution. I thought that in the eighties, Black men and women had declared a truce in the war between the sexes and that we had reached, or were striving to reach, a level where we could enjoy each other's company as equals.

2   I know now, however, that I hoped for much too much. Though I don't presume to paint all Black men with one broad brush stroke, it seems to me that there are men — too many — who, for reasons that only they and God understand, find it necessary to lie and pretend that they just love independent women. That's what they say at first, but as their relationships develop, it becomes painfully obvious that what they really want are women who work to help bring home the bacon but also cook, clean and take care of them and their babies on demand. These new men want women who are articulate and forceful when they're taking care of business — but who, behind closed doors, become simpering sycophants who heed their every wish.

3   I am an independent woman, and I'll tell anybody that what my mother and many of the women of her generation did to keep home and family together I won't do, not for love or money. Whenever I meet a man who says he's interested in me, I tell him up front that I don't do no windows. I don't love housework. I don't love to cook, and I certainly don't reach a climax thinking about having to clean up behind a bunch of kids and some mother's son. If a man wants somebody to make him

home bread and fresh collard greens every night, then I'm definitely not the girl of his dreams.

Now, I realize that I'm not every man's cup of tea. But take it or leave 　4
it, that's where I'm coming from. I'll gladly work every day to help bring home the money so that my man and I can pool our resources to go out to dinner every once in a while, take a few trips during the year and to pay somebody willing (or needing) to cook, clean and do laundry.

Surprisingly, my attitudes don't turn too many men off — in fact, 　5
brothers seem turned on by my honesty and independence. My ex-husband is one case in point. At the dawn of our relationship, he swore to me that I was just what the doctor ordered. Said he'd never met a woman like me — intelligent, witty, educated, self-sufficient and not all that hard on the eyes. He went on about how he was just so thrilled that I had "chosen" him.

At first, everything was wonderful. But soon after I acquired a sweet 　6
contract to write my first book, the shit was on. It occurred to me that my beloved husband was just a bit jealous of my success. Before I knew it, I realized that he got some kind of perverse pleasure out of trying to insult me and make me look small in the eyes of my friends and professional colleagues. I remember how one time, for no special reason, he got up and announced in front of my childhood friend, her husband and their children that I was "a stupid bitch." Now, he had already published a novel, and to me he was a fine writer who could handle the English language as smoothly as butter sliding down a hot roll. But my book, and the money I got, just seemed to set him off. Not surprisingly, the marriage was finished before the book hit the shelves.

Had what happened in my marriage been an isolated case, I might 　7
have concluded that it was just "my problem" — something we women tend to do a lot. But it wasn't isolated. All around me, women friends of mine were and still are bailing out of relationships with men who say one thing, then do another.

A friend of mine got married a few years ago to a man she'd been 　8
dating for more than a year. This was a marriage made in heaven, or so she and we thought. Both she and her husband were talented go-getters who seemed to want the same things out of life. When they first met, she says, he told her he didn't dig her just for her body but also for her sharp mind. Before long, however, it became clear that the only thing he wanted to do with her mind was to cause her to lose it. She says he wanted her to be dynamic by day and servile by night. Finally, after much verbal and physical abuse, she split. Thankfully, her memorable excursion into his insanity didn't last for long. Now she's recovering quite nicely.

Strong, dynamic, intelligent, independent women are what men of 　9
the eighties say they want. They claim they want their women to go that extra mile, but what they really mean is that we should work twice as hard but not forget our responsibilities at home. When a woman spends

time with *their* children, cleans the house or cooks for *their* family, it often goes unnoticed. No matter how tired she is after a demanding day at work, the expectation is that these are *her* responsibilities. But when a man spends time with *their* children, cooks food for *their* family or cleans *their* house once a month, he acts like he deserves an Academy Award.

10   Money is another area that has the brothers confused. For example, there are the men who say that if we women want to be truly liberated we should be willing, on occasion, to pick up the tab for dinner or for a night on the town. The fact that many of these same men often get their jaws wired when women, in the presence of a waiter or others at the table, reach for their wallet and pull out the cash or credit card says they're not ready for liberation. They don't mind women paying but would much prefer that they slip them the money under the table, the way women used to do.

11   And there are also the double-talking men who claim they can handle a woman who makes more money than they do. At first, everything is all right, but in order to assuage their egos, some men start thinking that "just because" they are men, they must exert control over their women's money and become personal financial managers of sorts. She's smart enough to make the money, he knows, but he believes she doesn't have enough sense to know how to spend it, invest it or manage it. "Are you sure you can afford this?" is a common question, but one rarely asked out of concern for a woman's finances. He knows she can afford it; he'd prefer to think she can't.

12   Many of the same men rattle on about how if we women want equality, we should buy gifts for them, as they allegedly have always done for us. Gift giving is nice, but for women, it can be a double-edged sword. One well-known singer tells the story of how she bought gifts for her man, which he gratefully accepted. But she says that after a time, the man got real nasty and told her that he couldn't be bought — he wasn't for sale.

13   And, of course, there are the men who seem to think that success drops out of the sky — that it doesn't require hard work and long hours. I've seen men hotly pursue women who they know are busy and then get bent out of shape if the sister pulls out her datebook to see when she's free. These women say they are tired of feeling guilty and trying to explain to some yo-yo that they can't just saunter off to dinner on the spur of the moment when they've got a report to finish or a meeting to attend.

14   Brothers are all for liberation when it works to their advantage. Yet, what we have found out is that when men don't want a serious commitment, they encourage us to be independent — to be open-minded enough to accept the terms of an "open relationship." But try that same rap on them, and we're in for trouble. Try saying, "Okay, baby, I don't want a commitment either"; or better yet, beat them to the punch. All of a sudden they've decided that they're in love and want to settle down. They get jealous and accuse us of "using" them.

And what about men who claim they want total honesty with their   15
women? For many men, total honesty means that they want the freedom
to talk openly about their prior involvements, including relating to their
women intimate details about how many other women they've slept
with or how many have aborted their babies. In return, a man like this
often demands that his woman tell all her business to keep things in
balance. Unfortunately, what many sisters have found—often after they
are laid out on a stretcher or when they've had their past sexual exploits
thrown in their faces in the heat of an argument—is that many men
can't handle total honesty, especially if it's sexual honesty. Many men
still seem to buy into the Madonna/whore syndrome. They still believe
that their peccadilloes are understandable because everyone knows that
"boys will be boys." Women, however, especially *their* women, are
supposed to be innocents who somehow, perhaps through osmosis,
instinctively know how to turn them on in bed.

There are dozens of other ways that men send out mixed signals to   16
the women in their lives and show, through their words and deeds, that
they really want it both ways. They want us to drive the car—but from
the backseat. Mostly what they want is for things to be the way they
used to be. That, however, is a pipe dream. Black women, like their
counterparts of other races, are liberating their minds and their bodies
from the shackles of the past. Increasingly, women are refusing to waste
their lives trying to decode men's mixed messages and buying into some
man's macho fantasies. Instead, many women who are or want to be
high achievers are accepting the fact that the price of success may be
temporary loneliness. And even that loneliness is relative, since many of
us have learned that having a man isn't all there is to life.

Questions For Discussion and Writing

1. If you are female, are you getting mixed messages from men who
say they want liberated women but really want traditional women? If
you are male, are you getting mixed messages from women?

2. What does being "feminine" mean? To what extend does being
"feminine" mean appealing to the male ego so that men will think
they are in charge?

3. How does Baye's experience with her ex-husband underscore her
assertion that men may say they want independent women who
make money and take the initiative but in reality cannot cope with
women who are true equals?

4. To what extent did Baye's husband's jealousy of her success lead to
their divorce? How does this experience illustrate male adherence to a
double standard?

5. How does Baye's discussion of the following two points support her thesis? (*a*) Although men insist on complete honesty when disclosing their past sexual relationships, they reject women who are equally honest about their past sexual relationships. (*b*) Men may say they are glad if women pay in restaurants, but really want women to slip them money under the table so they can be the one to pay the waiter.

6. What examples does Baye offer that illustrate how men give out mixed signals to women? How do these examples strengthen her argument? Do you find them to be typical or atypical, isolated cases or truly representative of modern male–female relationships?

7. If you are female, what don't you do because you will be rejected by men for "liberated behavior"? On the other hand, what do you do to flatter the male ego because you are rewarded for traditional behavior? How have things really changed aside from increased career opportunities for women?

8. How does Baye seem to feel about the subject? Is she regretful, bitter, wistful, indignant? What specific words or phrases communicate her attitude?

9. Analyze any ad for a product (perfume, cigarettes, and so on) that creates an image of a "superwoman" who does everything expected of women traditionally but who also has a career. What words and images contribute to creating this stereotype?

10. For some interesting reading, compare observations of Baye and Singletary to those made on the battle of the sexes by the American humorist James Thurber in *The Thurber Carnival* (1945), *Thurber Country* (1953), or his play *The Male Animal* (1940).

Donald Singletary

You New Women Want It All!

Donald Singletary is a free-lance writer and public relations consul-
tant in New York City. "You New Women Want It All!" originally
appeared in Essence *(July 1985). Singletary accuses modern young*
women of wanting all the advantages of being liberated women but
also wanting many of the advantages of being traditional women.

A: Why is it always *sex, sex, sex*? Can't a man talk to me as a   1
professional?

B: All men want to do is talk business; there's no romance.

A: These guys are together all day at work; now they come in the club   2
and they're still over there in a group talking to each other.

B: Damn, I can't even come in here to have a quiet drink with my
girlfriend without men coming around to hit on us.

A: I feel that as a woman today I can have just as much freedom as a   3
man. That means a casual affair is okay.

B: I don't understand men. They want to jump into bed as fast as
they can. They don't want any commitment.

In each of the above, statements A and B were made by the *same*   4
woman at different times. In the second example they were made in the
same evening.

Imagine eating in an expensive restaurant. You pick up the shaker   5
and it reads: "salt or sugar." Or picture the announcer's voice at the
beginning of a boxing match: "In this corner we have the liberated
woman. And in the *same* corner we have the woman who wants to be
'kept.'" Let's place the man in the role of referee: How does he judge this
fight? Yes, it is confusing, isn't it? Not to mention annoying. It is *very*
annoying. What we have here are examples of mixed messages, conflicting signals. And to put it bluntly, it is the women who are sending the
confusing signals and the men who are getting confused. Not to mention
angry.

In the last few years — since women began their quest for greater   6
personal independence, better jobs and pay comparable to men's and the
right to make decisions about what they do with their bodies — men
have struggled to understand this "new woman." The signals that we are
getting are that women want to take charge of their own destinies. They

want to compete alongside men for the fruits of success in society. They no longer wish to rely on men for the things that they want out of life. Instead they have opted to get it themselves. Although these changes do in fact create some anxiety among men, many feel that they will ultimately free men from some of the traditional male responsibilities society has imposed upon them. Ideally, this should mean men no longer have to carry the full burden of financial support, decision making and being the aggressor in romantic pursuits. Right?

7   Wrong! That's one message women send. But there is another message that says, "I'll have my cake and eat yours too."

8   A perplexed former coworker of mine once said, "You would think that a women making, say, $35,000 a year could go out with whoever she wants—even the guy in the mail room. But no, she wants somebody who makes $45,000 a year! Why? Because she's still looking to be taken care of."

9   For this man and for many others, the assumption is that once a woman has the necessary financial security, the need to form relationships on the basis of what a man earns is gone.

Not so.

10   It's what some of us call the "my money, *our* money" syndrome.

11   Here's a typical example: A man and woman meet through a mutual friend. Both single, they begin chatting about themselves. They are both professionals, make approximately the same money, and each has attended a good college.

12   SHE: *You're very nice to talk to. It's so refreshing. A lot of men these days can't deal with an independent woman. They seem to always want the upper hand, and if you are making the same bread, they become insecure. I think they still expect women to be impressed with what they* do.

HE: *That's true. I even see that in some of my own friends. But I like a professional woman, not one who's dependent on a man.*

SHE: *That's me. Hey, why don't we have dinner sometime? I know a great little place.*

13   They go out to dinner at an expensive restaurant that *she* chooses. *At last,* he thinks, *a woman who doesn't wait for the man to take the initiative, an independent woman! Wow, I never thought I'd be taken anyplace like this by a woman.*

14   The check comes, and she waits patiently for *him* to pick it up. Thank goodness our hero has his American Express card up to date. I know guys who've had to excuse themselves from the table and dash out into the streets in search of a bank cash machine. In fact, I've been one of those guys. It's tough. You have to run out in the bitter cold (it's *always*

cold) without your coat because you don't want the waiter to think you've left without paying. As one of my cronies put it, "Women want it all today, from soup to nuts—and the man has to pay for the meal."

No one is suggesting, least of all me, that women *have* to pay or date "dutch." But when one professes her liberation, as did this woman, the man has the right to expect her to follow through. The emerging new woman has not only created confusion for men; she has created some problems for women as well. At least one of them, as you might expect, is a paradoxical one. Now that women have more money and more mobility, there don't seem to be any men around. There is, they say, a shortage of men. Not *any* men, mind you, but those with the "right stuff." In conversations between women and men, women and women, coast to coast, the question "Where are all the men?" always rears its head. **15**

I defy you to find one man, one *real* man, who actually believes there is a shortage of men. Yes, I know what the statistics say. But what I and other men see is quite different. We see women who walk around as if they couldn't care less about a man. Women don't have time. **16**

One of my own former girlfriends once told me that she was having a difficult time deciding on what to do with her new status. She had recently passed the New York bar and had gotten a new job. "I don't know what I should be: a socialite, a hard-boiled attorney, or sort of work out a blend of my professional and social life," she mused. Curiously, none of the choices included me, so I asked, "Where do I fit in?" She stared blankly for a moment, as if she'd come home and discovered she'd forgotten to buy catsup. Then she said, "You know, Donald, sometimes I think you really have a place in my life, and sometimes I think if you walked out the door and never came back, it wouldn't faze me at all." **17**

I had to ask. **18**

Had it not been about nine below zero (it's *always* cold) that February night, I would have left right then. (I have since garnered lots more pride.) **19**

Women sit at tables in fours and fives wondering where all the men are, while the men sit a few feet away at the bar. The women almost never initiate anything. Believe me, if there were only ten eligible women in New York, I'd have two of them. If I didn't, it wouldn't be because I didn't try. **20**

It is baffling to men why women are not more aggressive. One has to assume that they are simply not interested. Here are some examples of what "eligible" men are saying. **21**

Women don't have time for you these days. I swear, making a date is like making a business appointment. Everybody's got calendars and datebooks. **22**

23   *While women are in their twenties, they party like crazy and tell you not to pressure them into relationships. Then all of a sudden they hit 30 and uh-oh! Everybody races the clock to get married and make that baby. What are we, sperm factories? I'm supposed to get married so you can have cut crystal?*

24   *It's quality I'm looking for, not quantity. I don't care how many women there are out there, it's quality I want. By the time you weed out the workaholics, the ones so bitter about their past lovers that they hate every man, the ones that want you only for your money/prestige, the druggies (yes, women do that too) and star seekers (noncelebrities need not apply) and ones who want fathers for their children, the margin really narrows.*

25   *I'll believe women are liberated when one walks up to me, says, 'Hey, good-lookin',' buys me dinner, pats me on the cakes and suggests we go to her place for a nightcap.*

26   It's ironic. Women are always telling me that men are intimidated by independent, assertive women. Where are they? On a recent *Donahue* show dedicated to single men, one man posed this question: "How many women out there would drive two hours to pick me up, take me out and spend $100, bring me back home and leave?" Yes, I'm certain some have done it. Just as I know there are some readers who have figured out the number of angels on the head of a pin. However, although the number of miles and dollar amount might seem exaggerated, the routine is one that is typical and expected of men.

27   I remember once being headed out the door at about 9:30 on a Saturday night when the phone rang. It was a woman I dated once in a while, and she invited me out that night. Already headed elsewhere, I respectfully declined. "Well, excuse me," she said, obviously miffed. "I guess I have to book ahead."

28   I remember that I really had something to do that night. I think it was open-heart surgery or something, so I explained that to her. She wouldn't have cared if it really had been open-heart surgery; she felt rejected, humiliated.

29   I hate to tell you this, but whenever you ask someone out, there is a possibility they will say no. Men know it, they live with it. I'll never like it, but I have gotten used to it.

30   Oh, you thought we had it easy, huh?

31   Women, I honestly think, believe it is easy for men to approach them. If that were true, I would be dating Jayne Kennedy *and* Diahann Carroll. Talking to a woman for the first time, especially without an introduction, is always a crap shoot. For me, it is worse. It is tantamount to walking down a dark alley knowing a psychopath with a big baseball bat and little mercy is in there. Approaching someone means you have to bare yourself and lay some of your cards on the table. That's not easy—

particularly with the "new woman" who waltzes into a room like it's the set of *Dynasty*. Thumbs up if she likes you; to the lions if not.

I'm certain that it's easier for many men. And I'm equally certain that 32 I've fooled lots of women with my cool, sophisticated facade. It comes with years of practice and experience.

What men are seeing and hearing from women, either directly or 33 indirectly, is that there is a very bad problem with self-image. I'm not quite sure why. It seems contradictory. There are more women than ever before who are well educated, have lucrative careers and are well dressed and good-looking.

Therein may lie the problem. Women are insecure not only about the 34 shortage of men but also about the increasing number of what they see as competition — other women.

I've said it myself. A woman walks into the room and I'm introduced 35 to her and I think, *Okay, you went to a good school, you've got a good job and look good. So what? So do most of the women in this room. In fact, so do most of the ones I meet.* Increasingly, there is nothing exceptional about being young, gifted and cute. It has, in many circles, become a given. Male friends of mine often say, "Why do women place so much emphasis on what they do professionally?" That automatically sets up a false criterion that men fall prey to. It creates a value system that emphasizes material things. Women, of course, are not solely responsible for that. Throughout history men have shown off their uniforms, three-piece suits and jobs since shepherding paid top dollar. However, at the same time, our criteria for women were based largely on hair, ankles, calves — you get the picture.

Nowadays we find ourselves asking more questions about education, 36 career goals and so on. These are valid questions for anyone to ask, mind you, but they are not by any means the sole criterion for what makes a good human being, let alone a good relationship. It does, on the other hand, keep the mind beyond the ankles, which is a step in the right direction.

Years ago men chose women who could cook, take care of a house 37 and raise children. Women chose men who would make good providers. Today more and more men do their own cooking and cleaning, are becoming closer to their children. Women, on the other hand, are becoming more self-supporting. This sounds to me like a marvelous opportunity for people to find some other reasons for relationships and shed some old ones. However, that does not seem to be happening.

It becomes extremely difficult to decipher the signals. One says, "I 38 want a man who's sensitive, caring, spiritual and warm." The other says, "I have this list of things that I feel I should have. I want a man who can help me achieve them and move up in society."

There is a curious other side to the pursuit of Mr. Right Stuff. When 39 women settle for less, it is *far* less. I'm talkin' triflin' here. But for some reason, Brother Rat seems to capture their attention. The story has become a tired soap opera.

40   I knew a woman, a professional, good school, good job, condo, the whole ball of wax. She could never find a guy good enough. She always broke off the relationships, saying that the men would feel bad because she made more money; their fragile egos would be crushed. She went out with a good guy. A professional, a nice person. They were to be married. At the last minute she shifted gears and decided she wanted more time as a career woman. She left him. She spent her days bemoaning the fact that she had nobody. Then she met a rogue. Not the charming, sophisticated, Billy Dee Williams type, but a sleazy, coke-dealing, never-had-an-honest-job type. She let him move into her apartment; he spent her money and left her in debt and with a great loss of self-esteem. Yet at a given opportunity, whenever he came through town, she would take him in for a few days and, yes, lend him money.

41   Figure it out.

42   I have spent nearly all my adult life in the communications business as a writer, journalist and media specialist, and ten years in corporate public relations. None of these things, however, prepared me for the biggest communications gap of all—that between men and women.

43   It happened so suddenly. Things hadn't changed very much for decades. Then came the middle sixties, while the Black movement was in full fury, and eventually people began questioning, challenging, their sexual roles. Age-old ideas about love, marriage, sex, family and children began to change for women—and for men as well.

44   When women were fragile little princesses (they never really were, but they played the part), it was a lot more palatable for men to play the role of Prince Charming.There is, at least among college-educated, professional women, little impetus for a man to feel he has to sweep you off your feet as you stand together, pinstripe to pinstripe, Gucci to Gucci, M.B.A. to M.B.A. But there you stand, waiting for him to open the door and take you to dinner. During the day he holds the door at work and she's furious. At night she stands in place until he opens it.

45   What's a guy to do?

46   How does one approach the new woman? Should he be forward? more aggressive and to the point? Or should he be more subtle? Should he try to appeal to her intellect through conversation? Or should he be more romantic? Can he assume she is more sexually liberated or that she is seeking only a "meaningful relationship?" How do you separate platonic friendships from romantic inclinations? Who pays the bill? Does the fact that she's "career oriented" mean that she doesn't want or have time for a relationship?

47   Women are facing a backlash from men that will rival the white blacklash of the seventies and eighties. And, like the white liberals in the sixties, the disenchanted men are the "nice guys"—the guys who feel they have been gentlemanly, supportive, considerate. All of a sudden the

message they are getting is one of distrust, as they're portrayed as abusers, ne'er-do-wells, drug abusers and cheats. And after struggling to survive the street, college and/or military service and the day-to-day strife of the work world, they are being sent messages that say women's struggles make theirs pale by comparison. Not only that — they are the ones responsible for it!

Liberation. Independence. They're words that imply hard-won, new-found freedom. Freedom from the shackles of the past. That should include the freedom to look at relationships in a new light. Taking one or two bad experiences into each relationship thereafter is not being liberated. It is being shackled, weighed down, by your past. Understanding that the changes that took place for women also changed the perspective of many men is important. It means that realignments in relationships are necessary.   48

I once had the experience of working with a group of five women. All of them had previously worked together and had been friends for some time. Their businesslike demeanor made me want to straighten my tie, let alone my files and desk. We would have group meetings prior to every division meeting. They would stress how we would go in as a group, pose a common front. But once inside the meeting, something interesting happened. They broke ranks, and each tried to impress the boss. How? By fluttering eyelashes, flashing toothy smiles and laughing at all his dumb jokes.   49

It caused one of my male coworkers to remark, "You know who the new woman is? She's the old woman, only she can't cook" — a sexist response evoked by a group of women who lapsed into a stereotypical role.   50

As bleak as some of this may seem, things are actually getting better. Change did move in very swiftly, and we are all, men and women alike, getting used to it. Certainly most of us over 30 grew up in an America where girls played nurse and boys played soldier. So it will take a while. But regardless of the changes, and the time it takes, there will always be a misread signal somewhere.   51

And it will *always* be on a cold night.   52

Questions for Discussion and Writing

1. How does Singletary use of contrasting statements made by the same woman to illustrate his claim that women are sending double messages to men and confusing them?

2. What is the "my money, *our* money" syndrome and how does it show itself in cases where a woman will wait for a man to pick up the check?

3. How does Singletary draw upon specific personal experiences to illustrate his claim that women are so caught up in their careers that commitment to a man is not part of their program?

4. Do you think Singletary has accurately observed a phenomenon that is occurring in society or is he just having trouble with women personally and projecting it onto all of society?

5. In the context of the overall development of his argument, what is the significance of Singletary's observations that some "new women" seem to prefer rogue and scoundrel types? How does his discussion on this point support his main thesis that women say one thing and do another?

6. In terms of overall strategies, why does Singletary reserve his description of working with five women for the end of his article? How does this episode support his assertion that women want to enjoy the advantages of being liberated without losing the advantages conferred by traditional sex roles?

7. Have you ever had an experience similar to those described by Singletary? In what ways did your experience correspond with Singletary's? Did you react in the same way?

8. When you go out on a date, who pays? Do you go dutch treat? If you are male, do women ask you out? If you are female, do men ask you out? If you are female, do you ask men out? If not, why not?

9. In your opinion, have the sexual revolution, the increasing number of women now working, and the women's liberation movement really changed the relationship between men and women?

10. Write an essay agreeing or disagreeing with either of the following statements. Also, to what extent is either statement an accurate description of the "new woman"?: (a) "I'll have my cake and eat yours too." (b) "The new woman is really the old woman who can't cook."

11. To what extent does Singletary bear out Baye's characterization of the man with the easily wounded ego? To what extent does Baye bear out Singletary's characterization of the new woman as uncaring and highly competitive?

12. In what way do Singletary's and Baye's essays mirror reflections of each other's complaints about the opposite sex?

13. Compare Singletary's and Baye's essays in terms of how each sees male and female sex roles as having changed in our society in the past two decades.

14. Despite disagreements on most other issues, Singletary and Baye do agree on what constitutes traditional male and female behavior. How does each define these traditional roles?

PORNOGRAPHY

Susan Brownmiller

Pornography Hurts Women

The founder of Women Against Pornography, Susan Brownmiller has written articles for The New York Times Magazine *and Book Review,* Esquire, Vogue, *and* Mademoiselle, *and is the author of several books, including* Femininity *(1984). This essay, "Pornography Hurts Women" from* Against Our Will *(1975), claims that rape is not so much a sexual as a political act by means of which men repress and seek to gain power over women. She develops her argument by drawing analogies between pornography and Nazi propaganda and argues that pornography can be censored since it is not a form of free speech entitled to protection under the First Amendment.*

1   Pornography has been so thickly glossed over with the patina of chic these days in the name of verbal freedom and sophistication that important distinctions between freedom of political expression (a democratic necessity), honest sex education for children (a societal good) and ugly smut (the deliberate devaluation of the role of women through obscene, distorted depictions) have been hopelessly confused. Part of the problem is that those who traditionally have been the most vigorous opponents of porn are often those same people who shudder at the explicit mention of any sexual subject. Under their watchful, vigilante eyes, frank and free dissemination of educational materials relating to abortion, contraception, the act of birth, and female biology in general is also dangerous, subversive and dirty. (I am not unmindful that frank and free discussion of rape, "the unspeakable crime," might well give these righteous vigilantes further cause to shudder.) Because the battle lines were falsely drawn a long time ago, before there was a vocal women's movement, the antipornography forces appear to be, for the most part, religious, Southern, conservative and right-wing, while the pro-porn forces are identified as Eastern, atheistic and liberal.

2   But a woman's perspective demands a totally new alignment, or at least a fresh appraisal. The majority report of the President's Commission on Obscenity and Pornography (1970), a report that argued strongly for the removal of all legal restrictions on pornography, soft and hard, made plain that 90 percent of all pornographic material is geared to the

male heterosexual market (the other 10 percent is geared to the male homosexual taste), that buyers of porn are "predominantly white, middle-class, middle-aged married males" and that the graphic depictions, the meat and potatoes of porn, are of the naked female body and of the multiplicity of acts done to that body.

Discussing the content of stag films, "a familiar and firmly established part of the American scene," the commission report dutifully, if foggily, explained, "Because pornography historically has been thought to be primarily a masculine interest, the emphasis in stag films seems to represent the preferences of the middle-class American male. Thus male homosexuality and bestiality are relatively rare, while lesbianism is rather common."   3

The commissioners in this instance had merely verified what purveyors of porn have always known: hard-core pornography is not a celebration of sexual freedom; it is a cynical exploitation of female sexual activity through the device of making all such activity, and consequently all females, "dirty." Heterosexual male consumers of pornography are frankly turned on by watching lesbians in action (although never in the final scenes, but always as a curtain raiser); they are turned off with the sudden swiftness of a water faucet by watching naked men act upon each other. One study quoted in the commission report came to the unastounding conclusion that "seeing a stag film in the presence of male peers bolsters masculine esteem." Indeed. The men in groups who watch the films, it is important to note, are *not* naked.   4

When male response to pornography is compared to female response, a pronounced difference in attitude emerges. According to the commission, "Males report being more highly aroused by depictions of nude females, and show more interest in depictions of nude females than [do] females." Quoting the figures of Alfred Kinsey, the commission noted that a majority of males (77 percent) were "aroused" by visual depictions of explicit sex while a majority of females (68 percent) were not aroused. Further, "females more often than males reported 'disgust' and 'offense.'"   5

From whence comes this female disgust and offense? Are females sexually backward or more conservative by nature? The gut distaste that a majority of women feel when we look at pornography, a distaste that, incredibly, it is no longer fashionable to admit, comes, I think, from the gut knowledge that we and our bodies are being stripped, exposed and contorted for the purpose of ridicule to bolster that "masculine esteem" which gets its kick and sense of power from viewing females as anonymous, panting playthings, adult toys, dehumanized objects to be used, abused, broken and discarded.   6

This, of course, is also the philosophy of rape. It is no accident (for what else could be its purpose?) that females in the pornographic genre are depicted in two cleanly delineated roles: as virgins who are caught and "banged" or as nymphomaniacs who are never sated. The most   7

popular and prevalent pornographic fantasy combines the two: an innocent, untutored female is raped and "subjected to unnatural practices"
that turn her into a raving, slobbering nymphomaniac, a dependent
sexual slave who can never get enough of the big, male cock.

8   There can be no "equality" in porn, no female equivalent, no turning
of the tables in the name of bawdy fun. Pornography, like rape, is a male
invention, designed to dehumanize women, to reduce the female to an
object of sexual access, not to free sensuality from moralistic or parental
inhibition. The staple of porn will always be the naked female body,
breasts and genitals exposed, because as man devised it, her naked body
is the female's "shame," her private parts the private property of man,
while his are the ancient, holy, universal, patriarchal instrument of his
power, his rule by force over *her*.

9   Pornography is the undiluted essence of anti-female propaganda. Yet
the very same liberals who were so quick to understand the method and
purpose behind the mighty propaganda machine of Hitler's Third Reich,
the consciously spewed-out anti-Semitic caricatures and obscenities that
gave an ideological base to the Holocaust and the Final Solution, the very
same liberals who, enlightened by blacks, searched their own conscience
and came to understand that their tolerance of "nigger" jokes and portrayals of shuffling, rolling-eyed servants in movies perpetuated the
degrading myths of black inferiority and gave an ideological base to the
continuation of black oppression — these very same liberals now fervidly
maintain that the hatred and contempt for women that find expression in
four-letter words used as expletives and in what are quaintly called
"adult" or "erotic" books and movies are a valid extension of freedom of
speech that must be preserved as a Constitutional right.

10   To defend the right of a lone, crazed American Nazi to grind out
propaganda calling for the extermination of all Jews, as the ACLU has
done in the name of free speech, is, after all, a self-righteous and not
particularly courageous stand, for American Jewry is not currently
threatened by storm troopers, concentration camps and imminent extermination, but I wonder if the ACLU's position might change if, come
tomorrow morning, the bookstores and movie theaters lining Forty-sec-
ond Street in New York City were devoted not to the humiliation of
women by rape and torture, as they currently are, but to a systematized,
commercially successful propaganda machine depicting the sadistic
pleasures of gassing Jews or lynching blacks?

11   Is this analogy extreme? Not if you are a woman who is conscious of
the ever-present threat of rape and the proliferation of a cultural ideology that makes it sound like "liberated" fun. The majority report of the
President's Commission on Obscenity and Pornography tried to pooh-
pooh the opinion of law enforcement agencies around the country that
claimed their own concrete experience with offenders who were caught
with the stuff led them to conclude that pornographic material is a
causative factor in crimes of sexual violence. The commission maintained

that it was not possible at this time to scientifically prove or disprove such a connection.

But does one need scientific methodology in order to conclude that   12 the antifemale propaganda that permeates our nation's cultural output promotes a climate in which acts of sexual hostility directed against women are not only tolerated but ideologically encouraged? A similar debate has raged for many years over whether or not the extensive glorification of violence (the gangster as hero; the loving treatment accorded bloody shoot-'em-ups in movies, books and on TV) has a causal effect, a direct relationship to the rising rate of crime, particularly among youth. Interestingly enough, in this area—nonsexual and not specifically related to abuses against women—public opinion seems to be swinging to the position that explicit violence in the entertainment media does have a deleterious effect; it makes violence commonplace, numbingly routine and no longer morally shocking.

More to the point, those who call for a curtailment of scenes of   13 violence in movies and on television in the name of sensitivity, good taste and what's best for our children are not accused of being pro-censorship or against freedom of speech. Similarly, minority group organizations, black, Hispanic, Japanese, Italian, Jewish, or American Indian, that campaign against ethnic slurs and demeaning portrayals in movies, on television shows and in commercials are perceived as waging a just political fight, for if a minority group claims to be offended by a specific portrayal, be it Little Black Sambo or the Frito Bandido, and relates it to a history of ridicule and oppression, few liberals would dare to trot out a Constitutional argument in theoretical opposition, not if they wish to maintain their liberal credentials. Yet when it comes to the treatment of women, the liberal consciousness remains fiercely obdurate, refusing to be budged, for the sin of appearing square or prissy in the age of the so-called sexual revolution has become the worst offense of all.

Questions for Discussion and Writing

1. How is the issue of obscenity and pornography related to the question of the boundaries of free speech? How does Brownmiller's argument depend on the assumption that pornography is not merely dirty and obscene but is a direct expression of violence against women and poses a threat sufficient to justify its suppression?

2. To what extent does Brownmiller deal with the counterargument that no causal relationship has been proved between socially injurious conduct and exposure to obscene and pornographic material? Does her argument come to terms with the question of whether society has a right to curb expressions that cannot be proved to be related to committed crimes?

3. In your opinion, has Brownmiller written her essay for an audience primarily of men or of women or of both? What word choices and argumentative strategies lead you to your conclusion?

4. How does Brownmiller's argument depend on the assumption that because women have no interest in seeing men sexually degraded there can be "no female equivalent" of male heterosexual pornography? Do you agree with her assumption? Explain your answer. If the opposite indeed were true, how would it affect the presumption of social threat on which her entire argument is based?

5. How does Brownmiller connect pornography with rape in the course of her argument?

6. Evaluate Brownmiller's use of analogy to link pornography with Nazi propaganda. To what extent does pornography, in Brownmiller's view, threaten society itself? In your opinion, does she make an effective case that the degraded view of women purveyed by pornography constitutes a threat to society as great as anti-Semitic or antiblack propaganda? Explain your answer. How does Brownmiller's argument depend on her belief that hard-core pornography affects males differently from the way that it affects females?

7. Write an essay that addresses the crucial question of whether pornography is or is not a form of free speech that ought to be constitutionally protected. Your assessment will depend on whether you agree with Brownmiller that pornography poses a "clear and present danger" to society (which, if proved, would exclude it from First Amendment protection). Does the degraded view of women purveyed by pornography constitute a threat to society sufficient to justify its suppression?

8. If you yourself are tolerant of pornography, would you adopt a more stringent standard for a younger sister or brother? Explain the implications of your answer.

9. If you are intolerant of pornography, would you adopt a less restrictive standard for masterpieces in art and literature? As part of this assignment you might wish to peruse James Joyce, *Ulysses*; D. H. Lawrence, *Lady Chatterley's Lover*; or Henry Miller, *Tropic of Cancer* and *Tropic of Capricorn*.

Susan Jacoby

A First Amendment Junkie

Susan Jacoby has written extensively about women's subjects for the New York Times and McCalls. Many of her essays have been reprinted in her book The Possible She *(1979). In the following essay, "A First Amendment Junkie," which originally was published in the "Hers" column of* The New York Times *(January 26, 1978), Jacoby formulates an effective evaluative comparison to argue that pornography should be a matter of individual not governmental responsibility.*

It is no news that many women are defecting from the ranks of civil 1
libertarians on the issue of obscenity. The conviction of Larry Flynt,
publisher of *Hustler* magazine — before his metamorphosis into a born-
again Christian — was greeted with unabashed feminist approval. Harry
Reems, the unknown actor who was convicted by a Memphis jury for
conspiring to distribute the movie *Deep Throat*, has carried on his legal
battles with almost no support from women who ordinarily regard
themselves as supporters of the First Amendment. Feminist writers and
scholars have even discussed the possibility of making common cause
against pornography with adversaries of the women's movement —
including opponents of the equal rights amendment and "right-to-life"
forces.

All of this is deeply disturbing to a woman writer who believes, as I 2
always have and still do, in an absolute interpretation of the First
Amendment. Nothing in Larry Flynt's garbage convinces me that the late
Justice Hugo L. Black was wrong in this opinion that "the Federal
Government is without any power whatsoever under the Constitution to
put any type of burden on free speech and expression of ideas of any
kind (as distinguished from conduct)." Many women I like and respect
tell me I am wrong; I cannot remember having become involved in so
many heated discussions of a public issue since the end of the Vietnam
War. A feminist writer described my views as those of a "First Amendment junkie."

Many feminist arguments for controls on pornography carry the 3
implicit conviction that porn books, magazines and movies pose a greater
threat to women than similarly repulsive exercises of free speech pose to
other offended groups. This conviction has, of course, been shared by
everyone — regardless of race, creed or sex — who has ever argued in
favor of abridging the First Amendment. It is the argument used by some

Jews who have withdrawn their support from the American Civil Liberties Union because it has defended the right of American Nazis to march through a community inhabited by survivors of Hitler's concentration camps.

4   If feminists want to argue that the protection of the Constitution should not be extended to *any* particularly odious or threatening form of speech, they have a reasonable argument (although I don't agree with it). But it is ridiculous to suggest that the porn shops on 42d Street are more disgusting to women than a march of neo-Nazis is to survivors of the extermination camps.

5   The arguments over pornography also blur the vital distinction between expression of ideas and conduct. When I say I believe unreservedly in the First Amendment, someone always comes back at me with the issue of "kiddie porn." But kiddie porn is not a First Amendment issue. It is an issue of the abuse of power—the power adults have over children—and not of obscenity. Parents and promoters have no more right to use their children to make porn movies than they do to send them to work in coal mines. The responsible adults should be prosecuted, just as adults who use children for back-breaking farm labor should be prosecuted.

6   Susan Brownmiller, in *Against Our Will: Men, Women and Rape*, has described pornography as "the undiluted essence of anti-female propaganda." I think this is a fair description of some types of pornography, especially of the brutish subspecies that equates sex with death and portrays women primarily as objects of violence.

7   The equation of sex and violence, personified by some glossy rock record album covers as well as by *Hustler*, has fed the illusion that censorship of pornography can be conducted on a more rational basis than other types of censorship. Are all pictures of naked women obscene? Clearly not, says a friend. A Renoir nude is art, she says, and *Hustler* is trash. "Any reasonable person" knows that.

8   But what about something between art and trash—something, say, along the lines of *Playboy* or *Penthouse* magazines? I asked five women for their reactions to one picture in *Penthouse* and got responses that ranged from "lovely" and "sensuous" to "revolting" and "demeaning." Feminists, like everyone else, seldom have rational reasons for their preferences in erotica. Like members of juries, they tend to disagree when confronted with something that falls short of 100 percent vulgarity.

9   In any case, feminists will not be the arbiters of good taste if it becomes easier to harass, prosecute and convict people on obscenity charges. Most of the people who want to censor girlie magazines are equally opposed to open discussion of issues that are of vital concern to women: rape, abortion, menstruation, contraception, lesbianism—in fact, the entire range of sexual experience from a women's viewpoint.

10   Feminist writers and editors and film makers have limited financial

resources: Confronted by a determined prosecutor, Hugh Hefner will fare better than Susan Brownmiller. Would the Memphis jurors who convicted Harry Reems for his role in *Deep Throat* be inclined to take a more positive view of paintings of the female genitalia done by sensitive feminist artists? *Ms.* magazine has printed color reproductions of some of those art works; *Ms.* is already banned from a number of high school libraries because someone considers it threatening and/or obscene.

Feminists who want to censor what they regard as harmful pornogra- 11 phy have essentially the same motivation as other would-be censors: They want to use the power of the state to accomplish what they have been unable to achieve in the marketplace of ideas and images. The impulse to censor places no faith in the possibilities of democratic persuasion.

It isn't easy to persuade certain men that they have better uses for 12 $1.95 each month than to spend it on a copy of *Hustler*? Well, then, give the men no choice in the matter.

I believe there is also a connection between the impulse toward 13 censorship on the part of people who used to consider themselves civil libertarians and a more general desire to shift responsibility from individuals to institutions. When I saw the movie *Looking for Mr. Goodbar*, I was stunned by its series of visual images equating sex and violence, coupled with what seems to me the mindless message (a distortion of the fine Judith Rossner novel) that casual sex equals death. When I came out of the movie, I was even more shocked to see parents standing in line with children between the ages of 10 and 14.

I simply don't know why a parent would take a child to see such a 14 movie, any more than I understand why people feel they can't turn off a television set their child is watching. Whenever I say that, my friends tell me I don't know how it is because I don't have children. True, but I do have parents. When I was a child, they did turn off the TV. They didn't expect the Federal Communications Commission to do their job for them.

I am a First Amendment junkie. You can't OD on the First Amend- 15 ment, because free speech is its own best antidote.

Questions for Discussion and Writing

1. How does Jacoby's argument revolve around the question of whether the individual or the state should have the ultimate power to decide whether certain materials should be censored?

2. What range of reasons does Jacoby offer to support her view that feminists are mistaken in advocating censorship of pornography?

3. Evaluate Jacoby's strategy of putting feminists who want to censor

pornography in the position of having to maintain that pornography, as such, poses a greater threat to women than other types of offensive speech pose to other groups. Thus, feminists would have to prove that pornography poses a greater threat to women than the speeches of American Nazis would pose to a community of concentration camp survivors.

4. Why does Jacoby believe that the issue of "kiddie porn" is not a First Amendment issue?

5. In what way, according to Jacoby, will feminists' support of censorship indirectly result in the censoring of discussions about issues of vital concern to women, such as rape and abortion? How does Jacoby use a "slippery slope" strategy in suggesting that feminists' support of censorship will trigger censorship of many other issues vitally important to women (including rape, abortion, contraception, and lesbianism)?

6. How does Jacoby choose to present herself to her audience? (This argument first appeared in her weekly newspaper column.) How does the title contribute to the reader's getting a certain picture of Jacoby?

7. In a short essay, contrast the respective arguments for and against censorship of pornography by Brownmiller and Jacoby. Who, in your opinion, makes a better case? Explain your answer using brief quotations from the two articles. Be sure to touch on the important issues that divide Brownmiller and Jacoby, such as the question of (*a*) whether the individual or the state should have the ultimate power to decide on matters of censorship, (*b*) whether pornography as such poses a "clear and present" danger to society, and (*c*) whether pornography is a form of free speech that ought to be protected under the First Amendment.

ABOMINABLE SNOWMAN

Edward W. Cronin, Jr.

The Yeti

Edward W. Cronin, Jr., is a distinguished zoologist who for three years was chief scientist for the Arun Valley Wildlife Expedition in the Himalayas. "The Yeti" originally appeared in the Atlantic Monthly *(November 1975). Cronin uses inductive reasoning and cites evidence from eyewitness reports in presenting a compelling case for the existence of the yeti.*

Each year the stories of the yeti, or Abominable Snowman, a monster man-ape roaming the snows, come rolling down out of the Himalayas like an avalanche. "We stared in amazement and disbelief at those huge, apelike impressions in the snow," a Polish mountaineer announced last spring. "Lhakpa said she got a good look at the beast as it ripped out the throat of her only cow and slaughtered her yaks by smashing their heads with its huge fists," was another recent statement. A "hardened" police officer told reporters, "I'm convinced the girl saw a yeti. No other beast I know of could have mutilated her animals that way. One yak had been ripped apart and savagely gnawed by a ferocious beast with phenomenal strength." A Frankenstein ogre incarnate? A vivid nightmare? But what about the yaks? And the police officer? 1

And so, tales, eyewitness reports, photographs of footprints, even plaster casts of prints accumulate each year into a morass of confusing information. There seems to be no end to the lore and its appeal. Why is there so much excitement about the hypothetical existence of the yeti? Certainly the sensationalism has something to do with it, but there is more to the phenomenon. 2

The interest, in part, has to do with the very confusion and mystery that surrounds the yeti. In an age when science, with heartless efficiency, has usurped religion to solve every enigma of life from the creation to our own evolution, here is one mystery that cannot be disposed of so readily. "Perhaps our science is good with rocket ships and microbiology," the yeti advocate can argue "but look, a large man-ape is alive on our crowded planet and we can't even find it!" For many, the yeti is a symbolic stone to hurl at science. 3

In part, also, the interest has to do with the creature itself. If there really is an unknown anthropoid of the yeti's description alive today, it 4 must be a close relative from our distant and forgotten past. Man is foremost interested in man, and the yeti would be the most significant zoological and anthropological discovery of the century, offering comparative insights into our own development, behavior, and prehistoric society. It would not be just another fossil ape, but a living, breathing creature that we could study in the flesh.

5   The largest part of the fascination, however, has to do with what the yeti represents emotionally. Such a creature triggers a primordial memory of the time when we had to face these competitors on equal terms with no more technology than a club. It would be the reality of our recurrent nightmares about man-monsters. It would be the embodiment of our cultural bogeyman, our attempts in legends and myths to put boundaries on the unknown. We might slay our nightmares by capturing the monster.

6   Indeed, the yeti might be so serviceable to our emotions and science that we should be hopeful that it exists. The evidence is far from conclusive, but it does raise questions.

7   During the past three years, I have been working in the Himalayas as chief scientist of the Arun Valley Wildlife Expedition. This multidisciplinary scientific expedition conducted the first ecological survey of the remote Arun Valley in far-eastern Nepal. The Arun is one of the world's deepest river valleys, an isolated haven for wildlife between the towering massifs of Everest and Kanchenjunga, the first and third highest mountains on the earth. Prior to our expedition, the valley had remained relatively unexplored because of the rugged topography, inaccessibility, and dense vegetation. Its unique fauna and flora had never been critically studied, and doubtless contained new species as yet unknown to man. Since numerous reports of the yeti came from this area, we were open to the possibility that it was inhabited by a hidden population of unknown apes. Before we entered the field, we made a comprehensive examination of the previous evidence for the yeti's existence; while in the field, we devoted special efforts to searching for it.

8   Reports of the yeti have come out of the Himalayas for over two hundred years. There is an eighteenth-century drawing of the yeti in a Chinese manuscript on Tibetan wildlife. If questioned, the local villagers of the Arun Valley will relate stories supposedly older, dating back many generations; such stories are often so ornamented and corrupted through retelling that they seem impossible. However, reports of villagers who claim to have recently seen yetis or their footprints are more specific and seem highly plausible. Also, if the villagers are asked about their local fauna, they often include the yeti as a matter of routine. They respond, "Yes, we have many wild animals here. There are bears, snow leopards, wolves, yetis, civets, serows, monkeys, rabbits, and many others."

9   The first Westerner to have published an account of the yeti was B. H. Hodgson in 1832. Since then, more than forty Westerners, including such reputable gentlemen as N. A. Tombazi, Sir John Hunt, H. W.

Tilman, Sir C. K. Howard-Bury, Don Whillans, Dr. Norman Dyhrenfurth, and Sir Edmund Hillary, have described sighting the yeti or its footprints. The primary question raised about these reports has always been the reliability of the witnesses. Perhaps some were excellent mountain climbers, but how qualified were they to examine spoor or interpret visual sightings? Were they tired or in some way affected by the high altitude? Did the powers of suggestion from a lengthy history of yeti lore convert otherwise explainable circumstances into confirmed yeti reports? Are the reports outright hoaxes, perpetrated for publicity and fame?

None of these accusations appear valid, given the personalities and 10 accomplishments of the witnesses. Many of them are respected public figures with illustrious careers who would have nothing to gain from further publicity. Many are competent naturalists and mountaineers familiar with the wildlife and field conditions in the Himalayas. Often, their first reactions to their discoveries have been to explain them in terms of exotic fauna, altitude sickness, or atmospheric aberrations, and it was only after discounting such possibilities that many witnesses were willing to suffer the abuse and doubt that accompany the report of a yeti. There is also the inescapable argument that even if all the reports are inaccurate except one, that one constitutes proof that the yeti does exist.

Together, the eyewitness reports construct a detailed description of 11 the yeti. Its body is stocky, apelike in shape, with a distinctly human quality to it, in contrast to that of a bear. It stands five and a half to six feet tall, and is covered with short coarse hair, reddish brown to black in color, sometimes with white patches on the chest. The hair is longest on the shoulders. The face is hairless and rather flat. The jaw is robust, the teeth are quite large, though fangs are not present, and the mouth is wide. The head is conically shaped, and comes to a pointed crown. The arms are long, reaching almost to the knees. The shoulders are heavy and hunched. There is no tail.

One of the most remarkable aspects of these descriptions by the 12 various eyewitnesses is their consistency; each one describes essentially the same creature. Those reports that can be considered reliable do not depict strange colors, unusual growths of hair, fangs, extraordinary proportions, or any of the likely elaborations that one would normally associate with a monster story. Rather, the reports show an uncanny zoological expertise in portraying a creature that is exactly what a scientist would expect.

The behavior described is even more familiar to the scientist. Local 13 villagers and Western observers relate the yeti's behavior with details that are easily recognized as displacement conflicts, aggressive posturing, and threat displays—patterns which scientists have recently found to be typical of wild ape behavior. The reports seem too good, too accurate, not to be true.

Although the sightings must be taken on faith, the photographs of 14 yeti footprints contribute concrete data. The most noteworthy discovery of footprints was made by Eric Shipton and Michael Ward during the 1951 British Mount Everest Reconnaissance. The prints were made on a thin layer of crystalline snow lying on firm ice, indicating that little erosion or melting had occurred. The photographs are exceptionally clear and sharp, showing that the yeti's foot is large, some twelve and a half inches wide, with the heel nearly as broad as the forepart. A conspicuous humanlike arch is absent. The great toe, or hallux, is quite large, with the second toe the longest and relatively thin, while the remaining three toes are short, stubby, and united toward their base. The hallux is separated from the second toe in an opposable manner, and suggests a more primitive condition than that of modern man. These photographs have since become the "type specimens" of yeti prints.

15   Possible identification of the yeti footprints as those of a known creature ranges from bears, langur monkeys, barefoot men, snow leopards, and wolves to eagles. The foot of man and the langur monkey can be easily discounted because of the markedly different proportions (especially length/width ratio) and structure of the yeti foot. And no serious investigator would entertain the possibility that the footprints are those of snow leopards or wolves (which have nearly round prints) or eagles (which have four narrow toes in a palmate structure). Of all these, bears, because of their size, habits, and habitat, are the most likely suspects. During the expedition's stay in the Arun Valley, we encountered numerous bear prints which the local villagers would occasionally identify as yeti. But the bear prints invariably showed the equal-sized, *symmetrical* arrangement of toes typical of the group. By contrast, Shipton's photographs show distinctively larger and smaller toes arranged in a characteristic *asymmetrical* pattern.

16   Like man, the yeti appears to use bipedal progression, that is, he walks on two rather than on four feet. Bipedalism in the yeti seems to have aroused the greatest controversy and source of disbelief among skeptics. It is often thought by the uninformed that bipedalism is unique to man among the primates, but, in fact, it is by no means rare among apes. Gibbons and orangutans, the most arboreal of the apes, consistently walk upright when on the ground. Recent studies have shown that gorillas occasionally revert to bipedal progression for short distances when traveling through wet vegetation, apparently to keep their hands dry. Similarly, captive chimpanzees frequently walk bipedally when there is snow on the ground to keep their hands from getting cold. In careful analysis, it seems not only possible but altogether likely that a primate that frequents the high snows of the Himalayas would be using bipedal progression.

17   Another point of serious controversy between the advocates and the skeptics has been the supposed yeti scalps. Several of the monasteries in the Himalayas are known to keep what are purported to be yeti scalps. An expedition sponsored by the World Book Encyclopedia managed to borrow one from the Khumjung monastery in the heart of yeti country: it

was taken directly to museums in Paris, London, and Chicago, where zoologists examined it carefully, comparing it to skins of known Himalayan animals. The verdict of the experts: a fake made from the skin of the serow, a wild goat antelope found in the Himalayas.

But the verdict was not unanimous. Dr. W. C. Osman Hill, a British 18 expert on primates, pointed out that the hairs from the Khumjung scalp had a simian quality despite their gross resemblance to serow hairs. Comparing the granules of pigments in the hairs, he detected an arrangement quite different from that of normal serow pigments. In addition, ectoparasites (small insects that feed on the exterior tissues) from the scalp were different from normal serow ectoparasites.

According to some of the Sherpas at the monastery, the scalp was 19 known to be at least several hundred years old, but none could vouch for its authenticity. Several of the Sherpas had insisted from the beginning that the Khumjung scalp was a fake, an imitation of the real scalps found at other monasteries, and made in order to enhance the reputation of the Khumjung monastery.

In reviewing yeti literature, it becomes increasingly obvious that the 20 biases of the scientists involved, rather than any inductive logic, determine the interpretation of the data. Responsible authorities operating with the same evidence and reports reach completely different conclusions. One notable scientist who visited the Himalayas stated flatly that, based on his discovery that known animal tracks can be melted by the sun into facsimiles of the yeti footprints, the "yeti does not exist." Not only is it a doubtful accomplishment to recognize that snow melts, it is also a serious insult to logic, ideally the tool-in-trade of the scientists, to assert that an unknown thing does not exist.

Comparison of the evidence for the existence of the yeti with ac- 21 cepted scientific ideas reveals the even deeper dilemma of the fine distinction between empirical evidence and accepted scientific fact. By studying a few fragments of fossilized bones, paleontologists are able to construct a specific account of an extinct creature's general morphology, ecology, and behavior. These accounts are highly theoretical constructions, yet we still rely on them. The yeti, by comparison, has been seen, for lengthy periods, on numerous occasions, in many different areas, by dozens of people. Why are we so quick to accept the evidence of a new fossil, but so reluctant to credit the reports of the yeti? Even at this late date, we seem to be hindered by a conservatism and parochialism that do disservice to the potential of science.

Any creature existing today must have ancestors, and it may be that 22 the antecedents of the yeti can be found among known fossil forms. Although there are numerous possibilities, one in particular, *Gigantopithecus*, seems especially likely. Remains of *Gigantopithecus* have been found in the foothills of the Himalayas, not far from where many of the modern sightings of the yeti have occurred; other remains have been found in Kwangsi Province of southern China, indicating an extensive range throughout South Asia. The dating of this material is as early as 9 million years ago, and as recent as 500,000 years ago, or middle Pleistocene age, which would make it a contemporary of *Homo erectus*.

23   *Gigantopithecus'* size and shape help make it a likely candidate, for it closely resembled the description of the yeti as given by eyewitnesses. Elwyn Simons and Peter Ettel of Yale University, who investigated the remains near the Himalayas, suggest that *Gigantopithecus* was an unusually large ape. It undoubtedly had the large jaw and teeth mentioned in the yeti descriptions, and, like the yeti, lacked conspicuous fangs or elongated canines. Also, the large mandible of *Gigantopithecus* meant extensive jaw muscles. In apes, this is often associated with a tall sagittal crest, which is required as an attachment point of these muscles, and would exactly duplicate the pointed head so consistently mentioned in the sightings of the yeti and observed in the scalp.

24   There are ecological reasons to suspect *Gigantopithecus.* It possibly came in contact with evolving man in India, and there would have been strong competitive pressure between them. A basic principle of population biology, the Competitive Exclusion Principle as stated by Hardin, explains that whenever two allied forms have a similar ecology and range, one will invariably gain a selective advantage over the other and displace it. The less successful form either becomes extinct or is forced to migrate. During the middle Pleistocene age, man had already learned about fire and had an extensive range of stone, bone, and wood tools; he would have been a powerful competitor. Meanwhile, *Gigantopithecus* would have been at a disadvantage, but assuredly had the behavioral flexibility to invade new habitats, such as those of the higher Himalayas. These mountains are noted for their ability to isolate populations of animals in steep valleys and protect them from outside competition. Today the Himalayas are truly a biological sanctuary, where creatures long extinct elsewhere continue to live in the inaccessible valleys. There is no valid reason to believe that they do not harbor a population of relict apes as they do harbor populations of other relict species.

25   How would *Gigantopithecus* have fitted into the Himalayas? It is a valuable question because it helps dispose of two common misconceptions about the yeti: 1) that the yeti is a resident of the harsh climate of the perennial snows; and 2) that it seems unlikely that a large primate could hide from the numerous investigators in such a small area as the Himalayas.

26   Our findings suggest that a yeti–*Gigantopithecus* form would not inhabit the snowlands. It would favor the dense vegetation of the steep valleys in the middle-altitude zone. The yeti is encountered in the snows because, like the mountaineers who discover its tracks, it uses the snowy passes as routes from one valley to the next. The topography of the Himalayas forces any animal traveling across the country to use the limited number of gaps, ridges, and passes as roads from one area to the next.

A creature like *Gigantopithecus* could easily survive in the lush forests 27
of the valleys. The abrupt changes in altitude produce a succession of
vegetational zones on the steep slopes, encompassing habitats ranging
from the tropic to the arctic. The heavy monsoons result in true cloud-
forest conditions in the middle levels. Forests of oak, magnolia, rhodo-
dendron, fir, alder, and beech, among others, provide an incredible
diversity and abundance of plants. Numerous large mammals enjoy the
rich conditions there and maintain sizable populations. In the mountains
of Africa, gorillas are known to inhabit areas of altitudes up to 12,800
feet. A large primate would do equally well in the Himalayas.

The yeti would have little trouble escaping detection in these steep 28
valleys. The dense vegetation presents a nearly impenetrable wall. During the years I lived in these forests, I repeatedly attempted to leave the
trails and travel through the thick, congested undergrowth. My movements were so constricted that I had to force my way through, at times
having to rely on a machete to cut a passage. Only a creature born in and
adapted to these conditions could travel through the vegetation with
ease. It would have been possible for a large mammal to hide within fifty
yards of me and remain unnoticed.

The irregular topography would also help conceal a large primate. In 29
the best monster tradition, the yeti could disappear among the numerous
gullies, canyons, cliffs, rock shelters, and varied slopes. A two-dimen-
sional map tends to disguise the enormous surface area that exists in the
three-dimensional terrain of the highest mountain range in the world.
The slopes fold back and forth upon themselves to include a prodigious
amount of land.

In addition, these forests are seldom visited by people. The moun- 30
taineers hurry to and from their icy peaks and keep on the main trails to
facilitate transport of their supplies. The villagers are primarily agricul-
turists and pastoralists who have little purpose in exploring the forests.
There have been surprisingly few naturalists who have spent any length
of time in the forests, and even they usually keep to the trails. As in
mountain country throughout the world, the trails follow the natural
signposts of the topography, the ridges and stream beds; the vast area of
the slope is virtually isolated.

Further, the ability of large mammals to escape documentation by 31
scientists is infamous. The kouprey, a large wild bison, was not discovered by Western science until 1936, when the first specimen was identified inside the Paris zoo. This animal does not frequent the forests, but
dwells in the open savanna and woodland areas of Cambodia, where the
terrain and vegetation leave him highly visible. Other creatures, such as
the mountain gorilla, pigmy hippopotamus, and giant panda, were all
known from villager reports and yet remained unknown to science for
years.

Finally, adding to the difficulty of discovery, the yeti is probably 32
nocturnal. Like many other large mammals that suffer from man's dis-

turbance of the wilderness, the yeti has probably developed the habit of hiding and sleeping during the day and confining its traveling and feeding to nighttime. Many elephant populations of South Asia have adopted this same strategy.

33   Thus, the sum total of evidence demonstrates that although there by no means exists the traditional zoological data required for naming a new species, there is no zoological, paleontological, or ecological reason to suppose that an unknown anthropoid does not exist in the Himalayas. There is, in fact, a significant body of data that warrants a more thorough field investigation.

34   In December, 1972, Dr. Howard Emery, expedition physician, and I decided to make a research trip to the high altitude areas around Kongmaa La mountain. The objective was to make our first reconnaissance of this remote, alpine area, and to investigate the winter conditions of the ecosystem.

35   We left base camp in the Kasuwa Khola sidevalley on December 14. The first days were a slow trek through an upper-temperate forest where a deciduous canopy of winter-bare branches cast twisted shapes against a gray sky. As we climbed, we encountered heavier snows, which made traveling difficult; our porters turned back because of the cold. On the seventeenth, accompanied by two Sherpa assistants, we emerged on a high alpine ridge connecting to Kongmaa La. The weather was beautiful, with a clear sky and warm sun. The icy summit of Makalu dominated the horizon to the northwest. In the late afternoon, we discovered a depression in the ridge at about 12,000 feet, offering a flat place with firm snow that was suitable for camp. The area was small, less than half an acre, a completely clear snowfield unmarked by animal prints.

36   The slopes on the side of the ridge were precipitous, falling several thousand feet to the Barun River on the north and the Kasuwa River on the south. We made camp, pitching two light tents, had dinner around an open fire, and retired just after dark. The evening was calm.

37   Shortly before dawn the next morning, Dr. Emery climbed out of our tent. He called excitedly. There, beside the trail we had made to our tents, was a new set of footprints. While we were sleeping, a creature had approached our camp and walked directly between our tents. The Sherpas identified the tracks without question as yeti footprints.

38   We immediately made a full photographic record of the prints before the sun touched them. Like the conditions Shipton had encountered, the surface consisted of crystalline snow, excellent for displaying the prints. These conditions were localized to our camp area, and were the result of the effects produced on the depression by the sun and the winds of the earlier days. The prints were clearest in the middle of the depression, directly beside our trail, where some ten to fifteen prints, both left and right feet, revealed the details of the toes and the general morphology of the creature's foot. Some of the right footprints were actually on our

previous trail, making them difficult to interpret; other prints of the right foot were distinct.

The prints measured approximately nine inches long by four and three quarters inches wide. The stride, or distance between individual prints, was surprisingly short, often less than one foot, and it appeared that the creature had used a slow, cautious walk along this section. The prints showed a short, broad, opposable hallux, an asymmetrical arrangement of the four remaining toes, and a wide, rounded heel. These features were present in all the prints made on firm snow, and we were impressed with their close resemblance to Shipton's prints. **39**

We then proceeded to explore the rest of the trail left by the creature. By the direction of the toes on the clear footprints, I determined that the creature had come up the north slope. I investigated these prints first, following the trail back down the slope. Because the north slope received less sun, it was covered with very deep snow, and the tracks consisted of large punch holes in the snow, revealing little detail. I descended several hundred yards, but the heavy snow made walking impossible, and I was forced to cling to the slope with my hands; the creature must have been exceptionally strong to ascend this slope in these conditions. From a vantage point, I could look down the trail, which continued toward the bottom of the valley in a direction generally perpendicular to the slope, but there seemed little advantage in climbing farther down, and I returned to the top of the ridge. **40**

From our camp, the tracks continued out onto the south slope, but here the increased exposure to the sun had melted most of the snow, and there were bare patches of rock and alpine scrub which made following the trail difficult. We walked farther up the ridge toward Kongmaa La to get a view of the trail from above, and discovered what appeared to be the prints of the same creature coming back onto the top of the ridge. They crossed back and forth several times. Here the ridge was covered with low bushes which enabled deeper snow to accumulate, and the prints were again confused punch holes. The trail then went back down onto the south slope, and we attempted to follow, but lost the prints on the bare rock and scrub. The slope was extremely steep, and searching for the prints was arduous and dangerous. We realized that whatever creature had made them was far stronger than any of us. **41**

We considered the possibility of a hoax perpetrated by our Sherpas, but discounted it, realizing that the Sherpas were not capable of making the full trail of prints we could see from the top of the ridge. They would not have had the time. We also doubted their ability to make prints which were so consistent with each other and which so closely matched the yeti footprints that we were familiar with from photographs. **42**

We sent word with one of the Sherpas down to the other members of the expedition. Jeffrey McNeely, expedition mammalogist, came up to the ridge later and made plaster casts of the prints. **43**

44   During the following three days, we kept a careful watch for the possible reappearance of the creature. We made a new camp farther up the ridge and spent the days examining other snowfields. At night, taking advantage of a bright moon that clearly illuminated the surrounding slopes, we watched from the front of our tent for possible nocturnal activity. There were no further signs.

45   Upon reflection, there are several aspects of this incident which constitute valuable additional information about the yeti:

46   1. The circumstances eliminate the hypothesis that all yeti prints are the function of melting by the sun or wind erosion. We know that the prints were made during the night of the seventeenth, or very early on the morning of the eighteenth. We photographed them before sunrise. We knew wind had not affected them, since a comparison of our own footprints made on the morning of the eighteenth with our footprints made on the seventeenth showed little, if any, distortion.

47   2. The prints are not referrable to a local animal. During the expedition, we devoted special efforts to examining all large mammal prints made in snow; we noted possible variations produced by different snow conditions, terrain, and activities of the animal (i.e. running, walking, etc.); a photographic record was made. As professional biologists with extensive experience in the Himalayas, we feel we can eliminate any possibility that the prints were made by any known, normal mammal.

48   3. The prints support the hypothesis that the various yeti reports refer to one species. The prints are similar to those photographed by Shipton, differing only in being smaller, with a shorter hallux, and perhaps indicating an immature or female yeti. (Sexual dimorphism, that is, difference in size between the sexes, is known from *Gigantopithecus* and many other primates.)

49   4. The prints support the hypothesis that the yeti is an ape. Like Shipton's photograph, our prints show a foot morphology typical of Pongidae.

50   5. The arrangement of the prints supports the hypothesis that the yeti uses bipedal progression. The prints demonstrated a left-right-left-right pattern; there was no overlapping; there was no indication that more than two appendages were used in making a lengthy series of prints.

51   6. The weight of the creature that made the prints is less than or equal to the weight of an average man. My footprints (I weighed approximately 185 pounds, including winter clothes and boots) were slightly deeper, suggesting that the creature weighed about 165 pounds.

52   7. The circumstances support the hypothesis that the yeti is nocturnal.

53   8. The creature displayed some inquisitiveness, since it made a detour along the ridge in order to enter our camp and pass between the tents. It is possibly significant that the creature appeared to be immature.

54   9. The track of the creature supports the hypothesis that the yeti

inhabits the forested regions. The tracks came from the heavily forested valley of the Barun, and rather than going in the direction of the higher snowfields, crossed the ridge and appeared to be continuing back down toward the forests of the Kasuwa.

10. The circumstances suggest that the yeti is very strong and well   55
adapted to traveling across the Himalayan topography.

11. The prints lend credibility to the general theory of the yeti. Their   56
resemblance to the numerous footprints previously reported, such as Shipton's, which were made twenty-one years before and a long distance from Kongmaa La, suggest a uniformity of data strongly indicating the existence of an unknown creature in the Himalayas.

Based on this experience, I believe that there is a creature alive today   57
in the Himalayas which is creating a valid zoological mystery. It is possibly a known species in a deformed or abnormal condition, although the evidence points to a new form of bipedal primate. Or perhaps an old form – a form that man once knew and competed with, and then forced to seek refuge in the seclusion of the Himalayas.

Even though I am intrigued with the yeti, both for its scientific   58
importance and for what it says about our own interests and biases, I would be deeply saddened to have it discovered. If it were to be found and captured, studied and confined, we might well slay our nightmares. But the mystery and imagination it evokes would also be slain. If the yeti is an old form that we have driven into the mountains, now we would be driving it into the zoos. We would gain another possession, another ragged exhibit in the concrete world of the zoological park, another Latin name to enter on our scientific ledgers. But what about the wild creature that now roams free of man in the forests of the Himalayas? Every time man asserts his mastery over nature, he gains something in knowledge, but loses something in spirit.

Questions for Discussion and Writing

1. How does Cronin use the Lhakpa incident to catch the reader's interest and raise the major issues associated with the yeti?

2. What hypothesis does Cronin present to explain why interest in the yeti continues to exist?

3. What credentials does Cronin possess or what kinds of research experience did he have that would make his argument more credible?

4. Why is it significant, according to Cronin, that villagers routinely refer to the Yeti as a part of their wildlife?

5. Describe the characteristics of the yeti as they are revealed by different accounts. Why is it significant that accounts tend to agree on a composite picture? Why is it important that few "monstrous" attributes have been ascribed to the yeti?

6. Why does Cronin draw attention to the distinctive shape and size of the yeti's footprint? How does it differ from footprints of bears or humans?

7. According to Cronin, to what extent is there a double standard in the readiness with which scientists accept hypotheses based on scant fossil records yet reject seemingly stronger evidence for the existence of the yeti?

8. What connection does Cronin see between the yeti and a fossil form known as *Gigantopithecus*? Why is this connection important to his argument?

9. How might the unusual ecology of densely forested plains account for the ability of the yeti to live in areas surrounding the Himalayas without being captured?

Sir Edmund Hillary

Epitaph to the Elusive Abominable Snowman

Sir Edmund Hillary, currently ambassador to Nepal from New Zealand, was the first explorer to climb Mount Everest (1953). "Epitaph to the Elusive Abominable Snowman" first appeared in Life *(January 13, 1961). In this article, Hillary describes extensive investigations he personally undertook that led him to the conclusion that he could find no credible evidence to support the claim that the "abominable snowman" (or yeti) ever existed.*

Does the yeti, or "abominable snowman," really exist? Or is it just a 1 myth without practical foundation? For the last four months our Himalayan scientific and mountaineering expedition has been trying to find out — and now we think we know the answer.

There has been a growing pile of evidence in favor of the creature's 2 existence: the tracks seen by many explorers on Himalayan glaciers, the complete conviction of the local people that yetis roam the mountains, the yeti scalps and hands kept as relics in the high monasteries, the many stories about people who claim to have seen them.

But despite the firm belief of many Himalayan explorers and of some 3 anthropologists, I began the search for the yeti with some skepticism. My own experience had been limited to two incidents. In 1951 a tough and experienced Sherpa (Sherpas are a mountain people of Tibetan stock) had told me with absolute conviction that he had seen a yeti and watched it for some time. In 1952 Explorer George Lowe and I had found a tuft of black hair at an altitude of 19,000 feet, a tuft that our Sherpas swore was yeti hair — and immediately threw away in obvious fear.

Last September we set off from Katmandu in Nepal and walked for a 4 hundred miles through rain and leeches to the 12,000-foot-high Sherpa village of Beding. For eight days we were immobilized by weather, but we made profitable use of our time by interrogating the villagers and the lamas in the local monastery. One of our expedition members, Desmond Doig, speaks the language of Nepal with great fluency and has the ability, quite unprecedented in my experience, to gain the confidence and liking of the local peoples.

We confirmed much that we already knew and learned more besides. 5 The Sherpas believe there are three types of yetis:

1. The chuteh: a vast, hairy, ginger-and-black creature, sometimes eight feet tall, generally vegetarian and not harmful to man unless disturbed or annoyed.
2. The miteh: usually four to five feet tall with a high, pointed skull. His feet are said to be placed back to front. He has a decidedly unpleasant temperament and delights in eating any humans who come his way.
3. The thelma: a small creature from 18 inches to two feet high who lives down in the jungle, has human features and takes great pleasure in piling sticks and stones into little mounds.

6   We couldn't find any Sherpa who had actually seen a yeti, but several had heard them — usually when the winter snowfalls lay deep on the ground and the villagers were confined to their houses. Then, one gathered, the sound of the yeti was frequently heard at night, and next morning tracks were seen by the frightened Sherpas.

7   One of our own Sherpas, Ang Temba, now proved to be a veritable Sherlock Holmes. He scoured the villages for information and brought us the exciting news that there was a yeti skin here, the prized possession of a lama and his wife. The lama was away, and at first the wife refused to show us the skin. But Ang Temba and Desmond Doig were a formidable combination, and after much persuasion and chinking of the rupees the skin became ours. In our opinion it was a fine specimen of the very rare Tibetan blue bear, but all our Sherpas disagreed emphatically. It wasn't a bear at all, they said, but undoubtedly the chuteh, or biggest type of yeti. Nothing we said could sway this belief.

8   When the weather cleared, we moved up the Rolwaling valley and began our search for signs of the yeti. Several weeks later our efforts were rewarded by the discovery of many tracks on the Ripimu glacier between 18,000 and 19,000 feet. These tracks were positively identified by our Sherpas as those of yetis, and they certainly fulfilled the required specifications: large broad feet with clear toe marks.

9   We devoted much care to the examination of these tracks and made some interesting discoveries. When we followed a line of tracks to a place where the footprints were in the shade of rocks or on the cold north side of a snow slope, the yeti tracks suddenly ceased to exist. In their place we found the small footprints of a fox or wild dog, bunched closely together as the animal bounded over the snow. Again and again we saw precise evidence of the effect of the sun on those bunches of small tracks. The warmth melted them out, ran them together, completely altered their contours and made as fine a yeti track as one could wish.

10   Probably the best known photographs of yeti tracks are those taken by explorer Eric Shipton and Dr. Michael Ward on the Menlung glacier in 1951. The tracks that we discovered were less than two miles from the Shipton tracks and at a similar height and time of the year. Dr. Ward, who came back to the Himalayas as a member of my physiological team,

said that among the yeti tracks on the Menlung glacier he and Shipton had noticed a number of small animal tracks, but at the time they had not thought them significant.

In November we continued our investigations in the Khumbu region **11** at the foot of Mt. Everest. In the villages of Namche Bazar and Khumjung we obtained two more blue bear skins. Whenever we showed these skins to a Sherpa, we got the confident reply, "Chuteh."

Doig and Marlin Perkins, our zoologist, carried out a thorough en- **12** quiry among the Khumbu villages and monasteries. All the Sherpas believed in the yeti, but it was practically impossible to find anyone who, under careful questioning, claimed to have seen one. Even in the Thyangboche monastery, traditionally the source of much yeti lore and many yeti sightings, we were unable to find anyone who had seen a yeti. In fact, the two oldest lamas, who had lived in the monastery since its founding over 40 years ago, said they had neither seen a yeti nor knew of anyone who had.

Relics of the yeti in the monasteries of Khumjung, Pangboche and **13** Namche Bazar came in for special attention. The bones of a hand in the Pangboche monastery were thought by our medical men to be those of a man—possibly the delicate hand of a lama. The yeti scalps we were shown in these monasteries were more of a puzzle. They were in the shape of high, pointed caps covered with coarse reddish and black hair and seemed to be very old. If they were authentic scalps, their very form indicated that they belonged to no known animal. Although they had no seams or needle marks, there was the chance that they had been cleverly fabricated many years before out of the molded skin of some other creature.

Doig and Perkins worked hard on this second possibility. Ang Temba **14** produced two skins which had hair similar in texture to the scalps. We made high, pointed molds out of blocks of wood. The skins were softened, then stretched over the molds and left to dry. The resultant scalps were similar enough to the yeti scalps we saw in the monastery to indicate that we might be on the right track.

We realized that unless we could get an authoritative answer on the **15** scalps, they would remain a constant challenge to any theories about the yeti. But the village elders of Khumjung firmly believed that their community would suffer a plague, earthquake, flood or avalanche if their relic scalp ever was removed. They insisted that it was the remains of a famous yeti slaughter that took place 240 years ago, when there were so many man-eating yetis about that the Sherpas resorted to ruse to eliminate them. The Sherpas pretended to get drunk and to kill each other with wooden swords. At night the Sherpas substituted real swords, which they left lying about. The yetis, who had been watching them were great imitators, proceeded to drink heavily also, slashed at each other with the real swords and killed each other off.

After much negotiation with the Khumjung elders, we persuaded **16** them to lend us the scalp for exactly six weeks. In exchange I promised I would try to raise money for a school which they will share with nearby Sherpa villages. To guarantee that we would bring the scalp back, the elders said they would hold as hostages our expedition's three head Sherpas, as well as their property and possessions.

17   Our faithful Sherpas unhesitatingly agreed. Then the villagers chose Kunjo Chumbi, the keeper of the village documents, to accompany us and bring the scalp back. For his first trip to the West, he wondered if he should take Sherpas traveling rations with him — a dried sheep carcass, wheat flour and some of the local brew. After talking it over with Doig, he settled instead on some cakes of Tibetan brick tea and his silver teacup.

18   He, Doig, Perkins and I covered the 170 miles of steep country to Katmandu in 9½ days. From there we flew to Chicago, Paris and London and showed the scalp and the chuteh skins to zoologists, anthropologists and other scientists. Their decision was unanimous: the yeti scalp was not a scalp at all. It had been molded out of some other skin, and the scientists agreed that it was the skin and hair of the serow, a rather uncommon Himalayan member of the large goat-antelope family. Also our chuteh skins were confirmed to be Tibetan blue bear.

19   We now know that a yeti track can be made by the sun melting the footprints of a small creature such as a fox or wild dog. The same effect could occur with the prints of snow leopards, bears and even humans. We know that the large furs so confidently described by our Sherpas as chutehs are in fact the Tibetan blue bear. There is the strong possibility that some of these big, unfamiliar creatures strayed down from their only known habitations in eastern Tibet and crossed the Himalayan range. The small thelma in its habits and description sounds very much like the rhesus monkey. And the pointed scalps of the miteh have proved to be made from the skin of the much less frightening serow.

20   There is still much to be explained. Our theory on the tracks does not cover every case. We have not yet found a satisfactory explanation for the noise of the yeti which many Sherpas claim to have heard. But all in all we feel we have solved some of the major problems surrounding this elusive creature. Of course, the yeti still remains a very real part of the mythology and tradition of the Himalayan people — and it is undoubtedly in the field of mythology that the yeti rightly belongs.

Questions for Discussion and Writing

1. Sir Edmund Hillary, known for scaling Mount Everest in 1953, set himself the task of discovering whether credible evidence could be found to support claims that the "abominable snowman" (or yeti) existed. How does Hillary's initial summary of previous evidence

(tracks, "yeti scalps and hands kept as relics," and reports of sightings) serve to put his own attempt to determine the truth in perspective?

2. How had Hillary's two previous experiences led him to begin his search "with some skepticism"? Is there any evidence within the article that Hillary was less than objective in the methods he used to discover the truth about the existence of the yeti or "abominable snowman?"

3. Based on the linguistic proficiency of Desmond Doig, what did Hillary find out concerning the different types of yetis that the Sherpas believed existed? Describe the important characteristics that differentiate one type of yeti from another.

4. Look carefully at the episode where Ang Temba and Desmond Doig were able to purchase the rare skin of what the Sherpas believed to be a yeti from the wife of a lama, or Tibetan priest. Hillary takes this to be evidence of the credulity of the Sherpas (guides drawn from the local people), but he seems to ignore some of the more obvious implications of the transaction itself. For example, is it probable that the wife of a priest would take it upon herself to sell a rare and valuable holy relic while her husband was away? What might be another explanation of her willingness to be persuaded to part with this relic?

5. What new evidence did Hillary's investigation of what supposedly were yeti tracks reveal?

6. What hypothesis does Hillary advance to account for what were believed to be the bones of a hand of a yeti, kept as a relic in a monastery?

7. Discuss the differences between the scientific research methods used by Hillary and his team and the explanations of the Sherpas, based on myths and legends. For example, how did the village elders of Khumjung account for the large-scale disappearance of the yetis as a species?

8. Summarize the elaborate steps that Hillary and his team (including Marlin Perkins, later to become the host of Mutual of Omaha's *Wild Kingdom*) took to bring what was believed to be a yeti scalp to the West for analysis. Based on the scientific analysis of "zoologists, anthropologists, and other scientists," what conclusion did Hillary reach as to the possible existence of the yeti in the present-day world? According to Hillary, what aspects of the yeti phenomenon still need satisfactory explanations?

9. In an essay, compare and contrast the kinds and quality of reasoning employed by Cronin and Hillary. Whose conclusion, based on the research methods and logic used in the respective arguments, strikes you as more sound? That is, who do you think makes a better objective case regarding the existence or nonexistence of the "abominable snowman"?

10. Although results of tests on presumed yeti scalps seem to support Hillary's conclusions, what additional evidence does Cronin provide to suggest that this case is not yet closed?

11. How does Cronin use his own personal experience around the Kongmaa La mountain to reexamine evidence pertaining to yeti footprints in snow? How does Cronin's account dispel certain objections raised by Hillary?

THE 1929 PARALLEL

John Kenneth Galbraith

The 1929 Parallel

John Kenneth Galbraith, a world-renowned economist and professor of economics at Harvard, is the author of the classic study The Great Crash of 1929. *"The 1929 Parallel" originally appeared in* The Atlantic Monthly *(January 1987). Galbraith argues that there are a number of modern counterparts to 1920s' investment trusts, leveraged instruments, and get-rich-quick investor psychology that will lead to a crash whose effects will be even more catastrophic than the one in 1929.*

SENATOR COUZENS:	Did Goldman, Sachs and Company organize the Goldman Sachs Trading Corporation?
MR. SACHS:	Yes, sir.
SENATOR COUZENS:	And it sold its stock to the public?
MR. SACHS:	A portion of it. The firms invested originally in ten per cent of the entire issue for the sum of ten million dollars.
SENATOR COUZENS:	And the other ninety per cent was sold to the public?
MR. SACHS:	Yes, sir.
SENATOR COUZENS:	At what price?
MR. SACHS:	At a hundred and four. That is the old stock . . . the stock was split two for one.
SENATOR COUZENS:	And what is the price of the stock now?
MR. SACHS:	Approximately one and three quarters.

—from the Senate Hearings on
Stock Exchange Practices, 1932

In March of 1929 Paul M. Warburg, a founding parent of the Federal Reserve System and an immensely prestigious banker in his time, called attention to the current orgy, as he said, of "unrestrained speculation" in the stock market and added that were it not brought to an end, there would be a disastrous collapse. His warning was badly received. It was

1

made clear that he did not appreciate the new era in economic well-being that the market was so admirably reflecting; he was said by one exceptionally articulate critic to be "sandbagging American prosperity." Less eloquent commentators voiced the thought that he was probably short in the market.

2   There was a decidedly more sympathetic response somewhat later that year to the still remembered observation of Professor Irving Fisher, of Yale, one of the most diversely innovative scholars of his time. Fisher said, "Stock prices have reached what looks like a permanently high plateau." Fisher was, in fact, long in the market and by some estimates lost between eight and ten million dollars in the almost immediately ensuing crash.

3   There is here a lesson about the larger constant as regards financial aberration and its consequences. There is a compelling vested interest in euphoria, even, or perhaps especially, when it verges, as in 1929, on insanity. Anyone who speaks or writes on current tendencies in financial markers should feel duly warned. There are, however, some controlling rules in these matters, which are ignored at not slight cost. Among those suffering most will be those who regard all current warnings with the greatest contempt.

4   The first rule—and our first parallel with 1929—has to do with the stock market itself and, as it may somewhat formally be called, the dynamics of speculation.

5   Any long-continued increase in stock prices, such as preceded the 1929 crash and such as we experienced at least until last September, brings a change in the purposes of the participants in the market. Initially the motivating force is from institutions and individuals who buy securities (and bid up prices) because of some underlying circumstance, actual or imagined, that is judged to affect values: The economy as a whole is improving. Inflation as a threat is pending or perhaps receding. The tax prospect seems favorable. Or, mercifully, a business-oriented Administration has come to power in Washington. Most of all, in a time when common-stock dividends are largely a fixed dole to stockholders, interest rates are thought likely to decline. This calls for a compensating increase in the value of stocks if they are to earn only the new going return. On such matters virtually all comment concerning the market, informed and often otherwise, centers.

6   But as the stock-market boom continues (the same can be true as regards a boom in real estate or even art), there is increasing participation by institutions and people who are attracted by the thought that they can take an upward ride with the prices and get out before the eventual fall. This participation, needless to say, drives up prices. And the prices so achieved no longer have any relation to underlying circumstance. Justifying causes for the increases will, also needless to say, be cited by the sadly vulnerable financial analysts and commentators and, alas, the

often vulnerable business press. This will persuade yet other innocents to come in for the loss that awaits all so persuaded.

For the loss will come. The market at this stage is inherently unstable. 7 At some point something—no one can ever know when or quite what —will trigger a decision by some to get out. The initial fall will persuade others that the time has come, and then yet others, and then the greater fall will come. Once the purely speculative component has been built into the structure, the eventual result is, to repeat, inevitable.

There will previously have been moments of unease from which 8 there was recovery. These are symptoms of the eventual collapse. In 1928 and through the winter, spring, and summer of 1929 the stock market divorced itself from all underlying reality in the manner just cited. Justification was, of course, asserted; the unique and enduring quality of Coolidge and Hoover prosperity; the infinitely benign effects of the supply-side tax reductions of Secretary of the Treasury Andrew W. Mellon, who was held to be the greatest in that office since Alexander Hamilton; the high-tech future of RCA, the speculative favorite of the time, which so far had not paid a dividend.

But mostly speculators, amateur and otherwise, were getting on for 9 the ride. In the spring of 1929 came the initial indication of instability— a very sharp break in the market. Prices recovered, and in the summer months they rocketed up. There was another bad break in September and further uneasy movements. Then, at the end of October, came the compelling rush to get out and therewith the crash. No one knows what precipitated it. No one ever will. A few—Bernard Baruch and, it has long been said, Joseph P. Kennedy—got out first. Most went down with the mob; to an extraordinary degree, this is a game in which there are mainly losers.

The question now, in the winter of 1987, is whether the stock market 10 is or has been repeating its history. There was, early last year, a period of very sharply appreciating prices following an earlier, slower ascent. Then, on September 11 and the days following, came a severe slump, the worst in any recent period. So far (as this is written) there has been no significant recovery. As to the further prospect, no one knows, despite the extreme willingness to say otherwise on the part of many who do not know. What is certain, however, is that once again there existed a speculative dynamic—of people and institutions drawn by the market rise to the thought that it would go up more, that they could ride the rise and get out in time. Perhaps last September signaled the end; perhaps it was an episode in a continuing speculative rise with a worse drop yet to come. What we do know is that speculative episodes never come gently to an end. The wise, though for most the improbable, course is to assume the worst.

Another stock-market collapse would, however—one judges—be 11 less traumatic in its larger effect than was the one in October of 1929.

The Great Crash had a shattering effect on investment and consumer spending and eventually on production and employment, leading to the collapse of banks and business firms. Now there are safety nets, as they are called. Unemployment compensation, pensions, farm-income support, and much else would have a general cushioning effect, along with government fiscal support to the economy. There is insurance of bank deposits and the further certainty that any large corporation, if in danger, would be bailed out. Modern socialism, as I've elsewhere said, is when the corporate jets come down on National and Dulles airports.

12   A second, rather stronger parallel with 1929 is the present commitment to seemingly imaginative, currently lucrative, and eventually disastrous innovation in financial structures. Here the similarity is striking and involves the same elements as before. In the months and years prior to the 1929 crash there was a wondrous proliferation of holding companies and investment trusts. The common feature of both the holding companies and the trusts was that they conducted no practical operations; they existed to hold stock in other companies, and these companies frequently existed to hold stock in yet other companies. Pyramiding, it was called. The investment trust and the utility pyramid were the greatly admired marvels of the time. Samuel Insull brought together the utility companies of the Midwest in one vast holding-company complex, which he did not understand. Similarly, the Van Sweringen brothers built their vast railroad pyramid. But equally admired were the investment trusts, the formations of Goldman, Sachs and Company and the United Founders Corporation, and — an exceptionally glowing example of the entrepreneurial spirit — those of Harrison Williams, who assembled a combined holding-company and investment-trust system that was thought to have a market value by the summer of 1929 of around a billion dollars. There were scores of others.

13   The pyramids of Insull and the Van Sweringens were a half dozen or more companies deep. The stock of the operating utility or railroad was held by a holding company. This company then sold bonds and preferred stock and common stock to the public, retaining for itself enough of the common stock for control. The exercise was then repeated — a new company, more bonds and stock to the public, control still retained in a majority or minority holding of the stock of the new creation. And so forth up the line, until an insignificant investment in the common stock of the final company controlled the whole structure.

14   The investment trusts were similar, except that their ultimate function was not to operate a railroad or a utility but only to hold securities. In December of 1928 Goldman, Sachs and Company created the Goldman Sachs Trading Corporation. It sold securities to the public but retained enough common stock for control. The following July the trading corporation, in association with Harrison Williams, launched the Shenandoah

Corporation. Securities were similarly sold to the public; a controlling interest remained with the trading corporation. Then Shenandoah, in the last days of the boom, created the Blue Ridge Corporation. Again preferred stock and common were sold to the public; the controlling wedge of common stock remained now with Shenandoah. Shenandoah, as before, was controlled by the trading corporation, and the trading corporation by Goldman Sachs. The stated purpose of these superior machinations was to bring the financial genius of the time to bear on investment in common stocks and to share the ensuing rewards with the public.

No institutions ever excited more admiration. The creators of the 15
investment trusts were men of conceded as well as self-admitted genius, and were believed to have a strong instinct for the public interest. John J. Raskob, the chairman of the Democratic National Committee in those days, thought an investment trust might be created in which the toiling masses would invest from their weekly earnings. He outlined the proposal in a *Ladies' Home Journal* article titled "Everybody Ought to Be Rich."

In all these operations debt was incurred to purchase common stock 16
that, in turn, provided full voting control. The debt was passive as to control; so was the preferred stock, which conferred no voting rights. The minority interests in the common stock sold to the public had no effect of power either. The remaining, retained investment in common stock exercised full authority over the whole structure. This was leverage. A marvelous thing. Leverage also meant that any increase in the earnings of the ultimate companies would flow back with geometric force to the originating company. That was because along the way the debt and preferred stock in the intermediate companies held by the public extracted only their fixed contractual share; any *increase* in revenue and value flowed through to the ultimate and controlling investment in common stock.

It was a grave problem, however, that in the event of failing earnings 17
and values, leverage would work fully as powerfully in reverse. All income and value, and in practice more, would be absorbed by the outer debt and preferred shares; for the originating company there would remain literally — very literally — nothing. But of this in 1929 no one, or not many, thought; a rising market combined with the managerial and investment genius of the men who built these structures made any such concern seem irrelevant in the extreme.

Here the parallel: after fifty-seven years investment trusts, called 18
closed-end funds, are now coming back into fashion, although still, I would judge, in a rather modest way as compared with 1929. The more exciting parallel is in the rediscovery of leverage. Leverage is again working its wonders. Not in utility pyramids: these in their full 1929 manifestation are forbidden by law. And the great investment houses, to be sure, still raise capital for new and expanding enterprises. But that is

not where the present interest and excitement lie. These lie in the wave of corporate takeovers, mergers, and acquisitions and the *leveraged* buy-outs. And in the bank loans and bond issues, not excluding the junk bonds, that are arranged to finance these operations.

19   The common feature of all these activities is the creation of debt. In 1985 alone some $139 billion dollars' worth of mergers and acquisitions was financed, much of it with new borrowing. More, it would appear, was so financed last year. Some $100 billion in admittedly perilous junk bonds (rarely has a name been more of a warning) was issued to more than adequately trusting investors. This debt has a first claim on earnings; in its intractable way, it will absorb all earnings (and claim more) at some astringent time in the future.

20   That time will come. Greatly admired for the energy and ingenuity it now and recently has displayed, this development (the mergers and their resulting debt), to be adequately but not unduly blunt, will eventually be regarded as no less insane than the utility and railroad pyramiding and the investment-trust explosion of the 1920s.

21   Ever since the Compagnie d'Occident of John Law (which was formed to search for the highly exiguous gold deposits of Louisiana); since the wonderful exfoliation of enterprises of the South Sea Bubble; since the outbreak of investment enthusiasm in Britain in the 1820s (a company "to drain the Red Sea with a view to recovering the treasure abandoned by the Egyptians after the crossing of the Jews"); and on down to the 1929 investment trusts, the offshore funds and Bernard Cornfeld, and yet on to Penn Square and the Latin American loans — nothing has been more remarkable than the susceptibility of the investing public to financial illusion and the like-mindedness of the most reputable of bankers, investment bankers, brokers, and free-lance financial geniuses. Nor is the reason far to seek. Nothing so gives the illusion of intelligence as personal association with large sums of money.

22   It is, alas, an illusion. The mergers, acquisitions, takeovers, leveraged buy-outs, their presumed contribution to economic success and market values, and the burden of debt that they incur are the current form of that illusion. They will one day — again, no one can say when — be so recognized. A fall in earnings will render the debt burden insupportable. A minor literature will marvel at the earlier retreat from reality, as is now the case with the Penn Square fiasco and the loans to Latin America.

23   The third parallel between present and past, which will be vividly and also painfully revealed, concerns one of the great constants of capitalism. That is its tendency to single out for the most ostentatious punishment those on whom it once seemed to lavish its greatest gifts.

24   In the years before the 1929 crash the system accorded fortune and prestige to a greatly featured group of men — to Arthur W. Cutten, M. J. Meehan, Bernard E. ("Sell 'em Ben") Smith, and Harry F. Sinclair, all

market operators of major distinction; also to Charles E. Mitchell, the head of the National City Bank as it then was, and Albert Wiggin, the head of the Chase National Bank, both deeply involved in the market on their own behalf; to Ivar Kreuger, the Match King, international financier (and sometime forger of government bonds); and to Richard Whitney, soon to become president of the New York Stock Exchange and its most uncompromising public defender.

All suffered a fearful fall after the crash. Called before a congressio- 25
nal committee, Cutten, Meehan, and Sinclair all had grave lapses of memory. Mitchell and Wiggin, the great bankers, were both sacked; Mitchell went through long and tedious proceedings for alleged income-tax evasion, and the large pension Wiggin had thoughtfully arranged for himself was revoked. Ivar Kreuger went out one day in Paris, bought a gun, and shot himself. Harry Sinclair eventually went to jail, and so, for embezzlement, did Richard Whitney. Whitney's passage into Sing Sing, in dignified, dark-vested attire, wearing, it has been said, the Porcellian pig of his Harvard club, was one of the more widely circulated news portraits of the time.

The young professionals now engaged in much-admired and no less 26
publicized trading, merger takeover, buy-back, and other deals, as they are called, will one day, we can be sadly sure, suffer a broadly similar fate. Some will go to jail; some are already on the way, for vending, buying, and using inside information. Given the exceptionally oblique line between legitimate and much-praised financial knowledge and wrongfully obtained and much-condemned inside information, more are known to be at risk. But for most the more mundane prospect is unemployment and professional obloquy, and for some, personal insolvency. Expensive apartments will become available on the upper East Side of Manhattan; there will be property transfers in the Hamptons. David Stockman, said by the press to have a car sent out for him to Connecticut each morning by his employer, may end up taking the train.

S. C. Gwynne, a young onetime banker, tells in his excellent book 27
Selling Money of his services in the late seventies and early eighties to the international division of Cleveland Trust, now AmeriTrust, a relatively conservative player on the world scene. He journeyed from Manila to Algiers and Riyadh in search of loans. It was a time of admiring reference to the recycling of funds on deposit from the OPEC countries to the capital-hungry lands. And he tells that

by December 31, 1982, more than $200 million in loans would be in trouble in Mexico, Brazil, Venezuela, Poland, and the Philippines. . . . By 1984, thirteen of the seventeen officers who had staffed the [international] division in 1980 would be gone, and Ben Bailey, [the] deputy manager, and most of the members of the senior credit committee that approved the foreign loans would take early retirements.

28   The end for those in the present play will come when either recession or a tight-money crunch to arrest inflation makes the debt load they have so confidently created no longer tolerable. Then there will be threats of default and bankruptcy, a drastic contraction in operations, no bonuses, a trimming of pay and payrolls, and numerous very, very early retirements. And from many who did not themselves foresee the result, there will be a heavy-handed condemnation of the failure to see that this would be the result. For those who engage in trading operations at the investment houses the day of reckoning could be when the market goes down seemingly without limit. Then will be rediscovered the oldest rule of Wall Street: financial genius is before the fall.

29   The final parallel with 1929 is a more general one; it has broadly to do with tax reduction and investment incentives. In the Coolidge years, as noted, Andrew Mellon reduced taxes on the affluent. The declared purpose was to stimulate the economy; more precise reference to saving, investment, and economic growth was for the future. The unannounced purpose was, as ever, to lessen the tax bite on the most bitten. By the summer of 1929 the economy was nonetheless, stagnant — even in slight recession. (To this, rather than to the built-in inevitabilities of speculation, some economists looking for deeper substance later attributed the crash.) There is every likelihood that a very large part of the enhanced personal revenues from the tax reduction simply went into the stock market, rather than into real capital formation or even improved consumer demand.

30   So again now. Funds have been flowing into the stock market to be absorbed by the deals aforementioned or the cost of making them. Some, perhaps much, of this money — no one, to be sure, knows how much — is from the supply-side tax reductions. Real capital spending is currently flat, even declining — a depressing fact.

31   From the mergers, acquisitions, and buy-backs, it is now reasonably well agreed, comes no increase at all in industrial competence. The young men who serve in the great investment houses render no service to investment decisions, product innovation, production, automation, or labor relations in the companies whose securities they shuffle. They have no real concern with such matters. They do float some issues for new ventures or expanded operations; one concedes this while noting again how dismal is the present showing on real capital investment. Mostly their operations absorb savings into an inherently sterile activity.

32   History may not repeat itself, but some of its lessons are inescapable. One is that in the world of high and confident finance little is ever really new. The controlling fact is not the tendency to brilliant invention; the controlling fact is the shortness of the public memory, especially when it contends with a euphoric desire to forget.

Questions for Discussion and Writing

1. How does Galbraith's inclusion of testimony from the Senate Hearings on Stock Exchange Practices, 1932, as an opening for his article emphasize the importance of the issue his article explores?

2. How does Galbraith's mentioning of Paul M. Warburg's testimony in March 1929 (and the objections raised to it at the time) serve as a precedent to make Galbraith's audience more receptive to his own argument?

3. Summarize the different phases of a stock market boom and bust cycle. According to Galbraith, what forces drive stock prices up and what psychological factors prevent participants from perceiving the truth until it is too late?

4. What specific parallels does Galbraith perceive operating today that lead him to believe that a crash like the one of 1929 will happen again? What are the modern equivalents of the 1929 (*a*) investment trusts, (*b*) investor "Everybody Ought to Be Rich" psychology, (*c*) belief in the advice of "financial geniuses," and (*d*) margins and leveraged investments?

5. Based on what happened to prominent financiers after the 1929 crash, what does Galbraith predict will happen to present-day inside traders and officers of financial institutions? To what extent have the Boesky affair and the prosecution of stock and bond brokers for illegal use of insider information begun to resemble what happened to their predecessors after the 1929 Wall Street crash?

6. What reasons does Galbraith present to support his thesis that the Reagan era tax reforms are similar to measures before 1929 that resulted in more stock market speculation than "real capital formation"?

7. Write an essay in which you evaluate the probability of Galbraith's predictions coming true in light of such modern safety nets as (*a*) unemployment compensation, (*b*) farm income support, (*c*) federal insurance of bank deposits (FDIC), and (*d*) any other government programs (Social Security, food stamps, welfare payments) that might have a cushioning effect. Would any or all of these be sufficient to prevent a crash of the magnitude of the one in 1929? If not, why not?

Norman Gall

The Ghost of 1929

Norman Gall is a business writer who wrote "The Ghost of 1929" for Forbes magazine (July 13, 1987). Gall describes what he believes are misconceptions surrounding the 1929 crash and argues that Herbert Hoover has been unjustly made a scapegoat for the Great Depression. Based on his comparison of important differences between 1929 and the present, including areas of consumer borrowing, home mortgages, and consumer credit, Gall claims that present-day safety nets (unemployment compensation, FDIC, Social Security, and so on) would mitigate the effects of any 1929 type of financial crash.

1   The Great Depression of the 1930s haunts not only the dwindling generations that experienced it, but successive generations who grew up hearing tales of the suffering it caused. It showed that, yes, our economy can collapse. Many of our laws and indeed our welfare state are products of that depression. And many of our economic attitudes.

2   We had recessions before, some quite severe, but none like this. From 1929 to 1933, the U.S. gross national product shrank by 31% in constant dollars. Unemployment grew from 1.6 million in 1929 to 12.8 million in 1933, from 3% to 25% of the civilian labor force.

3   Prices of farm products fell by half. In early 1933 machine tool orders were one-eighth their 1929 level. Crude oil was selling for a nickel a barrel. Federal government revenues fell by half, covering only 41% of 1932 spending. More than 9,000 banks closed, factories and mines were shut down, towns abandoned, farms sold for debt.

4   During the Great Depression people would walk miles, not because they needed the exercise, but because they couldn't afford the 5-cent trolley fare. Stew with real meat in it was a luxury for most. People lost their homes. Unfinished hotels and office buildings dotted big cities. The tax base of cities collapsed just as their welfare burdens mushroomed. A crash of that magnitude today would take the Dow Jones industrials down to 300, push unemployment to nearly 30 million and bankrupt most of our major cities.

5   Nevertheless, despite all that's been written about it in the course of half a century, despite its importance in American history and folklore, we're still in a great confusion about the Great Depression. Economists have bogged down in debates among themselves on technical issues, such as central bank policy, without paying enough attention to long-term forces that caused the calamity. Economists still disagree on what to

do if such a calamity threatens again. This confusion is dangerous. politicians and bureaucrats, making policy in the dark, are still afraid to cut credit and liquidate bad debt for fear of starting another major crisis. Thus, though so much has already been written on the subject, *Forbes* feels that the crash is worth a fresh look and some fresh conclusions.

A distance of half a century makes it clear that the Great Depression **6** was a calamity but not a catastrophe. Despite their suffering, people survived. From 1929 to 1933, death rates actually fell, continuing their downward trend. The Depression in the U.S. saw little revolt or violence. Society held together. Life and the political process went on.

Still, we don't want to go through it all again. To recognize the **7** symptoms one must examine the real causes. What led to the Great Depression?

There are plenty of theories. The best of them, however, are not **8** provided by today's economists but by the men who dealt with the calamity and whose views are grounded in historical experience. Most of them agree that the roots of the Great Depression lay in the profusion of debt that resulted from the First World War. We have plenty of testimony to this. As early as 1915, Germany's finance minister had warned: "How this [war] debt is cast off will be the biggest problem since the beginning of the world." Herbert Hoover, long after he had retired from the White House, wrote: "In the large sense the primary cause of the Great Depression was the War of 1914–18." Writing in 1939, the great economist Joseph Schumpeter declared: "Depressions were actually impending or in progress in 1914. . . . Public expenditure turned them into prosperity first and created untenable situations afterward."

The Great Depression was essentially a collapse of inflated asset **9** values. The most important were Wall Street stocks, German war-reparations obligations and the British pound. The overvaluing of all these assets was sustained by credit from the U.S. financial system.

Accelerated by the wartime Liberty Bond drives, American families **10** accumulated financial assets at an astonishing rate, from $72 billion in 1912 to $290 billion in 1929. Never before in the world economy had households accumulated assets on this scale. The basis was thus laid for the vast and credulous postwar market which culminated in the portentous speculation of 1928 and 1929.

For decades, Herbert Hoover was a scapegoat. It was fashionable to **11** say that he should have "done something." In fact, he was an activist by the standards of his times. Throughout the 1920s he had warned, passionately and insistently, against the dangers of easy money and stock market speculation. As Secretary of Commerce (1921–29), Hoover pioneered new methods of analyzing business cycles and softening recessions.

When the 1929 crash came, just seven months after he became **12** President, Hoover was ready with a plan. He quickly went into action with a three-pronged program to sustain demand and keep the economy moving: 1) more public works spending; 2) low interest rates to ease business investment and home-building — mortgage money could be had at 5%; 3) keeping wages high to prevent a collapse of consumer purchasing power.

13   Hoover persuaded Congress to enact a tax cut, persuaded business and labor leaders to hold the line on prices, wages and capital spending and got the Federal Reserve to ease credit by lowering interest rates from 4% to 1.75%, the lowest on record. As the Depression deepened, he organized the Reconstruction Finance Corp. Its loans to banks and railroads did much to save the financial system.

14   Plunging into his struggle against the Depression, Hoover also had to struggle against conventional wisdom. "Liquidate labor, liquidate stocks, liquidate the farmers, liquidate real estate," Treasury Secretary Andrew Mellon had counseled Hoover shortly after the crash. Mellon's was the conventional wisdom. "It will purge the rottenness from the system," he said, "High costs of living and high living will come down. People will work harder, live a more moral life. Values will be adjusted, and enterprising people will pick up the pieces."

15   Hoover listened to Mellon's advice but rejected it. Hoover felt that modern economic policy could do more.

16   At the start, Hoover's actions seemed adequate. The situation was serious but not critical. In 1930, after the stock market crashed and the first wave of plant closings and layoffs had occurred, most of the banks were still solvent. But in 1931, just when the U.S. Depression should have been bottoming, the whole world's economy collapsed, taking the U.S. with it.

17   If Hoover can be faulted, it is not for heartlessness but for allowing his commitment to the gold standard and a strong dollar to suck the U.S. into the collapse of the weird international debt and payments structure spawned by World War I. Here's what happened:

18   The Creditanstalt, the Rothschilds' Vienna bank and Austria's biggest, failed after the French pulled their loans in protest against a planned customs union between Germany and Austria. Half the Creditanstalt's $145 million deposits were foreign. The panic spread to Germany, which lost one-third of its gold and foreign exchange reserves in two months, forcing its whole banking system to shut down.

19   It was like throwing a match into a basket of oily rags. There was too much debt around, and debts were too interconnected. Europe was still trying to pay for debts incurred in fighting WWI, and one country's ability to pay depended on another's ability to meet obligations. Panic had to spread. The Bank for International Settlements found that $10 billion of short-term debt was floating around the world, with $5 billion in Central Europe alone.

20   Throughout the 1920s borrowing had continued. Lured by attractive spreads, London bankers had borrowed short term in French francs at

2% and re-lent the funds, changed into reichsmarks, to German industry and local governments at 8%. Such loans totaled $3.6 billion, more than five times the gold reserve of the Bank of England. Remember, in those days a billion was a big number. Translated to 1987 money, the $10 billion in short-term debt was comparable in size to what all developing countries owed short term at the time of the 1982 Mexico default.

As the German financial system collapsed under the impact of the   21 Creditanstalt failure, panic spread throughout Europe. Frightened, foreigners demanded gold for their British deposits, and Britain was forced to leave the gold standard in September.

By 1930 the U.S. had 39% of the world's gold reserves. But this began   22 to shrink when the still-solvent European countries — France, Switzerland, Belgium and Holland — withdrew deposits from London and then from the U.S. This started a drain of funds from the U.S. banking system, which by law maintained a 40% gold backing for money in circulation.

The European financial crisis of 1931 moved the Great Depression in   23 the U.S. into a new phase. Another 3 million U.S. workers lost their jobs, and the nation began to lose hope. Americans took to hoarding cash and gold under mattresses, and foreigners began taking away large amounts of bullion. By Feb. 7, 1932 Treasury Secretary Ogden Mills told Hoover that the U.S. was within two weeks of being forced off the gold standard.

The government acted. Within 20 days Congress passed the first   24 Glass-Steagall Act, enabling the Federal Reserve Board to use government securities to back the currency. When that easy-money decision was announced, the Dow rose by 20% in three days. Within three months, the Fed doubled its holdings of government securities.

But the momentum was too great. Amid rumors that President-elect   25 Roosevelt was going to take the U.S. off gold — which FDR refused to deny — the New York Fed lost nearly half its gold in just three days in March, leaving it with only $381 million against foreign deposits of $600 million. In his inaugural address, FDR blamed the bankers:

"The money changers have fled from their high places in the temple · 26 of our civilization." Two days later he closed all the country's banks.

To many it looked like Armageddon, or at least the final crisis of   27 capitalism so often predicted by Marxists. But the system didn't disintegrate. It remained remarkably stable. People coped, though painfully. In this sense, the Great Depression was a vindication, not a repudiation, of democracy and of the capitalist system upon which democracy rests.

Milton Friedman and his followers have faulted the Federal Reserve   28 Board for the deeper distress, arguing that it should have pumped credit into the system. The Fed, as it happened, did a great deal. It pumped money into the economy by buying government securities during the crash, tripling its holdings between August and December 1929, and then doubling its holdings again during the 1931 European financial crisis. As the economy touched bottom in early 1932, as a result of the gold panic's spreading from Europe, the Fed dropped its gold reserve requirement and again doubled its holdings of government paper.

29   The Depression didn't end with the New Deal—not even after FDR pumped billions of borrowed dollars into the economy and spread his myths about what had happened. It ended only with the coming of WWII. The war was followed by the greatest period of economic development the world has seen. The British economist Angus Maddison calls this the golden age of economic expansion.

30   From 1950 to 1973, real world output grew by 4.9% yearly, compared with 2.5% from 1870 to 1913, and 1.9% from 1913 to 1950. World export volume quadrupled, double the growth rate from 1870 to 1913, the previous golden age of world trade. With that, and improved nutrition and public health, worldwide life expectancy at birth rose by one-third after World War II.

31   The golden age of economic expansion ended with the 1973–74 oil crisis. Fears rose that another 1929 was at hand. It wasn't, but a crimp was put in the world growth rate. The U.S. and world economies have been growing by only 2.7% yearly since 1973.

32   Observe, though, that even as growth has slowed, liquidity has exploded. The International Monetary Fund says the world money supply multiplied seven times from 1970 to 1985. The Eurocurrency deposit market, basically an interbank lending system, has grown by 25% yearly from $90 billion in 1970 to $3 trillion today.

33   The oil crisis didn't bring on a world depression. Will this explosion of liquidity bring on a crash?

34   There are worrisome signs, certainly, and no one should ignore them. For example, in the 1920s the federal government ran surpluses and cut its debts by nearly one-third, becoming a net supplier of funds to credit markets. In sharp contrast, big federal deficits between 1982 and 1986 have sucked in 36.6% of all available credit.

35   In the 1920s consumer borrowing was in its infancy and home mortgages and consumer credit were taking only 18% of new credit at the time of the crash. From 1982 to 1986 these demands absorbed 42% of the total credit supply. In the 1920s households were big net suppliers of funds to credit markets. In 1986 they borrowed 2.5 times more than they saved.

36   Meanwhile, with takeovers and mergers and stock buybacks, U.S. corporations have been replacing equity with debt to the tune of roughly $500 billion since 1980. So there is a lot of debt around.

37   Currency trading in New York, London and Tokyo now amounts to roughly $200 billion daily or $48 trillion yearly, more than ten times the U.S. GNP. In debt and equity as well as currencies, the speed, scale and instant statistical analysis that is provided by computers have cut the cost of trading as floating currency and interest rates provide more trading opportunities.

The enormous growth in world liquidity is creating bull markets 38
everywhere. Tokyo is the leader, with a P/E around 60 and price gains of
42% this year. Yet the Japanese economy is in the doldrums, with
exports down, industrial production falling and profits of big companies
evaporating.

We worry about the fact that $7.2 billion in junk bonds are held by 39
our thrifts, those bastions of the common man's savings that hold $900
billion in deposits guaranteed by the federal government. Some 370 of
these 3,200 thrifts are hopelessly bust but can't be closed, because the
Federal Savings & Loan Insurance Corp. needs about $25 billion to clean
up these institutions. How many other of these "guarantees" are in
similar shape?

We also worry that the Japanese could liquidate a piece of their 40
half-trillion dollars in foreign assets if their own widely overpriced stock
market crashes, causing a major disturbance similar to Creditanstalt in
1931.

Are these parallels with 1929 compelling? 41

Anything is possible, but the facts do not support apocalypse now. 42
Take financial assets. Between 1922 and 1929 the value of all U.S.
equities rose from $76 billion to about $200 billion at the peak of the bull
market. This was a huge jump, from an amount equaling GNP in 1922 to
nearly twice 1929's GNP. This time? Quite a modest contrast. The total
value of stocks at the end of 1986, even after a five-year bull market, was
only 71% of GNP.

No economist, nor anybody else, has told us how the collapse of 43
1929's asset values was transmitted to the real economy, but it happened. Yet in 1974, after a crash that was almost as great, the economy
did not follow the stock market into the tank. And high as world stock
prices may look today, they haven't even matched the pre-oil-crisis
price/earnings peaks of December 1972, when the world average
reached 19.7, only to tumble to 7.7 after oil prices quadrupled the
following year.

Also on the credit side of the ledger: Our labor economy and wage 44
structure today are showing great flexibility, whereas 60 years ago they
were very rigid. The same with the financial structure. "Lenders were
unwilling to adjust the debts due to them for the severe price level
changes, and interest rates could not be said to have declined at all,"
observes Barrie A. Wigmore, a partner and corporate finance specialist at
Goldman, Sachs, in his penetrating new study The Crash and Its Aftermath. "Debtors accordingly had to bear debt burdens much greater in
real terms than they had bargained for." Today we have evolved ways of
scaling back debts without liquidating the underlying businesses and of
liquidating weak banks before their rottenness infects the whole system.

Most U.S. businesses, having survived the overvalued dollar and 45
import competition in the 1980s, have come out lean and mean. The

profit rate in manufacturing has almost doubled since 1982, comparative labor costs have fallen, and productivity has risen fast. The U.S. still is by far the world's leading knowledge center, a mecca for some of the brightest people in the world. And it is still at the cutting edge of innovation. By 2000, the U.S. will have the youngest population among the rich countries and should continue to have the biggest and most dynamic home market. Thus, our real economy is robust, flexible and stable.

46   In comparable fashion the Third World debt problem may be reaching a slow solution, what with the huge recent writeoffs by major banks. Drexel Burnham's Michael Milken . . . discusses making markets in Third World paper held by banks as a way of keeping the old loans liquid. There are plans afoot to scale down claims by developing countries by allowing banks to write off many of these loans gradually and convert some of them to equity.

47   Note this stark difference between the aftermath of the two wars: After WWI the victors tried to levy reparations on the losers, and the U.S. tried to get its allies to pay back what it had lent them. Thus, victors and losers were saddled with totally unproductive debts.

48   In 1946 the U.S., learning the lessons of the 1920s and 1930s, forgave all war debts and pumped new money into the world economy by giving aid for postwar reconstruction and by building a security network around the world. It also worked hard to knock down the trade barriers that had both impeded world prosperity and fostered international conflict. In short, the world did learn from the mistakes of 1919 and 1920.

49   In the 1920s most of the nations reverted to naked economic nationalism, with tariffs and nontariff barriers sharply restricting world trade. After World War II the victors wanted an end to world wars and understood that conquest in pursuit of trade was a major cause of war. So they set up a system of relatively free trade that endures to this day and was, then as now, underwritten by the U.S.

50   We still worry—and a good thing, because in 1929 we didn't worry enough. "No nation ever faced a business decline more optimistically than America did this one," wrote historian Samuel Eliot Morison of the early U.S. reaction to the onset of the Great Depression. Had Americans worried more, the speculation wouldn't have carried as far as it did for as long as it did. Politicians and bankers would have known better how to behave.

51   Now we are plenty worried. For every certified optimist today there is a certified pessimist, fretting about the trade deficit, the seemingly dizzy heights to which the stock markets of the world have climbed, about unemployment and foreign competition and what have you. The current bull market on Wall Street has, as they say, climbed a wall of worry. This kind of nervousness helps brake the financial expansion that otherwise might get out of hand. Are we on the brink of another 1929? No. Can we ignore its lessons? Definitely not.

Questions for Discussion and Writing

1. Norman Gall, writing on behalf of *Forbes* magazine, believes that many misconceptions surround the 1929 crash and the Great Depression. What are some of the misconceptions Gall intends to correct in his article?

2. What factors, according to Gall, played a role in creating the Great Depression? In what respects do the problem of Third World debt and Japanese investment in the United States represent parallels to situations that existed before the financial collapse of the 1920s?

3. What reasons and evidence does Gall present to support his thesis that Herbert Hoover has been unjustly made a scapegoat for the Great Depression? How, according to Gall, should history regard the part Hoover played?

4. What was the Glass-Steagall Act and what purpose was it supposed to serve?

5. According to Gall, what important differences in the areas of consumer borrowing, home mortgages, and consumer credit distinguish the economic situation in the 1920s from that of the 1980s?

6. What statistical evidence does Gall present to answer those who are concerned about ominous parallels between the 1920s and the present? For example, what difference does Gall discern between the treatment of debtor nations and the restriction of trade by means of tariffs after World War I and World War II?

7. Write an essay comparing and contrasting the cases made by Galbraith and Gall. Whose argument do you find more persuasive and more likely to come true?

ABORTION

Andrew Hacker

Of Two Minds
About Abortion

Andrew Hacker's "Of Two Minds about Abortion" first appeared in Harpers (September 1979). His books include The End of the American Era *(1970) and* Free Enterprise in America *(1977). The abortion issue was triggered by the now famous 1973 Roe v. Wade decision by the Supreme Court declaring that fetuses are not covered by the definition of person as used in the Fourteenth Amendment. Speaking for seven members of the Court, Justice Blackmun stated that "a right to privacy" gave a woman the right to terminate her pregnancy under specified circumstances. Hacker, a professor of political science at Queens College when he wrote this article, brings an unusual perspective to bear on the question of abortion; he examines the hidden agendas and psychological motivations of both advocates and opponents of abortion before making his own recommendation favoring abortion on an unrestricted basis.*

1   If opponents of abortion had their way, 1.3 million more babies would be born this year, for that is how many pregnancies are being artificially ended. If supporters of abortion had their way, there would be one million fewer births this year, for that is how many additional abortions could be performed were resources fully available.

2   Abortion has become the hardy perennial of our politics. It is a controversy with a life of its own, demanding a place on the public agenda no matter what other questions plague us. Of course there have been similar issues before, but none — not even Prohibition — has stirred so much soul-searching or ambiguity of feeling.

3   Not the least cause of confusion is that those most passionately embroiled in the struggle have defined the terms of debate. Thus we are asked to accept "Right to Life" and "Freedom of Choice" as the chief opposing principles. These slogans have been heard so often they need no rehearsing. ("A woman has the right to control her own body." "But not at the price of another life.") Yet being caught in a crossfire can help

to clear the mind. One might wonder if more is at stake than either side will admit. As it happens, the suspicion is correct.

In fact, abortion conceals a basic social conflict, but one we are not 4 prepared to discuss. The subject, of course, is sexual intercourse. But not in terms of attitudes or abstractions. At issue, rather, is the importance sexual pleasure is granted in our lives. For a growing number of Americans, full and frequent sexual activity is a vital source of enjoyment. Others see this development as endangering moral character and the survival of society. It is only in such a context that arguments over abortion become clear.

For this reason, it should be added that abortion is not the province of 5 any single religion. Though the majority of opponents are indeed Roman Catholic, many Protestants and Jews join in the outcry, and women of every religious background have availed themselves of abortions. Catholic tenets may be congruent with "the right to life," but the anti-abortion movement has less to do with doctrinal scruples than with the sensibility of a class and a generation.

Of the 5 million pregnancies that occurred last year, 3.3 million 6 resulted in live births, 1.3 million ended with abortions, and the remaining 400,000 were miscarriages or stillbirths. Supporters of abortion not only defend the 1.3 million terminations but would push the percentage higher. A recent study released by the Alan Guttmacher Institute — the main statistical source in this area — estimates that almost 600,000 women who wanted abortions last year were unable to obtain them because their region either lacked facilities or set onerous restrictions.

Some supporters go further. They claim that with suitable counseling, 7 many women now disposed to bearing their babies would come to change their minds. Even with abortion available, each year almost 250,000 teenage women have out-of-wedlock births. Unintended pregnancies precipitate many marriages. More than 300,000 teenage brides are pregnant at their weddings. Those who favor abortion feel more can and should be done to convince these women that having their babies would be a mistake. And were this goal attained, the number of abortions in the United States would match the number of annual births. Japan has already struck that balance. The Soviet Union even tips it on the side of abortion.

Of course, it is difficult to imagine a person who is literally "pro- 8 abortion." It is still a surgical procedure, requiring professional attention. Hence those who support abortion as an option speak of it as a last resort. Birth control, they say, is best. Abortion should be a recourse if contraception fails, or was never used at all.

Yet if this recourse has become increasingly necessary, the reasons 9 are not always the ones we hear. By and large, youth, poverty, ignorance are cited as the causes of unplanned pregnancies. While these are ob-

viously part of the explanation, statistics suggest other provocations as
well.

10   Two-thirds of all abortions are performed on women over the age of
twenty. Many are well-informed, middle-class persons, quite familiar
with contraceptive methods. Nor is unreliable equipment often the
cause. A significant reason women become unwillingly pregnant is that
even the best-educated bring mixed motives to bed.

11   Ambiguous feelings about conceiving come with the condition of
being a woman. To want and not want a baby at one and the same time
is an emotion most women have experienced or certainly understand.
Hence the high incidence of women reporting to their doctors that they
has simply "forgotten" to take a pill or put a diaphragm in place, or had
been certain that the "safe period" before ovulation had another day or
so to run. Thus far, researchers have avoided this subject, which is
probably just as well. We are dealing with sentiments even women
themselves find it difficult to articulate. To call such behavior illogical, as
men are apt to do, shows a failure of sympathy and imagination. Intercourse is not an act in which one is always in control or certain of one's
intent. Repeated insistence on women's right to control their own bodies
may itself be evidence of the ambivalence that attends surrender to
sexual pleasure, aside from the public and political content of this
phrase.

12   A woman can toy with the idea of becoming pregnant, without
wishing to see the pregnancy through to term. This is especially so with
younger women, curious about their capacities. Not only "Can I do it?"
but "What will be its effect on me?" are things every woman wonders.
No matter what else she does with her life—she can head a huge
corporation—having achieved conception is still part of being a woman.
And once that state has been attained, even if only for a fortnight, she
may reconsider where it will lead. Or tell herself having a baby is fine;
now is just not the time.

13   There are other forces at work. Women tend more than men to link
intercourse with romance. The more one plans precautions, the less
sublime it seems. Among women who do not have a steady sexual
partner, few use the pill on a regular basis or wear an intrauterine device.
Such ongoing protection is still relatively rare, even in our liberated age.
Even today, most women still like to believe that intercourse requires the
man's initiative. Not being prepared helps affirm that posture and adds
to the spontaneity. It is only after a month or so has passed that the
consequences must be faced.

14   There are instances where women obtain abortions to punish the
father, their parents, themselves. But here I find myself intruding on
territory I have no right or wish to enter. For whatever reason, it is
nonetheless a fact that many "unwanted" pregnancies were either desired in a halfhearted way or resulted from knowingly taking chances.

Such conceptions are as common among worldly women as among ingenuous girls in their teens.

The struggle to legalize abortion was conducted in the name of married women. The typical plaintiff ("Mrs. Roe") already had more children than the family budget could support. If allowed this one abortion, she would presumably ensure that it wouldn't happen again. 15

However, the chief clients for abortion have not been Mrs. Roe. Only one in six abortions is performed on women over thirty. And fewer than one in twelve is performed on mothers with more than three children. Fully 75 percent of all abortions are performed on unmarried women. A third of these women are still in their teens, and another third in their early twenties. In other words, the rising demand for abortion has attended the spread of youthful sexual activity. In fact, episodes of premarital intercourse were more common in the past than people admitted. What has changed is that once young people are initiated, they persist, usually with a steady partner. 16

A Guttmacher Institute survey of unmarried teenagers revealed that fewer than one in five of those deemed "sexually active" made consistent use of contraceptives. Fewer than half had protected themselves the last time they had intercourse, and only half of those used certifiably reliable methods. Moreover, some young women make pregnancy their goal. It is seen as a way of entering adulthood, of relieving an aimless life, of restoring self-esteem. Still, most teenagers are not equipped to be parents, and they have second thoughts when confronted with that fact of life. If they are not to be driven to abortion—as 400,000 annually are—then something must be done. But what? 17

Perhaps the most commonly heard solution is sex education in the schools. Supporters of abortion invariably invoke such programs in any remarks they make. The only problem is that "sex education" has become a vague and evasive symbol. Few who employ it have any idea what actually happens in the classroom, nor are they disposed to find out. Better to assume that experts know how to handle the niceties, as happens in driver training. 18

In fact, even the most liberal school districts allow little serious discussion of birth control. Teachers may mention various methods, but the descriptions are fairly summary. Not one school in a thousand will permit a diaphragm to be passed around, let alone give lessons how to unroll a condom. On a purely verbal level it can be said that some teenagers acquire "information." It is at the next step, where information becomes instruction and practice, that the schools abdicate. 19

While boys can buy condoms at a drugstore, it is a rare mid-teen girl who will approach a gynecologist on her own. Birth control services are increasingly available, especially on college campuses. The problem is reaching those who start sexual activity in their sophomore year of high 20

school. What passes for sex education will not prevent premarital pregnancies until schools shepherd groups of pupils over to nearby clinics,
with or without parental permission. Even progressive-minded parents
draw the line at such proposals. The idea persists that equipping an
adolescent can only encourage promiscuity. Once armored, she will
indulge in indiscriminate sex with an endless array of partners. This fear
may be universal, but it runs especially deep among parents of teenage
daughters. They prefer to hope their children will use good sense about
sex, whatever that may mean.

21   What emerges is that for young people abortion is not a "last resort"
at all. Rather, it is the first intervention of adult society. We are told it
must be available lest hundreds of thousands of young women be hob-
bled by early motherhood. Due to our chariness about sex education, we
are asked to accept a quick, surgical remedy rather than face our own
misgivings about providing preventive measures. It is only after a teenager has had an abortion that we feel we can give her the equipment she
clearly needed earlier. At this point it should be admitted that abortion
has become a major mode of birth control And it will continue to be one
until adults resolve their own dilemmas about teenage sexual experience.

22   With the advent of the abortion debate, a new word has entered
common usage. While people always knew what "fetus" meant, it was
not a term heard much in public. It belonged to biological science,
denoting animals in gestation. But now we hear it all the time, at least
among advocates of abortion. What is removed from a woman's womb is
invariably called a "fetus." Or occasionally an embryo. Or even a fertilized egg. But never, of course, a baby.

23   The reasons, while hardly mysterious, deserve explicit discussion.
Those who have had abortions are rarely unburdened of guilt. Even
active lobbyists have lingering feelings that their advocacy is wrong.
(The mention that someone has had, say, three abortions causes some
discomfort, even in sophisticated circles.) Sometimes this guilt is labeled
"ungrounded," an irrational emotion to be alleviated by therapy. Yet
regard for human life is considered a test of civilization. These doubts
have not been resolved, nor are they likely to be. Rather they are
screened from immediate consciousness by calling whatever it is a
"fetus." This is clearly a blindered solution, if it is any solution at all.

24   "Fetus" has another, more practical, use. It denotes something disposable, akin to an animal embryo discarded after a laboratory experiment. Here a "fetus" is construed as a growth within oneself, one of
several inconveniences that can arise from sexual activity. And like those
other annoyances, it has a prescribed mode of treatment.

25   Support for abortion comes primarily from men and women who
admit to enjoying sexual activity and want safeguards for that pleasure.
They have attained new realms of experience, which they have no wish
to abandon. Apart from a small minority, they are not swingers or

spouse-swappers or even necessarily unfaithful. They compose a new class of Americans, for whom intercourse is an important leisure pursuit. But it is also an activity that needs abortion as a backup.

And what of the babies who are aborted? Even fervent supporters of abortion cannot claim to know which particular children would be better off unborn. Only in rare instances do we say of certain persons — those who have suffered greatly or inflicted suffering on others — that it would have been preferable for everyone had they never lived at all. One knows of babies who were initially unwanted, yet brought joy to their parents' lives. There are infants who came perilously close to abortion, but went on to lives of real distinction. This is too tangled a subject for dispassionate analysis. Those who favor abortion prefer to avoid the issue by focusing on how a birth may affect the mother. Opponents resolve the dilemma by demanding that everyone be born. 26

Opponents of abortion base their case on principle, which allows for no exceptions. An abortion is a planned assault on life, a murder with no extenuating circumstances. Thus far the majority of Americans have not accepted this view. Victims of incest or rape enjoy special sympathy, as do women certain to deliver babies that will be deformed. For this reason, opponents have settled for restrictions rather than abolition. 27

Thus one national Right to Life campaign resulted in Congress's adoption of the Hyde Amendment, named for its sponsor, Henry Hyde, an Illinois Representative. Beginning in the summer of 1977, no further Medicaid funds could be spent on abortions unless childbirth risked the mother's life. In the previous year, 295,000 women with low incomes had abortions paid for with federal funds. The Hyde ban has proved all but total. In the twelve-month period following its passage, fewer than 3,000 women qualified for Medicaid abortions. 28

While individual states can still pay the bills, only nine now do so fully. Most of the rest accept the Hyde Amendment's limitations. Some go further. Massachusetts, for example, has removed abortion from the health coverage of employees on its payroll and their spouses. 29

At this writing, figures are not yet available on how many abortions will be blocked by the states' restrictions. Even women able to pay are subject to hardship. Some states now require hospitalization, which easily doubles the cost. Louisiana requires a court order for women under eighteen. It also makes physicians remind potential patients that "the unborn child is a human life," and then offer a graphic description of its "tactile sensitivity." This law, considered a model by abortion opponents, passed the Louisiana legislature by a 123–1 margin. Now a constitutional amendment is pending that would make it a federal crime to end any unborn life. 30

What makes opponents of abortion insist that every pregnant woman be made to bear her baby? Their own answer is well-known: that child has a right to experience whatever its life may hold in store. This would 31 suggest that opponents care deeply about the children they wish to save. Yet the record offers little concrete evidence of that professed concern.

32   This country has never claimed to offer equal opportunities to all its children. Those with privileged upbringings always stand a better chance than others. Still, with public education and a tolerance for talent, it could be argued that the odds allowed most youngsters hope for a decent start in life. However, recent years have seen the emergence of a generation of Americans who seem denied that hope, and destined by a host of disadvantages to careers of unfulfilled capacities. One of those disadvantages is early pregnancy, which writes a fairly predictable script for both mothers and children. Poor teenage girls who become pregnant generally quit school before they have the basic skills required for steady employment. Close to nine in ten keep their babies and enter the welfare rolls, where they remain as more children are born. Their infants begin with lower birth-weights and greater vulnerability to disease. In short, the children begin in settings similar to those where they were conceived.

33   To be sure, no one really knows to what degree society's intervention might improve their circumstances. Some very expensive programs (job training, for example) have had minimal effect. Still, there has been success in some cities. One program offers hostels for mothers while they finish high school, and day care for their children. Another adds to this counseling with job placement and frequent follow-ups. Needless to say, the high ratios needed of staff to constituency make these ventures very costly. Outlays can total five figures for each participant. Perhaps ultimately such services will be paid back, if mothers and their offspring become assets to society, but no one really knows.

34   What can be shown is that opponents of abortion have been conspicuously silent about services of this kind, particularly those funded by taxes. At best, they will point to a few homes for unwed mothers as a testament to their good will, and to services established to convince unmarried women that they ought to bear their babies. But as far as abortion opponents are concerned, once a child has been given its life it is on its own.

35   There is another reason for compelling the birth of a baby. It is a way to punish the mother. Chastening is what she deserves. She has had her hours of pleasure, and should be made to take the consequences, especially if those idylls were illicit. A baby as a burden sets limits on one's life, and one woman's forfeiture of freedom will be an example to others. When moral arguments go unheeded, motherhood remains a final threat.

36   Certainly, opponents of abortion want to see an end to youthful sexual intimacy. They make no pleas for birth-control instruction or providing contraceptives. Such safeguards will encourage the very acts they hope to halt. The aim is abstinence, at least until a couple has been married. Although these restraints are congruent with Catholic morals, the authority of the church alone does not seem to account for their persuasive power.

Nor is it only teenagers who require this stern attention. Too many   37
older women who should know better are casual about intercourse and
seek to avoid its responsibilities. Almost a quarter of all abortions are
being performed on women who have had one before. This, plus eagerness for a "morning-after" pill, shows a penchant for pleasure devoid of
moral sense. Only if abortion is no longer an option will these women
come to realize that bedding down is something to think about twice.

Opponents of abortion see the pursuit of pleasure as contaminating   38
our age. This view echoes a puritan as well as a Catholic heritage, which
says enjoyments should be earned. And even those who earn them
should take a slender ration. Needless to say, opponents of abortion do
not say they are opposed to sexual activity, only that it must be enjoyed
in marriage, and best on the sparing side.

People who oppose abortion see themselves as citizens who have   39
paid their dues. They have not only accepted parenthood, but have kept
their lusts in check. And they know — even envy — what they have
missed. The evidence is all around them, not least on prime-time television. At this point, the tensions take on social contours. Below them they
see the poor, engaging in carefree sex and then getting free abortions.
Above them stands a modish middle class, enjoying an array of partners
and putting abortions on credit cards. How can one keep one's own
children moral with so many examples around to the contrary?

Feminists argue that opposition to abortion reflects hostility to   40
women. Yet it happens that women — especially those married with
several children — are abortion's most active adversaries. There is, in
fact, a social division among women themselves. On one side are those
accustomed to frequent sexual enjoyment; on the other, those unsettled
by the notion of such indulgence. Were women alone to vote on abortion, the tally would still be close.

I feel I should end on a personal note. For my own part, I favor   41
making abortion available, on an unrestricted basis. My reasons are those
customarily given, and I have no new arguments to add. At the same
time, I am far from happy finding myself in this position.

Abortion is a taking of human life. No legal or scientific theorizing   42
can change that basic fact. My fear is that sanctioning abortion will direct
our sensibilities from moral principles to pragmatic matters of cost and
inconvenience. That aspect of abortion concerns me as much as anything
else.

Moreover, I find I have sympathy for those on the other side. Far   43
from being fanatics, they conceive of a social and moral order where
citizenship has its duties and passions are held in check. They believe
strongly in the family. Theirs may be a stern, even punitive, ethic, but
they are people who have contributed their share to society, at no small
cost to themselves.

I am not convinced that those supporting abortion have a parallel   44
vision. Theirs is a highly personal outlook, stressing freedom and choice
and pleasure. What is lacking is any sign of concern over the society we

will have, and the people we will be, once their ends are attained. A fully active sexual life may be fine. But we should consider where it can take us. Opponents of abortion have done just that. Its supporters prefer to avoid such questions.

Questions for Discussion and Writing

1. At what point does Hacker announce that his purpose in writing this essay is to go beyond the customary or usually heard slogans often repeated on both sides of the abortion issue?

2. What issue not usually identified does Hacker claim is crucial for understanding the context in which arguments over abortion take place?

3. How does Hacker use statistics to dramatize the additional hundreds of thousands of women whom abortion advocates intend to target?

4. According to Hacker, why are the explanations of youth, poverty, and ignorance traditionally cited as the causes of unplanned pregnancies not supported by the facts as to who really has abortions?

5. How does Hacker's discussion of women's subconscious attitudes, psychological factors, and attitudes toward sexual intercourse support his claim that "[a] significant reason women become unwillingly pregnant is that even the best-educated bring mixed motives to bed"? In your opinion, which of these unconscious predisposing factors seems to be the most plausible explanation? Which seems to be the least? Explain your answer.

6. In Hacker's view, why is it important to know that the 1973 landmark *Roe* v. *Wade* Supreme Court decision was atypical in many ways? What are some of the chief differences between Mrs. Roe's situation and the circumstances of the majority of women on whom abortions are performed? How does Hacker use the important differences to support his contention that "the rising demand for abortion has attended the spread of youthful sexual activity"?

7. How plausible do you find Hacker's descriptions of the reasons that many young women first become pregnant and then change their minds about having the baby?

8. According to Hacker, how does societal ambivalence toward sex education in the schools make it so ineffective that abortion winds up being used as "a major mode of birth control"?

9. What reasons does Hacker advance to support his claim that abortion advocates use the words *fetus* or *embryo* or *fertilized egg* as a means of distancing themselves psychologically from feelings of guilt?

10. Evaluate Hacker's characterization of the life-style of those who support abortion.

11. In Hacker's view, what is hypocritical about the demand by opponents of abortion that "every pregnant woman be made to bear her baby" on the grounds that every "child has a right to experience whatever its life may hold in store"? How does Hacker use analyses of day care and other child-support programs to support his views?

12. Evaluate the plausibility of Hacker's reasoning that opponents of abortion by and large do not care about the lives of children but simply want to punish the mothers. How accurate do you find Hacker's characterizations of (a) the role played by a desire to punish women for having sex, (b) resentment over the "poor, engaging in carefree sex and then getting free abortions," and (c) "even envy" over "what they have missed" as being the underlying motivations of abortion opponents?

13. How does Hacker's probing analysis of the hidden agendas and psychological undercurrents of both the advocates and opponents of abortion lend credibility to his own recommendation favoring making abortions available on an unrestricted basis? In essence, how has his analysis made it much more likely that Hacker is not lying to his readers or to himself?

14. How does Hacker's ability to empathize with those on both sides of the debate make his own recommendations more persuasive? How does the tone of his essay communicate that the purpose of his article is to try to understand the hidden social and psychological contexts in which arguments over abortion occur?

15. How does Hacker's arrangement of his argument—so that his own recommendations favoring abortion follow an extended analysis of both sides of the issue—increase the effectiveness of his case? How might his argument have been perceived had he put his own views first and then followed with an analysis of both sides?

16. For further reading, consult Kristin Luker, *Abortion and the Politics of Motherhood* (1984); on July 3, 1989, by a 5–4 vote, the United States Supreme Court placed new restrictions on when an abortion could be performed. States may now require doctors to determine whether a fetus, at least 20 weeks old, is capable of surviving outside the womb.

George F. Will

Discretionary Killing

George F. Will's "Discretionary Killing" first appeared in Newsweek *(September 20, 1976). Will's argument is not directly opposite to Hacker's position, although Hacker is for unrestricted abortion and Will is against it. What makes Will's argument intriguing is that he, like Hacker, looks at the moral issues surrounding abortion from an unusual perspective. This nationally syndicated columnist's argument against abortion on demand sketches a vivid picture outlining how present attitudes toward abortion will inevitably lead to a dehumanized society that will condone the discarding of "surplus embryos" and the extermination of genetically defective infants and old people.*

1   It is neither surprising nor regrettable that the abortion epidemic alarms many thoughtful people. Last year there were a million legal abortions in the U.S. and 50 million worldwide. The killing of fetuses on this scale is a revolution against the judgment of generations. And this revolution in favor of discretionary killing has not run its course.

2   That life begins at conception is not disputable. The dispute concerns when, if ever, abortion is a *victimless* act. A nine-week fetus has a brain, organs, palm creases, fingerprints. But when, if ever, does a fetus acquire another human attribute, the right to life?

3   The Supreme Court has decreed that *at no point* are fetuses "persons in the whole sense." The constitutional status of fetuses is different in the third trimester of pregnancy. States constitutionally can, but need not, prohibit the killing of fetuses after "viability" (24 to 28 weeks), which the court says is when a fetus can lead a "meaningful" life outside the womb. (The Court has not revealed its criterion of "meaningfulness.") But states cannot ban the killing of a viable fetus when that is necessary to protect a woman's health from harm, which can be construed broadly to include "distress." The essence of the Court's position is that the "right to privacy" means a mother (interestingly, that is how the Court refers to a woman carrying a fetus) may deny a fetus life in order that she may lead the life she prefers.

4   Most abortions kill fetuses that were accidentally conceived. Abortion also is used by couples who want a child, but not the one gestating. Chromosome studies of fetal cells taken from amniotic fluid enable prenatal diagnosis of genetic defects and diseases that produce physical and mental handicaps. Some couples, especially those who already have handicapped children, use such diagnosis to screen pregnancies.

New diagnostic techniques should give pause to persons who would   5
use a constitutional amendment to codify their blanket opposition to
abortion. About fourteen weeks after conception expectant parents can
know with virtual certainty that their child, if born, will die by age 4 of
Tay-Sachs disease, having become deaf, blind and paralyzed. Other
comparably dreadful afflictions can be detected near the end of the first
trimester or early in the second. When such suffering is the alternative to
abortion, abortion is not obviously the greater evil.

Unfortunately, morals often follow technologies, and new diagnostic   6
and manipulative skills will stimulate some diseased dreams. Geneticist
Bentley Glass, in a presidential address to the American Association for
the Advancement of Science, looked forward to the day when government may require what science makes possible: "No parents will in that
future time have a right to burden society with a malformed or a mentally incompetent child."

At a 1972 conference some eminent scientists argued that infants   7
with Down's syndrome (Mongolism) are a social burden and should be
killed, when possible, by "negative euthanasia," the denial of aid needed
for survival. It was the morally deformed condemning the genetically
defective. Who will they condemn next? Old people, although easier to
abandon, can be more inconvenient than unwanted children. Scientific
advances against degenerative diseases will enable old people to (as will
be said) "exist" longer. The argument for the discretionary killing of
these burdensome folks will be that "mere" existence, not "meaningful"
life, would be ended by euthanasia.

The day is coming when an infertile women will be able to have a   8
laboratory-grown embryo implanted in her uterus. Then there will be the
"surplus embryo problem." Dr. Donald Gould, a British science writer,
wonders: "What happens to the embryos which are discarded at the end
of the day—washed down the sink?" Dr. Leon R. Kass, a University of
Chicago biologist, wonders: "Who decides what are the grounds for
discard? What if there is another recipient available who wishes to have
the otherwise unwanted embryo? Whose embryos are they? The
woman's? The couple's? The geneticist's? The obstetrician's? The Ford
Foundation's? . . . Shall we say that discarding laboratory-grown embryos is a matter between a doctor and his plumber?"

But for now the issue is abortion, and it is being trivialized by cant   9
about "a woman's right to control her body." Dr. Kass notes that "the
fetus simply is not a mere part of a woman's body. One need only
consider whether a woman can ethically take thalidomide while pregnant to see that this is so." Dr. Kass is especially impatient with the
argument that a fetus with a heartbeat and brain activity "is indistinguishable from a tumor in the uterus, a wart on the nose, or a hamburger
in the stomach." But that argument is necessary to justify discretionary
killing of fetuses on the current scale, and some of the experiments that
some scientists want to perform on live fetuses.

10   Abortion advocates have speech quirks that may betray qualms. Homeowners kill crabgrass. Abortionists kill fetuses. Homeowners do not speak of "terminating" crabgrass. But Planned Parenthood of New York City, which suddenly regards abortion as just another form of birth control, has published an abortion guide that uses the word "kill" only twice, once to say what some women did to themselves before legalized abortion, and once to describe what some contraceptives do to sperm. But when referring to the killing of fetuses, the book, like abortion advocates generally, uses only euphemisms, like "termination of potential life."

11   Abortion advocates become interestingly indignant when opponents display photographs of the well-formed feet and hands of a nine-week-old fetus. People avoid correct words and object to accurate photographs because they are uneasy about saying and seeing what abortion is. It is *not* the "termination" of a hamburger in the stomach.

12   And the casual manipulation of life is not harmless. As Dr. Kass says: "We have paid some high prices for the technological conquest of nature, but none so high as the intellectual and spiritual costs of seeing nature as mere material for our manipulation, exploitation and transformation. With the powers for biological engineering now gathering, there will be splendid new opportunities for a similar degradation of our view of man. Indeed, we are already witnessing the erosion of our idea of man as something splendid or divine, as a creature with freedom and dignity. And clearly, if we come to see ourselves as meat, then meat we shall become."

13   Politics has paved the way for this degradation. Meat we already have become, at Ypres and Verdun, Dresden and Hiroshima, Auschwitz and the Gulag. Is it a coincidence that this century, which is distinguished for science and war and totalitarianism, also is the dawn of the abortion age?

Questions for Discussion and Writing

1. How does Will use statistics to underscore the extent of abortion both nationally and worldwide?

2. The first issue to which Will addresses himself is the question concerning precisely when a human individual or "person" is considered to exist. In the now famous 1973 *Roe* v. *Wade* decision, the Supreme Court declared that fetuses are not covered by the definition of *person* as used in the Fourteenth Amendment. Speaking for seven members of the Court, Justice Blackmun stated that a "right to privacy" gave a woman a right to terminate her pregnancy under specified circumstances. Before the end of the first trimester, the state may not interfere with a woman's decision to terminate a pregnancy.

After the first trimester, the state may regulate the abortion procedure only to protect the health of the mother. After the third trimester, as Will says, states can "constitutionally, but need not, prohibit the killing of fetuses after 'viability' (24 to 28 weeks), which the Court says is when a fetus can lead a 'meaningful' life outside the womb." Why is the question of personhood crucial in deciding whether (*a*) a fetus has a right to be carried to full term or (*b*) whether a woman's right to privacy is more important than a fetus's right to life?

3. Does Will mention any circumstances under which abortion is permissible? If so, what reasons does he give?

4. Summarize and evaluate Will's argument that the development of new diagnostic technologies, combined with the present attitude toward abortion, will inevitably lead to a dehumanized society that will condone the extermination of genetically defective infants and old people, and the discarding of "surplus embryos." How does Will use the testimony of various geneticists and biologists to develop his glimpse into a hypothetical future? In your opinion, is it a form of the "slippery slope," when Will suggests that the readiness to accept abortion will lead to the readiness to accept terminating genetically defective infants and old people who will be seen as burdensome, useless to society, and expendable? How is the idea of discretionary killing as stated in the title related to this phase of Will's argument?

5. How is the tone of Will's article related to his purpose of alerting his audience to the possibility that our age no longer views human beings as having freedom and dignity?

6. What fault does Will find with the words and phrases used by abortion advocates? Does his claim that abortion advocates use euphemisms because they feel shame and have guilty consciences strike you as persuasive?

7. Is Will's citation of Ypres, Verdun, Dresden, Hiroshima, Auschwitz, and the Gulag relevant or irrelevant to his argument? First, look up any of these references with which you may be unfamiliar and then explain your answer. To what extent is Will's attempt to link abortion with genocide an example of guilt by association?

8. What causal connection does Will suggest exists between the development in this century of science, totalitarianism, war, and abortions? That is, how, in Will's view, has the "technological conquest of nature" led to "discretionary killing"?

9. Both Will and Hacker examine attitudes toward abortion in the

context of the direction society as a whole may be taking. Write a short essay expressing your opinion of whose assessment of the situation you find more accurate, and why.

10. Both Will and Hacker speculate on the language used to describe abortions. What connections can you discover between their analyses of words and phrases used to describe the *fetus, fertilized egg, embryo, child,* or *baby?*

11. Will cites two sets of circumstances when abortions are desired: (*a*) "Most abortions kill fetuses that were accidentally conceived" and (*b*) "Abortion also is used by couples who want a child, but not the one gestating." What sets of circumstances besides these two mentioned by Will does Hacker discuss? Is there anything about Will's tone, presentation, or specific arguments that would suggest to you that he falls into what Hacker describes as the category of abortion opponents who are unaware of their real motivations and feel that women are selfish and should be made to bear the children they conceive? For example, Will says the "essence of the Court's position is that the 'right to privacy' means a mother (interestingly, that is how the Court refers to a woman carrying a fetus) may deny a fetus life in order that she may lead the life she prefers."

FEEDING THE HUNGRY MASSES

Garrett Hardin

Lifeboat Ethics: The Case against Helping the Poor

Garrett Hardin, the author of "Lifeboat Ethics: The Case against Helping the Poor," is a biologist who has been a professor of human ecology at the University of California at Santa Barbara. Hardin is the author of many books and articles including Nature and Man's Fate *(1959), "The Tragedy of the Commons" in* Science *(December 13, 1968), and* Exploring New Ethics for Survival *(1972). The following essay first appeared in* Psychology Today *(September 1974). In this article Hardin sets up an extended metaphor that asks the reader to see each rich nation as a lifeboat with a limited capacity that is already almost full of people. Outside the lifeboat are the poor and needy who wish to get in the boat. Hardin claims that the sharing ethic will lead to the swamping of the lifeboat unless its occupants maintain a safety factor and keep people out.*

Environmentalists use the metaphor of the earth as a "spaceship" in trying to persuade countries, industries and people to stop wasting and polluting our natural resources. Since we all share life on this planet, they argue, no single person or institution has the right to destroy, waste or use more than a fair share of its resources. 1

But does everyone on earth have an equal right to an equal share of its resources? The spaceship metaphor can be dangerous when used by misguided idealists to justify suicidal policies for sharing our resources through uncontrolled immigration and foreign aid. In their enthusiastic but unrealistic generosity, they confuse the ethics of a spaceship with those of a lifeboat. 2

A true spaceship would have to be under the control of a captain, since no ship could possibly survive if its course were determined by committee. Spaceship Earth certainly has no captain; the United Nations is merely a toothless tiger, with little power to enforce any policy upon its bickering members. 3

If we divide the world crudely into rich nations and poor nations, two thirds of them are desperately poor, and only one third comparatively rich, with the United States the wealthiest of all. Metaphorically each 4 nation can be seen as a lifeboat full of comparatively rich people. In the ocean outside each lifeboat swim the poor of the world, who would like to get in, or at least to share some of the wealth. What should the lifeboat passengers do?

5   First, we must recognize the limited capacity of any lifeboat. For example, a nation's land has a limited capacity to support a population and as the current energy crisis has shown us, in some ways we have already exceeded the carrying capacity of our land.

Adrift in a Moral Sea

6   So here we sit, say fifty people in our lifeboat. To be generous, let us assume it has room for ten more, making a total capacity of sixty. Suppose the fifty of us in the lifeboat see 100 others swimming in the water outside, begging for admission to our boat or for handouts. We have several options: We may be tempted to try to live by the Christian ideal of being "our brother's keeper," or by the Marxist ideal of "to each according to his needs." Since the needs of all in the water are the same, and since they can all be seen as "our brothers," we could take them all into our boat, making a total of 150 in a boat designed for sixty. The boat swamps, everyone drowns. Complete justice, complete catastrophe.

7   Since the boat has an unused excess capacity of ten more passengers, we could admit just ten more to it. But which ten do we let in? How do we choose? Do we pick the best ten, the neediest ten, "first come, first served"? And what do we say to the ninety we exclude? If we do let an extra ten into our lifeboat, we will have lost our "safety factor," an engineering principle of critical importance. For example, if we don't leave room for excess capacity as a safety factor in our country's agriculture, a new plant disease or a bad change in the weather could have disastrous consequences.

8   Suppose we decide to preserve our small safety factor and admit no more to the lifeboat. Our survival is then possible, although we shall have to be constantly on guard against boarding parties.

9   While this last solution clearly offers the only means of our survival, it is morally abhorrent to many people. Some say they feel guilty about their good luck. My reply is simple: "Get out and yield your place to others." This may solve the problem of the guilt-ridden person's conscience, but it does not change the ethics of the lifeboat. The needy person to whom the guilt-ridden person yields his place will not himself feel guilty about his good luck. If he did, he would not climb aboard. The net result of conscience-stricken people giving up their unjustly held seats is the elimination of that sort of conscience from the lifeboat.

10   This is the basic metaphor within which we must work out our solutions. Let us now enrich the image, step by step, with substantive

additions from the real world, a world that must solve real and pressing problems of overpopulation and hunger.

The harsh ethics of the lifeboat become even harsher when we   11
consider the reproductive differences between the rich nations and the poor nations. The people inside the lifeboats are doubling in numbers every eighty-seven years; those swimming around outside are doubling, on the average, every thirty-five years, more than twice as fast as the rich. And since the world's resources are dwindling, the difference in prosperity between the rich and the poor can only increase.

As of 1973, the U.S. had a population of 210 million people, who   12
were increasing by 0.8 percent per year. Outside our lifeboat, let us imagine another 210 million people (say the combined populations of Colombia, Ecuador, Venezuela, Morocco, Pakistan, Thailand and the Philippines), who are increasing at a rate of 3.3 percent per year. Put differently, the doubling time for this aggregate population is twenty-one years, compared to eighty-seven years for the U.S.

Multiplying the Rich and the Poor

Now suppose the U.S. agreed to pool its resources with those seven   13
countries, with everyone receiving an equal share. Initially the ratio of Americans to non-Americans in this model would be one-to-one. But consider what the ratio would be after eighty-seven years, by which time the Americans would have doubled to a population of 420 million. By then, doubling every twenty-one years, the other group would have swollen to 354 billion. Each American would have to share the available resource with more than eight people.

But, one could argue, this discussion assumes that current population   14
trends will continue, and they may not. Quite so. Most likely the rate of population increase will decline much faster in the U.S. than it will in the other countries, and there does not seem to be much we can do about it. In sharing with "each according to his needs," we must recognize that needs are determined by population size, which is determined by the rate of reproduction, which at present is regarded as a sovereign right of every nation, poor or not. This being so, the philanthropic load created by the sharing ethic of the spaceship can only increase.

The Tragedy of the Commons

The fundamental error of spaceship ethics, and the sharing it re-   15
quires, is that it leads to what I call "the tragedy of the commons." Under a system of private property, the men who own property recognize their responsibility to care for it, for if they don't they will eventually suffer. A

farmer, for instance, will allow no more cattle in a pasture than its carrying capacity justifies. If he overloads it, erosion sets in, weeds take over, and he loses the use of the pasture.

16   If a pasture becomes a commons open to all, the right of each to use it may not be matched by a corresponding responsibility to protect it. Asking everyone to use it with discretion will hardly do, for the considerate herdsman who refrains from overloading the commons suffers more than a selfish one who says his needs are greater. If everyone would restrain himself, all would be well; but it takes only one less than everyone to ruin a system of voluntary restraint. In a crowded world of less than perfect human beings, mutual ruin is inevitable if there are no controls. This is the tragedy of the commons.

17   One of the major tasks of education today should be the creation of such an acute awareness of the dangers of the commons that people will recognize its many varieties. For example, the air and water have become polluted because they are treated as commons. Further growth in the population or per-capita conversion of natural resources into pollutants will only make the problem worse. The same holds true for the fish of the oceans. Fishing fleets have nearly disappeared in many parts of the world, technological improvements in the art of fishing are hastening the day of complete ruin. Only the replacement of the system of the commons with a responsible system of control will save the land, air, water and oceanic fisheries.

The World Food Bank

18   In recent years there has been a push to create a new commons called a World Food Bank, an international depository of food reserves to which nations would contribute according to their abilities and from which they would draw according to their needs. This humanitarian proposal has received support from many liberal international groups, and from such prominent citizens as Margaret Mead, U.N. Secretary General Kurt Waldheim, and Senators Edward Kennedy and George McGovern.

19   A world food bank appeals powerfully to our humanitarian impulses. But before we rush ahead with such a plan, let us recognize where the greatest political push comes from, lest we be disillusioned later. Our experience with the "Food for Peace program," or Public Law 480, gives us the answer. This program moved billions of dollars' worth of U.S. surplus grain to food-short, population-long countries during the past two decades. But when P.L. 480 first became law, a headline in the business magazine *Forbes* revealed the real power behind it: "Feeding the World's Hungry Millions: How It Will Mean Billions for U.S. Business."

20   And indeed it did. In the years 1960 to 1970, U.S. taxpayers spent a total of $7.9 billion on the Food for Peace program. Between 1948 and

1970, they also paid an additional $50 billion for other economic-aid programs, some of which went for food and food-producing machinery and technology. Though all U.S. taxpayers were forced to contribute to the cost of P.L. 480, certain special interest groups gained handsomely under the program. Farmers did not have to contribute the grain; the Government, or rather the taxpayers, bought if from them at full market prices. The increased demand raised prices of farm products generally. The manufacturers of farm machinery, fertilizers and pesticides benefited by the farmers' extra efforts to grow more food. Grain elevators profited from storing the surplus until it could be shipped. Railroads made money hauling it to ports, and shipping lines profited from carrying it overseas. The implementation of P.L. 480 required the creation of a vast Government bureaucracy, which then acquired its own vested interest in continuing the program regardless of its merits.

Extracting Dollars

Those who proposed and defended the Food for Peace program in public rarely mentioned its importance to any of these special interests. The public emphasis was always on its humanitarian effects. The combination of silent selfish interests and highly vocal humanitarian apologists made a powerful and successful lobby for extracting money from taxpayers. We can expect the same lobby to push now for the creation of a World Food Bank. 21

However great the potential benefit to selfish interests, it should not be a decisive argument against a truly humanitarian program. We must ask if such a program would actually do more good than harm, not only momentarily but also in the long run. Those who propose the food bank usually refer to a current "emergency" or "crisis" in terms of world food supply. But what is an emergency? Although they may be infrequent and sudden, everyone knows that emergencies will occur from time to time. A well-run family, company, organization or country prepares for the likelihood of accidents and emergencies. It expects them, it budgets for them, it saves for them. 22

Learning the Hard Way

What happens if some organizations or countries budget for accidents and others do not? If each country is solely responsible for its own well-being, poorly managed ones will suffer. But they can learn from experience. They may mend their ways, and learn to budget for infrequent but certain emergencies. For example, the weather varies from year to year, and periodic crop failures are certain. A wise and competent government saves out of the production of the good years in anticipation 23 of bad years to come. Joseph taught this policy to Pharaoh in Egypt more than 2,000 years ago. Yet the great majority of the governments in the world today do not follow such a policy. They lack either the wisdom or the competence, or both. Should those nations that do manage to put something aside be forced to come to the rescue each time an emergency occurs among the poor nations?

24   "But it isn't their fault!" some kindhearted liberals argue. "How can we blame the poor people who are caught in an emergency? Why must they suffer for the sins of their governments?" The concept of blame is simply not relevant here. The real question is, what are the operational consequences of establishing a world food bank? If it is open to every country every time a need develops, slovenly rulers will not be motivated to take Joseph's advice. Someone will always come to their aid. Some countries will deposit food in the world food bank, and others will withdraw it. There will be almost no overlap. As a result of such solutions to food shortage emergencies, the poor countries will not learn to mend their ways, and will suffer progressively greater emergencies as their populations grow.

Population Control the Crude Way

25   On the average, poor countries undergo a 2.5 percent increase in population each year; rich countries, about 0.8 percent. Only rich countries have anything in the way of food reserves set aside, and even they do not have as much as they should. Poor countries have none. If poor countries received no food from the outside, the rate of their population growth would be periodically checked by crop failures and famines. But if they can always draw on a world food bank in time of need, their populations can continue to grow unchecked, and so will their "need" for aid. In the short run, a world food bank may diminish that need, but in the long run it actually increases the need without limit.

26   Without some system of worldwide food sharing, the proportion of people in the rich and poor nations might eventually stabilize. The overpopulated poor countries would decrease in numbers, while the rich countries that had room for more people would increase. But with a well-meaning system of sharing, such as a world food bank, the growth differential between the rich and the poor countries will not only persist, it will increase. Because of the higher rate of population growth in the poor countries of the world, 88 percent of today's children are born poor, and only 12 percent rich. Year by year the ratio becomes worse, as the fast-reproducing poor outnumber the slow-reproducing rich.

27   A world food bank is thus a commons in disguise. People will have more motivation to draw from it than to add to any common store. The less provident and less able will multiply at the expense of the abler and more provident, bringing eventual ruin upon all who share in the com-

mons. Besides, any system of "sharing" that amounts to foreign aid from the rich nations to the poor nations will carry the taint of charity, which will contribute little to the world peace so devoutly desired by those who support the idea of a world food bank.

As past U.S. foreign-aid programs have amply and depressingly 28 demonstrated, international charity frequently inspires mistrust and antagonism rather than gratitude on the part of the recipient nation.

Chinese Fish and Miracle Rice

The modern approach to foreign aid stresses the export of technology 29 and advice, rather than money and food. As an ancient Chinese proverb goes: "Give a man a fish and he will eat for a day; teach him how to fish and he will eat for the rest of his days." Acting on this advice, the Rockefeller and Ford Foundations have financed a number of programs for improving agriculture in the hungry nations. Known as the "Green Revolution," these programs have led to the development of "miracle rice" and "miracle wheat," new strains that offer bigger harvests and greater resistance to crop damage. Norman Borlaug, the Nobel Prize winning agronomist who, supported by the Rockefeller Foundation, developed "miracle wheat," is one of the most prominent advocates of a world food bank.

Whether or not the Green Revolution can increase food production as 30 much as its champions claim is a debatable but possibly irrelevant point. Those who support this well-intended humanitarian effort should first consider some of the fundamentals of human ecology. Ironically, one man who did was the late Alan Gregg, a vice president of the Rockefeller Foundation. Two decades ago he expressed strong doubts about the wisdom of such attempts to increase food production. He likened the growth and spread of humanity over the surface of the earth to the spread of cancer in the human body, remarking that "cancerous growths demand food; but, as far as I know, they have never been cured by getting it."

Overloading the Environment

Every human born constitutes a draft on all aspects of the environ- 31 ment: food, air, water, forests, beaches, wildlife, scenery and solitude. Food can, perhaps, be significantly increased to meet a growing demand. But what about clean beaches, unspoiled forests, and solitude? If we satisfy a growing population's need for food, we necessarily decrease its per-capita supply of the other resources needed by men.

India, for example, now has a population of 600 million, which 32 increases by 15 million each year. This population already puts a huge load on a relatively impoverished environment. The country's forests are now only a small fraction of what they were three centuries ago, and floods and erosion continually destroy the insufficient farmland that remains. Every one of the 15 million new lives added to India's population puts an additional burden on the environment, and increases the economic and social costs of crowding. However humanitarian our intent, every Indian life saved through medical or nutritional assistance from abroad diminishes the quality of life for those who remain, and for subsequent generations. If rich countries make it possible, through foreign aid, for 600 million Indians to swell to 1.2 billion in a mere twenty-eight years, as their current growth rate threatens, will future generations of Indians thank us for hastening the destruction of their environment? Will our good intentions be sufficient excuse for the consequences of our actions?

33   My final example of a commons in action is one for which the public has the least desire for rational discussion — immigration. Anyone who publicly questions the wisdom of current U.S. immigration policy is promptly charged with bigotry, prejudice, ethnocentrism, chauvinism, isolationism or selfishness. Rather than encounter such accusations, one would rather talk about other matters, leaving immigration policy to wallow in the crosscurrents of special interests that take no account of the good of the whole, or the interest of posterity.

34   Perhaps we still feel guilty about things we said in the past. Two generations ago the popular press frequently referred to Dagos, Wops, Polacks, Chinks and Krauts, in articles about how America was being "overrun" by foreigners of supposedly inferior genetic stock. But because the implied inferiority of foreigners was used than as justification for keeping them out, people now assume that restrictive policies could only be based on such misguided notions. There are no other grounds.

A Nation of Immigrants

35   Just consider the numbers involved. Our Government acknowledges a net inflow of 400,000 immigrants a year. While we have no hard data on the extent of illegal entries, educated guesses put the figure at about 600,000 a year. Since the natural increase (excess of births over deaths) of the resident population now runs about 1.7 million per year, the yearly gain from immigration amounts to at least 19 percent of the total annual increase, and may be as much as 37 percent if we include the estimate for illegal immigrants. Considering the growing use of birth-control devices, the potential effect of educational campaigns by such organizations as Planned Parenthood Federation of America and Zero Population Growth, and the influence of inflation and the housing shortage, the fertility rate of American women may decline so much that

immigration could account for all the yearly increase in population. Should we not at least ask if that is what we want?

For the sake of those who worry about whether the "quality" of the   36
average immigrant compares favorably with the quality of the average resident, let us assume that immigrants and nativeborn citizens are of exactly equal quality, however one defines that term. We will focus here only on quantity; and since our conclusions will depend on nothing else, all charges of bigotry and chauvinism become irrelevant.

Immigration vs. Food Supply

World food banks *move food to the people*, hastening the exhaustion of   37
the environment of the poor countries. Unrestricted immigration, on the other hand, *moves people to the food*, thus speeding up the destruction of the environment of the rich countries. We can easily understand why poor people should want to make this latter transfer, but why should rich hosts encourage it?

As in the case of foreign-aid programs, immigration receives support   38
from selfish interests and humanitarian impulses. The primary selfish interest in unimpeded immigration is the desire of employers for cheap labor, particularly in industries and trades that offer degrading work. In the past, one wave of foreigners after another was brought into the U.S. to work at wretched jobs for wretched wages. In recent years, the Cubans, Puerto Ricans and Mexicans have had this dubious honor. The interests of the employers of cheap labor mesh well with the guilty silence of the country's liberal intelligentsia. White Anglo-Saxon Protestants are particularly reluctant to call for a closing of the doors to immigration for fear of being called bigots.

But not all countries have such reluctant leadership. Most educated   39
Hawaiians, for example, are keenly aware of the limits of their environment, particularly in terms of population growth. There is only so much room on the islands, and the islanders know it. To Hawaiians, immigrants from the other forty-nine states present as great a threat as those from other nations. At a recent meeting of Hawaiian government officials in Honolulu, I had the ironic delight of hearing a speaker, who like most of his audience was of Japanese ancestry, ask how the country might practically and constitutionally close its doors to further immigration. One member of the audience countered: "How can we shut the doors now? We have many friends and relatives in Japan that we'd like to bring here some day so that they can enjoy Hawaii too." The Japanese-American speaker smiled sympathetically and answered: "Yes, but we have children now, and someday we'll have grandchildren too. We can bring more people here from Japan only by giving away some of the land that we hope to pass on to our grandchildren some day. What right do we have to do that?"

40   At this point, I can hear U.S. liberals asking: "How can you justify slamming the door once you're inside? You say that immigrants should be kept out. But aren't we all immigrants, or the descendants of immigrants? If we insist on staying, must we not admit all others?" Our craving for intellectual order leads us to seek and prefer symmetrical rules and morals: a single rule for me and everybody else; the same rule yesterday, today, and tomorrow. Justice, we feel, should not change with time and place.

41   We Americans of non-Indian ancestry can look upon ourselves as the descendants of thieves who are guilty morally, if not legally, of stealing this land from its Indian owners. Should we then give back the land to the now living American descendants of those Indians? However morally or logically sound this proposal may be, I, for one, am unwilling to live by it and I know no one else who is. Besides, the logical consequence would be absurd. Suppose that, intoxicated with a sense of pure justice, we should decide to turn our land over to the Indians. Since all our wealth has also been derived from the land, wouldn't we be morally obliged to give that back to the Indians too?

Pure Justice vs. Reality

42   Clearly, the concept of pure justice produces an infinite regression to absurdity. Centuries ago, wise men invented statutes of limitations to justify the rejection of such pure justice, in the interest of preventing continual disorder. The law zealously defends property rights, but only relatively recent property rights. Drawing a line after an arbitrary time has elapsed may be unjust, but the alternatives are worse.

43   We are all descendants of thieves, and the world's resources are inequitably distributed. But we must begin the journey to tomorrow from the point where we are today. We cannot remake the past. We cannot safely divide the wealth equitably among all peoples so long as people reproduce at different rates. To do so would guarantee that our grandchildren, and everyone else's grandchildren, would have only a ruined world to inhabit.

44   To be generous with one's own possessions is quite different from being generous with those of posterity. We should call this point to the attention of those who, from a commendable love of justice and equality, would institute a system of the commons, either in the form of a world food bank, or of unrestricted immigration. We must convince them if we wish to save at least some parts of the world from environmental ruin.

45   Without a true world government to control reproduction and the use of available resources, the sharing ethic of the spaceship is impossible. For the foreseeable future, our survival demands that we govern our actions by the ethics of a lifeboat, harsh though they may be. Posterity will be satisfied with nothing less.

Questions for Discussion and Writing

1. What measures does Hardin use to deal with his readers' emotional reluctance to think of themselves as the kind of people who would turn a deaf ear to pleas for help by the world's starving poor?

2. What extended metaphor does Hardin use as a graphic illustration of his thesis that affluent nations have no obligation to share their food and resources with the world's starving masses? How does this analogy function in the context of his argument?

3. What reasons, evidence, and statistics does Hardin advance to support his thesis that any attempts to help the world's starving masses would ultimately threaten the human species?

4. Why does Hardin believe that the state of being in need (of a person or of a starving nation) does not automatically create the obligation in others to fulfill these needs (for food, aid, money, or other resources)?

5. What does Hardin mean by the expression "the tragedy of the commons"? How is the idea underlying this phrase related to the assumption that human beings are not capable of responsible, voluntary restraint?

6. How does Hardin use Public Law 480, intended to set up a world food bank, to illustrate how past governmental programs have been exploited for private profit and have proved to be unworkable?

7. What function does Hardin's introduction of the concept of environmental quality of life serve in the development of his overall argument? For example, how is this issue related to his discussion of the effects of humanitarian assistance to India, and the consequences of legal and illegal immigration?

8. Where does Hardin state the arguments that opponents might raise against his position, and what reasons and examples does he give for rejecting these arguments? For instance, how does his account of "a recent meeting of Hawaiian government officials in Honolulu" serve as a specific example of what he believes should be adopted as a policy by the entire United States?

9. Evaluate the reasoning underlying Hardin's assertion that our obligations to future generations and to the human species make it imperative that we not help starving masses now.

10. In an essay, discuss your views of one or more of the following assumptions underlying Hardin's argument: (*a*) Aside from emergency famine or disaster relief, long-term assistance to Third World countries would ultimately do more harm than good; (*b*) Any attempt by the West to help the world's starving masses would ultimately threaten the entire human species; (*c*) Affluent nations have a moral obligation to the species and to future generations that takes precedence over helping starving masses in the present.

11. For a research project, investigate population control programs in those countries whose governments have taken an active role in trying to keep the birth rate down, such as in China and India. For example, in China, a country with the largest population on earth, the government has initiated a one-child-per-family program along with almost compulsory abortion for any second child—even at very late stages in the pregnancy.

12. To put Hardin's scenario into terms of a personal moral choice consider the following dilemma: Would you be willing to add five years to your lifespan even though it meant taking five years away from the lifespan of someone in the United States chosen by chance? How would it change your decision if you knew who the person was?

13. If you wish to do a research paper on this topic, you might read any of the following books: Susan George, *How the Other Half Dies: The Real Reasons for World Hunger* (1977); Onora O'Neill, *Faces of Hunger* (1985); Arline T. Golkin, *Famine: A Heritage of Hunger* (1987); or Peter G. Brown and Henry Shue, editors, *Food Policy: The Responsibility of the United States in the Life and Death Choices* (1977).

Richard A. Watson

Reason and Morality in a World of Limited Food

Richard A. Watson is a professor of philosophy. "Reason and Morality in a World of Limited Food" originally appeared in a collection of essays, World Hunger and Moral Obligation *(1977). Watson rejects any consideration of consequences as a basis for morality and argues for an absolute moral obligation of rich nations to share resources with the poor nations of the world. He asserts that nations have an obligation to behave morally even if the action may not be reasonable or practical. Watson uses deductive reasoning to argue that the claims of morality supersede those of reason. His conclusion that we must share follows inexorably from his major premiss that every human life is of equal value.*

A few years ago, President Johnson said: 1

There are 200 million of us and 3 billion of them and they want what we've got, but we're not going to give it to them.

In this essay I examine the conflict between reasonable and moral   2
behavior in a world of limited food. It appears to be unreasonable — and conceivably immoral — to share all food equally when this would result in everyone's being malnourished. Arguments for the morality of unequal distribution are presented from the standpoint of the individual, the nation, and the human species. These arguments fail because, although it is unreasonable to share limited food when sharing threatens survival, the moral principle of equity ranks sharing above survival. I accept the principle of equity, and conclude by challenging the ideological basis that makes sharing unreasonable.

The contrast of the moral with the reasonable depends on distin-   3
guishing people from things. Moral considerations pertain to behavior of individuals that affects other people by acting on them directly or by acting on things in which they have an interest. The moral context is broad, for people have interests in almost everything, and almost any behavior may affect someone.

If reasonable and moral behavior were coextensive, then there would   4
be no morality. Thus, there is no contrast at the extremes that bound the moral milieu, reason and morality being the same at one pole, and

morality not existing at the other. These extremes meet in evolutionary naturalism: If it is moral to treat people as animals surviving, then reason augmenting instinct is the best criterion for behavior, and a separate discipline of morality is extraneous. Only between the extremes can reason and morality conflict.

5   Between the extremes, some moralists use "rational" to indicate conclusions that tend toward moral behavior, and "practical" for conclusions that excusably do not. The use of these terms often constitutes special pleading, either to gain sympathy for a position that is not strictly reasonable but is "rational" (because it is "right"), or that is not strictly moral but is "practical" (because it "should" be done). These hedges hide the sharp distinction between people and things in the context of reason and morality. The rational and the practical are obviously reasonable in a way that they are not obviously either moral or immoral. Reasonable behavior is either moral, immoral, or amoral. When reason and morality conflict, there can be confusion, but no compromise.

6   Attacks on morality by reason disguised in practical dress are so common as to go almost without notice. The practical ousts morality as a determinant of behavior, particularly in industrialized nations. Many argue that the practical imperatives of survival preclude moral behavior even by those who want to be moral. If only it were practical to be moral, then all would gladly be so.

7   It is difficult to be moral in a world of limited food because the supreme moral principle is that of equity. The principle of equity is based on the belief that all human beings are moral equals with equal rights to the necessities of life. Differential treatment of human beings thus should be based only on their freely chosen actions and not on accidents of their birth and environment. Specific to this discussion, everyone has a right to an equal share of available food.

8   However, we find ourselves in a world about which many food and population experts assert the following:
1. One-third of the world's people (the West) consume two-thirds of the world's resources.
2. Two-thirds of the world's people (the Third World) are malnourished.
3. Equal distribution of the world's resources would result in everyone's being malnourished.

There is ample evidence that these statements are true, but for this discussion it is enough that many people in the West — particularly those who occupy positions of responsibility and power — understand and accept them.

9   These moral and factual beliefs drive one to this practical conclusion: Although morally we should share all food equally, and we in the West eat more than we need, equal sharing would be futile (unreasonable), for then no one would be well nourished. Thus, any food sharing is necessarily symbolic, for no practical action would alleviate the plight of the malnourished.

For example, practical action — moral as far as it goes — might be to   10
reduce food consumption until every Westerner is just well nourished.
But if the surplus were distributed equally to the other two-thirds of the
world's people, they would still be malnourished. Thus, an easy excuse
for not sharing at all is that it would neither solve the nourishment
problem nor change the moral situation. Two-thirds would still be malnourished, and one-third would still be consuming more than equal
shares of the world's food, to which everyone has equal rights.

Another argument for unequal distribution is as follows: All people   11
are moral equals. Because everyone has a right to be well nourished, it
would be immoral to take so much food from someone who has enough
as to leave him without enough. Anyone who takes the food would be
acting immorally, even if the taker is sharing. This argument can go two
ways. One could simply say that it would be immoral to deprive oneself
of what one has. But if one wanted to discredit morality itself, one could
claim that morality in this instance is self-contradictory. For if I behave
morally by distributing food equally, I behave immorally by depriving
someone (myself) of enough food to remain well nourished. And noticing that if all food were shared equally, everyone would be malnourished instead of just some, one might argue that it cannot be moral to
deprive one person of his right to enough food so that two people have
less than enough. Proper moral action must be to maintain the inequity,
so at least one person can enjoy his rights.

Nevertheless, according to the highest principles of traditional West-   12
ern morality, available food should be distributed equally even if everyone then will be malnourished. This is belabored by everyone who
compares the earth to a lifeboat, a desert island, or a spaceship. In these
situations, the strong are expected to take even a smaller share than the
weak. There is no need for us to go overboard, however. We shall soon
be as weak as anyone else if we just do our moral duty and distribute the
food equally.

Given this, the well-nourished minority might try to buttress its   13
position morally by attempting to solve the nourishment problem for
everyone, either by producing enough food for everyone, or by humanely reducing the world's population to a size at which equal distribution of food would nourish everyone adequately. The difficulty with
this is that national survival for the food-favored industrial nations
requires maintenance of political and economic systems that depend on
unequal distribution of limited goods.[1] In the present world context, it
would be unreasonable (disastrous) for an industrialized nation to attempt to provide food for everybody. Who would pay for it? And after
all, well-nourished citizens are obviously important to the survival of the
nation. As for humanely reducing the world's population, there are no
practical means for doing it. Thus, the practical expediencies of national
survival preclude actions that might justify temporary unequal distribution with the claim that it is essential for solving the nourishment prob-

lem. Equal distribution is impossible without total (impractical) economic and political revolution.

14   These arguments are morally spurious. That food sufficient for well-nourished survival is the equal right of every human individual or nation is a specification of the higher principle that everyone has equal right to the necessities of life. The moral stress of the principle of equity is primarily on equal sharing, and only secondarily on what is being shared. The higher moral principle is of human *equity per se.* Consequently, the moral action is to distribute all food equally, *whatever the consequences.* This is the hard line apparently drawn by such moralists as Immanuel Kant and Noam Chomsky—but then, morality is hard. The conclusion may be unreasonable (impractical and irrational in conventional terms), but it is obviously moral. Nor should anyone purport surprise; it has always been understood that the claims of morality—if taken seriously—supersede those of conflicting reason.

15   One may even have to sacrifice one's life or one's nation to be moral in situations where practical behavior would preserve it. For example, if a prisoner of war undergoing torture is to be a (perhaps dead) patriot even when reason tells him that collaboration will hurt no one, he remains silent. Similarly, if one is to be moral, one distributes available food in equal shares (even if everyone then dies). That an action is necessary to save one's life is no excuse for behaving unpatriotically or immorally if one wishes to be a patriot or moral. No principle of morality absolves one of behaving immorally simply to save one's life or nation. There is a strict analogy here between adhering to moral principles for the sake of being moral, and adhering to Christian principles for the sake of being Christian. The moral world contains pits and lions, but one looks always to the highest light. The ultimate test always harks to the highest principle—recant or die—and it is pathetic to profess morality if one quits when the going gets rough.

16   I have put aside many questions of detail—such as the mechanical problems of distributing food—because detail does not alter the stark conclusion. If every human life is equal in value, then the equal distribution of the necessities of life is an extremely high, if not the highest, moral duty. It is at least high enough to override the excuse that by doing it one would lose one's own life. But many people cannot accept the view that one must distribute equally even if the nation collapses or all people die.

17   If everyone dies, then there will be no realm of morality. Practically speaking, sheer survival comes first. One can adhere to the principle of equity only if one exists. So it is rational to suppose that the principle of survival is morally higher than the principle of equity. And though one might not be able to argue for unequal distribution of food to save a nation—for nations can come and go—one might well argue that unequal distribution is necessary for the survival of the human species.

That is, some large group—say one-third of the present world population—should be at least well-nourished for human survival.

However, from an individual standpoint, the human species—like 18 the nation—is of no moral relevance. From a naturalistic standpoint, survival does come first; from a moralistic standpoint—as indicated above—survival may have to be sacrificed. In the milieu of morality, it is immaterial whether or not the human species survives as a result of individual moral behavior.

A possible way to resolve this conflict between reason and morality is 19 to challenge the view that morality pertains only to the behavior of individual human beings. One way to do this is to break down the distinction between people and things. It would have to be established that such abstract things as "the people," "the nation," and "the human species" in themselves have moral status. Then they would have a right to survival just as human beings have a right to life: We should be concerned about the survival of these things not merely because human beings have an interest in them, but because it would be immoral *per se* to destroy them.

In the West, corporation law provides the theoretical basis for treating 20 things as people.[2] Corporate entities such as the State, the Church, and trading companies have long enjoyed special status in Western society. The rights of corporate entities are precisely defined by a legal fiction, the concept of the corporate person. Christopher D. Stone says that corporate persons enjoy as many legal rights as, and sometimes more than, do individual human persons.[3] Thus, while most of us are not tempted to confuse ordinary things like stones and houses with people, almost everyone concurs with a legal system that treats corporate entities as people. The great familiarity and usefulness of this system supports the delusion that corporate entities have rights in common with, and are the moral equals of, individual human beings.

On these grounds, some argue that because of size, importance, and 21 power of corporate entities, institutional rights have priority over the rights of individuals. Of course, to the extent that society is defined by the economy or the State, people are dependent on and subordinate to these institutions. Practically speaking, institutional needs come first; people's needs are satisfied perhaps coextensively with, but secondarily to, satisfying institutional needs. It is argued that to put individual human needs first would be both illogical and impractical, for people and their needs are defined only in the social context. Institutions come first because they are prerequisite to the very existence of people.

A difficulty with the above argument as a support for any given 22 institution is that it provides merely for the priority of *some* institutions over human individuals, not, say, for the priority of the United States or the West. But it does appear to provide an argument for the priority of the human species.

23   Given that the human species has rights as a fictional person on the analogy of corporate rights, it would seem to be rational to place the right of survival of the species above that of individuals. Unless the species survives, no individual will survive, and thus an individual's right to life is subordinate to the species' right to survival. If species survival depends on the unequal distribution of food to maintain a healthy breeding stock, then it is morally right for some people to have plenty while others starve. Only if there is enough food to nourish everyone well does it follow that food should be shared equally.

24   This might be true if corporate entities actually do have moral status and moral rights. But obviously, the legal status of corporate entities as fictional persons does not make them moral equals or superiors of actual human persons. Legislators might profess astonishment that anyone would think that a corporate person is a *person* as people are, let alone a moral person. However, because the legal rights of corporate entities are based on individual rights, and because corporate entities are treated so much like persons, the transition is often made.

25   Few theorists today would argue that the state or the human species is a personal agent.[4] But all this means is that idealism is dead in theory. Unfortunately, its influence lives, so it is worth giving an argument to show that corporate entities are not real persons.

26   Corporate entities are not persons as you and I are in the explicit sense that we are self-conscious agents and they are not. Corporate entities are not *agents* at all, let alone moral agents. This is a good reason for not treating corporate entities even as fictional persons. The distinction between people and other things, to generalize, is that people are self-conscious agents, whereas things are not.

27   The possession of rights essentially depends on an entity's being self-conscious, then it has a right to life. Self-consciousness is a necessary, but not sufficient, condition for an entity's also being a responsible moral agent as most human beings are. A moral agent must have the capacity to be responsible, i.e., the capacity to choose and to act freely with respect to consequences that the agent does or can recognize and accept as its own choice and doing. Only a being who knows himself as a person, and who can effect choices and accept consequences, is a responsible moral agent.

28   On these grounds, moral equality rests on the actuality of moral agency based on reciprocal rights and responsibilities. One is responsible to something only if it can be responsible in return. Thus, we have responsibilities to other people, and they have reciprocal rights. We have no responsibilities to things as such, and they have no rights. If we care for things, it is because people have interests in them, not because things in themselves impose responsibilities on us.

29   That is, as stated early in this essay, morality essentially has to do with relations among people, among persons. It is nonsense to talk of things that cannot be moral agents as having responsibilities; conse-

quently, it is nonsense to talk of whatever is not actually a person as having rights. It is deceptive even to talk of legal rights of a corporate entity. Those rights (and reciprocal responsibilities) actually pertain to individual human beings who have an interest in the corporate entity. The State or the human species have no rights at all, let alone rights superior to those of individuals.

The basic reason given for preserving a nation or the human species 30 is that otherwise the milieu of morality would not exist. This is false so far as specific nations are concerned, but it is true that the existence of individuals depends on the existence of the species. However, although moral behavior is required of each individual, no principle requires that the realm of morality itself be preserved. Thus, we are reduced to the position that people's interest in preserving the human species is based primarily on the interest of each in individual survival. Having shown above that the principle of equity is morally superior to the principle of survival, we can conclude again that food should be shared equally even if this means the extinction of the human race.

Is there no way to produce enough food to nourish everyone well? 31 Besides cutting down to the minimum, people in the West might quit feeding such nonhuman animals as cats and dogs. However, some people (e.g., Peter Singer) argue that mere sentience—the capacity to suffer pain—means that an animal is the moral equal of human beings.[5] I argue that because nonhuman animals are not moral agents, they do not share the rights of self-conscious responsible persons. And considering the profligacy of nature, it is rational to argue that if nonhuman animals have any rights at all, they include not the right to life, but merely the right to fight for life. In fact, if people in the West did not feed grain to cattle, sheep, and hogs, a considerable amount of food would be freed for human consumption. Even then, there might not be enough to nourish everyone well.

Let me remark that Stone and Singer attempt to break down the 32 distinction between people on the one hand, and certain things (corporate entities) and nonhuman animals on the other, out of moral concern. However, there is another, profoundly antihumanitarian movement also attempting to break down the distinction. All over the world, heirs of Gobineau, Goebbels, and Hitler practice genocide and otherwise treat people as nonhuman animals and things in the name of the State. I am afraid that the consequences of treating entities such as corporations and nonhuman animals—that are not moral agents—as persons with rights will not be that we will treat national parks and chickens the way we treat people, but that we will have provided support for those who treat people the way we now treat nonhuman animals and things.

The benefits of modern society depend in no small part on the 33 institution of corporation law. Even if the majority of these benefits are to the good—of which I am by no means sure—the legal fiction of corporate personhood still elevates corporate needs above the needs of people. In the present context, reverence for corporate entities leads to the spurious argument that the present world imbalance of food and resources is morally justified in the name of the higher rights of sovereign nations, or even of the human species, the survival of which is said to be more important than the right of any individual to life.

34   This conclusion is morally absurd. This is not, however, the fault of morality. We *should* share all food equally, at least until everyone is well-nourished. Besides food, *all* necessities of life should be shared, at least until everyone is adequately supplied with a humane minimum. The hard conclusion remains that we should share all food equally even if this means that everyone starves and the human species becomes extinct. But, of course, the human race would survive even equal sharing, for after enough people died, the remainder could be well-nourished on the food that remained. But this grisly prospect does not show that anything is wrong with the principle of equity. Instead, it shows that something is profoundly wrong with the social institutions in which sharing the necessities of life equally is "impractical" and "irrational."

35   In another ideological frame, moral behavior might also be practical and rational. As remarked above, equal sharing can be accomplished only through total economic and political revolution. Obviously, this is what is needed.

NOTES

1. See Richard Watson. "The Limits of World Order," *Alternatives: A Journal of World Policy*, I (1975), 487–513.

2. See Christopher D. Stone, *Should Trees Have Standing? Toward Legal Rights for Natural Objects* (Los Altos, Calif.: William Kaufman, 1974). Stone proposes that to protect such things as national parks, we should give them legal personhood as we do corporations.

3. Ibid., p. 47: "It is more and more the individual human being, with his consciousness, that is the legal fiction." Also: "The legal system does the best it can to maintain the illusion of the reality of the individual human being." (footnote 125) Many public figures have discovered that they have a higher legal status if they incorporate themselves than they do as individual persons.

4. Stone (ibid., p. 47) does say that "institutions . . . have wills, minds, purposes, and inertias that are in very important ways their own, i.e., that can transcend and survive changes in the consciousness of the individual humans who supposedly comprise them, and whom they supposedly serve," but I do not think Stone actually believes that corporate entities are persons like you and me.

5. See Peter Singer, *Animal Liberation* (New York: The New York Review of Books/Random House, 1975).

Questions for Discussion and Writing

1. What reasons does Watson present to support his thesis that people have a moral obligation to share food equally with the starving peoples of the world, even if the ultimate result of sharing is the extinction of the human species?

2. What fault does Watson find with arguments that seek to justify unequal distribution of food?

3. Why does Watson believe that the higher principle of morality supersedes utilitarian-based arguments even if the ultimate consequences of taking the morally correct action is not "reasonable"?

4. How is Watson's argument constructed around the assumption that every human life is of equal value? What is the relationship between this idea and Watson's argument in favor of an obligation to share food equally, regardless of any consequences?

5. Discuss features of deductive reasoning in Watson's essay. How does the assumption that every life is of equal value serve as one of the *premisses* in his argument? How does this *premiss* lead to the conclusion that everyone deserves an equal share, even if as a result the human species perishes.

6. Which of Hardin's arguments does Watson summarize in the course of developing his own essay? What counterarguments does he offer to each of Hardin's assertions? Specifically, what reasons does Watson give for not accepting Hardin's claim that "survival is higher than the principle of morality because we must exist to have morality"?

7. What function does Watson's rebuttal of the assumption that corporate or institutional entities "have rights in common with, and are the moral equals of, individual human beings" have in the overall structure of his argument? Why, according to Watson, does "the State or the human species have no rights at all, let alone rights superior to those of individuals"?

8. In a short essay, compare the "utilitarian" argument of Hardin with the "higher moral principle" argument of Watson. Which of the two arguments did you find more persuasive? Explain your answer using brief quotations drawn from Watson's and Hardin's articles.

CAPITAL PUNISHMENT

Perry M. Johnson

A Vote against Executions from a Man Who Knows Murderers

Perry M. Johnson was the director of the Michigan Department of Corrections. Faced with possible legislation that would have required him to administer the death penalty, Johnson argued against capital punishment, drawing on firsthand knowledge gained over twenty-seven years. This essay, "A Vote against Executions from a Man Who Knows Murderers," first appeared in The Christian Science Monitor *(October 7, 1982). Johnson is now assistant professor of criminal justice at Michigan State University.*

1   A petition drive to reinstate capital punishment in Michigan, where it was abolished in 1847, has fallen short of the signatures required to put the issue on this November's ballot. The public debate during the drive held special significance for me as director of the agency which would be required to carry out executions. What follows are the conclusions I have reached after much difficult and troubling reflection.

2   During my 27 years in corrections, I have learned more than I care to know about murder. I have reviewed the grisly details of many homicides — sometimes because I was responsible for supervising the murderer in prison, sometimes because the murder itself was committed there. I have personally known prisoners who later became victims of brutal killings. I have experienced sorrow and anger over the senseless prison slaying of a friend and loyal employee. I have come to know well many murderers who were serving out their adult lives in prisons, some as responsible, productive human beings, others as hopeless management problems.

3   Some of these people, in my opinion, deserved to die for their crimes. But I have come to the conclusion that we, as a civilized society, should not kill them.

4   We should not because the death penalty fails the two tests against which any just sanction must be measured.

No Protection Against Murder

The first test is that the sanction must be in our public self-interest. In   5
this instance that means that we protect our own lives by taking that of
another. In my profession public protection is my primary responsibility.
Therefore, if I had grounds for believing execution of convicted murderers saved the lives of innocent people, I would be obligated to endorse capital punishment.

But capital punishment does not protect. Few issues in criminal jus-   6
tice have seen as much research over the last 40 years as the deterrent
impact of executions, and there is no issue I am aware of in which the
balance of evidence weighs so heavily on the negative side. There is even
the possibility that some murderers see execution as a martyrdom which
will provide a dramatic end to a life of hatred for themselves and others;
Utah's Gary Gilmore may be an example.

It is sometimes said that even though an execution may not deter   7
others, it at least prevents the freeing of the murderer in a few years to
kill again. In Michigan, which has not executed anyone in nearly a
century and a half, we have no record of any person commuted from a
sentence of first-degree murder who repeated that crime. First-degree
murderers who do not die in prison serve an average of 25 years before
release, and their record thereafter is exemplary. To argue that we need
capital punishment for our own safety will not stand scrutiny; life imprisonment is as adequate for that purpose.

The second proper test of any penalty exacted by a civilized society is   8
that it can be applied with assurance of justice and fairness. Capital
punishment clearly fails this test as well.

It fails a test of social justice in that it has been disproportionately   9
applied to minorities. This disturbing aspect of the death penalty application remains a problem even today. A recent study in our own state
shows that both the race of the offender and the victim are factors in
determining whether a first-degree murderer will be charged and convicted as such, or of a lesser crime. Research in other states has consistently shown similar racial discrimination among death row prisoners.

There also is the ever-present possibility—and over time the   10
certainty—of the ultimate injustice: the socially approved execution of a
person who happens to be innocent. Despite all judicial safeguards, some
persons serving prison terms for murder in the first degree have been
subsequently found to have been wrongfully convicted. At that point a
prison term can at least be abridged, but a life cannot be restored.

Some argue for capital punishment on the grounds that it will save   11
money. This is unlikely, but even if true the taking of a human life
should not be based on so shallow a reason.

I am convinced capital punishment fails all proper criteria of an   12
effective and just response to homicide. But there is yet a strong reason

why we, as a civilized people, should not kill even the most heinous and undeserving of criminals. That is the brutalizing effect which the death penalty has on the public which imposes it. Deliberate, unnecessary killing cheapens the value of human life. The ultimate message we give by exacting this penalty is that it is all right to kill for convenience or for vengeance. That, as it happens, is what every unrepentant murderer I have ever known believes.

13   Once we recognize that the death penalty is neither a just nor effective response to murder, then only vengeance is left. Several years ago, Canada's Pierre Trudeau asked this question: "Are we so bankrupt as a society, so lacking in respect for ourselves, so lacking in hope for human betterment, so socially bankrupt that we are ready to accept vengeance as a penal philosophy?"

14   I am proud that Michigan continues to answer no to that question.

Questions for Discussion and Writing

1. How does the occasion mentioned in the first paragraph and the fact that Johnson as the director of corrections would have to supervise executions provide a framework for his argument?

2. To what extent does Johnson's firsthand familiarity with murderers and their victims undercut possible counterclaims that his views are merely theoretical?

3. How persuasive do you find Johnson's reasoning to support his view that capital punishment does not deter future murderers?

4. How does Johnson use the case of Gary Gilmore to support his view that some murderers have sick fantasies of being martyrs and therefore would not be deterred by the death penalty?

5. How does Johnson use records from the Michigan Department of Records to support his claim that life sentences would be as effective as capital punishment in preventing murderers from killing again?

6. What weight does Johnson give to studies showing that the death penalty is not applied in a just or evenhanded manner? How does he use this evidence in his argument?

7. Evaluate Johnson's rationale that the cost of administering life imprisonment for a convicted murderer should not be considered in the capital punishment debate.

8. To what extent does Johnson's argument depend on the assumption

that it is wrong for society to imbue citizens with the same disregard for human life held by unrepentant murderers? Evaluate the validity of this assumption. Would the death penalty send a message to society that it is all right to kill for convenience or for vengeance?

9. Does Johnson make his argument more persuasive by conceding that "some of these people in my opinion deserve to die for their crimes"?

10. How does Johnson's argument depend on the assumption that society has an obligation to live up to high moral standards and that capital punishment will lead to a lowering of these standards? How valid does this belief seem to be?

11. Does Johnson's job as director of Michigan's Department of Corrections make his argument more or less persuasive than it would otherwise be? Were you surprised that someone in his position holds these views?

12. How does this argument illustrate typical features of an ethical argument by exploring the conflict between Johnson's professional obligations and equally compelling moral principles? (You might wish to reread "Arguing in Ethics" in Chapter 2.)

13. Consider the following hypothetical scenario. What if Hitler had been caught alive after the conclusion of World War II and opponents of the death penalty had advocated putting him in prison for any of the reasons usually given: (*a*) to incapacitate him so that he would pose no further danger to society, (*b*) to deter others from doing what he did, or (*c*) to rehabilitate him through psychotherapy and work programs. How persuasive do you find any or all of these reasons? Would you agree with Johnson that although some people "deserve to die for their crimes," we as a civilized society should not kill them? Explain your answer in a short essay.

Frank B. Roome

An Insider's View of the Capital Punishment Controversy

Frank B. Roome is a convicted murderer who is presently serving his sentence at the Kansas Correctional Institution-Lansing. Contrary to what might be expected, Roome argues that "there must be a place for the death penalty in any rational system of justice," and builds his case with examples drawn from his unique perspective as a convicted murderer serving time. His article, "An Insider's View of the Capital Punishment Controversy," first appeared in The Kansas City Star *(May 21, 1981).*

1   I am a convicted murderer serving a sentence at the Kansas Correctional Institution-Lansing and I tell you that there must be a place for the death penalty in any rational system of justice. It is not to be applied casually or indiscriminately, but there are situations for which it is the only appropriate penalty, the only meaningful penalty.

2   It is an alternative that society naturally resists because it is unpleasant; blood is not lightly sought by any ethical human being. Yet a complex, contemporary society does take lives, far more lives than would ever be affected under any capital punishment law. Our young die in far off lands in defense of hazy, shifting foreign policy objectives; their only "crime" is being too young and too naively patriotic to evade their draft-defined responsibilities.

3   Our elderly, too, are cut down with statistical certainty by each leap of government-fed inflation that further weakens their already shaky existence; their only "crime" is a silent, proud poverty. Policy decisions in education, medicine, environment, safety—all affect not only the quality, but the very length of life for Americans. Society does kill, by action and by inaction.

4   Why, then, do we shrink from exacting the same penalty from a criminal that we will assign by lot to a blameless adolescent in an Asian rice paddy?

5   I suspect it is because the criminal is a visible human being, a "real" person. Someone must speak the words, take the responsibility on an individual basis, without the comforting buffer of statistical lot.

6   I doubt that we could carry on a war if it were known in advance exactly who must die to gain an objective. To make general predictions,

as our military attempts to do, that a particular offensive will cost a certain percentage of the men involved, is a far different matter emotionally from naming the doomed in advance. That sort of responsibility is a terrible weight. However, it is precisely the sort that we legitimately expect our chosen representatives to bear.

Particular Crimes

When should they be called upon to bear it? When should capital 7 punishment be applied? That is a question for more extended analysis than I can provide here, but I believe there are three obviously appropriate times: 1. When murder is committed for profit, to include robberies, kidnappings and killings for hire. 2. When murder is committed while institutionalized, whether involving staff or another prisoner. 3. Sequential acts of murder separated by meaningful periods of time.

The first category covers the cold-blooded crimes. Most murders are 8 sad acts of madly misplaced passion committed upon friends and relatives whose perpetrators deserve compassionate punishment, but there are others, callous men who kill without the slightest regard for human life. They are few in number, but they exist; I have lived among them.

In Kansas, the case for such a penalty is particularly acute. Profes- 9 sionals who make their living with a gun are quite aware that the peak sentences for armed robbery and the peak sentences for murder are often the same in practical terms. I have heard more than one bone-chilling discussion of the inadvisability of leaving any witnesses alive. Murder reduces the chances of apprehension and doesn't appreciably increase their probable penalty.

The second category is perhaps the most primitive. Plainly put, there 10 are men in prison who have absolutely nothing left to lose. They will probably spend the balance of their lives behind bars and a murder charge under current statutes means little. That fact can be a prime lever in some of the more brutish extortion efforts behind the walls.

An oldtimer can approach a young first-offender and tell him, "If you 11 don't do what I want, I can kill you for nothing. If you get lucky enough to kill me, that means you rot here for the rest of your life." Does it create substantial pressure? How would you respond?

The third category is essentially self-explanatory and covers those for 12 whom murder becomes an obscene hobby.

I support capital punishment for the categories I have mentioned 13 because it is needed and because I believe it to be just in principle. In that belief, I stand in good company.

Scholar Walter Berns noted that "No great political philosopher, with 14 the possible exception of Jeremy Bentham, has been opposed to the death penalty. . . . Plato, Aristotle, Aquinas, Thomas More and Locke favored capital punishment." The punishment should fit the crimes and there are some crimes so callous, so monstrous, as to make execution the only punishment that fits.

Life Imprisonment

15   Concurrently, I believe that in one sense capital punishment may actually be more humane than the probable alternative: life imprisonment without realistic possibility of parole. That would be the cruelest "death sentence" for any man with a vestige of humanity left. It forces a man to live without hope, to endure unending years in an environment that can grind the strongest down to the level of an animal.

16   Finally, I believe capital punishment is more efficient. This is a coldly calculated factor, and certainly not a primary justification, but it is a legitimate consideration.

17   We are finally beginning to realize that we have finite means. Government, at any level, cannot magically provide everything we would like. The national average cost per year of incarceration is now over $10,000 per individual. The $500,000 or more that may be spent on a prisoner before he dies is money that is not available to the elderly, not available to our schools or our hospitals.

18   After 20 years or so, when the inmate has become a real "old-timer," with access to drugs, booze, gambling, and a young car thief of his very own should he be sexually so inclined, would the wage earner who must sweat to earn the money which supports that inmate be impressed by his legislator's claim that "we're really punishing that guy!"?

19   One of the ironies of prison is that most of the punishment is accomplished in the first years. Prison only punishes while a man still dreams of the outside, while he still thinks of himself as a parent, a worker, a citizen with lost opportunities and lost contributions. Once he regards the prison as his home, as I have seen happen in a sad number of cases, he is beyond punishment. He has adjusted; he has become a "con."

20   That is why I do not support improbably long minimum sentences. They are costly in human and financial terms and, while execution can be a just punishment, a punishment that ultimately reduces a man to something less than human cannot be just.

21   I would offer one admonition. If you do implement a death penalty, ensure that it is carried out as an honest, open, serious expression of the judgment of the state. Do not hire an anonymous executioner who is driven by his own economic need to carry out your killings in the dark of night. If it is to be done, it must be done with candor and conviction, for it is the last lesson, the ultimate statement of society.

22   As Walter Berns declared, "Capital punishment does not deny human dignity, but recognizes it by holding us to the highest standards of human dignity. The deed should be witnessed, if not carried out, by

representatives of the jury which decreed it and the legislature which endorsed it as a matter of principle. Personal responsibility must be accepted to give it real legitimacy, not just as an abstract theory, but as a terrible, necessary part of our reality."

I am aware of the apparent irony of such arguments as I have presented coming from one in my position, and it is reasonable for those opposed in principle to the death penalty to wonder how I would have felt about receiving it as a sentence. Obviously, I could not have been entirely objective about that decision, but I would not have questioned the essential justice had it been rationally called for in my case. 23

Most simply, while I have lost much as a prisoner, I have forfeited neither my right to think nor my conscience. 24

Questions for Discussion and Writing

1. What effect does the information that Frank Roome is a "convicted murderer serving a sentence" have on the impact of his argument in favor of the death penalty? Does his situation make the logical case he presents more or less persuasive than it otherwise might be? Were you surprised that someone in this position holds these views?

2. Do Roome's discussions of apparently unrelated side issues such as the draft, American foreign policy, and the effect of inflation on the elderly support his *premiss* that "society does kill by action and by inaction?" Why must Roome gain acceptance for this general idea if he is to persuade his audience that the death penalty is justified in specific cases?

3. For which of the three specific circumstances warranting the death penalty does Roome make the strongest case? Which seems the least compelling?

4. If you favor the death penalty, are there other circumstances where you think it should be applied that Roome did not mention? What are they and why do you think they are applicable?

5. In terms of argumentative strategy, how does Roome use the viewpoints of noted scholars and philosophers to support his argument? What effect does this have on the persuasiveness of his case?

6. Both Roome and Johnson base their opposing arguments on differing concepts of justice. Write a short essay discussing how each writer develops a specific concept of justice that he then uses to support his particular position.

7. In your opinion, how satisfactorily does Roome confront the issue of whether he would still be in favor of the death penalty if he were going to be executed for the murder or murders he committed?

8. In a short essay, evaluate the merits of Roome's and Johnson's arguments. Who, in your opinion, makes a more persuasive case? Support your opinion with brief quotations from the two articles.

9. Evaluate the following arguments on the role played by race and economic status in determining who is executed among those convicted of capital crimes:

(*a*) Because of all these opportunities for arbitrary decision, only a small number of those convicted of capital crimes are actually executed . . . Inevitably, the death penalty has been imposed most frequently on the poor, and in this country it has been imposed in disproportionate numbers on blacks . . . Of 3,860 persons executed in the United States between 1930 and the present, 2,066, or 54 percent, were black. Although for a variety of reasons the per capita rate of conviction for most types of crime has been higher among the poor and the black, that alone cannot explain why a tenth of the population should account for more than half of those executed. Doubtless prejudice played a part. But no amount of goodwill and fair-mindedness can compensate for the disadvantage to those who cannot afford the highly skilled legal counsel needed to discern every loophole in the judicial process. (David Hoekema *Capital Punishment: The Question of Justification* [1979]).

(*b*) The business about the poor and the black suffering excessively from capital punishment is no argument against capital punishment. It is an argument against the *administration* of justice, not against the penalty. Any punishment can be unfairly or unjustly applied. Go ahead and reform the processes by which capital punishment is inflicted, if you wish; but don't confuse mal-administration with the merits of capital punishment. . . . (William F. Buckley, Jr. *Capital Punishment* [1975]).

10. Evaluate the following arguments about the presumed deterrent value of capital punishment. Whose reasoning do you find more persuasive?

(*a*) It is said that the example of capital punishment is needed to deter those who would otherwise commit murder . . . Surprisingly, none of the available empirical data shows any significant correlation between the existence or use of the death penalty and the incidence of capital crimes. When studies have compared the homicide rates for the past fifty years in states that employ the death penalty and in adjoining states that have abolished it, the numbers have in every case been quite similar: the death penalty has had no discernible effect on homicide rates. (David Hoekema *Capital Punishment: The Question of Justification* [1979]).

(*b*) Since we do not know for certain whether or not the death penalty adds deterrence, we have in effect the choice of two risks. Risk One: If we execute convicted murderers without thereby deterring prospective murderers beyond the deterrence that could have been achieved by life imprisonment, we may have vainly sacrificed the life of the convicted murderer. Risk Two: If we fail to execute a convicted murderer whose execution might have deterred an indefinite number of prospective murderers, our failure sacrifices an indefinite number of victims of future murderers. If we had certainty, we would not have risks. We do not have certainty. If we have risks — and we do — better to risk the life of the convicted man than risk the life of an indefinite number of innocent victims who might survive if he were executed. (William F. Buckley, Jr. *Capital Punishment* [1975]).

11. For further reading, you might wish to look into the arguments advanced by Walter Berns, *For Capital Punishment: Crime and the Morality of the Death Penalty* (1979).

GOVERNMENT

Thomas Paine

Rights of Man (excerpt)

Thomas Paine (1737–1809), following Benjamin Franklin's advice, left England and came to America in 1774. He served in the Revolutionary Army and supported the cause of the colonies through his influential pamphlets, Common Sense *(1776) and* The Crisis *(1776–1783). He also supported the French Revolution and wrote* The Rights of Man *(1791, 1792) and* The Age of Reason *(1793).* The Rights of Man *was written in reply to Edmund Burke's* Reflections upon the Revolution in France. *Paine disputes Burke's doctrine that one generation can compel succeeding ones to follow a particular form of government. He defines the inalienable "natural" and "civil" rights of mankind and expounds on society's obligation to protect these rights. In this excerpt from* The Rights of Man, *Paine displays his characteristically persuasive style.*

1   If any generation of men ever possessed the right of dictating the mode by which the world should be governed for ever, it was the first generation that existed; and if that generation did it not, no succeeding generation can show any authority for doing it, nor can set any up. The illuminating and divine principle of the equal rights of man, (for it has its origin from the Maker of man) relates, not only to the living individuals, but to generations of men succeeding each other. Every generation is equal in rights to the generations which preceded it, by the same rule that every individual is born equal in rights with his contemporary.

2   Every history of the creation, and every traditionary account, whether from the lettered or unlettered world, however they may vary in their opinion or belief of certain particulars, all agree in establishing one point, *the unity of man;* by which I mean, that men are all of *one degree,* and consequently that all men are born equal, and with equal natural right, in the same manner as if posterity had been continued by *creation* instead of *generation,* the latter being only the mode by which the former is carried forward; and consequently, every child born into the world must be considered as deriving its existence from God. The world is as new to him as it was to the first man that existed, and his natural right in it is of the same kind.

The Mosaic account of the creation, whether taken as divine author-   3
ity, or merely historical, is full to this point, *the unity or equality of man.*
The expressions admit of no controversy. "And God said, Let us make
man in our own image. In the image of God created he him; male and
female created he them." The distinction of sexes is pointed out, but no
other distinction is even implied. If this be not divine authority, it is at
least historical authority, and shows that the equality of man, so far from
being a modern doctrine, is the oldest upon record.

It is also to be observed, that all the religions known in the world   4
are founded, so far as they relate to man, on the *unity of man*, as being
all of one degree. Whether in heaven or in hell, or in whatever state
man may be supposed to exist hereafter, the good and the bad are the
only distinctions. Nay, even the laws of governments are obliged to slide
into this principle, by making degrees to consist in crimes, and not in
persons.

It is one of the greatest of all truths, and of the highest advantage to   5
cultivate. By considering man in this light, and by instructing him to
consider himself in this light, it places him in a close connexion with all
his duties, whether to his Creator, or to the creation, of which his is a
part; and it is only when he forgets his origin, or, to use a more fashionable phrase, his *birth and family*; that he becomes dissolute. It is not
among the least of the evils of the present existing governments in all
parts of Europe,that man, considered as man, is thrown back to a vast
distance from his Maker, and the artificial chasm filled up by a succession of barriers, or sort of turnpike gates, through which he has to pass. I
will quote Mr Burke's catalogue of barriers that he has set up between
man and his Maker. Putting himself in the character of a herald, he
says—"We fear God—we look with *awe* to kings—with affection to
parliaments—with duty to magistrates—with reverence to priests, and
with respect to nobility." Mr Burke has forgotten to put in "*chivalry.*" He
has also forgotten to put in Peter.

The duty of man is not a wilderness of turnpike gates, through which   6
he is to pass by tickets from one to the other. It is plain and simple, and
consists but of two points. His duty to God, which every man must feel;
and with respect to his neighbour, to do as he would be done by. If those
to whom power is delegated do well, they will be respected; if not, they
will be despised: and with regard to those to whom no power is delegated, but who assume it, the rational world can know nothing of them.

Hitherto we have spoken only (and that but in part) of the natural   7
rights of man. We have now to consider the civil rights of man, and to
show how the one originates from the other. Man did not enter into
society to become *worse* than he was before, nor to have fewer rights
than he had before, but to have those rights better secured. His natural
rights are the foundation of all his civil rights. But in order to pursue this

distinction with more precision, it will be necessary to mark the different qualities of natural and civil rights.

8   A few words will explain this. Natural rights are those which appertain to man in right of his existence. Of this kind are all the intellectual rights, or rights of the mind, and also all those rights of acting as an individual for his own comfort and happiness, which are not injurious to the natural rights of others. — Civil rights are those which appertain to man in right of his being a member of society. Every civil right has for its foundation, some natural right pre-existing in the individual, but to the enjoyment of which has individual power is not, in all cases, sufficiently competent. Of this kind are all those which relate to security and protection.

9   From this short review, it will be easy to distinguish between that class of natural rights which man retains after entering into society, and those which he throws into the common stock as a member of society.

10   The natural rights which he retains, are all those in which the *power* to execute is as perfect in the individual as the right itself. Among this class, as is before mentioned, are all the intellectual rights, or rights of the mind: consequently, religion is one of those rights. The natural rights which are not retained, are all those in which, though the right is perfect in the individual, the power to execute them is defective. They answer not his purpose. A man, by natural right, has a right to judge in his own cause; and so far as the right of mind is concerned; he never surrenders it: But what availeth it him to judge, if he has not power to redress? He therefore deposits this right in the common stock of society, and takes the arm of society, of which he is a part, in preference and in addition to his own. Society *grants* him nothing. Every man is a proprietor in society, and draws on the capital as a matter of right.

11   From these premises, two or three certain conclusions will follow.

12   First, That every civil right grows out of a natural right; or, in other words, is a natural right exchanged.

13   Secondly, that civil power, properly considered as such, is made up of the aggregate of that class of the natural rights of man, which becomes defective in the individual in point of power, and answers not his purpose; but when collected to a focus, becomes competent to the purpose of every one.

14   Thirdly, That the power produced from the aggregate of natural rights, imperfect in power in the individual, cannot be applied to invade the natural rights, which are retained in the individual, and in which the power to execute is as perfect as the right itself.

15   We have now, in a few words, traced man from a natural individual to a member of society, and shown, or endeavoured to show, the quality of the natural rights retained, and of those which are exchanged for civil rights. Let us now apply these principles to governments.

16   In casting our eyes over the world, it is extremely easy to distinguish the governments which have arisen out of society, or out of the social

compact, from those which have not: but to place this in a clearer light than what a single glance may afford, it will be proper to take a review of the several sources from which governments have arisen, and on which they have been founded.

They may be all comprehended under three heads. First, Supersti- 17 tion. Secondly, Power. Thirdly, The common interest of society, and the common rights of man.

Questions for Discussion and Writing

1. How does Paine use deductive reasoning in asserting that all men and women, as descendants of Adam and Eve, are born equal and that every child must be considered as "deriving its existence from God"? What consequence flows from the fact that, in Paine's view, these "natural rights" are God given and may not be abridged by any succeeding generation? What rationale supports Paine's assertion that all men and women possess certain natural rights? Where did these rights come from and who ordained them?

2. How does Paine make use of the biblical account of the Creation to support his claim that no generation has more rights than any other generation?

3. Given Paine's *premiss* that "all men are born equal, and with equal natural right," how does it then necessarily follow that no one generation can exercise authority over the next by any claim of superior right? How does Paine use this line of reasoning to justify the rejection of the barriers thrown up by "evils of the present existing governments in all parts of Europe"? It should be understood that these barriers include kings, parliaments, magistrates, priests, and the nobility, among others.

4. After defining what he considers to be man's inalienable natural rights, what reasons does Paine advance to support his claim that "every civil right has for its foundation, some natural right pre-existing in the individual"? By what process do civil rights arise, and what purposes are they designed to serve? For instance, how is a civil right everyone takes for granted, such as the right to vote, related to a corresponding natural right, as defined by Paine?

5. According to Paine, what kinds of functions justify the existence of the state and its ability to wield greater power than any one individual can?

6. How is Paine's argument constructed around the principal

assumption that the greater power of the state must never be used to overstep the boundaries of any person's natural, inalienable rights? How was this idea used as a rationale to justify rejecting British rule over the American colonies?

7. What features of style and tone add to the persuasiveness of Paine's argument? Discuss the particular word choices, connotations, images, and emotional appeals that make this essay particularly effective.

8. Compare this excerpt from *The Rights of Man* with Thomas Jefferson's draft of the Declaration of Independence. Which of Paine's words and phrases reappear in the latter work? How did Paine's *Rights of Man* provide the philosophical underpinnings for the Declaration of Independence? Keep in mind that Paine's argument follows from the *premiss* that every individual is born "equal in rights with his contemporary," although each individual shares his or her rights with society to protect all citizens. In Paine's view, the American colonists were simply withdrawing those natural rights that had been infringed upon by England. That is, since England had violated its part of the contract by overstepping the boundaries of the American colonists' natural, inalienable rights, Americans were free to withdraw their allegiance and set up their own form of government. For a research project, trace this line of argument through the text of the Declaration of Independence.

Mao Tse-Tung

The Rights of the Collective Take Precedence over the Rights of Individuals

"The Rights of the Collective Take Precedence Over the Rights of Individuals" is comprised of arguments made by Mao Tse-Tung (1983–1976), chairman of the Communist party in China, to the Central Committee of the Chinese Communist Party between 1947 and 1949 justifying the need for a "people's dictatorship." Mao argues that the rights of the collective take precedence over the rights of individuals.

"You are dictatorial." My dear sirs, what you say is correct. That is just what we are. All the experiences of the Chinese people, accumulated in the course of many successive decades, tell us to carry out a people's democratic dictatorship. 1

"You are not benevolent." Exactly. We definitely have no benevolent policies toward the reactionaries or the reactionary deeds of such classes. Our benevolent policy does not apply to such deeds or to such persons, who are outside the ranks of the people; it applies only to the people. 2

The job of reforming the reactionary classes can be handled only by a state having a people's dictatorship. 3

Our party is entirely different from the political parties of the bourgeoisie. They are afraid to speak of the elimination of classes, state power, and parties. We, however, openly declare that we are energetically striving to set up conditions just for the sake of eliminating these things. The Communist Party and the state power of the people's dictatorship constitute such conditions. 4

Communists everywhere are more competent than the bourgeoisie. They understand the law governing the existence and development of things. They understand dialetics and can see further ahead. 5

In this our land of China, the People's Liberation Army has already reversed the counterrevolutionary course. This is a turning point in history. This is a great event. 6

The victory of China's New Democratic revolution is impossible without the broadest united front. . . . But this is not all. This united 7 front must also be firmly led by the Chinese Communist party. Without the firm leadership of the Chinese Communist Party, no revolutionary united front can be victorious.

8   As long as their reactionary tendencies can still influence the masses, we must expose them among the masses who are open to their influence, and strike at their political influence in order to liberate the masses from it. But political blows are one thing and economic extermination is another. . . . The existence and development of small and middle capitalist elements is not at all dangerous. The same thing applies to the new-rich peasant economy, which, after agrarian revolution, will inevitably come into existence.

9   Many of China's conditions are identical with or similar to those of Russia before the October Revolution. Both had the same sort of feudal oppression. Economically and culturally they were similarly backward, though China was the more so.

10   We must take our destinies into our own hands. We must rid our ranks of all flabby and incompetent thinking. . . . We are well aware of the fact that there will still be all kinds of obstacles and difficulties in the path of our advance. . . . We must be up and doing!

11   They [the business men] have monopolized the economic life of the entire country. This monopoly capitalism, closely combined with foreign imperialism and the native landlord class and old type of rich peasants, becomes comprador-feudal, state-monopoly capitalism. This not only oppresses the workers and peasants but also oppresses the petty bourgeoisie and harms the middle bourgeoisie.

12   The Party must do its utmost to learn how to lead the urban people . . . and how to administer and build up the cities. The Plenary Session called on all Party comrades to devote all their energies to learning the technique and management of industrial production; and to learning commercial banking and other work closely related to production. If the Party is ignorant in production work the Party will fail.

13   We must overcome all difficulties and must learn the things we do not understand. We must learn to do economic work from all who know . . . (no matter who they are). We must respect them as teachers, learning from them attentively and earnestly. We must not pretend that we know when we do not know. We must not put on bureaucratic airs. If one bores into a subject for several months, for one year or two years, perhaps three years or four years, it can eventually be mastered.

14   The war of the People's Liberation Army is of a patriotic, just and revolutionary nature which must of necessity gain the support of the people. . . . the Communist Party seeks earnestly to unite the whole of the working class, the whole of the peasantry and the vast number of the revolutionary intelligentsia as the leading and foundation forces of this dictatorship.

15   On the basis of the experience of these twenty-eight years, we have

reached the same conclusions that Sun Yat-sen, in his will, mentioned gaining from "the experience of forty years." That is, "we must awaken the masses of the people and unite ourselves in a common struggle."

Internally, the people must be awakened.   16

Basing itself on the science of Marxism-Leninism, the Chinese Com-   17
munist Party clearly assessed the international and domestic situation.

Questions for Discussion and Writing

1. According to Mao-Tse-Tung, what is the task of government and why is it best handled, in his opinion, "only by a state having a people's dictatorship"? What assumptions about the proper relationship of the government to the people underlie Mao's argument?

2. In what ways is communism, according to Mao Tse-Tung, different from "the political parties of the bourgeoisie" and "more competent than the bourgeoisie"?

3. In what sections of his argument does Mao justify the paternalistic role of the Chinese Communist party in safeguarding the "masses" who otherwise might be duped by persisting "reactionary tendencies" of those who formerly held power? At the same time, why does Mao show a surprising tolerance for the "existence and development of small and middle capitalist elements"? Keep in mind his statement that the same tolerance will apply to "the new-rich peasant economy, which, after agrarian revolution, will inevitably come in existence." How does his rhetoric embody the carrot and stick approach in persuading his audience?

4. How does Mao use the historical parallel of "Russia before the October Revolution" to argue for full support of a "united front . . . firmly led by the Chinese Communist Party"? Specifically, how does Mao use the technique of arguing by analogy to bolster his position?

5. How does Mao handle the problem of denouncing "monopoly capitalism," on the one hand, while urging his followers (who were mainly peasants and workers) to learn the techniques and management "of industrial production" and "commercial banking"?

6. In a short essay, discuss Mao's change of tone between the beginning and end of his argument. Why does he begin with an uncompromising defense of the need for a "people's dictatorship" led by the

Communist party and claim that "Communists everywhere are more competent than the bourgeoisie," and then toward the end adopt a more flexible attitude toward commerce and admit "we must learn to do economic work from all who know, . . . We must not pretend we know when we do not know"? Plainly, these latter statements contradict assertions of "competence" made at the beginning, yet they serve a more important purpose in persuading his audience to accept his programs.

7. How does Mao's argument depend on his claim that there is a "science of Marx sm-Leninism" as the ultimate basis of authority? What connotations is the word *science* intended to have in persuading his audience?

8. In a short essay, discuss the influence that a charismatic leader such as Mao can have, and the various claims he makes for "a people's democratic dictatorship" in uniting a society that otherwise might have disintegrated. Keep in mind that when Mao came into power China was nearing the end of a decades-long struggle for competent leadership. In this context, Mao appeared to offer a viable means by which China could become economically self-sufficient and politically independent, by pursuing a pattern already successfully followed by the Soviet Union.

9. Write an essay comparing and contrasting Mao's argument that "the rights of the collective take precedence over the rights of individuals" with the excerpt from Thomas Paine's *Rights of Man*. What fundamentally different assumptions about human nature and the function of the state separate Paine's political theories from those of Mao? Support your analysis with short quotations from both articles.

10. How did the events of the summer of 1989 in China illustrate the extent to which Mao's political theories expressed in this article are still followed? Specifically, how did the clash between prodemocracy demonstrators and government soldiers in Beijing, in June of 1989, and the subsequent executions and imprisonment of students, workers, and other participants illustrate the conflict between the ideas of Mao and those of Paine?

BILINGUALISM

Richard Rodriguez

Aria: A Memoir of a Bilingual Childhood

Richard Rodriguez was born to Spanish-speaking Mexican-American parents in San Francisco in 1944. His many articles include those written for The American Scholar, Change, The Saturday Review, *and other magazines. He is also author of the collection of autobiographical essays,* Hunger of Memory *(1982). In "Aria: A Memoir of a Bilingual Childhood" (American* Scholar *[1980]) Rodriguez dramatizes the predicament often encountered by those who acquire a new language and culture at the expense of the traditional culture in which they were raised. This account expresses a number of thoughtful arguments against the concept of bilingual education.*

I remember, to start with, that day in Sacramento, in a California now 1
nearly thirty years past, when I first entered a classroom — able to understand about fifty stray English words. The third of four children, I had been preceded by my older brother and sister to a neighborhood Roman Catholic school. But neither of them had revealed very much about their classroom experiences. They left each morning and returned each afternoon, always together, speaking Spanish as they climbed the five steps to the porch. And their mysterious books, wrapped in brown shopping-bag paper, remained on the table next to the door, closed firmly behind them.

An accident of geography sent me to a school where all my class- 2
mates were white and many were the children of doctors and lawyers and business executives. On that first day of school, my classmates must certainly have been uneasy to find themselves apart from their families, in the first institution of their lives. But I was astonished. I was fated to be the "problem student" in class.

The nun said, in a friendly but oddly impersonal voice: "Boys and 3
girls, this is Richard Rodriguez." (I heard her sound it out: *Rich-heard Road-ree-guess.*) It was the first time I had heard anyone say my name in English. "Richard," the nun repeated more slowly, writing my name down in her book. Quickly I turned to see my mother's face dissolve in a watery blur behind the pebbled-glass door.

4   Now, many years later, I hear of something called "bilingual education"— a scheme proposed in the late 1960s by Hispanic-American social activists, later endorsed by a congressional vote. It is a program that seeks to permit non-English-speaking children (many from lower class homes) to use their "family language" as the language of school. Such, at least, is the aim its supporters announce. I hear them, and am forced to say no: It is not possible for a child, any child, ever to use his family's language in school. Not to understand this is to misunderstand the public uses of schooling and to trivialize the nature of intimate life.

5   Memory teaches me what I know of these matters. The boy reminds the adult. I was a bilingual child, but of a certain kind: "socially disadvantaged," the son of working-class parents, both Mexican immigrants.

6   In the early years of my boyhood, my parents coped very well in America. My father had steady work. My mother managed at home. They were nobody's victims.When we moved to a house many blocks from the Mexican-American section of town, they were not intimidated by those two or three neighbors who initially tried to make us unwelcome. ("Keep your brats away from my sidewalk!") But despite all they achieved, or perhaps because they had so much to achieve, they lacked any deep feeling of ease, of belonging in public. They regarded the people at work or in crowds as being very distant from us. Those were the others, *los gringos.* That term was interchangeable in their speech with another, even more telling: *los americanos.*

7   I grew up in a house where the only regular guests were my relations. On a certain day, enormous families of relatives would visit us, and there would be so many people that the noise and the bodies would spill out to the backyard and onto the front porch. Then for weeks no one would come. (If the doorbell rang, it was usually a salesman.) Our house stood apart—gaudy yellow in a row of white bungalows. We were the people with the noisy dog, the people who raised chickens. We were the foreigners on the block. A few neighbors would smile and wave at us. We waved back. But until I was seven years old, I did not know the name of the old couple living next door or the names of the kids living across the street.

8   In public, my father and mother spoke a hesitant, accented, and not always grammatical English. And then they would have to strain, their bodies tense, to catch the sense of what was rapidly said by *los gringos.* At home, they returned to Spanish. The language of their Mexican past sounded in counterpoint to the English spoken in public. The words would come quickly, with ease. Conveyed through those sounds was the pleasing, soothing, consoling reminder that one was at home.

9   During those years when I was first learning to speak, my mother and father addressed me only in Spanish; in Spanish I learned to reply. By contrast, English (*inglés*) was the language I came to associate with gringos, rarely heard in the house. I learned my first words of English overhearing my parents speaking to strangers. At six years of age, I knew

just enough words for my mother to trust me on errands to stores one block away—but no more.

I was then a listening child, careful to hear the very different sounds   10
of Spanish and English. Wide-eyed with hearing, I'd listen to sounds more than to words. First, there were English (gringo) sounds. So many words still were unknown to me that when the butcher or the lady at the drugstore said something, exotic polysyllabic sounds would bloom in the midst of their sentences. Often the speech of people in public seemed to me very loud, booming with confidence. The man behind the counter would literally ask, "What can I do for you?" But by being so firm and clear, the sound of his voice said that he was a gringo; he belonged in public society. There were also the high, nasal notes of middle-class American speech—which I rarely am conscious of hearing today because I hear them so often, but could not stop hearing when I was a boy. Crowds at Safeway or at bus stops were noisy with the birdlike sounds of *los gringos*. I'd move away from them all—all the chirping chatter above me.

My own sounds I was unable to hear, but I knew that I spoke English   11
poorly. My words could not extend to form complete thoughts. And the words I did speak I didn't know well enough to make distinct sounds. (Listeners would usually lower their heads to hear better what I was trying to say.) But it was one thing for *me* to speak English with difficulty; it was more troubling to hear my parents speaking in public: their high-whining vowels and guttural consonants; their sentences that got stuck with "eh" and "ah" sounds; the confused syntax; the hesitant rhythm of sounds so different from the way gringos spoke. I'd notice, moreover, that my parents' voices were softer than those of gringos we would meet.

I am tempted to say now that none of this mattered. (In adulthood I   12
am embarrassed by childhood fears.) And, in a way, it didn't matter very much that my parents could not speak English with ease. Their linguistic difficulties had no serious consequences. My mother and father made themselves understood at the county hospital clinic and at government offices. And yet, in another way, it mattered very much. It was unsettling to hear my parents struggle with English. Hearing them, I'd grow nervous, and my clutching trust in their protection and power would be weakened.

There were many times like the night at a brightly lit gasoline station   13
(a blaring white memory) when I stood uneasily hearing my father talk to a teenage attendant. I do not recall what they were saying, but I cannot forget the sounds my father made as he spoke. At one point his words slid together to form one long word—sounds as confused as the threads of blue and green oil in the puddle next to my shoes. His voice rushed through what he had left to say. Toward the end, he reached falsetto notes, appealing to his listener's understanding. I looked away at the lights of passing automobiles. I tried not to hear any more. But I

heard only too well the attendant's reply, his calm, easy tones. Shortly afterward, headed for home, I shivered when my father put his hand on my shoulder. The very first chance that I got, I evaded his grasp and ran on ahead into the dark, skipping with feigned boyish exuberance.

14   But then there was Spanish: *español*, the language rarely heard away from the house; *español*, the language which seemed to me therefore a private language, my family's language. To hear its sounds was to feel myself specially recognized as one of the family, apart from *los otros*. A simple remark, an inconsequential comment could convey that assurance. My parents would say something to me and I would feel embraced by the sounds of their words. Those sounds said: *I am speaking with ease in Spanish. I am addressing you in words I never use with los gringos. I recognize you as someone special, close, like no one outside. You belong with us. In the family. Ricardo.*

15   At the age of six, well past the time when most middle-class children no longer notice the difference between sounds uttered at home and words spoken in public, I had a different experience. I lived in a world compounded of sounds. I was a child longer than most. I lived in a magical world, surrounded by sounds both pleasing and fearful. I shared with my family a language enchantingly private — different from that used in the city around us.

16   Just opening or closing the screen door behind me was an important experience. I'd rarely leave home all alone or without feeling reluctance. Walking down the sidewalk, under the canopy of tall trees, I'd warily notice the (suddenly) silent neighborhood kids who stood warily watching me. Nervously, I'd arrive at the grocery store to hear there the sounds of the gringo, reminding me that in this so-big world I was a foreigner. But if leaving home was never routine, neither was coming back. Walking toward our house, climbing the steps from the sidewalk, in summer when the front door was open, I'd hear voices beyond the screen door talking in Spanish. For a second or two I'd stay, linger there listening. Smiling, I'd hear my mother call out, saying in Spanish, "Is that you, Richard?" Those were her words, but all the while her sounds would assure me: *You are home now. Come closer inside. With us.* "*Si,*" I'd reply.

17   Once more inside the house, I would resume my place in the family. The sounds would grow harder to hear. Once more at home, I would grow less conscious of them. It required, however, no more than the blurt of the doorbell to alert me all over again to listen to sounds. The house would turn instantly quiet while my mother went to the door. I'd hear her hard English sounds. I'd wait to hear her voice turn to soft-sounding Spanish, which assured me, as surely as did the clicking tongue of the lock on the door, that the stranger was gone.

18   Plainly it is not healthy to hear such sounds so often. It is not healthy to distinguish public from private sounds so easily. I remained cloistered by sounds, timid and shy in public, too dependent on the voices at home.

And yet I was a very happy child when I was at home. I remember many nights when my father would come back from work, and I'd hear him call out to my mother in Spanish, sounding relieved. In Spanish, his voice would sound the light and free notes that he never could manage in English. Some nights I'd jump up just hearing his voice. My brother and I would come running into the room where he was with our mother. Our laughing (so deep was the pleasure!) became screaming. Like others who feel the pain of public alienation, we transformed the knowledge of our public separateness into a consoling reminder of our intimacy. Excited, our voices joined in a celebration of sounds. *We are speaking now the way we never speak out in public—we are together*, the sounds told me. Some nights no one seemed willing to loosen the hold that sounds had on us. At dinner we invented new words that sounded Spanish, but made sense only to us. We pieced together new words by taking, say, an English verb and giving it Spanish endings. My mother's instructions at bedtime would be lacquered with mock-urgent tones. Or a word like *sí*, sounded in several notes, would convey added measures of feeling. Tongues lingered around the edges of words, especially fat vowels: And we happily sounded that military drum roll, the twirling roar of the Spanish *r*. Family language, my family's sounds: the voices of my parents and sisters and brother. Their voices insisting: *You belong here. We are family members. Related. Special to one another. Listen!* Voices singing and sighing, rising and straining, then surging, teeming with pleasure which burst syllables into fragments of laughter. At times it seemed there was steady quiet only when, from another room, the rustling whispers of my parents faded and I edged closer to sleep.

Supporters of bilingual education imply today that students like me 19
miss a great deal by not being taught in their family's language. What they seem not to recognize is that, as a socially disadvantaged child, I regarded Spanish as a private language. It was a ghetto language that deepened and strengthened my feeling of public separateness. What I needed to learn in school was that I had the right, and the obligation, to speak the public language. The odd truth is that my first-grade classmates could have become bilingual, in the conventional sense of the word, more easily than I. Had they been taught early (as upper middle-class children often are taught) a "second language" like Spanish or French, they could have regarded it simply as another public language. In my case, such bilingualism could not have been so quickly achieved. What I did not believe was that I could speak a single public language.

Without question, it would have pleased me to have heard my 20
teachers address me in Spanish when I entered the classroom. I would have felt much less afraid. I would have imagined that my instructors were somehow "related" to me; I would indeed have heard their Spanish as my family's language. I would have trusted them and responded with

ease. But I would have delayed—postponed for how long?—having to learn the language of public society. I would have evaded—and for how long?—learning the great lesson of school: that I had a public identity.

21   Fortunately, my teachers were unsentimental about their responsibility. What they understood was that I needed to speak public English. So their voices would search me out, asking me questions. Each time I heard them I'd look up in surprise to see a nun's face frowning at me. I'd mumble, not really meaning to answer. The nun would persist. "Richard, stand up. Don't look at the floor. Speak up. Speak to the entire class, not just to me!" But I couldn't believe English could be my language to use. (In part, I did not want to believe it.) I continued to mumble. I resisted the teacher's demands. (Did I somehow suspect that once I learned this public language my family life would be changed?) Silent, waiting for the bell to sound, I remained dazed, diffident, afraid.

22   Because I wrongly imagined that English was intrinsically a public language and Spanish was intrinsically private, I easily noted the difference between classroom language and the language at home. At school, words were directed to a general audience of listeners. ("Boys and girls . . .") Words were meaningfully ordered. And the point was not self-expression alone, but to make oneself understood by many others. The teacher quizzed: "Boys and girls, why do we use that word in this sentence? Could we think of a better word to use there? Would the sentence change its meaning if the words were differently arranged? Isn't there a better way of saying much the same thing?" (I couldn't say. I wouldn't try to say.)

23   Three months passed. Five. A half year. Unsmiling, ever watchful, my teachers noted my silence. They began to connect my behavior with the slow progress my brother and sisters were making. Until, one Saturday morning, three nuns arrived at the house to talk to our parents. Stiffly they sat on the blue living-room sofa. From the doorway of another room, spying on the visitors, I noted the incongruity, the clash of two worlds, the faces and voices of school intruding upon the familiar setting of home. I overheard one voice gently wondering, "Do your children speak only Spanish at home, Mrs. Rodriguez?" While another voice added, "That Richard especially seems so timid and shy."

24   *That Rich-heard!*

25   With great tact, the visitors continued, "Is it possible for you and your husband to encourage your children to practice their English when they are home?" Of course my parents complied. What would they not do for their children's well-being? And how could they question the Church's authority which those women represented? In an instant they agreed to give up the language (the sounds) which had revealed and accentuated our family's closeness. The moment after the visitors left, the change was observed. "*Ahora*, speak to us only *en inglés*," my father and mother told us.

At first, it seemed a kind of game. After dinner each night, the family 26
gathered together to practice "our" English. It was still then *inglés*, a
language foreign to us, so we felt drawn to it as strangers. Laughing, we
would try to define words we could not pronounce. We played with
strange English sounds, often overanglicizing our pronunciations. And
we filled the smiling gaps of our sentences with familiar Spanish sounds.
But that was cheating, somebody shouted, and everyone laughed.

In school, meanwhile, like my brother and sisters, I was required to 27
attend a daily tutoring session. I needed a full year of this special work. I
also needed my teachers to keep my attention from straying in class by
calling out, *"Rich-heard"* — their English voices slowly loosening the ties
to my other name, with its three notes, *Ri-car-do*. Most of all, I needed to
hear my mother and father speak to me in a moment of seriousness in
"broken" — suddenly heartbreaking — English. This scene was inevitable. One Saturday morning I entered the kitchen where my parents were
talking, but I did not realize that they were talking in Spanish until, the
moment they saw me, their voices changed and they began speaking
English. The gringo sounds they uttered startled me. Pushed me away. In
that moment of trivial misunderstanding and profound insight, I felt my
throat twisted by unsounded grief. I simply turned and left the room. But
I had no place to escape to where I could grieve in Spanish. My brother
and sisters were speaking English in another part of the house.

Again and again in the days following, as I grew increasingly angry, I 28
was obliged to hear my mother and father encouraging me: "Speak to us
en inglés." Only then did I determine to learn classroom English. Thus,
sometime afterward it happened: one day in school, I raised my hand to
volunteer an answer to a question. I spoke out in a loud voice and I did
not think it remarkable when the entire class understood. That day I
moved very far from being the disadvantaged child I had been only days
earlier. Taken hold at last was the belief, the calming assurance, that I
belonged in public.

Shortly after, I stopped hearing the high, troubling sounds of *los* 29
gringos. A more and more confident speaker of English, I didn't listen to
how strangers sounded when they talked to me. With so many English-
speaking people around me, I no longer heard American accents. Conversations quickened. Listening to persons whose voices sounded eccen-
trically pitched, I might note their sounds for a few seconds, but then I'd
concentrate on what they were saying. Now when I heard someone's
tone of voice — angry or questioning or sarcastic or happy or sad — I
didn't distinguish it from the words it expressed. Sound and word were
thus tightly wedded. At the end of each day I was often bemused, and
always relieved, to realize how "soundless," though crowded with
words, my day in public had been. An eight-year-old boy, I finally came
to accept what had been technically true since my birth: I was an
American citizen.

Questions for Discussion and Writing

1. Summarize Rodriguez's experiences, citing examples drawn from the account of his personal reminiscences and memories, as they illuminate the process by which he learned to speak English. For example, how did the nun's visit to his home change the way he and his parents communicated from then on?

2. What details effectively convey Rodriguez's awareness of himself as being different from the other children in his school and his family as being different from other families in the neighborhood? In your opinion, what part did these unusual circumstances play in motivating him to learn English?

3. What evidence can you cite of Rodriguez's unusual sensitivity to the various connotations and sounds of language? How does he use the descriptions of his sensitivity to the different sounds of English and Spanish to organize the rhetorical structure of this memoir so as to reflect his awareness of the sharp difference between public and private life?

4. How did Rodriguez's mastery of English have the unforeseen effect of lessening his parent's authority?

5. What reasons does Rodriguez present to advance recommendations opposing bilingualism? How does he use deductive reasoning to develop this section of his argument?

6. Like Rodriguez, many students discover that the experiences they have in school, although providing a sense of accomplishment, sometimes have the effect of undermining their parents' authority. Discuss an experience you had that made you realize this phenomenon was taking place.

7. What did this essay make you realize about the crucial role language plays in creating self-image and maintaining cultural identity?

8. What is your attitude toward the specific issue of the public schools' responsibility to provide bilingual education as part of its broader social mission of offering an appropriate education to everyone in a pluralistic society? If you are in favor of bilingualism on these grounds, how specifically do you think it should be put into action on a practical level?

Stan Steiner

The Shrunken Head of Pancho Villa

Stan Steiner's essay "The Shrunken Head of Pancho Villa" was taken from his book La Raza: The Mexican Americans *(1970). This essay presents an account of how the school systems in the Southwest have treated students who speak Spanish or speak English with Spanish accents. It supports the goals of bilingualism, namely, to instruct children in subjects taught in their native language while they learn English and to encourage them to continue speaking Spanish at home. Steiner believes that bilingual education will promote a positive attitude toward non-English-speaking people and, at the same time, will preserve native languages and family culture.*

The De-Education Schools

The boy waves his hand bashfully, and the teacher tells him to come 1
to her desk.

"Charles, what do you want?" 2

"I have to go," the boy whispers a little louder, in Spanish, "to the 3
bathroom."

"English!" the teacher rebukes him, growing impatient. "We speak 4
English in school, Carlos," she says in Spanish. "You ask in English, or
sit down."

The boy, who is maybe ten, and small, looks up at the teacher with 5
the awe and fear that the schoolchildren of his age have for authority. He
does not know what to say or do. Suddenly his eyes light up with a
mischievous thought.

"If you don't let me go to the bathroom," the boy exclaims, in 6
Spanish, "maybe I piss on your shoes."

Years later the grown man remembers the incident of his boyhood 7
humiliation without smiling. In his village the schoolhouse was closed
long ago, and the teacher is gone, but the conflict in the classroom is
indelible in his memory. "That teacher, she did not like us," he says.
"She was a good teacher, but for forty years she did not let children
speak Spanish in her classroom. She made us shamed." And the man of
fifty is angry, still.

"Why did that teacher shame us? Spanish is a cultured language. It 8
was here before English."

Children have been taught to forget the "foreign" ways of their 9 fathers. Children have been cajoled, enticed, threatened, and punished for speaking Spanish. Children have been beaten.

10   In one school in South Texas the children are forced to kneel in the playground and beg forgiveness for uttering a Spanish word. Some teachers have pupils who talk the forbidden language kneel before the entire class. A popular punishment is to have the offender stand facing the blackboard. Cesar Chavez, the farm workers' leader, vividly recalls being forced to stand in a corner for defying the order, "No Spanish in the classroom." That teaching method is still practiced in the rural schools. "Spanish detention" is another widely used punishment for speaking the native language. A wispy, white-haired teacher in Tucson, Arizona, proudly tells how she teaches English. The child who answers in Spanish walks to her desk and "he drops a penny in a bowl, for every Spanish word." She boasts, "It works! They come from poor families, you know."

11   One Rio Grande Valley school goes further. The teachers assign students to be "Spanish monitors," who guard its corridors, writing down the names of their fellow students who are heard speaking Spanish. The culprits are reprimanded or beaten.

12   Not all the methods of de-educating the Chicanos to forget their native language are nonviolent. Some of the largest school systems in the Southwest still sanction the beating of recalcitrant children if they persist in being "Spanish-speaking."

13   Even now, the schoolchildren of Los Angeles may be "paddled" with the official approval of the Board of Education.

14   When the barrio students walked out of the high schools of East Los Angeles to protest what they called "racist education," one of their pleas was that, "corporal punishment, which is carried on in the East Los Angeles schools, should be abolished throughout the district." The Los Angeles *Times* commented casually: "Corporal punishment is mostly in the form of paddling. . . . Authorization of corporal punishment at the discretion of school personnel is the board's [Los Angeles Board of Education] policy." The offhanded defense of "paddling" the Chicano high school students, by the second-largest school system in the country, was offered in the spring of 1968!

15   "We are teaching these kids with psychological guns pointed at their heads," angrily observed Sal Castro, a Los Angeles high school teacher. "If a kid speaks in Spanish, he is criticized. If a kid has a Mexican accent, he is ridiculed. If a kid talks back, in any language, he is arrested. If a kid wants to leave school, he is forced back. We have gun-point education. The school is a prison."

16   "Education in the barrio doesn't free the mind of the Chicano. It imprisons his mind," the teacher said.

17   One day that spring an honor student at the Sidney Lanier High School in San Antonio, Texas, was caught reciting his Spanish homework aloud, in the school cafeteria. He was taken to the principal's office

and beaten with a paddle; there were several cases of young people being beaten for speaking Spanish. "Just a gentle whack or two does them good," a teacher said. When the students complained about the paddling, they were threatened with the loss of their college scholarships and suspended. In frustration there was talk of a school strike. A meeting was hastily held by the city's Human Rights Commission in the hall of a local Catholic church, where the young Chicanos cited dozens of incidents of intimidation because they dared to talk in the mother tongue.

Educators listened in silence. There were no denials; everyone knew   18
that it had been this way for generations. Wasn't it everywhere? In Texas it is illegal, according to Section 288 of the State Penal Code, for a teacher, principal, or school superintendent to teach or conduct school business in any language but English. Textbooks have to be in English. By custom the language restriction has been stridently applied to the students as well.

The "sons of Zapata" County Commissioner Albert Pena extrava-   19
gantly praised the students: "Our generation didn't have the courage to speak out. You are brave," he told them.

In the San Antonio high schools there were months of turmoil,   20
meetings, student strikes, firings of teachers and even priests, newspaper headlines, and charges of infiltration by "Castro-trained extremists" before the high school students won the right to talk openly in their mother tongue. Until that triumph they had to whisper the language of Cervantes in the secrecy of the girls' locker room and the boys' urinals.

It was so everywhere. Language is a vital teaching tool in the de-edu-   21
cation process. The banning of Spanish in the classroom is not an arbitrary act of a callous teacher. In the metropolitan school systems and in the village schoolhouses the suppression of the Spanish language and the culture of La Raza reflects the de-education policy that has been dominant in the schools of the Southwest since the "Conquest" of the region.

In the small town of San Luis in the high mountains of southern   22
Colorado the people are mostly Spanish-speaking. Yet, there too the native language was prohibited inside the school gate.

"Until quite recently Spanish has been tacitly assumed to be an   23
inferior language by nearly all of us," writes a village teacher in San Luis, Alan Davis. "Its use has been forbidden in our classrooms, and on our playgrounds, until this month [February, 1969]." Of course, the teacher adds, "we offered no courses in Spanish."

The native language of the Chicano child was treated with colonialist   24
disdain. His voice was muted. "English is the national language of the United States, but it is not a native or indigenous language. It is one of the colonial languages," writes Dr. Vera John, in a comprehensive study of bilingualism in the schools of the Southwest. In a conquered land the institutions of culture—theaters, books, libraries, academics—may be visibly suppressed. It is more difficult to eradicate the spoken word.

Language then becomes the last resource of cultural survival. "If the language goes, the culture goes with it," writes a scholar of La Raza. And so, in the schools there are bitter skirmishes over the spoken word. The children have become combatants.

25   "They yell at our children in school, 'Do not speak Spanish!' You are a free man in the land of the free, but 'Do not speak Spanish!' English is the only language of freedom," Reies Tijerina, the prophet of cultural revival, tells a meeting in a village schoolhouse. "It's like the story of the man who took a bird from his cage, and set it free. But first he took the pair of scissors and clipped off its wings."

26   "Fly! Fly!" the man said.

27   "The blue-eyed cat, the Anglo, came and ate the poor, helpless bird," Tijerina says.

28   In the "migrant schools" proposed by the state of California's "master migrant plan," the process of de-education by which a Chicano child is stripped of his culture is bluntly outlined. The "sample migrant school curriculum" is explicit:

Physical education — English cultural games and activities . . .
Creative arts and crafts — Introduction to English culture, music and song . . .
Arithmetic — Concrete objects, English concept of arithmetic . . .
Social Studies — Developing knowledge of characteristics of English culture . . .

29   Nowhere in the curriculum is there a word on the Indian, Spanish, and Mexican cultures of the Southwest. In all the classes the emphasis is upon the de-education of the Chicano child.

30   He has to be de-educated before he can be re-educated — as "English"? The "English" cultural games he is taught may be the old Aztec sports of basketball and handball; the "English" music and song, Western style, may have originated in the vaquero music and song of the old West; and the "English" concept of arithmetic may be based on the sophisticated mathematics of the scholars of ancient Mexico. But none of these origins is mentioned in the textbooks or the curriculum. Education of the Chicano is de-education, first of all. The language and culture of the Southwest are seen by his teachers as a prime hindrance to his progress, not only in learning English, but in "becoming an American." In the better schools the ensuing conflict may be subtle, but in the poorer schools it is vulgar and cruel.

31   "Schools try to brainwash the Chicanos," says Maggie Alvarado, a student at St. Mary's University in San Antonio. "They try to make us forget our history, to be ashamed of being Mexicans, of speaking Spanish. They succeed in making us feel empty, and angry, inside."

De-education is a difficult process. The culture of La Raza and the   32
Spanish language were native to the country for hundreds of years
before the coming of the Anglo to the Southwest; they are not easy to
uproot. Every generation the attempt at de-education has to begin anew,
for the conflict of cultures in the schools of the Southwest is an unending
conflict between the conquered and the conqueror. Colonialism has
usurped the purposes of education. The schools have been one of the
most effective instruments of the "Conquest." "It is safe to say that the
school, more than barbed wire or the plowing up of the range, was
responsible for the decline of the vaquero," writes the venerable old
cowboy and settler of California, Arnold Rojas. The "Yankee school-
marm" was a more efficient conqueror of La Raza than the United States
Army, Rojas writes. "The children did not have a chance."

A child goes to school to wonder. The school is where he enters the   33
Anglo world with shy curiosity; it is a magical microcosm of society to
him. The teacher is his sorcerer, a mother who is worldly-wise, knowing
all sorts of facts and magic, powerful as the policeman, but human as an
aunt or uncle. In the beginning that is how school seems to the child.

He is lost at the thought that he cannot enter that wonderful world   34
because he speaks the wrong language or is the wrong color. The child is
proud of his father; he boasts of his barrio heritage. He doesn't know
that he is supposed to be "culturally deprived."

If the teacher ridicules the language of his father, his way of thinking,   35
the beliefs and behavior his mother taught him, the child is bewildered.
He is told he must choose between being "American" or "Mexican." It is
no choice for him, for he is neither but is both. He will argue, or grow
silent. Either way the child will be in conflict with the teacher. And his
idyl of education is ended.

Questions for Discussion and Writing

1. How is the tone of Steiner's article related to his purpose, which
is to denounce the way some teachers in the public schools treat
students who cannot speak English?

2. How does Steiner use California's "sample migrant school
curriculum" as an example of the "de-education" process, that is, as
part of an overall attempt to reprogram the way children think about
their native culture?

3. How do the examples offered by Steiner in the first few
paragraphs emphasize the psychologically destructive effects of
prohibiting students from speaking Spanish in elementary school?

4. What measures, both nonviolent and violent, have been employed

in the attempt to prevent children from speaking Spanish in schools? What function do these examples serve in the development of Steiner's argument?

5. How are phrases like "Castro-trained extremists" and "they had to whisper the language of Cervantes" examples of guilt by association and virtue by association, respectively?

6. Aside from the specific tactics employed to discourage the speaking of Spanish by children in the schools, how do assumptions about the Spanish language reveal, in Steiner's view, an underlying colonialist attitude?

7. What systematic attempts at "de-education" does Steiner cite as part of an overall attempt to reprogram the way children think about their native culture? How, according to Steiner, do these methods of "de-education" produce children who are "bewildered" and "must choose between being 'American' or 'Mexican'"?

8. Compare and contrast the memories and personal reminiscences of Rodriguez with cases mentioned by Steiner to determine how closely Rodriguez's experiences conform to the model of "de-education" described by Steiner. In your opinion, are Rodriguez's experiences closer to the norm than the examples Steiner uses to support his argument?

9. Whose views, Steiner's or Rodriguez's, seem more persuasive on the issue of bilingualism? How do both authors' arguments depend on the assumption that language confers a sense of self and defines one's personal and cultural identity? Discuss these issues in an essay.

10. What is your attitude toward the specific issue of the public school's responsibility to provide bilingual education as part of its broader social mission of offering an appropriate education to everyone in a pluralistic society? If you are in favor of bilingualism on these grounds, how specifically do you think it should be put into action on a practical level?

11. For further research, you might consult the Bilingual Education Act of 1978, Title VII of P.L. 95-561, and the accompanying arguments in the Congressional Record as well as read any of the following books: Christina B. Paulston, *Bilingual Education: Theories and Issues* (1980); Peter A. Hornby, editor, *Bilingualism: Social and Psychological Implications* (1977); and Josue Gonzalez, *Towards Equality in Bilingual Education* (1976).

SEXUAL HARASSMENT

Karen Sauvigne

Sexual Harassment and the Need for Legal Remedies

Karen Sauvigne is the program director and cofounder of the Working Woman's Institute. Sauvigne identifies typical cases of sexual harassment on the job and asserts that only government legislation can end this form of discrimination. Her views are contained in "Sexual Harassment and the Need for Legal Remedies," from Statement Submitted to the Committee on Labor and Human Resources, United States Senate, Hearings on Sexual Discrimination in the Workplace, 97th Congress, 1st Session, April 21, 1981. *Sauvigne develops her case by arguing for a broader definition of sexual harassment in employment as "any attention of a sexual nature in the context of the work situation which has the effect of making a woman uncomfortable on the job, impeding her ability to do her work or interfering with her employment opportunities."*

The Dilemma of Sexual Harassment

Equal and fair treatment of women on the job is as important to 1 achieving equal opportunity as access to jobs and equal pay. . . .

Research conducted by, among others, Working Women's Institute, 2 New Responses, Inc., *Redbook* magazine and the Illinois Task Force on Sexual Harassment, show that sexual harassment affects between half and three-quarters of working women. Indeed the 1980 Merit Systems Protection Board survey of federal employees found that over 40% of women in the survey reporting having been sexually harassed *during the previous two years.*[1] We characterize sexual harassment as the most widespread problem women face in the workforce.

Let me share with you the statements of some of those facing sexual 3 harassment to illustrate the problem:

Item: I was very excited when I first started working in advertising sales. There weren't many women in this field and I knew I'd be making more money than I ever had before. But I was not prepared for the sexual trips that the men I had to sell to put me through. Several of them came right out and said I'd get the sale if I slept with them — others weren't so out in the open but their insistence on dates and dinner were just as hard to deal with. I tried for a long time — but I've decided to quit the business. My superiors expected me to handle it — but I can't any longer. Even though the money's out there these guys wouldn't give me a chance. It was a big joke for them.

Item: The boss' son was just assigned to my department and he thinks he's God's gift to women. No matter how many times I tell him to cut it out he keeps on pestering me. His suggestive stories, the arm around the shoulder, the hugs, are starting to drive me crazy and my work is suffering. I loved my job until this and God knows I need the job — but I don't know what to do. I feel trapped.

Item: My daughter came home in tears last night after her boss cornered her in the hallway and tried to take advantage of her. It's her first real job and this has really frightened and confused her. My first impulse was to kill him. My wife and I are really upset, we don't know how to protect her and still give her the freedom to develop her own career.

4   Sexual harassment in employment is any attention of a sexual nature in the context of the work situation which has the effect of making a woman uncomfortable on the job, impeding her ability to do her work or interfering with her employment opportunities. It can be manifested by looks, touches, jokes, innuendoes, gestures, epithets or direct propositions. At one extreme, it is the direct demand for sexual compliance coupled with the threat of firing if a woman refuses. At the other, it is being forced to work in an environment in which, through various means, such as sexual slurs and/or the public display of derogatory images of women, or the requirement that she dress in revealing clothing, a woman is subjected to stress or made to feel humiliated because of her sex. Sexual harassment is behavior which becomes coercive because it occurs in the employment context, thus threatening both a woman's job satisfaction and security. . . .

5   A brief glance at the position of women in the economic hierarchy will serve to explain women's vulnerability to sexual harassment on the job. Women are overwhelmingly employed in low status, low paying, dead-end jobs, primarily in the clerical (35% of all women workers) and service (19.6% of all women workers) areas.[2] Less than 3% of engineers, 5% of dentists, 11% of physicians, 13% of attorneys, 19% of scientists and, perhaps most important, 25% of all salaried managers, officials and administrators, are women.[3] In economic terms, women earn $.59 for every $1.00 earned by comparably employed men; and the gap between male and female earnings has not decreased since the passage of the Title VII in 1964.

Viewed in the context of the employment realities of women, it 6
would be hard to underestimate the far-reaching and pervasive impact
that sexual harassment has had on circumscribing their work options and
opportunities. Whether it takes place in the office or the factory, sexual
harassment is the assertion of power by men over women who are
perceived to be in a vulnerable position with respect to male authority.[4]
Being an assertion of power,[5] sexual harassment serves to reinforce in
women the notion that, if they value their psychological and physical
integrity, they must function within certain limits, both in terms of work
choices and personal behavior. . . .

An example of this syndrome can clearly be seen in the experiences of 7
women who have obtained work in the traditionally male dominated
trades. Female craft apprentices report experiencing a combination of
sexual advances, allusions, teasing, jokes, horseplay, crude comments,
such as explicit offers of sex for money, and even physical assaults from
their fellow workers. At the same time, they complain of minute scrutiny
of their work and a "chivalry" which is used to deny them the opportunity to participate in work assignments.[6]

Sexual harassment is most commonly understood as a direct proposi- 8
tion from a superior with firing the penalty for refusal. Termination is
not however the only penalty that is inflicted on women by sexual
harassment and their response to it. Others include: negative job evaluations: poor personnel recommendations; denial of overtime; demotions;
injurious or undesired transfers; reassignment to less desirable shifts,
hours or locations of work; loss of job training; and being subjected to
impossible performance standards.

The situation is just as serious when the harassment comes from 9
co-workers. Peers can exert tremendous power over a woman's ability to
remain on the job. They can sabotage work directly and indirectly. Even
absent such overt undermining efforts, they can render the work environment so tense and intolerable or even hostile as to force a woman to
leave the job.

Clients and customers are unfortunately also a frequent source of 10
sexual harassment. This is often caused by an explicit requirement by the
employer that a woman wear revealing clothing or that she acquiesce in
the permissive environment of the workplace. Harassment from this
quarter is similar in its impact to that from coworkers. The work environment becomes increasingly stressful and degrading, thus interfering with
a woman's job performance and often resulting in her departure from
the job.

Sexual harassment thus impedes women's equal employment oppor- 11
tunity in direct and indirect ways. Directly, by conditioning advancement
or continued employment on accepting explicit propositions for sexual
compliance. Indirectly, through either denying women work opportunities based on the belief that they are sexual objects and therefore not real
workers; or actively impeding them in the performance of their jobs

through noncooperation, sabotage or the creation of an anti-woman work environment.

12   The experience of sexual harassment on the job has had a substantial negative impact on women's ability to achieve economic equality. Sexual harassment contributes directly to their lack of job advancement by causing them to be fired, lose promotions and/or raises, or be forced into resigning. Crull's study, undertaken for the Institute, found that 24% of the women responding were fired as a result of refusing and/or complaining about the sexual harassment they had experienced. Another 42% eventually resigned from their jobs, either because they could not stop the harassment or because their complaints led to retaliation or other forms of work harassment, such as negative performance evaluations, excessive work loads and jeopardized promotions. . . .

13   Sexual harassment interferes with a woman's ability to perform her job even when it does not result in her departure from work. It effects a cumulative disadvantage on her as she must devote time and energy to handling advances, remarks and/or situations that could otherwise be expended on her work. Crull's study found that 83% of the respondents felt that sexual harassment had interfered in some way with their ability to do their work. Some suffered a loss of self-confidence because they had come to doubt their ability to handle themselves professionally and socially. Many began to dread going to work and lost their desire to be successful.[7] The end result for women who remain on the job is a double bind situation. The very people who they must work with, who teach them their jobs and evaluate their performance, are the people they must avoid.

14   Not surprisingly, women who are the victims of sexual harassment at work experience stress symptoms similar to those experienced by persons working under conditions more commonly understood to cause stress, such as poor lighting, speed-up and inadequate ventilation.[8] Psychologically, these include feelings of powerlessness, fear, anger, nervousness, decreased job satisfaction and diminished ambition. These were reported by 95% of the women in Crull's study. In the case of 12% of those respondents, these stress symptoms were so severe that therapeutic help was sought. Physical stress symptoms, including headaches, nausea and weight change, were experienced by 63% of these women.[9] . . .

Legal Remedies for Sexual Harassment

15   A comprehensive legal framework now exists for combating the various manifestations of sexual harassment on the job. The heart of this problem lies in Title VII of the Civil Rights Act of 1964 and the stance of the EEOC which is empowered to enforce the Act. The progress women have made in terms of securing legal redress for sexual harassment has

been remarkable. Until 1975 there was not even a name which women could use to refer to the experience of sexual harassment. By 1977 the first landmark decisions had come down, in the cases of *Barnes* v. *Costle*, 561 F. 2d 983 (D.C. Cir. 1977) and *Tomkins* v. *Public Service Electric & Gas Co.*, 568 F 2d. 1044 (3rd Cir. 1977), holding that sexual harassment was impermissible employment discrimination within the meaning of Title VII.

The legal protections now available to women fall into four distinct   16
categories: sexual harassment by supervisors and other higher echelon management personnel; sexual harassment by co-workers; sexual harassment by clients, customers and the general public; and sexually degrading work environments.

1. *Sexual Harassment by Supervisors.* An employer will be absolutely   17
liable for sexual harassment by supervisory personnel where continued employment or advancement is implicitly or explicitly conditioned on acquiescence to the supervisor's sexual demands. The liability exists irrespective of whether the employer had any knowledge of the harassment and indeed, irrespective of whether the supervisor's conduct violated explicit company policy. See: *Barnes* v. *Costle*, 561 F. 2d 983 (D.C. Cir. 1977); *Miller* v. *Bank of America*, 600 F. 2d 211 (9th Cir. 1979); EEOC guidelines on sexual harassment sec. 1604.11(c), codified at 29 C.F.R. 1604 11(c).

2. *Sexual Harassment by Co-workers.* The employer will be liable for   18
sexual harassment by co-workers which has a negative impact on a woman's terms and conditions of employment, in those situations where the employer knew or should have known of the conduct and failed to take timely and appropriate corrective action. See: *Continental Can* v. *State of Minnesota*, 22 FEP 1809 (Minn. 1980), EEOC guidelines on sexual harassment sec. 1604 11 (d), codified at 29 C.F.R. 1604.11(d).

3. *Sexual Harassment by Clients and Customers.* An employer may be   19
liable for sexual harassment by clients, customers or the general public where it has actual or constructive knowledge of the harassment and failed to take appropriate and timely corrective action. In a decision issued in January 1981 by the federal district court for the Southern District of New York, *EEOC* v. *Sage Realty*, 24 FEP 1521 (SONY 1981), an employer was found liable for sexual harassment by members of the general public which resulted from a requirement that the plaintiff wear a revealing uniform. While this area of the law is still developing it seems clear that the employer has a duty to take corrective steps when an employee complains of sexual harassment by clients, customers and other non-employees.

4. *Sexually Degrading Work Environment.* In a landmark decision,   20
Bundy v. *Jackson*, 24 FEP 1155 (D.C. Cir. 1981), the D.C. Circuit has ruled that Title VII is violated where sexual advances, remarks and other verbal and non-verbal conduct create a substantially discriminating work

environment, regardless of whether the complaining employee lost any tangible benefits as a result of the sexual harassment. This decision represents an extension to the area of sex discrimination of a line of cases holding that racial discrimination generates a psychologically harmful work atmosphere. See: *Rogers* v. *EEOC,* 454 F. 2d 234 (5th Cir. 1971); *Gray* v. *Greyhound Lines, East,* 545 F. 2d 169 (D.C. Cir. 1976). The parameters of what constitutes a sexually degrading work environment will, of course, be determined over a period of time, as the courts and the EEOC consider more of these cases. The decisions of the courts and the EEOC in the racial atmosphere cases provide some guidance as to the types of conduct that may be included. Thus, for example, in *United States* v. *City of Buffalo,* 457 F. Supp. 612, 632-35 (W.D.N.Y. 1978), the court cited the following conduct as contributing to a work environment heavily charged with racial discrimination: racially derogatory materials, such as a drawing of a hooded rider with the legend "KKK Lives," displayed in work areas; the wearing of "Wallace for President" buttons by on-duty white police officers; a picture of Martin Luther King and his family with the words "A bunch of niggers" written across it posted in the work area; and a picture of Dr. King with a hole cut in the head and a live bullet placed in it on public display in the precinct house. It is not difficult to imagine analogous conduct targeted at women employees.

21   The breadth of legal protections available to combat sexual harassment on the job is in no small measure due to the foresight and diligence of the EEOC. The Commission has indeed long been sensitive to the impact of sexual harassment in the employment context. It recognized early on that sexual harassment was a form of employment discrimination and not simply a personal problem between a woman and her male supervisor. In the guidelines on sexual harassment it published in November 1980 the Commission formalized its position and affirmed the trend in the federal courts to recognize sexual harassment as a form of sex discrimination in violation of Title VII. As the courts have done, the EEOC also extended that concept to include sexual harassment from co-workers and working environments polluted by sexual harassment; the Commission has thus been an important force in women's efforts to achieve equality of opportunity in the workforce.

22   Both the EEOC and the majority of appellate courts which have considered complaints of sexual harassment have handled these in the same way that other complaints of employment discrimination are handled, and have held the employer strictly liable for sexual harassment by supervisory employees. This position represents an appropriate application of general Title VII law and principles to instances of sexual harassment. Thus in cases involving more generally recognized types of discrimination courts have held the employer liable for discriminatory conduct by supervisors and managers even in instances where: the employer had no knowledge of the discrimination; there were company-wide anti-discrimination policies in effect; the supervisor did not have

the authority to fire; and the supervisor had misrepresented company policy. Even where the employer had an exemplary record in terms of its anti-discrimination efforts at upper levels of management, liability has been found for discriminatory conduct by a lower echelon supervisor. See: *Young* v. *Southwestern Savings and Loan Assc*, 509 F. 2d 140 (5th Cir. 1975); *Anderson* v. *Methodist Evangelical Hospital*, 464 F. 2d 723 (6th Cir. 1972); *Tidwell* v. *American Oil Co.*, 332 F. Supp. 424 (D. Utah 1971). In a fundamental sense, this approach to employer liability under Title VII constitutes a recognition that little if any progress will be made toward eradicating discrimination if the employer is able to hide behind a shield of individual employee action.

Unfortunately the trial courts have too often deviated from applying   23
standard Title VII law to sexual harassment cases. In particular they have added a more stringent burden by inappropriately requiring actual notice of the harassment to the employer before it will be held responsible for the conduct even of supervisors. The extremes to which the trial courts have gone is illustrated by a case from the District of Columbia, *Vinson* v. *Taylor*, 22 E.P.D. ¶30, 708 (D.D.C. 1980). The plaintiff, a bank teller, alleged two years of sexual harassment, including sexual innuendoes and remarks, as well as rape and 40 to 50 incidents of coerced intercourse, by her supervisor, the branch manager, who was also an assistant Vice President at the Bank. The defendant denied all the allegations and alleged that the suit was the result of a dispute as to who should be appointed head teller. Their stories could hardly have been more opposed. The court's response however, was not to attempt to establish what had happened so much as to absolve the Bank of any liability; it held that her failure to report the harassment to higher level management nullified any liability on the part of the Bank.

The result the court reached is utterly at variance with Title VII law,   24
which holds the employer liable for the discriminatory acts of supervisory personnel such as branch managers and vice presidents. It points up the underlying problem that not all courts understand that sexual harassment is *employment discrimination* and are therefore reluctant to hold the employer responsible for what is considered personal misconduct by the supervisor. What gets overlooked in this analysis is that the impact of this so-called personal conduct is on the woman's employment.

As our introductory comments establish, sexual harassment also has a   25
deleterious and discriminatory effect when it comes from co-workers, clients, customers and/or the general public, or when it creates a hostile, intimidating, or degrading work atmosphere. The EEOC correctly follows developing case law by holding the employer liable for these forms of harassment. Indeed it is the position of Working Women's Institute that employers — who have the capacity to prevent these forms of sexual harassment by taking appropriate care in selecting, training and establishing rules for its employees and in determining the work environment — should be held strictly liable for these forms of harassment. Because

sexual harassment is such a widespread, pervasive phenomenon and has received so much public attention in recent years, all employers should be on notice that sexual harassment is occurring within their workforce.

26   The solution to sexual harassment is not to amend Title VII to include sexual harassment or to specify new standards for liability. Sexual harassment is a form of sex discrimination, which is already prohibited by Title VII. It is not something which stands apart from all the other forms of employment discrimination, on its own. To amend the statute will only reinforce the misconception of those who do not acknowledge that it is sex discrimination. The appellate court decisions, the recent promulgation of the EEOC guidelines on sexual harassment, and these public hearings should serve to educate the judiciary to the real discriminatory impact of sexual harassment on the job.

Conclusion

27   Sexual harassment in the workplace will not disappear by itself, the attitudes that foster it are too ingrained and pervasive in our society. Employers must take responsibility. They must issue policy statements condemning sexual harassment in writing to every employee, post them in conspicuous places in the workplace, and add them to affirmative action plans and union contracts. There must be on-going training programs for all employees describing sexual harassment and making it clear that it will not be tolerated in any form. Employees and agents (especially where women are in non-traditional jobs) should be made aware of specific disciplinary methods that will be used for violators. Grievance procedures for reporting, investigating, and hearing claims of sexual harassment should be instituted and publicized.

28   Employers, thus, must respond, investigate, and act, when a worker complains of sexual harassment. This will allow the worker to efficiently do her job without the added pressure presented by sexual harassment. While employers cannot be responsible for their workers' attitudes, they can be held responsible for the employment consequences resulting from their workers' actions. Employers must train and sensitize their male employees to the problem of sex discrimination and harassment, particularly where women workers enter non-traditional jobs. Government policy should encourage such action by employers. Only when sexual harassment is no longer implicitly sanctioned by inaction and inattention can the work environment become tolerable and nondiscriminatory for all workers.

FOOTNOTES

1. Merit Systems Protection Board, *Summary of Preliminary Findings on Sexual Harassment in the Federal Workplace* (September 1980).

2. U.S. Dept. of Labor, Bureau of Labor Statistics, *Employment and Earnings* (May 1980).

3. U.S. Dept. of Labor, Bureau of Labor Statistics, *Employment and Earnings* (Jan. 1980).

4. This perception of vulnerability is indeed accurate. In a study undertaken for Working Women's Institute, Crull found that of 92 women who had contacted Working Women's Institute for assistance with a sexual harassment problem on the job: more than 75% were single, separated, divorced or widowed; over 50% were the sole support of their families and/or themselves; 51% of those working full-time earned $150, or less per week before taxes; 53% were clerical workers; and 15% were service workers. Crull, *The Impact of Sexual Harassment on the Job: A Profile of the Experiences of 92 Women*, Working Women's Institute, Research Series, Report No. 3 (1979), 2 (hereinafter referred to as Crull). This perception is shared by many Fair Employment Practices Agencies which responded to a 1977 Working Women's Institute survey. See *Responses of Fair Employment Practices Agencies to Sexual Harassment Complaints: A Report and Recommendations*, Working Women's Institute, Research Series, Report No. 2 (1978).

5. Erving Goffman has written that superiors can often be recognized by their exercising of familiarities toward a subordinate, which the subordinate is not allowed to reciprocate. Such familiarities include touching, teasing, informal demeanor, using familiar address and asking for personal information. Goffman, The Nature of Deference and Demeanor, *LVIII American Anthropologist* 473 (1956). Likewise Argyle concluded that power is communicated to another by bodily contact, physical proximity and position, gestures, posture, nodding or smiling, and silences or interruptions. Argyle, *Psychology of Interpersonal Behavior* (1957). See also Henley which applies these theories to interactions between women and men. Henley, *Body Politics: Power, Sex and Non-Verbal Communication* (1977).

6. Goodman, Sexual Demands on the Job, 4 Civ. Lib. Rev. 55-56 (1978).

7. Crull, *supra* at 4.

8. Stellman and Daum, *Work is Dangerous to Your Health* (1973).

9. Crull, *supra*, at 4.

Questions for Discussion and Writing

1. In what way does sexual harassment interfere with the rights women have on the job?

2. How high is the percentage of working women subjected to sexual harassment?

3. What connection does Sauvigne draw between the relative lack of power women have on the job and sexual harassment?

4. What types of legal protections are available to women because of the Civil Rights Act (CRA) of 1964 and the Equal Employment Opportunity Commission (EEOC)?

5. What range of stress symptoms are reportedly experienced by victims of sexual harassment?

6. What narrow conception of "sexual harassment" does Sauvigne's argument attempt to refute? In what way does Sauvigne's broader definition of sexual harassment shift attention from specific acts to the whole range of effects, both objective and psychological, that such harassment can have on female employees?

7. How does Sauvigne's definition of sexual harassment (para. 4) establish the groundwork for her argument that such harassment not only means a *quid pro quo* of continued employment for sexual compliance but also includes such aspects as whether a woman is treated as a "real worker" or is subjected to an "anti-woman work environment"?

8. How do Sauvigne's examples of actual cases support her contention that sexual harassment is coercive and discriminatory?

9. In your opinion, is it fair or unfair to hold employers legally responsible for subjective perceptions of sexual harassment? Keep in mind that Sauvigne defines sexual harassment in the workplace as "any attention of a sexual nature in the context of the work situation which has the *effect* [emphasis added] of making a woman uncomfortable on the job, impeding her ability to do her work or interfering with her employment opportunities." Explain your reasoning. If you agree with Sauvigne, where would you draw the line?

10. Why does Sauvigne emphasize the problems posed by sexual harassment before discussing the means already provided, under Title VII of the Civil Rights Act, for dealing with the problem?

11. For a research project, you might wish to consult MacKinnon, *Sexual Harassment of Working Women: A Case of Discrimination* (1979), and A. Sachs and J. H. Wilson, *Sexism and the Law* (1978). You might also discuss how this issue was treated in the film *Nine to Five* (1981).

Phyllis Schlafly

Government Intrusion in the Workplace

Phyllis Schlafly is a politically conservative activist, lawyer, and publisher of The Phyllis Schlafly Report. *Her views are contained in "Government Intrusion in the Workplace," from Statement Submitted to the Committee on Labor and Human Resources, United States Senate,* Hearings on Sexual Discrimination in the Workplace, 97th Congress, 1st Session, April 21, 1981. *Schlafly argues that government intervention in the workplace is inappropriate, unworkable, and ineffective, and will subvert the traditional roles of women in society.*

Non-criminal sexual harassment on the job is not a problem for the 1 virtuous woman except in the rarest of cases. When a woman walks across the room, she speaks with a universal body language that most men intuitively understand. Men hardly ever ask sexual favors of women from whom the certain answer is "no."

The former Prime Minister of Israel, Golda Meir, once spoke frankly 2 about the relationship of men and women. She spent a lifetime working alongside of men, but she said no man ever told a dirty story in her presence. My experience has been similar to hers. Virtuous women are seldom accosted by unwelcome sexual propositions or familiarities, obscene talk, or profane language. . . .

The biggest problem of sex in the workplace is not harassment at all 3 but simply the chemistry that naturally occurs when women and men are put in close proximity day after day, especially if the jobs have other tensions. That chemistry has always been present; what's different today is that (a) there are many more women in the workplace, and (b) some women have abandoned the Commandments against adultery and fornication, and accepted the new notions that any sexual activity in or out of marriage is morally and socially acceptable. . . .

Andrew Hacker, a professor at Queens College in New York City, in 4 an article in *Harper's* magazine in September 1980, wrote: "Now husbands are increasingly apt to have as colleagues high-powered younger women who understand their professional problems in ways a wife never can. These affinities can emerge as easily in a patrol car as in planning a marketing campaign. Shared work, particularly under pressure, has aphrodisiac effects."

Sexual harassment can be the mischievous label applied in hate or 5 revenge when one party wants out of an extra-marital liaison between consenting adults. Neither Congress nor EEOC has the competence to sit in judgment on the unwitnessed events and decide who was harassing whom.

6   Sexual harassment can also occur when a non-virtuous woman gives off body language which invites sexual advances, but she chooses to give her favors to Man A but not to Man B, and he tries to get his share, too. On the U.S. missile test ship, the *Norton Sound*, a male petty officer was convicted of sexually harassing seven female sailors under his command. They said they were intimidated when he caught them alone on night watch. He was convicted. Two of the women were pregnant by other men. Another female sailor was mysteriously lost overboard at night.

7   Senators and Congressmen should heed the oft-quoted prayer, "Lord, help me to change the things I can change, to accept the things I cannot change, and give me the wisdom to know the difference." Congress cannot prevent or police the sexual attraction men and women have for each other. But Congress can:

8   (a) Stop the government-induced inflation which forces more and more women to join the labor force even though so many of them would prefer to be in the home.

9   (b) Keep women out of places where they don't belong, such as on ships of the U.S. Navy, and in military academy dormitories, and in military barracks where there is nothing between sleeping servicemen and servicewomen except maybe a curtain.

10   (c) Stop the Affirmative Action for women which forces women into jobs where the predictable effect is sex on the job and broken marriages.

11   The EEOC regulations for dealing with sexual harassment are ridiculous and unjust. They are ridiculous because there is no way to police the situation fairly, and they are fundamentally unjust because they penalize an innocent bystander, the employer, for an employee's act over which he had no control. Furthermore, the EEOC regulations are discriminatory because, although they prohibit sexual harassment by a supervisor using the power of his job to get sex, they do not prohibit an employee using the power of her sex to get job favors or promotions from her supervisor.

12   These one-sided, discriminatory regulations are not only unjust to the employer, but they result in substantial discrimination against the virtuous woman. She doesn't have a sex problem, but she may have a job problem; she will end up being discriminated against because the job or raise or promotion may go the female who uses her sex to get ahead. Look, for example, at the case of the promiscuous female Naval Academy cadet who was caught sexually entertaining so many male Academy cadets. Such women create real problems of morals, morale, discipline, work efficiency, and discrimination against virtuous women.

13   Sexual harassment in private industry no doubt causes real problems in some cases, but there isn't a shred of evidence that Congress or the EEOC can solve the problems or can even be fair in trying to cope with

them. Until Congress itself learns how to deal with the Paula Parkinsons of this world, it is presumptuous of Congress to presume to sit in judgment on private employers and to penalize them for not solving all the sex problems of their employees. Both Congress and the EEOC are unjust in setting up procedures which enable unscrupulous persons to file mischievous claims in order to wring unjust settlements out of employers or to wreak revenge on a discarded lover. . . .

Feminist Harassment of Motherhood via Affirmative Action

The feminist movement is sexually harassing the role of motherhood 14 and dependent wives (homemakers) by Affirmative Action for women. Affirmative Action in favor of women is grievously unjust to everyone, but most especially to the dependent wife and mother in the home whose breadwinner-husband is denied a job, a raise or a promotion he deserves or has earned, which is given instead to a less qualified woman, perhaps even to one who is the second wage-earner in the family.

Affirmative Action is a system of reverse discrimination in which an 15 employer is required to set minimal qualifications for each job category, and then to hire by quota from the pool of persons who meet the minimal qualifications. This denies the employer the right to hire the most qualified person, and it often results in hiring or promoting the less qualified woman in preference to the more qualified man. (Quotas are disguised as "goals," "intermediate targets," "timetables," or "profiles," but, since they are statistically expressed, everyone knows they are quotas. The process of passing over the more qualified applicants in order to select one from the favored quota is known as "dipping.")

The supposed rationale for the forced hiring of women is fundamen- 16 tally unjust because (a) it punishes a man who committed no wrong, and (b) it rewards a woman who was never wronged. The woman receiving the benefit today is not the one discriminated against a generation ago. There is no more justification for giving women preferential job treatment today than there is for giving women two votes since, a half century ago, many women were denied the suffrage.

Even worse than the unjust discrimination against the male worker is 17 the resulting discrimination against his dependent wife in the home. That is sexual harassment of the role of motherhood and of the traditional family lifestyle. All over the country, I meet women who tell me, "My husband has been told not to expect a promotion for ten years because the government says all the promotions must go to women."

The net effect is to reduce further the income of the one-wage-earner 18 family, which is already making financial sacrifices to provide children with a mother in the home. The economic result is to degrade the father-provider role and to induce the mother to enter the work force herself in order to protect her family against the ravages of inflation. That is exactly what the feminist movement and its federal-government allies want anyway. . . .

19   Affirmative Action was dramatized by a woman who phoned in when I was a guest on a Chicago radio talk show. She had an Affirmative Action job in production in the steel industry in Gary, Indiana (probably as a result of the EEOC settlement forced on the steel industry which mandated the hiring of 20 percent women in production). She said, "I'm making $18,000; my husband is making only $17,000." Why did she call in? In order to say it's the job of the government to provide child-care for her new baby. This situation shows how Affirmative Action is an attack on the economic and social integrity of the family unit. Affirmative Action induced a mother to abandon caring for her own baby and to take a job she didn't need and physically couldn't do, and took a job away from a steelworker trying to provide for his family, and then created an artificial demand for the government to take care of babies. Have you ever been through a steel plant? If you have, you would know that it is ridiculous to force a steel company to hire women in preference to the thousands of qualified unemployed steel workers.

20   Affirmative Action for women is so anti-family, so grievously unjust, and so financially costly to any enterprise that it is amazing that an impertinent bureaucracy has been allowed to force it on employers. When employers are forbidden to hire the most qualified person, man or woman, no wonder we have a decline in national productivity!

21   Feminist leaders have been able to put over Affirmative Action for women by the psychological device of making men feel guilty because there are not 50 percent women in every high-level job category. The principal reason why there is a low percentage of women in top positions in the professional, business and academic fields is that 20, 30, and 40 years ago, most educated and capable young women (like myself, who then had two degrees) chose a career which we then believed—and still believe—is more fulfilling and more worthwhile, namely, the career of motherhood and the role of a dependent wife in a traditional family with a provider husband.

22   If a man has been honorable in his dealings with women, and if he has fulfilled a husband-father-provider role, there is absolutely no reason for him to feel guilty because he hasn't moved over and given his job to a woman. It is time to reassert the dignity and social good of the male provider role. As George Gilder has so aptly shown in his best-selling new book WEALTH AND POVERTY, the traditional family unit with the male provider and the mother in the home is the surest and most successful formula for the creation of wealth and prosperity.

23   In addition to the social injustice of Affirmative Action for women,

and in addition to its attack on the economic integrity of the traditional family, Affirmative Action for women constitutes direct harassment of the moral integrity of the family in some particular fields of work. This effect is seen in those jobs which require close working conditions, over long or late hours, or on long trips away from home. It is absolutely intolerable the way that the military, the courts, and the federal bureaucracy have capitulated to feminist demands and ordered the hiring of women in work situations where putting men and women together is likely to result in fornication, adultery, divorce, or illegitimate births. Such orders are based on the notion that we must close our eyes to the immoral consequences and push women into every nontraditional job, even if it destroys families. We totally reject this notion.

The adverse effect on the family structure should be reason enough 24
to keep women off the ships and submarines of the U.S. Navy (even if there were no other good reasons, which there are). Many wives of our servicemen have tried to voice their complaints against present military policies in this regard, but they have been laughed at by those who have ruthlessly implemented the feminist demands at any cost.

The volunteer women in the armed services today are running a 25
pregnancy rate of 15 percent. There are no figures on the fornication and adultery that do not result in pregnancy. When General W. C. Westmoreland, U.S. Army (Ret.), Commander of U.S. Forces in Vietnam and former Army Chief of Staff, testified before the House Armed Services Committee, Military Personnel Subcommittee, on November 14, 1979, he commented on the pregnancy rate and said: "Many of the babies are born out of wedlock. But that makes no difference with the current Administration. The mother continues as a soldier in good standing. She is not discharged as was the previous practice. I believe this is the first time that our nation has by its official policy sanctioned an immoral practice." These problems are the result of the irrational feminist demands for the elimination of "sex discrimination"; these problems did not exist when service-women were separated from the men in the WACS and the WAVES.

Similar concerns for the moral integrity of their families have been 26
expressed by the wives of policemen and firemen who are forced to work in close quarters with Affirmative Action women, and by the wives of salesmen and others who are compelled to travel with Affirmative Action women.

The *Washington Post* reported the following typical comments made 27
at a 1976 seminar attended by the police chiefs of America's largest cities: "After we put 11 women on the street, three of the four married women among them subsequently filed for divorce, and four of the men who had been teamed with women also started divorce proceedings. . . . Under the tremendous stress of police work, you learn to depend on your partner. You're there eight hours a night side-by-side. You have to get to know your partner. You translate that to male-female

and you get sex. . . . If you put two women together in a squad car, they fight. If you put male and female together from 8:00 p.m. to 4:00 a.m., they fornicate. . . . We broke up marriages by assigning officers to the vice squad, where the incidence of divorce is three times as high." Should women be assigned to nontraditional jobs via Affirmative Action without regard to the effect on the family? No, say many police chiefs, because "the basic law of Western civilization is to preserve the family."

Feminist Harassment of Motherhood via the "59¢ Fraud"

28   Another type of sexual harassment of the role of motherhood is the current slogan known as the "59¢ fraud." Over the past year, a deceitful propaganda campaign has been orchestrated by the feminist movement which is designed to convince the American people that, when women take a paying job, they receive only 59¢ for every dollar paid to a man doing the same work.

29   As it is used by the feminists, the 59¢ figure is a lie—and worse. It is part of the feminists' harassment of the role of motherhood. The 59¢ propaganda slogan is designed explicitly to eliminate the role of motherhood by changing us into a society in which women are harnessed into the labor force both fulltime and lifetime.

30   "Equal pay for equal work" is the law of our land today. It is positively required by the Equal Employment Opportunity Act of 1972 and by many other federal statutes and executive orders. The Equal Employment Opportunity Commission is its aggressive enforcement agency, and has wrung multi-million dollar settlements against the largest companies in our land, such as the $38 million settlement imposed on AT&T.

31   We support equal pay for equal work. In all my travels, I have never met anyone who opposes equal pay for equal work. It is the single most noncontroversial concept in the country today. So why, then, do the feminists keep talking about it? Because they want you to believe that it should mean something which it doesn't mean at all.

32   Equal pay for equal work does not mean that the nurse should be paid the same as the doctor, or that the secretary should be paid the same as her boss—even if she works just as hard and thinks she is just as smart. Equal pay for equal work does not mean that the woman who has been on the job two years must be paid the same as a man who has been in his job for 30 years. Nor does it mean that a secretary must be paid the same as a plumber even if she has spent more years in school, or that the woman who works in an office or at a store counter must be paid equally with the man who works in a mine or in construction work.

33   Equal pay for equal work means that the man and woman must be paid equally if they are doing the same job for the same number of hours

with the same experience in the same type of industry in the same part of the country. That is the law today, and it has been very aggressively enforced by the Equal Employment Opportunity Commission.

The people who are carrying on the campaign to perpetrate the "59¢ fraud" obviously are not talking about violations of the Equal Employment Opportunity Act. They offer no suggestions for changing it. So where did they get the 59¢ figure?   34

The 59¢ figure is the average wage paid to all women as compared to the average wage paid to all men. That comparison doesn't prove anything at all about sex discrimination or the fairness with which anyone is paid on any job.   35

We certainly don't want a society in which the *average* wage paid to *all* women equals the *average* wage paid to *all* men because that would be a society which would have eliminated the role of motherhood. The career of motherhood is not recorded or compensated in cash wages in government statistics, but that doesn't make it any less valuable. It is the most socially useful role of all. We don't even want a society in which the average wage paid to all *working* women equals the average wage paid to all working men, because that would be a society in which working wives and mothers would be working in paid employment all their lives for as many hours a week as men. Most wives do not do this now, and they don't want to do it. By working fewer hours in the paid labor force, wives and mothers can give more time to their families and to the role of motherhood.   36

We want a society in which the average man earns more than the average woman so that his earnings can fulfill his provider role in providing a home and support for his wife who is nurturing and mothering their children. We certainly don't want feminist pressure groups to change public policy in order to force us into a society in which all women are locked into the work force on a lifetime basis, because that would mean forfeiting their precious years and hours as a mother.   37

Equal pay for equal work between a man and woman in any particular job is the law, and we support it. But when we *average* the wages of *all* women and compare them to the *average* wages of *all* men, the pay cannot and should not be equal because the work is not equal. The reasons why the average man earns more pay than the average woman are that he works longer hours, works more years on the same job, has more experience and education, and does harder or more dangerous work than the average woman. Therefore, it is only right and just that he earn more. Here are a few examples of why that pay differential exists: 38

1. The average man has far more work experience and far more seniority on his present job. The average woman has been in her present job only half as long as the average man. The average woman has more career interruptions; she is eleven times more likely to leave her job than the average man.   39

2. The average woman does not work as many hours per week as the   40

average man. Most wives do not work fulltime in paid employment, even if the statistics call it "fulltime," that does not mean 40 hours a week 12 months a year. Many women prefer and take part-time jobs. The new concept called "job sharing" is proving very attractive to wives compelled to enter the labor force. Many more men than women work overtime hours for premium pay; most women refuse overtime work if they can and resent it very much when they are "forced over" (the factory term for involuntary overtime).

41   3. Included in the figures for the average man are millions of men who do dangerous, heavy, he-man jobs which women cannot do, and for which women are unsuited and wouldn't take if they were offered three times the pay. These include such jobs as miners, steel and iron workers, high line electricians, lumberjacks, salvage divers, concrete finishers, millwrights, high explosive handlers, roofers, jack hammer operators, steeple jacks, tree trimmers, longshoremen, movers, and railroad and truck crews. The men in such jobs can and do receive good pay, and they deserve it. Attached to my testimony is an article from the *Wall Street Journal* of April 14, 1981, describing the job of an Arctic driller— and that certainly is a he-man job. It is absolutely unjust to think that the average woman should receive equal pay for the cleaner, safer, less demanding, less dangerous jobs that women prefer.

42   4. The *average* woman (not all women, of course) voluntarily declines the added responsibility, the long hours, and the lifetime commitment required for the high paying positions in the professional and business world. Here are some examples:

43   (a) The *Wall Street Journal* reported on March 18, 1981 that the differential in the earnings of male and female physicians is explained by the facts that [a] the average woman doctor sees 40 fewer patients per week than the average male doctor, and [b] the women choose the lower-earning specialties such as pediatrics and psychiatry over the more lucrative fields such as surgery which are chosen by men.

44   (b) Crain's *Chicago Business* of October 13, 1981, reported an interview with a woman who heads an executive search firm. She has found that "more women are starting to turn down job offers . . . because they refuse to make the same kind of commitment to their careers that a typical male executive would make." She gave many specific examples from her firm's experience of women who passed up good promotions because they were not willing to make the personal and family sacrifices needed to move up the corporate ladder.

45   (c) In colleges and universities, many women faculty members limit the number of hours they will teach and refuse to handle the other activities and counseling, all of which may add up to half the duties of a male professor.

46   (d) Women come out of law schools with high grades, but many are unwilling to work the long hours, the nights and weekends, which are

the typical life of a young male lawyer trying to build his career and become a partner.

(e) Wives will customarily decline a position that requires a move to 47
another city, and wives will customarily resign a position in order to accompany a husband's career move to another city. This is because keeping the family together is more important to most wives than career advancement.

The average man today has more years of education and more educa- 48
tion in more highly-paid specialties. That is why comparisons are irrelevant between young men and women today even if they have the same number of years of higher education. My daughter graduated from Princeton with honors in economics; my son graduated from Princeton with honors in electrical engineering. In the statistics, they will be reported as having the same number of years in college, but the differential between the starting salaries of those two specialties is about $8,000 per year. That is not sex discrimination, but the marketplace's recognition of the fact that electrical engineers have taken a more difficult academic course and are more in demand in our society today. Nobody discriminated against my daughter, she chose not to take engineering. . . .

Congress should reject all legislative proposals which harass, disad- 49
vantage, or discourage the role of motherhood and its essential complement, the role of male provider. Congress should reject all proposals which include financial inducements to wives to enter the labor force, or to mothers to assign care of their children to institutions.

Congress should not allow itself to become the conduit for feminist 50
harassment of those who believe in the role of motherhood, which is what this Committee has been doing for years in giving exclusive forums to the feminists to carry on their ideological and political campaign against the traditional sex roles freely chosen by the overwhelming majority of the American people.

Because the social problems resulting from the breakdown of family 51
life are of such tremendous concern today, and because the future of our nation depends on the next generation, we are asking the Congress to evaluate all proposed and recent legislation on this criterion: Is it an incentive or a disincentive to the role of motherhood? If it contains any disincentive to mothers caring for their own children, we must use our ingenuity to search for other ways to solve the problems.

However, one final comment must be added. The biggest single 52
assault on the role of motherhood today, as well as on the family unit, is government-caused inflation. The best thing you can do for mothers, fathers, singles, and children, is to cut taxes, cut spending, and let the great American private enterprise economy create the jobs and solve the problems which government is inherently incapable of solving.

Questions for Discussion and Writing

1. To what extent is Schlafly's claim that every woman who is sexually harassed gives off cues of body language that invite such sexual advances a form of blaming the victim?

2. What point is Schlafly trying to make about the need to distinguish between personal and work-related "harassment" when she says "neither Congress nor EEOC has the competence to sit in judgment on the unwitnessed events and decide who was harassing whom"?

3. Why does Schlafly blame the feminist movement and Affirmative Action for undermining the role of motherhood and "the traditional family life style"?

4. What reasons does Schlafly give to support her assertion that "it is only right and just that he [the average man] earn more" than the average woman?

5. Why is Schlafly against the passage of laws to counter the effects of sexual harassment?

6. How does Schlafly define "non-criminal sexual harassment" so as to make the woman to whom it happens responsible for provoking it? Evaluate her scenario that women give off sexual cues to attract the attention of one particular man but then, when they receive the unwanted attentions of many men, they press charges.

7. To what extent does Schlafly's characterization of the effects of Affirmative Action assume as true what her argument should exist to prove — that is, how does she beg the question or use circular reasoning?

8. Evaluate Schlafly's argument that the main reason that such a low percentage of women occupy professional positions is not due to employment discrimination but is rather the result of women choosing a career of motherhood.

9. How does Schlafly redefine sexual harassment so that the feminist movement and Affirmative Action are held accountable for societal discrimination against homemakers and dependent mothers?

10. In what way is Schlafly's reference to the female sailor who was "mysteriously lost overboard at night" a red herring? How does Schlafly use this incident to suggest, somewhat obliquely, that sexual misconduct is increasingly characteristic of the relationships between men and women in the navy?

11. Where, and for what purpose, in Schlafly's argument does she use emotionally loaded language such as "unscrupulous" or "mischievous" to attempt to manipulate her audience?

12. How does Schlafly strengthen her case by using examples (Golda Meir, steel workers, and so on) that might at first glance seem atypical? Would her argument lose its force if she used more commonplace examples?

13. How does the way in which Schlafly presents herself add to or detract from her argument?

14. Compare and contrast the attitudes of Sauvigne and Schlafly toward government intervention in the workplace to prevent sexual harassment. In your opinion, should the government actually get involved in trying to determine whether a given incident of sexual harassment was personal or work related? In essence, whose characterization and recommendations do you agree with, those of Schlafly or those of Sauvigne? Explain your reasons.

15. Discuss how Sauvigne and Schlafly both refer to the "59¢" earned by women for every dollar earned by men but interpret this figure in entirely different ways.

16. Discuss why Sauvigne and Schlafly differ on the issue of whether employers are to be held responsible in cases where they had no knowledge of any acts of sexual harassment.

UNANIMOUS JURIES

Charles Sevilla

The Case of the Non-Unanimous Jury

---

*Charles Sevilla's "The Case of the Non-Unanimous Jury" first ap-
peared in* The Los Angeles Times *(January 23, 1983). A former chief
deputy public defender for the state of California, Sevilla is now a trial
lawyer practicing in San Diego. Sevilla cites statistics to show that the
number of cases reaching trial that result in hung juries is so small
that it does not warrant losing the benefits of the unanimous verdict.
He also sketches out a "worst case scenario" if proposed reforms to
change the system were to go into effect.*

1   One of Henry Fonda's most memorable roles was as one of *Twelve
Angry Men* selected to determine the fate of a young Puerto Rican
accused of murdering his father. They were angry because the majority's
quest for a speedy verdict of guilty was frustrated by Fonda's lone vote
for acquittal. Without unanimity, a verdict could not be returned, and the
other jurors, anxious to get home to dinner or out to a ballgame, were
furious.

2   In real life, the lone dissenting juror on a first ballot almost always
succumbs to the pressure and joins ranks to return a verdict. Fonda's
character was different. He convinced the others to pause long enough to
discuss the evidence and hear him out. After all, he said, the defendant, a
slum youth, had been ignored most of his life. The jury owed him some
time for a just verdict.

3   In the next 90 tension-filled minutes Fonda argued the importance of
subtle points of testimony that the others had missed; he proved that the
murder weapon, a knife, was not as distinctive as the prosecutor had
insisted; he pointed out lapses in the defense attorney's presentation, all
the while importuning the others to reach a verdict through reason rather
than emotion. One by one, the others came around to join him, the last
capitulating only when his underlying motivation was revealed—the
defendant reminded him of his wayward son.

4   Hollywood melodrama though it was, the film's depiction of a jury
struggling to do its duty is a rare illustration of unanimity's function in
the difficult job of jury decisionmaking.

5   Perhaps nothing epitomizes the concept of American liberty as well

as the right to a trial by a jury. The jury is one of a handful of institutions that allow individual citizens, not government, to make important societal decisions. A crucial component of the jury trial is the rule that verdicts be unanimous. It has always been the rule in federal criminal trials, in the overwhelming majority of states.

Critics of the right to a unanimous verdict in serious criminal cases 6 see it as a costly medieval relic. Los Angeles new district attorney, Robert Philobosian, is the latest to join the chorus. He wants the verdict requirement shrunk from 12 jurors to 10 (in all but capital cases) so that one or two people will not be able to force a retrial.

Hung Juries

The costs of hung juries do not warrant losing the benefits of the 7 unanimous verdict. Statistically, jury trials play a minor role in the criminal-justice system. The vast majority of defendants plead guilty and have no trial. In 1981, only about 7 percent of accused felons had jury trials. The incidence of hung juries is thus but a fraction of the already small fraction of cases that go to trial.

Some money undoubtedly could be saved by such a reform. Even 8 more could be saved by abolishing jury trials altogether.

That juries occasionally are deadlocked does not demonstrate a flaw 9 in our criminal-justice system. Our concept of justice does not require juries to decide every case. Hung juries usually occur when the case is close—that is, when neither side has presented convincing evidence. Further, juries that wind up deadlocked with one or two members in dissent usually start with a more substantial minority of four or five which indicates that the evidence is not clear-cut.

Even though the requirement of unanimity may lead to an inconclu- 10 sive result from time to time, no verdict is better than a wrong one. Despite the protection of unanimous verdicts, we still manage to convict some innocent people each year. Eliminating the unanimity requirement would only increase the opportunity for mistakes. Unanimity guarantees give-and-take among jurors and filters out the biases of individuals. It makes the ultimate decision truly reflective of the community. Most important, it provides a better chance that the result will be correct by affording a counterbalance to the state's inherent advantages, such as the jurors' subconscious presumption that a defendant who is on trial must be guilty.

Consider what would have happened if the decision in *Twelve Angry* 11 *Men* could have been made by 10 jurors instead of 12. After the first ballot, the 11 who voted "guilty" could have put an end to the deliberations, without having to listen to Fonda.

What could be more fundamental to justice than verdicts that can be 12 trusted and respected? If even one juror has doubts, that is enough to undermine society's confidence that a proper verdict has been reached.

Questions for Discussion and Writing

1. Evaluate Sevilla's use of the classic film *Twelve Angry Men* to illustrate his thesis that "the jury is one of a handful of institutions that allow individual citizens, not government, to make important societal decisions. A crucial component of the jury trial is the rule that verdicts be unanimous." In what way does the action depicted in the film underscore the central point of Sevilla's argument? How does Sevilla's use of a worst case scenario, in the next to the last paragraph, dramatize what he fears might happen if proposed reforms were enacted?

2. Against what specific proposal is Sevilla arguing, and how would it change the present system?

3. What role does Sevilla's introduction of statistical evidence concerning the percentage of hung juries play in the overall development of his argument? How does this portion of his argument depend on the tactic of extending the opposition's stance to an extreme in order to refute it (reductio ad absurdum)?

4. What reasons does Sevilla present to support his assertion that because "juries occasionally are deadlocked does not demonstrate a flaw in our criminal-justice system"?

5. In an essay, discuss the validity of an important assumption underlying Sevilla's argument: keeping the existing system, which requires all twelve members of the jury to agree on a verdict, is superior to adopting a system that would allow a verdict to be reached if only ten of the twelve jurors agreed because, under the present system, jurors must publicly discuss and justify their decisions and, in the process, reveal latent personal motivations that might otherwise remain hidden. Points to consider in your evaluation include (*a*) whether the current system provides a better chance for a just result by offering lone dissenters the opportunity to argue subtle points in testimony that other jurors may have missed, (*b*) whether the doubt of even one juror should be enough to raise questions as to whether a proper verdict has been reached, and (*c*) whether the current requirement for a unanimous verdict encourages dissenting members of the jury to support their opinions, reveal their feelings, and disclose any possible biases or prejudices that may have influenced their reasoning in some way. If the obligation for dissenting jurors to justify their decisions was removed, would the system of justice be shortchanged as Sevilla claims?

Robert E. Jones

Justice Can Be Served Despite Dissenting Votes

Robert E. Jones has served as a criminal-felony trial judge on the Oregon Supreme Court for over twenty years. "Justice Can Be Served Despite Dissenting Votes" first appeared in The Los Angeles Times *(January 23, 1983). Jones uses inductive reasoning based on his extensive experience as a trial judge and on a series of mock trials to argue that the present jury system ought to be changed to allow for nonunanimous verdicts if ten out of the twelve jurors agree on a verdict.*

After sitting for 20 years as a criminal-felony trial judge in Oregon, where jurors in all but first-degree murder cases are allowed to return a verdict if 10 out of 12 agree, I believe that such a system delivers fair, if not perfect justice to both the state and the defendant. In my experience, no one who was convicted by a nonunanimous jury later was shown to have been innocent. 1

While unanimous verdicts are still required in federal trials, the U.S. Supreme Court ruled in 1972 that the Constitution does not require them in state trials. 2

Those who are opposed to allowing nonunanimous verdicts in criminal trials base their arguments on several assumptions: that the views of the minority will be given less consideration and that there will be less opportunity for persuasion: that jurors will be less inclined to engage in "earnest and robust argument" to quote the late U.S. Supreme Court Justice William O. Douglas; that there will be a less thorough examination of the facts; that jurors will not be as likely to review as much of the testimony or adhere as carefully to the judge's instructions and that the deliberations will be shorter, thereby making it easier to jump to conclusions. 3

Unfortunately for those who make such arguments, there is no scientific evidence to support those claims. 4

Many people cite the example of *Twelve Angry Men*, in which Henry Fonda played a holdout juror who managed to bring around 11 bigoted or misguided jurors to a verdict for the defense. I doubt that this occurs very often in real life, but stranger things have happened. 5

The main argument for nonunanimous verdicts is that no matter how carefully the jury is picked, a trial in which a unanimous verdict is required may be aborted by one or two kook jurors whose irrationality 6 does not blossom until after the jury is locked up for deliberations. I think this is a pretty convincing claim.

7   You have to wonder about the mentality or motives of certain jurors when you see cases, usually involving hardened criminals, in which the prosecution's witnesses remain unimpeached, the defense offers nothing and still the jury returns a guilty verdict of 11-1 or 10-2.

Experiment

8   In 1976, Alice Padawer-Singer and Allen Barton of Columbia University's Bureau of Applied Social Research set up an experiment with actual jurors participating in mock trials under different rules in order to compare unanimous and nonunanimous verdicts. The 23 12-member juries that were required to reach unanimous decisions returned 10 not-guilty and eight guilty verdicts with five winding up deadlocked. Of the 23 panels that were not required to reach unanimity, nine returned not guilty verdicts, nine guilty and five deadlocked. The average deliberation time for reaching a verdict was 178 minutes for the unanimous juries and 160 minutes for the nonunanimous.

9   From a statistical standpoint the differences between the two groups were insignificant. In short, the study did not prove that one system was better than the other. They were indistinguishable.

10   Last year I took a random sample of 164 felony cases tried before 12-person nonunanimous juries in Portland and found that 155 had resulted in verdicts—128 convictions and 27 acquittals. Of the convictions, 52 were unanimous, 35 were reached on a vote of 11-1 and 41 were 10-2. Of the acquittals, 9 were unanimous and 18 were split. Of those 18, seven were 11-1 and 11 were 10-2. Nine juries were deadlocked.

11   Chief Justice James Burns of the U.S. District Court in Oregon has had the rare opportunity to view both verdict systems in operation, first on our state court and then for the last decade on the federal trial court where unanimous verdicts are required. When I asked him to compare the two, his conclusion surprised me.

12   "I don't think it makes a bit of difference," he said. "A good or bad case will be spotted by either type of jury. The only difference seems to be that unanimous juries deliberate several minutes or sometimes several hours longer." He said that hung juries were rare—occurring only in about one out of 200 trials—something I have also observed in the Oregon state courts.

13   In sum, I believe that nonunanimous jury verdicts have no harmful consequences for our criminal-justice system. And, since such verdicts speed the jury-selection process and protect the system from irrational jurors, they provide a model that other states should follow.

Questions for Discussion and Writing

1. Initially, how does Jones draw upon his personal experience "as a criminal-felony trial judge" to support his thesis that nonunanimous jury verdicts are not incompatible with justice?

2. Evaluate Jones's summary of the opposition's viewpoint by comparing it with reasons Sevilla presents to support his thesis. Is it a fair restatement of Sevilla's argument and its underlying assumptions?

3. Discuss Jones's claim that "the main argument for nonunanimous verdicts is that no matter how carefully the jury is picked, a trial in which a unanimous verdict is required may be aborted by one or two kook jurors whose irrationality does not blossom until after the jury is locked up for deliberations." Where in his article does Jones present evidence of the number of times this situation has occurred (resulting in hung juries), either in his personal experience or in mock trials set up to compare unanimous versus nonunanimous jury verdicts.

4. Jones describes an experiment conducted by Alice Padawer-Singer and Allen Barton. What were the results of this experiment and how does Jones use them to support his thesis? Evaluate the design of this experiment and discuss whether or not it was constructed to test for the occasional irrational kook juror.

5. To what extent does Jones's argument depend on assertions and evidence that deadlocked juries occur with much greater frequency than Sevilla says they do? Cite the relevant passages from both articles in your answer.

6. What function does Jones's use of the testimony of Chief Justice James Burns have in supporting Jones's argument?

7. If you were a defendant on trial for murder, or another capital crime, which jury system would you want to decide upon your guilt or innocence (one requiring the unanimous consent of twelve jurors or one in which a guilty verdict could be returned by ten or eleven jurors)? Discuss your reasons in an essay, citing relevant arguments from either or both Sevilla's and Jones's articles.

ANIMAL EXPERIMENTATION

Peter Singer

Is Animal Experimentation Harming Society?

*The following essay, "Is Animal Experimentation Harming Society?"
was taken from Peter Singer's* Animal Liberation: A New Ethics for
Our Treatment of Animals *(1975). He is the director of the Monash
Center for Human Bio-Ethics and teaches in the department of philosophy at Monash University, Australia. Singer provides examples to
dramatize his claim that experimentation involving animals is unnecessary and should be stopped. He cites the thalidomide case and a host
of other specific examples to argue that much of animal experimentation is cruel, produces no clear benefit for humanity, and is inexcus-
able when alternative methodologies for obtaining knowledge via
tissue and cell cultures are now available.*

1   In July 1973 Congressman Les Aspin of Wisconsin learned through
an advertisement in an obscure newspaper that the United States Air
Force was planning to purchase 200 beagle puppies, with vocal chords
tied to prevent normal barking, for tests of poisonous gases. Shortly
afterward it became known that the army was also proposing to use
beagles — 400 this time — in similar tests.

2   Aspin began a vigorous protest, supported by antivivisection societies. Advertisements were placed in major newspapers across the country. Letters from an outraged public began pouring in. An aide from the
House of Representatives Armed Services Committee said that the committee received more mail on the beagles than it had received on any
other subject since Truman sacked General MacArthur, while an internal
Department of Defense memo released by Aspin said that the volume of
mail the department had received was the greatest ever for any single
event, surpassing even the mail on the bombings of North Vietnam and
Cambodia.[1] After defending the experiments initially, the Defense Department then announced that it was postponing them, and looking into
the possibility of replacing the beagles with other experimental animals.

3   All this amounted to a rather curious incident, curious because the
public furor over this particular experiment implied a remarkable igno-

rance of the nature of quite standard experiments performed by the armed services, research establishments, universities, and commercial firms of many different kinds. True, the proposed air force and army experiments were designed so that many animals would suffer and die without any certainty that this suffering and death would save a single human life, or benefit humans in any way at all; but the same can be said for tens of thousands of other experiments performed in the United States alone each year. For instance, limiting ourselves for the moment just to experiments done on beagles, the following should, one might think, have provoked as much protest as those planned by the air force and the army:

At the Lovelace Foundation, Albuquerque, New Mexico, experi- 4
menters forced sixty-four beagles to inhale radioactive strontium 90 as part of a larger "Fission Product Inhalation Program" which began in 1961 and has been paid for by the US Atomic Energy Commission. In this particular experiment twenty-five of the dogs eventually died. One of the deaths occurred during an epileptic seizure; another from a brain hemorrhage. Other dogs, before death, became feverish and anemic, lost their appetites, had hemorrhages and bloody diarrhea.

The experiments, in their published report, compared their results 5
with the results of other experiments at the University of Utah and at Argonne National Laboratory, in Illinois, in which beagles were injected with strontium 90. They concluded that the various experiments had led to similar results on the dose of strontium 90 needed to produce "early deaths" in 50 percent of a sample group of beagles, but that there was a difference in the number of deaths occurring later, because dogs injected with strontium 90 retain more of the radioactive substance than dogs forced to inhale it.[2]

At the University of Rochester School of Medicine a team of experi- 6
menters placed fifty beagles in wooden boxes and irradiated them with different levels of radiation by X-rays. Twenty-one of the dogs died between the ninth and thirty-ninth day after irradiation. The experimenters determined the dose at which 50 percent of the animals will die with "95 percent confidence." The irradiated dogs vomited, had diarrhea, and lost their appetites. Later they hemorrhaged from the mouth and the anus. In their report these experimenters summarized nine other experiments in which more than 700 beagles and other dogs were irradiated with X-rays, and they said that the injuries produced in their own experiments were "typical of those described for the dog."[3]

Experimenters working for the US Food and Drug Administration 7
gave thirty beagles and thirty pigs large amounts of methoxychlor (a pesticide) in their food, seven days a week for six months, "in order to ensure tissue damage." Within eight weeks, eleven dogs showed signs of "abnormal behavior" including nervousness, salivation, muscle tremors, spasms, and convulsions. Dogs in convulsions breathed as rapidly as 200 times a minute before lack of oxygen caused them to collapse. Upon

recovery from an episode of convulsion and collapse, the dogs were uncoordinated, apparently blind, and "any stimulus such as dropping a feed pan, squirting water, or touching the animals initiated another convulsion." After further experiments on an additional twenty beagles, the experimenters concluded that massive daily doses of methoxychlor produce different effects in dogs from those produced in pigs.[4]

8   These three examples should be enough to show that the air force beagle experiments were in no way exceptional. Note that all of these experiments, according to the experimenters' own reports, obviously caused the animals to suffer considerably before dying. No steps were taken to prevent this suffering, even when it was clear that the radiation or poison had made the animals extremely sick. Note, too, that these experiments are parts of series of similar experiments, repeated with only minor variations, that are being carried out all over the country. Note, finally, that these experiments do not save human lives. We already knew that strontium 90 was unhealthy before the beagles died; and the experimenters who poisoned dogs and pigs with methoxychlor knew beforehand that the large amounts they were feeding the animals (amounts no human would ever consume) would cause damage. In any case, as the differing results they obtained on dogs and pigs make clear, it is not possible to reach any firm conclusions about the effects of a substance on humans from tests on other species. The same is true of radioactive substances, and so the precision with which experimenters determine the dose necessary to make 50 percent of a sample group of beagles die has no application to humans.

9   Nor should we limit ourselves to dogs. People tend to care about dogs because they have dogs as pets; but other animals are as capable of suffering as dogs are. Dogs are only one species of many that are used in experiments. In Britain sentimental attachment to dogs and cats has gone so far that the law regulating experiments on animals requires an experimenter to obtain a special certificate for performing an experiment on unanesthetized dogs and cats; apes and monkeys, however, receive no such protection; nor, of course, does the common laboratory rat. Few people feel sympathy for rats. Yet the laboratory rat is an intelligent, gentle animal, the result of many generations of special breeding, and there can be no doubt that the rats are capable of suffering, and do suffer from the countless painful experiments performed on them.

10   The practice of experimenting on nonhuman animals as it exists today throughout the world reveals the brutal consequences of speciesism. Experiments are performed on animals that inflict severe pain without the remotest prospect of significant benefits for humans or any other animals. These are not isolated instances, but part of a major industry. In Britain, where experimenters are required to report the number of experiments performed, official government figures show that around 5 million experiments on animals are now performed each

year. In the United States there are no figures of comparable accuracy. . . .

An official of the US Department of Agriculture has stated that the number of rats and mice used annually for research purposes is estimated at 40 million.[5] In testimony before congressional committees in 1966, the Laboratory Animal Breeders Association estimated that the number of mice, rats, guinea pigs, hamsters, and rabbits used for experimental purposes in 1965 had totaled around 60 million; and they projected a figure of 97 million for these species by 1970. They estimated the number of dogs and cats used in 1965 as between 500,000 and 1 million.[6] A 1971 survey carried out by Rutgers University College of Agriculture and Environmental Sciences produced the following estimates of the number of animals used each year in U.S. laboratories: 85,000 primates, 500,000 dogs, 200,000 cats, 700,000 rabbits, 46,000 pigs, 23,000 sheep, 1.7 million birds, 45 million rodents, 15–20 million frogs, and 200,000 turtles, snakes, and lizards; a total of more than 63 million animals.[7]

These estimates are somewhat lower than the Laboratory Animal Breeders Association estimates for the species included in their survey for 1965; and much lower than their projections for 1970. These projections may, of course, have been over-optimistic expectations about the continued growth of the animal breeding industry, which had grown phenomenally in preceding years. Assuming then that the Rutgers University figures are a reasonable, and certainly not exaggerated, estimate, it is still clear that the official Animal Welfare Act report covers only a very small fraction of the animals experimented upon in the United States.

Of this vast number of experiments, only a few contribute to important medical research. Huge numbers of animals are used in university departments from Forestry to Psychology, and many more are used for commercial purposes, to test new cosmetics, shampoos, food coloring agents and other inessential items. All this can go on only because of our prejudice against taking seriously the suffering of a being that is not a member of our own species. The typical defender of experiments on animals does not deny that animals suffer. He cannot use this argument because he needs to stress the similarities between humans and other animals in order to claim that his experiment may have some relevance for human purposes. The researcher who forces rats to choose between starvation and electric shock to see if they develop ulcers (they do) does so because he knows that the rat has a nervous system very similar to man's, and presumably feels an electric shock in a similar way.

There has been opposition to experimenting on animals for a long time. This opposition has made little headway because experimenters, backed by commercial firms who profit by supplying laboratory animals and equipment, have been able to convince legislators and the public that opposition comes from sentimental cranks who consider the interests of animals more important than the interests of human beings. But to be opposed to what is going on now it is not necessary to insist that all experiments stop immediately. All that we need to say is that experiments serving no direct and urgent purpose should stop immediately, and in the remaining areas of research, methods involving animals should be replaced as soon as possible by alternative methods not involving animals. . . .

15   In Britain almost 100 new cosmetics and toiletries come onto the market every week, and it has been estimated that up to a million animals die annually in research connected with cosmetics alone.[8] The figure for the United States is not known, but could well be much higher. To this must be added the enormous numbers of animals used to test inessential foodstuffs—new coloring agents, new sweeteners or other flavoring agents, new preservatives, and so on. Any company that wants permission to market such a new substance must lodge with the Food and Drug Administration evidence of the product's safety. This evidence consists of a thick file full of reports of the experimental poisoning of animals.

16   It is not only products intended for consumption that are tested. All kinds of industrial and household goods are fed to animals and tested on their eyes. A reference book, *Clinical Toxicology of Commercial Products*, provides data, mostly from animal experiments, on how poisonous hundreds of commercial products are. The products include: insecticides, antifreeze, brake fluids, bleaches, Christmastree sprays, church candles, oven-cleaners, deodorants, skin fresheners, bubble baths, depilatories, eye make-up, fire extinguishers, inks, suntan oils, nail polish, mascara, hair sprays, paints, and zipper lubricants.[9]

17   Whenever the testing on animals of products intended for human use is criticized, someone brings up the tragic "thalidomide babies" in support of the claim that thorough testing is needed to protect the general public. This example is worth investigating. The lesson to be learned from it is not what most people expect.

18   The first thing to remember is that thalidomide was not an essential, lifesaving substance. It was a new kind of sleeping tablet, and while sleeping tablets may be more important than cosmetics, the animal suffering involved in testing a substance is in any case a high price to pay for the avoidance of sleeplessness. So doing without animal testing would not mean releasing substances like thalidomide untested; it would mean doing without it, and trying to become less dependent on drugs.

19   Second, and more important, is the fact that thalidomide *was* extensively tested on animals before it was released. These tests failed to show any abnormalities. Indeed, as the editor of a recent book on toxicology has stated: "the toxicity tests that had been carefully carried out on thalidomide without exception had demonstrated it to be an almost uniquely safe compound."[10] Even after the drug was suspected of causing deformities in human babies, tests on pregnant laboratory dogs, cats, rats, monkeys, hamsters, and chickens all failed to produce deformities.

Only when a particular strain of rabbit was tried were deformities produced.[11]

The thalidomide story underlines something that toxicologists have 20 known for a long time: species vary. Extrapolation from one species to another is a highly risky venture. Thalidomide is harmless to most animals. Insulin, on the other hand, can produce deformities in infant rabbits and mice, but not in humans.[12] And as another toxicologist has said: "If penicillin had been judged by its toxicity on guinea pigs it might never have been used on man."[13]

What we should learn from thalidomide, then, is not that animal 21 testing is necessary, but that it is unreliable; not that we need to poison more animals, but that we need to find alternative methods of testing, and until then we should make do without new nonessential drugs.

When experiments can be brought under the heading "medical" we 22 are inclined to think that any suffering they involve must be justifiable because the research is contributing to the alleviation of suffering. But the general label "medical research" can be used to cover research which is not directed toward the reduction of suffering, but is motivated by a general goalless curiosity that may be acceptable as part of a basic search for knowledge when it involves no suffering, but should not be tolerated if it causes pain. Very often this research has been going on for decades and much of it, in the long run, turns out to have been quite pointless. . . .

How can these things happen? How can a man who is not a sadist 23 spend his working day heating an unanesthetized dog to death, or driving a monkey into a lifelong depression, and then remove his white coat, wash his hands, and go home to dinner with his wife and children? How can taxpayers allow their money to be used to support experiments of this kind? And how can students go through a turbulent era of protest against injustice, discrimination, and oppression of all kinds, no matter how far from home, while ignoring the cruelties that are being carried out on their own campuses?

The answers to these questions stem from the unquestioned accept- 24 ance of speciesism. We tolerate cruelties inflicted on members of other species that would outrage us if performed on members of our own species. Speciesism allows researchers to regard the animals they experiment on as items of equipment, laboratory tools rather than living, suffering creatures. Sometimes they even refer to the animals in this way. Robert White of the Cleveland Metropolitan General Hospital, who has performed numerous experiments involving the transplanting of heads of monkeys, and the keeping alive of monkey brains in fluid, outside the body, has said in an interview that:

> Our main purpose here is to offer a living laboratory tool: a monkey "model" in which and by which we can design new operative techniques for the brain.

And the reporter who conducted the interview and observed White's experiments found his experience

> a rare and chilling glimpse into the cold, clinical world of the scientist, where the life of an animal has no meaning beyond the immediate purpose of experimentation.[14]

25   This "scientific" attitude to animals was exhibited to a large audience in December 1974 when the American public television network brought together Harvard philosopher Robert Nozick and three scientists whose work involves animals. The program was a follow-up to Fred Wiseman's controversial film *Primate*, which had taken viewers inside the Yerkes Primate Center, a research center in Atlanta, Georgia. Nozick asked the scientists whether the fact that an experiment will kill hundreds of animals is ever regarded, by scientists, as a reason for not performing it. One of the scientists answered: "Not that I know of." Nozick pressed his question: "Don't the animals count at all?" Dr. A. Perachio, of the Yerkes Center, replied: "Why should they?" while Dr. D. Baltimore, of the Massachusetts Institute of Technology, added that he did not think that experimenting on animals raised a moral issue at all.[15]

26   As well as the general attitude of speciesism which researchers share with other citizens there are some special factors operating to make possible the experiments I have described. Foremost among these is the immense respect that we still have for scientists. Although the advent of nuclear weapons and environmental pollution have made us realize that science and technology need to be controlled to some extent, we still tend to be in awe of anyone who wears a white coat and has a PhD. In a well-known series of experiments Stanley Milgram, a Harvard psychologist, has demonstrated that ordinary people will obey the directions of a white-coated research worker to administer what appears to be (but in fact is not) electric shock to a human subject as "punishment" for failing to answer questions correctly; and they will continue to do this even when the human subject cries out and pretends to be in great pain.[16] If this can happen when the participant believes he is inflicting pain on a human, how much easier is it for a student to push aside his initial qualms when his professor instructs him to perform experiments on animals? What Alice Heim has rightly called the "indoctrination" of the student is a gradual process, beginning with the dissection of frogs in school biology classes. When the budding medical student, or psychology student, or veterinarian, reaches the university and finds that to complete the course of studies on which he has set his heart he must experiment on living animals, it is difficult for him to refuse to do so, especially since he knows that what he is being asked to do is standard practice in the field.

27   Individual students will often admit feeling uneasy about what they are asked to do, but public protests are very rare. An organized protest

did occur in Britain recently, however, when students at the Welsh National School of Medicine in Cardiff complained publicly that a dog was unnecessarily injected with drugs more than 30 times to demonstrate a point during a lecture. The dog was then killed. One student said: "We learned nothing new. It could all have been looked up in textbooks. A film could be made so that only one dog dies and all this unnecessary suffering is stopped."[17] The student's comment was true; but such things happen routinely in every medical school. Why are protests so rare?

The pressure to conform does not let up when the student receives 28 his degree. If he goes on to a graduate degree in fields in which experiments on animals are usual, he will be encouraged to devise his own experiments and write them up for his PhD dissertation. . . . Naturally, if this is how students are educated they will tend to continue in the same manner when they become professors, and they will, in turn, train their own students in the same manner.

It is not always easy for people outside the universities to understand 29 the rationale for the research carried out under university auspices. Originally, perhaps, scholars and researchers just set out to solve the most important problems and did not allow themselves to be influenced by other considerations. Perhaps some are still motivated by these concerns. Too often, though, academic research gets bogged down in petty and insignificant details because the big questions have been studied already, and have either been solved or proven too difficult. So the researcher turns away from the well-ploughed fertile fields in search of virgin territory where whatever he learns will be new, although the connection with a major problem may be more remote. . . .

To return to the question of when an experiment might be justifiable. 30 It will not do to say: "Never!" In extreme circumstances, absolutist answers always break down. Torturing a human being is almost always wrong, but it is not absolutely wrong. If torture were the only way in which we could discover the location of a nuclear time bomb hidden in a New York City basement, then torture would be justifiable. Similarly, if a single experiment could cure a major disease, that experiment would be justifiable. But in actual life the benefits are always much, much more remote, and more often than not they are nonexistent. So how do we decide when an experiment is justifiable?

We have seen that the experimenter reveals a bias in favor of his own 31 species whenever he carries out an experiment on a nonhuman for a purpose that he would not think justified him in using a human being, even a retarded human being. This principle gives us a guide toward an answer to our question. Since a speciesist bias, like a racist bias, is unjustifiable, an experiment cannot be justifiable unless the experiment is so important that the use of a retarded human being would also be justifiable.

This is not an absolutist principle. I do not believe that it could *never* 32 be justifiable to experiment on a retarded human. If it really were possible to save many lives by an experiment that would take just one life, and there were *no other way* those lives could be saved, it might be right to do the experiment. But this would be an extremely rare case. Not one tenth of one percent of the experiments now being performed on animals would fall into this category. Certainly none of the experiments described in this chapter could pass this test. . . .

NOTES

1. *Air Force Times*, 28 November 1973; *New York Times*, 14 November 1973.

2. From a paper by R. Maclellan, B. Boecher, and others in M. Goldman and L. Bustad, eds., *Biomedical Implications of Radio-Strontium Exposure*, Atomic Energy Commission Symposium, Series #25, CONF-710201 (April 1972). The source for the starting date of these experiments is *Laboratory Animal Care*, 20 (1) p. 61 (1970).

3. K. Woodward, S. Michaelson, T. Noonan, and J. Howland; *International Journal of Radiation Biology*, 12 (3) p. 265 (1967).

4. A. Tegeris, F. Earl, H. Smalley, and J. Curtis, *Archives of Environmental Health*, 13, p. 776 (1966).

5. Personal communication to the author, 8 October 1974.

6. Hearings before the Subcommittee on Livestock and Feed Grains of the Committee on Agriculture (US House of Representatives, 1966), p. 63.

7. *Christian Science Monitor*, 18 July 1973.

8. *Sunday Mirror* (London), 24 February 1974, p. 10.

9. M.N. Gleason et al., eds., *Clinical Toxicology of Commercial Products* (Baltimore: Williams and Wilkins, 1969).

10. S.F. Paget, ed., *Methods in Toxicology* (Blackwell Scientific Publications, 1970), p. 4.

11. Ibid., pp. 134–139.

12. Ibid., p. 132.

13. G.F. Somers, *Quantitative Method in Human Pharmacology and Therapeutics* (Elmsford, New York: Pergamon Press, 1959); quoted by Richard Ryder, *Victims of Science*, p. 153.

14. *Scope* (Durban, South Africa), 30 March 1973.

15. "The Price of Knowledge," broadcast in New York, 12 December 1974, WNET/13; transcript supplied courtesy WNET/13 and Henry Spira.

16. S. Milgram, *Obedience to Authority* (New York: Harper & Row, 1974). Incidentally, these experiments were widely criticized on ethical grounds because they involved human beings without their consent. It is indeed questionable whether Milgram should have deceived participants in his experiments as he did; but when we compare what was done to them with what is commonly done to nonhuman animals, we can appreciate the double standard with which critics of the experiment operate.

17. *South Wales Echo*, 21 January 1974.

Questions for Discussion and Writing

1. How essential to Singer's argument is his assumption that many animals are used in experiments that cause them to "suffer and die without any certainty that this suffering and death would save a single human life, or benefit humans in any way at all"?

2. How does the attitude toward lower animals that Singer calls speciesism lead scientists involved in experimentation to rationalize their cruelty toward animals used in their tests? In your opinion, how would the attitude that animals are only "items of equipment" rather than living, sentient beings permit laboratory experimenters to destroy many more of them each year for research purposes than they might otherwise?

3. What function does Singer's citation of a 1971 Rutgers University survey serve in the overall structure of his argument? The survey put the number of animals used in U.S. laboratories each year at 63 million.

4. In what experiments cited by Singer is the animal's ability to suffer used as the basis of the experiment so that the results can be generalized to humans?

5. How much of animal experimentation is actually tied in with broader societal values that are geared toward the production of new, if inessential, products such as coloring and flavoring agents, sweeteners and preservatives? How does the fact that the majority of animals are sacrificed in testing nonessential products or luxury items illustrate speciesism, or the low value society places on animal life?

6. Why does Singer believe that the manner in which students are educated in the sciences exerts pressure on them to engage in unnecessary experimentation on animals?

7. Evaluate the test Singer would have experimenters apply to determine whether or not any particular experiment should be performed. The test stipulates "if it really were possible to save many lives by an experiment that would take just one life, and there were no other way those lives could be saved, it might be right to do the experiment." If you disagree with this test, what criteria would you propose to be applied instead?

8. What is Singer's purpose in shifting his focus from the public protest over planned air force tests involving beagle puppies to widespread, if generally unknown, tests routinely performed on beagles?

9. How do the many experiments Singer cites as examples support his assertion that very little useful medical knowledge is actually gained from the deluge of experiments on animals?

10. How does Singer use the example of thalidomide to undercut the assumption that results from animal experimentation can be generalized to humans? Keep in mind that the drug itself was inessential since it was intended simply as a sleeping aid.

11. How does Singer take into account the viewpoints of the opposition during the course of his argument against animal experimentation?

12. How do the interviews with the Yerkes Primate Center researchers illustrate the prevalence of what Singer calls speciesism?

13. Based on your own experience in lab courses, evaluate Singer's claim that one of the things that makes reform of animal experimentation so difficult is the enormous social pressure on students (whose field of study, and hopes of success, depend on animal experimentation) to acquiesce in the sacrifice of animals in order to obtain their degrees.

14. For further reading on the subject, see Hans Ruesch's books *Naked Empress: Or the Great Medical Fraud* (1982) and *Slaughter of the Innocent* (1978), which can be ordered through Civis/Civitas Publications, Box 26, Swain, New York 14884. For other reading materials and information, contact United Action for Animals, Inc., in New York City. Other books on antivivisection are Robert S. Mendelsohn, M.D., *Confessions of a Medical Heretic*; Peter Singer, *Practical Ethics* (1979); Henry Salt, *Animals' Rights Considered in Relation to Social Progress*; and Tom Regan, *The Case for Animal Rights*.

Maurice B. Visscher

The Ethics of the Use of Lower Animals in Scientific Study

Maurice B. Visscher, who wrote "The Ethics of the Use of Lower Animals in Scientific Study" (from Ethical Constraints and Imperatives in Medical Research, *[1975]*) *was a physiologist who taught at the University of Minnesota School of Medicine. He asserts that human beings, by virtue of their place at the top of the hierarchy of all species, have the right and the obligation to use living animals as research subjects to benefit humanity. Visscher interprets the thalidomide incident quite differently from Singer and uses deductive reasoning to argue that the doctrine of reverence for life, as stated originally by Albert Schweitzer, has been taken out of context to condemn all animal experimentation.*

There is a minority of the human race who categorically deny the 1 ethical propriety of the sacrifice of lower animal life under any conditions for the advancement of scientific knowledge. However, the numbers of these persons who call themselves antivivisectionists, and particularly their uncritical supporters, appear to be growing and consequently an analysis of the background of their positions seems to be essential. The analysis is also necessary today in view of the growing fraction of persons in the Western world who appear to have lost their bearings in ethical theory and practice.

In an earlier day in the Judeo-Christian world the authoritarian 2 dogma that lower animals were created for the service of man provided an adequate justification for their use in scientific study. Today, however, for large segments of society the situation has changed. No documentation is needed to sustain the assertion that the authority of Judeo-Christian cosmology has lost much popular ground in the last several centuries, and opinions regarding the origin and the place of man and other animals in the universe have also changed. The explosion in scientific knowledge and particularly the popularization of crucial aspects of it in relation to both cosmology and the evolution of life on our planet have resulted in a major revolution in background thinking about literalism in interpretation of ancient stories about creation which were once accepted by most of the literates and illiterates alike in the Western World as authoritative and reliable accounts. Today, for example, after everyone with a television set has seen men walking on the moon, and with spaceships sending us information about the other planets in our solar system, it has become difficult or impossible for anyone with much logical capacity to believe that the planet Earth is the center of the universe. In connection with the origin of the human race, comparable great shifts in views have occurred. Even a quarter of a century ago, although the statistical facts about overall genetic inheritance were known, the genetic coding mechanism was still a mystery. Today it is difficult for anyone who puts trust in observation and logic to doubt that the same basic mechanisms which control human heredity were in operation billions of years ago in less elaborate form controlling morphogenesis in primitive organisms. The kinship of man with other forms of life can be doubted only by those who reject the methods of science as useful and ultimately reliable in unravelling the secrets of nature.

3   The superior place of the genus *Homo sapiens* in the hierarchy of living things has not been altered, however. Scientific study of man in comparison with other, presumably earlier, forms of animal life has shown that the mutations which produced a brain with a neocortex capable of verbal communication, projective and abstract logic and other attributes not found in other animals, provides a basis for a view which still puts man at the pinnacle of evolution of animal life on earth.

4   The problem of man today is how to survive healthily on this planet. It has been that problem in different forms and contexts since the first examples of the genus Homo appeared. But the problem today has a new dimension, introduced by the rise of science and technology. The greatest problems are perhaps those of how to feed and otherwise care for an exploding population, how to limit that population, and especially how to prevent the destruction of the human race, and perhaps all life on the planet, by thermonuclear war. But the prevention and cure of disease are also prime desiderata. Scientific study, including study of living lower animals has been and will be indispensible to human survival and happiness. Even to solve the problems of overpopulation, animal experimentation has been and still is of prime importance. Therefore, clarifying a consensus concerning the ethics of animal experimentation is an important issue.

5   Man has, by virtue of his superior capacity for abstract and projective logic, a chance to do something about molding his environment and controlling his own behavior in rational ways. He can consider what he ought to do. Ethics is obviously that aspect of mental activity which deals with what individuals and societies at large think that they ought to do.

6   What people think they ought to do depends, of course, on value systems. This is where controversy enters. A person who starts, as for example Albert Schweitzer[1] did, with a value system that begins by asserting the theoretical equivalence of value of all life, from the protista to man, and giving to the life of a mosquito or a daisy the same absolute value as to the life of a human, is bound to encounter a hard time in his

logic. Schweitzer did. He spoke feelingly about never thoughtlessly crushing a flower or an earthworm, but he always ended up justifying the act of crushing countless plants and animals to meet a real human need, provided that one always cut a field of grain, for example, with a conscious sense of remorse that it had to be done. Likewise in his expressions about the sacrifice of lower animal life for medical research, he recognized the ethical propriety of such sacrifice but labored the need for conscious recognition that in each instance a judgment should be made. His exact words were, "Those who carry out scientific experiments with animals, in order to apply the knowledge gained to the alleviation of human ills, should never reassure themselves with the generality that their cruel acts serve a useful purpose. In each individual case they must ask themselves whether there is a real necessity for imposing such a sacrifice upon a living creature. They must try to reduce the suffering insofar as they are able."[2]

Schweitzer was a very complex personality who combined a broad 7 philosophic grasp of the realities of the natural world with a rigid personal ethic which grew out of his contemplation of the consequences of the "universal will to live" ideas of earlier philosophers. Furthermore, he recognized the dilemma in which he found himself, as is evident when he wrote, "The world is a ghastly drama of will to live divided against itself. One existence makes its way at the cost of another, one destroys the other. One will to live merely exerts its will against the other, and has no knowledge of it. But in me the will to live has come to know about other wills to live. There is in it a yearning to arrive at unity with itself, to become universal."[3]

The philosophy of reverence for life became an overriding philo- 8 sophic passion for Schweitzer in his later life, but his ideas about it began to appear as early as 1919. In a sermon he gave on February 23 of that year he expressed his conviction as to its great import for man while he detailed—with sorrow it would appear—the enormous gap between the facts of life in nature and his ideal. He said,

Reverence for life and sympathy with other lives is of supreme importance for this world of ours. Nature knows no similar reverence for life. It produces life a thousandfold in the most meaningful way and destroys it a thousandfold in the most meaningless way. In every stage of life, right up to the level of man, terrible ignorance lies over all creatures. They have the will to live but no capacity for compassion toward other creatures. They cannot feel what happens inside others. They suffer but have no compassion. The great struggle for survival by which nature is maintained is in strange contradiction with itself. Creatures live at the expense of other creatures. Nature permits the most horrible cruelties to be committed. It impels insects by their instincts to bore holes into other insects, to lay their eggs in them so that maggots may grow there and live off the caterpillar, thus causing it a slow and painful death. Nature lets ants band together to attack poor little creatures and hound them to death. Look at the spider. How gruesome is the craft that nature taught it!

Nature looks beautiful and marvelous when you view it from the outside. But when you read its pages like a book, it is horrible. And its cruelty is so senseless! The most precious form of life is sacrificed to the lowliest. A child breathes the germs of tuberculosis. He grows and flourishes but is destined to suffering and a premature death because these lowly creatures multiply in his vital organs. How often in Africa have I been overcome with horror when I examined the blood of a patient who was suffering from sleeping sickness. Why did this man, his face contorted in pain, have to sit in front of me, groaning, "Oh, my head, my head"? Why should he have to suffer night after night and die a wretched death? Because there, under the microscope were minute, pale corpuscles, one ten-thousandth of a millimeter long— not very many, sometimes such a very few that one had to look for hours to find them at all.

9   Nevertheless Schweitzer was, in his way, a pragmatist. In another of his essays he wrote, "Proceeding along that way, I have led you to this conclusion: that rational processes, properly pursued, must lead to the true ethic.

10   "Another commentary: What of this ethic? Is it absolute?

11   "Kant defines absolute ethics as that which is not concerned with whether it can be achieved. The distinction is not one of *absolute* as opposed to *relative*, but *absolute* as distinct from *practicable* in the ethical field. An absolute ethic calls for the creating of perfection in this life. It cannot be completely achieved; but that fact does not really matter. In this sense, reverence for life is an absolute ethic. It does not lay down specific rules for each possible solution. It simply tells us that we are responsible for the lives about us. It does not set either maximum or minimum limits to what we must do."[4]

12   Schweitzer was a gentle soul, with an unfulfilled yearning for logical consistency, who devoted his great talents to a practical exemplification of a life of service to the less fortunate. But he did not, as some appear to believe, think that moral scruples should, for example, prevent an ethical person from sacrificing the lives of animals in scientific study. In fact, although he did not develop the theme himself, the reverence for life principle can easily lead one to the logical conclusion that one has a moral duty to sacrifice life, if necessary, in scientific study, in order that the conditions of life generally can be improved.

13   A more pragmatic and more rationally consistent philosopher, the late John Dewey, wrote a definitive essay in 1909 on "The Ethics of Animal Experimentation." It was prepared as a reasoned argument against then impending antivivisection legislation. He wrote,

Scientific inquiry has been the chief instrumentality in bringing men from barbarism to civilization, from darkness to light, while it has incurred, at every step, determined opposition from the powers of ignorance, misunderstanding and jealousy. It is not so long ago, as years are reckoned, that a scientist in a physical or chemical laboratory was popularly regarded as a magician engaged in unlawful pursuits, or as in impious converse with evil spirits, about whom all sorts of detrimental stories were circulated and believed. Those days are gone. Generally speaking, the value of free scientific inquiry as an instrumentality of social progress and enlightenment is acknowledged. At the same time, it is still possible, by making irrelevant emotional appeals and obscuring the real issues to galvanize into life something of the old spirit of misunderstanding, envy and dread of science. The point at issue in the subjection of animal experimenters to special supervision and legislation is thus deeper than at first sight appears. In principle it involves the revival of the animosity to discovery and to the application to life of the fruits of discovery which, upon the whole, has been the chief foe of human progress, it behooves every thoughtful individual to be constantly on the alert against every revival of this spirit, in whatever guise it presents itself.[5]

Modern antivivisectionists have attempted to wrap the hallowed robes of Albert Schweitzer around themselves. They have taken his "reverence for life" philosophy out of context and are using it to justify new attacks upon animal experimentation. Recently a collection of essays edited by Stanley and Roslind Godlovitch and John Harris[6] has brought together the views of some British philosophers, novelists and humane society activists, along with one botanist, all of whom develop one or another aspect of the theme that the sacrifice of sentient animal life in biological, and particularly medical research is of very questionable ethical propriety. Their points of view can be summarized, as the philosopher Patrick Corbett did in the postscript to the volume, as follows: "Our conviction, for reasons we have given, is that *we* require *now* to extend the great principles of liberty, equality and fraternity over the lives of animals. Let animal slavery join human slavery in the graveyard of the past!" These viewpoints are not unique to the British. Catherine Roberts,[7] an American biologist, published in 1971 in the *American Scholar*, the organ of the United Chapters of Phi Beta Kappa, a long article defending the viewpoint that the taking of life from any sentient lower animal should be abhorrent to the scheme of morality of any decent person. She said,

Evolving life can therefore no longer tolerate the biological injustice of inflicting agony upon animals to ameliorate and prolong the physical existence of human lives. Brief respites from suffering and death made possible by the ruthlessness of scientists against lower life contribute nothing whatever to the spiritual ascent of mankind. Evolving life has need instead of gentle souls like Saint Francis and Gandhi to show us how to come together to live lives of nonviolence, in joy and peace with the whole of sentient creation. For the meek, strengthened and made wise in their decisions by divine sanction and their spiritual heritage, *shall* inherit the earth. The choice to abolish the sentient laboratory animal is evolutionary inevitability and a moral imperative.

15   The range of the positions of the newer antivivisectionists is from advocacy of regulations which would put the onus of responsibility for proof upon the scientist in each case that important needed new knowledge could not be obtained by the use of cell or tissue cultures, or computers, or more sophisticated mathematics, to outright prohibition of the use of animals. Common sense appears to be a scarce commodity among activist opponents of the use of animals in scientific research. The generally omnivorous human race sacrifices the lives of many billions of animals yearly for food, not to mention fur, leather and feathers. In 1973 in the U.S. alone, 2.5 billion chickens were killed for food. Hundreds of millions of other species were also used for human food. There are, of course, some antivivisectionists who do not eat meat, fish or fowl, and refrain from wearing animal skins or fur. But the fraction of the human race that is consistent on such scores is small.

16   On strictly logical grounds it would appear that no one who condones any sacrifice of aquatic or terrestrial animal life for food or clothing has a leg to stand on in criticizing the humane sacrifice of animal life in relatively very small numbers for the control of disease. It is possible for adults, and probably for children after the nursing period, to live entirely on vegetable matter, but it is totally impossible to advance certain kinds of knowledge essential to the control of cure or amelioration of disease without the use of living animals of various sorts.

17   The outright antiscience, antirational small core of antivivisectionists would not be a great problem, except for the fact that they form the nucleus for the crystallization of much larger numbers of ordinary pet lovers who can be mobilized to press for extremely restrictive and unwise legislation. In an affluent society, especially one with an aging population of lonely people who frequently distrust other humans and become more attached to lower animal pets than to humanity, there is a danger that a dominating majority will one day put an end to the era of progress in medicine and the rest of biological science, out of ignorance and prejudice. How this could happen in a society devoted to carnivorous eating habits may be hard to envision, but the near success of the bill in the British Parliament aimed at hobbling their biomedical researchers, shows that fears on this score are not paranoid.

18   The relation of this issue to the safe use of human subjects for

medical investigation can be made quite obvious. A new drug cannot be tested safely in man until it has been studied thoroughly in a variety of lower animals. Cell and tissue cultures are useful in analyzing some basic kinds of biochemical action, but drugs ordinarily do not act simply on one kind of cell or tissue, nor do they necessarily act the same way on isolated cells or even organs as they do when other cell types are present in an integrated system. Drug efficacy and safety must ordinarily be tested on numerous species of animal in order to be able to make reliable transferable predictions as to their actions in man. The majority of new drugs tested first in a number of species of animals have shown reliable transferability of information to man. Therefore, the U.S. Food and Drug Administration quite properly requires extensive animal testing before it will authorize even tentative small-scale tests on man. The same rule is applied in practically all countries in which a pharmaceutical industry exists.

The thalidomide tragedy is often brought up by antivivisectionists   19
and their allies as an example of a case in which the toxic effects on embryos in the human were not predicted by prior animal study and that therefore animal study is futile. The facts are that the animal studies on thalidomide were inadequate, and the reason for the inadequacy was simply that no tests for teratogenicity were made. Obviously, too few animal studies were performed. Thalidomide is therefore a prime example of the need for more, not less, preliminary study on lower animals before applications are made in human use. The experience with that drug should point up the ethical necessity of large-scale toxicity testing on animals.

The same general principle applies in other types of medical research.   20
No one would consider using an attenuated live virus vaccine without extensive study on lower animal models. Likewise with innumerable other innovations, very extensive investigation has preceded any human application. This is as it should be if humane ethics are to prevail. If there has been a defect in policy till recently, it is that too little rather than too much lower animal study has preceded trials on man.

An antivivisectionist today should be an anachronism. Most outright   21
antivivisectionists are actually misanthropic zoophiles. Some of them, as already noted, are dressing up their opposition to the use of animals in scientific study with the wholly illusory claim that the use of animals in research is obsolete in an era of advanced computer technology and other powerful mathematical tools. But some of the critics of animal experimentation go on to suggest that, if empirical data are really necessary, they should be acquired by the use of human rather than subhuman subjects. Often the suggestion is made that the human experimenter himself, rather than a dog, cat, monkey or mouse, should be the subject. Actually many scientists have made themselves the first guinea pigs when scientific necessity has required the use of human subjects, but it would seem to approach the absurd, not to say the insane, to suggest

seriously as some have done[8] that human subjects be routinely employed in order to avoid the use of lower animals in scientific study for human welfare, as in drug toxicity studies in the instance cited.

22   More than a century ago Claude Bernard[9] summarized the problem when he said,

> Have we the right to make experiments on animals and vivisect them? As for me, I think we have this right wholly and absolutely. It would be strange indeed if we recognized man's right to make use of animals in every walk of life, for domestic service, for food, and then forbade him to make use of them for his own instruction in one of the sciences most useful to humanity. No hesitation is possible; the science of life can be established only through experiment, and we can save living beings from death only after sacrificing others. Experiments must be made either on man or on animals. Now I think that physicians already make too many dangerous experiments on man, before carefully studying them on animals. I do not admit that it is moral to try more or less dangerous or active remedies on patients in hospitals, without first experimenting with them on dogs; for I shall prove, further on, that results obtained on animals may all be conclusive for man when we know how to experiment properly. If it is immoral, then, to make an experiment on man when it is dangerous to him, even though the result may be useful to others, it is essentially moral to make experiments on an animal, even though painful and dangerous to him, if they may be useful to man.

NOTES

1. Schweitzer, Albert: *Reverence for Life*, trans. by R.H. Fuller, New York, Harper & Row, 1969, pp. 120–121.

2. Schweitzer, Albert: *The Teaching of Reverence for Life*, trans. by R. and C. Winston. New York, Holt-Rinehart-Winston, 1965, p. 48.

3. Schweitzer, Albert: *The Philosophy of Civilization*, trans. by C.T. Campion. New York, Macmillan, 1950, p. 312.

4. Clark, Henry: *The Ethical Mysticism of Albert Schweitzer*. Boston, Beacon Press, 1962, Appendix I, pp. 186–187.

5. Visscher, M.B.: In Dewey, John: Medical research and ethics. *JAMA 199(9):*634, February 27, 1967.

6. Godlovitch, Stanley and Roslind, and Harris, John: *Animals, Men and Morals*. New York, Taplinger, 1972.

7. Roberts, Catherine: Animal experimentation and evolution. *The American Scholar*, Summer 1971.

8. Advertisement placed by United Action for Animals, Inc. *New York Times*, September 7, 1969.

9. Bernard, Claude: *Experimental Medicine*, trans. by Henry Copley Greene, U.S.A., Henry Schumann, 1949, p. 102.

Questions for Discussion and Writing

1. Why does Visscher believe that the doctrine of "reverence for life" has unjustifiably been used to frustrate the efforts of scientific research?

2. What qualities, according to Visscher, make humans superior to the lower animals and justify the use of laboratory animals in research for the benefit of man? How do these conclusions in turn form the basis of the further deduction that it is perfectly ethical to sacrifice some lower animals to benefit a greater number of human beings?

3. What ideas does Visscher say are implicit, although unexpressed, in Schweitzer's philosophy?

4. What inconsistency does Visscher object to in the opinions of those antivivisectionists who are not vegetarians?

5. How does Visscher cite the work of Albert Schweitzer to support his own thesis against followers of Schweitzer's "reverence for life" position?

6. How does Visscher use the process of deductive reasoning in arguing that if it is ethical to kill some animals to keep mankind alive, then to oppose killing other animals is to take an action against the welfare of mankind?

7. In terms of argumentative strategy, what means does Visscher use to discredit that segment of the public that is opposed to animal experimentation?

8. How does the persuasive technique of downplaying enter into the construction of both Visscher's and Singer's arguments? For example, Visscher neglects to state the figures of animals killed annually in experiments but supplies the numbers of animals killed yearly for food. By the same token, Singer does not mention the number of

animals killed yearly for food but does give full statistics of live animals killed in laboratories for experimental purposes. In an essay, discuss how each author downplays some facts while highlighting others whereas his opponent does the exact opposite. In what way did these two essays make you realize how authors use downplaying to select information that emphasizes the merits of their arguments to persuade their readers?

9. Where does Visscher use circular reasoning in his argument?

10. Both Singer and Visscher say "the opposition often brings up the tragic thalidomide incident" by way of introducing their own interpretations of this event. How do Singer's and Visscher's respective analyses of the thalidomide incident support their arguments by emphasizing completely different aspects, interpreting the events differently, and reaching completely different conclusions from the same data?

11. Compare the means used by Singer to dramatize the magnitude of the public outcry against research on live animals, on one hand, with the techniques (such as downplaying, guilt by association, labeling) used by Visscher to discredit, as he says, the "outright antiscience, antirational small core of antivivisectionists."

12. How do both Singer and Visscher omit viewpoints or facts (such as any cases where animal experimentation provided benefits to humanity, or conversely, examples of the slaughter of animals to produce hair dye, shampoos, mascara, and other nonmedical, inessential items) that would be damaging to their arguments? What aspects of Visscher's argument and attitude toward this subject might Singer perceive as the purest expression of what Singer terms speciesism? On the other hand, what aspects of Singer's argument and attitude might Visscher view as "antivivisectionist hypocrisy"?

13. Compare and contrast how Singer and Visscher characterize the moral relationship between animals and humans. How do the many differences between Singer's and Visscher's arguments flow directly from their diametrically opposite conceptions of the relationship between animals and humans?

14. As a field research assignment, interview those who make use of animals for either teaching or research purposes and then write up the results of your interviews either defending or attacking what you have discovered about the way animals are used for experimental purposes on your campus and/or in your community.

15. Write a short essay either pro or con the thesis that unwanted homeless dogs and cats that otherwise would be destroyed should be sold to research laboratories.

16. For further reading on the subject of why vivisection is beneficial, see R. G. Frey, *Interests and Rights: The Case Against Animals* (1980); Michael Allan Fox, *The Case for Animal Experimentation* (1986); *Ethics and Animals,* edited by Harlan B. Miller and William H. Williams (1983).

SOUTH AFRICA

Robert Slimp

The Bright Side of Dark Africa

Robert Slimp's account "The Bright Side of Dark Africa," which first appeared in The Manchester Union Leader *(March 22, 1984), is based on observations he made during a tour of South Africa. Slimp, a minister, claims that except for the unrest caused by outside agitators and communists the black majority would be content with the status quo. He argues that America's economic self-interest should lead it to support the current government in South Africa.*

1   Undoubtedly the most controversial country on the continent of Africa is the Republic of South Africa. This beautiful land, whose cities are as modern as our own, is a country of contrasts, contradictions and abundance.

2   South Africa is gifted with a myriad of assets which include immense mineral riches, enormous agricultural wealth, and an extraordinary and varied population.

3   Big booming bawdy Johannesburg, a city of nearly two million has been called the "New York" of Africa. Actually this ultra modern metropolis with its skyscrapers surrounded by huge mounds of dirt from its gold mines, more resembles Dallas or Denver than the Big Apple. Surprisingly it will celebrate only its 100th birthday next year. Cape Town with one million people looks a lot like San Francisco, and Pretoria, an extremely clean city filled with modern high rises, has a charm and distinction all its own.

4   South Africa is the OPEC of the mineral world. It supplies 65 percent of the world's gold, nearly 90 percent of its platinum and diamonds (the United States receives 98 percent of her industrial diamonds from South Africa). In addition South Africa supplies about half of the world's uranium, 42 percent of the world's vanadium and 81 percent of the world's chrome. She also has substantial deposits of copper, lead, plus 61 percent of the world's manganese. Certainly the West cannot afford to ignore this vast storehouse of mineral wealth. The strategic sea lanes around the Cape of Good Hope are so vital that Lenin once remarked that "the road to Berlin, Paris, London, and the United States runs

through Cape Town." Indeed we Americans receive 70 percent of our imported oil around the Cape. Hence South Africa is critically important to the survival of the West.

Small wonder that this fabulously wealthy country, though contain- 5 ing only 6 percent of Africa's population, generated 50 percent of the continent's electricity, manufactures 74 percent of its railway cars, 42 percent of its motor vehicles, and a whopping 94 percent of its books, magazines and newspapers.

And yet in spite of all her assets, South Africa is pictured by much of 6 the Western news media, the United Nations, the World Council of Churches, the Communist bloc and even by the Democratic Party Presidential hopefuls as a dictatorial police state where the white minority exercises cruel control of the black population. So widespread is this feeling, that it is difficult to put in a good word for South Africa without being called controversial or even "racist."

What are the facts: This country of 472,359 square miles has a history 7 very similar to our own. Today, those countries as told to me by George Matanzima, president of the Transkei, "We may not yet be recognized by the United States and Britain, but we are recognized by ITT, IBM, Coca Cola, Ford and even Kentucky Fried Chicken, and that's where the big bucks come from. That's the kind of recognition that counts."

In many ways the white man has been good to the black man. 8 Remember the whites were there first. It must be admitted in all candor, that everything that runs on two wheels, grows in two rows and stands more than two stories tall was brought to South Africa by the European. The black population has exploded because of the white man's medicine and because the white man stopped their tribal fighting. That is certainly a better record than we Americans enjoy. Our forefathers killed off most of our American Indians while winning the West. The Boer was more humanitarian.

But, in spite of this record, the rest of the world will not leave South 9 Africa alone to solve her own affairs. The whites thus far are the only ones who have the vote and although they represent only five million people out of 25 million, they hold the power and they govern. However, many South Africans feel that they are doing an extremely good job of taking care of their 17 million blacks, two million colored and 800,000 Indians and 200,000 other Asians, including 50,000 Malays.

There are beautiful housing areas for blacks, Indians, and coloreds. 10 The government spends 20 million annually on housing for blacks alone. Today, blacks have all the freedoms but one, and that is the right to vote, the right to govern himself outside of his homelands. And this right to vote is what is causing all of the problems. The outside world simply does not want to understand. Hence because of the bad press given to South Africa world wide, this country remains a pariah nation, or as Prime Minister Pieter Botha puts it: "We are the pole cat of the world."

Of course the Communists are exploiting this explosive situation. 11

They are stirring up unrest among the non whites and they are succeeding. "Our servants are sometimes a bit rebellious these days," says Shirley Bell, a Pinetown housewife. "Sometimes my maid goes to political meetings and then she is very sullen and hard to get along with for the next few days." Sometimes this rebellion breaks out in the open as was the case of the Soweto riots in 1976.

12   Is there a solution to this problem? The answer is no. What black nation to the north should a Black South Africa pattern herself after? Mozambique, Angola, Zimbabwe are all one party Marxist dictatorships. There is a grim joke in most of the black states north of the Limpopo, "one man one vote one time." What Rhodesians were promised at Lanchester House in London in 1979 was that they would have a future in a black ruled Zimbabwe. Dictator Mugabe has ignored this promise made for him by the British. The whites have not been allowed to have their own schools. They have been taxed out of their businesses, terrorized out of their farms. More whites have been killed since Mugabe took over in April, 1980 than lost their lives in the long bush war of 1974 to 1979. The slogan on Zimbabwean T shirts: "Kill a white a night" is no joke. Beautiful Rhodesia has been replaced by a ruin: Zimbabwe.

13   The future of South Africa seems to be unfolding like a three act play in which Act I was the destruction of Rhodesia, Act II is to be the destruction of South West Africa dubbed "Namibia" by the United Nations, and Act III, the grand finale, will be the destruction of the Republic of South Africa. This is the plan, not only of Moscow, but also the World Council of Churches and the liberal Democratic candidates for President of the United States. Even our own State Department in the person of African Affairs "expert" Chester Crocker is putting severe pressure on the South African government to capitulate and to give the blacks the vote now. Should this happen, the vast mineral wealth of this troubled land and the vital Sea Lanes around the Cape of Good Hope will fall into Marxist hands. If this happens, it will mean the end of the aircraft industry and will make it almost impossible to continue a viable defense system against our Soviet enemies.

14   Already the South Africans are fighting our battle against communism in Angola where the South Africans confront 30,000 Cubans and 3,000 East Germans. If the Reagan administration would put as much pressure on Moscow and Havana as it puts on Pretoria for a settlement, our future would be much brighter.

Questions for Discussion and Writing

1. How does Slimp, in the opening section of his article, use the technique of virtue by association to characterize the Republic of South Africa and its cities of Johannesburg and Cape Town? Why, in your opinion, does he choose to begin his article this way?

2. What role does the appeal to pragmatic economic self-interest play in Slimp's discussion of South Africa's mineral resources and strategic location?

3. What different kinds of evidence does Slimp offer to refute what he considers common misconceptions and misrepresentations about the quality of life for blacks in South Africa?

4. On whose testimony does Slimp base his contention that "many South Africans feel that they are doing an extremely good job of taking care of their 17 million blacks, two million colored and 800,000 Indians and 200,000 other Asians, including 50,000 Malays"? Is there any evidence that his characterization derives from any of those people being "taken care of" by the white government in power?

5. Slimp asserts that the white government has adequately cared for "blacks, Indians, and coloreds," what inconsistency is there in his logic? Since (*a*) "whites thus far are the only ones who have the vote," (*b*) "blacks have all the freedoms but one, and that is the right to vote, the right to govern himself outside of his homelands," and (*c*) this lack of a "right to vote is what is causing all of the problems," why shouldn't blacks be given the right to vote? According to Slimp's rosy characterization of life in South Africa, why wouldn't blacks simply vote to maintain the white government in power anyway?

6. Since Slimp rules out dissatisfaction among blacks themselves as a cause of social disorder, which group does he target as the cause of "unrest among the non whites"? Evaluate his use of the example of Shirley Bell, a Pinetown housewife, as an illustration of how whites perceive the effects of outside agitators stirring up blacks who would otherwise be satisfied with their lives. To what extent does the example backfire and actually illustrate something other than what Slimp intended?

7. What role does Slimp's discussion of the recent history of the country now called Zimbabwe play in supporting his view of what the future for South Africa would be like if whites relinquished their control? What reasons, evidence, and examples does Slimp give to uphold his arguments?

8. How does Slimp use the final paragraph to connect the United States' interests with those of South Africa? How does Slimp's purpose in stressing the nature of this connection differ from the similarities he pointed out originally (in the opening paragraphs)?

Anthony Lewis

Enough Is Enough

Anthony Lewis's "Enough Is Enough" first appeared in The New York Times *(February 5, 1984). Lewis, a columnist for the* Times, *seeks to dispel erroneous impressions created by an advertisement placed by the South African government in a number of American publications. Lewis cites a variety of examples and statistics to argue that while "disinvestment" will not by itself change the South African government's stand on apartheid it will prevent the United States from participating in an offensive racial policy.*

1   The South African Government had a beautiful advertisement in a number of American publications recently. "South Africa," it said, "is involved in a remarkable process of providing fair opportunities for all its population groups."

2   The ad told about how the Government is making houses available to black families at low prices—"an integrated part of its drive towards home ownership for everyone." At the bottom an attractive picture showed three black children playing outside a nice row house.

3   In the interest of completeness, South Africa might take another advertisement giving further details on those happy black children: on the realities they face as they grow up. Here are a few.

- They and other blacks, 70 percent of the population, may not vote for members of Parliament or take any other part in the country's government.

- They are barred from living in "white areas"—87 percent of South Africa—unless they are among the minority who qualify for permits under intricate laws.

- The police may stop them at any time and demand their passbooks showing where they may live. If they have the wrong stamp in the book, they will be fined or imprisoned after a trial lasting a few minutes—and then shipped to a desolate "homeland" where there are no jobs.

- They may be farmers in a black community that has owned the land for generations. But if that area is declared "white," they may suddenly be moved to a remote resettlement area where the only structures are rows of metal privies.

- If they join any serious movement to demand political rights for the majority of South Africans, they are likely to find themselves arrested, detained in solitary confinement without trial, tortured.

- Far from being "integrated" in the American sense of that word, their lives will be totally segregated. They will be confined to separate and grossly unequal schools, housing, trains, hospitals.

Advertisements notwithstanding, Americans are increasingly aware 4 of the realities of life in South Africa. More and more want to do something about the practice of massive institutionalized racism by a country that calls itself part of the "free world."

Those American feelings are taking concrete form in a spreading 5 legislative phenomenon. Three states — Massachusetts, Connecticut and Michigan — have passed laws forbidding the investment of public funds in companies that operate in South Africa. More than 20 cities, the largest Philadelphia, have similar laws. Many universities are under student pressure to take such action in regard to their funds.

Congress has taken a step of a more direct kind. Last fall, in passing 6 legislation to increase the U.S. contribution to the International Monetary Fund, it provided that the U.S. delegate must "actively oppose" any I.M.F. loan to South Africa unless the Secretary of the Treasury certifies in writing that a loan would benefit "the majority of the people," and meet other nonracial tests.

Then the House added significant amendments to the Export Admin- 7 istration Act. They would prohibit U.S. commercial bank loans to the South African Government except for nondiscriminatory housing, schools or hospitals; prohibit any further American private investment there; forbid the importation of Krugerrands, and make all U.S. companies in South Africa comply with the so-called Sullivan Code against discrimination. (Half the U.S. firms there now ignore the voluntary code.)

The Senate is to take up the export legislation shortly, and is expected 8 to pass it without considering South African issues. There will then be a fight in conference, with House members trying to keep some of the South African restrictions in the final version. If they succeed, it will be hard for President Reagan to veto a bill that includes essential trade provisions.

Legislative steps of that kind are not going to lead to a change of heart 9 by the South African Government: of course not. But they do keep Americans from participating in evil. And if there is anything that recent history teaches, it is the evil, the corrupting, dangerous evil, of racism.

10   The United States must continue diplomatic efforts in relation to South Africa's external policy: the effort to bring Namibia to independence, for example. But it is also necessary for Americans to make clear our opinion of internal South African policy. Those who rule the country will hear the message, and they do care what Americans think of them.

11   The ranking members of the House African subcommittee—Howard Wolpe, a liberal Democrat, and Gerald Solomon, a conservative Republican—were right when they wrote South Africa's Prime Minister that "there can never be a normal relationship between our two countries as long as the inhuman and destabilizing doctrine" of racial separation continues. It is time for Congress and other American institutions to tell South Africa: Enough is enough.

Questions for Discussion and Writing

1. How does Lewis use a recent advertisement, which the South African Government placed in a number of American publications, to alert his audience that his article will examine the assertions about the quality of black life that the ad presents?

2. What additional facts and circumstances does Lewis cite that put the rosy picture presented by the South African government in a more accurate, and realistic perspective? What specific counterarguments does Lewis give for each corresponding claim presented in the advertisement?

3. Discuss the rationale underlying the idea of "disinvestment." What goal is this policy "forbidding the investment of public funds in companies that operate in South Africa" designed to achieve?

4. What is the Sullivan code and how does it affect American corporations doing business in South Africa?

5. In light of Lewis's assertion that "legislative steps . . . are not going to lead to a change of heart by the South African Government," what reasons does he give to support his recommendations favoring these legislative provisions? Evaluate the assumptions underlying this rationale. Are they realistic or merely wishful thinking?

6. Write an essay comparing and contrasting Slimp's and Lewis's sharply different perceptions of the political and social climate of South Africa. For example, what would Slimp say in response to Lewis's recommendations, and how would Lewis respond to Slimp's explanation as to the real causes of the social unrest in South Africa?

7. Trace the recent history of this issue insofar as it involves your college's position on the issue of economic divestment from South Africa. Perhaps your campus newspaper has carried editorials, letters, and the results of interviews and surveys on this issue. If you wish to do further research on the issue you might consult recent volumes of the *Reader's Guide to Periodical Literature* and prepare your own position paper. Some related articles include, Richard E. Sincere, Jr., "The Churches and Investment in South Africa" in *America* (March 3, 1984); Gail Hovey, "Apartheid's New Clothes," available from the Africa Fund in New York City, and Justine De Lacy, "Western Investors Now Welcome" in the *Atlantic Monthly* (January 1984).

GENETIC ENGINEERING

President's Commission for the Study of Ethical Problems in Research

Splicing Life

"Splicing Life" was prepared by the President's Commission for the Study of Ethical Problems in Medicine and Biomedical and Behavioral Research (1983). This commission, established by Congress, opposes any ban on genetic engineering and claims that it is a legitimate area of research that presents no threat to future generations.

Concerns about "Playing God"

1   . . . Hardly a popular article has been written about the social and ethical implications of genetic engineering that does not suggest a link between "God-like powers" and the ability to manipulate the basic material of life. Indeed, a popular book about gene splicing is entitled *Who Should Play God?*, and in their June 1980 letter to the President, three religious leaders sounded a tocsin against the lack of a governmental policy concerning "those who would play God" through genetic engineering.

RELIGIOUS VIEWPOINTS

2   The Commission asked the General Secretaries of the three religious organizations to elaborate on any uniquely theological considerations underlying their concern about gene splicing in humans. . . .

3   In the view of the theologians, contemporary developments in molecular biology raise issues of responsibility rather than being matters to be prohibited because they usurp powers that human beings should not possess. The Biblical religions teach that human beings are, in some sense, co-creators with the Supreme Creator. Thus, as interpreted for the Commission by their representatives, these major religious faiths respect and encourage the enhancement of knowledge about nature as well as responsible use of that knowledge. Endorsement of genetic engineering,

which is praised for its potential to improve the human estate, is linked with the recognition that the misuse of human freedom creates evil and that human knowledge and power can result in harm.

While religious leaders present theological bases for their concerns, 4 essentially the same concerns have been raised—sometimes in slightly different words—by many thoughtful secular observers of contemporary science and technology. Concerns over unintended effects, over the morality of genetic manipulation in all its forms, and over the social and political consequences of new technologies are shared by religious and secular commentators. The examination of the various specific concerns need not be limited, therefore, to the religious format in which some of the issues have been raised.

FULLY UNDERSTANDING THE MACHINERY OF LIFE

Although it does not have a specific religious meaning, the objection 5 to scientists "playing God" is assumed to be self-explanatory. On closer examination, however, it appears to the Commission that it conveys several rather different ideas, some describing the power of gene splicing itself and some relating merely to its consequences.

At its heart, the term represents a reaction to the realization that 6 human beings are on the threshold of understanding how the fundamental machinery of life works. A full understanding of what are now great mysteries, and the powers inherent in that understanding, would be so awesome as to justify the description "God-like." In this view, playing God is not actually an objection to the research but an expression of a sense of awe—and concern.

Since the Enlightenment, Western societies have exalted the search 7 for greater knowledge, while recognizing its awesome implications. Some scientific discoveries reverberate with particular force because they not only open new avenues of research but also challenge people's entire understanding of the world and their place in it. Current discoveries in gene splicing—like the new knowledge associated with Copernicus and Darwin—further dethrone human beings as the unique center of the universe. By identifying DNA and learning how to manipulate it, science seems to have reduced people to a set of malleable molecules that can be interchanged with those of species that people regard as inferior. Yet unlike the earlier revolutionary discoveries, those in molecular biology are not merely descriptions, they give scientists vast powers for action.

ARROGANT INTERFERENCE WITH NATURE

By what standards are people to guide the exercise of this awe- 8 some new freedom if they want to act responsibly? In this context, the charge that human beings are playing God can mean that in "creating

new life forms" scientists are abusing their learning by interfering with
nature.

9   But in one sense *all* human activity that produces changes that otherwise would not have occurred interferes with nature. Medical activities
as routine as the prescription of eyeglasses for myopia or as dramatic as
the repair or replacement of a damaged heart are in this sense "unnatural." In another sense, human activity cannot interfere with nature — in
the sense of contravening it — since all human activities, including some
gene splicing, proceed according to the scientific laws that describe
natural processes. Ironically, to believe that "playing God" in this sense
is even possible would itself be hubris according to some religious
thought, which maintains that only God can interfere with the descriptive laws of nature (that is, perform miracles).

10   If, instead, what is meant is that gene splicing technology interferes
with nature in the sense that it violates God's prescriptive natural law or
goes against God's purposes as they are manifested in the natural order,
then some reason must be given for this judgment. None of the scholars
appointed to report their views by the three religious bodies that urged
the Commission to undertake this study suggested that either natural
reason or revelation imply that gene splicing technology as such is
"unnatural" in this prescriptive sense. Although each scholar expressed
concern over particular applications of gene splicing technology, they all
also emphasized that human beings have not merely the right but the
duty to employ their God-given powers to harness nature for human
benefit. To turn away from gene splicing, which may provide a means of
curing hereditary diseases, would itself raise serious ethical problems.

CREATING NEW LIFE FORMS

11   If "creating new life forms" is simply producing organisms with
novel characteristics, then human beings create new life forms frequently and have done so since they first learned to cultivate new
characteristics in plants and breed new traits in animals. Presumably the
idea is that gene splicing creates new life forms, rather than merely
modifying old ones, because it "breaches species barriers" by combining
DNA from different species — groups of organisms that cannot mate to
produce fertile offspring.

12   Genetic engineering is not the first exercise of humanity's ability to
create new life forms through nonsexual reproduction. The creation of
hybrid plants seems no more or no less natural than the development of
a new strain of *E. coli* bacteria through gene splicing. Further, genetic
engineering cannot accurately be called unique in that it involves the
creation of new life forms through processes that do not occur in nature
without human intervention. . . . Scientists have found that the transfer

of DNA between organisms of different species occurs in nature without human intervention. Yet, as one eminent scientist in the field has pointed out, it would be unwarranted to assume that a dramatic increase in the frequency of such transfers through human intervention is not problematic simply because DNA transfer sometimes occurs naturally.

In the absence of specific religious prohibitions, either revealed or   13
derived by rational argument from religious premises, it is difficult to see why "breaching species barriers" as such is irreligious or otherwise objectionable. In fact, the very notion that there are barriers that must be breached prejudges the issue. The question is simply whether there is something intrinsically wrong with intentionally crossing species lines. Once the question is posed in this way the answer must be negative— unless one is willing to condemn the production of tangelos by hybridizing tangerines and grapefruits or the production of mules by the mating of asses with horses.

There may nonetheless be two distinct sources of concern about   14
crossing species lines that deserve serious consideration. First, gene splicing affords the possibility of creating hybrids that can reproduce themselves (unlike mules, which are sterile). So the possibility of self-perpetuating "mistakes" adds a new dimension of concern, although here again, the point is not that crossing species lines is inherently wrong, but that it may have undesirable consequences and that these consequences may multiply beyond human control. As noted, the Commission's focus on the human applications of gene splicing has meant that it does not here address this important set of concerns, which lay behind the original self-imposed moratorium on certain categories of gene splicing research and which have been, and continue to be, addressed through various scientific and public mechanisms, such as RAC [Recombinant Advisory Committee].

Second, there is the issue of whether particular crossings of species   15
—especially the mixing of human and nonhuman genes—might not be illicit. The moral revulsion at the creation of human-animal hybrids may be traced in part to the prohibition against sexual relations between human beings and lower animals. Sexual relations with lower animals are thought to degrade human beings and insult their God-given dignity as the highest of God's creatures. But unease at the prospect of human-animal hybrids goes beyond sexual prohibitions.

The possibility of creating such hybrids calls into question basic   16
assumptions about the relationship of human beings to other living things. For example, those who believe that the current treatment of animals—in experimentation, food production, and sport—is morally suspect would not be alone in being troubled by the prospect of exploitive or insensitive treatment of creatures that possess even more human-like qualities than chimpanzees or porpoises do. Could genetic engineering be used to develop a group of virtual slaves—partly human, partly lower animal—to do people's bidding? Paradoxically, the very charac-

teristics that would make such creatures more valuable than any existing animals (that is, their heightened cognitive powers and sensibilities) would also make the moral propriety of their subservient role more problematic. Dispassionate appraisal of the long history of gratuitous destruction and suffering that humanity has visited upon the other inhabitants of the earth indicates that such concerns should not be dismissed as fanciful.

17   Accordingly, the objection to the creation of new life forms by crossing species lines (whether through gene splicing or otherwise) reflects the concern that human beings lack the God-like knowledge and wisdom required for the exercise of these God-like powers. Specifically, people worry that interspecific hybrids that are partially human in their genetic makeup will be like Dr. Frankenstein's monster. A striking lesson of the Frankenstein story is the uncontrollability and uncertainty of the consequences of human interferences with the natural order. Like the tale of the Sorcerer's apprentice or the myth of the golem created from lifeless dust by the 16th century rabbi, Loew of Prague, the story of Dr. Frankenstein's monster serves as a reminder of the difficulty of restoring order if a creation intended to be helpful proves harmful instead. Indeed, each of these tales conveys a painful irony: in seeking to extend their control over the world, people may lessen it. The artifices they create to do their bidding may rebound destructively against them—the slave may become the master.

18   Suggesting that someone lacks sufficient knowledge or wisdom to engage in an activity the person knows how to perform thus means that the individual has insufficient knowledge of the consequences of that activity or insufficient wisdom to cope with those consequences. But if this is the rational kernel of the admonition against playing God, then the use of gene splicing technology is not claimed to be wrong as such but wrong because of its potential consequences. Understood in this way, the slogan that crossing species barriers is playing God does not end the debate, but it does make a point of fundamental importance. It emphasizes that any realistic assessment of the potential consequences of the new technology must be founded upon a sober recognition of human fallibility and ignorance. At bottom, the warning not to play God is closely related to the Socratic injunction "know thyself"; in this case, acknowledge the limits of understanding and prediction, rather than assuming that people can foresee all the consequences of their actions or plan adequately for every eventuality.

19   Any further examination of the notion that the hybridization of species, at least when one of the species is human, is intrinsically wrong (and not merely wrong as a consequence of what is done with the hybrids) involves elaboration of two points. First, what characteristics are uniquely human, setting humanity apart from all other species? And second, does the wrong lie in bestowing some but not all of these characteristics on the new creation or does it stem from depriving the

being that might otherwise have arisen from the human genetic material of the opportunity to have a totally human makeup? The Commission believes that these are important issues deserving of serious study.

It should be kept in mind, however, that the information available to the Commission suggests that the ability to create interspecific hybrids of the sort that would present intrinsic moral and religious concerns will not be available in the foreseeable future. The research currently being done on experimentation with recombinant DNA techniques through the use of single human genes (for example, the insertion of a particular human hemoglobin gene into mouse cells at the embryonic stage) or the study of cellular development through the combining of human genetic material with that of other species in a way that does not result in a mature organism (for example, *in vitro* fusion of human and mouse cells) does not, in the Commission's view, raise problems of an improper "breaching of the barriers." . . . 20

EVOLUTIONARY IMPACT ON HUMAN BEINGS

Some critics warn against the dangers of attempting to control or interfere with the "wisdom of evolution" in order to satisfy scientific curiosity. Those who hold this view object in particular to crossing species lines by gene splicing because they believe that the pervasive inability of different species to produce fertile offspring by sexual reproduction must be an adaptive feature, that is, it must confer some significant survival advantage. Thus they view species lines as natural protective barriers that human beings may circumvent only at their peril, although the harm such barriers are supposed to shield people from remains unspecified. 21

Most proponents of genetic engineering argue that the benefits it will bring are more tangible and important and will affect more people than those objecting suggest. Further, the notion of the "wisdom of evolution" that apparently underlies this consequentialist version of the objection to crossing species lines is not well founded. As the scientific theory of evolution does not postulate a plan that the process of evolution is to achieve, evolutionary changes cannot be said to promote such a plan, wisely or unwisely. Moreover, evolutionary theory recognizes (and natural history confirms) that a "wise" adaptation at one time or place can become a lethal flaw when circumstances change. So even if it could be shown that species barriers have thus far played an important adaptive role, it would not follow that this will continue. An evolutionary explanation of any inherited characteristic can at most show that having that characteristic gave an organism's ancestors some advantage in enabling them to live long enough to reproduce and that the characteristic has not yet proved maladaptive for the offspring. 22

Furthermore, as a philosopher concerned with assessing the risks of 23 genetic engineering has recently noted, the ability to manipulate genes, both within and across species lines, may become a crucial asset for survival.

> There may . . . come a time when, because of natural or man-induced climatic change, the capacity to alter quickly the genetic composition of agricultural plants will be required to forestall catastrophic famine.

24   The consequentialist version of the warning against crossing species lines seems, then, to be no more a conclusive argument against genetic engineering than the admonition that to cross species lines is wrong because it is playing God. But it does serve the vital purpose of urging that, so far as this is possible, the evolutionary effects of any interventions are taken into account . . .

CHANGING THE MEANING OF BEING HUMAN

25   Some geneticists have seen in their field the possibility of benefit through improving human traits. Human beings have the chance to "rise above (their) nature" for "the first time in all time," as one leader in the field has observed:

> It has long been apparent that you and I do not enter this world as unformed clay compliant to any mold. Rather, we have in our beginnings some bent of mind, some shade of character. The origin of this structure—of the fiber in this clay—was for centuries mysterious . . . Today . . . we know to look within. We seek not in the stars but in our genes for the herald of our fate.

26   Will gene splicing actually make possible such changes in "human nature" for the first time? In some ways this question is unanswerable since there is great disagreement about which particular characteristics make up "human nature." For some people, the concept encompasses those characteristics that are uniquely human. Yet most human genes are actually found in other mammals as well; moreover, recent work by ethologists and other biologists on animal behavior and capacities is demonstrating that many characteristics once regarded as unique to human beings are actually shared by other animals, particularly by the higher primates, although an ability to record and study the past and to plan beyond the immediate future appears to be a singularly human trait.

27   Other people regard the critical qualities as those natural characteris-

tics that are common to all human beings, or at least all who fall within a certain "normal range." "Natural" here means characteristics that people are born with as opposed to those that result from social convention, education, or acculturation.

To consider whether gene splicing would allow the changing of 28 human nature thus breaks down into two questions. Which characteristics found in all human beings are inborn or have a large inborn basis? And will gene splicing techniques be able to alter or replace some of the genetic bases of those characteristics? As to the first, the history of religious, philosophical, and scientific thought abounds with fundamental disputes over human nature. Without a consensus on that issue the second question could only be answered affirmatively if it were clear that gene splicing will eventually allow the alteration of all natural characteristics of human beings.

As it is by no means certain that it will ever be possible to change the 29 genetic basis of all natural characteristics, it seems premature to assume that gene splicing will enable changes in human nature. At most, it can perhaps be said that this technology may eventually allow some aspects of what it means to be human to be changed. Yet even that possibility rightly evokes profound concern and burdens everyone with an awesome and inescapable responsibility—either to develop and employ this capability for the good of humanity or to reject it in order to avoid potential undesirable consequences.

The possibility of changing human nature must, however, be kept in 30 perspective. First, within the limits imposed by human beings' genetic endowment, there is already considerable scope by means other than gene splicing for changing some acquired characteristics that are distinctively human. For example, people's desires, values, and the way they live can be changed significantly through alterations in social and economic institutions and through mass education, indoctrination, and various forms of behavior control. Thus, even if gene splicing had the power that some people are concerned about, it would not be unique in its ability to produce major changes in what it means to be human— although it would be unusual in acting on the inheritable foundation of thoughts and actions. If the technology can ever be used in this way, the heritability of the changes ought probably to be regarded as significantly different from any changes now possible.

Second, according to the theory of evolution, the genetic basis of 31 what is distinctively human continually changes through the interplay of random mutation and natural selection. The concern, then, is that gene splicing will for the first time allow deliberate, selective, and rapid alterations to be made in the human genetic constitution.

Finally, concern about changing human nature may at bottom be still 32 more narrowly focused upon those characteristics of human beings— whether unique to the species or not—that are especially valued or cherished. Here, too, there may be disagreement as to which characteristics are most valuable and the value of a given characteristic may depend upon the social or natural environment in which it is manifested.

33   In sum, the question of whether gene splicing will enable changes in human nature—and the ethical, social, and philosophical significance of such changes—cannot be determined until much more is known about human genetics, specifically the exact contribution of heredity to many human physical and, more important, behavioral traits. Indeed, one of the most important contributions genetic engineering could make to the science of behavioral genetics may be that it will help resolve the age-old controversy of nature versus nurture. If designed changes were possible, society would have to confront whether such changes should be made, and, if they should, which ones. The problems created by uncertainty are particularly notable here since any decision about what characteristics are "desirable" would depend on the world that people will be living in, which is itself unknowable in advance. . . .

Continuing Concerns

34   A distinction has been drawn in this Report between two views: (1) that gene splicing technology is intrinsically wrong or contrary to important values and (2) that, while the technology is not inherently wrong, certain of its applications or consequences are undesirable. Regarding the latter, it has also been noted that genetic engineering involves an array of uncertainties beyond those usually found in technological developments. Not only is the occurrence of specific desirable or undesirable consequences impossible to predict but the application of gene splicing could have far-reaching consequences that could alter basic individual and social values.

35   The Commission could find no ground for concluding that any current or planned forms of genetic engineering, whether using human or nonhuman material, are intrinsically wrong or irreligious per se. The Commission does not see in the rapid development of gene splicing the "fundamental danger" to world safety or to human values that concerned the leaders of the three religious organizations. Rather, the issue that deserves careful thought is: by what standards, and toward what objectives, should the great new powers of genetic engineering be guided? . . .

Questions for Discussion and Writing

1. How is the President's Commission's claim that religious leaders are overreacting to the threat of gene splicing supported by their analysis of the technology of genetic engineering as simply a tool?

Evaluate their claim that since the Bible does not speak out against the practice and since scientists in no way could take God's place, genetic engineering poses no danger.

2. How does the President's Commission attempt to reassure its audience that the widespread fear of creating cross-species hybrids (for example, mixing human genes with animal genes to produce a slave species that could be exploited by humans) is baseless? How does the commission seek to minimize fears many people have that genetic engineering will create a "self-perpetuating mistake"?

3. Why does the President's Commission argue that genetic engineering does not pose as great a threat as religious leaders believe?

4. What reasons does the commission give to support the assertion that genetic engineering is not fundamentally different from other means (social or economic) that already are altering human behavior?

5. How does the commission's interpretation of the Bible support the assertion that genetic engineering is not a sacrilegious act despite the claim that scientists can serve as "co-creators" in the evolution of genetic alteration?

6. How effectively does the President's Commission take into account the views of the opposition? To what extent is the commission's overall argument weakened because it does not address the crucial issue of genetic diversity (that is, that by "playing God," genetic engineers are permanently altering the range of genetic variation for all future generations by imposing a certain "type" of human being)?

7. How does the commission argue by analogy by referring to past errors of religions concerning Copernicus' theories? The commission reminds the readers that it took the church many centuries to recognize the truth of Copernicus' theory that the earth and other planets move around the sun, and not vice versa.

8. How does the commission shape its argument by citing only positive examples of genetic manipulation while downplaying (undervaluing) those cases that could undermine their thesis?

9. Evaluate the commission's claim that the opposition should not be taken seriously because of the existence of so many diverse viewpoints. The commission suggests that the opposition's arguments must be weak since they have not coalesced around any central position.

10. In a specific case where the capability exists to correct a prenatal defect in the womb before the child is born, who should be given the right to make the final decision? Should the decision be made by the child's parents, the doctor, or the government? Precedents for this kind of dilemma have already been set in cases where the government through the courts has compelled the medical staff at a hospital to operate on an infant with multiple birth defects against the wishes of the parents.

11. For further reading on the subject, see Daniel J. Kevles, *In the Name of Eugenics* (1985); Robert Esbjornson, editor, *The Manipulation of Life* (1984); Jeremy Rifkin, *Algeny* (1983); and Ted Howard and Jeremy Rifkin, *Who Should Play God?* (1977). Also, the Office of Technology Assessment of the U.S. Congress has a report available titled *Human Gene Therapy* (1984).

Foundation on
Economic Trends

The Theological Letter concerning the Moral Arguments against Genetic Engineering of the Human Germline Cells

"The Theological Letter concerning the Moral Arguments against Genetic Engineering of the Human Germline Cells" was circulated by Jeremy Rifkin of the Foundation on Economic Trends (June 8, 1983). The foundation is an association comprised of officials of Jewish, Catholic, and Protestant church associations who oppose efforts to genetically engineer specific traits into the germline of the human species. They claim that no group or institution should have the right or authority to make decisions today that will permanently change the genetic makeup of future generations.

While the nation has begun to turn its attention to the dangers of nuclear war, little or no debate has taken place over the emergence of an entirely new technology which in time could very well pose as serious a threat to the existence of the human species as the bomb itself. We are referring to human genetic engineering. On July 22, 1982 the *New York Times* published a major editorial entitled "Whether to Make Perfect Humans." It will soon be possible, says the *Times*, to fundamentally alter the human species by engineering the genetic traits of the sex cells — the sperm and egg. Humanity's new found ability to engineer genetic traits could well lead to the creation of a new species, as different from homo-sapiens as we are to the higher apes. So grave is the threat of human genetic engineering that the *Times* suggests that we consider "the question of whether the human germline should be declared inviolable." 1

Programming genetic traits into human sex cells subjects the human species to the art of technological manipulation and architectural design. 2

With the arrival of human genetic engineering, humanity approaches a crossroads in its own technological history. It will soon be possible to engineer and produce human beings by the same technological design principles as we now employ in our industrial processes. 3

The wholesale design of human life, in accordance with technological 4 prerequisites, design specifications, and quality controls, raises a fundamental question. Nobel laureate biologist Dr. Salvador Lauria puts the question in its most succinct context when he asks "When does a repaired or manufactured man stop being a man . . . and become a robot, an object, an industrial product?"

5   The debate over genetic engineering is similar to the debate over nuclear power. For years the nuclear proponents argued that the potential benefits of nuclear power outweighed the potential harm. Today an increasingly skeptical public has begun to seriously question this basic presumption.

6   In a similar vein, proponents of human genetic engineering argue that the benefits outweigh the risks and that it would be irresponsible not to use this powerful new technology to eliminate serious "genetic disorders." The *New York Times* editorial board correctly addressed this conventional scientific argument by concluding in its editorial that once the scientists are able to repair genetic defects "it will become much harder to argue against adding genes that confer desired qualities, like better health, looks or brains." According to the *Times*, "There is no discernible line to be drawn between making inheritable repairs of genetic defects, and improving the species."

7   Once we decide to begin the process of human genetic engineering, there is really no logical place to stop. If diabetes, sickle cell anemia, and cancer are to be cured by altering the genetic make-up of an individual, why not proceed to other "disorders:" myopia, color blindness, left-handedness. Indeed, what is to preclude a society from deciding that a certain skin color is a disorder?

8   As knowledge about the genes increases, the bio-engineers will inevitably gain new insights into the functioning of more complex characteristics, such as those associated with behavior and thoughts. Many scientists are already contending that schizophrenia and other "abnormal" psychological states result from genetic disorders or defects. Others now argue that "antisocial" behavior, such as criminality and social protest, are also examples of malfunctioning genetic information. One prominent neurophysiologist has gone so far as to say "there can be no twisted thought without a twisted molecule." Many sociobiologists contend that virtually all human activity is in some way determined by our genetic make-up and that if we wish to change this situation, we must change our genes.

9   Whenever we begin to discuss the idea of genetic defects there is no way to limit the discussion to one or two or even a dozen so-called disorders because of a hidden assumption that lies behind the very notion of "defective." Ethicist Daniel Callahan penetrates to the core of the problem when he observes that "behind the human horror at genetic defectiveness lurks . . . an image of the perfect human being. The very language of 'defect,' 'abnormality,' 'disease,' and 'risk,' presupposes such an image, a kind of proto-type of perfection."

The question, then, is whether or not humanity should "begin" the 10
process of engineering future generations of human beings by technological design in the laboratory.

What is the price we pay for embarking on a course whose final goal 11
is the "perfection" of the human species?

First there is the ecological price to consider. It is very likely that in 12
attempting to "perfect" the human species we will succeed in engineering our own extinction. Eliminating so-called "bad genes" will lead to a
dangerous narrowing of diversity in the gene pool. Since part of the
strength of our gene pool consists in its very diversity, including defective genes, tampering with it might ultimately lead to extinction of the
human race. It should be recalled that in the 1950's genetic modifications
were made in wheat strains to create bumper crops of "super wheat."
When a new strain of disease hit the fields, farmers found that their
wheat was too delicate to resist. Within two years, virtually the entire
crop was destroyed.

We have no doubt that a similar effort to "perfect" the human species 13
by eliminating the so-called bad genes would prove equally destructive.
This simple biological fact is so patently obvious that one begins to
wonder why it is so conveniently ignored by so many of the "experts" in
the scientific community. Even Dr. Thomas Wagner, the scientist at Ohio
University who is responsible for the first successful transfer of a gene
trait from one mammalian species to the embryo of another mammalian
species, has gone on record as being opposed to genetic engineering of
the human germline cells because of the potentially devastating effect
that such narrowing of genetic diversity might have on the ability of the
human species to survive in the future. Dr. Wagner says,

> It is a terrible mistake to make a permanent, heritable change,
> even if it appears to be for the better, in a human being's genetic
> make-up. We don't know what the future brings, and we don't
> understand fully the process of evolution. Any species of animal
> needs a certain degree of diversity, some of which appears nega-
> tive, in order for it to survive into the future. I don't think we
> should be manipulating the genetic material beyond the individ-
> ual generation of the human involved.

Then there is the question of eugenics to carefully consider. Eugenics 14
is the inseparable ethical wing of the Age of Biotechnology. First coined
by Charles Darwin's cousin, Sir Francis Galton, eugenics is generally
categorized into two types, negative and positive. Negative eugenics
involves the systematic elimination of so called biologically undesirable
characteristics. Positive eugenics is concerned with the use of genetic
manipulation to "improve" the characteristics of an organism or species.

Eugenics is not a new phenomenon. At the turn of the century the 15
U.S. sported a massive eugenics movement. Politicians, celebrities, aca-

demicians and prominent business leaders joined together in support of a eugenic's program for the country. The frenzy over eugenics reached a fever pitch with many states passing sterilization statutes and the U.S. Congress passing a new emigration law in the 1920's based on eugenics considerations. As a consequence of the new legislation, thousands of American citizens were sterilized so they could not pass on their "inferior" traits and the federal government locked its doors to certain emigrant groups deemed biologically unfit by then existing eugenics standards.

16   While the Americans flirted with eugenics for the first thirty years of the twentieth century, their escapades were of minor historical account when compared with the eugenics program orchestrated by the Nazis in the 1930's and 40's. Millions of Jews and other religious and ethnic groups were gassed in the German crematoriums to advance the Third Reich's dream of eliminating all but the "Aryan" race from the globe. The Nazis also embarked on a "positive" eugenics program in which thousands of S.S. officers and German women were carefully selected for their "superior" genes and mated under the auspices of the state. Impregnated women were cared for in state facilities and their offspring were donated to the Third Reich as the vanguard for the new super race that would rule the world for the next millenium.

17   Eugenics lay dormant for nearly a quarter of a century after World War II. Then the spectacular breakthroughs in molecular biology in the 1960's raised the spectre of a eugenics revival once again. By the mid 1970's, many scientists were beginning to worry out loud that the potential for genetic engineering might lead to a return to the kind of eugenics hysteria that swept over America and Europe earlier in the century. Speaking at a National Academy of Science forum on recombinant DNA, Ethan Signer, a biologist at MIT, warned his colleagues that

> this research is going to bring us one more step closer to genetic engineering of people. That's where they figure out how to have us produce children with ideal characteristics. . . . Last time around, the ideal children had blonde hair, blue eyes and Aryan genes.

18   The concern over a re-emergence of eugenics is well-founded but misplaced. While professional ethicists watch out the front door for telltale signs of a resurrection of the Nazi nightmare, eugenics doctrine has quietly slipped in the back door. The new eugenics is commercial not social. In place of the shrill eugenic cries for racial purity, the new commercial eugenics talks in pragmatic terms of medical benefits and improvement in the quality of life. The old eugenics was steeped in political ideology and motivated by fear and hate. The new eugenics is grounded in medical advance and the spectre of extending the human life span.

Genetic engineering, then, is coming to us not as a threat, but as a   19
promise; not as a punishment but as a gift. And here is where the danger
lies. If the Brave New World comes, it will not be forced on us by an evil
cabal of self-serving scientists and Machiavellian politicians. On the
contrary, what makes opposition to the Brave New World so difficult is
the seductive path that leads to it. Every new advance in human genetic
engineering is likely to be heralded as a great stride forward, a boon for
humankind. Every one of the breakthroughs in genetic engineering will
be of benefit to someone, under some circumstance, somewhere in society. And step by step, advance by advance, we human beings might well
choose to trade away the spontaneity of natural life for the predictability
of technological design until the human species as we know it is transformed into a product of our own creation; a product that bears only a
faint resemblance to the original.

How important is it that we eliminate all the imperfections, all the   20
defects? What price are we willing to pay to extend our lives, to insure
our own health, to do away with all of the inconveniences, the irrita-
tions, the nuisances, the infirmities, the suffering, that are so much a part
of the human experience? Are we so enamored with the idea of physical
perpetuation at all costs that we are even willing to subject the human
species to rigid architectural design? Is guaranteeing our health worth
trading away our humanity?

What is the price we pay for medical advance, for securing our own   21
physical well being? If it means accepting the idea of reducing the
human species to a technologically designed product, then it is too dear a
price.

Ultimately, there is no security to be found in engineering the human   22
species, just as we have now learned that there is no security to be found
in building bigger, more sophisticated nuclear bombs.

Perhaps, if we had taken the time to look at the long-range implica-   23
tions of our work in nuclear physics forty years ago, we might well have
decided to restrict or prohibit the research and development of nuclear
weaponry. Today we have the opportunity to look ahead and envision
the final logical consequences of our work in genetic engineering. The
question is whether we will choose to do so.

It is our hope that this resolution will represent a watershed in our   24
thinking concerning science and technology. For the first time, it affirms
the right of humanity to say no to the application of its own scientific
knowledge. Just because something can be done is no longer an adequate
justification for assuming it should be done or that it can't be stopped
from being done.

We believe we have a sacred obligation to say no when the pursuit of   25
a specific technological path threatens the very existence of life itself.

It is with this thought in mind that we now turn to you for support of   26
this resolution.

Human genetic engineering presents the human race with the most   27 important political question it has ever had to contend with. Who do we entrust with the ultimate authority to decide which are the good genes that should be engineered into the human gene pool and which are the bad genes that should be eliminated?

28   Today the ultimate exercise of political power is within our grasp; the ability to control the future lives of human beings by engineering their characteristics in advance; making them a hostage of their own architecturally designed blueprints. Genetic engineering represents the power of authorship. Never before in history has such complete power over life been a possibility. The idea of imprisoning the life span of a human being by simply engineering its genetic blueprint at conception is truly awesome.

29   Aldous Huxley's spectre of a biologically designed caste system with its alphas, betas, gammas and deltas looms on the horizon. Our society must now ponder whether to give sanction to this fundamental departure in how human life is formed. In examining this issue, we would ask everyone to consider one simple question. Would we trust the Congress of the U.S. with the ultimate authority to decide which genes should be engineered into the human gene pool and which should be eliminated? Would we entrust the executive or judicial branch with such authority? Or the corporations and the marketplace? Or the scientists and the medical community?

30   Who do we designate to play God? The fact is, no individual, group, or set of institutions can legitimately claim the right or authority to make such decisions on behalf of the rest of the species alive today or for future generations.

31   Genetic engineering of the human germline cells represents a fundamental threat to the preservation of the human species as we know it, and should be opposed with the same courage and conviction as we now oppose the threat of nuclear extinction.

32   We would like your support for this proposed resolution to prohibit the engineering of genetic traits into the germline of the human species.

RESOLUTION

To express the conviction that engineering specific genetic traits into the human germline not be attempted.

Whereas molecular biologists have recently succeeded in altering the sex cells of a mammalian species through genetic engineering technology;

Whereas the new advances in genetic engineering technology now raise the possibility of altering the human species;

Whereas the ability to design and program specific physiological characteristics by engineering specific genetic traits into the sperm, egg, or embryo of a human being represents a fundamental alteration in the way a human being may be formed;

Whereas programming genetic traits directly into human sex cells subjects the human species to the art of technological manipulation and architectural design;

Whereas the redesign of the human species by genetic engineering technology irreversibly alters the composition of the gene pool for all future generations of human life;

Whereas engineering fundamental changes of human sex cells necessitates that decisions be made as to which genetic traits should be programmed into the human gene pool and which should be eliminated; and

Whereas no individual, group of individuals, or institutions can legitimately claim the right or authority to make such decisions on behalf of the rest of the species alive today or for future generations: Now, therefore, be it

Resolved, That efforts to engineer specific genetic traits into the germline of the human species should not be attempted.

Questions for Discussion and Writing

1. In what way is genetic engineering capable of producing more fundamental changes in the human species than other advances in biotechnology (such as artificial hearts, organ transplants)?

2. Why do the writers of the "Theological Letter" believe that one of the consequences of genetic engineering might be a reemergence of eugenics programs that would sacrifice the diversity of the human gene pool and produce a "technologically designed product"?

3. What connection do the writers draw between Aldous Huxley's *Brave New World* and the possibility that the government might use the capabilities of genetic engineering to create a biologically based caste system?

4. What specific policy changes do the writers of the letter recommend?

5. How do the writers of the "Theological Letter" use an editorial in the *New York Times* to support their argument?

6. What purpose do the writers have in equating or drawing a comparison between a modern commercial attempt to manufacture an improved human being and the Nazi attempt to create a perfect Aryan superrace that would take over the world and eliminate so-called racial undesirables? Evaluate their claim that once started, it would be all too easy for genetic engineering to serve existing prejudices (producing boys rather than girls, blue-eyed babies rather than brown-eyed babies, and so on). In what way might their argumentative strategy be construed as a case of guilt by association?

7. How do the writers argue by analogy in comparing genetic engineering with nuclear power? Are these two situations really comparable? Keep in mind that before nuclear power became part of everyday life the potential negative consequences were grossly underestimated.

8. In what way do the writers develop their argument by first comparing the development of genetic engineering with the growth of nuclear power and then illustrating possible misuses of biotechnology by comparing it with the eugenics program in Nazi Germany? Evaluate their claim that at first genetic engineering will be used to eliminate physical defects, but later inevitably it will be used to eradicate character traits, behavior patterns, and personality types that are considered socially undesirable.

9. How do the writers' analyses of the different meanings of the words *defect* and *perfection* illustrate that, when it comes to the question of designing an ideal human being, people will often disagree on what a psychological defect or perfection might be? More generally, how do the writers use language to undercut what they perceive as overly naive assumptions on the part of those who support genetic engineering?

10. How do the writers use the example of the production of "super wheat" to underscore their concerns regarding genetic engineering? Points to keep in mind are (*a*) that during the 1950s genetic modifications were made to a certain strain of wheat to create a superwheat that would make possible bumper crops of enormous proportions, (*b*) that the superwheat so created was inexplicably sensitive to a common disease to which other unimproved strains of wheat were immune, (*c*) that if all wheat were transformed into superwheat (as would naturally happen in the generations following an alteration of the germline) the unforeseen effects of disease would be capable of destroying the entire crop, and (*d*) that there would be no way to get back to the hardier strain of wheat with its own natural genetic diversity that was immune to the disease.

11. Based on the range of opinion expressed in arguments by the President's Commission and the writers of the "Theological Letter," discuss which kinds of particular genetic defects should be allowed to be corrected by gene splicing. Where should the line be drawn on correcting physical and mental traits that might be considered undesirable (such as antisocial behavior, dwarfism) but might also include variables such as skin color, height, gender, and so on.

12. Summarize the contrasting positions of both of these groups on the fundamental question of whether man has the right to alter the genetic inheritance or germline of the human species for all future generations.

13. Write a countercritique of the President's Commission from the viewpoint of the writers of the "Theological Letter." Show how the commission attempts to equate genetic engineering with social engineering when, in reality, gene splicing is very different in its permanent and irreversible effects.

PART THREE

Different Perspectives on Current Issues

8

Business: Is Business America's Only Business?

The philosophy underlying capitalism was presented by Adam Smith nearly 200 years ago in his *Wealth of Nations*. Smith's name has become synonymous with the free-market or laissez-faire economic system. Smith believed that human good followed from the free pursuit of self-interest. The opposite view was held by the German economist Karl Marx, who argued that the free-market theory Smith advocated was contrived by capitalist property owners to disguise their exploitation of workers.

A free-market system based on supply and demand is capable of producing a broad range of low-cost goods and services but has inherent problems with maintaining economic stability over long periods of time. For example, when it is working correctly, the farm economy is unparalleled. However, because farmers have very little control over the price at which they sell their crops, when the free-market system is not working well the farmers can suffer disastrously.

The tragic consequence of the lack of economic stability and equity for farmers is dramatized in a nonfiction chapter of John Steinbeck's classic novel *The Grapes of Wrath*. Steinbeck expresses his outrage at the plight of farmers who could not afford to have their crops harvested and had to leave them to rot in the fields while millions starved during the Great Depression of the 1930s. To deal with this kind of problem, the first farm price-support program, the Agricultural Adjustment Act of 1933, was enacted, based on the idea of *parity* (sustaining the value of farm output in comparison to other areas of the economy). This policy was designed to protect the family farm and, since then, price-support programs have played an enormous role in our economy.

Challenging this idea, free-market advocate Stephen Chapman argues that no further government subsidies should be used to preserve family farms "even if they are in danger of extinction." Chapman reasons that since the government doesn't take extraordinary measures to save "the family grocery store, the family pharmacy, or the family clothing store," it should not step in to preserve the family farm. By contrast, Congressman Byron Dorgan raises objections to government policies favoring huge agribusiness conglomerates. Dorgan claims that the free-market theory fails to work as anticipated and recommends continuing programs designed specifically to preserve the family farm.

The view that government should not attempt to regulate business is one also held by free-market economists. They believe that the market forces of supply and demand will produce the most good for the greatest number of people without government interference. Milton Friedman, following in Adam Smith's footsteps, argues that the only responsibility corporations have is to make as much money as possible without violating the law. In his view business managers are agents who would be remiss in their duty were they to distribute some of the firm's profits for social purposes. He says that corporate executives who wish to take socially responsible actions should use their own money, not that of the corporations they run.

Robert Almeder, on the other hand, claims that society must not approve corporate behavior that harms people, such as advertising cigarettes and marketing automobiles that cannot sustain moderate rear-end collisions. These profitable activities, although not illegal, symbolize the kind of behavior Almeder says society must not condone. His thesis is that society must regulate business until businesses have proved they can regulate themselves. This basic argument between Almeder and Friedman defines the framework for examining the kinds of responsibilities that corporations have in today's society, especially in the category of business practices that are not actually against the law but that demonstrate that companies are not living up to the ethical and moral obligations consumers now expect them to fulfill. The key question as to the nature of the obligations that corporations have to consumers and to society as a whole is nowhere more controversial than in the area of product safety.

The underlying *premiss* is that a business producing and marketing goods incurs certain moral and legal obligations to the consumer. The failure to meet these obligations is the theme of Judge Miles W. Lord's closing speech to officers of the A. H. Robins Company after a successful $4.6 million product-liability suit was brought against them for injuries caused by their product, the Dalkon Shield. Lord chastises the officers of the corporation and asks them to exhibit a "corporate conscience" not only by stopping sales and recalling devices already sold but by seeking out and warning women who may still be using the defective IUD (intrauterine device).

An argument against broadening product liability laws is made by a senior vice-president of R. J. Reynolds Industries. This tobacco company has never lost a liability suit directed against it. Harold L. Henderson argues that anyone who decides to smoke cigarettes in the face of "clear or widely claimed risks" cannot later sue the tobacco company for injuries suffered from using the product. In her opposing viewpoint, Elizabeth Whelan claims the tobacco companies have made a "conscious decision that their own economic well-being is far more important than the health of Americans."

It is difficult to draw the line on the question of corporate responsibility, especially when the causes and effects are geographically far removed from each other. A plant scientist argues that the ethic of "short term profitability" has led to the destruction of the tropical forests in Central America where cattle ranching produces cheap beef for export to fast-food hamburger chains in the United States. Skinner claims that the destruction of these forests accelerates the greenhouse effect.

The different perspectives on major issues presented in this chapter should provide new insights into basic questions such as: (1) Just what role should government play in business? (2) Is free trade good for our economy? (3) What should be done to ease the transition from an industrially based society to one based on information and services (as Americans in the past were faced with the challenge of moving from an agriculturally based economy to an industrial society)? The economic issues discussed in this section are more a part of our daily lives than ever before and certainly will remain so into the twenty-first century.

John Steinbeck

Hunger in a Land of Plenty

The distinguished American writer John Steinbeck is the author of many novels including Tortilla Flat *(1935),* Of Mice and Men *(1937),* Cannery Row *(1945),* East of Eden *(1952), and collections of short stories, such as* The Long Valley *(1938). "Hunger in a Land of Plenty" is one of the nonfiction chapters Steinbeck interwove with the narrative chapters of his Pulitzer Prize–winning novel* The Grapes of Wrath *(1939). This chapter poignantly expresses Steinbeck's outrage that small farmers could not afford to harvest and sell their crops while millions starved during the Great Depression of the 1930s.*

1   The spring is beautiful in California. Valleys in which the fruit blossoms are fragrant pink and white waters in a shallow sea. Then the first tendrils of the grapes, swelling from the old gnarled vines, cascade down to cover the trunks. The full green hills are round and soft as breasts. And on the level vegetable lands are the mile-long rows of pale green lettuce and the spindly little cauliflowers, the gray-green unearthly artichoke plants.

2   And then the leaves break out on the trees, and the petals drop from the fruit trees and carpet the earth with pink and white. The centers of the blossoms swell and grow and color: cherries and apples, peaches and pears, figs which close the flower in the fruit. All California quickens with produce, and the fruit grows heavy, and the limbs bend gradually under the fruit so that little crutches must be placed under them to support the weight.

3   Behind the fruitfulness are men of understanding and knowledge and skill, men who experiment with seed, endlessly developing the techniques for greater crops of plants whose roots will resist the million enemies of the earth: the molds, the insects, the rusts, the blights. These men work carefully and endlessly to perfect the seed, the roots. And there are the men of chemistry who spray the trees against pests, who sulphur the grapes, who cut out disease and rots, mildews and sicknesses. Doctors of preventive medicine, men at the borders, who look for fruit flies, for Japanese beetles, men who quarantine the sick trees and root them out and burn them, men of knowledge. The men who graft the young trees, the little vines, are the cleverest of all, for theirs is a surgeon's job, as tender and delicate; and these men must have surgeons' hands and surgeons' hearts to slit the bark, to place the grafts, to bind the wounds and cover them from the air. These are great men.

Along the rows, the cultivators move, tearing the spring grass and 4
turning it under to make a fertile earth, breaking the ground to hold the
water up near the surface, ridging the ground in little pools for the
irrigation, destroying the weed roots that may drink the water away from
the trees.

And all the time the fruit swells and the flowers break out in long 5
clusters on the vines. And in the growing year the warmth grows and the
leaves turn dark green. The prunes lengthen like little green bird's eggs,
and the limbs sag down against the crutches under the weight. And the
hard little pears take shape, and the beginning of the fuzz comes out on
the peaches. Grape blossoms shed their tiny petals and the hard little
beads become green buttons, and the buttons grow heavy. The men who
work in the fields, the owners of the little orchards, watch and calculate.
The year is heavy with produce. And men are proud, for of their knowledge they can make the year heavy. They have transformed the world
with their knowledge. The short, lean wheat has been made big and
productive. Little sour apples have grown large and sweet, and that old
grape that grew among the trees and fed the birds its tiny fruit has
mothered a thousand varieties, red and black, green and pale pink,
purple and yellow; and each variety with its own flavor. The men who
work in the experimental farms have made new fruits: nectarines and
forty kinds of plums, walnuts with paper shells. And always they work,
selecting, grafting, changing, driving themselves, driving the earth to
produce.

And first the cherries ripen. Cent and a half a pound. Hell, we can't 6
pick 'em for that. Black cherries and red cherries, full and sweet, and the
birds eat half of each cherry and the yellowjackets buzz into the holes
the birds made. And on the ground the seeds drop and dry with black
shreds hanging from them.

The purple prunes soften and sweeten. My God, we can't pick them 7
and dry and sulphur them. We can't pay wages, no matter what wages.
And the purple prunes carpet the ground. And first the skins wrinkle a
little and swarms of flies come to feast, and the valley is filled with the
odor of sweet decay. The meat turns dark and the crop shrivels on the
ground.

And the pears grow yellow and soft. Five dollars a ton. Five dollars 8
for forty fifty-pound boxes; trees pruned and sprayed, orchards
cultivated—pick the fruit, put it in boxes, load the trucks, deliver the
fruit to the cannery—forty boxes for five dollars. We can't do it. And the
yellow fruit falls heavily to the ground and splashes on the ground. The
yellowjackets dig into the soft meat, and there is a smell of ferment and
rot.

Then the grapes—we can't make good wine. People can't buy good 9
wine. Rip the grapes from the vines, good grapes, rotten grapes, wasp-
stung grapes. Press stems, press dirt and rot.

But there's mildew and formic acid in the vats. 10

11   Add sulphur and tannic acid.

12   The smell from the ferment is not the rich odor of wine, but the smell of decay and chemicals.

13   Oh, well. It has alcohol in it, anyway. They can get drunk.

14   The little farmers watched debt creep up on them like the tide. They sprayed the trees and sold no crop, they pruned and grafted and could not pick the crop. And the men of knowledge have worked, have considered, and the fruit is rotting on the ground, and the decaying mash in the wine vats is poisoning the air. And taste the wine—no grape flavor at all, just sulphur and tannic acid and alcohol.

15   This little orchard will be a part of a great holding next year, for the debt will have choked the owner.

16   This vineyard will belong to the bank. Only the great owners can survive, for they own the canneries too. And four pears peeled and cut in half, cooked and canned, still cost fifteen cents. And the canned pears do not spoil. They will last for years.

17   The decay spreads over the State, and the sweet smell is a great sorrow on the land. Men who can graft the trees and make the seed fertile and big can find no way to let the hungry people eat their produce. Men who have created new fruits in the world cannot create a system whereby their fruits may be eaten. And the failure hangs over the State like a great sorrow.

18   The works of the roots of the vines, of the trees, must be destroyed to keep up the price, and this is the saddest, bitterest thing of all. Carloads of oranges dumped on the ground. The people came for miles to take the fruit, but this could not be. How would they buy oranges at twenty cents a dozen if they could drive out and pick them up? And men with hoses squirt kerosene on the oranges, and they are angry at the crime, angry at the people who have come to take the fruit. A million people hungry, needing the fruit—and kerosene sprayed over the golden mountains.

19   And the smell of rot fills the country.

20   Burn coffee for fuel in the ships. Burn corn to keep warm; it makes a hot fire. Dump potatoes in the rivers and place guards along the banks to keep the hungry people from fishing them out. Slaughter the pigs and bury them, and let the putrescence drip down into the earth.

21   There is a crime here that goes beyond denunciation. There is a sorrow here that weeping cannot symbolize. There is a failure here that topples all our success. The fertile earth, the straight tree rows, the sturdy trunks, and the ripe fruit. And children dying of pellagra must die because a profit cannot be taken from an orange. And coroners must fill in the certificates—died of malnutrition—because the food must rot, must be forced to rot.

22   The people come with nets to fish for potatoes in the river, and the guards hold them back; they come in rattling cars to get the dumped oranges, but the kerosene is sprayed. And they stand still and watch the potatoes float by, listen to the screaming pigs being killed in a ditch and

covered with quicklime, watch the mountains of oranges slop down to a putrefying ooze; and in the eyes of the people there is the failure, and in the eyes of the hungry there is a growing wrath. In the souls of the people the grapes of wrath are filling and growing heavy, growing heavy for the vintage.

Questions for Discussion and Writing

1. How do paragraphs 1 and 2 create a vivid picture of a cornucopia of fruit and vegetables growing on every hillside, just waiting to be harvested? What function does Steinbeck's description of lush, abundant crops waiting to be harvested serve in the context of his argument?

2. How does paragraph 3 inform the reader that the present crops are the results of many years of skillful experimentation by scientists and agricultural engineers whose driving purpose has been the improvement of crop quality and quantity?

3. What rhetorical purpose is served by describing how much effort and skill is necessary to plow the earth, plant the seeds, water and nurture the plants, and combat weeds, insects, and blight to produce the crops described in paragraphs 1 and 2?

4. How does Steinbeck's description, interweaving images of natural bounty with images of crops rotting in the fields, underscore the idea that something is terribly wrong?

5. How does Steinbeck use a welter of voices to convey the idea that the small farmer must sell his produce at such a low price that he cannot afford to have his crop harvested and must allow fruit to rot in the fields? What advantage is there in having the reader "see" the situation before he or she "hears" these voices? Specifically, how do the cries "cherries. . . . Cent and a half a pound. . . . pears. . . . Five dollars a ton" explain why it would cost more to pick the crops than the farmers would receive?

6. What means does Steinbeck use to communicate the irony that the small farmers who cared for the crops must leave them to rot and go out of business while the big farmers with financial backing from industries can afford to can and store the fruit until prices rise again?

7. How does Steinbeck use the image of the harvest in his title — *The Grapes of Wrath* — in both its literal and its figurative sense to suggest the bitter repercussions of small farmers not being able to compete

with agricultural conglomerates that own both acreage and canning facilities?

8. As a research project, investigate how Steinbeck's description of the plight of the small farmers becoming poorer, of food being deliberately destroyed, and of hungry people being deprived of food that might have been fed them expresses an implicit argument against a social system in which displaced farmers from Oklahoma (called Okies) and elsewhere were forced to become migrant workers during the Great Depression.

Stephen Chapman

The Farmer on the Dole

———

Stephen Chapman served as associate editor of The New Republic *and as a columnist with* The Chicago Tribune. *"The Farmer on the Dole" first appeared in the October issue of* Harper's Magazine *(1982). Chapman, an advocate of free-market economics, argues against what he perceives to be the idealized myth of the American farmer. He claims that federal programs, incentives, and subsidies that were designed to help farmers have actually brought about the disastrous conditions they were designed to prevent. Chapman offers a wide range of statistical data to support his thesis that farmers are relatively well off, are not in imminent danger of bankruptcy, and therefore do not need further government subsidies.*

The family farmer is a durable feature of American folklore. From its 1
beginning America was regarded by Europeans as a pastoral Eden, shielded from the corrosive influences of city and commerce. American soil was cultivated, not by serfs and peasants as in the Old World, but by self-supporting landowners, thought to be the soul of a healthy democracy. In 1797 the *Encyclopaedia Britannica* stated that "in no part of the world are the people happier . . . or more independent than the farmers of New England." Thomas Jefferson frequently cited the blessings of America's agricultural character. "Those who labour in the earth are the chosen people of God, if ever he had a chosen people, whose breasts he has made his peculiar deposit for substantial and genuine virtue," he wrote in *Notes on the State of Virginia.* "Corruption of morals in the mass of cultivators is a phenomenon of which no age nor nation has furnished an example."

This vision of a nation of small farmers has always been largely 2
mythical. Jefferson urged his fellow Americans, "Let us never wish to see our citizens occupied at a workbench, or twirling a distaff," lost in the "mobs of great cities." When he wrote those lines, one in three of his countrymen already lived away from the farm. Many of the rest were on slaveholding farms and plantations in the South, not exactly compatible with Jefferson's ideal.

Today, only 2.8 percent of the American population lives on farms, 3
and fewer than half of these citizens depend on farming as their principal source of income. If independent family farmers are indeed the bedrock of the republic, that foundation has long since been eroded. But

the idealization of the family farm persists, along with the impulse to preserve it at whatever cost. These sentiments know none of the usual ideological or partisan boundaries.

4   Democrat Jim Hightower, a self-styled populist . . . quotes approvingly this characteristically apocalyptic complaint from the National Farmers Organization: "The farmhouse lights are going out all over America. And every time a light goes out, this country is losing something. It is losing the precious skills of a family farm system. And it is losing free men." Over on the other side of the political spectrum, conservative senator Robert Dole strikes a similar pose. "Family farms represent the very essence of what this country is about," he says. "They are the backbone of America." Like Hightower, Dole is worried about the decline of the family farm. "The farms are getting fewer, and the time has come for Congress to act," he argues.

5   Such emotionally charged pleas tend to strike a responsive chord in Congress, which, in fact, has been acting to protect the family farm for half a century. The array of programs ostensibly designed to preserve the nation's stock of sturdy yeomen has made agriculture the most heavily subsidized sector of our economy. The expense of these programs has grown even as the importance of farms in the economy has inexorably declined — from nearly a tenth of the nation's income in 1933, when most of the existing farm programs were initiated, to 2.6 percent in 1980. Last year the government spent over $11 billion on various forms of farm assistance — virtually all of them justified by pitchforkfuls of "save the family farm" rhetoric.

6   Even critics of the government's farm policies usually accept the goal of family-farm preservation, tending only to question whether the programs really help the beleaguered family farmer rather than his larger corporate competitors, or arguing simply that the expense has become excessive in a tight-budget era. These concerns are well founded, but they ignore the more basic question: why, exactly, does the tiny fraction of our population that chooses to practice family farming deserve all this solicitude in the first place?

7   So potent is the traditional image of the family farmer, and so unacquainted are most Americans with the real thing, that his actual characteristics are often ignored. For one thing, farm families are not worse off than their fellow citizens. Fifty years ago, the per capita income of farm dwellers was only 33 percent of the figure for nonfarmers; but since 1971 the recorded income of farm dwellers has amounted to 97 percent of that for nonfarmers, with the average farm family taking home $23,822 in 1980.

8   But the official figures undoubtedly underestimate the financial health of family farmers, given their ability, as self-employers, to underestimate their income when reporting it to the authorities (not to mention the favorable tax treatment those authorities accord what income farmers do report). Also, statistics on farm income typically include the nearly

two million farmers—often retirees or disenchanted urbanites—who farm more as a hobby than anything else. The average income of commercial farmers (those who actually do it for a living) is an impressive $34,000. And the typical farmer (even counting the hobbyists) has even greater wealth than income, largely because he owns, on average, 400 acres of land. That and other assets bring his family's net worth to about $300,000, approximately twice the average for other American households.

In short, today's family farmer is typically not a desperate home- 9 steader, but a sophisticated, relatively prosperous businessman. His success—which is simply the success of American agriculture—should not be resented, but it hardly makes him an obvious candidate for massive government assistance.

Why do we hear so much, then, about the family farmer's decline? 10 The most striking illustration of his plight, supposedly, is the continuing decrease in the number of farms and farmers. At the turn of the century, thirty million Americans lived on 5.7 million farms. By 1979, only 6.2 million people lived on 2.3 million farms. Projecting this trend far enough, it is easy to predict that soon there will be no farmers and no farms. This makes as much sense as assuming that because American fertility rates have declined steadily since the nation was founded, eventually no one will reproduce at all.

The decline of the farming sector is both perfectly natural and wholly 11 beneficial. It reflects two welcome phenomena: the increasing productivity of American farms and the rising living standards of all Americans. Seventy years ago, 106 man-hours of labor and seven acres of land were needed to produce 100 bushels of wheat; today it takes only nine man-hours and three acres. Technological improvements in machinery, fertilizer, pesticides, and seeds have made the difference. Hence fewer farmers cultivating roughly the same amount of land as in 1910 can feed a much larger number of people.

Then there is the effect of the growing affluence of the nation as a 12 whole. In a modern economy, the demand for food grows only about as fast as the population—a reflection of the fact that nearly everyone is adequately fed. The demand for other goods and services grows much faster, meaning that more and more people have to work to provide everything from television sets to medical care, while fewer and fewer have to grow food. It says something about the usual picture of farmers being driven off the land by factors beyond their control that the migration accelerates during times of prosperity, not during slumps. (During the Great Depression, the direction of the migration was actually reversed.) A shrinking agricultural population, far from being a sign of decay, is almost invariably a by-product of material progress. The only economies in which farming is stable are the poorest and most primitive, where most people farm because otherwise they wouldn't eat.

By itself, then, the decline in the number of farms, or farmers, is no 13 reason to worry. Some alarmists, however, blame it on the rise of big corporate farms—agribusiness, as the phenomenon is ominously labeled. True, farms have gotten bigger, as has nearly every other type of economic enterprise. They have done so in order to take advantage of the economies of scale offered by modern production techniques. Even so, the average farm has increased only 16 percent in size since 1969. There are still 2.4 million farms. In fact, only 8 percent of all U.S. farmland is farmed by corporations, set up mainly to avoid taxes. When you count only nonfamily corporations, the figure dips to one percent. So much for the fear that agriculture is being concentrated in a few corporate hands.

14   The number of federal programs directed at saving American farmers from extinction will come as a surprise to anyone familiar with the myth of the independent yeoman. Most farmers have their prices guaranteed by the federal price support program, which applies to wheat, corn, barley, oats, rye, sorghum, sugar, peanuts, soybeans, wool, rice, cotton, tobacco, and dairy products—just about everything, in fact. If the market price falls below the level set by the government, the Department of Agriculture in effect buys the farmer's crop. For many crops, it also provides an additional subsidy—"deficiency payments," which pay the farmer the difference between the market (or support) price and a higher "target price." This year, (1982) the support price for wheat is $3.55 a bushel. The target price is $4.05 a bushel. If the market price were $3.30 a bushel, the farmer could sell his crop to the government for $3.55, and then collect an additional fifty cents for each bushel. Most price subsidy programs also require farmers to "set aside" (that is, not plant) part of their land, in an attempt to hold prices up by restricting production.

15   It is widely but mistakenly assumed that Washington has gotten tough with farmers since Ronald Reagan took office. Last year Congress increased the support price for nearly every farm commodity covered by USDA programs, and provided for additional increases in subsequent years. The wheat price rose from $3.20 to $3.55 a bushel, corn from $2.40 to $2.55, peanuts from $455 to $550 a ton. Congress also enacted a new system of price supports for sugar, supplementing the existing protectionist tariffs on sugar imports. Reagan did propose abolishing "deficiency payments," but these too were kept, and most of the "target prices" were raised. Even the price support program for tobacco—the least defensible subsidy of all—was left alone.

16   The 1982 budget, the vehicle for so many well-publicized Reaganesque spending cuts, actually raised the Agriculture Department's spending by 45 percent. Reagan's 1983 budget would reduce it by almost that much, but less because of newfound austerity than because his advisers expect higher market prices to reduce the direct cost of various commodity programs. That expectation will almost c rtainly be proved wrong. And Congress is likely to overrule the administration and provide extra dollars to farmers, who, like everyone else, are suffering the effects of the recession.

Aside from the basic programs designed to guarantee farmers com-   17
fortably high prices, the government performs dozens of smaller special
favors. The USDA offers numerous loans to farmers — operating loans to
buy seed, fertilizer, and machinery; real-estate loans to finance purchases of land; homeownership loans to help low- and moderate-income
farmers buy houses; loans to help farmers recover from natural disasters,
like droughts; loans to finance soil and water conservation projects; even
loans to rural communities to pay for sewers. Most of these loans are
made at subsidized interest rates. Farmers can also get direct payments
(in addition to low-interest loans) to help them cope with disasters. They
can buy crop insurance from the government, again at prices subsidized
by the taxpayer. The Rural Electrification Administration, a relic of the
Great Depression, still runs a $5 billion subsidized loan program.
Farmers in most of the West get water from federal water projects at
absurdly low rates. So the government spends billions making arid land
fertile and then pays farmers to leave it idle.

Finally, the tax codes have often provided particularly rich soil for   18
cultivating farmers. To avoid imposing administrative burdens on
farmers, the tax law permits them to use the cash method of accounting.
This allows the quick deduction of capital expenses, while much farm
income — from the sale of cattle, for example — gets taxed as a long-term
capital gain, at 40 percent of the normal rates. True, farmers once had to
worry that the very land that made them wealthy might also subject
them to high federal estate taxes when the property passed to the next
generation — but their representatives in Washington have helped assuage these fears. Congress has decreed that the value of farmland, for
estate tax purposes, may be computed according to a special "use value"
formula, rather than by its ordinary market value. This formula cuts the
value of a farm estate by more than half, on average. The law also lets
farm heirs postpone payment of this reduced tax for up to five years, and
then pay in ten installments, on which interest accrues at the luxurious
rate of 4 percent.

The purpose of these provisions was to prevent family farmers from   19
having to sell their land to pay taxes. But in 1980 Congress (spurred by
farm-belt senators) repealed provisions in the income tax law that would
have taxed farmers who do sell their inherited land on the full increase in
its value since its purchase. (Now they need only pay taxes on any
increase in value since the land was inherited.) Finally, in 1981 — under
pressure from farmers who persisted in complaining about their onerous
tax burdens — Congress virtually eliminated the estate tax by creating a
flat $600,000 exemption (effective in 1985).

This welter of subsidies and privileges constitutes not a safety net for   20
farmers but a cocoon. Unfortunately, like recipients of most federal
benefits (Social Security beneficiaries, veterans, students with guaranteed loans), farmers have come to regard them as something they're
entitled to. When commodity prices fall below prosperous levels, farmers

pour into Washington to demand action; in 1979 one militant group, the American Agricultural Movement, set fire to a tractor in front of the Agriculture Department in protest. AAM also organized an unsuccessful "farm strike" in 1978 in an effort to extract higher prices for their crops. The reaction to the recession of 1981–82 has been equally predictable, as farm defenders in Congress have introduced a "farm crisis" bill that would increase crop subsidies still further, while restricting production in order to force prices up.

21   Ironically, the most serious threat to the family farm may come from the measures designed to preserve it. For example, tax treatment of farms has become so favorable that high-bracket nonfarm taxpayers—doctors, dentists, lawyers, and the like—now purchase farmland as a tax shelter. Farmers who own their own acreage are tempted to sell it to such absentee landlords—hardly grounds for pitying the farmers who cash in, but still a threat to the owner-operated farm as an institution. Equally important, the absentee tax shelterers frequently bid up the price of land so high that aspiring young farmers are unable to acquire it.

22   . . . The bigger and wealthier the farmer, and the more distant from the traditional image of the family farmer, the more help he gets from the government. Thirty percent of all government payments go to the 11 percent of farmers with the largest farms, measured in annual sales. This is an especially well-off bunch, with an average household income of nearly $46,894 in 1980 (a bad year, by the way), more than double the median family income in the U.S.

23   The incentives built into these price support programs aggravate the very problem they are supposed to alleviate. Market prices are lower than farmers would like, mainly because of chronic overproduction. Low prices inform farmers that they are producing too much of a given commodity and encourage them to stop. The artificially high prices established by the Agriculture Department send exactly the opposite signal, stimulating farmers to do more of what got them into trouble in the first place. The government tries to address this contradiction by limiting the amount of land each farmer can plant with a particular crop. But land is only one factor in the production equation. Each individual farmer can circumvent the acreage restrictions by cultivating the remaining acres more intensively. So when the government reduces the allowable cultivated land by 20 percent, it can normally expect to reduce total output by only half that much. Of course, the techniques of intensive cultivation that this system rewards—primarily the use of more machinery, water, pesticides, and fertilizer—are the very techniques in which larger farms are likely to enjoy an advantage over smaller farms.

24   Who pays to achieve these questionable goals? Price supports, the centerpiece of the farm programs, exact costs in two ways. Taxpayers have to bear the expense of whatever farm produce the Agriculture Department has to purchase when prices fall below the price support

level. (In the last fiscal year, these purchases, along with "deficiency payments," cost more than $7 billion.) But that isn't the end of it. The whole point of the program is to "support" market prices — to keep them artificially high — so as to minimize or even eliminate direct government expenses. So consumers pay higher prices in the grocery store for everything from bread to milk to peanut butter. Unfortunately, not all consumers suffer equally. The higher prices act as a regressive tax — placing the heaviest burden on the poor and the lightest on the rich. This is because the lower your income, the greater the share of it you have to spend on necessities like food. It is not an exaggeration to say that, under the price support system, slum children in Harlem go without milk so that dairy farmers in Wisconsin may prosper.

Even if family farms were in danger of extinction, and even if federal 25 farm programs served to preserve them, why should we? We don't try to preserve the family grocery store, the family pharmacy, or the family clothing store, and for good reason. In many industries and businesses, bigger has turned out to be better — better in the sense of providing more and better goods and services at a lower cost to consumers. In a relatively free market, large firms will drive out small ones only when their size allows greater efficiency. Such increases in efficiency are desirable because they raise living standards. If family farms were too inefficient to compete with huge corporate farms (which all evidence suggests they aren't), they would soon disappear in the absence of special aid. That might be unpleasant for family farmers. But it would increase the country's productivity, which tends to make everyone better off.

The usual rationale for aid to family farmers is that it preserves a 26 cherished American tradition of self-sufficiency — a supposed contrast to the gray conformity of life in the corporate sector. But the farm programs preserve the tradition's form without its content. Whatever the hardship and rigors of rural life, farmers are no longer rugged individualists, responsible to no one but themselves. They have become welfare addicts, protected and assisted at every turn by a network of programs paid for by their fellow citizens. In exchange, most farmers allow Washington to dictate much of what they do. They have abandoned independence for security. Today's family farms are to Jefferson's vision what government consultants are to Horatio Alger. If Americans still believe in the virtue of hardy rural self-reliance, they should tell Washington to get out of the way and let farmers practice it.

Questions for Discussion and Writing

1. In what way does the title of Chapman's article allude to a popular children's song? What in your opinion is the purpose of this reference?

2. What methods does Chapman use to discredit what he perceives to be an idealized myth of the American farmer? According to Chapman, how did this myth originate in the writings of Thomas Jefferson and in the way Europeans once viewed America?

3. What range of statistical evidence does Chapman provide to support his thesis that farmers are relatively well off, are not in imminent danger of bankruptcy, and therefore do not need further government subsidies? How does Chapman use the difference between average wages and total net worth to support his claim that the American farmer is not suffering nearly as badly as he is commonly thought to be?

4. What different kinds of reasons does Chapman present to justify his assertion that "the decline of the farming sector is both perfectly natural and wholly beneficial"? Specifically, what role does increased technology play—along with the greater number of people needed to work in other sectors of the economy—in causing the decline of the farming sector?

5. How does Chapman's analysis of the role played by lower farm prices in spurring extra production of crops support his claim that farmers themselves are to blame for the lower prices they get for their crops? Keep in mind that if prices were higher farmers would have to produce more of any crop in order to bring in the same revenue.

6. According to Chapman, how have the very same federal programs, incentives, and methods of taxation that were designed to help farmers actually brought about the conditions they were designed to prevent? Specifically, how do current tax laws encourage farmers to sell their land to nonfarmers? How do government incentives and subsidy programs cause lower market prices that then require farmers to grow more to get the same income they would have received at higher prices?

7. How does Chapman's philosophy of free-market economics explain why he urges that no extraordinary measures be taken to preserve family farms, even if they are "in danger of extinction"? What parallels does he draw between farming and "the family grocery store, the family pharmacy, or the family clothing store"? How does Chapman's argument depend on assumptions that (*a*) the greater efficiency of larger farms provides greater benefits for all, or (*b*) it is perfectly acceptable for big corporate farms to drive inefficient small family farms out of existence?

8. Evaluate Chapman's claim that people have an erroneous

impression that the family farm is a special case simply because of the persistence of the outdated Jeffersonian agrarian myth. Do you think it is foolish to protect the family farms because of traditions that may no longer exist?

9. How does Chapman's concluding paragraph return to themes stated in the opening paragraphs of his essay? What purpose is served by framing his argument against current government policies toward family arms in the context of these ideas? How does Chapman use the idea of rugged individualism (usually cited to defend family farms) to support his own recommendation that government subsidies be eliminated in order to let "true farmers" emerge—that is, those who have not gone bankrupt.

Byron Dorgan

America's Real Farm Problem: It Can Be Solved

Byron Dorgan is a Democratic congressman from North Dakota. In "America's Real Farm Problem: It Can Be Solved," first published in Washington Monthly *(April 1983), Dorgan argues that government policies favoring large corporate farms and agribusiness conglomerates ought to be changed in favor of preserving the family farm. Dorgan claims that the free-market theory of economics fails to work as anticipated and questions the desirability of large-scale farming.*

1   Recent scenes from America's farm belt seem like a grainy film clip from the thirties. Young families putting their home and farm machinery on the auction block. Men, choked with emotion, breaking down in tears as they describe their plight. Angry farmers organizing, getting madder and madder.

2   It's not as bad as the thirties yet; no governor has called out the National Guard to stop the foreclosures, the way North Dakota's William "Wild Bill" Langer did in 1933. But the pain is running deep. Losing a farm is not like having a new Chevrolet or a color TV repossessed. In many cases, what's lost is land that's been in the family for generations —and a way of life that for many is the only one they've ever known or wanted.

3   It's not that other victims of the recession deserve less sympathy. But there's an important difference between the plight of the farmer and that of other producers. What's happening in the farm belt is a far cry from what's happening in Pittsburgh and Detroit. Nobody is berating our farmers for falling behind the foreign competition and losing their edge, like the auto and steel industries. Nobody is shoving books on Japanese management into their faces. To the contrary, American farmers are our all-star economic performers. When other countries want to find out how to improve agriculture, they don't send their delegations to Tokyo. They send them to Iowa and Kansas and the Dakotas.

4   And the farmers' reward? Most North Dakota wheat farmers are getting $4 for a bushel of wheat that costs them $5.50 to grow. Farmers are making less in real income today than they did in 1934. Creditors are foreclosing in record numbers; the Farmers Home Administration alone

reports that at least 4,000 of its borrowers were forced out of business in 1982.

Rural Myths

Agriculture is a $140 billion-a-year industry, our nation's largest, far 5 bigger than steel, automobiles, or any other manufacturing enterprise. Farming and food-related businesses generate one out of five jobs in private industry and account for 20 percent of our GNP. Sooner or later the problems on the farm catch up with the rest of us, as the laid-off employees of International Harvester already know too well. Students of the Depression will also recall that it was long *before* the 1929 crash — while the market was still revving up — that farm income began falling. The troubles on the farm were a large part of the weight that ultimately dragged the entire economy down into the Depression.

If you read the editorial columns of *The Wall Street Journal*, you know 6 that some people have a simple explanation for the farmers' plight. Too much production is the problem, they say, and if government would only stop subsidizing overproduction by keeping prices artificially high, the free market would work its will and weed out the inefficient producers. What's more, many conservatives and liberals alike believe farmers are only getting their just deserts, having grown fat and happy on government price supports and double-digit inflation. You've seen the caricatures on "60 Minutes" — farmers driving big Cadillacs, spending their winters in Boca Raton — and still complaining that the government doesn't pay them enough not to grow certain crops.

Those aren't the farmers I know. But with less than four percent of all 7 Americans now living on farms, it's little surprise people have so many misconceptions about our farm program. Start with the "overproduction" argument. There are children and older people in this country who still don't have enough to eat, and roughly 450 million people in the world who go hungry most of the time. That people talk about "overproduction" rather than "underdistribution" is rather telling in itself. But more to the present point: almost from the time the early settlers planted their first row, American farmers have been growing more food than the nation could consume. The tendency toward producing surpluses is a perennial problem. It hardly explains the extraordinary difficulties our farmers now face.

As for the "60 Minutes" caricatures, they are just that — caricatures. 8 Last year (1982) the federal government paid farmers $1.5 billion in direct subsidies (it loaned another $11.4 billion that farmers must repay). Money from these federal programs came to about two percent of total receipts in 1982 for the average farmer, whose farm netted just $8,000. Add in what he and his family earned away from the farm, and his household still made less than a GS-11 civil servant and about half as much as a young lawyer on Wall Street. That's for working from morning to night and doing what many Americans no longer do—produce something the rest of us need.

9   But this is no blanket apology for the nation's farm policies—far from it. There *are* some farmers who get more than they deserve from the government, and nobody gets madder about that than the vast majority of farmers who bear no resemblance to them. Egregious abuses do exist, and it's time that representatives from the farm states (of which I'm one) begin to eliminate them. If we ignore such problems or dismiss them as inevitable, they will continue to act as lightning rods for attacks on all farm programs. Representatives of farm states must clean their own house for if they don't, I'm afraid, someone else will do it—hurting farmer and non-farmer alike.

10   The nation needs a federal farm program; to think otherwise in today's highly competitive international economy is self-defeating and naive. But we need the *right* kind of farm program, one that not only meets the test of fairness, but that promises to keep American agriculture second to none.

11   Unfortunately, that's not the kind of farm program we now have. Approaches that were fine in the thirties are no longer doing the job. In fact, what began as survival programs for family farmers are becoming the domain of extra-large producers who often elbow aside the very family farmers for whom these programs were originally intended. Congress must bear much of the blame for this. We continue to target most farm assistance not according to the circumstances of the individual farmer but largely according to the volume of the commodity he grows. While these federal programs have all been done in the name of the family farmer, the interests of the various commodity groups have not always been identical to those of the nation's family farmers.

12   This is not to criticize these groups, for everyone is entitled to his say. But it is to suggest that we in Congress have talked too much about programs for feed grains and wheat and corn and assorted "market prices" and "loan rates"—and not enough about the kind of agriculture that's best for the country. And we've done more than waste money in the process. For if our agricultural policy continues largely unchanged, I'm concerned the criticisms that now so tragically apply to the nation's automakers—that they became too big, too inflexible, and too inefficient to compete—may one day be appropriate for America's agriculture.

Farm Economics

13   To understand the failings of existing farm programs, it's important to understand the roots of the current farm crisis. At the heart of the problem is money—how much there is and how much it costs to borrow.

A farmer is a debtor almost by definition. In my own state, it's not   14
unusual for a wheat farmer with 1,000 acres to owe several hundred
thousand dollars for land and machinery. In addition to making payments on these loans, it's common for such a farmer to borrow about
$40,000 each spring to cover fertilizer, diesel fuel, seed, and other oper-
ating expenses. The months before the harvest will be anxious ones as
the farmer contemplates all the things that could bring financial hardship: bad weather, crop disease, insects, falling commodity prices. If he
has a good year, the farmer can repay his loans and retain some profit; in
a bad one, he can lose his whole farm.

Money thus becomes one of the farmer's biggest expenses. Most   15
consumers can find some refuge from high interest rates by postponing
large purchases like houses or cars. Farmers have no choice. In 1979, for
example, farmers paid $12 billion in interest costs while earning $32
billion; last year they paid $22 billion in interest costs, while earning only
$20 billion. In a business in which profit margins are small, $4,000 more
in interest can mean the difference between profit and loss. Since 1975,
100,000 family farms have disappeared, and while interest rates have
fallen recently, they still imperil the nation's farmers.

This is why the most basic part of our nation's farm policy is its   16
money and credit policy — which is set by Paul Volcker and the Federal
Reserve Board. The Federal Reserve Board's responsibility for nearly
ruining our economy is well-known. What's often overlooked is how the
board's policies have taken an especially devastating toll on farmers.
While high interest rates have increased farm expenses, they've also
undermined the export market farmers have traditionally relied on. High
interest rates, by stalling our economic engines, have been a drag on the
entire world's economy. Developing and third-world nations have been
particularly hard hit; struggling just to meet interest payments on their
loans from multinational banks, they have had little cash left over to buy
our farm products.

Even those countries that could still afford our farm products aban-   17
doned us for other producers. Our interest rates were so high they
attracted multinational bankers, corporations, and others who speculate
on currencies of different countries. These speculators were willing to
pay more for dollars in terms of pesos, yen, or marks because those rates
guaranteed them such a substantial return.

The news commentators called the result a "strong dollar," which   18
gave us a rush of pride. But what did this strong dollar really mean to the
farmer? It meant people in other countries found themselves suddenly
poorer when they went to buy something made or grown in America. In
1981, for example, West Germans paid 21 percent more for American
soybeans, even though our farmers were getting 11 percent less for those
very same soybeans than they had the previous year. Overall, our
"strong dollar" has been jacking up the price of American farm exports
by a full 25 percent, biting our potential foreign customer with a 25

percent surcharge the moment they start thinking of buying American. No wonder these exports have dropped for the first time in 12 years. This isn't a strong dollar, it's a big banker's dollar — and with a central bank like the Federal Reserve Board, who needs soil erosion, grasshoppers, or drought?

19   To be fair, interest rates aren't solely responsible for undercutting our farmers' export markets. President Carter's grain embargo did more than close the Russian market; it also drove away other foreign customers who wondered how dependable we were. Reagan has lifted the embargo, but to little avail, since he still refuses to sign a long-term grain contract with the Soviet Union. Meanwhile, our foreign competitors have quickly stepped into the breach, supporting their farmers with generous subsidies that make ours look miserly by comparison. Last September, for example, wheat from the U.S. and the Common Market countries was selling for almost the same price on the international market. But while the U.S. farmer was getting about $3.40 a bushel, his Common Market counterpart received $5.37.

20   Both the Federal Reserve Board's market-skewing policies and the hefty subsidies that foreign agriculture receives illustrate an important point. Those who say America should go back to a "free market" in agriculture are asking our farmers to go back to something that no longer exists. In today's world there's no free market in agriculture, just as there is none in steel, automobiles, or other major industries.

21   We learned during the Depression that agriculture, by its very nature, requires a moderating hand to smooth out the violent cycles that otherwise could destroy even the best farmers. No other producers have to confront the sudden price shifts with which farmers regularly contend. Automakers, for example, don't have to worry that prices for their product may drop 50 percent, as wheat prices did from 1974 to 1977. This is why even that bastion of freemarket orthodoxy, the Heritage Foundation, concedes the need for a government role in agriculture.

Home-Grown Depression

22   For the nation's first 150 years, there was no farm program as such. The Department of Agriculture wasn't created until 1862, and when President Lincoln proposed it to Congress he could applaud the nation's farmers as a "great interest so independent in its nature as to not have demanded and extorted more from government." For the next 70 years the department limited itself largely to statistics and research. Farmers received little in the way of subsidies; like all other consumers, they helped subsidize manufacturers through the tariffs they paid on imported goods.

23   Contrary to popular belief, the Depression hit our farms long before

the Okies started their desperate treks across the dust bowl in their sputtering Model T's. During World War I Europe bought our food like it was going out of style. Prices rose to record heights; farmers expanded their operations and borrowed heavily to do so.

Then the war ended. Export markets quickly dried up as European 24
countries started to rebuild their own agriculture. American farmers watched helplessly as prices plummeted, leaving many with huge debts to repay and no income with which to pay them. A rash of foreclosures followed, rehearsing a cycle that bears an eerie similarity to the current one. By 1932 farm income was less than one-third of what it had been in 1919. During this period, more than 1.5 million Americans left the farm. (The exodus was reversed during the Depression, when many returned to the farm in order to survive.)

Then, as now, the conventional economists and their camp followers 25
in Congress and the press found little alarming in this hardship. The "invisible hand," they said, would force farmers to produce less until prices returned to normal levels. The "weak" and the "inefficient" might be cut down in the process, but that was the way the free market was supposed to work. It didn't.

Unfortunately, someone forgot to tell the nation's farmers about the 26
economic etiquette that professors and journalists expected of them. As prices continued to fall, the farmers didn't produce less—they produced more. It's not hard to understand why. Farmers have certain set costs— such as debt—whether or not they plant a single seed. When prices dropped, many tried to produce more to make up the difference. Besides, to farm is to hope. The market may be terrible one year, but who knows what will happen next? Will there be drought in Europe? Blight in Russia? When you have to decide how much to plant in the spring, you have little idea what the market will really be in the fall. The worse things look, the more you pin your hopes on a sudden surge in prices. So you plant.

Those who put all the blame on government for today's excess pro- 27
duction and low prices are long on theory and short on history. We produced "too much" throughout the twenties, when there was no farm program to speak of. And it wasn't the weak and the inefficient who tumbled then. It was just about everybody.

Blind Generosity

The New Dealers recognized that when it comes to agriculture, the 28
invisible hand can end up shooting farmers in the foot. Their solution was straightforward—and effective. Remedies like the Agricultural Adjustment Act were begun to prop up the prices of certain commodities so that the farmers who grew them could count on at least a minimal

return. The main approach was to link government assistance to the farmers' agreement to cut production, thus forcing prices to rise according to the laws of supply and demand.

29   These relief programs were not geared to the circumstances of individual farmers. They were aimed at regulating the supply and price of certain commodities. Still, the commodity approach amounted to a relief program for the family farm because there just weren't many other kinds of farms around. In 1932 one of four Americans lived on a farm, and for that reason the commodity programs were a major part of the whole New Deal relief effort.

30   Over the last half century, this commodity approach has remained relatively unchanged, while American agriculture has changed radically. The number of farms today is one-third what it was during the Depression, and just seven percent of these control over half the farmland and account for over half the sales. Yet while farming has become more concentrated, the government still dispenses federal aid with a blindfold on, treating a multi-thousand-acre agrifactory giant as if it were a bedraggled Okie with a handcrank tractor and a cow. As a result, 29 percent of all federal farm benefits go to the top one percent of our farmers.

31   The government distributes this largess in a variety of ways. Some programs amount to government-guaranteed prices. For a few crops — tobacco and peanuts, for example — the government sanctions an allotment system by which the marketing of these is strictly controlled. The government also provides crop insurance, disaster relief, and subsidized loans for such things as purchasing more farmland and meeting operating expenses.

32   The traditional mainstay of the farm program is the "commodity loan." Each year the government establishes a loan rate for major crops, including wheat, corn, barley, sorghum, and soybeans. The rate for wheat, for example, was $3.55 per bushel in 1982. Early in the year, a farmer must decide whether he is going to sign up for the program; if he does, he may have to agree to cut back his production to help keep surpluses down. If the eventual market price goes above the loan-rate level, the farmer simply repays the loan, takes back his wheat, and sells it on the open market. But if the market price is below the loan rate, the farmer may take the money and leave the wheat with the government. In addition to the commodity loan, there is a "deficiency payment" that supposedly helps bridge the gap between what the farmer earns in the market and what his crop costs to produce.

33   It's important to understand two things about this price-support program. First, a guaranteed price is not a guaranteed profit. The loan rates and deficiency payments do not necessarily return the farmer's cost of production, and in recent years they haven't. In 1982, for example, the target price for wheat was more than a dollar less than the farmer's cost of production.

More important, the way these programs work, the more you have, 34
the more the government gives you. A wheat farmer with 250 acres
producing 30 bushels per acre gets a support loan of $26,625. A farmer
with 2,500 acres of similarly productive land gets approximately ten
times that much. The deficiency payments work in pretty much the same
way.

For deficiency payments there is a nominal $50,000 cap that in 35
practice does not have much effect. For support loans, there is no limitation at all. Thus, while smaller farmers get a little help, the largest farms
walk off with a bundle. In a recent editorial attacking all farm subsidies,
The Wall Street Journal fumed about a midwestern wheat grower who
received $68,760 last year from the government yet "rides around his
4,000-acre farm on a huge four-wheel-drive tractor with air conditioning
and a radio."

I'll bet the editorial writers of *The Wall Street Journal* have air condi- 36
tioning, radios, and a whole lot more in their offices; still, they do have a
point. As Don Paarlburg, a conservative agricultural economist who
toiled in the last three Republican administrations, has put it, the result
of the present federal farm program is that "average farm income is
increased by adding more dollars to those already well-off and adding
little or nothing to those at the low end of the income scale."

This bias toward bigness runs through most of the federal govern- 37
ment's farm program. One of the best illustrations is the Farmers Home
Administration, a case study of how a federal program that began to
help only those in need became a safety net for just about everybody
else.

The FmHA was created in the depths of the Depression as a lender of 38
last resort for small and beginning farmers who had a reasonable chance
to survive. For most of its life, the agency did serve family farmers
struggling to get their operation on its feet and unable to obtain credit
elsewhere. But in the 1970s, Congress tacked on something called the
Economic Emergency Loan program. To qualify for this new program
you didn't have to be small, needy, or even a family farmer. You just had
to be in economic trouble. Soon the "economic-emergency" loans were
pushing aside the kinds of loans the FmHA was originally intended to
provide. By 1980 FmHA was lending *four times* as much in such "emergency" assistance as it was in the so-called "limited-resource" loans for
needy farmers who were now receiving less than ten percent of the
agency's total. Ninety percent of these emergency loans went to bigger,
more established farms, many of which were unlikely candidates for
public philanthropy. One politician and judge with a net worth of
$435,000 and a nonfarm income of $70,000 a year received $266,000 in
such low-interest "emergency" loans.

After "60 Minutes" exposed a $17 million emergency loan to a 39
California agrifactory, an embarrassed Congress imposed a $400,000
limit on the program. Though this was an improvement, the still-gener-

ous limit enables the larger farms to eat up the bulk of FmHA's loan resources.

40   Showing nicely its concept of the "truly needy," the Reagan administration tried to abolish completely the limited-resource loan program that was targeted to the smaller farmers the agency was established to help in the first place. Congress wouldn't let it, so the Reaganites discovered the value of bureaucracy and gave it the redtape treatment. Nationwide, the FmHA in 1982 managed to lend only about half the money Congress had approved for these loans — this during the worst year for farmers in half a century.

41   In fairness, the administration has also stopped making economic-emergency loans. But that misses the point. Those loans should be made, but only to family farmers who need them. The FmHA's recent crackdown on delinquent borrowers, moreover, has fallen most heavily upon the smaller farmers. It's a cruel irony: having lavished so much money on the largest farmers, at least some of whom could have gotten credit elsewhere, the government now has too little left for smaller farmers who have nowhere else to turn. Not surprisingly, many are going under.

42   Meanwhile, the Reagan administration has introduced a Payment-In-Kind program that gives farmers government surplus commodities they in turn can sell, if they agree to take acreage out of production. PIK is thus a variation on traditional New Deal programs. But while the PIK program offers many beleaguered farmers some genuine help, it also embodies the same most-for-the-biggest approach.

Agricultural Bloat

43   Of course, some will argue there's nothing wrong with a farm policy that encourages bigger and bigger farms. This will only make them more efficient, so the argument goes, and past gains in agricultural productivity will continue indefinitely as farms get bigger.

44   To such people, a concern for the family-size farm seems a mushy and misplaced Jeffersonian nostalgia. In fact, it is anything but. Family farming is practical economics. Anyone who's looked recently at our automobile and steel industries knows that economies of scale stop beyond a certain point. When Thomas Peters and Robert Waterman examined successful American businesses for their book *In Search of Excellence*, what were the qualities they found? Small work units. Lean staffs. A minimum of management bureaucracy. Managers who get their hands into what they manage. Enterprises that stick to their knitting instead of using their assets to flit from one business to another.

45   It sounds like a profile of the American family farm. It's also a description of what we lose when we allow factory-in-the-field agglomerations to gobble up individual family farmers.

46   There's growing evidence to suggest that in agriculture, as in other

endeavors, the old "bigger is better" saying is a myth. A decade ago the Department of Agriculture was telling Congress the optimum size for a California vegetable farm was 400 acres, though 73 percent of the state's vegetables were already produced on farms much larger than that. A 1979 USDA study found that the average U.S. farm reaches 90 percent of maximum efficiency at just 314 acres; to attain 100 percent efficiency, the average size has to quadruple to 1,157 acres. Beyond that, farms don't get any better—they just get bigger. They may even become more bureaucratic and less efficient.

Consider, for example, the matter of debt. The very largest farms are 47 twice as debt-prone as smaller family farms. This is of little consequence when times are flush. But when trouble hits, as it has with Mr. Volcker's interest-rate policies, it's like sending a fleet of large sailing ships heading into a gale with twice the sail they normally carry.

Just as a rope of many strands is more flexible and resilient than a 48 single strand, a diverse agriculture of many relatively small units can adjust and change. Unlike the very largest operations, family farmers don't have so much capital tied up in what they did yesterday to keep them from doing what needs to be done tomorrow. Small farmers don't have to push paper through tedious chains of command. If they see a way of doing something better, they can do it right away. This kind of flexibility is important if sudden shifts in market conditions warrant different crops or production techniques.

There's also the question of rural communities. I grew up in Regent, 49 North Dakota, a farming community of 400 people. Family farms were and are the economic bloodstream of that town. When such farms are eaten up by larger ones, towns like Regent wither, and the government finds itself with a tax-consuming social problem instead of a healthy and taxproviding community.

In short, there is a link between the way we have farmed—in 50 traditional family-size units—and the extraordinary productivity of our agriculture as a whole. Yet our farm policies are pushing us towards a topheavy agriculture that threatens to mimic the same problems we are facing in other areas of our economy. The high interest rates of the last two years have made the problem even worse: whether family farmers go bankrupt or simply decide to sell out, the trend toward concentration is hastened.

Even worse, this trend feeds on itself. The alteration of the FmHA is 51 instructive. Having helped create large farms, the government felt compelled to keep them from failing. When a small family farmer bites the dust there may be a few condolences but nobody worries much. When a multi-thousand-acre agrifactory totters, its bankers and creditors get the jitters over the millions of dollars at stake. It's a prairie twist on the maxim familiar to international bankers: "Make a small loan and you create a debtor. Make a big loan and you create a partner."

Are we encouraging farms so big that we can't afford to let them fail? 52

I fear we are and I think it's an ominous prescription for slowly but inevitably undermining the very things that have made agriculture one of the few American industries still competitive in international markets. Despite high interest rates, agriculture still contributed more than $40 billion in export sales last year, helping defray the costs of our unhappy dependence on imported oil and automobiles.

Help for the Family Farmer

53   What does all this mean for our farm policies? Mr. Paarlburg recommends that we eliminate the current "tilt in favor of big farms" in our federal programs, and at least keep the playing field level. I agree with that, but would go a step further. For the reasons I've discussed, I think we should retarget the current programs toward family-size units. For example, we should put a cap on the commodity price-support loans to eliminate the exorbitant amounts going to the very largest farmers, thus freeing up more for those who need it more. In 1981, for example, I proposed capping these loans at $150,000, which would have affected less than ten percent of all farmers but would have enabled us to increase the support price by about 35 cents per bushel for the rest. (This new level, incidentally, would have still been below production costs.) Farmers could become as large as they wanted — the federal government just wouldn't pay them for doing so.

54   We should alter the FmHA loan program in similar fashion, restoring this agency to its original purpose of providing economic opportunity to beginning and smaller farmers. In the present crisis, the money saved should be used to extend loan deferrals to family farmers who have fallen behind on their FmHA loans because of economic circumstances beyond their control. At the same time, we should alter other federal policies, such as tax laws that invite lawyers and doctors to invest in farms as tax shelters, driving up land prices to the detriment of the beginning farmer.

55   Of course, it would not be fair to pull the plug suddenly on these larger farm operations. Many are essentially family farmers who overextended themselves during the 1970s, with a good deal of encouragement (including subsidized loans) from the government. Some of these farms may need emergency loans; the question is the direction in which our farm program goes from here.

56   These are the broad outlines of a farm program that I think would dispense agricultural benefits more fairly while promoting the right kind of agriculture. But the high interest rates of the last two years should serve as a stark reminder that the best farm program in the world will not do a great deal when a Federal Reserve Board accountable to no one can unleash an interest-rate tornado that levels the economic landscape. The best thing the government can do for the nation's farmer is not to

subsidize him, but to promote the kind of monetary policies that make credit available at a fair price. . . .

More than a century ago, President Abraham Lincoln warned us that 57 "the money power of this country will endeavor to prolong its reign until all wealth is aggregated in a few hands and the Republic is destroyed." While its policies have moderated somewhat in recent months, the board has taken us in precisely this direction. Money and credit should serve production, not the other way around. Regaining control over them is of utmost importance not only to the family farmer, but to all independent businessmen as well—not to mention the rest of us.

Questions for Discussion and Writing

1. In contrast to Chapman's characterization of the farm problem as unreal, Dorgan sees the situation of the family farmer as all too real. How are Dorgan's opening paragraphs designed to evoke a sympathetic response toward the farmer's plight?

2. Summarize the arguments to which Dorgan raises his own objections. How does he use statistics to refute many of the same points Chapman presented? What specific information does he offer on the issues of farmers' income and the role played by subsidies?

3. In what portions of his essay does Dorgan admit that some of what Chapman says may be true, but then recommend very different policies from those argued for by Chapman?

4. What purpose does the section "Farm Economics" play in enabling Dorgan's audience to understand the relationship between credit policies and the farmer's current plight? How does Dorgan introduce evidence drawn from history to support his argument?

5. Why, according to Dorgan, didn't the free-market or "invisible hand" theory of economics work as anticipated? Specifically, why is Dorgan concerned that if farms become bigger and bigger the "invisible hand" of the market can "end up shooting farmers in the foot"?

6. Although Dorgan agrees that the nature of agriculture has dramatically changed and now emphasizes huge agribusiness conglomerates, his views on the desirability of bigness clearly differ from Chapman's. What specific objections does he raise to large-scale farming, and what evidence does he offer to support his thesis that government policies ought to be geared specifically toward preservation of the family farm?

7. What specific policy recommendations does Dorgan propose, and what reasons does he offer to support these policy changes?

8. Who, in your opinion, makes a more persuasive case, Chapman or Dorgan? Explain your answer in an essay. To what extent is the debate between Dorgan and Chapman on the desirability of preserving the family farm dependent on what role government-sponsored farm programs ought to play in regulating the prices farmers get for goods? In drafting your essay, consider the following issues. Both Chapman and Dorgan use the criterion of efficiency. Chapman wants to eliminate government-sponsored programs even at the risk of eliminating small farms because he believes larger farms are more efficient. Dorgan, on the other hand, is opposed to continuing government subsidies to large farms and wants existing programs altered to help the family farmer. He believes that large farms are much less efficient and hence in greater danger of going under in tough times. Who, in your opinion, uses the idea of efficiency more effectively to develop his case?

9. Compare Chapman's use of connotative language and other techniques of persuasion with Dorgan's use of statistics. Whose argument was helped the most—aside from the issues argued—by the argumentative strategies the author chose to use?

Milton Friedman

The Social Responsibility of Business Is to Increase Its Profits

Milton Friedman is a spokesman for the conservative free-market theory of economics. Friedman has been Paul Snowden Russell Distinguished Service Professor at the University of Chicago and has won the Nobel Prize for economics (1975). "The Social Responsibility of Business Is to Increase Its Profits" first appeared in The New York Times Magazine *(September 13, 1970). In it Friedman examines and analyzes objections to his thesis that the sole responsibility of business is to increase its profits and that business firms have no obligation to take on social responsibility.*

When I hear businessmen speak eloquently about the "social respon- 1 sibilities of business in a free-enterprise system," I am reminded of the wonderful line about the Frenchman who discovered at the age of 70 that he had been speaking prose all his life. The businessmen believe that they are defending free enterprise when they declaim that business is not concerned "merely" with profit but also with promoting desirable "social ends; that business has a social conscience" and takes seriously its responsibilities for providing employment, eliminating discrimination, avoiding pollution and whatever else may be the catchwords of the contemporary crop of reformers. In fact they are—or would be if they or anyone else took them seriously—preaching pure and unadulterated socialism. Businessmen who talk this way are unwitting puppets of the intellectual forces that have been undermining the basis of a free society these past decades.

The discussions of the "social responsibilities of business" are notable 2 for their analytical looseness and lack of rigor. What does it mean to say that "business" has responsibilities? Only people can have responsibilities. A corporation is an artificial person and in this sense may have artificial responsibilities, but "business" as a whole cannot be said to have responsibilities, even in this vague sense. The first step toward clarity in examining the doctrine of the social responsibility of business is to ask precisely what it implies for whom.

Presumably, the individuals who are to be responsible are business- 3 men, which means individual proprietors or corporate executives. Most of the discussion of social responsibility is directed at corporations, so in what follows I shall mostly neglect the individual proprietor and speak of corporate executives.

4   In a free-enterprise, private-property system, a corporate executive is an employee of the owners of the business. He has direct responsibility to his employers. That responsibility is to conduct the business in accordance with their desires, which generally will be to make as much money as possible while conforming to the basic rules of the society, both those embodied in law and those embodied in ethical custom. Of course, in some cases his employers may have a different objective. A group of persons might establish a corporation for an eleemosynary purpose — for example, a hospital or a school. The manager of such a corporation will not have money profit as his objective but the rendering of certain services.

5   In either case, the key point is that, in his capacity as a corporate executive, the manager is the agent of the individuals who own the corporation or establish the eleemosynary institution, and his primary responsibility is to them.

6   Needless to say, this does not mean that it is easy to judge how well he is performing his task. But at least the criterion of performance is straightforward, and the persons among whom a voluntary contractual arrangement exists are clearly defined.

7   Of course, the corporate executive is also a person in his own right. As a person, he may have many other responsibilities that he recognizes or assumes voluntarily — to his family, his conscience, his feelings of charity, his church, his clubs, his city, his country. He may feel impelled by these responsibilities to devote part of his income to causes he regards as worthy, to refuse to work for particular corporations, even to leave his job, for example, to join his country's armed forces. If we wish, we may refer to some of these responsibilities as "social responsibilities." But in these respects he is acting as a principal, not an agent; he is spending his own money or time or energy, not the money of his employers or the time or energy he has contracted to devote to their purposes. If these are "social responsibilities," they are the social responsibilities of individuals, not of business.

8   What does it mean to say that the corporate executive has a "social responsibility" in his capacity as businessman? If this statement is not pure rhetoric, it must mean that he is to act in some way that is not in the interest of his employers. For example, that he is to refrain from increasing the price of the product in order to contribute to the social objective of preventing inflation, even though a price increase would be in the best interests of the corporation. Or that he is to make expenditures on reducing pollution beyond the amount that is in the best interests of the corporation or that is required by law in order to contribute to the social objective of improving the environment. Or that, at the expense of corporate profits, he is to hire "hard-core" unemployed instead of bet-

ter-qualified available workmen to contribute to the social objective of reducing poverty.

In each of these cases, the corporate executive would be spending 9 someone else's money for a general social interest. Insofar as his actions in accord with his "social responsibility" reduce returns to stockholders, he is spending their money. Insofar as his actions raise the price to customers, he is spending the customers' money. Insofar as his actions lower the wages of some employes, he is spending their money.

The stockholders or the customers or the employes could separately 10 spend their own money on the particular action if they wished to do so. The executive is exercising a distinct "social responsibility," rather than serving as an agent of the stockholders or the customers or the employes, only if he spends the money in a different way than they would have spent it.

But if he does this, he is in effect imposing taxes, on the one hand, 11 and deciding how the tax proceeds shall be spent, on the other.

This process raises political questions on two levels: principle and 12 consequences. On the level of political principle, the imposition of taxes and the expenditure of tax proceeds are governmental functions. We have established elaborate constitutional, parliamentary and judicial provisions to control these functions, to assure that taxes are imposed so far as possible in accordance with the preferences and desires of the public—after all, "taxation without representation" was one of the battle cries of the American Revolution. We have a system of checks and balances to separate the legislative function of imposing taxes and enacting expenditures from the executive function of collecting taxes and administering expenditure programs and from the judicial function of mediating disputes and interpreting the law.

Here the businessman—self-selected or appointed directly or indi- 13 rectly by stockholders—is to be simultaneously legislator, executive and jurist. He is to decide whom to tax by how much and for what purpose, and he is to spend the proceeds—all this guided only by general exhortations from on high to restrain inflation, improve the environment, fight poverty and so on and on.

The whole justification for permitting the corporate executive to be 14 selected by the stockholders is that the executive is an agent serving the interests of his principal. This justification disappears when the corporate executive imposes taxes and spends the proceeds for "social" purposes. He becomes in effect a public employee, a civil servant, even though he remains in name an employe of a private enterprise. On grounds of political principle, it is intolerable that such civil servants—insofar as their actions in the name of social responsibility are real and not just window-dressing—should be selected as they are now. If they are to be civil servants, then they must be selected through a political process. If they are to impose taxes and make expenditures to foster "social" objectives, then political machinery must be set up to guide the assessment of taxes and to determine through a political process the objectives to be served.

15   This is the basic reason why the doctrine of "social responsibility" involves the acceptance of the socialist view that political mechanisms, not market mechanisms, are the appropriate way to determine the allocation of scarce resources to alternative uses.

16   On the grounds of consequences, can the corporate executive in fact discharge his alleged "social responsibilities"? On the one hand, suppose he could get away with spending the stockholders' or customers' or employes' money. How is he to know how to spend it? He is told that he must contribute to fighting inflation. How is he to know what action of his will contribute to that end? He is presumably an expert in running his company—in producing a product or selling it or financing it. But nothing about his selection makes him an expert on inflation. Will his holding down the price of his product reduce inflationary pressure? Or, by leaving more spending power in the hands of his customers, simply divert it elsewhere? Or, by forcing him to produce less because of the lower price, will it simply contribute to shortages? Even if he could answer these questions, how much cost is he justified in imposing on his stockholders, customers and employes for this social purpose? What is the appropriate share and what is the appropriate share of others?

17   And, whether he wants to or not, can he get away with spending his stockholders', customers' or employes' money? Will not the stockholders fire him? (Either the present ones or those who take over when his actions in the name of social responsibility have reduced the corporation's profits and the price of its stock.) His customers and his employes can desert him for other producers and employers less scrupulous in exercising their social responsibilities.

18   This facet of "social responsibility" doctrine is brought into sharp relief when the doctrine is used to justify wage restraint by trade unions. The conflict of interest is naked and clear when union officials are asked to subordinate the interest of their members to some more general social purpose. If the union officials try to enforce wage restraint, the consequence is likely to be wildcat strikes, rank-and-file revolts and the emergence of strong competitors for their jobs. We thus have the ironic phenomenon that union leaders—at least in the U.S.—have objected to Government interference with the market far more consistently and courageously than have business leaders.

19   The difficulty of exercising "social responsibility" illustrates, of course, the great virtue of private competitive enterprise—it forces people to be responsible for their own actions and makes it difficult for them to "exploit" other people for either selfish or unselfish purposes. They can do good—but only at their own expense.

20   Many a reader who has followed the argument this far may be tempted to remonstrate that it is all well and good to speak of govern-

ment's having the responsibility to impose taxes and determine expenditures for such "social" purposes as controlling pollution or training the hard-core unemployed, but that the problems are too urgent to wait on the slow course of political processes, that the exercise of social responsibility by businessmen is a quicker and surer way to solve pressing current problems.

Aside from the question of fact—I share Adam Smith's skepticism 21
about the benefits that can be expected from "those who affected to trade for the public good" — this argument must be rejected on grounds of principle. What it amounts to is an assertion that those who favor the taxes and expenditures in question have failed to persuade a majority of their fellow citizens to be of like mind and that they are seeking to attain by undemocratic procedures what they cannot attain by democratic procedures. In a free society, it is hard for "good" people to do "good," but that is a small price to pay for making it hard for "evil" people to do "evil," especially since one man's good is another's evil.

I have, for simplicity, concentrated on the special case of the corpo- 22
rate executive, except only for the brief digression on trade unions. But precisely the same argument applies to the newer phenomenon of calling upon stockholders to require corporations to exercise social responsibility (the recent G.M. crusade, for example). In most of these cases, what is in effect involved is some stockholders trying to get other stockholders (or customers or employes) to contribute against their will to "social" causes favored by the activists. Insofar as they succeed, they are again imposing taxes and spending the proceeds.

The situation of the individual proprietor is somewhat different. If he 23
acts to reduce the returns of his enterprise in order to exercise his "social responsibility," he is spending his own money, not someone else's. If he wishes to spend his money on such purposes, that is his right, and I cannot see that there is any objection to his doing so. In the process, he, too, may impose costs on employes and customers. However, because he is far less likely than a large corporation or union to have monopolistic power, any such side effects will tend to be minor.

Of course, in practice the doctrine of social responsibility is frequently 24
a cloak for actions that are justified on other grounds rather than a reason for those actions.

To illustrate, it may well be in the long-run interest of a corporation 25
that is a major employer in a small community to devote resources to providing amenities to that community or to improving its government. That may make it easier to attract desirable employes, it may reduce the wage bill or lessen losses from pilferage and sabotage or have other worthwhile effects. Or it may be that, given the laws about the deductibility of corporate charitable contributions, the stockholders can contribute more to charities they favor by having the corporation make the gift than by doing it themselves, since they can in that way contribute an amount that would otherwise have been paid as corporate taxes.

26   In each of these—and many similar—cases, there is a strong temptation to rationalize these actions as an exercise of "social responsibility." In the present climate of opinion, with its widespread aversion to "capitalism," "profits," the "soulless corporation" and so on, this is one way for a corporation to generate goodwill as a by-product of expenditures that are entirely justified in its own self-interest.

27   It would be inconsistent of me to call on corporate executives to refrain from this hypocritical window-dressing because it harms the foundations of a free society. That would be to call on them to exercise a "social responsibility"! If our institutions, and the attitudes of the public make it in their self-interest to cloak their actions in this way, I cannot summon much indignation to denounce them. At the same time, I can express admiration for those individual proprietors or owners of closely held corporations or stockholders of more broadly held corporations who disdain such tactics as approaching fraud.

28   Whether blameworthy or not, the use of the cloak of social responsibility, and the nonsense spoken in its name by influential and prestigious businessmen, does clearly harm the foundations of a free society. I have been impressed time and again by the schizophrenic character of many businessmen. They are capable of being extremely far-sighted and clearheaded in matters that are internal to their businesses. They are incredibly short-sighted and muddle-headed in matters that are outside their businesses but affect the possible survival of business in general. This short-sightedness is strikingly exemplified in the calls from many businessmen for wage and price guidelines or controls or incomes policies. There is nothing that could do more in a brief period to destroy a market system and replace it by a centrally controlled system than effective governmental control of prices and wages.

29   The short-sightedness is also exemplified in speeches by businessmen on social responsibility. This may gain them kudos in the short run. But it helps to strengthen the already too prevalent view that the pursuit of profits is wicked and immoral and must be curbed and controlled by external forces. Once this view is adopted, the external forces that curb the market will not be the social consciences, however highly developed, of the pontificating executives; it will be the iron fist of Government bureaucrats. Here, as with price and wage controls, businessmen seem to me to reveal a suicidal impulse.

30   The political principle that underlies the market mechanisms is unanimity. In an ideal free market resting on private property, no individual can coerce any other, all cooperation is voluntary, all parties to such cooperation benefit or they need not participate. There are no "social" values, no "social" responsibilities in any sense other than the shared values and responsibilities of individuals. Society is a collection of individuals and of the various groups they voluntarily form.

31   The political principle that underlies the political mechanism is conformity. The individual must serve a more general social interest—

whether that be determined by a church or a dictator or a majority. The individual may have a vote and a say in what is to be done, but if he is overruled, he must conform. It is appropriate for some to require others to contribute to a general social purpose whether they wish to or not.

Unfortunately, unanimity is not always feasible. There are some respects in which conformity appears unavoidable, so I do not see how one can avoid the use of the political mechanism altogether. 32

But the doctrine of "social responsibility" taken seriously would extend the scope of the political mechanism to every human activity. It does not differ in philosophy from the most explicitly collectivist doctrine. It differs only by professing to believe that collectivist ends can be attained without collectivist means. That is why, in my book "Capitalism and Freedom," I have called it a "fundamentally subversive doctrine" in a free society, and have said that in such a society, "there is one and only one social responsibility of business — to use its resources and engage in activities designed to increase its profits so long as it stays within the rules of the game, which is to say, engages in open and free competition without deception or fraud." 33

Questions for Discussion and Writing

1. What reasons does Friedman present to support his thesis that business firms have no obligation to take on social responsibilities, and that the sole responsibility of business is to increase its profits?

2. How does Friedman's argument depend on the following assumptions: (*a*) All businessmen, including CEOs, are ultimately employees of owners of the firm and hence cannot spend shareholders' money on social programs. (*b*) Although individuals may voluntarily assume responsibilities outside the job to which they may dedicate time, effort, or money, they have no right to divert time, energy, or money belonging to the business to fulfill social responsibilities.

3. How does Friedman rhetorically structure his argument deductively to lead to conclusions that necessarily follow from assumptions taken as self-evident?

4. How does Friedman use the phrase "taxation without representation" ("one of the battle cries of the American Revolution") to support his view that the imposition of government regulations regarding the use of profits for social purposes would lead to a form of socialism? Keep in mind that taxation in this context means that profits that could have been used for wage increases or new

machinery are diverted to fulfill social responsibilities (whether imposed or chosen).

5. Rhetorically, what benefit does Friedman derive from linking his views with one of the rallying cries of the American Revolution?

6. What reasons does Friedman present to support his thesis that free-market mechanisms (that is, a free-market economy) rather than political mechanisms (that is, government regulations designed to allocate business profits for social purposes) are more efficient and a more "appropriate way to determine the allocation of scarce resources to alternative uses"? For example, how does Friedman's argument depend on the point that merely being given power to discharge social responsibilities does not qualify the corporate executive to decide how monies raised for these purposes should be spent?

7. What purpose does Friedman's discussion of trade unions have in the context of his overall argument? How does his discussion of wildcat strikes by these trade unions dramatize his fears about consequences of government interference in business?

8. According to Friedman, what role does guilt play in predisposing business people to feel responsible for redressing social inequities? Evaluate Friedman's claim that this process reveals, at least in business terms, "a suicidal impulse." According to Friedman, what sequence of events would lead businesses that undertake social responsibility in response to public opinion to find themselves under oppressive government control?

9. Write an essay evaluating Friedman's thesis and the quality of reasoning used in his argument. To what extent do you agree or disagree with the viewpoint he expresses? You might apply Friedman's views to a test case such as the 1989 decision by a leading manufacturer of deodorants to donate a portion of their profits from the sale of Sure® to aid the homeless.

10. As a research project, evaluate how Friedman's views are rooted in the philosophy of laissez-faire capitalism espoused by Adam Smith. In your opinion, is it in society's best interest for government to leave business alone?

Robert Almeder

Morality in the Marketplace

Robert Almeder is a professor of philosophy at Georgia State University and is the author of numerous philosophical essays and books including Beyond Death: The Evidence for Life After Death *(1987) and* The Philosophy of Charles Peirce *(1981). In "Morality in the Marketplace" from* Business Ethics *(1983), Almeder identifies inconsistencies in logic he perceives in Milton Friedman's argument and offers some pragmatic reasons why corporations should act in ways that are socially responsible.*

I. Introduction

In order to create a climate more favorable for corporate activity, International Telephone and Telegraph allegedly contributed large sums of money to "destabilize" the duly elected government of Chile. Even though advised by the scientific community that the practice is lethal, major chemical companies reportedly continue to dump large amounts of carcinogens into the water supply of various areas and, at the same time, lobby to prevent legislation against such practices. General Motors Corporation, other automobile manufacturers, and Firestone Tire and Rubber Corporation have frequently defended themselves against the charge that they knowingly and willingly marketed a product that, owing to defective design, had been reliably predicted to kill a certain percentage of its users and, moreover, refused to recall promptly the product even when government agencies documented the large incidence of death as a result of the defective product. Finally, people often say that numerous advertising companies happily accept, and earnestly solicit, accounts to advertise cigarettes knowing full well that as a direct result of their advertising activities a certain number of people will die considerably prematurely and painfully. We need not concern ourselves with whether these and other similar charges are true because our concern here is with what might count as a justification for such corporate conduct were it to occur. There can be no question that such behavior is frequently legal. The question is whether corporate behavior should be constrained by nonlegal or moral considerations. As things presently stand, it seems to be a dogma of contemporary capitalism that the sole responsibility of business is to make as much money as is legally possible. But the question is whether this view is rationally defensible.

2   Sometimes, although not very frequently, corporate executives will admit to the sort of behavior depicted above and then proceed proximately to justify such behavior in the name of their responsibility to the shareholders or owners (if the shareholders are not the owners) to make as much profit as is legally possible. Thereafter, less proximately and more generally, they will proceed to urge the more general utilitarian point that the increase in profit engendered by such corporate behavior begets such an unquestionable overall good for society that the behavior in question is morally acceptable if not quite praiseworthy. More specifically, the justification in question can, and usually does, take two forms.

3   The first and most common form of justification consists in urging that, as long as one's corporate behavior is not illegal, the behavior will be morally acceptable because the sole purpose of being in business is to make a profit; and the rules of the marketplace are somewhat different from those in other places and must be followed if one is to make a profit. Moreover, proponents of this view hasten to add that, as Adam Smith has claimed, the greatest good for society is achieved not by corporations seeking to act morally, or with a sense of social responsibility in their pursuit of profit, but rather by each corporation seeking to maximize its own profit, unregulated in that endeavor except by the laws of supply and demand along with whatever other laws are inherent to the competition process. Smith's view, that there is an invisible hand, as it were, directing an economy governed solely by the profit motive to the greatest good for society,[1] is still the dominant motivation and justification for those who would want an economy unregulated by any moral concern that would, or could, tend to decrease profits for some *alleged* social or moral good.

4   Milton Friedman, for example, has frequently asserted that the sole moral responsibility of business is to make as much profit as is legally possible; and by that he means to suggest that attempts to regulate or restrain the pursuit of profit in accordance with what some people believe to be socially desirable ends are in fact *subversive* of the common good since the greatest good for the greatest number is achieved by an economy maximally competitive and unregulated by moral rules in its pursuit of profit.[2] So, on Friedman's view, the greatest good for society is achieved by corporations acting legally, but with no further regard for what may be morally desirable; and this view begets the paradox that, *in business*, the greatest good for society can be achieved only by acting without regard for morality. Moreover, adoption of this position constitutes a fairly conscious commitment to the view that while one's personal life may well need governance by moral considerations, when pursuing profit, it is necessary that one's corporate behavior be unregulated by any moral concern other than that of making as much money as

is legally possible; curiously enough, it is only in this way that society achieves the greatest good. So viewed, it is not difficult to see how a corporate executive could consistently adopt rigorous standards of morality in his or her personal life and yet feel quite comfortable in abandoning those standards in the pursuit of profit. Albert Carr, for example, likens the conduct of business to that of playing poker.[3] As Carr would have it, moral busybodies who insist on corporations acting morally might do just as well to censure a good bluffer in poker for being deceitful. Society, of course, lacking a perspective such as Friedman's and Carr's, is only too willing to view such behavior as strongly hypocritical and fostered by an unwholesome avarice.

The second way of justifying, or defending, corporate practices that 5 may appear morally questionable consists in urging that even if corporations were to take seriously the idea of limiting profits because of a desire to be moral or more responsible to social needs, then corporations would be involved in the unwholesome business of selecting and implementing moral values that may not be shared by a large number of people. Besides, there is the overwhelming question of whether there can be any nonquestionable moral values or noncontroversial list of social priorities for corporations to adopt. After all, if ethical relativism is true, or if ethical nihilism is true (and philosophers can be counted upon to argue for both positions), then it would be fairly silly of corporations to limit profits for what may be a quite dubious reason, namely, for being moral, when there are no clear grounds for doing it, and when it is not too clear what would count for doing it. In short, business corporations could argue (as Friedman has done)[4] that corporate actions in behalf of society's interests would require of corporations an ability to clearly determine and rank in noncontroversial ways the major needs of society; and it would not appear that this could be done successfully.

Perhaps another, and somewhat easier, way of formulating this sec- 6 ond argument consists in urging that because philosophers generally fail to agree on what are the proper moral rules (if any), as well as on whether we should be moral, it would be imprudent to sacrifice a clear profit for a dubious or controversial moral gain. To authorize such a sacrifice would be to abandon a clear responsibility for one that is unclear or questionable.

If there are any other basic ways of justifying the sort of corporate 7 behavior noted at the outset, I cannot imagine what they might be. So, let us examine these two modes of justification. In doing this, I hope to show that neither argument is sound and, moreover, that corporate behavior of the sort in question is clearly immoral if anything is immoral —and if nothing is immoral, then such corporate behavior is clearly contrary to the long-term interest of a corporation. In the end, we will reflect on ways to prevent such behavior, and what is philosophically implied by corporate willingness to act in clearly immoral ways.

II.

8   Essentially, the first argument is that the greatest good for the greatest number will be, and can only be, achieved by corporations acting legally but unregulated by any moral concern in the pursuit of profit. As we saw earlier, the evidence for this argument rests on a fairly classical and unquestioning acceptance of Adam Smith's view that society achieves a greater good when each person is allowed to pursue her or his own self-interested ends than when each person's pursuit of self-interested ends is regulated in some way or another by moral rules or concern. But I know of no evidence Smith ever offered for this latter claim, although it seems clear that those who adopt it generally do so out of respect for the perceived good that has emerged for various modern societies as a direct result of the free enterprise system and its ability to raise the overall standard of living of all those under it.

9   However, there is nothing inevitable about the greatest good occurring in an unregulated economy. Indeed, we have good inductive evidence from the age of the Robber Barons that unless the profit motive is regulated in various ways (by statute or otherwise) untold social evil can (and some say *will*) occur because of the natural tendency of the system to place ever-increasing sums of money in ever-decreasing numbers of hands. If all this is so, then so much the worse for all philosophical attempts to justify what would appear to be morally questionable corporate behavior on the grounds that corporate behavior, unregulated by moral concern, is necessarily or even probably productive of the greatest good for the greatest number. Moreover, a utilitarian rule would not be very hard pressed to show the many unsavory implications to society as a whole if society were to take seriously a rule to the effect that, provided only that one acts legally, it is morally permissible to do whatever one wants to do to achieve a profit. Some of those implications we shall discuss below before drawing a conclusion.

10   The second argument cited above asserts that even if we were to grant, for the sake of argument, that corporations have social responsibilities beyond that of making as much money as is legally possible for the shareholders, there would be no noncontroversial way for corporations to discover just what these responsibilities are in the order of their importance. Owing to the fact that even distinguished moral philosophers predictably disagree on what one's moral responsibilities are, if any, it would seem irresponsible to limit profits to satisfy dubious moral responsibilities.

11   For one thing, this argument unduly exaggerates our potential for moral disagreement. Admittedly, there might well be important disagreements among corporations (just as there could be among philosophers) as to a priority ranking of major social needs; but that does not mean that most of us could not, or would not, agree that certain things ought not be done in the name of profit even when there is no law

prohibiting such acts. There will always be a few who would do anything for a profit; but that is hardly a good argument in favor of their having the moral right to do so rather than a good argument that they refuse to be moral. In sum, it is hard to see how this second argument favoring corporate moral nihilism is any better than the general argument for ethical nihilism based on the variability of ethical judgments or practices; and apart from the fact that it tacitly presupposes that morality is a matter of what we all in fact would, or should, accept, the argument is maximally counterintuitive (as I shall show) by way of suggesting that we cannot generally agree that corporations have certain clear social responsibilities to avoid certain practices. Accordingly, I would now like to argue that if anything is immoral, a certain kind of corporate behavior is quite immoral although it may not be illegal.

III.

Without caring to enter into the reasons for the belief, I assume we all   12
believe that it is wrong to kill an innocent human being for no other reason than that doing so would be more financially rewarding for the killer than if he were to earn his livelihood in some other way. Nor, I assume, should our moral feelings on this matter change depending on the amount of money involved. Killing an innocent baby for fifteen million dollars would not seem to be any less objectionable than killing it for twenty cents. It is possible, however that some self-professing utilitarian might be tempted to argue that the killing of an innocent baby for fifteen million dollars would not be objectionable if the money were to be given to the poor; under these circumstances, greater good would be achieved by the killing of the innocent baby. But, I submit, if anybody were to argue in this fashion, his argument would be quite deficient because he has not established what he needs to establish to make his argument sound. What he needs is a clear, convincing argument that raising the standard of living of an indefinite number of poor persons by the killing of an innocent person is a greater good for all those affected by the act than if the standard of living were not raised by the killing of an innocent person. This is needed because part of what we mean by having a basic right to life is that a person's life cannot be taken from him or her without a good reason. If our utilitarian cannot provide a convincing justification for his claim that a greater good is served by killing an innocent person in order to raise the standard of living for a large number of poor people, then it is hard to see how he can have the good reason he needs to deprive an innocent person of his or her life. Now, it seems clear that there will be anything but unanimity in the moral community on the question of whether there is a greater good achieved in raising the standard of living by killing an innocent baby than in leaving the standard of living alone and not killing an innocent baby.

Moreover, even if everybody were to agree that the greater good is achieved by the killing of the innocent baby, how could that be shown to be true? How does one compare the moral value of a human life with the moral value of raising the standard of living by the taking of that life? Indeed, the more one thinks about it, the more difficult it is to see just what would count as objective evidence for the claim that the greater good is achieved by the killing of the innocent baby. Accordingly, I can see nothing that would justify the utilitarian who might be tempted to argue that if the sum is large enough, and if the sum were to be used for raising the standard of living for an indefinite number of poor people, then it would be morally acceptable to kill an innocent person for money.

13   These reflections should not be taken to imply, however, that no utilitarian argument could justify the killing of an innocent person for money. After all, if the sum were large enough to save the lives of a large number of people who would surely die if the innocent baby were not killed, then I think one would as a rule be justified in killing the innocent baby for the sum in question. But this situation is obviously quite different from the situation in which one would attempt to justify the killing of an innocent person in order to raise the standard of living for an indefinite number of poor people. It makes sense to kill one innocent person in order to save, say, twenty innocent persons; but it makes no sense at all to kill one innocent person to raise the standard of living of an indefinite number of people. In the latter case, but not in the former, a comparison is made between things that are incomparable.

14   Given these considerations, it is remarkable and somewhat perplexing that certain corporations should seek to defend practices that are in fact instances of killing innocent persons for profit. Take, for example, the corporate practice of dumping known carcinogens into rivers. On Milton Friedman's view, we should not regulate or prevent such companies from dumping their effluents into the environment. Rather we should, if we like, tax the company after the effluents are in the water and then have the tax money used to clean up the environment.[5] For Friedman, and others, the fact that so many people will die as a result of this practice seems to be just part of the cost of doing business and making a profit. If there is any moral difference between such corporate practices and murdering innocent human beings for money, it is hard to see what it is. It is even more difficult to see how anyone could justify the practice and see it as no more than a business practice not to be regulated by moral concern. And there are a host of other corporate activities that are morally equivalent to deliberate killing of innocent persons for money. Such practices number among them contributing funds to "destabilize" a foreign government, advertising cigarettes, knowingly to market children's clothing having a known cancer causing agent, and refusing to recall (for fear of financial loss) goods known to be sufficiently defective to directly maim or kill a certain percentage of their unsuspecting users because of the defect. On this latter item, we are all

familiar, for example, with convincingly documented charges that certain prominent automobile and tire manufacturers will knowingly market equipment sufficiently defective to increase the likelihood of death as a direct result of the defect and yet refuse to recall the product because the cost of recalling and repairing would have a greater adverse impact on profit than if the product were not recalled and the company paid the projected number of predictably successful suits. Of course, if the projected cost of the predictably successful suits were to outweigh the cost of recall and repair, then the product would be recalled and repaired, but not otherwise. In cases of this sort, the companies involved may admit to having certain marketing problems or a design problem, and they may even admit to having made a mistake; but, interestingly enough, they do not view themselves as immoral or as murderers for keeping their product in the market place when they know people are dying from it, people who would not die if the defect were corrected.

The important point is not whether in fact these practices have occurred in the past, or occur even now; there can be no doubt that such practices have occurred and do occur. Rather the point is that when companies act in such ways as a matter of policy, they must either not know what they do is murder (i.e., unjustifiable killing of an innocent person), or knowing that it is murder, seek to justify it in terms of profit. And I have been arguing that it is difficult to see how any corporate manager could fail to see that these policies amount to murder for money, although there may be no civil statute against such corporate behavior. If so, then where such policies exist, we can only assume that they are designed and implemented by corporate managers who either see nothing wrong with murder for money (which is implausible) or recognize that what they do is wrong but simply refuse to act morally because it is more financially rewarding to act immorally. 15

Of course, it is possible that corporate executives would not recognize such acts as murder. They may, after all, view murder as a legal concept involving one noncorporate person or persons deliberately killing another noncorporate person or persons and prosecutable only under existing civil statute. If so, it is somewhat understandable how corporate executives might fail, at least psychologically, to see such corporate policies as murder rather than as, say, calculated risks, tradeoffs, or design errors. Still, for all that, the logic of the situation seems clear enough. 16

IV. Conclusion

In addition to the fact that the only two plausible arguments favoring the Friedman doctrine are unsatisfactory, a strong case can be made for the claim that corporations *do* have a clear and noncontroversial moral responsibility not to design or implement, for reasons of profit, policies 17 that they know, or have good reason to believe, will kill or otherwise seriously injure innocent persons affected by those policies. Moreover, we have said nothing about wage discrimination, sexism, discrimination in hiring, price fixing, price gouging, questionable but not unlawful competition, or other similar practices that some will think businesses should avoid by virtue of responsibility to society. My main concern has been to show that since we all agree that murder for money is generally wrong, and since there is no discernible difference between that and certain corporate policies that are not in fact illegal, then these corporate practices are clearly immoral (that is, they ought not to be done) and incapable of being morally justified by appeal to the Friedman doctrine since that doctrine does not admit of adequate evidential support. In itself, it is sad that this argument needs to be made and, if it were not for what appears to be a fairly strong commitment within the business community to the Friedman doctrine in the name of the unquestionable success of the free enterprise system, the argument would not need to be stated.

18   The fact that such practices do exist—designed and implemented by corporate managers who, for all intents and purposes, appear to be upright members of the moral community—only heightens the need for effective social prevention. Presumably, of course, any company willing to put human lives into the profit and loss column is not likely to respond to moral censure. Accordingly, I submit that perhaps the most effective way to deal with the problem of preventing such corporate behavior would consist in structuring legislation such that senior corporate managers who knowingly concur in practices of the sort listed above can effectively be tried, at their own expense, for murder, rather than censured and fined a sum to be paid out of corporate profits. This may seem a somewhat extreme or unrealistic proposal. However, it seems more unrealistic to think that aggressively competitive corporations will respond to what is morally necessary if failure to do so could be very or even minimally profitable. In short, unless we take strong and appropriate steps to prevent such practices, society will be reinforcing a destructive mode of behavior that is maximally disrespectful of human life, just as society will be reinforcing a value system that so emphasizes monetary gain as a standard of human success that murder for profit could be a corporate policy if the penalty for being caught at it were not too dear.

19   In the long run, of course, corporate and individual willingness to do what is clearly immoral for the sake of monetary gain is a patent commitment to a certain view about the nature of human happiness and success, a view that needs to be placed in the balance with Aristotle's reasoned argument and reflections to the effect that money and all that it brings is a means to an end, and not the sort of end in itself that will justify acting immorally to attain it. What that beautiful end is and why being moral allows us to achieve it, may well be the most rewarding and profitable subject a human being can think about. Properly understood

and placed in perspective, Aristotle's view on the nature and attainment of human happiness could go a long way toward alleviating the temptation to kill for money.

In the meantime, any ardent supporter of the capitalistic system will 20 want to see the system thrive and flourish; and this it cannot do if it invites and demands government regulation in the name of the public interest. A *strong* ideological commitment to what I have described above as the Friedman doctrine is counterproductive and not in anyone's long-range interest because it is most likely to beget an ever-increasing regulatory climate. The only way to avoid such encroaching regulation is to find ways to move the business community into the long-term view of what is in its interest, and effect ways of both determining and responding to social needs before society moves to regulate business to that end. To so move the business community is to ask business to regulate its own modes of competition in ways that may seem very difficult to achieve. Indeed, if what I have been suggesting is correct, the only kind of enduring capitalism is humane capitalism, one that is at least as socially responsible as society needs. By the same token, contrary to what is sometimes felt in the business community, the Friedman doctrine, ardently adopted for the dubious reasons generally given, will most likely undermine capitalism and motivate an economic socialism by assuring an erosive regulatory climate in a society that expects the business community to be socially responsible in ways that go beyond just making legal profits.

In sum, being socially responsible in ways that go beyond legal 21 profitmaking is by no means a dubious luxury for the capitalist in today's world. It is a necessity if capitalism is to survive at all; and, presumably, we shall all profit with the survival of a vibrant capitalism. If anything, then, rigid adherence to the Friedman doctrine is not only philosophically unjustified, and unjustifiable, it is also unprofitable in the long run, and therefore, downright subversive of the long-term common good. Unfortunately, taking the long-run view is difficult for everyone. After all, for each of us, tomorrow may not come. But living for today only does not seem to make much sense either, if that deprives us of any reasonable and happy tomorrow. Living for the future may not be the healthiest thing to do; but do it we must, if we have good reason to think that we will have a future. The trick is to provide for the future without living in it, and that just requires being moral.[6]

NOTES

1. Adam Smith, *The Wealth of Nations*, ed. Edwin Canaan (Modern Library, N.Y., 1937), p. 423.

2. See Milton Friedman, "The Social Responsibility of Business Is to Increase Its Profits" in *The New York Times Magazine* (September 13, 1970), pp. 33, 122–126

and "Milton Friedman Responds" in *Business and Society Review* (Spring, 1972, No. 1), p. 5 ff.

3. Albert Z. Carr, "Is Business Bluffing Ethical?" *Harvard Business Review* (January-February 1968).

4. Milton Friedman in "Milton Friedman Responds" in *Business and Society Review* (Spring 1972, No. 1), p. 10.

5. Milton Friedman in "Milton Friedman Responds" in *Business and Society Review* (Spring 1972, No. 1), p. 10.

6. I would like to thank C. G. Luckhardt, J. Humber, R. L. Arrington, and M. Snoeyenbos for their comments and criticisms of an earlier draft.

Shortly after this paper was initially written, an Indiana superior court judge refused to dismiss a homicide indictment against the Ford Motor Company. The company was indicted on charges of reckless homicide stemming from a 1978 accident involving a 1973 Pinto in which three girls died when the car burst into flames after being slammed in the rear. This was the first case in which Ford, or any other automobile manufacturer, had been charged with a criminal offense.

The indictment went forward because the state of Indiana adopted in 1977 a criminal code provision permitting corporations to be charged with criminal acts. At the time, twenty-two other states allowed as much.

The judge, in refusing to set aside the indictment, agreed with the prosecutor's argument that the charge was based not on the Pinto design fault, but rather on the fact that Ford had permitted the car "to remain on Indiana highways knowing full well its defects."

The case went to trial, a jury trial, and Ford Motor Company was found innocent of the charges. Of course, the increasing number of states that allow corporations to fall under the criminal code is an example of social regulation that could have been avoided had corporations and corporate managers not followed so ardently the Friedman doctrine.

Questions for Discussion and Writing

1. In light of Friedman's essay, to what extent does Almeder accurately summarize Friedman's argument in the opening section of his essay? Does Almeder's interpretation of Friedman's position ("it is only by acting without regard for morality that the greatest good for society can be achieved") represent the logical outcome of principles drawn from Friedman's essay? Why does Almeder begin his own counterargument in this fashion?

2. Summarize the specific counterarguments that Almeder presents that directly respond to corresponding arguments in Friedman's essay. Are there any of Friedman's arguments to which Almeder does not respond, or which he restates in a form that makes them easier to

refute? For example, how does Almeder answer Friedman's claim that businessmen have no knowledge of what society needs?

3. How does Almeder use the case of Robber Barons (unscrupulous industrialists of the 19th-century) to support his thesis that unless the profit motive is regulated in various ways great social evil will inevitably result?

4. Where in his essay does Almeder use specific strategies of argument such as (*a*) argument by analogy, (*b*) guilt by association, and (*c*) use of examples to get his points across? For instance, how does Almeder use the hypothetical example of $15 million being given to the poor for the sacrifice of an innocent baby to support his claim that business decisions must be made in the context of morality? What function does his mentioning of International Telephone and Telegraph, General Motors Corporation, Firestone Tire and Rubber Corporation, and the Ford Motor Company's Pinto case (in note no. 6) serve in the development of his overall argument? How does Almeder's discussion of these cases dramatize the destructive consequences when business sees profit-making as its sole responsibility?

5. Although it may not be obvious, Almeder's position does not rule out what Friedman calls a free-market economy. He does, however, say that there are some very good business reasons why corporations and firms should act in ways that are socially responsible. What are some of these pragmatic reasons and how do they add to the strength of Almeder's arguments based on ethics and morality?

6. In an essay, take a position midway between Friedman's and Almeder's arguments, drawing from each author those points you consider to be valid and emphasizing areas of agreement. In your synthesis, use short, direct quotes from both articles to develop your middle-of-the-road essay.

Judge Miles W. Lord

A Plea for Corporate Conscience

Judge Miles W. Lord is presiding judge of the Federal District Court of Minneapolis. This speech, "A Plea for Corporate Conscience" was delivered February 29, 1984, after Lord had approved a 4.6 million dollar product-liability suit against the A. H. Robins Company for injuries caused by one of its products, the Dalkon Shield Intra-Uterine Contraceptive Device (IUD). This decision covered only seven individual claims of the nine thousand total claims brought against the company. Lord made his comments to the firm's president, Mr. Robins, Mr. Lundsford, Senior vice-president for research and development and Mr. Forrest, vice-president and general counsel. Lord chastises the defendants for corporate irresponsibility and makes an impassioned plea to them to stop the sales of the Dalkon Shield, recall those already sold, and seek out and warn women who may still be using the deadly devices. The speech was later printed as an article in Harper's *(June 1984).*

1   Mr. Robins, Mr. Forrest, and Dr. Lunsford: After months of reflection, study, and cogitation — and no small amount of prayer — I have concluded that it is perfectly appropriate to make this statement, which will constitute my plea to you to seek new horizons in corporate consciousness and a new sense of personal responsibility for the activities of those who work under you in the name of the A.H. Robins Company.

2   It is not enough to say, "I did not know," "It was not me," "Look elsewhere." Time and again, each of you has used this kind of argument in refusing to acknowledge your responsibility and in pretending to the world that the chief officers and directors of your gigantic multinational corporation have no responsibility for its acts and omissions.

3   Today as you sit here attempting once more to extricate yourselves from the legal consequences of your acts, none of you has faced up to the fact that more than 9,000 women claim they gave up part of their womanhood so that your company might prosper. It has been alleged that others gave their lives so you might prosper. And there stand behind them legions more who have been injured but who have not sought relief in the courts of this land.

4   I dread to think what would have been the consequences if your victims had been men rather than women — women, who seem, through

some quirk of our society's mores, to be expected to suffer pain, shame, and humiliation.

If one poor young man were, without authority or consent, to inflict 5
such damage upon one woman, he would be jailed for a good portion of the rest of his life. Yet your company, without warning to women, invaded their bodies by the millions and caused them injuries by the thousands. And when the time came for these women to make their claims against your company, you attacked their characters. You inquired into their sexual practices and into the identity of their sex partners. You ruined families and reputations and careers in order to intimidate those who would raise their voices against you. You introduced issues that had no relationship to the fact that you had planted in the bodies of these women instruments of death, of mutilation, of disease.

Gentlemen, you state that your company has suffered enough, that 6
the infliction of further punishment in the form of punitive damages would cause harm to your business, would punish innocent shareholders, and could conceivably depress your profits to the point where you could not survive as a competitor in this industry. When the poor and downtrodden commit crimes, they too plead that these are crimes of survival and that they should be excused for illegal acts that helped them escape desperate economic straits. On a few occasions when these excuses are made and remorseful defendants promise to mend their ways, courts will give heed to such pleas. But no court will heed the plea when the individual denies the wrongful nature of his deeds and gives no indication that he will mend his ways. Your company, in the face of overwhelming evidence, denies its guilt and continues its monstrous mischief.

Mr. Forrest, you have told me that you are working with members of 7
the Congress of the United States to find a way of forgiving you from punitive damages that might otherwise be imposed. Yet the profits of your company continue to mount. Your last financial report boasts of new records for sales and earnings, with a profit of more than $58 million in 1983. And, insofar as this court has been able to determine, you three men and your company are still engaged in a course of wrongdoing. Until your company indicates that it is willing to cease and desist this deception and to seek out and advise the victims, your remonstrances to Congress and to the courts are indeed hollow and cynical. The company has not suffered, nor have you men personally. You are collectively being enriched by millions of dollars each year. There is no evidence that your company has suffered any penalty from these litigations. In fact, the evidence is to the contrary.

The case law suggests that the purpose of punitive damages is to 8
make an award that will punish a defendant for his wrongdoing. Punishment has traditionally involved the principles of revenge, rehabilitation, and deterrence. There is no evidence I have been able to find in my

review of these cases to indicate that any one of these objectives has been accomplished.

9   Mr. Robins, Mr. Forrest, Dr. Lundsford: You have not been rehabilitated. Under your direction, your company has continued to allow women, tens of thousands of them, to wear this device — a deadly depth charge in their wombs, ready to explode at any time. Your attorney denies that tens of thousands of these devices are still in women's bodies. But I submit to you that he has no more basis for denying the accusation than the plaintiffs have for stating it as truth. We simply do not know how many women are still wearing these devices because your company is not willing to find out. The only conceivable reasons that you have not recalled this product are that it would hurt your balance sheet and alert women who have already been harmed that you may be liable for their injuries. You have taken the bottom line as your guiding beacon and the low road as your route. That is corporate irresponsibility at its meanest. Rehabilitation involves an admission of guilt, a certain contrition, an acknowledgment of wrongdoing, and a resolution to take a new course toward a better life. I find none of this in you or your corporation. Confession is good for the soul, gentlemen. Face up to your misdeed. Acknowledge the personal responsibility you have for the activities of those who work under you. Rectify this evil situation. Warn the potential victims and recompense those who have already been harmed.

10   Mr. Robins, Mr. Forrest, Dr. Lunsford: I see little in the history of this case that would deter others. The policy of delay and obfuscation practiced by your lawyers in courts throughout this country has made it possible for you and your insurance company to put off the payment of these claims for such a long period that the interest you earned in the interim covers the cost of these cases. You, in essence, pay nothing out of your own pockets to settle these cases. What corporate officials could learn a lesson from this? The only lesson they might learn is that it pays to delay compensating victims and to intimidate, harass, and shame the injured parties.

11   Your company seeks to segment and fragment the litigation of these cases nationwide. The courts of this country are burdened with more than 3,000 Dalkon Shield cases. The sheer number of claims and the dilatory tactics used by your company's attorneys clog court calendars and consume vast amounts of judicial and jury time. Your company settles those cases out of court in which it finds itself in an uncomfortable position, a handy device for avoiding any proceeding that would give continuity or cohesiveness to this nationwide problem. The decision as to which cases are brought to trial rests almost solely at the whim and discretion of the A.H. Robins Company. In order to guarantee that no plaintiff or group of plaintiffs mounts a sustained assault upon your system of evasion and avoidance, you have time after time demanded that, as the price of settling a case, able lawyers agree not to bring a

Dalkon Shield case again and not to help less experienced lawyers with cases against your company.

Another of your callous legal tactics is to force women of little means   12
to withstand the onslaughts of your well-financed team of attorneys. You target your worst tactics at the meek and the poor.

If this court had the authority, I would order your company to make   13
an effort to locate each and every woman who still wears this device and recall your product. But this court does not. I must therefore resort to moral persuasion and a personal appeal to each of you. Mr. Robins, Mr. Forrest, and Dr. Lunsford: You are the people with the power to recall. You are the corporate conscience.

Please, in the name of humanity, lift your eyes above the bottom line.   14
You, the men in charge, must surely have hearts and souls and consciences.

Please, gentlemen, give consideration to tracing down the victims and   15
sparing them the agony that will surely be theirs.

Questions for Discussion and Writing

1. What evidence can you discover in Lord's speech that this is not the first time the defendants have appeared before him on such charges? How do you know that the A. H. Robins Company still refuses to recall the Dalkon Shield or even to take steps to advise people of its dangers? In what way does beginning his speech by summarizing the past and continuing misdeeds of the defendants contribute to its rhetorical effectiveness?

2. How does Lord structure his argument around the contrast between those who are weak, and thus need the law to defend them, and those who are powerful, and need the law to restrain them?

3. What words and phrases in Lord's argument reveal an appeal to pathos — that is, to the emotions of his audience?

4. Since the issue of what constitutes adequate punishment and what should serve as evidence of successful and earnest rehabilitation is at the very heart of this case, define *punishment* and *rehabilitation* and compare your definitions with Lords' use of the terms. To what extent does his use of these terms match what you have in mind, and to what degree does he seem to attach a slightly different meaning to them?

5. At what points in his speech does Lord make what he calls a "personal appeal"? What are the circumstances that compel him to go

beyond the jurisdiction of his court and make his plea for "corporate conscience"?

6. What kinds of actions, according to Lord, would serve as evidence that the officials of A. H. Robins took their corporate responsibility to the public seriously? On what underlying assumptions of corporate ethics and behavior does Lord base his expectations? Is there any indication that the A. H. Robins Company shares any of these assumptions?

7. Draft a reply on behalf of the three Robins officials in which they seek to defend themselves in answer to Lord's "plea." You may construct any kind of defense you wish. For example, you may argue that the real responsibility and, hence, accountability lies with the government agency that approved the sale of the IUD devices, or with the women who decided to use these devices, or with the physicians who recommended their use.

8. As a research project, evaluate how current developments (bankruptcy of A. H. Robins' parent company, establishment of a multi-billion dollar trust fund to compensate victims, nationwide solicitation by attorneys seeking to represent Dalkon Shield victims in recovery of damages) throw a new light on Judge Lord's plea made in 1984.

Joseph K. Skinner

Big Mac and the Tropical Forests

*Joseph K. Skinner is a 1979 graduate of the University of California
who majored in plant sciences. He reports that "in all of my course
work at the University of California at Davis, only once was brief
mention made of the biological calamity described in this article, and
even then no connection was made between it and U.S. economic
interests." "Big Mac and the Tropical Forests" first appeared in the*
Monthly Review *(December 1985). Skinner creates an intriguing
causal argument to show how tropical forests in Central and Latin
America are being destroyed in order to raise cattle to produce cheap
beef for companies such as McDonald's and Swift-Armour Meat Packing Co. Skinner claims that the failure to take responsibility on the
part of these and other corporations puts short-term profitability
ahead of catastrophic destruction of the tropical forests. In turn, this
destruction could well accelerate the greenhouse effect by permitting
rising levels of carbon dioxide to remain in the atmosphere.*

Hello, fast-food chains.   1

Goodbye, tropical forests.   2

Sound like an odd connection? The "free-market" economy has led   3
to results even stranger than this, but perhaps none have been as environmentally devastating.

These are the harsh facts: the tropical forests are being leveled for   4
commercial purposes at the rate of 150,000 square kilometers a year, an
area the size of England and Wales combined.[1]

At this rate, the world's tropical forests could be entirely destroyed   5
within seventy-three years. Already as much as a fifth or a quarter of the
huge Amazon forest, which constitutes a third of the world's total rain
forest, has been cut, and the rate of destruction is accelerating. And
nearly two thirds of the Central American forests have been cleared or
severely degraded since 1950.

Tropical forests, which cover only 7 percent of the Earth's land   6
surface (it used to be 12 percent), support half the species of the world's
living things. Due to their destruction, "We are surely losing one or more
species a day right now out of the five million (minimum figure) on
Earth," says Norman Myers, author of numerous books and articles on
the subject and consultant to the World Bank and the World Wildlife
Fund. "By the time ecological equilibrium is restored, at least one-quarter

of all species will have disappeared, probably a third, and conceivably even more. . . . If this pattern continues, it could mean the demise of two million species by the middle of next century." Myers calls the destruction of the tropical forests "one of the greatest biological debacles to occur on the face of the Earth." Looking at the effects it will have on the course of biological evolution, Myers says:

> The impending upheaval in evolution's course could rank as one of the greatest biological revolutions of paleontological time. It will equal in scale and significance the development of aerobic respiration, the emergence of flowering plants, and the arrival of limbed animals. But of course the prospective degradation of many evolutionary capacities will be an impoverishing, not a creative, phenomenon.[2]

7   In other words, such rapid destruction will vacate so many niches so suddenly that a "pest and weed" ecology, consisting of a relatively few opportunistic species (rats, roaches, and the like) will be created.

8   Beyond this—as if it weren't enough—such destruction could well have cataclysmic effects on the Earth's weather patterns, causing, for example, an irreversible desertification of the North American grain belt. Although the scope of the so-called greenhouse effect—in which rising levels of carbon dioxide in the atmosphere heat the planet by preventing infrared radiation from escaping into space—is still being debated within the scientific community, it is not at all extreme to suppose that the fires set to clear tropical forests will contribute greatly to this increase in atmospheric CO_2 and thereby to untold and possibly devastating changes in the world's weather systems.

Big Mac Attack

9   So what does beef, that staple of the fast-food chains and of the North American diet in general, have to do with it?

10   It used to be, back in 1960, that the United States imported practically no beef. That was a time when North Americans were consuming a "mere" 85 pounds of beef per person per year. By 1980 this was up to 134 pounds per person per year. Concomitant with this increase in consumption, the United States began to import beef, so that by 1981 some 800,000 tons were coming in from abroad, 17 percent of it from tropical Latin America and three fourths of that from Central America. Since fast-food chains have been steadily expanding and now are a $5-billion-a-year business, accounting for 25 percent of all the beef consumed in the United States, the connections between the fast-food empire and tropical beef are clear.

11   Cattle ranching is "by far the major factor in forest destruction in

tropical Latin America," says Myers. "Large fast-food outlets in the U.S. and Europe foster the clearance of forests to produce cheap beef."[3]

And cheap it is, compared to North American beef: by 1978 the 12 average price of beef imported from Central America was $1.47/kg, while similar North American beef cost $3.30/kg.

Cheap, that is, for North Americans, but not for Central Americans. 13 Central Americans cannot afford their own beef. Whereas beef production in Costa Rica increased twofold between 1959 and 1972, per capita consumption of beef in that country went down from 30 lbs. a year to 19. In Honduras, beef production increased by 300 percent between 1965 and 1975, but consumption decreased from 12 lbs. per capita per year to 10. So, although two thirds of Central America's arable land is in cattle, local consumption of beef is decreasing; the average domestic cat in the United States now consumes more beef than the average Central American.[4]

Brazilian government figures show that 38 percent of all deforesta- 14 tion in the Brazilian Amazon between 1966 and 1975 was attributable to large-scale cattle ranching. Although the presence of hoof-and-mouth disease among Brazilian cattle has forced U.S. lawmakers to prohibit the importation of chilled or frozen Brazilian beef, the United States imports $46 million per year of cooked Brazilian beef, which goes into canned products; over 80 percent of Brazilian beef is still exported, most of it to Western Europe, where no such prohibition exists.

At present rates, all remaining Central American forests will have 15 been eliminated by 1990. The cattle ranching largely responsible for this is in itself highly inefficient: as erosion and nutrient leaching eat away the soil, production drops from an average one head per hectare — measly in any case — to a pitiful one head per five to seven hectares within five to ten years. A typical tropical cattle ranch employs only one person per 2,000 head, and meat production barely reaches 50 lbs./ acre/year. In Northern Europe, in farms that do not use imported feed, it is over 500 lbs./acre/year.

This real-term inefficiency does not translate into bad business, how- 16 ever, for although there are some absentee landowners who engage in ranching for the prestige of it and are not particularly interested in turning large profits, others find bank loans for growing beef for export readily forthcoming, and get much help and encouragement from such organizations as the Pan American Health Organization, the Organization of American States, the U.S. Department of Agriculture, and U.S. AID, without whose technical assistance "cattle production in the American tropics would be unprofitable, if not impossible."[5] The ultimate big winner appears to be the United States, where increased imports of Central American beef are said to have done more to stem inflation than any other single government initiative.

"On the good land, which could support a large population, you have 17 the rich cattle owners, and on the steep slopes, which should be left in forest, you have the poor farmers," says Gerardo Budowski, director of the Tropical Agricultural Research and Training Center in Turrialba, Costa Rica. "It is still good business to clear virgin forest in order to fatten cattle for, say, five to eight years and then abandon it."[6]

18   (Ironically, on a trip I made in 1981 to Morazán, a Salvadoran province largely under control of FMLN guerrillas, I inquired into the guerilla diet and discovered that beef, expropriated from the cattle ranches, was a popular staple.)

Swift-Armour's Swift Armor

19   The rain forest ecosystem, the oldest on Earth, is extremely complex and delicate. In spite of all the greenery one sees there, it is a myth that rain forest soil is rich. It is actually quite poor, leached of all nutrients save the most insoluble (such as iron oxides, which give lateritic soil — the most common soil type found there — its red color). Rather, the ecosystem of the rain forest is a "closed" one, in which the nutrients are to be found in the biomass, that is, in the living canopy of plants and in the thin layer of humus on the ground that is formed from the matter shed by the canopy. Hence the shallow-rootedness of most tropical forest plant species. Since the soil itself cannot replenish nutrients, nutrient recycling is what keeps the system going.

20   Now, what happens when the big cattle ranchers, under the auspices of the Swift-Armour Meat Packing Co., or United Brands, or the King Ranch sling a huge chain between two enormous tractors, level a few tens of thousands of acres of tropical forest, burn the debris, fly a plane over to seed the ash with guinea grass, and then run their cattle on the newly created grasslands?[7]

21   For the first three years or so the grass grows like crazy, up to an inch a day, thriving on all that former biomass. After that, things go quickly downhill: the ash becomes eroded and leached, the soil becomes exposed and hardens to the consistency of brick, and the area becomes useless to agriculture. Nor does it ever regain anything near its former state. The Amazon is rising perceptibly as a result of the increased runoff due to deforestation.

22   Tractor-and-chain is only one way of clearing the land. Another common technique involves the use of herbicides such as Tordon, 2, 4-D, and 2,4,5-T (Agent Orange). The dioxin found in Agent Orange can be extremely toxic to animal life and is very persistent in the environment.

Tordon, since it leaves a residue deadly to all broad-leaved plants, renders the deforested area poisonous to all plants except grasses; consequently, even if they wanted to, ranchers could not plant soil-enriching legumes in the treated areas, a step which many agronomists recommend for keeping the land productive for at least a little longer.

23   The scale of such operations is a far cry from the traditional slash-

and-burn practiced by native jungle groups, which is done on a scale small enough so that the forest can successfully reclaim the farmed areas. Such groups, incidentally, are also being decimated by cattle interests in Brazil and Paraguay—as missionaries, human rights groups, and cattlemen themselves will attest.

Capital's "manifest destiny" has traditionally shown little concern for 24 the lives of trees or birds or Indians, or anything else which interferes with immediate profitability, but the current carving of holes in the gene pool by big agribusiness seems particularly short-sighted. Since the tropical forests contain two thirds of the world's genetic resources, their destruction will leave an enormous void in pool of genes necessary for the creation of new agricultural hybrids. This is not to mention the many plants as yet undiscovered—there could be up to 15,000 unknown species in South America alone—which may in themselves contain remarkable properties. (In writing about alkaloids found in the Madagascar periwinkle which have recently revolutionized the treatment of leukemia and Hodgkin's disease, British biochemist John Humphreys said: "If this plant had not been analyzed, not even a chemist's wildest ravings would have hinted that such structures would be pharmacologically active."[8] Ninety percent of Madagascar's forests have been cut.)

But there is no small truth in Indonesian Minister for Environment 25 and Development Emil Salim's complaint that the "South is asked to conserve genes while the other fellow, in the North, is consuming things that force us to destroy the genes in the South."[9]

Where's the Beef?

The marketing of beef imported into the United States is extremely 26 complex, and the beef itself ends up in everything from hot dogs to canned soup. Fresh meat is exported in refrigerated container ships to points of entry, where it is inspected by the U.S. Department of Agriculture. Once inspected, it is no longer required to be labeled "imported."[10] From there it goes into the hands of customhouse brokers and meat packers, often changing hands many times; and from there it goes to the fast-food chains or the food processors. The financial structures behind this empire are even more complex, involving governments and quasi-public agencies, such as the Export-Import Bank and the Overseas Private Investment Corporation, as well as the World Bank and the Inter-American Development Bank, all of which encourage cattle raising in the forest lands. (Brazilian government incentives to cattle ranching in Amazonia include a 50 percent income-tax rebate on ranchers' investments elsewhere in Brazil, tax holidays of up to ten years, loans with negative interest rates in real terms, and exemptions from sales taxes and import duties. Although these incentives were deemed excessive and since 1979 no longer apply to new ranches, they still continue for existing ones. This cost the Brazilian government $63,000 for each ranching job created.)

27   Beef production in the tropics may be profitable for the few, but it is taking place at enormous cost for the majority and for the planet as a whole. Apart from the environmental destruction, it is a poor converter of energy to protein and provides few benefits for the vast majority of tropical peoples in terms of employment or food. What they require are labor-intensive, multiple-cropping systems.

28   The world is obviously hostage to an ethic which puts short-term profitability above all else, and such catastrophes as the wholesale destruction of the tropical forests and the continued impoverishment of their peoples are bound to occur as long as this ethic rules.

NOTES

1. Jean-Paul Landley, "Tropical Forest Resources," *FAO Forestry Paper* 30 (Rome: FAO, 1982). This UN statistic is the most accurate to date. For further extrapolations from it, see Nicholas Guppy, "Tropical Deforestation: A Global View," *Foreign Affairs* 62, no. 4 (Spring 1984).

2. There are amazingly few scientists in the world with broad enough expertise to accurately assess the widest implications of tropical deforestation; Norman Myers is one of them. His books include *The Sinking Ark* (Oxford: Pergamon Press, 1979). See also *Conversion of Moist Tropical Forests* (Washington, D.C.: National Academy of Sciences, 1980), "The End of the Line." *Natural History* 94, no. 2 (February 1985), and "The Hamburger Connection," *Ambio* 10, no. 1 (1981). I have used Myers extensively in the preparation of this article. The quotes in this paragraph are from "The Hamburger Connection," pp. 3, 4, 5.

3. Myers, "End of the Line," p. 2.

4. See James Nations and Daniel I. Komer, "Rainforests and the Hamburger Society," *Environment* 25, no. 3 (April 1983).

5. Ibid., p. 17.

6. Catherine Caufield, "The Rain Forests," *New Yorker* (January 14, 1985), p. 42. This excellent article was later incorporated in a book, *In the Rainforest* (New York: Knopf, 1985).

7. Other multinationals with interests in meat packing and cattle ranching in tropical Latin America include Armour-Dial International, Goodyear Tire and Rubber Co., and Gulf and Western Industries, Inc. See Roger Burbach and Patricia Flynn, *Agribusiness in the Americas* (New York: Monthly Review Press, 1980).

8. Quoted in Caufield, "Rain Forests," p. 60.

9. Ibid., p. 100.

10. This is one way McDonald's, for example, can claim not to use foreign beef. For a full treatment of McDonald's, see M. Boas and S. Chain, *Big Mac: The Unauthorized Story of McDonald's* (New York: New American Library, 1976).

Questions for Discussion and Writing

1. How does Skinner's discussion of the consequences of cutting down the tropical forests set the stage for the role played by cattle ranching in raising cheap beef for export to North America? What factual evidence does Skinner offer as to the rate at which tropical forests are being destroyed and the complex ecological effects of deforestation?

2. What is the greenhouse effect and how is it related to the destruction of tropical forests?

3. How does Skinner use the contrast between increasing beef production and decreasing per capita consumption of beef in several Central American countries to support his claim that "Central Americans cannot afford their own beef"?

4. How does Skinner's discussion of the methods used by cattle ranchers to clear the land underscore his major concern over a business ethic that "puts short-term profitability above all else"? Specifically, how does the destruction of the "pool of genes necessary for the creation of new agricultural hybrids" illustrate the conflict between short-term gains and long-term biological resources? Keep in mind that 40 percent of modern drugs have been derived from plants whose value was previously unknown.

5. How does Skinner's discussion of the financial incentives offered to cattle ranchers support his thesis that such use of the tropics may be "profitable for the few, but it is taking place at enormous cost for the majority and for the planet as a whole"?

6. Evaluate the solutions Skinner proposes. Would they be effective in dealing with the problem he identifies?

7. Evaluate Skinner's article as a causal argument. How persuasively does he establish a causal link between hamburgers served in fast-food chains in North America and the destruction of tropical rain forests in Central America? How effectively does he use evidence in

the form of facts, statistics, and the testimony of experts to support his thesis?

8. How does Skinner organize his discussion to point up the unsuspected relationship between hamburgers and tropical forests? For example, how do the subjects covered in each of the four sections of his article and his alternate treatment of them help make his thesis clearer to his audience?

9. In a brief essay discuss how learning about this previously unknown causal relationship may have affected your attitude toward hamburgers served in fast-food chains.

10. To gain some insight into how food reaches the supermarket, investigate the steps a packaged food item such as steak or chicken goes through before it winds up on the supermarket shelves. For example, exactly what kinds of activities go on in a slaughterhouse and meat-packing plant? What stages might a pig go through before it winds up as bacon, canned ham, pork chops, and so forth?

11. As a research project, investigate any large public works project, such as a projected dam, whose construction came into conflict with the Endangered Species Act of 1973. For example, the Tellico Dam project in Tennessee was stopped because it posed a danger to the snail darter, an endangered species of fresh-water fish.

Elizabeth M. Whelan

Big Business vs. Public Health: The Cigarette Dilemma

Elizabeth M. Whelan is a physician and executive director of the American Council on Science and Health. In "Big Business vs. Public Health: The Cigarette Dilemma," from U.S.A. Today (May 1984), Whelan argues that although the big five tobacco companies publicly deny that cigarettes are devastating to health, there is no possibility that they are unaware of the risks associated with cigarette smoking. Whelan cites reasons, evidence, and testimony to support her claim that tobacco companies have "made a conscious decision that their own economic well-being is far more important than the health of Americans." Whelan's in-depth analysis substantiates the extent to which the national economy and the economy of entire regions of the country depend on tobacco as a cash crop. She explores the economic clout of the tobacco industry and relates this to why national women's organizations and magazines addressed to "liberated" women are strangely silent on an issue that so directly concerns the health of their readers.

What do the following have in common: dioxin in Missouri; chemical seepage at Love Canal; radioactive contamination at Three Mile Island; saccharin; hairdyes; formaldehyde; coffee; Red Dye #2? All of these topics have been extensively, and emotionally, covered by the media in recent years. All have been indicted as possible causes of cancer, birth defects, and other human maladies.

In recent months, we have witnessed dozens of television documentaries, magazine cover stories, and unsettling headlines focused on the theme, "America, the Poisoned." We have seen a dramatic increase in the use of scare verbs like "ooze," "seep," "brew," and "foul," and scare adjectives like "ominous," "sinister," and "horrific." We have come to believe that there is an environmental time bomb ticking, and that what we see today is only the tip of the iceberg. We are left with a guilt-provoking and anxiety-producing feeling that modern American technology is just now catching up with us, that we will ultimately pay the highest price for the conveniences we now enjoy—environmentally induced premature death.

The Environmental Protection Agency, Consumer Product Safety Commission, Food and Drug Administration, consumer groups, and home owners' associations have responded to—and indeed contributed to—this escalating fear of environmental sources of disease by demanding the banning of pesticides, food additives, urea formaldehyde foam insulation, and other products of modern industrial know-how. In the case of the Love Canal, Pres. Carter went so far as to declare an official state of emergency and order the costly relocation of more than 700 homeowners. In Missouri, the EPA was the subject of bitter criticism, and damning press coverage, for not evacuating families sooner from the dioxin-contaminated areas.

4   It is no surprise, then, that national surveys indicated that, in the 1980's, Americans are significantly more supportive than ever before of environmental legislation, efforts to clean up toxic wastes, and more stringent government control of food additives, pesticides, and a vast array of consumer products. All of this is *allegedly* in the interest of promoting health through the application of preventive measures to remove the suspected disease-causing agents.

5   Those topics listed above have something else in common as well. Although in some cases there was suggestive evidence to indicate a *potential* threat to human health, and there was just reason for vigilance, there is no solid evidence that exposure to these substances has caused either deaths or any deleterious long-term impact on human health! In other words, in retrospect, the swell of American anxiety about environmental contaminants, and the apparent mandate for action to control them, is based on very little evidence of the existence of a real problem.

6   Dioxin in Missouri was not the cause of any human disease. Indeed, the only known human effect to have occurred in other circumstances when humans have been exposed to dioxin is chloracne, a severe form of acne. Even chloracne was not noted in Missouri. New York Gov. Hugh Carey's blue ribbon physician panel, which examined the health status at Love Canal, concluded that "There has been no demonstration of acute health effects linked to exposure to hazardous wastes at Love Canal . . . chronic effects of hazardous waste exposure at Love Canal have neither been established nor ruled out. . . . " The same panel found no evidence to support claims of higher rates of miscarriage or birth defects among Love Canal residents. Rep. Mike McCormack (D. Wash.), chairman of a subcommittee that prepared a report on Three Mile Island, summed up the general feeling among scientists when he said, "the greatest harm from the TMI accident was its severe emotional impact on an ill-informed and easily frightened public." Saccharin, hairdyes, Red Dye #2, and formaldehyde have been shown in a limited number of experiments to increase cancer risk in laboratory animals. There is no evidence from human studies that these substances cause disease. Coffee consumption was linked with pancreatic cancer in one controversial epidemiological study, but other human studies have not confirmed this finding.

7   It is in this context that the cigarette stands out as the ultimate

paradox in American society. While magazines, newspapers, and the electronic media focus almost daily on the *hypothetical* risks posed by environmental chemical contamination and the techniques of modern food production and processing, and the American public is demanding that the government "do something" to prevent environmentally in- duced disease, there is a near complete lack of interest in the leading cause of premature death in the U.S. — the cigarette. *While no one died at Love Canal or Three Mile Island, some 400,000 Americans this year alone will die prematurely from diseases directly associated with cigarette smoke.*

A Malevolent Web

How can a product as dangerous as the cigarette continue to be   8 accepted — and indeed be heavily promoted by advertising — in such a health-conscious and demanding society? Why are there not frequent television documentaries, investigative reporting, outraged citizens groups, and concerned legislatures dealing with what is arguably the most dramatic and far-reaching public health threat of this century? Why do we have anxious scrutiny over traces of dioxin, yet apathy about cigarettes as a cause of disease? How, 30 years after it was definitely shown to be a health hazard, does the cigarette remain triumphant in its knowledge of a secure future? The answer lies in a malevolent web of five extrinsic and intrinsic factors:

- The happenstance of a cruel and unpredictable backfire in human innovation.

- The physically addictive nature of cigarettes, which keeps smokers hooked despite a desire to quit.

- The human tendency to reject the premise that, under some circumstances, we may be responsible for causing our own illness or death — the adaptive psychological defense mechanisms which allow the smoker to sublimate, repress, and disassociate himself from the bad news about cigarettes.

- The related reluctance of nonsmokers to bring up grim statistics when they know that the smoker is already overburdened with guilt and anxiety.

- The enormous and unprecedented economic clout exerted by the tobacco industry. Those dependent on it for their livelihood take great pains to ensure that their addicted and potentially addicted customers be shielded from frequent onslaughts of information about how harmful cigarette smoking is.

9   **Backfire.** It goes without saying that, if the cigarette were being considered for introduction today, there is no way it would meet the safety criteria of either the Food and Drug Administration or the Consumer Product Safety Commission, the two agencies which would seem most logical for approving and regulating it. Even without the dozens of human studies which we have today, the agencies would reject cigarettes because burned tobacco contains a significant number of cancer-causing agents and the immediate effects of tobacco inhalation (increased heart rate, increase in blood carbon monoxide levels, inhibition of stomach contractions) would be sufficient sources for concern. Whether it was the small businessman trying to have cigarettes approved or a large corporation's research department which had come up with this "brainstorm," today, the cigarette would not make its way out of the Federal testing laboratories, and the economic impact of the non-approval of cigarettes would be negligible.

10   However, the cigarette is *not* just being introduced; it has been around for approximately 100 years. (Tobacco, of course has been used for generations, but it was the invention of the cigarette manufacturing machine in the 1880's which resulted in a new and devastating form of behavior—inhalation of smoke on a regular basis, directly into the lungs.)

11   Through the first 60 years of its 100-year existence, the cigarette and the marketing techniques that went with it represented a stellar success for those who worked hard and cleverly in a free enterprise environment to sell a product that gave pleasure, prestige, and relaxation to millions of eager customers. During the first six decades, there was, of course, "controversy" about cigarettes, and eventually some impressive scientific evidence that cigarettes were hazardous. In general, however, the time period between 1890 and 1950 marked the golden age of the cigarette, the birth of a new symbol of the all-American man and, eventually, the all-American woman. That was the dream: the carefree life; the glamorous ads; the hints that cigarettes might not only be pleasurable, but even healthful; and the development of a major, successful economic base for millions of people, directly or indirectly financially dependent on the production, manufacture, sales, and advertising of cigarettes.

12   Then, in 1950, the dream became a nightmare. In a near explosion of medical data, smokers and nonsmokers alike were jolted by the reports of the devastating health impact of the pleasure-giving cigarette. The news was, quite decidedly, too frightening to fully digest, and indeed, through much of the 1950's, the most prevalent reaction of the medical profession, the press, and the general public was to downplay the evidence, demand "further data," point to alleged gaps and limitations of the "statistics," and run as far from the reality as possible. Human innovation had backfired, and people did not know what to do about it. For years, honest, hard-working, enterprising Americans had grown

tobacco, manufactured cigarettes, and promoted and distributed the product in a clever (and well-intentioned) manner. The tragedy here is that, by the time the bad news about cigarettes had accumulated, the cigarette had become socially desirable, enormous segments of the economic system—including the U.S. government—were dependent on the cigarette as a source of revenue, and a sizable portion of the American population was physically addicted to the product.

Addiction. Most Americans are well aware of the addictive proper- 13
ties of illegal "recreational" drugs like heroin. Many would be shocked to learn that Dr. Williams Polin, director of the National Institute on Drug Abuse, terms cigarette smoking "the most widespread drug dependence in our country." In general, the number of cigarettes consumed by the average smoker is 30 per day. Each inhaled puff delivers a dose of drug to the brain, resulting in 50,000 to 70,000 such doses per person every year. There is no other form of drug use which occurs with such frequency and regularity.

The evidence on the addictive nature of smoking is evident in na- 14
tional surveys which indicate that 90% of smokers would like to quit and that 85% have tried to quit, but failed. Cigarette smokers are physiological prisoners, their bodies in need of the substances in cigarette smoke in order to perform efficiently. Repeated studies indicate that tobacco is more addictive than heroin, producing very strong physical dependence. Cigarette withdrawal symptoms include significant body changes leading to decrease in heart rate, increase in appetite, disturbances in sleep patterns, anxiety, irritability, and aggressiveness.

When a smoker tells you that he has tried to stop smoking, but just 15
can't, he really means it. Moreover, of those who *are* able to give up smoking, some 70% resume the habit within three months—about the same recidivism rate as heroin. One can not overstate the contribution that this addictive nature has made to the continued use of the cigarette; indeed, it is an essential component of the tobacco industry's recipe for survival.

Psychological blackout. The survival of the cigarette in the 1980's is 16
a classical testimony to the existence of the psychological mechanisms which protect us from facts with which we can not cope. The classic response to cognitive dissonance, which occurs when people acquire new information that clashes with their current behavior or firmly held belief, was vividly evident during the 1950's, when retrospective and prospective human epidemiological studies around the world confirmed the extraordinary rates of lung cancer, heart disease, emphysema, and other ailments among smokers. People simply refused to incorporate this new information into their consciousness. During that entire decade, there was enormous resistance on the part of the media, legislators, and even physicians to believe the new findings, and a tendency to dismiss what was unacceptable. During the early 1950's, some 70% of American men from all walks of life smoked, had previously thought it was at

worst only slightly harmful, and could not deal with a different assessment.

17   Today's surveys show that 90% of Americans know cigarette smoking is hazardous to health (although most of them "know" it only in the rhetorical sense, unaware of the specific dangers). The clash here is between the reality of smoking and the evidence available that it is harmful. The two beliefs can not exist together, so it is the evidence that is repressed and in some cases sublimated.

WHAT ARE THE RISKS OF CIGARETTE SMOKING?

Americans may have heard the message "smoking is hazardous" hundreds of times, but rarely is it spelled out for them that regular smokers increase their risk of death from lung cancer by over 700%, while simultaneously assuming other staggeringly elevated risks of cancer of the larynx (500%), mouth (300%), esophagus (400%), bladder (100%), and pancreas (100%), as well as emphysema (1,300%) and coronary heart disease (100%). Moreover, all these risks are assumed *at the same time!*

(For example, when the smoker declares his "health consciousness" by joining an exercise club or shopping at a "health food" store.)

18   In plain English, smokers do not want to talk or think about the dangers of their habit. Currently, public service advertisements about the hazards of smoking are few and far between, so most smokers find it relatively easy to avoid mental dissonance. Cigarette smoking literally becomes an involuntary, automatic form of behavior, with no incentive for the smoker to reevaluate his decision to smoke from week to week.

19   **Nonsmokers' reluctance.** It would seem logical that the nonsmoker, unencumbered by the physiological addiction to cigarettes, would be an ideal source of encouragement for smoking cessation. However, it generally does not work that way, because some basic human psychological mechanisms are at work.

20   First, disease data on smoking are so horrifying that it may be difficult for a wife, for example, to allow herself to even imagine her husband experiencing an excruciating death from lung cancer, and a type of "secondhand" denial may set in. Second, she might meet major resistance and strike a chord of marital dissension should she attempt to focus her smoking husband on the subject. Third, in dealing with a friend, relative, or anyone else who smokes, many nonsmokers sense the smoker's depression, guilt, and unhappiness, sometimes masked by one-liners and grim humor, and feel reluctant to make a bad situation worse by bringing up a topic which is so depressing. There are, inevitably,

many relatives, friends, and employer seriously concerned about the health of their smoking friends, but simply baffled about how to tactfully, graciously, and effectively bring the topic up without incurring the wrath of the person they are trying to help. The irony today is that cigarette smoking is socially acceptable, while discussions of the health hazards of smoking are not.

The combination of the "guilt-ridden smoker's phenomenon" and 21 the helplessness of the nonsmoker in giving the advice may be one reason why certain institutions — like churches and synagogues — have generally ignored the topic. This is ironic since, while religious organizations across the country may differ widely in their codes of theology, all are united in their belief that human life is precious. Most probably would agree that it is a sin, however defined, to take one's own life. Many have taken formal stances on potentially life-threatening aspects of life-style. For example, the National Council of Churches of Christ has issued official policy statements on drug abuse, health care, and alcohol use, but it and almost all other formal religious sects in this country maintain silence on the subject of cigarettes and health. (A vivid exception here is the Seventh-Day Adventists Church, which issues a substantial quantity of literature about the dangers of smoking, complete with photographs of diseased lungs.)

Why would a clergyman who grimly warned you that shooting your- 22 self in the head with a loaded pistol would be contrary to God's wishes not warn you that slow-motion suicide was equally unacceptable and immoral? Why would the National Council of Churches take on the issue of infant formula in the Third World, claiming that it was life-threatening, and then turn their heads on an issue which kills hundreds of thousands of Americans — and is about to kill millions of new smokers in developing nations? The answer again indicates the physiological addiction process; the fact that a sizable minority of clergymen, like everyone else, smokes cigarettes; and that the smoking problem seems so deeprooted and hopeless that no effort is made to address the subject.

Part of the psychological cover-up on the subject of smoking might 23 be explained by the human eagerness to blame misfortune on anyone but ourselves. In the case of Third World-feeding practices, the "enemy" was the infant formula manufacturers; in the case of the anxiety about the health effects of dioxin or Red Dye #2, the "villain" was a chemical or a food company; in the case of the cigarette, the "villain" is the smoker or, as the cartoon figure Pogo once said, "We have met the enemy and he is us." It is far easier to focus one's attention and ire on health risks imposed by outside forces than it is to become introspective about one's own role in human disease. This rejection of introspection may, for example, explain the total lack of interest in the subject of cigarettes among the "women's movement," as represented by the National Organization for Women (NOW), Ms. magazine, and other groups which have a commitment to improving the quality of women's lives. The movement has been both active and successful in reducing on-the-job discrimination, fostering equal opportunity in advanced education, reducing the gap in compensation between males and females, proclaiming women's rights to control of their own bodies by encouraging availability of birth control services and abortion, and developing novel ways of effectively combining careers with family life. It thus seems a bit strange that there is a peculiar silence on the subject of women's smoking in feminist circles.

24   The feminist health "bible," *Our Bodies, Ourselves*, has only a passing reference to the subject of smoking. When asked about this, Judy Norsigian, a member of the Boston Women's Health Collective, which produced the original book, explained that they had intended to include a chapter on smoking, alcohol, and drugs, but "there was not sufficient room in the book, and we did not have the resources to do the research." NOW, which has taken a very active role in many women's health issues, has no comment on smoking, and in its 40-page submission to the 1979 Kennedy hearings on women's health, did not make a single reference to the problem. The National Women's Health Network, which represents about 1,000 American women's health organizations, has "no formal position on smoking." The San Francisco Women's Health Collective, an organization which describes itself as devoted to "women's health education," does not address the smoking issue because "it [is] not a priority in terms of health education."

25   Even the magazines of "liberated" women stand mute on this subject. *Ms.*, which claims to "serve women as people, not roles," has distinct opinions about what advertising they should accept and are on record as saying they will not accept advertising that is offensive to women (for example, they turned down ads for vaginal deodorants), but they freely advertise cigarettes and, since they began publication a decade ago, have *never* carried an article on smoking and health.

26   Why the silence here? In the case of the magazines, it is clear that the advertising revenue from tobacco companies plays some role, but there must be more to it than that. Feminist groups have a tradition of focusing on problems which they feel are unique to women, and perhaps they unconsciously decided that the cigarette problem affected everyone. However, in the 1980's, with lung cancer replacing breast cancer as the leading cause of cancer death in women and cigarettes being the major controllable threat to the health of unborn children, should not priorities be reexamined? That is where the addiction and "self-inflicted" nature of the cigarette nightmare come in. Once again, the major thrust of the women's movement has always been focused on what others (particularly the male of the species) are doing to women, as opposed to what they are doing to themselves. In order to effectively address the growing calamity of cigarettes in women's death and morbidity, the leaders of the

feminist movement must for once become introspective, acknowledging
that the cigarette problem is largely self-induced.

Economic clout. With some 35,000 medical citations in the literature   27
indicting tobacco use, particularly cigarette smoking, for a vast array of
human diseases, and with 90% of their customers, although physiologically hooked, desirous of giving up their product, it is necessary for the
tobacco industry to be constantly vigilant to ensure the survival of its
business. Tobacco, particularly in the form of cigarettes, *is* Big Business in
the U.S. With 640,000,000,000 cigarettes smoked in 1982 at a cost to
smokers of over $21,200,000,000, the economic stakes are very high. Not
only is tobacco grown in 22 American states and our sixth largest cash
crop, but there is a vast and complex tobacco supply network which
extends the chain of economic dependence on tobacco to include a full
spectrum of industries, including manufacturers of farm supplies and
equipment, transportation, advertising, and, in turn, those who depend
on these suppliers. Thus, the economic ripple effect extends from the
tobacco manufacturers, to Madison Avenue ad agencies, and finally to
newspapers and magazines which derive over $1,000,000,000 annually
in revenues from cigarette ads. In addition, any list of "cigarette depen-
dents" must include Federal, state, and local governments, which receive
more than $6,000,000,000 in cigarette sales and excise taxes each year.

There are four major ways that tobacco interests flex their economic   28
muscle when they perceive any threat to their most important product
—cigarettes. First, they rely on the corporate clout of their family companies. By buying soft drink, insurance, food, and alcoholic beverage companies, they have succeeded in spreading even further the economic
dependency on cigarettes, thus extending the reach of their corporate
teeth. For example, Del Monte, which operates canneries and specialty
plants, beverage operations, and seafood and frozen food plants around
the world, seemingly would have no interest in the sales of cigarettes.
However, Del Monte is part of the R.J. Reynolds family and thus has a
very definite interest in the success of the parent company. Similarly, it is
all-in-the-family for Miller beer and Seven-Up, with their "father," Philip Morris; and there is a partnership of Saks Fifth Avenue, Gimbels
department stores, and Brown and Williamson—all members of the
Batus family. Some of the family members seem most incompatible.
American Brands—makers of Lucky Strikes, Pall Mall, and Tareyton—
owns the Franklin Life Insurance company, which offers discounts on
policies to nonsmokers! There is no doubt that, when the tobacco men
are feeling pressure (for example, from Congress), they rally the "sibling" companies around the cigarette flag.

Second, tobacco executives know that businesses need clients, and   29
the tobacco empire is a very valuable client, one which businesses which
need accounts would do nothing to displease. Thus, a major chemical
company which produces agricultural chemicals is part of the tobacco

"family" too, because, if it became outspoken on the dangers of cigarettes, it might lose these affluent customers. The roots go even deeper; the suppliers of family companies (glass and container manufacturers) for Seven-Up, cans for Miller beer, sugar for Hawaiian Punch, flavoring agents for Patio Mexican foods and Chun King Oriental food) are dealing indirectly, but still significantly, with the tobacco empire.

30   Third, by teaming up with the manufacturers of other products that might be the subject of bad press or inhibiting government regulation, the cigarette manufacturers are constantly seeking potential allies who will stand by them in the name of Big Business and free enterprise. An analysis of the affiliation of the directors of the top tobacco companies is revealing, as it demonstrates how cigarette manufacturers have been successful in making corporate officers of other industries members of the tobacco team. For example, the R.J. Reynolds board includes Herschel H. Cudd, retired senior vice president of Standard Oil, Ronald Grierson from General Electric, John D. Macomber from Celanese, and John W. Hanley of Monsanto.

31   Fourth, the cigarette manufacturers demonstrate their economic clout through the use of some of the most elaborate and extravagant advertising and promotional budgets in American history. Although they deny publicly that cigarettes are devastating to health, there is no possibility that the decision-makers at the big five tobacco companies are unaware of the risk associated with their product. Thus, they have made a conscious decision that their own economic well-being is far more important than the health of Americans. Advertising is their primary mechanism for neutralizing the medical fears among smokers and keeping the "pleasures" of smoking in the public's mind.

32   For years, cigarette apologists have defended their advertising practices by claiming that they advertise only to foster competition among various brands, not to mislead smokers about the effects of their habit, or to lure new smokers to the ranks. However, an analysis of the current advertisements for cigarettes strongly suggest that what the ads are selling is not cigarettes, but the *social acceptance of cigarettes*. While smokers today are understandably very nervous and unsure of the legitimacy of their smoking behavior, cigarette advertising reinforces them by giving them reassurance when they need it and communicating that lots of goodlooking, healthy, young people smoke.

33   The heavy reliance on the low tar and low nicotine statistics represents an attempt to convey the misleading message that "everything is all right now," but, beyond that, tobacco industry documents reviewed by the FTC indicate that many cigarette advertising techniques are aimed at denigrating or undercutting the health warning. Documents from Brown and Williamson and one of its advertising agencies, Ted Bates and Company, Inc., focused on means of reducing the concern about health effects. As a result of its research, Bates reported to B&W that many

smokers perceive the habit as "dirty" and dangerous, a practice followed only by "very stupid people." The report concludes:

> Thus, the smokers have to face the fact that they are illogical, irrational, and stupid. People find it hard to go throughout life with such negative presentation and evaluation of self. The saviours are the *rationalization* and repression that end up and result in a defense mechanism that, as many of the defense mechanisms we use, has its own logic, its own rationale. (Emphasis theirs.)

The report goes on to recommend that good ad copy will "deemphasize the objections" to smoking. With specific regard to health issues, the Bates report recommends: "Start out from the basic assumption that cigarette smoking is dangerous to your health — try to go around it in an elegant manner, but don't try to fight it — it's a losing war."

Coping with Disaster

The complexity of the cigarette's ongoing devastation to public health in America sometimes appears overwhelming because of its intermeshing of human frailties with the existence of a dominant industry and many sub-industries which seem committed to serving the needs of that human frailty, no matter what the cost. However, there are a number of specific courses this country could take to begin to cope with this national health disaster.   34

First, and foremost, before we as a country can begin a plan of action to deal with the cigarette, we must face up to the enormity of the problem that cigarettes now pose. We have to cast aside that sense of resignation to cigarettes and death and recognize cigarettes for what they are — a unique problem that merits a unique solution.   35

One might initially be tempted to argue that cigarettes are not any different from alcohol or even food; that anything can be overused to the point of becoming a health threat. Actually, unlike other forms of legal recreation such as alcohol consumption, there is, for all practical purposes, no known safe level of use for cigarettes or any known health benefit. While there are those who abuse alcohol, either by drinking to the point it is physically damaging or combining drinking with driving an automobile, the majority of people who use alcohol consume it at levels that are harmless. The overwhelming majority of smokers, however, smoke at levels which are definitely detrimental to health. Due to their addictive nature, it is for all practical purposes not possible to smoke a "safe" number of cigarettes per day. Indeed, alcohol may offer some health benefits. Recently, a number of investigators have shown that moderate consumption of alcohol — one or two drinks a day — may offer   36 some protection against coronary heart disease by contributing to the elevation of high density lipoproteins.

37   Let us, as a country, make a policy decision one way or another on cigarettes. Given our experiences with Prohibition in the 1920's, a government attempt to deny access to a commodity that people want, the outlawing of cigarettes seems like an unrealistic option. However, we *can* remove our heads from the sand and face the ultimate question: Are the economic benefits of cigarettes important enough to this country that they justify the premature deaths of 400,000 Americans each year? [Smoking costs the nation about $11,000,000,000 in direct medical expenses and $36,000,000,000 in lost productivity due to illness and premature death each year. Cigarette smokers pay only $7,000,000,000 annually in excise taxes, however, and, even with the tobacco industry's direct contributions to the economy (about $22,000,000,000 per year), we still come up short.]

38   Even if the answer is yes, do we choose to continue to disperse the enormous costs of smoking throughout the entire population and, indeed, to subsidize the production of tobacco? Or, will we adopt the policy of letting people smoke cigarettes as they please, but no longer make the nonsmoking population foot the bill in terms of the costs of extensive medical care, lost workdays, fire damage, and increased life insurance costs?

39   Were we to face up to that question and familiarize American nonsmokers with the enormous amounts of money they are paying for the smoker's "right" to light up, we might have one of the answers to the cigarette dilemma in America—let those who wish to smoke do so, but also let the smokers and companies that market cigarettes assume all the economic responsibilities of the habit.

40   Second, both voluntary and government agencies should escalate their attempts to bring the warnings on the danger of smoking both to smokers and nonsmokers. In waging this war against more detailed cigarette health warnings, Sen. Wendell H. Ford (D.-Ky.) maintained that there was an "exceptionally high level of awareness" on the issue of smoking and the American public is bombarded with information on smoking." Indeed, a superficial look at recent Roper and Gallup polls seems to back him up, given that 90% of those surveyed knew that smoking could be "dangerous." However, the more-in-depth questions in these surveys noted that 30% of Americans were unaware that a 30-year-old man reduces his life expectancy by smoking a pack a day; 43% were unaware that smoking is a major cause of heart disease; and up to 80% of the population did not know that smoking causes most bronchitis and emphysema. Many anecdotal accounts from physicians indicate that nearly every patient who receives a diagnosis of lung cancer is shocked, angry, and indignant, claiming that he or she just didn't know that "only" a pack a day would cause this disease.

41   Although it would only be a small part of the effort to deal with the

effects of cigarettes, strengthening the warning label on the pack—and varying it occasionally to refer to specific diseases caused by ciagarettes —would serve the function of triggering some cognitive dissonance among smokers and might lead them to reevaluate their decision to continue smoking. Beyond that, a cigarette label which noted that the product was physiologically addictive would give the smoker the knowledge he needs for a true "freedom of choice." The best evidence that stronger labels might work is the fact that the tobacco industry and their spokesmen in Congress are dead set against it. For the tobacco business, the best consumer is an uninformed one.

Third, we could give some serious consideration to whether our society should encourage the production of increasingly brazen tobacco advertisements which associate smoking with glamour, youth, and good clean fun. It might be argued that cigarette advertisements perform a function by providing tar and nicotine levels, but this could be done without the Satin Doll, the macho cowboy, and the athlete putting his socks on in the locker room. Toning down the ads, and perhaps eliminating them entirely except at point of purchase, might have the additional benefit of removing the editorial hesitancy to cover the topic of cigarettes in popular magazines.   42

Fourth, the concept of cigarette addiction needs more attention than it has received. It is theoretically possible that a substance—a type of methadone for cigarettes—could be developed which could, when used with behavior modification, have a significant success rate in getting smokers unhooked. Such research—and the approval of any product that would break cigarette addiction—would no doubt be inhibited by the tobacco lobby. However, if we do truly believe in "freedom of choice," the suppression of such a life-saving measure would be inconsistent and indeed immoral.   43

The cigarette has been maligned by a series of critics through the ages, but, until 30 years ago, the attacks were primarily emotional, with heavy moral overtones. In the 1980s, we should not be moralizing about cigarettes, but simply facing up to the realities and asking ourselves, if we really want to win the war against environmental disease, why don't we start by identifying the number-one enemy?   44

It Takes Clout to Keep a Harmful Product on the Market

• A major American company which supplies processing materials to the cigarette industry [the company asked not to be named, lest it be the target of further ire from the tobacco companies] recently released a booklet on environmental causes of cancer. Naturally, the publication focused a good deal of attention cigarettes as the cause of many different malignancies and prominently featured a graph showing the enormous increase in lung cancer in the past 10 years. Shortly after the release of the publication, the chief executive officer of the chemical company received a letter from his counterpart at a large tobacco company, chastising him for citing cigarettes as a cause of disease and requesting that the publication be withdrawn. When the executive did not respond to the tobacco man's request, that cigarette company made it clear that it would look elsewhere for its supplies.

- Since 1964, there has been no major story on the health impact of cigarette smoking in any major U.S. popular publication (with the exception of *Reader's Digest, Good Housekeeping*, and *The New Yorker*). Freelance medical writers know well the rule, "it is not fair game to discuss cigarettes." Some 10–40% of advertising revenues for U.S. magazines comes from tobacco advertisements.

- Paul Maccabee, a reporter for the *Twin Cities Reader* in Minneapolis, covered a press conference announcing Brown and Williamson Tobacco Corporation's annual Kool Jazz Festival and inserted an unexpected twist in his story—a list of jazz greats who had died of lung cancer. The next day, he was fired.

- Joseph Califano, an outspoken critic of cigarettes while he was Secretary of Health, Education, and Welfare under Pres. Carter, reports in his book, *The Governing of America*, what happened when he invited the wife of Rep. Fred Rooney (D.-Pa.), who had been a "classmate" of Califano's at SmokeEnders, to join him on the stage during one of his speeches: "When a Tobacco Institute lobbyist saw her, he told her husband that he would never get another dollar from the industry." Rooney lost his bid for reelection.

- In the U.S. each year, thousands of people successfully sue major industries to collect damages resulting from everything from their exposure to asbestos, tampons, and cotton dust to injuries incurred while using toys and household products. Although numerous damage suits have been initiated against the tobacco industry for chronic health problems caused by smoking cigarettes, only 10 have ever made it to court and only two have ever gone to jury. Even though cigarettes—in contrast to those other products—are dangerous when used as intended, the cigarette industry has never lost a case or paid out one cent in compensation for tobacco-induced injuries.

- In September, 1976, 12,000,000 British viewers saw "Death in the West," frequently called "the most powerful anti-smoking film ever made." The film intercuts three types of footage: Marlboro commercials with cowboys lighting up around a camp fire; Philip Morris executives claiming that no one really knows if cigarettes cause cancer; and, finally, interviews with six real cowboys who have lung cancer and emphysema caused, their physicians say, by smoking. Philip Morris sued Thames Television, producers of the film, in British courts and obtained a court order preventing the film from being shown or even discussed by filmmakers. The court ordered that all copies of the film be destroyed or confiscated.

- "Death in the West" did, however, show up in San Francisco in mid 1982 and was shown on local television in that city. It stirred up a good deal of interest, so much so that the *Journal of the American Medical Association* commissioned a respected California public health authority, Dr. David Fletcher, to write a story on the documentary and the tobacco company's efforts to suppress it. As soon as it was submitted, however, the piece was killed because, in the words of a *JAMA* editor, "It was felt by the legal department that publication of a story on such a controversial subject would render the AMA vulnerable to legal action, possibly by Philip Morris, and that is not a chance that anyone here wanted to take."

Questions for Discussion and Writing

1. Although Whelan's article addresses the issue of cigarette use and the public health, she does not mention cigarettes, *per se*, until well into the article, after a long introduction discussing dangerous substances. What paradox does Whelan wish to highlight by beginning her article in this fashion?

2. Whelan proposes five answers to explain why, in such a health-conscious society, cigarettes are not the subject of "frequent television documentaries, investigative reporting, outraged citizens groups, and concerned legislatures dealing with what is unarguably the most dramatic and far-reaching public health threat of this century." According to Whelan, what are the five "extrinsic and intrinsic factors" responsible for this state of affairs?

3. What is the "backfire" effect and what role did advertising play in creating an image for cigarette smoking that could not be reversed,

even when medical data that surfaced in the 1950s pointed toward "the devastating health impact of the pleasure-giving cigarette"?

4. How does Whelan use (*a*) the testimony of Dr. Polin, (*b*) statistics as to the frequency with which cigarettes are used, and (*c*) evidence from national surveys to support her claim that cigarettes are addicting to those who use them? How does Whelan support her interpretation by discussing withdrawal symptoms of smokers who try to quit?

5. How does the psychological coping mechanism known as cognitive dissonance allow smokers to continue smoking despite "the evidence available that it is harmful"?

6. What reasons does Whelan present to explain why nonsmokers who are relatives or friends of smokers do not strenuously urge them to quit?

7. What irony does Whelan discover between the role played by religious institutions (churches and synagogues) for their congregations, and the surprising "silence on the subject of cigarettes and health" (with the exception of The Seventh-Day Adventists Church) that she would expect to be an issue clergymen would want to raise?

8. How does economic self-interest play a crucial role in explaining why national women's organizations and magazines addressed to the "liberated" woman are strangely silent on an issue that so directly concerns women's health? What facts, reasons, and evidence does Whelan offer to support this assertion? To what extent do you agree that the failure of such national women's organizations and women's magazines to condemn cigarette smoking is evidence of hypocrisy on the part of these groups?

9. What statistics does Whelan present to demonstrate the extent to which the national economy and the economy of entire regions of the country depend on tobacco as a cash crop? How does the ripple effect translate into money that goes to support advertising agencies, newspapers, magazines, and federal, state, and local governments? Specifically, what surprising interconnections exist that explain the economic clout of the tobacco industry and the tactics used in perpetuating the sale of cigarettes?

10. What evidence does Whelan present to support her claim that cigarette ads are carefully constructed so as to seem to convey one message while really conveying another? In an essay, analyze any cigarette ad to discover whether this is true. For example, how would

a cigarette ad appearing in a male-oriented magazine that warned that "cigarette smoking has been shown to pose a danger to pregnant women" reduce the probability that readers would apply this message to themselves?

11. What distinction does Whelan draw between alcohol consumption and cigarette smoking? How does this section of her article anticipate and answer proposals that cigarettes should be prohibited in the same way that the government attempted to deal with alcohol in the 1920s? By contrast, what specific recommendations does Whelan propose? Evaluate the effectiveness of these proposed changes. Which do you think would work?

12. As a research project, investigate the official U.S. Department of Agriculture policy of advocating the sale of domestically produced cigarettes to Asian countries, such as Japan, Taiwan, Korea, and Thailand. Cigarettes sold in these countries would not bear warning labels on the packages.

Harold L. Henderson

Where Do You Draw the Line on Product Liability?

Harold L. Henderson is the senior vice-president and general counsel for R. J. Reynolds Industries. He has never lost a liability suit brought against his company. Henderson uses hypothetical examples, analogies, and legal precedent to argue that product-liability laws should not be broadened to allow a person who decides to smoke cigarettes "in the face of clear or widely claimed risks" to later sue the tobacco company, as if to say, "I made the wrong choice—so pay me." "Where Do You Draw the Line on Product Liability?" first appeared in R.J. Reynolds Industries' RJR Report (fourth quarter 1985).

1 One factor distinguishing our legal system from those of many other countries is that ours is the product of judicial decision and interpretation as well as statutes, and as a result is constantly evolving. There is no better illustration of this than in the area of product liability law.

2 Not too long ago, it was assumed that if a company negligently manufactured a product, and such negligence harmed the user or another person, the company would be required by the law to pay damages for the injuries suffered. This seemed only fair.

3 In recent years, however, that simple proposition has been distorted to the point of unfairness. Some judges and plaintiff attorneys have sought to unduly broaden the interpretation of product liability laws in order to provide compensation in situations where none would have previously been available. At the same time, juries have returned awards for plaintiffs in ever increasing amounts, often in the millions of dollars and far beyond what would previously have been considered reasonable.

4 Broader interpretation of the law, and significant increase in jury awards, have encouraged more and more people to file product liability suits, often on spurious grounds. Between 1978 and 1984, for example, the number of product liability suits in federal courts doubled, bogging down an already overloaded civil court system. There was also a serious decline in the predictability of the outcome of litigation, a factor essential to the functioning of our economy and legal system. And there were astronomical increases in the cost of insurance coverage for large and for small companies alike.

These trends are of particular interest to our company because of the 5
considerable publicity generated by lawsuits against the tobacco industry
by persons claiming damages for disease or death allegedly due to smoking. Historically, several hundred such suits have been brought against
the industry over the years, and none has resulted in a settlement or
judgment in the plaintiff's favor. Although some of the recent publicity
has indicated that changes in product liability law may result in a different outcome in the cases now pending, the results in two recent cases
against R.J. Reynolds Tobacco Company indicate that common sense
may still prevail.

In the first case, the plaintiff, Floyd R. Roysdon, claimed that he had 6
suffered vascular disease and subsequent amputation of a leg as a result
of smoking cigarettes for many years. Two issues were of particular
significance in the *Roysdon* case: whether the warning labels on cigarette
packs as required by Congress can be found by a jury or court to be
inadequate; and whether cigarettes by their very nature are to be considered unreasonably dangerous products subjecting the manufacturer to
liability even when manufactured properly and used in a normal
manner.

Judge Thomas G. Hull, of the U.S. District Court for the Eastern 7
District of Tennessee, reached a decision favorable to Reynolds on both
issues and dismissed the plaintiff's suit. Regarding the adequacy of the
warning, Judge Hull, after considering the extensive legislative history,
ruled that Congress had fully considered what warning labels should go
on cigarette packages and that juries are not entitled to second-guess
Congress' determination in that regard. His views are summarized in the
following quote:

"If the courts were to impose any duty to go beyond the congression- 8
ally mandated labeling, this would thwart the stated intent of Congress
to have uniformity in the warnings. For this reason, the Court found any
such exposure incompatible with the intent of the legislation and dismissed any claim based on the adequacy of the warning label."

With respect to the issue of whether cigarettes are unreasonably 9
dangerous as a matter of Tennessee law, Judge Hull concluded that they
could not be, based on the fact that tobacco has been used for over 400
years, and adverse health claims are widespread and can be considered
part of the common knowledge of the community.

It is my considered judgment that Judge Hull's decision and analysis 10
should have a significant impact on similar cases now pending both in
Tennessee and other jurisdictions.

Another factor often cited as differentiating the current cases from 11
those successfully defended in the past is that of addiction. Plaintiff
lawyers now argue that cigarettes are addictive, and that, as a result,
their clients cannot be found to have voluntarily chosen to smoke. This
argument, while ingenious, flies in the face of reality. Cigarette smoking
simply does not meet the three standard tests for addiction: that the user

must increase the dosage to achieve the desired effect, that he suffers traumatic physical withdrawal upon quitting, and that his addiction interferes with normal social and work activities. Common sense and the fact that 35 million Americans have quit smoking also refute this position.

12   A successful result in another well-publicized suit against Reynolds Tobacco indicates that the addiction issue may also be one in which the common sense of juries will prevail. In that case, the widow and children of John Galbraith, represented by famed tort lawyer Melvin Belli, sued Reynolds claiming that Galbraith's smoking of the company's products over a long period had caused the disease that led to his death at almost 70. Belli argued throughout the trial, and in the media as well, that John Galbraith should not be held responsible for his own choice to smoke because he was "addicted."

13   After a five-week trial, the jury returned a verdict in Reynolds' favor. Although not required to make a specific finding on the addiction issue, post-trial comments by members of the jury clearly demonstrated that Belli had failed to convince the jury that John Galbraith was addicted and thus had not chosen to smoke of his own free will.

14   Ultimately, of course, these events are all facets of a major issue, critical to our whole civil liability system, and affecting many products other than tobacco, and that is what should be the proper role for freedom of choice and personal responsibility in our tort system. Few would argue the proposition that individuals have the right to smoke. And for hundreds of years, people have chosen to smoke because it gives them pleasure, much in the same manner as they have chosen to ride motorcycles, eat high cholesterol foods or red meats, and consume alcoholic beverages. If a person freely chooses to smoke or voluntarily enjoy other legal pleasures in the face of clear or widely claimed risks, should he or she then be permitted later to say, "I made the wrong choice — so pay me"?

15   The adverse consequences to our legal system and economy if such is to become the rule is now a matter of concern to prominent attorneys, legislators and persons within the academic community.

16   Professor Arthur Miller of the Harvard Law School said in a recent television interview that if a tobacco company can be held liable in such suits, "Then we would have alcohol cases, probably fatty food cases . . . we might even have diet pop cases. Once you start down the slippery slope of saying that even voluntary conduct can lead to product liability law — something for which there's no precedent in existing law — then you get a real problem of drawing lines."

17   The lines must be drawn, and they must be clear enough for every court in every state to rule by them consistently. I am encouraged by the results in both *Galbraith* and *Roysdon* that reason may prevail in this important area.

Questions for Discussion and Writing

1. Henderson begins his article by asserting that recent attempts to broaden "the interpretation of product liability laws" are unfair, unreasonable, and have increased the burden on "an already overloaded civil court system." What reasons and evidence does Henderson offer to support these assertions?

2. How does Henderson use statistics on the increasing number of liability suits to support his charge that larger negligence awards have caused more people to file spurious liability suits? In Henderson's view, why do lawyers of plaintiffs and certain judges bear the responsibility for this trend?

3. How does Henderson's discussion of recent trends in product-liability law relate to his role as chief legal counsel to a company that manufactures cigarettes and that must defend itself against lawsuits?

4. How does winning a case in the area of product liability depend on demonstrating that there was or was not a causal connection between the product and injuries sustained by using the product? In light of this, why does Henderson focus attention on the fact that, although several hundred lawsuits have been brought against the tobacco industry, "none has resulted in a settlement or judgment in the plaintiff's favor"?

5. Summarize the different kinds of arguments that have been advanced against the tobacco companies and discuss the specific reasons why each of these claims has been rejected. Why, for example, does Henderson believe that Judge Hull's analysis and decision should serve as a precedent for future cases?

6. In a short essay, compare and contrast Henderson's and Whelan's views on the issue of whether or not tobacco is an addictive substance. Who, in your opinion, presents a more persuasive argument on this issue? Keep in mind that Henderson cites statistics to prove that cigarettes cannot be addicting if 35 million Americans have quit smoking. When you are comparing Henderson's and Whelan's views, pay particular attention to (*a*) the issue of recidivism — that is, the number of people who start smoking again after quitting, (*b*) evidence for and against the existence of withdrawal symptoms, and (*c*) statistics related to lost productivity due to illness in smokers.

7. How does Henderson's introduction of the issue of free will widen the scope of his argument and return to the theme of the dangerous

consequences of a broader interpretation of product-liability law presented in the introduction? How does Henderson use comparisons between choosing to smoke and choosing to ride a motorcycle or eat high cholesterol foods to remove all responsibility from tobacco companies and place it firmly on those who choose to smoke? How is the crux of his argument contained in the statement: "If a person freely chooses to smoke or voluntarily enjoy other legal pleasures in the face of clear or widely claimed risks, should he or she then be permitted later to say, 'I made the wrong choice—so pay me'?"

9

Addictions: Why Can't Society Kick the Drug Habit?

Few people would disagree that drug abuse is one of the most serious problems facing American society. The dimensions of the problem are staggering, with thousands of deaths directly attributable to the effects of heroin, cocaine, and PCP, and billions of dollars lost to the economy because of crime, decreased worker productivity, and related medical costs.

Most segments of American life have been affected. Even children of grade school age are menaced by the drug problem. Through every level and stratum of society—including factory workers, professional athletes, Wall Street brokers, Hollywood producers, and business executives—the problem of drug abuse shows no signs of lessening its hold on our culture.

One of the basic issues of the drug dependency problem facing the United States centers around the question of why people use drugs. Some researchers suggest that the underlying cause stems from a basic desire of people to change their mental landscapes, have unusual experiences, and lose the sense of being trapped in an ego. Others believe that American society in particular encourages drug use through messages that all problems can be solved with a fast solution. In this view, the emphasis on competition and success at all costs coupled with a society-wide inability to tolerate frustration leads people to turn to drugs for a magic remedy. Whatever the cause, drug use escalated radically in the 1980s and is now endemic to Americans in every walk of life.

In the area of professional sports, the use of performance-enhancing drugs such as steroids has become widespread. Those who defend the practice claim that the policies aimed at prohibiting such drugs are ambiguous and that laws should not be made that deprive athletes of the right of free choice. Critics answer that many athletes are increasingly coerced into using drugs in order to remain competitive against athletes who are willing to risk addiction.

On Wall Street cocaine use has spread through the stock and commodity exchanges. Editorials in the *Wall Street Journal* decry the fact that some securities firms have provided cocaine for their brokers whereas other firms have tolerated cocaine abuse as long as the public remains unaware that billions of dollars in pension funds are traded by brokers who are high on it.

The solutions proposed to deal with the escalating drug problem have themselves become subjects of controversy. These solutions fall into two categories. The supply side solutions, aimed at halting the production of drugs in countries such as Bolivia, Peru, and Colombia, support pressuring these drug-producing countries to halt the export of illegal drugs or favor offering economic incentives to the countries to encourage crop substitution programs. Attempts to solve the problem from the demand side have focused on mandatory drug testing and plans for a comprehensive drug education program aimed at instituting preventive programs in the schools. Although widely implemented, the efficacy of the voluntary "just say no" campaign supported by Nancy Reagan and various antidrug organizations has been questioned, and the federal government thus far has shown little interest in funding programs for preventive education. The clash of viewpoints on these issues can be seen in the following chapter.

Supply side solutions aimed at halting the influx of illegal drugs from countries where they are produced fail to confront the reality that the economies of many countries in South and Central America are buoyed up by money derived from the production of cocaine-producing coca crops. Attempts to encourage farmers to switch to growing legal crops have failed because of the vastly greater sums that can be derived from growing coca plants. Demand side solutions aimed at eliminating the consumption of drugs have centered around mandatory drug testing on the grounds that it is a practical means of discouraging drug use. Critics question the reliability of drug testing and object to it on the grounds that it violates the Fourth Amendment guarantee against illegal search and seizure. The whole issue of privacy is closely related to the controversy surrounding drug testing. What concerns people is the possibility that test results, despite guarantees given by private employers or the state, could be divulged with resulting harm to employees.

In the schools, those recommending mandatory drug-testing programs see this as the only way to curb increasing drug use by teenagers, a group particularly vulnerable to pressure from their peers to take drugs. Those opposing the introduction of mandatory urinalysis tests cite the results of two court cases where attempts by local school systems to test students for drug use were declared unconstitutional.

The information and viewpoints contained in the selections that follow tackle the drug issue from a variety of perspectives and should help you get a clearer picture of this devastating threat to our country.

Andrew Weil and
Winifred Rosen

Chocolate to Morphine:
Understanding Mind Active Drugs

Andrew Weil received his M.D. degree from Harvard Medical School in 1968 and is currently research associate in ethnopharmacology at the Harvard Botanical Museum. He is the author of The Natural Mind *(1972) and* The Marriage of the Sun and Moon *(1980). Winifred Rosen was a high school teacher for several years before writing books for young people, including the Newbery Award nominee* Henrietta: The Wild Woman of Borneo *(1975). In this chapter from their book* Chocolate to Morphine: Understanding Mind Active Drugs *(1983) the authors explore how drugs are used in various societies and argue that human beings have an innate need to alter normal states of consciousness and obtain new sensory experiences through drug use. Weil and Rosen stress that experimentation should be limited to adults who are aware of the potential risks involved.*

The basic reason people take drugs is to vary their conscious experi- 1
ence. Of course there are many other ways to alter consciousness, such as listening to music, making music, dancing, fasting, chanting, exercising, surfing, meditating, falling in love, hiking in the wilderness (if you live in a city), visiting a city (if you live in the wilderness), having sex, daydreaming, watching fireworks, going to a movie or play, jumping into cold water after taking a hot sauna, participating in religious rituals. The list is probably endless, and includes nearly all the activities that people put most of their time, energy, and hard-earned money into. This suggests that changing consciousness is something people like to do.

Human beings, it seems, are born with a need for periodic variations 2
in consciousness. The behavior of young children supports this idea. Infants rock themselves into blissful states; many children discover that whirling, or spinning, is a powerful technique to change awareness; some also experiment with hyperventilation (rapid, deep breathing) followed by mutual chest-squeezing or choking, and tickling to produce paralyzing laughter. Even though these practices may produce some uncomfortable results, such as dizziness or nausea, the whole experience is so reinforcing that children do it again and again, often despite paren-

tal objections. Since children all over the world engage in these activities, the desire to change consciousness does not seem to be a product of a particular culture but rather to arise from something basically human. As children grow older they find that certain available substances put them in similar states. The attractiveness of drugs is that they provide an easy, quick route to these experiences.

3   Many drug users talk about getting high. Highs are states of consciousness marked by feelings of euphoria, lightness, self-transcendence, concentration, and energy. People who never take drugs also seek out highs. In fact, having high experiences from time to time may be necessary to our physical and mental health, just as dreaming at night seems to be vital to our well-being. Perhaps that is why a desire to alter normal consciousness exists in everyone and why people pursue the experiences even though there are sometimes uncomfortable side effects.

4   Although the desire for high states is at the root of drug-taking in both children and grownups, people also take drugs for other, more practical reasons. These include:

TO AID RELIGIOUS PRACTICES AND EXPLORE THE SELF

5   Throughout history, people have used drug-induced states to transcend their sense of separateness and feel more at one with nature, God, and the supernatural. Marijuana was used for this purpose in ancient India, and many psychedelic plants are still so used today by Indians in North and South America. Alcohol has been used for religious purposes in many parts of the world; the role of wine in Roman Catholic and Judaic rites persists as an example. Among primitive people, psychoactive plants are often considered sacred—gifts from gods and spirits to unite people with the higher realms.

6   Curious individuals throughout history have taken psychoactive substances to explore and investigate parts of their own minds not ordinarily accessible. One of the most famous modern examples was the British writer and philosopher Aldous Huxley, who experimented extensively with mescaline in the 1950s. He left us a record of his investigations in a book called *The Doors of Perception*. Some other well-known "explorers" are Oliver Wendell Holmes, the nineteenth-century American physician, poet, and author, who experimented with ether; William James, the Harvard psychologist and philosopher of the late nineteenth century, who used nitrous oxide; Sigmund Freud, the father of psychoanalysis, who took cocaine; William S. Burroughs, a contemporary American novelist and user of opiates; Richard Alpert (Ram Dass), a psychologist and guru, who has extensive experience with LSD and other psychedelics; and John Lilly, a medical researcher and philosopher, who has experimented with ketamine. Many others who have followed this path have done so privately, keeping their experiences to themselves, or sharing them only with intimate companions.

"Let's have a drink" is one of the most frequent phrases in use today.   7
It is an invitation to share time and communication around the consumption of a psychoactive drug. Like sharing food, taking drugs together is a ritual excuse for intimacy; coffee breaks and cocktail
("happy") hours are examples of the way approved drugs are used for
this purpose. Disapproved drugs may draw people together even more
strongly by establishing a bond of common defiance of authority. At the
big rock concerts and Vietnam War protests of the 1960s, strangers often
became instant comrades simply by passing a joint back and forth.

In different cultures other drugs perform the same function. For   8
example, South American Indians take coca breaks together, much as we
take coffee breaks, and chewing coca leaves with a friend establishes an
important social bond. For South Sea Islanders, drinking kava in groups
at night is the equivalent of an American cocktail party.

Aside from the ritual significance with which drugs are invested, their   9
pharmacological effects may also enhance social interaction. Because
alcohol lowers inhibitions in most people, businessmen and women have
drinks at lunch to encourage openness and congeniality. Similarly, on
dates people often drink to reduce anxiety and feelings of awkwardness.
By producing alertness and euphoria, stimulants, such as cocaine, promote easy conversation, even among strangers.

So important is this function of psychoactive drugs that many people   10
would find it difficult to relate to others if deprived of them.

TO ENHANCE SENSORY PLEASURE

Human beings are pleasure-seeking animals who are very inventive   11
when it comes to finding ways to excite their senses and gratify their
appetites. One of the characteristics of sensory pleasure is that it becomes
dulled with repetition, and there are only so many ways of achieving
pleasure. As much time, thought, and energy have gone into sex as into
any human activity, but the possibilities of sexual positions and techniques are limited. By making people feel different, psychoactive drugs
can make familiar experiences new and interesting again. The use of
drugs in combination with sex is as old as the hills, as is drug use with
such activities as dancing, eating, and listening to or playing music.
Drinking wine with meals is an example of this behavior that dates back
to prehistory and is still encouraged by society. Some men say that a
good cigar and a glass of brandy make a fine meal complete. Pot lovers
say that turning on is the perfect way for a fine meal to begin. Psychedelic drugs, especially, are intensifiers of experience and can make a
sunset more fascinating than a movie. (Of course, psychedelics can also
turn an unpleasant situation into a living nightmare.) Because drugs can,
temporarily at least, make the ordinary extraordinary, many people seek
them out and consume them in an effort to get more enjoyment out of
life.

Questions for Discussion and Writing

1. In addition to drugs, what are some other methods identified by the authors that have been used for altering consciousness? What underlying motivation do the authors propose to explain drug dependency?

2. According to Weil and Rosen, what are the three ways in which drugs are used in various societies, and what reasons and evidence do they advance to support their analysis?

3. How do Weil and Rosen use famous historical figures who have experimented with psychoactive substances in developing the overall structure of their argument? Specifically, how does the authors' discussion of historical figures who experimented with drugs strengthen their claim that drugs allow one to explore the inner self?

4. What attitude (negative, neutral, or positive) do Weil and Rosen take toward the phenomenon of drug use? How is this attitude reflected in words and images they use?

5. Evaluate the crucial argument that experimentation should be limited to adults who are aware of the potential risks. What reasons for and against this position can you think of to justify or refute it?

6. How successful as an argumentative strategy is Weil and Rosen's assertion that all drugs, along with many other substances as well as certain activities, can be included in the search to make the mundane more exciting and life more enjoyable?

7. How does Weil and Rosen's argument depend on the assumption that drug use should be tolerated in adults who have the capability to make rational choices and are aware of the dangers they may face? How would their argument have to be modified by taking into account that an addict, by definition, is no longer able to make rational choices?

8. Can you think of any objections to Weil and Rosen's claim that the use of drugs in religious rituals is identical to the individual's use of it to raise consciousness?

9. In an essay, define the boundary line between use and addiction for any substance. That is, at what point is a person addicted and not able to give up the substance because of dependency? If you or anyone you know ever began using any of the substances mentioned by Weil and Rosen, believing as they do, and only later discovered

there were unexpected negative effects, you may draw upon these experiences in your essay to illustrate your definition of *addiction*.

10. As a research project, you may wish to look into the life of any of the historical figures Weil and Rosen mention to discover the exact nature of the drug use involved. Evaluate Weil and Rosen's use of these cases. Are they accurate or do they distort what really happened in order to support their claim?

Philip Slater

Want-Creation Fuels
Americans' Addictiveness

*Philip Slater has been a professor of sociology at Harvard and is
author of* The Pursuit of Loneliness *(1970) and* Wealth-Addiction
*(1980). Slater argues that the premium Americans put on success
causes many people to resort to drugs to feel better about themselves
and cope with feelings of inadequacy. Slater, like Weil and Rosen,
constructs his essay to support a causal claim and cites a broad range
of examples from everyday life to demonstrate that advertisers exploit
societal pressures in order to sell products. The following article,
"Want-Creation Fuels Americans' Addictiveness," first appeared in
the* St. Paul Pioneer Press Dispatch *(September 6, 1984).*

1   Imagine what life in America would be like today if the surgeon
general convinced Congress that cigarettes, as America's most lethal
drug, should be made illegal.

2   The cost of tobacco would increase 5,000 percent. Law enforcement
budgets would quadruple but still be hopelessly inadequate to the task.
The tobacco industry would become mob-controlled, and large quantities of Turkish tobacco would be smuggled into the country through
New York and Miami.

3   Politicians would get themselves elected by inveighing against tobacco abuse. Some would argue shrewdly that the best enforcement
strategy was to go after the growers and advertisers — making it a capital
offense to raise or sell tobacco. And a great many Americans would try
smoking for the first time.

4   Americans are individualists. We like to express our opinions much
more than we like to work together. Passing laws is one of the most
popular pastimes, and enforcing them one of the least. We make laws
like we make New Year's resolutions — the impulse often exhausted by
giving voice to it. Who but Americans would have their food grown and
harvested by people who were legally forbidden to be in the country?

5   We are a restless, inventive, dissatisfied people. We like novelty. We
like to try new things. We may not want to change in any basic sense,
any more than other people, but we like the illusion of movement.

We like anything that looks like a quick fix — a new law, a new road,
a new pill. We like immediate solutions. We want the pain to stop, the

dull mood to pass, the problem to go away. The quicker the action, the better we like it. We like confrontation better than negotiation, antibiotics better than slow healing, majority rule better than community consensus, demolition better than renovation.

When we want something we want it fast and we want it cheap.   7
Obstacles and complications annoy us. We don't want to stop to think about side effects, the Big Picture, or how it's going to make things worse in the long run. We aren't too interested in the long run, as long as something brings more money, a promotion or a new status symbol in the short.

Our model for problem-solving is the 30-second TV commercial, in   8
which change is produced instantaneously and there is always a happy ending. The side effects, the pollution, the wasting diseases, the slow poisoning—all these unhappy complications fall into the great void outside that 30-second frame.

Nothing fits this scenario better than drugs—legal and illegal. The   9
same impatience that sees an environmental impact report as an annoying bit of red tape makes us highly susceptible to any substance that can make us feel better within minutes after ingesting it—whose immediate effects are more or less predictable and whose negative aspects are generally much slower to appear.

People take drugs everywhere, of course, and there is no sure way of   10
knowing if the United States has more drug abusers than other countries. The term "abuse" itself is socially defined.

The typical suburban alcoholic of the '40s and '50s and the wealthy   11
drunks glamorized in Hollywood movies of that period were not considered "drug abusers." Nor is the ex-heroin addict who has been weaned to a lifetime addiction to Methadone.

In the 19th century, morphine addicts (who were largely middle-   12
aged, middle-class women) maintained their genteel but often heavy addictions quite legally, with the aid of the family doctor and local druggist. Morphine only became illegal when its use spread to young, poor, black males. (This transition created some embarrassment for political and medical commentators, who argued that a distinction had to be made between "drug addicts" and "dope fiends.")

Yet addiction can be defined in a way that overrides these biases.   13
Anyone who cannot or will not let a day pass without ingesting a substance should be considered addicted to it, and by this definition Americans are certainly addiction-prone.

It would be hard to find a society in which so great a variety of   14
different substances have been "abused" by so many different kinds of people. There are drugs for every group, philosophy and social class: marijuana and psychedelics for the '60s counterculture, heroin for the hopeless of all periods, PCP for the angry and desperate, and cocaine for modern Yuppies and Yumpies.

Drugs do, after all, have different effects, and people select the effects   15 they want. At the lower end of the social scale people want a peaceful escape from a hopeless and depressing existence, and for this heroin is the drug of choice. Cocaine, on the other hand, with its energized euphoria and illusion of competence is particularly appealing to affluent achievers — those both obsessed and acquainted with success.

16   Addiction among the affluent seems paradoxical to outsiders. From the viewpoint of most people in the world an American man or woman making over $50,000 a year has everything a human being could dream of. Yet very few such people — even those with hundreds of millions of dollars — feel this way themselves. While they may not suffer the despair of the very poor, there seems to be a kind of frustration and hopelessness that seeps into all social strata in our society. The affluent may have acquired a great deal, but they seem not to have acquired what they wanted.

17   Most drugs — heroin, alcohol, cocaine, speed, tranquilizers, barbiturates — virtually all of them except the psychedelics and to some extent marijuana — have a numbing effect. We might then ask: Why do so many Americans need to numb themselves?

18   Life in modern society is admittedly harsh and confusing considering the pace for which our bodies were designed. Noise pollution alone might justify turning down our sensory volume: It's hard today even in a quiet suburb or rural setting to find respite from the harsh sound of "labor-saving" machines.

19   But it would be absurd to blame noise pollution for drug addiction. This rasping clamor that grates daily on our ears is only a symptom — one tangible consequence of our peculiar lifestyle. For each of us wants to be able to exert his or her will and control without having to negotiate with anyone else.

20   "I have a right to run my machine and do my work" even if it makes your rest impossible. "I have a right to hear my music" even if this makes it impossible to hear your music, or better yet, enjoy that most rare and precious of modern commodities: silence. "I have a right to make a profit" even if it means poisoning you, your children and your children's children. "I have a right to have a drink when I want to and drive my car when I want to" even if it means totaling your car and crippling your life.

21   This intolerance of any constraint or obstacle makes our lives rich in conflict and aggravation. Each day we encounter the noise, distress and lethal fallout of the dilemmas we brushed aside so impatiently the day before. Each day the postponed problems multiply, proliferate, metastasize — but this only makes us more aggravated and impatient than we were before. And since we're unwilling to change our ways it becomes more and more necessary to anesthetize ourselves to the havoc we've wrought.

22   We don't like the thought of attuning ourselves to nature or to a group or community. We like to fantasize having control over our lives,

and drugs seem to make this possible. With drugs you are not only master of your fate and captain of your soul, you are dictator of your body as well.

Unwilling to respond to its own needs and wants, you goad it into activity with caffeine in the morning and slow it down with alcohol at night. If the day goes poorly, a little cocaine will set it right, and if quiet relaxation and sensual enjoyment is called for, marijuana.   23

Cocaine or alcohol makes a party or a performance go well. Nothing is left to chance. The quality of experience is measured by how many drugs or drinks were consumed rather than by the experience itself. Most of us are unwilling to accept the fact that life has good days and bad days. We attempt—unsuccessfully but valiantly—to postpone all the bad days until that fateful moment when the body presents us with all our IOUs, tied up in a neat bundle called cancer, heart disease, cirrhosis or whatever.   24

Every great sage and spiritual leader throughout history has empha-sized that happiness comes not from getting more but from learning to want less. Clearly this is a hard lesson for humans, since so few have learned it.   25

But in our society we spend billions each year creating want. Cove-tousness, discontent and greed are taught to our children, drummed into them—they are bombarded with it. Not only through advertising, but in the feverish emphasis on success, on winning at all costs, on being the center of attention through one kind of performance or another, on being the first at something—no matter how silly or stupid ("The Guinness Book of Records"). We are an addictive society.   26

Addiction is a state of wanting. It is a condition in which the individ-ual feels he or she is incomplete, inadequate, lacking, not whole, and can only be made whole by the addition of something external.   27

This need not be a drug. It can be money, food, fame, sex, responsi-bility, power, good deeds, possessions, cleaning—the addictive impulse can attach itself to anything, real or symbolic. You're addicted to some-thing whenever you feel it completes you—that you wouldn't be a whole person without it. When you try to make sure it's always there, that there's always a good supply on hand.   28

Most of us are a little proud of the supposed personality defects that make addiction "necessary"—the "I can't . . . ," "I have to . . . ," "I always . . . ," "I never . . . " But such "lacks" are all delusional. It's fun to brag about not being able to live without something but it's just pomposity. We are all human, and given water, a little food, and a little warmth, we'll survive.   29

But it's very hard to hang onto this humanity when we're told every day that we're ignorant, misguided, inadequate, incompetent and unde-sirable and that we will emerge from this terrible condition only if we eat or drink or buy something, at which point we'll magically and instantly feel better.   30

31   We may be smart enough not to believe the silly claims of the individual ad, but can we escape the underlying message on which all of them agree? That you can only be made whole and healthy by buying or ingesting something? Can we reasonably complain about the amount of addiction in our society when we teach it every day?

32   A Caribbean worker once said, apropos of the increasing role of Western products in the economy of his country: "Your corporations are like mosquitoes. I don't so much mind their taking a little of my blood, but why do they have to leave that nasty itch in its place?"

33   It seems futile to spend hundreds of billions of dollars trying to intercept the flow of drugs—arresting and imprisoning those who meet the demand for them, when we activate and nourish that demand every day. Until we get tired of encouraging the pursuit of illusory fixes and begin to celebrate and refine what we already are and have, addictive substances will always proliferate faster than we can control them.

Questions for Discussion and Writing

1. To what extent is society's attitude—its approval of the quick fix to obtain results without overcoming obstacles—responsible for rampant drug abuse and addiction?

2. What relationship does Slater discover between financial and social status and drug use?

3. According to Slater, in what way do corporations fuel Americans' addiction to chemicals? What reasons and evidence does he present to support his assertion?

4. How does Slater use the analogy drawn between noise pollution and drug addiction to develop his argument?

5. How does Slater's argument depend on the assumption that corporations exploit the ever increasing frenetic pace of life in America through advertising to encourage obtaining quick fixes in the form of products? Locate and analyze an ad that does this. For example, cigarette ads for Marlboro show rural settings with wide-open spaces, yet billboards for this product are often placed on crowded highways —places of extreme stress.

6. Discuss Slater's objection to advertising on the grounds that advertisers give consumers the illusion of control while adding to their stress by creating a desire for still another product. Does Slater's argument suffer because he provides no statistical evidence to support

his claim that the essence of want-creation is the 30-second ad showing that you can be made better by the product?

7. In developing his unusual and arguable definition of addiction, what examples cited by Slater do you find the most effective in supporting his claim that people use drugs to gain a sense of control over their lives? Is this control real or illusory? In your answer, address the paradox of people using heroin, cocaine, alcohol, speed, or barbiturates to get a feeling of having control.

8. How does Slater use the example of people who make over $50,000 a year to support his thesis that wants do not disappear with higher incomes?

9. To what extent does Slater's argument depend on assumptions that (*a*) society pressures people to win, be first, be successful, while (*b*) advertisers set up hypothetical stressful situations and then push their products as a quick and easy way to relieve the stress?

10. What series of consequences does Slater believe will be the inevitable result of drug abuse?

11. What is the essential difference between Weil and Rosen's and Slater's claims as to why people take drugs? In an essay, evaluate the respective merits of Weil and Rosen's and Slater's arguments. Who, in your opinion, makes a better case as to the central nature of addiction? In your analysis be sure to identify and evaluate how well Weil and Rosen, on one hand, Slater, on the other, construct their essays as causation arguments. That is, how effectively do the writers establish both a means by which the effects they describe could have been produced and the probability (evidence, reasons, statistics) that these effects were produced by the causes they identify? To what extent do their different views of the phenomenon of drug use and addictiveness depend on their different explanations as to what causes people to use drugs in the first place?

Brian Noal Mittman

Teenagers Need Drug Testing

Brian Noal Mittman is a student at Dartmouth College. His article "Teenagers Need Drug Testing" first appeared in The Union Leader *(October 26, 1986). Other articles of his on a wide range of issues important to teenagers have been published in* U.S.A. Today, The New York Times, *and* The Dartmouth. *He also writes a weekly column for his hometown newspaper. The author describes instances of drug abuse on his campus and offers six reasons why the enactment of mandatory urinalysis-testing programs would reduce the problem of drug abuse by teenagers.*

1   As a recent high school graduate I've seen rampant drug use—in schools, where students take a few "hits" before entering class; at parties, from which many kids drive home completely stoned; and even at a high school prom, where cocaine usage was high. Today's younger generation is often too accepting of drugs as a part of its life, and adults are too unwilling to implement necessary anti-drug laws. With the massive drug problem that exists in our schools today, new legislation is necessary to discourage substance abuse. Cities in Texas, New York, California and Tennessee have already implemented mandatory drug testing in some of their public schools. Such a program is needed on a national scale.

2   Many adults who oppose mandatory drug testing in schools are completely oblivious to the severity of the problem. Students see signs of drug usage in school, with friends, and on the street far more often than their parents. In interviews conducted by USA Today, teenagers themselves were the strongest advocates of hardline legislation to handle drug abuse. Many parents fail to realize how rampant drug addiction is. It is no longer monopolized by problem-plagued students and inner-city schools—good students and promising athletes are often victims as well. I attended an academically-oriented, highly-competitive, affluent, suburban high school. The number of students dealing and using drugs was shocking. Parents of friends on drugs feel incapable of dealing with the problem, while others choose to ignore a child's addiction. Mandatory testing in schools would raise teenage consciousness about drug danger and could reduce students' abuse of toxic substances without depending upon their parents' guidance.

3   Most opponents of mandatory drug testing in schools argue that such

legislation is an invasion of students' privacy—the mere fact that so many teenagers do abuse drugs is sufficient evidence that they are not mature enough to handle such problems independently.

Mandatory school drug testing should be administered to students 4 beginning at the junior high level where many drug problems start. The test should be given by an outside organization, unassociated with our public schools. Without prior warning, testing should take place for all students at a given school on Mondays, when drugs ingested from weekend partying can still be detected. Repeated testing should be administered before reporting results to parents in order to reduce uncertainties inherent in the drug test itself. This would reduce unfounded parental suspicions of frequent use if a child simply "tried" a drug for the first time before the test date, had recently kicked a drug habit, or if the test result itself was inaccurate. Finally, all information should be kept confidential between parent, child and the administering agency. Results should be kept by the administering agency—not by the school—to lessen "leaks" of confidential information.

Such drug testing could reduce teen substance abuse in six ways. (1) 5 Younger, more immature students might be deterred from future drug abuse through junior high testing and heightened awareness. (2) Individuals might refrain from drugs due to embarrassment before drug testing personnel. (3) Students would fear that surprise drug testing could result in parent notification of abuse. (4) Parents notified of their children's drug problems would seek help for them. (5) Students already addicted, fearing they might be detected, might seek help on their own. (6) School administration could take action if heavy drug use over a long period of time is detected.

State laws (required inoculations against various diseases and peri- 6 odic medical checkups) have already affected health mandates for students. Today, drug abuse has become a terrible health menace in our public schools. Any attempt to reduce this growing disease should be implemented. It's time to institute drug testing for teens.

Questions for Discussion and Writing

1. What reasons does Mittman give to support his recommendation for new and stronger drug laws?

2. According to Mittman, under what circumstances and in what way should drug tests be administered?

3. What are the six ways by which mandatory testing could reduce drug abuse? Of these six, which in your opinion is the most realistic and effective and which is the least realistic and ineffective? Explain your assessment.

4. How does Mittman's argument that mandatory drug testing is necessary depend on the assumption that school officials will not have access to test results? To what extent does this assumption appear realistic? Identify and evaluate any other of Mittman's assumptions and explain how these act as warrants in the argument (justifying how he draws conclusions from reasons and evidence).

5. How does the fact that Mittman was a student when he wrote this affect your perception of his argument?

6. What is Mittman's attitude toward the subject? What words and phrases support this impression?

7. Evaluate the reasonableness of Mittman's conclusions that, with drug testing, students would refrain from drug abuse because of the embarrassment they would suffer. Is it credible they would really care about what the testers thought?

8. In your opinion, is the intrusion into students' privacy that Mittman recommends justified? Are there other factors that Mittman does not consider such as administrative costs or the conclusions students might draw about the ease with which their privacy can be invaded?

9. Does the school system or government have the right to violate citizens' rights in pursuing what it sees as a highly desirable goal? Explain your answer.

10. To what extent does Mittman appear to shift his ground by initially characterizing drug use as a disease but later treating it as a criminal offense? For example, he first says test results would be kept confidential but later allows for public disclosure of these test results and punitive action by school administrators "if heavy drug use over a long period of time is detected."

11. Do you think mandatory drug-testing should be instituted in your school? If so, should it be implemented in the way Mittman suggests or by some other means?

Thomas J. Flygare

De Jure: Courts Foil Schools' Efforts to Detect Drugs

Thomas J. Flygare is an attorney practicing in New Hampshire who describes two cases in different school districts where the courts found the attempts to search students for drugs was unconstitutional. This article shows that legal conclusions depend not only on the facts but on assumptions underlying the facts as well. In at least one of these cases the number of students who went for drug counseling out of the total school population was an important factor in the decision. "De Jure: Courts Foil Schools' Efforts to Detect Drugs" first appeared in the Phi Delta Kappan (December 1986).

Cracking down on drug use in the schools is a major theme for many 1 public officials these days, all the way from the President to members of local school boards. In their zeal to root out drugs, however, these officials must pay careful attention to the constitutional rights of students. Two recent cases demonstrate the difficulty of balancing the emphasis on drug detection with the privacy rights of students.

In August 1985 the Carlstadt-East Rutherford (New Jersey) Regional 2 Board of Education adopted a policy called "Comprehensive Medical Examination." This very carefully written policy, which appears to have been thoroughly reviewed by legal counsel, required all students to have physical examinations conducted by the school medical examiner. The policy stated that the purpose of the examinations was to determine whether students suffered from "any physical defects, illnesses, or communicable diseases." In addition, the policy stated:

> These complete physical examinations will help to identify any drug or alcohol use by pupils. The detection of drug and/or alcohol use will enable the Board of Education to enter the pupil into an appropriate rehabilitation program designed to help the student recognize the danger and to remedy any problem that exists.

Each student was to provide a urine sample, obtained by a "medically 3 appropriate method." The sample was to be tested for "the levels of protein, sugar, specific gravity, blood, and the existence or non-existence of controlled, dangerous substances, nonauthorized prescription drugs . . . , and alcohol."

4   A group of students brought suit in state court seeking to block the testing of urine samples for the presence of drugs. They argued, among other things, that the drug testing constituted a general search of their bodies that violated the constitutional ban against unreasonable searches and seizures under the subterfuge of a forced medical examination. The students pointed out that for the 1984–85 school year, from a student population of 520, only 28 students had asked about or had been referred to the student counselor for drug or alcohol assistance. Included in this number were some students who denied any involvement in either alcohol or drugs, as well as some who were currently drug- and alcohol-free but were receiving follow-up services.

5   School officials argued that the testing of the urine samples for the presence of drugs or alcohol was incidental to a number of traditional medical tests for which a urine sample is taken. Moreover, they argued, even if a student tested positive for either drugs or alcohol, no civil or criminal penalties would be imposed. In such cases, the doctor, parent, and student would discuss the problem and decide whether remedial actions were appropriate. The files maintained in accordance with the physical examination, including the drug and alcohol testing, would be kept confidential and separate from other school files. School officials emphasized their view that drug and alcohol abuse is an illness and not a criminal infraction. Therefore, they argued, the urine testing did not constitute an unreasonable search.

6   The state court sided with the students.[1] It found, without analysis, that performing drug and alcohol tests on students' urine samples constituted a search. Then, relying on the U.S. Supreme Court's 1985 decision in *New Jersey* v. *T.L.O.*, the court held that the search was not supported by reasonable suspicion:

> Assuming arguendo, that this is strictly and solely a medical examination to inquire into a medical condition, a position which this court does not accept, I would still find that the activities [of the school officials] violate the reasonable privacy expectations of school children. . . . the raw numbers and percentages of students referred to student counseling as compared with the total student body [are] not reasonably related in scope to the circumstances which justify the interference, urinalysis, in the first place.

7   The court also suggested that the drug tests might be an effort by school officials to circumvent the requirement that students be accorded due process prior to disciplinary action by the school. The court noted that school policy provided for suspension and expulsion of students as a disciplinary matter for drug activities only *after* a due process hearing. The court termed "unacceptable" any distinction between punishment

under that policy and similar treatment of students without due process "for medical reasons." The court found that

> in light of the Board of Education's proposed use of urinaly-
> sis . . . , this court suggests that the spectrum of items that could
> be approached simply by defining them as medical is limitless. To
> accept [the school officials'] position suggests that medical testing
> is without limit. The Board of Education's use of an exclusion to
> prohibit class attendance which does not provide for the due
> process mandated by [other cases] fails to pass constitutional
> muster.

The search for drugs was also an issue in a case from Howell, 8
Michigan, involving a 15-year-old high school sophomore named Ruth
Cales. At a time that Cales was required to be in school, she was
observed by a school security guard in the parking lot attempting to
avoid detection by ducking behind a car. When the security guard confronted her and asked for identification, she gave a false name. She was
taken to the office of the assistant principal, Daniel McCarthy, where she
was required to dump the contents of her purse on a desk. The purse
contained a number of "readmittance slips," which students were not
allowed to have. McCarthy directed another assistant principal, Mary
Steinhelper, and his secretary, Colleen Wise, to conduct a further search
of Cales for drugs.

When Cales was in the presence of only Steinhelper and Wise, she 9
was instructed to turn the pockets of her jeans inside out. She then
removed her jeans completely, although Steinhelper and Wise stated
that she was not ordered to do so. Steinhelper admitted that she ordered
Cales to bend over so she could look into Cales' brassiere. At no time was
Cales' body touched in any manner.

Cales sued the school system, as well as McCarthy, Steinhelper, and 10
Wise, for conducting an unreasonable and unconstitutional search. In
addressing some preliminary motions by the parties (the case has not yet
gone to trial), the court held that the search of Cales was not supported
by a reasonable suspicion that she was concealing drugs on her person.

> It is clear that plaintiff's conduct created reasonable grounds
> for suspecting that some school rule or law had been violated.
> However, it does not create a reasonable suspicion that a search
> would turn up evidence of drug usage. Plaintiff's conduct was
> clearly ambiguous. It could have indicated that she was truant, or
> that she was stealing hubcaps, or that she had left class to meet a
> boyfriend. In short, it could have signified that plaintiff had vio-
> lated any of an infinite number of laws or school rules. This court
> does not read *T.L.O.* so broadly as to allow a school administrator
> the right to search a student because that student acts in such a

way as to create a reasonable suspicion that the student has violated *some* rule or law.[2]

11   Educators had reason to be pleased when the U.S. Supreme Court held in early 1975 that a student could be searched by school officials on the basis of a reasonable suspicion (rather than on the higher standard of probable cause) that the student was concealing, in the place to be searched, evidence of conduct that was unlawful or that violated school rules. However, as these two cases demonstrate, school officials should not be cavalier in assuming that reasonable suspicion exists. *T.L.O.* provides that, if school officials have some reliable information about students' unlawful or improper conduct and make a "commonsense assumption" that evidence of that conduct will be concealed, reasonable suspicion should exist to support the search for the concealed evidence.

12   In the case discussed above, involving testing for drugs and alcohol in New Jersey, school officials had only "unparticularized" suspicion of drug use by students. It is always difficult to argue that such suspicion is adequate to support any type of student search. In the Michigan case, on the other hand, a single student was the particular focus of suspicion, but the evidence to assume that she was concealing drugs on her person was inadequate. She was not observed to be using or in possession of drugs, and the contents of her purse revealed no information suggesting that a search of her body would yield evidence of drugs. Thus, while the courts will judge cases involving student searches according to more relaxed standards than they did before *T.L.O.*, school officials must still try to determine whether a search is justified.

NOTES

1. *Odenheim* v. *Carlstadt-East Rutherford Regional School District*, 510 A. 1d 709 (N.J. Super. Ch. 1985).

2. *Cales* v. *Howell Public Schools*, 635 F. Supp. 454 (E.D. Mich. 1985).

Questions for Discussion and Writing

1. According to Flygare, what was the purpose of the medical examination proposed for the students of Carlstadt-East Rutherford?

2. What arguments, specifically, were presented on the students' behalf against the urinalysis testing?

3. What process of reasoning did the court follow, according to Flygare, in ruling in favor of the students?

4. Since most of Flygare's essay is an account of the Becton High School incident and subsequent court ruling, most of the explicit assumptions are drawn from the court decision. There are, however, a number of implicit assumptions underlying his argument. For example, how does Flygare's argument depend on assumptions that (*a*) substance abuse is a disease, not a criminal act, and cannot be used as the basis for an unreasonable search, and (*b*) students' constitutional rights should be protected?

5. Explain the rationale underlying the court's ruling that urinalysis tests must be construed as an effort by school officials to suspend students without granting them due process. (The assumption here is that all citizens are entitled to due process.)

6. Why was it important in the court's decision for the court to assume that the 28 students (out of the total of 520 students) who went for counseling were the total number abusing drugs and were not a large enough number to justify testing everyone in the school? How might the conclusion have been different if the obvious assumption had been successfully questioned? For example, perhaps all drug abusers did not go for counseling. Would it still have been a case of unwarranted search and seizure if the number who had come forward were, say, 450 out of the 520 students? Explain your answer by discussing how legal conclusions depend not only on the facts but on the assumptions underlying the facts. What do you think should have been done if 450 students had come forward initially?

7. How does the second case discussed by Flygare (involving a fifteen-year-old high school sophomore, Ruth Cales) also dramatize the issue of the permissible limits under which authorities can search students for drugs?

8. How is your perception of the credibility of this argument influenced by knowing that Flygare is a lawyer? If you had read Flygare's and Mittman's articles thinking that Mittman was a lawyer and Flygare was a student, how, if at all, would your perception have been altered?

9. In a short essay, evaluate the respective merits of Mittman's and Flygare's arguments. Who, in your opinion, makes a better case? In your analysis be sure to evaluate how well Mittman and Flygare construct their arguments as policy arguments recommending solutions to problems.

Anne Marie O'Keefe

The Case against Drug Testing

Anne Marie O'Keefe is a psychologist and a lawyer who specializes in health issues. In "The Case against Drug Testing," which first appeared in Psychology Today *(June 1987), O'Keefe draws on statistical evidence to support her claim that the technology on which drug testing is based is unreliable and produces "false positive results." She also delves into the historical background of the Fourth Amendment in order to support her claim that drug testing violates the Fourth Amendment's guarantee against "illegal search and seizure."*

1   During 1986, the nation's concern over illegal drug use reached almost hysterical proportions. The U.S. House of Representatives passed legislation that, had the Senate agreed, would have suspended certain Constitutional protections and required the death penalty for some drug offenses. The President issued an executive order calling for the mass drug testing of federal employees in "sensitive" positions. Federal courts have deemed such testing to be illegal for some classes of federal workers; however, these decisions are still being appealed, and the administration is determined to forge ahead with its drug-testing program. And private employers have turned increasingly to chemical laboratories to determine who is fit for hiring, promotion and continuing employment. Between 1982 and 1985, the estimated proportion of Fortune-500 companies conducting routine urinalysis rose from 3 to nearly 30 percent—a figure expected to reach 50 percent by this year or next year.

2   While there are issues of legitimate concern about drug use and public safety, the speed and enthusiasm with which many of our elected representatives and business leaders have embraced drug testing as a panacea has left many questions unanswered. Why did our national drug problem so rapidly become the focus of political and business decisions? Did this change reflect a sudden, serious worsening of the problem? Why did mass drug testing suddenly gain favor? Was it shown to be particularly effective in detecting and deterring illegal drug use? And finally, what are the costs of making employees and job applicants take urine tests?

3   Our country has a serious drug problem. The National Institute on Drug Abuse (NIDA) estimates that nearly two-thirds of those now entering the work force have used illegal drugs—44 percent within the past year. But ironically, the drug-testing craze has come just when most

types of drug use are beginning to wane. NIDA reports that for all drugs except cocaine, current rates are below those of 1979, our peak year of drug use.

Why the furor now? The drug-testing fad might be viewed as the   4
product of both election-year posturing and well-timed and well-financed marketing efforts by test manufacturers. During the 1970s, the relatively low-cost chemical assay (called EMIT) that promised to detect drugs in urine was first manufactured. In the beginning, these tests were used only by crime laboratories, drug-treatment programs and the military. By the early 1980s, a handful of private employers were also using them. But more recently, sales of drug tests have gotten a big boost from the attitudes and edicts of the Reagan administration. On March 3, 1986, the President's Commission on Organized Crime recommended that all employees of private companies contracting with the federal government be regularly subjected to urine testing for drugs as a condition of employment. Then came the President's executive order on September 15, requiring the head of each executive agency to "establish a program to test for the use of illegal drugs by employees in sensitive positions." It remains unclear how many millions of federal workers will be subject to such testing if the President gets his way.

Strangely, drug testing is becoming widespread despite general   5
agreement that the results of mass tests are often highly inaccurate. Error rates reflect both inherent deficiencies in the technology and mistakes in handling and interpreting test results. In a series of studies conducted by the federal Centers for Disease Control (CDC) and NIDA, urine samples spiked with drugs were sent periodically to laboratories across the country serving methadone treatment centers. Tests on these samples, which the labs knew had come from CDC, revealed drug-detection error rates averaging below 10 percent. However, when identical samples subsequently were sent to the same laboratories, but not identified as coming from CDC, error rates increased to an average of 31 percent, with a high of 100 percent. These errors were "false negatives," cases in which "dirty" urine samples were identified as "clean."

Independent studies of laboratory accuracy have also confirmed high   6
error rates. One group of researchers reported a 66.5 percent rate of "false positives" among 160 urine samples from participants in a methadone treatment center. False-positive mistakes, identifying a "clean" urine sample as containing an illegal drug, are far more serious in the context of worker screening than are false-negative mistakes. This is because false positives can result in innocent people losing their jobs. Ironically, since the error rates inherent in the drug tests are higher than the actual rate of illegal drug use in the general working population, as reported by NIDA, the tests are more likely to label innocent people as illegal drug users than to identify real users.

Many of the false-positive results stem from a phenomenon known   7
as "cross-reactivity." This refers to the fact that both over-the-counter

and prescription drugs, and even some foods, can produce false-positive results on the tests. For example, Contac, Sudafed, certain diet pills, decongestants and heart and asthma medications can register as amphetamines on the tests. Cough syrups containing dextromethorphan can cross-react as opiates, and some antibiotics show up as cocaine. Anti-inflammatory drugs and common painkillers, including Datril, Advil and Nuprin, mimic marijuana. Even poppy seeds, which actually contain traces of morphine, and some herbal teas containing traces of cocaine can cause positive test results for these drugs.

8   Commercial testing companies almost always claim very high accuracy and reliability. But because these laboratories are not uniformly regulated, employers who buy their services may find it hard to confirm these claims or even to conduct informed comparative shopping. Companies that mass-market field-testing kits such as EMITs (which cost an estimated $15 to $25 per test) usually recommend that positive test results be confirmed with other laboratory procedures, which can run from $100 to $200 per test. But relatively few employers seem to be using the expensive back-up procedures before firing employees who test positive. Even when employers do verify positive results, employees who turn out to be drug-free upon retesting will already be stigmatized.

9   The tests have other critical failings, particularly their limited sensitivity to certain drugs, a shortcoming the drug-test manufacturers readily admit. Consider cocaine, for example. Despite great concern in the 1980s over the use of cocaine, the only illicit drug whose use is on the rise, this is the drug to which the tests are least sensitive since its chemical traces dissipate in a few days. Alcohol, which is legal but potentially detrimental to job performance, is also hard to detect, since traces disappear from within 12 to 24 hours. By contrast, urine testing is, if anything, overly sensitive to marijuana; it can detect the drug's chemical byproducts (not its active ingredient) for weeks after its use and can even pick up the residue of passive inhalation. Drug testing does not indicate the recency of use, nor does it distinguish between chronic and one-time use. Most important, though urinalysis can reveal a lot about off-the-job activities, it tells nothing about job performance.

10   Mass drug testing is expensive, but its greatest costs are not financial and cannot be neatly quantified. The greatest costs involve violations of workers' rights and the poor employee morale and fractured trust that result when workers must prove their innocence against the presumption of guilt.

11   The most important cost of drug testing, however, may be the invasion of workers' privacy. Urinalysis may be highly inaccurate in detecting the use of illegal drugs, but it can reveal who is pregnant, who has asthma and who is being treated for heart disease, manic-depression, epilepsy, diabetes and a host of other physical and mental conditions.

12   In colonial times, King George III justified having his soldiers break into homes and search many innocent people indiscriminately on the

grounds that the procedure might reveal the few who were guilty of crimes against the Crown. But the founders of our nation chose to balance things quite differently. An important purpose and accomplishment of the Constitution is to protect us from government intrusion. The Fourth Amendment is clear that "the right of the people to be secure in their persons . . . against unreasonable searches and seizures, shall not be violated. . . . " Searches are permitted only "upon probable cause, supported by Oath or affirmation, and particularly describing the place to be searched, and the persons or things to be seized."

The U.S. Supreme Court has ruled that extracting bodily fluids constitutes a search within the meaning of this Amendment. Therefore, except under extraordinary circumstances, when the government seeks to test an employee's urine, it must comply with due process and must first provide plausible evidence of illegal activity. People accused of heinous crimes are assured of this minimum protection from government intrusion. Because employees in our government work force deserve no less, most courts reviewing proposals to conduct mass tests on such employees have found these programs to be illegal.   13

Unfortunately, workers in the private sector are not as well protected. The Constitution protects citizens only from intrusions by government (county, state and federal); it does not restrict nongovernmental employers from invading workers' privacy, although employers in the private sector are subject to some limitations. The constitutions of nine states have provisions specifically protecting citizens' rights to privacy and prohibiting unreasonable searches and seizures. Several private lawsuits against employers are now testing the applicability of these shields. Local governments, can, if they wish, pass legislation to protect private employees from unwarranted drug tests; in fact, San Francisco has done so. In addition, union contracts and grievance procedures may give some workers protection from mass drug testing, and civil-rights laws could block the disproportionate testing of minorities. Nonetheless, private employees have relatively little legal protection against mandatory drug testing and arbitrary dismissal.   14

Civil libertarians claim that as long as employees do their work well, inquiries into their off-duty drug use are no more legitimate than inquiries into their sex lives. Then why has drug testing become so popular? Perhaps because it is simple and "objective"—a litmus test. It is not easily challenged because, like the use of lie detectors, it relies on technology that few understand. It is quicker and cheaper than serious and sustained efforts to reduce illegal drug use, such as the mass educational efforts that have successfully reduced cigarette smoking. And finally, while drug testing may do little to address the real problem of drug use in our society, it reinforces the employer's illusion of doing something.   15

Apparently some employers would rather test their employees for drugs than build a relationship with them based on confidence and loyalty. Fortunately, there are employers, such as the Drexelbrook Engi-   16 neering Company in Pennsylvania, who have decided against drug testing because of its human costs. As Drexelbrook's vice president put it, a relationship "doesn't just come from a paycheck. When you say to an employee, 'you're doing a great job; just the same, I want you to pee in this jar and I'm sending someone to watch you,' you've undermined that trust."

Questions for Discussion and Writing

1. What reasons and evidence does O'Keefe provide to support her thesis that the use of drug tests to evaluate employees (when no shortcoming in job performance is evident) constitutes a breech of civil rights?

2. How does O'Keefe use statistical evidence to support her claim that drug testing has been shown to be inaccurate and can produce false positive results? How do many over-the-counter drugs like Contac and Datril produce test results that, when unconfirmed, lead to unwarranted conclusions and subsequent loss of employment?

3. According to O'Keefe, why are employees in the private sector particularly vulnerable to violation of their Fourth Amendment rights against illegal search and seizure? Why does O'Keefe go into the historical perspective tracing the origin of the Fourth Amendment?

4. How did an increasing percentage of the nation's workforce using illegal drugs and the development of tests that could be used to detect illegal drugs in urine lead to the institution of required drug-testing programs for government employees?

5. How does the administration of drug-testing programs put the burden on government employees to prove that they are innocent? How has technology reversed the usual presumption of innocent until proven guilty?

6. How compelling do you find the reasons O'Keefe presents to support her thesis that drug testing invades privacy by revealing to employers who is pregnant, asthmatic, diabetic, or epileptic?

7. What objections might someone who agreed with O'Keefe raise to the following argument: O'Keefe objects to drug testing on the grounds that such tests violate an individual's right to privacy. She fails to acknowledge that society routinely invades the privacy of individuals for the common good. A blood test is required to obtain a marriage license, an eye test is required to get a driver's license, and

prospective employees are routinely required by large corporations and the government to take lie-detector tests. In these cases, the rights of the group take precedence over those of individuals; since drugs pose a major threat to society, mandatory drug-testing should be instituted even if it does invade the privacy of individuals.

In formulating your counterargument, be sure to consider the essential question as to how drug testing differs, if at all, from blood, eye, and lie-detector tests and why these differences are significant.

8. If you had to take a drug test to get or keep a job, would you object? If so, why? If not, why not?

9. What negative psychological effects described by O'Keefe are viewed by Mittman as a positive way of deterring drug use?

10. Drawing on O'Keefe's article and the essays by Mittman and Flygare, discuss how all three writers shed light on the issue of the conflict between individual rights and rights of the group or society as a whole to protect itself from the dangers posed by widespread drug use. In your view, does society have this right and how far can it go in limiting the rights of individuals?

Thomas H. Murray

The Coercive Power of Drugs in Sports

Thomas H. Murray is a professor of ethics and public policy at the Institute for the Medical Humanities at the University of Texas Medical Branch in Galveston. In "The Coercive Power of Drugs in Sports," that appeared in The Hastings Center Report *(August 1983), Murray argues that the use of performance-enhancing drugs such as steroids should be banned because athletes are often coerced into using them despite the known health risks. Murray's argument depends on the value claim that the performance-enhancing drugs are morally wrong because they give athletes willing to risk their health an unfair advantage over those who do not wish to risk harm and possible addiction in order to remain competitive. He recommends that coaches who influence athletes to take drugs should be punished along with the athletes who use the drugs.*

1   Our images of the nonmedical drug user normally include the heroin addict nodding in the doorway, the spaced-out marijuana smoker, and maybe, if we know that alcohol is a drug, the wino sprawled on the curb. We probably do not think of the Olympic gold medalist, the professional baseball player who is a shoo-in for the Hall of Fame, or the National Football League lineman. Yet these athletes and hundreds, perhaps thousands of others regularly use drugs in the course of their training, performance, or both. I am talking not about recreational drug use — athletes use drugs for pleasure and relaxation probably no more or less than their contemporaries with comparable incomes — but about a much less discussed type of drug use: taking drugs to enhance performance.

2   It is a strange idea. Most of us think of drugs in one of two ways. Either they are being properly used by doctors and patients to make sick people well or at least to stem the ravages of illness and pain, or they are being misused — we say "abused" — by individuals in pursuit of unworthy pleasures. Performance-enhancing drug use is so common and so tolerated in some forms that we often fail to think of it as "drug" use. The clearest example is the (caffeinated) coffee pot, which is as much a part of the American workplace as typewriters and timeclocks. We drink coffee (and tea and Coke) for the "lift" it gives us. The source of "that Pepsi feeling" and the "life" added by Coke is no mystery — it is caffeine or some of its close chemical relatives, potent stimulants to the human central nervous system. Anyone who has drunk too much coffee and felt

caffeine "jitters," or drunk it too late at night and been unable to sleep can testify to its pharmacological potency. Caffeine and its family, the xanthines, can stave off mental fatigue and help maintain alertness, very important properties when we are working around a potentially dangerous machine, fighting through a boring report, or driving for a long stretch.

Caffeine, then, is a performance-enhancing drug. Using caffeine to keep alert is an instance of the nonmedical use of a drug. So, too, is consuming alcohol at a cocktail party for the pleasure of a mild inebriation, or as a social lubricant to enable you to be charming to people you find intolerably boring when you are sober. In the first case, alcohol is a pleasure-enhancer; in the second, it is a performance-enhancer. What the drug is used for and the intention behind the use — not the substance itself — determines whether we describe it as medical or nonmedical; as pleasure, performance-, or health-enhancing. 3

The area of human endeavor that has seen the most explosive growth in performance-enhancing drug use is almost certainly sport. At the highest levels of competitive sports, where athletes strain to improve performances already at the limits of human ability, the temptation to use a drug that might provide an edge can be powerful. Is this kind of drug use unethical? Should we think of it as an expression of liberty? Or do the special circumstances of sport affect our moral analysis? In particular, should liberty give way when other important values are threatened, and when no one's good is advanced? These questions frame the discussion that follows. . . . 4

May athletes use drugs to enhance their athletic performance? The International Olympic committee [IOC] has given an answer of sorts by flatly prohibiting "doping" of any kind. This stance creates at least as many problems as it solves. It requires an expensive and cumbersome detection and enforcement apparatus, turning athletes and officials into mutually suspicious adversaries. It leads Olympic sports medicine authorities to proclaim that drugs like steroids are ineffective, a charge widely discounted by athletes, and thereby decreases the credibility of Olympic officials. Drug use is driven underground, making it difficult to obtain sound medical data on drug side effects. 5

The enforcement body, in an attempt to balance firmness with fairness, bans athletes "for life" only to reinstate them a year later, knowing that what distinguishes these athletes from most others is only that they were caught. 6

Any argument for prohibiting or restricting drug use by Olympic athletes must contend with a very powerful defense based on our concept of individual liberty. We have a strong legal and moral tradition of individual liberty that proclaims the right to pursue our life plans in our own way, to take risks if we so desire and, within very broad limits, do with our own bodies what we wish. This right in law has been extended unambiguously to competent persons who wish to refuse even life-sav- 7 ing medical care. More recently, it has been extended to marginally competent persons who refuse psychiatric treatment. Surely, competent and well-informed athletes have a right to use whatever means they desire to enhance their performance.

8   Those who see performance-enhancing drug use as the exercise of individual liberty are unmoved by the prospect of some harm. They believe it should be up to the individual, who is assumed to be a rational, autonomous, and uncoerced agent, to weigh probable harms against benefits, and choose according to his or her own value preferences. It would be a much greater wrong, they would say, to deny people the right to make their own choices. Why should we worry so much about some probabilistic future harm for athletes while many other endeavors pose even greater dangers? High-steel construction work and coal-mining, mountain-climbing, hang-gliding, and auto-racing are almost certainly more dangerous than using steroids or other common performance-enhancing drugs.

9   Reasons commonly given to limit liberty fall into three classes: those that claim that the practice interferes with capacities for rational choice; those that emphasize harms to self; and those that emphasize harm to others. The case of performance-enhancing drugs and sport illustrates a fourth reason that may justify some interference with liberty, a phenomenon we can call "inherent coerciveness." But first the other three reasons.

10   There is something paradoxical about our autonomy: we might freely choose to do something that would compromise our future capacity to choose freely. Selling oneself into slavery would be one way to limit liberty, by making one's body the property of another person. If surrendering autonomous control over one's body is an evil and something we refuse to permit, how much worse is it to destroy one's capacity to *think* clearly and independently? Yet that is one thing that may happen to people who abuse certain drugs. We may interfere with someone's desire to do a particular autonomous act if that act is likely to cause a general loss of the capacity to act autonomously. In this sense, forbidding selling yourself into slavery and forbidding the abuse of drugs likely to damage your ability to reason are similar *restrictions* on liberty designed to *preserve* liberty.

11   This argument applies only to things that do in fact damage our capacity to reason and make autonomous decisions. While some of the more powerful pleasure-enhancing drugs might qualify, no one claims that performance-enhancing drugs like the steroids have any deleterious impact on reason. This argument, then, is irrelevant to the case of performance-enhancing drugs. . . .

12   A second class of reasons to limit liberty says that we may interfere with some actions when they result in wrong to others. The wrong done may be direct — lying, cheating, or other forms of deception are unavoidable when steroid use is banned. Of course, we could lift the ban, and

then the steroid use need no longer be deceptive; it could be completely open to the same extent as other training aids. Even with the ban forcing steroids into the pale of secrecy, it would be naive to think that other athletes are being deceived when they all know that steroids are in regular use. The public may be deceived, but not one's competitors. There is no lie when no one is deceived. Using steroids may be more like bluffing in poker than fixing the deck, at least for your competitors.

The wrong we do to others may be indirect. We could make ourselves incapable of fulfilling some duty we have to another person. For example, a male athlete who marries and promises his wife that they will have children makes himself sterile with synthetic anabolic steroids (a probable side effect). He has violated his moral duty to keep a promise. This objection could work, but only where the duty is clearly identifiable and not overly general, and the harm is reasonably foreseeable. Duties to others must have a limited, clear scope or become absurdly general or amorphous. We may believe that parents have the duty to care for their children, but we do not require parents to stay by their children's bedside all night, every night, to prevent them from suffocating in their blankets. The duty is narrower than that. In order to avoid being too vague, we would have to be able to specify what the "duty to care for one's children" actually includes. Except for cases like the sterile athlete reneging on his promise, instances where athletes make themselves incapable of fulfilling some specific duty to others would probably be rare. In any case, we cannot get a general moral prohibition on drug use in sports from this principle, only judgments in particular cases. **13**

We may also do a moral wrong to others by taking unnecessary risks and becoming a great burden to family, society, or both. The helmetless motorcyclist who suffers severe brain damage in an accident is a prototype case. Increasingly, people are describing professional boxing in very similar terms. While this might be a good reason to require motorcyclists to wear helmets or to prohibit professional boxing matches, it is not a sound reason to prohibit steroid use. No one claims that the athletes using steroids are going to harm themselves so grievously that they will end up seriously brain-damaged or otherwise unable to care for themselves. **14**

Olympic and professional sport, as a social institution, is an intensely competitive endeavor, and there is tremendous pressure to seek a competitive advantage. If some athletes are believed to have found something that gives them an edge, other athletes will feel pressed to do the same, or leave the competition. Unquestionably, coerciveness operates in the case of performance-enhancing drugs and sport. Where improved performance can be measured in fractions of inches, pounds, or seconds, and that fraction is the difference between winning and losing, it is very difficult for athletes to forego using something that they believe improves their competitors' performance. Many athletes do refuse; but **15** many others succumb; and still others undoubtedly leave rather than take drugs or accept a competitive handicap. Under such pressure, decisions to take performance-enhancing drugs are anything but purely "individual" choices.

16   Can we say that "freedom" has actually been diminished because others are using performance-enhancing drugs? I still have a choice whether to participate in the sport at all. In what sense is my freedom impaired by what the other athletes may be doing? If we take freedom or liberty in the very narrow sense of noninterference with my actions, then my freedom has not been violated, because no one is prohibiting me from doing what I want, whether that be throwing the discus, taking steroids, or selling real estate. But if we take freedom to be one of a number of values, whose purpose is to support the efforts of persons to pursue reasonable life plans without being forced into unconscionable choices by the actions of others, then the coerciveness inherent when many athletes use performance-enhancing drugs and compel others to use the same drugs, accept a competitive handicap, or leave the competition can be seen as a genuine threat to one's life plan. When a young person has devoted years to reach the highest levels in an event, only to find that to compete successfully he or she must take potentially grave risks to health, we have as serious a threat to human flourishing as many restrictions on liberty.

17   At this point it might be useful to consider the social value we place on improved performance in sport. It is a truism that you win a sports event by performing better than any of your competitors. The rules of sport are designed to eliminate all influences on the outcome except those considered legitimate. Natural ability, dedication, cleverness are fine; using an underweight shot-put, taking a ten-yard head start, fielding twelve football players are not. The rules of sport are man-made conventions. No natural law deems that shot-puts shall weigh sixteen pounds, or that football teams shall consist of eleven players. Within these arbitrary conventions, the rules limit the variations among competitors to a small set of desired factors. A willingness to take health risks by consuming large quantities of steroids is *not* one of the desired, legitimate differences among competitors.

18   Changing the rules of a sport will alter performances, but not necessarily the standing of competitors. If we use a twelve-lb. shot-put, everyone will throw it farther than the sixteen-lb. one, but success will still depend on strength and technique, and the best at sixteen pounds will probably still be best at twelve pounds. Giving all shot-putters 10 mg. of Dianabol [a steroid] a day will have a similar impact, complicated by variations in physiological response to the drug. Noncatastrophic changes in the rules may shift some rankings, but will generally preserve relations among competitors. Changes that do not alter the nature of a sport, but greatly increase the risk to competitors are unconscionable.

Changes that affirmatively tempt athletes to take the maximum health risk are the worst. Lifting the ban on performance-enhancing drugs would encourage just that sort of brinksmanship. On the other hand, an effective policy for eliminating performance-enhancing drug use would harm no one, except those who profit from it.

My conclusions are complex. First, the athletes who are taking per-   19 formance-enhancing drugs that have significant health risks are engaging in a morally questionable practice. They have turned a sport into a sophisticated game of "chicken." Most likely, each athlete feels pressed by others to take drugs, and does not feel he or she is making a free choice. The "drug race" is analogous to the arms race.

Second, since the problem is systemic, the solution must be too. The   20 IOC has concentrated on individual athletes, and even then it has been inconsistent. This is the wrong place to look. Athletes do not use drugs because they like them, but because they feel compelled to. Rather than merely punishing those caught in the social trap, why not focus on the system? A good enforcement mechanism should be both ethical and efficient. To be ethical, punishment should come in proportion to culpability and should fall on *all* the guilty parties—not merely the athletes. Coaches, national federations, and political bodies that encourage, or fail to strenuously discourage, drug use are all guilty. Current policy punishes only the athlete.

To be efficient, sanctions should be applied against those parties who   21 can most effectively control drug use. Ultimately, it is the athlete who takes the pill or injection, so he or she ought to be one target of sanctions. But coaches are in an extraordinarily influential position to persuade athletes to take or not to take drugs. Sanctions on coaches whose athletes are caught using drugs could be very effective. Coaches, not wanting to be eliminated from future competitions, might refuse to take on athletes who use performance-enhancing drugs.

Finally, although I am not in a position to elaborate a detailed plan to   22 curtail performance-enhancing drug use in sports, I have tried to establish several points. Despite the claims of individual autonomy, the use of performance-enhancing drugs is ethically undesirable because it is coercive, has significant potential for harm, and advances no social value. Furthermore, any plan for eliminating its use should be just and efficient, in contrast to current policies.

Can we apply this analysis of drug use in sports to other areas of life?   23 One key variable seems to be the social value that the drug use promotes, weighed against the risks it imposes. If we had a drug that steadied a surgeon's hand and improved her concentration so that surgical errors were reduced at little or no personal risk, I would not fault its use. If, on the other hand, the drug merely allowed the surgeon to operate more quickly and spend more time on the golf course with no change in surgical risk, its use would be at best a matter of moral indifference. Health, in the first case, is an important social value, one worth spending money and effort to obtain. A marginal addition to leisure time does not carry anywhere near the same moral weight.

24   A careful, case-by-case, practice-by-practice weighing of social value gained against costs and risks appears to be the ethically responsible way to proceed in deciding on the merits of performance-enhancing drugs.

Questions for Discussion and Writing

1. Although Murray never explicitly defines *performance-enhancing* drugs, most readers will understand what he means by this term. How would you define it? Illustrate your definition with examples.

2. What reasons does Murray present to support his contention that an argument based on personal liberty doesn't justify the use of drugs in sports?

3. Why does Murray believe that performance-enhancing drugs are essentially coercive?

4. Evaluate Murray's conclusion that performance-enhancing drugs are morally wrong because they give athletes willing to take risks an unfair advantage over those who do not want to risk harm and addiction in order to remain competitive.

5. Evaluate Murray's claim that the nature of athletic competition should not allow for an individual to risk his or her health by taking drugs and should preclude even those athletes who just want to win and don't care about their health.

6. To what extent does Murray's argument depend on the concept of impaired judgment?

7. Do you agree with Murray's recommendation that coaches who influence athletes to take drugs should be punished along with the athletes who actually use the drugs?

8. Evaluate Murray's claim that by restricting liberty of athletes to use performance-enhancing drugs we can help preserve it; is this a sufficient reason to take away the athlete's freedom of choice? Discuss the underlying assumption that we can limit an athlete's liberty in the present to prevent him or her from suffering harm in the future.

9. In what way have many of the issues discussed by Murray been brought home more forcefully by the numbers of athletes who were disqualified from competing, or from receiving medals, in the 1988

Summer Olympics in Seoul, Korea? Tests revealed that these athletes had taken prohibited substances, including steroids.

10. If you have ever participated in athletic competition or been on a team where you were faced with the choice of taking performance-enhancing drugs, tell what you decided and discuss the reasons for your decision.

11. Analyze how Murray defines the key terms *coercion* and *freedom* in his argument. To what extent has he defined these terms in a way that is favorable to his thesis?

Norman Fost

Banning Drugs in Sports: A Skeptical View

Norman Fost is the director of the Program in Medical Ethics at the University of Wisconsin. In "Banning Drugs in Sports: A Skeptical View," in The Hastings Center Report *(August 1986), Fost argues that policies aimed at deciding between ethical and unethical uses of performance-enhancing drugs are ambiguous and laws should not deprive athletes of the right to choose whether or not to use these drugs. To support his case, Fost draws a distinction between restorative and addictive drugs. He also argues that taking performance-enhancing drugs is no worse than taking vitamins.*

1   Nearly everyone condemns the use of drugs—amphetamines, cocaine, steroids, and narcotics—in sports. But other drugs—antibiotics, insulin, vitamins, and aspirin—are quite acceptable. The basis for these distinctions is not obvious, nor is it self-evident why there should be any restrictions on the use of drugs in sports. Drugs can be used for various purposes: to restore a person with a disease to normal function; to improve function in a healthy person; to relieve pain; and to give pleasure, with no expected effects on performance.

2   Let me emphasize my personal distaste for drugs in sports, particularly performing-enhancing and recreational drugs. As an athlete, I would not use them. As a physician, I would not prescribe them. As a father, I would urge my children to avoid them. As a citizen, I deplore their widespread use. But these are merely preferences and not a sufficient basis for a national policy that claims to be based on ethical considerations.

3   In the 1972 Olympics, Rick DeMont, an American long-distance swimmer, had to give up a gold medal when it was discovered he had taken his routine antiasthmatic medications before the race. He apparently was unaware that the medicine contained a prohibited substance —ephedrine. Presumably the punishment was imposed for the procedural error of failing to comply with regulations, rather than for the substantive error of improperly enhancing performance.

4   It is probably irrelevant whether he took the banned drug to relieve an asthma attack and thereby restore his pulmonary function, or to gain whatever additive effect the ephedrine might provide. The presumed

purpose of banning certain drugs was not to proscribe or punish bad intentions, but to prevent an athlete from gaining unfair advantage. DeMont's problem was complicated by the possible double-effect, restorative and additive, of ephedrine. But let me consider the premise that a drug with purely restorative actions — insulin, for example — would be permissible.

The policy of allowing an athlete to use a drug that combats a disease,   5 illness, or disability is ambiguous in two regards. First, it presupposes a consensus or rational basis for defining disease, and for distinguishing diseases that may acceptably be treated before competition from those that may not. Suppose, for example, an athlete suffering from the ailment "narcotic withdrawal" desired treatment to restore himself to a normal or baseline state. Apart from moralistic statements about the importance of not empathizing with such a disease, how can we distinguish such an illness from asthma, diabetes, or endogenous depression? One might point out its social or personal causation, rather than some intrinsic or uncontrollable etiology. Such a distinction would be specious, since many diseases and disabilities result from an interaction of volitional and involuntary forces. The asthmatic might not wheeze if he did not exercise, or if he stayed away from substances that provoked an attack.

Second, and more important, allowing an athlete to restore his func-   6 tion to "normal" or "baseline" fails to address the ambiguity of those concepts. The Olympic athlete can hardly consider his strength or speed normal. In fact, his functioning in a diseased state may be closer to what we would generally consider normal. DeMont, wheezing or not, could swim laps around me. What the athlete seeks through restorative drugs is not normal function, in a statistical sense, but something closer to his personal baseline. But even personal baseline is not what the world-class athlete seeks. He wants to be beyond his baseline or normal level, preferably at a level of performance that is supernormal even for him. In these settings the distinction between restorative and additive is unclear.

One might try to distinguish restorative from additive drugs by dis-   7 tinguishing needs from wants. The restorative drug is presumably given because of a medical need; the additive drug is hardly needed in the medical sense, but is devoutly wanted as an adjunct to performance. This distinction also assumes an ability to distinguish wants from needs in a value-free way, as if these were purely medical judgments. The mild asthmatic does not need medication for normal daily functions, or to enjoy the pleasures of sport, or even to compete in a variety of contests other than world-class events. He uses drugs not because he is sick or disabled, but because being very good is not enough. He wants, not needs, to be as good as he possibly can be.

Similarly, the athlete who asks for anabolic steroids is commonly   8 already a superhuman, but wants to be one notch better. If there is a distinction between a mild asthmatic and nonasthmatic Olympian, it is not that one is sick or subnormal. They are both "supernormal." The asthmatic is limited by pulmonary function that prevents him from achieving his maximal performance. The nonasthmatic might be limited by insufficient strength or speed. Neither seeks normality but both seek maximal possible performance. Suggesting that physical limitations that interfere with such maximization necessarily connote illness distorts our customary understanding of that concept.

9   Claims of additive powers of drugs are often exaggerated, based on hearsay, or, at least, unproven. But some drugs, such as anabolic steroids, probably do enhance performance in some individuals. Why should effective additives be proscribed? The simple answer is that they give unfair advantage. There are two problems with this argument.

10   First, even if drugs did enhance performance, that alone would not be a sufficient reason for considering such enhancement unfair. Inequality *per se* is not unfair. Many endogenous and exogenous factors enhance performance without raising such concern. It is not unfair that Kareem Abdul-Jabbar is taller, quicker, and smarter than his opponents on a basketball court, or that Martina Navratilova is stronger and faster on the tennis court. Some of their superiority is earned, the reward for long hours of practice and the willingness to endure pain and other deprivations; but much of it is unearned, the result of unequal genetic endowment. No amount of commitment would enable most athletes to play professional sports. But since this genetic lottery is not the result of human choice, we do not usually consider it immoral, or perhaps even unfair.

11   In some sports, however, unequal genetic endowment is considered unfair. Boxers and wrestlers do not compete against bigger or stronger opponents. Considerable effort is invested in matching opponents by size. Then why not arrange events that reward speed or height so that the slow compete against the slow, the short against the short? The answer lies partly in the financial burden of underwriting fair competition in all areas. The public is not interested in a professional basketball league made up of six-footers. The existence of 150-pound football and separate women's leagues reflects an awareness that fair competition requires approximate matching according to genetic endowment.

12   Questions of unfairness arise more commonly when inequality is the result of conscious human decision, but that alone does not make inequality unfair. Much of Abdul-Jabbar's advantage results from his deliberate effort to gain such an advantage by practicing long hours. We do not consider such deliberate oneupsmanship immoral; it is the essence of fair competition. The challenge is to define the characteristics of unfair advantage. The current campaign to label performance-enhancing or additive drugs as unfair, without explaining why, is a policy without a justification.

13   Even if we were to concede, for the moment, that the use of some performance-enhancing drugs is unfair, there are inconsistencies that

suggest confusion about which additives are permissible and why. Many exogenous "additives" are ingested with the specific intent of improving performance. Special diets, vitamins, fluids, electrolytes, and even placebos are lawfully ingested for the specific intent of improving performance. The distinction between the banned and the permitted is presumably not based on relative efficacy, since there is agreement that some legal substances enhance performance. Since all such substances are chemicals, we need some other basis for distinguishing good from bad.

Nor does it help to distinguish foods from drugs, for the conventional 14 definitions do not do so. The FDA defines a drug as " . . . articles (other than food) intended to affect the structure or any function of the body." Food means "articles used for food," a tautology of no help here.

If the concern for exogenous additives were centered on fairness, we 15 could avoid the problem by making efficacious substances available to all. Legalizing all drugs, or even distributing them free at the training table or at game time, would moot charges of unfairness. Athletes would be free to eschew such aids, just as they are free to avoid training hard, or risking injury through weight-training. However, they could no longer claim their opponents' advantage was unfair.

If the unfairness argument fails, perhaps there is another rational 16 basis for prohibiting certain drugs, or for distinguishing the banned from the permitted. Perhaps the banned list is considered more toxic, but such a paternalistic justification would require considerable argument and would be disingenuous. In many sports, the risk of competing is greater than the risk of taking certain banned substances. We cannot plausibly argue that we prohibit professional football players from using steroids or amphetamines because of concern for their health, when the sport itself permanently disables a high proportion of participants. The number of deaths from boxing, football, or auto racing far exceeds even the speculative harms from presently used drugs. Yet those who are most concerned about the harms of drug use are relatively tolerant of these more dangerous activities.

Even if toxicity from drugs exceeded harm from the sport itself, it 17 would be beside the point. We tolerate the high risk of some sports because spectators and participants enjoy them. We also tolerate death and disability because of the high value we place on autonomy and personal freedom. Whether or not a competent person seeks pleasure or financial gain involving risk is a personal decision. So long as the activity is not imposing burdens involuntarily on others, we reject paternalistic interference with risky behavior. Many jobs and recreational pursuits involve risks, often death, but most people would oppose regulations prohibiting competent persons from weighing those risks and benefits according to their own values.

Sometimes the concern for toxicity shifts from pure paternalism to a 18 claim that world-class athletes are not really free to choose and need protection from a system that forces them to take drugs. According to this view, athletes are required to keep up with competitors' techniques if they want to compete effectively. Calling this situation coercion fails to distinguish between an offer and a threat. Coercion normally refers to situations in which a person will be worse off by failing to act in the suggested way. An example is the person confronted by a robber who demands: "Your money or your life."

19   Athletes confronting the choice of whether to use steroids face an opportunity to be better than they are admittedly at some risk, but with no loss of property, health, or basic rights if they refuse. The worst consequence is that they might fail to gain some extraordinary honor, such as a gold medal or a financial reward. Great opportunities are typically accompanied by extraordinary demands and risks. We would not lament for the athlete who complains he wants to win a gold medal in the discus but doesn't want to endure the risks of weight-lifting, or the swimmer who says she doesn't want the social costs of practicing long hours. Imagine a candidate for professional football who argues he is being coerced into risking knee injury. Such individuals are free to refuse these opportunities and attendant risks with no loss of anything to which they are entitled.

20   It is certainly true, as Thomas Murray points out, that "it is very difficult for athletes to forego using something that they believe improves their competitors' performance" and that "under such pressure, decisions to take performance-enhancing drugs are anything but purely 'individual' choices." However, these difficulties and pressures are inherent in all risk-taking decisions. In trying to define the limits of permissible pressures, Murray concludes: "When . . . to compete successfully (a person) must take potentially grave risks to health, we have as serious a threat to human flourishing as many restrictions on liberty." This, of course, describes the decision to participate in sport as well as the decision to use additive drugs.

21   What, then, is left as a rational basis for opposing additive drugs? The inchoate feeling remains that there is an important distinction between "natural" and "unnatural" assists. Ideally, we want athletic competition to be based on intrinsic qualities, such as speed, strength, endurance, and character. Unnatural chemicals, it is claimed, obscure or diminish the importance of the "real" person. Even a horse race is less interesting if we know that one of the entrants (or all of them) is doped. But this feeling does not explain why many unnatural drugs are on the acceptable list and some natural ones, such as testosterone, are banned. If marijuana enhanced performance, we would not be persuaded to allow it just because it grows in the athlete's garden. Nor do we oppose the use of manufactured vitamins.

22   While the yearning for natural competition is understandable and possibly laudable, it does not explain the present distinctions between banned and permitted drugs. The training techniques and diets used by

athletes are unnatural in many ways, some of which have come to be accepted after initial resistance. The use of a fiberglass pole instead of a bamboo pole by pole-vaulters was initially resisted because of the obvious advantage it gave to those who had it. The response was not to ban it, but to make it available to everyone. This produced a different sport, perhaps less natural than its predecessor, but not one that is inherently immoral.

Some athletes say, "If I lose, I want it to be because my opponent is   23 better than I, not because of some chemicals he took." Consider a special diet, developed by a nutritional scientist, proven to enhance performance. Would we suggest that victories aided by such a diet were corrupt, or that athletes who used such information to enhance their performance were immoral? Would it matter whether the diet used "artificial" food, made in factories and packaged in cans, or "natural" foods, eaten fresh from the farm, with or without chemical fertilizers? Would we establish testing procedures to ensure no athlete used such a diet? The difference between this kind of chemical assistance and drugs is unclear.

There is another sense in which drugs may be considered unnatural;   24 namely, that they distort the nature of the sport. The rules of sport are, of course, not natural but man-made conventions. Many innovations have altered a sport more radically than drugs: the fiberglass vaulting pole, the lively baseball, and the elimination of the center jump after each field goal in basketball. It would be meaningless to talk of these alterations in moral terms. If we were genuinely concerned about changes that distort the nature of football and increase the risk, we might concentrate on the forward pass.

Questions for Discussion and Writing

1. In what sense, according to Fost, are current policies on the use of drugs in sports unclear and ambiguous?

2. By what means does Fost draw a distinction between restorative and additive drugs? What is the essential difference he identifies?

3. What reasons does Fost present to support his claim that inequality is not in itself necessarily unfair in the field of sports?

4. What is Fost's attitude toward this subject? How is this attitude reflected in words and images he uses?

5. To what extent does Fost base his argument on the *premiss* that taking drugs to produce better performances is no worse than taking vitamins or foods for the same purpose and poses no higher health risks? Evaluate these assertions.

6. To what extent does Fost's argument depend on the assumption that the decision to take drugs, like the decision to participate in the sport, should be a matter of free choice?

7. How does Fost's argument revolve around the central issue of the difficulty in distinguishing between drugs needed medically and those that the athlete simply wants to use? Why does he find it ironic that athletes cannot take anything for asthma but might receive drugs for symptoms of narcotic withdrawal?

8. Compare the positions on drug use and the strategies by which Murray and Fost make their respective cases. Who, in your opinion, constructs a better argument? Keep in mind that Murray sees athletes as being coerced into using drugs by the pressure to compete whereas Fost claims that athletes always have free choice about whether or not to use drugs.

Peter Gent

Between the White Lines: The NFL Cocaine War

Peter Gent played for the Dallas Cowboys (1964–1968) and is the author of the 1984 novel North Dallas Forty *(subsequently made into a movie starring Nick Nolte),* The Texas Celebrity Turkey Trot *(1978), and* The Franchise *(1984). "Between the White Lines: The NFL Cocaine War" first appeared in* The Dallas Times Herald Magazine *(September 4, 1983). In it, Gent discusses why football players resort to using drugs and claims that the NFL's attempts to deal with the "cocaine war" is only a cosmetic attempt to manage an "Image Problem."*

In September 1978 as my second book, *Texas Celebrity Turkey Trot,* 1
was reaching the bookstores, *Sport* magazine asked me to write a January cover story on the Dallas Cowboys. America's Team, as usual, was expected to win the Super Bowl. I had to have the story to the magazine by late October because lead time in magazine publishing is often several months. I packed up and left Hays County for Dallas, unaware that simultaneously someone had carried a copy of *TCTT* into the Dallas team plane for their return flight following a West Coast game.

Arriving in Dallas, I called Joe Bailey, then Cowboys assistant general 2
manager, but he never accepted nor returned my call. When I played with the Cowboys, Bailey was the ball boy and seemed like a decent 15-year-old; his father was a prominent Washington, D.C., heart specialist and a fine man. But when the ex-ball boy doesn't return your call, expect trouble.

In *TCTT* there was a short scene that took place in the locker room of 3
the Los Angeles Coliseum. The Coliseum's locker room is divided into semiprivate dressing stalls that are usually shared by two real players or three rookies. The scene in *TCTT* involved the protagonist, Mabry Jenkins, walking into the stall occupied by his two good friends just as they were snorting cocaine from a small bottle with a tiny spoon. When Jenkins shut the door, a gush of air blew the coke off the spoon and all over the floor. It was a slightly funny scene, meant more for humor than social comment.

But on the Cowboy team plane, up in the first-class section where 4
management and the Big Money groupies sit, the intimation of cocaine use raised quite a stir, I was later told. I am not sure whether it was shock

or outrage that the players weren't sharing their coke with the people in first class. Or if it was the mention of cocaine linked with football that caused the fuss. Maybe it was all those "cats" in fur coats seeming to be having so much fun back in the tourist section.

5   Several days after the plane touched down, I was still having no luck reaching anyone in the Cowboy front office. I called *Sport* magazine, and the editor informed me that Cowboy president Tex Schramm had called in a rage saying that they would never cooperate with *Sport* doing any story I wrote. Normally, that would be enough to put me off and send me back to Hays County, to sit on the porch of the Dinner Bell with Sonny the JP and J.C. Burchfield, the barber. But, at this particular time I NEEDED THE MONEY. *TCTT* had earned $3,000, not the $300,000 my agent had estimated, and I had just signed a note for an expensive house.

6   I had to confront Tex in one of his legendary rages. . . . I didn't want to, but I didn't have much choice. You can't just quit; Everson Walls is proof of that.

7   My calls to Bailey proved fruitless, and I was still unable to reach Tex. So I went to the practice field and started looking for a player or players who would talk to me.

8   There weren't many. But because God loves me as he does all major sinners, he sent forth Thomas Henderson. Thomas and I talked and continued the conversation at his locker.

9   At noon, in walked Tex. He worked out every lunch hour at the practice field, and when he saw me with Henderson huddling together and laughing, it must have turned his stomach.

10   "Pete. . . ." Tex walked straight to me. . . . "We better talk in my office right after lunch."

11   "Exactly what time Tex." I pinned him down, knowing that this could easily be a ploy to merely separate two bad boys and then disappear back into the woodwork.

12   "Well . . . I'm . . . going back . . . " Tex always talked extra slow when he was really trying to screw me. He did it on three contracts and a trade to the New York Giants " . . . as soon as . . . I finish my workout . . . I got a short meeting then we . . . can . . . get . . . together."

13   "Fine Tex," I said. "Then I'll just wait here and watch you workout." Remembering the old saw about fatigue and cowardice, I figured to stay right in Tex's face while he wore himself out; I would try and convince him that I was doing it. I followed him into the coaches' dressing room and watched him change clothes, making certain to gaze in wonder at *all* parts of his naked body. These are little tricks you learn after 20 years in this business.

14   I watched his complete workout—the laps, the exercises—and I stood directly over him as he did his bench presses. I talked all the time. It's a nervous habit of mine.

When he quit and returned to the showers, I followed, again staring   15
and gaping and talking. Then, I drove behind him back to the Cowboy
tower on North Central Expressway and waited in the outer office while
he conducted his short meeting.

During that time defensive coach Ernie Stautner saw me, gave me a   16
big handshake and a nice "hello," and invited me to his home for dinner.
It seemed strange and a little overenthusiastic, but I had to eat. So I
accepted.

Then Danny Reeves and Mike Ditka, both now NFL head coaches,   17
came out of an offensive meeting and offered their greetings. While
Stautner had just said hello, Danny and Mike called me by name.

When Stautner heard Reeves and Ditka call my name, he blanched.   18

"Jesus, Pete, I'm sorry," Stautner said, slapping himself on the fore-   19
head, a blow that would have stunned an ox. "I thought you were Dick
Lynch." Nothing more was said about dinner.

Tex finally summoned me into his office, and I saw that he had   20
reworked himself into a rage. But I couldn't figure out why. It was five
years since *North Dallas Forty* had been published, the movie was a year
away from going into release and *Texas Celebrity Turkey Trot* had very
little football in it at all. It mainly was a book about unemployment and
loss of identity.

Tex was mad about *TCTT*. They had been reading sections of it to him   21
on the plane, I learned.

"Pete, I've been in this business a long damn time! . . . " There was   22
no mistaking his tone " . . . and I may not know everything that goes
on, but I'll be goddamned if I have ever been on a football team where
the players were snuffling cocaine."

The National Football League's drug troubles began when the league   23
drove drugs underground. When the NFL denied its own abuses in
dispensing drugs to players, it was only an Image Problem. But it set the
standard of behavior now being reaped in the NFL Cocaine War. The
NFL powers turned their heads, closed their eyes, denied reality, and
their little children grew up to be just like them. Once, NFL Commissioner Pete Rozelle even blamed players' wives for giving them "diet
pills." Every player married a fat woman that year.

Alcohol has always been a problem drug in society, and it is the same   24
in football. Men seek lost self-esteem in the bottom of the bottle.

Only the cocaine bottles are smaller, and the contents more expen-   25
sive. In addition, cocaine suffers from a severe quality-control problem
and worse, puts the user outside of the law.

To live outside the law, one must be honest.   26

The Cowboys' attempts to deal with The Cocaine War are not any   27
more effective nor much different than the rest of the NFL—with the
exception of hiring ex-FBI agent Larry Wansley as security director after

five Cowboys were mentioned in a federal cocaine investigation. Wansley, who describes himself as the "Ultimate Cowboy Fan," says the drug problem is "very critical" and that the "Image Problem is big."

28   Remember, this is not a human problem nor a drug problem nor even a communist conspiracy. It's just another Image Problem.

29   Coach Tom Landry says Wansley was hired because "we are the Dallas Cowboys . . . and because of that people are more likely to notice."

30   Hindsight shows the error of hiring an ex-FBI agent to deal with "image." You can't "deep six" players; some scream when you toss them off the bridge. Besides, the five players mentioned under investigation are damn good football players — Tony Dorsett, Tony Hill, Larry Bethea, Harvey Martin and Ron Springs.

31   Lauiberto Ignacio, who went on trial in early August for allegedly conspiring to import and distribute Brazilian cocaine in the metroplex, claimed that Drug Enforcement Administration agents were trying to make a sensational federal case by using the Dallas Cowboys to attract publicity and do what all bureaucrats do: justify their existence. Having played one mediocre soccer season with the Dallas Tornado and trying out in 1974 with the Cowboys, Ignacio is obviously not as big a catch as the Cowboys. He had subpoenaed Hill and Martin as defense witnesses, although they were never called to testify. He believed they would refute the testimony of his accusers. However, Ignacio was found guilty on six of seven cocaine charges on August 12. He faced a 68 year prison term at his early September sentencing.

32   As an Image Problem, the Cowboys could say this was a case of a kicking caravan gone bad. Now, the Image Problem has become a "distraction."

33   And how does Pete Rozelle react to the NFL's Image Problem? He suspends four league players. His act resembles a general in the French Army executing four men chosen at random from the ranks in an attempt to "boost morale."

34   If anything, the Cowboys' inability to handle cocaine and its big-money dangers for high-profile athletes is pure Pollyanna. I don't believe they really comprehend the size of the abyss they are gazing into. Wondering what's tugging at their shirt sleeves, Tex and Tom stand at the edge of this black hole, this collapsing star, toss in pebbles and listen vainly for the sound of them to hit bottom.

35   Cocaine, from beginning to end, is a big-money criminal enterprise. A dangerous, expensive drug peddled by dangerous people to unsophisticated lower- and middle-class workers (athletes), who suddenly find themselves wealthy and terrified of the fall. The players think coke is an escape from the post-game come down.

36   It is a painful drop from the high of performing, but fall they will at an increasing rate and speed.

37   Drugs and sports go hand in hand. If you don't agree, we are proba-

bly just splitting hairs on definitions of drugs. This is a drug culture, and drugs are a very effective technology.

The body does not heal according to a seven-day schedule. Inside 38 sprains usually take longer to heal and hurt more than outside sprains. There are many treatments and technological techniques for speeding the recovery of a professional athlete. All are keyed to one overriding consideration: How soon can the athlete play again?

Drugs are very effective in returning the injured athlete to action, and 39 I find nothing morally reprehensible in that. The guy's got a job to do, and he wants to do it. As long as his doctor is being honest and treating him to the best of his ability, drugs have a rightful place in sports medicine.

On the other hand, when a team, such as the Cowboys, knowingly 40 misleads kicker Raphael Septien about the extent of his "muscle pull" (actually a hernia) and Danny White, the team's quarterback, admits publicly that were he in Septien's situation, he "wouldn't want to know," I believe it is more than an Image Problem and may have the makings of a serious disaster or a good musical comedy.

We players certainly have no slight comprehension of the great 41 dangers. Bob Lilly understood it well.

"You have to sacrifice your body," Lilly would say. 42

But that didn't mean you had to sacrifice it to the team doctor. Lilly 43 treated himself. He played for years on a knee he taped himself, constantly refusing surgical intervention by eager orthopods. As far as I knew, he took a few aspirin and not much else. He played defensive tackle as well as it has ever been played. He sacrificed his body, but he kept his mind.

So did his roommate George Andrie. 44

In the '60s, when I was with the Cowboys, the trainers would bring 45 your medication to your hotel room the night before the game. Empirin compound for men in pain, amphetamine for men expecting pain, specialty drugs for players with chronic injuries, experimental drugs for those who had little body left to sacrifice, including Butazolidin for joint pain (a drug also used to treat horses) and, of course, sleeping pills.

Lots of guys took sleeping pills. Others drank. The trainers made you 46 promise not to do both.

Andrie, Lilly's roommate, took sleeping pills the night before the 47 game and amphetamine the day of the game. If you have to ask why, I suggest you watch the interior line play closely. Nobody likes to go into The Pit alone.

The trainers brought the pills in small white boxes in carefully mea- 48 sured doses. Andrie was already in bed with the lights out anxious for sleep to bring Sunday and the God-awful war that awaited him on the field.

In the dark, Andrie dug in the box for his sleeping pill and popped 49 the capsule in his mouth washing it quickly down with water, then lay back waiting for blessed rest. It was around 3 or 4 a.m. when he realized that in the darkness, he had knocked down about 15 milligrams of Dexadrine instead of his sleeping pill.

50 This was no great disaster. Although Andrie was a little sleepy at halftime, the slack was made up by the tremendous lift the team got from Lilly's recounting of Andrie's sleepless night.

51 "Bob? . . . Bob, you awake? Jesus . . . I can't sleep . . . Bob? Goddammit Lilly, wake up . . . "

52 *"Cocaine's for horses, not for men*
they say it'll kill you
but they don't say when."

—*Cocaine*
—*By Rev. Gary Davis*

53 In professional football, cocaine is not the only horse medicine used, nor is it the only one that will kill. For example, Butazolidin, which has been used with an almost arrogant and alarming impunity, has been known to cause a potentially deadly condition called aplastic anemia. I took a bushel-basket full of Butazoldin, along with cortisone, and I know it certainly knocks out joint pain. I also know the life expectancy of a professional football player is 55. Maybe that's the reason our pension starts then. The old double nickel.

54 The pharmacological arsenal of exotic-and-varied pills and needles, hormones and narcotics all takes its toll. All have the potential to help or harm.

55 I also learned in my years with the Cowboys—times of semi-obscurity, high four-figure and low five-figure salaries—that my continual stream of "new best friends" attaching themselves like barnacles, were usually there to rip me off for what they could. Then, it was fifths of whiskey and the latest Beach Boys or Janis Joplin album. Now, the stakes are higher, and the rip-off artists are more numerous and thus, according to the principles set down by Darwin, more deadly at taking players off. It is done every day.

56 But what would they do for $40,000 worth of cocaine or the rumor of a $40,000 stash? I saw what they did in '68 for my Beatles white album.

57 These people have refined their techniques and sharpened their knives, but the object is the same: Get the SOB for as much as you can for as long as you can, then break his back so he won't be able to use the phone to call for help or a cheese pizza.

58 Daytrippers.
59 Front Runners.
60 Groupies.

61 They are all there for the same reason: to tear chunks out of the

player and go through his pockets even as he falls, grabbing his watch when he hits the ground and then getting the hell out before he starts to stink and draw a curious crowd.

Players drink with *them*, become friends, lovers, business partners 62 and some even marry *them*. Usually the wife skims for years, nibbling away until D-day. I know one player who married a Daytripper, went home alone for 15 years and didn't even know it until she thought he lost a step and cleaned him out before he lost another.

Enter THE LADY. Cocaine. 63

The Daytripper's latest weapon is an already vast arsenal supple- 64 mented by better intelligence supplied in great quantities by the press, the grapevine and the player himself. Seldom does his or her plan of attack change! A sneak attack on The Ego. Stroke the SOB to the floor or onto the bed. Run the Lady up his nose a few rails at a time, and the old Ego arches and purrs like a kitten rubbing up against anybody's calf. Anybody's. After that, it is a short fast ride on the cocaine train. Even those with sense enough to get off are bruised badly in the jump.

If a Daytripper shows up at a Player's door with a .44 magnum and 65 demands his $40,000 worth of cocaine, the player better have it. Six Janis Joplin records ain't gonna get it. Even if Tony Dorsett autographs them.

Hide a flaw, and the world imagines the worst . . . stitch up a 66 wound with the dirt still in it, and you infect the whole body. Dishonesty breeds dishonesty . . . disabling creates dissemblers.

Today, athletes created for a system that encourages tactile feeling, 67 but discourages intellectual growth, individual thought. Tomorrow. . . .

Adolescents in mink coats snorting houses, cars, families, in the 68 hopeless attempt to keep away the inevitable come down. The end *will come*. It always has. Maybe the Cowboys will end worse than most because they continually, sadly, return to this concern with their IMAGE. "Image" and "Esteem" are not synonyms.

America's Team allegedly has a South American connection, yet the 69 IMAGE is not *machismo*.

Players must respect themselves and their teammates. Where do the 70 Dallas Cowboy players stand on the drug problem? What about other NFL players?

Most are lining up behind National Football League Player's Associa- 71 tion executive director Gene Upshaw, who is waiting his turn behind the Commissioner to mouth some homilies about law and rules and stiffer punishment and urinalysis. I'll urinate in the bottle the day they make all the fans, owners, coaches, and general managers do the same. Urinalysis is just another way of saying, "Are you now? Or have you ever been?"

If the players don't protect each other's rights, who will? 72

Coming from the generation of professional football when wide 73 receivers still used single pencil-bar face masks and the nose was often considered the point of attack, I have had many things run up my nostrils and several that ran back out. In following from a distance the antics of this generation of football player, all of whom hide inside cages of elaborate design, I find the cocaine culture phrase "enjoy the pigeon hole" particularly apt. Make the most of your cage.

74   Cocaine is one way a growing segment of our society is finding escape from the tedium of daily life. And fame and stardom can be just as tedious as anything else. It is, after all, just a job . . . a job with little security . . . yards of hard work . . . no future and no past. It is only The Moment. Today's players seem to be using cocaine to avoid the awful pain of coming down after the tremendous high of game day.

75   Well, if the going up *ain't* worth the coming down, the Indian Rope Trick would offer a better solution than cocaine. Because sooner or later Issac Newton will be proven right again. What goes up must come down . . . the higher they go . . . the longer they stay . . . the harder they fall.

76   The league can send around reformed junkies, alkies and cokeheads to counsel and warn against the dangers of drug dependency and abuse, but until the NFL looks its own monster in the face they are just giving make work to ex-players who can't do anything else but snitch themselves down and look ashamed.

77   It is not a solution, it is delusion . . . illusion. But then professional sports is show business.

78   And there is no business like show business unless you're a general in the Bolivian Air Force flying cocaine into the United States. But not everybody can get that job.

79   *"I took a shot of cocaine and I shot my woman down. I went right home and I went to bed with that .44 smokeless under my head . . . "*

> —*Cocaine Blues*
> —*By T.J. Arnold*

80   I personally see no escape for the current players caught up in the NFL Cocaine War. They'll either be victims, or they'll be scapegoats. Incidently, the Greek word for scapegoat is *Pharmakos*.

81   That the NFL Cocaine War has yet to claim a known victim is one of the small miracles of our time.

82   Don't expect it to last forever.

83   Nothing lasts . . . not even if you are buying it by the kilo.

Questions for Discussion and Writing

1. How did the reactions of Tex Schramm, president of the Dallas Cowboys, reveal to Gent that he had touched a raw nerve in some of the scenes of the novel *Texas Celebrity Turkey Trot?*

2. How is Gent's credibility enhanced by the readers' knowledge that Gent himself formerly played with the Dallas Cowboys and was the author of *North Dallas Forty* (which subsequently was made into a movie starring Nick Nolte and Mac Davis)?

3. What reasons and evidence does Gent produce to support his explanations as to why football players resort to using drugs and why the Cowboys' (as well as the rest of the NFL's) attempts to deal with "The Cocaine War" are largely ineffective?

4. In a short paragraph discuss and evaluate Gent's rationale when he writes "Drugs are very effective in returning the injured athlete to action. . . . As long as his doctor is being honest and treating him to the best of his ability, drugs have a rightful place in sports medicine." Keep in mind that Gent is opposed to the use of drugs only in specific circumstances: what are these?

5. Do you feel Gent is exploiting his past fame as a player with the Dallas Cowboys? Has he betrayed the confidence of his teammates by disclosing behind-the-scenes drug use?

6. How is Gent's argument strengthened by his ability as a novelist to support his argument with realistic re-creations of conversations?

7. Before the start of the 1988 football season, Lawrence Taylor of the Giants was suspended for several weeks because tests detected the presence of cocaine. Discuss this event from any or all of the following perspectives: a fan who has season tickets, a teenager who sees Taylor as a role model, an NFL official, Taylor's family, other members of the Giants whose ability to win games is lessened because of Taylor's absence, and Taylor himself.

8. Analyze Gent's article in relation to the arguments of Murray and of Fost. Who has the best grasp, in your opinion, of the issues involved? Discuss to what extent some of Gent's views align him with either Fost or Murray. Be sure to address the central issue of whether drug use gives an unfair advantage to the user, thereby compelling other athletes to take drugs also.

The Wall Street Journal

High Fliers: Use of Cocaine Grows Among Top Traders in Financial Centers

―――――――

"High Fliers: Use of Cocaine Grows Among Top Traders In Financial Centers" appeared on the front page of The Wall Street Journal *(September 12, 1983). This article draws from real life experiences, case histories, the testimony of psychiatrists, and surveys to document the extent to which cocaine has become a widespread problem in the financial centers of the United States. The staff reporters Stephen J. Sansweet, Thomas Petzinger, Jr., and Gary Putka, claim that those who manage brokerage houses tolerate cocaine abuse so long as the investors remain unaware that their losses may have been caused by the cocaine-clouded judgment of their brokers.*

1   Mike is 28, a bond trader with a major Wall Street firm, and makes more than $100,000 in a good year. He likes his job. He likes cocaine too, off the job and sometimes on it.

2   He claims he isn't addicted to the costly white powder (at least $100 a gram); he just enjoys, he says, the sense of omnipotence it gives him. Mike buys most of his own but occasionally is given a gram or two by brokers who want to keep his friendship—and business.

3   "Sometimes, say when I've just made the company $20,000, I tell myself: You deserve a treat today," Mike says. "It makes me feel mildly indestructible and gives me a shot of energy, sort of like a bull snorting and hoofing the ground ready to attack a matador."

4   Interviews with dozens of users (whose real names aren't given, at their request) and professionals who monitor drug abuse reveal that cocaine use is extensive, accepted and steadily growing in financial centers from coast to coast. Employers in the securities, commodities and financial-services industry either don't want to acknowledge the problem, possibly out of fear that public trust in their employees' judgments will be damaged, or try to minimize it. But it is clear that the increasing use of the drug is exacting a price.

Wrecked Careers

Some of the brokers, dealers, traders, lawyers and executives snorting   5
it—most of them young males with high-pressure jobs and high incomes to match—are making costly mistakes in business judgment.
Sometimes they end up wrecking promising careers. Sometimes they end
up dead.

Like Timothy Anderson, a whiz at trading Treasury bond futures in   6
Chicago for Donaldson, Lufkin & Jenrette Securities Corp. He left the
firm early last December to become an independent order-filler at the
Chicago Board of Trade, and seemed to be doing well. But on Jan. 14 Mr.
Anderson died from "acute cocaine toxicity," according to the Cook
County medical examiner. Mr. Anderson was 26.

Cocaine first became the drug of choice in the financial community in   7
the middle to late 1970s. Some users and others believe its use was
declining—or was less visible—until the 1982–1983 bull market. With
volume up and the market climbing, there has been a lot more money
around (along with increased stress and tension) and thousands of new,
young brokers and dealers to spend it.

Surveys on Wall Street

"There isn't any question that cocaine use is spreading even among   8
more conservative and corporate types," says Douglas S. Lipton, deputy
director for research and evaluation of the New York State Division of
Substance Abuse Services. His office has done street checks and surveys
that indicate a high degree of cocaine use among white-collar workers on
Wall Street.

"We're talking about the core of the financial structure of this coun-   9
try," Mr. Lipton says. "But the banks and brokerage houses close their
eyes to the problem and are loath to share information even informally
because of the vast amounts of public money being invested and the real
fear that any publicity would undermine confidence. Would you invest
your money if you knew your broker was stoned more than half the
time?"

Peter, the head of corporate finance at one New York securities firm,   10
says, "Every trading desk on Wall Street is full of cocaine." Peter himself
spent nine weeks at an expensive New York clinic to kick his $1,500-a-
week habit. Prior to treatment, his typical day started with an early-
morning snort to get going, frequent use during the day to keep up his
energy and "social" use in the evening, usually while entertaining
clients.

Misplaced Confidence

11   "There's a lot of pressure in carrying big stock positions, and I wasn't a disciplined guy," says Peter, who really wasn't aware that cocaine had begun to fog his trading decisions. "The market could go down 15 points in one day, and I'd be out a million dollars. Yet I was still confident that I was doing the right thing, losses or no losses."

12   In Chicago, cocaine use is spreading in the city's commodities trading and financial centers. "A few people take a toot before the trading session and maybe a few times during the day," says one member of the Chicago Board of Trade, himself a user. "It's like drinking coffee." He estimates that 10% of the traders and brokers he knows use cocaine on the job.

13   Several Chicago-area psychiatrists specializing in drug abuse say that cocaine now trails only alcohol as an addictive substance and that securities professionals account for a significant portion of their practices. In New York, psychiatrist Richard Resnick adds: "I'm seeing more and more businessmen, particularly stockbrokers."

14   At the Lutheran Center for Substance Abuse in Park Ridge, Ill., the steady admission of traders and brokers enables medical director Donald W. Sellers to assemble a profile of a typical securities professional with a cocaine problem. He says nearly all are male, married, 30 to 45, and "very energetic, very imaginative and very intelligent . . . highly ambitious, competitive and self-confident."

15   (Cocaine isn't the only problem. In addition to alcohol and marijuana, users often take coke in combination with other illicit drugs, including Quaaludes, amphetamines and barbiturates. Heroin also seems to be taking hold in the financial community. "They get too frenzied and hyper if they don't cut cocaine with a sedative, and heroin appears to be the sedative of choice," says one researcher.)

16   Cocaine is a powerful energizer, and users describe a "rush" of sensory arousal that lasts for about 10 to 30 minutes, as well as a feeling of Herculean stamina and a surge of self-assuredness. While the drug isn't physically addicting like heroin and other opium derivatives, it can quickly become psychologically addicting, a crutch.

'It's Showtime'

17   "You go to war every day in this business," says Richard, a former brokerage-house officer and reformed cocaine user who has a background in stocks, options and commodities. For him, cocaine was strength. "You do a line (of cocaine) and you think, 'It's showtime! I'm ready, fans!'" he says.

18   Samuel, an ex-user who worked for a half-dozen West Coast brokerage firms in less than a decade, says cocaine was widely used at each.

While it initially seemed to help him and others think more clearly, says Samuel, before long more and more was needed to achieve the same effect—and occasional use turned into compulsive habit. That habit can eventually ruin the addict's career and his life.

"I have seen 20 guys blow themselves out of this business because of   19 cocaine," says the head of a small New York brokerage firm. Several West Coast users concede that snorting cocaine until 3 or 4 in the morning means that they are in no shape to get up at 5 to be at their desks in time for the New York market openings.

Strange Allergies

Paul, a 41-year-old former partner in a risk arbitrage firm, sought   20 help a few years ago when his cocaine-centered drug habit was costing him about $2,500 a week. "Money wasn't ever a problem," he says. "But I began missing about two days of work a week, telling everyone I had a lot of allergies. That was easy, with all the sneezing I was doing."

Paul says he lost "millions" for his firm because of his drug-clouded   21 judgment, part of it in last year's takeover battle for Marathon Oil Co. by U.S. Steel Corp. (Arbitragers buy and sell securities in different markets to take advantage of small differences in prices, and takeover fights can generate tidy profits for them.) "I set up a lot of funny strategies with put and call options, and they became pretty hard to unwind," he adds.

Paul dropped out of the securities business before he was ruined   22 financially, but he has been suffering from unstoppable weight loss and rising blood pressure. There was a painful separation from his wife, and he isn't sure he has permanently controlled his cocaine habit.

Rash Decisions

Under the influence of the drug, brokers and traders may make rash   23 decisions and refuse to alter them because they cannot believe they could be wrong. "When a position goes against you, you may double your exposure rather than get out of the market," says Frank, a professional trader in Chicago who speculates for his own account. Good money chasing after bad recently cost another trader $8,500 in 15 minutes. "Adding to a losing trade violates the No. 1 rule of trading," this man says, "but I was real coked up."

The habitual, heavy user may eventually descend into the paranoia   24 called cocaine psychosis. The characteristic gregariousness of a trader, for example, often turns to suspicion and isolation. The once-manageable expense of his habit balloons out of control.

Jack, a former brokerage official who is currently undergoing psycho-   25 therapy to help him stay off cocaine, alcohol and other drugs, was consuming a quarter-ounce of cocaine daily—about $500 worth. Indebted to his supplier, he collateralized his exchange membership to get a bank loan and lost the seat when the bank foreclosed.

26   There are lots of people like Jack, but it doesn't seem to matter. Cocaine is in. "It's a calling card, a way of saying, 'I'm cool, I'm hip, I'm successful,'" says a broker. It is used at Christmas parties from brokerage firms with a view of the Battery to those with a view of the San Francisco Bay. In Chicago, traders use the edges of their plastic identification badges to chop up "lines" of cocaine on the tops of toilet-paper dispensers in exchange bathrooms. Others use rolled-up dollar bills or hollowed-out Bic pens. And some snort it right on the exchange floor through nasal inhalers that don't hold medicine.

27   Cocaine has become a medium of exchange itself, as good as and sometimes better than cash. Business inducements—sometimes outright bribes—are given in the form of cocaine. In Chicago, a financial futures trader tells of commodity executives who use cocaine to entice business from New York–based institutional portfolio managers. In New York, a puckish bond trader says he wants to set up an independent company to cater to trader's whims. He would call it "Limos, Bimbos & Lines," providing, as he claims securities firms do informally, a limousine, a woman in a hotel room, and cocaine for customers.

28   Sometimes the coke passes in the opposite direction, from traders to securities dealers. "I have seen people get discounts on commissions through a passing of the bindle" (a folded piece of paper containing cocaine), says a former West Coast broker.

Industry's Indifference

29   For the most part, the reaction of the securities industry to growing drug abuse seems to range from indifference to ostrichlike denial. There are exceptions, such as the Los Angeles securities firm that recently called in undercover police to catch a suspected cocaine user-dealer among its brokers, but mostly the industry doesn't want to know what's happening or pooh-poohs the extent of cocaine abuse—at least publicly.

30   Four years ago the Chicago Board Options Exchange, the nation's largest stock-option marketplace, expressed anger at law enforcers when 30 federal agents arrested 10 suspected cocaine dealers on the trading floor as television crews filmed the action. Subsequent arrests by Chicago police of dealers from the CBOE and other exchanges have occurred away from the trading floors in a cooperative attempt to minimize bad publicity that could chase business away.

31   At the Chicago Board of Trade, the world's largest commodity exchange, Executive Vice President George Sladoje says, "We don't feel we have a problem." Anyone using cocaine at the exchange, he says, is a low-level clerical employee. But interviews with users make it clear that

the cocaine trade flourishes among professionals even on the exchange floors, with dealing a profitable sideline for some clerks and runners who deliver orders and messages. Buying cocaine is "like ordering a pizza," says a financial futures trader. Chicago police agree. A recent undercover investigator at a major exchange was able to make a cocaine connection on his first day.

Attention on Clerks

New York's largest securities firms deny in chorus that drug use is a major problem. The New York Stock Exchange has fired several employees in the past year because of on-the-job drug use, but a spokesman maintains that cocaine abuse there isn't any greater than in society at large. American Stock Exchange officials agree, although the Amex has taken steps to prevent drug use on the trading floor. And the Securities Industry Association, the largest trade group, is sponsoring a drug-abuse and -prevention seminar next month — but says the program is mainly a response to growing drug use among *clerical* employees.   32

Kingsley Barham, a former broker and reformed cocaine abuser, says the securities industry is deluding itself if it thinks the problem either is negligible or only affects lower-level employees. "They talk about a 'Know Your Client' rule, but they don't know their own brokers," he says. "In a sense, that protects the firms and exchanges, but it perpetuates the cocaine abuse; they would rather discharge a broker than try to salvage him."   33

Mr. Barham recently organized a basketball marathon in San Francisco as a way to raise both money and public awareness about cocaine abuse. But the event lost money, mainly because the expected support from the securities industry and other businesses never materialized. Undaunted, Mr. Barham says he will try again next year.   34

Questions for Discussion and Writing

1. In what respects does the attitude of executives in the securities, commodities, and financial services industry bear a striking resemblance to the reaction of owners of NFL teams toward athletes who use cocaine? To investigate these parallels, you might consider under what conditions cocaine use is tolerated. Once the widespread existence of drug use is disclosed to the general public, how does management react?

2. How do the writers use examples drawn from real life and case histories to provide effective insights into the widespread problem of

cocaine use? Does the fact that some interviews protect the identity of the individual being quoted lessen the credibility of the information?

3. How do the staff reporters use the testimony of psychiatrists in developing their argument?

4. How do the staff reporters use statistics to document the extent of the problem of cocaine use on Wall Street?

5. Based on the case histories presented, what are the reasons that cocaine use is growing among the top traders in financial centers?

6. How does the discussion of the extent to which cocaine itself has become a "medium of exchange" enable you to understand why drugs have become as important as money?

7. Which do you find more disturbing; the widespread use of drugs by sports figures or drug use by financiers on Wall Street? Explain your reaction.

Dollars & Sense

White Lines, Bottom Lines: Profile of a Mature Industry

"White Lines, Bottom Lines: Profile of a Mature Industry" appeared as an editorial in Dollars and Sense *(December 1986). The editors offer a wide range of statistical evidence to support their argument that there is little chance to curtail the supply side of cocaine production because the economies of Bolivia, Peru, and Colombia are dependent on the billions of dollars produced by this cash crop. They argue that the government policies designed to deal with the demand side of the drug problem have also proved to be largely ineffective.*

The media recently have focused a great deal of attention on a small 1
but rapidly growing industry, one dominated by a few foreign-based multinationals. This industry's sales in the United States have grown at an impressive rate, with shipments up by 325% between 1976 and 1984, despite U.S. government attempts to establish a strict quota on imports. Yearly retail sales in the business are estimated at $40 billion.

The industry's goods are particularly popular with the 18-to-25-year- 2
old crowd: one person in six in this age group used them last year. However, the U.S. market for the products appears to be nearing saturation. U.S. market prices for the products have been falling since 1982. As a result, firms in the industry are trying out new products and searching for new markets.

The industry, in case you haven't guessed, is cocaine. Like any big 3
business, the cocaine industry follows certain economic principles. A Miami attorney told *The Wall Street Journal*, "more than any other business I know, the drug business is pure capitalism, pure supply and demand."

Successful Multinational

Most cocaine is grown from coca plants, then refined in Bolivia, 4
Colombia, and Peru. These countries are economically dependent on the cocaine industry, one which Peru's President Alan Farcia calls Latin America's "only successful multinational." However, the bulk of the profits from the industry never reaches these countries. American supplier countries to the coca plant and its chemical derivatives could be

called "supply-side dependency." Cocaine proceeds are estimated to account for one-quarter of Bolivia's gross national product, exceeding legal exports by $200 million or more. The cocaine industry employs as many as 100,000 Bolivians.

5   While Bolivia is an extreme case, Peru and Colombia are also "hooked." The drug trade brings $800 million annually into Peru — twice as much as copper exports. Colombia gains $600 million to $1 billion a year from cocaine exports.

6   That is not to say that these Latin American countries are getting rich. Cocaine follows a lengthy route from grower to consumer. Of the $75 street price of a gram of cocaine, about $60 goes to U.S. wholesalers and retailers. Only $2 per gram actually ends up in the hands of Latin American peasants and employees. Most of the remaining $13 earned by the Latin American cocaine entrepreneurs goes to foreign banks for laundering and safekeeping. One estimate is that Colombia's $1 billion in cocaine revenues is the result of trade worth $30 billion.

7   Meanwhile, these countries have experienced falling prices for other commodities, wiping out jobs. For example, Bolivia's revenues from tin and natural gas fell 70% in 1985 alone, and the Bolivian government has proposed sharply cutting back on employment in the tin mines.

8   At the base of the cocaine-production pyramid, the peasants and workers face few alternative sources of income. Even the $2 or less (per gram of cocaine) that peasants can earn represents much more than they can make otherwise. A peasant woman in the coca-growing region of Bolivia told the *New York Times* that her family earned ten times as much growing coca as they had earned with other crops. She added, "We couldn't live if it wasn't for the coca."

9   While U.S. crop-substitution programs offer Bolivian peasants $140 an acre to cultivate other crops, they can earn $2,000 to $4,000 an acre from coca. Sometimes U.S. trade and aid policies even spur drug production, as in Belize where cuts in U.S. sugar import quotas have turned a sugar-producing area into a marijuana-producing zone.

10   In addition to employment and earnings, a number of other threads tie Latin American countries to cocaine production. Foreigners' demand for pesos with which to buy cocaine keeps the value of the local currency up. When the Bolivian army launched its first raid into coca territory in 1984, the black market value of the peso dropped by two-thirds.

11   Cocaine serves political purposes, too. Producers use their wealth to win — or at least buy off — allies. With monthly salaries for police officers in Bolivia running as low as $25, buying complicity from the local police is not difficult. And some of the cocaine producers — such as reputed Colombian kingpin Pablo Escobar, who funded a slum redevelopment program — have won a reputation as "Robin Hoods." Finally, the *narcotraficantes* have their own armies, and can use the threat of assassination to pressure government officials.

Across the Border

According to the National Institute on Drug Abuse (NIDA, a division   12
of the National Institutes of Health), over 20 million Americans have
tried cocaine. But this fact alone does not constitute a "drug crisis."

Cocaine-related deaths, such as those of actor John Belushi and   13
college basketball great Len Bias, have helped to propel cocaine into the
headlines. But the 613 deaths due to cocaine last year pale in comparison
to the 100,000 deaths due to alcohol (over 30 times the amount attributed to all illegal drugs taken together) and to the 350,000 deaths blamed
on tobacco.

While cocaine use increased dramatically in the late 1970s, the per-   14
centage of the U.S. population who report using cocaine in the past year
has remained roughly fixed since then. In fact, use of other illegal drugs
is holding steady or declining, creating an overall *decline* in the rate of
illicit drug use.

Cocaine is highly addictive. The National Narcotics Intelligence Con-   15
sumers Commission estimated in 1981 that 6% of U.S. cocaine users
consumed 60% of the cocaine, using cocaine an average of 234 times a
year. The demand for cocaine appears to be relatively inelastic—that is,
cocaine use is unresponsive to changes in price. Heavy users would
presumably pay almost anything to keep obtaining the drug.

Despite this inelastic demand, the street price of cocaine has been   16
falling. Cocaine prices are currently almost 40% below their peak in
1982. All evidence points to a glut of cocaine on the U.S. market: supply
has outrun demand. Cocaine has become a "mature industry."

In response, the cocaine industry has begun to diversify and expand.   17
One of the new products is crack—cocaine in solid, smokable form.
Arnold Washton, a psychopharmacologist at Fair Oaks Hospital in New
Jersey, told *Newsweek*, "Crack itself is a marketing effort. Like fast food,
it's a quick-sale product. [Because] it transforms the occasional user into
an addictive user, it is much more likely to yield a repeat customer."
Crack dealers are reaching out to a youth market, with prices of $10 to
$15 per dose.

Enter the Feds

In theory, government policies to reduce drug use could target either   18
the supply- or demand-side of the cocaine market. So far, the Reagan
administration's policies have focused primarily on the supply-side. But
when demand is inelastic, decreasing the supply can be expected simply
to drive prices up, attracting new suppliers into the market without
significantly reducing the quantity consumed. Examination of the results

of three supply-side policies—interdiction, eradication, and enforcement—confirms this expectation.

19   Interdiction—stopping drugs at a country's borders—has been somewhat effective at stopping marijuana imports, resulting in a shift to domestic cultivation of cannabis. A second result of interdiction efforts has been to lead smugglers to switch their operations from marijuana to cocaine, a substance which is less bulky, easier to conceal, and which brings a much higher price per ounce with little difference in the legal penalties for getting caught. A third outcome of the federal government's focus on interdiction has led cocaine importers in south Florida to move to supply routes across the Mexican border. The federal Drug Enforcement Agency claims that interdiction captures about a quarter of the cocaine entering the United States, but this figure is probably inflated.

20   Eradication involves ending the cultivation and refinement of drugs in their source countries. Again, there is a "success" story: during the 1970s, under U.S. pressure, Mexico wiped out much of its marijuana and heroin crops. But as a result, Colombia simply took Mexico's place in the marijuana business, and opened up the cocaine market to Colombian producers as well.

21   The recent raids on Bolivian cocaine refineries by Bolivian and U.S. troops have been fiascos. Understandably, not everyone in the Bolivian government and the armed forces supported the elimination of Bolivia's major export, and leaks allowed drug producers to clear out before the strike forces arrived. One effect of the raids has been to establish a precedent for intervention by U.S. armed forces, and many Bolivians are angered by them. When over 100 Bolivian and American drug agents raided the town of Santa Ana in October 1985, 3,000 of the town's 5,000 people rushed to the town square, rallied by the ringing of church bells. Shouting "Kill the Yankees," they surrounded the agents and chased them out of town.

22   Even if the cocaine business was driven out of Bolivia, Colombia, and Peru, there are plenty of other poor Latin American and Caribbean countries that would be hard put to refuse the dollars that the industry brings. Already, coca cultivation is spreading to Brazil, Ecuador, and Venezuela.

23   A final supply-side strategy is law enforcement—jailing drug dealers. Despite the clamor made by the President and Congress about imposing harsh sentences and even the death penalty for dealers, this strategy is unlikely to make much of a dent in the cocaine trade. Overworked police departments, clogged courts, and overcrowded prisons simply can't accommodate large numbers of dealers—except by letting other crimes go. And street-level dealers (the ones who get caught) are easily replaced. The most likely consequence of stepped-up enforcement is increased repression in poor communities, without much decrease in the flow of drugs.

24   What about government intervention on the demand side? Two key

elements of a strategy to cut demand for cocaine would have to be drug treatment programs (to help heavy users) and preventive education. The Reagan administration has substantially cut funding for both. The Department of Education's drug education budget fell from $14 million in 1981 to less than $3 million in 1985. Reagan has proposed allotting an additional $100 million for drug treatment programs, but advocates for these programs point out that this "addition" would only bring their funding back up to 1980 levels.

Instead of these programs, the administration has made "voluntary" 25 drug testing and Nancy Reagan's "Just Say No" clubs the real center pieces of its demand-side strategy. The clubs have about 200,000 high school age members, but nobody knows just how many of them are actually saying "no" outside the club meetings.

The drug tests introduce a new level of surveillance without much 26 promise of eliminating drug use. Inexpensive versions of the urine test have a 20% rate of "false positives" — test results that falsely show drug use. And without access to treatment programs, people "caught" using cocaine may be more likely to lose their jobs than to quit the drug.

In short, the Reagan administration's strategy for the "war on drugs" 27 is more repression: repression in the producer countries of Latin America, on the borders, in the streets, and in the workplaces. But between supply-side dependency and inelastic demand, this strategy is unlikely to reduce drug use.

Up in Smoke

The NIDA claims that a larger proportion of young people use illegal 28 drugs in the United States than in any other industrialized country. Why do so many people turn to illegal drugs? Certainly part of the reason is that our culture condones and, even glorifies, the use of other (legal) addictive substances such as alcohol, nicotine, and caffeine.

Another reason is that drugs are a distraction from the tedium and 29 alienation of jobs, schools, and living environments. "I don't know if you've had the opportunity to stand in a pit and turn a screwdriver over your head hour after hour, but I have," Dr. Douglas Talbott, president of the American Academy of Additionology, commented to *Newsweek*. "It's almost like torture. These people bring mind-altering drugs to ease the boredom, the tension, and the stress of doing their job." Dr. Wesley Westman, head of the alcohol and drug dependency center at the Miami Veteran Administration hospital was quoted in *Time* as saying that "Cocaine is the drug of choice by people who are into the American dream —'I love my job, I am successful'—except that they don't and they're not." And in the inner city, especially among low-income people of color, the wide-spread use of crack means that the drug has evolved into much more than a suburbanite fix: It is helping to destroy the social fabric of these communities.

30   But the leaders of the crusade against illegal drug use seem oblivious to these issues. Like the U.S. government's "war on poverty," the "war on drugs" is a determined assault on a set of symptoms, combined with an equally determined disregard for its underlying causes.

Questions for Discussion and Writing

1. What statistical evidence do the editors offer to support their assertion that Bolivia, Peru, and Colombia are "hooked" because of their economic dependency on coca crops?

2. What explanation do the editors offer for the emergence of crack?

3. What reasons, evidence, and examples do the editors present to support their assertion that attacking the supply-side policies (interdiction, eradication, and enforcement) has been largely ineffective?

4. To what extent does the editors' argument depend on the assumptions that (*a*) the governments of drug-producing countries are corrupt, and (*b*) the local populations do not object to growing coca for cocaine?

5. Why, according to the editors, have government policies designed to deal with the demand side also proved to be useless?

6. Evaluate the editors' conclusions (in the section titled "Up in Smoke") about why "so many people turn to illegal drugs." What different kinds of explanations do they offer? Which appears to be the most persuasive explanation and which the least in explaining the widespread use of drugs?

7. How does the editors' detailed analysis of the supply and demand side of drug use enhance your understanding of the role played by drugs in society? To what extent does the editors' analysis complement or provide a context for understanding the arguments of any of the other writers in this chapter? For example, what in the editors' analysis clarifies what Gent says about drug use in the NFL, or what *The Wall Street Journal* reports about drugs on Wall Street?

8. In a short essay, evaluate how well the editors support their argument with specific quotations from authorities and how effectively they use facts and figures to build their case. Did they convince you

that cocaine use would remain a serious problem no matter what the government tries to do?

9. What recent events reported on the news did this argument enable you to understand better? In a short essay, discuss the content of the news report (for example, President Bush's September 1989 speech proclaiming a war on drugs, interception of drug shipments, arrests of drug dealers, debates over whether the military should be used to control drug trafficking, international political ramifications of other governments that sanction exporting drugs) and how this article helped you to better understand it.

10

Media: Is the Medium Really the Message?

Today's society depends so heavily on the flow of information that the mass media's impact on our society has often been taken for granted. Critics decry the fact that the media have become so influential and have gone far beyond the mere communication of information to the actual shaping of beliefs and attitudes. The "medium" has indeed, in Marshall McLuhan's famous phrase, "become the message." To place the issue in perspective, this chapter begins with an essay written by Joseph Addison in 1710 for *The Tatler* wherein he describes how the addiction to news of royalty and the heads of state led a man to neglect the welfare of his "own family" and "nearest relations." Addison would no doubt recognize in today's radio and television talk shows or in "Lifestyles of the Rich and Famous" the electronic equivalent of eighteenth-century coffeehouse discussions of princes and monarchs.

The impact of the media on American culture is a rich source of argument on a broad range of issues. One area that has been recently under public scrutiny has been the phenomenon of "media ministries." In part this is due to the shenanigans of Jim Bakker and his wife Tammy, the doleful laments of Jimmy Swaggart, and the umbrage taken by Pat Robertson at Tom Brokaw's comment during Robertson's run for the presidency in 1988 that Robertson was a former "television evangelist" (he said he wished to be called a "religious broadcaster"). But, as one commentator makes clear, long before television, radio evangelists pioneered a wide range of marketing strategies and psychological techniques to maintain profitable "media ministries."

Although perhaps less obvious than in the case of religious broadcasts, the media not only entertain and inform the public but influence social change by highlighting some issues and downplaying others, making some political candidates and destroying others. For example, television not only provides information but sells products and shapes attitudes for millions of adults and children. Some researchers question the extent to which television presents an accurate picture of the real world and believe it reinforces stereotypical attitudes toward women, minorities, and the elderly and projects a grossly distorted picture of American society. Representatives of organizations like Action for Children's Television (ACT) cite studies to support their claim that young children, especially, cannot distinguish reality from television fantasy and are consistently fooled by deceptive product claims. These critics advocate that the First Amendment guarantee of freedom of speech and press that applies to all forms of expression, including television, should be suspended when it comes to advertising directed toward children under the age of eight. Opponents of the ACT's proposed censorship also protest the insertion of "pro-social" behavior management messages in programming for children. They make the case that traditional stories and fairy tales give children the chance to develop inner resources in dealing with evil; by contrast, pro-social or "pro-child" programming teaches that the group will rescue the individual.

Aside from First Amendment issues, the central issue at the heart of most debates regarding the media concerns the question of how powerful television is in influencing attitudes, values, and behavior. Some writers contend that an increase in teenage suicides and pregnancies can be directly tied in to violence and sadomasochism featured in rock videos. Others dispute this claim on the grounds that innovations in music have been attacked as subversive to morality for centuries and assert that the negative effects of rock music and rock videos have been greatly exaggerated.

The arguments in this chapter will help you address basic questions as to whether television has an unsuspected damaging effect on the viewing public, whether the government should step in to regulate advertising for children, and whether the violence and sex depicted by rock videos should be protected by First Amendment guarantees.

Joseph Addison

The Political Upholsterer

Joseph Addison was one of the most brilliant literary figures of the eighteenth century. With his journalistic partner, Richard Steele, he created The Tatler *(1709–1710) and* The Spectator *(1711–1712, 1714), among other publications. He also had a distinguished career as a diplomat, member of Parliament, and secretary of state. He is best known today for his sparkling and perceptive essays. "The Political Upholsterer" first appeared in* The Tatler *(Thursday, April 6, 1710). This still-pertinent essay depicts the irony and pathos of people who live vicariously through coffeehouse discussions of the latest news about heads of state while they fail to concern themselves with the welfare of their own families. Addison would doubtless discern today's talk shows on radio and television as the electronic versions of "three or four very odd fellows sitting together upon the bench."*

1   There lived some years since within my neighbourhood a very grave person, an Upholsterer, who seemed a man of more than ordinary application to business. He was a very early riser, and was often abroad two or three hours before any of his neighbours. He had a particular carefulness in the knitting of his brows, and a kind of impatience in all his motions, that plainly discovered he was always intent on matters of importance. Upon my enquiry into his life and conversation, I found him to be the greatest newsmonger in our quarter; that he rose before day to read the Postman; and that he would take two or three turns to the other end of the town before his neighbours were up, to see if there were any Dutch mails come in. He had a wife and several children; but was much more inquisitive to know what passed in Poland than in his own family, and was in greater pain and anxiety of mind for King Augustus's welfare than that of his nearest relations. He looked extremely thin in a dearth of news, and never enjoyed himself in a westerly wind. This indefatigable kind of life was the ruin of his shop; for about the time that his favourite prince left the crown of Poland, he broke and disappeared.

2   This man and his affairs had been long out of my mind, till about three days ago, as I was walking in St. James's Park, I heard somebody at a distance hemming after me: and who should it be but my old neighbour the Upholsterer? I saw he was reduced to extreme poverty, by certain shabby superfluities in his dress; for notwithstanding that it was a very sultry day for the time of the year, he wore a loose greatcoat and a

muff, with a long campaign wig out of curl; to which he had added the ornament out of a pair of black garters buckled under the knee. Upon his coming up to me, I was going to enquire into his present circumstances; but was prevented by his asking me, with a whisper, Whether the last letters brought any accounts that one might rely upon from Bender? I told him, None that I heard of; and asked him, whether he had yet married his eldest daughter? He told me, No. 'But pray,' says he, 'tell me sincerely, what are your thoughts of the King of Sweden'? For though his wife and children were starving, I found his chief concern at present was for this great monarch. I told him, that I looked upon him as one of the first heroes of the age. 'But pray,' says he, 'do you think there is any thing in the story of his wound'? And finding me surprized at the question — 'Nay,' says he, 'I only propose it to you.' I answered, that I thought there was no reason to doubt of it. 'But why in the heel,' says he, 'more than any other part of the body'? — 'Because,' said I, 'the bullet chanced to light there.'

This extraordinary dialogue was no sooner ended, but he began to   3
launch out into a long dissertation upon the affairs of the North; and after having spent some time on them, he told me he was in great perplexity how to reconcile the Supplement with the English Post, and had been just now examining what the other papers say upon the same subject. 'The Daily Courant,' says he, 'has these words; "We have advices from very good hands, that a certain prince has some matters of great importance under consideration." This is very mysterious; but the Post-boy leaves us more in the dark, for he tells us "That there are private intimations of measures taken by a certain prince, which time will bring to light." Now the Postman,' says he, 'who used to be very clear, refers to the same news in these words: "The late conduct of a certain prince affords great matter of speculation." This certain prince, says the Upholsterer, 'whom they are all so cautious of naming, I take to be ———.' Upon which, though there was nobody near us, he whispered something in my ear, which I did not hear, or think worth my while to make him repeat.

We were now got to the upper end of the Mall, where were three or   4
four very odd fellows sitting together upon the bench. These I found were all of them politicians, who used to sun themselves in that place every day about dinner-time. Observing them to be curiosities in their kind, and my friend's acquaintance, I sat down among them.

The chief politician of the bench was a great asserter of paradoxes. He   5
told us, with a seeming concern, That by some news he had lately read from Muscovy, it appeared to him that there was a storm gathering in the Black Sea, which might in time do hurt to the naval forces of this nation. To this he added, That for his part, he could not wish to see the Turk driven out of Europe, which he believed could not but be prejudicial to our woollen manufacture. He then told us, That he looked upon those extraordinary revolutions which had lately happened in those parts of

the world, to have risen chiefly from two persons who were not much talked of; 'And those,' says he, 'are Prince Menzikoff, and the Duchess of Mirandola.' He backed his assertions with so many broken hints, and such a show of depth and wisdom, that we gave ourselves up to his opinions.

6   The discourse at length fell upon a point which seldom escapes a knot of true-born Englishmen. Whether, in case of a religious war, the Protestants would not be too strong for the Papists? This we unanimously determined on the Protestant side. One who sat on my right hand, and, as I found by his discourse, had been in the West Indies, assured us, That it would be a very easy matter for the Protestants to bear the Pope at sea; and added, That whenever such a war does break out, it must turn to the good the Leeward Islands. Upon this, one who sat at the end of the bench, and, as I afterwards found, was the geographer of the company, said, that in case the Papists should drive the Protestants from these parts of Europe, when the worst came to the worst, it would be impossible to beat them out of Norway and Greenland, provided the Northern crowns hold together, and the Czar of Muscovy stand neuter. He further told us, for our comfort, that there were vast tracts of land about the Pole, inhabited neither by Protestants nor Papists, and of greater extent than all the Roman Catholic dominions in Europe.

7   When we had fully discussed this point, my friend the Upholsterer began to exert himself upon the present negotiations of peace; in which he deposed princes, settled the bounds of kingdoms, and balanced the power of Europe, with great justice and impartiality.

8   I at length took my leave of the company, and was going away; but had not gone thirty yards, before the Upholsterer hemmed again after me. Upon his advancing towards me, with a whisper, I expected to hear some secret piece of news, which he had not thought fit to communicate to the bench; but instead of that, he desired me in my ear to lend him half a crown. In compassion to so needy a statesman, and to dissipate the confusion I found he was in, I told him, if he pleased, I would give him five shillings, to receive five pounds of him when the Great Turk was driven out of Constantinople; which he very readily accepted, but not before he had laid down to me the impossibility of such an event, as the affairs of Europe now stand.

9   This paper I design for the particular benefit of those worthy citizens who live more in a coffee-house than in their shops, and whose thoughts are so taken up with the affairs of the Allies, that they forget their customers.

Questions for Discussion and Writing

1. Describe the nature of the Upholsterer's addiction to keeping up with the latest news. What effects does this have on his family? Why is it ironic that a person with his troubles should fail to concern

himself with the welfare of his "own family" and "nearest relations" and think only of the comings and goings of world leaders?

2. How do the increasingly distressed circumstances in which Addison encounters the Upholsterer make his continuing obsession with news concerning monarchs and heads of state all the more pathetic?

3. In what way does Addison's encounter with "three or four very odd fellows sitting together upon the bench" emphasize the idea that the Upholsterer's predisposition to live vicariously through the news is a pervading malady that has afflicted many people?

4. How does Addison use the contrast between the Upholsterer's powerlessness to improve his own life or the condition of his family with the sweeping rearrangements of political and military alliances that the Upholsterer constantly discusses? For example, right after the Upholsterer "deposed princes, settled the bounds of kingdoms, and balanced the power of Europe, with great justice and impartiality" he whispered to Addison "to lend him half a crown."

5. In an essay, discuss your responses to Addison's essay as it applies to present-day manifestations of the same phenomenon. Some illustrations might include (*a*) fans who follow the activities of movie celebrities, rock stars, and sports figures and live vicariously through these figures or imagine a relationship between themselves and these people where none exists, (*b*) people who, like the Upholsterer, are addicted to being up on and constantly discussing the latest world news, to the detriment of their own interests, (*c*) talk radio and television shows that are electronic versions of the "three or four very odd fellows sitting together upon the bench," and (*d*) shows like "Lifestyles of the Rich and Famous" that encourage vicarious participation on the part of their audiences. Addison might find any or all of these cases ample illustration of "those worthy citizens who live more in a coffee-house than in their shops."

William C. Martin

The God-Huckslers of the Radio

William C. Martin, a professor of sociology at Rice University, has written numerous articles on various aspects of popular culture for Esquire, Harper's, and The Atlantic, where "The God-Hucksters of the Radio" first appeared (June 1970). Martin analyzes the marketing strategies and psychological techniques radio evangelists use in their broadcasts to create and maintain successful media ministries. Martin contends that some religious broadcasters are little more than "God hucksters" who exploit the poor, the uneducated, and the infirm.

1   You have heard them, if only for a few seconds at a time. Perhaps you were driving cross-country late at night, fiddling with the radio dial in search of a signal to replace the one that finally grew too weak as you drew away from Syracuse, or Decatur, or Amarillo. You listened for a moment until you recognized what it was, then you dialed on, hoping to find *Monitor* or *Music Till Dawn*. Perhaps you wondered if, somewhere, people really listen to these programs. The answer is, they do, by the tens and hundreds of thousands. And they not only listen; they believe and respond. Each day, on local stations that cater to religious broadcasting and on the dozen or so "superpower" stations that can be picked up hundreds of miles away during the cool nighttime hours, an odd-lot assortment of radio evangelists proclaims its version of the gospel to the Great Church of the Airwaves.

2   Not all who produce religious broadcasts, of course, are acceptable to the scattered multitude for whom "gospel radio" is a major instrument of instruction and inspiration. Denominational programs and Billy Graham are regarded as too Establishment. Billy James Hargis and his Christian Anti-Communist Crusade are too political. Even faith healer Oral Roberts, once a favorite out there in radioland, has become suspect since he founded a university and joined the Methodist Church. For these believers, the true vessels of knowledge, grace, and power are people like Brother Al ("That's A-L, Brother Al"), the Reverend Frederick B. Eikerenkoetter II, better known to millions as "Reverend Ike"; C. W. Burpo ("Spelled 'B,' as in Bible . . . "); Kathryn Kuhlman ("Have . . . you . . . been . . . waiting . . . for . . . me"?); and the two giants of radio religion, healer A. A. Allen (of Miracle Valley, Arizona) and teacher Garner Ted Armstrong, who can be heard somewhere at this very moment proclaiming The Plain Truth about The World Tomorrow.

The format of programs in this genre rarely makes severe intellectual 3 demands on either pastor or flock. C. W. Burpo (Dr. Burpo accents the last syllable; local announcers invariably stress the first) and Garner Ted Armstrong usually give evidence of having thought about the broadcast ahead of time, though their presentations are largely extemporaneous. Some of the others seem simply to turn on the microphone and shout. Occasionally there is a hint of a sermon. J. Charles Jessup of Gulfport, Mississippi, may cite Herodias's directing her daughter to ask for the head of John the Baptist as illustrating how parents set a bad example for their children. David Terrell may, in support of a point on the doctrine of election, note that God chose Mary for his own good reasons, and not because she was the only virgin in Palestine—"There was plenty of virgins in the land. Plenty of 'em. Mucho virgins was in the land." Evangelist Bill Beeny of St. Louis, Missouri (Period. Beeny regards the Zip Code as a plot to confuse the nation), may point to the flea's ability to jump 200 times his own length as proof that God exists. Often, however, a program consists of nothing more than a canned introduction, a taped segment from an actual "healing and blessing" service (usually featuring testimonials to the wondrous powers of the evangelist), and a closing pitch for money.

The machinery for broadcasting these programs is a model of effi- 4 ciency. A look at station XERF in Ciudad Acuã, Coahuila, Mexico, just across the border from Del Rio, Texas, illustrates the point. Freed from FCC regulations that restrict the power of American stations to 50,000 watts, XERF generates 250,000 watts, making it the most powerful station in the world. On a cold night, when high-frequency radio waves travel farthest, it can be heard from Argentina to Canada. Staff needs are minimal; less than a dozen employees handle all duties, from the front office to equipment maintenance. The entire fourteen hours of programming, from 6:00 P.M. to 8:00 A.M., are taped. Each week the evangelists send their tapes to the station, with a check for the air time they will use.

All announcing is done by Paul Kallinger, "Your Good Neighbor 5 along the way." A pleasant, gregarious man, Kallinger has been with XERF since 1949. In the fifties, he performed his duties live. At present he operates a restaurant in Del Rio and tapes leads and commercials in a small studio in his home; he has not been to the station in years. A lone technician switches back and forth between the preachers and Kallinger from dusk till dawn. Kallinger recognizes the improbability of some of the claims made by the ministers and acknowledges that their motives may not be entirely altruistic. Still, he figures that, on balance, they do more good than harm, and he does his best to impress listeners with the fact that "these are faith broadcasts and need your tithes and love offerings if they are to remain on the air with this great message."

Who listens to these evangelists, and why? No single answer will 6 suffice. Some, doubtless, listen to learn. Garner Ted Armstrong discusses

current problems and events—narcotics, crime, conflict, space exploration, pollution—and asserts that biblical prophecy holds the key to
understanding both present and future. C. W. Burpo offers a conservative mixture of religion, morals, and politics. Burpo is foursquare in favor
of God, Nixon, and constitutional government, and adamantly opposed
to sex education, which encourages the study of materials "revealing the
basest part of human nature."

7   Others listen because the preachers promise immediate solutions to
real, tangible problems. Although evidence is difficult to obtain, one gets
the definite impression, from the crowds that attend the personal appearances of the evangelists, from the content and style of oral and
written testimonials, from studies of storefront churches with similar
appeals, and from station executives' analyses of their listening population, that the audience is heavily weighted with the poor, the uneducated, and others who for a variety of reasons stand on the margins of
society. These are the people most susceptible to illness and infirmity, to
crippling debts, and to what the evangelists refer to simply as "troubles."
At the same time, they are the people least equipped to deal with these
problems effectively. Some men in such circumstances turn to violence
or radical political solutions. Others grind and are ground away, in the
dim hope of a better future. Still others, like desperate men in many
cultures, succumb to the appeal of magical solutions. For this group,
what the preachers promise is, if hardly the Christian gospel, at least
good news.

8   The "healers and blessers," who dominate the radio evangelism
scene, address themselves to the whole range of human problems: physical, emotional, social, financial, and spiritual. Like their colleagues in the
nonmiraculous healing arts some evangelists develop areas of special
competence, such as the cure of cancer or paralysis. Brother Al is something of a foot specialist—"God can take corns, bunions, and tired feet,
and massage them with his holy love and make them well." A. A. Allen
tells of disciples who have received silver fillings in their teeth during his
meetings and asks, sensibly enough, "Why not let God be your dentist?"
But most are general practitioners. On a single evening's set of programs,
hope is extended to those suffering from alcoholism, arthritis, asthma,
birth defects, blindness, blood pressure (high and low), bunions, calluses,
cancer (breast, eye, lung, skin, stomach, and throat), corns, death, diabetes, dope, eye weakness, gallstones, heart disease, insomnia, kidney
trouble, leukemia, mental retardation, mononucleosis, nervous breakdown, nervous itch, nicotine addiction, obesity, pain, paralysis, polio,
pregnancy, respiratory problems, rheumatic fever, tuberculosis, tumors
(brain, abdominal, and miscellaneous), ulcers, useless limbs, and water
in the veins.

9   The continually fascinating aspect of the healing and blessing ministries is that they do produce results. Some of the reported healings are
undoubtedly fraudulent. One station canceled a healer's program after

obtaining an affidavit from individuals who admitted posing as cripples and being "healed" by the touch of the pastor's hand. Police officers have occasionally reported seeing familiar vagrants in the healing lines of traveling evangelists, apparently turning newly discovered disorders into wine. But these blatant frauds are probably rare, and a faith healer need not depend on them to sustain his reputation. He can rely much more safely on psychological, sociological, and psychotherapeutic mechanisms at work among his audience.

The testimonials that fill the broadcasts and publications of the 10 healers point to two regularities in a large percentage — not all — of the reported cures. First, the believer had suffered from his condition for some time and had been unable to gain relief from medical or other sources. Long illness or disability can weaken emotional and mental resistance to sources of help that one would not consider in other circumstances. Second, most of the cures occur at actual healing services, when the deep desire to be made whole is transformed into eager expectation by a frenzied whirl of noise, anxiety, and promise, and the pervasive power of the gathered group of true believers.

In recent years, the miracle-workers have turned their attention to 11 financial as well as physical needs. They promise better jobs, success in business, or in lieu of these, simple windfalls. A. A. Allen urges listeners to send for his book *Riches and Wealth, the Gift of God*. Reverend Ike fills his publications and broadcasts with stories of financial blessings obtained through his efforts — "This Lady Blessed with New Cadillac," "How God Blessed and Prospered Mrs. Rena Blige" (he revealed to her a secret formula for making hair grow), "Sister Rag Muffin Now Wears Mink to Church," and "Blessed with New Buick in 45 Minutes." Forty-five minutes is not, apparently, unusually fast for Reverend Ike. He regularly assures his listeners, "The moment you get your offering [and] your prayer requests into the mail, start looking up to God for your blessing because it will be on the way."

These men of God realize, of course, that good health and a jackpot 12 prize on the Big Slot Machine in the Sky are not all there is to life. They promise as well to rid the listener of bad habits, quiet his doubts and fears, soothe his broken heart, repair his crumbling marriage, reconcile his fussing kinfolk, and deliver him from witches and demons. No problem is too trivial, too difficult, or past redemption. Brother Al will help women "that wants a ugly mouth cleaned out of their husband." A. A. Allen claims to have rescued men from the electric chair. Glenn Thompson promises "that girl out there 'in trouble' who's trying to keep it from Dad and Mother" that if she will "believe and doubt not, God will perform a miracle."

The radio evangelists do not cast their bread upon the waters, how- 13 ever, without expecting something in return. Though rates vary widely, a fifteen-minute daily program on a local radio station costs, on the average, about $200 per week. On a superpower station like XERF the rate may run as high as $600. The evangelists pay this fee themselves, but they depend on their radio audience to provide the funds. For this reason, some take advantage of God's Precious Air Time to hawk a bit of sacred merchandise. Much of it is rather ordinary — large-print Bibles, calendars, greeting cards, Bible-verse yo-yos, and ball-point pens with an inspirational message right there on the side. Other items are more unusual. Bill Beeny, who tends to see the darker side of current events, offers $25-contributors a Riot Pack containing a stove, five fuel cans, a rescue gun, a radio, and the marvelous Defender, a weapon that drives an attacker away and covers him with dye, making him an easy target for police. Ten dollars will buy a blue-steel, pearl-handled, tear-gas pistol, plus the informative and inspirational Truth-Pac No. 4. Or, for the same price, Evangelist Beeny will send his own album of eighteen songs about heaven, together with the Paralyzer, "made by the famous Mace Company." Presumably, it is safer to turn the other cheek if one has first paralyzed one's enemy.

14   The most common items offered for sale, however, are the evangelist's own books and records. Brother Al's current book is *The Second Touch:* "It's wrote in plain, down-to-earth language, and has big print that will heal any weak eyes that reads it." For a $5-offering C. W. Burpo will send his wonderful recording of "My America," plus a bonus bumper sticker advertising his program, The Bible Institute of the Air — "Be a moving billboard for God and Country." Don and Earl, "two young Christian singers from Fort Worth, Texas," offer for only $3 "plus a extra quarter to pay the postage back to your house," albums of heart-touching songs and stories that include such old favorites as "Just One Rose Will Do," "A Tramp on the Streets," "Lord, Build Me a Cabin in Heaven," "Streamline to Glory," "Remember Mother's God," "A Soldier's Last Letter," "That Little Pair of Half-worn Shoes," "Just a Closer Walk with Thee" (featuring the gospel whistling of Don), and that great resurrection hymn, "There Ain't No Grave Gonna Keep My Body Down."

15   In keeping with St. Paul's dictum that "those who proclaim the gospel should get their living by the gospel," the radio ministers do not always offer merchandise in return for contributions. In fact, the books and records and magazines probably function primarily as a link that facilitates the more direct appeals for money almost sure to follow.

16   Brother Al, sounding like a pathetic Andy Devine, asks the faithful to send "God's Perfect Offering — $7.00. Not $6.00, not $8.00, but $7.00." An offering even more blessed is $77, God's two perfect numbers, although any multiple of seven is meritorious. "God told me to ask for this. You know I don't talk like this. It's got to be God. God told me he had a lot of bills to pay. Obey God — just put the cash inside the envelope." In addition to cash, Brother Al will also accept checks, money orders, and American Express — surely he means traveler's checks. Seven's perfection stems from its prominence in the Bible: the seven

deadly sins, the seven churches of Asia, and so forth. Radio Pastor David Epley also believes God has a perfect number, but he has been reading about the apostles and the tribes of Israel. Quite understandably, he seeks a $12-offering, or the double portion offering of $24.

Brother Glenn Thompson, who also names God as his co-solicitor, 17 claims that most of the world's ills, from crabgrass and garden bugs to Communism and the Bomb, can be traced to man's robbing God. "You've got God's money in your wallet. You old stingy Christian. No wonder we've got all these problems. You want to know how you can pay God what you owe? God is speaking through me. God said, 'Inasmuch as you do it unto one of these, you do it unto me.' God said, 'Give all you have for the gospel's sake.' My address is Brother Glenn, Paragould, Arkansas."

In sharp contrast, Garner Ted Armstrong makes it quite clear that all 18 publications offered on his broadcasts are absolutely free. There is no gimmick. Those who request literature never receive any hint of an appeal for funds unless they specifically ask how they might contribute to the support of the program. Garner Ted's father, Herbert W. Armstrong, began the broadcast in 1937, as a vehicle for spreading a message that features a literalistic interpretation of biblical prophecy. The program has spawned a college with campuses in California, Texas, and London, and a church of more than 300,000 members. Characteristically, the ministers of the local churches, which meet in rented halls and do not advertise, even in the telephone book, will not call on prospective members without a direct invitation. This scrupulous approach has proved quite successful. *The World Tomorrow*, a half-hour program, is heard daily on more than four hundred stations throughout the world, and a television version is carried by sixty stations.

Several evangelists use their radio programs primarily to promote 19 their personal appearance tours throughout the country, and may save the really high-powered huckstering for these occasions. A. A. Allen is both typical and the best example. An Allen Miracle Restoration Revival Service lasts from three to five hours and leaves even the inhibited participant observer quite spent. On a one-night stand in the Houston Music Hall, Allen and the Lord drew close to a thousand souls, in approximately equal portions of blacks, whites, and Mexican-Americans. As the young organist in a brown Nehru [jacket] played gospel rock, hands shot into the air and an occasional tambourine clamored for joy. Then, without announcement, God's Man of Faith and Power came to pulpit center. Allen does not believe in wearing black; that's for funerals. On this night he wore a green suit with shiny green shoes.

For the better part of an hour, he touted his book that is turning the 20 religious world upside down, *Witchcraft, Wizards, and Witches*, and a record, pressed on 100 percent pure vinyl, of his top two soul-winning sermons.

To prepare the audience for the main pitch, Allen went to great 21 lengths to leave the impression that he was one of exceedingly few faithful men of God still on the scene. He lamented the defection from the ministry: "In the last few years, 30 percent of the preachers have stopped preaching; 70 percent fewer men are in training for the ministry. A cool 100 percent less preachers than just a few years ago." He chortled over the fate of rival evangelists who had run afoul of the law or justifiably irate husbands. At another service, he used this spot to describe the peril of opposing his ministry. He told of a student who tried to fool him by posing as a cripple; God struck him dead the same night. A man who believed in Allen's power, but withheld $100 God had told him to give the evangelist, suffered a stroke right after the meeting. And on and on.

22   When he finished, Brother Don Stewart, Allen's associate in the ministry of fund-raising, took the microphone to begin a remarkable hour of unalloyed gullery. At the end of his recitation, approximately 135 people pledged $100 apiece, and others emptied bills and coins into large plastic wastebaskets that were filled and replaced with astonishing regularity. And all the while Brother Don walked back and forth shouting to the point of pain, "Vow and pay, vow and pay, the scripture does say, vow and pay."

23   Despite the blatantly instrumental character of much radio religion, it would be a mistake to suppose that its only appeal lies in the promise of health and wealth, though these are powerful incentives. The fact is that if the world seems out of control, what could be more reassuring than to discover the road map of human destiny? This is part of the appeal of Garner Ted Armstrong, who declares to listeners, in a tone that does not encourage doubt, that a blueprint of the future of America, Germany, the British Commonwealth, and the Middle East, foolproof solutions for the problems of child-rearing, pollution, and crime in the streets, plus a definitive answer to the question, "Why Are You Here?" can all be theirs for the cost of a six-cent stamp. On a far less sophisticated level, James Bishop Carr, of Palmdale, California, does the same thing. Brother Carr believes that much of the world's ills can be traced to the use of "Roman time" (the Gregorian calendar) and observances of religious holidays such as Christmas. He has reckoned the day and hour of Christ's second coming but is uncertain of the year. Each Night of Atonement, he awaits the Eschaton with his followers, the Little Flock of Mount Zion. Between disappointments, he constructs elaborate charts depicting the flow of history from Adam's Garden to Armageddon, complete with battle plans for the latter event. Others deal in prophecy on more of an *ad hoc* basis, but are no less confident of their accuracy. David Terrell, the Endtime Messenger, recently warned that "even today, the sword of the Lord is drawed" and that "coastal cities shall be inhabited by strange creatures from the sea, yea, and there shall be great sorrow in California. . . . God has never failed. Who shall deny when these things happen that

a prophet was in your midst? Believest thou this and you shall be blessed."

To become a disciple of one of these prophet-preachers is, by the 24 evangelists' own admission, to obtain a guide without peer to lead one over life's uneven pathway. Though few of them possess standard professional credentials, they take pains to assure their scattered flocks that they have divine recognition and approval. Some associate themselves with leading biblical personalities, as when A. A. Allen speaks of the way "God has worked through his great religious leaders, such as Moses and myself," or when C. W. Burpo intones, "God loves you and I love you." Several report appearances by heavenly visitors. According to David Terrell, Jesus came into his room on April 17, about eight-thirty at night and told him there was too much junk going around. "Bring the people unto me." Though some receive angels regularly, they do not regard their visits lightly. "If you don't think that it'll almost tax your nervous system to the breaking point," says the Reverend Billy Walker, Jr., "let an angel come to you." Other evangelists simply promise, as does Brother Al, "I can get through to God for you." In support of such claims, they point to the testimony of satisfied disciples and to their own personal success; the flamboyance in dress affected by some of the men obviously capitalizes on their followers' need for a hero who has himself achieved the success denied them.

In the fiercely competitive struggle for the listeners' attention and 25 money, most of the evangelists have developed a novel twist or gimmick to distinguish them from their fellow clerics. C. W. Burpo does not simply pray; he goes into the "throne room" to talk to God. The door to the throne room can be heard opening and shutting. David Epley's trademark is the use of the gift of "discernment." He not only heals those who come to him, but "discerns" those in his audience who need a special gift of healing, in the manner of a pious Dunninger. A. A. Allen emphasizes witchcraft on most of his current broadcasts, blaming everything from asthma to poverty on hexes and demons. In other years he has talked of holy oil that flowed from the hands of those who were being healed, or crosses of blood that appeared on their foreheads. David Terrell frequently calls upon his gift of "tongues." Terrell breaks into ecstatic speech either at the peak of an emotional passage or at points where he appears to need what is otherwise known as "filler." Certain of his spirited words tend to recur repeatedly. *Ralpha, nissi*, and *honda bahayah* are three favorites. The first two may be derived from the Hebrew words for healing and victory. Unless the third is a Hebrew term having to do with motorcycles, its meaning is known only to those with the gift of interpretation. Terrell defends his "speaking in the Spirit" over the radio on the grounds that he is an apostle — "not a grown-up apostle like Peter or Paul; just a little boy apostle that's started out working for Jesus."

26   Once one has made contact with a radio evangelist, preferably by a letter containing a "love offering," one is usually bombarded with letters and publications telling of what God has recently wrought through his servant, asking for special contributions to meet a variety of emergencies, and urging followers to send for items personally blessed by the evangelist and virtually guaranteed to bring the desired results. One runs across holy oil, prosperity billfolds, and sacred willow twigs, but the perennial favorite of those with talismaniacal urges is the prayer cloth.

Prayer cloths come in several colors and sizes, and are available in muslin, sackcloth, terrycloth, and for a limited time only, revival-tent cloth. As an optional extra, they can be anointed with water, oil, or ashes. My own model is a small (2½ × 2½ inches) unanointed rectangle of pinked cloth. The instructions state that it represents the man of God who sent it, and that it can be laid upon those with an ailment, hidden in the house to bring peace and blessings, carried in the purse or pocketbook for financial success, and even taken to court to assure a favorable outcome. One woman told Reverend Ike that she had cut her cloth in two and placed a piece under the separate beds of a quarreling couple. She declared the experiment an unqualified success, to the delight of Reverend Ike — "You did that? You rascal, you! Let's all give God a great big hand!"

27   These scraps of paper and cloth serve to bind preacher and people together until the glorious day when a faithful listener can attend a live service at the civic auditorium or the coliseum, or under the big tent at the fairgrounds. It is here, in the company of like-minded believers, that a person loses and perhaps finds himself as he joins the shouting, clapping, dancing, hugging, weeping, rejoicing throng. At such a service, a large Negro lady pointed into the air and jiggled pleasantly. Beside her, a sad, pale little woman, in a huge skirt hitched up with a man's belt, hopped tentatively on one foot and looked for a moment as if she might have found something she had been missing. On cue from the song leader, all turned to embrace or shake hands with a neighbor and to assure each other that "Jesus is *all right!*" Old men jumped about like mechanical toys. Two teen-age boys "ran for Jesus." And in the aisles a trim, gray-haired woman in spike heels and a black nylon dress, danced sensuously all over the auditorium. She must have logged a mile and a half, maybe a mile and three quarters, before the night was over. I couldn't help wondering if her husband knew where she was. But I was sure she liked where she was better than where she had been.

28   If a radio evangelist can stimulate this kind of response, whether he is a charlatan (as some undoubtedly are) or sincerely believes he is a vessel of God (as some undoubtedly do) is secondary. If he can convince his listeners that he can deliver what he promises, the blend of genuine need, desperate belief, reinforcing group—and who knows what else? —can move in mysterious ways its wonders to perform. And, for a long time, that will likely be enough to keep those cards and letters coming in.

Questions for Discussion and Writing

1. What would one be able to infer about Martin's essay from the title?

2. How does Martin structure his analysis (beginning with representative examples of the "God-Hucksters," followed by a discussion of the mechanics of religious broadcasting, and ending with a close look at the listeners who are manipulated by these broadcasts) to support his conclusion about these activities? What exactly is Martin's view of these media ministers, especially with respect to the means radio evangelists use to raise funds?

3. How, according to Martin, is the popularity of these evangelists related to their ability to speak for the poor and the disenfranchised in our society?

4. How does Martin use evidence drawn from demographic profiles of audiences, and excerpts form various radio sermons offering relief from "troubles" in return for "tithes and love offerings," to support his characterization of the God-hucksters as exploiters of the poor, uneducated, and infirm?

5. What effect does Martin achieve by listing the extensive catalogue of problems dealt with by media ministers in alphabetical order, rather than in order of seriousness ("death" appears under the d's)?

6. What sources does Martin draw from for evidence as to who listens to these broadcasts? Does the widespread range of sources enhance the credibility of his conclusion?

7. How does the medical profession provide the role model for many radio evangelists? Why do these media ministers choose the methods of the medical profession as a basis for their own specialized areas of healing?

8. To what extent are evangelists' claims that God has appointed them or that they communicate with figures from the Bible an illustration of the persuasive technique known as virtue by association?

9. How does the marketing of survivalist items by radio evangelists relate to a recurrent theme in their broadcasts? To what extent does success in marketing these products depend on the audience's belief that they are members of an elect group who would survive a nuclear holocaust or worldwide catastrophe? In realistic terms, how useful would powdered food concentrates, compasses, weapons, and tents be under those circumstances?

10. Why, according to Martin, is it important for evangelists, like doctors, to look successful? Why would this prove reassuring to an evangelist's followers even when many of them are far less well off than the minister appears to be? Why would his flock see him as standing in for them, take great satisfaction in contributing to his well-being, and not see themselves as being ripped off?

11. As a research project, keep a log of the subjects discussed and any distinctive qualities of showmanship or tone for several broadcasts by a media evangelist. Based on your observations, evaluate Martin's analyses and decide whether the conclusions he reaches are justified. Does the format of the shows you monitored interweave testimony from believers with requests for donations? Do these shows promise a physical souvenir (pin, piece of parchment, or other memorabilia) in return for money? Most important, what sort of value or benefit do you feel the audience members believe they are getting for their donation? You might wish to compare any of the broadcasts you study with a fictionalized treatment such as Sinclair Lewis's novel *Elmer Gantry* (1927).

Rob Lamp

The World of "Dark Rock": In the shadow of death and despair

Rob Lamp is an editor of Rock Music Update Newsletter *and* Inside Rock, *as well as a musician, record producer, and music director at the Great Commission Church in Silver Spring, Maryland. Lamp cites a wide variety of sources including testimony of psychiatrists and interviews with rock stars to support his thesis that rock music and rock videos are directly responsible for an increase in teenage suicides and pregnancies. "The World of 'Dark Rock'" first appeared in* The New American *(February 17, 1986).*

On October 27, 1984, nineteen-year-old John McCollum shot himself   1
in the head in his father's home in Indio, California. According to the
coroner's report, McCollum committed suicide "while listening to devil
music."

Now, more than a year later, Jack McCollum, the dead youth's father,   2
has filed suit against a British heavy metal rock musician, Ozzy Osbourne, and his two record companies, CBS Records and Jet Records.
McCollum charges that his son's decision to kill himself was precipitated
by listening to an Ozzy Osbourne song "Suicide Solution."

CBS Records released Osbourne's albums "with the knowledge that   3
such would, or at the very least, could promote suicide," McCollum's
lawyer Thomas Anderson told a California news conference last month.
Anderson said the suit seeks unspecified compensatory and punitive
damages that could amount to millions of dollars.

"The record companies and rock stars know exactly what effect this   4
type of music has on young people," Jack McCollum insisted to reporters. "They know they are encouraging young people to commit
suicide."

Of course, Ozzy Osbourne has disputed McCollum's charges. "These   5
comments are slanderous; they are preposterous and . . . ludicrous allegations made against an artist who clearly had nothing remotely related to such thoughts in mind when writing or performing his songs,"
said Howard Weitzman, Osbourne's attorney.

Osbourne, former lead singer for the band Black Sabbath, says that   6
McCollum and his lawyer have misinterpreted the meaning of his song.
"This song wasn't written for suicide, it was anti-suicide," he said.

"It was about a friend of mine (Bon Scott, lead singer of the heavy   7 metal group AC-DC) who killed himself on alcohol and drugs," Osbourne continued. "It means suicide solution as a liquid; not as a solution or a way out."

8   Yet, despite the claims of Ozzy Osbourne, the suicide of John McCollum is another link in the chain tying certain types of rock music to incidents of witchcraft, death and suicide across the nation. For example, the names of Ozzy Osbourne and his former band, Black Sabbath, were found spray-painted along with satanic symbols in Northport, New York—the scene of the mutilation-slaying of seventeen-year-old Gary Lauwers. Charged with the murder was seventeen-year-old Richard Kasso, who was reported to be involved in drugs, séances, animal sacrifices, grave digging and other satanic activities.

9   Attorney William Keahon, who investigated the murder, reported a strong correlation between the tragic events surrounding the murder and the satanic image of certain rock performers. Keahon admitted: "I look at it as a reasonable person; I know what I see in these rock videos, and I know what I see and hear from these kids who watch these videos and do these drugs. I believe there is an acting out of the same outrageous behavior as what the kids see up there on the stage."

10   It is no wonder that parent groups, psychologists, and even some recording artists are reacting strongly against what some are calling "dark rock." Critics identify dark rock as popular music that promotes violent and sexually explicit messages in the lyrics. No longer heard by only a few, these pervasive messages have now crept into the mainstream of American music and are constantly blaring through the stereos of vulnerable teens and pre-teen listeners.

11   No one blames rock music entirely for the 300 percent rise in adolescent suicides or the seven percent increase in teenage pregnancies. There are certainly many causes for these social problems. However, many observers have become convinced that potent messages "aimed" at children that promote and glorify suicide, rape, and sadomasochism at least have to be considered a possible "contributing factor."

12   Ozzie Osbourne once defended himself to *Circus* magazine by protesting, "As much as the kids love to hear me sing, 'Satan is Lord' and 'I Love You Devil,' I am no satanist—I'm a rock 'n roll rebel." The rock star's wife and manager, Sharon Osbourne, explains: "Ozzy isn't into Satanism . . . that's a marketing campaign we invented for him. He doesn't take it seriously."

13   But Kerry Livgren, former guitarist for the band Kansas, admits that teenagers do take what he and others say in their music quite seriously. "I've run across many people who worshipped our band and other bands," Livgren commented. "When it got to the point with Kansas when I realized what I was writing in my songs was becoming an actual standard by which people lived—that thousands of kids were looking to me as if I was some type of guru—I knew it had gotten way out of my hands."

Many professionals who study adolescent behavior have been so- 14
bered by the effects of dark rock on their patients. Dr. David Guttman,
Professor of Psychiatry at Northwestern University told the *Washington
Post*, "Rock has so often been involved in these things [violence, teen
suicide, etc.] many of us in psychiatry have had to take it more
seriously."

Dr. Joseph Novello, a psychiatrist and director of "Gateway," a drug 15
treatment center in Washington DC, often asks teenagers what kind of
music they listen to. "It's clear that kids define themselves to a large
extent by the artists and music that they like," says Novello. "There is a
small and vulnerable group of youngsters who are inclined to drug abuse
who tend to identify with the heavy metal and satanic kind of music."

Other psychiatrists have cited rock videos as contributors to the rise 16
of violence among students. Thomas Radecki, chairman for the National
Coalition on Television Violence (NCTV), estimated that 45 percent of
some 1200 rock videos monitored were of a violent nature.

A large number of rock videos were rated "extremely violent" by the 17
NCTV. For example, the Rolling Stones amputation video entitled "Too
Much Blood" is a take-off of the Texas Chainsaw Massacre. "They sing
about chopping a woman's head off, putting her pieces in the refrigerator, then taking them out and eating them," Radecki commented.

A similar theme appears in Tom Petty's music video, "Don't Come 18
Around Here No More." In it, a woman turns into a cake which Petty
slices up with a knife while she is screaming. The final scene shows Petty
putting the last piece of cake in his mouth and then burping. "That type
of image is really quite harmful. It endorses a hostility and revengeful
type of thinking between the sexes," Radecki warns.

In another video by Twisted Sister entitled "We're Not Gonna Take 19
It," a boy decides he's not going to put up with an angry father, so he
hurls Dad out the window. Proponents have said that these videos are
just tongue-in-cheek or cartoon-like. Unfortunately, a young man in
New Mexico took Twisted Sister somewhat seriously when he murdered
his father in a similar fashion. The homicide was reported to have been
inspired by the Twisted Sister video.

Scientific research also backs up the assertion that violent videos can 20
have harmful effects on their young viewers. In various surveys done
with college students, Dr. Radecki reported a "desensitizing of individuals who watch violent videos."

Advertisers certainly enjoy rock stars like Michael Jackson endorsing 21
their soft drinks. Pepsi paid Jackson $5 million to say "This is the Pepsi
Generation." That fantasy helped Pepsi spurt to a $20 million gain in
sales last year. Radecki concludes, "If the little thirty- and sixty-second
commercials can sell, certainly the three- and four-minute videos
themselves — which are really promoting things of violence, making
them seem fun and acceptable, normal, and healthy — will be much
more influential."

22   Not only has violence and occult activity become prevalent in today's dark rock, but sexual themes have moved from mere innuendos to blatant profanity.

23   [We would prefer to end any discussion of eroticism in rock lyrics by simply noting that it exists—abundantly. But that would fail to show the reader how perverse an influence it is on its young audiences. With apologies for the offensive nature, therefore, some less extreme examples follow. —Ed.]

24   Sexuality in popular music has come a long way from Cole Porter's "Birds do it; bees do it. . . . " Popular top forty artists like Cindy Lauper in her song "She Bop" encourage masturbation for teenagers. In "She Bop," Lauper tells her adolescent followers that it won't make you blind and "there ain't no law against it yet."

25   Prince, described by *Rolling Stone* magazine as the most influential musician of the 1980s, has crossed lines that once were considered taboo in rock. In one of his earlier albums, "Dirty Minds," Prince sings about incest in his song called "Sister" and oral sex in another song entitled "Head."

26   His film, *Purple Rain*, was a box-office smash and crowned him as rock's new king of sex. Although Prince has toned down his erotic image since the days of "Dirty Minds," he did not completely lose his sexual taint in *Purple Rain*. In the film, Prince thrusts the stage with his body and sings about "a girl named Nikki . . . a sex fiend" whom he "met . . . in a hotel lobby masturbating."

27   Madonna was voted in some polls as the top female performer of 1985. Her hit single, "Like a Virgin," was number one on *Billboard*'s list of The Top One Hundred songs for the year. Her nude photos in *Playboy* and *Penthouse* and her confessions to *Time* magazine reveal that a virgin she is not.

28   Madonna-style clothing and accessories are very popular among young girls. Her exposed belly button and "Boy Toy" belt buckle are standard trademarks of the Madonna image. Kendis Moore counsels pregnant teenagers in the Los Angeles area. She told the *Los Angeles Times*, "I know how impressionable these girls are. Rock stars like Madonna, Sheila E., and Vanity are important to them. They buy their records, sing their songs, and dress like them. They get the message of what it means to have sex, and it puts a lot of pressure on them to live up to that image."

29   The Kinsey Report discovered that, in 1940, 33 percent of all women lost their virginity by age 25. Today, 30 percent have lost it before age sixteen. According to the *Journal of Sex Research*, most women in the 1980s have their first sexual experience between the ages of sixteen and nineteen. A rock magazine headline described the situation appropriately, "The Sexual Revolution is Over! (Sex Won)."

30   However, some parent groups have not given up the fight. The battle between parent groups (like the National PTA and the Parents Music

Resource Center) and the record industry is still raging. The NPTA sent letters to most of the major record companies inviting them to attend a conference where they could discuss this issue of explicit song lyrics. The *Washington Times* reports that many did not even acknowledge the letter, and only one record company, a gospel music company, said they would attend.

More pressure came when two Washington DC women, Mrs. James 31 Baker and Mrs. Tipper Gore, co-founded the Parents Music Resource Center (PMRC). Appearances on NBC's *Today Show*, the *Phil Donahue Show*, and other popular discussion programs brought the issue of "dark rock" to national attention.

Mrs. Gore, wife of Senator Albert Gore (R-TN) and the mother of 32 four, explained her concerns on the *Phil Donahue Show:* "Right now, there are really no boundaries. We're not talking about putting anyone in jail or censorship. We're saying, since the material is this explicit and this violent, for those of us who care and don't want our younger children inadvertently bringing it home or listening to it, give us information. Give us a tool, a general rating on an album that the material is violent and sexually explicit. . . ."

Mrs. Gore added, "I don't think it's unreasonable to ask the music 33 industry to exercise some self-restraint and to give me, as a parent, more information so I can do my job better in my home. That's not abridging anybody's rights."

Dr. Radecki of the NCTV makes a similar plea regarding rock videos. 34 "If they are going to show the violent videos, they should be segregated. The NPTA and others have called for ratings of rock music videos. Let's lump them together so we have non-violent videos in a non-violent hour. If they want to have the violent ones, have those in [a certain time period]," suggests Radecki. "If you're discriminating and you don't want to get the degrading sexual images and the very violent sadistic images, at least you can choose."

Parent groups found a sympathizer in the person of George David 35 Weiss, president of the Songwriters Guild and a recent inductee into the Songwriters Hall of Fame. In the June 29th issue of *Billboard Magazine*, Weiss calls for a voluntary "self-restraint" by the record companies who produce explicit material.

In his commentary, Weiss praises the efforts of so many artists who 36 raised millions of dollars with their recording of "We Are the World." The concern over physical health is admirable, but he asks, "What about the moral health of children in America? Aren't their emotional health and developing values also worth our attention?"

The issue of labeling or rating records with explicit lyrics culminated 37 when the PMRC and various participants from the recording industry met before the Senate Commerce Committee last September. After hearing testimony from musicians Frank Zappa, John Denver, and Twisted Sister's Dee Snider, the committee insisted that there would be no legislation if the musicians and record companies would just "clean up their act."

38   Six weeks after the Senate hearings, the PMRC and the Recording Industry Association of America agreed to a compromise. Individual record companies would decide what material was considered "blatant explicit lyric content" and print a warning label marked "Explicit Lyrics Parental Advisory" on the back cover of the album or tape. Record companies would also have the option of printing the song lyrics on a sheet of paper inserted between the album and the outside plastic wrap. Consumers then could either investigate the lyrics themselves or heed the warning label.

39   PMRC was very pleased with the November 1st agreement and saw it as "an important step," said a PMRC representative. Both sides agreed to monitor the impact of the agreement on consumers. This decision was to be carried out "in good faith" by all the participating record companies. PMRC will, however, continue to assert more pressure on the few companies who will not provide the warning label or song lyrics.

40   The agreement does not necessarily mean that rock musicians will now change their tune. Record companies, like other providers of entertainment, have learned that "sex and violence sells," and this is still the bottom line. Most observers recognize that it is the parents who must take control of the situation and determine what is healthy and unhealthy music for their children.

41   Dr. Novello and others agree that parents should be the ones to sit down and discuss the messages of rock songs with their children. "If parents were doing their job in the home, kids wouldn't seek other role models," says Novello. Dr. Radecki also urges that parents lay a foundation of religious morals that will help their children develop into more discerning and loving individuals.

Questions for Discussion and Writing

1. How does the suicide of John McCollum typify the kinds of negative effects supposedly produced, according to Lamp, by listening to "dark rock"?

2. How does Ozzy Osbourne's defense against the charge depend on the different meanings of the word *solution*? How credible does this explanation seem to be to you?

3. In what way does the case of seventeen-year-old Gary Lauwers, who was murdered at a site where spray-painted "satanic symbols" and the names of Ozzy Osbourne and his former band Black Sabbath were found, illustrate either a convincing circumstantial case or the use of guilt by association? Explain your interpretation.

4. What different explanations are offered to explain exactly how "dark rock" acts as either a primary or contributing cause to witchcraft, death, and suicide? Summarize these hypotheses and identify the assumptions that underlie them about how teenagers are influenced by this kind of music and the rock stars who perform it. How plausible do you find these hypotheses? Explain your answer.

5. How does Lamp use statements by Kerry Livgren to refute counterarguments that Ozzy Osbourne uses satanism as simply a "marketing campaign"?

6. How does Lamp use the testimony of psychiatrists to support his claim? In what way does their testimony shed light on the means by which rock music influences teenagers?

7. Evaluate the specific examples of rock videos given to support the claim that these videos produce violence in teenagers. To what extent are these examples typical or representative of the entire category of rock videos? Discuss the extent to which Lamp's argument is either strengthened or weakened by using examples that might be perceived as atypical.

8. Examine the logic underlying Radecki's claim that "if the little thirty- and 60-second commercials can sell, certainly the three- and four-minute videos themselves—which are really promoting things of violence, making them seem fun and acceptable, normal, and healthy—will be much more influential." How strong or weak do you find Lamp's argument by analogy?

9. What evidence does Lamp provide to support his claim that the trend in rock music lyrics is away from innuendo to "blatant profanity"?

10. Examine Lamp's discussion of how the clothing worn by Madonna and other rock stars can be correlated with a trend toward earlier sexual activity by teenage girls. Does this correlation appear to be inductively sound?

11. What actions do groups like the National PTA and the Parents Music Resource Center recommend as a solution to what they see as the problem of "dark rock"? Which, if any, of these recommended actions appears to you to be the most feasible, practical, and reasonable?

12. What principle of rhetorical organization underlies the order in which Lamp raises issues within his argument? Does he move from most controversial to least or vice versa? Or does he use some other

principle of organization? How does the order in which issues are presented support Lamp's purpose in writing this article?

13. In a short essay, discuss your position on the issues raised by Lamp in this article. Do you think the solution worked out as a compromise among the NPTA, PMRC, and the recording industry was fair? In your opinion, should some form of labeling or censorship be imposed because some lyrics are perceived as offensive, sexually explicit, and dangerous? In your argument, be sure to take into account the explanations given by McCollum's lawyer, Thomas Anderson, attorney William Keahon, former guitarist Kerry Livgren, D. Joseph Novello, and Thomas Radecki as to how teenagers are actually influenced by "dark rock."

Leo N. Miletich

Rock Me with a Steady Roll

Leo N. Miletich is a former disc jockey and writer whose articles have appeared in Playboy, Cosmos, *and* The Library Journal. *Miletich uses a chronological pattern of organization to document his claim that musical innovations down through the ages have been greeted with the same degree of outrage now directed toward rock music. "Rock Me With a Steady Roll" appeared in* Reason *(March 1987).*

> *Rock music is a purveyor
> of drugs, alcoholism,
> fornication, adultery,
> necrophilia, beastiality [sic],
> homosexuality and every
> other debilitating influence. . . . It
> is satanic. . . . In a more
> subtle way, country music
> is just as bad.*

1

> —Evangelist Jimmy Swaggart

Music hath more than the power to charm wild beasts; according to some people, it can drive the beast in you wild.

2

After Jimmy Swaggart denounced Wal-Mart stores in a televised sermon condemning rock music, Wal-Mart leaped on the bluenose bandwagon. Just days later—and less than two weeks after the Meese pornography commission's call for a porn purge—Wal-Mart ordered the removal of certain records and rock-oriented magazines (including *Rolling Stone*) from its 900 stores.

3

Wal-Mart spokesmen later said Swaggart had nothing to do with the decision, though the company did ask for a copy of the sermon and Swaggart relishes taking responsibility for this moral enlightenment. (As in the case of 7-Eleven and other convenience stores being browbeaten into removing *Playboy* and *Penthouse* from their racks, intimidation tactics often reveal deep reservoirs of timidity among the nation's retailers.)

4

The current knee-jerk, overreactive surge of antimusic mania, fueled by preachers, "concerned parents," and exploitative politicians, may seem like something dreadfully new, a threat unparalleled in world history. In fact, the hysteria is as old as music itself. As Tolstoy said: "The older generation almost always fails to understand the younger one—

5

they think their own immutable values the only ones. . . . And so the older generation barks like a dog at what they don't understand." The barking has been going on a long time.

6   *Sing of good things, not bad,*
                    *Sing of happy, not sad.**

                                        —Joe Raposo, "Sing"

7   In the fourth century before Christ, Greek historian Ephorus warned, "Music was invented to deceive and delude mankind." This suspicion is reflected in the works of Aristotle ("The flute is not an instrument which has a good moral effect; it is too exciting") and Plato ("Musical innovation is full of danger to the State, for when modes of music change, the laws of the State always change with them"). The centuries that followed featured variations on those themes.

8   In 1572 a Vienna ordinance on public dancing laid down the law: "Ladies and maidens are to compose themselves with chastity and modesty and the male persons are to refrain from whirling and other such frivolities."

9   By 1595 "voluptuous turning, jumping, or running hither and yon" were also banned. (Apparently, "hither" was snuggling somewhere beneath the bandstand while "yon" was out in the dark Vienna woods.) A sermon of the time denounced dancers for "letting themselves be swung around and allowing themselves to be kissed and mauled about. . . . They cannot be honest while each entices the other to harlotry and offers a sop to the devil."

10   In *A Short View of the Immorality and Profaneness of the English Stage,* Jeremy Collier (1650–1726) decreed that "Musick is almost as dangerous as Gunpowder; and it may be requires looking after. . . . 'Tis possible a publick Regulation might not be amiss."

11   And in *An Irreverent and Thoroughly Incomplete Social History of Almost Everything,* Frank Muir describes the effect of the waltz when it was introduced into England from Germany in 1812: "Guardians of public morality immediately pronounced the waltz to be 'will-corrupting,' 'disgusting,' 'immodest'; an 'outright romp in which the couples not only embrace throughout the dance but, flushed and palpitating, whirl about in the posture of copulation.'"

12   In 1957, Meredith Wilson's *The Music Man* had Professor Harold Hill warning the people of River City, Iowa, about the evils inherent in ragtime (but you'll have to go listen to the record; permission to quote the passage was denied). Contemporary audiences laughed, but in fact, ragtime—perhaps because of its origins in bawdyhouse parlors, per-

formed by itinerant black musicians like Jelly Roll Morton and Scott Joplin—was no joke at the turn of the century.

The *Musical Courier* exclaimed in 1899: "A wave of vulgar, filthy and   13
suggestive music has inundated the land. Nothing but ragtime prevails, and the cake-walk with its obscene posturings, its lewd gestures. . . . Our children, our young men and women are continually exposed to its contiguity, to the monotonous attrition of this vulgarizing music. It is artistically and morally depressing and should be suppressed by press and pulpit."

> *I am heartily in favor of*   14
> *a board of censorship for the*
> *unspeakably depraved modern*
> *popular song. Its effect on*
> *young folk is shocking.*
> *The vicious song is allowed in*
> *the home by parents, who, no*
> *doubt, have not troubled*
> *themselves to look at the words.*
> *As a result, the suggestive*
> *meanings are allowed to play*
> *upon immature minds at a*
> *dangerous age.*
> *It is from the popular song that*
> *the popular suggestive dances*
> *spring. Together and apart,*
> *they are a menace to the*
> *social fabric.*

Pop Quiz: The above quote was delivered by: 15

(a) Jimmy Swaggart

(b) Jerry Falwell

(c) Jesse Helms

(d) Tipper Gore

To would-be censors, the social fabric is always on the brink of unraveling. The answer to the pop quiz is: (e) None of the above. That hysterical call for musical censorship came from violinist Maude Powell, speaking before the National Federation of Musical Clubs in Chicago—in 1913. A whole lot of unraveling hasn't happened yet.

Four years later, the New Orleans *Times-Picayune* editorialized   16
against what is now a trademark of its city. Jazz, said the paper's June 17

issue, "is the indecent story syncopated and counterpointed," a form of "musical vice" with no value, "and its possibilities of harm are great."

17   Meanwhile, back on the Continent, things weren't going too well either. Friedrich Nietzsche wrote of the music of Richard Wagner: "He contaminates everything he touches — he had made music sick."

18   In *Degeneration,* critic Max Nordau accused Wagner's music of things Jimmy Swaggart might only imagine while in the throes of religious ecstasy: "The lovers of his pieces behave like tom-cats gone mad, rolling in contortions and convulsions over a root of valerian. They reflect a state of mind which is . . . a form of Sadism. It is the love of those degenerates   who,   in   sexual   transport   become   like   wild beasts . . . which leads coarse nature to murder and lust."

19   Morris L. Ernst advanced the appropriate defense against such attacks. Fighting censorship of a play in 1930 which had been banned for its E-flat background music, Ernst asked: "Was there such a thing as a special gonadic key? Or did each person have a special key? Or were extroverts susceptible to one key and introverts to another?" The music was approved.

20   In 1986 the parents of a teenage boy who killed himself while listening to heavy-metal rocker Ozzy Osbourne's "Suicide Solution" sued the singer. They argued that a low-noise hum on the record had a disturbing influence on the boy and made him lyrically pliable. The courts recently dismissed the suit, giving First Amendment protection to the song. Thanks to the ruling, listeners are now responsible for their own behavior.

21   The Osbourne case was not the first time music has been said to cause suicide. There was a trend, of a sort, in "death rock" in the early '60s, epitomized by morbid teen songs like "Deadman's Curve" and "Last Kiss."

22   But before death rock came "Gloomy Sunday." According to David Ewen's *All the Years of American Popular Music,* the song was "promoted by its publishers as a 'suicide song' because it was reputed to have encouraged the suicidal tendencies of the tormented and the harassed of the early thirties." Written by Rezso Seress and translated by Sam M. Lewis, "Gloomy Sunday" was an import from equally gloomy Hungary. Billie Holiday recorded it in 1936 after it had been widely sung in concerts by Paul Robeson.

23   From that somber dirge of the Great Depression, America leaped into the "swing" era — and that too was roundly condemned. On October 25, 1938, the Archbishop of Dubuque, the Most Reverend Francis J. L. Beckman, labeled the swing music of Benny Goodman and others "a degenerated and demoralizing musical system" that had been "turned loose to gnaw away the moral fiber of young people." William E. Miles reports in *Damn It!* that the cleric told his flock that "jam sessions, jitterbugs and cannibalistic rhythmic orgies are wooing our youth along the primrose path to Hell!"

One of the most actively banned composers of the modern age was 24 Cole Porter. From his first 1928 hits, "Let's Do It" and "Let's Misbehave," Porter's saucy lyrics have been deleted and banned with amazing consistency. "I get no kick from champagne" was originally "I get no kick from cocaine," but that was deemed too strong for the mass audience. "I'm a Gigolo," "You've Got That Thing," "My Heart Belongs to Daddy," and "Love for Sale" were often attacked and kept off the airwaves.

Rodgers and Hammerstein also came in for Hollywood cleansing. In 25 the 1956 version of *Carousel*, "My Boy Bill' was sanitized and its impact lessened when "damn" was changed to "darn" and "skinny-lipped virgin" to "skinny-lipped lady."

When Porter's *Out of This World* opened in Boston in 1950, the 26 licensing division of the mayor's office sent a letter to the theater demanding the removal of "all irreverent use of 'God,'" various costume changes to render them "less suggestive," and the dropping of a lyric line that went, "saving my urgin's for vestal virgins." Also, the "ballet at end of Act 1 to be greatly modified" and the song lyric "goosing me" eliminated. The letter ended with a thanks for the theater's "past cooperation."

But at a congressional debate in 1957 about network censoring of 27 Stephen Foster songs ("darkies" and other such terms being by then seen as racial slurs), Rep. Frank Chelf left his old Kentucky home to remind his colleagues: "Whenever any group of people in this nation, or any other nation, take it upon themselves to set up rules and regulations by and through which they can arbitrarily control what songs shall or shall not be heard — and get away with it — then they can censor speech, censor religion, censor or even control the press."

> *If we are to change every* 28
> *song that has something in*
> *it that somebody does not like,*
> *there are not enough rewrite*
> *men in America to even get*
> *the project started.*

— Rep. Frank Chelf

When rock and roll burst upon the scene, it almost immediately 29 became the censors' prime target. Elvis and his twitching, pumping pelvis; almost anything by the Rolling Stones; even the insipid "Puff, the Magic Dragon" by Peter, Paul, and Mary became the focus of conservative outrage.

"Puff," the 1963 flip side of "Blowin' in the Wind," was interpreted 30 as a metaphorical celebration of pot smoking. As late as 1972 this was still a live issue — a radio station I worked for received angry letters when we played an *instrumental* version of the song. Ironically, ol' Puff is now a cartoon dragon seen on Saturday morning television.

31   Those who think that contemporary rock has gone "too far" along whatever personal highway to hell they're monitoring ought to look back 20 years—to the heyday of The Fugs. The name came from Norman Mailer's euphemism "Fug you" in *The Naked and the Dead.* Lillian Roxon's *Rock Encyclopedia* describes the group as "freaky-looking poets" from New York's East Village who "went out of their way to be 'offensive.'" She calls them "comics and satirists" and likens them to Lenny Bruce. It was, she notes, "like Henry Miller's novels set to music."

32   The Fugs's titles included: "Boobs a Lot," "Group Grope," "Dirty Old Man," "Kill For Peace," "New Amphet Amine Shriek," "I Command the House of the Devil," "Coca Cola Douche," "Wet Dream," "I Saw the Best Minds of My Generation Rot," and "Exorcising the Evil Spirits from the Pentagon." All prior to 1970.

33   It could probably be argued that Richard Nixon's Watergate exploits had a more disastrous influence on public ethics and morality in the '70s than did the music of The Fugs in the '60s or AC/DC in the '80s. And will be remembered longer.

34   Still, as Jimmy Swaggart's ministry has proven, some people will believe anything if it's screeched at them from a pulpit. In April 1986, according to the American Library Association's *Newletter on Intellectual Freedom,* the Reverends Steven W. Timmons of Beloit, Wisconsin, and William A. Riedel, pastor of the Westwood United Pentecostal Church in Jackson, Michigan, spoke hell-raising sermons against "satanic" rock groups. Named as part of Lucifer's legion were such innocuous songsmiths as Abba, The Eagles, Stevie Nicks, and "probably the most powerful figure in this," John Denver.

35   Timmons told a flock of young people that "Rocky Mountain High" teaches "witchcraft." (But wasn't it Sinatra who recorded "Witchcraft"? Or maybe it was "That Old Black Magic"? Or "That Old Devil Moon"?) The parishioners, worked up to a lather, buried a batch of rock records (and some Harlequin romance novels) under a tombstone that reads, "Never to rise again."

36   That same month, down in Ohio, a South Point evangelist named Jim Brown told his congregation that the theme song of TV's "Mr. Ed" contains hidden messages from Satan. He says he played the song backwards and heard, "the source is Satan." While singing "Oh, How I Love Jesus," the sappy psalmsters set about burning rock and country records and tapes. (If you want to check out the devil in Mr. Ed without rewiring your $1,200 Mitsubishi, use a reel-to-reel tape deck. Record the suspect song on the tape and then, without rewinding, take off the reels and place them on the opposite spindles. Then hit "Play.")

37   You hear what you listen for, of course. But it's a certainty that if it was possible to put backwards messages on records and have them subliminally influence forward-thinking listeners, people like Swaggart

would be loading gospel records with injunctions to "Praise the Lord" and "Send the Money."

> *If we think to regulate*   **38**
> *Printing, thereby to*
> *rectify manners, we must*
> *regulate all recreations*
> *and passions, all that is*
> *delightful to man. . . . And*
> *who shall silence all airs*
> *and madrigals?*

— John Milton

In 1985 there emerged a new group of neopuritans enraged by song **39** lyrics and album art—the Parents Music Resource Center (PMRC). All of its founders were mothers (in the biological sense, of course), and all were well connected to powerful politicians—even to the unseemly extreme of sleeping with them (though only in the Meese pornography commission's preferred state of conjugal bliss).

Like the porn commission's emphasis on the most shocking kinds of **40** smut, the record molesters circulate copies of the most explicit rock lyrics in order to work people up to a froth of indignation. While it is certainly true that "offensive," as Vladimir Nabokov said, "is frequently but a synonym for 'unusual,'" this stuff is as warped as a disk left in the trunk on a hot summer day. Just look at this filth:

> *I'm wild about that thing,*
> *It makes me to laugh and sing.*
> *Give it to me, papa,*
> *I'm wild about that thing.*
>
> *Give ev'ry bit of it else I'll die,*
> *I'm wild about that thing.*
>
> *What's the matter, papa?*
> *Please don't stall!*
> *Don't you know I love it*
> *And I wants it all!*
>
> *Yes, give my bell a ring,*
> *You press my button,*
> *I'm wild about that thing.*
> *Mmmmm, if you want to satisfy my soul*
> *Come on and rock me with a steady roll,*
> *I'm wild about that thing.*

41   And what about this one from the same depraved singer:

> *Lovin' is the thing I crave*
> *For your love I'd be your slave,*
> *You gotta give me some. . . .*
> *Said Mrs. Jones to ol' Butcher Pete,*
> *I want a piece of your good ol' meat. . . .*
> *I crave your round steak,*
> *You gotta give me some.*

Why, if that song reached the tender ears of our young people, our whole value system would collapse like . . . uh, just a second . . . I'm sorry, those aren't on the PMRC list. They were recorded by Bessie Smith in 1929.

42   Okay, this one's a rocker, and one feminists hate: "Honey, come in this house and stop all that yakety-yak./Don't make me nervous cause I'm holdin' a baseball bat."* Clearly a call for female degradation and violent wife abuse! Has this singer no shame? Your guess is as good as mine: it was recorded in the late 1950s by Pat Boone, who now spends much of his time lobbying for prayer in the public schools.

43   Speaking of violent imagery in oft-heard songs, sample this lyric: "The havoc of war and the battle's confusion . . . their blood has washed out their foul footsteps' pollution." That's verse three; you might be more familiar with verse one, which includes: "And the rocket's red glare, the bombs bursting in air."

44   It's bad enough that our national anthem is set to the tune of a rowdy beer-drinking song—such a bad example for impressionable youth— but to encourage them to sing of such violent goings-on might inspire them to who-knows-what murderous actions!

45   It becomes obvious that if you really want to shield kids from sex and violence—from life itself—*everything* better have a warning label on it. And if music is going to be blamed for antisocial behavior, you'd better ban the Bible too. On August 22, 1986, an 18-year-old Miami high-school student named Alejandro Martinez stabbed his grandmother to death. He told police she interrupted him while he was reading the Bible and he thought she was the devil. For the well-being of the world's grandmothers, better prohibit sales of that book to minors.

46   But there's at least one cry common to all would-be censors, the PMRC being no exception: they all claim they are not censors. In a letter to *Film Comment*, Tipper Gore, cofounder of PMRC and the wife of Sen. Albert

---

*"Honey Hush" by Lou Willie Turner.
Copyright (c) 1954, 1963 by Progressive Music Publishing Co.
Copyright (c) Renewed, assigned to Unichappell Music Inc. (Rightsong Music, publisher).
International Copyright Secured. ALL RIGHTS RESERVED. Used by permission.

Gore (D-Tenn.), responded to the charge of advocating censorship by flatly claiming, "We are doing just the opposite." All PMRC wants, she wrote, is lyrics printed on the outside of albums that will allow "consumers to know what they are getting before they buy it." (Given the nature of kids, the dirtiest albums will thus be assured of brisk sales.)

Despite Mrs. Gore's protests to the contrary, though, PMRC actions   47
suggest a desire for censorship. For one thing, she was successful in getting the Senate Commerce Committee to hold a widely publicized hearing on rock lyrics, at which rockers Frank Zappa, Dee Snider of the band Twisted Sister, and John Denver defended the First Amendment against a horde of outraged senators. That's called government intimidation of artists.

Mrs. Gore later told *Newsweek*, "We're determined to wipe out the   48
pervasive message in music that to be hip and cool you have to have sex." Wipe out, as in eradicate, as in throttle and suppress that idea before anyone can express or hear it. That's called censorship.

Another thing would-be censors have in common is that they never   49
stop at the most lurid examples of what they find offensive but keep redrawing their line (like Libya's "Line of Death") ever backwards, from satanism to heavy petting. "Consider Madonna," wrote syndicated columnist Michael J. McManus in August 1985. "She mocks virginity and Christianity!" As if she doesn't have a right to! Shakespeare mocked virginity (*All's Well That Ends Well*); should he too be censored?

And in *America*, a Catholic-oriented magazine, Richard W. Chilson   50
quoted a Bob Dylan lyric that "praised his savior as 'a shot of love.' Anyone who knows and loves the man from Galilee," wrote Chilson (who obviously neither knows nor loves poetic vision) "should find this image scandalous and obscene." Obscenity, according to the Supreme Court, can be legally banned. Bye bye, Dylan.

> *There is perhaps no*   51
> *phenomenon which contains*
> *so much destructive feeling*
> *as moral indignation, which*
> *permits envy or hate*
> *to be acted out under*
> *the guise of virtue.*

> — Eric Fromm

Lewd and obscene waltzes; scandalous ragtime and jazz; showtunes   52
and blues red-penciled by bluenoses; Mr. Ed an agent of Satan; John Denver a warlock. Truly, it's a depressing catalog of narrow-minded boobery at work. Censors are people disturbed by what they perceive around them, who either don't understand the problem or who have manufactured a problem where none exists. They don't know what else

to do but feel they have to do *something*. And censorship (no matter what other name they give it) of what they find offensive seems so quick, so easy. Out of sight, out of mind. You might just as well ban cars because some people drive drunk.

53   Calls for banning this or that seem to occur in cycles. There are clots of oversensitive, overreactive people in every generation, people resistant to and scared by change. Instead of thinking for themselves, they'll let their self-appointed leaders do it for them.

54   Thinking for yourself *is* dangerous. It carries with it the possibility of error as well as the weight of personal responsibility. For some people, that's too heavy a burden. They certainly have the right to denounce anything they don't like. But when they move to take what they don't like away from you, away from me, that's un-American. That's censorship.

55   If I could choose one song lyric to play for the censors, it would be Maxwell Anderson's "How Can You Tell An American," from the 1938 stage musical *Knickerbocker Holiday*:

> *It's just that he hates and eternally*
> *despises*
> *The policeman on his beat, and the judge*
> *with his assizes,*
> *The sheriff with his warrants and the*
> *bureaucratic crew,*
> *For the sole and simple reason that they*
> *tell him what to do.*
> *And he insists on eating,*
> *He insists on drinking,*
> *He insists on reading,*
> *He insists on thinking —*
> *Free of governmental snooping or a governmental plan,*
> *And that's an American!†*

Or would that song now be banned as fostering disrespect for law and authority?

Questions for Discussion and Writing

1. How does Miletich use a quotation by evangelist Jimmy Swaggart to illustrate the kind of argument that his article is intended to refute?

---

†"How Can You Tell An American" by Maxwell Anderson and Kurt Weill. Copyright (c) 1938 by DeSylva, Brown & Henderson Inc. Copyright Renewed. Assigned to Chappell & Co. Inc. and Hampshire House Publishing Corp. for the USA only. International copyright secured. ALL RIGHTS RESERVED. Used by permission.

2. In what way does Miletich's organization of his article—using a chronological pattern to document the objections with which all musical innovations have been greeted down through the ages—support his argument against censorship of rock music? That is, how does putting the latest objections in a historical context work to his advantage and make his argument more persuasive?

3. Which of the examples of pre-twentieth-century criticism of music did you find the most effective?

4. To what extend does Miletich's argument depend on the assumption that the latest developments in contemporary rock music and in rock lyrics are opposed by critics who are against whatever they cannot understand?

5. How is Miletich's use of examples of music now considered to be traditional, along with criticisms of them made at the time they came out, intended to cut the ground from under today's critics of rock music?

6. Is Miletich's reference to Richard Nixon and the Watergate era relevant to his argument? To what extent is it a red herring? Do any of the following qualify as red herrings: phrases from the national anthem, the incident of Alejandro Martinez, the role played by the Bible, and Miletich's reference to Shakespeare's *All's Well that Ends Well?*

7. How does Miletich use the report by the American Library Association's *Newsletter on Intellectual Freedom* to question the ability of critics to differentiate "satanic" rock groups from "innocuous" performers? How does undercutting the credibility of this association's judgments serve Miletich's purpose? How does the example of the supposedly satanic theme song from the television program "Mr. Ed" serve the same argumentative purpose?

8. How does Miletich use a quotation by John Milton to set the debate in the context of a defense of free speech?

9. Are there any places in Miletich's article where his tone becomes so sarcastic that he might risk alienating those members of his audience who were neutral on the issue? For example, consider this paragraph:

> In 1985 there emerged a new group of neopuritans enraged by song lyrics and album art—the Parents Music Resource Center (PMRC). All of its founders were mothers (in the biological sense, of course), and all were well connected to powerful politicians—even to the unseemly extreme of sleeping with them (though only in the Meese pornography commission's preferred state of conjugal bliss).

10. How does Miletich use excerpts from songs sung by Bessie Smith in 1929 to support his claim?

11. To what extent might Miletich's definition of censors be perceived as an example of an either/or fallacy? He defines them thus: "Censors are people disturbed by what they perceive around them, who either don't understand the problem or have manufactured a problem where none exists." How is this stipulative definition intended to serve as a persuasive definition of the term *censor*?

12. Compare Miletich's account of the Senate Commerce Committee's meeting on rock lyrics with that given by Rob Lamp. Whose description of the role played by Frank Zappa, John Denver, and Dee Snider (of the band Twisted Sister) gives a more accurate picture of how these particular musicians testified? If you can spot any omissions or distortions, how might this relate to the particular author's purpose?

13. Rhetorically, how does Miletich use a framing technique to bring his argument back to his opening thesis?

14. Write an essay comparing and contrasting the argumentative strategies used by Lamp and Miletich. Who, in your opinion, makes a better case and uses identifiable rhetorical techniques to better advantage?

Donna Woolfolk Cross

Shadows on the Wall

Donna Woolfolk Cross, a former advertising copywriter, currently teaches at Onondaga Community College in Syracuse, New York. She is the author of Word Abuse: How the Words We Use Use Us *(1979) and* Mediaspeak: How Television Makes Up Your Mind *(1983), from which "Shadows on the Wall" was taken. This essay grew out of Cross's desire to help her students defend themselves against manipulation by admen, politicians, and the media. She offers evidence that children find television more exciting and more real than their own lives. Cross also cites research to show that adult audiences cannot distinguish reality from television fantasy and believe that fictionalized docudramas accurately portray real events.*

I see no virtue in having a public that cannot distinguish fact from fantasy. When you start thinking fantasy is reality you have a serious problem. People can be stampeded into all kinds of fanaticism, folly and warfare.

Isaac Asimov

Why sometimes I've believed as many as six impossible things before breakfast.

Queen to Alice in Lewis Carroll's
Through the Looking Glass

In Book Four of *The Republic*, Plato tells a story about four prisoners who since birth have been chained inside a cave, totally isolated from the world outside. They face a wall on which shadows flicker, cast by the light of the fire. The flickering shadows are the only reality they know. Finally, one of the prisoners is released and permitted to leave the cave. Once outside, he realizes that the shadows he has watched for so long are only pale, distorted reflections of a much brighter, better world. He returns to tell the others about the world outside the cave. They listen in disbelief, then in anger, for what he says contradicts all they have known. Unable to accept the truth, they cast him out as a heretic.

Today, our picture of the world is formed in great part from television's flickering shadows. Sometimes that picture is a fairly accurate reflection of the real world; sometimes it is not. But either way, we accept it as real and we act upon it as if it were reality itself. "And that's the way it is," Walter Cronkite assured us every evening for over nineteen years, and most of us did not doubt it.

3   A generation of Americans has grown up so dependent on television that its images appear as real to them as life itself. On a recent trip to a widely advertised amusement park, my husband, daughter, and I rode a "white-water" raft through manufactured "rapids." As we spun and screamed and got thoroughly soaked, I noticed that the two young boys who shared our raft appeared rather glum. When the ride ended, I heard one remark to the other, "It's more fun on television."

4   As an experiment, Jerzy Kosinski gathered a group of children, aged seven to ten years, into a room to show them some televised film. Before the show began, he announced, "Those who want to stay inside and watch the films are free to remain in the classroom, but there's something fascinating happening in the corridor, and those who want to see it are free to leave the room." Kosinski describes what happened next:

> No more than 10 percent of the children left. I repeated, "You know, what's outside is really fantastic. You have never seen it before. Why don't you just step out and take a look?"
> And they always said, "No, no, no, we prefer to stay here and watch the film." I'd say, "But you don't know what's outside." "Well, what is it?" they'd ask. "You have to go find out." And they'd say, "Why don't we just sit here and see the film first? . . . " They were already too corrupted to take a chance on the outside. (Sohn, 1975, pp. 20–21)

5   In another experiment, Kosinski brought a group of children into a room with two giant video screens mounted on the side walls. He stood in the front of the room and began to tell them a story. Suddenly, as part of a prearranged plan, a man entered and pretended to attack Kosinski, yelling at him and hitting him. The entire episode was shown on the two video screens as it happened. The children did not respond, but merely watched the episode unfold on the video screens. They rarely glanced at the two men struggling in the front of the room. Later, in an interview with Kosinski, they explained that the video screens captured the event much more satisfactorily, providing close-ups of the participants, their expressions, and such details as the attacker's hand on Kosinski's face (Sohn, 1975, p. 22).

6   Some children can become so preoccupied with television that they are oblivious to the real world around them. UPI filed a report on a burglar who broke into a home and killed the father of three children, aged nine, eleven, and twelve. The crime went unnoticed until ten hours later, when police entered the apartment after being called by neighbors and found the three children watching television just a few feet away from the bloody corpse of their father.

7   Shortly after this report was released, the University of Nebraska

conducted a national survey in which children were asked which they would keep if they had to choose — their fathers or their televisions sets. *Over half* chose the television sets!

Evidence of this confusion between reality and illusion grows daily. Trial lawyers, for example, complain that juries have become conditioned to the formulas of televised courtroom dramas.

Former Bronx District Attorney Mario Merola (1981) says,

> All they want is drama, suspense — a confession. Never in all my years as a prosecutor have I seen someone cry from the witness stand, "I did it! I did it — I confess!" But that's what happens on prime-time TV — and that's what the jurors think the court system is all about. (p. 17)

He adds, "Such misconceptions make the work of a district attorney's office much harder than it needs to be" (p. 17). Robert Daley describes one actual courtroom scene in which the defendant was subjected to harsh and unrelenting cross-examination: "I watched the jury," he says.

> It seemed to me that I had seen this scene before, and indeed I had dozens of times — on television. On television the murderer always cracks eventually and says something like "I can't take it any more." He suddenly breaks down blubbering and admits his guilt. But this defendant did not break down, he did not admit his guilt. He did not blubber. It seemed to me I could see the jury conclude before my eyes: ergo, he cannot be guilty — and indeed the trial ended in a hung jury. . . . Later I lay in bed in the dark and brooded about the trial. . . . If [television courtroom dramas] had never existed, would the jury have found the defendant guilty even though he did not crack? (Mankiewicz, 1978, p. 272)

Television actors are frequently treated by their fans as though they actually were the characters they are paid to portray. Confusion of the actor with his role occurs at the very highest levels. Consider the following examples:

— Robert Young, the actor who played Marcus Welby on the long-running television series, is asked to deliver the commencement address at Harvard Medical School.

— Norman Fell, the actor who played landlord Mr. Roper on *Three's Company*, is hired to appear in a series of commercials promoting tenants' class action suits against the Department of Housing and Urban Development.

— Michelle Nichols, former ballerina, supperclub singer, and actress in the old *Star Trek* series, is made a member of the Board of Directors of the National Space Institute, and a consultant for NASA.

— John Gavin, an actor whose command of Spanish resulted in a lucrative series of television spots advertising rum in South America, is appointed United States Ambassador to Mexico.

11   Television drama seems to be trying to blur further the fading distinctions between reality and fiction. In the minds of millions of Americans, the television production of *Shōgun* became an accurate account of Japanese history, tradition, and thought. Yet Professor Henry Smith, a specialist in Japanese history, who was in Japan at the time the show aired there, reported that the Japanese found the program to be "bad if not insulting" (Bernstein, 1981, p. 90). Before the first broadcast in Japan, Yoko Shimada, the actress who played the lead role of Mariko, and former U.S. Ambassador to Japan Edwin O. Reischauer appeared on the screen to appeal for audience indulgence toward this naive and error-ridden "Western view" of Japan. But most Americans readily accepted that view, because, as *The New York Times* (1981) suggested, it "provided stereotypes that Americans could recognize, feel comfortable with, and accept as authentic" (p. 90).

12   At least the television drama of *Shōgun*, derived from James Clavell's best-selling novel, never claimed to be anything but a work of fiction. But other forms of entertainment, such as "fact-based" or "docu-" dramas, are far less clear about where fact ends and fiction begins. Originally, fact-based dramas were imaginative reconstructions of great historical events, of the kind satirized by Russell Baker (1980):

> The army of the Israelites is gazing at a distant city. "Hath yonder distant city a name, O Joshua?"
> "That, sergeant, is a place called — JERICHO!"

* * *

> Behind his desk in the Oval Office Franklin Roosevelt glances up from dispatches. "Well, bless my soul," he says to a man entering, "if it isn't HARRY HOPKINS, THE MOST CONTROVERSIAL FIGURE IN THE NEW DEAL."
> "I hear there is bad news, chief."
> "True, my CONTROVERSIAL YET CLOSE FRIEND. The Japanese have bombed a place."
> "What place, chief?"
> "A place called — PEARL HARBOR!"

* * *

> "General Washington," asks Colonel Travers, "what is that town ahead?"
> "Scaggsville, Maryland, if you must know, and hereafter I'll thank you not to ask me that question again until we come to a certain place in southeastern Virginia."
> "Do you mean a place called — "

"That's my line," says Washington. "A place called—YORKTOWN!"

"My dream, Colonel, is of a place called—

"Do you ever dream of the future, General?"

"My dream, Colonel, is of a place called—THE UNITED STATES OF AMERICA—a place where, FOURSCORE AND SEVEN YEARS FROM NOW we will be called—OUR FOREFATHERS." (p. 12)

13

The popularity of this form of entertainment proved to be so great that rights to "real life" properties were bought up at an astonishing rate. Promising news events were "dramatized" even as they unfolded. The story of Jean Harris, the school headmistress convicted of murdering diet doctor Herman Tarnower, was written, produced, and broadcast less than four months after her trial ended. On the very afternoon *Newsweek* published a story on the death of a Los Angeles college student during a fraternity hazing, four dramatized versions of the story were filed with the Writers Guild. Last year alone, three news features from CBS's *60 Minutes* were turned into television docudramas. Writer Lance Morrow (1978) comments,

> At times television seems a kind of history-devouring machine scooping up great sections of reality and then reconstituting them, made for TV. . . . Dozens of public events, issues, and figures have been filtered through the sophisticated docudramatizing process. In millions of viewers' minds the televised account has now become surrogate reality. (p. 19)

Many docudramas invite this reaction by deliberately trying to create 14
a "real-life" atmosphere. *The Rideout Case*, a dramatization of the widely publicized court case in which a wife sued her husband for rape, used documentary techniques such as providing the exact hour and date for specific scenes—"October 6, 1978, 2:30 P.M." Other "fact-based" dramas assure viewers, "The names have been changed. But the story is true."

Bill Moyers comments, 15

> Docudramas cross the line between art and reality without telling you that they have done so. They are done for the sake of commerce instead of illumination and are a very disturbing mélange of fact and fantasy. Without discriminating respect for what actually happened, they can set back the cause of public understanding by giving an *illusion* of what happened. They are done hastily with little regard for the nuances and subtleties that make history intelligible. (Morrow, 1978, p. 20)

16   They also permit opinion to masquerade as fact. The producers and writers of docudramas can, in effect, ensure that their interpretation of the meaning of events will be seen as the "correct" one. History Professor Eric Foner says,

> I think the first thing that ought to be done by people who are involved in the docudramas is to realize that your selection of the facts is an interpretation. The very subject you choose to present is itself a political decision. (Levinson, 1981, p. 42)

17   Given the social and economic status of television's illusionmakers, it is not surprising that their interpretation of history is often pro-Establishment. Take, for example, *The Missiles of October*, a docudramatization of John F. Kennedy's handling of the Cuban missile crisis. The program depicted Kennedy as a Lincolnesque hero capable of making difficult decisions and sticking by them. For millions of people, that vision has become the reality, though libraries are filled with books that give very different—and less favorable—interpretations of Kennedy's actions and motives.

18   Or there is the example of *The Marva Collins Story*, a docudrama based on the experiences of a black schoolteacher who, disgusted with the inadequacies of the ghetto public schools, quit and set up her own highly successful private school. The program clearly identified the reason for the public schools' dismal failure adequately to educate ghetto children: teachers so overwhelmed with bureaucratic regulations and unnecessary paperwork that they have no time left "for our *real* jobs— teaching!" All the other social and economic factors that might cause the inadequacy of ghetto schooling were entirely overlooked. This left a clear political message: We should leave the school system exactly as it is, but try to cut down on unnecessary and harmful regulation by the federal government.

19   Still another example of pro-Establishment propaganda was seen in the docudrama series *Backstairs at the White House*, which dealt with the intimate personal lives of twentieth-century American presidents: Teddy Roosevelt, Taft, Wilson, Harding, Coolidge, Hoover, and Franklin Roosevelt. Ostensibly based on "the facts" about these men, much of the dialogue necessarily had to be invented, because it consisted of private conversations between family members. Yet many people regarded these conversations as matters of factual record. After the broadcast, I questioned a group of my freshmen college students about their understanding of what they had seen:

Q: How much of it do you think actually happened?
A: All of it. I mean, it said it was based on the facts, didn't it?
Q: How do you think the writers knew exactly what President Wilson said to his wife at that point?

A: I don't know. I guess maybe they interviewed people and stuff like that. And aren't all White House conversations recorded on tape?

A: Maybe those weren't the *exact* words they said, but they must have said something very close to it or else they couldn't get away with saying it was a "true story."

As far as these students were concerned, the dialogue was real, not 20 invented. The invented dialogue portrayed the presidents as benign statesmen with no identifiable party affiliations or political convictions beyond an altruistic concern for the welfare of the nation. Critic Frank Rich comments,

> I'm willing to accept the premise that every fact in *Backstairs at the White House* was accurate, but what was that show telling us? What did they do with those facts? It was telling us that all the presidents in this century were a bunch of cuddly guys . . . and they had no particular strong political positions. It wasn't clear how they got us in the wars and took us out of the wars and so on. That show was a complete disservice to history. . . . (Levinson, 1981, p. 142).

Responding to remarks made by docudrama producer Alan Lands- 21 burg, journalist Richard Reeves said,

> [This was] one of the most extraordinary statements I've ever heard. . . . What he said was that he had toiled in the vineyards of documentaries and he got terribly frustrated by photographing the outside of the White House and not being allowed in the Oval Office to find out what happened. Then he said, "Thank God docudrama came along . . . and allowed me to guess what was happening in the Oval Office." He then continued to say what a marvelous opportunity this was and ended by saying, "And now I can tell the truth. I can tell what's really going on in the Oval Office." That to me is a political story — that many Americans are going to be told one man's guess. (Levinson, 1981, p. 143)

Docudramas and similar forms of entertainment that mix fact and 22 fiction allow storytellers to propagandize for established political and social viewpoints. No one alerts viewers that this is what they are doing. As psychologist Victor Cline explains,

> The very real danger of docudrama films is that people take it for granted that they're true and — unlike similar fictionalized history in movies and theater — they are seen on a medium which also presents straight news. No matter how much they call these movies "drama," they're really advocacy journalism. They can't

help reflecting the point of view of the writer or the studio or the network. (Davidson, 1978, p. 62)

23   The impact of such propagandizing is enormous because so many of us accept what we see as truth, not illusion. Writer Paddy Chayevsky railed against this kind of folly in his award-winning movie *Network*:

> Television is not the truth. . . . We lie like hell. . . . We deal in illusions, man. None of it is true. But *you* people sit there day after day, night after night. . . . We're all you know. You're beginning to believe the illusions we're spinning here. You're beginning to think that the tube is reality and that your own lives are unreal. You *do* whatever the tube tells you. You dress like the tube, you eat like the tube, you raise your children like the tube. This is mass madness, you maniacs. In God's name, *you* people are the real thing; *we're* the illusion! (Hedrin, 1976, p. 151)

24   Looking back through history, it is easy to see how people erred because the "pictures in their heads" did not correspond with reality. Because they believed God was offended by "pagan" art, Egyptian Christians burned the greatest repository of knowledge in the ancient world, the library at Alexandria. Because they believed that witches walked the earth, the Salem settlers drowned old women and children. Because they believed a disastrous economy and mounting social problems were caused by a lack of racial "purity," Nazis exterminated six million Jews.

25   Today we view the illusions on which these irrational actions were based as ludicrous. We flatter ourselves that our own mental maps are far more accurate guides to the actual territory. Yet the discrepancy between the pictures in our heads and the world outside is just as wide as that of our predecessors. We revere our founding fathers as "patriots," when in fact they were revolutionaries who overthrew an existing government and replaced it with a new one; we pride ourselves on our Constitution and Bill of Rights, though in fact we often disapprove the practice of its fundamental tenets; we accuse "big government" of being the source of our economic and social woes, though in fact we suffer and complain when government funds and services are withdrawn; we believe we are the champions of liberty throughout the world, though in fact we actively support oppressive governments.

26   We are the victims of the most extravagant of all illusions: that every kind of human distress can be solved with an appropriate pill, and that a simple and easy solution exists for even the most complex problem.

27   A poster popular during the time of the hostage crisis in Iran pictured actor Clint Eastwood as "Dirty Harry" holding a .44 magnum gun to the head of the Ayatollah Khomeini and saying, "Say goodnight, Khomeini." This type of "poster thinking" reduces the complexity of world

affairs to the level of understanding of a five-year-old child. And five-year-old children, charming and funny as they are, are not equipped to deal with the intricacies of foreign policy. Daniel Boorstin comments,

> Now, in the height of our power, we are threatened by a new and peculiarly American menace. It is not the menace of class war . . . of poverty, of disease, of illiteracy. . . . It is the menace of unreality. We risk being the first people in history to make their illusions so vivid, so persuasive, so "realistic" that we can live in them. (Boorstin, 1962, p. 240)

There is a great danger whenever simplistic illusions displace reality. 28
The manufacturers of those illusions acquire enormous power over the rest of us. Semanticist Alfred Korzybski says, "Human beings are a symbolic class of life. Those who rule our symbols rule us." The danger is magnified when, as with television broadcasting, the illusionmakers constitute a very small and unrepresentative social group. Jerry Mander (1978) says,

> Television technology is inherently anti-democratic. Because of its cost, the limited kind of information it can disseminate, the way it transforms the people who use it, and the fact that a few speak while millions absorb, television is suitable for use only by the most powerful corporate interests in the country. They inevitably use it to redesign human minds. . . . (p. 349)

It is still possible to free ourselves from this insidious manipulation of 29
our minds. Commercial broadcasters do not, after all, *own* the airwaves; they license them. The mechanisms for revoking those licenses if broadcasters fail to serve "the public interest" are clearly defined in the Federal Communications Act. These mechanisms have not been used, not because they won't work, but because powerful groups are opposed to having them work.

There is much that can be done. An important first step is to accept 30
the fact that change is possible, that the current state of affairs does not represent a fixed and immovable order. All of this century's important political achievements, from women's suffrage to civil rights legislation, appeared at the outset to be mere tilting at windmills. To start with a small, easily achieved goal: Antitrust proceedings can be instituted to compel networks to sell the five stations each now owns and operates outright. As journalist and television critic Jeff Greenfield (1978) asks, "Should suppliers of programming also have instant control over a quarter of the American viewing population" (p. 34)?

Further antitrust action can be taken to require networks to accept 31
news stories and programs from freelance agencies. Networks argue that they use news features they produce themselves because they must be

sure of their accuracy and truthfulness. In reality this is another way to consolidate their control over the free flow of information. Important documentaries have been made by independent producers, and many more have been proposed, only to be kept from the public view by the network blackout of outside news sources.

32   The number of hours that any one licensee uses on a given channel can be legally restricted. Greenfield (1978) says,

> There is no reason why Channel 2 in New York must be pro-
> grammed from dawn to dawn, seven days a week, by the same
> corporation, particularly when a broadcast band represents a gov-
> ernment-licensed monopoly of a terribly scarce and enormously
> valuable "property." (p. 34)

Broadcast time could be shared by groups of licensees occupying alter-
nating time periods. Such a move would be in keeping with the Supreme Court ruling that truly democratic communication requires a variety of information from "diverse and antagonistic sources."

33   Obviously, so thorough a shaking of The Powers That Be will not come about without a struggle. But it is a struggle well worth waging. What is at stake is not merely the issue of who will control the media but who, ultimately, will control America. Consider the words of former FCC Chairman Nicholas Johnson (1970), who believed that the mass media should not hold us hostage to our old dreams but lead us toward new ones:

> The issue before us ought to be stated quite starkly. It is, quite
> simply, who is to retain the potential to rule America. We know, if
> we are honest with ourselves, which segments of the economic
> and social structure have the loudest voices. . . . But the poten-
> tial for popular check remains. It remains, however, only so long
> as the people can obtain education and information, only so long
> as they can communicate with each other, only so long as they
> can retain potential control over the mass media of this country.
> So long as we preserve the people's *potential* to rule — their po-
> tential opportunity to participate in the operation of their mass
> media — there is some hope, however small, that some future
> generation — perhaps the next — will use this potential to rebuild
> America. (p. 219)

WORKS CITED

Baker, Russell. "Sunday Observer," *New York Times Magazine* 15 June 1980: 12.

Bernstein, Paul. "Making of a Literary Shogun," *New York Times Magazine* 13 Sept. 1981: 46+.

Boorstin, Daniel. *The Image, or What Happened to the American Dream*. New York: Atheneum, 1962.

Davidson, Bill. "Docudrama: Fact or Fiction?" *Celebrity*. Ed. James Monaco. New York: Delta, 1978. 62–67.

Greenfield, Jeff. "TV is *Not* the World," *Columbia Journalism Review* 17 (May 1978): 29–34.

Hedrin, Sam. *Network*. (Screenplay by Paddy Chayevsky.) New York: Pocket Books, 1976.

Johnson, Nicholas. *How to Talk Back to Your TV Set*. Boston: Little, Brown, 1970.

Levinson, Richard, and William Link. *Stay Tuned: An Inside Look at the Making of Prime-Time Television*. New York: St. Martin's, 1981.

Mander, Jerry. *Four Arguments for the Elimination of TV*. New York: Morrow, 1978.

Mankiewicz, Frank, and Joel Swerdlow. *Remote Control: TV and the Manipulation of American Life*. New York: Times, 1978.

Merola, Mario. "Who'd Beat on a Suspect While the Camera's Running?" *TV Guide* 25 July 1981: 17–20.

Morrow, Lance. "The History-Devouring Machine: Television and the Docudrama," *Media and Methods* Oct. 1978: 18+.

Sohn, David. "A Nation of Videots: An Interview with Jerzy Kosinski."

Questions for Discussion and Writing

1. Explain the relationship of Cross's title, "Shadows on the Wall," and her summary of Plato's allegory of the cave to her assertions about the nature and effects of television.

2. To what extent does Cross's argument depend on the assumption that people depend on television not only for entertainment but for values and instruction on how to look, act, and present themselves?

3. How does Cross show that adults are just as vulnerable as children to confusing television's version of reality with the real world?

4. In what way, according to Cross, does television have a "pro-Establishment" bias and serve the interests of those in power?

5. How does Cross use the examples of docudramas (fact-based television stories) to show that audiences unquestionably accept stories that bear only a slight resemblance to actual events?

6. What significance does Cross find in the results of one study that found that adults serving on a jury were confused and disappointed when the defendant did not jump up and confess to the crime, since most television programs depict people behaving that way in courtroom scenes?

7. In a short essay, discuss how this article exemplifies the methodology discussed in Chapter six about how to go about writing a research paper from different sources. What different kinds of sources does Cross draw on and how does she use them (for example, interviews and surveys)? Analyze her decisions as to when to quote directly, when to paraphrase, and when to summarize. Evaluate her essay within the framework of what a good argument research paper should do.

8. Discuss the implications of one finding or set of findings cited by Cross that you find especially significant. To help your readers understand your analysis, be sure to state your own assumptions clearly. You might consider any of the following: (*a*) when given the choice of watching television or experiencing something new, wonderful, and exciting, 90 per cent of the children in the experiment chose to watch television; (*b*) when given the choice of watching an actual fight or watching the same fight on television, children in the study chose to watch the televised version; or (*c*) when asked to choose between giving up their fathers or their television, most children in a study chose to give up their fathers rather than their television sets.

9. As a reading assignment, read Jerzy Kosinski's novella *Being There* (1971) and analyze how the main character, Chauncey Gardiner, depends on television for guidance in all situations.

10. In an essay, evaluate Cross's recommendations. Which of these proposed changes seems to you to be more feasible and which seems to be less realistic, less workable, or less desirable? Explain your assessment.

Peggy Charren

Should We Ban TV Advertising to Children? YES

Peggy Charren is president of Action for Children's Television (ACT), a national consumers' group. "Should We Ban TV Advertising to Children? YES" appeared in National Forum: The Phi Kappa Phi Journal *(1979). Charren cites studies proving that young children are consistently fooled by deceptive product claims because they are unable to evaluate the nature and intent of advertising. Charren argues that the First Amendment protection of freedom of expression should be suspended in the case of television ads directed at children under the age of eight.*

It is beyond dispute that television is a major element in the lives of all Americans, especially children. Recent statistics bear this out. As of September, 1977, 98 percent of American households, 72.9 million homes, had at least one television set; 46 percent of those had more than one set; and 78 percent of television households have color sets. Approximately 33.3 million children between the ages of two and eleven live in households with television sets. The average household viewing time is six hours and ten minutes per day. Children age six to eleven view, on the average, 24 hours and 25 minutes of television per week.[1] Two-to-five-year-olds view an average of 27 hours and 25 minutes of television per week. Daily television viewing of six-to-eleven-year-old children peaks at eight p.m., when 44 percent of the six-to-eleven-year-olds in television-owning households are watching television. The viewing of two-to-five-year-olds peaks at ten a.m. Saturday morning, when 36 percent are watching television.[2]   1

It has been estimated that two-to-five-year-olds view, on average, 20,746 television commercials per year, and that six-to-eleven-year-olds see 19,236 commercials a year.[3] The average two-to-eleven-year-old child is exposed to approximately five hours of advertising per week.   2

Television broadcast revenues were $5,889,000,000 in 1977.[4] It has been estimated that $660,765,000 of that amount was generated by television advertising of products which have strong appeal to children: candy, soft drinks, cereals, and toys.[5] It is clear that these expenditures would not continue to be made if they did not result in increased sales of the advertised products.   3

Figures of this magnitude raise significant questions. First, are chil-   4 dren who request parents to purchase specific products capable of evaluating product claims made in advertisements? Second, are they basing their requests on factual information derived from advertisements or are their requests based on emotional appeals in the advertisements which are calculated to generate unreasoning responses? Finally, is it feasible to place upon parents the full responsibility for evaluating the products advertised to children and then mediating between children and television advertising?

5   *The child as consumer.* Advertisers who sell to children are asking the most impressionable and least experienced members of the audience to make complex and reasoned consumer judgments. In order to make a meaningful purchase decision, the child, whose skills of analysis and judgment are still in a developmental stage, must answer an intricate series of questions: Is the product as it appears in the TV commercials? Is the product more desirable than other products in its category? Does the desire or need for the product justify its price? Does the product have limitations or potential harmful effects which should be considered? Is the price a reasonable and/or affordable one?

6   At every step of the consumer reasoning process, the child is at a disadvantage. Analysis of child-oriented commercials suggests that children are given little true consumer information, few facts about the price, durability, or nutritional value of a given product.[6] However, even if advertisers were to radically alter the commercial presentation of products, research on child development and consumer socialization indicates that most children would not be able to understand or evaluate commercials in a reasonable manner.

7   Central to the child's inability to evaluate commercial messages is the lack of comprehension of the promotional or selling intent inherent in advertising. The report of the National Science Foundation, *Research on the Effects of Television Advertising on Children: A Review of the Literature and Recommendations for Future Research*, summarizes the findings:

> Younger children, particularly those below ages 8 or 9, either express confusion or base their discrimination of commercials on effect or on superficial perceptual cues, such as a commercial's shorter length. . . . A substantial proportion of children, particularly those below 8 years, express little or no comprehension of the persuasive intent of commercials.[7]

8   Since most young children do not comprehend an advertiser's motives, they lack the reasonable skepticism which adults exhibit when evaluating commercials. Research findings have revealed that as many as half of all preschool children believe that all commercials are true in a literal sense.[8] Findings such as these reflect the child's incomplete con-

ception of the world. The egocentric nature of the young child as described in cognitive development theory suggests that he cannot see into the minds of others and that he cannot imagine that others see the world differently than he does.

Even though older children — ages 9 through 12 — display some understanding of advertising messages as qualitatively distinct from other broadcast announcements, a strikingly small percentage of this age group understands commercials in adult terms. In research conducted at the Graduate School of Business at the University of Texas with children in the fourth and sixth grades, generally ages 8 through 11, less than 15 percent of the children questioned were able to differentiate between programs and commercials on the basis that "television commercials sell; make money."[9]   9

The cynicism manifested by some 9-to-12-year olds concerning TV   10
advertising may reflect no more than a lingering inability to comprehend the true nature of commercials. T. G. Bever, professor of psychology and linguistics at Columbia University and a former associate of Piaget's Institute Scientifique D'Education in Geneva, describes his research with 10 year olds:

> Rather than attempt to use skills that they recognize are too limited to differentiate effectively between the subtleties of truth and falsehood, right and wrong, the 10-year-olds resolve the conflict by adopting a rigid moral stance and an overgeneralized view of the world. They simplify the problem by assuming that advertising . . . always "lies!"[10]

Fantasy in child-directed advertising. The inability of children, particu-   11
larly that of preschoolers, to detect or comprehend the persuasive intent of commercials makes them especially vulnerable to the aspects of fantasy contained in many child-directed advertisements. Barbara Fowles, director of Children's Television Workshop, describes a preschool child's perception of television fantasy:

> The child sees no boundaries between his own fantasies and objective reality. . . . A television reality, like a young child's thoughts, can flow freely between reality and fantasy.[11]

The common inclusion of imaginary beings and magical transforma-   12
tion of reality in many merchandising campaigns manipulate the preschool child's undeveloped sense of reality to promote desires for particular products. Fowles further defines the concept:

> No four-year-old gives a second thought to the appearance of Tony the Tiger at the breakfast table of an ordinary child. This is

not so much because he is jaded by television, as it is because, to his way of thinking, this is perfectly reasonable. If it can happen in his imagination, it can happen in fact.[12]

13   Research by Charles K. Atkin for Public Advocates, Inc. illustrates the impact that advertising appeals from imaginary television characters can have on young viewers. Interviews with one hundred children, ages 4–5 and 7–8, indicated that children recognized and liked the characters of Fred Flintstone and Barney Rubble utilized by General Foods to market its Cocoa Pebbles cereal. Moreover, half of the preschool children and three-quarters of the children from a low-income Mexican-American group believed that Fred and Barney would like them more if they ate Cocoa Pebbles.[13]

14   Although children cannot evaluate commercials in a meaningful manner, there is little question that advertising does teach children to desire and request advertised products, but Donald Hendon, professor of business administration at Texas A & I University, notes, "Commercials are teaching something which may have little or no value, except to the companies involved."[14]

15   The disproportionate number of child-directed ads for highly sugared and/or nutritionally questionable foods has generated mounting concern among doctors, dentists, parents, and other child-care providers. Adults may be able to inform themselves about the potential nutritional value of food products advertised to them, and consequently make more reasonable food choices. Children, however, do not have this advantage.

16   With the advent of child-directed TV advertising, family nutrition education has been challenged by commercial suppliers who may or may not recognize their role as health educators. Dr. Joan Gussow, assistant professor of nutrition and education at Teachers' College, Columbia University, points out:

> The diet sold to children by television . . . is so impoverished that it makes it impossible for a child not to go wrong. Thus, whatever one may think of individual products or of individual commercials, it is clear that the diet children's television commercials are promoting is an imbalanced one.[15]

17   Although some members of the food industry have acknowledged that children do need additional education in order to make reasoned food choices, efforts to supply these lessons on television has been, to this date, half-hearted. The disclosure by cereal advertisers that their product is "part of a balanced breakfast," rather than a complete meal in itself, constitutes no more than five seconds in most 30-second ads.

18   Research by Charles Atkin on the effectiveness of the "balanced breakfast" tag line found that most children could not remember the components of a balanced breakfast, and that "only one child in seven

could provide an adequate definition of the concept."[16] Moreover, two-thirds of the preschoolers tested believed that a bowl of cereal alone constituted a balanced meal, a misconception shared by two-thirds of the children under eight years old from a predominantly low-income Mexican-American sample population.

The emotional appeal of TV advertising. Children are at an emotional, 19 as well as a rational disadvantage, in facing the TV advertising on-slaught. Since any true assessment of advertising requires that children understand only the reality of the advertised product, but also the role it can reasonably play in their lives, and since children lack the experience and developed world view to make such judgments, they may be manipulated by the advertiser's insistence. As Richard Feinbloom, Medical Director of the Family Health Care Program of Harvard Medical School, comments:

> To children, normally impulsive, advertisements for appealing things demand immediate gratification. An advertisement has the quality of an order, not a suggestion. The child lacks the ability to set priorities, to determine relative importance, and to reject some directives as inappropriate.[17]

Advertisers use children to carry messages about products to adult 20 consumers, a practice which often creates conflict for children who receive opposing messages from adults on television and adults in the home. Decisions about appropriate food and toy purchases have always required negotiation between parents and children, but the advent of child-directed TV advertising has markedly increased the incidence of these conflict situations.

Several studies have documented the experience of children who are 21 the target of commercials for desirable products, but who are unable to persuade their parents to purchase the advertised items. Research by Charles K. Atkin of Michigan State University and John Rossiter and Thomas Robertson of the University of Pennsylvania suggests that these children experience considerable disappointment and unhappiness.[18] A recent study by Marvin E. Goldberg and Gerald J. Gorn confirms the role commercials play in producing frustration among children.[19] In this study, exposure to a toy commercial was shown significantly to change children's preferences from playing with friends in a sandbox to playing with the toy, even when it was postulated to the children that their mothers wished them to play with a tennis ball rather than the advertised toy.

Problems related to TV advertising are frequently cited by parents 22 and other childcare providers as a source of familial conflict. A national survey of over 1200 families by Yankelovich, Skelly, and White for "The General Mills American Family Report, 1976–77," concluded:

Advertising is regarded as an industry which is not living up to its responsibilities to parents and children. One out of four parents mentions the "gimmies"—children always asking for things that they see advertised—as a major problem in raising children.[20]

23   The extent of parental displeasure over child-directed TV advertising is also evaluated in the *NSF Report* which cites research compiled by Ward, Wackman, and Wartella in 1975. Almost 75 percent of the over 600 parents indicated "negative" or "strongly negative" responses to children's commercials.[21]

24   The continual recurrence of family conflict generated by TV commercials may be particularly stressful among low-income families. Selling to children wrongly presupposes that children understand the value of money and are cognizant of their family's economic level. Moreover, since products currently advertised to children could be marketed directly to adults—consumers who have the necessary cognitive skills to make reasoned purchasing judgments—using children for their "pester power" is unconscionable and unnecessary.

25   Freedom to communicate messages, commercial or otherwise, is founded on the existence of a free-thinking, independent and non-captive audience. While modern television, with its intrusiveness and omnipresence, was obviously not envisioned by the founding fathers when they framed the first amendment, the content of programs broadcast over the airwaves clearly deserves free speech protection. But commercial speech, on television elsewhere, has less constitutional protection, and none, the Supreme Court tells us, if the commercial message is unfair or deceptive.

26   It is advertising directed to children that Action for Children's Television is most concerned with. It is believed that advertising directed to very young children is inherently deceptive and unfair and should be stopped. ACT believes that such a government-ordered restriction would not in any way violate the first amendment. It is unquestioned that the FTC has, by virtue of its charge from Congress, the power to prohibit advertisers from promoting their products by means of unfair or deceptive practices. A ban on television advertising directed to very young children, at least under age eight, would comply with the Commission's standard of unfairness and deception now recognized as valid, and thus would be a valid restriction on commercial speech.

27   For these reasons—and others not detailed in this abbreviated article—Action for Children's Television supports a ban on television ads directed to children too young to understand the selling or persuasive intent of commercials, proposed by the Federal Trade Commission.

28   Robert Choate, president of the Council on Children, Media, and Merchandising, has succinctly expressed the point of view we have tried to defend as follows:

Advertising to children much resembles a tug of war between 200-pound men and 60-pound youngsters. Whether called an unfair practice or though subject to fairness doctrine interpretation, the fact remains that any communication that has a $1,000-per commercial scriptwriter, actors, lighting technicians, sound effects specialists, electronic editors, psychological analysts, focus groups, and motivational researchers with a $50,000 budget on one end and the 8-year-old mind (curious, spongelike, eager, gullible) with 50 cents on the other *inherently represents an unfair contest.*

REFERENCES

1. A. C. Nielsen Co., *Nielsen Television 78* (1978), pp. 5, 6, 8, 10, 11.

2. *The Media Book 1978* (New York: Min-Mid Publishing, 1978), pp. 301, 302.

3. National Science Foundation *Research on the Effects of Television Advertising on Children* (1977), pp. 14, 15. Hereinafter called *NSF Report.*

4. Television/Radio Age (September 25, 1978), p. 40.

5. *Broadcasting* (February 27, 1978), p. 27.

6. See Charles Atkin and Gary Herald, "The Content of Children's Toy and Food Commercials," *Journal of Communication,* Vol. 27, No. 1 (Winter, 1977), pp. 107–114.

7. *NSF Report,* pp. 30, 31.

8. Scott Ward, et al., *Children Learning to Buy: The Development of Consumer Information Processing Skills* (Cambridge: Marketing Science Institute, 1976).

9. Clara Ferguson, *Preadolescent Children's Attitudes Toward Television Commercials* (Austin, Texas: The University of Texas, 1975), p. 30.

10. T. F. Bever, et al., "Young Viewers' Troubling Response to TV Ads," *Harvard Business Review* (November/December, 1975), p. 116.

11. Barbara Fowles, "A Child and His Television Set: What is the Nature of the Relationship?" *Education and Urban Society,* Vol. 10, No. 1 (November, 1977), p. 93.

12. *Ibid.*

13. Charles K. Atkin and Wendy Gibson, *Children's Responses to Cereal Commercials,* report to Public Advocates, Inc. (San Francisco, 1978), p. 5.

14. Donald W. Hendon, Anthony F. McGann, and Brenda Hendon, "Children's Age, Intelligence and Sex as Variables Mediating Reactions to TV Commercials," *Journal of Advertising*, Vol. 7, No. 3 (Summer, 1978), p. 10.

15. Joan Gussow, "Counternutritional Messages of TV Ads Aimed at Children," *Journal of Nutritional Education* (Spring 1972), p. 50.

16. Atkin and Gibson, *Children's Responses to Cereal Commercials*, p. 2.

17. Richard I. Feinbloom, Statement submitted to the Federal Trade Commission, November, 1971, quoted by Charren in Hearings on Broadcast Advertising and Children Before House Committee on Interstate and Foreign Commerce, 94th Congress, 1st Session (July, 1975), p. 29.

18. Charles K. Atkin, "Parent-Child Communication in Supermarket Breakfast Cereal Selection," *Effects of Television Advertising on Children* (East Lansing, Michigan: Michigan State University, 1975); Thomas Robertson and John Rossiter, "Children's Consumer Satisfaction," Center for Research in Media and Children, University of Pennsylvania.

19. Marvin E. Goldberg and Gerald J. Gorn, "Some Unintended Consequences of TV Advertising to Children," *Journal of Consumer Research* 5 (June, 1978).

20. Yankelovich, Skelly and White, Inc. *Raising Children in a Changing Society: The General Mills American Family Report, 1976–1977* (Minneapolis, MN: General Mills, Inc., 1977), p. 36.

21. *NSF Report*, p. 134.

Questions for Discussion and Writing

1. On the average, how much television do children between the ages of six to eleven watch every week and how many television commercials are seen by most children every year? How does Charren use these statistics to provide a framework for the development of her argument?

2. What reasons and evidence does Charren give to demonstrate that children (*a*) lack the necessary intellectual development to be able to evaluate commercial messages directed at them and (*b*) do not understand that these ads are designed to sell products? How does Charren use these results to justify her claim that "commercial speech" (that is, ads on television) should not receive the same protections under the Constitution accorded "non-commercial speech"?

3. How does Charren use the results of the studies and surveys to support her assertions that (*a*) children are consistently fooled by

deceptive product claims because they are unable to realistically evaluate ads, and (*b*) the use of children by advertisers "to carry messages about products" to their parents increases conflicts between parents and children? Do the surveys and studies cited by Charren meet the standards of reliable evidence in the way they were conducted and in the way the results were interpreted?

4. Explain the rationale behind Charren's argument that deceptive television advertising directed toward children should not receive the same degree of First Amendment protection as a form of free expression as do other forms of speech and expression of opinion in print. How does the crux of her proposal (banning television advertising directed at children under the age of eight) depend on her argument that young children are simply unable to evaluate the nature and intent of advertising?

5. How does Charren's argument depend on the assumption that television advertisers not only exploit children but undermine the family structure and parental authority in precisely those areas of society where maintaining a strong family is crucial? Discuss how this assumption is used in her recommendation that the federal government should intervene to prevent children from being exploited.

6. Analyze the extent to which evidence turned up by Charren that children cannot "detect or comprehend the persuasive intent of commercials" supports Donna Woolfolk Cross's thesis that children are unable to distinguish fantasy from reality.

7. Discuss your responses to the question of whether the traditional First Amendment protection of freedom of expression in all media should be modified in the case of commercial messages directed toward children under the age of eight. One of the key issues is whether the ominous situation Charren describes justifies changing the First Amendment. Whether you agree or disagree with Charren, be sure to present your reasons in a clear and consistent manner, taking into account any objections that could be made by someone who did not agree with you. For example, if you agree with Charren, how would you reply to the counterargument that in the final analysis having parents, not the federal government, decide what is best for the child is preferable to rewriting the First Amendment?

Walter Karp

Where the Do-Gooders Went Wrong

Walter Karp is a contributing editor for Channels of Communication *and is the author of several books on American life and politics including* The Center: A History and Guide to Rockefeller Center. *In "Where the Do-Gooders Went Wrong," first published in* Channels *(March-April 1984), Karp argues against ACT's advocacy of the insertion of "pro-social" messages into children's programming. He claims that traditional "pro-child" fairy tales, such as Hansel and Gretel, help children develop inner resources in dealing with evil whereas pro-social programs deceive children by promising them that individuals will always be rescued by the group.*

1   There is something distinctly sinister about the world of children's television. I discovered this quite by accident while trying to resolve a difference of opinion: my children like Saturday-morning children's television; the critics loathe it. "A monstrous mess," Gary Grossman calls it in his 1981 study, *Saturday Morning TV.* "An animated world of meanness and mayhem," is how it appears to Peggy Charren, founder and head of Action of Children's Television. The critics especially deplore "outdated" cartoons such as *Bugs Bunny.* My children like Bugs Bunny best of all.

2   Intrigued by a difference of opinion so sharp, I decided to spend a few Saturday mornings judging for myself the merits and defects of children's television. Here I made the first of many curious discoveries. I thought judging the merits of children's television would be comparatively easy. Instead I found it virtually impossible. I simply had no standard for judging what I saw. One episode of the *Smurfs,* a blue-skinned race of dwarflets, convinced me of that.

3   In the episode, a trumpet-playing Smurf, feeling spurned by his fellows, blows a loud blast on his trumpet, unwittingly disclosing to the evil wizard the whereabouts of the Smurf village. What, if anything, did the plot signify? I certainly didn't know. The wizard looked to me far more comical than menacing, but was he? How can an adult know what a child will find fearsome? The wizard chases the tiny Smurf up hill and down dale, but in vain. His back aches, he gasps for breath. He is an *out-of-shape* wizard. A witty idea, I thought, but I wondered whether it was not perhaps too adult an idea. Do children really think big hulking adults are too weak to harm them? I suspected not, but what did it signify one way or the other?

Ultimately the exhausted wizard winds up hanging from a log slung   4
over a ravine. Instead of shoving him to his doom, the Smurf decides
that vengeance is "un-Smurflike" and mercifully spares the wicked wizard. When the Grimm brothers' Gretel had the witch at her mercy, she
shoved her into a hot oven. Was Smurf mercy "better" for children than
Hansel and Gretel's grisly justice? Again, I simply did not know, and I
think most people don't know. My own knowledge of children is exactly
the common knowledge: once I was one of them, now I have two of
them. The common knowledge does not suffice. That leaves a vacuum
and a politically perilous one, for the ignorance of a free people endan-
gers their freedom.

Trying hard to fill that vacuum are the various critics of children's   5
television. They include organized parents, educators, enlightened (usually public) broadcasters, pediatricians, child psychologists, and professors of human development. They have also included a few powerful
politicians, but that I did not know until much later.

The critics (whom I now began to read in earnest) have evolved a   6
stringent standard of judgment. They believe that good children's television teaches children to be cooperative, hard-working, and peace-loving
members of society. Programs that carry such lessons are praised as
"pro-social." The critics regard as defective those programs that appear
to encourage selfishness, self-assertiveness, and aggression. After an
experimental group of young children watched *Superman* and *Batman*,
which are deemed to be "aggressive" shows, they demonstrated a
heightening of aggressive tendencies, according to two professors of
human development at the University of Pennsylvania. After watching
Mr. Rogers' Neighborhood, a much-lauded "pro-social" program, young
children reportedly demonstrated greater "observance of the rules, tolerance of delays, and persistence in tasks."

In order to serve the pro-social ideal of peaceful, unselfish, coopera-   7
tive behavior, pro-social programming would feature, for example, "television characters who solve problems in nonaggressive ways" and "television characters who cooperate with each other, who openly express
their feelings, who devote their energies to helping other people." Pro-
social programming would alter, often drastically, traditional storytelling
devices. In the *ACT Guide to Children's Television*, which was written
"with the cooperation of the American Academy of Pediatrics," Evelyn
Kaye points out that "constructive" children's stories would show superior evil forces overcome by means of "thoughtfulness, cooperation, or
reason," rather than by "magic, cunning, or cheating" — traditional
modes of besting giants and wizards who violate the pro-social rules.

Group-minded, industrious, and self-effacing, the pro-social child   8
envisioned by the critics of children's television bears a curious resemblance to those Japanese workers so much admired of late by American
businessmen.

Determined to "socialize" children and provide them with "strategies   9 for coping with an increasingly complex world," the critics of children's television also prefer factuality to fantasy and realism to rowdy comedy. Slapstick, for one thing, is excessively aggressive, while fantasy the critics tend to regard as deceiving. As Peggy Charren puts it in *Changing Channels:* "Children need to understand that many of the things they see on TV do not happen in real life. Real people do not fly or disappear or walk through walls." The critics prefer programs that "reflect our own reality" — programs, for example, that would make children more aware of the people "who carry out the basic tasks of American society," such as blue-collar workers and sales personnel. They also prefer stories that show black and Hispanic characters in positions of leadership.

10   This kind of sanitized "realism" bears a striking resemblance to what was taught in the "progressive" schools of the 1940s, described by David Reisman in his celebrated work *The Lonely Crowd* as "agencies for the destruction of fantasy," where "fairy tales are replaced by stories about trains, telephones, and grocery stores and later by material on race relations or the United Nations or 'our Latin-American neighbors.'"

11   Lastly, the critics of children's television have taken great pains to demonstrate to the nation's parents that whatever is not pro-social is physically and mentally *harmful* to their children. Working closely with pediatricians and child psychologists, the critics contend that frightening stories and fearsome villains make children "anxious" and give them nightmares. Citing studies that show "some children" cannot distinguish an animated cartoon from real life, the critics demand the elimination of rowdy or unreal actions that a deluded child might imitate at his peril, as in the extreme instance of children jumping off roofs thinking they are Superman. In this way the critics can demand on the grounds of safety the curtailment of "aggressive" actions that they disfavor, in any case, on pro-social grounds.

12   More persistently, the critics of children's television have tried to marshal incontrovertible scientific proof that viewing violent action on television incites violent behavior in children. The proof has not been forthcoming. The most positive conclusions are hedged and cautious, as in the assertion that "there is evidence to support the theory that watching destructive cartoons leads to destructive play." Other studies give exactly the opposite results. As Cecily Truett, a former PBS official, ruefully noted in *Television & Children*, "Studies on the effects of violence on children's behavior are inconsistent and inconclusive." Completely undaunted by these disappointing results, the critics of children's television remain determined to root out televised violence and destruction.

13   In their hostility to violent deeds and powerful emotions, the critics of children's television bear a remarkable resemblance to those bowdlerizing turn-of-the-century schoolmarms who used to march through Grimms' fairy tales snipping out cruelty and cutting down ogres in the name of "mental hygiene."

That resemblance, more than anything, made me suspicious of the   14
pro-social standard. In defending the fairy tales from the censorious
schoolmarms, England's G. K. Chesterton offered a memorable insight
into the psychology of children and of the ancient children's stories.
"Fairy tales," wrote Chesterdon, "do not give the child the idea of the
evil or the ugly; that is in the child already because it is in the world
already. Fairy tales do not give the child his first idea of bogey. What
fairy tales give the child is his first clear idea of the possible defeat of
bogey." Instead of protecting children from unhealthy fears, the bowd-
lerizers of the fairy tales were depriving them of much-needed hope, the
hope that the ghouls beneath their beds and the monsters in their closets
have forms and faces, and that there is a champion who can best them, if
not by "thoughtfulness, cooperation, reason," then somehow or other—
perhaps with a sword. The fairy tales, as Chesterton understood them,
exposed the schoolmarms as the children's false friends. I strongly suspected that they might shed the same merciless light on today's pro-social critics and, more important, on the real merits and defects of children's television.

I thought I knew where such light could be found. In 1976 Bruno   15
Bettelheim, an eminent child psychologist and one of the shining spirits
of our time, published a book entitled *The Uses of Enchantment: The
Meaning and Importance of Fairy Tales.* It is a rich and difficult work
(especially after reading the banalities of the pro-social), the fruit of high
intelligence, long reflection, and deep compassion for children—the
work of an "informed heart," to borrow the title of Dr. Bettelheim's own
account of what he learned about himself and his fellow man in the
hell-hole of a Nazi concentration camp.

In *The Uses of Enchantment,* Bettelheim shows how irrelevant to the   16
real needs of children the pro-social enterprise turns out to be. "Since the
child at every moment of his life is exposed to the society in which he
lives, he will certainly learn to cope with its conditions, provided his
inner resources permit him to do so." In concentrating on mere outward
behavior (cooperating, helping others), proponents of the pro-social neglect the child himself—the fearful, struggling child "with his immense
anxieties about what will happen to him and his aspirations." The
difficulties a child faces seem to him so great, his fears so immense, his
sense of failure so complete, says Bettelheim, that without encouragement of the most powerful kind he is in constant danger of falling prey to
despair, "of completely withdrawing into himself, away from the
world." What children urgently need from children's stories are not
lessons in cooperative living but the life-saving "assurance that one can
succeed"—that monsters can be slain, injustice remedied, and all obstacles overcome on the hard road to adulthood.

Fairy tales can help provide the inner strength to grow up, notes   17
Bettelheim, only because they are fantasies. The menace of despair
weighs so heavily on a child that "only exaggerated hopes and fantasies

of future achievement can balance the scales so that the child can go on living and striving." "Realistic" stories, he says, cannot give children inner strength because they can offer only pedestrian hopes and mundane triumphs. They inform without nourishing, like the "educational reports" and "social studies" that the pro-social critics demand of children's television as part of their curious campaign to make blissful Saturday a sixth day of school.

18   Fairy tales can "come to the rescue" of children, moreover, only because their fearsome, fantastic dangers are rooted in a child's real fears—the fear of being lost or abandoned; the dread of monsters, which represent to the child, says Bettelheim, the monstrous side of himself, the side he must learn how to master. Fairy tales, in a word, are meant to be scary. If they do not frighten, they do not work, for overcoming a flimsy danger gives a child no real assurance.

19   In the fairy tales, the hero of the story struggles alone. This, too, is an essential feature, for without it the fairy tales could not fulfill their task of helping the child "go on living and striving." The lonely hero offers the child "the image of the isolated man who is nevertheless capable of meaningful achievement." His isolation mirrors the isolation every child feels in the face of his real terrors. The hero's ultimate triumph provides the heartswelling promise that the child, too, will find inner strength when he ventures forth on his own.

20   Lastly, the fairy tales help rescue the child from despair with their triumphantly happy endings—gaining a kingdom, winning a peerless spouse, vanquishing all foes. "Without such encouraging conclusions, the child, after listening to the story, will feel that there is indeed no hope of extricating himself from the despairs of life." No happy ending is complete, moreover, unless the wicked are severely punished. To a child, says Bettelheim, only severe punishment truly fits the terrible crimes he believes are committed against *him*—which, in his own view, go utterly unpunished. The punishment of the wicked is welcome proof to the child that he, too, will find justice one day; the great world will not let him down. "The more severely those bad ones are dealt with, the more secure the child feels." Thus, the fairy tales (speaking through Bettelheims's deep, tender analysis) answered my question about the significance of mercy in a children's story. Quite simply, it is adulteration: something adults foist upon children at the children's expense.

21   By conjuring up fearful dangers, lonely trials, and justice triumphant, the fairy tales give children strength for their arduous journey to the kingdom of adulthood. Like wise and loving parents, these ancient, universal tales serve the true interests of children as distinct from the interests of society, which cares nothing about the inner strength of its members, but only about their outward conformity. The fairy tales are not pro-social. What they are is pro-child. They stand guard against the adulteration of childhood by society's overzealous agents.

How pro-child would children's television turn out to be, I wondered, 22
when at last I felt ready to return to the animated cartoon world of
Saturday-morning television? With eyes sharpened by *The Uses of Enchantment*, I discovered the astonishing answer quickly enough. Every
essential element that makes it possible for fairy tales to give children
inner strength, hope, and security is absent today from children's
television.

The hero of children's television is not a person at all. It is the 23
ubiquitous group. The group is five dogs roaming the world; two frogs
and a turtle solving crimes; two teenagers and two dogs unmasking
villains; a team of young gymnasts and their ghetto-smart leader; three
chipmunks; an explorer, his niece, and a cowardly lion; a village of
minuscule dwarfs; an island of minuscule monkeys; a team of tree-
dwelling elves.

In this group-dominated world, deeds are group deeds, and motives, 24
group motives. It is the group that faces the dangers and the group that
emerges triumphant, demonstrating its invincible strength. The sources
of group strength are constantly made clear through social backchat
among the group members. Their discussions of tolerance, teamwork,
and the evils of vanity and selfishness often rival, and sometimes over-
whelm, the action. The sources of group weakness are also made clear. In
Saturday's group-minded world, the nonconformist is an obnoxious
complainer. In the *Smurfs*, he is Grouchy. In *Dungeons and Dragons*, he is
Eric, the sneering sourpuss who constantly derides the group's judgment.
In every conceivable way, children are taught the pro-social virtues of
cooperation, self-effacement, and subservience to the group.

The "image of the isolated man who is nonetheless capable of mean- 25
ingful achievement" — so important to the child, so useless to society —
rarely crosses the screen on Saturday morning. Even when the group
must split up to perform special tasks, nobody goes forth alone. Like an
army unit, the group, when it splits, divides into squads. That an isolated
being may be capable of meaningful achievement is an idea kept from
the children as though it were a secret of state. If, as the fairy tales tell us,
a child learns to have faith in his own inner strength through fantastic
tales of lone heroes, then children's television systematically deprives
children of that faith.

What is even worse, it actively subverts a child's faith in his own 26
inner strength. On Saturday-morning television, practically the only
thing a lone being can do is fall prey to wizards, wicked adults, and
master criminals. On Saturday-morning television, the most vivid
"image of the isolated man" is that of a hapless victim whom the group
decides to rescue. The group-rescue motif is one of the main devices of
children's television, and its primary message is perfectly plain: the lone
individual is weak and helpless; the group is strong and kind. Several
programs dramatize this seductive message by making one of the group's

members a slightly comical coward whom the group treats with bemused toleration; the group has strength enough for all.

27   This kind of reassurance is sweet consolation to children (including my own), but it is treacherous and baseless, the most insidious kind of false comfort. In real life, no gang can help a child master the deep anxieties that beset him. In real life, cowardice is not in the least comical, for every child knows in his heart how desperately he needs courage. Like the sugary cereals the pro-social critics are forever assailing, this kind of sugary, pro-social reassurance sweetens subservience and weakens the child.

28   Children's television doles out equally poisonous comfort with its treatment of danger. Whereas the fairy tales confront the terrors of childhood by showing great perils overcome, children's television deals with those terrors by making light of them. The out-of-shape wizard who had puzzled me at first proved to be merely one example of television's massive falsifying of children's fears. With the consistent exception of two programs, *Dungeons and Dragons* and *The Littles*, the bogeys and perils of Saturday-morning television have little or no power to frighten.

29   Often the villains are deliberately portrayed as inept clowns. The Grumplins are manifestly too silly to do the Monchichis any harm. Dragons are drawn with goofy faces, or they trip over their tails as soon as they breathe fire. "Isn't danger funny!" these shows seem to say.

30   On the more "realistic" programs, children's fears are mocked outright: a disguised villain, seemingly scary and phantasmal, is unmasked at the end, revealing a run-of-the-mill crook. The two teenagers and two dogs on *Scooby-Doo* reveal that the "Hound of the Baskervilles" is only the caretaker disguised. Richie Rich reveals that the "Phantom of TV" is merely a security guard at the broadcasting studio. This kind of unmasking is petty rationalism at its worst. It does no good whatever to call a child's fears groundless. It only makes his demons all the more terrible, since the child sees no way to overcome them.

31   These cartoons seldom present the kinds of dangers that spring from the real fears of childhood. Bank robbers and master criminals are not rooted in children's primordial fears. They are merely cartoon copies of adult television. Wicked witches and evil stepmothers *do* rise up from childhood's primordial depths, but during many, many hours of watching Saturday television, I saw not a one of them. Rooted in the child's passionate life in the family, these mother figures (as Dr. Bettelheim shows) are much too potent, it seems, for the antiseptic world of children's television. In the great majority of children's shows, the family does not exist at all, perhaps because it is the only group that deeply matters to the child. The characters in most children's television shows dwell in kinless, bloodless limbo drained of all real emotion.

32   Even the pro-social campaign against "aggression" and "violence" ends by betraying the real interests of children. Out of fear of encourag-

ing "aggressive" behavior, it deprives children of the very promise of justice itself. In the sanitized world of children's television, the wicked are merely foiled, the scene quickly changes, and they are left scot-free, presumably because punishment would be too "violent." So children's television, which gives children no faith in their own inner strength, which gives them no hope that their demons will be bested, robs them of the precious assurance that justice will be theirs when they, too, venture into the great world. You must put no faith in yourself, says children's television: you must put no faith in an unjust world; the group alone can save you. This is a very strange lesson to teach a free people's children.

When I first read the pro-social critics, I assumed that they were   33
lonely voices in the video wilderness. Yet nothing could be further from the truth. The pro-social standard dominated children's television. As one veteran children's shows producer, David de Patie, put it four years ago: "The greatest changes [in children's television] are because of the ladies in Boston — Action for Children's Television. I think they have exerted a great influence." Rigid network codes, I learned, rigorously enforce the pro-social standard by eliminating "aggression" and emasculating danger. "Today, networks red-pencil any prolonged action that would so much as make a palm sweat," notes Gary Grossman in *Saturday Morning TV.* One network code rules that if a building is damaged in the course of an episode it must be repaired by the episode's end. The networks' "program practices" departments — the censors — also enforce with rigor the pro-social stricture against dangerously "imitable" behavior. One network cut out a scene showing a pussy-cat character hiding from a monster in a dish of spaghetti on the grounds that some child might dunk his cat into pasta as well. "I can't even have a character throw a pie in somebody's face anymore," says Joseph Barbera, the most prolific producer of children's carton shows. "The reason is simple. It's imitable, and the networks say we can't do anything bad that a child might imitate. It's gone that far."

The pro-social may not be esteemed, but it is certainly feared. When I   34
interviewed a children's programming executive, she quickly assured me (supposing me to be a snoop from pro-social headquarters) that her network was dedicated to promoting "positive values" such as "cooperation as a group," "teamwork," and "working together," and that it dutifully showed characters "resolving conflicts within the group" while scrupulously putting "selfishness" and "bellyaching" in a "negative" light. Only when I hinted that my preferences lay elsewhere did she feel free to tell me how "browbeaten" by the codes the scriptwriters felt and how hard it was, under the rules, to establish "emotional contact with the child." The pro-social has become a despotic little orthodoxy.

Interestingly enough, you would never know this from reading the   35
pro-social literature. When a leading critic assails Saturday-morning television in 1982 as an "animated world of meanness and mayhem," who

would ever suspect that the networks had paid the pro-social any heed whatever?

36   This, too, struck me as a little strange, because it cuts off a question that would arise naturally in people's minds if they knew how thoroughly the pro-social forces have triumphed. The question is: How did a band of pedagogues, "ladies in Boston," and professors of human development manage to wield so much power? The question would open up interesting lines of inquiry. It would lead back from the pro-social critics to the real wielders of power who have promoted the pro-social cause. It would lead, as I discovered, to powerful federal officials such as the Federal Communication Commission member who, in 1968, invited parents to *sue* the networks if they thought television had harmed their children—an invitation to the most overwrought, irresponsible, and censorious parents to help the government bowdlerize children's television. It would lead back to still more powerful political figures, such as Senator John Pastore of Rhode Island, a former chairman of the Senate Commerce Committee's powerful communications subcommittee. In 1972 Senator Pastore put the frightened networks on notice that he and his senatorial colleagues would no longer tolerate television's "endless repetition of the message that conflict may be resolved by aggression." It was behind Pastore's well-organized assault on televised aggression, begun in 1968, that the pro-social critics gathered their forces. His victory became their victory.

37   Interestingly enough, while Senator Pastore was forcing the networks to cut down on "aggression" for the sake of the children, he remained a diehard supporter of the Vietnam War. Here was a powerful public man who approved of B-52 bombers blowing women and children to bits while frowning on Bugs Bunny as an incitement to violence. Nor was Pastore the first bellicose senator to campaign against televised violence. His predecessor in this work was the infamous Thomas Dodd of Connecticut, who was as determined to rid television of "aggression" as he was to see America girded for war in every corner of the globe.

38   That those two senators should have worried so greatly about televised violence struck me, I confess, as a very odd coincidence. Pondering that coincidence brought dark suspicions to my mind. I wondered whether the Dodds and the Pastores were really worried about televised "aggression" at all, or whether, perhaps, they harbored concerns of a very different kind. Their timing alone was worth considering. While these two war-minded worthies were fretting over fisticuffs on *Wagon Train*, a vast rebellion *against* official violence and official aggression was taking place in America, a vast protest in the cause of peace, a vast uprising against the war policies that the Dodds and the Pastores had so ardently supported for so many long years. For the first time in more than half a century, private citizens in America were demonstrating that they still had the inner strength to think for themselves, to judge for themselves, and to act for themselves. That demonstration profoundly

shocked the established political leaders of the country, especially old-line machine politicians like Senator Pastore.

Entrenched in power for fifty years, unchallenged by a people grown 39 pliant and credulous, the nation's startled leaders suddenly found themselves facing a great democratic revolt against their power and prerogatives. It was plain enough that the nation's leaders needed to put their challenged power on a more secure and lasting basis. They needed a citizenry more prone to obedience and less prone to act for themselves than young Americans so surprisingly had turned out to be. It was clear, too, that the traditional anarchy of children's television, with its knockabout comedy, irreverent clowns, and headstrong heroes, had done nothing to aid and abet the nation's leaders. It seemed to me, therefore, that when Pastore struck his decisive blow for pro-social children's television, what he was really asking the networks to do was make a more positive contribution to the indoctrination of America's children, to play a more systematic role in modeling a more docile and subservient people.

Such was my suspicion, and it seems to me far from groundless, for 40 this is precisely what pro-social television attempts to accomplish. It is systematic training for personal weakness and social subservience. It promotes conformity and saps inner strength. It teaches the children of a free people (whose ignorance thus menaces their liberty) to look to the group for their opinions and to despise those who do not do the same. Out of a pretended fear of "aggressiveness," it would deprive a free people of the very inner force and self-assurance they need to stand up and fight for their rights.

Is this not a little sinister? 41

Questions for Discussion and Writing

1. What reasons does Karp present to justify his opposition to children's programs that carry "pro-social" messages teaching the social ideal of peaceful, unselfish, cooperative behavior?

2. How does pro-social children's programming filter out certain genres that are not considered suitable?

3. According to Karp, how have critics of children's television supported their views with testimony of pediatricians and child psychologists? What fault does Karp find with this expert opinion? Why is Karp not persuaded by critics of children's television?

4. What reasons does Karp give for defending continued retelling of traditional fairy tales even though they don't exclude (as pro-social programs do) the evil or the ugly?

5. How does Karp use the work of Bruno Bettleheim to support his thesis that pro-social children's programs unnecessarily censor evil, thereby depriving children of important opportunities to develop inner resources?

6. Specifically, in what ways do "pro-child" fairy tales help children develop inner resources in a fashion that pro-social programs can never accomplish?

7. When Karp viewed the animated cartoon world of Saturday morning children's television from his newly acquired perspective, what deficiencies did he observe in the structure of the stories, the character of the heroes, and the messages conveyed? How do pro-social and pro-child types of programming divide on the issues of individual versus group achievement and the theme that true satisfaction results only from team effort?

8. How is Karp's objection to the persistent message of children's television that the individual must always be subservient to the group related to the theme that the group will rescue the individual? Why does Karp believe that this is a deceptive message?

9. Evaluate Karp's analysis of the role played by the FCC invitation to parents to sue television networks that harmed children and Senator Pastore's role in the enactment of pro-social children's television to produce "a docile, subservient people." Does Karp's steering of the discussion to support a condemnation of America's Vietnam policy seem relevant to the argument he has been developing?

10. What is Karp's attitude toward the issue of pro-social programming for children? How is this attitude reflected in the tone of the article? What specific words, phrases, and images support your impression? Where does Karp use language with emotional connotations to influence his readers?

11. Karp attacks pro-social censors both for what material they remove and for what they add. Cite an example that you found effective in illustrating how the program content was altered by censorship either adding or deleting something. How does this example dramatize what Karp sees as the excesses of pro-social censorship?

12. What traditional fairy tales were your favorites when you were a child? What television shows did you watch on Saturday mornings? If

you had to choose between your favorite Saturday morning television show and your favorite fairy tale, which would you have picked and why?

13. Compare the positions of Charren and Karp on what children should be allowed to see on television, be it programs or advertising. Who constructs a better argument and creates a more persuasive case?

Glossary

Abstract—designating qualities or characteristics apart from specific objects or events; opposite of **concrete**.

Analogy—a process of reasoning that assumes if two subjects share a number of specific observable qualities then they may be expected to share qualities that have not been observed; the process of drawing a comparison between two things based on a partial similarity of like features.

Argument—a process of reasoning and putting forth evidence on controversial issues; a statement or fact presented in support of a point.

Assumption—an idea or belief taken for granted; see **warrant**.

Audience—the people who read or hear an argument.

Authority—a person who is accepted as a source of reliable information because of his or her expertise in the field.

Backing—authority providing the assurance that the body of experience relied on to establish the warrant is appropriate and justified.

Claim—the assertion that the arguer wishes the audience to discover as the logical outcome of the case being presented.

Cliché—a timeworn expression that through overuse has lost its power to evoke concrete images.

Concrete—pertaining to actual things, instances, or experiences; opposite of **abstract**.

Connotation—the secondary or associative meanings of a word as distinct from its explicit or primary meaning; the emotional overtones of a word or phrase; opposite of **denotation**.

Deduction—a method of reasoning that infers the validity of a particular case from general statements or **premisses** taken to be true.

Definition—the method of identifying distinguishing characteristics of an idea, term, or process to establish its meaning.

Denotation—the literal explicit meaning of a word or expression; opposite of **connotation**.

Enthymeme—an abbreviated syllogism in which the major or minor **premiss** is not explicitly stated.

Euphemism—from the Greek word meaning *to speak well of*; the substitution of an inoffensive, indirect, or agreeable expression for a word or phrase perceived as socially unacceptable or unnecessarily harsh.

Evidence—all material, including testimony of experts, statistics, cases whether real, hypothetical, or analogical, and reasons brought forward to support a claim.

Exception—an extraordinary instance or circumstance in which an otherwise valid claim would not hold true.

Fallacy—errors of psuedoreasoning caused by incorrect interpretations of evidence and incorrectly drawn inferences.
   Ad hominem—an attack against the character of the person instead of the issue.
   Ad misericordiam—an attempt to manipulate the audience through an appeal to pity.
   Ad populum—an emotional appeal to the audience's feelings for country, class, national identity, or religious affiliation. Variations include *bandwagon, patriotic appeal, just plain folks, common practice* or *appeal to tradition*, and *appeal to status*.
   Appeal to force—an attempt to intimidate the audience into compliance by holding up a threat of force to compel acceptance of a claim; also known as *scare tactics*.
   Argument from ignorance—an erroneous belief that the failure to draw a conclusion can be used as evidence to support a claim.
   Begging the question—a pseudoargument that offers as proof the claim that the argument itself exists to prove; also known as *circular reasoning*.
   Fallacy of accent—an erroneous impression created by misplaced emphasis or by taking words out of context.
   Fallacy of accident—a failure to take into account cases that are clearly exceptions to the rule. Also called *sweeping generalization*.
   Fallacy of amphiboly—an unintended meaning arising from faulty syntax, confusing grammatical structure, or faulty punctuation.
   Fallacy of complex question—sometimes called the *loaded question*. Occurs when the arguer poses a question ("Have you stopped beating your wife?") in a way that assumes that an implicit first question has already been answered.
   Fallacy of composition—a failure to recognize that qualities of the individual parts do not automatically characterize the whole.
   Fallacy of division—an erroneous inference drawn about qualities of the parts based on what is valid for the whole.
   Fallacy of equivocation—a misleading impression created by using a word that has a double meaning.

False dilemma—a simplistic characterization suggesting that there are only two choices in a particular situation; also known as the *either/or dilemma*.

Faulty analogy—an unwarranted assumption that two things similar in some respects are also similar in all other ways.

Faulty use of authority—a citing of an authority outside the field of his or her relevant expertise.

Hasty generalization—an erroneous judgment based on too few instances, atypical or inadequate examples.

Non sequitur—meaning *it does not follow*; the introduction of irrelevant evidence to support a claim.

Post hoc ergo propter hoc—meaning *after this, therefore because of this*; the incorrect inference that simply because B *follows* A, A *caused* B.

Red herring—the bringing in of a tangential or irrelevant point to divert attention from the real issue.

Slippery slope—a failure to provide evidence to support predictions that one event will lead to a whole chain of events, usually catastrophic.

Straw man—the using of an easily refuted objection to divert attention from the real issue.

Grounds—specific facts relied on to support a given claim.

Hypothesis—a provisional thesis, subject to revision, accepted as a working **premiss** in an argument.

Induction—a process of reasoning that reaches a generalization by drawing inferences from particular cases.

Inference—the process of reaching conclusions drawn from the interpretation of facts, circumstances, or statements.

Irony—a way of drawing the reader into a secret collaboration where the writer means something quite opposite to what is being literally said.

Jargon—from the fifteenth-century French term *jargoun*, meaning *twittering* or *jibberish*; usually refers to a specialized language providing a shorthand method of quick communication between people in the same field. Often used to disguise the inner workings of a particular trade or profession from public scrutiny.

Metaphor—applying a word or phrase to an object it does not literally connote to suggest a comparison that evokes a vivid picture in the imagination of the audience.

Persuasion—according to Aristotle, the act of winning acceptance of a claim achieved through the combined effects of the audience's confidence in the speaker's character (*ethos*), appeals to reason (*logos*), and to the audience's emotional needs and values (*pathos*).

Picturesque language—words or phrases that evoke vivid images or pictures in the minds of the audience.

Plagiarism—using someone's words or ideas without giving proper credit.

Premiss (premise)—statements or generalizations in deductive reasoning taken as self-evidence that have been previously established through the process of inductive reasoning.

Qualifier—a restriction that may have to be attached to a particular claim to indicate its relative strength or certainty.

Rebuttal—a special circumstance or extraordinary instance that challenges the claim being made.

Refutation—showing a position to be false or erroneous in order to lessen its credibility.

Rhetoric—according to Aristotle, the process of discovering all the available means of persuasion in any situation where the truth cannot be known for certain; includes seeking out the best arguments, arranging them in the most effective way, and presenting them in a manner calculated to win agreement from a particular audience.

Satire—an enduring form of argument that uses parody, irony, and caricature to poke fun at a subject, idea, or person.

Simile—a comparison of one object or experience to another using the words *like* or *as* to create a vivid picture.

Slanting—the presentation of information in such a way as to reflect a particular point of view.

Stereotype—labeling a person or a group in terms of a single character trait, usually pejorative.

Support—all the evidence the writer brings forward to enhance the probability of a claim being accepted; can include evidence in the form of testimony of experts, statistics, examples from personal experience, hypothetical cases, appeals to the audience's emotions and values, and the speaker's own character or personality.

Syllogism—a classic form of deductive reasoning illustrating the relationship between a major and a minor **premiss** and a conclusion in which the validity of a particular case is drawn from statements assumed to be true or self-evident.

Thesis—an expression of the claim, assertion, or position the writer wishes the audience to accept.

Tone—the voice the writer has chosen to project in order to adapt the argument for a specific occasion and a particular audience; produced by the combined effect of word choice, sentence structure, and the writer's attitude toward the subject.

Values—moral or ethical principles or beliefs that express standards or criteria by which actions may be considered right or wrong, good or bad, acceptable or unacceptable, appropriate or unseemly; value arguments supply ethical, moral, aesthetic, or utilitarian criteria against which proposed actions may be evaluated.

Warrant—according to Stephen Toulmin, warrants are general statements that express implicit or explicit assumptions as to how the agreed-upon facts of a particular case are connected to the claim or conclusion being offered.

Acknowledgments

Edward Abbey, "The Right to Arms." From *Abbey's Road* by Edward Abbey. Copyright ©
1979 by Edward Abbey. Reprinted by permission of the publisher, E. P. Dutton, a division
of NAI Penguin Inc.

Joseph Addison, "The Political Upholsterer," from "The Tatler No. 155. Thursday, April 6,
1710." From *Selections From Addison and Steele*, Edited by Will D. Howe. From *The Modern
Student's Library. Selections From Addison and Steele*. Copyright 1921 Charles Scribner's
Sons; copyright renewed. Reprinted with the permission of Charles Scribner's Sons, a
division of Macmillan, Inc.

Gordon W. Allport, excerpt from *The Nature of Prejudice*, © 1979, Addison-Wesley Publishing Co., Inc. Reading, Massachusetts. Reprinted with permission.

Robert Almeder, "Morality in the Marketplace." From *Business Ethics*, ed. by M.
Snoeyenbos, Robert Almeder, and James Humber. Prometheus Press, Buffalo, N.Y., 1983.
Reprinted with permission of the author.

Issac Asimov, "Science and Beauty." Reprinted from "Science and Beauty," in Issac
Asimov's *The Roving Mind* with permission of Prometheus Books, Buffalo, N.Y., 1983.

James Baldwin, "If Black English Isn't a Language, Then Tell Me, What Is?" *The New York
Times*, July 29, 1979, Op-ed. Copyright © 1979 by The New York Times Company.
Reprinted by permission.

Betty Winson Baye, "You Men Want It Both Ways." Copyright © 1985 [July] by *Essence*
Communications, Inc. Reprinted by permission.

Robert Benchley, "Opera Synopsis." From *The Benchley Roundup* by Robert Benchley.
Copyright 1954 by Nathaniel Benchley. Reprinted by permission of Harper and Row,
Publishers, Inc.

Harold W. Bernard, Jr., "The Greenhouse Effect." From *The Greenhouse Effect*. Copyright
1980 by Harold W. Bernard, Jr. Reprinted by permission of Ballinger Division, Harper &
Row, Publishers, Inc.

Walter Berns, "Crime and the Morality of the Death Penalty." From *For Capital Punishment: Crime and the Morality of the Death Penalty*, by Walter Berns. Copyright © 1979 by Walter Berns. Reprinted by permission of Basic Books, Inc., Publishers.

Suzanne Britt, "That Lean and Hungry Look." First published in *Newsweek Magazine*, October 9, 1978. Reprinted by permission of the author.

Susan Brownmiller, "Pornography Hurts Women." From *Against Our Will*. Copyright 1975 by Susan Brownmiller. Reprinted by permission of Simon & Schuster, Inc.

Patrick J. Buchanan and J. Gordon Muir, "Gay Times and Diseases." First published in *The American Spectator*, August 1984. Reprinted by permission of Patrick J. Buchanan.

David Burnham, "Surveillance." From *The Rise of the Computer State* by David Burnham, 1984. Random House, New York. Reprinted with permission.

Gilbert Cant, "Deciding When Death is Better than Life." Copyright 1973 Time Inc. All rights reserved. Reprinted by permission from TIME.

Stephen Chapman, "The Farmer on the Dole." Copyright © 1982 by *Harper's Magazine*. All rights reserved. Reprinted from the October issue by special permission.

Stephen Chapman, "The Prisoner's Dilemma." Reprinted by permission of *The New Republic*, © 1980, The New Republic, Inc.

Peggy Charren, "Should We Ban TV Advertising to Children? YES." *National Forum: The Phi Kappa Phi Journal*, Vol. LIX, No. 4, Fall 1979. Reprinted with permission from Action for Children's Television, and permission of the author.

Consumers' Research Magazine, "The Suzuki Rolls Over Too Easily." Copyright 1988 by Consumers Union of the United States, Inc., Mount Vernon, N. Y. 10553. Excerpted by permission from *Consumer Reports*, July 1988.

Edward W. Cronin, Jr., "The Yeti," as originally published in the November 1975 issue of *The Atlantic Monthly*, Vol. 236, No. 5. Reprinted with permission of the author.

Donna Woolfolk Cross, "Shadows on the Wall." From *Mediaspeak: How Television Makes Up Your Mind*. The Putnam Publishing Group, N. Y., 1983. Reprinted with permission. Reprinted with permission of the author. Copyright © 1983 by Donna Woolfolk Cross.

Dollars & Sense magazine editorial, "White Lines, Bottom Lines: Profile of a Mature Industry?" Reprinted with permission from *Dollars & Sense* magazine (December 1986). Subscriptions: $19.50/yr. (10 issues) from Dollars & Sense, 1 Summer St., Somerville, MA 02143.

Byron Dorgan, "America's Real Farm Problem: It Can Be Solved," April 1983. Reprinted with permission from *The Washington Monthly*. Copyright by *The Washington Monthly Co.*, 1711 Connecticut Avenue, NW, Washington, D. C. 20009. (202) 462-0128.

Barbara Ehrenreich, Elizabeth Hess, and Gloria Jacobs, excerpt from *Re-Making Love: The Feminization of Sex*. Copyright © 1986 by Barbara Ehrenreich, Elizabeth Hess, and Gloria Jacobs. Reprinted by permission of Doubleday, a division of Bantam, Doubleday, Dell Publishing Group, Inc.

Loren C. Eiseley, "Using a Plague to Fight a Plague." *Saturday Review*, September 29, 1962. Copyright © 1962 *Saturday Review* magazine. Reprinted by permission.

Willard R. Espy. From *The Garden of Eloquence: A Rhetorical Bestiary*, Harper & Row, Publishers, Inc. 1983. Reprinted with permission.

Thomas J. Flygare, "De Jure: Courts Foil Schools' Efforts to Detect Drugs." From *Phi Delta Kappan*, December 1986. Reprinted with permission.

Norman Fost, "Banning Drugs in Sports: A Skeptical View." From *The Hastings Center Report*, August 1986, pp. 5–10. Reproduced by permission. © The Hastings Center.

Foundation on Economic Trends, from "The Theological Letter Concerning the Moral Arguments against Genetic Engineering of the Human Germline Cells," June 8, 1983. Reprinted with permission from the Foundation on Economic Trends.

Monroe Freedman, "Lawyers Ethics in an Adversary System." Bobbs Merrill, 1975. Reprinted by permission of the author.

Milton Friedman, "The Social Responsibility of Business is to Increase Its Profits." *The New York Times Magazine*, September 13, 1970. Copyright © 1970 by The New York Times Company. Reprinted by permission.

Paul Fussell, "Notes on Class." Reprinted by permission of *The New Republic*, © 1980, The New Republic, Inc.

John Kenneth Galbraith, "The 1929 Parallel." First appeared in *The Atlantic Monthly*, January 1987. Reprinted by permission of the author.

Norman Gall, "The Ghost of 1929." Reprinted by permission of *Forbes* magazine, July 13, 1987. © Forbes, Inc., 1987.

Peter Gent, "Between the White Lines: The NFL Cocaine War." First appeared in the *Dallas Times Herald*, Magazine Section, September 4, 1983. Reprinted with permission of the author.

Richard N. Goodwin, "Money Has Corrupted the Legislative Process." *The Los Angeles Times*, December 12, 1985. Reprinted with permission.

Andrew Hacker, "Of Two Minds about Abortion." Copyright © 1979 by *Harper's Magazine*. All rights reserved. Reprinted from the September issue by special permission.

Garrett Hardin, "Lifeboat Ethics: The Case Against Helping the Poor." Reprinted with permission from *Psychology Today Magazine*. Copyright © 1974 American Psychological Association.

Michael Harrington, excerpt from *The Other America: Poverty in the United States*. Reprinted with permission from Macmillan Publishing Co. Copyright © 1962 by Michael Harrington.

Arthur D. Hasler and James A. Larsen, "The Homing Salmon." *Scientific American*, August 1955, p. 75. Reprinted with permission.

Denis Hayes, "Nuclear Power: The Fifth Horseman." *Worldwatch Paper #6*, May, 1976. Reprinted with permission.

Harold L. Henderson, "Where do you draw the line on product liability?" Editorial RJR Report, Fourth Quarter 1985. R. J. Reynolds Industries, Inc. Reprinted with permission of the RJR Nabisco Co.

David Hilfiker, "A Doctor's View of Modern Medicine." *The New York Times Magazine*, February 23, 1986. Copyright © 1986 by The New York Times Company. Reprinted by permission.

Sir Edmund Hillary, "Epitaph to the Elusive Abominable Snowman," *Life*, January 13, 1961, Vol. 50. Reprinted with permission of the author.

Gerald L. Houseman, "The Merger Game Starts with Deception." *Challenge*, September/October 1986. Reprinted with permission of the author and of the publisher, M. E. Sharpe, Inc. 80 Business Park Drive, Armonk, N.Y. 10504 USA, from the September/October 1986 issue of *Challenge*.

Darrell Huff and Irving Geis, excerpt from *How to Lie with Statistics*. Reprinted from *How to Lie with Statistics* by Darrell Huff, pictures by Irving Geis, by permission of W. W. Norton & Co., Inc. Copyright 1954 by Darrell Huff and Irving Geis. Copyright renewed 1982 by Darrell Huff and Irving Geis. Reprinted with permission of W. W. Norton & Co., Inc.

Michael R. Jackman, "Enabling the Disabled: Paternalism Is Enemy No. 1." *Perspectives,* Winter/Spring 1983. Reprinted with permission of the author.

Susan Jacoby, "Confessions of a First Amendment Junkie." First published in *The New York Times,* Hers column, 1978. Reprinted by permission of Susan Jacoby. Copyright © 1978. Reprinted by permission of Georges Borchardt Agency.

Susan Jacoby, "Unfair Game." First published in *The New York Times,* Hers column, 1978. Reprinted by permission of Susan Jacoby. Copyright © 1978. Reprinted by permission of Georges Borchardt Agency.

Jennifer James, "The Prostitute as Victim." From *The Victimization of Women,* edited by Jane Roberts Chapman and Margaret Gates, Sage Publications, 1978. Reprinted with permission of the author.

Perry M. Johnson, "A Vote Against Executions from a Man Who Knows Murderers." *The Christian Science Monitor,* October 7, 1982. Reprinted with permission of the author.

Robert E. Jones, "Justice Can Be Served Despite Dissenting Votes." *The Los Angeles Times,* January 23, 1983. Reprinted by permission of the author.

Walter Karp, "Where the Do-Gooders Went Wrong." Copyright *Channels,* 1984 [March-April]. Reprinted by permission.

C. Everett Koop, excerpt from the proceedings of the International Conference on Infanticide and Handicapped Newborns, sponsored by Americans United for Life. Legal Defense Fund, Chicago, 1980. Copyright © 1982, Americans United for Life. Reprinted by permission.

Rob Lamp, "The World of 'Dark Rock.'" *The New American,* February 17, 1986. Reprinted by permission.

Michael Levin, "The Case for Torture." Copyright 1982 by Newsweek, Inc. Reprinted by permission of the author.

Anthony Lewis, "Enough Is Enough." *The New York Times,* February 5, 1984. Copyright © 1984 by The New York Times Company. Reprinted by permission.

Miles Lord, "A Plea for Corporate Conscience." Copyright © 1984 by *Harper's Magazine.* All rights reserved. Reprinted from the June issue by special permission.

Marilyn Machlowitz, "Workaholics." From *Workaholics,* by Marilyn M. Machlowitz, Ph.D. (Addison-Wesley, 1980). Reprinted with permission of the author.

William C. Martin, "The God-Hucksters of the Radio." Originally published in *The Atlantic Monthly,* June 1970. Reprinted with permission of the author.

Terence McLaughlin, excerpt from *Dirt: A Social History as Seen through the Uses and Abuses of Dirt.* Stein and Day Publishers, 1971. Copyright © by Terence McLaughlin. Reprinted with permission of Stein and Day Publishers.

Leo N. Miletich, "Rock Me with a Steady Roll." *Reason.* Reprinted with permission, from the March 1987 issue of *Reason* magazine. Copyright © 1988 by the Reason Foundation, 2716 Ocean Park Blvd., Suite 1062, Santa Monica, California 90405.

John Milton, extract from *Areopagitica,* Everyman's Library text. J.M. Dent & Sons Ltd. Reprinted with permission.

Brian Noal Mittman, "Teenagers Need Drug Testing." From *The Union Leader,* October 26, 1986. Reprinted with permission of the author.

Thomas H. Murray, "The Coercive Power of Drugs in Sports." From *The Hastings Center Report,* August 1983, pp. 24–30. Reproduced by permission. © The Hastings Center.

Anne Marie O'Keefe, "The Case Against Drug Testing." Reprinted with permission from *Psychology Today Magazine*. Copyright © 1987 [June], American Psychological Association.

Kenneth W. Payne and Stephen J. Risch. "The Politics of Aids." From *Science for the People*, Vol. 16, No. 5, September/October 1984. Reprinted with permission by Science Resource Center, Inc. and the authors.

Quarterley Review of Doublespeak, edited by William Lutz. Reprinted with permission of William Lutz and the National Council of Teachers of English.

Hugh Rank, "Teaching about Public Persuasion: Rationale and a Schema," by Hugh Rank. From *Teaching About Doublespeak*, edited by Daniel Dieterich. Copyright 1976 by the National Council of Teachers of English. Reprinted with permission of NCTE and Hugh Rank.

Judith L. Rapoport, excerpt from *The Boy Who Couldn't Stop Washing*, E. P. Dutton, 1989. Reprinted with permission.

Richard Rodriguez, "Aria: A Memoir of a Bilingual Childhood." Reprinted by permission of Georges Borchardt, Inc. for Richard Rodriguez. Copyright © 1980 by Richard Rodriguez. First published in *The American Scholar*.

Anne Wilson Schaef, excerpt from *When Society Becomes An Addict*, Harper & Row, 1987. Copyright © 1987 by Anne Wilson Schaef. Reprinted with permission.

Charles M. Sevilla, "The Case of the Unanimous Jury." From *The Los Angeles Times*, January 23, 1983. Reprinted with permission of the author.

John Simon "Playing Tennis Without a Net." Reprinted from *Paradigms Lost* by John Simon. Copyright © 1976, 1977, 1978, 1979, 1980 by John Simon. Used by permission of Clarkson N. Potter, Inc.

John Simon, "Why Reed Can't Write." Reprinted from *Paradigms Lost* by John Simon. Copyright © 1976, 1977, 1978, 1979, 1980 by John Simon. Used by permission of Random House, Inc.

Peter Singer, "Is Animal Experimentation Harming Society?" From *Animal Liberation: A New Ethics for Our Treatment of Animals*, by Peter Singer. Copyright 1975 by Peter Singer. Reprinted by permission of the author.

Peter Singer, "Rich and Poor." From *Practical Ethics*, 1979. Reprinted with the permission of Cambridge University Press.

Donald Singletary, "You New Women Want It All!" Copyright © 1985 [July] by *Essence* Communications, Inc. Reprinted by permission.

Joseph K. Skinner, "Big Mac and the Tropical Forests." From *Monthly Review*. Copyright © 1985 by Monthly Review Inc. Reprinted by permission of Monthly Review Foundation.

Philip Slater, "Want-Creation Fuels Americans' Addictiveness." First published in the *St. Paul Pioneer Press Dispatch*, September 6, 1984. Reprinted by permission of the author.

Robert L. Slimp, "The Bright Side of Dark Africa." Originally appeared in the *Manchester Union Leader*, 1984. Reprinted with permission of the author.

Adam Smith, "Fifty Million Handguns." Reprinted with permission from *Esquire*. Copyright © 1981 [April] by Esquire Associates.

Bruce Springsteen, "Rock and Roll Hall of Fame Induction of Roy Orbison." Speech delivered on January 21, 1987. Reprinted with permission of the author and Jon Landau Management, Inc.

John Steinbeck, "Hunger in a Land of Plenty." From *The Grapes of Wrath*, by John

Index

A

Instructor's Manual

Strategies
of Argument

___

STUART HIRSCHBERG

Rutgers: The State University
of New Jersey, Newark

Macmillan Publishing Company

NEW YORK

CONTENTS

PART I   STRATEGIES FOR TEACHING ARGUMENTATIVE WRITING

PART II   SUGGESTED ANSWERS TO QUESTIONS (and supplementary sources for further reading)

DIFFERENT PERSPECTIVES ON CURRENT ISSUES

STRATEGIES FOR TEACHING ARGUMENTATIVE WRITING

Strategies of Argument is designed to meet the needs of instructors teaching composition courses whose focus is the critical reading and writing of arguments. Students are shown why argument is important for the papers they will be writing in school. They can also learn a valuable method of reasoning through which they can critically evaluate events and communicate their opinions, value judgments, and solutions to problems.

Claims   35-55 (text pages)

The first chapter gives students a good foundation in the important skills of summarizing, paraphrasing, and critical reading. Chapter two introduces students to a method of reasoning based on Stephen Toulmin's model. This method makes it possible for students to get a clear grasp of how arguments are put together. Teachers should make every effort to ensure that students understand the principles underlying the Toulmin model. Extra effort spent at this point will prevent misunderstandings or misinterpretations later. Students need to understand the rationale behind the Toulmin approach before they can analyze other people's arguments or formulate their own.

Teachers find that the Toulmin model permits students to grasp the essential features of argumentation. Many students are already familiar with the legal model of claim and support (or evidence) on which Toulmin's model is based.

A useful way to introduce students to the different kinds of claims presented in arguments is to begin the discussion with factual claims. Factual claims establish the nature or characteristics of something. The class can then move on to explanations of causal claims and claims of consequence. These kinds of claims point out possible effects or possible causes of how things got to be the way they are. Then the class might consider value claims, that is, claims that measure a subject against some known criteria. Last, the class can study policy claims that propose solutions to problems. Students should be informed that this classification is artificial since many arguments contain claims of different kinds. For example, the set of pro and con arguments on the merits of genetic engineering (#16 in ch. 7) contain factual claims about how the problem should be defined, claims about what caused the problem, claims about what consequences genetic manipulation will produce, value claims making moral judgments, and policy claims recommending different legislative solutions. Teachers who wish to direct the attention of the class to selections illustrating these types of claims might wish to consult the following list of readings, presented alphabetically by author:

I. Readings that illustrate Factual Claims (that define, describe, characterize, or identify the most important feature).

Cronin	Sauvigne
Dollars & Sense	Schlafly
Hillary	Singer
Machlowitz	Visscher
Martin	

II. A. Selections that exemplify Causal Claims.

Buchanan & Muir	Slater
Burnham	Weil & Rosen
Henderson	Whelan
Payne & Risch	

B. Selections that exemplify Claims about Consequences.

Brownmiller
Cross
Galbraith
Gall
Jacoby ("Unfair Game")

III. Readings that illustrate Value Claims.

Addison   Karp
Almeder   Lord
Baldwin   Mao
Britt   Murray
Cant   Paine
Cooke   Simon
Chapman ("The Prisoner's Dilemma")   Steinbeck
Fost   Watson
Friedman   Will
Hacker
Hardin

IV. Readings that illustrate Policy Claims recommending solutions to
problems.

Abbey   Lewis
Chapman ("The Farmer on the Dole")   Milton
Charren   Mittman
Dorgan   O'Keefe
Flygare   Rodriguez
Jackman   Roome
Jacoby ("Unfair Game")   Sevilla
Johnson   Slimp
Jones   Smith
                                            Steiner

Support 55-72 (text pages)

Chapter two introduces students to the importance of different kinds
of support or evidence. Support in the Toulmin model is important
because it shows students how writers go beyond the real, but limited
evidence of personal experience in developing opinions. Students can
see that writers base their beliefs on a range of written sources of
information--case histories, testimony of experts, and statistics
compiled by reputable organizations.

Teachers can help students observe that writers use sources in drawing
legitimate conclusions. Writers also draw upon sources to enhance the
credibility and persuasiveness of their personal opinions. The
"support" section of chapter 2 not only introduces students to
different kinds of evidence but shows them how to critically evaluate
the reliability of information. The discussion offers guidelines and
practice in discovering whether information is objectively verifiable
or has been misrepresented to support the writer's position.

Teachers who wish to focus the classes' attention on the role specific
kinds of evidence play in supporting a claim may wish to draw on the
following selections:

Readings that use examples drawn from real experience.

Addison   Rodriguez
Abbey   Roome
Baye   Singletary
Cronin   Steinbeck
Cross   Steiner
Gent   Wall Street Journal

Hillary
Jacoby ("Unfair Game")
Johnson
Jones

Readings that draw analogies or use hypothetical examples.

Almeder
Fost
Hardin
Henderson
Milton
Simon

Readings that use the testimony of experts as evidence.

Charren   Jones
Cross   Karp
Hacker   Lamp
Henderson

Readings that rely on statistics as evidence.

Buchanan & Muir   O'Keefe
Chapman   Sevilla
Charren   Singer
Dollars & Sense   Smith
Dorgan   Visscher
Gall   Whelan

Students should have little trouble with real and hypothetical
examples, or the testimony of experts, but may need intensive work on
how writers use statistics.

Warrants 72-84 (text pages)

For some students, the most mysterious feature of the Toulmin model is
the warrant. For practical purposes, warrants can be explained as if
they were assumptions. The discussion in the text shows how arguments
rely on warrants of different kinds to justify using evidence to
support a claim. The following diagram might be put on the board to
illustrate the text's discussion of the Generalization Warrant:

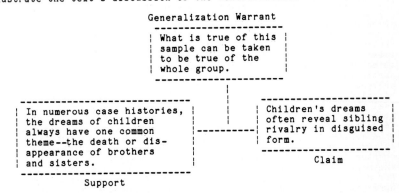

Generalization Warrant
```
----------------------
¦ What is true of this ¦
¦ sample can be taken  ¦
¦ to be true of the    ¦
¦ whole group.         ¦
----------------------
                          ¦
----------------------------        ----------------------
¦ In numerous case histories, ¦ ¦ ¦   ¦ Children's dreams    ¦
¦ the dreams of children       ¦ ¦ ¦   ¦ often reveal sibling ¦
¦ always have one common       ¦----------¦ rivalry in disguised ¦
¦ theme--the death or dis-     ¦ ¦   ¦ form.                ¦
¦ appearance of brothers       ¦        ----------------------
¦ and sisters.                 ¦                 Claim
----------------------------
         Support
```

An effective way to introduce students to the idea of assumptions is
to draw on a real case or invent a hypothetical one. The case should
challenge them to think critically about their beliefs, values, or

3

ideas they take for granted. For example, students might be asked their opinion about the following dilemma. Recently, historians have discovered that Nazi doctors in concentration camps amassed much information by performing sadistic experiments on prisoners. In one experiment, doctors killed scores of people trying to discover how long human beings could remain alive in freezing water. Although the circumstances under which the information was obtained was immoral, the data itself might be used to save lives today. Researchers who wish to use the data to enhance the ability of sailors to survive in freezing water over various periods of time argue that there are no other sources for this essential information. Concentration camp survivors are divided on the issue. Some think the data is so stained with blood it should never be used. Others feel that by using the data to save lives, the victims will not have died in vain. Students who voice their own opinion can be asked to examine assumptions that led them to their views. This kind of exercise can be used to introduce warrants. Students can see the importance of assumptions when they critically evaluate what they know and ask themselves how they know it.

Teachers can use many end-of-selection questions to encourage students to become aware of how writers bring assumptions, expectations, and prejudices to their arguments. By seeing how assumptions shape a writer's outlook, students can become aware of their own expectations, especially when these values and beliefs conflict with the assumptions of the argument they are reading. The best arguments are those that challenge them to think deeply about their own values, assumptions and beliefs. By allowing the discussion of argument to go backstage, as it were, Toulmin made it possible for students to focus on underlying assumptions, make them explicit, and evaluate the role that they play in connecting the evidence to the claim of the argument.

Audience 84-91 (text pages)

The Toulmin model makes it possible to understand more accurately the role the audience plays in determining how an argument is put together. Students should be aware that argument is designed for an immediate audience, even when that audience is the general public. An understanding of the role played by audience is crucial in argument. Instructors accustomed to teaching rhetorical modes are pleasantly surprised to discover that teaching argument is easier than they anticipated. This is because students become the audience for others in class when they evaluate the quality of reasoning used by fellow students. Likewise, students respond to an immediate audience when they formulate counterarguments to arguments others present. The atmosphere in classes that teach argument also differs from that of traditional writing classes. Students see, often for the first time, that their opinions count. They also see they will have to meet certain standards of reasoning when expressing their views in writing or in open discussion.

Toulmin's model of reasoning takes audience into account through the ideas of backing, qualifier, and exception (or rebuttal). These are terms given to strategies writers use to adapt their argument for a particular audience. Some audiences might require the writer to provide additional information (backing) and would remain skeptical of the claim if the writer did not do so. In other cases, writers might feel that a particular audience might not accept the claim unless it were extensively qualified. For other audiences, the writer might sense the need to include exceptions where the claim would not hold true as literally stated. Still other circumstances might require the writer to bring forward and provide a rebuttal to significant counterarguments. The Toulmin model makes it possible to analyze an argument in terms of those things writers do to adapt their position for real audiences. For example, here is how the speech by Bruce Springsteen (discussed in ch. 2) at the induction of Roy Orbison into the Rock and Roll Hall of Fame might appear:

Backing, in the form of personal experiences
```
----------------------------------------------
| I carry his records with me when I       |
| go on tour today, and I'll always        |
| remember what he means to me and what    |
| he meant to me when I was young and      |
| afraid to love.                          |
----------------------------------------------
```

Warrant
```
-----------------------------------
| Great rock 'n' roll ballads let |
| you know you are not alone.      |
-----------------------------------
```

but, for me
```
                                      --------------
                                      | Qualifier
-----------------------------            -------------------------
| His arrangements were com- |          | Roy's ballads were    |
| plex and operatic ... they |          | always best when you  |
| addressed the underside of |----------| were alone and in the |
| pop romance. They were     |          | dark.                 |
| scary. His voice was un-   |            -------------------------
| earthly ... He made a      |                  Claim
| little town in New Jersey  |          -------------------------
| feel as big as the sound   |          | Some rock 'n' roll rein- |
| of his records.            |          | forces friendship and    |
-----------------------------            | community.               |
Evidence to support the claim           -------------------------
                                              Exception
```

Arguing Across the Disciplines   91-112 (text pages)

The next section of chapter 2, "Arguing Across the Disciplines,"
extends the Toulmin model to the role audience plays in shaping a
writer's rhetorical strategy. Communities comprising the broad areas
of the curriculum function as audiences. Each discipline has its own
needs, aims, interests, expectations, and sets standards about what
constitutes acceptable reasoning. For example here is how the
veterinary diagnosis made by James Herriot cited in the text might
look:

Warrant drawn from experience
```
---------------------------------
| A cow that swallows a foreign |
| body like a nail can be ex-   |
| pected to show symptoms of    |
| sudden fall in milk yield.    |
---------------------------------
```
```
---------------------                    -------------------
| Sudden fall in milk |                  | The cow needs a |
| yield, loss of cud- |------------------| rumenotomy to re- |
| ding...nails miss-  |                  | move the foreign |
| ing used to repair  |                  | body.            |
| loose boards in a   |                  -------------------
| hen house in the    |                  Claim (as diagnosis)
| cow pasture.        |
---------------------                    ---------------------------
Grounds (facts of the case)             | Unless it can be establish- |
                                        | ed that the cow definitely  |
                                        | did not swallow one of the  |
                                        | loose nails.                |
                                        ---------------------------
                                        Qualifier or Exception
```

5

First year students should understand the significant differences in methods of reasoning of different fields of study. Here, too, the Toulmin model is useful in showing students how reasoning and standards of evidence differ between the arts, ethics, history, law, business, social sciences and sciences. For example, students might observe how, in a business argument, a change in the underlying warrant would produce a completely opposite conclusion:

A traditional warrant

```
---------------------------------
| The dependence of a society   |
| on fossil fuel for energy re- |
| quires the exploitation of any|
| domestic energy source that is|
| discovered.                   |
---------------------------------
```

```
---------------------------                    ----------------------
| The Alaska reserves of  |                    | Oil companies must |
| untapped oil constitute |                    | be granted the right|
| the largest single re-  |--------------------| to drill for oil in |
| maining source of energy-|                   | the Alaska oil re-  |
| producing fossil fuel left|                  | serve.              |
| available to the U. S.  |                     ----------------------
---------------------------                              Claim
        Grounds
```

A new warrant, based on social responsibility

```
---------------------------------
| The long-term impact of the   |
| burning of fossil fuels on    |
| the environment ("greenhouse  |
| effect"), and the danger of   |
| oil spills requires oil com-  |
| panies to act in such a way   |
| that harm is not caused to    |
| society as a whole.           |
---------------------------------
```

```
---------------------------                    ----------------------
| The Alaska reserves of  |                    | Oil companies must |
| untapped oil constitute |                    | NOT be granted the |
| the largest single re-  |--------------------| right to drill for |
| maining source of energy-|                   | oil in the Alaska  |
| producing fossil fuel left|                  | oil reserve.       |
| available to the U. S.  |                     ----------------------
---------------------------                          A new claim
      Grounds (unchanged)
```

Logic   137-162 (text pages)

Chapter 3 introduces students to the traditional methods of reasoning that until recently were the only approaches to logic students could expect in a course on argument. The discussion supplements the traditional presentations of logic by emphasizing the often overlooked relationship between inductive and deductive reasoning.

Teachers who wish to focus the attention of the class on essays featuring deductive reasoning can use the following list:

Brownmiller   Mao Tse-Tung
Cooke   Milton
Flygare   Paine

6

Friedman   Slater
Hardin   Visscher
Jacoby ("First Amendment Junkie") Watson

The following readings, presented alphabetically by author, illustrate
arguments developed by inductive reasoning:

Cronin   Singer
Jacoby   Singletary
Jones   Smith
Martin   Steinbeck
Miletich   Whelan

Logical fallacies are discussed in the context of the Toulmin model.
That is, fallacies are classified and presented to illustrate failures
to meet the Toulmin criteria of claim, warrant, and support. Students
can see that fallacies result when (1) no real evidence is presented,
(2) when the evidence is not relevant, or (3) when insufficient
evidence is offered to support a claim. They also learn that fallacies
result from (4) inappropriate warrants or from (5) ambiguous
definitions of important terms.

Students might be encouraged to identify specific fallacies in the
following readings:

Ad Hominem - Visscher
Begging the Question - Schlafly, Vilar
Blaming the Victim - Schlafly
False Dilemma - Hillary, Watson
Faulty Analogy - Foundation
Hasty Generalization - Jacoby ("Unfair Game"), Lamp
Slippery Slope - Foundation, Visscher, Will
Straw Man - Henderson
Reductio ad Absurdum - Sevilla, Miletich
Scare Tactics - Abbey, Buchanan & Muir, Burnham, Hardin,
     Mittman, and Will.
Guilt by Association - Abbey, Brownmiller, Foundation,
     Lamp, and Visscher.
Virtue by Association - Cooke, Mao Tse-Tung,
     Paine, Slimp and Steiner.

Language   172-191 (text Pages)

Chapter 4 introduces students to the important role language plays in
arguments. First, students see the importance of defining key terms
and concepts. Writers define key terms in ways designed to gain
acceptance for their arguments. The following list identifies
arguments that depend on definitions of key terms:

Baldwin   Sauvigne
Baye   Schlafly
Cant   Singer
Cooke   Singletary
Hacker   Visscher
Machlowitz   Will

It is important for students to realize that arguments based on
definitions often attack stereotypes. Readings that assail the process
of labeling people and events are by:

Britt
Chapman
Jackman
Machlowitz
Miletich

Teachers know that the persuasive effect of arguments is due as much
to the quality of language the authors use as to the quality of

7

reasoning. This chapter examines how style and the author's voice are integral parts of persuading an audience. Some writers project themselves into the forefront of their arguments, whereas others retire and let the facts of the case speak for them. The discussion explores how writers use irony and satire in arguments. Essays that illustrate diverse uses of parody, satire, irony, and caricature include:

Addison
Benchley
Britt
Gent
Martin

Language and Persuasion   191-212 (text pages)

This chapter also introduces students to the strategies of language writers use to affect audiences. Students can observe the connotative use of language, emotionally-loaded terms, euphemisms, slogans, slanted language and propaganda techniques. Selections that illustrate these strategies include:

Cant	Miletich
Cooke	Schlafly
Foundation	Simon
Lamp	Visscher
Martin	

Students enjoy analyzing the language used to express claims by advertisers and politicians. They see how language is used to influence thinking and behavior. Understanding these strategies of linguistic persuasion gives them a measure of freedom from being manipulated by those who expertly use language to deceive.

The discussion relies on the pioneering work of Hugh Rank of Governors State University and the Quarterly Review of Doublespeak, edited by William Lutz of Rutgers, to illustrate the perennial rhetorical objectives shared by all acts of persuasion. These hidden agendas follow the pattern identified by George Orwell in "The Politics and the English Language." To introduce the ideas of "downplaying/intensifying" to students, teachers might draw upon the events in China during the summer of 1989. Students can bring in articles from newspapers and magazines and analyze them to discover how techniques identified by Rank, and illustrated by QRD, were used to alter perceptions of reality. For example, pro-democracy demonstrators were labeled by the government as "hooligans" or "counter-revolutionaries." The government downplayed their use of tanks and the massacres in Beijing. They fabricated events, denied or suppressed the existence of other events, purged leaders and paraded students in show trials before executing them. They made it a crime to remember events as they really happened. Every technique Rank discusses can be illustrated from events during this period.

Teachers might also introduce students to the idea that language includes all icons and images that constitute symbolic forms of speech. Teachers might find the United States Supreme Courts' June 1989 ruling that burning of the American flag is a form of political speech protected by the First Amendment an ideal way to introduce students to this concept. Pro and con arguments could be considered on the merits of introducing a Constitutional Amendment that would nullify the Supreme Court ruling and outlaw flag burning.

Strategies for Writing Arguments   227-256 (text pages)

Chapter 5 brings together prior discussions of critical reading, language study, and the analytical framework of the Toulmin model to show students how to generate their own arguments. Students learn proven invention strategies. They are shown how to select, arrange and organize what they have to say, and adapt their arguments for particular audiences.

At first glance, the emphasis on prewriting strategies in this chapter may seem excessive. Students, however, seem to appreciate knowing about a wide variety of strategies. Prewriting strategies are important as new ways for students to discover what they have to say on any subject. These strategies allow them to see issues from many different perspectives before they choose any particular one. The discussion of invention strategies places special emphasis on the role developing pro and con perspectives should play in the prewriting stage of the writing process. The sixteen pro and con debates on a wide range of issues that comprise chapter 7 provide informative and lively applications of these strategies.

Teachers should try to structure classroom instruction of these strategies to create situations where students can have practice using them on a range of topics, testing their first impressions, critically evaluating what they have produced, and getting a feel for which strategies they prefer. The process-oriented approach realistically reflects how writers solve problems. This chapter emphasizes the role critical thinking plays at the invention stage of the writing process. The discussion shows students how the process of evaluating someone else's argument requires them to understand the difference between opinion and fact, be sensitive to their own preconceptions, and base their judgments on objective evidence. It is especially important that they be aware of assumptions they bring to the analysis of particular arguments. Their assumptions may clash with the opinions or ideology of the writer they are evaluating.

Discussion of critical thinking emphasizes how all arguments arise in specific contexts. They can see that the rhetorical features of arguments depend on strategies of selection, organization, arrangement, and style required to persuade a particular audience. Teachers should feel free to adapt all or any of the strategies in this chapter to meet the needs of the students responding to the writing suggestions.

Writing a Research Paper 289-335 (text pages)

Chapter 6 provides students with information needed to write the library or research paper traditionally assigned in second-semester composition courses. Teachers should try to schedule an orientation tour of the library to coincide with this chapter. Students need to be shown the value of serious systematic research. However deeply a student may feel about a particular issue and no matter how thoroughly these feelings are anchored in memories and experiences, students must know how to take advantage of the wider sources of information libraries can provide. Each selection includes a number of writing suggestions designed to lead students towards a topic for their end-of-term papers. Even if the course does not require a formal library paper, this chapter is valuable for giving students techniques for locating information they may need to more fully understand any issue. Lacking this information, on any topic from disinvestment to genetic engineering, students will be less able to understand the structure and fine points of the arguments. Despite the effort to give necessary information in the headnotes, teachers should find out what students do not know about an issue before beginning a detailed analysis of the argument.

This chapter encourages students to transform topics into problems to which they can propose solutions. Teachers may wish to have the library paper follow the rhetorical structure of the problem-solution format. Instructors may wish to have the paper take the form of a recommendation sent to an official on campus proposing the best way to solve a problem. Writing the research paper elevates students into resident experts on particular problems. Some students may even wish to conduct their own surveys, interviews and field research along with reading, summarizing and synthesizing information from many sources.

Writing a research paper requires students to focus on a topic and use the storehouse of information in the library in writing, revising,

9

rewriting, researching and drafting the final paper. For many
students, this is the single most compelling assignment they complete
for a freshman composition course. Teachers who wish to enhance the
process might consider asking students to keep a log of their research
and prepare a short narrative of the steps they went through in the
course of doing their paper. Students might explain how they became
interested in the topic. They can describe how the research process
required them to rethink their initial stance and reformulate their
thesis. They might tell of obstacles they faced in gathering source
materials and the tactics they used to overcome them. Students might
be asked to describe how the paper changed in the process of repeated
drafts and conferences. They can describe changes that made it easier
for readers to follow their argument. Writing a narrative account
based on keeping a notebook, diary, journal, or research log, can be
enormously helpful in developing students' confidence in handling
research projects in other courses. By gaining insight into their own
thinking processes, students see what problem-solving strategies work
for them that they can rely on in the future.

Pro and Con Arguments   343-576 (text pages)

The pro and con arrangement makes it possible for teachers to
introduce students to an extraordinarily wide range of issues,
forcefully articulated by equally-matched arguers. In many of these
selections, the two writers specifically address their arguments to
each other.

Teachers can use the pro-con format as a model for setting up debates
or discussions in the classroom, of the kind presented on Point
Counterpoint (CNN). Half the class can prepare one side of an issue
and the other half of the class can prepare the opposing viewpoint.
Conversely, teachers can set up debates based on responses students
have prepared before coming to class. Follow-up assignments can allow
students to refine their own positions or answer objections raised by
students arguing on the other side.

Teachers may also wish to have students exchange papers with those
holding opposing views. The peer review process works well in
composition classes teaching argument since it provides students with
a real and immediate audience. Students know they will be challenged
if they fail to develop points or do not offer enough relevant
supporting evidence. Teachers, too, should know they will be expected
to voice opinions and defend them in open discussion. Instructors
should be prepared to be participants, not just referees.

Different Perspectives on Current Issues   577-795 (text pages)
(Business, Addictions, and Media)

The multiple perspectives on current issues of the thematic clusters
emphasize controversial issues that have more than two sides. These
groups of readings are intended to encourage students to see single
issues from different standpoints. By realizing that there are many
legitimate ways of seeing things, students can develop tolerance, and
even generosity of spirit, towards opposing viewpoints.

The readings can also serve as jumping-off points for research papers
dealing with business, addictions, and media. The three clusters
strike a balance between subjective, personal issues and those that
affect all of society. Business and non-business majors throughout the
country should be interested in the problems today's businesses face
in meeting their corporate responsibilities toward employees,
consumers, the environment, and society. As a topic, drugs should need
no justification. Students can draw on personal experiences in
relating to the insights provided by some of these essays. The
relationship of students to the world of media that envelops them is
rather like fish swimming in the tank unaware of the surrounding
water. Students enjoy being given the opportunity to think critically
about the persuasive messages directed at them at every turn by radio,
television, rock music, advertising, newspapers, magazines and the

print and electronic media. Within these topic areas, students will confront basic issues in business, science and technology, social sciences, humanities and education.

Teachers can use the multiple perspectives of these readings to familiarize students with the Rogerian form of non-confrontational argument presented in the "audience" section of chapter 2. Students using the Rogerian technique can be asked to summarize the views of an opponent. The fairness of the summary can be tested by asking students on the opposite side whether they would agree that these were accurate statements of their positions.

The readings in this text are intended to meet a wide range of needs. For courses which place special emphasis on (a) liberal arts and education, (b) sciences, computers and medicine, or (c) law, business and politics, the following syllabi may be useful:

Liberal Arts & Education   Sciences, Computers & Medicine

Cant vs Cooke   Buchanan & Muir vs Payne & Risch
Jacoby ("Unfair Game")   Burnham
Milton   Cronin vs Hillary
Machlowitz   Hacker vs Will
Benchley   Singer vs Visscher
Britt   President's Commission vs Foundation
Jackman   & the Addictions Cluster
Baldwin vs Simon
Baye vs Singletary
Rodriguez vs Steiner
& the Media Cluster

Business, Law, and Politics

Chapman ("Prisoner's Dilemma")
Abbey vs Smith
Brownmiller vs Jacoby
Galbraith vs Gall
Hardin vs Watson
Johnson vs Roome
Paine vs Mao Tse-Tung
Sauvigne vs Schlafly
Sevilla vs Jones
Slimp vs Lewis
& the Business Cluster

Taking a composition course on argument can be a rare opportunity for college students to think critically and write coherently. The manual follows the sequence of the book's questions. Titles of supplemental readings usually appear at the end of the answers for that selection. Answers to questions offered in this manual are intended, like opening moves in a chess game, to start rather than settle class discussions on the issues.

PART I

THE ELEMENTS OF ARGUMENT

Chapter One   Understanding Arguments

Patrick J. Buchanan & J. Gordon Muir
"Gay Times and Diseases"

1. Buchanan and Muir characterize the gay lifestyle as one of "random, repeated, anonymous sex [and] runaway promiscuity" (para.1). They refer to AIDS as a consequence of homosexuality. That is, many AIDS victims are gay and homosexual contact transmits the disease. For them, the spread of AIDS is ample proof that the gay lifestyle is immoral and destructive.

2. Buchanan and Muir quote Dr. Kinsey who estimates that the average homosexual has nearly 1,000 sexual partners over a lifetime. They cite a quotation from the Village Voice which places the figure at almost 1,600 partners for additional support for their contention that gays are promiscuous. They also mention that group-sex is a frequent activity.

3. Buchanan and Muir wish to portray themselves as not making moral judgments, but primarily concerned with the public health ramifications of AIDS. In essence, they assert they are simply pointing to an obvious relationship between the spread of AIDS and homosexuality. However, at various points in their argument, Buchanan and Muir do make moral judgments.

4. Buchanan and Muir view homosexuals afflicted with AIDS and other sexually-related diseases as victims of the Gay Rights Movement and its leaders. Buchanan and Muir do this in order to show themselves as sympathetic to those who are victims of AIDS. They structure the argument to present first the terrible effects of AIDS on the homosexual community and then cite the slogans and mottoes encouraging gay sexual liberation promulgated by the Gay Rights Organizations. They classify homosexuals into duped followers and culpable leaders.

5. The authors suggest that the medical system was slow in presenting advice against homosexual practices. Doctors were overly cautious because they were unwilling to be perceived as being moralistic. Doctors' reluctance to advise against homosexual practices permitted AIDS to advance much more rapidly in the gay community than otherwise would have been the case.

6. Buchanan and Muir fail to mention exact sources chiefly in paragraphs 2 (where they refer to an unnamed activist and his research), 4 (a reference to an unnamed gay author), 8 (they cite an anonymous physician) and especially in para. 17 where they draw a conclusion from undocumented evidence.

7. The APA's decision to rescind their definition that homosexuality indicates mental disease resulted from lobbying by gay activists' groups. They use this as evidence that the "intense pressure to recognize homosexuality...as normal human behavior" (para.14) contributed to the present AIDS threat. The AMA's reluctance to speak out and the APA's reversal of their definition were not legitimate medical and psychological judgments. These organizations acted as they did because they were afraid they would look biased against homosexuals. The assumption is that doctors who would normally alert the public to health threats in this case were silent.

8. Paragraph 15 is a concise version of the contents of Buchanan and Muir's entire essay. If homosexuality is normal behavior, why, ask Buchanan and Muir, do impartial observers find evidence of a connection between many different diseases and male homosexuality. The authors ask rhetorically: can it be that homosexuals suffer from so many sex-related diseases because these diseases are the natural consequences of homosexual behavior? The authors then put this question in the context of references to injunctions against

homosexuality contained in the Bible.

9. Buchanan and Muir trace the presence of AIDS among homosexuals and intravenous drug-users, examine how it spreads, and speculate about the future. The authors suggest that AIDS entered the United States mainland population via male prostitutes in Haiti and their sexual contacts with vacationing United States' gays. This group then carried the disease into the homosexual community where it spread to intravenous drug-users, hemophiliacs, bi-sexual males, women who had contact with bi-sexual males, and children of these women. Buchanan and Muir suggest that a promiscuous sexual lifestyle is the main cause of the rapid growth of the disease within the gay community. They forecast that unless a "dramatic behavioral change" (para. 18) occurs, the gay community will be wiped out.

10. By discussing the possible mutation of the AIDS virus into a more virulent strain and by raising the spectre of contamination of the national blood supply, Buchanan and Muir are using "scare tactics." They attempt to shock and alarm their audiences into readily accepting recommendations that otherwise would appear too harsh (barring homosexuals from all food-handling positions, or working in health services). Many measures they recommend violate current right-to-work laws. Without the extreme perils dramatized by Buchanan and Muir, these proposals would seem to be an overreaction to the problem.

11. The authors' discussion of other sexually transmitted diseases prevalent in the gay community support the authors' thesis that AIDS is not an isolated occurrence. It is only a more dangerous disease arising from the extreme promiscuity the authors see as characteristic of the gay community. Buchanan and Muir blame sexually transmitted epidemics on promiscuous sex and societal leniency toward homosexual behavior.

12. Buchanan and Muir state that "common sense" (para. 31) suggests homosexuals should be barred from food service, health service, day care and other occupations where they would have physical contact with food or people, or jobs involving children. This proposal conflicts with existing right-to-work laws that prohibit employment discrimination based on sexual preference.

13. Paragraph 34 restates the author's position on homosexuality concisely: homosexual practices pose a threat to the general public. Paragraph 35 restates the author's claim that societal leniency toward homosexuality has contributed to the present AIDS crisis. The authors see this societal acquiescence most visible in portrayals by Hollywood and the media. Thus, Hollywood's depiction of gays as regular guys "who happen to be gay" (para.36) has encouraged promiscuity which has, in turn, produced a sexually transmitted epidemic threatening society.

Kenneth W. Payne & Stephen J. Risch "The Politics of AIDS"

1. For reference, students might take another look at the short summary which restates main ideas from two paragraphs from Payne and Risch's argument.

2. The authors believe that the commitment of medical resources, and society's response to disease is profoundly influenced by the value society attaches to its victims. This is what Payne and Risch mean by "the politics of AIDS." Since homosexual AIDS victims are condemned for their gay lifestyle and since intravenous drug-users and minorities are viewed as disposable citizens, victims of AIDS are doubly stigmatized. In short, the extent to which proper medical treatment and research dollars are committed depends not on the disease but rather on the moral status of its victims.

3. Although many different groups suffer from AIDS (homosexuals, bi-sexuals, IV drug-users, Haitians and hemophiliacs), society views only hemophiliacs as being the "innocent victims of AIDS." Other AIDS victims are perceived as receiving just punishment for what most heterosexuals consider wrongful activity. That is, people feel the disease seeks out its "proper victims" (para.9) and establishes a

close fit between the disease and its victims. This approach of
"blaming the victim" sees AIDS as punishment for a deviant lifestyle
and blames the victim for having brought the disease on himself.

4. The authors claim that because AIDS victims are seen as responsible
for their disease they will receive "less than optimal care" (para.19)
from hospitals and medical clinics. Because of the very real, although
low statistical risk of contracting AIDS, health care professionals
are reluctant to treat AIDS patients. Moreover, the special medical
care required for AIDS is very expensive and hospitals are aware that
many insurance companies will not give health insurance to those who
have been diagnosed as having the HTLV-3 virus.

5. Homophobia can be defined as an irrational fear of homosexuals.
Apprehension that homosexuals can transmit AIDS to the general public
has increased homophobia. As soon as AIDS became known as a "gay
disease" (para.13) various groups, according to Payne and Risch, began
to propose legislation that would have discriminated against
homosexuals. For example, a bill proposed in Texas, against homosexual
activity invoked the threat of AIDS as an epidemic that could "destroy
the public health" (para.10) Payne and Risch find it ironic that civil
rights gained by gays during the 1960's and 1970's are in danger of
being curtailed because of the emergence of the AIDS issue in the
1980's. They see this as an example of the ease with which latent
homophobia can rise to the surface.

6. Payne and Risch state that gay groups have been forced, in
self-defense, to monitor the media's presentation of information on
AIDS for accuracy and timeliness. The argumentative strategy they
follow is first to present their position, then state the opponents'
viewpoint and then comment on the inaccuracy of their opponents'
arguments. For example, they present evidence showing how the media
has erroneously presented AIDS as a strictly "gay disease." They also
note that while AIDS is often characterized as a "gay plague" evidence
suggests that it "barely constitutes an epidemic, let alone a plague"
(para.12). The authors' counterarguments center on showing that
because 95% of AIDS victims are already stigmatized, medical research
is proceeding at a snail's pace. Although they don't say so, the
assumption here (later proved correct) is that medical research into
AIDS would increase dramatically when AIDS was perceived as a threat
to the heterosexual population. They dispute the charge that
discrimination against homosexuals is "reasonable" (para.20) since
homosexuals place their own health and the health of society at risk;
their answer is that smokers and alcoholics could also be accused of
risking their own and society's health, yet are not discriminated
against in receiving adequate medical care.

7. As evidence supporting their thesis that different groups in
society distort AIDS to suit their own agendas, Payne and Risch cite
evidence that:

(1) the media uses AIDS for its headline potential but rarely follow
up with later stories.
(2) politicians use AIDS to score political points with voters against
homosexuals (for example, in California, a state senator used the
threat of AIDS to defeat a bill that would have placed homosexuals
under the protection of the fair employment act as a discriminated
against minority).
(3) preachers use AIDS to score moral points against homosexuals with
their congregations.
(4) medical researchers fail to share their research findings in hopes
of competing for research funds, wealth, and international
recognition.
All these groups use AIDS "politically" to further their own agendas.

8. Payne's background in medical anthropology is apparent in the
discussion why medical care for AIDS patients is substandard and based
on the moral status of the victims. The difference in quality of
health care is dramatized by comparing medical assistance given to
AIDS patients with that routinely given to those suffering from
anorexia nervosa. The case of a California state senator using the

threat of AIDS to defeat a bill that would have accorded homosexuals
equal employment protection is a clear example of how AIDS has become
a political football. Risch's background as a biologist is apparent in
the discussion that deals with the AIDS outbreak, the procedures that
should be followed in searching for a cure, and in his knowledge of
specialized techniques such as LAV.

For students thinking of doing a research paper on the topic of AIDS
some interesting sources are: AIDS and Its Metaphors by Susan Sontag
(1988), AIDS and the New Puritanism by Dennis Altman (1987), The AIDS
Cover Up? by Gene Antonio (1986), "AIDS and Eros" by Julia Kristeva,
Harper's Magazine, October 1987, And the Band Played On: Politics,
People and the AIDS Epidemic, by Randy Shilts (1988), "Senate Fails to
Extend AIDS Drug Program," The New York Times, March 18, 1989.

Chapter Two   Strategies of Argument

Mike Jackman   "Enabling the Disabled"

1. Examples cited by Jackman of frustrating obstacles disabled people
must face in every day life include: not being able to see the numbers
in the elevator (para. 1), the inability to tell a doctor you are
allergic to medicine the doctor is about to administer (para. 2),
being turned away from various public places because you are
considered a fire hazard, trying to rent an apartment. This strategy
enables Jackman's readers to instantly empathize with those who must
cope with these situations every day.

2. Jackman uses the opening paragraphs (para.1-3) to present a graphic
picture of the physical and emotional obstacles facing the disabled
person. He then summarizes (para.4) how society's perceptions of the
disabled promotes discrimination. First, the disabled are faced with
physical barriers and outdated legislation. Second, society
perpetrates a subtle but insidious form of discrimination by viewing
the disabled as incompetent. In a vicious cycle, society first
prohibits the disabled from becoming productive, and discourages them
from trying. When the disabled fail to overcome these barriers,
society then discriminates psychologically by sending out the message
that the disabled are bound to fail since they are inferior.
Tragically, many disabled people accept this judgment and begin to see
themselves as helpless, fulfilling society's expectations. This
vicious cycle justifies society's belief that they are helpless. One
of the purposes of Jackman's article is to help disabled people break
this vicious cycle by being made aware of it.

3. Jackman feels that society has stereotyped the disabled and sees
them as being incompetent and even unintelligent. As proof, Jackman
cites the experiences of people who were in no way disabled, or
discriminated against, and shows how attitudes shifted after they
became disabled. Even though their disabilities in no way affected
their ability to do jobs at which they were already quite competent,
society was blind to everything but the disability. For example, a
woman who developed a speech impairment after two years of college was
prevented from graduating. The speech impairment does not show
decreased intelligence, yet she was treated as though it did.
Jackman's point in this and other cases is that people who were
capable and subsequently became handicapped were treated with the same
prejudices as those who were born disabled.

4. The belief that the disabled are "flawed and incapable of caring
for themselves" (para.21) repeatedly confronts the disabled. Thus,
ironically, because of the many barriers placed in their way, disabled
people are unable to perform as well as the non-disabled. This only
serves to justify societal stereotypes and reinforce a
self-perpetuating vicious cycle.

5. One of the most shocking examples is the quarantine requirement for
guide dogs for blind people when they visit Hawaii. The quarantine
period is 120 days and requires the blind owner to pay a $466 bill.
Why, Jackman asks, should a blind person be denied the right to use

his or her guide dog upon entering the state. Other examples of
shocking regulations include the cases of the evicted schizophrenic
(para.12), the prohibition against motorized wheelchairs (para. 38),
and the denial of voting rights (para. 44).

6. Jackman uses a variety of statistics. The total number of disabled
people in the United States is 36 million or about 13% of the
population. This shows that the disabled are a significant percentage
of the population whose problems ought to receive greater public
attention. Jackman observes that many television programs are not
closed captioned for the deaf despite the fact that there are 11
million people with hearing problems. He observes that for every
dollar a non-disabled person makes, a white disabled male makes 60
cents and a black disabled woman makes only 12 cents (para.54). These
statistics collectively support his thesis that the disabled face
pervasive discrimination.

7. Section 504 of the 1973 Rehabilitation Act "guaranteed specific
civil rights for disabled people" (para.25). This Act recognized that
"disabled people... were being discriminated against" (para.35) and
made it somewhat easier for the disabled to enter the work force.
Section 504 makes discrimination against the disabled as illegal as it
is against other minorities. Jackman says that because this bill was
negligently enforced at first, the disabled formed a coalition (DREDF)
to educate the disabled on their legal rights in the work place,
school, and society. Some victories have been won, but many barriers
to employment, education, and social services remain.

8. The title "Enabling the Disabled" suggests how paternalism
perpetuates societal stereotypes about the disabled and shows how they
can rid themselves of these stereotypes and lead normal lives. The
article is also a plea to the general public to become aware of a
problem that many people think has already been solved.

9. By refuting erroneous societal stereotypes, Jackman hopes to
persuade his readers to accept the disabled as being able to take care
of themselves and competent to hold jobs. The general public will gain
a greater awareness of the conditions that disabled people must endure
and will be prompted to treat the disabled in less prejudiced and
stereotyped ways. Jackman's article is not only addressed to
able-bodied people who have no idea what life as a disabled person
would be like, but to the handicapped as well. This article urges the
disabled to believe in themselves, and see themselves as competent to
deal with their own lives and take care of themselves. For both
audiences, this is an effective argument.

10. Most people have had the experience at one time or another of
experiencing a disability. A broken ankle that takes twelve weeks to
heal, broken fingers that make it impossible to drive, or any other
physical impairment dramatizes Jackman's point. The simplest physical
activity becomes inconvenient. Being disabled, even temporarily, will
make the person feel how disapproving society is of those who are not
able-bodied. Anyone who has ever experienced a disability will be
able to empathize with many of the things Jackman discusses. For those
who have not experienced a disability, the way in which society treats
the elderly and infirm will provide a significant insight into the
same type of problem.

Arguing in Ethics: Euthanasia

The opposing arguments by Cant and Cooke dramatically illustrate the
distinctive features of arguments in ethics. They should be
accompanied by a class discussion of the "Arguing in Ethics" section
of Arguing Across the Disciplines in chapter two. Ethical arguments
address conflicts that arise between professional or societal roles
and basic questions of right or wrong.

Gilbert Cant   "Deciding When Death Is Better Than Life"

In diagram form, Cant's argument appears as follows:

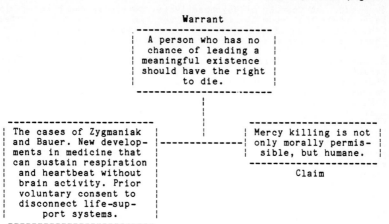

Warrant

```
-----------------------
¦ A person who has no  ¦
¦ chance of leading a  ¦
¦ meaningful existence ¦
¦ should have the right¦
¦      to die.         ¦
-----------------------
```

```
-------------------------         ----------------------
¦ The cases of Zygmaniak ¦        ¦ Mercy killing is not ¦
¦ and Bauer. New develop-¦--------¦ only morally permis- ¦
¦ ments in medicine that ¦        ¦ sible, but humane.   ¦
¦ can sustain respiration¦        ----------------------
¦ and heartbeat without  ¦               Claim
¦ brain activity. Prior  ¦
¦ voluntary consent to   ¦
¦ disconnect life-sup-   ¦
¦     port systems.      ¦
-------------------------
            Grounds
```

1. The two cases of Zygmaniak and Bauer dramatize the issues involved in the euthanasia debate. The cases illustrate two extremes. One death was violently brought about whereas the other was the result of a non-violent, but still lethal act--an injection of potassium chloride into Bauer's veins (para.2). In both cases, the "murderers" believed they were saving others from more pain and did what they did out of compassion. Both cases dramatize the controversy at the center of the issue of euthanasia or mercy killing--that is, the unlawful taking of a life versus the "right to die" (para.3).

2. In para.15 Cant says "while legal definitions of death lag far behind medical advances, today's criterion is, in most instances, the absence of brain activity for 24 hours." This new definition is required because heart and lung activity can be artificially maintained. Black's Law Dictionary (1979) defines death as occurring with "a total and irreversible cessation of brain function" (p. 360).

3. Even though the response to this will be personal, students interested in further research might wish to read Joanne Lynn, M.D., ed. By No Extraordinary Means: The Choice to Forgo Life-Sustaining Food and Water (1986) or James Rachels' The End of Life (1986).

4. Advances in biomedical technology make it possible for people to continue to live even when there is no hope of a recovery. Sometimes it becomes difficult to determine when a person should be considered "dead." "Active" (para.8) euthanasia involves accelerating the death of one who is terminally ill or taking direct means to produce a "mercy killing" (para.3). "Passive" (para.10) euthanasia entails disconnecting vital life support systems and letting nature take its course, even if circumstances where death might be temporarily avoided if extraordinary measures were taken.

5. In Pope Pius XII's view, life should never be prolonged by "extraordinary means" (para.16) and should only be sustained by ordinary means such as "feeding, usual drug treatment, care, and shelter" (para.17). Cant cites this statement to illustrate that some of the clergy support his position.

6. Father McCormick says that permitting decisions regarding death is the same as passing judgment on the quality of a person's life. This, for him, would be equal to passing judgment on what kinds of lives are not worth living. For McCormick, this kind of judgment leads inevitably to the mentality that prevailed in Nazi Germany. Once death decisions are based on quality of life judgments, extermination of physical and mental defectives and entire races becomes possible.

7. Freud, the founder of psychoanalysis, developed mouth cancer in his later years that made it impossible for him to live a normal life. Cant cites Freud as an example of someone who "died with dignity" (para.22) because Freud made arrangements to die when he wanted to.

8. Advocates of euthanasia or "mercy killing" claim that it allows a person to "die with dignity." Those opposed to this practice argue that euthanasia is simply murder under a different name. Euthanasia raises the basic question about who should decide whether a specific life should be ended. This dilemma was dramatized in the play <u>Whose Life Is It Anyway?</u> when an artist paralyzed in a car accident <u>finds</u> that he will not be allowed to decide whether he should live or die. The doctors attending him keep him alive despite his wishes to the contrary. The crucial question is whether a person should be allowed to choose death if life would be little more than a continued tortured existence. Another issue is who has the right to decide when a patient cannot make his or her wishes known. Supporters of euthanasia say that doctors, along with the patient's family, should be able to choose when to end the patient's life.

Terence Cardinal Cooke   "Address Delivered to the First
                          Annual American Health Congress"

In diagram form, Cooke's argument appears as follows:

Warrant
```
----------------------------
| Permitting a patient's    |
| life to be terminated on  |
| the grounds that it is    |
| meaningless is against    |
| the law of God and should |
| be justly labeled as "mur-|
| dering a human being."    |
----------------------------
```

```
----------------------              ----------------------
| "Death with dignity" |            | Health care pro-    |
| now part of health   |            | fessionals should   |
| care workers duties  |------------| not be party to     |
| since legislature    |            | "death with dignity."|
| passed a bill grant- |            ----------------------
| ing it, if three     |                     Claim
| physicians concur.   |
----------------------
        Grounds
```

1. Students need to look closely at the assumption underlying Cooke's argument to decide whether the conclusion he draws necessarily follows from the stated (and implied) premises. This line of reasoning also forms the basis for George Will's article "Discretionary Killing" (see chapter 7).

2. Cooke attempts to draw his audience into the argument by addressing them using the editorial we ("we must never lose sight of those values," "we must not allow," "we have seen far too many") and through an almost chant-like repetition of phrases (para. 6-9). Cooke's style is balanced, with a biblical quality in its cadences: "you see it comes swiftly and unexpectedly; you see it come slowly and lingeringly" (para.11). The voice he projects is one that takes the "high ground," morally speaking, and is addressed to the conscience of each member of the audience.

3. Cooke reminds us that ever since the beginning of the Catholic Church, the clergy has acknowledged that life is "a God-given gift" (para.20). Because life is given by God, its value is changeless and cannot be lessened by changing social values. Thus, no human has the right to take the life of another regardless of the circumstances.

4. Health care professionals should think about the moral issues involved because if new legislation is passed ("the so-called model

bill" para.16), physicians and medical professionals would be able to "play God" with the lives of the insane, deformed and diseased. If this bill were to be passed into law, Cooke is concerned that doctors and nurses around the country would become responsible for deciding which people should live. This is not a right, says Cooke, that medical professionals should be able to exercise.

5. The essential issue underlying Cooke's reference to the Declaration of Independence is that life is bestowed by a higher power. Cooke uses language drawn from the Declaration of Independence to suggest that euthanasia is not only a crime against God, but goes against fundamental tenets of American society.

6. Cooke says that new cures may be discovered for the diseases afflicting terminally ill patients (para.21). This argument appeals to hope and the possibility of future cures that could help people only if they were still alive. In essence, life should not be taken because the possible discovery of a cure, however slight the chance, should not be discounted.

7. and 8. For Cooke "death with dignity" means that a patient should be respected as he or she approaches death. A patient should be given a chance to be at peace, pain should be lessened and he or she should not be subjected to any unnecessary procedures. Cooke's use of the phrase is diametrically opposite to Gilbert Cant's use of "death with dignity" to mean that a person should be allowed "to die comfortably when death is inevitable." Cooke's argumentative strategy is to attempt a victory "by definition."

9. Some considerations to weigh in the balance include: (1) consideration of medical costs, (2) consideration of the feelings of family and friends, (3) the desire not to be dependent on others or (4) a fear of becoming totally helpless and losing control over one's intellectual and physical faculties.

Chapter Three   The Role of Logic in Argument

Inductive Reasoning

Susan Jacoby "Unfair Game"

In diagram form, Jacoby's argument appears as follows:

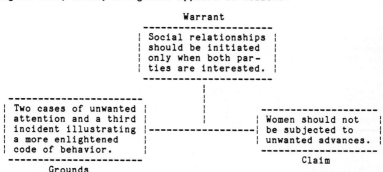

1. Jacoby uses the title to communicate the main idea of her argument: most men consider unescorted women as "fair game" (para.6) to be approached or picked up. However, since not all unescorted women want to be picked up, they are not "fair game" and the prevalent attitude in our society is "unfair" to women.

2. Jacoby supports her argument with examples drawn from her everyday

19

experience. Once on an airplane trip she was immersed in work and the man sitting next to her boorishly insisted on making a pass. In the Oak Room at the Plaza Hotel, she and her friend wished to talk privately while having drinks and were accosted by a man who would not leave them alone. Jacoby asserts that a woman sitting alone in a bar or restaurant is constantly subjected to male assumptions that women are always looking for escorts for the evening.

3. Jacoby presents herself as an independent, confident woman who is not afraid to state her views. She feels that her experience is typical: women are constantly bothered by men who approach them simply because they are unescorted. Jacoby is indignant that this attitude in society results in women constantly being pestered by men trying to pick them up. In terms of argumentative strategy, the conclusion of her argument is especially important in establishing her as a trustworthy observer. She describes an incident when someone tried to pick her up and after she refused, simply accepted the fact and left. Thus, she shows that she is not objecting to men picking up women, but to the attitude of discourtesy and their refusal to take no for an answer. This example lends objectivity to her essay and leads the reader to trust her as an observer.

4. Jacoby's description of a "code of feminine politeness" (para.17) may have been more true in the past; women today are taught to be independent and to initiate relationships in ways that would have been discouraged in the past. It is just as true that the code of basic human decency in relationships that Jacoby argues for is never out-of-date.

5. The sexual revolution has changed relationships between men and women so that now women are independent and take the initiative. Because of this, men perceive women as more open and flirtatious and view a refusal as a rejection that they think (incorrectly) should not be part of the new social rules. Unfortunately, they do not see past their own desire, fail to respect a woman's privacy, and then blame women's liberation for their own inappropriate behavior. In many ways, men are still operating according to the old rules where women were taught to hint they were interested even though they said "no." Then, men could take "no" for an answer since it might really have meant "yes." Now the case is the opposite and communication is much clearer; "yes" means "yes" and "no" means "no."

6. It is characteristic of inductive reasoning to reach a conclusion that generalizes from specific representative events. Using herself as a typical woman, Jacoby draws on personal experiences of different incidents with men in her life to reach a conclusion about the way men treat women in public. Some readers may fault her for only citing two real examples from her experience, while other readers may see these cases as entirely typical. Both these cases and her description of an incident at the Stanhope Hotel support her thesis that a woman should have the right to be left alone if she so chooses.

7. During the incident at the Stanhope Hotel, the man expressed an interest in Jacoby but when she politely rejected him, he simply apologized and left her alone. She applauds this behavior since she says that social relationships should be initiated only when both parties are interested. By honoring Jacoby's rejection, neither he nor Jacoby was insulted since they both were playing the same game by a civilized set of rules.

8. Some students have found it helpful to write out the dialogue that might take place in one of these encounters, and then try to determine the basic assumptions operating in the situation.

Deductive Reasoning

John Milton   Areopagitica: Defense of Books

1. Milton begins his defense by conceding that it is important for the Church and the Commonwealth to "have a vigilant eye" (para.1) on books; that is, it is important for the church and state to be aware

of works printed in this society. By agreeing to this proposition, Milton gains leverage by allowing the validity of the opponent's point of view before beginning his own argument. In this way, he leads the discussion away from a direct confrontation so that he can present good reasons with which his audience will agree. His argumentative strategy is quite sound.

2. Milton's premiss (or statement expressing a self-evident truth) is: books are not inanimate objects since they are filled with the "potency of life," (para.1); that is, books contain and express the essential thoughts of those who wrote them. They are also alive because ideas may spring from them in much the same way as armed soldiers, in mythology, sprang from dragon's teeth. In some ways, a book that embodies living truth may more effectively transmit thoughts than the author would have been capable of doing in person.

3. Milton's argument relies upon his analogy between killing a man and killing a book (through censorship, prevention of publication, withdrawal from circulation, etc.). Milton claims that killing a book that is a vehicle to express ideas does just as much harm as killing a man. In some ways, says Milton, killing a book might be worse. He reasons that men are mortal and fated to die while books contain the immortal spirit of the creator (as he phrases it, they contain "reason itself" para.1). Thus, when a book "dies" the whole world loses ideas that might have been of enormous value to society.

4. Milton's argument that some books are worth more than some lives is effective both because of and despite the essential outrageousness of his claim. Because the assertion is so outrageous, audiences really consider his thesis. Some students doubtless will agree unless of course it was a choice between them and a particular book. This question becomes interesting when students are asked to pick those books they would nominate for rescue. Some observant students may realize that medical textbooks and scientific books would be capable of forestalling epidemics.

5. Milton contrasts the idea of "license" (para.2) (permissiveness) with "licensing," or censorship. The pun here is somewhat fanciful and for some readers may detract from the force of Milton's argument.

6. Milton is arguing by analogy using historical precedent. In Athens, the types of books that were censored were those that were blasphemous or libelous. Of other types of writing, Milton says, "they took no heed" (para.3). This is why we have so many writings of the Greeks still surviving. Thus, the Athenian practice of censorship should serve modern-day Englishmen as a precedent. Milton gives two examples of censored works (the books of Protagoras and the vetus Comoedia) and many examples of works of authors whose works were not censored. These writers, including Epicurus and Aristophanes, would not have been known by audiences of Milton's time if their works had been censored by the Greeks. Thus, Milton urges his contemporaries to seek a position midway between those seeking complete freedom of publication and those who are concerned with what they see as the dangerous content in many books. In effect, Milton's position is a reasonable one, saying to his contemporaries that they should emulate the policy of the Greeks and censor only those books that are atheistic or libelous. Surprisingly, most people believe Milton's argument on this issue is to be against all censorship and to be in favor of all public communication in print, which is not the case.

7. Major premiss: some books, although inanimate, embody truth in a way that makes them worth more than the lives of some human beings.
  Minor premiss: censorship of a book, through prevention of publication or withdrawal from circulation, is akin to "homicide" (para.3).
  Conclusion: censorship of some books is a kind of murder that is worse than homicide.

8. This question will elicit a wide range of opinions. One view will stress individual responsibility and favor providing a freedom of choice to accept or reject any published idea. The opposite view will

168-221 (text pages)
center on the idea of protecting people by eliminating the chance they
will ever come in contact with corrupting, dangerous, or offensive
published materials. For students interested in studying the
historical aspect of this document, some good sources are: David A.
Lowenstein "Areopagitica and the Dynamics of History, Studies in
English Literature, 1500-1900 Winter 1988, 28 (1): 77-93, Michael
Wilding, "Milton's Areopagitica: Liberty for the Sects," Prose
Studies, September 1986 9 (2): 7-38, and Christopher Kendrick, "Ethics
and the Orator in Areopagitica," ELH, Winter 1983, 50 (4): 655-691.

Chapter Four   The Role of Language in Argument

The Definition Essay

Marilyn Machlowitz   "What Is Workaholism?"

In diagram form, Machlowitz's argument appears as follows:

```
                            Warrant
              ---------------------------------
              | It is unfair to characterize  |
              | productive behavior as if it  |
              | were as addictive, debilitat- |
              | ing, and detrimental as alco- |
              | holism.                       |
              ---------------------------------
                             |
 -------------------------   |   ----------------------
 | Examples showing that  |  |   | Workaholics should  |
 | workaholics do not     |  |   | not be subjected to |
 | work to please bosses, |-----| ridicule or stereo- |
 | earn promotions, but   |  |   | typed as obsessive  |
 | work only to satisfy   |  |   | killjoys.           |
 | themselves.            |  |   ----------------------
 -------------------------           Claim
         Grounds
```

1. Machlowitz's main reason for discussing workaholism is to dispel
negative connotations of the word and prove that being a workaholic is
not necessarily bad. A better understanding of the term would make
people less anxious about being called workaholics and better able to
deal with those who are.

2. Machlowitz states that in certain governmental, professional, and
academic circles, workaholism is viewed with disapproval. The term
acquired its negative connotations according to Machlowitz, by
association with alcoholism, and because workaholics are incorrectly
portrayed as having miserable personal lives. This bias stems from
non-workaholics who feel that such excessive devotion to work is
abnormal or who fear that something is wrong with them because they do
not love work as fervently as do workaholics. Workaholism is depicted
as an addiction, like drug addiction, alcoholism and smoking.
Machlowitz is honest in showing that home life and family suffer, yet
disputes the popular ideas of workaholism as an addiction. Her
research suggests "workaholics are... happy... doing exactly what they
love--work--and they cannot seem to get enough of it... workaholics
can be astonishingly productive" (para.23).

3. Workaholics are more willing to settle for excellence in one
endeavor and admit that they are inept and disinterested in anything
else. American cultural norms dictate that we are supposed to lead a
balanced and "normal" life, working during the day and participating
in other activities, hobbies and pastimes, in the evenings and on
weekends. American society expects people to dislike their jobs and
paradoxically, disapproves of workaholics because they love their
jobs.

4. Labeling fixes a set of characteristics in a stereotyped way that concentrates on certain traits to the exclusion of all others. People labelled as workaholics are stereotyped as obsessive killjoys and are subject to ridicule. Machlowitz's article is intended to refute many of these negative connotations. Other examples of labeling are the use of "sanitation engineer" or "landscape engineer" for a garbage collector or a gardener. In these cases, the label makes the job sound more appealing and more prestigious.

5. Machlowitz depicts workaholics as people who love their job so much they do not want to take time off. To illustrate her point, she presents several examples including a surgeon who would not be happy if he could not operate each day (para.16-18), a janitor who has no time for conversation because he is so busy working (para.20), a playwright (para.8) who has no real wish to do anything else, and a senator who becomes unhappy when he has less work to do (para.14). These examples show that workaholics do not work to please their boss, earn promotions, or meet deadlines. Workaholics see work as the most natural kind of activity possible and work only to satisfy themselves.

6. Machlowitz's reference to many famous, well-known and respected people such as Neil Simon (para.8), Dick Vermeil (para.13), and William Proxmire (para.14), supports her thesis that workaholism should not be considered a bad habit or an addiction. Her examples prove that workaholics often lead productive and successful lives.

7. The range of examples Machlowitz supplies proves that workaholism is not restricted to any job classification, sex or social class. She dispels the common misconception that workaholics cannot be blue-collar workers. She proves that the concept can be applied to the entire work force and by applying it so widely gives a greater validity. The effect of her argumentative strategy here is to answer a question in her audience's mind who might have been wondering if the concept applied to themselves as well.

8. The basic difference between the workaholic and the "super woman" is that whereas workaholics concentrate all their efforts on work alone, "superwomen" try to be "super moms," "super wives" and "super workers" (para.20). Whereas the workaholic has but one job, "superwoman" attempts to fulfill all her roles with equal fervor. Machlowitz feels that "superwomen" scatter their energies and contrasts this with the more focused effort of workaholics.

9. Some students will recoil at the very notion of such excessive zeal while others will happily characterize themselves as workaholics who now have a banner to fly. An interesting response would be from a student who is a workaholic but doesn't want to be one.

10. This question can provoke lively debate and is an interesting one for students because it makes them think about what is really important to them for their futures.

11. If this question does not work with the amount given, try changing it to either greater or lesser amounts so that it triggers a real psychological dilemma for the students.

Tone: Satire

Robert Benchley   "Opera Synopsis"

1. Benchley's short piece satirizes the pompous nature of classical opera and the conventions of Germanic opera in particular. Benchley ridicules these customs by having his opera take place in ridiculous, anachronistic surroundings. Benchley reverses the expectation that treasure is located in some inaccessible exotic place and punctures the convention by having it hidden in the familiar and decidedly common bureau drawer. He pokes fun at the convoluted, often absurd story line of grand opera by parodying the "synopsis" that usually accompanies opera programs.

2. Benchley's tone is humorous and witty. His readers, even if they have not seen Germanic opera, cannot help but laugh with him at the absurdities of grand opera. The author gleefully satirizes many of the outer trappings of classical opera to get his audience to view this monument of high culture with less solemnity. Opera lovers would respond that they go to operas primarily for the music, the staging and the performances and not for the story line or characters.

3. One aspect of opera that Benchley satirizes is the plot. Most German operas have plots that introduce new characters whose intentions and purposes are not clear to the audience ("where did he come from?" or "what is he doing there?"). Benchley's synopsis parodies this feature by introducing characters with absurd occupations and names into strange situations. The first act explores and parodies the ridiculous premises that govern many classical operas. The supposed basis of this particular opera is to tell "how the whale got his stomach" (para.1) but Benchley's characters and their actions do not explain this in any way.

4. Benchley's listing of characters parodies how opera draws on myths and legends. In ancient mythology, there were gods for practically everything and that is what his characters' names portray. For example, the four dwarfs are named "Hot Water, Cold Water, Cool and Cloudy" (para.2). Even the name of the sword "assistance in emergency" parodies the Anglo-Saxon kenning that characterizes an object by describing its function.

5. The ending of the synopsis "Immergluck Never Marries" (para.9) has nothing whatsoever to do with the rest of the story. Since the name Immergluck means "always happy" and no mention was made previously of her desire to get married, the ending was completely incongruous. Benchley satirizes the fact that the endings of operas are often incongruous and have little to do with the rest of the plot.

6. Benchley satirizes the names of characters in opera by giving his characters the German names of foods such as Strudel and Schmaltz and by juxtaposing the unpretentious and contemporary name Betty side by side with these names.

7. In traditional opera, characters play the role of servants to the gods. In Benchley's opera synopsis, he introduces Dampfboot, the tinsmith of the gods, Ragel, the papercutter of the gods, and Zweiback, the druggist of the gods. Their roles parody characters found in legends and myths.

8. Benchley also ridicules the magic concoctions and powers that are so much a part of grand opera. Instead of achieving expected results they produce the exact opposite. Hymns are sung for the dying of crops, love potions make young couples hate each other. When Benchley introduces Immergluck's magic cap and ring, he gives these possessions powers contrary to mythological tradition. Rather than giving the wearer powers that would normally be considered desirable, these possessions inflict insensibility and confuse the wearer. Benchley parodies the traditional assumption in opera that if a character changes their appearance, they immediately become unrecognizable to everyone else on the stage. Immergluck does this when she changes her hair style.

9. Benchley's use of Germanic names of foods parodies the grandiose names given to characters in Wagnerian operas.

10. Sources that might work well for this assignment include any of the television soap operas or traditional fairy tales. For students interested in critical studies on Benchley, some sources are: Eric Solomon's "Notes Towards a Definition of Robert Benchley's 1930s New Yorker Humor" in Studies in American Humor, Spring 1984 3 (1): 34-46 and Gerald Weales' "Robert Benchley as Guy Fawkes" in Sewanee Review, Fall 1985 93 (4): 601-609.

Chapter Five   Strategies for Writing Arguments

Three Short Arguments for Analysis

Suzanne Britt   "That Lean and Hungry Look"

1. Britt uses the phrase "that lean and hungry look," from
Shakespeare's play <u>Julius Caesar</u>, to spotlight her assertion that thin
people are not to be trusted. She confirms this at the start of her
essay with "Caesar was right" (para.1). She refers to thin people as
being "dangerous," (para.1) and "not fun" (para.2). The original
phrase "keep watch over him, he has that lean and hungry look" was
said by Caesar of Cassius implying that Cassius had the lean look of
someone hungry for power:

               Julius Caesar

     Let me have men about me that are fat;
     Sleek-headed men, and such as sleep o' nights:
     Yond Cassius has a lean and hungry look;
     He thinks too much: such men are dangerous   (I.ii.192-6)

Britt's agreement with Caesar's opinion that thin people should not be
trusted sets the tone for this delightful defense of "chubbies"
(para.4).

2. Syllogisms drawn from her essay might appear as follows:
Major <u>premiss</u>: a fun person is someone who knows how to
     clown around.
Minor <u>premiss</u>: thin people do not know how to clown around.
Conclusion: thin people are not fun.

A second example would be:
Major <u>premiss</u>: math and logic make people "downers."
Minor <u>premiss</u>: thin people like math and logic.
Conclusion: thin people are "downers."

3. Britt argues that thin people turn "surly, mean and hard" (para.4)
at a young age because they cannot release tension, and that thin
people are dull, oversimplify things and see the world in a rigidly
organized manner. In her view, the way a fat person conducts him or
herself leads to a longer and more rewarding life. Britt's point is a
good one. Although all fat people are not lazy, they are stereotyped
and perceived in this way. She believes that fat people, unlike thin
people, are cheerful and gregarious.

4. Britt disputes the validity of negative stereotypes by arguing that
fat people are happy and therefore must be doing something right. Her
strategy is to take a negative stereotype (fat people are lazy) and
show that, in reality, fat people have their priorities straight, and
are the true realists, who enjoy life, unlike thin people.

5. Britt states that fat people have the ability to see all sides of
an issue where thin people can only see one view, their own. She
claims that fat people have a better grasp of reality than do thin
people because thin people believe in logic and in simplistic answers
to complex problems. Fat people are also better adjusted since they
see that most "problems" are truly not worth worrying about.

6. According to Britt, thin people are: not fun, surly, believers in
logic, oppressive, and downers. Fat people, on the other hand, are:
jolly, knowledgeable, well equipped to deal with the mystery of life
and convivial. This question may produce varying opinions. Consider
the terms used to describe thin people: trim, suave, debonair,
elegant. Contrast these with terms like ponderous, unwieldy,
cumbersome, and bulky used to describe fat people. This question can
produce a lively debate and a range of varying opinions.

7. Responses to this question will vary. Some will see excessive thinness or obesity as symptomatic of an emotional disorder that should be addressed. Qualities other than physical appearance such as warmth, compassion, kindness, sense of humor, etc. would, for many, be more important than any change in physique.

8. Every culture has different definitions of what constitutes fat or thin and what is attractive or unattractive. Throughout the centuries, artists have presented women as being desirable only if they were voluptuous, and the decades of the late 1940's and 1950's aspired to an ideal of feminine beauty that was distinctly on the hefty side. In the 1980's, like the "roaring" twenties, "thin is in," although presumably the cycle will once more rotate back to the fully developed figure. What is most important here is that students give some thought to how cultural attitudes shape perceptions.

9. Britt's playful approach is compassionate and witty. Her essay expresses the kind of attitude for which she praises fat people, that is, she makes allowances, is non-judgmental, and does not hold others to impossibly high standards.

Stephen Chapman "The Prisoner's Dilemma"

1. Punishment in Eastern cultures differs from their Western counterparts in several significant ways. In Eastern cultures, punishment is public whereas punishment in Western cultures is private. In Eastern cultures, the accused must undergo public humiliation and punishment. The punishment is often violent and often follows methods decreed by the religion of the country. In Western cultures, offenders are sent to prison where they are kept out of the mainstream and are confined for varying periods of time. Punishment in the East tends to stress physical acts such as beating whereas punishment in the West is based on the idea of confinement. Interestingly, both forms of punishment are intended to serve as a deterrent and both systems have evolved within their respective cultures.

NOTE TO INSTRUCTOR

Included in this presentation copy is an excerpt of the Instructor's Manual to accompany STRATEGIES OF ARGUMENT. To obtain a copy of the complete Instructor's Manual, please contact your local Macmillan representative or call 1-800-428-3750.